מסורה

ArtScroll Mesorah Series

Rabbi Nosson Scherman/Rabbi Meir Zlotowitz
General Editors

באור על התורה לרבי עובדיה ספורנו

COMMENTARY ON THE TORAH

Published by

Mesorah Publications, ltd

SFORNO

Translation and explanatory notes
by Rabbi Raphael Pelcovitz

FIRST EDITION
First Impression . . . May, 1989

Published and distributed by
MESORAH PUBLICATIONS, Ltd.
Brooklyn, New York 11232

Distributed in Israel by
MESORAH MAFITZIM / J. GROSSMAN
Rechov Harav Uziel 117
Jerusalem, Israel

Distributed in Europe by
J. LEHMANN HEBREW BOOKSELLERS
20 Cambridge Terrace / Gateshead
Tyne and Wear / England NE8 1RP

THE ARTSCROLL MESORAH SERIES ®
SFORNO — COMMENTARY ON THE TORAH
Volume II: Vayikra/Bamidbar/Devarim

4401 Second Avenue / Brooklyn, N.Y. 11232 / (718) 921-9000

ISBN: 0-89906-240-7 (hard cover)
0-89906-241-5 (paperback)

Typography by CompuScribe at ArtScroll Studios, Ltd.
4401 Second Avenue / Brooklyn, N.Y. 11232 / (718) 921-9000

Printed by Moriah Offset U.S.A.
Bound by Sefercraft, Inc., Brooklyn, NY

Volume II:

ספר ויקרא

Vayikra/Leviticus

ספר במדבר

Bamidbar/Numbers

ספר דברים

Devarim/Deuteronomy

This is the first volume to be published
at our new home, at
4401 Second Avenue, Brooklyn, New York

Upon this occasion, we express our gratitude
to all those who were instrumental
in making this move possible, especially:

MR. AND MRS. LAURENCE A. TISCH

MR. AND MRS. JAMES S. TISCH

MR. THOMAS J. TISCH

MR. AND MRS. JUDAH SEPTIMUS, ESQ.

and

MR. AND MRS. NATHAN B. SILBERMAN

In the merit of their devotion to the
dissemination of Torah,
may Hashem Yisborach shower His blessings
upon them;
and may He enable us to make the new location
a wellspring of His Word.

Mesorah Publications, ltd

May 1989/Iyar 5749

◆§ Author's Acknowledgments

The first volume of the Sforno's commentary on the Torah, covering the Books of Bereishis and Sh'mos, was well received by a large number of readers, among whom are respected Rabbonim, educators and learned laymen. I have found this acceptance and approval on their part to be most gratifying, and I wish to thank all those who were kind enough to share their feelings with me, and express their appreciation to me.

In the preparation of this second volume, which completes the Sforno's commentary on the Chumash, I was assisted by a number of individuals whom I wish to thank. I am indebted to my dear daughter Ethel Gottlieb for her careful reading of the manuscript and to Belle Koenigsberg for her secretarial assistance during the editing and rewriting process. Above all, I am beholden to my dear wife Shirley שתחי׳ for her tremendous help in editing and refining the final version of this second volume. She gave me the strength, support and inspiration I needed, during a difficult period in my life, helping me to bring this work to its completion. Her Torah erudition, coupled with a gifted, graceful command of the English language, proved to be of considerable help to me. I am profoundly grateful to her.

Rabbi Avie Gold of Mesorah Publications, was extremely helpful to me during the final phases of this publication, as were the editors of the ArtScroll Series, Rabbi Nosson Scherman and Rabbi Meir Zlotowitz, and Rabbi Sheah Brander who designed the beautiful layout of this work.

At the completion of a Sefer of Torah on Shabbos, we stand up and recite חזק חזק ונתחזק — *Be strong, be strong and let us strengthen ourselves.* My prayer to Hashem is, that He grant me the strength to continue to disseminate Torah, through the spoken and written word, in tranquility, good health and with peace of mind.

Raphael Pelcovitz

Adar II, 5749

ספר ויקרא
Vayikra/Leviticus

Sforno's Introduction

In this third book we are told how various sacrifices were ordered so as to secure (God's) Presence in their midst. Among them were sin-offerings, guilt-offerings and communal-drink offerings to eliminate the evil (consequences) of communal and private transgressions (*Parshiyos Vayikra-Tzav*). We are then cautioned regarding various defilements caused by reproduction, by ethical and moral (errors), through (prohibited) food and by contact, carrying and resting beneath the same roof (*Parshiyos Tazria-Metzora*). (Then follows) the order of the festivals (and) holy convocations for the purpose of gathering (the people) together on special days in the service of God, the Blessed One (*Parashas Emor*). (Next follows) the order of the *Shemittah* (Sabbatical year) and the *Yovel,* (Jubilee) through which (Israel) will merit to inherit God's land, which has been prepared for His service (*Parashas Behar*) and in which He designated (all) material things necessary for temporal life (lit. life of the hour) so that they might support themselves painlessly, and that their hearts be unencumbered, enabling them to serve Him — as it says, וַיִּתֵּן לָהֶם אַרְצוֹת גּוֹיִם וַעֲמַל לְאֻמִּים יִירָשׁוּ בַּעֲבוּר יִשְׁמְרוּ חֻקָּיו, *And He gave them the lands of the nations and they inherited the toil of nations, that they might observe His statutes* (*Psalms* 105:44-45). Regarding all this, He imposed an oath upon them after they nullified His first covenant through their sin (of the Golden Calf), and at the end of the curses we are told of the redemption of Israel after (their) despair (*Parashas Bechukosai*), and thus the third book concludes.

פרשת ויקרא
Parashas Vayikra

א א־ב וַיִּקְרָא אֶל־מֹשֶׁה וַיְדַבֵּר יהוה אֵלָיו מֵאֹהֶל מוֹעֵד לֵאמֹר: דַּבֵּר אֶל־בְּנֵי
יִשְׂרָאֵל וְאָמַרְתָּ אֲלֵהֶם אָדָם כִּי־יַקְרִיב מִכֶּם קָרְבָּן לַיהוה מִן־הַבְּהֵמָה

I

1. וַיִּקְרָא אֶל מֹשֶׁה — *And He called to Moses.* Constantly from the midst of the cloud, similar to (the experience at) Mt. Sinai, as it says, וַיִּקְרָא אֶל מֹשֶׁה בַּיּוֹם הַשְּׁבִיעִי מִתּוֹךְ הֶעָנָן, *He called to Moses, on the seventh day, out of the midst of the cloud* (*Exodus* 24:16), for he (Moses) would never enter there without permission.

מֵאֹהֶל מוֹעֵד — *Out of the Tent of Meeting.* Moses did not enter the Tent of Meeting then, while the glory (of God) was there, which was on the day Moses completed erecting the *Mishkan,* at which time the glory descended to sanctify the place and its servants, as it says, וְנֹעַדְתִּי שָׁמָּה לִבְנֵי יִשְׂרָאֵל וְנִקְדַּשׁ בִּכְבֹדִי. וְקִדַּשְׁתִּי אֶת אֹהֶל מוֹעֵד וְאֶת הַמִּזְבֵּחַ וְאֶת אַהֲרֹן וְאֶת בָּנָיו, *And there I will meet with the Children of Israel and* (*the Tent*) *shall be sanctified by My glory. And I will sanctify the Tent of Meeting and the altar; also Aaron and his sons* (*Exodus* 29:43,44). And so He did in Solomon's Temple as it says, וְלֹא יָכְלוּ הַכֹּהֲנִים לַעֲמֹד לְשָׁרֵת מִפְּנֵי הֶעָנָן, כִּי מָלֵא כְבוֹד ה׳ אֶת בֵּית ה׳, *The Kohanim could not stand to minister because of the cloud, for the glory of* HASHEM *filled the house of* HASHEM (*I Kings* 8:11) and thus He sanctified the place, as it says, הִקְדַּשְׁתִּי אֶת הַבַּיִת הַזֶּה אֲשֶׁר בָּנִתָה, *I have hallowed this house which you have built* (ibid. 9:3). From that first day forward, however, Moses entered the Tent of Meeting outside the veil and the word (of God) came to him from above the ark cover, as it says, וּבְבֹא מֹשֶׁה אֶל אֹהֶל מוֹעֵד לְדַבֵּר אִתּוֹ וַיִּשְׁמַע אֶת הַקּוֹל מִדַּבֵּר אֵלָיו מֵעַל הַכַּפֹּרֶת, *And when Moses went into the Tent of Meeting that He might speak with him, then he heard the Voice speaking to him from above the ark cover* (*Numbers* 7:89).

2. אָדָם כִּי יַקְרִיב מִכֶּם — *When any man of you brings an offering ...* when he sacrifices himself (lit., from yourself) through confession and submission, akin to, וּנְשַׁלְּמָה פָרִים שְׂפָתֵינוּ, *So we will offer the words of our lips instead of calves* (*Hosea* 14:3) and as it says, זִבְחֵי אֱלֹהִים רוּחַ נִשְׁבָּרָה, *The sacrifices of God are a broken spirit*

NOTES

I

1. וַיִּקְרָא אֶל מֹשֶׁה ... מֵאֹהֶל מוֹעֵד — *And He called to Moses ... out of the Tent of Meeting.* The Book of *Exodus* ends with a description of the cloud covering the אֹהֶל מוֹעֵד, *Tent of Meeting,* and the glory of God filling the *Mishkan* in such a manner that Moses could not enter, but remained standing outside. Therefore, God had to call to him *from* the אֹהֶל מוֹעֵד, the meaning of the verse being *And He called from the Tent of Meeting to Moses and spoke to him* (as the *Rashbam* explains). Now this only happened on the day that the *Mishkan* was completed. After that first day, as the *Sforno* explains, Moses could enter the Tent and God would speak to him from the other side of the veil from above the ark cover. However, the cloud of glory hovered over the Tent at all times when they were encamped in the wilderness, and God would *always* call to Moses from the midst of the cloud, as both the *Sforno* and *Rashi* explain, based on the *Sifra.* The phenomena of the intensity of the cloud coming to rest on the first day after completion of the *Mishkan,* as well as on the day Solomon's Temple was inaugurated, is explained by the *Sforno* as a Divine act of sanctification of the holy place and the *Kohanim,* as explicitly stated in *Exodus* 29:43,44 and in *I Kings* 9:3.

2. אָדָם כִּי יַקְרִיב מִכֶּם — *When any man of you brings an offering.* The phrase מִכֶּם means *'from you,'* i.e., from yourself. When one brings a sacrifice it is symbolic of offering himself to God in the sense of submitting his will to the will of God. By doing so, he manifests repentance for any actions which were in defiance of God's will. This interpreta-

(*Psalms* 51:19), for He has no desire for fools who bring offerings without a (sense) of prior submission (to God), and our Sages have already said, 'מִכֶּם, *From you*, and not all of you, to exclude the apostate' (*Chullin* 8a).

מִן הַבְּהֵמָה — *Of the cattle.* If he sacrifices an animal it shall be only from the species of herd or flock but not from the species of beasts, even though they are included in (the term) בְּהֵמָה, *animal*, as it says, זֹאת הַבְּהֵמָה אֲשֶׁר תֹּאכֵלוּ . . . אַיָּל וּצְבִי, *These are the animals which you may eat . . . the hart and the deer* (*Deut.* 14:4,5). Now the intent of these chapters is to explain the categories of *those who bring* sacrifices, of those (animals) that can be offered, the types of sacrifices and the reason for (various) offerings. He (first) explains that free-will offerings are accepted from every man, even from heathens (lit., the nations) as is explained later on, when (the Torah) says, *Neither from the hand of a foreigner shall you offer the bread of your God of any of these, because their corruption is in them, there is a blemish in them* (22:25). Now behold that apostates (מְשׁוּמָּדִים) are worse than heathens, especially those who are idolaters or desecrate the Sabbath in public. (The Torah then) explains that the species of sacrifices are herd and flock among the cattle, turtledoves and young pigeons from the fowl, and fine flour, oil and frankincense (for a meal offering). (The Torah then) explains the types of sacrifices, among them burnt offerings, peace offerings and meal offerings which can at times be brought as a free will offering, and (others) among them are sin offerings and guilt offerings which are only brought if obligated to do so. From this (i.e., the above) the affair of Cain can be clarified (explained) when it says, וְאֶל קַיִן וְאֶל מִנְחָתוֹ לֹא שָׁעָה, *But to Cain and to his offering He did not turn* (*Genesis* 4:5), for he was of the class of heretics, as the end of the story shows (lit., whose conclusion proves the beginning), from whom offerings are not accepted, and (also) his offering was from a kind not fitting for sacrifice. Also by Noah (we find) when it says, וַיָּרַח ה' אֶת רֵיחַ הַנִּיחֹחַ, *And HASHEM smelled the pleasing aroma* (*Genesis* 8:21), meaning that He (God) accepted those parts of his offerings which were fitting to be a pleasing aroma, being that they were from the species fitting to be sacrificed, but He did not accept all his offerings which were מִכֹּל הַבְּהֵמָה הַטְּהֹרָה וּמִכֹּל הָעוֹף הַטָּהוֹר, *of every tahor* (i.e., kosher) *animal and of every tahor* (i.e., kosher) *bird* (ibid. v. 20). We can (now) also understand what is meant by the statement, זֶבַח וּמִנְחָה לֹא חָפַצְתָּ אָזְנַיִם כָּרִיתָ לִּי, *You do not desire sacrifice nor meal offering, You have opened my ears* (*Psalms* 40:7), and when it states, לָמָּה לִּי רֹב זִבְחֵיכֶם, *To what purpose is the multitude of your sacrifices?* (*Isaiah* 1:11) and many more such (verses) in holy books, for indeed it is proper that he who brings the offering be a man acceptable to do so, choosing from the species fitting for sacrifice, which are suitable for attaining the purpose for which he brought the offering. He should lay his hand on the sacrifice, as though he was falling down and praying (to God) that his iniquity be on the head of the sacrifice, similar to the scapegoat (16:21), and thus he will manifest the submissive thoughts of repentance which are in his heart.

NOTES

tion is not in conflict with the Sages' exclusion of the apostate from the privilege of bringing sacrifices, for an apostate cannot meet these requirements and comply with the true purpose and motivation which must underlie all offerings, as already explained.

מִן הַבְּהֵמָה — *Of the cattle.* The term בְּהֵמָה is an all-inclusive generic one, as the *Sforno* proves from the verse in *Deuteronomy*, since a hart and a deer are חַיּוֹת, *beasts*, yet are included in the general class of בְּהֵמָה, *animals.* Nonetheless, the Torah, by specifying בָּקָר, *herd*, and

א ג מִן־הַבָּקָר וּמִן־הַצֹּאן תַּקְרִיבוּ אֶת־קָרְבַּנְכֶם׃ אִם־עֹלָה קָרְבָּנוֹ מִן־הַבָּקָר
זָכָר תָּמִים יַקְרִיבֶנּוּ אֶל־פֶּתַח אֹהֶל מוֹעֵד יַקְרִיב אֹתוֹ לִרְצֹנוֹ לִפְנֵי יהוה׃
ד־ה וְסָמַךְ יָדוֹ עַל רֹאשׁ הָעֹלָה וְנִרְצָה לוֹ לְכַפֵּר עָלָיו׃ וְשָׁחַט אֶת־בֶּן הַבָּקָר
לִפְנֵי יהוה וְהִקְרִיבוּ בְּנֵי אַהֲרֹן הַכֹּהֲנִים אֶת־הַדָּם וְזָרְקוּ אֶת־הַדָּם
ו עַל־הַמִּזְבֵּחַ סָבִיב אֲשֶׁר־פֶּתַח אֹהֶל מוֹעֵד׃ וְהִפְשִׁיט אֶת־הָעֹלָה וְנִתַּח אֹתָהּ
ז לִנְתָחֶיהָ׃ וְנָתְנוּ בְּנֵי אַהֲרֹן הַכֹּהֵן אֵשׁ עַל־הַמִּזְבֵּחַ וְעָרְכוּ עֵצִים עַל־הָאֵשׁ׃
ח וְעָרְכוּ בְּנֵי אַהֲרֹן הַכֹּהֲנִים אֵת הַנְּתָחִים אֶת־הָרֹאשׁ וְאֶת־הַפָּדֶר עַל־הָעֵצִים
ט אֲשֶׁר עַל־הָאֵשׁ אֲשֶׁר עַל־הַמִּזְבֵּחַ׃ וְקִרְבּוֹ וּכְרָעָיו יִרְחַץ בַּמָּיִם וְהִקְטִיר
י הַכֹּהֵן אֶת־הַכֹּל הַמִּזְבֵּחָה עֹלָה אִשֵּׁה רֵיחַ־נִיחוֹחַ לַיהוה׃ וְאִם־
מִן־הַצֹּאן קָרְבָּנוֹ מִן־הַכְּשָׂבִים אוֹ מִן־הָעִזִּים לְעֹלָה זָכָר תָּמִים יַקְרִיבֶנּוּ׃
יא וְשָׁחַט אֹתוֹ עַל יֶרֶךְ הַמִּזְבֵּחַ צָפֹנָה לִפְנֵי יהוה וְזָרְקוּ בְּנֵי אַהֲרֹן הַכֹּהֲנִים
יב אֶת־דָּמוֹ עַל־הַמִּזְבֵּחַ סָבִיב׃ וְנִתַּח אֹתוֹ לִנְתָחָיו וְאֶת־רֹאשׁוֹ וְאֶת־פִּדְרוֹ
יג וְעָרַךְ הַכֹּהֵן אֹתָם עַל־הָעֵצִים אֲשֶׁר עַל־הָאֵשׁ אֲשֶׁר עַל־הַמִּזְבֵּחַ׃ וְהַקֶּרֶב
וְהַכְּרָעַיִם יִרְחַץ בַּמָּיִם וְהִקְרִיב הַכֹּהֵן אֶת־הַכֹּל וְהִקְטִיר הַמִּזְבֵּחָה עֹלָה הוּא
אִשֵּׁה רֵיחַ נִיחֹחַ לַיהוה׃

---

4. וְנִרְצָה לוֹ לְכַפֵּר עָלָיו — *And it shall be accepted for him to make atonement for him.* Now being that the kinds of sin (are varied), some being only in the thoughts of (man's) heart, while some are also in deed, (therefore) to atone for the thoughts of the heart, it is proper that those parts of the sacrifice which are burnt, namely the עוֹלָה, *burnt offering,* the אֵימוּרִים, *limbs of the sacrifice which are burnt,* and the מַזְכֶּרֶת הַמִּנְחָה, *the memorial of the meal offerings,* be consumed by the flames of the altar. (However) to atone for (sinful) deeds, it is proper that certain parts of the

NOTES

צֹאן, *flock*, disqualifies חַיּוֹת from the altar.

Three areas are covered in these chapters. The first is the מַקְרִיב, *he who brings the offering,* i.e., his qualifications. The second are the species of animals and birds that are acceptable and the third are the types of sacrifices, which vary in accordance with the purpose for which they are offered. The *Sforno,* commenting on the first three chapters of *Leviticus* makes the following points:

(a) The reason God did not accept Cain's offering is because he was not qualified to bring a sacrifice since he proved to be a heretic after the murder of his brother, as reflected in his answers to God (see *Genesis* 4:9 and the *Sforno* there). The second reason for God's rejection was the fact that Cain's offering was unworthy and not fitting to be brought to God (see the *Sforno, Genesis* 4:5).

(b) After the flood Noah brought sacrifices from *all* the clean animals and birds, including those which the Torah here does not consider acceptable for the purpose of קָרְבָּן, *sacrifice.* The *Sforno* interprets the verse, *smelled the pleasing aroma,* as applying only to those animals and fowl which were acceptable as offerings. It is interesting to note that the *Sforno* on *Genesis* 8:21 comments that God accepted *all* of Noah's sacrifices since at that time (before the giving of the Torah) all clean animals and birds were acceptable and only after the giving of the Torah were some qualified and others not. It is possible that the *Sforno* here retreats from his original opinion or perhaps the text there is incorrect and should read as it does here, *Those that were fitting to be accepted for a pleasing aroma.*

(c) Being that there are restrictions regarding both the one who brings the offering and the types of animals and fowl offered, the verses cited by the *Sforno* from *Psalms* and *Isaiah* become clear and understandable. God is not rejecting sacrifices out of hand, as some latter-day critics would have it; He is rejecting only those which do not meet His standards.

4. וְנִרְצָה לוֹ לְכַפֵּר עָלָיו — *And it shall be accepted for him to make atonement for him.* The ceremony of *semichah,* in which the

שני יד וְאִם מִן־הָעוֹף עֹלָה קָרְבָּנוֹ לַיהוָה וְהִקְרִיב מִן־הַתֹּרִים אוֹ מִן־בְּנֵי הַיּוֹנָה
טו אֶת־קָרְבָּנוֹ׃ וְהִקְרִיבוֹ הַכֹּהֵן אֶל־הַמִּזְבֵּחַ וּמָלַק אֶת־רֹאשׁוֹ וְהִקְטִיר
טז הַמִּזְבֵּחָה וְנִמְצָה דָמוֹ עַל קִיר הַמִּזְבֵּחַ׃ וְהֵסִיר אֶת־מֻרְאָתוֹ בְּנֹצָתָהּ וְהִשְׁלִיךְ
יז אֹתָהּ אֵצֶל הַמִּזְבֵּחַ קֵדְמָה אֶל־מְקוֹם הַדָּשֶׁן׃ וְשִׁסַּע אֹתוֹ בִכְנָפָיו לֹא יַבְדִּיל
וְהִקְטִיר אֹתוֹ הַכֹּהֵן הַמִּזְבֵּחָה עַל־הָעֵצִים אֲשֶׁר עַל־הָאֵשׁ עֹלָה הוּא אִשֵּׁה
ב א רֵיחַ נִיחֹחַ לַיהוָה׃ וְנֶפֶשׁ כִּי־תַקְרִיב קָרְבַּן מִנְחָה לַיהוָה
ב סֹלֶת יִהְיֶה קָרְבָּנוֹ וְיָצַק עָלֶיהָ שֶׁמֶן וְנָתַן עָלֶיהָ לְבֹנָה׃ וֶהֱבִיאָהּ אֶל־בְּנֵי
אַהֲרֹן הַכֹּהֲנִים וְקָמַץ מִשָּׁם מְלֹא קֻמְצוֹ מִסָּלְתָּהּ וּמִשַּׁמְנָהּ עַל כָּל־לְבֹנָתָהּ
ג וְהִקְטִיר הַכֹּהֵן אֶת־אַזְכָּרָתָהּ הַמִּזְבֵּחָה אִשֵּׁה רֵיחַ נִיחֹחַ לַיהוָה׃ וְהַנּוֹתֶרֶת
ד מִן־הַמִּנְחָה לְאַהֲרֹן וּלְבָנָיו קֹדֶשׁ קָדָשִׁים מֵאִשֵּׁי יהוָה׃ וְכִי
תַקְרִב קָרְבַּן מִנְחָה מַאֲפֵה תַנּוּר סֹלֶת חַלּוֹת מַצֹּת בְּלוּלֹת בַּשֶּׁמֶן וּרְקִיקֵי
ה מַצּוֹת מְשֻׁחִים בַּשָּׁמֶן׃ וְאִם־מִנְחָה עַל־הַמַּחֲבַת קָרְבָּנֶךָ
ו סֹלֶת בְּלוּלָה בַשֶּׁמֶן מַצָּה תִהְיֶה׃ פָּתוֹת אֹתָהּ פִּתִּים וְיָצַקְתָּ עָלֶיהָ שָׁמֶן
שלישי ז מִנְחָה הִוא׃ וְאִם־מִנְחַת מַרְחֶשֶׁת קָרְבָּנֶךָ סֹלֶת בַּשֶּׁמֶן
ח תֵּעָשֶׂה׃ וְהֵבֵאתָ אֶת־הַמִּנְחָה אֲשֶׁר יֵעָשֶׂה מֵאֵלֶּה לַיהוָה וְהִקְרִיבָהּ
ט אֶל־הַכֹּהֵן וְהִגִּישָׁהּ אֶל־הַמִּזְבֵּחַ׃ וְהֵרִים הַכֹּהֵן מִן־הַמִּנְחָה אֶת־אַזְכָּרָתָהּ
י וְהִקְטִיר הַמִּזְבֵּחָה אִשֵּׁה רֵיחַ נִיחֹחַ לַיהוָה׃ וְהַנּוֹתֶרֶת מִן־הַמִּנְחָה לְאַהֲרֹן
יא וּלְבָנָיו קֹדֶשׁ קָדָשִׁים מֵאִשֵּׁי יהוָה׃ כָּל־הַמִּנְחָה אֲשֶׁר תַּקְרִיבוּ לַיהוָה לֹא

---

sacrifice be given to the *Kohanim*, the servants of God who occupy themselves with His service, as a symbolic exchange of the limbs of the sinner which were used for evildoing, as it says, *He has given it to you to bear the iniquity of the congregation, to make atonement for them* (10:17). And so our Sages say that 'the *Kohanim* eat (from the sacrifice) and the owners gain atonement' (*Pesachim* 59b). Now being that the evil acts which are fitting to be atoned for through a sacrifice are of two categories, some connected with serious iniquities such as (those) which incur the penalty of *kares, excision,* while some are lighter than those but do (cause) desecration of the holy, then behold, for the first (type) of sin, a sin offering is suitable, to cleanse (purge) the soul defiled by a sin incurring *kares*, as it says, וְנִכְרְתָה הַנֶּפֶשׁ הַהִוא, *that soul shall be cut off* (*Exodus* 31:14); and (as for) the second type, a guilt offering is suitable to remove the desecration of which he is guilty. This (shall be) through (his) submission as manifested through the sacrifice, coupled with repentance; and there is one law for both of them (i.e., sin offering and guilt offering). However, peace offerings associate the owners with the servants of God *to serve Him in one accord* (based on *Zephaniah* 3:9). Now being that sinners are of divergent degrees, some of them more prone to stumble into sin, (while) others are further removed from it and it is rare that they (will sin), therefore (the Torah) addresses itself to them in different ways and their sacrifices are (also) diverse, and thus regarding the anointed *Kohen*, because he is unlikely to slip into sin, it says . . .

NOTES

person who brings the offering lays his hands on its head, is explained by the *Sforno* as being not only symbolic of the transference of his sin to the animal but also a manifestation of his submission to God and a sign of his desire to repent.

תַעֲשֶׂה חָמֵץ כִּי כָל־שְׂאֹר וְכָל־דְּבַשׁ לֹא־תַקְטִירוּ מִמֶּנּוּ אִשֶּׁה לַיהוָה׃
יב קָרְבַּן רֵאשִׁית תַּקְרִיבוּ אֹתָם לַיהוָה וְאֶל־הַמִּזְבֵּחַ לֹא־יַעֲלוּ לְרֵיחַ נִיחֹחַ׃
יג וְכָל־קָרְבַּן מִנְחָתְךָ בַּמֶּלַח תִּמְלָח וְלֹא תַשְׁבִּית מֶלַח בְּרִית אֱלֹהֶיךָ מֵעַל
יד מִנְחָתֶךָ עַל כָּל־קָרְבָּנְךָ תַּקְרִיב מֶלַח׃ וְאִם־תַּקְרִיב מִנְחַת
בִּכּוּרִים לַיהוָה אָבִיב קָלוּי בָּאֵשׁ גֶּרֶשׂ כַּרְמֶל תַּקְרִיב אֵת מִנְחַת בִּכּוּרֶיךָ׃
טו-טז וְנָתַתָּ עָלֶיהָ שֶׁמֶן וְשַׂמְתָּ עָלֶיהָ לְבֹנָה מִנְחָה הִוא׃ וְהִקְטִיר הַכֹּהֵן אֶת־
אַזְכָּרָתָהּ מִגִּרְשָׂהּ וּמִשַּׁמְנָהּ עַל כָּל־לְבֹנָתָהּ אִשֶּׁה לַיהוָה׃
רביעי א וְאִם־זֶבַח שְׁלָמִים קָרְבָּנוֹ אִם מִן־הַבָּקָר הוּא מַקְרִיב אִם־זָכָר אִם־נְקֵבָה
ב תָּמִים יַקְרִיבֶנּוּ לִפְנֵי יהוה׃ וְסָמַךְ יָדוֹ עַל־רֹאשׁ קָרְבָּנוֹ וּשְׁחָטוֹ פֶּתַח אֹהֶל
ג ג מוֹעֵד וְזָרְקוּ בְּנֵי אַהֲרֹן הַכֹּהֲנִים אֶת־הַדָּם עַל־הַמִּזְבֵּחַ סָבִיב׃ וְהִקְרִיב מִזֶּבַח
הַשְּׁלָמִים אִשֶּׁה לַיהוָה אֶת־הַחֵלֶב הַמְכַסֶּה אֶת־הַקֶּרֶב וְאֵת כָּל־הַחֵלֶב
ד אֲשֶׁר עַל־הַקֶּרֶב׃ וְאֵת שְׁתֵּי הַכְּלָיֹת וְאֶת־הַחֵלֶב אֲשֶׁר עֲלֵהֶן אֲשֶׁר
ה עַל־הַכְּסָלִים וְאֶת־הַיֹּתֶרֶת עַל־הַכָּבֵד עַל־הַכְּלָיוֹת יְסִירֶנָּה׃ וְהִקְטִירוּ אֹתוֹ
בְנֵי־אַהֲרֹן הַמִּזְבֵּחָה עַל־הָעֹלָה אֲשֶׁר עַל־הָעֵצִים אֲשֶׁר עַל־הָאֵשׁ אִשֵּׁה
רֵיחַ נִיחֹחַ לַיהוָה׃
ו וְאִם־מִן־הַצֹּאן קָרְבָּנוֹ לְזֶבַח שְׁלָמִים לַיהוָה זָכָר אוֹ נְקֵבָה תָּמִים יַקְרִיבֶנּוּ׃
ז-ח אִם־כֶּשֶׂב הוּא־מַקְרִיב אֶת־קָרְבָּנוֹ וְהִקְרִיב אֹתוֹ לִפְנֵי יהוה׃ וְסָמַךְ אֶת־יָדוֹ
עַל־רֹאשׁ קָרְבָּנוֹ וְשָׁחַט אֹתוֹ לִפְנֵי אֹהֶל מוֹעֵד וְזָרְקוּ בְּנֵי אַהֲרֹן אֶת־דָּמוֹ
ט עַל־הַמִּזְבֵּחַ סָבִיב׃ וְהִקְרִיב מִזֶּבַח הַשְּׁלָמִים אִשֶּׁה לַיהוָה חֶלְבּוֹ הָאַלְיָה
תְמִימָה לְעֻמַּת הֶעָצֶה יְסִירֶנָּה וְאֶת־הַחֵלֶב הַמְכַסֶּה אֶת־הַקֶּרֶב וְאֵת
י כָּל־הַחֵלֶב אֲשֶׁר עַל־הַקֶּרֶב׃ וְאֵת שְׁתֵּי הַכְּלָיֹת וְאֶת־הַחֵלֶב אֲשֶׁר עֲלֵהֶן
יא אֲשֶׁר עַל־הַכְּסָלִים וְאֶת־הַיֹּתֶרֶת עַל־הַכָּבֵד עַל־הַכְּלָיֹת יְסִירֶנָּה׃ וְהִקְטִירוֹ
הַכֹּהֵן הַמִּזְבֵּחָה לֶחֶם אִשֶּׁה לַיהוָה׃
יב-יג וְאִם עֵז קָרְבָּנוֹ וְהִקְרִיבוֹ לִפְנֵי יהוה׃ וְסָמַךְ אֶת־יָדוֹ עַל־רֹאשׁוֹ וְשָׁחַט אֹתוֹ
יד לִפְנֵי אֹהֶל מוֹעֵד וְזָרְקוּ בְּנֵי אַהֲרֹן אֶת־דָּמוֹ עַל־הַמִּזְבֵּחַ סָבִיב׃ וְהִקְרִיב
מִמֶּנּוּ קָרְבָּנוֹ אִשֶּׁה לַיהוָה אֶת־הַחֵלֶב הַמְכַסֶּה אֶת־הַקֶּרֶב וְאֵת כָּל־הַחֵלֶב
טו אֲשֶׁר עַל־הַקֶּרֶב׃ וְאֵת שְׁתֵּי הַכְּלָיֹת וְאֶת־הַחֵלֶב אֲשֶׁר עֲלֵהֶן אֲשֶׁר
טז עַל־הַכְּסָלִים וְאֶת־הַיֹּתֶרֶת עַל־הַכָּבֵד עַל־הַכְּלָיֹת יְסִירֶנָּה׃ וְהִקְטִירָם הַכֹּהֵן
יז הַמִּזְבֵּחָה לֶחֶם אִשֶּׁה לְרֵיחַ נִיחֹחַ כָּל־חֵלֶב לַיהוָה׃ חֻקַּת עוֹלָם לְדֹרֹתֵיכֶם
בְּכֹל מוֹשְׁבֹתֵיכֶם כָּל־חֵלֶב וְכָל־דָּם לֹא תֹאכֵלוּ׃
ד חמישי א-ב וַיְדַבֵּר יהוה אֶל־מֹשֶׁה לֵּאמֹר׃ דַּבֵּר אֶל־בְּנֵי יִשְׂרָאֵל לֵאמֹר נֶפֶשׁ כִּי־
תֶחֱטָא בִשְׁגָגָה מִכֹּל מִצְוֹת יהוה אֲשֶׁר לֹא תֵעָשֶׂינָה וְעָשָׂה מֵאַחַת מֵהֵנָּה׃
ג אִם הַכֹּהֵן הַמָּשִׁיחַ יֶחֱטָא לְאַשְׁמַת הָעָם וְהִקְרִיב עַל חַטָּאתוֹ אֲשֶׁר חָטָא

IV

3. אִם הַכֹּהֵן הַמָּשִׁיחַ יֶחֱטָא לְאַשְׁמַת הָעָם — *If the anointed Kohen shall sin* (*due*) *to the guilt of the people.* That is to say, he will not sin (even) inadvertently except for *the people that ensnare* (based on *Job* 34:30), as (our Sages) say, 'He who prays and makes a mistake, it is a bad omen for himself; and if he is the messenger of the congrega-

ד פַּר בֶּן־בָּקָר תָּמִים לַיהוָה לְחַטָּאת׃ וְהֵבִיא אֶת־הַפָּר אֶל־פֶּתַח אֹהֶל מוֹעֵד
ה לִפְנֵי יְהוָה וְסָמַךְ אֶת־יָדוֹ עַל־רֹאשׁ הַפָּר וְשָׁחַט אֶת־הַפָּר לִפְנֵי יְהוָה׃ וְלָקַח
ו הַכֹּהֵן הַמָּשִׁיחַ מִדַּם הַפָּר וְהֵבִיא אֹתוֹ אֶל־אֹהֶל מוֹעֵד׃ וְטָבַל הַכֹּהֵן אֶת־
אֶצְבָּעוֹ בַּדָּם וְהִזָּה מִן־הַדָּם שֶׁבַע פְּעָמִים לִפְנֵי יְהוָה אֶת־פְּנֵי פָּרֹכֶת
ז הַקֹּדֶשׁ׃ וְנָתַן הַכֹּהֵן מִן־הַדָּם עַל־קַרְנוֹת מִזְבַּח קְטֹרֶת הַסַּמִּים לִפְנֵי יְהוָה
אֲשֶׁר בְּאֹהֶל מוֹעֵד וְאֵת ׀ כָּל־דַּם הַפָּר יִשְׁפֹּךְ אֶל־יְסוֹד מִזְבַּח הָעֹלָה
ח אֲשֶׁר־פֶּתַח אֹהֶל מוֹעֵד׃ וְאֶת־כָּל־חֵלֶב פַּר הַחַטָּאת יָרִים מִמֶּנּוּ אֶת־הַחֵלֶב
ט הַמְכַסֶּה עַל־הַקֶּרֶב וְאֵת כָּל־הַחֵלֶב אֲשֶׁר עַל־הַקֶּרֶב׃ וְאֵת שְׁתֵּי הַכְּלָיֹת
וְאֶת־הַחֵלֶב אֲשֶׁר עֲלֵיהֶן אֲשֶׁר עַל־הַכְּסָלִים וְאֶת־הַיֹּתֶרֶת עַל־הַכָּבֵד עַל־
י הַכְּלָיוֹת יְסִירֶנָּה׃ כַּאֲשֶׁר יוּרַם מִשּׁוֹר זֶבַח הַשְּׁלָמִים וְהִקְטִירָם הַכֹּהֵן עַל
יא מִזְבַּח הָעֹלָה׃ וְאֶת־עוֹר הַפָּר וְאֶת־כָּל־בְּשָׂרוֹ עַל־רֹאשׁוֹ וְעַל־כְּרָעָיו וְקִרְבּוֹ
יב וּפִרְשׁוֹ׃ וְהוֹצִיא אֶת־כָּל־הַפָּר אֶל־מִחוּץ לַמַּחֲנֶה אֶל־מָקוֹם טָהוֹר אֶל־שֶׁפֶךְ
הַדֶּשֶׁן וְשָׂרַף אֹתוֹ עַל־עֵצִים בָּאֵשׁ עַל־שֶׁפֶךְ הַדֶּשֶׁן יִשָּׂרֵף׃
יג וְאִם כָּל־עֲדַת יִשְׂרָאֵל יִשְׁגּוּ וְנֶעְלַם דָּבָר מֵעֵינֵי הַקָּהָל וְעָשׂוּ אַחַת מִכָּל־
יד מִצְוֹת יְהוָה אֲשֶׁר לֹא־תֵעָשֶׂינָה וְאָשֵׁמוּ׃ וְנוֹדְעָה הַחַטָּאת אֲשֶׁר חָטְאוּ עָלֶיהָ
וְהִקְרִיבוּ הַקָּהָל פַּר בֶּן־בָּקָר לְחַטָּאת וְהֵבִיאוּ אֹתוֹ לִפְנֵי אֹהֶל מוֹעֵד׃
וְסָמְכוּ זִקְנֵי הָעֵדָה אֶת־יְדֵיהֶם עַל־רֹאשׁ הַפָּר לִפְנֵי יְהוָה וְשָׁחַט אֶת־הַפָּר
לִפְנֵי יְהוָה׃ וְהֵבִיא הַכֹּהֵן הַמָּשִׁיחַ מִדַּם הַפָּר אֶל־אֹהֶל מוֹעֵד׃ וְטָבַל הַכֹּהֵן

---

tion (ש״ץ), it is a bad omen for those who sent him' (*Berachos* 34b). (Now) his offering is burnt but the *Kohen* gets no part of it, and therefore the phrase וְאָשֵׁם, *and he is guilty*, is not written in this instance as it is written regarding all other sinners, for when it states וְאָשֵׁם it indicates an admonition to repent, but this is not applicable to the anointed *Kohen* for he did not sin on his own (lit., from his heart) whatsoever, but it happened *due to the guilt of the people*. (Now) regarding the inadvertent sin of the Sanhedrin (court), which is also a far-removed (occurrence), it says . . .

13. יִשְׁגּוּ וְנֶעְלַם דָּבָר מֵעֵינֵי הַקָּהָל — *Shall err, the thing being hidden from the eyes of the assembly.* For being that they are the eyes of the assembly (the public) who should see for others, they themselves did not look (observe) well, and of them it is also said (וְאָשֵׁמוּ, *and are guilty*).

NOTES

IV

3. אִם הַכֹּהֵן הַמָּשִׁיחַ יֶחֱטָא לְאַשְׁמַת הָעָם — *If the anointed Kohen shall sin (due) to the guilt of the people.* The *Sforno* interprets the phrase אָשֵׁם, *guilty*, as implying the need for repentance. In this fashion, he explains the reason for the Torah's inclusion or exclusion of this phrase in subsequent verses. See 4:3,21,22,27. The *Sforno* is of the opinion that the *Kohen Gadol*, High Priest (the anointed one), as the representative of the people, is himself above suspicion, but he may sin without intent because of their sins. Therefore, it is not he who is guilty and must repent, but the people. This explains the absence of the word וְאָשֵׁם, *and he is guilty*, from this portion, as explained above.

13. יִשְׁגּוּ וְנֶעְלַם דָּבָר מֵעֵינֵי הַקָּהָל — *Shall err, the thing being hidden from the eyes of the assembly.* The Sanhedrin, unlike the *Kohen Gadol*, are considered to be an integral part of the people. When they err there is direct personal involvement and responsibility; hence both they and the people are guilty (וְאָשֵׁמוּ).

יח אֶצְבָּעוֹ מִן־הַדָּם וְהִזָּה שֶׁבַע פְּעָמִים לִפְנֵי יהוה אֶת־פְּנֵי הַפָּרֹכֶת׃ וּמִן־הַדָּם
יִתֵּן ׀ עַל־קַרְנֹת הַמִּזְבֵּחַ אֲשֶׁר לִפְנֵי יהוה אֲשֶׁר בְּאֹהֶל מוֹעֵד וְאֵת כָּל־הַדָּם
יט יִשְׁפֹּךְ אֶל־יְסוֹד מִזְבַּח הָעֹלָה אֲשֶׁר־פֶּתַח אֹהֶל מוֹעֵד׃ וְאֵת כָּל־חֶלְבּוֹ יָרִים
כ מִמֶּנּוּ וְהִקְטִיר הַמִּזְבֵּחָה׃ וְעָשָׂה לַפָּר כַּאֲשֶׁר עָשָׂה לְפַר הַחַטָּאת כֵּן יַעֲשֶׂה־
כא לּוֹ וְכִפֶּר עֲלֵהֶם הַכֹּהֵן וְנִסְלַח לָהֶם׃ וְהוֹצִיא אֶת־הַפָּר אֶל־מִחוּץ לַמַּחֲנֶה
וְשָׂרַף אֹתוֹ כַּאֲשֶׁר שָׂרַף אֵת הַפָּר הָרִאשׁוֹן חַטַּאת הַקָּהָל הוּא׃
כב אֲשֶׁר נָשִׂיא יֶחֱטָא וְעָשָׂה אַחַת מִכָּל־מִצְוֺת יהוה אֱלֹהָיו אֲשֶׁר לֹא־
כג תֵעָשֶׂינָה בִּשְׁגָגָה וְאָשֵׁם׃ אוֹ־הוֹדַע אֵלָיו חַטָּאתוֹ אֲשֶׁר חָטָא בָּהּ וְהֵבִיא
כד אֶת־קָרְבָּנוֹ שְׂעִיר עִזִּים זָכָר תָּמִים׃ וְסָמַךְ יָדוֹ עַל־רֹאשׁ הַשָּׂעִיר וְשָׁחַט
כה אֹתוֹ בִּמְקוֹם אֲשֶׁר־יִשְׁחַט אֶת־הָעֹלָה לִפְנֵי יהוה חַטָּאת הוּא׃ וְלָקַח הַכֹּהֵן
מִדַּם הַחַטָּאת בְּאֶצְבָּעוֹ וְנָתַן עַל־קַרְנֹת מִזְבַּח הָעֹלָה וְאֶת־דָּמוֹ יִשְׁפֹּךְ
כו אֶל־יְסוֹד מִזְבַּח הָעֹלָה׃ וְאֶת־כָּל־חֶלְבּוֹ יַקְטִיר הַמִּזְבֵּחָה כְּחֵלֶב זֶבַח
הַשְּׁלָמִים וְכִפֶּר עָלָיו הַכֹּהֵן מֵחַטָּאתוֹ וְנִסְלַח לוֹ׃
ששי כז וְאִם־נֶפֶשׁ אַחַת תֶּחֱטָא בִשְׁגָגָה מֵעַם הָאָרֶץ בַּעֲשֹׂתָהּ אַחַת מִמִּצְוֺת יהוה
כח אֲשֶׁר לֹא־תֵעָשֶׂינָה וְאָשֵׁם׃ אוֹ הוֹדַע אֵלָיו חַטָּאתוֹ אֲשֶׁר חָטָא וְהֵבִיא
כט קָרְבָּנוֹ שְׂעִירַת עִזִּים תְּמִימָה נְקֵבָה עַל־חַטָּאתוֹ אֲשֶׁר חָטָא׃ וְסָמַךְ אֶת־
ל יָדוֹ עַל רֹאשׁ הַחַטָּאת וְשָׁחַט אֶת־הַחַטָּאת בִּמְקוֹם הָעֹלָה׃ וְלָקַח הַכֹּהֵן

---

21. חַטַּאת הַקָּהָל הוּא — *It is the sin offering for the assembly.* For this does not occur except for the iniquity of the generation as well. However, here (v. 13) (the Torah) writes וְאָשֵׁמוּ, *and are guilty,* to caution them to repent before the offering is brought. Their sin offering is also burnt and due to the severity of both (the sins of the anointed *Kohen* and of the Sanhedrin), the blood (of their sacrifices) was brought to the inner sanctuary. Now regarding the transgression of the king it says . . .

22. אֲשֶׁר נָשִׂיא יֶחֱטָא — *When a ruler sins.* For, indeed, this event is prone (to happen) that he sin, as it says, וַיִּשְׁמַן יְשֻׁרוּן וַיִּבְעָט, *But Yeshurun waxed fat and kicked* (*Deut.* 32:15), and here it says, וְאָשֵׁם, *and is guilty,* i.e., he himself will acknowledge his sin.

23. אוֹ הוֹדַע אֵלָיו — *Or it is made known to him* . . . through others. The (long vowel) *cholam* (וֹ) in the word הוֹדַע is in place of the *shuruk* (ֻ). It then says regarding the common people . . .

27. וְאִם נֶפֶשׁ אַחַת תֶּחֱטָא בִשְׁגָגָה מֵעַם הָאָרֶץ — *And if any one of the common people sin through error.* For it is a likely possibility that one of the common people will sin. Now here, and regarding the sin of the ruler it says וְאָשֵׁם, *and is guilty,* which is an admonition to repent prior to the (bringing of the) sacrifice. In both of these (cases) and by all guilt offerings, a portion is given to the *Kohanim,* for the eating of the *Kohanim* is beneficial for the atonement of the sinners.

NOTES

22. אֲשֶׁר נָשִׂיא יֶחֱטָא — *When a ruler sins.* נָשִׂיא refers to the king. It is not unusual for a man of power and wealth to sin, hence he must repent (וְאָשֵׁם). However, as a king, others need not accuse him. He will be big enough to acknowledge his own sin. There will be occasions, however, when he will be unaware and at such times it should be made known to him.

23. אוֹ הוֹדַע אֵלָיו — *Or it is made known to him.* The *Sforno* explains that the word הוֹדַע spelled with the long vowel *cholam* (וֹ) should be read as though it is written with a *shuruk* (ֻ), i.e.,

מִדָּמָהּ בְּאֶצְבָּעוֹ וְנָתַן עַל־קַרְנֹת מִזְבַּח הָעֹלָה וְאֶת־כָּל־דָּמָהּ יִשְׁפֹּךְ
לא אֶל־יְסוֹד הַמִּזְבֵּחַ׃ וְאֶת־כָּל־חֶלְבָּהּ יָסִיר כַּאֲשֶׁר הוּסַר חֵלֶב מֵעַל זֶבַח
הַשְּׁלָמִים וְהִקְטִיר הַכֹּהֵן הַמִּזְבֵּחָה לְרֵיחַ נִיחֹחַ לַיהוָה וְכִפֶּר עָלָיו הַכֹּהֵן
וְנִסְלַח לוֹ׃
לב-לג וְאִם־כֶּבֶשׂ יָבִיא קָרְבָּנוֹ לְחַטָּאת נְקֵבָה תְמִימָה יְבִיאֶנָּה׃ וְסָמַךְ אֶת־יָדוֹ עַל
רֹאשׁ הַחַטָּאת וְשָׁחַט אֹתָהּ לְחַטָּאת בִּמְקוֹם אֲשֶׁר יִשְׁחַט אֶת־הָעֹלָה׃
לד וְלָקַח הַכֹּהֵן מִדַּם הַחַטָּאת בְּאֶצְבָּעוֹ וְנָתַן עַל־קַרְנֹת מִזְבַּח הָעֹלָה
לה וְאֶת־כָּל־דָּמָהּ יִשְׁפֹּךְ אֶל־יְסוֹד הַמִּזְבֵּחַ׃ וְאֶת־כָּל־חֶלְבָּהּ יָסִיר כַּאֲשֶׁר יוּסַר
חֵלֶב־הַכֶּשֶׂב מִזֶּבַח הַשְּׁלָמִים וְהִקְטִיר הַכֹּהֵן אֹתָם הַמִּזְבֵּחָה עַל אִשֵּׁי יְהוָה
וְכִפֶּר עָלָיו הַכֹּהֵן עַל־חַטָּאתוֹ אֲשֶׁר־חָטָא וְנִסְלַח לוֹ׃
א וְנֶפֶשׁ כִּי־תֶחֱטָא וְשָׁמְעָה קוֹל אָלָה וְהוּא עֵד אוֹ רָאָה אוֹ יָדָע אִם־לוֹא יַגִּיד
ב וְנָשָׂא עֲוֺנוֹ׃ אוֹ נֶפֶשׁ אֲשֶׁר תִּגַּע בְּכָל־דָּבָר טָמֵא אוֹ בְנִבְלַת חַיָּה טְמֵאָה אוֹ
בְּנִבְלַת בְּהֵמָה טְמֵאָה אוֹ בְּנִבְלַת שֶׁרֶץ טָמֵא וְנֶעְלַם מִמֶּנּוּ וְהוּא טָמֵא
ג וְאָשֵׁם׃ אוֹ כִי יִגַּע בְּטֻמְאַת אָדָם לְכֹל טֻמְאָתוֹ אֲשֶׁר יִטְמָא בָּהּ וְנֶעְלַם
ד מִמֶּנּוּ וְהוּא יָדַע וְאָשֵׁם׃ אוֹ נֶפֶשׁ כִּי תִשָּׁבַע לְבַטֵּא בִשְׂפָתַיִם לְהָרַע ׀ אוֹ
לְהֵיטִיב לְכֹל אֲשֶׁר יְבַטֵּא הָאָדָם בִּשְׁבֻעָה וְנֶעְלַם מִמֶּנּוּ וְהוּא־יָדַע וְאָשֵׁם
ה לְאַחַת מֵאֵלֶּה׃ וְהָיָה כִי־יֶאְשַׁם לְאַחַת מֵאֵלֶּה וְהִתְוַדָּה אֲשֶׁר חָטָא עָלֶיהָ׃
ו וְהֵבִיא אֶת־אֲשָׁמוֹ לַיהוָה עַל חַטָּאתוֹ אֲשֶׁר חָטָא נְקֵבָה מִן־הַצֹּאן כִּשְׂבָּה
ז אוֹ־שְׂעִירַת עִזִּים לְחַטָּאת וְכִפֶּר עָלָיו הַכֹּהֵן מֵחַטָּאתוֹ׃ וְאִם־לֹא תַגִּיעַ יָדוֹ
דֵּי שֶׂה וְהֵבִיא אֶת־אֲשָׁמוֹ אֲשֶׁר חָטָא שְׁתֵּי תֹרִים אוֹ־שְׁנֵי בְנֵי־יוֹנָה לַיהוָה
ח אֶחָד לְחַטָּאת וְאֶחָד לְעֹלָה׃ וְהֵבִיא אֹתָם אֶל־הַכֹּהֵן וְהִקְרִיב אֶת־אֲשֶׁר
ט לַחַטָּאת רִאשׁוֹנָה וּמָלַק אֶת־רֹאשׁוֹ מִמּוּל עָרְפּוֹ וְלֹא יַבְדִּיל׃ וְהִזָּה מִדַּם
הַחַטָּאת עַל־קִיר הַמִּזְבֵּחַ וְהַנִּשְׁאָר בַּדָּם יִמָּצֵה אֶל־יְסוֹד הַמִּזְבֵּחַ חַטָּאת
י הוּא׃ וְאֶת־הַשֵּׁנִי יַעֲשֶׂה עֹלָה כַּמִּשְׁפָּט וְכִפֶּר עָלָיו הַכֹּהֵן מֵחַטָּאתוֹ
ה שביעי יא אֲשֶׁר־חָטָא וְנִסְלַח לוֹ׃ וְאִם־לֹא תַשִּׂיג יָדוֹ
לִשְׁתֵּי תֹרִים אוֹ לִשְׁנֵי בְנֵי־יוֹנָה וְהֵבִיא אֶת־קָרְבָּנוֹ אֲשֶׁר חָטָא עֲשִׂירִת
הָאֵפָה סֹלֶת לְחַטָּאת לֹא־יָשִׂים עָלֶיהָ שֶׁמֶן וְלֹא־יִתֵּן עָלֶיהָ לְבֹנָה כִּי
יב חַטָּאת הִוא׃ וֶהֱבִיאָהּ אֶל־הַכֹּהֵן וְקָמַץ הַכֹּהֵן ׀ מִמֶּנָּה מְלוֹא קֻמְצוֹ
יג אֶת־אַזְכָּרָתָהּ וְהִקְטִיר הַמִּזְבֵּחָה עַל אִשֵּׁי יְהוָה חַטָּאת הִוא׃ וְכִפֶּר עָלָיו
הַכֹּהֵן עַל־חַטָּאתוֹ אֲשֶׁר־חָטָא מֵאַחַת מֵאֵלֶּה וְנִסְלַח לוֹ וְהָיְתָה לַכֹּהֵן
יד-טו כַּמִּנְחָה׃ וַיְדַבֵּר יְהוָה אֶל־מֹשֶׁה לֵּאמֹר׃ נֶפֶשׁ כִּי־תִמְעֹל
מַעַל וְחָטְאָה בִּשְׁגָגָה מִקָּדְשֵׁי יְהוָה וְהֵבִיא אֶת־אֲשָׁמוֹ לַיהוָה אַיִל תָּמִים
טז מִן־הַצֹּאן בְּעֶרְכְּךָ כֶּסֶף־שְׁקָלִים בְּשֶׁקֶל־הַקֹּדֶשׁ לְאָשָׁם׃ וְאֵת אֲשֶׁר חָטָא
מִן־הַקֹּדֶשׁ יְשַׁלֵּם וְאֶת־חֲמִישִׁתוֹ יוֹסֵף עָלָיו וְנָתַן אֹתוֹ לַכֹּהֵן וְהַכֹּהֵן יְכַפֵּר
עָלָיו בְּאֵיל הָאָשָׁם וְנִסְלַח לוֹ׃

NOTES

הֻדַע, for then the conjugation would be in הָפְעַל which is the *passive* of הִפְעִיל, *the causative*. The meaning would then be *it is made known to him*.

יז וְאִם־נֶפֶשׁ כִּי תֶחֱטָא וְעָשְׂתָה אַחַת מִכָּל־מִצְוֺת יהוה אֲשֶׁר לֹא תֵעָשֶׂינָה
יח וְלֹא־יָדַע וְאָשֵׁם וְנָשָׂא עֲוֺנוֹ: וְהֵבִיא אַיִל תָּמִים מִן־הַצֹּאן בְּעֶרְכְּךָ לְאָשָׁם
אֶל־הַכֹּהֵן וְכִפֶּר עָלָיו הַכֹּהֵן עַל שִׁגְגָתוֹ אֲשֶׁר־שָׁגָג וְהוּא לֹא־יָדַע וְנִסְלַח לוֹ:
יט אָשָׁם הוּא אָשֹׁם אָשַׁם לַיהוה:
כ-כא וַיְדַבֵּר יהוה אֶל־מֹשֶׁה לֵּאמֹר: נֶפֶשׁ כִּי תֶחֱטָא וּמָעֲלָה מַעַל בַּיהוה וְכִחֵשׁ
כב בַּעֲמִיתוֹ בְּפִקָּדוֹן אוֹ־בִתְשׂוּמֶת יָד אוֹ בְגָזֵל אוֹ עָשַׁק אֶת־עֲמִיתוֹ: אוֹ־מָצָא
אֲבֵדָה וְכִחֶשׁ בָּהּ וְנִשְׁבַּע עַל־שָׁקֶר עַל־אַחַת מִכֹּל אֲשֶׁר־יַעֲשֶׂה הָאָדָם
כג לַחֲטֹא בָהֵנָּה: וְהָיָה כִּי־יֶחֱטָא וְאָשֵׁם וְהֵשִׁיב אֶת־הַגְּזֵלָה אֲשֶׁר גָּזָל אוֹ אֶת־
הָעֹשֶׁק אֲשֶׁר עָשָׁק אוֹ אֶת־הַפִּקָּדוֹן אֲשֶׁר הָפְקַד אִתּוֹ אוֹ אֶת־הָאֲבֵדָה אֲשֶׁר
מפטיר כד מָצָא: אוֹ מִכֹּל אֲשֶׁר־יִשָּׁבַע עָלָיו לַשֶּׁקֶר וְשִׁלַּם אֹתוֹ בְּרֹאשׁוֹ וַחֲמִשִׁתָיו יֹסֵף
כה עָלָיו לַאֲשֶׁר הוּא לוֹ יִתְּנֶנּוּ בְּיוֹם אַשְׁמָתוֹ: וְאֶת־אֲשָׁמוֹ יָבִיא לַיהוה אַיִל
כו תָּמִים מִן־הַצֹּאן בְּעֶרְכְּךָ לְאָשָׁם אֶל־הַכֹּהֵן: וְכִפֶּר עָלָיו הַכֹּהֵן לִפְנֵי יהוה
וְנִסְלַח לוֹ עַל־אַחַת מִכֹּל אֲשֶׁר־יַעֲשֶׂה לְאַשְׁמָה בָהּ:

V

17. וְאָשֵׁם וְנָשָׂא עֲוֺנוֹ — *He is guilty and shall bear his iniquity.* Our Sages know from tradition that this (verse) speaks of an אָשָׁם תָּלוּי, *guilt offering for a doubtful transgression.* He is not certain if he sinned or not, and regarding this it says, *And he shall bear his iniquity,* i.e., in accordance with what is fitting for him, whether he sinned inadvertently or (perhaps) did not lapse into sin (at all). But his transgression was that he was not careful and slipped into doubt; according to his iniquity he shall bear the punishment.

19. אָשָׁם הוּא — *It is a guilt offering.* Although at times this sacrifice (אָשָׁם תָּלוּי) may be brought and (in reality) he never stumbled into that sin, let him not think that he is bringing a secular (animal) to the courtyard (of the Temple) for indeed it is nonetheless a guilt offering, even though he did not stumble in that sin of which he is in doubt. The reason is because ...

אָשֹׁם אָשַׁם לַה׳ — *He is certainly guilty to* H*ASHEM* ... when he wasn't careful in this matter until (he reached a point) that he was in doubt.

23-25. וְהֵשִׁיב אֶת הַגְּזֵלָה ... וְאֶת אֲשָׁמוֹ יָבִיא — *And he shall restore that which he took ... and he shall bring his guilt offering.* The sacrifice cannot atone unless he first recompenses (appeases) the injured party before he brings the offering, as our Sages say, 'If one brings his guilt offering before he repays what he stole, he has not fulfilled his obligation' (*Bava Kama* 110a).

NOTES

V

19. אָשָׁם הוּא אָשֹׁם אָשַׁם לַה׳ — *It is a guilt offering he is certainly guilty to* H*ASHEM*. The *Sforno* explains the difficult wording of this verse in the following manner. One can be guilty of *actually* violating a precept of the Torah or one can be guilty of conducting himself in such a careless manner that he is unaware of his actions and cannot determine whether or not he transgressed. The latter heedless action requires atonement no less than the former overt act of transgression.

23-25. וְהֵשִׁיב אֶת הַגְּזֵלָה ... וְאֶת אֲשָׁמוֹ יָבִיא — *And he shall restore that which he took ... and he shall bring his guilt offering.* Man will not be forgiven by God for the sin committed against Him until he has rid himself of ill-begotten (stolen) gains and compensated his victim. This is similar to the last Mishnah in *Yoma* which states that Yom Kippur will not atone for man's sins against God unless one has first appeased those whom he has harmed.

פרשת צו
Parasahas Tzav

ו א-ב וַיְדַבֵּר יהוה אֶל־מֹשֶׁה לֵּאמֹר: צַו אֶת־אַהֲרֹן וְאֶת־בָּנָיו לֵאמֹר זֹאת תּוֹרַת
הָעֹלָה הִוא הָעֹלָה עַל מוֹקְדָה עַל־הַמִּזְבֵּחַ כָּל־הַלַּיְלָה עַד־הַבֹּקֶר וְאֵשׁ
ג הַמִּזְבֵּחַ תּוּקַד בּוֹ: וְלָבַשׁ הַכֹּהֵן מִדּוֹ בַד וּמִכְנְסֵי־בַד יִלְבַּשׁ עַל־בְּשָׂרוֹ וְהֵרִים
אֶת־הַדֶּשֶׁן אֲשֶׁר תֹּאכַל הָאֵשׁ אֶת־הָעֹלָה עַל־הַמִּזְבֵּחַ וְשָׂמוֹ אֵצֶל הַמִּזְבֵּחַ:
ד וּפָשַׁט אֶת־בְּגָדָיו וְלָבַשׁ בְּגָדִים אֲחֵרִים וְהוֹצִיא אֶת־הַדֶּשֶׁן אֶל־מִחוּץ
ה לַמַּחֲנֶה אֶל־מָקוֹם טָהוֹר: וְהָאֵשׁ עַל־הַמִּזְבֵּחַ תּוּקַד־בּוֹ לֹא תִכְבֶּה וּבִעֵר
עָלֶיהָ הַכֹּהֵן עֵצִים בַּבֹּקֶר בַּבֹּקֶר וְעָרַךְ עָלֶיהָ הָעֹלָה וְהִקְטִיר עָלֶיהָ חֶלְבֵי
ו-ז הַשְּׁלָמִים: אֵשׁ תָּמִיד תּוּקַד עַל־הַמִּזְבֵּחַ לֹא תִכְבֶּה: וְזֹאת
ח תּוֹרַת הַמִּנְחָה הַקְרֵב אֹתָהּ בְּנֵי־אַהֲרֹן לִפְנֵי יהוה אֶל־פְּנֵי הַמִּזְבֵּחַ: וְהֵרִים

VI

2. צַו אֶת אַהֲרֹן . . . זֹאת תּוֹרַת הָעֹלָה הִיא הָעֹלָה — *Command Aaron . . . this is the law of the burnt offering, it is that which goes up.* After telling (us) the work of the sacrifices, (the Torah) now states the laws applicable to each one of them, (including) their analytical aspects. Without a doubt, there are great differences among 'the children of the living God' (based on *Hosea* 2:1) in their works and intents, similar to the differences in the various kinds of sacrifices. (The Torah) makes mention that the entire burnt offering is brought on the altar as a sweet savor (to God); however (only) part of it *goes up* in the flame of the altar, (and of that part) it is said that it truly is הָעוֹלָה, *'the' olah.* And part of it is *beside the altar* (v. 3), namely the דֶּשֶׁן, *ashes,* which still retain some moisture in such a manner that the fire can burn within it together with the authentic (central) part of the *olah,* as it says . . .

3. הַדֶּשֶׁן אֲשֶׁר תֹּאכַל הָאֵשׁ אֶת הָעֹלָה — *The ashes of the burnt offering which the fire consumed.* And some of it is totally ashes which is brought out . . .

4. אֶל מִחוּץ לַמַּחֲנֶה אֶל מָקוֹם טָהוֹר — *Outside the camp to a clean place.* (With the *Kohen* wearing) inferior garments, nonetheless it is brought to a *clean place.*

7. תּוֹרַת הַמִּנְחָה . . . לִפְנֵי ה׳ אֶל פְּנֵי הַמִּזְבֵּחַ — *The law of the meal offering . . . before* HASHEM *in front of the altar.* (The Torah) then makes mention of the law of the

NOTES

VI

2-4. הִיא הָעֹלָה . . . הַדֶּשֶׁן אֲשֶׁר תֹּאכַל הָאֵשׁ אֶת הָעֹלָה . . . אֶל מִחוּץ לַמַּחֲנֶה אֶל מָקוֹם טָהוֹר — *It is that which goes up . . . the ashes of the burnt offering which the fire consumed . . . outside the camp to a clean place.* The *Sforno* explains that there are three parts of the burnt offering (עוֹלָה), the disposition of which are indicated in these verses. The principal part is that which is totally consumed and goes up, hence the term עוֹלָה (lit., going up). The second part consists of the ashes which still retain some fat of the animal and are burnt together with the first part. Thus the words אֶת הָעוֹלָה (v. 3) are to be translated *with* the *olah.* The third part consists of the ashes carried out of the camp by the *Kohen* after he changed his priestly garments for clothes of inferior quality, since he would be occupied with a non-holy duty. Nonetheless, the ashes are still treated with respect and placed in a מָקוֹם טָהוֹר, *clean place,* as we find in chapter 4:12, *A clean place, where the ashes are poured out* (שֶׁפֶךְ הַדֶּשֶׁן).

7. תּוֹרַת הַמִּנְחָה . . . לִפְנֵי ה׳ אֶל פְּנֵי הַמִּזְבֵּחַ — *The law of the meal offering . . . before* HASHEM *in front of the altar.* The מִנְחָה, *meal offering,* is eaten by the *Kohen*. However, a קֹמֶץ, *handful,* is brought on the altar as a רֵיחַ נִיחֹחַ, *sweet savor,* to God. The *Sforno* explains that although the *major* part of the offering is

מִמֶּנּוּ בְּקֻמְצוֹ מִסֹּלֶת הַמִּנְחָה וּמִשַּׁמְנָהּ וְאֵת כָּל־הַלְּבֹנָה אֲשֶׁר עַל־הַמִּנְחָה
ט וְהִקְטִיר הַמִּזְבֵּחַ רֵיחַ נִיחֹחַ אַזְכָּרָתָהּ לַיהוָה: וְהַנּוֹתֶרֶת מִמֶּנָּה יֹאכְלוּ אַהֲרֹן
י וּבָנָיו מַצּוֹת תֵּאָכֵל בְּמָקוֹם קָדֹשׁ בַּחֲצַר אֹהֶל־מוֹעֵד יֹאכְלוּהָ: לֹא תֵאָפֶה
חָמֵץ חֶלְקָם נָתַתִּי אֹתָהּ מֵאִשָּׁי קֹדֶשׁ קָדָשִׁים הִוא כַּחַטָּאת וְכָאָשָׁם:
יא כָּל־זָכָר בִּבְנֵי אַהֲרֹן יֹאכְלֶנָּה חָק־עוֹלָם לְדֹרֹתֵיכֶם מֵאִשֵּׁי יְהוָה כֹּל
אֲשֶׁר־יִגַּע בָּהֶם יִקְדָּשׁ:
שני יב־יג וַיְדַבֵּר יְהוָה אֶל־מֹשֶׁה לֵּאמֹר: זֶה קָרְבַּן אַהֲרֹן וּבָנָיו אֲשֶׁר־יַקְרִיבוּ לַיהוָה
בְּיוֹם הִמָּשַׁח אֹתוֹ עֲשִׂירִת הָאֵפָה סֹלֶת מִנְחָה תָּמִיד מַחֲצִיתָהּ בַּבֹּקֶר
יד וּמַחֲצִיתָהּ בָּעָרֶב: עַל־מַחֲבַת בַּשֶּׁמֶן תֵּעָשֶׂה מֻרְבֶּכֶת תְּבִיאֶנָּה תֻּפִינֵי
טו מִנְחַת פִּתִּים תַּקְרִיב רֵיחַ־נִיחֹחַ לַיהוָה: וְהַכֹּהֵן הַמָּשִׁיחַ תַּחְתָּיו מִבָּנָיו
טז יַעֲשֶׂה אֹתָהּ חָק־עוֹלָם לַיהוָה כָּלִיל תָּקְטָר: וְכָל־מִנְחַת כֹּהֵן כָּלִיל תִּהְיֶה
לֹא תֵאָכֵל:
יז־יח וַיְדַבֵּר יְהוָה אֶל־מֹשֶׁה לֵּאמֹר: דַּבֵּר אֶל־אַהֲרֹן וְאֶל־בָּנָיו לֵאמֹר זֹאת
תּוֹרַת הַחַטָּאת בִּמְקוֹם אֲשֶׁר תִּשָּׁחֵט הָעֹלָה תִּשָּׁחֵט הַחַטָּאת לִפְנֵי יְהוָה
יט קֹדֶשׁ קָדָשִׁים הִוא: הַכֹּהֵן הַמְחַטֵּא אֹתָהּ יֹאכְלֶנָּה בְּמָקוֹם קָדֹשׁ תֵּאָכֵל

---

meal offering and states that all of it be brought close *before HASHEM in front of the altar*, for to God, the Blessed One, alone does the person making the offering bring his entire sacrifice, and the *Kohanim* 'receive their (portion) from the heavenly (lit., higher) table' (*Beitzah* 21a) while a small part of the total is chosen (to be offered as) a *sweet savor* (v. 8). The priestly portion also atones and (hence) is also prevented from becoming leavened similar to the Divine portion. (And we also are taught that) the meal offering of the *Kohen* is offered totally to (the One) on High, not just a small part thereof, as is (true) regarding the meal offerings of the masses.

18. זאת תורת החטאת — *This is the law of the sin offering.* (The Torah then) makes mention of the law of the sin offering, stating in regard to that (particular) sin offering that due to the severity of the sin (for which it is brought), it cannot atone unless its blood is brought into the inner sanctuary. Unlike other sin offerings, it does not (attain) atonement through the eating of the *Kohanim*, but by being burnt.

NOTES

consumed by the *Kohanim* and not by the fire of the altar, initially, the entire meal offering is brought close to the altar to indicate that the *Kohen's* portion is not given to him directly but, as it were, by God from His table. This concept is clearly stated in verse 10. Therefore, the portion eaten by the *Kohanim* must be unleavened since all that is related to offerings on the altar must be מַצָּה and the *Kohen's* share is granted to him from God's table. As mentioned above (4:27), the eating of the sacrifice by the *Kohanim* is considered part of the atonement. The reason that the *Kohen's* own meal offering is wholly burnt on the altar, and not eaten by him, as is the case regarding the מִנְחָה of the Israelite, is explained by the *Rambam* in his *Guide* [and brought here (v. 10) by the *Ramban*]. Were the *Kohen* to eat his own meal offering, since only a handful is brought on the altar, it would be considered as though he had offered naught, hence he must bring it all on the altar to be consumed there by the holy fire.

18. זאת תורת החטאת — *This is the law of the sin offering*. The *Sforno* is referring to the sin offerings of the anointed *Kohen* and the Sanhedrin, brought when they sin through an error in judgment, as well as to the bull and goat brought on Yom Kippur, the flesh of which must not be eaten but burnt as the Torah states explicitly in verse 23.

כ בַּחֲצַ֥ר אֹ֣הֶל מוֹעֵ֑ד: כֹּ֛ל אֲשֶׁר־יִגַּ֥ע בִּבְשָׂרָ֖הּ יִקְדָּ֑שׁ וַאֲשֶׁ֨ר יִזֶּ֤ה מִדָּמָהּ֙
כא עַל־הַבֶּ֔גֶד אֲשֶׁ֨ר יִזֶּ֤ה עָלֶ֙יהָ֙ תְּכַבֵּ֣ס בְּמָק֣וֹם קָדֹ֑שׁ: וּכְלִי־חֶ֜רֶשׂ אֲשֶׁ֤ר
כב תְּבֻשַּׁל־בּוֹ֙ יִשָּׁבֵ֔ר וְאִם־בִּכְלִ֤י נְחֹ֙שֶׁת֙ בֻּשָּׁ֔לָה וּמֹרַ֥ק וְשֻׁטַּ֖ף בַּמָּֽיִם: כָּל־זָכָ֧ר
כג בַּכֹּהֲנִ֛ים יֹאכַ֥ל אֹתָ֖הּ קֹ֣דֶשׁ קָֽדָשִׁ֥ים הִֽוא: וְכָל־חַטָּ֡את אֲשֶׁר֩ יוּבָ֨א מִדָּמָ֜הּ
אֶל־אֹ֧הֶל מוֹעֵ֛ד לְכַפֵּ֥ר בַּקֹּ֖דֶשׁ לֹ֣א תֵאָכֵ֑ל בָּאֵ֖שׁ תִּשָּׂרֵֽף:

ז

א-ב וְזֹ֥את תּוֹרַ֖ת הָאָשָׁ֑ם קֹ֥דֶשׁ קָֽדָשִׁ֖ים הֽוּא: בִּמְק֗וֹם אֲשֶׁ֤ר יִשְׁחֲטוּ֙ אֶת־הָ֣עֹלָ֔ה
ג יִשְׁחֲט֖וּ אֶת־הָאָשָׁ֑ם וְאֶת־דָּמ֛וֹ יִזְרֹ֥ק עַל־הַמִּזְבֵּ֖חַ סָבִֽיב: וְאֵ֥ת כָּל־חֶלְבּ֖וֹ
ד יַקְרִ֣יב מִמֶּ֑נּוּ אֵ֚ת הָֽאַלְיָ֔ה וְאֶת־הַחֵ֖לֶב הַֽמְכַסֶּ֥ה אֶת־הַקֶּֽרֶב: וְאֵת֙ שְׁתֵּ֣י
הַכְּלָיֹ֔ת וְאֶת־הַחֵ֙לֶב֙ אֲשֶׁ֣ר עֲלֵיהֶ֔ן אֲשֶׁ֖ר עַל־הַכְּסָלִ֑ים וְאֶת־הַיֹּתֶ֙רֶת֙
ה עַל־הַכָּבֵ֔ד עַל־הַכְּלָיֹ֖ת יְסִירֶֽנָּה: וְהִקְטִ֨יר אֹתָ֤ם הַכֹּהֵן֙ הַמִּזְבֵּ֔חָה אִשֶּׁ֖ה לַֽיהֹוָ֑ה
ו אָשָׁ֖ם הֽוּא: כָּל־זָכָ֥ר בַּכֹּהֲנִ֖ים יֹאכְלֶ֑נּוּ בְּמָק֤וֹם קָדוֹשׁ֙ יֵֽאָכֵ֔ל קֹ֥דֶשׁ קָֽדָשִׁ֖ים
ז הֽוּא: כַּֽחַטָּאת֙ כָּֽאָשָׁ֔ם תּוֹרָ֥ה אַחַ֖ת לָהֶ֑ם הַכֹּהֵ֛ן אֲשֶׁ֥ר יְכַפֶּר־בּ֖וֹ ל֥וֹ יִהְיֶֽה:
ח וְהַ֨כֹּהֵ֔ן הַמַּקְרִ֖יב אֶת־עֹ֣לַת אִ֑ישׁ ע֤וֹר הָֽעֹלָה֙ אֲשֶׁ֣ר הִקְרִ֔יב לַכֹּהֵ֖ן ל֥וֹ יִהְיֶֽה:
ט וְכָל־מִנְחָ֗ה אֲשֶׁ֤ר תֵּֽאָפֶה֙ בַּתַּנּ֔וּר וְכָל־נַֽעֲשָׂ֥ה בַמַּרְחֶ֖שֶׁת וְעַל־מַֽחֲבַ֑ת לַכֹּהֵ֛ן
י הַמַּקְרִ֥יב אֹתָ֖הּ ל֥וֹ תִֽהְיֶֽה: וְכָל־מִנְחָ֥ה בְלוּלָֽה־בַשֶּׁ֖מֶן וַֽחֲרֵבָ֑ה לְכָל־בְּנֵ֧י אַֽהֲרֹ֛ן
תִּֽהְיֶ֖ה אִ֥ישׁ כְּאָחִֽיו:

שלישי יא-יב וְזֹ֥את תּוֹרַ֖ת זֶ֣בַח הַשְּׁלָמִ֑ים אֲשֶׁ֥ר יַקְרִ֖יב לַֽיהֹוָֽה: אִ֣ם עַל־תּוֹדָה֮ יַקְרִיבֶ֒נּוּ֒

VII

1. וְזֹאת תּוֹרַת הָאָשָׁם — *And this is the law of the guilt offering.* Although the guilt offering is not brought (to atone) for a sin punishable by excision (כָּרֵת), as is (true of) a sin offering, nonetheless, since his sin is a trespass against the holy, one law shall apply to them (see v. 7). (The Torah then) says . . .

11. וְזֹאת תּוֹרַת זֶבַח הַשְּׁלָמִים — *And this is the law of the sacrifice of peace offerings.* (The Torah) tells us that even though all peace offerings are (in the category of) קָדָשִׁים קַלִּים, (sacrifices belonging to) *a lesser level of sanctity*, nonetheless, there are differences among them. (For example) if one is brought as a תּוֹדָה, a *thanksgiving offering*, then bread is to be brought with it, including leavened loaves, for indeed, the cause of the danger (which he experienced and was delivered from) for which he

---

NOTES

VII

1. וְזֹאת תּוֹרַת הָאָשָׁם — *And this is the law of the guilt offering.* The five cases where the Torah imposes the obligation to bring a guilt offering (אָשָׁם) is discussed in chapter 5. In this chapter (v. 7), the Torah equates the sin offering and the guilt offering (כַּחַטָּאת כָּאָשָׁם תּוֹרָה אַחַת) regarding the laws regulating the eating of the flesh, the place where it can be eaten and the status of purity of the Kohen.

11. וְזֹאת תּוֹרַת זֶבַח הַשְּׁלָמִים — *And this is the law of the sacrifice of peace offerings.* As mentioned above (note 6:7), nothing leavened is brought on the altar, except on some infrequent occasions. One of these exceptions are the ten loaves of leavened bread brought in conjunction with the thanksgiving offering. The *Sforno* explains that this exception is to symbolize what our Sages call שְׂאוֹר שֶׁבָּעִסָּה, *the leaven in the dough (Berachos 17a). Rashi* there states that this expression refers to the evil inclination in the heart of man. Now a

וְהִקְרִיב | עַל־זֶבַח הַתּוֹדָה חַלּוֹת מַצּוֹת בְּלוּלֹת בַּשֶּׁמֶן וּרְקִיקֵי מַצּוֹת
יג מְשֻׁחִים בַּשָּׁמֶן וְסֹלֶת מֻרְבֶּכֶת חַלֹּת בְּלוּלֹת בַּשָּׁמֶן: עַל־חַלֹּת לֶחֶם
יד חָמֵץ יַקְרִיב קָרְבָּנוֹ עַל־זֶבַח תּוֹדַת שְׁלָמָיו: וְהִקְרִיב מִמֶּנּוּ אֶחָד מִכָּל־
טו קָרְבָּן תְּרוּמָה לַיהוָה לַכֹּהֵן הַזֹּרֵק אֶת־דַּם הַשְּׁלָמִים לוֹ יִהְיֶה: וּבְשַׂר
טז זֶבַח תּוֹדַת שְׁלָמָיו בְּיוֹם קָרְבָּנוֹ יֵאָכֵל לֹא־יַנִּיחַ מִמֶּנּוּ עַד־בֹּקֶר: וְאִם־
נֶדֶר | אוֹ נְדָבָה זֶבַח קָרְבָּנוֹ בְּיוֹם הַקְרִיבוֹ אֶת־זִבְחוֹ יֵאָכֵל וּמִמָּחֳרָת
יז וְהַנּוֹתָר מִמֶּנּוּ יֵאָכֵל: וְהַנּוֹתָר מִבְּשַׂר הַזָּבַח בַּיּוֹם הַשְּׁלִישִׁי בָּאֵשׁ
יח יִשָּׂרֵף: וְאִם הֵאָכֹל יֵאָכֵל מִבְּשַׂר־זֶבַח שְׁלָמָיו בַּיּוֹם הַשְּׁלִישִׁי לֹא
יֵרָצֶה הַמַּקְרִיב אֹתוֹ לֹא יֵחָשֵׁב לוֹ פִּגּוּל יִהְיֶה וְהַנֶּפֶשׁ הָאֹכֶלֶת מִמֶּנּוּ עֲוֹנָהּ
יט תִּשָּׂא: וְהַבָּשָׂר אֲשֶׁר־יִגַּע בְּכָל־טָמֵא לֹא יֵאָכֵל בָּאֵשׁ יִשָּׂרֵף וְהַבָּשָׂר
כ כָּל־טָהוֹר יֹאכַל בָּשָׂר: וְהַנֶּפֶשׁ אֲשֶׁר־תֹּאכַל בָּשָׂר מִזֶּבַח הַשְּׁלָמִים אֲשֶׁר
כא לַיהוָה וְטֻמְאָתוֹ עָלָיו וְנִכְרְתָה הַנֶּפֶשׁ הַהִוא מֵעַמֶּיהָ: וְנֶפֶשׁ כִּי־תִגַּע
בְּכָל־טָמֵא בְּטֻמְאַת אָדָם אוֹ | בִּבְהֵמָה טְמֵאָה אוֹ בְּכָל־שֶׁקֶץ טָמֵא וְאָכַל
כב מִבְּשַׂר־זֶבַח הַשְּׁלָמִים אֲשֶׁר לַיהוָה וְנִכְרְתָה הַנֶּפֶשׁ הַהִוא מֵעַמֶּיהָ: וַיְדַבֵּר
כג יְהוָה אֶל־מֹשֶׁה לֵּאמֹר: דַּבֵּר אֶל־בְּנֵי יִשְׂרָאֵל לֵאמֹר כָּל־חֵלֶב שׁוֹר וְכֶשֶׂב
כד וָעֵז לֹא תֹאכֵלוּ: וְחֵלֶב נְבֵלָה וְחֵלֶב טְרֵפָה יֵעָשֶׂה לְכָל־מְלָאכָה וְאָכֹל לֹא
כה תֹאכְלֻהוּ: כִּי כָּל־אֹכֵל חֵלֶב מִן־הַבְּהֵמָה אֲשֶׁר יַקְרִיב מִמֶּנָּה אִשֶּׁה לַיהוָה
כו וְנִכְרְתָה הַנֶּפֶשׁ הָאֹכֶלֶת מֵעַמֶּיהָ: וְכָל־דָּם לֹא תֹאכְלוּ בְּכֹל מוֹשְׁבֹתֵיכֶם
כז לָעוֹף וְלַבְּהֵמָה: כָּל־נֶפֶשׁ אֲשֶׁר־תֹּאכַל כָּל־דָּם וְנִכְרְתָה הַנֶּפֶשׁ הַהִוא
מֵעַמֶּיהָ:
כח־כט וַיְדַבֵּר יְהוָה אֶל־מֹשֶׁה לֵּאמֹר: דַּבֵּר אֶל־בְּנֵי יִשְׂרָאֵל לֵאמֹר הַמַּקְרִיב אֶת־

---

is now thanking God was the 'leaven in the dough'. Nonetheless, those cakes which are unleavened outnumber them (i.e., the leavened ones). Now, through the many cakes and the increased number of those who eat, the miracle will become well known. All of the תּוֹדָה must be eaten in the time limitation of קָדְשֵׁי קָדָשִׁים, *holy of holies*, namely for a day and a night (v. 15). However, when one brings regular peace offerings other than a תּוֹדָה, the time (in which it must be consumed) is two days and one night (v. 16).

Now, since they are all קָדָשִׁים קַלִּים, it is prohibited to be eaten by one who is *tamei*, unclean, and also prohibited to be eaten if the flesh is *tamei*. The punishment of excision, however, applies only to a *tamei* person who eats the *tahor*, flesh of an offering, for he who is *tamei*, and approaches to eat from the holy which is *tahor*, has desecrated the holy (vs. 19-21).

NOTES

תּוֹדָה, *thanksgiving sacrifice*, is brought by one delivered from peril. The very fact that he was exposed to danger indicates that he was vulnerable due to his spiritual shortcomings. However, God in His mercy saved him. This is symbolized by the loaves of leavened bread (see the *Sforno* on 23:17).

The *Sforno* explains why the punishment for one who eats unclean sanctified flesh is lighter than the punishment imposed on an unclean person who consumes clean holy meat. The reason is that the latter is guilty of חִלּוּל הַקּוֹדֶשׁ, *desecration of the holy*, which is not so in the case of the former.

ל זֶבַח שְׁלָמָיו לַיהוָה יָבִיא אֶת־קָרְבָּנוֹ לַיהוָה מִזֶּבַח שְׁלָמָיו: יָדָיו תְּבִיאֶינָה
אֵת אִשֵּׁי יהוָה אֶת־הַחֵלֶב עַל־הֶחָזֶה יְבִיאֶנּוּ אֵת הֶחָזֶה לְהָנִיף אֹתוֹ תְּנוּפָה
לא לִפְנֵי יהוָה: וְהִקְטִיר הַכֹּהֵן אֶת־הַחֵלֶב הַמִּזְבֵּחָה וְהָיָה הֶחָזֶה לְאַהֲרֹן וּלְבָנָיו:
לב-לג וְאֵת שׁוֹק הַיָּמִין תִּתְּנוּ תְרוּמָה לַכֹּהֵן מִזִּבְחֵי שַׁלְמֵיכֶם: הַמַּקְרִיב אֶת־דַּם
לד הַשְּׁלָמִים וְאֶת־הַחֵלֶב מִבְּנֵי אַהֲרֹן לוֹ תִהְיֶה שׁוֹק הַיָּמִין לְמָנָה: כִּי אֶת־חֲזֵה
הַתְּנוּפָה וְאֵת ׀ שׁוֹק הַתְּרוּמָה לָקַחְתִּי מֵאֵת בְּנֵי־יִשְׂרָאֵל מִזִּבְחֵי שַׁלְמֵיהֶם
לה וָאֶתֵּן אֹתָם לְאַהֲרֹן הַכֹּהֵן וּלְבָנָיו לְחָק־עוֹלָם מֵאֵת בְּנֵי יִשְׂרָאֵל: זֹאת
מִשְׁחַת אַהֲרֹן וּמִשְׁחַת בָּנָיו מֵאִשֵּׁי יהוָה בְּיוֹם הִקְרִיב אֹתָם לְכַהֵן לַיהוָה:
לו אֲשֶׁר צִוָּה יהוָה לָתֵת לָהֶם בְּיוֹם מָשְׁחוֹ אֹתָם מֵאֵת בְּנֵי יִשְׂרָאֵל חֻקַּת
לז עוֹלָם לְדֹרֹתָם: זֹאת הַתּוֹרָה לָעֹלָה לַמִּנְחָה וְלַחַטָּאת וְלָאָשָׁם וְלַמִּלּוּאִים
לח וּלְזֶבַח הַשְּׁלָמִים: אֲשֶׁר צִוָּה יהוָה אֶת־מֹשֶׁה בְּהַר סִינָי בְּיוֹם צַוֺּתוֹ אֶת־בְּנֵי
יִשְׂרָאֵל לְהַקְרִיב אֶת־קָרְבְּנֵיהֶם לַיהוָה בְּמִדְבַּר סִינָי:
ח רביעי א-ב וַיְדַבֵּר יהוָה אֶל־מֹשֶׁה לֵּאמֹר: קַח אֶת־אַהֲרֹן וְאֶת־בָּנָיו אִתּוֹ וְאֵת הַבְּגָדִים
וְאֵת שֶׁמֶן הַמִּשְׁחָה וְאֵת ׀ פַּר הַחַטָּאת וְאֵת שְׁנֵי הָאֵילִים וְאֵת סַל הַמַּצּוֹת:

---

30. יָדָיו תְּבִיאֶינָה אֵת אִשֵּׁי ה׳ — *His own hands shall bring the fire-offerings of HASHEM.* Being that the rest belongs to the owners, the act of waving (by the owners) will indicate that they are giving everything, the fat and breast, to God, while the *Kohanim receive their portion from the Higher Table.*

אֵת הֶחָזֶה לְהָנִיף אֹתוֹ — *That the breast may be waved.* Even though the fat is placed on the breast when it is waved, nonetheless, the principle purpose of waving is to demonstrate that the breast is offered on High, whereas it is already known that the fat belongs to God, for it is offered on the altar.

32. וְאֵת שׁוֹק הַיָּמִין תִּתְּנוּ תְרוּמָה לַכֹּהֵן — *And the right thigh you shall give as an offering to the Kohen* ... from the portion of the owners, (as though) they are greeting the servants (of the king) with a gift in honor of the king.

VIII

2. וְאֵת פַּר הַחַטָּאת וְאֵת שְׁנֵי הָאֵילִים — *And the bull of the sin offering and the two rams.* The bull of the sin offering precedes (the burnt offering) as our Sages say, 'Every sin offering precedes the burnt offering brought with it' (*Pesachim* 59a), because until the sin is expiated, the burnt offering serves no purpose at all, as it says עוֹלָה וַחֲטָאָה לֹא שָׁאָלְתָּ, *burnt offering and sin offering You have not required* (*Psalms* 40:7). Now, his sin offering after his anointment was a bull in accordance

NOTES

30. יָדָיו תְּבִיאֶינָה אֵת אִשֵּׁי ה׳ — *His own hands shall bring the offerings of HASHEM.* See 6:7 regarding the *Kohen's* portion coming from the *Higher Table* of God.

32. וְאֵת שׁוֹק הַיָּמִין תִּתְּנוּ תְּרוּמָה לַכֹּהֵן — *And the right thigh you shall give as an offering to the Kohen.* The right shoulder is not given to the *Kohanim* from 'God's table,' rather it is an offering (תְּרוּמָה) given to them by the owners as a gesture of respect to the servants of the king.

VIII

2. וְאֵת פַּר הַחַטָּאת וְאֵת שְׁנֵי הָאֵילִים — *And the bull of the sin offering and the two rams.* To bring the blood of a sacrifice into the קֹדֶשׁ, *the*

ג-ד וְאֵת כָּל־הָעֵדָה הַקְהֵל אֶל־פֶּתַח אֹהֶל מוֹעֵד׃ וַיַּעַשׂ מֹשֶׁה כַּאֲשֶׁר צִוָּה יהוה
ה אֹתוֹ וַתִּקָּהֵל הָעֵדָה אֶל־פֶּתַח אֹהֶל מוֹעֵד׃ וַיֹּאמֶר מֹשֶׁה אֶל־הָעֵדָה זֶה
ו הַדָּבָר אֲשֶׁר־צִוָּה יהוה לַעֲשׂוֹת׃ וַיַּקְרֵב מֹשֶׁה אֶת־אַהֲרֹן וְאֶת־בָּנָיו וַיִּרְחַץ
ז אֹתָם בַּמָּיִם׃ וַיִּתֵּן עָלָיו אֶת־הַכֻּתֹּנֶת וַיַּחְגֹּר אֹתוֹ בָּאַבְנֵט וַיַּלְבֵּשׁ אֹתוֹ
אֶת־הַמְּעִיל וַיִּתֵּן עָלָיו אֶת־הָאֵפֹד וַיַּחְגֹּר אֹתוֹ בְּחֵשֶׁב הָאֵפֹד וַיֶּאְפֹּד לוֹ בּוֹ׃
ח-ט וַיָּשֶׂם עָלָיו אֶת־הַחֹשֶׁן וַיִּתֵּן אֶל־הַחֹשֶׁן אֶת־הָאוּרִים וְאֶת־הַתֻּמִּים׃ וַיָּשֶׂם
אֶת־הַמִּצְנֶפֶת עַל־רֹאשׁוֹ וַיָּשֶׂם עַל־הַמִּצְנֶפֶת אֶל־מוּל פָּנָיו אֵת צִיץ הַזָּהָב
י נֵזֶר הַקֹּדֶשׁ כַּאֲשֶׁר צִוָּה יהוה אֶת־מֹשֶׁה׃ וַיִּקַּח מֹשֶׁה אֶת־שֶׁמֶן הַמִּשְׁחָה
יא וַיִּמְשַׁח אֶת־הַמִּשְׁכָּן וְאֶת־כָּל־אֲשֶׁר־בּוֹ וַיְקַדֵּשׁ אֹתָם׃ וַיַּז מִמֶּנּוּ עַל־הַמִּזְבֵּחַ
שֶׁבַע פְּעָמִים וַיִּמְשַׁח אֶת־הַמִּזְבֵּחַ וְאֶת־כָּל־כֵּלָיו וְאֶת־הַכִּיֹּר וְאֶת־כַּנּוֹ
יב לְקַדְּשָׁם׃ וַיִּצֹק מִשֶּׁמֶן הַמִּשְׁחָה עַל רֹאשׁ אַהֲרֹן וַיִּמְשַׁח אֹתוֹ לְקַדְּשׁוֹ׃
יג וַיַּקְרֵב מֹשֶׁה אֶת־בְּנֵי אַהֲרֹן וַיַּלְבִּשֵׁם כֻּתֳּנֹת וַיַּחְגֹּר אֹתָם אַבְנֵט וַיַּחֲבֹשׁ
חמישי יד לָהֶם מִגְבָּעוֹת כַּאֲשֶׁר צִוָּה יהוה אֶת־מֹשֶׁה׃ וַיַּגֵּשׁ אֵת פַּר הַחַטָּאת וַיִּסְמֹךְ
טו אַהֲרֹן וּבָנָיו אֶת־יְדֵיהֶם עַל־רֹאשׁ פַּר הַחַטָּאת׃ וַיִּשְׁחָט וַיִּקַּח מֹשֶׁה אֶת־
הַדָּם וַיִּתֵּן עַל־קַרְנוֹת הַמִּזְבֵּחַ סָבִיב בְּאֶצְבָּעוֹ וַיְחַטֵּא אֶת־הַמִּזְבֵּחַ וְאֶת־
טז הַדָּם יָצַק אֶל־יְסוֹד הַמִּזְבֵּחַ וַיְקַדְּשֵׁהוּ לְכַפֵּר עָלָיו׃ וַיִּקַּח אֶת־כָּל־הַחֵלֶב
אֲשֶׁר עַל־הַקֶּרֶב וְאֵת יֹתֶרֶת הַכָּבֵד וְאֶת־שְׁתֵּי הַכְּלָיֹת וְאֶת־חֶלְבְּהֶן וַיַּקְטֵר
יז מֹשֶׁה הַמִּזְבֵּחָה׃ וְאֶת־הַפָּר וְאֶת־עֹרוֹ וְאֶת־בְּשָׂרוֹ וְאֶת־פִּרְשׁוֹ שָׂרַף בָּאֵשׁ
יח מִחוּץ לַמַּחֲנֶה כַּאֲשֶׁר צִוָּה יהוה אֶת־מֹשֶׁה׃ וַיַּקְרֵב אֵת אֵיל הָעֹלָה וַיִּסְמְכוּ

---

with the rule (regarding) the anointed *Kohen* (subsequent to his installation — 4:3). But the blood was not brought into the inner sanctum because his sin was not on such a level of evil as to necessitate it, as is necessary with the (erroneous) decision of the anointed *Kohen* and the (erroneous) verdict of a court, (or) the bull and goat of Yom Kippur which come to atone for the impurity of the Sanctuary and (to expiate) sins, iniquities and transgressions, as explained in chapter 16.

18. וַיַּקְרֵב אֵת אֵיל הָעֹלָה — *And the ram of the burnt offering was presented.* The burnt offering preceded the ram of consecration because the burnt offering also came for some expiation, as it says, *And it shall be accepted for him to make atonement for him* (1:4). After the atonement was complete, they became worthy to 'fill their hand' and perfect it for the service (of God).

NOTES

holy, is an indication of the severity of the sin which the sacrifice is meant to expiate. Since Aaron was now anointed as *Kohen Gadol*, his sin offering (for his role in the sin of the Golden Calf) conformed with the ritual of the sacrifice brought by the anointed *Kohen* (4:3) except for the sprinkling of the blood in front of the veil of the Sanctuary (4:6). The *Sforno* is of the opinion that Aaron's involvement in the Golden Calf was minimal (see *Sforno* on *Exodus* 32:24); hence, the procedure here did not include bringing the blood of his bull into *the holy*, as is the case of those transgressions mentioned by the *Sforno*, which were of a more serious nature.

18. וַיַּקְרֵב אֵת אֵיל הָעֹלָה — *And the ram of the burnt offering was presented.* The first of the two rams brought for the ceremony of induction was meant to atone for sins committed by Aaron and his sons other than that of the Golden Calf. Therefore, it preceded the offer-

יט אַהֲרֹן וּבָנָיו אֶת־יְדֵיהֶם עַל־רֹאשׁ הָאָיִל׃ וַיִּשְׁחָט וַיִּזְרֹק מֹשֶׁה אֶת־הַדָּם עַל־
כ הַמִּזְבֵּחַ סָבִיב׃ וְאֶת־הָאַיִל נִתַּח לִנְתָחָיו וַיַּקְטֵר מֹשֶׁה אֶת־הָרֹאשׁ וְאֶת־
כא הַנְּתָחִים וְאֶת־הַפָּדֶר׃ וְאֶת־הַקֶּרֶב וְאֶת־הַכְּרָעַיִם רָחַץ בַּמָּיִם וַיַּקְטֵר מֹשֶׁה
אֶת־כָּל־הָאַיִל הַמִּזְבֵּחָה עֹלָה הוּא לְרֵיחַ־נִיחֹחַ אִשֶּׁה הוּא לַיהוָה כַּאֲשֶׁר
ששי כב צִוָּה יְהוָה אֶת־מֹשֶׁה׃ וַיַּקְרֵב אֶת־הָאַיִל הַשֵּׁנִי אֵיל הַמִּלֻּאִים וַיִּסְמְכוּ אַהֲרֹן
כג וּבָנָיו אֶת־יְדֵיהֶם עַל־רֹאשׁ הָאָיִל׃ וַיִּשְׁחָט ׀ וַיִּקַּח מֹשֶׁה מִדָּמוֹ וַיִּתֵּן עַל־
תְּנוּךְ אֹזֶן־אַהֲרֹן הַיְמָנִית וְעַל־בֹּהֶן יָדוֹ הַיְמָנִית וְעַל־בֹּהֶן רַגְלוֹ הַיְמָנִית׃
כד וַיַּקְרֵב אֶת־בְּנֵי אַהֲרֹן וַיִּתֵּן מֹשֶׁה מִן־הַדָּם עַל־תְּנוּךְ אָזְנָם הַיְמָנִית וְעַל־
בֹּהֶן יָדָם הַיְמָנִית וְעַל־בֹּהֶן רַגְלָם הַיְמָנִית וַיִּזְרֹק מֹשֶׁה אֶת־הַדָּם עַל־
כה הַמִּזְבֵּחַ סָבִיב׃ וַיִּקַּח אֶת־הַחֵלֶב וְאֶת־הָאַלְיָה וְאֶת־כָּל־הַחֵלֶב אֲשֶׁר עַל־
הַקֶּרֶב וְאֵת יֹתֶרֶת הַכָּבֵד וְאֶת־שְׁתֵּי הַכְּלָיֹת וְאֶת־חֶלְבְּהֶן וְאֵת שׁוֹק הַיָּמִין׃
כו וּמִסַּל הַמַּצּוֹת אֲשֶׁר ׀ לִפְנֵי יְהוָה לָקַח חַלַּת מַצָּה אַחַת וְחַלַּת לֶחֶם שֶׁמֶן
כז אַחַת וְרָקִיק אֶחָד וַיָּשֶׂם עַל־הַחֲלָבִים וְעַל שׁוֹק הַיָּמִין׃ וַיִּתֵּן אֶת־הַכֹּל עַל
כח כַּפֵּי אַהֲרֹן וְעַל כַּפֵּי בָנָיו וַיָּנֶף אֹתָם תְּנוּפָה לִפְנֵי יְהוָה׃ וַיִּקַּח מֹשֶׁה אֹתָם

---

25. וְאֵת שׁוֹק הַיָּמִין — *And the right thigh.* Behold, from all peace offerings the right thigh belongs to the *Kohanim* (7:32), but from the *nazir's* peace offering the thigh and arm, i.e., the foot and hand, are given to the *Kohen* (*Numbers* 6:19,20). (However), the thigh of the consecration ram was put on the altar (25-28). For indeed, when an Israelite (lit., stranger) brings his sacrifice, he generally gives the thigh, together with the foot, to the *Kohen,* who can enter beyond the partition allowable to the Israelite who is bringing the sacrifice. The *nazir* also gives the arm,

NOTES

ing of the second ram which was the ram of consecration. Only after expiation from sin could Aaron and his sons be fully (מָלֵא) and completely (שָׁלֵם) inducted into the priestly office (see *Rashi* on v. 22).

25. וְאֵת שׁוֹק הַיָּמִין — *And the right thigh.* The *Sforno* explains the significance and symbolism of the thigh of the peace offerings given to the *Kohen,* and the additional gift of the arm from the peace offering of the *nazir,* in the following manner. The thigh is connected to the foot while the arm is connected to the hand. Since the *Kohen* can enter where the Israelite who brings the peace offering cannot, he is entitled to the thigh (foot). The *nazir* adds the arm (hand) to indicate that heretofore his actions and deeds were restricted by his vow,

מֵעַל כַּפֵּיהֶם וַיַּקְטֵר הַמִּזְבֵּחָה עַל־הָעֹלָה מִלֻּאִים הֵם לְרֵיחַ נִיחֹחַ אִשֶּׁה
כט הוּא לַיהוה: וַיִּקַּח מֹשֶׁה אֶת־הֶחָזֶה וַיְנִיפֵהוּ תְנוּפָה לִפְנֵי יהוה מֵאֵיל
שביעי ל הַמִּלֻּאִים לְמֹשֶׁה הָיָה לְמָנָה כַּאֲשֶׁר צִוָּה יהוה אֶת־מֹשֶׁה: וַיִּקַּח מֹשֶׁה מִשֶּׁמֶן
הַמִּשְׁחָה וּמִן־הַדָּם אֲשֶׁר עַל־הַמִּזְבֵּחַ וַיַּז עַל־אַהֲרֹן עַל־בְּגָדָיו וְעַל־בָּנָיו
וְעַל־בִּגְדֵי בָנָיו אִתּוֹ וַיְקַדֵּשׁ אֶת־אַהֲרֹן אֶת־בְּגָדָיו וְאֶת־בָּנָיו וְאֶת־בִּגְדֵי
לא בָנָיו אִתּוֹ: וַיֹּאמֶר מֹשֶׁה אֶל־אַהֲרֹן וְאֶל־בָּנָיו בַּשְּׁלוּ אֶת־הַבָּשָׂר פֶּתַח
אֹהֶל מוֹעֵד וְשָׁם תֹּאכְלוּ אֹתוֹ וְאֶת־הַלֶּחֶם אֲשֶׁר בְּסַל הַמִּלֻּאִים כַּאֲשֶׁר
לב צִוֵּיתִי לֵאמֹר אַהֲרֹן וּבָנָיו יֹאכְלֻהוּ: וְהַנּוֹתָר בַּבָּשָׂר וּבַלָּחֶם בָּאֵשׁ תִּשְׂרֹפוּ:
מפטיר לג וּמִפֶּתַח אֹהֶל מוֹעֵד לֹא תֵצְאוּ שִׁבְעַת יָמִים עַד יוֹם מְלֹאת יְמֵי מִלֻּאֵיכֶם
לד כִּי שִׁבְעַת יָמִים יְמַלֵּא אֶת־יֶדְכֶם: כַּאֲשֶׁר עָשָׂה בַּיּוֹם הַזֶּה צִוָּה יהוה לַעֲשֹׂת
לה לְכַפֵּר עֲלֵיכֶם: וּפֶתַח אֹהֶל מוֹעֵד תֵּשְׁבוּ יוֹמָם וָלַיְלָה שִׁבְעַת יָמִים
לו וּשְׁמַרְתֶּם אֶת־מִשְׁמֶרֶת יהוה וְלֹא תָמוּתוּ כִּי־כֵן צֻוֵּיתִי: וַיַּעַשׂ אַהֲרֹן וּבָנָיו
אֵת כָּל־הַדְּבָרִים אֲשֶׁר־צִוָּה יהוה בְּיַד־מֹשֶׁה:

---

meaning the hand, as though he were transmitting to the *Kohen* the work of his hands which until now were kept (reserved) for God. However, (since) the consecration (ram) is a preparatory offering for the *Kohen* with which to enter within, (therefore) the thigh was placed on the altar.

35. יוֹמָם וָלַיְלָה — *Day and night* . . . because the curtains were not dismantled, as explained above.

NOTES

i.e., given over to קֹדֶשׁ, the holy — but now the hand is once again in his domain and control. Since the consecration sacrifice is unique, symbolizing the preparation of the *Kohen* to minister in the Sanctuary, the thigh (foot) was rightfully placed on the altar.

35. יוֹמָם וָלַיְלָה — *Day and night.* The curtains are called *mishkan* (see *Sforno* — *Exodus* 40:18). They remained in place during the seven days of consecration, even though the other parts of the Sanctuary were erected and dismantled during that period (*Yerushalmi Yoma* 1:1). The *Sforno* explains how the *Kohanim* were able to abide at the door of the Tent of Meeting during these seven days. They were able to do so since the curtains remained in place and were not dismantled.

פרשת שמיני

Parashas Shemini

ט
א-ב וַיְהִי בַּיּוֹם הַשְּׁמִינִי קָרָא מֹשֶׁה לְאַהֲרֹן וּלְבָנָיו וּלְזִקְנֵי יִשְׂרָאֵל: וַיֹּאמֶר אֶל־
אַהֲרֹן קַח־לְךָ עֵגֶל בֶּן־בָּקָר לְחַטָּאת וְאַיִל לְעֹלָה תְּמִימִם וְהַקְרֵב לִפְנֵי
ג יהוה: וְאֶל־בְּנֵי יִשְׂרָאֵל תְּדַבֵּר לֵאמֹר קְחוּ שְׂעִיר־עִזִּים לְחַטָּאת וְעֵגֶל
ד וָכֶבֶשׂ בְּנֵי־שָׁנָה תְּמִימִם לְעֹלָה: וְשׁוֹר וָאַיִל לִשְׁלָמִים לִזְבֹּחַ לִפְנֵי יהוה
ה וּמִנְחָה בְּלוּלָה בַשָּׁמֶן כִּי הַיּוֹם יהוה נִרְאָה אֲלֵיכֶם: וַיִּקְחוּ אֵת אֲשֶׁר צִוָּה
ו מֹשֶׁה אֶל־פְּנֵי אֹהֶל מוֹעֵד וַיִּקְרְבוּ כָּל־הָעֵדָה וַיַּעַמְדוּ לִפְנֵי יהוה: וַיֹּאמֶר
ז מֹשֶׁה זֶה הַדָּבָר אֲשֶׁר־צִוָּה יהוה תַּעֲשׂוּ וְיֵרָא אֲלֵיכֶם כְּבוֹד יהוה: וַיֹּאמֶר
מֹשֶׁה אֶל־אַהֲרֹן קְרַב אֶל־הַמִּזְבֵּחַ וַעֲשֵׂה אֶת־חַטָּאתְךָ וְאֶת־עֹלָתֶךָ וְכַפֵּר
בַּעַדְךָ וּבְעַד הָעָם וַעֲשֵׂה אֶת־קָרְבַּן הָעָם וְכַפֵּר בַּעֲדָם כַּאֲשֶׁר צִוָּה יהוה:
ח-ט וַיִּקְרַב אַהֲרֹן אֶל־הַמִּזְבֵּחַ וַיִּשְׁחַט אֶת־עֵגֶל הַחַטָּאת אֲשֶׁר־לוֹ: וַיַּקְרִבוּ בְּנֵי
אַהֲרֹן אֶת־הַדָּם אֵלָיו וַיִּטְבֹּל אֶצְבָּעוֹ בַּדָּם וַיִּתֵּן עַל־קַרְנוֹת הַמִּזְבֵּחַ וְאֶת־
י הַדָּם יָצַק אֶל־יְסוֹד הַמִּזְבֵּחַ: וְאֶת־הַחֵלֶב וְאֶת־הַכְּלָיֹת וְאֶת־הַיֹּתֶרֶת מִן־
יא הַכָּבֵד מִן־הַחַטָּאת הִקְטִיר הַמִּזְבֵּחָה כַּאֲשֶׁר צִוָּה יהוה אֶת־מֹשֶׁה: וְאֶת־
יב הַבָּשָׂר וְאֶת־הָעוֹר שָׂרַף בָּאֵשׁ מִחוּץ לַמַּחֲנֶה: וַיִּשְׁחַט אֶת־הָעֹלָה וַיַּמְצִאוּ
יג בְּנֵי אַהֲרֹן אֵלָיו אֶת־הַדָּם וַיִּזְרְקֵהוּ עַל־הַמִּזְבֵּחַ סָבִיב: וְאֶת־הָעֹלָה הִמְצִיאוּ
יד אֵלָיו לִנְתָחֶיהָ וְאֶת־הָרֹאשׁ וַיַּקְטֵר עַל־הַמִּזְבֵּחַ: וַיִּרְחַץ אֶת־הַקֶּרֶב וְאֶת־

IX

4. כִּי הַיּוֹם ה׳ נִרְאָה אֲלֵיכֶם — *For today* HASHEM *appeared unto you.* He already appeared in the work of your hands, as it says, וּכְבוֹד ה׳ מָלֵא אֶת הַמִּשְׁכָּן, *And the glory of* HASHEM *filled the Mishkan* (*Exodus* 40:34), therefore it is fitting that you honor Him with this offering (in recognition of) the revelation of His Divine Presence (*Shechinah*).

6. זֶה הַדָּבָר אֲשֶׁר צִוָּה ה׳ תַּעֲשׂוּ — *This is the thing which* HASHEM *has commanded that you do* . . . to lay your hands on the communal sin offering and burnt offering.

וְיֵרָא אֲלֵיכֶם כְּבוֹד ה׳ — *That the glory of* HASHEM *may appear to you.* Besides (in addition to) the revelation of the Divine Presence in the *Mishkan,* as it says, *And the glory of* HASHEM *appeared to all the people* (v. 23).

12. וַיַּמְצִאוּ . . . אֵלָיו — *And* (*they*) *delivered . . . to him . . .* to be trained (in the method) by occupying themselves in their father's sacrifice.

NOTES

IX

4. ה׳ נִרְאָה אֲלֵיכֶם — HASHEM *appeared unto you.* The *Sforno* interprets the word נִרְאָה in the past tense, i.e., He already appeared to you; therefore it is fitting that you bring this offering in recognition of His revelation at the time that the *Mishkan* was completed.

6. זֶה הַדָּבָר אֲשֶׁר צִוָּה ה׳ תַּעֲשׂוּ — *This is the thing which* HASHEM *has commanded that you do.* Since the glory of God had already filled the Sanctuary, the act of *laying the hands* (סְמִיכָה) at this time will merit an additional revelation of God's glory, as the Torah indeed records in verse 23. The *Sforno* explains the obscure phrase, זֶה הַדָּבָר, *this is the thing,* as referring to the ritual of סְמִיכָה.

12. וַיַּמְצִאוּ . . . אֵלָיו — *And* (*they*) *delivered . . . to him.* The purpose of having Aaron's sons participate in the service of the burnt offering as well as the peace offering (v. 18) was to teach and train them in these functions which they as *Kohanim* would be charged with in the future.

טו הַכְּרָעָיִם וַיַּקְטֵר עַל־הָעֹלָה הַמִּזְבֵּחָה: וַיַּקְרֵב אֵת קָרְבַּן הָעָם וַיִּקַּח אֶת־
טז שְׂעִיר הַחַטָּאת אֲשֶׁר לָעָם וַיִּשְׁחָטֵהוּ וַיְחַטְּאֵהוּ כָּרִאשׁוֹן: וַיַּקְרֵב אֶת־הָעֹלָה
שני יז וַיַּעֲשֶׂהָ כַּמִּשְׁפָּט: וַיַּקְרֵב אֶת־הַמִּנְחָה וַיְמַלֵּא כַפּוֹ מִמֶּנָּה וַיַּקְטֵר עַל־הַמִּזְבֵּחַ
יח מִלְּבַד עֹלַת הַבֹּקֶר: וַיִּשְׁחַט אֶת־הַשּׁוֹר וְאֶת־הָאַיִל זֶבַח הַשְּׁלָמִים אֲשֶׁר
יט לָעָם וַיַּמְצִאוּ בְּנֵי אַהֲרֹן אֶת־הַדָּם אֵלָיו וַיִּזְרְקֵהוּ עַל־הַמִּזְבֵּחַ סָבִיב: וְאֶת־
הַחֲלָבִים מִן־הַשּׁוֹר וּמִן־הָאַיִל הָאַלְיָה וְהַמְכַסֶּה וְהַכְּלָיֹת וְיֹתֶרֶת הַכָּבֵד:
כ־כא וַיָּשִׂימוּ אֶת־הַחֲלָבִים עַל־הֶחָזוֹת וַיַּקְטֵר הַחֲלָבִים הַמִּזְבֵּחָה: וְאֵת הֶחָזוֹת
כב וְאֵת שׁוֹק הַיָּמִין הֵנִיף אַהֲרֹן תְּנוּפָה לִפְנֵי יהוה כַּאֲשֶׁר צִוָּה מֹשֶׁה: וַיִּשָּׂא
אַהֲרֹן אֶת־יָדָו אֶל־הָעָם וַיְבָרְכֵם וַיֵּרֶד מֵעֲשֹׂת הַחַטָּאת וְהָעֹלָה וְהַשְּׁלָמִים:
כג וַיָּבֹא מֹשֶׁה וְאַהֲרֹן אֶל־אֹהֶל מוֹעֵד וַיֵּצְאוּ וַיְבָרְכוּ אֶת־הָעָם וַיֵּרָא כְבוֹד־
שלישי כד יהוה אֶל־כָּל־הָעָם: וַתֵּצֵא אֵשׁ מִלִּפְנֵי יהוה וַתֹּאכַל עַל־הַמִּזְבֵּחַ אֶת־
י א הָעֹלָה וְאֶת־הַחֲלָבִים וַיַּרְא כָּל־הָעָם וַיָּרֹנּוּ וַיִּפְּלוּ עַל־פְּנֵיהֶם: וַיִּקְחוּ בְנֵי־
אַהֲרֹן נָדָב וַאֲבִיהוּא אִישׁ מַחְתָּתוֹ וַיִּתְּנוּ בָהֵן אֵשׁ וַיָּשִׂימוּ עָלֶיהָ קְטֹרֶת

---

15. כָּרִאשׁוֹן — *As the first.* It was burnt, although it was an 'outer' sin offering.

16. כַּמִּשְׁפָּט — *According to the ordinance.* The sons of Aaron sprinkled (the blood), prepared (the wood on the altar) and burnt (the sacrifice).

17. מִלְּבַד עֹלַת הַבֹּקֶר — *Besides the burnt offering of the morning* . . . besides the meal offering of the (daily) morning burnt offering.

18. וַיַּמְצִאוּ — *And (they) delivered to him.* They were also trained in (the method) of the communal peace offerings.

X

1. וַיִּקְחוּ בְנֵי אַהֲרֹן . . . אִישׁ מַחְתָּתוֹ — *And the sons of Aaron (took) . . . each of them his censer.* They were under the impression that (just) as the incense came after the daily offering whereby the *Shechinah* manifested itself, as it says, עֹלַת תָּמִיד לְדֹרֹתֵיכֶם פֶּתַח אֹהֶל מוֹעֵד לִפְנֵי ה׳ אֲשֶׁר אִוָּעֵד לָכֶם שָׁמָּה, *It shall be a continual burnt offering throughout your generations at the door of the Tent of Meeting before* HASHEM, *where I will meet with you* (Exodus 29:42), so it would be proper to burn additional incense now that the Divine Glory had been revealed to all the people and the fire had descended, therefore they offered it . . .

NOTES

15. כָּרִאשׁוֹן — *As the first.* As *Rashi* points out, although those sin offerings whose blood was sprinkled on the outer altar were not burnt, and the *Kohanim* were entitled to eat the flesh, this sin offering and the one of the consecration ceremony as well *were* burnt. These were exceptions to the rule and the *Sforno* explains the verse accordingly.

17. עֹלַת הַבֹּקֶר — *The burnt offering of the morning.* The *Sforno,* following the commentary of the *Ramban,* interprets the words עֹלַת הַבֹּקֶר as referring to the *meal offering* of the daily morning sacrifice.

X

1. וַיִּקְחוּ בְנֵי אַהֲרֹן . . . אִישׁ מַחְתָּתוֹ — *And the sons of Aaron (took) . . . each of them his censer.* The *Sforno* explains what prompted Nadav and Avihu to bring the incense at this particular time. However, their reasoning was faulty and they erred for two reasons. Firstly, no incense may be brought on the inner altar except at those times specified by the Torah, and secondly, even if one were to argue that this day was different, as indeed it was, for we see that certain ordinary regulations were not operative the day of the consecration,

ב וַיַּקְרִיבוּ לִפְנֵי יהוה אֵשׁ זָרָה אֲשֶׁר לֹא צִוָּה אֹתָם: וַתֵּצֵא אֵשׁ מִלִּפְנֵי יהוה
ג וַתֹּאכַל אוֹתָם וַיָּמֻתוּ לִפְנֵי יהוה: וַיֹּאמֶר מֹשֶׁה אֶל־אַהֲרֹן הוּא אֲשֶׁר־דִּבֶּר
ד יהוה ׀ לֵאמֹר בִּקְרֹבַי אֶקָּדֵשׁ וְעַל־פְּנֵי כָל־הָעָם אֶכָּבֵד וַיִּדֹּם אַהֲרֹן: וַיִּקְרָא
מֹשֶׁה אֶל־מִישָׁאֵל וְאֶל אֶלְצָפָן בְּנֵי עֻזִּיאֵל דֹּד אַהֲרֹן וַיֹּאמֶר אֲלֵהֶם קִרְבוּ
ה שְׂאוּ אֶת־אֲחֵיכֶם מֵאֵת פְּנֵי־הַקֹּדֶשׁ אֶל־מִחוּץ לַמַּחֲנֶה: וַיִּקְרְבוּ וַיִּשָּׂאֻם
ו בְּכֻתֳּנֹתָם אֶל־מִחוּץ לַמַּחֲנֶה כַּאֲשֶׁר דִּבֶּר מֹשֶׁה: וַיֹּאמֶר מֹשֶׁה אֶל־אַהֲרֹן
וּלְאֶלְעָזָר וּלְאִיתָמָר ׀ בָּנָיו רָאשֵׁיכֶם אַל־תִּפְרָעוּ ׀ וּבִגְדֵיכֶם לֹא־תִפְרֹמוּ
וְלֹא תָמֻתוּ וְעַל כָּל־הָעֵדָה יִקְצֹף וַאֲחֵיכֶם כָּל־בֵּית יִשְׂרָאֵל יִבְכּוּ אֶת־
ז הַשְּׂרֵפָה אֲשֶׁר שָׂרַף יהוה: וּמִפֶּתַח אֹהֶל מוֹעֵד לֹא תֵצְאוּ פֶּן־תָּמֻתוּ כִּי־
שֶׁמֶן מִשְׁחַת יהוה עֲלֵיכֶם וַיַּעֲשׂוּ כִּדְבַר מֹשֶׁה:
ח־ט וַיְדַבֵּר יהוה אֶל־אַהֲרֹן לֵאמֹר: יַיִן וְשֵׁכָר אַל־תֵּשְׁתְּ ׀ אַתָּה ׀ וּבָנֶיךָ אִתָּךְ
י בְּבֹאֲכֶם אֶל־אֹהֶל מוֹעֵד וְלֹא תָמֻתוּ חֻקַּת עוֹלָם לְדֹרֹתֵיכֶם: וּלֲהַבְדִּיל בֵּין

לִפְנֵי ה׳ — *Before HASHEM* . . . on the inner altar, of which (the Torah) said, לֹא תַעֲלוּ עָלָיו קְטֹרֶת זָרָה, *You shall offer no strange incense on it* (*Exodus* 30:9). Now even if it was the proper thing to do had they (but) been commanded to do so, (nevertheless) they sinned by doing it presently (since) . . .

אֲשֶׁר לֹא צִוָּה אֹתָם — *Which He had not commanded them* . . . as our Sages say, 'They decided the law in the presence of Moses their teacher' (*Eruvin* 63a).

3. וַיִּדֹּם אַהֲרֹן — *And Aaron was silent* . . . comforting himself (in the thought) that God was sanctified through their death.

5. בְּכֻתֳּנֹתָם אֶל מִחוּץ לַמַּחֲנֶה — *In their shirts out of the camp.* They were not concerned about removing their holy (priestly) tunics, since they were already *tamei.*

6. רָאשֵׁיכֶם אַל תִּפְרָעוּ — *Let not the hair of your heads grow* (*long*). Although the deceased were relatives for whom an ordinary *Kohen* could defile himself (21:2), (the law) for them was more stringent because they were anointed (that day) as it says, *For the anointing oil of HASHEM is upon you* (v. 7).

כָּל בֵּית יִשְׂרָאֵל יִבְכּוּ — *The whole house of Israel will bewail* . . . that two great pious men are now lacking (from Israel), and therefore *honor, of the dead* (based on *Sanhedrin* 46b) will not be denied.

10-11. וּלְהַבְדִּיל . . . וּלְהוֹרֹת — *And that you may differentiate . . . and that you may teach* . . . because יַיִן וְתִירוֹשׁ יִקַּח לֵב, *Wine and new wine take away the heart* (*Hosea* 4:11), as it says, אַל לַמְלָכִים שְׁתוֹ יָיִן וּלְרוֹזְנִים אֵי שֵׁכָר פֶּן יִשְׁתֶּה וְיִשְׁכַּח מְחֻקָּק, *It is not for kings to drink wine, nor for princes to say, where is strong drink? Lest he drink and forget the decree* (*Proverbs* 31:4,5).

NOTES

nonetheless they were not empowered to determine the law in the presence of their teacher Moses.

3. וַיִּדֹּם אַהֲרֹן — *And Aaron was silent.* See *Rashi's* commentary on this verse where the concept of קִדּוּשׁ ה׳, *sanctification of God's Name,* mentioned by the *Sforno,* is elaborated upon.

6. רָאשֵׁיכֶם אַל תִּפְרָעוּ . . . כָּל בֵּית יִשְׂרָאֵל יִבְכּוּ — *Let not the hair of your heads grow* (*long*) . . . *The whole house of Israel will bewail.* Since they were anointed that day, they had the

יא הַקֹּדֶשׁ וּבֵין הַחֹל וּבֵין הַטָּמֵא וּבֵין הַטָּהוֹר: וּלְהוֹרֹת אֶת־בְּנֵי יִשְׂרָאֵל אֵת
כָּל־הַחֻקִּים אֲשֶׁר דִּבֶּר יהוה אֲלֵיהֶם בְּיַד־מֹשֶׁה:
רביעי יב וַיְדַבֵּר מֹשֶׁה אֶל־אַהֲרֹן וְאֶל אֶלְעָזָר וְאֶל־אִיתָמָר | בָּנָיו הַנּוֹתָרִים קְחוּ
אֶת־הַמִּנְחָה הַנּוֹתֶרֶת מֵאִשֵּׁי יהוה וְאִכְלוּהָ מַצּוֹת אֵצֶל הַמִּזְבֵּחַ כִּי קֹדֶשׁ
יג קָדָשִׁים הִוא: וַאֲכַלְתֶּם אֹתָהּ בְּמָקוֹם קָדוֹשׁ כִּי חָקְךָ וְחָק־בָּנֶיךָ הִוא מֵאִשֵּׁי
יד יהוה כִּי־כֵן צֻוֵּיתִי: וְאֵת חֲזֵה הַתְּנוּפָה וְאֵת | שׁוֹק הַתְּרוּמָה תֹּאכְלוּ בְּמָקוֹם
טָהוֹר אַתָּה וּבָנֶיךָ וּבְנֹתֶיךָ אִתָּךְ כִּי־חָקְךָ וְחָק־בָּנֶיךָ נִתְּנוּ מִזִּבְחֵי שַׁלְמֵי בְּנֵי
טו יִשְׂרָאֵל: שׁוֹק הַתְּרוּמָה וַחֲזֵה הַתְּנוּפָה עַל אִשֵּׁי הַחֲלָבִים יָבִיאוּ לְהָנִיף
תְּנוּפָה לִפְנֵי יהוה וְהָיָה לְךָ וּלְבָנֶיךָ אִתְּךָ לְחָק־עוֹלָם כַּאֲשֶׁר צִוָּה יהוה:
חמישי טז וְאֵת | שְׂעִיר הַחַטָּאת דָּרֹשׁ דָּרַשׁ מֹשֶׁה וְהִנֵּה שֹׂרָף וַיִּקְצֹף עַל־אֶלְעָזָר
יז וְעַל־אִיתָמָר בְּנֵי אַהֲרֹן הַנּוֹתָרִם לֵאמֹר: מַדּוּעַ לֹא־אֲכַלְתֶּם אֶת־הַחַטָּאת
בִּמְקוֹם הַקֹּדֶשׁ כִּי קֹדֶשׁ קָדָשִׁים הִוא וְאֹתָהּ | נָתַן לָכֶם לָשֵׂאת אֶת־עֲוֺן
יח הָעֵדָה לְכַפֵּר עֲלֵיהֶם לִפְנֵי יהוה: הֵן לֹא־הוּבָא אֶת־דָּמָהּ אֶל־הַקֹּדֶשׁ
יט פְּנִימָה אָכוֹל תֹּאכְלוּ אֹתָהּ בַּקֹּדֶשׁ כַּאֲשֶׁר צִוֵּיתִי: וַיְדַבֵּר אַהֲרֹן אֶל־מֹשֶׁה
הֵן הַיּוֹם הִקְרִיבוּ אֶת־חַטָּאתָם וְאֶת־עֹלָתָם לִפְנֵי יהוה וַתִּקְרֶאנָה אֹתִי

---

15. יָבִיאוּ לְהָנִיף . . . וְהָיָה לְךָ וּלְבָנֶיךָ — *They shall bring to wave . . . and it shall be yours and your sons.* You shall not acquire them till after the waving; then you will acquire them from the *Higher Table.*

16. וְאֵת שְׂעִיר הַחַטָּאת — *And the goat of the sin offering* . . . that goat which was for an everlasting statute, namely, the 'goat of the New Moon,' a holy (sacrifice) for future generations.

17. וְאֹתָהּ נָתַן לָכֶם לָשֵׂאת אֶת עֲוֺן הָעֵדָה — *And He has given it to you to bear the iniquity of the congregation.* Although it was given to you, you had no permission to burn it because it was given to you to eat (in order) *to bear the iniquity of the congregation.*

19. הֵן הַיּוֹם הִקְרִיבוּ — *If this day they had offered.* This is similar to, הֵן יְשַׁלַּח אִישׁ אֶת אִשְׁתּוֹ, *If a man send away his wife* (*Jeremiah* 3:1); הֵן יִשָּׂא אִישׁ בְּשַׂר קֹדֶשׁ, *If one carries consecrated meat* (*Chaggai* 2:12). His reasoning was: if the situation were such that they were sacrificing their obligatory sin offering and their freewill burnt

NOTES

status of a *Kohen Gadol,* and as such were not permitted to defile themselves or manifest mourning for a brother. However, lest we think that their abstinence from involvement with their deceased brothers be viewed as a denial of כְּבוֹד הַמֵּת, *honor of the dead,* the Torah tells us that *all* of Israel will mourn for these great men, thereby granting them the proper respect.

15. יָבִיאוּ לְהָנִיף — *They shall bring to wave.* The act of הֲנָפָה, *waving,* qualifies the *Kohen* to partake of the offering. The expression מִשֻּׁלְחַן גָּבוֹהַּ זָכוּ, *to merit acquisition from the Higher Table,* (i.e., of God) is used throughout the Talmud to indicate that the *Kohanim* do not receive their portion *directly* from the owner of the sacrifice, but are like sons or servants who take their portion from the table of their Father and King.

16-19. וְאֵת שְׂעִיר הַחַטָּאת . . . וְאֹתָהּ נָתַן לָכֶם לָשֵׂאת אֶת עֲוֺן הָעֵדָה . . . הֵן הַיּוֹם הִקְרִיבוּ — *And the goat of the sin offering . . . and He has given it to you to bear the iniquity of the congregation . . . if this day they had offered.* The discussion between Moses and Aaron is explained by the *Sforno* as follows. The eighth day (from which

כ כָּאֵלֶּה וְאָכַלְתִּי חַטָּאת֙ הַיּ֔וֹם הַיִּיטַ֖ב בְּעֵינֵ֣י יְהוָ֑ה וַיִּשְׁמַ֣ע מֹשֶׁ֔ה וַיִּיטַ֖ב
בְּעֵינָֽיו:

יא שׁשׁי א־ב וַיְדַבֵּ֤ר יְהוָה֙ אֶל־מֹשֶׁ֣ה וְאֶֽל־אַהֲרֹ֔ן לֵאמֹ֖ר אֲלֵהֶֽם: דַּבְּר֛וּ אֶל־בְּנֵ֥י יִשְׂרָאֵ֖ל
ג לֵאמֹ֑ר זֹ֤את הַֽחַיָּה֙ אֲשֶׁ֣ר תֹּֽאכְל֔וּ מִכָּל־הַבְּהֵמָ֖ה אֲשֶׁ֥ר עַל־הָאָֽרֶץ: כֹּ֣ל |
מַפְרֶ֣סֶת פַּרְסָ֗ה וְשֹׁסַ֤עַת שֶׁ֨סַע֙ פְּרָסֹ֔ת מַעֲלַ֥ת גֵּרָ֖ה בַּבְּהֵמָ֑ה אֹתָ֖הּ תֹּאכֵֽלוּ:
ד אַ֤ךְ אֶת־זֶה֙ לֹ֣א תֹֽאכְל֔וּ מִֽמַּעֲלֵי֙ הַגֵּרָ֔ה וּמִמַּפְרִיסֵ֖י הַפַּרְסָ֑ה אֶֽת־הַ֠גָּמָל כִּֽי־
ה מַעֲלֵ֨ה גֵרָ֜ה ה֗וּא וּפַרְסָה֙ אֵינֶ֣נּוּ מַפְרִ֔יס טָמֵ֥א ה֖וּא לָכֶֽם: וְאֶת־הַשָּׁפָ֗ן
ו כִּֽי־מַעֲלֵ֤ה גֵרָה֙ ה֔וּא וּפַרְסָ֖ה לֹ֣א יַפְרִ֑יס טָמֵ֥א ה֖וּא לָכֶֽם: וְאֶת־הָֽאַרְנֶ֗בֶת
ז כִּֽי־מַעֲלַ֤ת גֵּרָה֙ הִ֔וא וּפַרְסָ֖ה לֹ֣א הִפְרִ֑יסָה טְמֵאָ֥ה הִ֖וא לָכֶֽם: וְאֶת־הַ֠חֲזִיר
כִּֽי־מַפְרִ֨יס פַּרְסָ֜ה ה֗וּא וְשֹׁסַ֥ע שֶׁ֨סַע֙ פַּרְסָ֔ה וְה֖וּא גֵּרָ֣ה לֹֽא־יִגָּ֑ר טָמֵ֥א ה֖וּא

---

offering, even though these sacrifices are not permanent communal holy offerings,
and we were to have eaten the sin offering today while in a state of *aninus*,
mourning, would it have been pleasing in the sight of God that in a state of *aninus*
we should (also) eat a sacrifice which is obligatory upon all generations? It is well
known that if a *Kohen* who is an *onein* eats an offering with knowledge and intent,
it cannot atone, as it says regarding קָדָשִׁים קַלִּים (*the lesser holy*), לֹא אָכַלְתִּי בְאֹנִי
מִמֶּנּוּ, *I have not eaten thereof in my mourning* (Deut. 26:14). Although you
commanded us to eat the meal offering which is of transitory sanctity, even in a
state of mourning, it does not follow that this ruling also applies in the case of
permanent sacrifices.

20. וַיִּיטַב בְּעֵינָיו — *It was pleasing in his eyes.* He rejoiced in the good reasoning of
his brother and his sons who understood and taught (decided the law) so well.

XI

2. זֹאת הַחַיָּה אֲשֶׁר תֹּאכְלוּ — *These are the living things which you may eat.* Behold,
after Israel removed their spiritual crowns (ornaments) which they had attained at
the time of the giving of the Torah, and through which they were deemed worthy
that the Divine Presence dwell in their midst without (the need for) any
intermediary, as it says, בְּכָל הַמָּקוֹם אֲשֶׁר אַזְכִּיר אֶת שְׁמִי אָבוֹא אֵלֶיךָ וּבֵרַכְתִּיךָ, *In every*

NOTES

Sforno as follows. The eighth day (from which
this Torah portion takes its name) was *Rosh
Chodesh* (the New Moon of) Nissan. The sin
offering which the *Kohanim* had burned was
that of the New Moon sacrifice which Moses
felt had to be eaten if it was to serve its
purpose of atonement. Aaron, however, argued that an *onen* (a mourner from the time of
his relative's death until nightfall following
the burial), in which category they all were,
may not partake of any sacrifice, especially a
communal one which is incumbent upon
Israel to offer for all time. Even if an exception
was made by Moses regarding the meal
offering of consecration, this dispensation
could not apply to the sin offering of the New

Moon which is an obligation for all generations, unlike that meal offering which was
only קָדָשִׁי שָׁעָה, a one-time transitory offering.
Therefore, they were justified in burning the
sin offering, given their state of *aninus*
(mourning). Moses accepted Aaron's reasoning and was pleased to see the clarity and logic
of his brother's thinking which was not
beclouded by the tragic death of his two sons.

XI

2. זֹאת הַחַיָּה אֲשֶׁר תֹּאכְלוּ — *These are the living
things which you may eat.* God's original
intent was to dwell in the midst of the Jewish
people without the medium of a Sanctuary or

ח־ט לָכֶם: מִבְּשָׂרָם לֹא תֹאכֵלוּ וּבְנִבְלָתָם לֹא תִגָּעוּ טְמֵאִים הֵם לָכֶם: אֶת־זֶה
תֹּאכְלוּ מִכֹּל אֲשֶׁר בַּמָּיִם כֹּל אֲשֶׁר־לוֹ סְנַפִּיר וְקַשְׂקֶשֶׂת בַּמַּיִם בַּיַּמִּים
י וּבַנְּחָלִים אֹתָם תֹּאכֵלוּ: וְכֹל אֲשֶׁר אֵין־לוֹ סְנַפִּיר וְקַשְׂקֶשֶׂת בַּיַּמִּים
וּבַנְּחָלִים מִכֹּל שֶׁרֶץ הַמַּיִם וּמִכֹּל נֶפֶשׁ הַחַיָּה אֲשֶׁר בַּמָּיִם שֶׁקֶץ הֵם לָכֶם:
יא־יב וְשֶׁקֶץ יִהְיוּ לָכֶם מִבְּשָׂרָם לֹא תֹאכֵלוּ וְאֶת־נִבְלָתָם תְּשַׁקֵּצוּ: כֹּל אֲשֶׁר
יג אֵין־לוֹ סְנַפִּיר וְקַשְׂקֶשֶׂת בַּמָּיִם שֶׁקֶץ הוּא לָכֶם: וְאֶת־אֵלֶּה תְּשַׁקְּצוּ מִן־
יד הָעוֹף לֹא יֵאָכְלוּ שֶׁקֶץ הֵם אֶת־הַנֶּשֶׁר וְאֶת־הַפֶּרֶס וְאֵת הָעָזְנִיָּה: וְאֶת־
טו־טז הַדָּאָה וְאֶת־הָאַיָּה לְמִינָהּ: אֵת כָּל־עֹרֵב לְמִינוֹ: וְאֵת בַּת הַיַּעֲנָה וְאֶת־
יז הַתַּחְמָס וְאֶת־הַשָּׁחַף וְאֶת־הַנֵּץ לְמִינֵהוּ: וְאֶת־הַכּוֹס וְאֶת־הַשָּׁלָךְ וְאֶת־
יח־יט הַיַּנְשׁוּף: וְאֶת־הַתִּנְשֶׁמֶת וְאֶת־הַקָּאָת וְאֶת־הָרָחָם: וְאֵת הַחֲסִידָה הָאֲנָפָה

---

place where I cause My Name to be mentioned I will come to you and bless you (*Exodus* 20:21), and which shall be in the future (end of days), as it says, *And I will set My Mishkan among you, and My soul shall not abhor you* (26:11), God, the Blessed One, afterward refused to have His Presence dwell among them at all, as it says, כִּי לֹא אֶעֱלֶה בְּקִרְבְּךָ, *For I will not go up in the midst of you* (*Exodus* 33:3). Moses our Teacher (however) achieved through his prayer some amelioration that the Divine Presence would abide among them through the medium of the *Mishkan* (Sanctuary), its furnishings, attendants (servants) and sacrifices, and they merited and attained (the level of) *And the glory of* HASHEM *appeared unto all the people* (9:23) and to the fire descending from heaven (9:24). Therefore, (God) considered (the need) to remedy their temperament that it be predisposed to be illuminated with the light of everlasting life. This (was to be done) through the regulation (lit., repair) of food and (laws regarding) the reproductive system. (The Torah) prohibits foods which defile (man's) (moral) characteristics and (mental) powers, as it says, *And you shall be defiled through them* (11:43), and as it says, *You shall not make yourselves detestable* (v. 43), and as it says, *Neither shall you defile yourselves with any manner of swarming things, because I am* HASHEM *that brought you up out of the land of Egypt to be your God; you shall therefore be holy* (vs. 44-45), namely, everlasting, comparable to the Creator, Blessed be He, as it says, *for I am holy* (ibid.). And (He) prohibited a *niddah* (menstruant), a *zavah* (one who has an issue) and a *yoledes* (woman who gave birth) so as to sanctify the seed (of Israel) and purify it

NOTES

any other form of intermediary between Israel and God. Were it not for the sin of the Golden Calf this would have come to pass and Israel, as a holy nation, would never have withered or perished but would have been everlasting (see notes to the *Sforno* on *Exodus* 19:6). After this grand plan was thwarted, God originally refused to cause His Presence to dwell in the midst of Israel until Moses prevailed upon Him through his prayers to dwell in the Sanctuary. Our Sages teach us that the laws enumerated in this portion of the Torah (*Shemini*) and those which follow (*Tazria-Metzora*) serve to refine and purify the collective soul and character of Israel, thereby preparing them to receive the *Shechinah*, Divine Presence. The laws of *Kashrus* and the laws of *Niddah*, as well as the laws of purity and uncleanness, are all meant to sanctify the people of Israel, thereby bringing them to a level of holiness which reflects the Holy One Himself. This is the thrust of the *Sforno's* commentary on this verse, and verses 43-44. The *Sforno* then proceeds to explain the difference between the expressions *tamei*, unclean, and שֶׁקֶץ, *detestable*. He submits that only that which can convey defilement through contact or carrying is referred to as טָמֵא while that which is prohibited but does not physically defile is referred to as שֶׁקֶץ.

כ לְמִינָהּ וְאֶת־הַדּוּכִיפַת וְאֶת־הָעֲטַלֵּף: כֹּל שֶׁרֶץ הָעוֹף הַהֹלֵךְ עַל־אַרְבַּע

כא שָׁקֶץ הוּא לָכֶם: אַךְ אֶת־זֶה תֹּאכְלוּ מִכֹּל שֶׁרֶץ הָעוֹף הַהֹלֵךְ עַל־אַרְבַּע

°לו ק׳ כב אֲשֶׁר־°לֹא כְרָעַיִם מִמַּעַל לְרַגְלָיו לְנַתֵּר בָּהֵן עַל־הָאָרֶץ: אֶת־אֵלֶּה מֵהֶם

תֹּאכֵלוּ אֶת־הָאַרְבֶּה לְמִינוֹ וְאֶת־הַסָּלְעָם לְמִינֵהוּ וְאֶת־הַחַרְגֹּל לְמִינֵהוּ

כג וְאֶת־הֶחָגָב לְמִינֵהוּ: וְכֹל שֶׁרֶץ הָעוֹף אֲשֶׁר־לוֹ אַרְבַּע רַגְלָיִם שֶׁקֶץ הוּא

כד־כה לָכֶם: וּלְאֵלֶּה תִּטַּמָּאוּ כָּל־הַנֹּגֵעַ בְּנִבְלָתָם יִטְמָא עַד־הָעָרֶב: וְכָל־הַנֹּשֵׂא

כו מִנִּבְלָתָם יְכַבֵּס בְּגָדָיו וְטָמֵא עַד־הָעָרֶב: לְכָל־הַבְּהֵמָה אֲשֶׁר הִוא מַפְרֶסֶת

פַּרְסָה וְשֶׁסַע ׀ אֵינֶנָּה שֹׁסַעַת וְגֵרָה אֵינֶנָּה מַעֲלָה טְמֵאִים הֵם לָכֶם כָּל־הַנֹּגֵעַ

כז בָּהֶם יִטְמָא: וְכֹל ׀ הוֹלֵךְ עַל־כַּפָּיו בְּכָל־הַחַיָּה הַהֹלֶכֶת עַל־אַרְבַּע טְמֵאִים

כח הֵם לָכֶם כָּל־הַנֹּגֵעַ בְּנִבְלָתָם יִטְמָא עַד־הָעָרֶב: וְהַנֹּשֵׂא אֶת־נִבְלָתָם יְכַבֵּס

כט בְּגָדָיו וְטָמֵא עַד־הָעָרֶב טְמֵאִים הֵמָּה לָכֶם: וְזֶה לָכֶם

ל הַטָּמֵא בַּשֶּׁרֶץ הַשֹּׁרֵץ עַל־הָאָרֶץ הַחֹלֶד וְהָעַכְבָּר וְהַצָּב לְמִינֵהוּ: וְהָאֲנָקָה

לא וְהַכֹּחַ וְהַלְּטָאָה וְהַחֹמֶט וְהַתִּנְשָׁמֶת: אֵלֶּה הַטְּמֵאִים לָכֶם בְּכָל־הַשָּׁרֶץ כָּל־

לב הַנֹּגֵעַ בָּהֶם בְּמֹתָם יִטְמָא עַד־הָעָרֶב: וְכֹל אֲשֶׁר־יִפֹּל־עָלָיו מֵהֶם ׀ בְּמֹתָם

יִטְמָא מִכָּל־כְּלִי־עֵץ אוֹ בֶגֶד אוֹ־עוֹר אוֹ שָׂק כָּל־כְּלִי אֲשֶׁר־יֵעָשֶׂה מְלָאכָה

שביעי לג בָּהֶם בַּמַּיִם יוּבָא וְטָמֵא עַד־הָעֶרֶב וְטָהֵר: וְכָל־כְּלִי־חֶרֶשׂ אֲשֶׁר־יִפֹּל מֵהֶם

לד אֶל־תּוֹכוֹ כֹּל אֲשֶׁר בְּתוֹכוֹ יִטְמָא וְאֹתוֹ תִשְׁבֹּרוּ: מִכָּל־הָאֹכֶל אֲשֶׁר יֵאָכֵל

אֲשֶׁר יָבוֹא עָלָיו מַיִם יִטְמָא וְכָל־מַשְׁקֶה אֲשֶׁר יִשָּׁתֶה בְּכָל־כְּלִי יִטְמָא:

לה וְכֹל אֲשֶׁר־יִפֹּל מִנִּבְלָתָם ׀ עָלָיו יִטְמָא תַּנּוּר וְכִירַיִם יֻתָּץ טְמֵאִים הֵם

לו וּטְמֵאִים יִהְיוּ לָכֶם: אַךְ מַעְיָן וּבוֹר מִקְוֵה־מַיִם יִהְיֶה טָהוֹר וְנֹגֵעַ בְּנִבְלָתָם

לז־לח יִטְמָא: וְכִי יִפֹּל מִנִּבְלָתָם עַל־כָּל־זֶרַע זֵרוּעַ אֲשֶׁר יִזָּרֵעַ טָהוֹר הוּא: וְכִי

לט יֻתַּן־מַיִם עַל־זֶרַע וְנָפַל מִנִּבְלָתָם עָלָיו טָמֵא הוּא לָכֶם: וְכִי

יָמוּת מִן־הַבְּהֵמָה אֲשֶׁר־הִיא לָכֶם לְאָכְלָה הַנֹּגֵעַ בְּנִבְלָתָהּ יִטְמָא

מ עַד־הָעָרֶב: וְהָאֹכֵל מִנִּבְלָתָהּ יְכַבֵּס בְּגָדָיו וְטָמֵא עַד־הָעָרֶב וְהַנֹּשֵׂא

---

from all *tumah*, uncleanness, as it says, *You shall separate the children of Israel from their tumah that they die not in their tumah when they defile My Mishkan that is in the midst of them* (15:31). And (the Torah) makes mention of (utilizes) the term *tumah* regarding the carcass of a non-kosher animal and beast (vs. 26-28) and regarding the eight swarming things (vs. 29-38) and regarding the carcass of a kosher animal (vs. 39-40) because each of these has (laws of) *tumah* through contact and some through carrying. However, (regarding) those which only defile the soul, and do not make one *tamei* through contact at all, such as fish, fowl, locusts and other crawling things, the term used is שִׁקּוּץ, *detestable*, as it says, *They are a detestable thing to you* (vs. 10-13), and *Is a detestable thing, it shall not be eaten* (v. 41) and *For they are a detestable thing* (v. 42).

מא אֶת־נִבְלָתָהּ יְכַבֵּס בְּגָדָיו וְטָמֵא עַד־הָעָרֶב׃ וְכָל־הַשֶּׁרֶץ הַשֹּׁרֵץ עַל־הָאָרֶץ
מב שֶׁקֶץ הוּא לֹא יֵאָכֵל׃ כֹּל הוֹלֵךְ עַל־גָּחוֹן וְכֹל ׀ הוֹלֵךְ עַל־אַרְבַּע עַד
כָּל־מַרְבֵּה רַגְלַיִם לְכָל־הַשֶּׁרֶץ הַשֹּׁרֵץ עַל־הָאָרֶץ לֹא תֹאכְלוּם כִּי־שֶׁקֶץ
מג הֵם׃ אַל־תְּשַׁקְּצוּ אֶת־נַפְשֹׁתֵיכֶם בְּכָל־הַשֶּׁרֶץ הַשֹּׁרֵץ וְלֹא תִטַּמְּאוּ בָּהֶם
מד וְנִטְמֵתֶם בָּם׃ כִּי אֲנִי יהוה אֱלֹהֵיכֶם וְהִתְקַדִּשְׁתֶּם וִהְיִיתֶם קְדֹשִׁים כִּי קָדוֹשׁ
מפטיר מה אָנִי וְלֹא תְטַמְּאוּ אֶת־נַפְשֹׁתֵיכֶם בְּכָל־הַשֶּׁרֶץ הָרֹמֵשׂ עַל־הָאָרֶץ׃ כִּי ׀ אֲנִי
יהוה הַמַּעֲלֶה אֶתְכֶם מֵאֶרֶץ מִצְרַיִם לִהְיֹת לָכֶם לֵאלֹהִים וִהְיִיתֶם קְדֹשִׁים
מו כִּי קָדוֹשׁ אָנִי׃ זֹאת תּוֹרַת הַבְּהֵמָה וְהָעוֹף וְכֹל נֶפֶשׁ הַחַיָּה הָרֹמֶשֶׂת בַּמָּיִם
מז וּלְכָל־נֶפֶשׁ הַשֹּׁרֶצֶת עַל־הָאָרֶץ׃ לְהַבְדִּיל בֵּין הַטָּמֵא וּבֵין הַטָּהֹר וּבֵין הַחַיָּה
הַנֶּאֱכֶלֶת וּבֵין הַחַיָּה אֲשֶׁר לֹא תֵאָכֵל׃

43-44. וְלֹא תִטַּמְּאוּ בָּהֶם וְנִטְמֵתֶם בָּם . . . כִּי אֲנִי ה׳ אֱלֹהֵיכֶם וְהִתְקַדִּשְׁתֶּם — *You shall not make yourselves tamei through them that you shall become tamei thereby . . . For I am HASHEM your God; sanctify yourselves.* Do not make yourselves unclean through them in a manner (that will result in) your becoming unclean and vacuous. This will occur if you eat them; for since *I am your God* I desire that you sanctify yourselves and prepare yourselves for holiness.

וִהְיִיתֶם קְדֹשִׁים כִּי קָדוֹשׁ אָנִי — *And be holy, for I am holy* . . . in order that you be holy and everlasting by acknowledging your Creator and walking in His ways. Now this I desire so that you shall become similar to Me, *for I am holy.* All this you will realize when you sanctify yourselves and take care (not to partake) of prohibited foods, as (our Sages) say, 'A man sanctifies himself a little, and he is sanctified (by God) in great measure' (*Yoma* 39a).

45. כִּי אֲנִי ה׳ הַמַּעֲלֶה אֶתְכֶם מֵאֶרֶץ מִצְרַיִם לִהְיֹת לָכֶם לֵאלֹהִים — *For I am HASHEM Who brought you up out of the land of Egypt to be your God.* And it is proper that you make this effort to sanctify (yourselves) and to be holy so as to fulfill My desire, for indeed, My intent in bringing you out from the land of Egypt was that you attain this (degree of holiness), that I shall be a God to you without any intermediary, and you (in turn) shall be holy and everlasting, resembling Me in characteristics (conduct) and concepts, *for I am holy.*

46. זֹאת תּוֹרַת הַבְּהֵמָה וְהָעוֹף — *This is the law of the beast and of the fowl.* This is the purpose and reason for the food prohibitions enumerated (mentioned) above.

NOTES

44. וִהְיִיתֶם קְדֹשִׁים — *And be holy.* The concept that holiness insures the everlasting nature of Israel was developed by the *Sforno* in *Exodus* 15:11 and 19:6. See his commentary and notes there which elucidate his commentary here.

45. כִּי אֲנִי ה׳ הַמַּעֲלֶה אֶתְכֶם מֵאֶרֶץ מִצְרַיִם לִהְיֹת לָכֶם לֵאלֹהִים — *For I am HASHEM Who brought you up out of the land of Egypt to be your God.* Since God wishes us to be holy, thereby 'imitating him,' He gave us the laws of food and of purity which help us lead holy lives. That was His intention in bringing us out of Egypt. Redemption was for the purpose of becoming a *holy nation.*

פרשת תזריע
Parashas Tazria

יב א־ב וַיְדַבֵּר יהוה אֶל־מֹשֶׁה לֵּאמֹר: דַּבֵּר אֶל־בְּנֵי יִשְׂרָאֵל לֵאמֹר אִשָּׁה כִּי
ג תַזְרִיעַ וְיָלְדָה זָכָר וְטָמְאָה שִׁבְעַת יָמִים כִּימֵי נִדַּת דְּוֺתָהּ תִּטְמָא: וּבַיּוֹם
ד הַשְּׁמִינִי יִמּוֹל בְּשַׂר עָרְלָתוֹ: וּשְׁלֹשִׁים יוֹם וּשְׁלֹשֶׁת יָמִים תֵּשֵׁב בִּדְמֵי טָהֳרָה

XII

2. אִשָּׁה כִּי תַזְרִיעַ וְיָלְדָה זָכָר — *If a woman caused fructification of seed and gives birth to a male.* (Our Sages) have said, 'If a woman emits seed first she bears a male' (*Niddah* 31a). This means that the seed of the woman, which is the liquid emitted by her at times during intercourse, plays no role in the formation of the male fetus at all; rather her (uterine) blood is worked upon and jells in the seed of the male. When (however) her liquid seed enters her jelled blood, there is an excess of liquid (seed) and the child will be female.

כִּימֵי נִדַּת דְּוֺתָהּ — *As the days of the niddos (impurity) of the sickness.* Because in the initial seven days, the *niddah* blood, which has not yet degenerated nor lost its form of *tumah,* is stimulated.

3. וּבַיּוֹם הַשְּׁמִינִי יִמּוֹל — *And on the eighth day there shall be circumcised.* For then the unclean *niddah* blood from which the child received his nourishment in the womb of his mother, has been consumed (lit., digested), and the child is now (sufficiently) pure to enter the holy covenant.

NOTES

XII

2. אִשָּׁה כִּי תַזְרִיעַ וְיָלְדָה זָכָר — *If a woman caused fructification of seed and gives birth to a male.* The saying of our Sages, quoted by the *Sforno,* is based upon their interpretation of this verse. If a woman emits seed (תַזְרִיעַ) first, then the result will be that she will give birth to a male child (וְיָלְדָה זָכָר). The *Sforno,* who was a doctor, explains the reason for this as follows: at the time of ovulation, the woman releases her seed which loses a degree of potency as it jells in the seed of the male, being more dominant since it is released later than hers. However, if she ovulates after the male has emitted his seed, her liquid seed is dominant and will result in the conception of a female.

Recent medical research has established that the acid in the vaginal canal can destroy the male Y chromosome, resulting in the male X chromosome impregnating the egg whereby the offspring will be a female. However, at the time of ovulation, the alkaline which is secreted by the female neutralizes the acid, thereby permitting the Y chromosome to come into play and impregnate the woman, resulting in a male offspring. This bears out the statement of our Sages that if the woman emits her seed first (i.e., ovulates and thereby ejects alkaline), the chances of a male child being conceived are far greater. [I am indebted to Dr. Fred Rosner and Rabbi David Cohen for their assistance in the preparation of this note.]

כִּימֵי נִדַּת דְּוֺתָהּ — *As the days of the niddos (impurity) of the sickness.* The *Sforno* explains the reason for the seven-day period of impurity. Being that the impure blood is still viable, the woman remains *tamei.* This also explains the reason for the twofold expression וְטָמְאָה, *and she shall be in an impure condition,* and תִּטְמָא which has the same meaning and is seemingly redundant. However, the meaning of these two expressions is : she is in an impure state (וְטָמְאָה) for seven days because her blood has as yet not been purified, and therefore תִּטְמָא — she remains in an impure state since her condition has not changed.

3. וּבַיּוֹם הַשְּׁמִינִי יִמּוֹל — *And on the eighth day there shall be circumcised.* The *Sforno* explains why the Torah finds it necessary to mention *bris milah, the covenant of circumcision,* in this *parashah* which deals with the ritual laws pertaining to the woman, not the child! His answer is that the nature of the mother's blood, which is the subject of this chapter, also has an effect upon the status and readiness of the child. Only after the impure blood from which the child received his nourishment in the womb has been eliminated is he fit to enter the holy covenant of circumcision.

בְּכָל־קֹדֶשׁ לֹא־תִגָּע וְאֶל־הַמִּקְדָּשׁ לֹא תָבֹא עַד־מְלֹאת יְמֵי טָהֳרָהּ׃
ה וְאִם־נְקֵבָה תֵלֵד וְטָמְאָה שְׁבֻעַיִם כְּנִדָּתָהּ וְשִׁשִּׁים יוֹם וְשֵׁשֶׁת יָמִים תֵּשֵׁב
ו עַל־דְּמֵי טָהֳרָה׃ וּבִמְלֹאת ׀ יְמֵי טָהֳרָהּ לְבֵן אוֹ לְבַת תָּבִיא כֶּבֶשׂ בֶּן־שְׁנָתוֹ
ז לְעֹלָה וּבֶן־יוֹנָה אוֹ־תֹר לְחַטָּאת אֶל־פֶּתַח אֹהֶל־מוֹעֵד אֶל־הַכֹּהֵן׃ וְהִקְרִיבוֹ
לִפְנֵי יהוה וְכִפֶּר עָלֶיהָ וְטָהֲרָה מִמְּקֹר דָּמֶיהָ זֹאת תּוֹרַת הַיֹּלֶדֶת לַזָּכָר אוֹ
ח לַנְּקֵבָה׃ וְאִם־לֹא תִמְצָא יָדָהּ דֵּי שֶׂה וְלָקְחָה שְׁתֵּי־תֹרִים אוֹ שְׁנֵי בְּנֵי יוֹנָה
אֶחָד לְעֹלָה וְאֶחָד לְחַטָּאת וְכִפֶּר עָלֶיהָ הַכֹּהֵן וְטָהֵרָה׃
יג א־ב וַיְדַבֵּר יהוה אֶל־מֹשֶׁה וְאֶל־אַהֲרֹן לֵאמֹר׃ אָדָם כִּי־יִהְיֶה בְעוֹר־בְּשָׂרוֹ
שְׂאֵת אוֹ־סַפַּחַת אוֹ בַהֶרֶת וְהָיָה בְעוֹר־בְּשָׂרוֹ לְנֶגַע צָרָעַת וְהוּבָא

---

4. בִּדְמֵי טָהֳרָה — *In the blood of purification.* Because the *niddah* blood is not from her present menstrual period, but from those periods which preceded her pregnancy, (and they) already degenerated and no longer have the form of the blood (from) those periods of *tumah.*

5. שְׁבֻעַיִם — *Two weeks.* For the aftereffects (of birth) are increased (prolonged) with the birth of a female.

8. וְכִפֶּר עָלֶיהָ — *Shall make atonement for her.* Because all the days that her unclean (blood) flows, her thoughts are concentrated on the reproductive organs and their functioning, (hence) she is not worthy (prepared or geared) to (enter) the Temple or (come into contact) with its sacred objects — until she brings her atonement (offering) and turns (her thoughts) to the holy.

XIII

2. אָדָם כִּי יִהְיֶה בְעוֹר בְּשָׂרוֹ — *When a man shall have in the skin of his flesh.* Now this happens most frequently if the seed does not become purified from the unclean blood (lit., blood of *niddos*).

שְׂאֵת אוֹ סַפַּחַת אוֹ בַהֶרֶת — *A rising or a scab or a bright spot.* These are all types of leprosy and their appearance is white, as tradition teaches us. Among them there is no variety of leprosy discussed by doctors (today), except for the *morphia albaram*

NOTES

4. בִּדְמֵי טָהֳרָה — *In the blood of purification.* The *Sforno* explains the reason for this law that any blood seen by the woman during the thirty-three-day period after the birth of a male child is considered טָהוֹר, *clean, pure.* See *Rashi.* [This passage does not reflect the *halachah* in practice today.]

8. וְכִפֶּר עָלֶיהָ — *Shall make atonement for her.* The *Sforno* explains the reason for this waiting period before the woman can bring her sacrifices and once again qualify to enter the Temple precincts and come into contact with the sacred. Although she is physically ready and ritually clean, mentally she is not yet geared to concentrate on the holy. Since the sacred demands כַּוָּנָה, *intent,* she must wait until her thoughts are sufficiently predisposed to focus on the non-physical, namely, the spiritual and the holy.

XIII

2. אָדָם כִּי יִהְיֶה בְעוֹר בְּשָׂרוֹ — *When a man shall have in the skin of his flesh.* The *Sforno* is explaining the link between the previous chapter, which discusses the status of the woman who has given birth, with this chapter which deals with various נְגָעִים, *afflictions.*

שְׂאֵת אוֹ סַפַּחַת אוֹ בַהֶרֶת — *A rising or a scab or a bright spot.* The *Sforno* explains that the afflictions of leprosy which make a person *tamei,* unclean, are not connected with those afflictions which may be far more severe

ג אֶל־אַהֲרֹן הַכֹּהֵן אוֹ אֶל־אַחַד מִבָּנָיו הַכֹּהֲנִים: וְרָאָה הַכֹּהֵן אֶת־הַנֶּגַע
בְּעוֹר־הַבָּשָׂר וְשֵׂעָר בַּנֶּגַע הָפַךְ ׀ לָבָן וּמַרְאֵה הַנֶּגַע עָמֹק מֵעוֹר בְּשָׂרוֹ נֶגַע
ד צָרַעַת הוּא וְרָאָהוּ הַכֹּהֵן וְטִמֵּא אֹתוֹ: וְאִם־בַּהֶרֶת לְבָנָה הִוא בְּעוֹר בְּשָׂרוֹ

(white mole) and the scall. Indeed, (regarding) other types of severe leprosy of which they (the doctors) have told us, (such as) cancerous spreading over the entire body, which tend (in color) toward red and black, the Torah does not (declare) them *tamei* at all. For only these four appearances (of leprosy) of which our Sages tell us — namely a *rising*, and its sub-species, a *bright spot*, and its sub-species — come as an admonition for iniquity, as (our Sages) state, 'Any person who has one of these four appearances (of leprosy), it is naught but an altar of atonement' (*Berachos* 5b). But other types of leprosy which the doctors speak of are not (considered) as an altar of atonement among our people, (but are a result) of ultimate debasement, God forbid, as are the other evil diseases of Egypt (*Deut.* 7:15) or they are due to (improper) deviations in (one's) eating and drinking habits (lit., behavior) and other (similar aberrations); (but) these are not (considered) *tamei* at all.

וְהוּבָא — *Then he shall be brought.* (Regarding) one who goes to a place to be worked upon (i.e., to receive the act of another) the term בָּא, *come*, is not used; rather it is termed מוּבָא, *to be brought*, similar to, תּוּבַל לַמֶּלֶךְ . . . רֵעוֹתֶיהָ מוּבָאוֹת לָךְ, *She shall be brought to the king . . . her companions shall be brought to you* (*Psalms* 45:15), (also) וְהִגִּישׁוֹ אֲדֹנָיו, *Then his master shall bring him* (*Exodus* 21:6), (also) וְהֵבִיא הָאִישׁ אֶת אִשְׁתּוֹ, *Then shall the man bring his wife* (*Numbers* 5:15). The reverse (being) וְנִגְּשׁוּ אֶל הַמִּשְׁפָּט, *And they 'come' unto judgment* (*Deut.* 25:1) (and) וְנִקְרַב בַּעַל הַבַּיִת, *The master of the house 'shall come' near* (*Exodus* 22:7) (and) עַד הָאֱלֹהִים יָבֹא דְּבַר שְׁנֵיהֶם, *The cause of both parties 'shall come' before the judges* (ibid. 8).

3. נֶגַע צָרַעַת הוּא — *It is an affliction of leprosy.* Behold, at times (the Torah) says, נֶגַע צָרַעַת הוּא, *It is an affliction of leprosy*, and at other times, צָרַעַת הִיא, *It is leprosy* (v. 8) and at times, צָרַעַת נוֹשֶׁנֶת הִוא, *It is an old leprosy* (v. 11) and at times נֶגַע הוּא,

NOTES

physically (in nature) than the four which our Sages have listed as causing *tumah*, uncleanness. One must not confuse *tumah* with physical illness. They are separate, distinct and unrelated. *Tumah* is caused only by those afflictions which the Torah has ordained. As the *Sforno* will explain later, these four types of leprosy are visited upon man, as are the afflictions of garments and houses, for the purpose of alerting him to his shortcomings in the hope that he will repent and improve his behavior. That is why the Sages refer to them as 'an altar of atonement,' for through the suffering experienced by the victim, he will repent and God will forgive him.

וְהוּבָא — *Then he shall be brought.* The word וְהוּבָא is interpreted by the *Sforno* as being in the *huphal* form — the passive recipient of the causative *hiphil*. The afflicted person does not 'come' on his own volition to the *Kohen* — he is brought. However, he is brought for his own benefit, to be cleansed and purified. The examples cited by the *Sforno* all refer to instances where a person is brought by another, unwillingly in certain cases such as the Hebrew slave and the wife suspected of infidelity, but ultimately for their own good as in the case of the leper. The *Sforno* points out that when the Torah speaks of one who comes voluntarily, and not necessarily for his own benefit, the verb used is not in the *hiphil* or the *huphal* but in the *kal* or *niphal*, i.e., ונקרב ונגשו, יבא.

3. נֶגַע צָרַעַת הוּא — *It is an affliction of leprosy.* The *Sforno* amplifies the thought developed in v. 2 that the period of הֶסְגֵּר, when the afflicted person is 'shut up' and isolated from society, is for the purpose of contemplation and self-ex-

וְעָמֹק אֵין־מַרְאֶהָ מִן־הָעוֹר וּשְׂעָרָה לֹא־הָפַךְ לָבָן וְהִסְגִּיר הַכֹּהֵן אֶת־הַנֶּגַע
ה שִׁבְעַת יָמִים: וְרָאָהוּ הַכֹּהֵן בַּיּוֹם הַשְּׁבִיעִי וְהִנֵּה הַנֶּגַע עָמַד בְּעֵינָיו לֹא־פָשָׂה
שני ו הַנֶּגַע בָּעוֹר וְהִסְגִּירוֹ הַכֹּהֵן שִׁבְעַת יָמִים שֵׁנִית: וְרָאָה הַכֹּהֵן אֹתוֹ בַּיּוֹם

It is an affliction (v. 22). (The reason for this) is that leprosy, as is true of other illnesses, has periods of inception, of increase and of completeness and when the ailment is cured, (it is preceded by) a period of recession. The inception is called נֶגַע, *affliction*; when it worsens it is called נֶגַע צָרַעַת, *affliction of leprosy*; when full-blown it is called צָרַעַת, *leprosy*; when it becomes established (lit., old) it is called צָרַעַת נוֹשֶׁנֶת, *an old leprosy*, and when it recedes it is said נִרְפָּא הַנָּגַע, *the affliction is healed* (14:48), and נִרְפָּא הַנֶּתֶק, *the scall is healed* (v. 37). Now since this kind of ailment (is inflicted) as a punishment, as our Sages say, 'It is only an altar of atonement' (*Berachos* 5b), a time of isolation is given to arouse him to repent, as it says, וַיִּגֶל אָזְנָם לַמּוּסָר וַיֹּאמֶר כִּי יְשׁוּבוּן מֵאָוֶן, *He opens also their ear to discipline and commands that they return from iniquity* (*Job* 36:10).

4. וְעָמֹק אֵין מַרְאֶהָ מִן הָעוֹר — *And the appearance thereof is not deeper than the skin.* Although (our Sages) said, 'Every white color is deep, just as anything illuminated by the sun is deeper than the shadow' (*Shevuos* 6b); nonetheless, since the skin is also, to an extent, part of the white, (hence) not every white (affliction) is deeper than it (the skin) unless it is a whiter shade than the skin. (The result is) that the whiteness of the skin relative to it (the affliction) will be as that of the shadow to the sunlight.

5. וְרָאָהוּ הַכֹּהֵן — *And the Kohen shall look on him.* It is an enactment of Scriptures (גְּזֵרַת הַכָּתוּב) that the (declaration) of uncleanness and purification of afflictions be pronounced only by the mouth of a *Kohen* (*Sifra*) — כִּי שִׂפְתֵי כֹהֵן יִשְׁמְרוּ דַעַת, *For the Kohen's lips should keep knowledge* (*Malachi* 2:7) — and they will instruct the afflicted one to examine his deeds, and he will pray for himself and the *Kohen* will also pray on his behalf. Additionally, since all afflictions (are decided) by their 'mouths,' they will gain expertise regarding the (various) levels of appearance, (thereby being able) to differentiate between one affliction and another.

NOTES

amination, which brings him eventually to תְּשׁוּבָה, *repentance.*

4. וְעָמֹק אֵין מַרְאֶהָ מִן הָעוֹר — *And the appearance thereof is not deeper than the skin.* The *Sforno* resolves the seeming discrepancy between verses 3 and 4. *Rashi*, commenting on verse 4, says: 'I do not know the meaning of this.' He refers to the fact that in verse 3 he had stated that the white spot is *always* deeper in appearance than the surrounding skin, therefore he cannot understand why verse 4 speaks of an instance of the white spot *not* being deeper in appearance than the skin. The *Sforno*, however, explains that it depends upon the relative shades of whiteness between the skin and the נֶגַע, *affliction*. Only if the skin is darker will the white spot appear deeper but if the skin also takes on the white hue of the affliction, then the נֶגַע will not appear deeper than the skin.

5. וְרָאָהוּ הַכֹּהֵן — *And the Kohen shall look on him.* The *Sforno* gives two reasons for empowering the *Kohen* to determine whether the afflicted person is *tamei* or *tahor*. Firstly, as mentioned above, since leprosy is visited upon the person to awaken him to examine his ways and redirect them, the most suitable person to assist him through prayer and instruction is the *Kohen*, who is charged to be the teacher of the people of Israel. Secondly, since the *Kohen* gains experience through constant practice, he becomes the expert who can distinguish between different appearances and thereby determine the status of each case.

הַשְּׁבִיעִי֙ שֵׁנִ֔ית וְהִנֵּ֗ה כֵּהָ֤ה הַנֶּ֙גַע֙ וְלֹא־פָשָׂ֤ה הַנֶּ֙גַע֙ בָּע֔וֹר וְטִהֲר֥וֹ הַכֹּהֵ֖ן

ז מִסְפַּ֣חַת הִ֑וא וְכִבֶּ֥ס בְּגָדָ֖יו וְטָהֵֽר: וְאִם־פָּשֹׂ֨ה תִפְשֶׂ֤ה הַמִּסְפַּ֙חַת֙ בָּע֔וֹר אַחֲרֵ֣י

ח הֵרָאֹת֥וֹ אֶל־הַכֹּהֵ֖ן לְטָהֳרָת֑וֹ וְנִרְאָ֥ה שֵׁנִ֖ית אֶל־הַכֹּהֵֽן: וְרָאָה֙ הַכֹּהֵ֔ן וְהִנֵּ֛ה פָּשְׂתָ֥ה הַמִּסְפַּ֖חַת בָּע֑וֹר וְטִמְּא֥וֹ הַכֹּהֵ֖ן צָרַ֥עַת הִֽוא:

ט-י נֶ֣גַע צָרַ֔עַת כִּ֥י תִהְיֶ֖ה בְּאָדָ֑ם וְהוּבָ֖א אֶל־הַכֹּהֵֽן: וְרָאָ֣ה הַכֹּהֵ֗ן וְהִנֵּ֤ה שְׂאֵת־

יא לְבָנָה֙ בָּע֔וֹר וְהִ֕יא הָפְכָ֖ה שֵׂעָ֣ר לָבָ֑ן וּמִֽחְיַ֛ת בָּשָׂ֥ר חַ֖י בַּשְׂאֵֽת: צָרַ֨עַת נוֹשֶׁ֜נֶת

יב הִ֗וא בְּע֤וֹר בְּשָׂרוֹ֙ וְטִמְּא֣וֹ הַכֹּהֵ֔ן לֹ֥א יַסְגִּרֶ֖נּוּ כִּ֥י טָמֵ֥א הֽוּא: וְאִם־פָּר֜וֹחַ תִּפְרַ֤ח הַצָּרַ֙עַת֙ בָּע֔וֹר וְכִסְּתָ֣ה הַצָּרַ֗עַת אֵ֚ת כָּל־ע֣וֹר הַנֶּ֔גַע מֵרֹאשׁ֖וֹ וְעַד־רַגְלָ֑יו

יג לְכָל־מַרְאֵ֖ה עֵינֵ֥י הַכֹּהֵֽן: וְרָאָ֣ה הַכֹּהֵ֗ן וְהִנֵּ֨ה כִסְּתָ֤ה הַצָּרַ֙עַת֙ אֶת־כָּל־בְּשָׂר֔וֹ

יד וְטִהַ֖ר אֶת־הַנָּ֑גַע כֻּלּ֛וֹ הָפַ֥ךְ לָבָ֖ן טָה֥וֹר הֽוּא: וּבְי֨וֹם הֵרָא֥וֹת בּ֛וֹ בָּשָׂ֥ר חַ֖י

טו יִטְמָֽא: וְרָאָ֧ה הַכֹּהֵ֛ן אֶת־הַבָּשָׂ֥ר הַחַ֖י וְטִמְּא֑וֹ הַבָּשָׂ֥ר הַחַ֛י טָמֵ֥א ה֖וּא צָרַ֥עַת

טז-יז הֽוּא: א֣וֹ כִ֥י יָשׁ֛וּב הַבָּשָׂ֥ר הַחַ֖י וְנֶהְפַּ֣ךְ לְלָבָ֑ן וּבָ֖א אֶל־הַכֹּהֵֽן: וְרָאָ֙הוּ֙ הַכֹּהֵ֔ן וְהִנֵּ֛ה נֶהְפַּ֥ךְ הַנֶּ֖גַע לְלָבָ֑ן וְטִהַ֧ר הַכֹּהֵ֛ן אֶת־הַנֶּ֖גַע טָה֥וֹר הֽוּא:

שלישי יח-יט וּבָשָׂ֕ר כִּֽי־יִהְיֶ֥ה בֽוֹ־בְעֹר֖וֹ שְׁחִ֑ין וְנִרְפָּֽא: וְהָיָ֞ה בִּמְק֤וֹם הַשְּׁחִין֙ שְׂאֵ֣ת לְבָנָ֔ה א֥וֹ

כ בַהֶ֖רֶת לְבָנָ֣ה אֲדַמְדָּ֑מֶת וְנִרְאָ֖ה אֶל־הַכֹּהֵֽן: וְרָאָ֣ה הַכֹּהֵ֗ן וְהִנֵּ֤ה מַרְאֶ֙הָ֙ שָׁפָ֣ל מִן־הָע֔וֹר וּשְׂעָרָ֖הּ הָפַ֣ךְ לָבָ֑ן וְטִמְּא֧וֹ הַכֹּהֵ֛ן נֶֽגַע־צָרַ֥עַת ה֖וּא בַּשְּׁחִ֥ין פָּרָֽחָה:

כא וְאִ֣ם ׀ יִרְאֶ֣נָּה הַכֹּהֵ֗ן וְהִנֵּ֤ה אֵֽין־בָּהּ֙ שֵׂעָ֣ר לָבָ֔ן וּשְׁפָלָ֥ה אֵינֶ֖נָּה מִן־הָע֑וֹר וְהִ֣יא

כב כֵהָ֑ה וְהִסְגִּיר֥וֹ הַכֹּהֵ֖ן שִׁבְעַ֥ת יָמִֽים: וְאִם־פָּשֹׂ֥ה תִפְשֶׂ֖ה בָּע֑וֹר וְטִמֵּ֥א הַכֹּהֵ֖ן

כג אֹת֖וֹ נֶ֣גַע הִֽוא: וְאִם־תַּחְתֶּ֜יהָ תַּעֲמֹ֤ד הַבַּהֶ֙רֶת֙ לֹ֣א פָשָׂ֔תָה צָרֶ֥בֶת הַשְּׁחִ֖ין הִ֑וא

רביעי כד וְטִהֲר֖וֹ הַכֹּהֵֽן: א֣וֹ בָשָׂ֔ר כִּֽי־יִהְיֶ֥ה בְעֹר֖וֹ מִכְוַת־אֵ֑שׁ וְהָֽיְתָ֞ה

כה מִֽחְיַ֣ת הַמִּכְוָ֗ה בַּהֶ֛רֶת לְבָנָ֥ה אֲדַמְדֶּ֖מֶת א֣וֹ לְבָנָֽה: וְרָאָ֣ה אֹתָ֣הּ הַכֹּהֵ֗ן וְהִנֵּ֨ה נֶהְפַּ֤ךְ שֵׂעָ֤ר לָבָן֙ בַּבַּהֶ֔רֶת וּמַרְאֶ֖הָ עָמֹ֣ק מִן־הָע֑וֹר צָרַ֣עַת הִ֔וא בַּמִּכְוָ֖ה פָּרָ֑חָה

כו וְטִמֵּ֤א אֹתוֹ֙ הַכֹּהֵ֔ן נֶ֥גַע צָרַ֖עַת הִֽוא: וְאִ֣ם ׀ יִרְאֶ֣נָּה הַכֹּהֵ֗ן וְהִנֵּ֤ה אֵֽין־בַּבַּהֶ֙רֶת֙ שֵׂעָ֣ר לָבָ֔ן וּשְׁפָלָ֥ה אֵינֶ֖נָּה מִן־הָע֛וֹר וְהִ֥וא כֵהָ֑ה וְהִסְגִּיר֥וֹ הַכֹּהֵ֖ן שִׁבְעַ֥ת יָמִֽים:

כז וְרָאָ֥הוּ הַכֹּהֵ֖ן בַּיּ֣וֹם הַשְּׁבִיעִ֑י אִם־פָּשֹׂ֤ה תִפְשֶׂה֙ בָּע֔וֹר וְטִמֵּ֤א הַכֹּהֵן֙ אֹת֔וֹ נֶ֥גַע

כח צָרַ֖עַת הִֽוא: וְאִם־תַּחְתֶּ֩יהָ֩ תַעֲמֹ֨ד הַבַּהֶ֜רֶת לֹא־פָשְׂתָ֤ה בָעוֹר֙ וְהִ֣וא כֵהָ֔ה שְׂאֵ֥ת הַמִּכְוָ֖ה הִ֑וא וְטִהֲרוֹ֙ הַכֹּהֵ֔ן כִּֽי־צָרֶ֥בֶת הַמִּכְוָ֖ה הִֽוא:

חמישי כט-ל וְאִישׁ֙ א֣וֹ אִשָּׁ֔ה כִּֽי־יִהְיֶ֥ה ב֖וֹ נָ֑גַע בְּרֹ֖אשׁ א֥וֹ בְזָקָֽן: וְרָאָ֤ה הַכֹּהֵן֙ אֶת־הַנֶּ֔גַע

---

19. וְהָיָ֞ה בִּמְק֤וֹם הַשְּׁחִין֙ שְׂאֵ֣ת לְבָנָ֔ה — *And in the place of the boil there is a white rising.* That place is not judged by the (same) signs as the skin mentioned above (nor) the place of the *burning by fire* either (v. 24), for indeed, the natural skin destroyed by the boil or burn cannot be restored as it was originally. Instead, in its place something similar to skin develops, but the skin (itself) is not renewed, as (our Sages) tell us (*Niddah* 55a) and as the doctors have related (to us).

NOTES

19. וְהָיָ֞ה בִּמְק֤וֹם הַשְּׁחִין֙ שְׂאֵ֣ת לְבָנָ֔ה — *And in the place of the boil there is a white rising.* The *Sforno* explains why the law concerning a *white rising* (שְׂאֵת) in the place of a boil, or a

bright spot (בַּהֶרֶת) in a place burnt by fire, is different than when these appearances occur in normal skin. The new skin which grows in these areas is not the same as the original, as

וְהִנֵּה מַרְאֵ֙הוּ עָמֹק֙ מִן־הָע֔וֹר וּב֛וֹ שֵׂעָ֥ר צָהֹ֖ב דָּ֑ק וְטִמֵּ֙א אֹת֤וֹ הַכֹּהֵן֙ נֶ֣תֶק ה֔וּא

לא צָרַ֧עַת הָרֹ֛אשׁ א֥וֹ הַזָּקָ֖ן הֽוּא: וְכִֽי־יִרְאֶ֨ה הַכֹּהֵ֜ן אֶת־נֶ֣גַע הַנֶּ֗תֶק וְהִנֵּ֤ה אֵין־

מַרְאֵ֙הוּ֙ עָמֹ֣ק מִן־הָע֔וֹר וְשֵׂעָ֥ר שָׁחֹ֖ר אֵ֣ין בּ֑וֹ וְהִסְגִּ֧יר הַכֹּהֵ֛ן אֶת־נֶ֥גַע הַנֶּ֖תֶק

לב שִׁבְעַ֥ת יָמִֽים: וְרָאָ֨ה הַכֹּהֵ֣ן אֶת־הַנֶּגַע֮ בַּיּ֣וֹם הַשְּׁבִיעִי֒ וְהִנֵּה֙ לֹא־פָשָׂ֣ה הַנֶּ֔תֶק

לג וְלֹא־הָ֥יָה ב֖וֹ שֵׂעָ֣ר צָהֹ֑ב וּמַרְאֵ֤ה הַנֶּ֙תֶק֙ אֵ֣ין עָמֹ֔ק מִן־הָעֽוֹר: וְהִתְגַּלָּ֔ח וְאֶת־

לד הַנֶּ֖תֶק לֹ֣א יְגַלֵּ֑חַ וְהִסְגִּ֨יר הַכֹּהֵ֧ן אֶת־הַנֶּ֛תֶק שִׁבְעַ֥ת יָמִ֖ים שֵׁנִֽית: וְרָאָה֩ הַכֹּהֵ֨ן

אֶת־הַנֶּ֜תֶק בַּיּ֣וֹם הַשְּׁבִיעִי֒ וְהִנֵּ֙ה לֹא־פָשָׂ֤ה הַנֶּ֙תֶק֙ בָּע֔וֹר וּמַרְאֵ֕הוּ אֵינֶ֥נּוּ עָמֹ֖ק

לה מִן־הָע֑וֹר וְטִהַ֤ר אֹתוֹ֙ הַכֹּהֵ֔ן וְכִבֶּ֥ס בְּגָדָ֖יו וְטָהֵֽר: וְאִם־פָּשֹׂ֥ה יִפְשֶׂ֛ה הַנֶּ֖תֶק

לו בָּע֑וֹר אַחֲרֵ֣י טָהֳרָת֑וֹ: וְרָאָ֙הוּ֙ הַכֹּהֵ֔ן וְהִנֵּ֛ה פָּשָׂ֥ה הַנֶּ֖תֶק בָּע֑וֹר לֹֽא־יְבַקֵּ֧ר הַכֹּהֵ֛ן

לז לַשֵּׂעָ֥ר הַצָּהֹ֖ב טָמֵ֣א הֽוּא: וְאִם־בְּעֵינָיו֩ עָמַ֨ד הַנֶּ֜תֶק וְשֵׂעָ֧ר שָׁחֹ֛ר צָֽמַח־בּ֖וֹ

לח נִרְפָּ֥א הַנֶּ֖תֶק טָה֣וֹר ה֑וּא וְטִהֲר֖וֹ הַכֹּהֵֽן: וְאִישׁ֙ אֽוֹ־אִשָּׁ֔ה כִּֽי־

לט יִֽהְיֶ֧ה בְעוֹר־בְּשָׂרָ֛ם בֶּהָרֹ֖ת בֶּהָרֹ֣ת לְבָנֹ֑ת וְרָאָ֣ה הַכֹּהֵ֗ן וְהִנֵּ֧ה בְעוֹר־בְּשָׂרָ֛ם

ששי [שלישי] מ בֶּהָרֹ֛ת כֵּה֥וֹת לְבָנֹ֖ת בֹּ֣הַק ה֑וּא פָּרַ֥ח בָּע֖וֹר טָה֥וֹר הֽוּא: וְאִ֕ישׁ

מא כִּ֥י יִמָּרֵ֖ט רֹאשׁ֑וֹ קֵרֵ֥חַ ה֖וּא טָה֣וֹר הֽוּא: וְאִם֙ מִפְּאַ֣ת פָּנָ֔יו יִמָּרֵ֖ט רֹאשׁ֑וֹ גִּבֵּ֥חַ

מב ה֖וּא טָה֣וֹר הֽוּא: וְכִֽי־יִהְיֶ֤ה בַקָּרַ֙חַת֙ א֣וֹ בַגַּבַּ֔חַת נֶ֥גַע לָבָ֖ן אֲדַמְדָּ֑ם צָרַ֤עַת

מג פֹּרַ֙חַת֙ הִ֔וא בְּקָרַחְתּ֖וֹ א֥וֹ בְגַבַּחְתּֽוֹ: וְרָאָ֣ה אֹתוֹ֮ הַכֹּהֵן֒ וְהִנֵּ֤ה שְׂאֵת־הַנֶּ֙גַע֙

מד לְבָנָ֣ה אֲדַמְדֶּ֔מֶת בְּקָרַחְתּ֖וֹ א֥וֹ בְגַבַּחְתּ֑וֹ כְּמַרְאֵ֥ה צָרַ֖עַת ע֣וֹר בָּשָֽׂר: אִישׁ־

מה צָר֥וּעַ ה֖וּא טָמֵ֣א ה֑וּא טַמֵּ֧א יְטַמְּאֶ֛נּוּ הַכֹּהֵ֖ן בְּרֹאשׁ֥וֹ נִגְעֽוֹ: וְהַצָּר֜וּעַ אֲשֶׁר־בּ֣וֹ

הַנֶּ֗גַע בְּגָדָ֞יו יִהְי֤וּ פְרֻמִים֙ וְרֹאשׁוֹ֙ יִהְיֶ֣ה פָר֔וּעַ וְעַל־שָׂפָ֖ם יַעְטֶ֑ה וְטָמֵ֥א ׀ טָמֵ֖א

מו יִקְרָֽא: כָּל־יְמֵ֞י אֲשֶׁ֨ר הַנֶּ֥גַע בּ֛וֹ יִטְמָ֖א טָמֵ֣א ה֑וּא בָּדָ֣ד יֵשֵׁ֔ב מִח֥וּץ לַֽמַּחֲנֶ֖ה

מז מֽוֹשָׁבֽוֹ:   וְהַבֶּ֕גֶד כִּֽי־יִהְיֶ֥ה ב֖וֹ נֶ֣גַע צָרָ֑עַת בְּבֶ֣גֶד צֶ֔מֶר א֖וֹ

---

30. נֶ֣תֶק ה֑וּא — *It is a scall.* If in the area of hair there be a place from which the hair fell out due to infection (lit., power of illness), and not due to (the action of) man or because of a drug, and even though there is no (aberrant) appearance, as our Sages have taught us [this is considered a נֶ֣תֶק, *scall*]. This condition is also considered to be a form of leprosy by the doctors. (The Torah) therefore says that even though there are unclean appearances or spreading in the area of the scall, (a condition) which otherwise would have (established) a definitive decision (of uncleanness) were it not in the area of the hair, (in our case) the black hair in the area of hair, overrides (lit., saves) the appearance of *white* and spreading (which usually denotes uncleanness).

39. כֵּה֥וֹת לְבָנֹ֖ת — *Dull white* ... a degree lesser (in whiteness) than that of the membrane surrounding the egg, of which our Sages have taught.

47. וְהַבֶּ֕גֶד כִּֽי־יִהְיֶ֥ה ב֖וֹ נֶ֣גַע צָרָ֑עַת — *And when an affliction of leprosy is in a garment.* There is no doubt that this (phenomena) cannot possibly be a natural one, for these strange colors (appearances) cannot occur in a garment except through (1) the work

---

NOTES

our Sages tell us in Tractate *Niddah*; therefore the regulation and ordinances are also not similar.

47. וְהַבֶּ֕גֶד כִּֽי־יִהְיֶ֥ה ב֖וֹ נֶ֣גַע צָרָ֑עַת — *And when a affliction of leprosy is in a garment.* The *Sforno*, in his lengthy commentary on this

א

מח בְּבֶגֶד פִּשְׁתִּים: אוֹ בִשְׁתִי אוֹ בְעֵרֶב לַפִּשְׁתִּים וְלַצָּמֶר אוֹ בְעוֹר אוֹ בְּכָל־
מט מְלֶאכֶת עוֹר: וְהָיָה הַנֶּגַע יְרַקְרַק | אוֹ אֲדַמְדָּם בַּבֶּגֶד אוֹ בָעוֹר אוֹ־בַשְּׁתִי
נ אוֹ־בָעֵרֶב אוֹ בְכָל־כְּלִי־עוֹר נֶגַע צָרַעַת הוּא וְהָרְאָה אֶת־הַכֹּהֵן: וְרָאָה
נא הַכֹּהֵן אֶת־הַנָּגַע וְהִסְגִּיר אֶת־הַנֶּגַע שִׁבְעַת יָמִים: וְרָאָה אֶת־הַנֶּגַע בַּיּוֹם
הַשְּׁבִיעִי כִּי־פָשָׂה הַנֶּגַע בַּבֶּגֶד אוֹ־בַשְּׁתִי אוֹ־בָעֵרֶב אוֹ בָעוֹר לְכֹל אֲשֶׁר־
נב יֵעָשֶׂה הָעוֹר לִמְלָאכָה צָרַעַת מַמְאֶרֶת הַנֶּגַע טָמֵא הוּא: וְשָׂרַף אֶת־הַבֶּגֶד
אוֹ אֶת־הַשְּׁתִי | אוֹ אֶת־הָעֵרֶב בַּצֶּמֶר אוֹ בַפִּשְׁתִּים אוֹ אֶת־כָּל־כְּלִי הָעוֹר
נג אֲשֶׁר־יִהְיֶה בוֹ הַנָּגַע כִּי־צָרַעַת מַמְאֶרֶת הִוא בָּאֵשׁ תִּשָּׂרֵף: וְאִם יִרְאֶה
הַכֹּהֵן וְהִנֵּה לֹא־פָשָׂה הַנֶּגַע בַּבֶּגֶד אוֹ בַשְּׁתִי אוֹ בָעֵרֶב אוֹ בְּכָל־כְּלִי־עוֹר:

---

strange colors (appearances) cannot occur in a garment except through (1) the work (of the dyer) using various colors, by some error which happened with the color dyes intentionally or unintentionally; or (2) the dyer's (lit., workman's) performance; or (3) the (chemical) reaction in the garment being colored. Now we have a tradition that these laws of נִגְעֵי בְּגָדִים, *afflictions of garments*, do not apply except to white, uncolored garments. In truth, the Torah is attesting that at times this wonder (phenomena) will occur in garments and in houses so as to awaken (open) the ear of the owners to their transgressions, as (our Sages) tell us regarding שְׁבִיעִית, *the Sabbatical year*, as they say, 'Come and see the far-reaching results of violating the laws of the seventh year. A man who trades in seventh-year produce must eventually sell his movables . . . if he disregards this, he eventually sells his estates' (*Kiddushin* 20a). All this is because of God's compassion for His people.

Also (our Sages) received a tradition that the garments of gentiles do not become *tamei* through (these) afflictions (*Negaim* 11:1). This is so, for in truth the human species represents the ultimate purpose intended (by the Creator) in all existence, particularly among mortal beings, for he alone among all (creatures) is predisposed to be like the Creator in intellect and deed, as He, the Blessed One, testifies saying, בְּצַלְמֵנוּ כִּדְמוּתֵנוּ, *In our image after our likeness* (*Genesis* 1:26). Now this is justly so regarding all humans (who possess) human reason, which is called 'the image of God,' and (who possess) the power of free will which is called 'God's likeness,' for among all creation man alone possesses free will. When (man) is aroused to reflect upon the existence of his Creator, His greatness and goodness, in Whom there is abundant kindness and truth, through (which) He performs righteousness and

NOTES

section dealing with נִגְעֵי בְגָדִים, *afflictions of garments*, including as well the chapter (14:34-53) which discusses נִגְעֵי בָתִּים, *afflictions of houses*, makes the following points:

(1) Since the discolorations mentioned in verse 49, namely green and red, can only appear in a garment for one of the three reasons listed by the *Sforno*, and since the laws regarding the affliction of garments only apply to a white neutral garment, then it is impossible for this discoloration to happen naturally.

(2) It therefore follows that this phenomenon is heaven-sent for the purpose of alerting the owner of the garment or house to take stock and repent for his sins, as the *Rambam* states (*Hilchos Tumas Tzaraas* 16:10), 'These changes stated (in the Torah) regarding garments and houses . . . are not according to the natural order of the world, but they are a sign and wonder for Israel, cautioning them to abstain from the evil tongue.'

(3) The fact that these laws do not apply to gentiles serves as a springboard for the *Sforno* to stress once again, as he already did at the

נד וְצִוָּה֙ הַכֹּהֵ֔ן וְכִ֨בְּס֔וּ אֵ֥ת אֲשֶׁר־בּ֖וֹ הַנָּ֑גַע וְהִסְגִּיר֥וֹ שִׁבְעַת־יָמִ֖ים שֵׁנִֽית׃
שביעי [רביעי] נה וְרָאָ֨ה הַכֹּהֵ֜ן אַחֲרֵ֣י ׀ הֻכַּבֵּ֣ס אֶת־הַנֶּ֗גַע וְ֠הִנֵּה לֹא־הָפַ֨ךְ הַנֶּ֤גַע אֶת־עֵינוֹ֙ וְהַנֶּ֣גַע
נו לֹא־פָשָׂ֔ה טָמֵ֣א ה֔וּא בָּאֵ֖שׁ תִּשְׂרְפֶ֑נּוּ פְּחֶ֣תֶת הִ֔וא בְּקָרַחְתּ֖וֹ א֥וֹ בְגַבַּחְתּֽוֹ׃
וְאִם֮ רָאָ֣ה הַכֹּהֵן֒ וְהִנֵּה֙ כֵּהָ֣ה הַנֶּ֔גַע אַחֲרֵ֖י הֻכַּבֵּ֣ס אֹת֑וֹ וְקָרַ֣ע אֹת֗וֹ מִן־הַבֶּ֙גֶד֙
נז א֣וֹ מִן־הָע֔וֹר א֥וֹ מִן־הַשְּׁתִ֖י א֥וֹ מִן־הָעֵֽרֶב׃ וְאִם־תֵּרָאֶ֨ה ע֜וֹד בַּבֶּ֗גֶד אֽוֹ־בַשְּׁתִ֤י
אֽוֹ־בָעֵ֙רֶב֙ א֣וֹ בְכָל־כְּלִי־ע֔וֹר פֹּרַ֖חַת הִ֑וא בָּאֵ֣שׁ תִּשְׂרְפֶ֔נּוּ אֵ֥ת אֲשֶׁר־בּ֖וֹ
מפטיר נח הַנָּֽגַע׃ וְהַבֶּ֡גֶד אֽוֹ־הַשְּׁתִ֨י אֽוֹ־הָעֵ֜רֶב אֽוֹ־כָל־כְּלִ֤י הָעוֹר֙ אֲשֶׁ֣ר תְּכַבֵּ֔ס וְסָ֥ר
נט מֵהֶ֖ם הַנָּ֑גַע וְכֻבַּ֥ס שֵׁנִ֖ית וְטָהֵֽר׃ זֹ֠את תּוֹרַ֨ת נֶֽגַע־צָרַ֜עַת בֶּ֣גֶד הַצֶּ֣מֶר ׀ א֣וֹ
הַפִּשְׁתִּ֗ים א֤וֹ הַשְּׁתִי֙ א֣וֹ הָעֵ֔רֶב א֖וֹ כָּל־כְּלִי־ע֑וֹר לְטַהֲר֖וֹ א֥וֹ לְטַמְּאֽוֹ׃

---

justice; and after perceiving and recognizing (all) this he will walk in His ways, making His will as his own (will). Behold, in this manner he becomes, without a doubt, like unto his Creator more so than all other creatures, and this is the ultimate purpose intended from the Creator who brought (all) into existence as it says, וְצַדִּיק יְסוֹד עוֹלָם, *And the righteous one is the foundation of the world* (*Proverbs* 10:25). (But) when a deceived heart turned man aside from this (path) for he listened (instead) to the power of physical temptations in all, or some, of his actions, (causing him) to be lax in (fulfilling) the will of his Maker or to rebel against Him, then his punishment was everlasting or transitory according to Divine judgment as it says, כִּי לֹא אַצְדִּיק רָשָׁע, *For I will not justify the wicked* (*Exodus* 23:7). Now when this occurs to man, who sins in error, he will suffer pain (or loss) in his possessions or physical being, according to Divine wisdom, to alert his ear, as it says, וַיִּגֶל אָזְנָם לַמּוּסָר, *He opens also their ear to discipline* (*Job* 36:10). However, those who slumber and are not awakened at all to know any of these things, these being the gentiles and the majority of the Israelite nation save an elite few, (hence) they, without a doubt, are under the control (lit., conduct) of nature and the heavenly forces, which are superior to these human beings, similar to other living creatures who are not subject to God's providence individually but only in terms of their species, for through them (i.e., the species as a whole) the intent of their Creator, Blessed is He, is fulfilled. And He chose the Israelite nation as it says, בְּךָ בָּחַר ה׳ אֱלֹהֶיךָ לִהְיוֹת לוֹ לְעַם סְגֻלָּה, *HASHEM, your God has chosen you to be His own treasure* (*Deut.* 7:6), and this (He did) because the hopeful intent of (God) the Blessed One was more likely (to be realized) among the men of this nation than among other

NOTES

beginning of *Genesis*, that man is indeed the crown of creation chosen to imitate God through his power of reason and freedom of choice. However, the bulk of mankind did not realize this awesome responsibility except for the people of Israel. Even among them only a relatively small number attained the level of excellence which God had ordained for them, and even they must be reminded, when they falter and deviate, to mend their ways and return to God. One of the methods used by God to awaken them from their periodic slumber is that of נְגָעִים, *afflictions*. It therefore is understandable that these laws would not apply to gentiles, for נְגָעִים are a miraculous lesson reserved only for those who understand their ultimate purpose and act accordingly.

(4) Based upon the above, the *Sforno* explains that the visiting of these afflictions upon Israel is motivated by God's compassion for them and His desire that they repent and accept their historic mission to be a holy people. The special providence enjoyed by Israel is manifested by His ongoing attention and concern which, ironically, also carries with it these special reminders. It is precisely

men, for the existence of God and His unity was known partially and accepted among all (of Israel) from their ancestors, as it says, נוֹדָע בִּיהוּדָה אֱלֹהִים בְּיִשְׂרָאֵל גָּדוֹל שְׁמוֹ, *In Judah is God known, His name is great in Israel* (*Psalms* 76:2). He (therefore) wrote and taught them the Torah, which is the intellectual (analytical) portion, and the commandment which is the section of deeds, as He testifies saying, וְהַתּוֹרָה וְהַמִּצְוָה אֲשֶׁר כָּתַבְתִּי לְהוֹרֹתָם, *And the Torah and the commandment which I have written that you may teach them* (*Exodus* 24:12). He (then) warned that if they deviate from this path, He will awaken their ears through suffering, as it says, אִם שָׁמוֹעַ תִּשְׁמַע . . . כָּל הַמַּחֲלָה אֲשֶׁר שַׂמְתִּי בְמִצְרַיִם לֹא אָשִׂים עָלֶיךָ, *If you will hearken . . . I will put none of the diseases upon you which I have put upon Egypt* (*Exodus* 15:26), and in His compassion for them (at such a time) when the majority of them will be viewed favorably before Him, He resolved to alert a select few among them, first through afflictions of garments, regarding which we have a tradition that the garments of gentiles do not become defiled through these afflictions, and when this does not suffice to alert them, (then He shall visit) afflictions on their houses, and (in this case) also, no affliction of leprosy can come naturally at all. Therefore, it is appropriate that the garments and houses of gentiles are not defiled by these afflictions, as our Sages have received from tradition. But when (subsequent) generations did not attain the proper level which would make them worthy of this compassion, there is no (longer) any memory of these early (phenomena) of the affliction of houses, bringing some Sages to state that they never ever happened!

NOTES

because Israel reached a high level of holiness that their sins create such vulnerability. Once Israel descended from that exalted plateau, they no longer were worthy to be singled out for such direct, wondrous Divine reminders as נְגָעִים. That is why we do not witness these phenomena today, nor have we heard of them for many generations.

פרשת מצורע
Parashas Metzora

יד

א־ב וַיְדַבֵּ֥ר יהו֖ה אֶל־מֹשֶׁ֥ה לֵּאמֹֽר: זֹ֤את תִּֽהְיֶה֙ תּוֹרַ֣ת הַמְּצֹרָ֔ע בְּי֖וֹם טׇהֳרָת֑וֹ

ג וְהוּבָ֖א אֶל־הַכֹּהֵֽן: וְיָצָא֙ הַכֹּהֵ֔ן אֶל־מִח֖וּץ לַמַּחֲנֶ֑ה וְרָאָה֙ הַכֹּהֵ֔ן וְהִנֵּ֛ה נִרְפָּ֥א

ד נֶֽגַע־הַצָּרַ֖עַת מִן־הַצָּרֽוּעַ: וְצִוָּה֙ הַכֹּהֵ֔ן וְלָקַ֧ח לַמִּטַּהֵ֛ר שְׁתֵּֽי־צִפֳּרִ֥ים חַיּ֖וֹת

ה טְהֹר֑וֹת וְעֵ֣ץ אֶ֔רֶז וּשְׁנִ֥י תוֹלַ֖עַת וְאֵזֹֽב: וְצִוָּה֙ הַכֹּהֵ֔ן וְשָׁחַ֖ט אֶת־הַצִּפּ֣וֹר הָאֶחָ֑ת

ו אֶל־כְּלִי־חֶ֖רֶשׂ עַל־מַ֥יִם חַיִּֽים: אֶת־הַצִּפֹּ֤ר הַֽחַיָּה֙ יִקַּ֣ח אֹתָ֔הּ וְאֶת־עֵ֤ץ הָאֶ֨רֶז֙

וְאֶת־שְׁנִ֣י הַתּוֹלַ֔עַת וְאֶת־הָֽאֵזֹ֑ב וְטָבַ֣ל אוֹתָ֗ם וְאֵ֣ת ׀ הַצִּפֹּ֣ר הַֽחַיָּ֗ה בְּדַם֙

ז הַצִּפֹּ֣ר הַשְּׁחֻטָ֔ה עַ֖ל הַמַּ֥יִם הַֽחַיִּֽים: וְהִזָּ֗ה עַ֧ל הַמִּטַּהֵ֛ר מִן־הַצָּרַ֖עַת שֶׁ֣בַע

ח פְּעָמִ֑ים וְטִ֣הֲר֔וֹ וְשִׁלַּ֥ח אֶת־הַצִּפֹּ֛ר הַֽחַיָּ֖ה עַל־פְּנֵ֥י הַשָּׂדֶֽה: וְכִבֶּס֩ הַמִּטַּהֵ֨ר

אֶת־בְּגָדָ֜יו וְגִלַּ֣ח אֶת־כׇּל־שְׂעָר֗וֹ וְרָחַ֤ץ בַּמַּ֨יִם֙ וְטָהֵ֔ר וְאַחַ֖ר יָב֣וֹא אֶל־הַֽמַּחֲנֶ֑ה

ט וְיָשַׁ֛ב מִח֥וּץ לְאׇהֳל֖וֹ שִׁבְעַ֣ת יָמִֽים: וְהָיָה֩ בַיּ֨וֹם הַשְּׁבִיעִ֜י יְגַלַּ֣ח אֶת־כׇּל־שְׂעָר֗וֹ

אֶת־רֹאשׁ֤וֹ וְאֶת־זְקָנוֹ֙ וְאֵת֙ גַּבֹּ֣ת עֵינָ֔יו וְאֶת־כׇּל־שְׂעָר֖וֹ יְגַלֵּ֑חַ וְכִבֶּ֣ס

י אֶת־בְּגָדָ֗יו וְרָחַ֧ץ אֶת־בְּשָׂר֛וֹ בַּמַּ֖יִם וְטָהֵֽר: וּבַיּ֣וֹם הַשְּׁמִינִ֗י יִקַּ֤ח שְׁנֵֽי־כְבָשִׂים֙

תְּמִימִ֔ים וְכַבְשָׂ֥ה אַחַ֖ת בַּת־שְׁנָתָ֣הּ תְּמִימָ֑ה וּשְׁלֹשָׁ֣ה עֶשְׂרֹנִ֗ים סֹ֤לֶת מִנְחָה֙

יא בְּלוּלָ֣ה בַשֶּׁ֔מֶן וְלֹ֥ג אֶחָ֖ד שָֽׁמֶן: וְהֶעֱמִ֞יד הַכֹּהֵ֣ן הַֽמְטַהֵ֗ר אֵ֛ת הָאִ֥ישׁ הַמִּטַּהֵ֖ר

יב וְאֹתָ֑ם לִפְנֵ֣י יהו֔ה פֶּ֖תַח אֹ֥הֶל מוֹעֵֽד: וְלָקַ֨ח הַכֹּהֵ֜ן אֶת־הַכֶּ֣בֶשׂ הָֽאֶחָ֗ד

שני יג וְהִקְרִ֥יב אֹת֛וֹ לְאָשָׁ֖ם וְאֶת־לֹ֣ג הַשָּׁ֑מֶן וְהֵנִ֥יף אֹתָ֛ם תְּנוּפָ֖ה לִפְנֵ֣י יהו֑ה: וְשָׁחַ֞ט

XIV

2. וְהוּבָא אֶל הַכֹּהֵן — *He shall be brought to the Kohen* . . . to a nearby place outside the camp, where the *Kohen* can go to see him in a dignified manner, and without excessive exertion.

7. וְטִהֲרוֹ — *And pronounce him clean* . . . from the (regulations) of rent clothing and the loose hair (of the leper) (13:45).

8. וְרָחַץ בַּמַּיִם וְטָהֵר — *And he shall bathe himself in water and he shall be clean* . . . from the (restriction) of *'Outside the camp shall be his dwelling'* (13:46).

9. וְרָחַץ אֶת בְּשָׂרוֹ בַּמַּיִם וְטָהֵר — *And he shall bathe his flesh in water and he shall be clean* . . . from the (restriction) of *'But he shall dwell outside his tent'* (v. 8).

12. וְהִקְרִיב אֹתוֹ לְאָשָׁם — *And offer it as a guilt offering.* As already explained, the guilt offering is brought when one misappropriates holy things, just as the sin

---

NOTES

XIV

2. וְהוּבָא אֶל הַכֹּהֵן — *He shall be brought to the Kohen.* In the previous chapter (13:2), the expression וְהוּבָא, *and he shall be brought*, is also used, but whereas there it means literally *he shall be brought to Aaron* (within the camp), here it cannot mean that the מְצֹרָע, *leper*, is brought to the *Kohen into* the camp, since he is still prohibited to enter therein. The *Sforno*, therefore, interprets the phrase וְהוּבָא in this instance to mean that he will be brought to a place *near* the camp, and the

Kohen will go out to examine him, as it clearly states in the next verse (3).

7. וְטִהֲרוֹ — *And pronounce him clean.* The leper is cleansed in stages. First, the regulations of *rent clothing* and *loose hair* are waived. The second step is permission to come back into the camp. Third, he may enter his tent and will not be restricted to dwell outside. Finally, he is allowed to enter the environs of the Holy and partake of קָדָשִׁים, *sacred meat*, once he has brought his offerings. These four stages are indicated by the four expressions of טׇהֳרָה,

אֶת־הַכֶּ֫בֶשׂ בִּמְק֞וֹם אֲשֶׁ֨ר יִשְׁחַ֧ט אֶת־הַחַטָּ֛את וְאֶת־הָעֹלָ֖ה בִּמְק֣וֹם הַקֹּ֑דֶשׁ
יד כִּ֡י כַּחַטָּ֨את הָאָשָׁ֥ם הוּא֙ לַכֹּהֵ֔ן קֹ֥דֶשׁ קָֽדָשִׁ֖ים הֽוּא׃ וְלָקַ֣ח הַכֹּהֵן֮ מִדַּ֣ם הָֽאָשָׁם֒
וְנָתַן֙ הַכֹּהֵ֔ן עַל־תְּנ֛וּךְ אֹ֥זֶן הַמִּטַּהֵ֖ר הַיְמָנִ֑ית וְעַל־בֹּ֤הֶן יָדוֹ֙ הַיְמָנִ֔ית וְעַל־בֹּ֥הֶן
טו רַגְל֖וֹ הַיְמָנִֽית׃ וְלָקַ֥ח הַכֹּהֵ֖ן מִלֹּ֣ג הַשָּׁ֑מֶן וְיָצַ֛ק עַל־כַּ֥ף הַכֹּהֵ֖ן הַשְּׂמָאלִֽית׃
טז וְטָבַ֤ל הַכֹּהֵן֙ אֶת־אֶצְבָּע֣וֹ הַיְמָנִ֔ית מִן־הַשֶּׁ֕מֶן אֲשֶׁ֥ר עַל־כַּפּ֖וֹ הַשְּׂמָאלִ֑ית
יז וְהִזָּ֨ה מִן־הַשֶּׁ֧מֶן בְּאֶצְבָּע֛וֹ שֶׁ֥בַע פְּעָמִ֖ים לִפְנֵ֥י יהוה׃ וּמִיֶּ֨תֶר הַשֶּׁ֜מֶן אֲשֶׁ֣ר עַל־
כַּפּ֗וֹ יִתֵּ֤ן הַכֹּהֵן֙ עַל־תְּנ֞וּךְ אֹ֤זֶן הַמִּטַּהֵר֙ הַיְמָנִ֔ית וְעַל־בֹּ֤הֶן יָדוֹ֙ הַיְמָנִ֔ית וְעַל־
יח בֹּ֥הֶן רַגְל֖וֹ הַיְמָנִ֑ית עַ֖ל דַּ֥ם הָאָשָֽׁם׃ וְהַנּוֹתָ֗ר בַּשֶּׁ֙מֶן֙ אֲשֶׁר֙ עַל־כַּ֣ף הַכֹּהֵ֔ן יִתֵּ֖ן
יט עַל־רֹ֣אשׁ הַמִּטַּהֵ֑ר וְכִפֶּ֥ר עָלָ֛יו הַכֹּהֵ֖ן לִפְנֵ֥י יהוה׃ וְעָשָׂ֤ה הַכֹּהֵן֙ אֶת־הַ֣חַטָּ֔את
כ וְכִפֶּ֕ר עַל־הַמִּטַּהֵ֖ר מִטֻּמְאָת֑וֹ וְאַחַ֖ר יִשְׁחַ֥ט אֶת־הָעֹלָֽה׃ וְהֶעֱלָ֧ה הַכֹּהֵ֛ן אֶת־
שלישי [חמישי] כא הָעֹלָ֥ה וְאֶת־הַמִּנְחָ֖ה הַמִּזְבֵּ֑חָה וְכִפֶּ֥ר עָלָ֛יו הַכֹּהֵ֖ן וְטָהֵֽר׃ וְאִם־
דַּ֣ל ה֗וּא וְאֵ֣ין יָדוֹ֮ מַשֶּׂ֒גֶת֒ וְ֠לָקַח כֶּ֣בֶשׂ אֶחָ֥ד אָשָׁ֛ם לִתְנוּפָ֖ה לְכַפֵּ֣ר עָלָ֑יו

---

offering is brought for (a sin which is) punishable by excision. Now, (our Sages) have said that צָרַעַת, *leprosy,* (comes as a punishment) for evil talk and for haughtiness, both of which are (akin to) misappropriation of the holy, for indeed, evil talk is principally spoken in secret, as one who 'seeks deeply to hide counsel from HASHEM' (based on *Isaiah* 29:15), as (our Sages) said, 'When anyone commits a transgression in secret, it is as though he has thrust aside the feet of the Divine Presence' (*Chagigah* 16a). And as for one who is haughty it says, גְּבַהּ עֵינַיִם וּרְחַב לֵבָב אֹתוֹ לֹא אוּכָל, *He that has a haughty look and a proud heart I will not tolerate* (*Psalms* 101:5). "The Holy One, Blessed is He, says, 'This one steals My raiment. He and I cannot abide in one world' " (*Sotah* 5a). And the Scriptures have already told us of Uzziyahu, saying, וּכְחֶזְקָתוֹ גָּבַהּ לִבּוֹ עַד לְהַשְׁחִית וַיִּמְעַל בַּה׳ אֱלֹהָיו . . . וְהַצָּרַעַת זָרְחָה בְמִצְחוֹ, *But when he was strong his heart was lifted up to his destruction; for he trespassed against HASHEM his God . . . the leprosy broke out on his forehead* (*II Chronicles* 26:16, 19).

20. וְכִפֶּר עָלָיו הַכֹּהֵן וְטָהֵר — *And the Kohen shall make atonement for him and he shall be clean . . .* for (the purpose of) eating sacred things (קָדָשִׁים) and to enter the Holy, as our Sages have said, 'Once he brings his offerings (lit., his atonements) he may partake of the Holy (flesh)' (*Negaim* 14:3).

NOTES

cleansing, which appear in verses 7 (וְטִהֲרוֹ), 8, 9 and 20 (וְטָהֵר).

12. וְהִקְרִיב אֹתוֹ לְאָשָׁם — *And offer it as a guilt offering.* The *Sforno* already explained (1:2) that an אָשָׁם, *guilt offering,* is brought to make amends for the unlawful use of sacred property (מְעִילָה). He now points out that our Sages have taught us that leprosy comes as a punishment for evil talk and for haughtiness. The former is considered a form of מְעִילָה, for by slandering his fellow secretly one acts as though God is unaware of his transgression and thus he encroaches on the Almighty's omniscience. As for the latter sin, he misappropriates God's exclusive right to גֵּאוּת, *majesty,* which is related to גַּאֲוָה, *pride.* Here again, he intrudes on God's domain. In both cases he is guilty of trespassing which obligates him to bring a guilt offering. The *Sforno* demonstrates the link between haughtiness and מְעִילָה by citing the episode of King Uzziyahu who, in his arrogance, entered the Temple to burn incense upon the altar although he was not a *Kohen*. The verse in *Chronicles* refers to this act as מְעִילָה and he was punished for it with leprosy.

כב וְעִשָּׂרוֹן סֹלֶת אֶחָד בָּלוּל בַּשֶּׁמֶן לְמִנְחָה וְלֹג שָׁמֶן: וּשְׁתֵּי תֹרִים אוֹ שְׁנֵי בְּנֵי
כג יוֹנָה אֲשֶׁר תַּשִּׂיג יָדוֹ וְהָיָה אֶחָד חַטָּאת וְהָאֶחָד עֹלָה: וְהֵבִיא אֹתָם בַּיּוֹם
כד הַשְּׁמִינִי לְטָהֳרָתוֹ אֶל־הַכֹּהֵן אֶל־פֶּתַח אֹהֶל־מוֹעֵד לִפְנֵי יהוה: וְלָקַח הַכֹּהֵן
אֶת־כֶּבֶשׂ הָאָשָׁם וְאֶת־לֹג הַשָּׁמֶן וְהֵנִיף אֹתָם הַכֹּהֵן תְּנוּפָה לִפְנֵי יהוה:
כה וְשָׁחַט אֶת־כֶּבֶשׂ הָאָשָׁם וְלָקַח הַכֹּהֵן מִדַּם הָאָשָׁם וְנָתַן עַל־תְּנוּךְ
אֹזֶן־הַמִּטַּהֵר הַיְמָנִית וְעַל־בֹּהֶן יָדוֹ הַיְמָנִית וְעַל־בֹּהֶן רַגְלוֹ הַיְמָנִית:
כו־כז וּמִן־הַשֶּׁמֶן יִצֹק הַכֹּהֵן עַל־כַּף הַכֹּהֵן הַשְּׂמָאלִית: וְהִזָּה הַכֹּהֵן בְּאֶצְבָּעוֹ
כח הַיְמָנִית מִן־הַשֶּׁמֶן אֲשֶׁר עַל־כַּפּוֹ הַשְּׂמָאלִית שֶׁבַע פְּעָמִים לִפְנֵי יהוה: וְנָתַן
הַכֹּהֵן מִן־הַשֶּׁמֶן ׀ אֲשֶׁר עַל־כַּפּוֹ עַל־תְּנוּךְ אֹזֶן הַמִּטַּהֵר הַיְמָנִית וְעַל־בֹּהֶן
כט יָדוֹ הַיְמָנִית וְעַל־בֹּהֶן רַגְלוֹ הַיְמָנִית עַל־מְקוֹם דַּם הָאָשָׁם: וְהַנּוֹתָר
מִן־הַשֶּׁמֶן אֲשֶׁר עַל־כַּף הַכֹּהֵן יִתֵּן עַל־רֹאשׁ הַמִּטַּהֵר לְכַפֵּר עָלָיו לִפְנֵי
ל יהוה: וְעָשָׂה אֶת־הָאֶחָד מִן־הַתֹּרִים אוֹ מִן־בְּנֵי הַיּוֹנָה מֵאֲשֶׁר תַּשִּׂיג יָדוֹ:
לא אֵת אֲשֶׁר־תַּשִּׂיג יָדוֹ אֶת־הָאֶחָד חַטָּאת וְאֶת־הָאֶחָד עֹלָה עַל־הַמִּנְחָה
לב וְכִפֶּר הַכֹּהֵן עַל הַמִּטַּהֵר לִפְנֵי יהוה: זֹאת תּוֹרַת אֲשֶׁר־בּוֹ נֶגַע צָרָעַת אֲשֶׁר
לֹא־תַשִּׂיג יָדוֹ בְּטָהֳרָתוֹ:
רביעי לג־לד וַיְדַבֵּר יהוה אֶל־מֹשֶׁה וְאֶל־אַהֲרֹן לֵאמֹר: כִּי תָבֹאוּ אֶל־אֶרֶץ כְּנַעַן אֲשֶׁר
[ששי] לה אֲנִי נֹתֵן לָכֶם לַאֲחֻזָּה וְנָתַתִּי נֶגַע צָרַעַת בְּבֵית אֶרֶץ אֲחֻזַּתְכֶם: וּבָא אֲשֶׁר־
לו לוֹ הַבַּיִת וְהִגִּיד לַכֹּהֵן לֵאמֹר כְּנֶגַע נִרְאָה לִי בַּבָּיִת: וְצִוָּה הַכֹּהֵן וּפִנּוּ אֶת־
הַבַּיִת בְּטֶרֶם יָבֹא הַכֹּהֵן לִרְאוֹת אֶת־הַנֶּגַע וְלֹא יִטְמָא כָּל־אֲשֶׁר בַּבָּיִת
לז וְאַחַר כֵּן יָבֹא הַכֹּהֵן לִרְאוֹת אֶת־הַבָּיִת: וְרָאָה אֶת־הַנֶּגַע וְהִנֵּה הַנֶּגַע

---

36. וּפִנּוּ אֶת הַבַּיִת בְּטֶרֶם יָבֹא הַכֹּהֵן — *And they shall empty the house before the Kohen comes.* But he shall not come before this (is done). In the interim, there will be time for the owners to pray and repent (as well as) time for the *Kohen's* prayers. The period of 'shutting up' is given for this (purpose, as well) (13:3). In the *Midrash* (*Vayikra Rabbah, Metzora*), it is said that all this alludes to the first destruction (of the Holy Temple), its remedy (restoration) in the Second (Temple), and its demolishment in the second destruction, and its purification through the third construction, may it be built and established speedily in our days, Amen.

NOTES

36. וּפִנּוּ אֶת הַבַּיִת בְּטֶרֶם יָבֹא הַכֹּהֵן — *And they shall empty the house before the Kohen comes.* Consistent with his commentary in the previous chapter (13:47), the *Sforno* explains that the purpose of נִגְעֵי בָתִּים, *afflictions of a house,* is to arouse the owner to examine his conduct and repent his sins, therefore an opportunity is given to him to do so *before* the *Kohen* comes to pronounce the house *tamei,* unclean.

The Midrash cited by the *Sforno* interprets this *parashah* in a symbolic manner as alluding to the destruction of the First Temple, the construction and subsequent destruction of the Second Temple and the eventual rebuilding of the Third Temple. *The house in the land of your possession* (v. 34) introduces the theme of the Temple, the House of God. *He that owns the house* (v. 35) refers to God. The dismantling of the house (vs. 40-41) symbolizes the destruction of the Temple and *Casting them ... outside the city* (v. 40) indicates the exile of Israel. Taking other stones and rebuilding the house (v. 42) symbolizes the rebuilding of the Temple when the people return from Babylonia, but verse 45 indicates that the house will once again be destroyed. The expression *So shall he make atonement for the house and it shall be clean* (v. 53) alludes to the Third Temple which shall be everlasting.

בְּקִירֹת הַבָּיִת שְׁקַעֲרוּרֹת יְרַקְרַקֹּת אוֹ אֲדַמְדַּמֹּת וּמַרְאֵיהֶן שָׁפָל מִן־הַקִּיר:
לח וְיָצָא הַכֹּהֵן מִן־הַבַּיִת אֶל־פֶּתַח הַבָּיִת וְהִסְגִּיר אֶת־הַבַּיִת שִׁבְעַת יָמִים:
לט-מ וְשָׁב הַכֹּהֵן בַּיּוֹם הַשְּׁבִיעִי וְרָאָה וְהִנֵּה פָּשָׂה הַנֶּגַע בְּקִירֹת הַבָּיִת: וְצִוָּה הַכֹּהֵן
וְחִלְּצוּ אֶת־הָאֲבָנִים אֲשֶׁר בָּהֵן הַנָּגַע וְהִשְׁלִיכוּ אֶתְהֶן אֶל־מִחוּץ לָעִיר אֶל־
מא מָקוֹם טָמֵא: וְאֶת־הַבַּיִת יַקְצִעַ מִבַּיִת סָבִיב וְשָׁפְכוּ אֶת־הֶעָפָר אֲשֶׁר הִקְצוּ
מב אֶל־מִחוּץ לָעִיר אֶל־מָקוֹם טָמֵא: וְלָקְחוּ אֲבָנִים אֲחֵרוֹת וְהֵבִיאוּ אֶל־תַּחַת
מג הָאֲבָנִים וְעָפָר אַחֵר יִקַּח וְטָח אֶת־הַבָּיִת: וְאִם־יָשׁוּב הַנֶּגַע וּפָרַח בַּבַּיִת
מד אַחַר חִלֵּץ אֶת־הָאֲבָנִים וְאַחֲרֵי הִקְצוֹת אֶת־הַבַּיִת וְאַחֲרֵי הִטּוֹחַ: וּבָא
הַכֹּהֵן וְרָאָה וְהִנֵּה פָּשָׂה הַנֶּגַע בַּבָּיִת צָרַעַת מַמְאֶרֶת הִוא בַּבַּיִת טָמֵא
מה הוּא: וְנָתַץ אֶת־הַבַּיִת אֶת־אֲבָנָיו וְאֶת־עֵצָיו וְאֵת כָּל־עֲפַר הַבָּיִת וְהוֹצִיא
מו אֶל־מִחוּץ לָעִיר אֶל־מָקוֹם טָמֵא: וְהַבָּא אֶל־הַבַּיִת כָּל־יְמֵי הִסְגִּיר אֹתוֹ
מז יִטְמָא עַד־הָעָרֶב: וְהַשֹּׁכֵב בַּבַּיִת יְכַבֵּס אֶת־בְּגָדָיו וְהָאֹכֵל בַּבַּיִת יְכַבֵּס
מח אֶת־בְּגָדָיו: וְאִם־בֹּא יָבֹא הַכֹּהֵן וְרָאָה וְהִנֵּה לֹא־פָשָׂה הַנֶּגַע בַּבַּיִת
מט אַחֲרֵי הִטֹּחַ אֶת־הַבָּיִת וְטִהַר הַכֹּהֵן אֶת־הַבַּיִת כִּי נִרְפָּא הַנָּגַע: וְלָקַח
נ לְחַטֵּא אֶת־הַבַּיִת שְׁתֵּי צִפֳּרִים וְעֵץ אֶרֶז וּשְׁנִי תוֹלַעַת וְאֵזֹב: וְשָׁחַט
נא אֶת־הַצִּפֹּר הָאֶחָת אֶל־כְּלִי־חֶרֶשׂ עַל־מַיִם חַיִּים: וְלָקַח אֶת־עֵץ־הָאֶרֶז
וְאֶת־הָאֵזֹב וְאֵת ׀ שְׁנִי הַתּוֹלַעַת וְאֵת הַצִּפֹּר הַחַיָּה וְטָבַל אֹתָם בְּדַם הַצִּפֹּר
נב הַשְּׁחוּטָה וּבַמַּיִם הַחַיִּים וְהִזָּה אֶל־הַבַּיִת שֶׁבַע פְּעָמִים: וְחִטֵּא אֶת־
הַבַּיִת בְּדַם הַצִּפּוֹר וּבַמַּיִם הַחַיִּים וּבַצִּפֹּר הַחַיָּה וּבְעֵץ הָאֶרֶז וּבָאֵזֹב
נג וּבִשְׁנִי הַתּוֹלָעַת: וְשִׁלַּח אֶת־הַצִּפֹּר הַחַיָּה אֶל־מִחוּץ לָעִיר אֶל־פְּנֵי
חמישי נד הַשָּׂדֶה וְכִפֶּר עַל־הַבַּיִת וְטָהֵר: זֹאת הַתּוֹרָה לְכָל־נֶגַע הַצָּרַעַת וְלַנָּתֶק:

---

54. זאת הַתּוֹרָה — *This is the law.* He who comes to instruct regarding the afflictions must know how to differentiate between two kinds (of afflictions), even though they are of one class, as it says, וּבֵין נֶגַע לָנֶגַע, *Between affliction and affliction* (*Deut.* 17:8).

לְכָל נֶגַע הַצָּרַעַת וְלַנָּתֶק — *For all manner of affliction of leprosy and for a scall.* Although they are both a leprosy on the skin of man, nonetheless, they are different in that the scall is judged not by its appearance, but by that hair which falls out and by black hair (Chapter 13). All other types of leprosy are (however) always judged through appearance.

55. וּלְצָרַעַת הַבֶּגֶד וְלַבָּיִת — *And for the leprosy of a garment and for a house.* Although they are similar regarding their green or red appearance, and both are (afflicted) in an unnatural manner (see *Sforno* 13:47), nonetheless, they are

NOTES

54-56. זאת הַתּוֹרָה ... הַצָּרַעַת וְלַנָּתֶק: וּלְצָרַעַת הַבֶּגֶד וְלַבָּיִת: וְלַשְׂאֵת — *This is the law ... of leprosy and for a scall. And for the leprosy of a garment and for a house. And for a rising.* The phrase זאת הַתּוֹרָה, the introductory phrase of these three verses, is interpreted by the *Sforno* as emphasizing the need for the *Kohen* to be expert in these laws because there are so many subtle variations of *halachah* and differentiations between one affliction and another, as he explains in his commentary. The combining of certain afflictions in the same verse is explained by the *Sforno* as the listing of afflictions which possess similarities, yet are different. For example, *leprosy and scall* (v. 54), *leprosy of a garment and a house* (v. 55),

נה־נו וּלְצָרַעַת הַבֶּגֶד וְלַבָּיִת׃ וְלַשְׂאֵת וְלַסַּפַּחַת וְלַבֶּהָרֶת׃ לְהוֹרֹת בְּיוֹם הַטָּמֵא
וּבְיוֹם הַטָּהֹר זֹאת תּוֹרַת הַצָּרָעַת׃

טו א־ב וַיְדַבֵּר יהוה אֶל־מֹשֶׁה וְאֶל־אַהֲרֹן לֵאמֹר׃ דַּבְּרוּ אֶל־בְּנֵי יִשְׂרָאֵל וַאֲמַרְתֶּם
ג אֲלֵהֶם אִישׁ אִישׁ כִּי יִהְיֶה זָב מִבְּשָׂרוֹ זוֹבוֹ טָמֵא הוּא׃ וְזֹאת תִּהְיֶה טֻמְאָתוֹ

---

differentiated in the following fashion: If (the affliction) in the garment has spread by the end of the first week, the (garment) must be burnt in its entirety (13:51,52), but (if the affliction) has spread in a house by the end of the first week, the stones are taken out, scraped and plastered and a (further) week is granted (to determine whether the affliction will return or not) (vs. 39-42).

56. וְלַשְׂאֵת וְלַסַּפַּחַת וְלַבֶּהָרֶת — *And for a rising, and for a scab and for a bright spot.* Although they are similar (in many ways) — each one is white, they have similar laws and they (can be) combined (to effect the needed size) — as (our Sages) have received the tradition, nonetheless, he who comes to instruct regarding (these) afflictions must be expert in the different degrees of whiteness and their location. For (whereas) the place of a boil and a burn is judged by mixed appearances, a scab and a hairy area are not judged by appearance at all.

57. זאת תורת הַצָּרָעַת — *This is the law of leprosy.* One must not be extra strict in pronouncing *tamei* other afflictions of the skin and flesh, even though there are many more types of leprosy among us, as it says, אַל תּוֹסְףְּ עַל דְּבָרָיו, *Add not to his words* (*Proverbs* 30:6). For indeed, even with all their severity we cannot apply the laws of leprosy to them at all, just as the (Torah) pronounces him *tahor*, clean, when the afflicted skin turns entirely white (13:13) for the leprosy has crossed utterly over the boundary of *tumah* to (a level of) evil, similar to *tamei* (holy meat) which is burnt and (thereby) its form is obliterated.

XV

2. זָב מִבְּשָׂרוֹ — *An issue from his flesh.* (We) have learned from tradition that *from his flesh* (implies) 'not due to an accident,' meaning that the issue's flow is caused by *his flesh,* which is an euphemism for the male organ or reproductive system, but not by any other cause which aroused the emission. (Our Sages) here explained that this

NOTES

and *a rising, a scab and a bright spot* (v. 56) have common characteristics but there is diversity in their laws. For the *Kohen* to know how to decide these questions, he must possess great expertise.

57. זאת תורת הַצָּרָעַת — *This is the law of leprosy.* The *Sforno* in the previous chapter (13:2) explained that it is not the severity of the physical ailment which determines the cleanness or *tumah* of the affliction. Since it is a גְּזֵרַת הַכָּתוּב, *a Scriptural decree,* only those ordained by God as being *tamei* are considered to be so. Therefore, it follows that only those enumerated by the Torah in these chapters are deemed צָרַעַת, *leprosy.* Thus, the laws of leprosy cannot be understood logically by man. One cannot, with pure reason, grasp why a white spot causes *tumah* whereas the *total* spreading of white over one's skin is deemed *tahor*! The *Sforno* does, however, suggest a reason. When holy meat (קָדָשִׁים) becomes *tamei,* and is burnt, the ashes are no longer considered as being *tamei,* nor do they have the stringencies of holy meat for the form has been changed. So too, with the affliction; when it covers the entire body it is as though the skin has been consumed and thereby transformed.

XV

2. זָב מִבְּשָׂרוֹ — *An issue from his flesh.* The *Sforno* explains that זִיבָה, *an abnormal issue,*

בְּזוֹבוֹ רָר בְּשָׂרוֹ אֶת־זוֹבוֹ אוֹ־הֶחְתִּים בְּשָׂרוֹ מִזּוֹבוֹ טֻמְאָתוֹ הִוא׃
ד כָּל־הַמִּשְׁכָּב אֲשֶׁר יִשְׁכַּב עָלָיו הַזָּב יִטְמָא וְכָל־הַכְּלִי אֲשֶׁר־יֵשֵׁב עָלָיו
ה יִטְמָא׃ וְאִישׁ אֲשֶׁר יִגַּע בְּמִשְׁכָּבוֹ יְכַבֵּס בְּגָדָיו וְרָחַץ בַּמַּיִם וְטָמֵא
ו עַד־הָעָרֶב׃ וְהַיֹּשֵׁב עַל־הַכְּלִי אֲשֶׁר־יֵשֵׁב עָלָיו הַזָּב יְכַבֵּס בְּגָדָיו וְרָחַץ
ז בַּמַּיִם וְטָמֵא עַד־הָעָרֶב׃ וְהַנֹּגֵעַ בִּבְשַׂר הַזָּב יְכַבֵּס בְּגָדָיו וְרָחַץ בַּמַּיִם וְטָמֵא
ח עַד־הָעָרֶב׃ וְכִי־יָרֹק הַזָּב בַּטָּהוֹר וְכִבֶּס בְּגָדָיו וְרָחַץ בַּמַּיִם וְטָמֵא
ט־י עַד־הָעָרֶב׃ וְכָל־הַמֶּרְכָּב אֲשֶׁר יִרְכַּב עָלָיו הַזָּב יִטְמָא׃ וְכָל־הַנֹּגֵעַ בְּכֹל
אֲשֶׁר יִהְיֶה תַחְתָּיו יִטְמָא עַד־הָעָרֶב וְהַנּוֹשֵׂא אוֹתָם יְכַבֵּס בְּגָדָיו וְרָחַץ
יא בַּמַּיִם וְטָמֵא עַד־הָעָרֶב׃ וְכֹל אֲשֶׁר יִגַּע־בּוֹ הַזָּב וְיָדָיו לֹא־שָׁטַף בַּמָּיִם וְכִבֶּס
יב בְּגָדָיו וְרָחַץ בַּמַּיִם וְטָמֵא עַד־הָעָרֶב׃ וּכְלִי־חֶרֶשׂ אֲשֶׁר־יִגַּע־בּוֹ הַזָּב יִשָּׁבֵר
יג וְכָל־כְּלִי־עֵץ יִשָּׁטֵף בַּמָּיִם׃ וְכִי־יִטְהַר הַזָּב מִזּוֹבוֹ וְסָפַר לוֹ שִׁבְעַת יָמִים
יד לְטָהֳרָתוֹ וְכִבֶּס בְּגָדָיו וְרָחַץ בְּשָׂרוֹ בְּמַיִם חַיִּים וְטָהֵר׃ וּבַיּוֹם הַשְּׁמִינִי
יִקַּח־לוֹ שְׁתֵּי תֹרִים אוֹ שְׁנֵי בְּנֵי יוֹנָה וּבָא ׀ לִפְנֵי יהוה אֶל־פֶּתַח אֹהֶל מוֹעֵד
טו וּנְתָנָם אֶל־הַכֹּהֵן׃ וְעָשָׂה אֹתָם הַכֹּהֵן אֶחָד חַטָּאת וְהָאֶחָד עֹלָה וְכִפֶּר עָלָיו
ששי [שביעי] טז הַכֹּהֵן לִפְנֵי יהוה מִזּוֹבוֹ׃ וְאִישׁ כִּי־תֵצֵא מִמֶּנּוּ שִׁכְבַת־זָרַע
יז וְרָחַץ בַּמַּיִם אֶת־כָּל־בְּשָׂרוֹ וְטָמֵא עַד־הָעָרֶב׃ וְכָל־בֶּגֶד וְכָל־עוֹר אֲשֶׁר־
יח יִהְיֶה עָלָיו שִׁכְבַת־זָרַע וְכֻבַּס בַּמַּיִם וְטָמֵא עַד־הָעָרֶב׃ וְאִשָּׁה אֲשֶׁר יִשְׁכַּב
אִישׁ אֹתָהּ שִׁכְבַת־זָרַע וְרָחֲצוּ בַמַּיִם וְטָמְאוּ עַד־הָעָרֶב׃

---

issue (looks like) the white of an addled egg. Now, when this occurs *from his flesh,* caused solely by an ailment of the reproductive organ, behold, this indicates a weakness and lack in its assimilative ability which usually happens because of overindulgence in sexual intercourse and his preoccupation (with these matters), as a result of which the folly of his lewd sinfulness does not cease. Therefore, it is fitting that he count seven clean (days) (v. 13) in which to erase his preoccupation from his heart, (after which) he immerses himself, (thereby removing) his (state of) *tumah* and finds atonement through sin and burnt offerings (vs. 14-15) for his deeds and thoughts.

18. וְאִשָּׁה אֲשֶׁר יִשְׁכַּב אִישׁ אֹתָהּ — *The woman also with whom a man shall lie carnally.* It is not written אִישׁ כִּי יִשְׁכַּב אֶת אִשָּׁה, *If a man lies with a woman,* for (the Torah) attests that a woman does not become unclean from any issue unless it is red or from a seminal emission, as does a man. However the *tumah* of a woman through semen only results when a man lies with her, even though (the semen) is in (her) concealed chamber.

NOTES

which some interpret to mean gonorrhea, is caused by impure thoughts and unbridled sexual indulgence. Therefore, two sacrifices must be brought by the זָב when he is ready for atonement. One is the חַטָּאת, *sin offering,* which atones for overt sinful acts, while the second is the עוֹלָה, *burnt offering,* which atones for man's thoughts, as the *Sforno* explained above (1:2).

18. וְאִשָּׁה אֲשֶׁר יִשְׁכַּב אִישׁ אֹתָהּ — *The woman also with whom a man shall lie carnally.* A woman becomes טְמֵאָה, *unclean,* in one of two ways: if blood flows from her, or through

יט וְאִשָּׁה֙ כִּֽי־תִהְיֶ֣ה זָבָ֔ה דָּ֛ם יִהְיֶ֥ה זֹבָ֖הּ בִּבְשָׂרָ֑הּ שִׁבְעַ֤ת יָמִים֙ תִּהְיֶ֣ה בְנִדָּתָ֔הּ
כ וְכָל־הַנֹּגֵ֥עַ בָּ֖הּ יִטְמָ֥א עַד־הָעָֽרֶב׃ וְכֹל֩ אֲשֶׁ֨ר תִּשְׁכַּ֥ב עָלָ֛יו בְּנִדָּתָ֖הּ יִטְמָ֑א
כא וְכֹ֛ל אֲשֶׁר־תֵּשֵׁ֥ב עָלָ֖יו יִטְמָֽא׃ וְכָל־הַנֹּגֵ֖עַ בְּמִשְׁכָּבָ֑הּ יְכַבֵּ֥ס בְּגָדָ֛יו וְרָחַ֥ץ
כב בַּמַּ֖יִם וְטָמֵ֥א עַד־הָעָֽרֶב׃ וְכָל־הַנֹּגֵ֔עַ בְּכָל־כְּלִ֖י אֲשֶׁר־תֵּשֵׁ֣ב עָלָ֑יו יְכַבֵּ֥ס
כג בְּגָדָ֛יו וְרָחַ֥ץ בַּמַּ֖יִם וְטָמֵ֥א עַד־הָעָֽרֶב׃ וְאִ֨ם עַֽל־הַמִּשְׁכָּ֜ב ה֗וּא א֛וֹ עַֽל־הַכְּלִ֛י
כד אֲשֶׁר־הִ֥וא יֹשֶֽׁבֶת־עָלָ֖יו בְּנָגְעוֹ־ב֑וֹ יִטְמָ֖א עַד־הָעָֽרֶב׃ וְאִ֡ם שָׁכֹב֩ יִשְׁכַּ֨ב אִ֜ישׁ
אֹתָ֗הּ וּתְהִ֤י נִדָּתָהּ֙ עָלָ֔יו וְטָמֵ֖א שִׁבְעַ֣ת יָמִ֑ים וְכָל־הַמִּשְׁכָּ֛ב אֲשֶׁר־יִשְׁכַּ֥ב עָלָ֖יו
כה יִטְמָֽא׃ וְאִשָּׁ֡ה כִּֽי־יָזוּב֩ ז֨וֹב דָּמָ֜הּ יָמִ֣ים רַבִּ֗ים בְּלֹא֙ עֶת־נִדָּתָ֔הּ
א֥וֹ כִֽי־תָז֖וּב עַל־נִדָּתָ֑הּ כָּל־יְמֵ֞י ז֣וֹב טֻמְאָתָ֗הּ כִּימֵ֧י נִדָּתָ֛הּ תִּהְיֶ֖ה טְמֵאָ֥ה
כו הִֽוא׃ כָּל־הַמִּשְׁכָּ֞ב אֲשֶׁר־תִּשְׁכַּ֤ב עָלָיו֙ כָּל־יְמֵ֣י זוֹבָ֔הּ כְּמִשְׁכַּ֥ב נִדָּתָ֖הּ יִֽהְיֶה־
כז לָּ֑הּ וְכָל־הַכְּלִי֙ אֲשֶׁ֣ר תֵּשֵׁ֣ב עָלָ֔יו טָמֵ֣א יִהְיֶ֔ה כְּטֻמְאַ֖ת נִדָּתָֽהּ׃ וְכָל־הַנּוֹגֵ֥עַ בָּ֖ם
כח יִטְמָ֑א וְכִבֶּ֧ס בְּגָדָ֛יו וְרָחַ֥ץ בַּמַּ֖יִם וְטָמֵ֥א עַד־הָעָֽרֶב׃ וְאִֽם־טָהֲרָ֖ה מִזּוֹבָ֑הּ
שביעי כט וְסָ֥פְרָה לָּ֛הּ שִׁבְעַ֥ת יָמִ֖ים וְאַחַ֥ר תִּטְהָֽר׃ וּבַיּ֣וֹם הַשְּׁמִינִ֗י תִּֽקַּֽח־לָהּ֙ שְׁתֵּ֣י תֹרִ֔ים
ל א֥וֹ שְׁנֵ֖י בְּנֵ֣י יוֹנָ֑ה וְהֵבִיאָ֤ה אוֹתָם֙ אֶל־הַכֹּהֵ֔ן אֶל־פֶּ֖תַח אֹ֥הֶל מוֹעֵֽד׃ וְעָשָׂ֣ה
הַכֹּהֵ֗ן אֶת־הָֽאֶחָד֙ חַטָּ֔את וְאֶת־הָאֶחָ֖ד עֹלָ֑ה וְכִפֶּ֨ר עָלֶ֤יהָ הַכֹּהֵן֙ לִפְנֵ֣י יהוה
מפטיר לא מִזּ֖וֹב טֻמְאָתָֽהּ׃ וְהִזַּרְתֶּ֥ם אֶת־בְּנֵֽי־יִשְׂרָאֵ֖ל מִטֻּמְאָתָ֑ם וְלֹ֤א יָמֻ֙תוּ֙ בְּטֻמְאָתָ֔ם

---

19. וְאִשָּׁה כִּי תִהְיֶה זָבָה דָּם — *And if a woman have an issue of blood.* (The Torah) teaches the laws of a נִדָּה, *menstruant*, and a זָבָה, *woman that has a flow many days*, imposing (the obligation) upon a זָבָה (to bring) a sin and a burnt offering. Thus (the Torah) testifies that this does not (normally) occur with the daughters of His people, except to alert them (lit., awaken their ear) to the 'early rebellion' in deed and in thought, for it is, in actuality, (merely) an extension of the punishment with which Eve was punished for her deed and thought, included in His saying, הַרְבָּה אַרְבֶּה עִצְּבוֹנֵךְ, *I will greatly multiply your pain* (*Genesis* 3:16). Therefore, it is fitting that she count seven clean days until a spirit of repentance and purity 'pours over her,' and then she will immerse herself and achieve atonement for (her) misdeeds through the sin offering, and from her (evil) thoughts through the burnt offering.

NOTES

semen (שִׁכְבַת זֶרַע) which has entered her body through sexual intercourse. The latter law, however, is difficult to understand since there is a principle that טוּמְאַת בֵּית הַסְּתָרִים, *tumah in a concealed region*, does not render her unclean. The Talmud (*Niddah* 41b) therefore states that, in this case, it is a Scriptural ordinance (גְּזֵרַת הַכָּתוּב). The *Sforno* explains that our Sages understanding of this *halachah* is derived from the phraseology of our verse — i.e., אִשָּׁה אֲשֶׁר יִשְׁכַּב אִישׁ אֹתָהּ, rather than אִישׁ כִּי יִשְׁכַּב.

19. וְאִשָּׁה כִּי תִהְיֶה זָבָה דָּם — *And if a woman have an issue of blood.* The *Sforno* in his commentary on *Genesis* 3:16 interprets עִצְּבוֹנֵךְ, *your pain*, as referring to menstruation. זִיבָה, *an abnormal flow*, is, in his opinion, an extension (in terms of the pain endured) of this 'early' punishment of Eve. Hence, when a woman is thus afflicted it is meant to spur her to repentance, as is the case with all afflictions; such as leprosy of the body, garments, and houses. She also must bring a sin and a burnt offering for the reasons given in verse 2 (see the note there), and in verse 32 (see the *Sforno's* commentary).

32. זֹאת תּוֹרַת הַזָּב — *This is the law of one who has an issue.* The *Sforno* interprets this phrase

לב בְּטַמְּאָם אֶת־מִשְׁכָּנִי אֲשֶׁר בְּתוֹכָם: זֹאת תּוֹרַת הַזָּב וַאֲשֶׁר תֵּצֵא מִמֶּנּוּ
לג שִׁכְבַת־זֶרַע לְטָמְאָה־בָהּ: וְהַדָּוָה בְּנִדָּתָהּ וְהַזָּב אֶת־זוֹבוֹ לַזָּכָר וְלַנְּקֵבָה
וּלְאִישׁ אֲשֶׁר יִשְׁכַּב עִם־טְמֵאָה:

---

32. זאת תורת הַזָּב — *This is the law of one who has an issue.* This is what is proper to reflect upon in all these (laws): Firstly, since a זָב is obligated to bring a sin offering (and burnt offering), it indicates that they are brought (to atone for) for that which is sinful, both in deed and in thought.

וַאֲשֶׁר תֵּצֵא מִמֶּנּוּ שִׁכְבַת זֶרַע לְטָמְאָה בָהּ — *And of one from whom the flow of seed issues forth so that he is unclean thereby.* (And secondly), because the reason for the *tumah* resulting from a nocturnal emission is that the intent of the one who emitted it was *to become tamei thereby,* (which was caused by) the 'instigation of the serpent' (based on *Bava Basra* 17a), and not for the perpetuation of the species; otherwise, there would be no *tumah* (connected) with semen just as there is no *tumah* in excrement and urine.

33. וְהַדָּוָה בְּנִדָּתָהּ — *And of she who is sick with her menstruation.* The term דְּוֹתָהּ, *her sickness* (12:2), implies that this is (due) to sin, and therefore she becomes *tamei.*

וְהַזָּב — *And of those who have an issue . . .* and to consider the matter of a *zav,* which is to alert one (lit., awaken the ear) to the sin which preceded it.

אֶת זובו לַזָּכָר וְלַנְּקֵבָה — *The issue of a man and of a woman.* And (in connection) with this, it is fitting to discern the differences (in law) regarding the issue of a man and the issue of a woman, for the issue of a woman is only *tamei* if it is red, (whereas) the issue of a man is only *tamei* if it is *not* red.

וּלְאִישׁ אֲשֶׁר יִשְׁכַּב עִם טְמֵאָה — *And of the man that lies with her that is unclean.* It is also proper to consider that regarding a man who lies with an unclean (woman), (the Torah) says, *and her niddos shall be upon him* (v. 24), whereas this is not said of a clean woman who lies with a *zav,* because (the Torah) is teaching us that a male is more impaired by lying with a 'sick woman' (i.e., נִדָּה) than a woman is impaired by lying with a 'sick man' (i.e., זָב), as we find from experience regarding leprous women and similar cases.

NOTES

in the context of the *learning* of certain lessons. One lesson is elucidated through the reason for the bringing of two offerings, as explained above (to expiate the evil act and thought). The second lies in the fact that the only emission from the human body which makes a man unclean (and a woman as well under certain circumstances) is semen. The reason for this is that this emission, although involuntary, is connected to impure thoughts; yet is not for reproductive purposes. The Torah exhorts us to contemplate the laws discussed in this chapter so that we may better understand their significance and better appreciate the different levels of *tumah,* as well as the importance of examining our thoughts and deeds which cause these abnormal ailments.

פרשת אחרי מות
Parashas Acharei Mos

טז א וַיְדַבֵּר יהוה אֶל־מֹשֶׁה אַחֲרֵי מוֹת שְׁנֵי בְּנֵי אַהֲרֹן בְּקָרְבָתָם לִפְנֵי־יהוה
ב וַיָּמֻתוּ׃ וַיֹּאמֶר יהוה אֶל־מֹשֶׁה דַּבֵּר אֶל־אַהֲרֹן אָחִיךָ וְאַל־יָבֹא בְכָל־עֵת
אֶל־הַקֹּדֶשׁ מִבֵּית לַפָּרֹכֶת אֶל־פְּנֵי הַכַּפֹּרֶת אֲשֶׁר עַל־הָאָרֹן וְלֹא יָמוּת כִּי
ג בֶּעָנָן אֵרָאֶה עַל־הַכַּפֹּרֶת׃ בְּזֹאת יָבֹא אַהֲרֹן אֶל־הַקֹּדֶשׁ בְּפַר בֶּן־בָּקָר

XVI

1. וַיְדַבֵּר ה׳ אֶל מֹשֶׁה אַחֲרֵי מוֹת — *And HASHEM spoke to Moses after the death.* Behold, the word וַיְדַבֵּר, *and he spoke*, in the holy tongue does not usually introduce a particular statement but refers to a general course of communication. Therefore, the expression וַיְדַבֵּר, *and he spoke,* is usually followed by the word וַיֹּאמֶר, which indicates a particular statement. Hence, the sense of the verse is, *And HASHEM spoke to Moses after the death,* (v. 1) ... *and said to him, 'Speak to Aaron your brother'* (v. 2). But because (v. 1) speaks at length about the death of Aaron's sons which is a particular subject, (the Torah) does not simply state *and said to him* (in v. 2) but repeats the name of God, the Blessed One, Who is the speaker, and Moses, who is the listener.

However, according to some of our Sages, of blessed memory, these (two verses) represent two statements. The sense of the verses (will then be) *And HASHEM spoke to Moses and said, 'Speak to Aaron ... that he come not ... that he die not.'* And (secondly) *after the death of the two sons of Aaron,* He said to Moses *'Speak to Aaron ... that he come not,'* that he should not enter (the Holy) except when he is so commanded *'that he die not,'* as his sons did when they persisted in offering incense beyond that which had been commanded. This (second statement) is meant to put him on guard more so than the first (statement).

2. כִּי בֶּעָנָן אֵרָאֶה — *For I will appear in a cloud* ... to speak with Moses in this generation, and in other generations to call those who are prepared for prophecy, similar to Samuel, about whom (the Torah) says, וּשְׁמוּאֵל שֹׁכֵב בְּהֵיכַל ה׳ אֲשֶׁר שָׁם אֲרוֹן אֱלֹהִים, וַיִּקְרָא ה׳ אֶל שְׁמוּאֵל, *And Samuel was lying in the temple of HASHEM, where the ark of God was and HASHEM called to Samuel* (*I Samuel* 3:3,4).

3. בְּזֹאת יָבֹא ... בְּפַר בֶּן בָּקָר — *With this* (*Aaron*) *shall come ... with a young bull.* (He shall come) with the sanctification of the bull as a sin offering and a ram as a

NOTES

XVI

1-2. וַיְדַבֵּר ה׳ אֶל מֹשֶׁה — *And HASHEM spoke to Moses.* Although verse 1 begins וַיְדַבֵּר ה׳, *And HASHEM spoke,* verse 2 nevertheless begins וַיֹּאמֶר ה׳, *And HASHEM said,* a seeming repetition. The *Sforno* explains that the two are not redundant. The former phrase refers to God's general communication with a prophet whereas the latter phrase refers to the exact nature of that communication. There is, however, a difficulty regarding these two verses since the Torah could have simply written in verse 2, ... וַיֹּאמֶר, דַּבֵּר, *And He said, 'Speak ...'* Why was it necessary to repeat the Name of God and the name of Moses? The *Sforno* answers that since there is an interruption in verse 1 where the Torah tells us about the death of Aaron's sons and the circumstances surrounding that incident, the Torah finds it necessary to repeat, once again, the name of the communicator (God) and the name of the recipient of that communication (Moses). The *Sforno* also suggests another interpretation of these two verses, as does *Rashi,* based on the *Sifra* that there were two orders and commandments which Moses was told to give to Aaron. The first was simply to warn Aaron not to enter the Holy (i.e., the Sanctuary) at will, but only at specifically ordained times, lest he die. The second was to underscore the peril of doing so by telling him that this was indeed the

ד לְחַטָּאת וְאַיִל לְעֹלָה: כְּתֹנֶת־בַּד קֹדֶשׁ יִלְבָּשׁ וּמִכְנְסֵי־בַד יִהְיוּ עַל־בְּשָׂרוֹ
וּבְאַבְנֵט בַּד יַחְגֹּר וּבְמִצְנֶפֶת בַּד יִצְנֹף בִּגְדֵי־קֹדֶשׁ הֵם וְרָחַץ בַּמַּיִם
ה אֶת־בְּשָׂרוֹ וּלְבֵשָׁם: וּמֵאֵת עֲדַת בְּנֵי יִשְׂרָאֵל יִקַּח שְׁנֵי־שְׂעִירֵי עִזִּים
ו לְחַטָּאת וְאַיִל אֶחָד לְעֹלָה: וְהִקְרִיב אַהֲרֹן אֶת־פַּר הַחַטָּאת אֲשֶׁר־לוֹ
ז וְכִפֶּר בַּעֲדוֹ וּבְעַד בֵּיתוֹ: וְלָקַח אֶת־שְׁנֵי הַשְּׂעִירִם וְהֶעֱמִיד אֹתָם לִפְנֵי יהוה
ח פֶּתַח אֹהֶל מוֹעֵד: וְנָתַן אַהֲרֹן עַל־שְׁנֵי הַשְּׂעִירִם גֹּרָלוֹת גּוֹרָל אֶחָד לַיהוָה
ט וְגוֹרָל אֶחָד לַעֲזָאזֵל: וְהִקְרִיב אַהֲרֹן אֶת־הַשָּׂעִיר אֲשֶׁר עָלָה עָלָיו הַגּוֹרָל
י לַיהוָה וְעָשָׂהוּ חַטָּאת: וְהַשָּׂעִיר אֲשֶׁר עָלָה עָלָיו הַגּוֹרָל לַעֲזָאזֵל יָעֳמַד־חַי

---

burnt offering and the wearing of the linen (garments), which have no color, nor artificial design. For, indeed, the *Kohen Gadol* must not postpone his entrance to the inner (room) until after the sacrifice of the burnt offering, but must enter to burn the incense immediately after the slaughtering of the sin offering.

4. בִּגְדֵי קֹדֶשׁ הֵם — *They are holy garments.* In similar garments do angels appear to the prophets, for they (also) appear in linen garments.

5. שְׁנֵי שְׂעִירֵי עִזִּים לְחַטָּאת — *Two he-goats for a sin offering.* The first (goat) is to (atone) for sins committed in connection with the Sanctuary, and the (second) is sent away (to expiate) the other sins of the community which, due to the excess of its *tumah,* is not fit to be sacrificed and (even) defiles the one through whom it is sent.

8. גֹּרָלוֹת — *Lots.* Because the lot, particularly through the hand of His pious one, is considered as if the one who casts it is seeking the word of God, as it says, בַּחֵיק יוּטַל אֶת הַגּוֹרָל וּמֵה׳ כָּל מִשְׁפָּטוֹ, *The lot is cast into the lap, but the whole of its decision is from* HASHEM (*Proverbs* 16:33).

9. וְעָשָׂהוּ חַטָּאת — *And make it a sin offering.* The lot designates (makes) the goat as a sin offering, as (our Sages) say, 'It is the lot that makes the sin offering, not the calling of the Name which makes it a sin offering' (*Yoma* 40b).

NOTES

cause of his sons' death, thereby putting Aaron on guard. See *Rashi* who brings the words of Rabbi Elazar ben Azariah and the parable used by him regarding this second statement.

3. בְּזֹאת יָבֹא — *With this* (*Aaron*) *shall come.* The word בְּזֹאת, *with this,* is ambiguous. The *Midrash* offers numerous interpretations as to its meaning. The *Sforno* explains that it simply means that with *these* offerings (sin and burnt offerings) and *this* wearing of simple, unadorned, white linen garments, the *Kohen Gadol* is deemed worthy to enter the Holy of Holies to offer the incense in honor of God. (See the *Sforno's* commentary on verse 12.) Since the Torah tells us (vs. 23-24) that the linen garments were removed *before* the burnt offering was brought, the *Sforno* stresses that his entrance into the inner sanctum must have perforce preceded the burnt offering.

4. בִּגְדֵי קֹדֶשׁ הֵם — *They are holy garments.* The first part of this verse already stated that the linen tunic was *holy* (כְּתֹנֶת בַּד קֹדֶשׁ), hence what is the purpose of repeating the phrase קֹדֶשׁ הֵם, *they are holy?* The *Sforno* explains that the Torah is telling us that white linen garments in general are holy, being that angels appear in prophetic visions wearing these same kinds of garments. (See *Ezekiel* 9:3 and *Daniel* 12:6).

8. גֹּרָלוֹת — *Lots.* The expression 'pious one' used by the *Sforno* is based on *Deut.* 33:8, referring there specifically to Aaron, and in general to the tribe of Levi. The *Sforno,* in his commentary on that verse, calls the tribe of Levi, שֵׁבֶט הֶחָסִיד, *the pious tribe.* Since we believe that nothing happens by chance (see *Sforno, Genesis* 24:14), the *Sforno* explains that a lot cast by a pious, righteous man is akin to seeking out God's decision.

9. וְעָשָׂהוּ חַטָּאת — *And make it a sin offering.* The expression וְעָשָׂהוּ is usually translated *and*

יא לִפְנֵי יהוה לְכַפֵּר עָלָיו לְשַׁלַּח אֹתוֹ לַעֲזָאזֵל הַמִּדְבָּרָה: וְהִקְרִיב אַהֲרֹן
אֶת־פַּר הַחַטָּאת אֲשֶׁר־לוֹ וְכִפֶּר בַּעֲדוֹ וּבְעַד בֵּיתוֹ וְשָׁחַט אֶת־פַּר הַחַטָּאת
יב אֲשֶׁר־לוֹ: וְלָקַח מְלֹא־הַמַּחְתָּה גַּחֲלֵי־אֵשׁ מֵעַל הַמִּזְבֵּחַ מִלִּפְנֵי יהוה וּמְלֹא
יג חָפְנָיו קְטֹרֶת סַמִּים דַּקָּה וְהֵבִיא מִבֵּית לַפָּרֹכֶת: וְנָתַן אֶת־הַקְּטֹרֶת
עַל־הָאֵשׁ לִפְנֵי יהוה וְכִסָּה | עֲנַן הַקְּטֹרֶת אֶת־הַכַּפֹּרֶת אֲשֶׁר עַל־הָעֵדוּת
יד וְלֹא יָמוּת: וְלָקַח מִדַּם הַפָּר וְהִזָּה בְאֶצְבָּעוֹ עַל־פְּנֵי הַכַּפֹּרֶת קֵדְמָה וְלִפְנֵי
טו הַכַּפֹּרֶת יַזֶּה שֶׁבַע־פְּעָמִים מִן־הַדָּם בְּאֶצְבָּעוֹ: וְשָׁחַט אֶת־שְׂעִיר הַחַטָּאת
אֲשֶׁר לָעָם וְהֵבִיא אֶת־דָּמוֹ אֶל־מִבֵּית לַפָּרֹכֶת וְעָשָׂה אֶת־דָּמוֹ כַּאֲשֶׁר
טז עָשָׂה לְדַם הַפָּר וְהִזָּה אֹתוֹ עַל־הַכַּפֹּרֶת וְלִפְנֵי הַכַּפֹּרֶת: וְכִפֶּר עַל־הַקֹּדֶשׁ
מִטֻּמְאֹת בְּנֵי יִשְׂרָאֵל וּמִפִּשְׁעֵיהֶם לְכָל־חַטֹּאתָם וְכֵן יַעֲשֶׂה לְאֹהֶל מוֹעֵד
יז הַשֹּׁכֵן אִתָּם בְּתוֹךְ טֻמְאֹתָם: וְכָל־אָדָם לֹא־יִהְיֶה | בְּאֹהֶל מוֹעֵד בְּבֹאוֹ
לְכַפֵּר בַּקֹּדֶשׁ עַד־צֵאתוֹ וְכִפֶּר בַּעֲדוֹ וּבְעַד בֵּיתוֹ וּבְעַד כָּל־קְהַל יִשְׂרָאֵל:
שני יח וְיָצָא אֶל־הַמִּזְבֵּחַ אֲשֶׁר לִפְנֵי־יהוה וְכִפֶּר עָלָיו וְלָקַח מִדַּם הַפָּר וּמִדַּם
יט הַשָּׂעִיר וְנָתַן עַל־קַרְנוֹת הַמִּזְבֵּחַ סָבִיב: וְהִזָּה עָלָיו מִן־הַדָּם בְּאֶצְבָּעוֹ שֶׁבַע
כ פְּעָמִים וְטִהֲרוֹ וְקִדְּשׁוֹ מִטֻּמְאֹת בְּנֵי יִשְׂרָאֵל: וְכִלָּה מִכַּפֵּר אֶת־הַקֹּדֶשׁ
כא וְאֶת־אֹהֶל מוֹעֵד וְאֶת־הַמִּזְבֵּחַ וְהִקְרִיב אֶת־הַשָּׂעִיר הֶחָי: וְסָמַךְ אַהֲרֹן

---

11. וְכִפֶּר בַּעֲדוֹ — *And shall make atonement for himself.* We know from tradition that the two atonements for himself (v. 6 and here) are atonements achieved through the words of confession. Therefore, they precede the slaughter of the sin offering.

12. וְלָקַח מְלֹא הַמַּחְתָּה — *And he shall take a censer full.* For immediately after the sin offering has been slaughtered and he has confessed and his iniquity has been removed, he is prepared to be illuminated by the light of the King's countenance. Now, behold, the King will appear to all who are prepared (to receive) His light, as it says, *For in a cloud I will appear* (v. 2). And it is proper to honor Him with incense, which is the case after the daily sacrifices (have been offered) as it says, עֹלַת תָּמִיד לְדֹרֹתֵיכֶם פֶּתַח אֹהֶל מוֹעֵד לִפְנֵי ה׳ אֲשֶׁר אִוָּעֵד לָכֶם שָׁמָּה, *It shall be a continual burnt offering throughout your generations at the door of the Tent of Meeting before* HASHEM *where I will meet with you* (*Exodus* 29:42). And this was the error of the sons of Aaron who offered (incense) *which He had not commanded them* (10:1).

15. הַחַטָּאת אֲשֶׁר לָעָם — *The sin offering that is for the people.* (This took place) after he completed his own atonement through his sin offering, similar to הִתְקוֹשְׁשׁוּ וָקוֹשׁוּ, *Gather yourselves together, and assemble together* (*Zephaniah* 2:1); with (all) this, the countenance of the King will appear.

NOTES

offer him. The *Sforno* stresses that the correct translation should be *and make him.* The lot actually converts that particular goat into a חַטָּאת, *sin offering.*

12. וְלָקַח מְלֹא הַמַּחְתָּה — *And he shall take a censer full.* The portion dealing with the incense altar (*Exodus* 30) follows the portion dealing with the daily sacrifices, indicating that whenever God appears, whether on Yom Kippur or on an ordinary weekday, it is proper to offer incense in His honor.

15. הַחַטָּאת אֲשֶׁר לָעָם — *The sin offering that is for the people.* The *Sforno* cites the verse from *Zephaniah* because of the commentary of our

אֶת־שְׁתֵּ֣י יָדָ֗ו עַל־רֹ֣אשׁ הַשָּׂעִיר֮ הַחַי֒ וְהִתְוַדָּ֣ה עָלָ֗יו אֶת־כָּל־עֲוֹנֹת֙ בְּנֵ֣י
יִשְׂרָאֵ֔ל וְאֶת־כָּל־פִּשְׁעֵיהֶ֖ם לְכָל־חַטֹּאתָ֑ם וְנָתַ֤ן אֹתָם֙ עַל־רֹ֣אשׁ הַשָּׂעִ֔יר
כב וְשִׁלַּ֛ח בְּיַד־אִ֥ישׁ עִתִּ֖י הַמִּדְבָּֽרָה׃ וְנָשָׂ֨א הַשָּׂעִ֥יר עָלָ֛יו אֶת־כָּל־עֲוֹנֹתָ֖ם
כג אֶל־אֶ֣רֶץ גְּזֵרָ֑ה וְשִׁלַּ֥ח אֶת־הַשָּׂעִ֖יר בַּמִּדְבָּֽר׃ וּבָ֤א אַהֲרֹן֙ אֶל־אֹ֣הֶל מוֹעֵ֔ד
כד וּפָשַׁט֙ אֶת־בִּגְדֵ֣י הַבָּ֔ד אֲשֶׁ֥ר לָבַ֖שׁ בְּבֹא֣וֹ אֶל־הַקֹּ֑דֶשׁ וְהִנִּיחָ֖ם שָֽׁם׃ וְרָחַ֨ץ
אֶת־בְּשָׂר֤וֹ בַמַּ֙יִם֙ בְּמָק֣וֹם קָד֔וֹשׁ וְלָבַ֖שׁ אֶת־בְּגָדָ֑יו וְיָצָ֗א וְעָשָׂ֤ה אֶת־עֹֽלָתוֹ֙
שלישי [שני] כה וְאֶת־עֹלַ֣ת הָעָ֔ם וְכִפֶּ֥ר בַּֽעֲד֖וֹ וּבְעַ֥ד הָעָֽם׃ וְאֵ֛ת חֵ֥לֶב הַֽחַטָּ֖את יַקְטִ֥יר
כו הַמִּזְבֵּֽחָה׃ וְהַֽמְשַׁלֵּ֤חַ אֶת־הַשָּׂעִיר֙ לַֽעֲזָאזֵ֔ל יְכַבֵּ֣ס בְּגָדָ֔יו וְרָחַ֥ץ אֶת־בְּשָׂר֖וֹ
כז בַּמָּ֑יִם וְאַחֲרֵי־כֵ֖ן יָב֥וֹא אֶל־הַֽמַּחֲנֶֽה׃ וְאֵת֩ פַּ֨ר הַֽחַטָּ֜את וְאֵ֣ת ׀ שְׂעִ֣יר הַֽחַטָּ֗את
אֲשֶׁ֨ר הוּבָ֤א אֶת־דָּמָם֙ לְכַפֵּ֣ר בַּקֹּ֔דֶשׁ יוֹצִ֖יא אֶל־מִח֣וּץ לַֽמַּחֲנֶ֑ה וְשָׂרְפ֣וּ
כח בָאֵ֔שׁ אֶת־עֹרֹתָ֥ם וְאֶת־בְּשָׂרָ֖ם וְאֶת־פִּרְשָֽׁם׃ וְהַשֹּׂרֵ֣ף אֹתָ֔ם יְכַבֵּ֣ס בְּגָדָ֔יו
כט וְרָחַ֥ץ אֶת־בְּשָׂר֖וֹ בַּמָּ֑יִם וְאַחֲרֵי־כֵ֖ן יָב֥וֹא אֶל־הַֽמַּחֲנֶֽה׃ וְהָיְתָ֥ה לָכֶ֖ם לְחֻקַּ֣ת
עוֹלָ֑ם בַּחֹ֣דֶשׁ הַ֠שְּׁבִיעִ֠י בֶּֽעָשׂ֨וֹר לַחֹ֜דֶשׁ תְּעַנּ֣וּ אֶת־נַפְשֹֽׁתֵיכֶ֗ם וְכָל־

---

23. וְהִנִּיחָם שָׁם — *And shall leave them there.* For he has offered them before God and thus they became sanctified with an extra sanctity; (therefore), it is not proper that they (be used), even by the *Kohen Gadol*, after this exalted hour has passed.

24. וְרָחַץ אֶת בְּשָׂרוֹ — *And he shall bathe his flesh* . . . after placing his hands on the goat sent (to the wilderness).

וְעָשָׂה אֶת עֹלָתוֹ — *And offer his burnt offering*. . . after he has atoned for himself through his sin offering, and for the people through the two sin offerings, the goat sent away (also) being called *sin offering*, as it says, *two he-goats for a sin offering* (v. 5). And both of them precede the burnt offering of the people, according to the rule that every sin offering precedes a burnt offering, as we know from tradition.

וְכִפֶּר בַּעֲדוֹ וּבְעַד הָעָם — *And make atonement for himself and for the people* . . . atonement for the evil thoughts of the heart as is fitting for those that are נְקִי כַפַּיִם וּבַר לֵבָב, *clean of hands and pure of heart* (*Psalms* 24:4), and this is (accomplished) through the burnt offering.

29. לְחֻקַּת עוֹלָם — *A statute forever.* Even when there is a Sanctuary for the service (of Yom Kippur), nonetheless, you must also observe (the laws of) rest and affliction.

NOTES

Sages on that phrase, 'Chastise yourself (first) and afterward chastise others' (*Sanhedrin* 18a).

23. וְהִנִּיחָם שָׁם — *And shall leave them there.* The garments used on Yom Kippur were not to be used again, even on a subsequent Yom Kippur, as *Rashi* comments. The *Sforno* explains the reason for this law. Once used, they became holy to God for that specific service at that specific time; hence, they may no longer be used.

24. וְרָחַץ אֶת בְּשָׂרוֹ — *And he shall bathe his flesh.* The *Sforno* in verse 5 stated that the goat sent away to the wilderness carried with it excessive *tumah*, so much so that he who brought it there became *tamei*. Therefore, since the *Kohen Gadol* had *laid his hands on the head of this goat* (v. 21), it was necessary for him to bathe his flesh before bringing his burnt offering.

29. לְחֻקַּת עוֹלָם — *A statute forever.* This term appears here and in verses 31 and 34. The *Sforno* explains that each comes to teach us a different lesson. The first refers to a time when Israel had a Temple service but nonetheless

ל מְלָאכָה֙ לֹ֣א תַעֲשׂ֔וּ הָֽאֶזְרָ֔ח וְהַגֵּ֖ר הַגָּ֣ר בְּתֽוֹכְכֶֽם: כִּֽי־בַיּ֥וֹם הַזֶּ֛ה יְכַפֵּ֥ר עֲלֵיכֶ֖ם
לא לְטַהֵ֣ר אֶתְכֶ֑ם מִכֹּל֙ חַטֹּ֣אתֵיכֶ֔ם לִפְנֵ֥י יְהוָ֖ה תִּטְהָֽרוּ: שַׁבַּ֨ת שַׁבָּת֥וֹן הִיא֙
לב לָכֶ֔ם וְעִנִּיתֶ֖ם אֶת־נַפְשֹֽׁתֵיכֶ֑ם חֻקַּ֖ת עוֹלָֽם: וְכִפֶּ֨ר הַכֹּהֵ֜ן אֲשֶׁר־יִמְשַׁ֣ח אֹת֗וֹ
וַאֲשֶׁ֤ר יְמַלֵּא֙ אֶת־יָד֔וֹ לְכַהֵ֖ן תַּ֣חַת אָבִ֑יו וְלָבַ֛שׁ אֶת־בִּגְדֵ֥י הַבָּ֖ד בִּגְדֵ֥י
לג הַקֹּֽדֶשׁ: וְכִפֶּר֙ אֶת־מִקְדַּ֣שׁ הַקֹּ֔דֶשׁ וְאֶת־אֹ֧הֶל מוֹעֵ֛ד וְאֶת־הַמִּזְבֵּ֖חַ יְכַפֵּ֑ר וְעַ֧ל
לד הַכֹּֽהֲנִ֛ים וְעַל־כָּל־עַ֥ם הַקָּהָ֖ל יְכַפֵּֽר: וְהָֽיְתָה־זֹּ֨את לָכֶ֜ם לְחֻקַּ֣ת עוֹלָ֗ם לְכַפֵּ֞ר
עַל־בְּנֵ֣י יִשְׂרָאֵ֗ל מִכָּל־חַטֹּאתָ֛ם אַחַ֖ת בַּשָּׁנָ֑ה וַיַּ֕עַשׂ כַּאֲשֶׁ֛ר צִוָּ֥ה יְהוָ֖ה
אֶת־מֹשֶֽׁה:

יז רביעי א-ב וַיְדַבֵּ֥ר יְהוָ֖ה אֶל־מֹשֶׁ֥ה לֵּאמֹֽר: דַּבֵּ֨ר אֶל־אַהֲרֹ֜ן וְאֶל־בָּנָ֗יו וְאֶ֨ל כָּל־בְּנֵ֣י

---

30. כִּי בַיּוֹם הַזֶּה יְכַפֵּר — *For on this day shall atonement be made.* The reason that you will also need, in addition (to the service), rest (from labor) and affliction (of the soul) is because the *Kohen* through his service can merely atone, the purpose of this atonement being to mitigate the sin and prepare (the sinner) to receive forgiveness.

לִפְנֵי ה' תִּטְהָרוּ — *You shall be clean before HASHEM.* But the attainment of (spiritual) purification and complete forgiveness can only be *before HASHEM,* through confession and repentance, for He alone knows their sincerity — and therefore . . .

31. שַׁבַּת שַׁבָּתוֹן הִיא לָכֶם — *It is a Sabbath of Sabbaths unto you* . . . the reverse of הֵן בְּיוֹם צֹמְכֶם תִּמְצְאוּ חֵפֶץ, *Behold, on the day of your fast you pursue your business* (Isaiah 58:3).

חֻקַּת עוֹלָם — *A statute forever.* Even when the Temple no longer stands, you must (still) observe (the Sabbath of) rest and affliction (fasting).

32. וַאֲשֶׁר יְמַלֵּא אֶת יָדוֹ . . . וְלָבַשׁ — *And who shall be consecrated . . . and shall put on.* Even (a *Kohen Gadol* who is only distinguished by) a greater number of official garments can also atone.

34. וְהָיְתָה זֹּאת לָכֶם לְחֻקַּת עוֹלָם — *And this shall be an everlasting statute to you* . . . that the day itself atone, even though there is no Temple or service, as (our Sages) say, 'Repentance suspends punishment and Yom Kippur atones' (*Yoma* 86a).

NOTES

were obligated to refrain from labor and fast on Yom Kippur. The second teaches us that these laws apply even when there is no Temple. The third comes to tell us that Yom Kippur itself has the power to atone even when the Temple is destroyed and there is no עֲבוֹדַת יוֹם הַכִּפּוּרִים, *service of Yom Kippur.*

31. שַׁבַּת שַׁבָּתוֹן — *Sabbath of Sabbaths.* The *Sforno* interprets the phrase שַׁבַּת שַׁבָּתוֹן as meaning *absolute*; total rest, abstinence from labor and all material pursuits, as opposed to the kind of fast which Isaiah criticized because it was only ceremonial and in no way affected their behavior.

32. וַאֲשֶׁר יְמַלֵּא אֶת יָדוֹ . . . וְלָבַשׁ — *And who shall be consecrated . . . and shall put on.* There are two ways a *Kohen Gadol* is invested into his office. One is through anointment with the oil of anointing (שֶׁמֶן הַמִּשְׁחָה), and the second is by clothing him in eight garments as compared to the four worn by ordinary *Kohanim.* This is called מְרוּבֶּה בְּגָדִים. In the days of King Josiah, the flask of anointing oil was concealed (*Horayos* 12a) and subsequently a *Kohen Gadol* was consecrated by putting the additional priestly garments on him. The verse here teaches us that regardless of the method, the *Kohen Gadol* can function in his office on Yom Kippur and attain atonement for Israel.

ג יִשְׂרָאֵל וְאָמַרְתָּ אֲלֵיהֶם זֶה הַדָּבָר אֲשֶׁר־צִוָּה יהוה לֵאמֹר: אִישׁ אִישׁ
מִבֵּית יִשְׂרָאֵל אֲשֶׁר יִשְׁחַט שׁוֹר אוֹ־כֶשֶׂב אוֹ־עֵז בַּמַּחֲנֶה אוֹ אֲשֶׁר יִשְׁחַט
ד מִחוּץ לַמַּחֲנֶה: וְאֶל־פֶּתַח אֹהֶל מוֹעֵד לֹא הֱבִיאוֹ לְהַקְרִיב קָרְבָּן לַיהוה
לִפְנֵי מִשְׁכַּן יהוה דָּם יֵחָשֵׁב לָאִישׁ הַהוּא דָּם שָׁפָךְ וְנִכְרַת הָאִישׁ הַהוּא
ה מִקֶּרֶב עַמּוֹ: לְמַעַן אֲשֶׁר יָבִיאוּ בְּנֵי יִשְׂרָאֵל אֶת־זִבְחֵיהֶם אֲשֶׁר הֵם זֹבְחִים
עַל־פְּנֵי הַשָּׂדֶה וֶהֱבִיאֻם לַיהוה אֶל־פֶּתַח אֹהֶל מוֹעֵד אֶל־הַכֹּהֵן וְזָבְחוּ זִבְחֵי
ו שְׁלָמִים לַיהוה אוֹתָם: וְזָרַק הַכֹּהֵן אֶת־הַדָּם עַל־מִזְבַּח יהוה פֶּתַח אֹהֶל
ז מוֹעֵד וְהִקְטִיר הַחֵלֶב לְרֵיחַ נִיחֹחַ לַיהוה: וְלֹא־יִזְבְּחוּ עוֹד אֶת־זִבְחֵיהֶם
לַשְּׂעִירִם אֲשֶׁר הֵם זֹנִים אַחֲרֵיהֶם חֻקַּת עוֹלָם תִּהְיֶה־זֹּאת לָהֶם לְדֹרֹתָם:

XVII

2. זֶה הַדָּבָר — *This is the thing.* When (God) said, *Thus shall you separate the Children of Israel from their tumah* (15:31), He was also warning that they be separated from the *tumah* of the spirit of impurity and the demons.

4. דָּם יֵחָשֵׁב לָאִישׁ הַהוּא — *Blood shall be imputed to that man.* (The rule here) is as it was prior to the Flood, when they were not permitted to slaughter any living creature for human consumption.

7. חֻקַּת עוֹלָם תִּהְיֶה זֹּאת — *This shall be a statute forever.* That they may not sacrifice unto the satyrs (demons), even though they do not accept them in any way as gods, but (only) desire their companionship so that the demons will be their servants and assist them in their affairs or as messengers to (be sent to) a distant land, as (the Sages) make mention regarding יוֹסֵף שֵׁידָא, *Joseph the Demon* (*Eruvin* 43a), and the demon that frequented the house of Rav Ashi (*Chullin* 105b).

However, regarding the demons, whose creation is not mentioned (in the Torah), it is proper to study (consider) them. Our Sages, of blessed memory, called them מַזִּיקִים, *injurers,* and mention (the fact) that they eat, drink, reproduce and die (*Chagigah* 16a). Still and all, they can see but are not visible! Now this cannot properly be (understood) unless they are composed of an (extremely) fine substance

NOTES

XVII

2. זֶה הַדָּבָר — *This is the thing.* The *Sforno* explains this phrase as referring back to the concluding section of chapter 15 (end of *parashas Metzora*) where Moses is urged to separate Israel from *tumah.* Now the Torah tells us that just as we are to separate ourselves from the *tumah* of the body, so is Israel to reject the רוּחַ הַטּוּמְאָה, *spirit of tumah,* engendered by demons.

4. דָּם יֵחָשֵׁב לָאִישׁ הַהוּא — *Blood shall be imputed to that man.* From the time of Creation until the Flood, man was not permitted to slaughter any living creature and eat its flesh. Such slaughter was tantamount to shedding blood. However, after the Flood, God permitted the flesh of animals to Noah and his children, provided they did not violate other laws ordained by God in the process of slaughtering. If they were to do so, then it would be as if they had shed blood unnecessarily. The *Sforno* explains that this is the meaning of the words *blood shall be imputed to that man.*

7. חֻקַּת עוֹלָם תִּהְיֶה זֹאת — *This shall be a statute forever.* Our Sages treated the existence of שֵׁדִים, *demons,* as a fact of life. Apparently, at the time when the Torah was given people attempted to court the demons' favor and fraternize with them, 'so that they (would) come to him and let him know future events' (*Guide* 3:46). Maimonides tells us further that the Sabians believed that these

אמישי (שלישי) ח וַאֲלֵהֶם תֹּאמַר אִישׁ אִישׁ מִבֵּית יִשְׂרָאֵל וּמִן־הַגֵּר אֲשֶׁר־יָגוּר בְּתוֹכָם
ט אֲשֶׁר־יַעֲלֶה עֹלָה אוֹ־זָבַח׃ וְאֶל־פֶּתַח אֹהֶל מוֹעֵד לֹא יְבִיאֶנּוּ לַעֲשׂוֹת אֹתוֹ

which is invisible. And since they eat and drink, their food perforce must be of a substance composed of (something) extremely fine which is assimilated into the organism consuming it. Now there are no compositions known to us more refined than the 'vapor' of blood from which the spirit, which carries the life force, exists. This force being carried is the soul of life through which (every creature) lives, and since this force cannot be without this 'carrier,' at times it is called נֶפֶשׁ, *life*, as it says, כִּי הַדָּם הוּא הַנָּפֶשׁ, *For the blood is the life* (*Deut.* 12:23). Being that this (i.e., blood) is the food of demons, consequently he who offers them blood, which is (the source) of their substance and which they are powerless to take (on their own), as our Sages say, 'We have no permission to take anything which is closed, sealed, measured or counted' (*Chullin* 105b), (he) will gain their love, and he who eats it (blood) will acquire a temperament which tends toward their nature and (therefore) they will long for his company. Now since many desired the companionship of demons and their love, so that (the demons) would assist them in acquiring futile pleasures (which are sweet, but without practical benefit) — the identical desire which was attained by the eating from the tree of knowledge — (hence) they would bring blood as an offering to the demons and eat it (themselves) in order to join together with them. Some would eat (the blood) adjacent to a pool of blood, where they believed that the satyrs danced, so as to attract their love and fraternize with them. When God, the Blessed One, sanctified us and distanced His people as much as possible from pursuing futile pleasures, He distanced them from the demons and their company, since they are, in truth, 'injurers' as our Sages named them. He (also) prohibited blood (which He made) punishable by כָּרֵת, *excision*, similar to the penalty of death (imposed on man) for partaking of the tree of knowledge (*Genesis* 2:17) and gave as the reason for this, *For the life of the flesh is in the blood* (v. 10), because the force which is the living spirit is carried in the mist-like delicate part of the blood, and that mist-like part, which is also called נֶפֶשׁ, *life*, is essentially found in all blood. He then additionally states, *And I have given it to you upon the altar* (v. 11), (and) I have not chosen it (the blood) to atone because it is beloved to Me, but rather because it is, to a certain extent, נֶפֶשׁ, *life*, (therefore) it atones for the נֶפֶשׁ (of the one who brings the offering) similar to the burning (on the altar) of the various limbs of the sacrifices which atones for the limbs of the one who is making the sacrifice (see the *Sforno* on 1:2).

NOTES

demons, whom they called *jinn*, assumed the form of goats, and that blood was their only food. Hence, 'whoever ate it (blood) fraternized with the *jinn*' by gathering at a pool of blood. The *Sforno* has a similar approach in his commentary on this verse while adding that these demons, once befriended, could also serve as messengers and assistants to those who knew how to attract them. The Torah, however, admonishes Israel not to *sacrifice to the* שְׂעִירִים, i.e., the שֵׁדִים, *demons*, who, as mentioned above, took on the form of goats (שָׂעִיר in Hebrew means 'goat'). The *Sforno* proceeds to link this prohibition to that of blood, which follows (vs. 10-14). Since blood was the food of the demons, those who desired their friendship would provide it for them and join with them in partaking of the blood. In order to dissuade Israel from this practice, the Torah forbids blood to them totally, except for the blood brought to the altar of God, and also blood used for a special purpose such as the consecration of the *Kohanim*. The reason why God commands Israel to offer blood on the

י לַיהוָה וְנִכְרַת הָאִישׁ הַהוּא מֵעַמָּיו: וְאִישׁ אִישׁ מִבֵּית יִשְׂרָאֵל וּמִן־הַגֵּר הַגָּר
בְּתוֹכָם אֲשֶׁר יֹאכַל כָּל־דָּם וְנָתַתִּי פָנַי בַּנֶּפֶשׁ הָאֹכֶלֶת אֶת־הַדָּם וְהִכְרַתִּי
יא אֹתָהּ מִקֶּרֶב עַמָּהּ: כִּי נֶפֶשׁ הַבָּשָׂר בַּדָּם הִוא וַאֲנִי נְתַתִּיו לָכֶם עַל־הַמִּזְבֵּחַ
יב לְכַפֵּר עַל־נַפְשֹׁתֵיכֶם כִּי־הַדָּם הוּא בַּנֶּפֶשׁ יְכַפֵּר: עַל־כֵּן אָמַרְתִּי לִבְנֵי
יִשְׂרָאֵל כָּל־נֶפֶשׁ מִכֶּם לֹא־תֹאכַל דָּם וְהַגֵּר הַגָּר בְּתוֹכְכֶם לֹא־יֹאכַל דָּם:
יג וְאִישׁ אִישׁ מִבְּנֵי יִשְׂרָאֵל וּמִן־הַגֵּר הַגָּר בְּתוֹכָם אֲשֶׁר יָצוּד צֵיד חַיָּה
יד אוֹ־עוֹף אֲשֶׁר יֵאָכֵל וְשָׁפַךְ אֶת־דָּמוֹ וְכִסָּהוּ בֶּעָפָר: כִּי־נֶפֶשׁ כָּל־בָּשָׂר דָּמוֹ
בְנַפְשׁוֹ הוּא וָאֹמַר לִבְנֵי יִשְׂרָאֵל דַּם כָּל־בָּשָׂר לֹא תֹאכֵלוּ כִּי נֶפֶשׁ

---

13. אֲשֶׁר יָצוּד צֵיד — *That takes in hunting.* The places (where animals) are usually hunted are deserted and predisposed to be frequented by demons, as it says, וְשָׁכְנוּ שָׁם בְּנוֹת יַעֲנָה וּשְׂעִירִים יְרַקְּדוּ שָׁם, *And ostriches shall dwell there and satyrs dance there* (*Isaiah* 13:21). (Therefore), He prohibited (us) to leave blood exposed, and commanded (us) to cover it with dirt to forestall the tendancy of demons to frequent (that place), and He said ...

14. כִּי נֶפֶשׁ כָּל בָּשָׂר דָּמוֹ בְנַפְשׁוֹ הוּא — *As for the life of all flesh, its blood is with the life thereof.* Because the *life* (נֶפֶשׁ) of (every) living creature is *its blood* — i.e., the mist-like substances of blood with the life force carried in it (בְּנַפְשׁוֹ), for indeed this fine vapor-like (part) of the blood carries the force of life, and being the thinnest and most insubstantial of all material things, it (therefore qualifies) without a doubt to be the food (sustenance) of demons and those who seek their company.

וָאֹמַר לִבְנֵי יִשְׂרָאֵל — *Therefore, I said to the Children of Israel.* And besides this (i.e., the reason given above), even though I permitted (blood) to the sons of Noah, I prohibited it to Israel (as stated) above in *parashas Tzav* (7:26) because (when) the soul of life (blood) is (ingested) into one's body (lit., his life), the (nature) of the one fed by it returns to its animalistic nature.

NOTES

altar is because it represents the life force (the נֶפֶשׁ) of man, and just as the limbs of the animal are offered on the altar symbolizing those of the מַקְרִיב, *he who brings the sacrifice*, so too, the blood of the animal fulfills the same symbolic purpose. The *Sforno* also offers a reason for blood being the food of the demons. According to our Sages, demons live, breed and die — hence they need sustenance. We are also told that they are invisible. To explain this phenomenon, the *Sforno* discusses the property of blood in light of 16th-century medical knowledge. What he terms אֵיד הַדָּם (based on the word אֵד in *Genesis* 2:6), *the vapor of the blood*, must refer to oxygen which is conveyed to the tissues by hemoglobin — the red blood corpuscles. Since oxygen is a gaseous substance it is the least substantial of all compositions known to man; in other words it is mist-like (אֵד), made up of minute particles (דַּק), and invisible, but life giving! Hence, the demons who subsist on the oxygen component of the blood are also invisible, for 'we are what we eat.' Based on this premise, the *Sforno* explains the word נֶפֶשׁ used by the Torah in conjunction with blood as referring to the oxygen carried by the blood, which is indeed the supporter of life. Although oxygen was not recognized as a separate element in the *Sforno's* time, nonetheless he knew there was such an element within the blood, carried by it, as we see from his commentary here. For further commentary of the *Sforno* on שֵׁדִים, see his כַּוָּנוֹת הַתּוֹרָה כ״ב.

14. כִּי נֶפֶשׁ כָּל בָּשָׂר דָּמוֹ בְנַפְשׁוֹ הוּא — *As for the life of all flesh, its blood is with the life thereof.* See notes on verse 7 for clarification of the *Sforno's* commentary. The *Sforno* gives two reasons for the prohibition of blood. One is to prevent Israel from associating with the demons, as explained above. Second, by consuming the blood of the animal, man will take

טו כָּל־בָּשָׂר דָּמוֹ הוּא כָּל־אֹכְלָיו יִכָּרֵת: וְכָל־נֶפֶשׁ אֲשֶׁר תֹּאכַל נְבֵלָה וּטְרֵפָה
טז בָּאֶזְרָח וּבַגֵּר וְכִבֶּס בְּגָדָיו וְרָחַץ בַּמַּיִם וְטָמֵא עַד־הָעֶרֶב וְטָהֵר: וְאִם לֹא
יְכַבֵּס וּבְשָׂרוֹ לֹא יִרְחָץ וְנָשָׂא עֲוֹנוֹ:

יח א־ב וַיְדַבֵּר יְהוָֹה אֶל־מֹשֶׁה לֵּאמֹר: דַּבֵּר אֶל־בְּנֵי יִשְׂרָאֵל וְאָמַרְתָּ אֲלֵהֶם אֲנִי
ג יְהוָֹה אֱלֹהֵיכֶם: כְּמַעֲשֵׂה אֶרֶץ־מִצְרַיִם אֲשֶׁר יְשַׁבְתֶּם־בָּהּ לֹא תַעֲשׂוּ
וּכְמַעֲשֵׂה אֶרֶץ־כְּנַעַן אֲשֶׁר אֲנִי מֵבִיא אֶתְכֶם שָׁמָּה לֹא תַעֲשׂוּ וּבְחֻקֹּתֵיהֶם
ד לֹא תֵלֵכוּ: אֶת־מִשְׁפָּטַי תַּעֲשׂוּ וְאֶת־חֻקֹּתַי תִּשְׁמְרוּ לָלֶכֶת בָּהֶם אֲנִי יְהוָֹה
ה אֱלֹהֵיכֶם: וּשְׁמַרְתֶּם אֶת־חֻקֹּתַי וְאֶת־מִשְׁפָּטַי אֲשֶׁר יַעֲשֶׂה אֹתָם הָאָדָם וָחַי
ששי ו בָּהֶם אֲנִי יְהוָֹה: אִישׁ אִישׁ אֶל־כָּל־שְׁאֵר בְּשָׂרוֹ לֹא תִקְרְבוּ

---

15. וְכָל נֶפֶשׁ אֲשֶׁר תֹּאכַל נְבֵלָה וּטְרֵפָה — *And every soul (i.e., individual) that eats
that which dies of itself or that which is torn by beasts.* After writing of the
prohibition of blood which attracts the company of demons, (the Torah) now
speaks of the eating of that which dies of itself (נְבֵלָה) and of that which is torn by
beasts (טְרֵפָה), for this predisposes (a person) for a spirit of *tumah* to dwell upon him,
as (our Sages) say, 'The verse וְדֹרֵשׁ אֶל הַמֵּתִים, *One who consults the dead* (*Deut.*
18:11), refers to one who starves himself and spends the night in a cemetery so that
an unclean spirit may rest upon him' (*Sanhedrin* 65b).

16. וְנָשָׂא עֲוֹנוֹ — *Then he shall bear his iniquity . . .* according to (the severity) of his
sin of *tumah*; whether he ate holy things, merely touched them or defiled *tahor*
non-holy things.

XVIII

6. אִישׁ אִישׁ אֶל כָּל שְׁאֵר בְּשָׂרוֹ לֹא תִקְרְבוּ — *None of you shall approach to any one
that is near of kin to him.* Behold, that (regarding) the offspring of relatives, since
the active and passive (parties) are close (to each other) in temperament, it would
properly (follow) that (these children) be more worthy and compatible, as happened
with the birth of Moses, Aaron and Miriam (born of) Amram and his aunt
Yocheved, and as (our Sages) said in regard to marrying a sister's daughter
(*Yevamos* 62b). Now, this assumption would be so if the active and passive parties
were to have as their sole intent the fulfillment of their Creator's will. However, this
rarely occurs, for indeed, what happens with all human beings, or the majority of
them in these (matters) is only the desire to (find) pleasure (in the act of intimacy),

NOTES

on the characteristics of the animal since blood
is the essence of the animal's life force.

15. וְכָל נֶפֶשׁ אֲשֶׁר תֹּאכַל נְבֵלָה וּטְרֵפָה — *And
every soul that eats that which dies of itself or
that which is torn by beasts.* The *Sforno*
explains that after issuing a prohibition
against blood, the Torah now forbids נְבֵלָה
וּטְרֵפָה which, if partaken of, convey a spirit of
tumah.

16. וְנָשָׂא עֲוֹנוֹ — *Then he shall bear his
iniquity.* The expression *he shall bear his*

iniquity is indefinite. The *Sforno* explains it to
mean that the severity of the punishment
depends on the extent of his transgression. To
eat holy things in a state of *tumah* is a more
serious infraction than touching them, and to
defile non-holy things which are *tahor* is a
lesser sin than the former two infractions.

XVIII

6. אִישׁ אִישׁ אֶל כָּל שְׁאֵר בְּשָׂרוֹ לֹא תִקְרְבוּ — *None
of you shall approach to any one that is near of
kin to him.* The *Sforno* explains the prohibition

ז לְגַלּוֹת עֶרְוָה אֲנִי יְהוָה׃ עֶרְוַת אָבִיךָ וְעֶרְוַת אִמְּךָ לֹא תְגַלֵּה
ח אִמְּךָ הִוא לֹא תְגַלֶּה עֶרְוָתָהּ׃ עֶרְוַת אֵשֶׁת־אָבִיךָ לֹא תְגַלֵּה
ט עֶרְוַת אָבִיךָ הִוא׃ עֶרְוַת אֲחוֹתְךָ בַת־אָבִיךָ אוֹ בַת־אִמֶּךָ מוֹלֶדֶת
י בַּיִת אוֹ מוֹלֶדֶת חוּץ לֹא תְגַלֶּה עֶרְוָתָן׃ עֶרְוַת בַּת־בִּנְךָ אוֹ בַת־
יא בִּתְּךָ לֹא תְגַלֶּה עֶרְוָתָן כִּי עֶרְוָתְךָ הֵנָּה׃ עֶרְוַת בַּת־אֵשֶׁת
יב אָבִיךָ מוֹלֶדֶת אָבִיךָ אֲחוֹתְךָ הִוא לֹא תְגַלֶּה עֶרְוָתָהּ׃ עֶרְוַת
יג אֲחוֹת־אָבִיךָ לֹא תְגַלֵּה שְׁאֵר אָבִיךָ הִוא׃ עֶרְוַת אֲחוֹת־אִמְּךָ

---

as it says, הֵן בְּעָווֹן חוֹלָלְתִּי וּבְחֵטְא יֶחֱמַתְנִי אִמִּי, *Behold I was shaped in iniquity and in sin did my mother conceive me* (*Psalms* 51:7). Now being that relatives are very accessible, and the (lewd) thoughts and pleasure in this matter are very great, hence if they would both think that their union was not prohibited, these thoughts would increase and their (sexual) union would be only (for the purpose) of pleasure. Thereby, they would fornicate and desist from reproducing and the earth would be filled with lewdness. Therefore it states . . .

לְגַלּוֹת עֶרְוָה — *To uncover their nakedness* . . . because, in the majority of these cases, the intimate relationship (lit., uncovering of nakedness) is intended only to attain pleasure. Therefore, the Torah prohibited unions among relatives of common ancestry (lit., common offspring), including relatives (who are) of the same line on one level. These levels of relationship are enumerated by the Torah as they apply to the male, and a wife is considered as her husband (regarding these regulations). Therefore, (the Torah) prohibited a sister of one's father since she is on the first level with the father but permitted the daughter of one's brother (a niece) since she is on a second level (in relationship) to him. (The Torah) forbade the wife of one's father, the wife of a brother, and the wife of an uncle even after the husband is deceased, although they are in no manner related, because they are considered as being on the same level as their husbands. In this manner the prohibition of all other relatives can (also) be understood.

NOTES

of marriage between שְׁאֵר בָּשָׂר, *near of kin*, in a similar vein to that of the *Rambam* in his *Guide* (3:49). The *Rambam* states, 'All illicit unions with (related) females have one thing in common . . . they are easily accessible to him . . . and if it were possible to marry them . . . most people would have . . . fornicated with them.' However, since the Torah forbids them, 'their thoughts are turned away from them.' The *Sforno*, however, includes a most unique point in his commentary on this chapter of consanguineous unions. Contrary to the opinion of some that children born of such unions would be defective, the *Sforno* suggests the opposite. He is of the opinion that children born to parents who are similar in temperament and who come from a common ancestry may well be exceptional and even superior! He cites as proof the fact that Moses, Aaron and Miriam — all great personalities — were the offspring of Amram and Yocheved. The latter, who was Amram's aunt, was permitted to him prior to the giving of the Torah. Similarly, the Talmud lauds one who marries his sister's daughter, noting that he is deserving of the blessing which appears in *Isaiah* (58:9), *Then shall you call and* HASHEM *will answer*. *Tosfos* explains that this is because they are especially suited for one another, precisely because of their close relationship. The *Sforno*, however, qualifies this as being so only if one marries 'for the sake of heaven.' Since in most cases this is not so, for their attraction is not a spiritual but a physical one, the Torah prohibited these unions for the reason given by the *Sforno* and the *Rambam* in his *Guide*. The Torah alludes to this base motivation by using the expression *to uncover their nakedness* throughout the chapter, rather than a more delicate phrase.

יד לֹא תְגַלֵּה כִּי־שְׁאֵר אִמְּךָ הִוא׃ עֶרְוַת אֲחִי־אָבִיךָ לֹא תְגַלֵּה
טו אֶל־אִשְׁתּוֹ לֹא תִקְרָב דֹּדָתְךָ הִוא׃ עֶרְוַת כַּלָּתְךָ לֹא תְגַלֵּה
טז אֵשֶׁת בִּנְךָ הִוא לֹא תְגַלֶּה עֶרְוָתָהּ׃ עֶרְוַת אֵשֶׁת־אָחִיךָ לֹא
יז תְגַלֵּה עֶרְוַת אָחִיךָ הִוא׃ עֶרְוַת אִשָּׁה וּבִתָּהּ לֹא תְגַלֵּה אֶת־
בַּת־בְּנָהּ וְאֶת־בַּת־בִּתָּהּ לֹא תִקַּח לְגַלּוֹת עֶרְוָתָהּ שַׁאֲרָה הֵנָּה זִמָּה הִוא׃
יח וְאִשָּׁה אֶל־אֲחֹתָהּ לֹא תִקָּח לִצְרֹר לְגַלּוֹת עֶרְוָתָהּ עָלֶיהָ בְּחַיֶּיהָ׃
יט־כ וְאֶל־אִשָּׁה בְּנִדַּת טֻמְאָתָהּ לֹא תִקְרַב לְגַלּוֹת עֶרְוָתָהּ׃ וְאֶל־אֵשֶׁת עֲמִיתְךָ
כא לֹא־תִתֵּן שְׁכָבְתְּךָ לְזָרַע לְטָמְאָה־בָהּ׃ וּמִזַּרְעֲךָ לֹא־תִתֵּן לְהַעֲבִיר לַמֹּלֶךְ
שביעי [רביעי] כב וְלֹא תְחַלֵּל אֶת־שֵׁם אֱלֹהֶיךָ אֲנִי יהוה׃ וְאֶת זָכָר לֹא תִשְׁכַּב מִשְׁכְּבֵי אִשָּׁה

---

17. וְזִמָּה הִוא — *It is lewdness* . . . a union resulting only from sinful thoughts.

18. לֹא תִקָּח לִצְרֹר — *You shall not take to be a rival to her*. (The Torah) says that were it not for this (problem of rivalry), the sister of one's wife would not be forbidden since she is not the offspring of this woman (the wife) and the woman herself is permitted. However, she is prohibited so that they shall not become rivals. Therefore, (the Torah) only forbids her during the lifetime of her sister, unlike other forbidden relatives (who are permanently forbidden).

21. וּמִזַּרְעֲךָ לֹא תִתֵּן לְהַעֲבִיר לַמֹּלֶךְ וְלֹא תְחַלֵּל אֶת שֵׁם אֱלֹהֶיךָ — *And you shall not give any of your seed to set them apart to Molech and you shall not profane the Name of your God*. For indeed, when you offer other living creatures (i.e., animals) to God, the Blessed One, and you offer your son to the Molech, then behold it would appear that the Molech is superior to Him — God forbid!

אֲנִי ה׳ — *I am* HASHEM. Unchanging — and I vowed to be your God when I said to Abraham, לִהְיוֹת לְךָ לֵאלֹהִים וּלְזַרְעֲךָ אַחֲרֶיךָ, *To be a God to you and to your seed after you* (*Genesis* 17:7). Now since He speaks (i.e., commands) concerning prohibited relatives so as to prepare the seed (of Israel) that they be worthy that (God's) great Name dwell upon them, (therefore) He speaks of the Molech whose worshipers thought that by serving him they would prepare their other seed for (the blessing) of success. (That is why the Torah) says that by serving him (the Molech), there will be desecration of God and (that will) cause the Divine Presence to abandon their other children (lit., seed).

NOTES

21. וּמִזַּרְעֲךָ לֹא תִתֵּן לְהַעֲבִיר לַמֹּלֶךְ וְלֹא תְחַלֵּל אֶת שֵׁם אֱלֹהֶיךָ אֲנִי ה׳ — *And you shall not give any of your seed to set them apart to Molech and you shall not profane the Name of your God, I am God*. To serve the Molech is obviously an act of עֲבוֹדָה זָרָה, *idolatry*. Why then does the Torah have to give the added reason, *you shall not profane the Name of your God?* It is also necessary to understand the concluding phrase, *I am* HASHEM. The *Sforno* explains both of these additions in the following manner: When one worships the Molech he is guilty of a most serious offense, for not only does he serve a strange god but he also denigrates and desecrates God's Holy Name by acknowledging the superiority of the Molech. This is manifested by the offering of his son to the Molech, whereas when he worships God, he 'only' sacrifices animals! This is a חִלּוּל הַשֵּׁם, *profanation of the Name of God*. Secondly, by serving the Molech, one accomplishes precisely the reverse of his intention. Those who offered one of their offspring to the Molech did so in the false hope that the Molech would bless their other children. This was of course patently false. Were Israel to serve God, as they were commanded to do, and keep Abraham's

כג תּוֹעֵבָה הִוא: וּבְכָל־בְּהֵמָה לֹא־תִתֵּן שְׁכָבְתְּךָ לְטָמְאָה־בָהּ וְאִשָּׁה
כד לֹא־תַעֲמֹד לִפְנֵי בְהֵמָה לְרִבְעָהּ תֶּבֶל הוּא: אַל־תִּטַּמְּאוּ בְּכָל־אֵלֶּה כִּי
כה בְכָל־אֵלֶּה נִטְמְאוּ הַגּוֹיִם אֲשֶׁר־אֲנִי מְשַׁלֵּחַ מִפְּנֵיכֶם: וַתִּטְמָא הָאָרֶץ
כו וָאֶפְקֹד עֲוֺנָהּ עָלֶיהָ וַתָּקִא הָאָרֶץ אֶת־יֹשְׁבֶיהָ: וּשְׁמַרְתֶּם אַתֶּם אֶת־חֻקֹּתַי
וְאֶת־מִשְׁפָּטַי וְלֹא תַעֲשׂוּ מִכֹּל הַתּוֹעֵבֹת הָאֵלֶּה הָאֶזְרָח וְהַגֵּר הַגָּר
כז בְּתוֹכְכֶם: כִּי אֶת־כָּל־הַתּוֹעֵבֹת הָאֵל עָשׂוּ אַנְשֵׁי־הָאָרֶץ אֲשֶׁר לִפְנֵיכֶם
מפטיר כח וַתִּטְמָא הָאָרֶץ: וְלֹא־תָקִיא הָאָרֶץ אֶתְכֶם בְּטַמַּאֲכֶם אֹתָהּ כַּאֲשֶׁר קָאָה

---

24. אַל תִּטַּמְּאוּ בְּכָל אֵלֶּה — *Do not defile yourselves in any of these things* . . . even to draw nigh to uncover nakedness.

כִּי בְכָל אֵלֶּה נִטְמְאוּ הַגּוֹיִם — *For in all these the nations defiled themselves* . . . for the beginning of these nations' transgressions in (the area) of prohibited unions was not in the actual uncovering of nakedness, but only in the coming close (to the forbidden partner).

25. וַתִּטְמָא הָאָרֶץ — *And the land was defiled.* Drawing nigh resulted in the defilement of the land through actual uncovering of nakedness.

26. וּשְׁמַרְתֶּם אַתֶּם אֶת חֻקֹּתַי — *You shall therefore keep My statutes* . . . that you shall not draw nigh to uncover any (forbidden) nakedness.

וְאֶת מִשְׁפָּטַי — *And My ordinances* . . . to punish the sinners.

וְלֹא תַעֲשׂוּ מִכֹּל הַתּוֹעֵבֹת — *And you shall not do any of these abominations.* And in this manner you will not commit even one of these abominable statutes.

27. כִּי אֶת כָּל הַתּוֹעֵבֹת הָאֵל עָשׂוּ אַנְשֵׁי הָאָרֶץ — *For all these abominations have the men of the land done.* For the nations that did not guard themselves from drawing nigh (to these immoralities) and who did not inflict punishment upon those who sinned by uncovering prohibited nakedness, (eventually) they did all (these) abominations, for they proceeded from evil to evil. And so shall you also (transgress) if you do not observe all these statutes and ordinances; therefore keep them!

28. וְלֹא תָקִיא הָאָרֶץ אֶתְכֶם . . . כַּאֲשֶׁר קָאָה אֶת הַגּוֹי — *That the land not vomit you out . . . as it vomited out the nation.* And in this manner the land will not vomit you out in the same evil way that it now vomits out the (other) nations.

NOTES

covenant with Him, they and their children would receive blessings from on High. However, by deserting God and following the Molech, they deny themselves the Divine blessing which is granted through God's presence in their midst, a presence which is removed when Israel deviates from God's laws. This is why the verse concludes with the phrase, *'I am God,'* to underscore that only from Him do blessings for his children emanate.

24-28. אַל תִּטַּמְּאוּ בְּכָל אֵלֶּה . . . וַתִּטְמָא הָאָרֶץ . . . וּשְׁמַרְתֶּם אַתֶּם אֶת חֻקֹּתַי . . . וְלֹא תָקִיא הָאָרֶץ אֶתְכֶם . . . כַּאֲשֶׁר קָאָה אֶת הַגּוֹי — *Do not defile yourselves in any of these things . . . And the land was defiled . . . You shall therefore keep My statutes . . . That the land not vomit you out . . . as it vomited out the nation.* The *Sforno,* sensitive to the subtle differences within the terminology used by the Torah in these verses, explains their progression as follows: One does not usually violate the prohibition of incest immediately. The first step is one of close association which starts a trend that culminates in ultimate iniquity. The Torah therefore cautions Israel to erect a protective moral fence so as to avoid an initial transgression. This is referred to by the indefinite term אֵלֶּה, *these things* (v. 24). The failure to do so leads

כט אֶת־הַגּוֹי אֲשֶׁר לִפְנֵיכֶם: כִּי כָּל־אֲשֶׁר יַעֲשֶׂה מִכֹּל הַתּוֹעֵבוֹת הָאֵלֶּה
ל וְנִכְרְתוּ הַנְּפָשׁוֹת הָעֹשֹׂת מִקֶּרֶב עַמָּם: וּשְׁמַרְתֶּם אֶת־מִשְׁמַרְתִּי לְבִלְתִּי
עֲשׂוֹת מֵחֻקּוֹת הַתּוֹעֵבֹת אֲשֶׁר נַעֲשׂוּ לִפְנֵיכֶם וְלֹא תִטַּמְּאוּ בָּהֶם אֲנִי יהוה
אֱלֹהֵיכֶם:

---

29. כִּי כָּל אֲשֶׁר יַעֲשֶׂה מִכֹּל הַתּוֹעֵבֹת הָאֵלֶּה וְנִכְרְתוּ הַנְּפָשׁוֹת — *For whosoever shall do any of these abominations, these souls shall be cut off.* The reason that the land will vomit you out in this evil fashion if you do *even* one of these (sins) is because each one of these sins alone is worthy to be punished with excision.

30. וּשְׁמַרְתֶּם אֶת מִשְׁמַרְתִּי לְבִלְתִּי עֲשׂוֹת מֵחֻקּוֹת הַתּוֹעֵבֹת — *And you shall keep My charge that you not do any of these abominable statutes.* Also observe the commandments I commanded to serve as a safeguard and a fence so that you do not stumble over all these (sins), such as: prohibited foods; the *tumah* of *niddah; zavah; yoledes* (a woman who gives birth); and similar cases (of *tumah*). For in this manner *you will not make yourselves tamei therein.*

NOTES

inevitably to the land casting out its sinful inhabitants. Had the original inhabitants imposed stern and prompt punishments, thereby not permitting the early, less severe transgressions to proceed and proliferate, the progression of abominations would not have reached a point where the inhabitants would have to be expelled from the Land of Canaan. This, as the *Sforno* sees it, is the burden of admonition given to Israel in these five verses.

29. כִּי כָּל אֲשֶׁר יַעֲשֶׂה מִכֹּל הַתּוֹעֵבֹת הָאֵלֶּה וְנִכְרְתוּ הַנְּפָשׁוֹת — *For whosoever shall do any of these abominations, these souls shall be cut off.* The *Sforno* interprets the expression מִכֹּל הַתּוֹעֵבֹת to mean *any 'one' of these abominations.* The reason why merely one infraction carries with it the punishment of כָּרֵת, *excision*, is because of the severity of immoral sexual acts.

30. וּשְׁמַרְתֶּם אֶת מִשְׁמַרְתִּי — *And you shall keep My charge.* The *Sforno* interprets מִשְׁמַרְתִּי, *My charge*, as including more than just the laws of prohibited marriage relationships listed in this chapter. To insure a life of restraint, purity and sanctity, one must discipline himself in this total area as well as in all other aspects of his life. Hence, this warning to keep God's charge through self-discipline is all-inclusive. It ranges from the laws of *Niddah* to the dietary laws; from the laws of a יוֹלֶדֶת (a woman after childbirth) to that of a זָבָה (a woman who has an abnormal flow). Only by training oneself, and establishing a pattern of discipline in these varied areas, will Israel be able to observe the laws enumerated in the *parashah* of עֲרָיוֹת, *prohibited marriages.* This verse is not an additional admonition. Rather, it is one of assurance. By keeping the charge, they will assuredly not follow (לְבִלְתִּי עֲשׂוֹת) the abominable customs of the nations whom they are displacing.

פרשת קדושים
Parashas Kedoshim

יט א-ב וַיְדַבֵּר יהוה אֶל־מֹשֶׁה לֵּאמֹר: דַּבֵּר אֶל־כָּל־עֲדַת בְּנֵי־יִשְׂרָאֵל וְאָמַרְתָּ
ג אֲלֵהֶם קְדֹשִׁים תִּהְיוּ כִּי קָדוֹשׁ אֲנִי יהוה אֱלֹהֵיכֶם: אִישׁ אִמּוֹ וְאָבִיו תִּירָאוּ

XIX

2. דַּבֵּר אֶל כָּל עֲדַת . . . קְדֹשִׁים תִּהְיוּ — *Speak unto all the congregation . . . you shall be holy.* After (God) had caused His Divine Presence to abide in the midst of Israel, so as to sanctify them for everlasting life, as was (His) intent when He said, וְאַתֶּם תִּהְיוּ לִי מַמְלֶכֶת כֹּהֲנִים וְגוֹי קָדוֹשׁ, *And you shall be unto Me a kingdom of Kohanim and a holy nation* (*Exodus* 19:6), and when He said, *For I am HASHEM that brought you up out of the land of Egypt to be your God; you shall therefore be holy* (11:45); and (after) He separated them from the defilement of (prohibited) food (ch. 11) and the *tamei* seed of a *niddah* (ch. 15) and the afflictions which emanate from her; and from the *tumah* of the זָבָה (a woman who has an issue); and the defilement of sins, as it says, *From all your sins shall you be clean before HASHEM* (16:30) and from the company of demons, and the spirit of *tumah* and from the *tumah* of prohibited unions (עֲרָיוֹת) as it says, *Defile not yourselves in any of these things* (18:24) — (after all this) He now says that the intent (purpose) of all these warnings is that they be holy. This is in order that they may imitate their Creator as much as possible, as was the original intent when man was created, as it says, נַעֲשֶׂה אָדָם בְּצַלְמֵנוּ כִּדְמוּתֵנוּ, *Let us make man in our image, after our likeness* (*Genesis* 1:26). This he now explains saying . . .

כִּי קָדוֹשׁ אֲנִי ה׳ אֱלֹהֵיכֶם — *For I HASHEM your God am holy.* And it is fitting that you be like Me, as much as possible in mind and in deed. Now to attain this identification (with God), He explains that we must observe the commandments which are written on the First Tablet (of the Ten Commandments), for their entire purpose is to (attain) eternal life, as explained at their conclusion where it says, לְמַעַן יַאֲרִכוּן יָמֶיךָ, *that your days may be long* (*Exodus* 20:12), as was explained there. (The Torah) begins now to explain the subject of honoring one's father and mother, saying . . .

3. אִישׁ אִמּוֹ וְאָבִיו תִּירָאוּ — *You shall fear, every man, his mother and his father.* This teaches (us) that the honoring of them shall not be in an arrogant manner, even though one honors them by supplying them with food, drink and clothing, as (our Sages) mention, saying, 'One can give his father pheasant to eat, yet drive him out of the world (make him desperate)' (*Kiddushin* 31a), but (rather) his honoring them shall be as one who honors revered people who are superior to himself. Following this, (the Torah) explains the subject of Shabbos, saying . . .

NOTES

XIX

2. דַּבֵּר אֶל כָּל עֲדַת . . . קְדֹשִׁים תִּהְיוּ — *Speak unto all the congregation . . . you shall be holy. Rashi*, quoting the *Sifra*, states that this section of the Torah (*parashas Kedoshim*) contains 'most of the fundamental teachings of the Torah.' The *Sforno*, however, explains that the Torah is now summing up the purpose of all the laws presented in the portions of *Shemini, Tazria, Metzora and Acharei* (chs. 9-18), that purpose being to attain a state of קְדוּשָׁה, *holiness*, as a people and as individuals. He also interprets the opening verses of this chapter (vs. 3-7) as mirroring the basic ideas of the first five commandments of the Ten Commandments — in reverse order — starting with the fifth commandment (honor your father and mother) and concluding with the first commandment, אָנֹכִי (*I am HASHEM your*

ד וְאֶת־שַׁבְּתֹתַי תִּשְׁמֹרוּ אֲנִי יְהוָה אֱלֹהֵיכֶם: אַל־תִּפְנוּ אֶל־הָאֱלִילִים וֵאלֹהֵי
ה מַסֵּכָה לֹא תַעֲשׂוּ לָכֶם אֲנִי יְהוָה אֱלֹהֵיכֶם: וְכִי תִזְבְּחוּ זֶבַח שְׁלָמִים לַיהוָה
ו לִרְצֹנְכֶם תִּזְבָּחֻהוּ: בְּיוֹם זִבְחֲכֶם יֵאָכֵל וּמִמָּחֳרָת וְהַנּוֹתָר עַד־יוֹם הַשְּׁלִישִׁי
ז־ח בָּאֵשׁ יִשָּׂרֵף: וְאִם הֵאָכֹל יֵאָכֵל בַּיּוֹם הַשְּׁלִישִׁי פִּגּוּל הוּא לֹא יֵרָצֶה: וְאֹכְלָיו
עֲוֹנוֹ יִשָּׂא כִּי־אֶת־קֹדֶשׁ יְהוָה חִלֵּל וְנִכְרְתָה הַנֶּפֶשׁ הַהִוא מֵעַמֶּיהָ:
ט וּבְקֻצְרְכֶם אֶת־קְצִיר אַרְצְכֶם לֹא תְכַלֶּה פְּאַת שָׂדְךָ לִקְצֹר וְלֶקֶט קְצִירְךָ
י לֹא תְלַקֵּט: וְכַרְמְךָ לֹא תְעוֹלֵל וּפֶרֶט כַּרְמְךָ לֹא תְלַקֵּט לֶעָנִי וְלַגֵּר תַּעֲזֹב

וְאֶת שַׁבְּתֹתַי תִּשְׁמֹרוּ — *And you shall keep My Sabbaths.* It is not the Sabbath of Creation (i.e., the seventh day of every week) alone in regard to which (the Torah) cautions, but regarding every kind of Sabbath, namely the Sabbath of Creation and the Sabbath of the Land (i.e., the Sabbatical Year) with the nullification of monetary (debts), all of which testify to the (Divine) origin of the world (lit., the new 'beginning' of the world, i.e., that is created by God), as He says later . . .

4. אַל תִּפְנוּ אֶל הָאֱלִילִם — *Turn not to the idols (nonentities).* (The Torah) explains that when (He) warned and said, לֹא תַעֲשֶׂה לְךָ פֶסֶל, *You shall not make for yourself a graven image* (*Exodus* 20:4), this was not only a prohibition to accept it as a god but it forbade (us) to honor them or to make talismen at specific hours to attain illusionary material success or other (similar) things through them.

5. וְכִי תִזְבְּחוּ — *And when you offer.* (The Torah) explains that when He said, אָנֹכִי ה' אֱלֹהֶיךָ, *I am* HASHEM *your God* (*Exodus* 20:2), (it was meant) that they should accept only Him as a God, as they accepted Him when they left Egypt when they said, זֶה אֵלִי וְאַנְוֵהוּ אֱלֹהֵי אָבִי וַאֲרֹמְמֶנְהוּ, *This is my God and I will glorify Him, my father's God and I will exalt Him* (*Exodus* 15:2). Not only did they say that they would observe His commandments and exalt Him, as it is fitting for one accepted as king, and that they would pray to Him alone (for assistance) in all their troubles, but they are (now) cautioned to be very concerned for His honor in such a manner that His holy things are not profaned even in thought.

9-10. וּבְקֻצְרְכֶם . . . לֶעָנִי וְלַגֵּר תַּעֲזֹב אֹתָם — *And when you reap . . . you shall leave them for the poor and the stranger.* (The Torah) explains that since we have accepted Him as God, it is proper that we walk in His ways, to do righteousness and justice, and among the (various) categories of righteousness are gleanings, forgotten sheaves and the corner of the field mentioned in this chapter. And this is explained by His saying . . .

NOTES

God). Verses 5-7 are interpreted by the *Sforno* as amplifying the first commandment of אָנֹכִי. To accept God is to honor Him and refrain from profaning קֹדֶשׁ, *holy things*, even in thought (i.e., פִּגּוּל). Verses 3 and 4 amplify the second, third, fourth and fifth commandments. To reject other gods means also rejecting talismen even though one doesn't actually worship them (v.4). To keep שַׁבָּת, *the Sabbath*, includes festivals and the Sabbatical year (v. 3). To honor parents, one must not merely meet their material needs, but respect and revere them as well (v. 3).

For clarification of many of the thoughts expressed by the *Sforno* on this verse, see the *Sforno* and notes on *Genesis* 1:26, *Exodus* 20:12 regarding length of days, *Leviticus* 11:2 and 45 and 13:47.

יא אַתָּ֖ם אֲנִ֣י יהוה אֱלֹהֵיכֶֽם: לֹ֖א תִּגְנֹ֑בוּ וְלֹא־תְכַחֲשׁ֥וּ וְלֹֽא־תְשַׁקְּר֖וּ אִ֥ישׁ
יב בַּֽעֲמִיתֽוֹ: וְלֹֽא־תִשָּֽׁבְע֥וּ בִשְׁמִ֖י לַשָּׁ֑קֶר וְחִלַּלְתָּ֛ אֶת־שֵׁ֥ם אֱלֹהֶ֖יךָ אֲנִ֥י יהוֹה:
יג לֹֽא־תַֽעֲשֹׁ֤ק אֶת־רֵֽעֲךָ֙ וְלֹ֣א תִגְזֹ֔ל לֹֽא־תָלִ֞ין פְּעֻלַּ֥ת שָׂכִ֛יר אִתְּךָ֖ עַד־בֹּֽקֶר:
יד לֹֽא־תְקַלֵּ֣ל חֵרֵ֔שׁ וְלִפְנֵ֣י עִוֵּ֔ר לֹ֥א תִתֵּ֖ן מִכְשֹׁ֑ל וְיָרֵ֥אתָ מֵּֽאֱלֹהֶ֖יךָ אֲנִ֥י יהוֹה:
שני [חמישי] טו לֹֽא־תַֽעֲשׂ֥וּ עָ֨וֶל֙ בַּמִּשְׁפָּ֔ט לֹֽא־תִשָּׂ֣א פְנֵי־דָ֔ל וְלֹ֥א תֶהְדַּ֖ר פְּנֵ֣י גָד֑וֹל בְּצֶ֖דֶק
טז תִּשְׁפֹּ֥ט עֲמִיתֶֽךָ: לֹֽא־תֵלֵ֤ךְ רָכִיל֙ בְּעַמֶּ֔יךָ לֹ֥א תַֽעֲמֹ֖ד עַל־דַּ֣ם רֵעֶ֑ךָ אֲנִ֥י יהוֹה:

אֲנִי ה׳ אֱלֹהֵיכֶם — *I am HASHEM your God.* That is to say: Since I am your God and all My ways are kindness and truth, (hence), it is fitting that you observe these categories of righteousness which are desirable before Me Afterwards, (the Torah) continues to explain categories of justice, some of which (deal) with individuals comprising the populace, some (with matters) between the judge and the populace, while others (pertain to matters) regarding the leaders of the people. In the category regarding individuals of the populace, (the Torah) cautions against one man harming another in matters of money, which is to say . . .

11. לֹא תִּגְנֹבוּ וְלֹא תְכַחֲשׁוּ וְלֹא תְשַׁקְּרוּ — *You shall not steal, neither shall you deal falsely nor lie.* All this refers to money, and similarly when it says . . .

12. וְלֹא תִשָּׁבְעוּ בִשְׁמִי לַשָּׁקֶר — *And you shall not swear by My Name falsely* . . . so as to be acquitted from a monetary obligation. Therefore (the verse) adds and states . . .

וְחִלַּלְתָּ אֶת שֵׁם אֱלֹהֶיךָ — *And profane the Name of your God.* That is to say; Besides harming your friend by acquitting yourself falsely, behold, you (also) profane the name of your God. Following this, (the Torah) cautions (us) not to harm him by debasing his honor; this is stated by saying . . .

14. לֹא תְקַלֵּל חֵרֵשׁ — *You shall not curse the deaf.* After which (the Torah) warns us not to cause a person harm, stating, וְלִפְנֵי עִוֵּר לֹא תִתֵּן מִכְשֹׁל, *Do not put a stumbling block before the blind,* (meaning that) although you do not harm him directly (lit., with your hands), still you can cause him damage. After (all this), He explains that area of justice which concerns the relationship between the judges and the populace, stating . . .

15. לֹא תַעֲשׂוּ עָוֶל בַּמִּשְׁפָּט — *You shall do no unrighteousness in judgment.* Do not be lenient toward one (party) and harsh with the other (*Kesuvos* 46a), (or) make one stand while the other sits (*Shevuos* 30a), and (situations) similar to these. After this, the (Torah) relates the portion (of laws) pertaining to judges and leaders of the people which involve hatred and talebearing to the king; similar to the episode of Doeg and his comrades who informed on David to Saul, resulting in (Saul's) bearing a grudge, seeking vengeance and attempting to have (David) killed, as the Prophet attests saying, אַנְשֵׁי רָכִיל הָיוּ בָךְ לְמַעַן שְׁפָךְ דָּם, *In your midst were men of slander for the purpose of shedding blood* (Ezekiel 22:9). He then teaches (us) a great principle regarding these (admonitions) by saying . . .

NOTES

15. לֹא תַעֲשׂוּ עָוֶל בַּמִּשְׁפָּט — *You shall do no unrighteousness in judgment. Unrighteousness in judgment* (עָוֶל בַּמִּשְׁפָּט) is not to be understood literally. Rather, it is an admonition to refrain from treating the parties in a dispute in a disparate fashion, thereby showing partiality. The *Sforno* interprets verse 16 as referring to men in power who can influence a ruler in

יז לֹא־תִשְׂנָא אֶת־אָחִיךָ בִּלְבָבֶךָ הוֹכֵחַ תּוֹכִיחַ אֶת־עֲמִיתֶךָ וְלֹא־תִשָּׂא עָלָיו
יח חֵטְא: לֹא־תִקֹּם וְלֹא־תִטֹּר אֶת־בְּנֵי עַמֶּךָ וְאָהַבְתָּ לְרֵעֲךָ כָּמוֹךָ אֲנִי יהוה:
יט אֶת־חֻקֹּתַי תִּשְׁמֹרוּ בְּהֶמְתְּךָ לֹא־תַרְבִּיעַ כִּלְאַיִם שָׂדְךָ לֹא־תִזְרַע כִּלְאָיִם
כ וּבֶגֶד כִּלְאַיִם שַׁעַטְנֵז לֹא יַעֲלֶה עָלֶיךָ: וְאִישׁ כִּי־יִשְׁכַּב אֶת־אִשָּׁה
שִׁכְבַת־זֶרַע וְהִוא שִׁפְחָה נֶחֱרֶפֶת לְאִישׁ וְהָפְדֵּה לֹא נִפְדָּתָה אוֹ חֻפְשָׁה לֹא
כא נִתַּן־לָהּ בִּקֹּרֶת תִּהְיֶה לֹא יוּמְתוּ כִּי־לֹא חֻפָּשָׁה: וְהֵבִיא אֶת־אֲשָׁמוֹ לַיהוה

18. וְאָהַבְתָּ לְרֵעֲךָ כָּמוֹךָ — *And you shall love your neighbor as yourself.* You should desire for your neighbor that which you would desire (lit., love) for yourself, were you in his position.

Now being that included in one's reverence of God, the Blessed One, is the keeping of the statutes, for indeed those who observe them in order not to sin against Him do so because they have come to recognize His greatness and goodness, and know that He did not command (anything) except that which is worthy and good, (hence) it is not proper to disobey His word, even though the reason for the commandment is not known; (therefore), He says . . .

19. אֶת חֻקֹּתַי תִּשְׁמֹרוּ — *You shall keep My statutes.* (The Torah) mentions statutes regarding the work of animals, agricultural labor, clothing, breeding, food and drink and foretelling the future, for all these were representative of their lifestyle at that time. Many of these statutes are prohibitions meant to eliminate practices which are contrary to the nature of things as intended and ordered by God, the Exalted One. However, regarding a שִׁפְחָה חֲרוּפָה, *a designated bondwoman* (v.20), although it is also a statute, considering that *she* receives lashes whereas *he* does not, and also in that *he* brings an offering even for an intentional transgression (מֵזִיד) and that both these laws (lashes only for the woman and bringing a sacrifice for מֵזִיד) are not found regarding any other *mitzvos* in the Torah (hence it is certainly a חֹק), nonetheless, some explanation is given for this statute (in the next verse) where it says . . .

20. כִּי לֹא חֻפָּשָׁה — *Because she was not free.* The sin (of the perpetrator) is (relatively) light because the act of betrothal (of this bondwoman) is not totally valid and the principal aspect of the sin committed lies in his being intimate with one who is partially a bondwoman (חֲצִי שִׁפְחָה), thereby profaning the sanctity of God. Now,

NOTES

such a way that their talebearing can lead to bloodshed. That is why he cites the episode of Doeg, Saul and David, and why he quotes the verse from Ezekiel. This explains the continuity of verse 16 — *do not bear tales* and *do not stand idly by the blood of your neighbor.*

18. וְאָהַבְתָּ לְרֵעֲךָ כָּמוֹךָ — *And you shall love your neighbor as yourself.* The *Sforno*, among many other commentators, does not translate the phrase וְאָהַבְתָּ לְרֵעֲךָ כָּמוֹךָ to mean *love your neighbor 'as' yourself*, for then the Torah would have written אֶת רֵעֲךָ. In general, this is an unrealistic expectation. Rather, man is being told to love and to treat his fellowman as he would desire others to treat him. This is precisely what Hillel meant when he said to the non-Jew who wished to convert, 'What is hateful to you, do it not to your friend' (*Shabbos* 31a); however, since he was speaking to a non-Jew he expressed it in the negative sense.

19-20. אֶת חֻקֹּתַי תִּשְׁמֹרוּ . . . כִּי לֹא חֻפָּשָׁה — *You shall keep My statutes . . . Because she was not free.* Statutes are laws commanded by God which defy logical explanation and must be accepted on faith. However, the *Sforno* feels that not all חֻקִּים are equal. Some appear more understandable than others since their pur-

כב אֶל־פֶּתַח אֹהֶל מוֹעֵד אֵיל אָשָׁם׃ וְכִפֶּר עָלָיו הַכֹּהֵן בְּאֵיל הָאָשָׁם לִפְנֵי
יְהוָה עַל־חַטָּאתוֹ אֲשֶׁר חָטָא וְנִסְלַח לוֹ מֵחַטָּאתוֹ אֲשֶׁר חָטָא׃
שלישי כג וְכִי־תָבֹאוּ אֶל־הָאָרֶץ וּנְטַעְתֶּם כָּל־עֵץ מַאֲכָל וַעֲרַלְתֶּם עָרְלָתוֹ אֶת־פִּרְיוֹ
כד שָׁלֹשׁ שָׁנִים יִהְיֶה לָכֶם עֲרֵלִים לֹא יֵאָכֵל׃ וּבַשָּׁנָה הָרְבִיעִת יִהְיֶה כָּל־פִּרְיוֹ
כה קֹדֶשׁ הִלּוּלִים לַיהוָה׃ וּבַשָּׁנָה הַחֲמִישִׁת תֹּאכְלוּ אֶת־פִּרְיוֹ לְהוֹסִיף לָכֶם
כו תְּבוּאָתוֹ אֲנִי יְהוָה אֱלֹהֵיכֶם׃ לֹא תֹאכְלוּ עַל־הַדָּם לֹא תְנַחֲשׁוּ וְלֹא
כז־כח תְעוֹנֵנוּ׃ לֹא תַקִּפוּ פְּאַת רֹאשְׁכֶם וְלֹא תַשְׁחִית אֵת פְּאַת זְקָנֶךָ׃ וְשֶׂרֶט
לָנֶפֶשׁ לֹא תִתְּנוּ בִּבְשַׂרְכֶם וּכְתֹבֶת קַעֲקַע לֹא תִתְּנוּ בָּכֶם אֲנִי יְהוָה׃
כט אַל־תְּחַלֵּל אֶת־בִּתְּךָ לְהַזְנוֹתָהּ וְלֹא־תִזְנֶה הָאָרֶץ וּמָלְאָה הָאָרֶץ זִמָּה׃

---

being that this deed on the human level represents an impairment of the honor of the man (the active participant) and not of the honor of the woman (the passive participant), we must assume that she enticed him and therefore she deserves to receive the lashes. (As for the bringing of a guilt offering) this intentional trangression (מֵזִיד), whereby he so foolishly profaned himself, borders on an unintentional act; שׁוֹגֵג, hence he brings a guilt offering for profaning the holy.

26. לֹא תֹאכְלוּ עַל הַדָּם לֹא תְנַחֲשׁוּ וְלֹא תְעוֹנֵנוּ — *You shall not eat with the blood, neither shall you practice divination nor soothsaying.* All these methods (were practiced) among them to predict the future (in the process of) turning aside from the spirit of *taharah* and prophecy to the way of the spirit of *tumah*. And being that the ways of revering and honoring God (include) the prohibition of physically profaning His people whom He hallowed to serve Him, (the Torah) says . . .

27-29. לֹא תַקִּפוּ . . . אַל תְּחַלֵּל אֶת בִּתְּךָ — *You shall not round . . . do not profane your daughter.* And He commanded that we are not to profane (our bodies) by rounding the corners of the head as is the practice of fools, drunkards or heathen priests and (also) not to shave the beard, as our Sages say, 'The beard is the dignity (beauty) of the face' (*Shabbos* 152a), nor to *make a cutting in the flesh* (v. 28), thereby attaching excessive importance to man's death, and mourning excessively over it. (He also prohibited us) *to imprint any marks on the body* (tattooing) so as not to have any sign on our flesh other than the sign of the covenant, (בְּרִית מִילָה), and to make one's daughter a harlot (v. 29) even though she be unmarried, for it profanes her and her

NOTES

pose is to maintain the balance and order of nature ordained by God, the Creator. However, some not only seem to lack rationale but contain seemingly contradictory elements. One such example is שִׁפְחָה חֲרוּפָה, *a designated bondwoman*, as the *Sforno* explains. Paradoxically, in this instance, the Torah *does* indicate some reason for the statute. The guilt of the maidservant lies in the fact that, having nothing to lose in regard to her reputation, she feels she may as well be the seductress; hence she is punished. The man, on the other hand, is a prisoner of passion and closer to שׁוֹגֵג, *unintentional transgression*, than to מֵזִיד, *intentional;* therefore, he can atone with a sacrifice.

26. לֹא תֹאכְלוּ עַל הַדָּם — *You shall not eat with the blood.* See the *Sforno* and the notes on 17:7 regarding the link between blood and the demons who were courted by people in the hope of having future events revealed to them.

27-28. לֹא תַקִּפוּ — *You shall not round.* The *Sforno* explains that the concept of, קְדוּשָׁה, *sanctity*, extends to the care of ones body which must be treated with respect and dignity. One way this is manifested is through one's refraining from imprinting any perma-

ל-לא אֶת־שַׁבְּתֹתַי תִּשְׁמֹרוּ וּמִקְדָּשִׁי תִּירָאוּ אֲנִי יהוה: אַל־תִּפְנוּ אֶל־הָאֹבֹת
לב וְאֶל־הַיִּדְּעֹנִים אַל־תְּבַקְשׁוּ לְטָמְאָה בָהֶם אֲנִי יהוה אֱלֹהֵיכֶם: מִפְּנֵי שֵׂיבָה
רביעי (ששי) לג תָּקוּם וְהָדַרְתָּ פְּנֵי זָקֵן וְיָרֵאתָ מֵּאֱלֹהֶיךָ אֲנִי יהוה: וְכִי־יָגוּר
לד אִתְּךָ גֵּר בְּאַרְצְכֶם לֹא תוֹנוּ אֹתוֹ: כְּאֶזְרָח מִכֶּם יִהְיֶה לָכֶם הַגֵּר | הַגָּר

---

father, similar to *If she profanes herself by playing the harlot, she profanes her father* (21:9). (Now), after warning (us) regarding those things which are a profanation, He commands (us) to honor the holy days, places and people — saying . . .

30. אֶת שַׁבְּתֹתַי תִּשְׁמֹרוּ — *You shall keep My Sabbaths* . . . which means the Shabbos and all the holy convocations.

וּמִקְדָּשִׁי תִּירָאוּ — *And revere My Sanctuary* . . . which means every place hallowed for Torah, prayer and service (of God). (Now) being that inquiring of the אֹבֹת (a form of necromancy) among the nations was (considered) as a divine search, (appealing) to the dead on behalf of the living, (the Torah) states . . .

31. אַל תִּפְנוּ אֶל הָאֹבֹת — *Do not turn to the 'ovos'*. Do not turn toward them, but show them (lit., give them) the back of your neck and not your face. Needless to say, do not honor them.

אַל תְּבַקְשׁוּ לְטָמְאָה בָהֶם — *Do not seek them out to be defiled by them.* Do not seek them out in order to be defiled through them, but you may seek them to know their nature so as to teach, as (our Sages say) (*Shabbos* 75a), 'Do not learn (these subjects) in order to perform them, but you may learn them to understand and to teach.'

32. מִפְּנֵי שֵׂיבָה תָּקוּם — *You shall rise up before the hoary head.* But you shall honor the 'holy ones of the Most High' (based on *Daniel* 7:18) of whom most are hoary heads, as it says, עֲטֶרֶת תִּפְאֶרֶת שֵׂיבָה בְּדֶרֶךְ צְדָקָה תִּמָּצֵא, *The hoary head is a crown of glory, it is found in the way of righteousness* (*Proverbs* 16:31).

וְהָדַרְתָּ פְּנֵי זָקֵן — *And honor the face of the elder.* These are the Torah scholars (lit., who hold the Torah), as our Rabbis, of blessed memory, say, 'A *zaken* is none other than one who has acquired wisdom' (*Kiddushin* 32b). After cautioning (us) regarding the honor of the holy ones, (the Torah) warns us not to shame the lowly ones, saying . . .

33. וְכִי יָגוּר אִתְּךָ גֵּר . . . לֹא תוֹנוּ אֹתוֹ — *And if a stranger sojourn with you . . . you shall not do him wrong* . . . even by vexing him with words . . . (the Torah) then additionally says . . .

NOTES

nent mark on his body. The one notable exception is that of the בְּרִית מִילָה demonstrates the Jew's identification with his God and his people.

30. אֶת שַׁבְּתֹתַי תִּשְׁמֹרוּ — *You shall keep My Sabbaths.* The term שַׁבְּתֹתַי, *My Sabbaths,* is in the plural, therefore the *Sforno* interprets it as including, in addition to Shabbos, festivals and the *Shemittah* (seventh year) as well. (See verse 3.) And just as *My Sabbaths* is all-inclusive, so does the term מִקְדָּשִׁי, *My Sanctuary,* include every holy place designated for prayer and Torah study, which must be treated with reverence.

32. מִפְּנֵי שֵׂיבָה תָּקוּם — *You shall rise up before the hoary head.* Whereas the status of שֵׂיבָה is determined by age, that of a זָקֵן is established by Torah scholarship, regardless of one's chronological age.

אִתְּכֶם וְאָהַבְתָּ לוֹ כָּמוֹךָ כִּי־גֵרִים הֱיִיתֶם בְּאֶרֶץ מִצְרָיִם אֲנִי יהוה
לה־לו אֱלֹהֵיכֶם׃ לֹא־תַעֲשׂוּ עָוֶל בַּמִּשְׁפָּט בַּמִּדָּה בַּמִּשְׁקָל וּבַמְּשׂוּרָה׃ מֹאזְנֵי צֶדֶק
אַבְנֵי־צֶדֶק אֵיפַת צֶדֶק וְהִין צֶדֶק יִהְיֶה לָכֶם אֲנִי יהוה אֱלֹהֵיכֶם
לז אֲשֶׁר־הוֹצֵאתִי אֶתְכֶם מֵאֶרֶץ מִצְרָיִם׃ וּשְׁמַרְתֶּם אֶת־כָּל־חֻקֹּתַי וְאֶת־כָּל־
מִשְׁפָּטַי וַעֲשִׂיתֶם אֹתָם אֲנִי יהוה׃
כ חמישי א־ב וַיְדַבֵּר יהוה אֶל־מֹשֶׁה לֵּאמֹר׃ וְאֶל־בְּנֵי יִשְׂרָאֵל תֹּאמַר אִישׁ אִישׁ מִבְּנֵי
יִשְׂרָאֵל וּמִן־הַגֵּר ׀ הַגָּר בְּיִשְׂרָאֵל אֲשֶׁר יִתֵּן מִזַּרְעוֹ לַמֹּלֶךְ מוֹת יוּמָת עַם

---

35. לֹא תַעֲשׂוּ עָוֶל בַּמִּשְׁפָּט בַּמִּדָּה בַּמִּשְׁקָל וּבַמְּשׂוּרָה — *You shall do no unrighteousness concerning judgment in land measurement, in weight or in measure.* Being that אוֹנָאָה (*wrongdoing* — misleading a person) also includes money matters, namely, liquid and dry measures and weights, (the Torah) cautions against general wrongdoing toward the native and the stranger.

37. וּשְׁמַרְתֶּם אֶת כָּל חֻקֹּתַי וְאֶת כָּל מִשְׁפָּטַי — *And you shall observe all My statutes and all My ordinances.* Analyze them and recognize that they are worthy.

וַעֲשִׂיתֶם אֹתָם — *And do them.* And in this way (i.e., through studying them and recognizing their great worth), you will do them.

אֲנִי ה׳ — *I am HASHEM.* (The Torah) explains that it is proper to keep the statutes and ordinances without adding (to) or diminishing (them) because, indeed, the works of God and His commandments are the ultimate in perfection, and עָלָיו אֵין לְהוֹסִיף וּמִמֶּנּוּ אֵין לִגְרוֹעַ, *Nothing can be added to it nor anything taken from it* (*Koheles* 3:14).

XX

2. אֲשֶׁר יִתֵּן מִזַּרְעוֹ לַמֹּלֶךְ — *That gives of his seed to Molech.* After explaining the Godly intent to sanctify Israel so that they shall be like Him as much as possible, and (after) teaching them the way through which the intended goal of God, the Exalted One, shall be attained, and (after) cautioning against acting contrary (to these teachings), He now speaks of the punishment (of those who) become *tamei* with one of three types of *tumah* which are the antithesis of the aforementioned holiness. The first is *tumah* in the area of דֵּעוֹת (philosophical opinions) such as that of the Molech which is said *to defile My sanctuary* (v. 3) and that of *ovos* and familiar spirits of which it was said earlier, *Seek them not out to be defiled by them* (19:31). The second is *tumah* regarding one's seed (i.e., offspring), which is עֲרָיוֹת (prohibited sexual relations) of which (the Torah) stated above, *Defile not yourselves in any of these things, for in all these the nations are defiled . . . and the land was defiled* (18:24,25). And the third *tumah* is (contracted through the consumption) of prohibited foods, of which it is said at the conclusion of this chapter, *Which I have set apart for you to consider tamei* (v. 25). However, in

NOTES

37. וּשְׁמַרְתֶּם אֶת כָּל חֻקֹּתַי . . . וַעֲשִׂיתֶם אֹתָם — *And you shall observe all My statutes . . . and do them.* The *Sforno* explains that וּשְׁמַרְתֶּם and וַעֲשִׂיתֶם are not redundant. The former does not refer to *observance* but to study and analysis, which leads to *keeping* and *doing.*

XX

2. . . . אֲשֶׁר יִתֵּן מִזַּרְעוֹ לַמֹּלֶךְ — *That gives of his seed to Molech.* The *Sforno* explains the concluding section of *parashas Kedoshim* in the following manner. The numerous laws set

ג הָאָרֶץ יִרְגְּמֻהוּ בָאָבֶן: וַאֲנִי אֶתֵּן אֶת־פָּנַי֙ בָּאִישׁ הַהוּא וְהִכְרַתִּי אֹתוֹ מִקֶּרֶב
עַמּוֹ כִּי מִזַּרְעוֹ֙ נָתַן לַמֹּלֶךְ לְמַעַן טַמֵּא֙ אֶת־מִקְדָּשִׁי וּלְחַלֵּל אֶת־שֵׁם קָדְשִׁי:
ד וְאִם הַעְלֵם יַעְלִימוּ עַם הָאָרֶץ אֶת־עֵינֵיהֶם֙ מִן־הָאִישׁ הַהוּא בְּתִתּוֹ מִזַּרְעוֹ
ה לַמֹּלֶךְ לְבִלְתִּי הָמִית אֹתוֹ: וְשַׂמְתִּי אֲנִי אֶת־פָּנַי בָּאִישׁ הַהוּא וּבְמִשְׁפַּחְתּוֹ
וְהִכְרַתִּי אֹתוֹ וְאֵת | כָּל־הַזֹּנִים אַחֲרָיו לִזְנוֹת אַחֲרֵי הַמֹּלֶךְ מִקֶּרֶב עַמָּם:
ו וְהַנֶּפֶשׁ אֲשֶׁר תִּפְנֶה אֶל־הָאֹבֹת֙ וְאֶל־הַיִּדְּעֹנִים לִזְנוֹת אַחֲרֵיהֶם וְנָתַתִּי

---

parashas Emor, (the Torah) speaks of the *tumah* (caused) by a dead person, the profanation of (one's) seed, of blemishes (how they relate to the laws of *Kohanim* and of sacrifices) and of מְעִילָה (*trespass* — forbidden enjoyment of the holy), topics which pertain only to holy items and persons. Now (the Torah) begins to speak of Molech, saying —

עַם הָאָרֶץ יִרְגְּמֻהוּ בָאָבֶן — *The people of the land shall stone him with stones.* Thus the populace shall do in their zealousness (to defend) the honor of their Creator. This shall be when there are witnesses and a warning.

3. וַאֲנִי אֶתֵּן אֶת פָּנַי בָּאִישׁ הַהוּא — *I will set My face against that man* ... if he does not repent of his wickedness, and in this manner his death will not be an atonement.

וְהִכְרַתִּי אֹתוֹ — *And I will cut him off.* This must perforce be understood as an allusion to the World to Come, for after he is stoned he can no longer be cut off from This World.

לְמַעַן טַמֵּא אֶת מִקְדָּשִׁי — *To defile My Sanctuary.* (This caused) the *Shechinah* (Divine Presence) to depart from Israel, (therefore) it is fitting that they stone him.

וּלְחַלֵּל אֶת שֵׁם קָדְשִׁי — *And to profane My holy Name.* Therefore, I will set My face against him, though it (the Molech) is not an (actual) idol.

5. וּבְמִשְׁפַּחְתּוֹ — *And against his family.* For the people of the land would not have hidden their eyes (to this evil) except for fear of his family who support him.

NOTES

forth in this portion of the Torah are meant to refine and sanctify the Jewish people. The antithesis of קְדוּשָׁה, *holiness,* is טוּמְאָה, *impurity.* The *Sforno* calls our attention to the fact that the term טוּמְאָה is used in connection with laws regulating food, sexual relationships and the occult. This is the common denominator of the subjects which comprise the concluding section of *Kedoshim.* They all represent the opposite of the ideal which the Torah demands of us, i.e., *you shall be holy.*

3. וַאֲנִי אֶתֵּן אֶת פָּנַי בָּאִישׁ הַהוּא — *I will set My face against that man.* The *Sforno* teaches us two important concepts in his commentary on this verse. One is that a person's death is a כַּפָּרָה, *atonement,* only if he repents beforehand and the second is that the term כָּרֵת, *excision,* in this case alludes not to עוֹלָם הַזֶּה, *This World,* but to עוֹלָם הַבָּא, *the World to Come.*

לְמַעַן טַמֵּא אֶת מִקְדָּשִׁי וּלְחַלֵּל — *To defile My Sanctuary and to profane.* Giving one's seed to the Molech is an act which both defiles and desecrates. It defiles by causing the *Shechinah* to depart, leaving a spiritual vacuum which is filled by טוּמְאָה. By offering one's child to the Molech, a man profanes God's Name, even though he does not accept the Molech as a god.

5. וּבְמִשְׁפַּחְתּוֹ — *And against his family.* To punish the family of the sinner seems contrary to the teaching that *each man shall die for his own sin* (אִישׁ בְּחֶטְאוֹ יָמוּת). The *Sforno* explains, however, that the family shares in the blame for supporting the sinner and shielding him.

ז אֶת־פָּנַי֙ בַּנֶּ֣פֶשׁ הַהִ֔וא וְהִכְרַתִּ֥י אֹת֖וֹ מִקֶּ֥רֶב עַמּֽוֹ׃ וְהִ֨תְקַדִּשְׁתֶּ֔ם וִהְיִיתֶ֖ם
ששי [שביעי] ח קְדֹשִׁ֑ים כִּ֛י אֲנִ֥י יְהוָ֖ה אֱלֹהֵיכֶֽם׃ וּשְׁמַרְתֶּם֙ אֶת־חֻקֹּתַ֔י וַעֲשִׂיתֶ֖ם אֹתָ֑ם אֲנִ֥י
ט יְהוָ֖ה מְקַדִּשְׁכֶֽם׃ כִּֽי־אִ֣ישׁ אִ֗ישׁ אֲשֶׁ֨ר יְקַלֵּ֧ל אֶת־אָבִ֛יו וְאֶת־אִמּ֖וֹ מ֣וֹת יוּמָ֑ת
י אָבִ֧יו וְאִמּ֛וֹ קִלֵּ֖ל דָּמָ֥יו בּֽוֹ׃ וְאִ֗ישׁ אֲשֶׁ֤ר יִנְאַף֙ אֶת־אֵ֣שֶׁת אִ֔ישׁ אֲשֶׁ֥ר יִנְאַ֖ף
יא אֶת־אֵ֣שֶׁת רֵעֵ֑הוּ מֽוֹת־יוּמַ֥ת הַנֹּאֵ֖ף וְהַנֹּאָֽפֶת׃ וְאִ֗ישׁ אֲשֶׁ֤ר יִשְׁכַּב֙ אֶת־אֵ֣שֶׁת
יב אָבִ֔יו עֶרְוַ֥ת אָבִ֖יו גִּלָּ֑ה מֽוֹת־יוּמְת֥וּ שְׁנֵיהֶ֖ם דְּמֵיהֶ֥ם בָּֽם׃ וְאִ֗ישׁ אֲשֶׁ֤ר יִשְׁכַּב֙
יג אֶת־כַּלָּת֔וֹ מ֥וֹת יוּמְת֖וּ שְׁנֵיהֶ֑ם תֶּ֥בֶל עָשׂ֖וּ דְּמֵיהֶ֥ם בָּֽם׃ וְאִ֗ישׁ אֲשֶׁ֨ר יִשְׁכַּ֤ב

---

7. וְהִתְקַדִּשְׁתֶּם — *Sanctify yourselves* ... by separating yourselves from sexual immorality.

וִהְיִיתֶם קְדֹשִׁים — *And you shall be holy* ... that your offspring (lit., seed) be predisposed for the *Shechinah* to dwell in their midst, as (our Sages) say, 'The *Shechinah* only dwells upon families of distinguished ancestry in Israel' (*Kiddushin* 70b).

כִּי אֲנִי ה׳ אֱלֹהֵיכֶם — *For I am* HASHEM *your God* ... who said to Abraham, לִהְיוֹת לְךָ לֵאלֹהִים וּלְזַרְעֲךָ אַחֲרֶיךָ, *To be a God to you and to your seed after you* (*Genesis* 17:7), i.e., (only) to seed descended from your ancestral line, as (our Sages) explained (*Midrash Bamidbar Rabbah* 12:4).

8. וּשְׁמַרְתֶּם אֶת חֻקֹּתַי וַעֲשִׂיתֶם אֹתָם — *And keep My statutes and do them.* In this manner, namely, that you sanctify yourselves through separation from forbidden unions, you will thereby *keep* and *do them* for (future) generations. (But) if you do not sanctify yourselves, your descendants will undoubtedly also rebel (against these laws) since they will have been born in sin, as we find in הֵן בְּעָווֹן חוֹלָלְתִּי, *Behold, I was shaped in iniquity* (*Psalms* 51:7).

אֲנִי ה׳ מְקַדִּשְׁכֶם — *I am* HASHEM *Who sanctifies you.* For, in truth, I have prohibited (these) forbidden unions (to you) to sanctify you to my service.

9. כִּי אִישׁ אִישׁ אֲשֶׁר יְקַלֵּל אֶת אָבִיו וְאֶת אִמּוֹ — *For any man there be that curses his father or his mother.* As an indication (lit., sign) that I am extremely exacting regarding the sanctity of your offspring is the fact that I ordained capital punishment (lit., death sentence by the court) for whosoever curses his parents. Now this occurs, in most cases, when there is a flaw in one's offspring, for then he is not predisposed to that which is written, שְׁמַע בְּנִי מוּסַר אָבִיךָ, *My son, hear the instruction of your father* (*Proverbs* 1:8). And a man such as this will (also) not keep the statutes and ordinances, for he will utterly refuse to accept them from his father and mother.

NOTES

7. וְהִתְקַדִּשְׁתֶּם — *Sanctify yourselves.* Unlike *Rashi,* who interprets וְהִתְקַדִּשְׁתֶּם as referring to rejection of idolatry, the *Sforno* applies it to rejection of immorality. For only through proper moral conduct is Israel fit for the *Shechinah* to dwell in its midst. Their children, in turn, by perpetuating this way of life, are thereby worthy to have God as their God and also to have the *Shechinah* abide with them. The *Sforno's* commentary on the following verse (8) continues this theme.

8-9. וּשְׁמַרְתֶּם אֶת חֻקֹּתַי וַעֲשִׂיתֶם אֹתָם ... כִּי אִישׁ אִישׁ אֲשֶׁר יְקַלֵּל אֶת אָבִיו וְאֶת אִמּוֹ — *And keep My statutes and do them ... For any man there be that curses his father or his mother.* The *Sforno* points out the link connecting the chastity of family life, the obligation of children to have respect for parental authority,

יד אֶת־זָכָר מִשְׁכְּבֵי אִשָּׁה תּוֹעֵבָה עָשׂוּ שְׁנֵיהֶם מוֹת יוּמָתוּ דְּמֵיהֶם בָּם: וְאִישׁ
אֲשֶׁר יִקַּח אֶת־אִשָּׁה וְאֶת־אִמָּהּ זִמָּה הִוא בָּאֵשׁ יִשְׂרְפוּ אֹתוֹ וְאֶתְהֶן
טו וְלֹא־תִהְיֶה זִמָּה בְּתוֹכְכֶם: וְאִישׁ אֲשֶׁר יִתֵּן שְׁכָבְתּוֹ בִּבְהֵמָה מוֹת יוּמָת
טז וְאֶת־הַבְּהֵמָה תַּהֲרֹגוּ: וְאִשָּׁה אֲשֶׁר תִּקְרַב אֶל־כָּל־בְּהֵמָה לְרִבְעָה אֹתָהּ
יז וְהָרַגְתָּ אֶת־הָאִשָּׁה וְאֶת־הַבְּהֵמָה מוֹת יוּמָתוּ דְּמֵיהֶם בָּם: וְאִישׁ אֲשֶׁר־יִקַּח
אֶת־אֲחֹתוֹ בַּת־אָבִיו אוֹ בַת־אִמּוֹ וְרָאָה אֶת־עֶרְוָתָהּ וְהִיא תִרְאֶה
אֶת־עֶרְוָתוֹ חֶסֶד הוּא וְנִכְרְתוּ לְעֵינֵי בְּנֵי עַמָּם עֶרְוַת אֲחֹתוֹ גִּלָּה עֲוֹנוֹ יִשָּׂא:
יח וְאִישׁ אֲשֶׁר־יִשְׁכַּב אֶת־אִשָּׁה דָּוָה וְגִלָּה אֶת־עֶרְוָתָהּ אֶת־מְקֹרָהּ הֶעֱרָה
יט וְהִוא גִּלְּתָה אֶת־מְקוֹר דָּמֶיהָ וְנִכְרְתוּ שְׁנֵיהֶם מִקֶּרֶב עַמָּם: וְעֶרְוַת אֲחוֹת
כ אִמְּךָ וַאֲחוֹת אָבִיךָ לֹא תְגַלֵּה כִּי אֶת־שְׁאֵרוֹ הֶעֱרָה עֲוֹנָם יִשָּׂאוּ: וְאִישׁ
כא אֲשֶׁר יִשְׁכַּב אֶת־דֹּדָתוֹ עֶרְוַת דֹּדוֹ גִּלָּה חֶטְאָם יִשָּׂאוּ עֲרִירִים יָמֻתוּ: וְאִישׁ
אֲשֶׁר יִקַּח אֶת־אֵשֶׁת אָחִיו נִדָּה הִוא עֶרְוַת אָחִיו גִּלָּה עֲרִירִים יִהְיוּ:
כב וּשְׁמַרְתֶּם אֶת־כָּל־חֻקֹּתַי וְאֶת־כָּל־מִשְׁפָּטַי וַעֲשִׂיתֶם אֹתָם וְלֹא־תָקִיא
שביעי כג אֶתְכֶם הָאָרֶץ אֲשֶׁר אֲנִי מֵבִיא אֶתְכֶם שָׁמָּה לָשֶׁבֶת בָּהּ: וְלֹא תֵלְכוּ בְּחֻקֹּת
כד הַגּוֹי אֲשֶׁר־אֲנִי מְשַׁלֵּחַ מִפְּנֵיכֶם כִּי אֶת־כָּל־אֵלֶּה עָשׂוּ וָאָקֻץ בָּם: וָאֹמַר
לָכֶם אַתֶּם תִּירְשׁוּ אֶת־אַדְמָתָם וַאֲנִי אֶתְּנֶנָּה לָכֶם לָרֶשֶׁת אֹתָהּ אֶרֶץ זָבַת
חָלָב וּדְבָשׁ אֲנִי יְהוָה אֱלֹהֵיכֶם אֲשֶׁר־הִבְדַּלְתִּי אֶתְכֶם מִן־הָעַמִּים:
מפטיר כה וְהִבְדַּלְתֶּם בֵּין־הַבְּהֵמָה הַטְּהֹרָה לַטְּמֵאָה וּבֵין־הָעוֹף הַטָּמֵא לַטָּהֹר
וְלֹא־תְשַׁקְּצוּ אֶת־נַפְשֹׁתֵיכֶם בַּבְּהֵמָה וּבָעוֹף וּבְכֹל אֲשֶׁר תִּרְמֹשׂ הָאֲדָמָה
כו אֲשֶׁר־הִבְדַּלְתִּי לָכֶם לְטַמֵּא: וִהְיִיתֶם לִי קְדֹשִׁים כִּי קָדוֹשׁ אֲנִי יְהוָה
כז וָאַבְדִּל אֶתְכֶם מִן־הָעַמִּים לִהְיוֹת לִי: וְאִישׁ אוֹ־אִשָּׁה כִּי־יִהְיֶה בָהֶם אוֹב
אוֹ יִדְּעֹנִי מוֹת יוּמָתוּ בָּאֶבֶן יִרְגְּמוּ אֹתָם דְּמֵיהֶם בָּם:

---

25. וְלֹא תְשַׁקְּצוּ אֶת נַפְשֹׁתֵיכֶם בַּבְּהֵמָה וּבָעוֹף וּבְכֹל אֲשֶׁר תִּרְמֹשׂ הָאֲדָמָה — *And you shall not make your souls detestable by beast, or by fowl, or by anything which creeps on the ground* . . . from the species which are unclean (i.e., non-kosher) which I have set apart for you from the ones that are clean (i.e., kosher).

לְטַמֵּא — *To make you unclean.* The manner in which the detestable (species) shall make the soul unclean is exclusively by eating them, not merely by touching or carrying them.

27. וְאִישׁ אוֹ אִשָּׁה כִּי יִהְיֶה בָהֶם אוֹב אוֹ יִדְּעֹנִי — *A man or a woman that divines by a necromancy or a familiar spirit.* Since the intent of all these (commandments) is to sanctify Israel, hence, he who veers from this (through utilization of) a necromancy or a familiar spirit, a practice which is entirely steeped in the spirit of *tumah*, the very opposite of (God's) intent, (that man) undoubtedly deserves to be stoned.

NOTES

and the observance of God's commandments. Only when the people of Israel exercise discipline and thereby safeguard the nobility of their moral character will they merit offspring who will honor and obey their parents and accept their instruction which, in turn, will shape them into servants of God.

25. לְטַמֵּא — *To make you unclean.* The *Sforno* explains that *tumah* can be contracted not only by touching a דָּבָר טָמֵא but also by ingesting it.

פרשת אמור
Parashas Emor

כא א וַיֹּאמֶר יהוה אֶל־מֹשֶׁה אֱמֹר אֶל־הַכֹּהֲנִים בְּנֵי אַהֲרֹן וְאָמַרְתָּ אֲלֵהֶם לְנֶפֶשׁ
ב לֹא־יִטַּמָּא בְּעַמָּיו: כִּי אִם־לִשְׁאֵרוֹ הַקָּרֹב אֵלָיו לְאִמּוֹ וּלְאָבִיו וְלִבְנוֹ
ג וּלְבִתּוֹ וּלְאָחִיו: וְלַאֲחֹתוֹ הַבְּתוּלָה הַקְּרוֹבָה אֵלָיו אֲשֶׁר לֹא־הָיְתָה לְאִישׁ
°יִקְרְחוּ ק׳ ד־ה לָהּ יִטַּמָּא: לֹא יִטַּמָּא בַּעַל בְּעַמָּיו לְהֵחַלּוֹ: לֹא־°יקרחה קָרְחָה בְּרֹאשָׁם

XXI

1. אֱמֹר אֶל הַכֹּהֲנִים — *Speak to the Kohanim* ... regarding that which was said above, to understand and to teach (the laws of) the various types of *tumos* and to differentiate between those animals and birds which are clean (i.e., kosher) and those which are unclean (i.e., non-kosher). Now this (role) is most appropriate for the *Kohanim*, as it says, *To differentiate between the holy and the profane, and between the tamei and the tahor, and that you may teach* (10:10 and 11).

וְאָמַרְתָּ אֲלֵהֶם — *And you shall say to them* ... that they must also exercise caution, in addition to these (laws), (to distance themselves) from *tumah* contracted through contact with the dead and the profanation of their offspring, these being higher levels of holiness for *Kohanim* alone.

לְנֶפֶשׁ לֹא יִטַּמָּא בְּעַמָּיו — *He shall not defile himself for the dead among his people.* No *Kohen* shall defile himself for a dead (person) among his people; (implying) any dead person from among the populace who is not related to him, but is only *from his people.*

4. לֹא יִטַּמָּא בַּעַל בְּעַמָּיו לְהֵחַלּוֹ — *He shall not defile himself, being a chief among his people, to profane himself.* The reason that a *Kohen* should not defile himself except for a relative, is because a *Kohen* is indeed a chief among his people, (whose task is) to learn (lit., understand) and to teach, כִּי שִׂפְתֵי כֹהֵן יִשְׁמְרוּ דַעַת וְתוֹרָה יְבַקְשׁוּ מִפִּיהוּ, *for the Kohen's lips should preserve knowledge, and they should seek Torah from his mouth* (*Malachi* 2:7); (therefore), it is proper that such a man conduct himself as a prince 'so that his words will be listened to' (based on *Gittin* 52b). It is improper for him to profane his readiness toward the (service) of the Sanctuary and its holy things for the purpose of honoring the dead who are not his relatives, as (our Sages), of blessed memory, say that the burial of, and eulogy for, a dead person is יְקָרָא דִשְׁכִבֵי, *in honor of the dead* (*Sanhedrin* 47a). However, for one's relatives, (the Torah) permitted (the *Kohen*) to defile himself, for their honor is also his.

NOTES

XXI

1. אֱמֹר אֶל הַכֹּהֲנִים ... וְאָמַרְתָּ אֲלֵהֶם — *Speak to the Kohanim ... and you shall say to them.* The repetition of the verb *say* (אֱמֹר־וְאָמַרְתָּ) is explained by our Sages (*Yevamos* 114a) as emphasizing the responsibility of adult *Kohanim* to teach and caution their young sons to observe these laws. The *Sforno*, however, interprets the first verb (אֱמֹר) as referring to the concluding section of the previous *parashah* (קְדוֹשִׁים). The laws of *tumah* and the differences between animals and birds which are kosher and non-kosher mentioned there are to be mastered by the *Kohanim* whose mission it is to be the scholars, teachers and arbiters of Torah law. The second verb (וְאָמַרְתָּ) is an admonition that they are to guard their sanctity as *Kohanim* and observe an added dimension of *taharah* by refraining from defilement through contact with those dead who are non-relatives, and through certain marital restrictions.

4. לֹא יִטַּמָּא בַּעַל בְּעַמָּיו לְהֵחַלּוֹ — *He shall not defile himself, being a chief among his people, to profane himself.* The expression בַּעַל בְּעַמָּיו is interpreted by the *Sifra* (and so quoted by

ו וּפְאַת זְקָנָם לֹא יְגַלֵּחוּ וּבִבְשָׂרָם לֹא יִשְׂרְטוּ שָׂרָטֶת: קְדֹשִׁים יִהְיוּ
לֵאלֹהֵיהֶם וְלֹא יְחַלְּלוּ שֵׁם אֱלֹהֵיהֶם כִּי אֶת־אִשֵּׁי יהוה לֶחֶם אֱלֹהֵיהֶם הֵם
ז מַקְרִיבִם וְהָיוּ קֹדֶשׁ: אִשָּׁה זֹנָה וַחֲלָלָה לֹא יִקָּחוּ וְאִשָּׁה גְּרוּשָׁה מֵאִישָׁהּ לֹא
ח יִקָּחוּ כִּי־קָדֹשׁ הוּא לֵאלֹהָיו: וְקִדַּשְׁתּוֹ כִּי־אֶת־לֶחֶם אֱלֹהֶיךָ הוּא מַקְרִיב
ט קָדֹשׁ יִהְיֶה־לָּךְ כִּי קָדוֹשׁ אֲנִי יהוה מְקַדִּשְׁכֶם: וּבַת אִישׁ כֹּהֵן כִּי תֵחֵל
י לִזְנוֹת אֶת־אָבִיהָ הִיא מְחַלֶּלֶת בָּאֵשׁ תִּשָּׂרֵף: וְהַכֹּהֵן
הַגָּדוֹל מֵאֶחָיו אֲשֶׁר־יוּצַק עַל־רֹאשׁוֹ | שֶׁמֶן הַמִּשְׁחָה וּמִלֵּא אֶת־יָדוֹ לִלְבֹּשׁ

---

5. לֹא יִקְרְחוּ — *They shall not make baldness.* Although I have permitted them to defile themselves with their dead relatives for their own honor, I have not permitted them to mourn excessively so as to increase honor for their dead through 'baldness' and 'cuttings,' as our Sages state, 'As the case there (applies to baldness made) for the dead, so here too it applies to the dead' (*Makkos* 20a).

6. וְלֹא יְחַלְּלוּ שֵׁם אֱלֹהֵיהֶם — *And not profane the name of their God.* Although all these (acts) are for his (i.e., the priest's) honor, he has no permission to forgo God's honor, for indeed, the intent (of the Torah) in honoring the *Kohanim* is for (the purpose of enhancing) the honor of God, the Blessed One; hence, by forgoing their own honor they thereby profane His Name.

7. כִּי קָדֹשׁ הוּא לֵאלֹהָיו — *For he is holy to his God.* All the offspring of the priesthood, who are (in the category of) *chief among his people*, are sanctified to their God, and if a *Kohen* marries one of these women, he profanes his honor and his offspring, for they (the children) will not be worthy of that holiness.

NOTES

Rashi) to mean that a *Kohen* who is married to a woman halachically unfit for him may not defile himself with her corpse, providing she has others to bury her and therefore is not a מֵת מִצְוָה (a dead person who has no one to bury him or her; hence it becomes a *mitzvah* to do so). The term בַּעַל, according to this interpretation, means 'husband.' The *Sforno*, however, interprets this word (בַּעַל) as *master* or *chief*, namely a leader among his people (בְּעַמָּיו). Hence the Torah, in this verse, is giving a *reason* for the prohibition of a *Kohen* to defile himself through involvement with a corpse. Were the burial and eulogy meant to honor the living, as some of our Sages assert (יְקָרָא דְחַיֵּי), the *Kohen* would be permitted to take part. However, the final decision in the Talmud is that it is to honor the dead (יְקָרָא דְשָׁכְבֵי); therefore, the *Kohen's* main concern must be to uphold the dignity due his station of leadership. Occupying himself with a corpse would only serve to impede his ability to do so. Only if it is on behalf of a close relative do we consider his involvement as an extension of his own honor and it would therefore be permitted since the prohibition is transcended by the honor given to the *Kohen* himself.

5-6. לֹא יִקְרְחוּ ... וְלֹא יְחַלְּלוּ שֵׁם אֱלֹהֵיהֶם ... — *They shall not make baldness ... and not profane the name of their God.* Since the Torah makes an exception for a *Kohen* in the case of the burial of a relative because he enhances his own honor, one might think that *all* restrictive laws of mourning are waived, including those which prohibit קָרְחָה (tearing out one's hair in grief) and שָׂרֶטֶת (making a cutting in one's flesh); therefore, the Torah must specifically state that it is forbidden to do so. This comment of the *Sforno* also explains the need for reiterating this dual prohibition for the *Kohanim*, inasmuch as the law applies equally to *all* Israel (see *Deut.* 14:1). The Torah then proceeds to explain the reason for this prohibition. Although it may be honorable for the *Kohen* to perform these acts, nonetheless he is forbidden since by doing so he profanes the name of God, who confers this special honor upon the *Kohanim*.

יא אֶת־הַבְּגָדִים אֶת־רֹאשׁוֹ לֹא יִפְרָע וּבְגָדָיו לֹא יִפְרֹם: וְעַל כָּל־נַפְשֹׁת מֵת
יב לֹא יָבֹא לְאָבִיו וּלְאִמּוֹ לֹא יִטַּמָּא: וּמִן־הַמִּקְדָּשׁ לֹא יֵצֵא וְלֹא יְחַלֵּל אֵת
יג מִקְדַּשׁ אֱלֹהָיו כִּי נֵזֶר שֶׁמֶן מִשְׁחַת אֱלֹהָיו עָלָיו אֲנִי יהוה: וְהוּא אִשָּׁה
יד בִבְתוּלֶיהָ יִקָּח: אַלְמָנָה וּגְרוּשָׁה וַחֲלָלָה זֹנָה אֶת־אֵלֶּה לֹא יִקָּח כִּי
טו אִם־בְּתוּלָה מֵעַמָּיו יִקַּח אִשָּׁה: וְלֹא־יְחַלֵּל זַרְעוֹ בְּעַמָּיו כִּי אֲנִי יהוה
שני טז־יז מְקַדְּשׁוֹ: וַיְדַבֵּר יהוה אֶל־מֹשֶׁה לֵּאמֹר: דַּבֵּר אֶל־אַהֲרֹן
לֵאמֹר אִישׁ מִזַּרְעֲךָ לְדֹרֹתָם אֲשֶׁר יִהְיֶה בוֹ מוּם לֹא יִקְרַב לְהַקְרִיב לֶחֶם
יח אֱלֹהָיו: כִּי כָל־אִישׁ אֲשֶׁר־בּוֹ מוּם לֹא יִקְרָב אִישׁ עִוֵּר אוֹ פִסֵּחַ אוֹ חָרֻם אוֹ
יט־כ שָׂרוּעַ: אוֹ אִישׁ אֲשֶׁר־יִהְיֶה בוֹ שֶׁבֶר רָגֶל אוֹ שֶׁבֶר יָד: אוֹ־גִבֵּן אוֹ־דַק אוֹ
כא תְּבַלֻּל בְּעֵינוֹ אוֹ גָרָב אוֹ יַלֶּפֶת אוֹ מְרוֹחַ אָשֶׁךְ: כָּל־אִישׁ אֲשֶׁר־בּוֹ מוּם
מִזֶּרַע אַהֲרֹן הַכֹּהֵן לֹא יִגַּשׁ לְהַקְרִיב אֶת־אִשֵּׁי יהוה מוּם בּוֹ אֵת לֶחֶם
כב אֱלֹהָיו לֹא יִגַּשׁ לְהַקְרִיב: לֶחֶם אֱלֹהָיו מִקָּדְשֵׁי הַקֳּדָשִׁים וּמִן־הַקֳּדָשִׁים
כג יֹאכֵל: אַךְ אֶל־הַפָּרֹכֶת לֹא יָבֹא וְאֶל־הַמִּזְבֵּחַ לֹא יִגַּשׁ כִּי־מוּם בּוֹ וְלֹא
כד יְחַלֵּל אֶת־מִקְדָּשַׁי כִּי אֲנִי יהוה מְקַדְּשָׁם: וַיְדַבֵּר מֹשֶׁה אֶל־אַהֲרֹן וְאֶל־בָּנָיו
וְאֶל־כָּל־בְּנֵי יִשְׂרָאֵל:
כב א־ב וַיְדַבֵּר יהוה אֶל־מֹשֶׁה לֵּאמֹר: דַּבֵּר אֶל־אַהֲרֹן וְאֶל־בָּנָיו וְיִנָּזְרוּ מִקָּדְשֵׁי
בְנֵי־יִשְׂרָאֵל וְלֹא יְחַלְּלוּ אֶת־שֵׁם קָדְשִׁי אֲשֶׁר הֵם מַקְדִּשִׁים לִי אֲנִי יהוה:

---

12. וּמִן הַמִּקְדָּשׁ לֹא יֵצֵא — *He shall not go out of the Sanctuary* ... on behalf of the dead person.

וְלֹא יְחַלֵּל אֵת מִקְדַּשׁ אֱלֹהָיו — *Nor profane the Sanctuary of his God* ... (for) thereby he will demonstrate that he esteems the honor of the dead more than the honor of the Sanctuary and the holy which has been (entrusted) to him.

18. כִּי כָל אִישׁ אֲשֶׁר בּוֹ מוּם לֹא יִקְרָב — *For any man that has a blemish shall not approach* ... to stand to serve in the Name of God, similar to כִּי אֵין לָבוֹא אֶל שַׁעַר הַמֶּלֶךְ בִּלְבוּשׁ שָׂק, *No one may enter the king's gate clothed with sackcloth* (*Esther* 4:2).

אִישׁ עִוֵּר — *A blind man.* These are blemishes from birth, due to a physical deficiency or the imaginative powers (of the parents).

19. שֶׁבֶר רָגֶל — *A broken foot.* These are blemishes which are caused by external happenings (mishaps).

20. אוֹ גִבֵּן — *Or one whose eyebrows overhang his eyes.* These are blemishes which are caused through deficiences in the body's chemical makeup.

NOTES

12. וְלֹא יְחַלֵּל אֵת מִקְדַּשׁ אֱלֹהָיו — *Nor profane the Sanctuary of his God.* The *Kohen Gadol*, in addition to his dignified station as a *Kohen*, is also the guardian of the Sanctuary. As such, he cannot abandon his special charge and defile himself, even on behalf of his father or mother, for the reason given by the *Sforno*.

18-20. אִישׁ עִוֵּר ... שֶׁבֶר רָגֶל ... אוֹ גִבֵּן — *A blind man ... a broken foot ... Or one whose eyebrows overhang his eyes.* The *Sforno* explains that there are three categories of blemishes which disqualify a *Kohen*. The first is congenital, the second category is the result of an accident, while the third relates to physical deformities resulting from illnesses subsequent to birth.

ג אֱמֹ֣ר אֲלֵהֶ֡ם לְדֹרֹ֣תֵיכֶם֩ כָּל־אִ֨ישׁ ׀ אֲשֶׁר־יִקְרַ֜ב מִכָּל־זַרְעֲכֶ֣ם אֶל־הַקֳּדָשִׁים֩
אֲשֶׁ֨ר יַקְדִּ֤ישׁוּ בְנֵי־יִשְׂרָאֵל֙ לַֽיהֹוָ֔ה וְטֻמְאָת֖וֹ עָלָ֑יו וְנִכְרְתָ֞ה הַנֶּ֤פֶשׁ הַהִוא֙

ד מִלְּפָנַ֖י אֲנִ֣י יְהֹוָֽה: אִ֣ישׁ אִ֞ישׁ מִזֶּ֣רַע אַֽהֲרֹ֗ן וְה֤וּא צָר֨וּעַ֙ א֣וֹ זָ֔ב בַּקֳּדָשִׁים֙ לֹ֣א
יֹאכַ֔ל עַ֖ד אֲשֶׁ֣ר יִטְהָ֑ר וְהַנֹּגֵ֨עַ֙ בְּכָל־טְמֵא־נֶ֔פֶשׁ א֣וֹ אִ֔ישׁ אֲשֶׁר־תֵּצֵ֥א מִמֶּ֖נּוּ

ה שִׁכְבַת־זָֽרַע: אוֹ־אִ֗ישׁ אֲשֶׁ֤ר יִגַּע֙ בְּכָל־שֶׁ֔רֶץ אֲשֶׁ֥ר יִטְמָא־ל֖וֹ א֣וֹ בְאָדָם֙

ו אֲשֶׁ֣ר יִטְמָא־ל֔וֹ לְכֹ֖ל טֻמְאָת֑וֹ נֶ֚פֶשׁ אֲשֶׁ֣ר תִּגַּע־בּ֔וֹ וְטָֽמְאָ֖ה עַד־הָעָ֑רֶב וְלֹ֣א

ז יֹאכַל֙ מִן־הַקֳּדָשִׁ֔ים כִּ֥י אִם־רָחַ֛ץ בְּשָׂר֖וֹ בַּמָּ֑יִם: וּבָ֤א הַשֶּׁ֨מֶשׁ֙ וְטָהֵ֔ר וְאַחַר֙

ח יֹאכַ֣ל מִן־הַקֳּדָשִׁ֔ים כִּ֥י לַחְמ֖וֹ הֽוּא: נְבֵלָ֧ה וּטְרֵפָ֛ה לֹ֥א יֹאכַ֖ל לְטָמְאָה־בָ֑הּ

ט אֲנִ֖י יְהֹוָֽה: וְשָֽׁמְר֣וּ אֶת־מִשְׁמַרְתִּ֗י וְלֹֽא־יִשְׂא֤וּ עָלָיו֙ חֵ֔טְא וּמֵ֥תוּ ב֖וֹ כִּ֣י יְחַלְּלֻ֑הוּ

י אֲנִ֥י יְהֹוָ֖ה מְקַדְּשָֽׁם: וְכָל־זָ֖ר לֹא־יֹ֣אכַל קֹ֑דֶשׁ תּוֹשַׁ֥ב כֹּהֵ֛ן וְשָׂכִ֖יר לֹא־יֹ֥אכַל

XXII

2. וְיִנָּֽזְרוּ מִקָּדְשֵׁי בְּנֵי יִשְׂרָאֵל — *That they separate themselves from the holy things of the Children of Israel.* Let them not think that on account of their exalted status, the holy things of the people may be considered as profane (חולין) to them, similar to 'one excommunicated by the disciple need not be treated as such by the teacher' (*Moed Kattan* 16a).

וְלֹא יְחַלְּלוּ אֶת שֵׁם קָדְשִׁי אֲשֶׁר הֵם מַקְדִּשִׁים לִי — *And that they do not profane My holy Name which they sanctify unto Me* ... that they do not profane the name of holiness which Israel sanctified to Me by declaring it holy.

7. כִּי לַחְמוֹ הוּא — *Because it is his bread.* He need not wait for his atonement before eating his bread, as our Sages said, 'When the sun sets, he eats *terumah* (heave offering)' (*Pesachim* 35a).

9. אֲנִי ה' מְקַדְּשָׁם — *I am HASHEM Who sanctify them.* Since Israel sanctified (these holy things) I (also) sanctified them, therefore, it is fitting that those *Kohanim* who profane them be punished.

NOTES

XXII

2. וְיִנָּֽזְרוּ מִקָּדְשֵׁי בְּנֵי יִשְׂרָאֵל וְלֹא יְחַלְּלוּ אֶת שֵׁם קָדְשִׁי ... — *That they separate themselves from the holy things of the Children of Israel and that they do not profane My holy Name* ... The Talmud (*Moed Katan* 16a) differentiates between a ban imposed by a teacher and one imposed by a disciple. In the former case, the ban must be respected by the disciple as well, whereas in the latter case, although the ban is in effect, the teacher is not obligated to honor it. From this *halachah*, we learn that there are degrees of stringency in law which one might mistakenly assume can be likened to degrees of sanctity. Just as the disciple's ban doesn't carry enough authority so as to be binding on his teacher since the teacher is superior to him, so too, the status of holiness

declared by an Israelite over an animal or object should not be binding upon the *Kohen*, since the Israelite is inferior to him. Therefore, the Torah stresses that this analogy is incorrect and the sanctity of all things is binding on the *Kohen* as well. The reason for this is because the act of sanctification by Israel is sanctioned by God Who hallows these things Himself, and therefore must be honored by the *Kohen* as well. See the *Sforno's* commentary on verses 9 and 16. Also see *Rashi* who interprets this verse differently.

7. כִּי לַחְמוֹ הוּא — *Because it is his bread.* The Torah is explaining why the *Kohen* who was *tamei* and immersed himself need only wait until sunset to eat his *terumah*, even though he has not yet brought his offerings. The reason is *because it is his bread* and he depends upon it for his basic sustenance.

יא קֹדֶשׁ: וְכֹהֵן כִּי־יִקְנֶה נֶפֶשׁ קִנְיַן כַּסְפּוֹ הוּא יֹאכַל בּוֹ וִילִיד בֵּיתוֹ הֵם יֹאכְלוּ
יב בְלַחְמוֹ: וּבַת־כֹּהֵן כִּי תִהְיֶה לְאִישׁ זָר הִוא בִּתְרוּמַת הַקֳּדָשִׁים לֹא תֹאכֵל:
יג וּבַת־כֹּהֵן כִּי תִהְיֶה אַלְמָנָה וּגְרוּשָׁה וְזֶרַע אֵין לָהּ וְשָׁבָה אֶל־בֵּית אָבִיהָ
יד כִּנְעוּרֶיהָ מִלֶּחֶם אָבִיהָ תֹּאכֵל וְכָל־זָר לֹא־יֹאכַל בּוֹ: וְאִישׁ כִּי־יֹאכַל קֹדֶשׁ
טו בִּשְׁגָגָה וְיָסַף חֲמִשִׁיתוֹ עָלָיו וְנָתַן לַכֹּהֵן אֶת־הַקֹּדֶשׁ: וְלֹא יְחַלְּלוּ אֶת־קָדְשֵׁי
טז בְּנֵי יִשְׂרָאֵל אֵת אֲשֶׁר־יָרִימוּ לַיהוָה: וְהִשִּׂיאוּ אוֹתָם עֲוֺן אַשְׁמָה בְּאָכְלָם
אֶת־קָדְשֵׁיהֶם כִּי אֲנִי יהוָה מְקַדְּשָׁם:
שלישי יז־יח וַיְדַבֵּר יהוָה אֶל־מֹשֶׁה לֵּאמֹר: דַּבֵּר אֶל־אַהֲרֹן וְאֶל־בָּנָיו וְאֶל כָּל־בְּנֵי
יִשְׂרָאֵל וְאָמַרְתָּ אֲלֵהֶם אִישׁ אִישׁ מִבֵּית יִשְׂרָאֵל וּמִן־הַגֵּר בְּיִשְׂרָאֵל אֲשֶׁר
יַקְרִיב קָרְבָּנוֹ לְכָל־נִדְרֵיהֶם וּלְכָל־נִדְבוֹתָם אֲשֶׁר־יַקְרִיבוּ לַיהוָה לְעֹלָה:

---

16. וְהִשִּׂיאוּ אוֹתָם עֲוֹן אַשְׁמָה — *And so cause them to bear the iniquity of guilt.* They themselves, when they sanctified the holy things, brought about their own guilt at such time that they would trespass and have enjoyment from it — and we do not (apply the principle), הַפֶּה שֶׁאָסַר הוּא הַפֶּה שֶׁהִתִּיר, *The mouth which prohibited is the mouth which (now) permits* (*Demai* 6:11), the reason for this being . . .

כִּי אֲנִי ה׳ מְקַדְּשָׁם — *For I am* HASHEM *Who sanctifies them* . . . since they sanctified this thing, I God likewise sanctified it, and they have no power to rescind its sanctity.

18. אֲשֶׁר יַקְרִיב קָרְבָּנוֹ — *That brings his offering.* After (the Torah) tells us of the *Kohanim* who offer (the sacrifices) and their sanctity, it now speaks of the conditions (regulating) the offerings, saying . . .

לְכָל נִדְרֵיהֶם וּלְכָל נִדְבוֹתָם — *Whether it be any of their vows, or any of their free-will offerings.* Although they are free-will offerings, hence one might think that whatever he contributes, even a blemished animal, is acceptable since that which he gives is not obligatory, as (indeed) some Israelites thought, and the prophet (therefore) had to show them their error, saying, וְכִי תַגִּשׁוּן עִוֵּר לִזְבֹּחַ אֵין רָע וְכִי תַגִּישׁוּ פִּסֵּחַ וְחֹלֶה אֵין רָע הַקְרִיבֵהוּ נָא לְפֶחָתֶךָ, *And if you offer the blind for sacrifice, is it not evil? And if you offer a lame or sick animal, is that not evil? Offer it now to your governor* (*Malachi* 1:8).

NOTES

16. וְהִשִּׂיאוּ אוֹתָם עֲוֹן אַשְׁמָה . . . כִּי אֲנִי ה׳ מְקַדְּשָׁם — *And so cause them to bear the iniquity of guilt . . . for I am* HASHEM *Who sanctifies them.* There is a fundamental principle in *halachah* that one who establishes (creates) an איסור, *prohibition*, is empowered to remove it as well. For example, if a woman declares that she is married and subsequently states that she received a divorce, if there is no other evidence, her testimony is accepted, for 'the mouth which prohibited is the mouth which now permits.' This, however, is not the case regarding הֶקְדֵּשׁ, *sanctifying an object*. Although the one who sanctified transformed a secular object (חולין) into a holy one, nonetheless, that same person is not empowered to declare it חולין once again. The reason is because, as mentioned above (verse 2), God has joined in the act of sanctification, thereby removing the power of the מַקְדִּישׁ (he who sanctified it originally) to change it back to its original status.

18. לְכָל נִדְרֵיהֶם וּלְכָל נִדְבוֹתָם — *Whether it be any of their vows, or any of their free-will offerings.* The *Sforno's* commentary clarifies the verse in *Malachi*. How could any Israelite think that it would be proper to bring a blind or lame animal as an offering to God, as alluded to by the prophet in cautioning them against such a practice? The answer given by

יט־כ לִרְצֹנְכֶם תָּמִים זָכָר בַּבָּקָר בַּכְּשָׂבִים וּבָעִזִּים: כֹּל אֲשֶׁר־בּוֹ מוּם לֹא
כא תַקְרִיבוּ כִּי־לֹא לְרָצוֹן יִהְיֶה לָכֶם: וְאִישׁ כִּי־יַקְרִיב זֶבַח־שְׁלָמִים לַיהוָה
לְפַלֵּא־נֶדֶר אוֹ לִנְדָבָה בַּבָּקָר אוֹ בַצֹּאן תָּמִים יִהְיֶה לְרָצוֹן כָּל־מוּם לֹא
כב יִהְיֶה־בּוֹ: עַוֶּרֶת אוֹ שָׁבוּר אוֹ־חָרוּץ אוֹ־יַבֶּלֶת אוֹ גָרָב אוֹ יַלֶּפֶת
כג לֹא־תַקְרִיבוּ אֵלֶּה לַיהוָה וְאִשֶּׁה לֹא־תִתְּנוּ מֵהֶם עַל־הַמִּזְבֵּחַ לַיהוָה: וְשׁוֹר
כד וָשֶׂה שָׂרוּעַ וְקָלוּט נְדָבָה תַּעֲשֶׂה אֹתוֹ וּלְנֵדֶר לֹא יֵרָצֶה: וּמָעוּךְ וְכָתוּת

---

19. לִרְצֹנְכֶם — *That you may be accepted* ... as an offering which will be acceptable on your behalf, and not for (the purpose of) *repair of the House* (the Sanctuary) (בֶּדֶק הַבַּיִת).

תָּמִים זָכָר — *A male without blemish.* It (the sacrifice) must be perfect (without blemish), for *the Rock, His work is perfect* (*Deut.* 32:4); (therefore) He desires perfection. This (the Torah) explains, saying ...

20. כֹּל אֲשֶׁר בּוֹ מוּם לֹא תַקְרִיבוּ כִּי לֹא לְרָצוֹן יִהְיֶה לָכֶם — *But whatsoever has a blemish you shall not bring, for it shall not be acceptable for you.* This is similar to הֲיִרְצְךָ אוֹ הֲיִשָּׂא פָנֶיךָ, *Will he be pleased with you or will he show you favor* (*Malachi* 1:8). After (the Torah) cautions us regarding a burnt-offering, which is (in the category of) קָדְשֵׁי קָדָשִׁים, *sacrifices of major sanctity,* and which must be a male and without blemish, it is explained that these restrictions are only obligatory regarding cattle and sheep, as our Sages say, 'The law requiring an unblemished male (for a burnt-offering) only applies to animals, not to fowl' (*Kiddushin* 24b). (The Torah now) says ...

21. וְאִישׁ כִּי יַקְרִיב זֶבַח שְׁלָמִים לַה׳ — *And whosoever brings a sacrifice of peace offerings to HASHEM.* (The Torah) states that although these are (in the category of) קָדָשִׁים קַלִּים, *sacrifices of lesser sanctity,* and they do not require a male animal, as explained above when it stated, *whether male or female* (3:1); nonetheless, they may not have a blemish. (The Torah) explains the reason for this by stating, *You shall not offer these to HASHEM* (v. 22), i.e., it is improper to offer a blemished animal to God, the Blessed One. (The Torah) then adds a second reason, saying, *Nor make from them an offering by fire upon the altar to HASHEM* (ibid.), (meaning) if the blemish developed after the owners sanctified it, one is not to offer the אֵימוּרִים, *ordained parts,* on the altar, for it is not fitting that there be a blemish, which is despised by Him, in (any) offering.

23. נְדָבָה תַּעֲשֶׂה אֹתוֹ — *You may make it a free-will offering.* Although these are blemishes which are extremely visible, and one might think that these animals are unsuitable even for *repair of the House* (בֶּדֶק הַבַּיִת), (the Torah) says that they *are* fit for contribution towards בֶּדֶק הַבַּיִת, as tradition teaches us, since the altar has no share in them, and their sanctity is only in terms of their monetary value (קְדוּשַּׁת דָּמִים), i.e., they are to be sold and thereby they become profane (חוּלִּין).

NOTES

the *Sforno* is that since it is a *free-will offering* (נְדָבָה), and not an *obligatory offering* (חוֹבָה), one might think that any animal is acceptable. That is why the prophet concludes, *Offer it now to your governor; will he be pleased?*

19-23. תָּמִים זָכָר ... נְדָבָה תַּעֲשֶׂה אֹתוֹ — *A male without blemish ... You may make it a free-will offering.* A blemish-free animal of the proper sex (a male in the case of a burnt offering) may be brought as an offering on the

כה וְנָתוּק וְכָרוּת לֹא תַקְרִיבוּ לַיהוָה וּבְאַרְצְכֶם לֹא תַעֲשׂוּ: וּמִיַּד בֶּן־נֵכָר לֹא
תַקְרִיבוּ אֶת־לֶחֶם אֱלֹהֵיכֶם מִכָּל־אֵלֶּה כִּי מָשְׁחָתָם בָּהֶם מוּם בָּם לֹא יֵרָצוּ
כו־כז לָכֶם: וַיְדַבֵּר יהוָה אֶל־מֹשֶׁה לֵּאמֹר: שׁוֹר אוֹ־כֶשֶׂב

---

24. וּמָעוּךְ וְכָתוּת — *That which has its stones bruised or crushed.* After telling us of accidental blemishes, which affect only קָדָשִׁים, *sanctified animals,* making them prohibited to be offered on the altar, and of the prohibition to impose any blemish on them after they have been sanctified, (the Torah) now speaks of artificial blemishes which are prohibited to be inflicted even on a profane animal.

25. וּמִיַּד בֶּן נֵכָר לֹא תַקְרִיבוּ — *Neither from the hand of a foreigner shall you offer.* Although we accept vows and free-will offerings from them, we are not (permitted) to accept blemished animals from them, even those castrated which, in their opinion, are better (superior), and hence there is no deficiency of הַקְרִיבֵהוּ נָא לְפֶחָתֶךָ, *Would you offer it to your governor?* (*Malachi* 1:8). Now the reason why a castrated animal is not fit for the altar is 'because their impairment is in them.' Even though it is a concealed blemish, it impairs (lit., corrupts) their intended שְׁלֵימוּת, *completeness,* which is the capacity to reproduce in their likeness.

27. שׁוֹר אוֹ כֶשֶׂב — *A bull or a sheep.* After mentioning the various types of blemishes which invalidate קָדָשִׁים, *sanctified animals,* from being offered on the altar, even though at times the perfect (animal) may be worth a *sela* while the blemished one, because of its size and fat, is worth two; and at times the blemish may even be considered an advantage, as when brought as a gift to a human king; (still, it is invalid as a sacrifice to God) because הַצּוּר תָּמִים פָּעֳלוֹ, *the Rock His work is perfect* (*Deut.* 32:4). He desires the perfection and completeness of the offering and of the one who offers it; the offering must possess its natural completeness and the one who offers it must possess Divine completeness, to be like his Creator as much as it is possible. (Now the Torah) says similarly, regarding the limits of time which God established, that one is not permitted to add or subtract from them. (The Torah) mentions the prohibition of מְחוּסַר זְמַן (sacrificing an animal without waiting the minimum period from birth), the prohibition of slaughtering אוֹתוֹ וְאֶת בְּנוֹ, *it and its young* on the same day and the prohibition against intending to eat the sacrifices חוּץ לִזְמַנּוֹ, *beyond the allotted time,* which includes even קָדָשִׁים קַלִּים, *sacrifices of lesser sanctity.* (The Torah) then mentions the thanksgiving offering, for even though it is included in (the category) of peace offerings, its time limit (for consumption) is only one day and one night, not two days and one night as is true of other peace offerings.

NOTES

altar. One which is blemished, although not qualified to be offered to God on the altar (whether the blemish occurred before or after its sanctification), may, however, be designated as קְדוּשַּׁת דָּמִים, *sanctified for its monetary value.* This is the case even if blemished excessively.

The *Sforno* proceeds to explain the reason for the Torah's insistence upon תְּמִימוּת, *perfection,* in an offering. Since God is perfect, one cannot offer any animal to Him which is less than perfect. This explains the disqualification of a סָרִיס, *an emasculated animal,* whose blemish is concealed but is incapable of fulfilling its primary purpose as a living creature of God, i.e., to reproduce its own kind. As the *Sforno* points out (in these verses and verse 27 as well), the criteria for selecting an offering to be brought to a human king is not the same as that offered to God on the altar in His Sanctuary. The standards and rationale are totally different.

אוֹ־עֵז כִּי יִוָּלֵד וְהָיָה שִׁבְעַת יָמִים תַּחַת אִמּוֹ וּמִיּוֹם הַשְּׁמִינִי וָהָלְאָה
כח יֵרָצֶה לְקָרְבַּן אִשֶּׁה לַיהוָה: וְשׁוֹר אוֹ־שֶׂה אֹתוֹ וְאֶת־בְּנוֹ לֹא תִשְׁחֲטוּ
כט־ל בְּיוֹם אֶחָד: וְכִי־תִזְבְּחוּ זֶבַח־תּוֹדָה לַיהוָה לִרְצֹנְכֶם תִּזְבָּחוּ: בַּיּוֹם הַהוּא
לא יֵאָכֵל לֹא־תוֹתִירוּ מִמֶּנּוּ עַד־בֹּקֶר אֲנִי יהוָה: וּשְׁמַרְתֶּם מִצְוֹתַי וַעֲשִׂיתֶם
לב אֹתָם אֲנִי יהוָה: וְלֹא תְחַלְּלוּ אֶת־שֵׁם קָדְשִׁי וְנִקְדַּשְׁתִּי בְּתוֹךְ בְּנֵי יִשְׂרָאֵל
לג אֲנִי יהוָה מְקַדִּשְׁכֶם: הַמּוֹצִיא אֶתְכֶם מֵאֶרֶץ מִצְרַיִם לִהְיוֹת לָכֶם לֵאלֹהִים
אֲנִי יהוָה:

29-30. לִרְצֹנְכֶם תִּזְבָּחוּ . . . בַּיּוֹם הַהוּא יֵאָכֵל — *You shall sacrifice it, that you may be accepted . . . On the same day it shall be eaten.* It must be your will and intention at the time you bring the sacrifice that it be eaten that day, and this is because . . .

אֲנִי ה׳ — *I am* HASHEM. I perform My deeds with perfection and set a limit to completeness without tolerating anything more or less.

32. וְלֹא תְחַלְּלוּ אֶת שֵׁם קָדְשִׁי — *And you shall not profane My holy Name.* Since you see the completeness of My work, therefore, you who are sanctified to walk in My ways, *do not profane My holy Name* through faulty and disgraceful deeds, similar to, וַיָּבוֹא אֶל הַגּוֹיִם אֲשֶׁר בָּאוּ שָׁם וַיְחַלְּלוּ אֶת שֵׁם קָדְשִׁי, *And when they came to the nations, into which they came, they profaned My holy Name* (*Ezekiel* 36:20).

וְנִקְדַּשְׁתִּי בְּתוֹךְ בְּנֵי יִשְׂרָאֵל — *And I will be sanctified among the Children of Israel . . .* to perform wonders for them as I vowed, saying, הִנֵּה אָנֹכִי כֹּרֵת בְּרִית נֶגֶד כָּל עַמְּךָ אֶעֱשֶׂה נִפְלָאֹת, *Behold I make a covenant, before all your people I will do marvels* (*Exodus* 34:10); the reason for this is (because) indeed — אֲנִי ה׳ מְקַדִּשְׁכֶם, *I am* HASHEM *Who sanctifies you.*

33. הַמּוֹצִיא אֶתְכֶם מֵאֶרֶץ מִצְרַיִם לִהְיוֹת לָכֶם לֵאלֹהִים — *Who brought you out of the land of Egypt to be your God . . .* to lead you without any intermediary, as is the rule with those 'separated from corporeality' (i.e., angels), providing you walk in My holy ways, as it says, אֶל דֶּרֶךְ הַגּוֹיִם אַל תִּלְמָדוּ וּמֵאֹתוֹת הַשָּׁמַיִם אַל תֵּחָתּוּ, *Learn not the way of the nations and be not dismayed at the signs of heaven* (*Jeremiah* 10:2).

אֲנִי ה׳ — *I am* HASHEM . . . (Who is) unchangeable, and I will act towards you as in the past as long as your sins do not create a barrier between you and your God, as it says, כִּימֵי צֵאתְךָ מֵאֶרֶץ מִצְרָיִם אַרְאֶנּוּ נִפְלָאוֹת, *As in the days of your coming out of the land of Egypt I will show him marvelous things* (*Micah* 7:15).

NOTES

27-30. שׁוֹר אוֹ כֶשֶׂב . . . לִרְצֹנְכֶם תִּזְבָּחוּ . . . בַּיּוֹם הַהוּא יֵאָכֵל — *A bull or a sheep . . . you shall sacrifice it, that you may be accepted . . . On the same day it shall be eaten.* The Torah sets time limits regarding sacrifices just as it establishes rules regarding blemishes which disqualify either the *Kohen* who officiates or the animal brought to God. The *Sforno* explains that the time factor regulates the minimum age of the animal (v. 27); the offering of an animal and its young on the same day (v. 28); the intent in the mind of the *Kohen* who brings the קָרְבָּן as to when the sacrifice will be eaten (v. 29), which also explains why the תּוֹדָה, the thanksgiving offering, is singled out; and finally (v. 30) the law of נוֹתָר (the meat of a sacrifice *remaining* past the allotted time).

32-33. וְלֹא תְחַלְּלוּ . . . וְנִקְדַּשְׁתִּי בְּתוֹךְ בְּנֵי יִשְׂרָאֵל — הַמּוֹצִיא אֶתְכֶם מֵאֶרֶץ מִצְרַיִם לִהְיוֹת לָכֶם לֵאלֹהִים — *And you shall not profane . . . and I will be sanctified among the Children of Israel . . . Who brought you out of the land of Egypt to be your God.* The Almighty becomes sanctified in the eyes of mankind when He manifests

כג רביעי א־ב וַיְדַבֵּר יהוה אֶל־מֹשֶׁה לֵּאמֹר: דַּבֵּר אֶל־בְּנֵי יִשְׂרָאֵל וְאָמַרְתָּ אֲלֵהֶם מוֹעֲדֵי
ג יהוה אֲשֶׁר־תִּקְרְאוּ אֹתָם מִקְרָאֵי קֹדֶשׁ אֵלֶּה הֵם מוֹעֲדָי: שֵׁשֶׁת יָמִים

XXIII

2. מוֹעֲדֵי ה׳ אֲשֶׁר תִּקְרְאוּ אֹתָם מִקְרָאֵי קֹדֶשׁ — *The appointed seasons of HASHEM which you shall proclaim to be holy convocations.* After (the Torah) speaks regarding the offerings and those who bring these offerings, the purpose of which is to cause the Divine Presence to dwell in Israel, as it says, עֹלַת תָּמִיד לְדֹרֹתֵיכֶם פֶּתַח אֹהֶל מוֹעֵד לִפְנֵי ה׳ אֲשֶׁר אִוָּעֵד לָכֶם שָׁמָּה, *A continual burnt-offering throughout your generations at the door of the Tent of Meeting before HASHEM, where I will meet with you* (*Exodus* 29:42), it now speaks of the appointed seasons wherein one's intent should be to cease from doing common work, some of which involve a total abstention such as Shabbos and Yom Kippur, and to occupy (oneself) during all of them with Torah and holy concerns, as it says, שֵׁשֶׁת יָמִים תַּעֲבֹד ... וְיוֹם הַשְּׁבִיעִי שַׁבָּת לַה׳ אֱלֹהֶיךָ, *Six days shall you labor ... but the seventh day is a Sabbath to HASHEM your God* (*Exodus* 20:9,10), (when) you shall rest from your work and your occupation shall be totally with God your God. During some (of these festivals), you shall rest only from servile work, as it is true of (all) other appointed seasons.

Now their intent (and purpose) is that, through the rejoicing on the day (itself) when Israel will rejoice with its Maker, (the festival shall be spent) at least partially in (pursuing) holy concerns, as (our Sages) say, '(Divide the) *Yom Tov* — half is for God and half is for you' (*Pesachim* 68b), and in this manner, undoubtedly, the Divine Presence will dwell in Israel, as it states, אֱלֹהִים נִצָּב בַּעֲדַת אֵל, *God stands in the congregation of El* (*God*) (*Psalms* 82:1). (Therefore the Torah) mentions those appointed seasons which you will proclaim as *holy convocations*, meaning a gathering of the people for holy concerns — for a gathering of the people is called מִקְרָא, *an assembly*, similar to חֹדֶשׁ וְשַׁבָּת קְרֹא מִקְרָא, *New Moons, and Sabbaths and the calling of assemblies* (*Isaiah* 1:13), and also, עַל כָּל מְכוֹן הַר צִיּוֹן וְעַל מִקְרָאֶהָ, *Upon every dwelling place of Mt. Zion and upon her assemblies* (ibid. 4:5) ...

אֵלֶּה הֵם מוֹעֲדָי — *These are My appointed seasons.* These are the appointed seasons which I desire. However, when you do not proclaim them as *holy convocations*, but as mundane gatherings devoted to the transitory pleasures of man, then they will not be (considered) מוֹעֲדָי, *'My'* appointed seasons; rather they will be (in the category of) וּמוֹעֲדֵיכֶם שָׂנְאָה נַפְשִׁי, *Your appointed feasts My soul hates* (ibid. 1:14).

NOTES

His power and might on behalf of His people. He did so at the time of the Exodus and has promised to do so in the future as well, providing that Israel is worthy and fulfills its mission to be a holy people. The expression 'separated from corporeality' refers to those who never perish and are everlasting. The *Sforno* in *Genesis* 17:7 explains the special relationship between God and Abraham's descendants, which is a direct one without need for an intermediary, as he explains in this verse as well. See the *Sforno's* commentary there and the notes.

XXIII

2. מוֹעֲדֵי ה׳ ... מִקְרָאֵי קֹדֶשׁ אֵלֶּה הֵם מוֹעֲדָי — *The appointed seasons of HASHEM ... holy convocations, these are My appointed seasons.* The *Sforno* explains the link between the previous chapter, which speaks of offerings, and this chapter which discusses the various festivals. Both represent that which causes God's presence to dwell in the midst of Israel. Although the prohibition of labor on the Sabbath is not identical to that of the festivals, the latter being less stringent insofar as אוֹכֶל נֶפֶשׁ, work

תֵּעָשֶׂה מְלָאכָה֮ וּבַיּוֹם הַשְּׁבִיעִי שַׁבַּת שַׁבָּתוֹן֙ מִקְרָא־קֹדֶשׁ כָּל־מְלָאכָה
לֹא תַעֲשׂוּ שַׁבָּת הִוא֙ לַיהוָה בְּכֹל מוֹשְׁבֹתֵיכֶם׃
ד-ה אֵלֶּה מוֹעֲדֵי יהוה מִקְרָאֵי קֹדֶשׁ אֲשֶׁר־תִּקְרְאוּ אֹתָם בְּמוֹעֲדָם׃ בַּחֹדֶשׁ
ו הָרִאשׁוֹן בְּאַרְבָּעָה עָשָׂר לַחֹדֶשׁ בֵּין הָעַרְבָּיִם פֶּסַח לַיהוָה׃ וּבַחֲמִשָּׁה עָשָׂר

3. שַׁבָּת הוּא לַה׳ בְּכֹל מוֹשְׁבֹתֵיכֶם — *It is a Sabbath to* HASHEM *in all your dwelling places.* He who formed light and created darkness (based on *Isaiah* 45:7) determines (fixes) them (the Sabbaths) for *all your dwelling places,* even though the beginning of the day and the night changes in accordance with the time span (of day and night) in a particular geographical region. Whereas the first Sabbath was measured according to some special singular time span (of day and night), nonetheless, the beginning and end of the Sabbath in each region (is determined) for its inhabitants according to the (local) beginning of the day and the night in that region.

4. אֵלֶּה מוֹעֲדֵי ה׳ — *These are the appointed seasons of* HASHEM. After (the Torah) speaks of the Sabbath whose time is already fixed, as (our Sages) say, 'It is the Sabbath whose time is fixed' (*Pesachim* 117b), (the Torah) now begins the subject of the appointed seasons whose appointed time (is determined) by the proclamation of the court, as we have it from tradition, אַתֶּם אֲפִילוּ שׁוֹגְגִין אַתֶּם אֲפִילוּ מְזִידִין אַתֶּם אֲפִילוּ מוּטְעִין, *By you, even if (you err) unintentionally; by you, even if (you err) with intention; by you, even if you are mistaken* (*Rosh Hashanah* 25a).

5. בֵּין הָעַרְבָּיִם פֶּסַח לַה׳ — *At dusk, is* HASHEM*'s Pesach.* (The Torah) mentions the subject of the *Pesach* (i.e., the sacrifice of the *Pesach* lamb on the 14th day of Nissan) even though that day is not a *holy convocation,* because it is the cause of changes in the times of the appointed seasons. For, indeed, it is (God's intent) that the time of the sacrifice of the *Pesach* (lamb) for all generations shall coincide with the time of the sacrifice when (the original) 'passing over' took place exactly at that midnight. This is the reason that the court is empowered to decide intercalations and

NOTES

connected with food preparation, is concerned, nonetheless, in both cases the cessation of labor is for the purpose of assembling Israel together to occupy themselves with Torah study and holy activities. Only in this manner will these appointed seasons be worthy to be called מוֹעֲדַי, *'My' appointed seasons;* otherwise they are totally man's and rejected by God (See *Rambam, Mishneh Torah, Hilchos Yom Tov* 6:18-20).

3. שַׁבָּת הוּא לַה׳ בְּכֹל מוֹשְׁבֹתֵיכֶם — *It is a Sabbath to* HASHEM *in all your dwelling places.* As the *Sforno* explained in *Genesis* 1:4-5, the terms *day* and *night* as we understand them were not applicable during the six days of creation; therefore, the beginning and end of the first Sabbath were also perforce unique. However, once the laws of nature regulating the spheres and their movements were established, the times of the beginning and end of Shabbos would be determined by local conditions of longitude and latitude. This is the meaning of *'in all your dwelling places.'*

4. אֵלֶּה מוֹעֲדֵי ה׳ — *These are the appointed seasons of* HASHEM. The commentators give various explanations for the repetition of the phrase אֵלֶּה מוֹעֲדֵי ה׳, *these are the appointed seasons,* in this verse, since practically the identical phrase appears in verse 2 (אֵלֶּה הֵם מוֹעֲדָי) The *Sforno* explains it by emphasizing the concluding portion of the verse — *which 'you' shall proclaim.* The Sabbath, which is commanded in the previous verse, is set by heaven, whereas *these appointed seasons* are set by the Sanhedrin (the Supreme Religious Court) who are empowered to determine the day of ראשׁ חֹדֶשׁ, *the New Moon.* See *Rashi's* commentary on this verse.

5. בֵּין הָעַרְבָּיִם פֶּסַח לַה׳ — *At dusk, is* HASHEM*'s Pesach.* The *Sforno* explains why the Torah begins the *parashas Hamoadim* (the chapter

ז יוֹם לַחֹדֶשׁ הַזֶּה חַג הַמַּצּוֹת לַיהוָה שִׁבְעַת יָמִים מַצּוֹת תֹּאכֵלוּ: בַּיּוֹם
הָרִאשׁוֹן מִקְרָא־קֹדֶשׁ יִהְיֶה לָכֶם כָּל־מְלֶאכֶת עֲבֹדָה לֹא תַעֲשׂוּ:
ח וְהִקְרַבְתֶּם אִשֶּׁה לַיהוָה שִׁבְעַת יָמִים בַּיּוֹם הַשְּׁבִיעִי מִקְרָא־קֹדֶשׁ
כָּל־מְלֶאכֶת עֲבֹדָה לֹא תַעֲשׂוּ:

(other) calculations, as explained (by the Torah) saying, שָׁמוֹר אֶת חֹדֶשׁ הָאָבִיב וְעָשִׂיתָ פֶּסַח לַה׳ אֱלֹהֶיךָ כִּי בְּחֹדֶשׁ הָאָבִיב הוֹצִיאֲךָ ה׳ אֱלֹהֶיךָ מִמִּצְרַיִם לָיְלָה, *Observe the month of Aviv and keep the Pesach unto HASHEM your God; for in the month of Aviv, HASHEM your God brought you forth out of Egypt by night* (Deut. 16:1). Tradition dictates that (the court) shall so fix the calendar that the New Moon of *Pesach* shall fall in the *Aviv*.

8. וְהִקְרַבְתֶּם אִשֶּׁה לַה׳ שִׁבְעַת יָמִים — *And you shall bring an offering made by fire to HASHEM for seven days.* (This comes) to tell us that חוֹל הַמּוֹעֵד, *the intermediate days of the festival*, are not completely חוֹל, *profane*, i.e., regular weekdays, for since a communal offering is offered at that time in addition to the daily offering, as on a day of holy assembly, undoubtedly, it is considered part of the festival. (The Torah), however, does not explain here the subject of *Mussafim*, the additional offerings, for that is not its intent presently, just as it does not explain that subject by the other festivals. In a similar manner, (the Torah) writes, *And you shall bring for seven days*, regarding the festival of Succos (verse 36), to indicate the holiness of the intermediate days. As for Rosh Hashanah, אִשֶּׁה לַה׳, *an offering made by fire*, is also mentioned, to teach us that there is an extra מוּסָף besides that of the New Moon, as it says, מִלְּבַד עֹלַת הַחֹדֶשׁ וּמִנְחָתָהּ, *Beside the burnt-offering of the New Moon and the meal-offering thereof* (Numbers 29:6). However, (in the sections of) Shabbos, the festival of Shavuos and Yom Kippur, the subject of *Mussafim* is not mentioned at all, for that which is written regarding Yom Kippur, *And you shall bring an offering made by fire to HASHEM* (v. 27), refers (not to *Mussaf* but) to the burnt-offerings and sin-offerings of the *Kohen Gadol* and of the congregation as explained in *parashas Acharei Mos.*

NOTES

of the festivals) with the *Pesach* lamb sacrificed on the fourteenth day of Nissan (*erev Pesach*), although the fourteenth is not, itself, a *Yom Tov* (festival). Nonetheless, as the *Sforno* points out, it is a pivotal date affecting all the מוֹעֲדִים. Since Israel's is a lunar year, it is inevitable that the festivals will in fall different seasons with the passing of time. To solve this problem, an extra month is inserted seven times in every cycle of nineteen years. The authority to intercalate the year is based on the verse in *Deut.* 16:1 where the Torah commands Israel to observe the festival of *Pesach* in the season when the ears become ripe (*Aviv*). The *Sforno* explains that the reason we are careful to adjust the calendar so as to bring the lunar and solar years into alignment is not only because of seasonal fluctuation but also for the purpose of having the *Pesach* sacrifice offered at a time which coincides with the 'passing over' by God when He punished Egypt with the plague of the first-born, namely on the fourteenth of Nissan. Hence, it is proper to begin this section of the festivals with the *Pesach* sacrifice brought on the fourteenth day of the first month, considering that all calendar calculations are determined by that particular date.

8. וְהִקְרַבְתֶּם אִשֶּׁה לַה׳ שִׁבְעַת יָמִים — *And you shall bring an offering made by fire to HASHEM for seven days.* On a festival, a קָרְבַּן מוּסָף, *additional sacrifice*, is offered besides the קָרְבַּן תָּמִיד, *daily offering*. The laws of *Mussafim* are recorded in the Book of *Numbers, parashas Pinchas*. The *Sforno* states that the only reason this sacrifice is mentioned here in *Emor* is to explain the significance of the intermediate

ט־י וַיְדַבֵּר יְהוָה אֶל־מֹשֶׁה לֵּאמֹר: דַּבֵּר אֶל־בְּנֵי יִשְׂרָאֵל וְאָמַרְתָּ אֲלֵהֶם
כִּי־תָבֹאוּ אֶל־הָאָרֶץ אֲשֶׁר אֲנִי נֹתֵן לָכֶם וּקְצַרְתֶּם אֶת־קְצִירָהּ וַהֲבֵאתֶם
יא אֶת־עֹמֶר רֵאשִׁית קְצִירְכֶם אֶל־הַכֹּהֵן: וְהֵנִיף אֶת־הָעֹמֶר לִפְנֵי יְהוָה
יב לִרְצֹנְכֶם מִמָּחֳרַת הַשַּׁבָּת יְנִיפֶנּוּ הַכֹּהֵן: וַעֲשִׂיתֶם בְּיוֹם הֲנִיפְכֶם אֶת־הָעֹמֶר

(The Torah) introduces Shabbos, the *Pesach* (sacrifice) and the Festival of Matzos (unleavened bread) with one all-inclusive דבור, *statement*, (וַיְדַבֵּר ה׳ — verse 1) because the three of them were commanded prior to the giving of the Torah, but for each of the other *appointed seasons*, (lit.) (the Torah) allocates a separate דבור for each festival (vs. 9,23,26,33).

Now (the Torah) introduces the statement (regarding) the festival of Shavuos with the *Omer* because that is when the harvest of the *Omer* begins, and with the counting of the weeks, both of which relate to the festival that is called *the harvest festival* and the Feast of Weeks, at which time thanks is given to God, the Blessed One, for *the appointed weeks of the harvest which He kept for us* (based on *Jeremiah* 5:24). For indeed, the purpose of the festivals is (to occupy oneself with) prayer and thanksgiving, just as the appointed season of the month of *Aviv* is (for the purpose) of praying to God for the ripening of the ears and to give thanks for our freedom. And being that the success of the harvest depends on the climate of the season from the time of ripening until the harvest, as it says, שְׁבֻעֹת חֻקֹּת קָצִיר יִשְׁמָר לָנוּ, *The appointed weeks of the harvest He keeps for us* (*Jeremiah* 5:24), (therefore) the *Omer* is a thanksgiving for the *Aviv*, as though one is offering the first fruits of the field to the owner. The offering which accompanies it (verses 12,13), serves as a prayer for the future, and the counting is a remembrance of prayer each day, (while) the harvest festival is (an occasion for giving) thanks for the good harvest, (and) the festival of ingathering (Succos) is for the goodness of the ingathering.

NOTES

days of Pesach and Succos. Since each of these days requires a קָרְבָּן מוּסָף, this indicates that they have festival status. There is a different reason for the קָרְבָּן מוּסָף being mentioned in conjunction with Rosh Hashanah. Since Rosh Hashanah is also ראשׁ חֹדֶשׁ, *the New Moon*, it is necessary for the Torah to teach us that, in addition to the regular New Moon sacrifice, an additional offering is brought to mark Rosh Hashanah. As for Yom Kippur, the אִשֶּׁה לַה׳ does not refer to the *Mussaf* offering but to the sin and burnt offerings of the *Kohen Gadol* and of the people, peculiar to that day.

The expression וַיְדַבֵּר ה׳ אֶל מֹשֶׁה, *And* HASHEM *spoke to Moses*, appears as an introductory phrase in verses 1,9,23,26 and 33. Following the first וַיְדַבֵּר, the Torah discusses the Sabbath, the *Pesach* sacrifice and the festival of Pesach. The phrase is then repeated to introduce the festivals of Shavuos, Rosh Hashanah, Yom Kippur and Succos. The *Sforno* explains the grouping of the first three (Sabbath, the *Pesach* sacrifice and Pesach festival) as having in common the fact that they all preceded Sinai; the others, however, were commanded at Sinai and are therefore discussed independently.

The *Omer*, which is a measure equal to a tenth of an *ephah*, was brought on the sixteenth day of Nissan. The festival of Shavuos, or the חַג הַקָּצִיר, the *harvest festival*, is celebrated seven weeks later. The *Sforno* explains why the Torah begins the discussion of Shavuos with the commandments regarding the *Omer*, the animal offering and *Sefirah*, the counting of the weeks. Since the observance of every festival is for the purpose of thanksgiving on the past and prayer for the future, hence the prerequisite for the harvest is the bringing of the *Omer* which is our manner of giving thanks for the *Aviv*, namely the ripening of the barley which is reaped at that time. In the same vein, the animal offering is a prayer for the future while the counting is meant to remind Israel to pray for God's providence daily during these seven critical weeks leading up to the wheat harvest.

יג כֶּבֶשׂ תָּמִים בֶּן־שְׁנָתוֹ לְעֹלָה לַיהוָה: וּמִנְחָתוֹ שְׁנֵי עֶשְׂרֹנִים סֹלֶת בְּלוּלָה
יד בַשֶּׁמֶן אִשֶּׁה לַיהוָה רֵיחַ נִיחֹחַ וְנִסְכֹּה יַיִן רְבִיעִת הַהִין: וְלֶחֶם וְקָלִי וְכַרְמֶל
לֹא תֹאכְלוּ עַד־עֶצֶם הַיּוֹם הַזֶּה עַד הֲבִיאֲכֶם אֶת־קָרְבַּן אֱלֹהֵיכֶם חֻקַּת
טו עוֹלָם לְדֹרֹתֵיכֶם בְּכֹל מֹשְׁבֹתֵיכֶם: וּסְפַרְתֶּם לָכֶם מִמָּחֳרַת
הַשַּׁבָּת מִיּוֹם הֲבִיאֲכֶם אֶת־עֹמֶר הַתְּנוּפָה שֶׁבַע שַׁבָּתוֹת תְּמִימֹת תִּהְיֶינָה:
טז עַד מִמָּחֳרַת הַשַּׁבָּת הַשְּׁבִיעִת תִּסְפְּרוּ חֲמִשִּׁים יוֹם וְהִקְרַבְתֶּם מִנְחָה חֲדָשָׁה
יז לַיהוָה: מִמּוֹשְׁבֹתֵיכֶם תָּבִיאוּ | לֶחֶם תְּנוּפָה שְׁתַּיִם שְׁנֵי עֶשְׂרֹנִים סֹלֶת
יח תִּהְיֶינָה חָמֵץ תֵּאָפֶינָה בִּכּוּרִים לַיהוָה: וְהִקְרַבְתֶּם עַל־הַלֶּחֶם שִׁבְעַת
כְּבָשִׂים תְּמִימִם בְּנֵי שָׁנָה וּפַר בֶּן־בָּקָר אֶחָד וְאֵילִם שְׁנָיִם יִהְיוּ עֹלָה לַיהוָה
יט וּמִנְחָתָם וְנִסְכֵּיהֶם אִשֵּׁה רֵיחַ־נִיחֹחַ לַיהוָה: וַעֲשִׂיתֶם שְׂעִיר־עִזִּים אֶחָד
כ לְחַטָּאת וּשְׁנֵי כְבָשִׂים בְּנֵי שָׁנָה לְזֶבַח שְׁלָמִים: וְהֵנִיף הַכֹּהֵן | אֹתָם עַל לֶחֶם
הַבִּכֻּרִים תְּנוּפָה לִפְנֵי יהוה עַל־שְׁנֵי כְּבָשִׂים קֹדֶשׁ יִהְיוּ לַיהוָה לַכֹּהֵן:

---

14. בְּכֹל מֹשְׁבֹתֵיכֶם — *In all your dwellings.* The prohibition of חָדָשׁ, *new grain*, (is still in effect) until the sixteenth day of Nissan even though the sacrifice (of the *Omer)* and the Temple are no more.

17. חָמֵץ תֵּאָפֶינָה בִּכּוּרִים לַה׳ — *They shall be baked with leaven, as first fruits to* HASHEM. The *Omer* was the first fruit of barley, whereas (these loaves) are the first fruits of the wheat harvest, and for this reason the festival is called יוֹם הַבִּכּוּרִים, *the Day of the first-fruits,* as it says, וּבְיוֹם הַבִּכּוּרִים בְּהַקְרִיבְכֶם מִנְחָה חֲדָשָׁה, *Also in the day of the first-fruits when you bring a new meal offering* (*Numbers* 28:26); and (the Torah) states, לַה׳, *to* HASHEM, because from that time onward, the חָדָשׁ is permitted to be brought as an offering (to God).

Now, being that (these loaves) are the means of giving thanks for *the appointed weeks of the harvest* (*Jeremiah* 5:24) at which time the grain is endangered, (therefore) the two loaves, brought with the he-lambs (offered as) a peace-offering, are leavened, similar to the שַׁלְמֵי תוֹדָה, *thanksgiving peace-offering,* (which is offered) *with loaves of leavened bread* (7:13).

NOTES

14. בְּכֹל מֹשְׁבֹתֵיכֶם — *In all your dwellings.* This phrase appears again in verses 21 and 31. In all three cases, it comes to teach us that certain laws apply even when circumstances have changed. For example, חָדָשׁ, *new grain,* is prohibited until the sixteenth day of Nissan even subsequent to the Temple's destruction when the *Omer* sacrifice could no longer be offered. The second case (v. 21) deals with the *mitzvah* of *Sefiras HaOmer*, the Counting of the *Omer*, and the observance of Shavuos as a *Yom Tov.* Both are operative even when the two loaves cannot be brought to the Temple. The third case is that of Yom Kippur (v. 31). The Torah tells us that work is prohibited on the tenth day of Tishrei even when the service of Yom Kippur cannot be held in the Temple. Hence, the expression *in all your dwellings* teaches us that changing circumstances and locales do not effect these laws, prohibitions and *mitzvos*.

17. חָמֵץ תֵּאָפֶינָה בִּכּוּרִים לַה׳ — *They shall be baked with leaven, as first fruits to* HASHEM. The Torah tells us that כָּל שְׂאֹר וְכָל דְּבַשׁ לֹא תַקְטִירוּ מִמֶּנּוּ אִשֶּׁה לַה׳, *You shall burn no leaven or honey as a smoke offering to* HASHEM (*Leviticus* 2:11). The two loaves brought on Shavuos are an exception to this rule, as is the תּוֹדָה, *thanksgiving offering*, when leavened cakes are brought together with unleavened cakes and wafers (7:12-13). The *Sforno* suggests that the reason leavened bread is offered on this *Yom Tov* is because it is the means by which Israel gives thanks to the Almighty for protecting the grain during the

כא וּקְרָאתֶם בְּעֶצֶם ׀ הַיּוֹם הַזֶּה מִקְרָא־קֹדֶשׁ יִהְיֶה לָכֶם כָּל־מְלֶאכֶת עֲבֹדָה
כב לֹא תַעֲשׂוּ חֻקַּת עוֹלָם בְּכָל־מוֹשְׁבֹתֵיכֶם לְדֹרֹתֵיכֶם׃ וּבְקֻצְרְכֶם אֶת־קְצִיר
אַרְצְכֶם לֹא־תְכַלֶּה פְּאַת שָׂדְךָ בְּקֻצְרֶךָ וְלֶקֶט קְצִירְךָ לֹא תְלַקֵּט לֶעָנִי
וְלַגֵּר תַּעֲזֹב אֹתָם אֲנִי יהוה אֱלֹהֵיכֶם׃
חמישי כג־כד וַיְדַבֵּר יהוה אֶל־מֹשֶׁה לֵּאמֹר׃ דַּבֵּר אֶל־בְּנֵי יִשְׂרָאֵל לֵאמֹר בַּחֹדֶשׁ
הַשְּׁבִיעִי בְּאֶחָד לַחֹדֶשׁ יִהְיֶה לָכֶם שַׁבָּתוֹן זִכְרוֹן תְּרוּעָה מִקְרָא־קֹדֶשׁ׃

---

21. חֻקַּת עוֹלָם בְּכָל מוֹשְׁבֹתֵיכֶם — *A statute forever in all your dwellings.* Although no sacrifices are brought in your dwellings that are in exile (outside *Eretz Yisrael*), the concepts of *Sefirah* (counting) and the (holding of) a holy convocation shall not cease.

22. וּבְקֻצְרְכֶם — *And when you reap.* After giving thanks for the success of the harvest, (the Torah) cautions (us) regarding those commandments which will preserve the wealth attained thereby, i.e., by commanding (us) regarding לֶקֶט, *the gleanings* and פֵּאָה, *the corner* of the field, as (our Sages) say, 'To salt (preserve) wealth, deduct from it; and others say, (do acts of) kindness' (*Kesuvos* 66b).

אֲנִי ה׳ אֱלֹהֵיכֶם — *I am HASHEM your God.* The God of the harvesters and the God of those poor who collect from the gleanings and corners of the field, and I shall be good to those who are good to them, (motivated to) do My will.

24. זִכְרוֹן תְּרוּעָה — *A memorial of a blast of horns.* A memorial of the trumpet-signal for the king (based on *Numbers* 23:21) by which the people rejoice in their king, as it says, הַרְנִינוּ לֵאלֹהִים עוּזֵּנוּ הָרִיעוּ, *Sing aloud to God our strength, make a joyful noise* (הָרִיעוּ) (*Psalms* 81:2). This is (done) because He sits on the throne of justice, as we know from tradition (*Rosh Hashanah* 8b), (and) as it says, תִּקְעוּ בַחֹדֶשׁ שׁוֹפָר בַּכֶּסֶה לְיוֹם חַגֵּנוּ כִּי חֹק לְיִשְׂרָאֵל הוּא מִשְׁפָּט לֵאלֹהֵי יַעֲקֹב, *Blow a shofar at the New Moon, at the full moon of our festival day; for this is a statute for Israel, an ordinance of the God of Jacob* (*Psalms* 81:4,5). It is (therefore) fitting that we rejoice more so at this time when He is our King who will lean towards (being) kindly and judging us favorably, as it says, כִּי ה׳ שֹׁפְטֵנוּ ה׳ מְחֹקְקֵנוּ ה׳ מַלְכֵּנוּ הוּא יוֹשִׁיעֵנוּ, *For HASHEM is our Judge, HASHEM is our Ruler, HASHEM is our King, He will save us* (*Isaiah* 33:22).

NOTES

critical period from Pesach until this time. (See notes on verse 8.)

21. חֻקַּת עוֹלָם בְּכָל מוֹשְׁבֹתֵיכֶם — *A statute forever in all your dwellings.* See note on verse 14.

22. וּבְקֻצְרְכֶם — *And when you reap.* It is difficult to understand why the commandments regarding gifts to the poor are inserted in this section of the festivals, especially since they already appeared in chapter 19:9. While various answers are given by the commentators (see *Rashi*), the *Sforno* offers this explanation. Since the offerings on Shavuos are brought in order to give thanks to God for the blessings of the harvest, the Torah now teaches us how to insure and conserve that blessing. It is through acts of righteousness and kindness and through sharing our bounty with the less fortunate that we can preserve our wealth. As our Sages say in the aphorism cited by the *Sforno*, just as salt preserves food, so do acts of kindness and sharing one's bounty preserve one's possessions.

24. זִכְרוֹן תְּרוּעָה — *A memorial of a blast of horns.* The *Sforno* interprets the word תְּרוּעָה, *blast*, (as in trumpet signal) as indicating the role played by God on the Day of Judgment. This function of God as King is one which causes Israel to rejoice, for He shall surely judge His children with compassion and love.

כה-כו כָּל־מְלֶאכֶת עֲבֹדָה לֹא תַעֲשׂוּ וְהִקְרַבְתֶּם אִשֶּׁה לַיהוָה: וַיְדַבֵּר
כז יְהוָה אֶל־מֹשֶׁה לֵּאמֹר: אַךְ בֶּעָשׂוֹר לַחֹדֶשׁ הַשְּׁבִיעִי הַזֶּה יוֹם הַכִּפֻּרִים
הוּא מִקְרָא־קֹדֶשׁ יִהְיֶה לָכֶם וְעִנִּיתֶם אֶת־נַפְשֹׁתֵיכֶם וְהִקְרַבְתֶּם אִשֶּׁה
כח לַיהוָה: וְכָל־מְלָאכָה לֹא תַעֲשׂוּ בְּעֶצֶם הַיּוֹם הַזֶּה כִּי יוֹם כִּפֻּרִים הוּא לְכַפֵּר
כט עֲלֵיכֶם לִפְנֵי יְהוָה אֱלֹהֵיכֶם: כִּי כָל־הַנֶּפֶשׁ אֲשֶׁר לֹא־תְעֻנֶּה בְּעֶצֶם
ל הַיּוֹם הַזֶּה וְנִכְרְתָה מֵעַמֶּיהָ: וְכָל־הַנֶּפֶשׁ אֲשֶׁר תַּעֲשֶׂה כָּל־מְלָאכָה בְּעֶצֶם
לא הַיּוֹם הַזֶּה וְהַאֲבַדְתִּי אֶת־הַנֶּפֶשׁ הַהִוא מִקֶּרֶב עַמָּהּ: כָּל־מְלָאכָה לֹא

---

27. אַךְ בֶּעָשׂוֹר לַחֹדֶשׁ הַשְּׁבִיעִי — *Nonetheless on the tenth day of the seventh month.* Although on all other holy convocations, it is proper to rejoice and to enjoy food and drink, as it says, אִכְלוּ מַשְׁמַנִּים וּשְׁתוּ מַמְתַקִּים וְשִׁלְחוּ מָנוֹת לְאֵין נָכוֹן לוֹ כִּי קָדוֹשׁ הַיּוֹם לַאֲדֹנֵינוּ, *Eat fat (meat), and drink sweet beverages and send portions to those for whom nothing is prepared, for this day is holy to our Master* (*Nechemiah* 8:10), nonetheless, the tenth day is a day of atonement (wherein one) shall confess and (every) man shall bemoan his sins (based on *Lamentations* 3:39), (therefore) it is not a day of joy and pleasure but a day of affliction, as it says . . .

וְעִנִּיתֶם אֶת נַפְשֹׁתֵיכֶם וְהִקְרַבְתֶּם אִשֶּׁה — *And you shall afflict your souls; and you shall bring an offering made by fire.* This אִשֶּׁה consists of the offerings of the *Kohen Gadol* and the offerings of the congregation, which are brought for atonement.

28. וְכָל מְלָאכָה לֹא תַעֲשׂוּ . . . כִּי יוֹם כִּפֻּרִים הוּא — *And you shall do no manner of work . . . for it is a day of atonement.* Because it is fitting on this day to turn away from other pursuits and to concentrate on attaining forgiveness and atonement, as opposed to, הֵן בְּיוֹם צֹמְכֶם תִּמְצְאוּ חֵפֶץ וְכָל עַצְּבֵיכֶם תִּנְגֹּשׂוּ, *Behold, on the day of your fast you pursue your business and exact all your payments* (*Isaiah* 58:3). Now since most who sin by not afflicting themselves do so only because of their physical appetites, while the majority of those who sin by doing work do so to be provocative; (therefore, the Torah) imposes the punishment of כָּרֵת, *excision,* upon one who does not afflict (his soul) (verse 29) while imposing the punishment of destruction of the soul upon one who works (v. 30).

NOTES

27. אַךְ בֶּעָשׂוֹר לַחֹדֶשׁ הַשְּׁבִיעִי — *Nonetheless on the tenth day of the seventh month.* The word אַךְ lends itself to various interpretations. *Rashi* interprets it in a restrictive sense. The *Ramban* translates it as *surely.* The *Sforno,* however, explains it to mean אַף עַל פִּי, *although,* i.e., although all festivals have the common characteristics of מִשְׁתֶּה וְשִׂמְחָה, *feasting and rejoicing,* Yom Kippur is the exception to this rule since the stress is on confession and affliction. Regarding the *Sforno's* explanation of the אִשֶּׁה לַה׳, *offering made by fire,* see the note on verse 8.

28. וְכָל מְלָאכָה לֹא תַעֲשׂוּ . . . כִּי יוֹם כִּפֻּרִים הוּא — *And you shall do no manner of work . . . for it is a day of atonement.* The *Sforno* explains why the punishment for eating on Yom Kippur is a lesser one than that imposed for working. The former, he submits, is caused by human weakness, i.e., by man's difficulty in controlling his physical cravings. The latter, however, is a case of לְהַכְעִיס, *an intent to anger God.* When one sits idle, his inborn desires do not tempt him to get up and begin working. Thus, one who works on Yom Kippur does so in blatant defiance of God's will. For this

לב תַּעֲשׂוּ חֻקַּת עוֹלָם לְדֹרֹתֵיכֶם בְּכֹל מֹשְׁבֹתֵיכֶם: שַׁבַּת שַׁבָּתוֹן הוּא לָכֶם
וְעִנִּיתֶם אֶת־נַפְשֹׁתֵיכֶם בְּתִשְׁעָה לַחֹדֶשׁ בָּעֶרֶב מֵעֶרֶב עַד־עֶרֶב תִּשְׁבְּתוּ
שַׁבַּתְּכֶם:
ששי לג-לד וַיְדַבֵּר יהוה אֶל־מֹשֶׁה לֵּאמֹר: דַּבֵּר אֶל־בְּנֵי יִשְׂרָאֵל לֵאמֹר בַּחֲמִשָּׁה עָשָׂר
לה יוֹם לַחֹדֶשׁ הַשְּׁבִיעִי הַזֶּה חַג הַסֻּכּוֹת שִׁבְעַת יָמִים לַיהוה: בַּיּוֹם הָרִאשׁוֹן
לו מִקְרָא־קֹדֶשׁ כָּל־מְלֶאכֶת עֲבֹדָה לֹא תַעֲשׂוּ: שִׁבְעַת יָמִים תַּקְרִיבוּ אִשֶּׁה
לַיהוה בַּיּוֹם הַשְּׁמִינִי מִקְרָא־קֹדֶשׁ יִהְיֶה לָכֶם וְהִקְרַבְתֶּם אִשֶּׁה לַיהוה
לז עֲצֶרֶת הִוא כָּל־מְלֶאכֶת עֲבֹדָה לֹא תַעֲשׂוּ: אֵלֶּה מוֹעֲדֵי יהוה

---

31. בְּכֹל מֹשְׁבֹתֵיכֶם — *In all your dwellings.* Although atonement is no longer attained through the altar, it is (still) an obligation of the day, as (indeed) it is, in (our) Exile.

36. עֲצֶרֶת הִוא — *It is a day of solemn assembly* (lit., *restraint*). The concept of עֲצִירָה, *restraint,* is not only in order to rest from ordinary labor, but it is also a warning to spend some time in holy places, serving God, the Blessed One, through Torah or prayer or Divine service, similar to, וְשָׁם אִישׁ מֵעַבְדֵי שָׁאוּל בַּיּוֹם הַהוּא נֶעְצָר לִפְנֵי ה׳, *Now a certain man of the servants of Saul was there that day detained before* HASHEM (*I Samuel* 21:8), and it is also said, קַדְּשׁוּ צוֹם קִרְאוּ עֲצָרָה, *Sanctify a fast, call a solemn assembly* (עֲצָרָה) (*Joel* 1:14), and in this manner Yehu said, קַדְּשׁוּ עֲצָרָה לַבַּעַל, *Sanctify a solemn assembly for the Baal* (*II Kings* 10:20).

(The Torah) therefore says that this day following the festival of Succos, wherein the joy of all the festivals reaches its climax, is to be sanctified as a day of solemn assembly, to remain (i.e., spend time) in the holy places, and that his (Israel's) joy be that of rejoicing with the Torah and good deeds as it says, יִשְׂמַח יִשְׂרָאֵל בְּעֹשָׂיו, *Let Israel rejoice in Him who made him* (*Psalms* 149:2). This is similar to, וַיְהִי כִּי הִקִּיפוּ יְמֵי הַמִּשְׁתֶּה וַיִּשְׁלַח אִיּוֹב וַיְקַדְּשֵׁם וְהִשְׁכִּים בַּבֹּקֶר וְהֶעֱלָה עֹלוֹת מִסְפַּר כֻּלָּם כִּי אָמַר אִיּוֹב אוּלַי חָטְאוּ בָנַי, *And when the days of their feasting were completed, Job sent and sanctified them, and rose up early in the morning and offered burnt offerings according to their complete number, for Job said, 'It may be that my sons have sinned . . .'* (*Job* 1:5), all this due to the previous rejoicing.

Now, being that on the seventh day of Pesach Israel stood together with Moses to sing to God, the Blessed One, as it says, אָז יָשִׁיר מֹשֶׁה וּבְנֵי יִשְׂרָאֵל, *Then sang Moses*

NOTES

rebellion, he is liable to a far harsher punishment.

31. בְּכֹל מֹשְׁבֹתֵיכֶם — *In all your dwellings.* See note on verse 14.

36. עֲצֶרֶת הִוא — *It is a day of solemn assembly.* Three festival days are called עֲצֶרֶת: the seventh day of Pesach, the eighth day of Succos, and Shavuos. The latter is only called as such by our Sages, not by the Torah. The *Sforno* explains the reason for calling these three festivals, עֲצֶרֶת, which implies being detained for the purpose of a solemn assembly. On Shemini Atzeres, Israel gathers to rejoice with the Torah and the performance of good deeds, as a culmination of the week of rejoicing which preceded it, as the *Sforno* explains. On the seventh day of Pesach, Israel joined Moses in singing to God in gratitude for their deliverance from the Egyptians at the Sea of Reeds, and on Shavuos, the people gathered together to receive the Torah. The reason, however, that the Torah itself refrains from calling Shavuos by the name עֲצֶרֶת is because Israel sinned with the Golden Calf and forfeited their special status as מַמְלֶכֶת כֹּהֲנִים וְגוֹי קָדוֹשׁ, a *kingdom of Kohanim and holy nation.* Regarding the seventh day of

אֲשֶׁר־תִּקְרְא֣וּ אֹתָ֔ם מִקְרָאֵ֖י קֹ֑דֶשׁ לְהַקְרִ֨יב אִשֶּׁ֜ה לַֽיהוֹ֗ה עֹלָ֧ה וּמִנְחָ֛ה זֶ֥בַח

לח וּנְסָכִ֖ים דְּבַר־י֣וֹם בְּיוֹמֽוֹ: מִלְּבַ֖ד שַׁבְּתֹ֣ת יְהֹוָ֑ה וּמִלְּבַ֣ד מַתְּנֽוֹתֵיכֶ֗ם וּמִלְּבַ֤ד

לט כָּל־נִדְרֵיכֶם֙ וּמִלְּבַד֙ כָּל־נִדְבֹ֣תֵיכֶ֔ם אֲשֶׁ֥ר תִּתְּנ֖וּ לַֽיהוֹֽה: אַ֡ךְ בַּחֲמִשָּׁה֩ עָשָׂ֨ר

י֜וֹם לַחֹ֣דֶשׁ הַשְּׁבִיעִ֗י בְּאָסְפְּכֶם֙ אֶת־תְּבוּאַ֣ת הָאָ֔רֶץ תָּחֹ֥גּוּ אֶת־חַג־יְהֹוָ֖ה

מ שִׁבְעַ֣ת יָמִ֑ים בַּיּ֤וֹם הָֽרִאשׁוֹן֙ שַׁבָּת֔וֹן וּבַיּ֥וֹם הַשְּׁמִינִ֖י שַׁבָּתֽוֹן: וּלְקַחְתֶּ֨ם לָכֶ֜ם

בַּיּ֣וֹם הָרִאשׁ֗וֹן פְּרִ֨י עֵ֤ץ הָדָר֙ כַּפֹּ֣ת תְּמָרִ֔ים וַעֲנַ֥ף עֵץ־עָבֹ֖ת וְעַרְבֵי־נָ֑חַל

מא וּשְׂמַחְתֶּ֗ם לִפְנֵ֛י יְהֹוָ֥ה אֱלֹֽהֵיכֶ֖ם שִׁבְעַ֥ת יָמִֽים: וְחַגֹּתֶ֤ם אֹתוֹ֙ חַ֣ג לַֽיהֹוָ֔ה

שִׁבְעַ֥ת יָמִ֖ים בַּשָּׁנָ֑ה חֻקַּ֤ת עוֹלָם֙ לְדֹרֹ֣תֵיכֶ֔ם בַּחֹ֥דֶשׁ הַשְּׁבִיעִ֖י תָּחֹ֥גּוּ אֹתֽוֹ:

מב-מג בַּסֻּכֹּ֥ת תֵּשְׁב֖וּ שִׁבְעַ֣ת יָמִ֑ים כָּל־הָֽאֶזְרָח֙ בְּיִשְׂרָאֵ֔ל יֵשְׁב֖וּ בַּסֻּכֹּֽת: לְמַ֙עַן֙

---

and the Children of Israel (Exodus 15:1); therefore, that day was hallowed to be עֲצֶרֶת לַה׳, an assembly to God, even though the salvation did not occur at the beginning of the day (i.e., the preceding night). This is explained in מִשְׁנֵה תוֹרָה (Deuteronomy) where it says, וּבַיּוֹם הַשְּׁבִיעִי עֲצֶרֶת לַה׳ אֱלֹהֶיךָ לֹא תַעֲשֶׂה מְלָאכָה, And on the seventh day shall be a solemn assembly to HASHEM your God; you shall do no work therein (Deut. 16:8).

And since the fiftieth day after the Exodus from Egypt was the day the Torah was given, at which time Israel remained together in the service of God, the Blessed One, (therefore) our Sages of blessed memory called it עֲצֶרֶת (remaining in a certain place) (Pesachim 68b). The Torah, however, does not mention this name (עֲצֶרֶת) at all, because Israel impaired the goal (lit., attainment) of that solemn assembly, and וַיִּתְנַצְּלוּ אֶת עֶדְיָם מֵהַר חוֹרֵב, removed their ornaments from Mt. Horeb (Exodus 33:6).

39. אַךְ בַּחֲמִשָּׁה עָשָׂר יוֹם — However, on the fifteenth day. After (God) mentions the regulations common to all the festivals, namely that all are holy convocations and require an additional offering, as it says, These are the appointed seasons of HASHEM which you shall proclaim to be holy convocations, to bring an offering made by fire (v. 37), He now says, However, on the fifteenth day, etc., telling us that the festival of Succos is distinguished from the other appointed seasons (in a number of ways). The first is in that the eighth day (i.e., the day following Succos) is a holy assembly, as it says, And on the eighth day shall be a solemn rest (v.39) (שַׁבָּתוֹן), as distinct from the days of the week and the days of the Festival of Matzos and the months and years, where the seventh is holy instead of the eighth. Secondly, this festival requires a change of residence (i.e., dwelling in booths) as it says, You shall dwell in booths (v. 42), and thirdly, (there is) the waving of the four species, as it says, And you shall take to yourself on the first day the fruit of goodly trees (v. 40).

NOTES

Pesach, the Sforno points out that although the actual miracle did not occur until morning, as it says in Exodus 14:27, nonetheless, the significance of the observance of this day begins the night before as is true of the Sabbath and all festivals.

39. אַךְ בַּחֲמִשָּׁה עָשָׂר יוֹם — However, on the fifteenth day. The Sforno interprets the word אַךְ in this verse (unlike his translation

of this word in verse 27) as meaning however. The sense of the verse is: The various festivals enumerated above have two things in common; they are holy convocations and require a מוּסָף, additional offering. However, the festival of Succos is different in three ways: in the manner of dwelling, in the added mitzvah of the four species and the designation of the eighth day as a day of solemn assembly.

מג יֵדְעוּ דֹרֹתֵיכֶם כִּי בַסֻּכּוֹת הוֹשַׁבְתִּי אֶת־בְּנֵי יִשְׂרָאֵל בְּהוֹצִיאִי אוֹתָם
מֵאֶרֶץ מִצְרָיִם אֲנִי יהוה אֱלֹהֵיכֶם: וַיְדַבֵּר מֹשֶׁה אֶת־מֹעֲדֵי יהוה אֶל־בְּנֵי
יִשְׂרָאֵל:

כד שביעי א־ב וַיְדַבֵּר יהוה אֶל־מֹשֶׁה לֵּאמֹר: צַו אֶת־בְּנֵי יִשְׂרָאֵל וְיִקְחוּ אֵלֶיךָ שֶׁמֶן זַיִת
ג זָךְ כָּתִית לַמָּאוֹר לְהַעֲלֹת נֵר תָּמִיד: מִחוּץ לְפָרֹכֶת הָעֵדֻת בְּאֹהֶל מוֹעֵד
יַעֲרֹךְ אֹתוֹ אַהֲרֹן מֵעֶרֶב עַד־בֹּקֶר לִפְנֵי יהוה תָּמִיד חֻקַּת עוֹלָם לְדֹרֹתֵיכֶם:
ד עַל הַמְּנֹרָה הַטְּהֹרָה יַעֲרֹךְ אֶת־הַנֵּרוֹת לִפְנֵי יהוה תָּמִיד:

---

43. אֲנִי ה׳ אֱלֹהֵיכֶם — *I am* HASHEM *your God.* He explains that all these (festivals) are for the purpose intended by Him, the Blessed One, i.e., for our benefit because He is our God Who does not remove His watchful eye from us.

XXIV

2. צַו אֶת בְּנֵי יִשְׂרָאֵל וְיִקְחוּ אֵלֶיךָ שֶׁמֶן — *Command the Children of Israel to bring you oil.* After the oil which was contributed at the time of the building of the Sanctuary was depleted, (God) commanded them to bring it for all generations.

3. יַעֲרֹךְ אֹתוֹ אַהֲרֹן — *Shall Aaron arrange.* Though the kindling of the lamps and the burning of the incense of the daily (i.e., continual) sacrifice could be performed by an ordinary *Kohen* in future generations as (our Sages) received (this law) from tradition, nonetheless, Aaron's name is mentioned in conjunction with both acts. (This is) because during all the days (that Israel was in) the wilderness, the status of the Sanctuary on a daily basis was akin to that of Yom Kippur in future generations of which it says, *For I appear in the cloud upon the ark cover* (16:2), and during the period of the wilderness it says, כִּי עֲנַן ה׳ עַל הַמִּשְׁכָּן יוֹמָם וְאֵשׁ תִּהְיֶה לַיְלָה בּוֹ, *For the cloud of* HASHEM *was upon the Sanctuary by day and there was fire therein by night* (*Exodus* 40:38). Therefore, it was fitting for the act of the burning of the incense and the kindling of the lamps, which were performed within (the Holy), to be done by the *Kohen Gadol*, as it was done on Yom Kippur in future generations.

NOTES

XXIV

2. צַו אֶת בְּנֵי יִשְׂרָאֵל וְיִקְחוּ אֵלֶיךָ שֶׁמֶן — *Command the Children of Israel to bring you oil.* The Children of Israel were commanded to bring pure olive oil for the light when the Sanctuary's construction was completed, as recorded in *Exodus* 27:20. *Rashi* explains that the verse in *Exodus* is referring to the eventual issue of this command at some future date, while the *actual* command regarding the lamps appears here. The *Sforno*, however, explains these two verses thus: When the Sanctuary was completed, a certain amount of oil was contributed. At that time, Moses was told that when the original oil would be depleted, he was to command the Children of Israel to bring additional oil. This was necessary to be said by God lest Moses think that the kindling of the menorah was only a *mitzvah* at that time (see the *Sforno* on *Exodus* 27:20). In our verse, the time had come to command Israel to bring new oil since the original supply had been exhausted.

3. יַעֲרֹךְ אֹתוֹ אַהֲרֹן — *Shall Aaron ararnge.* The *Sforno* explains why the Torah specifies Aaron, the *Kohen Gadol*, as being the one to arrange the lamps, since a כֹּהֵן הֶדְיוֹט, *an ordinary priest*, is also qualified to do so. The same question can be asked on the verse in *Exodus* 30:7 regarding the קְטֹרֶת, *burning of the incense*, where Aaron is also specifically mentioned as being in charge. The answer of the *Sforno* is that during the years when Israel was in the wilderness, the daily status of the Sanctuary was equal to its status on Yom Kippur after Israel came into *Eretz Yisrael*, in that the cloud of glory was continuously present. Later, this was only true on Yom

ה וְלָקַחְתָּ סֹלֶת וְאָפִיתָ אֹתָהּ שְׁתֵּים עֶשְׂרֵה חַלּוֹת שְׁנֵי עֶשְׂרֹנִים יִהְיֶה הַחַלָּה
ו הָאֶחָת: וְשַׂמְתָּ אוֹתָם שְׁתַּיִם מַעֲרָכוֹת שֵׁשׁ הַמַּעֲרָכֶת עַל הַשֻּׁלְחָן הַטָּהֹר
ז לִפְנֵי יהוה: וְנָתַתָּ עַל־הַמַּעֲרֶכֶת לְבֹנָה זַכָּה וְהָיְתָה לַלֶּחֶם לְאַזְכָּרָה אִשֶּׁה
ח לַיהוה: בְּיוֹם הַשַּׁבָּת בְּיוֹם הַשַּׁבָּת יַעַרְכֶנּוּ לִפְנֵי יהוה תָּמִיד מֵאֵת
ט בְּנֵי־יִשְׂרָאֵל בְּרִית עוֹלָם: וְהָיְתָה לְאַהֲרֹן וּלְבָנָיו וַאֲכָלֻהוּ בְּמָקוֹם קָדֹשׁ כִּי
י קֹדֶשׁ קָדָשִׁים הוּא לוֹ מֵאִשֵּׁי יהוה חָק־עוֹלָם: וַיֵּצֵא
בֶּן־אִשָּׁה יִשְׂרְאֵלִית וְהוּא בֶּן־אִישׁ מִצְרִי בְּתוֹךְ בְּנֵי יִשְׂרָאֵל וַיִּנָּצוּ בַּמַּחֲנֶה
יא בֶּן הַיִּשְׂרְאֵלִית וְאִישׁ הַיִּשְׂרְאֵלִי: וַיִּקֹּב בֶּן־הָאִשָּׁה הַיִּשְׂרְאֵלִית אֶת־הַשֵּׁם
וַיְקַלֵּל וַיָּבִיאוּ אֹתוֹ אֶל־מֹשֶׁה וְשֵׁם אִמּוֹ שְׁלֹמִית בַּת־דִּבְרִי לְמַטֵּה־דָן:
יב וַיַּנִּיחֻהוּ בַּמִּשְׁמָר לִפְרֹשׁ לָהֶם עַל־פִּי יהוה:
יג־יד וַיְדַבֵּר יהוה אֶל־מֹשֶׁה לֵּאמֹר: הוֹצֵא אֶת־הַמְקַלֵּל אֶל־מִחוּץ לַמַּחֲנֶה
וְסָמְכוּ כָל־הַשֹּׁמְעִים אֶת־יְדֵיהֶם עַל־רֹאשׁוֹ וְרָגְמוּ אֹתוֹ כָּל־הָעֵדָה:
טו וְאֶל־בְּנֵי יִשְׂרָאֵל תְּדַבֵּר לֵאמֹר אִישׁ אִישׁ כִּי־יְקַלֵּל אֱלֹהָיו וְנָשָׂא חֶטְאוֹ:
טז וְנֹקֵב שֵׁם־יהוה מוֹת יוּמָת רָגוֹם יִרְגְּמוּ־בוֹ כָּל־הָעֵדָה כַּגֵּר כָּאֶזְרָח

---

5. וְלָקַחְתָּ סֹלֶת — *And you shall take fine flour.* It seems (to me) that this also was said after the appropriation (of flour) for the showbread, offered at the time of the Sanctuary's completion, was exhausted (lit., completed), as explained in the narrative of וַיָּבִיאוּ אֶת הַמִּשְׁכָּן אֶל מֹשֶׁה, *and they brought the Sanctuary to Moses* (*Exodus* 39:33).

10. וְהוּא בֶּן אִישׁ מִצְרִי — *And he was the son of an Egyptian man* ... and therefore he was impudent and blessed (an euphemism for cursed) 'the Name' (of God), for an Israelite would not be 'that unrestrained (lawless),' (based on *Sanhedrin* 60a).

15. כִּי יְקַלֵּל אֱלֹהָיו — *Whosoever curses his God* . . . and transgresses the prohibition of אֱלֹהִים לֹא תְקַלֵּל, *You shall not curse* (*revile*) *the judges* (*Exodus* 22:27) [אֱלֹהִים meaning *judges*].

וְנָשָׂא חֶטְאוֹ — *Shall bear his sin.* He shall bear a punishment fitting (the status of) the one who curses, and he who is cursed, providing if he does not curse with God's Name, or if he only insults and degrades (the judges), as the *Targum* (*Onkelos*) translates, 'You shall not curse the judges.'

16. וְנֹקֵב שֵׁם ה׳ מוֹת יוּמָת — *And he that blasphemes the Name of* HASHEM *shall surely be put to death.* But the punishment for one who blasphemes the Name of God shall not be the same as for one who curses other אֱלֹהִים, *judges*, nor shall it be from the same category of punishment, even though their number is great (i.e., he cursed many judges); (rather) it shall be the death penalty.

NOTES

Kippur. Hence, these rituals (arranging the lamps and burning the incense) were only performed by the *Kohen Gadol* during their sojourn in the wilderness, for only he was permitted to perform these services on Yom Kippur.

5. וְלָקַחְתָּ סֹלֶת — *And you shall take fine flour.* Compare the *Sforno's* commentary here to his commentary on verse 2 and the notes there.

15-16. כִּי יְקַלֵּל אֱלֹהָיו וְנָשָׂא חֶטְאוֹ: וְנֹקֵב שֵׁם ה׳ מוֹת יוּמָת . . . כַּגֵּר כָּאֶזְרָח — *Whosoever curses his*

יז־יח בְּנָקְבוֹ־שֵׁם יוּמָת: וְאִישׁ כִּי יַכֶּה כָּל־נֶפֶשׁ אָדָם מוֹת יוּמָת: וּמַכֵּה
יט נֶפֶשׁ־בְּהֵמָה יְשַׁלְּמֶנָּה נֶפֶשׁ תַּחַת נָפֶשׁ: וְאִישׁ כִּי־יִתֵּן מוּם בַּעֲמִיתוֹ כַּאֲשֶׁר
כ עָשָׂה כֵּן יֵעָשֶׂה לּוֹ: שֶׁבֶר תַּחַת שֶׁבֶר עַיִן תַּחַת עַיִן שֵׁן תַּחַת שֵׁן כַּאֲשֶׁר
כא יִתֵּן מוּם בָּאָדָם כֵּן יִנָּתֶן בּוֹ: וּמַכֵּה בְהֵמָה יְשַׁלְּמֶנָּה וּמַכֵּה אָדָם יוּמָת:

כַּגֵּר כָּאֶזְרָח — *As well for the stranger as for the homeborn (citizen).* This punishment now being given to this blasphemer is not because he is a stranger (i.e., the son of an Egyptian), for a native (Israelite) would be equal to him in this instance, were he to blaspheme the Name.

17. וְאִישׁ כִּי יַכֶּה כָּל נֶפֶשׁ אָדָם — *And a man that smites any person mortally.* Being that blasphemy among some (heathen) nations is treated most lightly, as it says, וְהִתְקַצַּף וְקִלֵּל בְּמַלְכּוֹ וּבֵאלֹהָיו, *They shall become angry and curse their king and their god* (*Isaiah* 8:21), and as (our Sages) say, 'If one hears God's Name pronounced by a heathen (in a blasphemous manner) he is not obligated to rent his garment, for were (the law) so, one's garment would be totally rent' (*Sanhedrin* 60a), hence, considering this, it would appear that the words of the blasphemer should be considered null and void since every curse is as naught relative to the existence of God, the Blessed One. (The Torah, however,) explains the reason (for the severe punishment exacted) thus: When the 'subject' (really the object) of an evil act varies, even though the act is the same, the punishment (for that act) varies (also) according to the standing of the particular subject so that the punishment for a sin in certain cases will be physical punishment or capital punishment, whereas in other cases where the subject is inferior, the punishment is monetary compensation. (The Torah proceeds) to give three examples (lit., proofs): Firstly, regarding killing; if one murders a man, he receives the death penalty whereas if he kills his friend's animal, he is only liable to monetary payment. Secondly, regarding injury; if one injures (another) person it would have been proper to punish him physically were it not for

NOTES

God shall bear his sin. And he that blasphemes the Name of HASHEM shall surely be put to death ... as well for the stranger as for the homeborn (citizen). The *Sforno* in his commentary on *Genesis* 1:1 explains that the word אֱלֹהִים, at times, means *judges.* He also interprets the phrase אֱלֹהִים לֹא תְקַלֵּל as meaning *you shall not curse the judges* (*Exodus* 22:27). The meaning, therefore, of these two verses is: He who reviles a judge, or even a number of judges, shall be punished in accordance with the laws of damages which cover בֹּשֶׁת (the shaming or embarrassing of another person). The Talmud teaches us that these damages are determined according to the status of both the מְבַיֵּישׁ וּמִתְבַּיֵּישׁ, the one who shames and the one embarrassed (*Bava Kamma* 83b). This is the meaning of the ambiguous term *he shall bear his sin,* for the Torah cannot be exact or precise in this kind of case. However, if one blasphemes God, who is (also) called אֱלֹהִים (God), his punishment is far more severe. He shall be put to death, whether he is a native Israelite or a proselyte.

17. וְאִישׁ כִּי יַכֶּה כָּל נֶפֶשׁ אָדָם — *And a man that smites any person mortally.* The *Sforno* explains the linkage and continuity of verses 15-21 which, at first reading, is most difficult to comprehend. What connection is there between the laws of murder and damages with cursing and blasphemy? The *Sforno,* however, explains the meaning of these verses as follows: Although the heathens treated blasphemy most lightly, the Torah demands the death penalty for this grave sin. This is not because a man's curse in any way diminishes God's honor, but since the object of his blasphemy is God, this sinful act is extremely serious and is therefore punishable by death. The Torah then proceeds to show how a similar injurious act calls for the imposition of different degrees of punishment, depending upon the one towards whom that action is

כב־כג מִשְׁפַּט אֶחָד יִהְיֶה לָכֶם כַּגֵּר כָּאֶזְרָח יִהְיֶה כִּי אֲנִי יהוה אֱלֹהֵיכֶם: וַיְדַבֵּר
מֹשֶׁה אֶל־בְּנֵי יִשְׂרָאֵל וַיּוֹצִיאוּ אֶת־הַמְקַלֵּל אֶל־מִחוּץ לַמַּחֲנֶה וַיִּרְגְּמוּ אֹתוֹ
אָבֶן וּבְנֵי־יִשְׂרָאֵל עָשׂוּ כַּאֲשֶׁר צִוָּה יהוה אֶת־מֹשֶׁה:

---

our inability to measure precisely (the degree of punishment), as our Sages learn from tradition (*Bava Kamma* 84a); therefore, it is necessary to (substitute) monetary punishment. The payment, however, is considerable since one is obligated to pay five items (damages, suffering, medical costs, forced unemployment and shame), as (our Sages) learned from tradition. (However,) if one injures an animal, minimal monetary payment shall be his punishment. The third (proof) is in the case of inflicting injury on a person. If one injures his father or his mother, he is liable to capital punishment, whereas when one injures another man he is obligated to compensate (him) monetarily, and certainly if one inflicts injury on an animal, his punishment is quite minimal. (The Torah) does not mention the cursing of a father or mother because it is dissimilar to this curse (blasphemy) which is a totally ineffective statement, unlike the cursing of (one's) father.

22. כַּגֵּר כָּאֶזְרָח יִהְיֶה — *As well for the stranger as for the homeborn it shall be . . .* because *I am HASHEM your God*, the God of the stranger and the God of the citizen (as it says), וְלֹא נִכַּר שׁוֹעַ לִפְנֵי דָל, *Nor regards the rich more than the poor* (*Job* 34:19).

23. וּבְנֵי יִשְׂרָאֵל עָשׂוּ כַּאֲשֶׁר צִוָּה ה׳ אֶת מֹשֶׁה — *And the Children of Israel did as HASHEM commanded Moses.* They did not stone him due to hatred because he was a stranger who quarreled with a citizen, but they did so to fulfill the commandment (of God).

NOTES

directed. For example, whether one kills a man or an animal, the means (i.e., the act of violence) and the end are the same, but a different punishment is imposed in each case, as is true when one injures a man as opposed to an animal. Parenthetically, the *Sforno* explains that the *lex talionis* (an eye for an eye, etc.) was interpreted by our Sages as meaning monetary compensation because it would be impossible to inflict *exactly* the same degree of physical damage upon the perpetrator as that suffered by the victim, and the consequences could also be far different, depending upon the person's physical condition. The *Sforno* also explains why cursing one's parent is omitted here. It is precisely because these verses speak of blasphemy regarding God, that the Torah does not choose to discuss the cursing of one's parents, so as to differentiate between the two.

22. כַּגֵּר כָּאֶזְרָח יִהְיֶה — *As well for the stranger as for the homeborn it shall be . . .* Although the nature of the punishment varies with different sinful acts, the law itself applies equally to the citizen and the stranger.

23. וּבְנֵי יִשְׂרָאֵל עָשׂוּ כַּאֲשֶׁר צִוָּה ה׳ אֶת מֹשֶׁה — *And the Children of Israel did as HASHEM commanded Moses.* The Torah stresses the motivation of the people when they executed the sinner. It was not inspired by hatred but by a desire to carry out the law.

פרשת בהר
Parasbas Behar

כה א־ב וַיְדַבֵּ֤ר יהוה֙ אֶל־מֹשֶׁ֔ה בְּהַ֥ר סִינַ֖י לֵאמֹֽר׃ דַּבֵּ֞ר אֶל־בְּנֵ֤י יִשְׂרָאֵל֙ וְאָמַרְתָּ֣
אֲלֵהֶ֔ם כִּ֤י תָבֹ֙אוּ֙ אֶל־הָאָ֔רֶץ אֲשֶׁ֥ר אֲנִ֖י נֹתֵ֣ן לָכֶ֑ם וְשָׁבְתָ֣ה הָאָ֔רֶץ

XXV

1. וַיְדַבֵּר ה׳ אֶל מֹשֶׁה בְּהַר סִינַי — *And* HASHEM *spoke to Moses on Mount Sinai.*
Consider that the Torah does not mention the place where any commandment was
given unless something unique (lit., new) occurred at that place. However, (here the
verse) explains that when God, the Exalted One, said at Sinai, וְהַשְּׁבִיעִת תִּשְׁמְטֶנָּה
וּנְטַשְׁתָּהּ וְאָכְלוּ אֶבְיֹנֵי עַמֶּךָ וְיִתְרָם וכו׳, *But the seventh year you shall let it rest and lie
fallow, that the poor of your people may eat; and what they leave,* etc. (*Exodus*
23:11), He explained to Moses all the laws of the Seventh Year which were set forth
(lit., said) here. This is to teach (us) and to make us understand that likewise, with all
other *mitzvos,* although there is little written regarding some of them, the
explanation (however) is broad and well explained, as our Sages say, 'What
connection is there between the *Shemittah* (Sabbatical year) and Mt. Sinai? (It comes
to teach us) that just as (this law of) *Shemittah* was told to us at Sinai with its
general rules, minute details and explanations, so all the commandments were told
(to us) at Sinai with their general rules, minute details and explanations' (*Sifra*).

Now, Moses our Teacher mentions this chapter here because he thought that they
would immediately enter the Land, as he stated (lit., testified) saying, נֹסְעִים אֲנַחְנוּ אֶל
הַמָּקוֹם, *We are journeying to the place* (*Numbers* 10:29). He (therefore) is
particularly careful to emphasize the resting of the Land, for if they were to
transgress in the matter of this observance they would be exiled from it, as the
(Torah) testifies, saying, *Then shall the land appease* (the wrath of God) *for the
neglect of her Sabbaths* (*Leviticus* 26:34), and so it is (also) testified to at the end of
Chronicles, where it says, עַד רָצְתָה הָאָרֶץ אֶת שַׁבְּתוֹתֶיהָ, *Until the Land had been
appeased (paid) for her Sabbaths* (II *Chronicles* 36:21).

2. כִּי תָבֹאוּ אֶל הָאָרֶץ — *When you come into the land . . .* to גְּלִיל הַגּוֹיִם, *the district of
nations* (based on *Isaiah* 8:23).

וְשָׁבְתָה הָאָרֶץ — *And the land shall rest . . .* those lands which are prepared for
agricultural work.

NOTES

XXV

1. וַיְדַבֵּר ה׳ אֶל מֹשֶׁה בְּהַר סִינַי — *And*
HASHEM *spoke to Moses on Mount Sinai.*
Similar to *Rashi* in his commentary on this
verse based upon the *Sifra,* the *Sforno* explains
why the Torah specifies the location where
God spoke to Moses. תּוֹרָה שֶׁבִּכְתָב, the *Written
Torah,* is presented in somewhat of a short-
hand fashion. It is the תּוֹרָה שֶׁבְּעַל פֶּה, the *Orul
Torah,* which elaborates upon the *Written
Torah,* filling in the missing pieces, so to
speak, of what is implied in its brief, succinct
words. Hence, what was done regarding the
detailed laws of the Sabbatical year is true of
all other commandments as well.

The *Sforno* adds an additional point beyond

that which was mentioned in *Rashi's* commentary. He states that the reason Moses
placed this chapter toward the end of *Leviticus,* which is the concluding section that
discusses the commandments given to Moses
at Mt. Sinai (see 27:34), is because he believed
that Israel was on the threshold of entering the
Land. Moses understood that the way in
which to insure their continued stay in *Eretz
Yisrael* was to observe the laws of the
Sabbatical year, as is indicated in the verses in
Leviticus and *Chronicles* quoted by the *Sforno.*

2. כִּי תָבֹאוּ אֶל הָאָרֶץ — *When you come into
the land.* The area mentioned by the *Sforno*
refers to the land first conquered by the
Israelites after crossing the Jordan River. The

ג שַׁבָּת לַיהוָה: שֵׁשׁ שָׁנִים תִּזְרַע שָׂדֶךָ וְשֵׁשׁ שָׁנִים תִּזְמֹר כַּרְמֶךָ וְאָסַפְתָּ
ד אֶת־תְּבוּאָתָהּ: וּבַשָּׁנָה הַשְּׁבִיעִת שַׁבַּת שַׁבָּתוֹן יִהְיֶה לָאָרֶץ שַׁבָּת לַיהוָה
ה שָׂדְךָ לֹא תִזְרָע וְכַרְמְךָ לֹא תִזְמֹר: אֵת סְפִיחַ קְצִירְךָ לֹא תִקְצוֹר
ו וְאֶת־עִנְּבֵי נְזִירֶךָ לֹא תִבְצֹר שְׁנַת שַׁבָּתוֹן יִהְיֶה לָאָרֶץ: וְהָיְתָה
שַׁבַּת הָאָרֶץ לָכֶם לְאָכְלָה לְךָ וּלְעַבְדְּךָ וְלַאֲמָתֶךָ וְלִשְׂכִירְךָ וּלְתוֹשָׁבְךָ
ז הַגָּרִים עִמָּךְ: וְלִבְהֶמְתְּךָ וְלַחַיָּה אֲשֶׁר בְּאַרְצֶךָ תִּהְיֶה כָל־תְּבוּאָתָהּ
ח לֶאֱכֹל: וְסָפַרְתָּ לְךָ שֶׁבַע שַׁבְּתֹת שָׁנִים שֶׁבַע שָׁנִים
שֶׁבַע פְּעָמִים וְהָיוּ לְךָ יְמֵי שֶׁבַע שַׁבְּתֹת הַשָּׁנִים תֵּשַׁע וְאַרְבָּעִים שָׁנָה:

שַׁבָּת לַה׳ — *A Sabbath to* H*ASHEM*. The entire year, which shall be devoid of agricultural work, will (instead) be one devoted to His service, as was the intent of the Sabbath of *Bereishis* (*Genesis*) as it says, שַׁבָּת לַה׳ אֱלֹהֶיךָ, *A Sabbath to* H*ASHEM your God* (*Exodus* 20:10).

3. שֵׁשׁ שָׁנִים תִּזְרַע שָׂדֶךָ — *Six years shall you sow your field*. You will then be able to plant the same field for six consecutive years, unlike the usual practice of agricultural labor which is to allow (a field) to lie fallow one year and plant it the next year, as mentioned by our Sages (*Bava Basra* 36b).

וְאָסַפְתָּ אֶת תְּבוּאָתָהּ — *And gather in its produce . . .* unlike the usual tendency of agricultural labor whereby if the same portion (field) is planted in consecutive years it loses its productivity (lit., no longer gives of its strength).

4. שַׁבַּת שַׁבָּתוֹן יִהְיֶה לָאָרֶץ — *A Sabbath of Sabbaths shall it be to the Land . . .* including, as well, all agricultural preparations such as besmearing the saplings, and smearing (with oil) and piercing unripe figs and other fruits, as mentioned by our Sages (*Avodah Zarah* 50b).

שַׁבָּת לַה׳ — *A Sabbath to* H*ASHEM*. Landworkers, who will rest during that year, will also be awakened (aroused) to seek God in some manner.

8. וְהָיוּ לְךָ יְמֵי שֶׁבַע שַׁבְּתֹת הַשָּׁנִים — *And there shall be to you the days of seven Sabbaths of years.* For (determining) the Jubilee, you shall not count years

NOTES

land on the east bank of the river (עֵבֶר הַיַּרְדֵּן — *Trans-Jordan*) is only Rabbinically obligated to observe the laws of the Sabbatical year and not by Torah law (see *Rambam, Mishneh Torah, Shemittah VeYovel* 4:28). The phrase הָאָרֶץ, *'the' land*, using the definite article, comes to teach this law.

שַׁבָּת לַה׳ — *A Sabbath to* H*ASHEM*. The expression שַׁבָּת לַה׳ is used here, and again in verse 4. Here it is a general statement teaching us that the Sabbatical year is meant to be utilized to seek out and serve God, similar to the purpose of the weekly Sabbath. In verse 4, it is repeated to emphasize that even the simple land laborer whose Torah knowledge is minimal will also be afforded the opportunity to seek God on his own simple level.

3. שֵׁשׁ שָׁנִים תִּזְרַע שָׂדֶךָ — *Six years shall you sow your field*. The Torah assures Israel that if the laws of *Shemittah* are kept, the fields will not lose their productivity even though they will be sown for six consecutive years rather than alternately, as was common agricultural practice.

4. שַׁבַּת שַׁבָּתוֹן — *A Sabbath of Sabbaths*. The expression שַׁבַּת שַׁבָּתוֹן, which is translated a *Sabbath of Sabbaths* or *a Sabbath of solemn rest*, is used here to indicate *absolute* rest, i.e., cessation of all agricultural work and commercial use of the produce yielded by the fields.

8. וְהָיוּ לְךָ יְמֵי שֶׁבַע שַׁבְּתֹת הַשָּׁנִים — *And there shall be to you the days of seven Sabbaths of years*. The word *year* and *years* is repeated four times in this verse. This is meant to teach

ט וְהַעֲבַרְתָּ שׁוֹפַר תְּרוּעָה בַּחֹדֶשׁ הַשְּׁבִעִי בֶּעָשׂוֹר לַחֹדֶשׁ בְּיוֹם הַכִּפֻּרִים
י תַּעֲבִירוּ שׁוֹפָר בְּכָל־אַרְצְכֶם: וְקִדַּשְׁתֶּם אֵת שְׁנַת הַחֲמִשִּׁים שָׁנָה וּקְרָאתֶם
דְּרוֹר בָּאָרֶץ לְכָל־יֹשְׁבֶיהָ יוֹבֵל הִוא תִּהְיֶה לָכֶם וְשַׁבְתֶּם אִישׁ אֶל־אֲחֻזָּתוֹ
יא וְאִישׁ אֶל־מִשְׁפַּחְתּוֹ תָּשֻׁבוּ: יוֹבֵל הִוא שְׁנַת הַחֲמִשִּׁים שָׁנָה תִּהְיֶה לָכֶם לֹא
יב תִזְרָעוּ וְלֹא תִקְצְרוּ אֶת־סְפִיחֶיהָ וְלֹא תִבְצְרוּ אֶת־נְזִרֶיהָ: כִּי יוֹבֵל הִוא
יג קֹדֶשׁ תִּהְיֶה לָכֶם מִן־הַשָּׂדֶה תֹּאכְלוּ אֶת־תְּבוּאָתָהּ: בִּשְׁנַת הַיּוֹבֵל הַזֹּאת

---

according to the calculation of twelve lunar months per year, but rather include the regular as well as the intercalated (months) as ordained by the Sages, so that it (may) correspond to forty-nine solar years, as this undoubtedly is (also how we determine) the Sabbatical year which is linked to ploughing and sowing, as explained in (the portion of the Torah) pertaining to it.

9. שׁוֹפַר תְּרוּעָה — *The blast of the shofar* . . . (as a sign) of joy for the emancipation of the slaves and the return of fields to their (original) owners.

10. יוֹבֵל הִוא תִּהְיֶה לָכֶם — *It shall be a Jubilee to you.* You shall also be free from the servitude of the nations, as opposed to אַתֶּם לֹא שְׁמַעְתֶּם אֵלַי לִקְרֹא דְרוֹר אִישׁ לְאָחִיו וְאִישׁ לְרֵעֵהוּ הִנְנִי קֹרֵא לָכֶם דְּרוֹר נְאֻם ה׳ אֶל הַחֶרֶב אֶל הַדֶּבֶר וְאֶל הָרָעָב, '*You have not hearkened to Me to proclaim liberty every man to his brother and every man to his neighbor; behold, I proclaim for you liberty,' says God, 'to the sword, to the pestilence and to the famine'* (*Jeremiah* 34:17).

11. יוֹבֵל הִוא שְׁנַת הַחֲמִשִּׁים שָׁנָה תִּהְיֶה לָכֶם — *A Jubilee shall the fiftieth year be to you.* Just as the land was liberated from the hands of the buyer, so shall it not be controlled by the returning owners, i.e., they shall not make use of it during that year in the (usual) manner of owners.

12. קֹדֶשׁ תִּהְיֶה לָכֶם מִן הַשָּׂדֶה תֹּאכְלוּ — *It shall be holy to you; you shall eat from the field.* Although I have prohibited the owners to use the (field) for sowing and reaping as well as for the gathering of (its) fruit which is done in other years, as it

NOTES

us that only after forty-nine complete years of solar months, and not twelve lunar months, shall the fiftieth year mark the Jubilee. The seven cycles of seven years must reflect the seasons of planting and harvesting; hence they are determined by the solar calendar, not the lunar one. The extra months of the intercalated years must therefore be included in the calculations.

10. יוֹבֵל הִוא תִּהְיֶה לָכֶם — *It shall be a Jubilee to you.* This phrase seems to be superfluous. The proclamation of liberty has been mentioned; the return of each man to his possession and to his family is also specifically noted. Hence, what is the meaning of this phrase? The *Sforno*, quoting from *Jeremiah*, explains that it refers to the national independence of Israel who will be free from onslaught of war and the ravages of famine and pestilence.

11. יוֹבֵל הִוא שְׁנַת הַחֲמִשִּׁים שָׁנָה תִּהְיֶה לָכֶם — *A Jubilee shall the fiftieth year be to you.* The *Sforno* explains why the phrase, . . . **יוֹבֵל הִוא לָכֶם**, *It shall be a Jubilee . . . to you*, which appears in the previous verse as well, is not superfluous or repetitious. The land which was liberated from the purchaser and returned to the original owner shall also be liberated from *his* mastery and control. Thus, the *Sforno's* interpretation is buttressed by the concluding portion of this verse, *you shall not sow, neither reap . . . nor gather, etc.* Consequently there are two consecutive rest years, the forty-ninth, which is *Shemittah* and the fiftieth, which is the Jubilee.

12. קֹדֶשׁ תִּהְיֶה לָכֶם מִן הַשָּׂדֶה תֹּאכְלוּ — *It shall be holy to you; you shall eat from the field.* The *Sforno* interprets this verse to mean: although the produce of this year has a status of

שני יד תָּשֻׁבוּ אִישׁ אֶל־אֲחֻזָּתוֹ: וְכִי־תִמְכְּרוּ מִמְכָּר לַעֲמִיתֶךָ אוֹ קָנֹה מִיַּד עֲמִיתֶךָ
טו אַל־תּוֹנוּ אִישׁ אֶת־אָחִיו: בְּמִסְפַּר שָׁנִים אַחַר הַיּוֹבֵל תִּקְנֶה מֵאֵת עֲמִיתֶךָ

---

says, *Neither reap that which grows of itself nor gather the grapes* (v. 11); (nonetheless,) I did not prohibit the eating of the fruit by the owners. They are permitted to partake like everyone else, just as in the Sabbatical year.

13. תָּשֻׁבוּ אִישׁ אֶל אֲחֻזָּתוֹ — *Every man shall return to his possession.* The returning owner is permitted to take possession of (the land) and use it to build houses, dovecotes, sheep enclosures and other (structures), but not for agricultural work (of the field) and guarding its fruit.

14. וְכִי תִמְכְּרוּ — *And if you sell.* There shall be no kind of deceit in any transaction (lit., sale), as (our Sages) state, 'One must not pick out the refuse from the top of the bin, because its only purpose is to deceive the eye' (*Bava Metzia* 60a).

אוֹ קָנֹה — *Or buy* . . . when the seller is not aware of the value of the article, even though it was in his possession (lit., hand) and he had time to show it to a merchant or his relative.

אַל תּוֹנוּ — *Do not deceive.* Although (our Sages) taught us that deceit does not apply to land (*Kesubos* 99b), nonetheless . . .

15. בְּמִסְפַּר שָׁנִים . . . תִּקְנֶה — *According to the number of the years . . . you shall buy.* There must not be any deceit regarding the number of the years (till the Jubilee), as (our Sages) say, 'Any (fraud) in measure, weight or number, even if less than the standard of אוֹנָאָה, *deceit*, one can withdraw' (*Bava Metzia* 56b).

אַחַר הַיּוֹבֵל תִּקְנֶה — *After the Jubilee you shall buy.* For it is improper to buy land during the Jubilee year in a manner which will, at times, result in depriving the returning owners any time (to possess it), and hence it will be as though they never returned to their possession at all.

NOTES

'holiness,' nonetheless, it may be eaten by the owners, and others as well.

13. תָּשֻׁבוּ אִישׁ אֶל אֲחֻזָּתוֹ — *Every man shall return to his possession.* Since, as explained in verse 11, the original owner is not permitted to use the land for agricultural purposes during the Jubilee year, then in what way does he *return to his possession?* The answer given by the *Sforno* is that he will *return to his possession* in the sense that he will be able to build various types of structures there.

14. וְכִי תִמְכְּרוּ . . . אוֹ קָנֹה . . . אַל תּוֹנוּ — *And if you sell . . . or buy . . . do not deceive.* The law cited by the *Sforno* from *Bava Metzia* 60a prohibits the seller to pick out the refuse from the top of the bin and mix it in with the grain beneath, for this is patently deceptive. By the same token, the Torah cautions the buyer not to take unfair advantage of the seller's lack of knowledge regarding the true value of the article he is selling.

15. בְּמִסְפַּר שָׁנִים . . . תִּקְנֶה — *According to the number of the years . . . you shall buy.* The *Sforno* links this verse with the preceding one. At the conclusion of verse 14, he comments that although the law of אוֹנָאָה, *overreaching,* does not apply to fields or land (קַרְקַע), nonetheless, the Torah admonishes one, upon establishing the sale price of his field, to take into consideration the amount of years left till the Jubilee. The reason, he explains, is because we are dealing with the amount of time that the buyer can enjoy the use of the field, and that which is numbered or measured (דָּבָר שֶׁבְּמִנְיָן וּבְמִדָּה) is, without exception, covered by the law of אוֹנָאָה, *overreaching.* Therefore, if the buyer is unaware of the number of years until the Jubilee, this knowledge must be shared with him.

אַחַר הַיּוֹבֵל תִּקְנֶה — *After the Jubilee you shall buy.* Were the Torah merely telling us here to set a fair price for the field by calculating the

טז בְּמִסְפַּר שְׁנֵי־תְבוּאֹת יִמְכָּר־לָךְ: לְפִי ׀ רֹב הַשָּׁנִים תַּרְבֶּה מִקְנָתוֹ וּלְפִי
יז מְעֹט הַשָּׁנִים תַּמְעִיט מִקְנָתוֹ כִּי מִסְפַּר תְּבוּאֹת הוּא מֹכֵר לָךְ: וְלֹא תוֹנוּ
יח אִישׁ אֶת־עֲמִיתוֹ וְיָרֵאתָ מֵאֱלֹהֶיךָ כִּי אֲנִי יהוה אֱלֹהֵיכֶם: וַעֲשִׂיתֶם
אֶת־חֻקֹּתַי וְאֶת־מִשְׁפָּטַי תִּשְׁמְרוּ וַעֲשִׂיתֶם אֹתָם וִישַׁבְתֶּם עַל־הָאָרֶץ

שְׁנֵי תְבוּאֹת — *Years of the crops* . . . but not years of blast or drought, as is the case (lit., law) with leasing or tenancy (of land).

16. תַּרְבֶּה מִקְנָתוֹ — *You shall increase the price thereof.* You shall buy it for a higher (price) than one would pay for leasing it on a yearly basis, because, indeed, when one buys it many years prior to the Jubilee, during that time he can construct there sheep enclosures, dovecotes and similar (structures), besides (using its) produce.

תַּמְעִיט מִקְנָתוֹ — *You shall diminish its price.* You shall not buy according to the calculation of one who leases, and certainly not of a short-term buyer (lit., a few years), the reason being . . .

כִּי מִסְפַּר תְּבוּאֹת הוּא מֹכֵר לָךְ — *For according to the amount of produce he sells it to you* . . . because when you buy it for a few years you can only use it for its produce, and may not (plant) that which impoverishes the land, (that is) in a manner which does not permit the field to regain its strength (productivity) when it reverts to its owner, as (our Sages) say, 'If a man leases a field for but a few years, he must not sow it with flax' (*Bava Metzia* 109a).

17. וְלֹא תוֹנוּ — *And you shall not wrong* . . . even through speech, (or) misleading (lit., stealth of mind) information or improper advice, although there is no money at stake.

כִּי אֲנִי ה' אֱלֹהֵיכֶם — *For I am* HASHEM *your God.* The God of the buyer and the God of the seller and I object to the wronging of either of them.

18. וַעֲשִׂיתֶם אֶת חֻקֹּתַי — *And you shall do My statutes* . . . in the matter of the Sabbatical year and the Jubilee.

וְאֶת מִשְׁפָּטַי תִּשְׁמְרוּ — *And keep My ordinances* . . . (in the) matter of selling and buying according to the number (of years till) the Jubilee, and similar matters, that there be no deceit.

NOTES

number of years that the field will remain in the hands of the buyer, it would have stated עַד, *until*; not אַחַר, *after*. The choice of the word אַחַר implies that one should only purchase land *after* the Jubilee, not during it, for the reason given by the *Sforno*.

16. תַּרְבֶּה מִקְנָתוֹ . . . תַּמְעִיט מִקְנָתוֹ — *You shall increase the price thereof* . . . *you shall diminish its price.* Increasing or diminishing the price is not to be understood only as reflecting the number of years that the buyer will be able to use the field. It also is to be understood relative to the amount normally paid for leasing a similar field. Purchase, as compared to leasing, makes for less restrictions while offering greater opportunity for the buyer if it is bought for a long period, and greater restrictions with lesser opportunity if purchased for a shorter period. All this must be taken into consideration when the purchase price is set.

18. וַעֲשִׂיתֶם אֶת חֻקֹּתַי וְאֶת מִשְׁפָּטַי תִּשְׁמְרוּ — *And you shall do My statutes and keep My ordinances.* A חֹק, *statute*, is a law enacted by God which is not always understood by man's limited reasoning. A מִשְׁפָּט, *ordinance*, is that which appears logical and reasonable. Hence, the *Sforno* interprets the phrase *My statutes* as referring to the laws of *Shemittah* and Jubilee, whereas *My ordi-*

שלישי [שני] יט לָבֶטַח׃ וְנָתְנָה הָאָרֶץ פִּרְיָהּ וַאֲכַלְתֶּם לָשֹׂבַע וִישַׁבְתֶּם לָבֶטַח עָלֶיהָ׃
כ וְכִי תֹאמְרוּ מַה־נֹּאכַל בַּשָּׁנָה הַשְּׁבִיעִת הֵן לֹא נִזְרָע וְלֹא נֶאֱסֹף אֶת־
כא תְּבוּאָתֵנוּ׃ וְצִוִּיתִי אֶת־בִּרְכָתִי לָכֶם בַּשָּׁנָה הַשִּׁשִּׁית וְעָשָׂת אֶת־הַתְּבוּאָה
כב לִשְׁלֹשׁ הַשָּׁנִים׃ וּזְרַעְתֶּם אֵת הַשָּׁנָה הַשְּׁמִינִת וַאֲכַלְתֶּם מִן־הַתְּבוּאָה יָשָׁן
כג עַד ׀ הַשָּׁנָה הַתְּשִׁיעִת עַד־בּוֹא תְּבוּאָתָהּ תֹּאכְלוּ יָשָׁן׃ וְהָאָרֶץ לֹא תִמָּכֵר
כד לִצְמִתֻת כִּי־לִי הָאָרֶץ כִּי־גֵרִים וְתוֹשָׁבִים אַתֶּם עִמָּדִי׃ וּבְכֹל אֶרֶץ

וִישַׁבְתֶּם עַל הָאָרֶץ לָבֶטַח — *And you shall dwell in the land in safety* . . . so that you won't be exiled from it, as opposed to *And the land shall be paid her Sabbaths* (26:43), and to בַּעֲוֹן בִּצְעוֹ קָצַפְתִּי, *For the iniquity of his unjust gain I was angered* (*Isaiah* 57:17).

19. וַאֲכַלְתֶּם לָשֹׂבַע — *And you shall eat until you are satiated.* The fruits' nutritional value shall be plentiful, similar to the measures (of manna) which sufficed for adult and child alike, as (our Sages) state, 'One eats a little and it is blessed in his intestines' (*Sifra*), (so that) the produce of the sixth year will suffice also for the seventh.

וִישַׁבְתֶּם לָבֶטַח עָלֶיהָ — *And dwell therein in safety.* You will not bear the shame of hunger among the nations for you will not have to travel to their lands to buy produce.

20. וְכִי תֹאמְרוּ מַה נֹּאכַל — *And if you shall say, 'What shall we eat?'* Now, if you will doubt this assurance and will not trust (the promise) that the small (amount of food) will satisfy qualitatively . . .

21. וְעָשָׂת אֶת הַתְּבוּאָה — *And it shall bring forth grain* . . . in such a manner as to satisfy (your) eye from what it sees, and (you) shall see that the quantity is sufficient.

23. וְהָאָרֶץ לֹא תִמָּכֵר לִצְמִתֻת — *And the land shall not be sold in perpetuity* . . . i.e., land that is cultivated.

כִּי לִי הָאָרֶץ — *For the Land is Mine.* This region (i.e., *Eretz Yisrael*) is the land of God.

כִּי גֵרִים וְתוֹשָׁבִים אַתֶּם עִמָּדִי — *For you are strangers and settlers with Me* . . . in that region, for it is not included in the general principle of וְהָאָרֶץ נָתַן לִבְנֵי אָדָם, *But the earth He has given to mankind* (*Psalms* 115:16).

NOTES

nances refer to the prohibition against אוֹנָאָה, *deceit.*

18-19. וִישַׁבְתֶּם עַל הָאָרֶץ לָבֶטַח . . . וִישַׁבְתֶּם לָבֶטַח עָלֶיהָ — *And you shall dwell in the land in safety . . . and dwell therein in safety.* The assurance that Israel shall dwell on its land in safety (לָבֶטַח), as a reward for observing the aforementioned laws is repeated twice in these two verses. The *Sforno* explains that the first refers to national security while the second is a promise of economic stability.

20-21. וְכִי תֹאמְרוּ מַה נֹּאכַל . . . וְעָשָׂת אֶת הַתְּבוּאָה — *And if you shall say, 'What shall we eat . . .?' and it shall bring forth grain.* To the person of faith, God's assurance that the earth will yield enough produce to nourish Israel for the sixth, seventh and eighth years is sufficient. However, if one lacks faith in the Almighty, asking, 'What shall we eat?', it is necessary to *show* him that there is enough to satisfy his needs. God will grant him the ability to see that the seemingly small quantity contains a lot!

23. וְהָאָרֶץ לֹא תִמָּכֵר לִצְמִתֻת כִּי לִי הָאָרֶץ — *And the land shall not be sold in perpetuity, for the land is Mine.* The phrase הָאָרֶץ, *the land,* appears twice in this verse. The *Sforno* explains the first as meaning cultivated land which is not to be sold in perpetuity. The second refers to the unique status of *Eretz*

רביעי כה אֲחֻזַּתְכֶם גְּאֻלָּה תִּתְּנוּ לָאָרֶץ׃ כִּי־יָמוּךְ אָחִיךָ וּמָכַר
כו מֵאֲחֻזָּתוֹ וּבָא גֹאֲלוֹ הַקָּרֹב אֵלָיו וְגָאַל אֵת מִמְכַּר אָחִיו׃ וְאִישׁ כִּי לֹא
כז יִהְיֶה־לּוֹ גֹּאֵל וְהִשִּׂיגָה יָדוֹ וּמָצָא כְּדֵי גְאֻלָּתוֹ׃ וְחִשַּׁב אֶת־שְׁנֵי מִמְכָּרוֹ
כח וְהֵשִׁיב אֶת־הָעֹדֵף לָאִישׁ אֲשֶׁר מָכַר־לוֹ וְשָׁב לַאֲחֻזָּתוֹ׃ וְאִם לֹא־מָצְאָה
יָדוֹ דֵּי הָשִׁיב לוֹ וְהָיָה מִמְכָּרוֹ בְּיַד הַקֹּנֶה אֹתוֹ עַד שְׁנַת הַיּוֹבֵל וְיָצָא בַּיֹּבֵל
חמישי [שלישי] כט וְשָׁב לַאֲחֻזָּתוֹ׃ וְאִישׁ כִּי־יִמְכֹּר בֵּית־מוֹשַׁב עִיר חוֹמָה
ל וְהָיְתָה גְּאֻלָּתוֹ עַד־תֹּם שְׁנַת מִמְכָּרוֹ יָמִים תִּהְיֶה גְאֻלָּתוֹ׃ וְאִם לֹא־יִגָּאֵל
עַד־מְלֹאת לוֹ שָׁנָה תְמִימָה וְקָם הַבַּיִת אֲשֶׁר־בָּעִיר אֲשֶׁר־לֹא חֹמָה
לא לַצְּמִיתֻת לַקֹּנֶה אֹתוֹ לְדֹרֹתָיו לֹא יֵצֵא בַּיֹּבֵל׃ וּבָתֵּי הַחֲצֵרִים אֲשֶׁר
אֵין־לָהֶם חֹמָה סָבִיב עַל־שְׂדֵה הָאָרֶץ יֵחָשֵׁב גְּאֻלָּה תִּהְיֶה־לּוֹ וּבַיֹּבֵל יֵצֵא׃
לב-לג וְעָרֵי הַלְוִיִּם בָּתֵּי עָרֵי אֲחֻזָּתָם גְּאֻלַּת עוֹלָם תִּהְיֶה לַלְוִיִּם׃ וַאֲשֶׁר יִגְאַל
מִן־הַלְוִיִּם וְיָצָא מִמְכַּר־בַּיִת וְעִיר אֲחֻזָּתוֹ בַּיֹּבֵל כִּי בָתֵּי עָרֵי הַלְוִיִּם הִוא
לד אֲחֻזָּתָם בְּתוֹךְ בְּנֵי יִשְׂרָאֵל׃ וּשְׂדֵה מִגְרַשׁ עָרֵיהֶם לֹא יִמָּכֵר כִּי־אֲחֻזַּת עוֹלָם
לה הוּא לָהֶם׃ וְכִי־יָמוּךְ אָחִיךָ וּמָטָה יָדוֹ עִמָּךְ וְהֶחֱזַקְתָּ בּוֹ
לו גֵּר וְתוֹשָׁב וָחַי עִמָּךְ׃ אַל־תִּקַּח מֵאִתּוֹ נֶשֶׁךְ וְתַרְבִּית וְיָרֵאתָ מֵאֱלֹהֶיךָ וְחֵי
לז אָחִיךָ עִמָּךְ׃ אֶת־כַּסְפְּךָ לֹא־תִתֵּן לוֹ בְּנֶשֶׁךְ וּבְמַרְבִּית לֹא־תִתֵּן אָכְלֶךָ׃
לח אֲנִי יהוה אֱלֹהֵיכֶם אֲשֶׁר־הוֹצֵאתִי אֶתְכֶם מֵאֶרֶץ מִצְרָיִם לָתֵת לָכֶם
ששי [רביעי] לט אֶת־אֶרֶץ כְּנַעַן לִהְיוֹת לָכֶם לֵאלֹהִים׃ וְכִי־יָמוּךְ אָחִיךָ

---

24. וּבְכֹל אֶרֶץ אֲחֻזַּתְכֶם גְּאֻלָּה תִּתְּנוּ לָאָרֶץ — *And in all the land of your possession you shall grant redemption to the land.* However, outside the Land (of Israel) the laws of the Sabbatical year and the Jubilee do not apply.

35. וְהֶחֱזַקְתָּ בּוֹ — *Then you shall uphold him* . . . to support him.

36. אַל תִּקַּח מֵאִתּוֹ — *Do not take interest from him* . . . because the proper way to support him is to lend him (money) without interest or increase.

וְחֵי אָחִיךָ עִמָּךְ — *That your brother may live with you.* And you shall do this when you have sufficient (means) for your own livelihood while (still) lending him, as (our Sages) say, 'Your life takes precedence over the life of your friend' (*Bava Metzia* 62a).

38. לִהְיוֹת לָכֶם לֵאלֹהִים — *To be your God* . . . that His intended purpose be attained by all, and therefore it is proper that you organize your social and political order in such a manner that everyone can live together and assist each other so as to fulfill (God's) intent.

NOTES

Yisrael. Unlike other lands which God apportioned to various nations (*He set the borders of the people* — *Deut.* 32:8), the Land of Israel was not given to Israel unconditionally. They are *strangers and settlers* with God, Who is the true owner and master of the land called *Eretz Yisrael.* Therefore the laws of the Sabbatical year and the Jubilee apply only to the Land of Israel itself and not to חוּץ לָאָרֶץ, *outside the Land,* as the *Sforno* explains in verse 24.

38. לִהְיוֹת לָכֶם לֵאלֹהִים — *To be your God.* The preceding verses appear in the singular form. This verse, however, appears in the plural form to indicate that only when all Jews feel responsible for one another can these laws be fulfilled and God's purpose in creating man realized.

מ עִמָּךְ וְנִמְכַּר־לָךְ לֹא־תַעֲבֹד בּוֹ עֲבֹדַת עָבֶד: כְּשָׂכִיר כְּתוֹשָׁב יִהְיֶה עִמָּךְ
מא עַד־שְׁנַת הַיֹּבֵל יַעֲבֹד עִמָּךְ: וְיָצָא מֵעִמָּךְ הוּא וּבָנָיו עִמּוֹ וְשָׁב
מב אֶל־מִשְׁפַּחְתּוֹ וְאֶל־אֲחֻזַּת אֲבֹתָיו יָשׁוּב: כִּי־עֲבָדַי הֵם אֲשֶׁר־הוֹצֵאתִי אֹתָם
מג מֵאֶרֶץ מִצְרָיִם לֹא יִמָּכְרוּ מִמְכֶּרֶת עָבֶד: לֹא־תִרְדֶּה בוֹ בְּפָרֶךְ וְיָרֵאתָ
מד מֵאֱלֹהֶיךָ: וְעַבְדְּךָ וַאֲמָתְךָ אֲשֶׁר יִהְיוּ־לָךְ מֵאֵת הַגּוֹיִם אֲשֶׁר סְבִיבֹתֵיכֶם
מה מֵהֶם תִּקְנוּ עֶבֶד וְאָמָה: וְגַם מִבְּנֵי הַתּוֹשָׁבִים הַגָּרִים עִמָּכֶם מֵהֶם תִּקְנוּ
וּמִמִּשְׁפַּחְתָּם אֲשֶׁר עִמָּכֶם אֲשֶׁר הוֹלִידוּ בְּאַרְצְכֶם וְהָיוּ לָכֶם לַאֲחֻזָּה:
מו וְהִתְנַחַלְתֶּם אֹתָם לִבְנֵיכֶם אַחֲרֵיכֶם לָרֶשֶׁת אֲחֻזָּה לְעֹלָם בָּהֶם תַּעֲבֹדוּ
שביעי מז וּבְאַחֵיכֶם בְּנֵי־יִשְׂרָאֵל אִישׁ בְּאָחִיו לֹא־תִרְדֶּה בוֹ בְּפָרֶךְ: וְכִי
תַשִּׂיג יַד גֵּר וְתוֹשָׁב עִמָּךְ וּמָךְ אָחִיךָ עִמּוֹ וְנִמְכַּר לְגֵר תּוֹשָׁב עִמָּךְ אוֹ
מח לְעֵקֶר מִשְׁפַּחַת גֵּר: אַחֲרֵי נִמְכַּר גְּאֻלָּה תִּהְיֶה־לּוֹ אֶחָד מֵאֶחָיו יִגְאָלֶנּוּ:
מט אוֹ־דֹדוֹ אוֹ בֶן־דֹּדוֹ יִגְאָלֶנּוּ אוֹ־מִשְּׁאֵר בְּשָׂרוֹ מִמִּשְׁפַּחְתּוֹ יִגְאָלֶנּוּ אוֹ־הִשִּׂיגָה
נ יָדוֹ וְנִגְאָל: וְחִשַּׁב עִם־קֹנֵהוּ מִשְּׁנַת הִמָּכְרוֹ לוֹ עַד שְׁנַת הַיֹּבֵל וְהָיָה כֶּסֶף
נא מִמְכָּרוֹ בְּמִסְפַּר שָׁנִים כִּימֵי שָׂכִיר יִהְיֶה עִמּוֹ: אִם־עוֹד רַבּוֹת בַּשָּׁנִים לְפִיהֶן

---

40. כְּשָׂכִיר כְּתוֹשָׁב יִהְיֶה עִמָּךְ — *As a hired servant and as a settler he shall be with you.* He who is purchased for six years will have the status of a servant hired annually, and he who is purchased (for the time period) until the Jubilee will have the status of a servant who has settled with you (in your employ) for many years.

42. כִּי עֲבָדַי הֵם — *For they are My servants.* Although this person went and took a master upon himself (and) is (therefore) deserving of total servitude, nonetheless, since he is My servant, it is not in his hand to sell himself as an absolute slave.

48. אַחֲרֵי נִמְכַּר גְּאֻלָּה תִּהְיֶה לּוֹ — *After he is sold, he may be redeemed.* (Our Sages) have explained, "Lest you say, 'since he went and became an acolyte in the service of idolatry, I will cast a stone after the fallen,' the Torah says, *After he is sold, he may be redeemed*" (*Kiddushin* 20b).

50. וְחִשַּׁב עִם קוֹנֵהוּ — *And he shall reckon with the one who bought him.* Though the gentile buyer in your control (lit., under your hand) bought (this Israelite) improperly, (nonetheless) you shall not withdraw and release him (i.e., without payment).

51. אִם עוֹד רַבּוֹת בַּשָּׁנִים — *If there be yet many years.* Without a doubt, after the slave has been in his master's house for a lengthy period, his work will be more valuable than it was when he first entered his service. Therefore, (the Torah) tells (us) that even though there is yet a long time until the end of his sale, and there is no question that his work in the future (years) will improve even more if he serves out the entire time, nonetheless, (we) deduct from the cost of the sale according to

NOTES

40. כְּשָׂכִיר כְּתוֹשָׁב יִהְיֶה עִמָּךְ — *As a hired servant and as a settler he shall be with you.* A שָׂכִיר is one who is employed for a short period while a תּוֹשָׁב is one who is hired for many years.

42. כִּי עֲבָדַי הֵם — *For they are My servants.* This statement is an explanation of verses 40-41. No Israelite can sell himself permanently since he is the servant of God. Therefore, his servitude ceases on the Jubilee and he

נב יָשִׁיב גְּאֻלָּתוֹ מִכֶּסֶף מִקְנָתוֹ: וְאִם־מְעַט נִשְׁאַר בַּשָּׁנִים עַד־שְׁנַת הַיֹּבֵל
נג וְחִשַּׁב־לוֹ כְּפִי שָׁנָיו יָשִׁיב אֶת־גְּאֻלָּתוֹ: כִּשְׂכִיר שָׁנָה בְּשָׁנָה יִהְיֶה עִמּוֹ
נד לֹא־יִרְדֶּנּוּ בְּפֶרֶךְ לְעֵינֶיךָ: וְאִם־לֹא יִגָּאֵל בְּאֵלֶּה וְיָצָא בִּשְׁנַת הַיֹּבֵל הוּא
מפטיר נה וּבָנָיו עִמּוֹ: כִּי־לִי בְנֵי־יִשְׂרָאֵל עֲבָדִים עֲבָדַי הֵם אֲשֶׁר־הוֹצֵאתִי אוֹתָם
כו א מֵאֶרֶץ מִצְרָיִם אֲנִי יְהוָה אֱלֹהֵיכֶם: לֹא־תַעֲשׂוּ לָכֶם אֱלִילִם וּפֶסֶל וּמַצֵּבָה

---

the (original) cost when he was sold, as (the Sages) state, 'If his value increases, then (his redemption shall be) from the money he was bought for' (*Kiddushin* 20b).

52. וְאִם מְעַט נִשְׁאַר — *And if there remain but few* . . . in such a manner that the hire for the work of the good years which have passed exceeds the expected value according to the sale price, then one deducts that which is appropriate for the labor of the years which passed, as (the Sages) say there, 'If his value decreases, then (we reckon) according to his years' (ibid.).

XXVI

1. לֹא תַעֲשׂוּ לָכֶם — *You shall not make for yourselves.* Although you will be subjected to the nations, similar to the one who sold himself to the gentiles, (nonetheless) do not exchange your honor for that which does not profit (based on *Jeremiah* 2:11). This (is said) so that they should not err, as (our Sages) mention that many did err at the time of the exile and said to the prophets, 'If a master sells his slave or a husband divorces his wife, has one a claim upon the other?' (*Sanhedrin* 105a). This is so because even after subjugation (to the nations), you are My servants, as (our Sages) tell us that the prophets answered them, saying: 'דָּוִד עַבְדִּי, *David My servant* (*II Samuel* 3:18) and נְבֻכַדְנֶאצַּר . . . עַבְדִּי, *Nebuchadnezzar My servant* (*Jeremiah* 43:10) . . . When a servant acquires property — to whom does the servant belong and to whom the property?' (ibid.).

NOTES

returns to his own family.

51-52. אִם עוֹד רַבּוֹת בַּשָּׁנִים . . . וְאִם מְעַט נִשְׁאַר — *If there be yet many years . . . And if there remain but few.* The principle established in the Talmud (*Kiddushin* 20b) is as follows: Although a slave's work is more valuable to his master after several years since he has gained experience, nonetheless, when the slave is redeemed one gives back the price paid minus the years worked. Conversely, if the slave's value has depreciated with time due to advanced age, one only pays the estimated value of the remaining years. The *Sforno's* explanation is to be understood based upon this principle. Accordingly, the phrase רַבּוֹת בַּשָּׁנִים, *many years,* implies increased value, while the phrase מְעַט בַּשָּׁנִים, *few years,* implies diminished value. In each case the Torah is lenient with the Israelite slave, making his redemption less difficult.

XXVI

1. לֹא תַעֲשׂוּ לָכֶם . . . כִּי אֲנִי ה׳ אֱלֹהֵיכֶם — *You shall not make for yourselves . . . for I am*

לֹא־תָקִימוּ לָכֶם וְאֶבֶן מַשְׂכִּית לֹא תִתְּנוּ בְּאַרְצְכֶם לְהִשְׁתַּחֲוֹת עָלֶיהָ כִּי
ב אֲנִי יהוה אֱלֹהֵיכֶם: אֶת־שַׁבְּתֹתַי תִּשְׁמֹרוּ וּמִקְדָּשִׁי תִּירָאוּ אֲנִי יהוה:

כִּי אֲנִי ה׳ אֱלֹהֵיכֶם — *For I am* HASHEM *your God.* Even in the period of your servitude as it says, *And yet for all that . . . I will not reject them . . . for I am* HASHEM *their God* (v. 44).

2. אֶת שַׁבְּתֹתַי תִּשְׁמֹרוּ — *You shall keep My Sabbaths* ... in the period of servitude as well, even though the quietude (of the Sabbath) is a remembrance of freedom.

וּמִקְדָּשִׁי תִּירָאוּ — *And revere My Sanctuary.* (This refers to) those sanctified places in exile, namely Houses of Assembly (synagogues) and Houses of Study, even though the Temple is destroyed, as it says, וָאֱהִי לָהֶם לְמִקְדָּשׁ מְעַט, *And I shall be to them as a little sanctuary* (*Ezekiel* 11:16). And (in regard to this) (the Sages) say, 'these are Houses of Assembly (for prayer) and Houses of Study' (*Megillah* 29a).

NOTES

HASHEM your God. The *Sforno* explains the connection between this verse and the previous chapter. The concluding portion of chapter 25 speaks of an Israelite slave who sold himself to one who ministers to עֲבוֹדָה זָרָה, *idolatry*, in a heathen temple, and becomes his helper. Nonetheless, as explained in verse 48, he must not be rejected but should be redeemed. The Torah, in our verse, speaks of the people of Israel in exile among the nations who in despair may argue that it matters not whether they remain loyal to their faith or accept the religion of their masters. Hence, they are admonished not to make idols nor bow down to existing ones, for God is still their Master and they are still His servants. Nebuchadnezzar, the king of Babylonia, is called God's servant, not in a complimentary sense but to stress that even though he has conquered Israel, they are not his, for what a servant owns belongs to his master, and so the people of Israel still belong to God as His servants. As such, He still retains His claim over them. The verse therefore concludes, *I am HASHEM your God*, emphasizing this point, and the *Sforno* links this statement to verse 44 where the Torah explicitly states that, in spite of having driven Israel into exile, God has not rejected them and is still their God. Just as the Israelite sold to the heathen priest can still be redeemed, so the people of Israel, though in exile, shall be redeemed.

2. אֶת שַׁבְּתֹתַי תִּשְׁמֹרוּ וּמִקְדָּשִׁי תִּירָאוּ — *You shall keep My Sabbaths and revere My Sanctuary.* This verse continues the theme of Israel in exile among the nations. Although they are no longer free and are subjugated to others, they are commanded to continue to keep the Sabbath, and although their Holy Temple is destroyed, the Houses of Prayer and Study in exile are miniature sanctuaries wherein God still dwells in their midst.

פרשת בחוקותי
Parashas Bechukosai

ג־ד אִם־בְּחֻקֹּתַי תֵּלֵכוּ וְאֶת־מִצְוֺתַי תִּשְׁמְרוּ וַעֲשִׂיתֶם אֹתָם: וְנָתַתִּי גִשְׁמֵיכֶם
ה בְּעִתָּם וְנָתְנָה הָאָרֶץ יְבוּלָהּ וְעֵץ הַשָּׂדֶה יִתֵּן פִּרְיוֹ: וְהִשִּׂיג לָכֶם דַּיִשׁ
אֶת־בָּצִיר וּבָצִיר יַשִּׂיג אֶת־זָרַע וַאֲכַלְתֶּם לַחְמְכֶם לָשֹׂבַע וִישַׁבְתֶּם לָבֶטַח
שני ו בְּאַרְצְכֶם: וְנָתַתִּי שָׁלוֹם בָּאָרֶץ וּשְׁכַבְתֶּם וְאֵין מַחֲרִיד וְהִשְׁבַּתִּי חַיָּה רָעָה
ז מִן־הָאָרֶץ וְחֶרֶב לֹא־תַעֲבֹר בְּאַרְצְכֶם: וּרְדַפְתֶּם אֶת־אֹיְבֵיכֶם וְנָפְלוּ
ח לִפְנֵיכֶם לֶחָרֶב: וְרָדְפוּ מִכֶּם חֲמִשָּׁה מֵאָה וּמֵאָה מִכֶּם רְבָבָה יִרְדֹּפוּ וְנָפְלוּ
ט אֹיְבֵיכֶם לִפְנֵיכֶם לֶחָרֶב: וּפָנִיתִי אֲלֵיכֶם וְהִפְרֵיתִי אֶתְכֶם וְהִרְבֵּיתִי אֶתְכֶם

---

3. אִם בְּחֻקֹּתַי תֵּלֵכוּ — *If you walk in My statutes.* Statutes are decrees of the king by which man should conduct the endeavors of his life, and such conduct is called 'walking,' as it says, *And you shall not walk in their statutes* (18:3), and also, *And My statutes you shall keep to walk therein* (18:4), and also בְּחֻקּוֹת הַחַיִּים הָלָךְ, *Walk in the statutes of life* (*Ezekiel* 33:15).

וְאֶת מִצְוֺתַי תִּשְׁמְרוּ — *And keep My commandments.* Behold, the keeping of commandments (denotes) scrupulous care in the manner that they are done and in their intent, (which comes about through) proper reflection as (our Sages) say, " 'To keep' implies (the need for) constant repetition (מִשְׁנָה)" (*Sifre* on *Deut.* 12:28). (The Torah) is therefore saying: If you conduct (yourselves) in the ways of God, the Blessed One, which are incorporated into the pragmatical portion of His Torah, and you will reflect upon the commandments so as to know the manner in which they are done and their purpose, you will thereby fully (realize) His intent so that you may make yourselves in His image and likeness.

וַעֲשִׂיתֶם אֹתָם — *And do them.* Then you shall acquire this perfection in such a manner that you shall do them (i.e., the *mitzvos*) as good laborers (who do so) willingly; not as those who are commanded and do (so) out of a sense of fear (though) the doer is inspired somewhat. (Rather), you shall do (them) out of a sense of love, desiring to fulfill the will of God, the Blessed One, as (our Sages) say, עֲשֵׂה רְצוֹנוֹ כִּרְצוֹנְךָ, *Do His will as if it were your will* (*Avos* 2:4).

7. וּרְדַפְתֶּם אֶת אֹיְבֵיכֶם — *And you shall pursue your enemies* ... beyond your borders.

וְנָפְלוּ לִפְנֵיכֶם לֶחָרֶב — *And they shall fall before you by the sword* ... without your waging war, as it says, כִּי בָאֵשׁ ה׳ נִשְׁפָּט וּבְחַרְבּוֹ אֶת כָּל בָּשָׂר וְרַבּוּ חַלְלֵי ה׳, *For by fire will HASHEM contend, and by His sword with all flesh, and the slain of HASHEM shall be many* (*Isaiah* 66:16).

9. וּפָנִיתִי אֲלֵיכֶם — *And I will turn unto you* ... after the destruction of the nations,

NOTES

XXVI

3. אִם בְּחֻקֹּתַי תֵּלֵכוּ וְאֶת מִצְוֺתַי תִּשְׁמְרוּ וַעֲשִׂיתֶם אוֹתָם — *If you walk in My statutes and keep My commandments and do them.* This verse uses three different verbs — *to walk, to keep* and *to do.* The *Sforno* explains the first as referring to man's behavior and conduct, the second is applicable both to one's understanding of and obedience to God's commandments, while the third is not meant as an admonition (*to do the commandments*), but is to be understood as an *assurance* that if one obeys the first two (*walking in the statutes* and *keeping the commandments*), then he shall do God's will with enthusiasm and love.

7. וּרְדַפְתֶּם אֶת אֹיְבֵיכֶם וְנָפְלוּ לִפְנֵיכֶם לֶחָרֶב — *And you shall pursue your enemies and they*

שלישי [חמישי] י וַהֲקִמֹתִ֥י אֶת־בְּרִיתִ֖י אִתְּכֶֽם: וַאֲכַלְתֶּ֥ם יָשָׁ֖ן נוֹשָׁ֑ן וְיָשָׁ֕ן מִפְּנֵ֥י חָדָ֖שׁ תּוֹצִֽיאוּ:

---

as it says, כִּי אֶעֱשֶׂה כָלָה בְּכָל הַגּוֹיִם . . . וְאֹתְךָ לֹא אֶעֱשֶׂה כָלָה, *For I will make a full end of all the nations . . . but I will not make a full end of you* (*Jeremiah* 46:28).

וַהֲקִימֹתִי אֶת בְּרִיתִי — *And I will establish My covenant* . . . that covenant wherein I said, לִהְיוֹת לְךָ לֵאלֹהִים וּלְזַרְעֲךָ אַחֲרֶיךָ, *to be a God unto you and to your seed after you* (*Genesis* 17:7).

אִתְּכֶם — *With you*. I shall fulfill it with you, in your (own) merit, besides the fact that I will remember for you the covenant of the Fathers, as it says, וְכָרַתִּי לָהֶם בְּרִית שָׁלוֹם בְּרִית עוֹלָם יִהְיֶה אוֹתָם, *I will make a covenant of peace with them, it shall be an everlasting covenant with them* (*Ezekiel* 37:26), and as it says, וּבְרִית שְׁלוֹמִי לֹא תָמוּט, *Neither shall My covenant of peace be removed* (*Isaiah* 54:10).

10. וַאֲכַלְתֶּם יָשָׁן נוֹשָׁן — *And you shall eat old store long kept*. After the nations will be diminished, (including) *their* (lit., *your*) *plowmen and vinedressers* (based on *Isaiah* 61:5), the annual corn will (last) for years in order that the few (laborers) from the remnant of the nations will be able to serve you by gathering the produce and other (goods) so that you shall be sustained without suffering, similar to, יְהִי פִסַּת בַּר בָּאָרֶץ בְּרֹאשׁ הָרִים יִרְעַשׁ כַּלְּבָנוֹן פִּרְיוֹ, *May he be as a rich cornfield in the land upon the top of the mountains; may his fruit rustle like Lebanon* (*Psalms* 72:16), and as (our Sages) say, '*Eretz Yisrael is destined to bring forth cakes and woolen robes*' (*Shabbos* 30b).

וְיָשָׁן מִפְּנֵי חָדָשׁ תּוֹצִיאוּ — *And you shall bring forth the old from before the new*. You will have sufficient (produce) from the old (store) for your needs, although you will supply sustenance from the old (crop) to those who escape from the nations, as it says, כִּי הַגּוֹי וְהַמַּמְלָכָה אֲשֶׁר לֹא יַעַבְדוּךָ יֹאבֵדוּ, *For that nation and kingdom that will not serve you shall perish* (*Isaiah* 60:12). Now the reason that you will export (even) items which are life's necessities from your land to the nations, is because the new (harvest) will have come and you will (therefore) have no need to worry for lack — as (our Sages) say, 'One must not carry out of *Eretz Yisrael* things which are life's necessities such as wine, oil and flour' (*Bava Basra* 90b).

NOTES

shall fall before you by the sword. (a) The previous verse states that there will be *peace in the land* and that *no sword shall pass through the land*. How is it relevant to say that we shall *pursue the enemy?* The *Sforno* explains that this pursuit shall be *beyond* the borders. (b) The *Sforno's* commentary on the latter part of this verse is unlike that of *Rashi* who explains it to mean, 'each man by the sword of his companion.' Rather, it is to be understood as God intervening, thereby obviating the need for Israel to wage war themselves.

9. וַהֲקִימֹתִי אֶת בְּרִיתִי אִתְּכֶם — *And I will establish My covenant with you*. *Rashi* explains the phrase *My covenant* as referring to a new covenant which, unlike the original one, will never be nullified. The *Sforno*, however, interprets it to mean the original covenant made between the Almighty and Abraham which was never abrogated! And since the Torah here stresses אִתְּכֶם, *with you*, we are being told that this covenant will be fulfilled in our own merit, as well as in the merit of our forefathers.

10. וַאֲכַלְתֶּם יָשָׁן נוֹשָׁן וְיָשָׁן מִפְּנֵי חָדָשׁ תּוֹצִיאוּ — *And you shall eat old store long kept and you shall bring forth the old from before the new*. The *Sforno* interprets this *parashah* as referring to the *end of days*, the Messianic age. At that time, only a remnant will remain from among the nations and they will be dependent upon Israel for their sustenance. They will also serve Israel as necessary laborers. Now according to Torah law, one is not permitted to export life's necessities such as flour, oil or

יא־יב וְנָתַתִּי מִשְׁכָּנִי בְּתוֹכְכֶם וְלֹא־תִגְעַל נַפְשִׁי אֶתְכֶם: וְהִתְהַלַּכְתִּי בְּתוֹכְכֶם
יג וְהָיִיתִי לָכֶם לֵאלֹהִים וְאַתֶּם תִּהְיוּ־לִי לְעָם: אֲנִי יהוה אֱלֹהֵיכֶם אֲשֶׁר

---

11. וְנָתַתִּי מִשְׁכָּנִי בְּתוֹכְכֶם — *And I will set My Sanctuary* (*Presence*) *among you.* My Divine Presence (שְׁכִינָה) will dwell in your midst, wherever you shall be, as was intended before the (sin of the) Golden Calf when (*God*) said, בְּכָל הַמָּקוֹם אֲשֶׁר אַזְכִּיר אֶת שְׁמִי אָבוֹא אֵלֶיךָ, *In every place where I cause My Name to be mentioned I will come to you* (Exodus 20:21).

וְלֹא תִגְעַל נַפְשִׁי אֶתְכֶם — *And My soul will not abhor you.* Never — as it says, לֹא יוֹסִיף לְהַגְלוֹתֵךְ, *He will not exile you again* (Lamentations 4:22), and as it says, כֵּן נִשְׁבַּעְתִּי מִקְּצֹף עָלַיִךְ וּמִגְּעָר בָּךְ, *So have I sworn that I would not be angry with you, nor rebuke you* (Isaiah 54:9).

12. וְהִתְהַלַּכְתִּי בְּתוֹכְכֶם — *And I will walk among you.* The term מִתְהַלֵּךְ (*to walk* — in the reflexive form) signifies walking from place to place (lit., hither and yon), not only to one place. The (verse) therefore states, *I will walk among you,* because the Divine glory will not only descend into one place which was (the case) in the *Mishkan* and the Holy Temple, as it says, וְעָשׂוּ לִי מִקְדָּשׁ וְשָׁכַנְתִּי בְּתוֹכָם, *And let them make Me a Sanctuary that I may dwell among them* (*Exodus* 25:8). (This means to say) that only in that place and in that manner shall I dwell among them; and this is explained when He said, אֲשֶׁר אִוָּעֵד לְךָ שָׁמָּה, *Where I will meet with you* (ibid. 30:6) (and also) וְנֹעַדְתִּי שָׁמָּה לִבְנֵי יִשְׂרָאֵל, *And there I will meet with the Children of Israel* (ibid. 29:43). Rather, I will walk among you and My glory will be seen wherever you will be, for indeed, wherever the righteous of (each) generation are to be found, that (place) is קְדֹשׁ מִשְׁכְּנֵי עֶלְיוֹן, *the holiest dwelling place of the Most High* (*Psalms* 46:5), where His (original) intent is fulfilled as it says, הַשָּׁמַיִם כִּסְאִי וְהָאָרֶץ הֲדֹם רַגְלָי . . . וְאֶל זֶה אַבִּיט אֶל עָנִי וּנְכֵה רוּחַ וְחָרֵד עַל דְּבָרִי, *The heaven is My throne and the earth is My footstool . . . but to this* (*man*) *will I look, to him who is poor and of contrite spirit and trembles at My word* (*Isaiah* 66:1,2).

וְהָיִיתִי לָכֶם לֵאלֹהִים — *And I will be unto you as God.* I will be God exclusively for you and you will have no other God or leader besides Me. Therefore, the everlasting nature of your existence will emanate from Me with no intermediary, as is the case of all separate (entities) who are everlasting; for you will then be (a people) in My image and likeness, as was the (original) intent in the creation of man and in the giving of the Torah. This is (the meaning) of the statement, וְלָקַחְתִּי אֶתְכֶם לִי לְעָם וְהָיִיתִי לָכֶם לֵאלֹהִים, *And I will take you to Me for a people, and I will be to you as God* (*Exodus* 6:7). For through the giving of the Torah, had they not become corrupted, the intent would have been to establish them on the level of Messianic days and of the World to Come which (is indicated) without a doubt as an objective in this portion (*Bechukosai*). However, in the

NOTES

wine from *Eretz Yisrael* to other lands unless they are in surplus. The *Sforno* interprets this verse to mean that even earlier harvests will provide this surplus food supply for many years, and that since the new crops will grow and be harvested while the old store is not yet exhausted, Israel will be able to feed other nations from their granaries.

11-12. וְנָתַתִּי מִשְׁכָּנִי בְּתוֹכְכֶם ... וְהִתְהַלַּכְתִּי בְּתוֹכְכֶם וְהָיִיתִי לָכֶם לֵאלֹהִים — *And I will set My Sanctuary* (*Presence*) *among you . . . and I will*

הוֹצֵאתִי אֶתְכֶם מֵאֶרֶץ מִצְרַיִם מִהְיֹת לָהֶם עֲבָדִים וָאֶשְׁבֹּר מֹטֹת עֻלְּכֶם
וָאוֹלֵךְ אֶתְכֶם קוֹמְמִיּוּת׃
יד־טו וְאִם־לֹא תִשְׁמְעוּ לִי וְלֹא תַעֲשׂוּ אֵת כָּל־הַמִּצְוֹת הָאֵלֶּה׃ וְאִם־בְּחֻקֹּתַי

---

portion of *Nitzavim* (*Deut.* 29:12), the intent stated there is that He will establish them (Israel) as a people so that He shall be (their) God, but it was not destined to come to pass at that time. However, the continuous functioning of the Sanctuary, (of which the Torah) says, וְשָׁכַנְתִּי בְּתוֹךְ בְּנֵי יִשְׂרָאֵל וְהָיִיתִי לָהֶם לֵאלֹהִים, *And I will dwell among the Children of Israel and will be their God* (*Exodus* 29:45), (does appear) as an objective in this chapter. In other passages (of the Torah), however, the expressions used are, *To be unto you as God* and *You shall be unto Me as a people,* that is, their exclusive desire shall be to do My will and to serve Me *with one consent* (based on *Zephaniah* 3:9), as it befits every people to (conduct themselves) toward their king in truth.

13. קוֹמְמִיּוּת — *Upright.* The reverse of, אָמְרוּ לְנַפְשֵׁךְ שְׁחִי וְנַעֲבֹרָה וַתָּשִׂימִי כָאָרֶץ גֵּוֵךְ, *have said to your soul, 'Bow down that we may go over, and you have laid your back as the ground'* (*Isaiah* 51:23).

14. וְאִם לֹא תִשְׁמְעוּ לִי — *But if you will not hearken to Me . . .* to walk in My statutes, as explained above.

וְלֹא תַעֲשׂוּ אֵת כָּל הַמִּצְוֹת הָאֵלֶּה — *And will not do all these commandments.* Since you will not walk in My statutes, then you will not do *all* the commandments, rather you will only do those which are favorable in your eyes.

15. וְאִם בְּחֻקֹּתַי תִּמְאָסוּ — *And if you shall reject My statutes . . .* not only to nullify them but to reject (despise) them.

NOTES

walk among you and I will be unto you as God. The original intent of God was that all mankind should reach the level of צֶלֶם אֱלֹהִים, *the image of God,* which was frustrated when Adam and Eve sinned. When the Torah was given at Sinai, God's purpose was to communicate with all Israel in a prophetic manner, similar to His communication with Moses (see the *Sforno's* commentary, on *Exodus* 19:9). The sin of the Golden Calf, however, thwarted this plan and the Divine Presence limited itself to the Sanctuary alone. In the end of days, the original plan — that God dwell actually in our very midst — will come to pass, and this chapter speaks of that time. Hence, according to the explanation of the *Sforno,* the phrase וְנָתַתִּי מִשְׁכָּנִי בְּתוֹכְכֶם does not refer to the Holy Temple as *Rashi* states, but it means that the Divine Presence will dwell in the *midst of Israel.* וְהִתְהַלַּכְתִּי בְּתוֹכְכֶם, *And I will walk among you,* means that the Divine glory will radiate everywhere and not just confine itself to the Sanctuary. The phrase וְהָיִיתִי לָכֶם לֵאלֹהִים, *And I will be unto you as God,* is to be understood as the direct relationship of God with Israel, with no need for any intermediary. This, in turn, will insure their everlasting existence as a people.

The *Sforno,* however, draws a distinction between various verses where the expression *To be unto you as God* is used. In some instances, it refers to the *end of days,* as is the case in this chapter, and is therefore interpreted to mean a special direct relationship, while in others (such as *Nitzavim*) it refers to the relationship of a nation to its king, namely one of subservience, discipline and respect.

14. וְאִם לֹא תִשְׁמְעוּ לִי וְלֹא תַעֲשׂוּ — *But if you will not hearken to Me and will not do.* The *Sforno* reconciles the apparent redundancy of this verse (*not hearken* and *not do*) by explaining that if one rejects the statutes (which are not readily understood), then he shall ultimately become selective and perform only those commandments which appeal to him.

תִּמְאָסוּ וְאִם אֶת־מִשְׁפָּטַי תִּגְעַל נַפְשְׁכֶם לְבִלְתִּי עֲשׂוֹת אֶת־כָּל־מִצְוֹתַי
טז לְהַפְרְכֶם אֶת־בְּרִיתִי: אַף־אֲנִי אֶעֱשֶׂה־זֹּאת לָכֶם וְהִפְקַדְתִּי עֲלֵיכֶם בֶּהָלָה
אֶת־הַשַּׁחֶפֶת וְאֶת־הַקַּדַּחַת מְכַלּוֹת עֵינַיִם וּמְדִיבֹת נָפֶשׁ וּזְרַעְתֶּם לָרִיק
יז זַרְעֲכֶם וַאֲכָלֻהוּ אֹיְבֵיכֶם: וְנָתַתִּי פָנַי בָּכֶם וְנִגַּפְתֶּם לִפְנֵי אֹיְבֵיכֶם וְרָדוּ בָכֶם

וְאִם אֶת מִשְׁפָּטַי תִּגְעַל נַפְשְׁכֶם — *And if your soul abhor My ordinances.* You will abhor them, similar to one who intentionally causes (himself) to vomit, for it is not logical (lit., customary) to abhor them (i.e., the ordinances) since they are reasonable and proper.

לְבִלְתִּי עֲשׂוֹת אֶת כָּל מִצְוֹתַי — *So that you will not do all My commandments.* This abhorrence of the ordinances is (motivated) only for the purpose of casting off the yoke of all the commandments from yourselves, as (our Sages) said, 'Israel knew that the idols were nonentities but they engaged in idolatry only that they might satisfy (lit., permit to themselves) in public their immoral sexual desires' (*Sanhedrin* 63b), and the prophet also attests (to this) when he says, לֹא יִתְּנוּ מַעַלְלֵיהֶם לָשׁוּב אֶל אֱלֹהֵיהֶם כִּי רוּחַ זְנוּנִים בְּקִרְבָּם, *Their actions will not allow them to return to their God for the spirit of harlotry is within them* (Hosea 5:4).

לְהַפְרְכֶם אֶת בְּרִיתִי — *To break My covenant* . . . so as to be like the other nations who reign in this world without any yoke of Torah and *mitzvos* (commandments), as it says, וְהָעֹלָה עַל רוּחֲכֶם הָיוֹ לֹא תִהְיֶה אֲשֶׁר אַתֶּם אֹמְרִים נִהְיֶה כַגּוֹיִם כְּמִשְׁפְּחוֹת הָאֲרָצוֹת לְשָׁרֵת עֵץ וָאָבֶן, *And that which enters your mind shall not be of any consequence at all; in that you say we will be as the nations, as the families of the lands, to serve wood and stone* (Ezekiel 20:32).

16. אַף אֲנִי אֶעֱשֶׂה זֹּאת לָכֶם — *I also will do this unto you.* I will do what you thought to do, namely, the covenant will be abrogated and nullified by Me as well, as I said that (only) when you will be a people to Me will I be a God to you, without any intermediary.

וְהִפְקַדְתִּי עֲלֵיכֶם בֶּהָלָה — *I will appoint terror over you.* I will appoint over you officials of terror, similar to, וּלְאֵלֶּה אָמַר בְּאָזְנַי עִבְרוּ בָעִיר אַחֲרָיו וְהַכּוּ אַל תָּחֹס עֵינְכֶם וְאַל תַּחְמֹלוּ, *And to these He said in my hearing, go through the city after him and smite; let not your eye spare, neither have pity* (Ezekiel 9:5).

וַאֲכָלֻהוּ אֹיְבֵיכֶם — *For your enemies shall eat it* . . . as it came to pass in the days of the Judges, as it says, וְהָיָה אִם זָרַע יִשְׂרָאֵל וְעָלָה מִדְיָן וַעֲמָלֵק וּבְנֵי קֶדֶם, *When Israel had sown, the Midianites came up and the Amalekites and the children of the east* (Judges 6:3).

NOTES

15. וְאִם בְּחֻקֹּתַי תִּמְאָסוּ וְאִם אֶת מִשְׁפָּטַי תִּגְעַל נַפְשְׁכֶם לְבִלְתִּי עֲשׂוֹת — *And if you shall reject My statutes and if your soul abhor My ordinances so that you will not do.* The motivation to reject a חֹק, *statute,* is perhaps understandable but to *abhor* a מִשְׁפָּט, *ordinance* which is logical and reasonable is beyond comprehension. The *Sforno* therefore explains that the answer lies in the Torah's choice of the word גָּעַל, *abhor,* which is not based upon reason but is willful repudiation, similar to self-induced regurgitation. Now this is done in order to live a life of licentiousness and to indulge one's most base desires and appetites without any restraints or inhibitions, as the *Sforno* cites from the words of the Prophets and our Sages.

16-33. אַף אֲנִי אֶעֱשֶׂה זֹּאת לָכֶם — *I also will do this unto you* . . . that which you planned to do

יח שֹׂנְאֵיכֶם וְנַסְתֶּם וְאֵין־רֹדֵף אֶתְכֶם׃ וְאִם־עַד־אֵלֶּה לֹא תִשְׁמְעוּ לִי וְיָסַפְתִּי
יט לְיַסְּרָה אֶתְכֶם שֶׁבַע עַל־חַטֹּאתֵיכֶם׃ וְשָׁבַרְתִּי אֶת־גְּאוֹן עֻזְּכֶם וְנָתַתִּי
כ אֶת־שְׁמֵיכֶם כַּבַּרְזֶל וְאֶת־אַרְצְכֶם כַּנְּחֻשָׁה׃ וְתַם לָרִיק כֹּחֲכֶם וְלֹא־תִתֵּן
כא אַרְצְכֶם אֶת־יְבוּלָהּ וְעֵץ הָאָרֶץ לֹא יִתֵּן פִּרְיוֹ׃ וְאִם־תֵּלְכוּ עִמִּי קֶרִי וְלֹא
כב תֹאבוּ לִשְׁמֹעַ לִי וְיָסַפְתִּי עֲלֵיכֶם מַכָּה שֶׁבַע כְּחַטֹּאתֵיכֶם׃ וְהִשְׁלַחְתִּי בָכֶם
אֶת־חַיַּת הַשָּׂדֶה וְשִׁכְּלָה אֶתְכֶם וְהִכְרִיתָה אֶת־בְּהֶמְתְּכֶם וְהִמְעִיטָה
כג אֶתְכֶם וְנָשַׁמּוּ דַּרְכֵיכֶם׃ וְאִם־בְּאֵלֶּה לֹא תִוָּסְרוּ לִי וַהֲלַכְתֶּם עִמִּי קֶרִי׃
כד וְהָלַכְתִּי אַף־אֲנִי עִמָּכֶם בְּקֶרִי וְהִכֵּיתִי אֶתְכֶם גַּם־אָנִי שֶׁבַע עַל־
כה חַטֹּאתֵיכֶם׃ וְהֵבֵאתִי עֲלֵיכֶם חֶרֶב נֹקֶמֶת נְקַם־בְּרִית וְנֶאֱסַפְתֶּם אֶל־עָרֵיכֶם
כו וְשִׁלַּחְתִּי דֶבֶר בְּתוֹכְכֶם וְנִתַּתֶּם בְּיַד־אוֹיֵב׃ בְּשִׁבְרִי לָכֶם מַטֵּה־לֶחֶם וְאָפוּ
עֶשֶׂר נָשִׁים לַחְמְכֶם בְּתַנּוּר אֶחָד וְהֵשִׁיבוּ לַחְמְכֶם בַּמִּשְׁקָל וַאֲכַלְתֶּם וְלֹא
כז תִשְׂבָּעוּ׃ וְאִם־בְּזֹאת לֹא תִשְׁמְעוּ לִי וַהֲלַכְתֶּם
כח עִמִּי בְּקֶרִי׃ וְהָלַכְתִּי עִמָּכֶם בַּחֲמַת־קֶרִי וְיִסַּרְתִּי אֶתְכֶם אַף־אָנִי שֶׁבַע
כט-ל עַל־חַטֹּאתֵיכֶם׃ וַאֲכַלְתֶּם בְּשַׂר בְּנֵיכֶם וּבְשַׂר בְּנֹתֵיכֶם תֹּאכֵלוּ׃ וְהִשְׁמַדְתִּי
אֶת־בָּמֹתֵיכֶם וְהִכְרַתִּי אֶת־חַמָּנֵיכֶם וְנָתַתִּי אֶת־פִּגְרֵיכֶם עַל־פִּגְרֵי

---

19. וְשָׁבַרְתִּי אֶת גְּאוֹן עֻזְּכֶם — *And I will break the pride of your powers.* (This refers to) the destruction of the Sanctuary at Shiloh, as it says, וַיִּתֵּן לַשְּׁבִי עֻזּוֹ, *And delivered His strength into captivity* (*Psalms* 78:61).

25. וְהֵבֵאתִי עֲלֵיכֶם חֶרֶב — *And I will bring a sword upon you* . . . as occurred in the days of the kings of Israel, as it says, כִּי יָדַעְתִּי אֵת אֲשֶׁר תַּעֲשֶׂה לִבְנֵי יִשְׂרָאֵל רָעָה מִבְצְרֵיהֶם תְּשַׁלַּח בָּאֵשׁ וּבַחֻרֵיהֶם בַּחֶרֶב תַּהֲרֹג, *Because I know the evil that you will do to the Children of Israel; you will set their strongholds on fire and you will slay their young men with the sword* (*II Kings* 8:12).

נֹקֶמֶת נְקַם בְּרִית — *That shall execute the vengeance of the covenant* . . . executing that vengeance which is written in the Book of the Covenant (i.e., the Torah), as (our Sages) state, 'Although the Sanhedrin ceased, the judgment of the four forms of capital punishment has not ceased' (*Kesubos* 30a).

וְנִתַּתֶּם בְּיַד אוֹיֵב — *And you shall be delivered into the hand of the enemy* . . . as was the case with the Ten Tribes (who were delivered) into the hand of the king of Assyria.

30. וְנָתַתִּי אֶת פִּגְרֵיכֶם עַל פִּגְרֵי גִּלּוּלֵיכֶם — *And cast your carcasses upon the carcasses of your idols.* (This refers to) when the city was besieged, as we are told regarding Elijah the Righteous One who found a child languishing with hunger, and when he said to him, "Recite 'Hear O Israel' and you shall live," (the child) retorted, 'Be silent,' and don't mention the name of God.' He then brought forth his idol from his bosom, kissed it and fell dead upon it (see *Sanhedrin* 63b).

NOTES

is what I shall, in turn, do, i.e., I will abrogate the covenant.

Beginning with this verse, the *Sforno* interprets the dire predictions and promises (recorded through verse 33) as referring to specific historic periods and events. For example, וַאֲכָלֻהוּ אֹיְבֵיכֶם, *For your enemies shall eat* (*your plantings*), refers to the period following the era of Deborah, while verses 19 and 25 refer to the destruction of the Sanctuary in

לא גִּלּוּלֵיכֶם וְגָעֲלָה נַפְשִׁי אֶתְכֶם: וְנָתַתִּי אֶת־עָרֵיכֶם חָרְבָּה וַהֲשִׁמּוֹתִי
לב אֶת־מִקְדְּשֵׁיכֶם וְלֹא אָרִיחַ בְּרֵיחַ נִיחֹחֲכֶם: וַהֲשִׁמֹּתִי אֲנִי אֶת־הָאָרֶץ וְשָׁמְמוּ
לג עָלֶיהָ אֹיְבֵיכֶם הַיֹּשְׁבִים בָּהּ: וְאֶתְכֶם אֱזָרֶה בַגּוֹיִם וַהֲרִיקֹתִי אַחֲרֵיכֶם חָרֶב
לד וְהָיְתָה אַרְצְכֶם שְׁמָמָה וְעָרֵיכֶם יִהְיוּ חָרְבָּה: אָז תִּרְצֶה הָאָרֶץ
אֶת־שַׁבְּתֹתֶיהָ כֹּל יְמֵי הָשַּׁמָּה וְאַתֶּם בְּאֶרֶץ אֹיְבֵיכֶם אָז תִּשְׁבַּת הָאָרֶץ
לה וְהִרְצָת אֶת־שַׁבְּתֹתֶיהָ: כָּל־יְמֵי הָשַּׁמָּה תִּשְׁבֹּת אֵת אֲשֶׁר לֹא־שָׁבְתָה
לו בְּשַׁבְּתֹתֵיכֶם בְּשִׁבְתְּכֶם עָלֶיהָ: וְהַנִּשְׁאָרִים בָּכֶם וְהֵבֵאתִי מֹרֶךְ בִּלְבָבָם
בְּאַרְצֹת אֹיְבֵיהֶם וְרָדַף אֹתָם קוֹל עָלֶה נִדָּף וְנָסוּ מְנֻסַת־חֶרֶב וְנָפְלוּ וְאֵין
לז רֹדֵף: וְכָשְׁלוּ אִישׁ־בְּאָחִיו כְּמִפְּנֵי־חֶרֶב וְרֹדֵף אָיִן וְלֹא־תִהְיֶה לָכֶם תְּקוּמָה
לח-לט לִפְנֵי אֹיְבֵיכֶם: וַאֲבַדְתֶּם בַּגּוֹיִם וְאָכְלָה אֶתְכֶם אֶרֶץ אֹיְבֵיכֶם: וְהַנִּשְׁאָרִים
מ בָּכֶם יִמַּקּוּ בַּעֲוֹנָם בְּאַרְצֹת אֹיְבֵיכֶם וְאַף בַּעֲוֹנֹת אֲבֹתָם אִתָּם יִמָּקּוּ: וְהִתְוַדּוּ
אֶת־עֲוֹנָם וְאֶת־עֲוֹן אֲבֹתָם בְּמַעֲלָם אֲשֶׁר מָעֲלוּ־בִי וְאַף אֲשֶׁר־הָלְכוּ עִמִּי

---

31. וְנָתַתִּי אֶת עָרֵיכֶם חָרְבָּה — *And I will make your cities a waste* . . . through the king of Babylonia and his lords.

וַהֲשִׁמּוֹתִי אֶת מִקְדְּשֵׁיכֶם — *And bring your sanctuaries to desolation* . . . through Nebuzradan.

וְלֹא אָרִיחַ בְּרֵיחַ נִיחֹחֲכֶם — *And I will not smell the savor of your sweet odors.* Even though the sons of Zadok the Kohen were then (functioning as) *Kohanim* in (the Temple), whose sacrifices, without a doubt, had the savor of sweet odors, nonetheless, they were not acceptable due to the guilt of the people.

33. וְאֶתְכֶם אֱזָרֶה בַגּוֹיִם — *And I will scatter you among the nations* . . . when they go down to Egypt after the destruction (of the Temple). (See *II Kings* 25:26.)

וַהֲרִיקֹתִי אַחֲרֵיכֶם חָרֶב — *And I will draw out the sword after you.* The sword of Nebuchadnezzar (will overtake you) in Egypt, as it says, הַחֶרֶב אֲשֶׁר אַתֶּם יְרֵאִים מִמֶּנָּה שָׁם תַּשִּׂיג אֶתְכֶם בְּאֶרֶץ מִצְרָיִם, *The sword of which you are afraid shall overtake you there in the land of Egypt* (*Jeremiah* 42:16).

34. אָז תִּרְצֶה הָאָרֶץ — *Then shall the land be appeased* (*be paid*) . . . will be paid and will be remitted.

אֶת שַׁבְּתֹתֶיהָ — *Her Sabbaths.* (This refers to) Sabbatical years and Jubilees, as it is explained when it says, עַד רָצְתָה הָאָרֶץ אֶת שַׁבְּתוֹתֶיהָ כָּל יְמֵי הָשַּׁמָּה שָׁבָתָה לְמַלֹּאת שִׁבְעִים שָׁנָה, *Until the land had been paid her Sabbaths; for as long as she lay desolate she kept the Sabbath to fulfill seventy years* (*II Chronicles* 36:21).

40. וְהִתְוַדּוּ אֶת עֲוֹנָם — *And they shall confess their iniquity.* (This means) a number of them such as Daniel, Ezra and others.

NOTES

Shiloh, the period of the Northern Kingdom (מַלְכוּת יִשְׂרָאֵל) and the exile of the Ten Tribes. Verses 31 through 33 refer to the fate of the Southern Kingdom (מַלְכוּת יְהוּדָה), including the destruction of the Holy Temple in Jerusalem and the flight of the Jews to Egypt where the sword of Nebuchadnezzar, king of Babylonia, overtook them.

34. אָז תִּרְצֶה הָאָרֶץ אֶת שַׁבְּתֹתֶיהָ — *Then shall the land be appeased* (*be paid*) *her Sabbaths.* Because the people failed to allow the land to

מא בְקֶרִי: אַף־אֲנִי אֵלֵךְ עִמָּם בְּקֶרִי וְהֵבֵאתִי אֹתָם בְּאֶרֶץ אֹיְבֵיהֶם אוֹ־אָז
מב יִכָּנַע לְבָבָם הֶעָרֵל וְאָז יִרְצוּ אֶת־עֲוֺנָם: וְזָכַרְתִּי אֶת־בְּרִיתִי יַעֲקוֹב וְאַף
מג אֶת־בְּרִיתִי יִצְחָק וְאַף אֶת־בְּרִיתִי אַבְרָהָם אֶזְכֹּר וְהָאָרֶץ אֶזְכֹּר:
וְהָאָרֶץ תֵּעָזֵב מֵהֶם וְתִרֶץ אֶת־שַׁבְּתֹתֶיהָ בָּהְשַׁמָּה מֵהֶם וְהֵם יִרְצוּ אֶת־
מד עֲוֺנָם יַעַן וּבְיַעַן בְּמִשְׁפָּטַי מָאָסוּ וְאֶת־חֻקֹּתַי גָּעֲלָה נַפְשָׁם: וְאַף־גַּם־זֹאת
בִּהְיוֹתָם בְּאֶרֶץ אֹיְבֵיהֶם לֹא־מְאַסְתִּים וְלֹא־גְעַלְתִּים לְכַלֹּתָם לְהָפֵר
מה בְּרִיתִי אִתָּם כִּי אֲנִי יְהוָה אֱלֹהֵיהֶם: וְזָכַרְתִּי לָהֶם בְּרִית רִאשֹׁנִים אֲשֶׁר
מו הוֹצֵאתִי־אֹתָם מֵאֶרֶץ מִצְרַיִם לְעֵינֵי הַגּוֹיִם לִהְיוֹת לָהֶם לֵאלֹהִים אֲנִי יְהוָה:

---

41. וְהֵבֵאתִי אֹתָם בְּאֶרֶץ אֹיְבֵיהֶם — *And bring them into the land of their enemies.* When the exiles returned to the Land of Israel at the command of Cyrus the Persian king, the land was under the rule of the nations, as it says, וְהָאָרֶץ אֲשֶׁר נָתַתָּה לַאֲבֹתֵינוּ לֶאֱכֹל אֶת פִּרְיָהּ וְאֶת טוּבָהּ הִנֵּה אֲנַחְנוּ עֲבָדִים עָלֶיהָ. וּתְבוּאָתָהּ מַרְבָּה לַמְּלָכִים אֲשֶׁר נָתַתָּה עָלֵינוּ בְּחַטֹּאותֵינוּ, *And as for the land that You gave to our fathers to eat its fruit and the good thereof, behold we are servants on it. And it yields much produce to the kings whom You have set over us because of our sins* (*Nehemiah* 9:36-37).

42. וְזָכַרְתִּי אֶת בְּרִיתִי — *And I will remember My covenant* ... with the building of the Second Temple.

43. וְהָאָרֶץ תֵּעָזֵב מֵהֶם — *For the land shall lie forsaken without them* ... when destroyed.

45. וְזָכַרְתִּי לָהֶם — *And I shall remember for their sake* ... when I gather the exiles.

אֲשֶׁר הוֹצֵאתִי ... לִהְיוֹת לָהֶם לֵאלֹהִים — *Whom I brought forth ... to be a God to them.* (For) I brought them forth to be their God, as it says, וְאַתֶּם תִּהְיוּ לִי מַמְלֶכֶת כֹּהֲנִים וְגוֹי קָדוֹשׁ, *And you shall be unto Me a kingdom of Kohanim and a holy nation* (*Exodus* 19:6). And what they then destroyed shall be reestablished after the ingathering of the exiles in the days of Messiah and the World to Come.

אֲנִי ה׳ — *I am HASHEM* ... who does not change (based on *Malachi* 3:6). The impairment (deterioration) was due to them alone, (but) I will fulfill my (original) intent when their impairment will be removed at the end of days (lit., in the future time).

NOTES

lie fallow during the Sabbatical and Jubilee years, the land will demand its due and remain desolate for those same number of years before the people can return to *Eretz Yisrael* from Babylonia.

41. וְהֵבֵאתִי אֹתָם בְּאֶרֶץ אֹיְבֵיהֶם — *And bring them into the land of their enemies.* Unlike other commentators, the *Sforno* interprets this verse as applying to Israel's *return* to the Land of Israel, not their exile *from* it to the land of their enemies. The difficulty, however, is in the word בְּאֶרֶץ, *into the land*, rather than מֵאֶרֶץ, *from the land*. The *Sforno* resolves this difficulty by explaining that even after their return to *Eretz Yisrael* in the time of Cyrus, they were not free but were still subjected to alien rule.

42-45. וְזָכַרְתִּי אֶת בְּרִיתִי ... וְהָאָרֶץ תֵּעָזֵב מֵהֶם ... וְזָכַרְתִּי לָהֶם ... לִהְיוֹת לָהֶם לֵאלֹהִים — *And I will remember My covenant ... for the land shall lie forsaken without them ... and I shall remember for their sake ... to be a God to them.* The *Sforno*, consistent with his running commentary on this chapter, interprets these verses as representing the culmination of the Jewish people's journey through history. They shall return to the land, rebuild the Temple, be exiled once again but ultimately they will return to the Land of Israel in the Messianic time and the end of days when they will

מו אֵ֣לֶּה הַֽחֻקִּ֣ים וְהַמִּשְׁפָּטִים֮ וְהַתּוֹרֹת֒ אֲשֶׁר֙ נָתַ֣ן יְהוָ֔ה בֵּינ֕וֹ וּבֵ֖ין בְּנֵ֣י יִשְׂרָאֵ֑ל

בְּהַ֥ר סִינַ֖י בְּיַד־מֹשֶֽׁה:

כז

רביעי [ששי] א־ב וַיְדַבֵּ֥ר יְהוָ֖ה אֶל־מֹשֶׁ֥ה לֵּאמֹֽר: דַּבֵּ֞ר אֶל־בְּנֵ֤י יִשְׂרָאֵל֙ וְאָמַרְתָּ֣ אֲלֵהֶ֔ם אִ֕ישׁ

ג כִּ֥י יַפְלִ֖א נֶ֑דֶר בְּעֶרְכְּךָ֥ נְפָשֹׁ֖ת לַֽיהוָֽה: וְהָיָ֤ה עֶרְכְּךָ֙ הַזָּכָ֔ר מִבֶּן֙ עֶשְׂרִ֣ים שָׁנָ֔ה

וְעַ֖ד בֶּן־שִׁשִּׁ֣ים שָׁנָ֑ה וְהָיָ֣ה עֶרְכְּךָ֗ חֲמִשִּׁ֛ים שֶׁ֥קֶל כֶּ֖סֶף בְּשֶׁ֥קֶל הַקֹּֽדֶשׁ:

ד־ה וְאִם־נְקֵבָ֖ה הִ֑וא וְהָיָ֥ה עֶרְכְּךָ֖ שְׁלֹשִׁ֥ים שָֽׁקֶל: וְאִ֨ם מִבֶּן־חָמֵ֜שׁ שָׁנִ֗ים וְעַד֙

בֶּן־עֶשְׂרִ֣ים שָׁנָ֔ה וְהָיָ֧ה עֶרְכְּךָ֛ הַזָּכָ֖ר עֶשְׂרִ֣ים שְׁקָלִ֑ים וְלַנְּקֵבָ֖ה עֲשֶׂ֥רֶת

ו שְׁקָלִֽים: וְאִ֣ם מִבֶּן־חֹ֗דֶשׁ וְעַד֙ בֶּן־חָמֵ֣שׁ שָׁנִ֔ים וְהָיָ֤ה עֶרְכְּךָ֙ הַזָּכָ֔ר חֲמִשָּׁ֥ה

ז שְׁקָלִ֖ים כָּ֑סֶף וְלַנְּקֵבָ֣ה עֶרְכְּךָ֔ שְׁלֹ֥שֶׁת שְׁקָלִ֖ים כָּֽסֶף: וְאִ֣ם מִבֶּן־שִׁשִּׁ֣ים שָׁנָ֩

וָמַ֨עְלָה אִם־זָכָ֜ר וְהָיָ֣ה עֶרְכְּךָ֗ חֲמִשָּׁ֥ה עָשָׂ֖ר שָׁ֑קֶל וְלַנְּקֵבָ֖ה עֲשָׂרָ֥ה שְׁקָלִֽים:

ח וְאִם־מָ֣ךְ הוּא֮ מֵֽעֶרְכֶּךָ֒ וְהֶֽעֱמִידוֹ֙ לִפְנֵ֣י הַכֹּהֵ֔ן וְהֶעֱרִ֥יךְ אֹת֖וֹ הַכֹּהֵ֑ן עַל־פִּ֗י

ט אֲשֶׁ֤ר תַּשִּׂיג֙ יַ֣ד הַנֹּדֵ֔ר יַעֲרִיכֶ֖נּוּ הַכֹּהֵֽן: וְאִם־בְּהֵמָ֗ה אֲשֶׁ֨ר

י יַקְרִ֧יבוּ מִמֶּ֛נָּה קָרְבָּ֖ן לַֽיהוָ֑ה כֹּל֩ אֲשֶׁ֨ר יִתֵּ֥ן מִמֶּ֛נּוּ לַֽיהוָ֖ה יִֽהְיֶה־קֹּֽדֶשׁ: לֹ֣א

יַחֲלִיפֶ֗נּוּ וְלֹֽא־יָמִ֥יר אֹת֛וֹ ט֥וֹב בְּרָ֖ע אוֹ־רַ֣ע בְּט֑וֹב וְאִם־הָמֵ֨ר יָמִ֤יר בְּהֵמָה֙

יא בִּבְהֵמָ֔ה וְהָֽיָה־ה֥וּא וּתְמוּרָת֖וֹ יִֽהְיֶה־קֹּֽדֶשׁ: וְאִם֙ כָּל־בְּהֵמָ֣ה טְמֵאָ֔ה אֲשֶׁ֡ר

יב לֹֽא־יַקְרִ֩יבוּ֩ מִמֶּ֨נָּה קָרְבָּ֜ן לַֽיהוָ֗ה וְהֶֽעֱמִ֥יד אֶת־הַבְּהֵמָ֖ה לִפְנֵ֥י הַכֹּהֵֽן: וְהֶעֱרִ֤יךְ

יג הַכֹּהֵן֙ אֹתָ֔הּ בֵּ֥ין ט֖וֹב וּבֵ֣ין רָ֑ע כְּעֶרְכְּךָ֥ הַכֹּהֵ֖ן כֵּ֥ן יִהְיֶֽה: וְאִם־גָּאֹ֖ל יִגְאָלֶ֑נָּה

יד וְיָסַ֥ף חֲמִֽישִׁת֖וֹ עַל־עֶרְכֶּֽךָ: וְאִ֗ישׁ כִּֽי־יַקְדִּ֨שׁ אֶת־בֵּית֥וֹ קֹ֨דֶשׁ֙ לַֽיהוָ֔ה וְהֶעֱרִיכוֹ֙

טו הַכֹּהֵ֔ן בֵּ֥ין ט֖וֹב וּבֵ֣ין רָ֑ע כַּאֲשֶׁ֨ר יַעֲרִ֥יךְ אֹת֛וֹ הַכֹּהֵ֖ן כֵּ֥ן יָקֽוּם: וְאִם־הַמַּקְדִּ֗ישׁ

חמישי [שביעי] טז יִגְאַל֙ אֶת־בֵּית֔וֹ וְ֠יָסַף חֲמִישִׁ֧ית כֶּֽסֶף־עֶרְכְּךָ֛ עָלָ֖יו וְהָ֣יָה לֽוֹ: וְאִ֣ם ׀ מִשְּׂדֵ֣ה

אֲחֻזָּתוֹ֮ יַקְדִּ֣ישׁ אִישׁ֒ לַֽיהוָ֔ה וְהָיָ֥ה עֶרְכְּךָ֖ לְפִ֣י זַרְע֑וֹ זֶ֛רַע חֹ֥מֶר שְׂעֹרִ֖ים

---

46. אֵלֶּה הַֽחֻקִּים — *These are the statutes.* All the commandments given (lit., said) before the beginning of the portion of *Bechukosai* (fall into the categories of) the statutes, ordinances and laws upon which the covenant was made with the blessings and curses. This is the covenant mentioned when (the Torah) says, מִלְּבַד הַבְּרִית אֲשֶׁר כָּרַת אִתָּם בְּחֹרֵב, *Beside the covenant which He made with them in Horeb* (Deuteronomy 28:69).

בֵּינוֹ וּבֵין בְּנֵי יִשְׂרָאֵל — *Between Him and the Children of Israel.* The Exalted One vowed (to fulfill) the blessings when they would so merit, and they accepted the curses upon themselves in the event that they would not hearken. However, (the laws of) human valuation and those of sanctification of houses and fields and of a

NOTES

finally bring to fruition the original plan of God for mankind in general, and the people of Israel in particular.

46. אֵלֶּה הַֽחֻקִּים — *These are the statutes.* The *Sforno* explains that *the statutes, ordinances and laws* mentioned in this verse refer to all

יז בַּחֲמִשִּׁים שֶׁקֶל כָּסֶף׃ אִם־מִשְּׁנַת הַיֹּבֵל יַקְדִּישׁ שָׂדֵהוּ כְּעֶרְכְּךָ יָקוּם׃
יח וְאִם־אַחַר הַיֹּבֵל יַקְדִּישׁ שָׂדֵהוּ וְחִשַּׁב־לוֹ הַכֹּהֵן אֶת־הַכֶּסֶף עַל־פִּי הַשָּׁנִים
יט הַנּוֹתָרֹת עַד שְׁנַת הַיֹּבֵל וְנִגְרַע מֵעֶרְכֶּךָ׃ וְאִם־גָּאֹל יִגְאַל אֶת־הַשָּׂדֶה
כ הַמַּקְדִּישׁ אֹתוֹ וְיָסַף חֲמִשִׁית כֶּסֶף־עֶרְכְּךָ עָלָיו וְקָם לוֹ׃ וְאִם־לֹא יִגְאַל
כא אֶת־הַשָּׂדֶה וְאִם־מָכַר אֶת־הַשָּׂדֶה לְאִישׁ אַחֵר לֹא יִגָּאֵל עוֹד׃ וְהָיָה הַשָּׂדֶה
ששי כב בְּצֵאתוֹ בַיֹּבֵל קֹדֶשׁ לַיהוָה כִּשְׂדֵה הַחֵרֶם לַכֹּהֵן תִּהְיֶה אֲחֻזָּתוֹ׃ וְאִם
כג אֶת־שְׂדֵה מִקְנָתוֹ אֲשֶׁר לֹא מִשְּׂדֵה אֲחֻזָּתוֹ יַקְדִּישׁ לַיהוָה׃ וְחִשַּׁב־לוֹ הַכֹּהֵן
אֵת מִכְסַת הָעֶרְכְּךָ עַד שְׁנַת הַיֹּבֵל וְנָתַן אֶת־הָעֶרְכְּךָ בַּיּוֹם הַהוּא קֹדֶשׁ
כד לַיהוָה׃ בִּשְׁנַת הַיּוֹבֵל יָשׁוּב הַשָּׂדֶה לַאֲשֶׁר קָנָהוּ מֵאִתּוֹ לַאֲשֶׁר־לוֹ אֲחֻזַּת
כה הָאָרֶץ׃ וְכָל־עֶרְכְּךָ יִהְיֶה בְּשֶׁקֶל הַקֹּדֶשׁ עֶשְׂרִים גֵּרָה יִהְיֶה הַשָּׁקֶל׃
כו אַךְ־בְּכוֹר אֲשֶׁר־יְבֻכַּר לַיהוָה בִּבְהֵמָה לֹא־יַקְדִּישׁ אִישׁ אֹתוֹ אִם־שׁוֹר
כז אִם־שֶׂה לַיהוָה הוּא׃ וְאִם בַּבְּהֵמָה הַטְּמֵאָה וּפָדָה בְעֶרְכֶּךָ וְיָסַף חֲמִשִׁתוֹ
כח עָלָיו וְאִם־לֹא יִגָּאֵל וְנִמְכַּר בְּעֶרְכֶּךָ׃ אַךְ־כָּל־חֵרֶם אֲשֶׁר יַחֲרִם אִישׁ לַיהוָה
מִכָּל־אֲשֶׁר־לוֹ מֵאָדָם וּבְהֵמָה וּמִשְּׂדֵה אֲחֻזָּתוֹ לֹא יִמָּכֵר וְלֹא יִגָּאֵל
שביעי כט כָּל־חֵרֶם קֹדֶשׁ־קָדָשִׁים הוּא לַיהוָה׃ כָּל־חֵרֶם אֲשֶׁר יָחֳרַם מִן־הָאָדָם לֹא
ל יִפָּדֶה מוֹת יוּמָת׃ וְכָל־מַעְשַׂר הָאָרֶץ מִזֶּרַע הָאָרֶץ מִפְּרִי הָעֵץ לַיהוָה הוּא
לא קֹדֶשׁ לַיהוָה׃ וְאִם־גָּאֹל יִגְאַל אִישׁ מִמַּעַשְׂרוֹ חֲמִשִׁיתוֹ יֹסֵף עָלָיו׃
מפטיר לב וְכָל־מַעְשַׂר בָּקָר וָצֹאן כֹּל אֲשֶׁר־יַעֲבֹר תַּחַת הַשָּׁבֶט הָעֲשִׂירִי יִהְיֶה־קֹּדֶשׁ
לג לַיהוָה׃ לֹא יְבַקֵּר בֵּין־טוֹב לָרַע וְלֹא יְמִירֶנּוּ וְאִם־הָמֵר יְמִירֶנּוּ וְהָיָה־הוּא
לד וּתְמוּרָתוֹ יִהְיֶה־קֹּדֶשׁ לֹא יִגָּאֵל׃ אֵלֶּה הַמִּצְוֹת אֲשֶׁר צִוָּה יְהוָה אֶת־מֹשֶׁה
אֶל־בְּנֵי יִשְׂרָאֵל בְּהַר סִינָי׃

---

firstling and bans and the animal tithe (chapter 27) were all said (i.e., commanded) *after* this covenant (was made) even though they were also said on Mount Sinai, as it says . . .

XXVII

34. אֵלֶּה הַמִּצְוֹת אֲשֶׁר צִוָּה ה׳ אֶת מֹשֶׁה אֶל בְּנֵי יִשְׂרָאֵל בְּהַר סִינָי — *These are the commandments which HASHEM commanded Moses to the Children of Israel on Mount Sinai.* But they were not given as (part of the) covenant between Him and the Children of Israel.

NOTES

the laws preceding this chapter, which are all part of the covenant between God and Israel. However, the laws of the next chapter (27) are not part of the covenant even though they were also commanded on Mount Sinai as were the preceding ones.

ספר במדבר

Bamidbar/Numbers

Sforno's Introduction

In this fourth book it is related how, (because) He desired (to bestow) kindness (upon Israel), He arranged their flags similar to (the arrangement of) the (Divine) chariot as seen in the vision of His prophets, the intent being that just as they encamped so would they journey, thereby entering the Land immediately without need to resort to weapons.[1] Now to merit this, He arranged the charge of the *Kohanim* and Levites,[2] separated all those who were *tamei* from their camps,[3] and set down the laws (lit. 'the subject') of the *sotah* (a woman suspected of infidelity) and the *nazir*,[4] in order to remove all bastardy (from their midst) and to sanctify a number of their sons as *nazirim*. Through all this, they became worthy (to receive) the Priestly Blessings.[5]

And therefore, (the Torah) makes mention of the merits of Israel by which they became worthy to enter the Land in this manner (i.e., without opposition). These are the dedication of the altar;[6] their efforts towards the *taharah* of the Levites [7] and the (preparation of the) *Pesach*,[8] and their (willingness) to follow Him in the wilderness.

He (then) commanded (regarding) the trumpets (which alerted) the camps to journey, to battle and for other (purposes).[9] He then led them on three journeys in the great and awesome wilderness until Kadesh Barnea. (However) they, in the manner of (fallible) mortals, transgressed His covenant and behaved treacherously in the episode of the spies,[10] thereby subverting their (own) interests. It was therefore decreed that they perish in the wilderness and that their children would go into exile for (many) generations at the ordained time.[11] As a result (of this sin), their children encircled the lands of the nations for forty years and did not enter the land without a struggle.

The third part (of this book) relates that, in spite of all this, the mercy of God did not cease in arranging the affairs of His children as much as

1. See the *Sforno's* commentary on 1:2.
2. Chapter 4.
3. 5:1-4.
4. 5:11-31; 6:1-21.
5. 6:22-27.
6. Chapter 7.
7. 8:5-14.
8. 9:1-8.
9. 10:1-10.
10. Chapter 13.
11. See the *Sforno's* commentary on 14:28.

possible, and He commanded regarding the libations (נְסָכִים) of an offering made by an individual, and the (separation of) *challah*, and the goat (sacrifice) to atone for idolatry,[12] all this instituted from (the time of) the (episode of) the spies and beyond.[13] He (also) sanctified them unto Himself through the commandment of *tzitzis*.[14] In spite of all this, Korach and his congregation did not hesitate to rebel against His honored leaders.[15] Indeed, they transgressed and were punished, (but) He had compassion on the rest of the masses and mended the breach, as symbolized by the firepans and the rod[16] and the priestly gifts[17] so that they should not revert to their reckless ways (lit., 'foolishness').

(The Torah) then mentions the *taharah* process of one rendered *tamei* through contact with a dead person, by means of water (mixed with the ashes of the Red Cow).[18] (Now) when they entered that portion of the land of the Emorites which is identified with Sichon and Og, He also gave them the order of dividing the land on the other side of the Jordan and beyond.[19] All this (took place) after the despair of their fathers, due to the impairment of the spies. Thus the fourth book concludes.

---

12. 15:1-31.
13. See the *Sforno's* commentary there.
14. 15:37-41.
15. Chapter 16 — (Korach).
16. Chapter 17.
17. 18:8-20.
18. Chapter 19 — (Chukas).
19. *Parashios Pinchas, Mattos, Maasei.*

פרשת במדבר
Parashas Bamidbar

א

א וַיְדַבֵּר יְהוָה אֶל־מֹשֶׁה בְּמִדְבַּר סִינַי בְּאֹהֶל מוֹעֵד בְּאֶחָד לַחֹדֶשׁ הַשֵּׁנִי
ב בַּשָּׁנָה הַשֵּׁנִית לְצֵאתָם מֵאֶרֶץ מִצְרַיִם לֵאמֹר: שְׂאוּ אֶת־רֹאשׁ כָּל־עֲדַת
בְּנֵי־יִשְׂרָאֵל לְמִשְׁפְּחֹתָם לְבֵית אֲבֹתָם בְּמִסְפַּר שֵׁמוֹת כָּל־זָכָר לְגֻלְגְּלֹתָם:
ג מִבֶּן עֶשְׂרִים שָׁנָה וָמַעְלָה כָּל־יֹצֵא צָבָא בְּיִשְׂרָאֵל תִּפְקְדוּ אֹתָם לְצִבְאֹתָם
ד אַתָּה וְאַהֲרֹן: וְאִתְּכֶם יִהְיוּ אִישׁ אִישׁ לַמַּטֶּה אִישׁ רֹאשׁ לְבֵית־אֲבֹתָיו
ה הוּא: וְאֵלֶּה שְׁמוֹת הָאֲנָשִׁים אֲשֶׁר יַעַמְדוּ אִתְּכֶם לִרְאוּבֵן אֱלִיצוּר

I

1. וַיְדַבֵּר ה׳ אֶל מֹשֶׁה — *And HASHEM spoke to Moses.*

2. שְׂאוּ אֶת רֹאשׁ — *Take you the sum . . .* to organize them so that they might enter the Land immediately, each man according to his standard (i.e., flag or banner), without having to wage war. Rather, the nations will depart (voluntarily), as the (Torah) testifies in regard to some who did when it says, כַּעֲזוּבַת הַחֹרֶשׁ וְהָאָמִיר אֲשֶׁר עָזְבוּ מִפְּנֵי בְּנֵי יִשְׂרָאֵל, *Which were forsaken from before the Children of Israel after the manner of woods and lofty forests* (*Isaiah* 17:9). Perhaps these were the families of the Girgoshi of whom (our Sages) say that they arose and left of their own volition (see *Rashi, Exodus* 33:2). (However) because of the impairment of the Spies, the seven nations increased their evil (ways) for forty years and it was (therefore) necessary to destroy them.

בְּמִסְפַּר שֵׁמוֹת — *According to the number of names . . .* for at that time every one of that generation was designated by his name which indicated and reflected stature and character, similar to, וָאֵדָעֲךָ בְּשֵׁם, *And I know you by name* (*Exodus* 33:17). It was not so regarding (the people of) the generation which entered the Land, and therefore, they were not counted by the number of names. Only the heads of families were mentioned and the number of men (chapter 26). This tells us that the (original) intent was that these selfsame men should live to inherit the Land, without exception.

4. אִישׁ רֹאשׁ לְבֵית אֲבֹתָיו — *Every one head of his fathers' house.* The reason that they should be with you is because each one is the head of his fathers' house and will (therefore) be knowledgeable regarding the lineage of each individual.

NOTES

I

2. שְׂאוּ אֶת רֹאשׁ — *Take you the sum.* The *Sforno* is of the opinion, stated here as well as in his commentary later in this Book (9:1 and 10:35), that had the Israelites not sinned in the episode of the spies (*parashas Shlach*) they would have entered the Promised Land much earlier in the course of their journey, without having to wage war, and would not have been compelled to wander in the wilderness for close to forty years. The seven nations would have forsaken the land on their own, as indeed one of them (the Girgoshi) did, as *Rashi* tells us in *Exodus* 33:2 where only six of the seven nations are mentioned because one had already left voluntarily. However, since the Israelites sinned, the inhabitants of the land intensified their evil ways during the forty years of Israel's wanderings, thereby necessitating a prolonged war of conquest by Joshua and the Israelite army. The original intent of taking the census and organizing the tribes under their individual ensigns was not for military purposes, but rather to lead them to *Eretz Yisrael* in an organized and dignified manner. The verse from Isaiah cited by the *Sforno* alludes to the nature of the conquest, when cities were forsaken in the manner of woods and forests which are uninhabited.

בְּמִסְפַּר שֵׁמוֹת — *According to the number of*

ו־ז בֶּן־שְׁדֵיאוּר: לְשִׁמְעוֹן שְׁלֻמִיאֵל בֶּן־צוּרִישַׁדָּי: לִיהוּדָה נַחְשׁוֹן בֶּן־עַמִּינָדָב:
ח־י לְיִשָּׂשכָר נְתַנְאֵל בֶּן־צוּעָר: לִזְבוּלֻן אֱלִיאָב בֶּן־חֵלֹן: לִבְנֵי יוֹסֵף לְאֶפְרַיִם
יא אֱלִישָׁמָע בֶּן־עַמִּיהוּד לִמְנַשֶּׁה גַּמְלִיאֵל בֶּן־פְּדָהצוּר: לְבִנְיָמִן אֲבִידָן
יב־יד בֶּן־גִּדְעֹנִי: לְדָן אֲחִיעֶזֶר בֶּן־עַמִּישַׁדָּי: לְאָשֵׁר פַּגְעִיאֵל בֶּן־עָכְרָן: לְגָד
°קְרוּאֵי ק׳ טו־טז אֶלְיָסָף בֶּן־דְּעוּאֵל: לְנַפְתָּלִי אֲחִירַע בֶּן־עֵינָן: אֵלֶּה °קריאי הָעֵדָה
יז נְשִׂיאֵי מַטּוֹת אֲבוֹתָם רָאשֵׁי אַלְפֵי יִשְׂרָאֵל הֵם: וַיִּקַּח מֹשֶׁה וְאַהֲרֹן אֵת
יח הָאֲנָשִׁים הָאֵלֶּה אֲשֶׁר נִקְּבוּ בְּשֵׁמוֹת: וְאֵת כָּל־הָעֵדָה הִקְהִילוּ בְּאֶחָד
לַחֹדֶשׁ הַשֵּׁנִי וַיִּתְיַלְדוּ עַל־מִשְׁפְּחֹתָם לְבֵית אֲבֹתָם בְּמִסְפַּר שֵׁמוֹת מִבֶּן
יט עֶשְׂרִים שָׁנָה וָמַעְלָה לְגֻלְגְּלֹתָם: כַּאֲשֶׁר צִוָּה יהוה אֶת־מֹשֶׁה וַיִּפְקְדֵם
שני כ בְּמִדְבַּר סִינָי: וַיִּהְיוּ בְנֵי־רְאוּבֵן בְּכֹר יִשְׂרָאֵל
תּוֹלְדֹתָם לְמִשְׁפְּחֹתָם לְבֵית אֲבֹתָם בְּמִסְפַּר שֵׁמוֹת לְגֻלְגְּלֹתָם כָּל־זָכָר
כא מִבֶּן עֶשְׂרִים שָׁנָה וָמַעְלָה כֹּל יֹצֵא צָבָא: פְּקֻדֵיהֶם לְמַטֵּה רְאוּבֵן שִׁשָּׁה
וְאַרְבָּעִים אֶלֶף וַחֲמֵשׁ מֵאוֹת:
כב לִבְנֵי שִׁמְעוֹן תּוֹלְדֹתָם לְמִשְׁפְּחֹתָם לְבֵית אֲבֹתָם פְּקֻדָיו בְּמִסְפַּר שֵׁמוֹת
כג לְגֻלְגְּלֹתָם כָּל־זָכָר מִבֶּן עֶשְׂרִים שָׁנָה וָמַעְלָה כֹּל יֹצֵא צָבָא: פְּקֻדֵיהֶם
לְמַטֵּה שִׁמְעוֹן תִּשְׁעָה וַחֲמִשִּׁים אֶלֶף וּשְׁלֹשׁ מֵאוֹת:
כד לִבְנֵי גָד תּוֹלְדֹתָם לְמִשְׁפְּחֹתָם לְבֵית אֲבֹתָם בְּמִסְפַּר שֵׁמוֹת מִבֶּן עֶשְׂרִים
כה שָׁנָה וָמַעְלָה כֹּל יֹצֵא צָבָא: פְּקֻדֵיהֶם לְמַטֵּה גָד חֲמִשָּׁה וְאַרְבָּעִים אֶלֶף
וְשֵׁשׁ מֵאוֹת וַחֲמִשִּׁים:
כו לִבְנֵי יְהוּדָה תּוֹלְדֹתָם לְמִשְׁפְּחֹתָם לְבֵית אֲבֹתָם בְּמִסְפַּר שֵׁמֹת מִבֶּן

---

18. וַיִּתְיַלְדוּ עַל מִשְׁפְּחֹתָם — *And they declared their pedigrees according to their families* ... because the purpose of this census was to enable the army to go out to war; hence, the intent was to protect their pedigree since the merit of their fathers would assist them (see *Kiddushin* 76b). Thus (our Sages) have stated, 'We make no investigation of one who was recorded among the king's list of officers' (*Kiddushin* 76a), and this is in accordance with the statement, 'The Divine Presence rests only upon families of pure birth in Israel' (*Kiddushin* 70b).

20. בְּכֹר יִשְׂרָאֵל — *Israel's firstborn.* For he (Reuben) did not fall from his elevated status according to the law of heaven because he repented, as we find, וַיִּהְיוּ בְנֵי יַעֲקֹב שְׁנֵים עָשָׂר בְּנֵי לֵאָה בְּכוֹר יַעֲקֹב רְאוּבֵן, *And the sons of Jacob were twelve; the sons of Leah, Jacob's firstborn, Reuben* (*Genesis* 35:22, 23); even though he fell from this status according to the law (i.e., perspective) of man.

NOTES

names. The significance of names is established by the *Sforno* in his commentary on *Exodus* 1:1.

18. וַיִּתְיַלְדוּ עַל מִשְׁפְּחֹתָם — *And they declared their pedigrees according to their families* ... Although the original and primary purpose of the census was to lead them into the Land in an orderly fashion, as explained above; nonetheless it was also for the purpose of organizing them into a disciplined, efficient army. As such, their יִחוּס, *lineage,* was an extremely important factor, for in the merit of their familial purity God would protect them.

20. בְּכֹר יִשְׂרָאֵל — *Israel's firstborn.* See *Genesis* 35:23, the *Sforno's* commentary on that verse and the explanatory note.

כז עֶשְׂרִ֥ים שָׁנָ֖ה וָמַ֑עְלָה כֹּ֖ל יֹצֵ֥א צָבָֽא׃ פְּקֻדֵיהֶ֖ם לְמַטֵּ֣ה יְהוּדָ֑ה אַרְבָּעָ֧ה
וְשִׁבְעִ֛ים אֶ֖לֶף וְשֵׁ֥שׁ מֵאֽוֹת׃
כח לִבְנֵ֣י יִשָּׂשכָ֔ר תּוֹלְדֹתָ֥ם לְמִשְׁפְּחֹתָ֖ם לְבֵ֣ית אֲבֹתָ֑ם בְּמִסְפַּ֣ר שֵׁמֹ֗ת מִבֶּ֨ן
כט עֶשְׂרִ֤ים שָׁנָה֙ וָמַ֔עְלָה כֹּ֖ל יֹצֵ֥א צָבָֽא׃ פְּקֻדֵיהֶ֖ם לְמַטֵּ֣ה יִשָּׂשכָ֑ר אַרְבָּעָ֧ה
וַחֲמִשִּׁ֛ים אֶ֖לֶף וְאַרְבַּ֥ע מֵאֽוֹת׃
ל לִבְנֵ֣י זְבוּלֻ֔ן תּוֹלְדֹתָ֥ם לְמִשְׁפְּחֹתָ֖ם לְבֵ֣ית אֲבֹתָ֑ם בְּמִסְפַּ֣ר שֵׁמֹ֗ת מִבֶּ֨ן
לא עֶשְׂרִ֤ים שָׁנָה֙ וָמַ֔עְלָה כֹּ֖ל יֹצֵ֥א צָבָֽא׃ פְּקֻדֵיהֶ֖ם לְמַטֵּ֣ה זְבוּלֻ֑ן שִׁבְעָ֧ה וַחֲמִשִּׁ֛ים
אֶ֖לֶף וְאַרְבַּ֥ע מֵאֽוֹת׃
לב לִבְנֵ֤י יוֹסֵף֙ לִבְנֵ֣י אֶפְרַ֔יִם תּוֹלְדֹתָ֥ם לְמִשְׁפְּחֹתָ֖ם לְבֵ֣ית אֲבֹתָ֑ם בְּמִסְפַּ֣ר שֵׁמֹ֗ת
לג מִבֶּ֨ן עֶשְׂרִ֤ים שָׁנָה֙ וָמַ֔עְלָה כֹּ֖ל יֹצֵ֥א צָבָֽא׃ פְּקֻדֵיהֶ֖ם לְמַטֵּ֣ה אֶפְרָ֑יִם אַרְבָּעִ֥ים
אֶ֖לֶף וַחֲמֵ֥שׁ מֵאֽוֹת׃
לד לִבְנֵ֣י מְנַשֶּׁ֔ה תּוֹלְדֹתָ֥ם לְמִשְׁפְּחֹתָ֖ם לְבֵ֣ית אֲבֹתָ֑ם בְּמִסְפַּ֣ר שֵׁמ֗וֹת מִבֶּ֨ן
לה עֶשְׂרִ֤ים שָׁנָה֙ וָמַ֔עְלָה כֹּ֖ל יֹצֵ֥א צָבָֽא׃ פְּקֻדֵיהֶ֖ם לְמַטֵּ֣ה מְנַשֶּׁ֑ה שְׁנַ֧יִם וּשְׁלֹשִׁ֛ים
אֶ֖לֶף וּמָאתָֽיִם׃
לו לִבְנֵ֣י בִנְיָמִ֔ן תּוֹלְדֹתָ֥ם לְמִשְׁפְּחֹתָ֖ם לְבֵ֣ית אֲבֹתָ֑ם בְּמִסְפַּ֣ר שֵׁמֹ֗ת מִבֶּ֨ן
לז עֶשְׂרִ֤ים שָׁנָה֙ וָמַ֔עְלָה כֹּ֖ל יֹצֵ֥א צָבָֽא׃ פְּקֻדֵיהֶ֖ם לְמַטֵּ֣ה בִנְיָמִ֑ן חֲמִשָּׁ֧ה וּשְׁלֹשִׁ֛ים
אֶ֖לֶף וְאַרְבַּ֥ע מֵאֽוֹת׃
לח לִבְנֵ֣י דָ֔ן תּוֹלְדֹתָ֥ם לְמִשְׁפְּחֹתָ֖ם לְבֵ֣ית אֲבֹתָ֑ם בְּמִסְפַּ֣ר שֵׁמֹ֗ת מִבֶּ֨ן עֶשְׂרִ֤ים
לט שָׁנָה֙ וָמַ֔עְלָה כֹּ֖ל יֹצֵ֥א צָבָֽא׃ פְּקֻדֵיהֶ֖ם לְמַטֵּ֣ה דָ֑ן שְׁנַ֧יִם וְשִׁשִּׁ֛ים אֶ֖לֶף וּשְׁבַ֥ע
מֵאֽוֹת׃
מ לִבְנֵ֣י אָשֵׁ֔ר תּוֹלְדֹתָ֥ם לְמִשְׁפְּחֹתָ֖ם לְבֵ֣ית אֲבֹתָ֑ם בְּמִסְפַּ֣ר שֵׁמֹ֗ת מִבֶּ֨ן עֶשְׂרִ֤ים
מא שָׁנָה֙ וָמַ֔עְלָה כֹּ֖ל יֹצֵ֥א צָבָֽא׃ פְּקֻדֵיהֶ֖ם לְמַטֵּ֣ה אָשֵׁ֑ר אֶחָ֧ד וְאַרְבָּעִ֛ים אֶ֖לֶף
וַחֲמֵ֥שׁ מֵאֽוֹת׃
מב בְּנֵ֣י נַפְתָּלִ֔י תּוֹלְדֹתָ֥ם לְמִשְׁפְּחֹתָ֖ם לְבֵ֣ית אֲבֹתָ֑ם בְּמִסְפַּ֣ר שֵׁמֹ֗ת מִבֶּ֨ן עֶשְׂרִ֤ים
מג שָׁנָה֙ וָמַ֔עְלָה כֹּ֖ל יֹצֵ֥א צָבָֽא׃ פְּקֻדֵיהֶ֖ם לְמַטֵּ֣ה נַפְתָּלִ֑י שְׁלֹשָׁ֧ה וַחֲמִשִּׁ֛ים אֶ֖לֶף
וְאַרְבַּ֥ע מֵאֽוֹת׃
מד אֵ֣לֶּה הַפְּקֻדִ֡ים אֲשֶׁר֩ פָּקַ֨ד מֹשֶׁ֤ה וְאַהֲרֹן֙ וּנְשִׂיאֵ֣י יִשְׂרָאֵ֔ל שְׁנֵ֥ים עָשָׂ֖ר אִ֑ישׁ
מה אִישׁ־אֶחָ֥ד לְבֵית־אֲבֹתָ֖יו הָיֽוּ׃ וַיִּהְי֛וּ כָּל־פְּקוּדֵ֥י בְנֵֽי־יִשְׂרָאֵ֖ל לְבֵ֣ית אֲבֹתָ֑ם
מו מִבֶּ֨ן עֶשְׂרִ֤ים שָׁנָה֙ וָמַ֔עְלָה כָּל־יֹצֵ֥א צָבָ֖א בְּיִשְׂרָאֵֽל׃ וַיִּֽהְיוּ֙ כָּל־הַפְּקֻדִ֔ים
מז שֵׁשׁ־מֵא֥וֹת אֶ֖לֶף וּשְׁלֹ֣שֶׁת אֲלָפִ֑ים וַחֲמֵ֥שׁ מֵא֖וֹת וַחֲמִשִּֽׁים׃ וְהַלְוִיִּ֖ם לְמַטֵּ֣ה
אֲבֹתָ֑ם לֹ֥א הָתְפָּקְד֖וּ בְּתוֹכָֽם׃

---

44. אֵלֶּה הַפְּקֻדִים — *These are those that were numbered.* Each one of these was counted by Moses and Aaron.

45. וַיִּהְיוּ כָּל פְּקוּדֵי . . . כָּל יֹצֵא צָבָא בְּיִשְׂרָאֵל — *And all those that were numbered . . . all that were able to go forth to war in Israel . . .* not including those over sixty years of age who no longer went forth to war, as (our Sages) mention regarding Yair the son of Menashe and others (*Bava Basra* 121b). Now, without them, the total was that which is written later (in the following verse).

מח-מט וַיְדַבֵּ֥ר יְהֹוָ֖ה אֶל־מֹשֶׁ֥ה לֵּאמֹֽר: אַ֣ךְ אֶת־מַטֵּ֤ה לֵוִי֙ לֹ֣א תִפְקֹ֔ד וְאֶת־
נ רֹאשָׁ֖ם לֹ֣א תִשָּׂ֑א בְּת֖וֹךְ בְּנֵ֥י יִשְׂרָאֵֽל: וְאַתָּ֗ה הַפְקֵ֤ד אֶת־הַלְוִיִּם֙ עַל־מִשְׁכַּ֣ן
הָעֵדֻ֗ת וְעַ֤ל כָּל־כֵּלָיו֙ וְעַ֣ל כָּל־אֲשֶׁר־ל֔וֹ הֵ֜מָּה יִשְׂא֤וּ אֶת־הַמִּשְׁכָּן֙
נא וְאֶת־כָּל־כֵּלָ֔יו וְהֵ֖ם יְשָׁרְתֻ֑הוּ וְסָבִ֥יב לַמִּשְׁכָּ֖ן יַחֲנֽוּ: וּבִנְסֹ֣עַ הַמִּשְׁכָּן֮ יוֹרִ֣ידוּ
נב אֹתוֹ֙ הַלְוִיִּ֔ם וּבַחֲנֹת֙ הַמִּשְׁכָּ֔ן יָקִ֥ימוּ אֹת֖וֹ הַלְוִיִּ֑ם וְהַזָּ֥ר הַקָּרֵ֖ב יוּמָֽת: וְחָנ֖וּ בְּנֵ֣י
נג יִשְׂרָאֵ֑ל אִ֧ישׁ עַֽל־מַחֲנֵ֛הוּ וְאִ֥ישׁ עַל־דִּגְל֖וֹ לְצִבְאֹתָֽם: וְהַלְוִיִּ֗ם יַחֲנ֣וּ סָבִיב֮

---

47. לֹא הָתְפָּקְדוּ בְּתוֹכָם — *Were not numbered among them.* They were not numbered by the census takers nor did they count themselves, for they did not prepare themselves, as did the others, by gathering (in order to establish their) lineage. Now this was *before* God, the Blessed One, said to Moses, *Nevertheless, the tribe of Levi you shall not number* (v. 49), because they waited to see what God would command them (to do) since the tribe of Levi was not mentioned with the other tribes when He said, *And with you there shall be a man from every tribe* (v. 4).

49. אַךְ אֶת מַטֵּה לֵוִי — *Nevertheless, the tribe of Levi.* Even though I said, *Take you the sum of all the congregation of the Children of Israel* (v. 2), and the Levites are included among them to be counted as well, nonetheless, they are separated from the rest of the people of Israel (in two ways): Firstly, regarding the count, that the counting of their men (is different), and (also in that) their sum total shall not be included with the rest of the people.

לֹא תִפְקֹד — *You shall not number.* The counting of their individuals shall not be from twenty years old and higher, as was the case with the counting of the rest of the people.

וְאֶת רֹאשָׁם לֹא תִשָּׂא — *Neither shall you take their sum.* When you take the total count of all the tribes (of Israel), the total of the tribe of Levi shall not be included (with them).

50. וְאַתָּה הַפְקֵד — *And you shall appoint.* Secondly, they shall be separated from the rest of the people regarding their appointments, for only they shall be assigned the sacred appointments.

53. וְהַלְוִיִּם יַחֲנוּ סָבִיב לַמִּשְׁכָּן — *But the Levites shall pitch round about the Sanctuary.* Thirdly, they shall be separated from the rest of the people in their encampment, for they alone shall encamp round about the Sanctuary, while the others shall encamp each one with his own standard.

NOTES

47. לֹא הָתְפָּקְדוּ בְּתוֹכָם — *Were not numbered among them.* The expression הָתְפָּקְדוּ, *numbered,* is written in the הִתְפַּעֵל (reflexive form), suggesting that they themselves (the Levites) were the ones doing the act of counting, as well as being the referents. The *Sforno,* therefore, explains that they were neither counted by the census takers nor did they gather and prepare themselves for a count as did the others. Since the tribe of Levi was not

included when God told Moses to take a representative from each tribe with whom to take the census, the Levites realized that their counting was to be different — and separate — from that of the rest of Israel.

49-53. אַךְ אֶת מַטֵּה לֵוִי לֹא תִפְקֹד ... וְאַתָּה הַפְקֵד ...וְהַלְוִיִּם יַחֲנוּ סָבִיב לַמִּשְׁכָּן — *Nevertheless, the tribe of Levi you shall not number ... And you shall appoint ... But the Levites shall pitch*

לְמִשְׁכַּן הָעֵדֻת וְלֹא־יִהְיֶה קֶצֶף עַל־עֲדַת בְּנֵי יִשְׂרָאֵל וְשָׁמְרוּ הַלְוִיִּם
נד אֶת־מִשְׁמֶרֶת מִשְׁכַּן הָעֵדוּת: וַיַּעֲשׂוּ בְּנֵי יִשְׂרָאֵל כְּכֹל אֲשֶׁר צִוָּה יְהוָה
אֶת־מֹשֶׁה כֵּן עָשׂוּ:
ב שלישי א־ב וַיְדַבֵּר יְהוָה אֶל־מֹשֶׁה וְאֶל־אַהֲרֹן לֵאמֹר: אִישׁ עַל־דִּגְלוֹ בְאֹתֹת לְבֵית
ג אֲבֹתָם יַחֲנוּ בְּנֵי יִשְׂרָאֵל מִנֶּגֶד סָבִיב לְאֹהֶל־מוֹעֵד יַחֲנוּ: וְהַחֹנִים קֵדְמָה
מִזְרָחָה דֶּגֶל מַחֲנֵה יְהוּדָה לְצִבְאֹתָם וְנָשִׂיא לִבְנֵי יְהוּדָה נַחְשׁוֹן
ד־ה בֶּן־עַמִּינָדָב: וּצְבָאוֹ וּפְקֻדֵיהֶם אַרְבָּעָה וְשִׁבְעִים אֶלֶף וְשֵׁשׁ מֵאוֹת: וְהַחֹנִים
ו עָלָיו מַטֵּה יִשָּׂשכָר וְנָשִׂיא לִבְנֵי יִשָּׂשכָר נְתַנְאֵל בֶּן־צוּעָר: וּצְבָאוֹ וּפְקֻדָיו
ז אַרְבָּעָה וַחֲמִשִּׁים אֶלֶף וְאַרְבַּע מֵאוֹת: מַטֵּה זְבוּלֻן וְנָשִׂיא לִבְנֵי זְבוּלֻן
ח אֱלִיאָב בֶּן־חֵלֹן: וּצְבָאוֹ וּפְקֻדָיו שִׁבְעָה וַחֲמִשִּׁים אֶלֶף וְאַרְבַּע מֵאוֹת:
ט כָּל־הַפְּקֻדִים לְמַחֲנֵה יְהוּדָה מְאַת אֶלֶף וּשְׁמֹנִים אֶלֶף וְשֵׁשֶׁת־אֲלָפִים
י וְאַרְבַּע־מֵאוֹת לְצִבְאֹתָם רִאשֹׁנָה יִסָּעוּ: דֶּגֶל מַחֲנֵה רְאוּבֵן
יא תֵּימָנָה לְצִבְאֹתָם וְנָשִׂיא לִבְנֵי רְאוּבֵן אֱלִיצוּר בֶּן־שְׁדֵיאוּר: וּצְבָאוֹ וּפְקֻדָיו
יב שִׁשָּׁה וְאַרְבָּעִים אֶלֶף וַחֲמֵשׁ מֵאוֹת: וְהַחוֹנִם עָלָיו מַטֵּה שִׁמְעוֹן וְנָשִׂיא לִבְנֵי
יג שִׁמְעוֹן שְׁלֻמִיאֵל בֶּן־צוּרִישַׁדָּי: וּצְבָאוֹ וּפְקֻדֵיהֶם תִּשְׁעָה וַחֲמִשִּׁים אֶלֶף
יד־טו וּשְׁלֹשׁ מֵאוֹת: וּמַטֵּה גָּד וְנָשִׂיא לִבְנֵי גָד אֶלְיָסָף בֶּן־רְעוּאֵל: וּצְבָאוֹ
טז וּפְקֻדֵיהֶם חֲמִשָּׁה וְאַרְבָּעִים אֶלֶף וְשֵׁשׁ מֵאוֹת וַחֲמִשִּׁים: כָּל־הַפְּקֻדִים
לְמַחֲנֵה רְאוּבֵן מְאַת אֶלֶף וְאֶחָד וַחֲמִשִּׁים אֶלֶף וְאַרְבַּע־מֵאוֹת וַחֲמִשִּׁים
יז לְצִבְאֹתָם וּשְׁנִיִּם יִסָּעוּ: וְנָסַע אֹהֶל־מוֹעֵד מַחֲנֵה הַלְוִיִּם בְּתוֹךְ
יח הַמַּחֲנֹת כַּאֲשֶׁר יַחֲנוּ כֵּן יִסָּעוּ אִישׁ עַל־יָדוֹ לְדִגְלֵיהֶם: דֶּגֶל

II

17. וְנָסַע אֹהֶל מוֹעֵד . . . בְּתוֹךְ הַמַּחֲנֹת — *Then the Tent of Meeting traveled . . . in the midst of the camps* . . . between the two aforementioned standards (Judah and Reuben).

כַּאֲשֶׁר יַחֲנוּ — *As they encamped.* So that when half of all the standards arrive, the Sanctuary will be completely standing in their midst, for immediately following the standard of Reuben traveled the Kehathites who carried the holy (articles) which are the central (feature) of the (Tent of) Meeting, as it says, וְנוֹעַדְתִּי לְךָ שָׁם וְדִבַּרְתִּי אִתְּךָ מֵעַל הַכַּפֹּרֶת, *And there I will meet with you and I will speak with you from above the Ark cover* (Exodus 25:22).

כַּאֲשֶׁר יַחֲנוּ כֵּן יִסָּעוּ — *As they encamp, so they shall journey* . . . and therefore, the entire (*Mishkan*) was in the midst of all the camps, even when they journeyed.

NOTES

round about the Sanctuary. The Levites were distinct from the rest of the Israelites in three ways. Since they were counted from the age of thirty days rather than twenty years, their total number was not included in the sum total of all the tribes. Secondly, they alone were charged with the sacred service connected with the Sanctuary, and thirdly, they alone encamped around the Sanctuary, unlike the other tribes who encamped as distinct units under their individual banners. The reason for this differentiation and separation was because they were exempt from military service, for their mission was to serve in the Sanctuary.

II

17. וְנָסַע אֹהֶל מוֹעֵד . . . בְּתוֹךְ הַמַּחֲנֹת — *Then the Tent of Meeting traveled . . . in the midst of the*

מַחֲנֵ֥ה אֶפְרַ֛יִם לְצִבְאֹתָ֖ם יָ֑מָּה וְנָשִׂיא֙ לִבְנֵ֣י אֶפְרַ֔יִם אֱלִישָׁמָ֖ע בֶּן־עַמִּיהֽוּד׃
יט־כ וּצְבָא֖וֹ וּפְקֻדֵיהֶ֑ם אַרְבָּעִ֥ים אֶ֖לֶף וַחֲמֵ֥שׁ מֵאֽוֹת׃ וְעָלָ֖יו מַטֵּ֣ה מְנַשֶּׁ֑ה
כא וְנָשִׂיא֙ לִבְנֵ֣י מְנַשֶּׁ֔ה גַּמְלִיאֵ֖ל בֶּן־פְּדָהצֽוּר׃ וּצְבָא֖וֹ וּפְקֻדֵיהֶ֑ם שְׁנַ֧יִם
כב וּשְׁלֹשִׁ֛ים אֶ֖לֶף וּמָאתָֽיִם׃ וּמַטֵּ֖ה בִּנְיָמִ֑ן וְנָשִׂיא֙ לִבְנֵ֣י בִנְיָמִ֔ן אֲבִידָ֖ן בֶּן־גִּדְעֹנִֽי׃
כג־כד וּצְבָא֖וֹ וּפְקֻדֵיהֶ֑ם חֲמִשָּׁ֧ה וּשְׁלֹשִׁ֛ים אֶ֖לֶף וְאַרְבַּ֥ע מֵאֽוֹת׃ כָּֽל־הַפְּקֻדִ֞ים
לְמַחֲנֵ֣ה אֶפְרַ֗יִם מְאַ֥ת אֶ֛לֶף וּשְׁמֹנַת־אֲלָפִ֥ים וּמֵאָ֖ה לְצִבְאֹתָ֑ם וּשְׁלִשִׁ֖ים
כה יִסָּֽעוּ׃ דֶּ֣גֶל מַחֲנֵ֥ה דָ֛ן צָפֹ֖נָה לְצִבְאֹתָ֑ם וְנָשִׂיא֙ לִבְנֵ֣י דָ֔ן
כו אֲחִיעֶ֖זֶר בֶּן־עַמִּישַׁדָּֽי׃ וּצְבָא֖וֹ וּפְקֻדֵיהֶ֑ם שְׁנַ֧יִם וְשִׁשִּׁ֛ים אֶ֖לֶף וּשְׁבַ֥ע מֵאֽוֹת׃
כז־כח וְהַחֹנִ֥ים עָלָ֖יו מַטֵּ֣ה אָשֵׁ֑ר וְנָשִׂיא֙ לִבְנֵ֣י אָשֵׁ֔ר פַּגְעִיאֵ֖ל בֶּן־עָכְרָֽן׃ וּצְבָא֖וֹ
כט וּפְקֻדֵיהֶ֑ם אֶחָ֧ד וְאַרְבָּעִ֛ים אֶ֖לֶף וַחֲמֵ֥שׁ מֵאֽוֹת׃ וּמַטֵּ֖ה נַפְתָּלִ֑י וְנָשִׂיא֙ לִבְנֵ֣י
ל נַפְתָּלִ֔י אֲחִירַ֖ע בֶּן־עֵינָֽן׃ וּצְבָא֖וֹ וּפְקֻדֵיהֶ֑ם שְׁלֹשָׁ֧ה וַחֲמִשִּׁ֛ים אֶ֖לֶף וְאַרְבַּ֥ע
לא מֵאֽוֹת׃ כָּל־הַפְּקֻדִים֙ לְמַחֲנֵ֣ה דָ֔ן מְאַ֣ת אֶ֗לֶף וְשִׁבְעָ֧ה וַחֲמִשִּׁ֛ים אֶ֖לֶף וְשֵׁ֣שׁ
מֵא֑וֹת לָאַחֲרֹנָ֥ה יִסְע֖וּ לְדִגְלֵיהֶֽם׃
לב אֵ֛לֶּה פְּקוּדֵ֥י בְנֵֽי־יִשְׂרָאֵ֖ל לְבֵ֣ית אֲבֹתָ֑ם כָּל־פְּקוּדֵ֤י הַֽמַּחֲנֹת֙ לְצִבְאֹתָ֔ם
לג שֵׁשׁ־מֵא֤וֹת אֶ֙לֶף֙ וּשְׁלֹ֣שֶׁת אֲלָפִ֔ים וַחֲמֵ֥שׁ מֵא֖וֹת וַחֲמִשִּֽׁים׃ וְהַ֨לְוִיִּ֔ם לֹ֣א
לד הָתְפָּקְד֔וּ בְּת֖וֹךְ בְּנֵ֣י יִשְׂרָאֵ֑ל כַּאֲשֶׁ֛ר צִוָּ֥ה יְהֹוָ֖ה אֶת־מֹשֶֽׁה׃ וַֽיַּעֲשׂ֖וּ בְּנֵ֣י
יִשְׂרָאֵ֑ל כְּכֹל֩ אֲשֶׁר־צִוָּ֨ה יְהֹוָ֜ה אֶת־מֹשֶׁ֗ה כֵּֽן־חָנ֤וּ לְדִגְלֵיהֶם֙ וְכֵ֣ן נָסָ֔עוּ אִ֥ישׁ
לְמִשְׁפְּחֹתָ֖יו עַל־בֵּ֥ית אֲבֹתָֽיו׃

---

33. וְהַלְוִיִּם לֹא הָתְפָּקְדוּ — *But the Levites were not numbered . . .* in the sum total of all the other tribes, as well.

כַּאֲשֶׁר צִוָּה ה׳ אֶת מֹשֶׁה — *As* HASHEM *commanded Moses.* As He said, *Neither shall you take their sum among the Children of Israel* (1:49).

NOTES

camps. It would seem from *Rashi's* commentary on this verse that he is of the opinion that after the camps of Judah and Reuben had set off, the Tent of Meeting with the Levites immediately began to move, followed by the remaining two camps. (see the *Sifsai Chachomim* on this *Rashi*). The *Sforno*, however, is of the opinion that immediately following Judah's departure, the Tent of Meeting with the Levites followed, *after which* the camp of Reuben set out. In chapter 10, verse 17, *Rashi* also seems to accept this interpretation (although he does not state so clearly). He states there that the encampment broke up in the following order: After the departure of the division of Judah, Aaron and his sons went into the Tabernacle and covered the Ark and all the other holy vessels which were in the charge of the Kehathites. Then the Gershonites and the Merarites dismantled the *Mishkan*, loaded it on the wagons, and started off behind Judah. Next came the division of Reuben and after them the Kehathites with the holy objects. All this is clearly stated in chapter 10 verses 17 and 21. The *Sforno's* interpretation of our verse is consistent with the order written in *Behaaloscha.*

כַּאֲשֶׁר יַחֲנוּ — *As they encamp.* The Kehathites were charged with carrying the Ark (3:31). The *Sforno*, therefore, refers to their arrival at the encampment as representing עִיקָּר אֹהֶל מוֹעֵד (the central, important feature of the Tent of Meeting), for God spoke to Moses above the Ark cover. Now, since they followed immediately after the section of Reuben which was the second group after Judah, one half of all the camps were now in place, with the Tabernacle set up in the middle by the Gershonites and Merarites when the Kehathites arrived with the ark. (See *Rashi* on 10:21 for a fuller description of the sequence followed during Israel's journeying and encamping.)

ג רביעי א־ב וְאֵ֣לֶּה תְּוֹלְדֹ֤ת אַהֲרֹן֙ וּמֹשֶׁ֔ה בְּי֗וֹם דִּבֶּ֧ר יְהוָ֛ה אֶת־מֹשֶׁ֖ה בְּהַ֣ר סִינָֽי: וְאֵ֛לֶּה
ג שְׁמ֥וֹת בְּנֵ֣י־אַהֲרֹ֖ן הַבְּכֹ֣ר ׀ נָדָ֑ב וַאֲבִיה֛וּא אֶלְעָזָ֖ר וְאִיתָמָֽר: אֵ֗לֶּה שְׁמוֹת֙ בְּנֵ֣י
ד אַהֲרֹ֗ן הַכֹּֽהֲנִים֙ הַמְּשֻׁחִ֔ים אֲשֶׁר־מִלֵּ֥א יָדָ֖ם לְכַהֵֽן: וַיָּ֣מָת נָדָ֣ב וַאֲבִיה֣וּא לִפְנֵ֣י
יְהוָ֡ה בְּהַקְרִבָם֩ אֵ֨שׁ זָרָ֜ה לִפְנֵ֤י יְהוָה֙ בְּמִדְבַּ֣ר סִינַ֔י וּבָנִ֖ים לֹא־הָי֣וּ לָהֶ֑ם וַיְכַהֵ֤ן
אֶלְעָזָר֙ וְאִ֣יתָמָ֔ר עַל־פְּנֵ֖י אַהֲרֹ֥ן אֲבִיהֶֽם:

III

1. וְאֵלֶּה תוֹלְדֹת אַהֲרֹן וּמֹשֶׁה בְּיוֹם דִּבֶּר ה׳ אֶת מֹשֶׁה — *Now these are the generations of Aaron and Moses on the day that HASHEM spoke to Moses.* At the time that (God) separated the tribe of Levi, some to carry (the Tabernacle) and some to serve Him and bless His name, (at that time) Nadav and Avihu were among them.

2. וְאֵלֶּה שְׁמוֹת בְּנֵי אַהֲרֹן — *And these are the names of the sons of Aaron.* Each one of them was important in his own right besides (the fact that) he was the son of Aaron.

3. הַכֹּהֲנִים הַמְּשֻׁחִים — *The Kohanim that were anointed* ... unlike future generations when a כֹּהֵן הֶדְיוֹט, *an ordinary priest*, was never anointed during the lifetime of the *Kohen Gadol* — the reason being ...

אֲשֶׁר מִלֵּא יָדָם לְכַהֵן — *Whom he consecrated to minister in the Kohen's office* ... for at that time they required the anointing, without which they would never have become *Kohanim* at all since they were born before Aaron was chosen to function as a *Kohen*, as was the case (also) with Pinchas before he killed Zimri (see 25:13).

4. בְּהַקְרִבָם אֵשׁ זָרָה — *When they offered strange fire.* This was the only (sin) they had committed.

וּבָנִים לֹא הָיוּ לָהֶם — *And they had no children.* For if they would have had children to succeed them, they (the offspring) would have inherited the prominent positions fitting for their fathers.

וַיְכַהֵן אֶלְעָזָר וְאִיתָמָר — *And Elazar and Ithamar ministered in the Kohen's office.* They were appointed to exercise authority in the Sanctuary by the command of God, the Blessed One.

עַל פְּנֵי אַהֲרֹן אֲבִיהֶם — *In the presence of Aaron their father.* During Aaron's lifetime, his sons were anointed, two of whom died and two of whom gained

NOTES

III

2. וְאֵלֶּה שְׁמוֹת — *And these are the names.* The *Sforno* explains why the expression *These are the names* is repeated twice — in this verse and in verse 3; it is to emphasize the importance of each son in his own right, not only as the son of an illustrious father. For the significance of a 'name', see 1:2 above and the beginning of the Book of Exodus.

3. הַכֹּהֲנִים הַמְּשֻׁחִים — *The Kohanim that were anointed.* The son of a *Kohen* inherits the status of priesthood from his father, provided

he was born after his father already attained that status himself. The sons of Aaron required anointing to be consecrated as *Kohanim* since they were born before Aaron had been designated as the *Kohen Gadol*. This was also the case with Pinchas to whom God gave *the covenant of eternal priesthood* (25:13) for, as *Rashi* explains there, 'He was born before his father (Elazar) was designated as a *Kohen*;' hence, he could not attain priesthood through his lineage alone.

4. וּבָנִים לֹא הָיוּ לָהֶם — *And they had no children.* The *Sforno* explains the parenthetical

ה־ו וַיְדַבֵּר יְהוָה אֶל־מֹשֶׁה לֵּאמֹר: הַקְרֵב אֶת־מַטֵּה לֵוִי וְהַעֲמַדְתָּ אֹתוֹ לִפְנֵי
ז אַהֲרֹן הַכֹּהֵן וְשֵׁרְתוּ אֹתוֹ: וְשָׁמְרוּ אֶת־מִשְׁמַרְתּוֹ וְאֶת־מִשְׁמֶרֶת כָּל־הָעֵדָה
ח לִפְנֵי אֹהֶל מוֹעֵד לַעֲבֹד אֶת־עֲבֹדַת הַמִּשְׁכָּן: וְשָׁמְרוּ אֶת־כָּל־כְּלֵי אֹהֶל
ט מוֹעֵד וְאֶת־מִשְׁמֶרֶת בְּנֵי יִשְׂרָאֵל לַעֲבֹד אֶת־עֲבֹדַת הַמִּשְׁכָּן: וְנָתַתָּה אֶת־

---

authority; yet (all this took place) without his sanction even though he was the *Kohen Gadol*. Now this would not continue throughout the generations, for (there would come a time that) there would be no anointing of an ordinary *Kohen*, nor any appointment during the lifetime of the *Kohen Gadol* without his authorization.

6. וְשֵׁרְתוּ אֹתוֹ — *That they may minister unto him.* For the entire guardianship (of the Sanctuary) is vested in him, as it says, *You and your sons and your father's house with you shall bear the iniquity (i.e., responsibility) of the Sanctuary, and you and your sons with you shall bear the iniquity (i.e., responsibility) of your priesthood* (18:1). Therefore, the work of the Levites (was) to serve the *Kohen Gadol* in the area incumbent upon him, i.e., to guard the Sanctuary and its vessels, while the guarding of the priesthood, that no stranger should draw close, was incumbent only upon Aaron and his sons.

7. וְאֶת מִשְׁמֶרֶת כָּל הָעֵדָה לִפְנֵי אֹהֶל מוֹעֵד לַעֲבֹד אֶת עֲבֹדַת הַמִּשְׁכָּן — *And the charge of the whole congregation before the Tent of Meeting to do the service of the Sanctuary* ... to minister to the needs of the (Divine) service, which would have been the privilege of the members of the Sanhedrin, were it not for the sin of the Golden Calf.

8. מִשְׁמֶרֶת בְּנֵי יִשְׂרָאֵל לַעֲבֹד אֶת עֲבֹדַת הַמִּשְׁכָּן — *The charge of the Children of Israel to do the service of the Sanctuary* . . . to carry (the components of the *Mishkan*) and to sing (chant) which was (originally) the privilege of all Israel.

NOTES

insertion of the phrase *and they had no children* as the reason for Elazar and Ithamar succeeding to the priesthood following the death of their older brothers. If Nadav and Avihu would have had children, those children would have inherited their father's positions rather than Elazar and Ithamar.

עַל פְּנֵי אַהֲרֹן אֲבִיהֶם — *In the presence of Aaron their father.* The addition of this phrase is to be understood, as *Rashi* comments, in the sense of 'in his lifetime.' The Torah stresses this to teach us that only at that period in Jewish history was this so, i.e., that children attained positions of authority in the priesthood even while the *Kohen Gadol* was alive, yet without his sanction. In later generations, this would not be the case, as the *Sforno* explains.

6. וְשֵׁרְתוּ אֹתוֹ — *That they may minister unto him.* The *Sforno* draws a subtle distinction between the guardianship of the Sanctuary and its vessels, to which role the Levites were assigned to assist the *Kohen Gadol* (whose primary responsibility this was), and that of preventing any זָר, non-*Kohen*, from 'drawing close,' i.e., assuming the role reserved for the *Kohanim* alone, which is the *sole* responsibility of the *Kohanim* and did not require the Levites' intervention.

7. וְאֶת מִשְׁמֶרֶת כָּל הָעֵדָה לִפְנֵי אֹהֶל מוֹעֵד לַעֲבֹד אֶת עֲבֹדַת הַמִּשְׁכָּן — *And the charge of the whole congregation before the Tent of Meeting to do the service of the Sanctuary.* The phrase עֵדָה, *congregation*, in Biblical usage refers to the Sanhedrin. The *Sforno*, therefore, explains this verse as implying that, were it not for the sin of the Golden Calf, the members of the Sanhedrin would have been worthy to perform certain aspects of the service of the *Mishkan*, which are now assumed by the Levites.

י הַלְוִיִּם לְאַהֲרֹן וּלְבָנָיו נְתוּנִם נְתוּנִם הֵמָּה לוֹ מֵאֵת בְּנֵי יִשְׂרָאֵל: וְאֶת־אַהֲרֹן
וְאֶת־בָּנָיו תִּפְקֹד וְשָׁמְרוּ אֶת־כְּהֻנָּתָם וְהַזָּר הַקָּרֵב יוּמָת:
יא־יב וַיְדַבֵּר יְהוָה אֶל־מֹשֶׁה לֵּאמֹר: וַאֲנִי הִנֵּה לָקַחְתִּי אֶת־הַלְוִיִּם מִתּוֹךְ בְּנֵי
יג יִשְׂרָאֵל תַּחַת כָּל־בְּכוֹר פֶּטֶר רֶחֶם מִבְּנֵי יִשְׂרָאֵל וְהָיוּ לִי הַלְוִיִּם: כִּי לִי
כָּל־בְּכוֹר בְּיוֹם הַכֹּתִי כָל־בְּכוֹר בְּאֶרֶץ מִצְרַיִם הִקְדַּשְׁתִּי לִי כָל־בְּכוֹר

---

9. נְתוּנִם נְתוּנִם הֵמָּה לוֹ — *They are given, they are given to him.* All their (involvement with the Divine service) shall be exclusively according (to the instruction) of Aaron and his sons exclusively.

מֵאֵת בְּנֵי יִשְׂרָאֵל — *From the Children of Israel ...* who are obligated to give them the first tithe in exchange for their (participation in the Divine) service.

10. וְשָׁמְרוּ אֶת כְּהֻנָּתָם — *And they shall guard their priesthood ...* regarding everything (associated) with the altar and (the service) within the veil, that the Levites shall not draw nigh (to participate or enter).

וְהַזָּר הַקָּרֵב — *And the stranger* (*i.e., non-Levite or non-Kohen*) *that draws nigh ...* to the service of the Levites or the priesthood.

12. תַּחַת כָּל בְּכוֹר — *Instead of every firstborn ...* as a redemption.

וְהָיוּ לִי הַלְוִיִּם — *And the Levites shall be mine ...* for (My) service.

13. כִּי לִי כָּל בְּכוֹר — *For all the firstborn are Mine.* Originally, the service (of God) was done by the firstborn.

בְּיוֹם הַכֹּתִי כָל בְּכוֹר בְּאֶרֶץ מִצְרַיִם הִקְדַּשְׁתִּי לִי כָל בְּכוֹר בְּיִשְׂרָאֵל — *On the day that I smote all the firstborn in the land of Egypt, I sanctified unto Me all the firstborn in Israel.* Indeed, (at the time) of the smiting of the firstborn, the firstborn (of Israel) also deserved to be punished for the sins of that generation being that they were the most honored (members of the community); and they were not worthy of being saved from the plague visited on the community, similar to פֶּן תִּסָּפֶה בַּעֲוֹן הָעִיר, *Lest you be swept away in the iniquity of the city* (*Genesis* 19:15). But I saved them by sanctifying them unto Me; thus they are prohibited from engaging in ordinary (secular) labor, as is the law regarding sacred animals who may not be sheared or

NOTES

9. נְתוּנִם נְתוּנִם הֵמָּה לוֹ מֵאֵת בְּנֵי יִשְׂרָאֵל — *They are given, they are given to him from the Children of Israel.* The *Sforno's* interpretation is similar to that of *Rashi's* commentary on verse 8, except that *Rashi* understands מֵאֵת בְּנֵי יִשְׂרָאֵל as meaning the Levites were chosen and separated from the midst of Israel while the *Sforno* interprets this phrase as meaning that Israel is obligated to support the Levites in exchange for their ministration, which was originally meant to be performed by the entire people.

For a fuller understanding of the *Sforno's* interpretation of the phrase נְתוּנִם נְתוּנִם, *they are given, they are given,* see his commentary on 8:16-19.

13. בְּיוֹם הַכֹּתִי כָל בְּכוֹר בְּאֶרֶץ מִצְרַיִם הִקְדַּשְׁתִּי לִי כָל בְּכוֹר בְּיִשְׂרָאֵל — *On the day that I smote all the firstborn in the land of Egypt, I sanctified unto Me all the firstborn in Israel.* Originally, the firstborn son of each family was charged with the responsibility of spiritual leadership which included *avodah*, the service of God. See *Rashi* on *Genesis* 25:31 regarding the sale of the birthright by Esau to Jacob. As such, they were also responsible for the behavior of the members of their family, and hence were held accountable for the sins of their generation. Consequently, because of their special status, even the Jewish firstborn were vulnerable during the plague of the firstborn in Egypt. Only by sanctifying them

בְּיִשְׂרָאֵל מֵאָדָם עַד־בְּהֵמָה לִי יִהְיוּ אֲנִי יהוה:
חמישי יד־טו וַיְדַבֵּר יהוה אֶל־מֹשֶׁה בְּמִדְבַּר סִינַי לֵאמֹר: פְּקֹד אֶת־בְּנֵי לֵוִי לְבֵית
טז אֲבֹתָם לְמִשְׁפְּחֹתָם כָּל־זָכָר מִבֶּן־חֹדֶשׁ וָמַעְלָה תִּפְקְדֵם: וַיִּפְקֹד אֹתָם מֹשֶׁה
יז עַל־פִּי יהוה כַּאֲשֶׁר צֻוָּה: וַיִּהְיוּ־אֵלֶּה בְנֵי־לֵוִי בִּשְׁמֹתָם גֵּרְשׁוֹן וּקְהָת וּמְרָרִי:
יח־יט וְאֵלֶּה שְׁמוֹת בְּנֵי־גֵרְשׁוֹן לְמִשְׁפְּחֹתָם לִבְנִי וְשִׁמְעִי: וּבְנֵי קְהָת לְמִשְׁפְּחֹתָם
כ עַמְרָם וְיִצְהָר חֶבְרוֹן וְעֻזִּיאֵל: וּבְנֵי מְרָרִי לְמִשְׁפְּחֹתָם מַחְלִי וּמוּשִׁי אֵלֶּה הֵם
כא מִשְׁפְּחֹת הַלֵּוִי לְבֵית אֲבֹתָם: לְגֵרְשׁוֹן מִשְׁפַּחַת הַלִּבְנִי וּמִשְׁפַּחַת הַשִּׁמְעִי
כב אֵלֶּה הֵם מִשְׁפְּחֹת הַגֵּרְשֻׁנִּי: פְּקֻדֵיהֶם בְּמִסְפַּר כָּל־זָכָר מִבֶּן־חֹדֶשׁ וָמָעְלָה
כג פְּקֻדֵיהֶם שִׁבְעַת אֲלָפִים וַחֲמֵשׁ מֵאוֹת: מִשְׁפְּחֹת הַגֵּרְשֻׁנִּי אַחֲרֵי הַמִּשְׁכָּן
כד־כה יַחֲנוּ יָמָּה: וּנְשִׂיא בֵית־אָב לַגֵּרְשֻׁנִּי אֶלְיָסָף בֶּן־לָאֵל: וּמִשְׁמֶרֶת בְּנֵי־גֵרְשׁוֹן
כו בְּאֹהֶל מוֹעֵד הַמִּשְׁכָּן וְהָאֹהֶל מִכְסֵהוּ וּמָסַךְ פֶּתַח אֹהֶל מוֹעֵד: וְקַלְעֵי הֶחָצֵר
וְאֶת־מָסַךְ פֶּתַח הֶחָצֵר אֲשֶׁר עַל־הַמִּשְׁכָּן וְעַל־הַמִּזְבֵּחַ סָבִיב וְאֵת מֵיתָרָיו
כז לְכֹל עֲבֹדָתוֹ: וְלִקְהָת מִשְׁפַּחַת הָעַמְרָמִי וּמִשְׁפַּחַת

---

worked with. (Now) in order for them to be permitted to occupy (themselves in secular pursuits) redemption is necessary, as is the rule with all sacred objects (or animals) which are transformed into profane (objects), as it says, וְכֹל בְּכוֹר אָדָם בְּבָנֶיךָ תִּפְדֶּה, *And all the firstborn of man among your sons, you shall redeem* (*Exodus* 13:13). However, they were not absolved from (God's) service as a result of this redemption; only now that they sinned (with the Golden Calf), I rejected them and redeemed them by taking the Levites in their place.

מֵאָדָם עַד בְּהֵמָה לִי יִהְיוּ — *Both man and animal they shall be Mine* . . . both now and in the future — man for redemption and animals for sacrifice.

אֲנִי ה׳ — *I am* HASHEM. I did not change (based on *Malachi* 3:6), when I rejected the firstborn, for this change did not originate with Me but with them when they sinned. And so (also) the reason that I wanted the Levites to redeem the firstborn in this generation (only) and not in the future is because in this generation they are of sufficient worth to (redeem them) but they will not be so in the future.

NOTES

at that time were they saved by God, as the *Sforno* explains here and elaborates in his commentary on 8:17. Once sanctified however, they were not permitted to occupy themselves with non-sacred labor and therefore needed פִּדְיוֹן, *redemption*, as is the case with all *kodesh*, holy articles, as explained in *Exodus* 13:13. After the sin of the Golden Calf, the firstborn were relieved of their duties in the service of God, and this privilege was transferred to the Levites, who had remained steadfast in their loyalty to God at that time. The law of redemption, however, was unaffected, since their status of *kedushah* still remained. See the notes on 8:17 as well as the *Sforno's* commentary and the notes on *Exodus* 13:2.

אֲנִי ה׳ — *I am* HASHEM. The expression אֲנִי ה׳, *I am* HASHEM, at the conclusion of this verse requires explanation since there is no commandment given in this verse. It is to be understood, therefore, as an explanatory statement regarding the firstborn and the Levites. It is meant to stress the fact that although God, Who is unchanging, originally chose the firstborn to be His servants, a change in *their* status took place as a result of their participation in the sin of the Golden Calf. The *Sforno* also points out that Hashem determined that only in this generation were the Levites considered worthy to redeem the firstborn, but not in later generations. This is a second reason for the phrase אֲנִי ה׳ used at the conclusion of the verse.

הַיִּצְהָרִ֗י וּמִשְׁפַּ֙חַת֙ הַחֶבְרֹנִ֔י וּמִשְׁפַּ֖חַת הָעָזִּיאֵלִ֑י אֵ֥לֶּה הֵ֖ם מִשְׁפְּחֹ֥ת הַקְּהָתִֽי:

כח בְּמִסְפַּר֙ כָּל־זָכָ֔ר מִבֶּן־חֹ֖דֶשׁ וָמָ֑עְלָה שְׁמֹנַ֤ת אֲלָפִים֙ וְשֵׁ֣שׁ מֵא֔וֹת שֹׁמְרֵ֖י

כט-ל מִשְׁמֶ֥רֶת הַקֹּֽדֶשׁ: מִשְׁפְּחֹ֥ת בְּנֵי־קְהָ֖ת יַחֲנ֑וּ עַ֛ל יֶ֥רֶךְ הַמִּשְׁכָּ֖ן תֵּימָ֑נָה: וּנְשִׂ֣יא

לא בֵֽית־אָ֔ב לְמִשְׁפְּחֹ֖ת הַקְּהָתִ֑י אֱלִֽיצָפָ֖ן בֶּן־עֻזִּיאֵֽל: וּמִשְׁמַרְתָּ֗ם הָאָרֹ֤ן וְהַשֻּׁלְחָן֙

וְהַמְּנֹרָ֣ה וְהַֽמִּזְבְּחֹ֔ת וּכְלֵ֣י הַקֹּ֔דֶשׁ אֲשֶׁ֥ר יְשָׁרְת֖וּ בָּהֶ֑ם וְהַ֨מָּסָ֔ךְ וְכֹ֖ל עֲבֹֽדָתֽוֹ:

לב וּנְשִׂיא֙ נְשִׂיאֵ֣י הַלֵּוִ֔י אֶלְעָזָ֖ר בֶּן־אַֽהֲרֹ֣ן הַכֹּהֵ֑ן פְּקֻדַּ֕ת שֹׁמְרֵ֖י מִשְׁמֶ֥רֶת הַקֹּֽדֶשׁ:

לג לִמְרָרִ֕י מִשְׁפַּ֙חַת֙ הַמַּחְלִ֔י וּמִשְׁפַּ֖חַת הַמּוּשִׁ֑י אֵ֥לֶּה הֵ֖ם מִשְׁפְּחֹ֥ת מְרָרִֽי:

לד וּפְקֻֽדֵיהֶם֙ בְּמִסְפַּ֣ר כָּל־זָכָ֔ר מִבֶּן־חֹ֖דֶשׁ וָמָ֑עְלָה שֵׁ֥שֶׁת אֲלָפִ֖ים וּמָאתָֽיִם:

לה וּנְשִׂ֣יא בֵֽית־אָ֗ב לְמִשְׁפְּחֹת֙ מְרָרִ֔י צוּרִיאֵ֖ל בֶּן־אֲבִיחָ֑יִל עַ֣ל יֶ֧רֶךְ הַמִּשְׁכָּ֛ן יַחֲנ֖וּ

לו צָפֹֽנָה: וּפְקֻדַּ֣ת מִשְׁמֶרֶת֮ בְּנֵ֣י מְרָרִי֒ קַרְשֵׁי֙ הַמִּשְׁכָּ֔ן וּבְרִיחָ֖יו וְעַמֻּדָ֣יו וַאֲדָנָ֑יו

לז וְכָל־כֵּלָ֔יו וְכֹ֖ל עֲבֹֽדָתֽוֹ: וְעַמֻּדֵ֧י הֶחָצֵ֛ר סָבִ֖יב וְאַדְנֵיהֶ֑ם וִיתֵֽדֹתָ֖ם וּמֵֽיתְרֵיהֶֽם:

לח וְהַחֹנִ֣ים לִפְנֵ֣י הַמִּשְׁכָּ֡ן קֵ֣דְמָה לִפְנֵי֩ אֹֽהֶל־מוֹעֵ֨ד ׀ מִזְרָ֜חָה מֹשֶׁ֣ה ׀ וְאַֽהֲרֹ֣ן וּבָנָ֗יו

שֹֽׁמְרִים֙ מִשְׁמֶ֣רֶת הַמִּקְדָּ֔שׁ לְמִשְׁמֶ֖רֶת בְּנֵ֣י יִשְׂרָאֵ֑ל וְהַזָּ֥ר הַקָּרֵ֖ב יוּמָֽת:

לט כָּל־פְּקוּדֵ֨י הַלְוִיִּ֜ם אֲשֶׁר֩ פָּקַ֨ד מֹשֶׁ֧ה וְאַֽהֲרֹ֛ן עַל־פִּ֥י יְהֹוָ֖ה לְמִשְׁפְּחֹתָ֑ם

ששי מ כָּל־זָכָר֙ מִבֶּן־חֹ֣דֶשׁ וָמַ֔עְלָה שְׁנַ֥יִם וְעֶשְׂרִ֖ים אָֽלֶף: וַיֹּ֨אמֶר

יְהֹוָ֜ה אֶל־מֹשֶׁ֗ה פְּקֹ֨ד כָּל־בְּכֹ֤ר זָכָר֙ לִבְנֵ֣י יִשְׂרָאֵ֔ל מִבֶּן־חֹ֖דֶשׁ וָמָ֑עְלָה וְשָׂ֕א

מא אֵ֖ת מִסְפַּ֣ר שְׁמֹתָֽם: וְלָקַחְתָּ֨ אֶת־הַלְוִיִּ֥ם לִי֙ אֲנִ֣י יְהֹוָ֔ה תַּ֥חַת כָּל־בְּכֹ֖ר בִּבְנֵ֣י

מב יִשְׂרָאֵ֑ל וְאֵת֙ בֶּֽהֱמַ֣ת הַלְוִיִּ֔ם תַּ֣חַת כָּל־בְּכ֔וֹר בְּבֶֽהֱמַ֖ת בְּנֵ֥י יִשְׂרָאֵֽל: וַיִּפְקֹ֣ד

מג מֹשֶׁ֗ה כַּאֲשֶׁ֛ר צִוָּ֥ה יְהֹוָ֖ה אֹת֑וֹ אֶֽת־כָּל־בְּכ֖וֹר בִּבְנֵ֣י יִשְׂרָאֵֽל: וַֽיְהִ֣י כָל־בְּכ֣וֹר

זָכָ֗ר בְּמִסְפַּ֥ר שֵׁמֹ֛ת מִבֶּן־חֹ֥דֶשׁ וָמַ֖עְלָה לִפְקֻֽדֵיהֶ֑ם שְׁנַ֤יִם וְעֶשְׂרִים֙ אֶ֔לֶף

שְׁלֹשָׁ֥ה וְשִׁבְעִ֖ים וּמָאתָֽיִם:

מד-מה וַיְדַבֵּ֥ר יְהֹוָ֖ה אֶל־מֹשֶׁ֥ה לֵּאמֹֽר: קַ֣ח אֶת־הַלְוִיִּ֗ם תַּ֤חַת כָּל־בְּכוֹר֙ בִּבְנֵ֣י

מו יִשְׂרָאֵ֔ל וְאֶת־בֶּהֱמַ֥ת הַלְוִיִּ֖ם תַּ֣חַת בְּהֶמְתָּ֑ם וְהָיוּ־לִ֥י הַלְוִיִּ֖ם אֲנִ֣י יְהֹוָֽה: וְאֵת֙

פְּדוּיֵ֣י הַשְּׁלֹשָׁ֔ה וְהַשִּׁבְעִ֖ים וְהַמָּאתָ֑יִם הָעֹֽדְפִים֙ עַל־הַלְוִיִּ֔ם מִבְּכ֖וֹר בְּנֵ֥י

מז יִשְׂרָאֵֽל: וְלָקַחְתָּ֗ חֲמֵ֧שֶׁת חֲמֵ֛שֶׁת שְׁקָלִ֖ים לַגֻּלְגֹּ֑לֶת בְּשֶׁ֤קֶל הַקֹּ֙דֶשׁ֙ תִּקָּ֔ח

מח עֶשְׂרִ֥ים גֵּרָ֖ה הַשָּֽׁקֶל: וְנָתַתָּ֣ה הַכֶּ֔סֶף לְאַֽהֲרֹ֖ן וּלְבָנָ֑יו פְּדוּיֵ֕י הָעֹֽדְפִ֖ים בָּהֶֽם:

מט-נ וַיִּקַּ֣ח מֹשֶׁ֔ה אֵ֖ת כֶּ֣סֶף הַפִּדְי֑וֹם מֵאֵת֙ הָעֹ֣דְפִ֔ים עַ֖ל פְּדוּיֵ֥י הַלְוִיִּֽם: מֵאֵ֗ת בְּכ֛וֹר

בְּנֵ֥י יִשְׂרָאֵ֖ל לָקַ֣ח אֶת־הַכָּ֑סֶף חֲמִשָּׁ֤ה וְשִׁשִּׁים֙ וּשְׁלֹ֣שׁ מֵא֔וֹת וָאֶ֖לֶף בְּשֶׁ֥קֶל

נא הַקֹּֽדֶשׁ: וַיִּתֵּ֨ן מֹשֶׁ֜ה אֶת־כֶּ֧סֶף הַפְּדֻיִ֛ם לְאַֽהֲרֹ֥ן וּלְבָנָ֖יו עַל־פִּ֣י יְהֹוָ֑ה כַּֽאֲשֶׁ֛ר

צִוָּ֥ה יְהֹוָ֖ה אֶת־מֹשֶֽׁה:

שביעי א-ב וַיְדַבֵּ֣ר יְהֹוָ֔ה אֶל־מֹשֶׁ֥ה וְאֶֽל־אַהֲרֹ֖ן לֵאמֹֽר: נָשֹׂ֗א אֶת־רֹאשׁ֙ בְּנֵ֣י קְהָ֔ת מִתּ֖וֹךְ

ד בְּנֵ֣י לֵוִ֑י לְמִשְׁפְּחֹתָ֖ם לְבֵ֥ית אֲבֹתָֽם: מִבֶּ֨ן שְׁלֹשִׁ֤ים שָׁנָה֙ וָמַ֔עְלָה וְעַ֕ד

ד בֶּן־חֲמִשִּׁ֖ים שָׁנָ֑ה כָּל־בָּא֙ לַצָּבָ֔א לַֽעֲשׂ֥וֹת מְלָאכָ֖ה בְּאֹ֥הֶל מוֹעֵֽד: זֹ֣את

ה עֲבֹדַ֥ת בְּנֵֽי־קְהָ֖ת בְּאֹ֣הֶל מוֹעֵ֑ד קֹ֖דֶשׁ הַקֳּדָשִֽׁים: וּבָ֨א אַהֲרֹ֤ן וּבָנָיו֙ בִּנְסֹ֣עַ

NOTES

Although the *Sforno* does not give a reason for this decision, we can surmise that since the Levites of that generation responded to the call of Moses in the aftermath of the sin of the Golden Calf, they were deemed worthy not only to *replace* the firstborn in the service of God, but also to *redeem* them.

ו הַמַּחֲנֶה וְהוֹרִדוּ אֵת פָּרֹכֶת הַמָּסָךְ וְכִסּוּ־בָהּ אֵת אֲרֹן הָעֵדֻת: וְנָתְנוּ עָלָיו
ז כְּסוּי עוֹר תַּחַשׁ וּפָרְשׂוּ בֶגֶד־כְּלִיל תְּכֵלֶת מִלְמָעְלָה וְשָׂמוּ בַּדָּיו: וְעַל ׀
שֻׁלְחַן הַפָּנִים יִפְרְשׂוּ בֶּגֶד תְּכֵלֶת וְנָתְנוּ עָלָיו אֶת־הַקְּעָרֹת וְאֶת־הַכַּפֹּת
ח וְאֶת־הַמְּנַקִּיֹּת וְאֵת קְשׂוֹת הַנָּסֶךְ וְלֶחֶם הַתָּמִיד עָלָיו יִהְיֶה: וּפָרְשׂוּ עֲלֵיהֶם
ט בֶּגֶד תּוֹלַעַת שָׁנִי וְכִסּוּ אֹתוֹ בְּמִכְסֵה עוֹר תָּחַשׁ וְשָׂמוּ אֶת־בַּדָּיו: וְלָקְחוּ ׀
בֶּגֶד תְּכֵלֶת וְכִסּוּ אֶת־מְנֹרַת הַמָּאוֹר וְאֶת־נֵרֹתֶיהָ וְאֶת־מַלְקָחֶיהָ
י וְאֶת־מַחְתֹּתֶיהָ וְאֵת כָּל־כְּלֵי שַׁמְנָהּ אֲשֶׁר יְשָׁרְתוּ־לָהּ בָּהֶם: וְנָתְנוּ אֹתָהּ
יא וְאֶת־כָּל־כֵּלֶיהָ אֶל־מִכְסֵה עוֹר תָּחַשׁ וְנָתְנוּ עַל־הַמּוֹט: וְעַל ׀ מִזְבַּח הַזָּהָב
יב יִפְרְשׂוּ בֶּגֶד תְּכֵלֶת וְכִסּוּ אֹתוֹ בְּמִכְסֵה עוֹר תָּחַשׁ וְשָׂמוּ אֶת־בַּדָּיו: וְלָקְחוּ
אֶת־כָּל־כְּלֵי הַשָּׁרֵת אֲשֶׁר יְשָׁרְתוּ־בָם בַּקֹּדֶשׁ וְנָתְנוּ אֶל־בֶּגֶד תְּכֵלֶת וְכִסּוּ
יג אוֹתָם בְּמִכְסֵה עוֹר תָּחַשׁ וְנָתְנוּ עַל־הַמּוֹט: וְדִשְּׁנוּ אֶת־הַמִּזְבֵּחַ וּפָרְשׂוּ עָלָיו
יד בֶּגֶד אַרְגָּמָן: וְנָתְנוּ עָלָיו אֶת־כָּל־כֵּלָיו אֲשֶׁר יְשָׁרְתוּ עָלָיו בָּהֶם אֶת־
הַמַּחְתֹּת אֶת־הַמִּזְלָגֹת וְאֶת־הַיָּעִים וְאֶת־הַמִּזְרָקֹת כֹּל כְּלֵי הַמִּזְבֵּחַ וּפָרְשׂוּ
טו עָלָיו כְּסוּי עוֹר תַּחַשׁ וְשָׂמוּ בַדָּיו: וְכִלָּה אַהֲרֹן־וּבָנָיו לְכַסֹּת אֶת־הַקֹּדֶשׁ
וְאֶת־כָּל־כְּלֵי הַקֹּדֶשׁ בִּנְסֹעַ הַמַּחֲנֶה וְאַחֲרֵי־כֵן יָבֹאוּ בְנֵי־קְהָת לָשֵׂאת
טז וְלֹא־יִגְּעוּ אֶל־הַקֹּדֶשׁ וָמֵתוּ אֵלֶּה מַשָּׂא בְנֵי־קְהָת בְּאֹהֶל מוֹעֵד: וּפְקֻדַּת
אֶלְעָזָר ׀ בֶּן־אַהֲרֹן הַכֹּהֵן שֶׁמֶן הַמָּאוֹר וּקְטֹרֶת הַסַּמִּים וּמִנְחַת הַתָּמִיד וְשֶׁמֶן
הַמִּשְׁחָה פְּקֻדַּת כָּל־הַמִּשְׁכָּן וְכָל־אֲשֶׁר־בּוֹ בְּקֹדֶשׁ וּבְכֵלָיו:
מפטיר יז־יח וַיְדַבֵּר יהוה אֶל־מֹשֶׁה וְאֶל־אַהֲרֹן לֵאמֹר: אַל־תַּכְרִיתוּ אֶת־שֵׁבֶט מִשְׁפְּחֹת
יט הַקְּהָתִי מִתּוֹךְ הַלְוִיִּם: וְזֹאת ׀ עֲשׂוּ לָהֶם וְחָיוּ וְלֹא יָמֻתוּ בְּגִשְׁתָּם אֶת־קֹדֶשׁ

IV

5. בִּנְסֹעַ הַמַּחֲנֶה — *When the camp journeys* ... after the (Divine) cloud removes itself, because prior to that it is prohibited to enter (the Holy of Holies).

10. וְנָתְנוּ עַל הַמּוֹט — *And shall put it upon a bar* ... and (only) then shall the Levites be allowed to carry (them).

16. וּפְקֻדַּת אֶלְעָזָר — *And the charge of Elazar* ... to command which (articles of the Sanctuary) each one should carry.

פְּקֻדַּת כָּל הַמִּשְׁכָּן — *And the charge of the entire Sanctuary.* During the time of their journeying and encampment, his charge was to command them (i.e., the Kehathites) regarding the erection, dismantling and setting up (of the items entrusted to them) in their proper places.

18. אַל תַּכְרִיתוּ — *Do not cause to be cut off.* Do not (simply) put down the objects (to be carried) in such a way that the one who takes them first will merit (to carry them), for in this manner it may happen that one will push another (in their eagerness to carry the holy objects) and thereby profane the Holy. This (in turn) will cause their being 'cut off,' as (our Sages) tell us that this occurred with the 'offering of the ashes' (see *Yoma* 22, 23).

הַקֳּדָשִׁים אַהֲרֹן וּבָנָיו יָבֹאוּ וְשָׂמוּ אוֹתָם אִישׁ אִישׁ עַל־עֲבֹדָתוֹ וְאֶל־מַשָּׂאוֹ׃
כ וְלֹא־יָבֹאוּ לִרְאוֹת כְּבַלַּע אֶת־הַקֹּדֶשׁ וָמֵתוּ׃

---

19. וְשָׂמוּ אוֹתָם אִישׁ אִישׁ עַל עֲבֹדָתוֹ וְאֶל מַשָּׂאוֹ — *And appoint each one of them to his service and to his burden.* And it shall not be that those who arrive earlier shall merit (to choose), but each one must wait to be commanded and then he shall act.

20. וְלֹא יָבֹאוּ לִרְאוֹת — *But they shall not enter to observe.* In this manner, they will not enter to observe when the *Kohen* covers the sacred articles (in such a manner) as to be able to precede the others, and (thereby) they will (avoid the pitfall of) conducting themselves in a frivolous fashion, bringing upon themselves the death penalty.

NOTES

IV

18-20. אַל תַּכְרִיתוּ . . . וְשָׂמוּ אוֹתָם אִישׁ אִישׁ עַל עֲבֹדָתוֹ וְאֶל מַשָּׂאוֹ. וְלֹא יָבֹאוּ לִרְאוֹת . . . — *Do not cause to be cut off . . . and appoint each one of them to his service and to his burden. But they shall not enter to observe* The Torah tells us that specific assignments were given by Elazar to the Kehathites as to which articles they were to carry since it was not permitted for them to do so on a 'first come first serve' basis. The *Sforno* explains the reason for this strictness by citing the Mishnah in tractate *Yoma* (22a and 23a) where we are told that the *Kohanim* originally would race up the ramp to the top of the altar for the privilege of removing the ashes. Once, in his zeal to be first, one *Kohen* pushed his colleague off the ramp and he broke his leg. On another occasion, two *Kohanim* reached the top together and one stabbed the other. After these incidents, a lottery was instituted so as to eliminate such dangerous competition. In a similar vein, in order to protect the Levites from being 'cut off' (i.e., exposed to danger) due to frivolous conduct in the Sanctuary, the Torah ordained that all assignments were to be given by Elazar in an orderly fashion. Since there was nothing to be gained by being there first, the Kehathites would not be tempted to enter the Holy of Holies while the *Kohanim* were covering the holy objects and preparing them to be carried. In this manner they would avoid wrongdoing and its consequent punishment.

פרשת נשא
Parashas Nasso

כא-כב וַיְדַבֵּ֥ר יְהֹוָ֖ה אֶל־מֹשֶׁ֥ה לֵּאמֹֽר: נָשֹׂ֗א אֶת־רֹ֛אשׁ בְּנֵ֥י גֵרְשׁ֖וֹן גַּם־הֵ֑ם לְבֵ֥ית
כג אֲבֹתָ֖ם לְמִשְׁפְּחֹתָֽם: מִבֶּן֩ שְׁלֹשִׁ֨ים שָׁנָ֜ה וָמַ֗עְלָה עַ֛ד בֶּן־חֲמִשִּׁ֥ים שָׁנָ֖ה תִּפְקֹ֣ד
כד אוֹתָ֑ם כָּל־הַבָּא֙ לִצְבֹ֣א צָבָ֔א לַעֲבֹ֥ד עֲבֹדָ֖ה בְּאֹ֥הֶל מוֹעֵֽד: זֹ֣את עֲבֹדַ֗ת
כה מִשְׁפְּחֹ֖ת הַגֵּרְשֻׁנִּ֑י לַעֲבֹ֖ד וּלְמַשָּֽׂא: וְנָֽשְׂא֞וּ אֶת־יְרִיעֹ֤ת הַמִּשְׁכָּן֙ וְאֶת־אֹ֣הֶל
מוֹעֵ֔ד מִכְסֵ֕הוּ וּמִכְסֵ֛ה הַתַּ֥חַשׁ אֲשֶׁר־עָלָ֖יו מִלְמָ֑עְלָה וְאֶ֨ת־מָסַ֔ךְ פֶּ֖תַח אֹ֥הֶל
כו מוֹעֵֽד: וְאֵת֩ קַלְעֵ֨י הֶחָצֵ֜ר וְאֶת־מָסַ֣ךְ ׀ פֶּ֗תַח ׀ שַׁ֤עַר הֶֽחָצֵר֙ אֲשֶׁ֣ר עַל־הַמִּשְׁכָּ֤ן
וְעַל־הַמִּזְבֵּ֨חַ֙ סָבִ֔יב וְאֵת֙ מֵ֣יתְרֵיהֶ֔ם וְאֶֽת־כָּל־כְּלֵ֖י עֲבֹדָתָ֑ם וְאֵ֨ת כָּל־אֲשֶׁ֧ר
כז יֵעָשֶׂ֛ה לָהֶ֖ם וְעָבָֽדוּ: עַל־פִּי֩ אַהֲרֹ֨ן וּבָנָ֜יו תִּהְיֶ֗ה כָּל־עֲבֹדַת֙ בְּנֵ֣י הַגֵּֽרְשֻׁנִּ֔י
לְכָל־מַשָּׂאָ֔ם וּלְכֹ֖ל עֲבֹדָתָ֑ם וּפְקַדְתֶּ֤ם עֲלֵהֶם֙ בְּמִשְׁמֶ֔רֶת אֵ֖ת כָּל־מַשָּׂאָֽם:
כח זֹ֣את עֲבֹדַ֗ת מִשְׁפְּחֹ֛ת בְּנֵ֥י הַגֵּרְשֻׁנִּ֖י בְּאֹ֣הֶל מוֹעֵ֑ד וּמִ֨שְׁמַרְתָּ֔ם בְּיַד֙ אִֽיתָמָ֔ר
כט בֶּֽן־אַהֲרֹ֖ן הַכֹּהֵֽן: בְּנֵ֖י מְרָרִ֑י לְמִשְׁפְּחֹתָ֥ם לְבֵית־אֲבֹתָ֖ם
ל תִּפְקֹ֣ד אֹתָ֑ם מִבֶּן֩ שְׁלֹשִׁ֨ים שָׁנָ֜ה וָמַ֗עְלָה וְעַ֛ד בֶּן־חֲמִשִּׁ֥ים שָׁנָ֖ה תִּפְקְדֵ֑ם
לא כָּל־הַבָּא֙ לַצָּבָ֔א לַעֲבֹ֕ד אֶת־עֲבֹדַ֖ת אֹ֣הֶל מוֹעֵֽד: וְזֹאת֙ מִשְׁמֶ֣רֶת מַשָּׂאָ֔ם
לב לְכָל־עֲבֹדָתָ֖ם בְּאֹ֣הֶל מוֹעֵ֑ד קַרְשֵׁי֙ הַמִּשְׁכָּ֔ן וּבְרִיחָ֖יו וְעַמּוּדָ֣יו וַאֲדָנָֽיו: וְעַמֻּדֵי֩
הֶחָצֵ֨ר סָבִ֜יב וְאַדְנֵיהֶ֗ם וִיתֵֽדֹתָם֙ וּמֵ֣יתְרֵיהֶ֔ם לְכָל־כְּלֵיהֶ֖ם וּלְכֹ֣ל עֲבֹדָתָ֑ם
לג וּבְשֵׁמֹ֣ת תִּפְקְד֔וּ אֶת־כְּלֵ֖י מִשְׁמֶ֥רֶת מַשָּׂאָֽם: זֹ֣את עֲבֹדַ֗ת מִשְׁפְּחֹת֙ בְּנֵ֣י
לד מְרָרִ֔י לְכָל־עֲבֹדָתָ֖ם בְּאֹ֣הֶל מוֹעֵ֑ד בְּיַד֙ אִ֣יתָמָ֔ר בֶּֽן־אַהֲרֹ֖ן הַכֹּהֵֽן: וַיִּפְקֹ֨ד
מֹשֶׁ֧ה וְאַהֲרֹ֛ן וּנְשִׂיאֵ֥י הָעֵדָ֖ה אֶת־בְּנֵ֣י הַקְּהָתִ֑י לְמִשְׁפְּחֹתָ֖ם וּלְבֵ֥ית אֲבֹתָֽם:
לה מִבֶּן֩ שְׁלֹשִׁ֨ים שָׁנָ֜ה וָמַ֗עְלָה וְעַ֛ד בֶּן־חֲמִשִּׁ֥ים שָׁנָ֖ה כָּל־הַבָּא֙ לַצָּבָ֔א לַעֲבֹדָ֖ה
לו בְּאֹ֥הֶל מוֹעֵֽד: וַיִּהְי֥וּ פְקֻדֵיהֶ֖ם לְמִשְׁפְּחֹתָ֑ם אַלְפַּ֕יִם שְׁבַ֥ע מֵא֖וֹת וַחֲמִשִּֽׁים:

---

24. לַעֲבֹד וּלְמַשָּׂא — *In serving and in bearing burdens.* 'Serving' (refers to) when they are encamped and 'bearing burdens' to when they are on a journey. Now, since the Torah stated above (3:25), *And the charge of the sons of Gershon in the Tent of Meeting* in reference to their charge at the time (Israel) encamped, (therefore) it states here that all the work in their charge at the time of encampment, was also in their charge when (carrying) burdens at the time of journeying.

26. וְעָבָדוּ — *Therein shall they serve.* At the time of encampment, their charge shall be over all these vessels and (also) over all the implements *concerning that which is to be done to them* and for them in order to do the work, such as pliers and mallets to set in the pegs and to extract them.

27. לְכָל מַשָּׂאָם — *In all their burden* ... when they journey.

וּלְכֹל עֲבֹדָתָם — *And in all their service* ... when they encamp.

NOTES

24. לַעֲבֹד וּלְמַשָּׂא — *In serving and in bearing burdens.* The *Sforno* explains throughout this section (vs. 24-49) that the assignment of the Levites was a two-fold one: to carry the various parts of the Tabernacle when the Israelites journeyed, which the Torah refers to as מַשָּׂא, *burden*; and also to assume responsibility for these same parts, vessels and instruments when they encamped, which the Torah

refers to as עֲבוֹדָה, *serving*.

26. וְעָבָדוּ — *Therein shall they serve.* The phrase וְעָבָדוּ is translated by the *Sforno* as meaning 'in order to do their work.' Hence, it applies to the implements such as those necessary to drive in the pegs and remove them. Compare this to the *Sforno's* commentary on *Exodus* 27:19.

לז אֵ֣לֶּה פְקוּדֵי֩ מִשְׁפְּחֹ֨ת הַקְּהָתִ֜י כָּל־הָעֹבֵ֗ד בְּאֹ֣הֶל מוֹעֵ֔ד אֲשֶׁ֥ר פָּקַ֖ד מֹשֶׁ֣ה

שני לח וְאַהֲרֹ֑ן עַל־פִּ֥י יהו֖ה בְּיַד־מֹשֶֽׁה: וּפְקוּדֵ֖י בְּנֵ֥י גֵרְשׁ֑וֹן

לט לְמִשְׁפְּחוֹתָ֖ם וּלְבֵ֣ית אֲבֹתָ֑ם מִבֶּן֩ שְׁלֹשִׁ֨ים שָׁנָ֤ה וָמַ֙עְלָה֙ וְעַ֣ד בֶּן־חֲמִשִּׁ֣ים

מ שָׁנָ֔ה כָּל־הַבָּא֙ לַצָּבָ֔א לַעֲבֹדָ֖ה בְּאֹ֣הֶל מוֹעֵֽד: וַיִּֽהְיוּ֙ פְּקֻ֣דֵיהֶ֔ם לְמִשְׁפְּחֹתָ֖ם

מא לְבֵ֣ית אֲבֹתָ֑ם אַלְפַּ֕יִם וְשֵׁ֥שׁ מֵא֖וֹת וּשְׁלֹשִֽׁים: אֵ֣לֶּה פְקוּדֵי֮ מִשְׁפְּחֹת֮ בְּנֵ֣י

גֵרְשׁוֹן֒ כָּל־הָעֹבֵ֖ד בְּאֹ֣הֶל מוֹעֵ֑ד אֲשֶׁ֨ר פָּקַ֥ד מֹשֶׁ֛ה וְאַהֲרֹ֖ן עַל־פִּ֥י יהוֽה:

מב־מג וּפְקוּדֵ֕י מִשְׁפְּחֹ֖ת בְּנֵ֣י מְרָרִ֑י לְמִשְׁפְּחֹתָ֖ם לְבֵ֣ית אֲבֹתָ֑ם מִבֶּן֩ שְׁלֹשִׁ֨ים שָׁנָ֤ה

מד וָמַ֙עְלָה֙ וְעַ֣ד בֶּן־חֲמִשִּׁ֣ים שָׁנָ֔ה כָּל־הַבָּא֙ לַצָּבָ֔א לַעֲבֹדָ֖ה בְּאֹ֣הֶל מוֹעֵֽד: וַיִּֽהְי֣וּ

מה פְקֻ֣דֵיהֶ֔ם לְמִשְׁפְּחֹתָ֑ם שְׁלֹ֥שֶׁת אֲלָפִ֖ים וּמָאתָ֑יִם: אֵ֣לֶּה פְקוּדֵ֖י מִשְׁפְּחֹ֣ת בְּנֵ֣י

מו מְרָרִ֑י אֲשֶׁ֨ר פָּקַ֜ד מֹשֶׁ֤ה וְאַהֲרֹן֙ עַל־פִּ֣י יהו֔ה בְּיַד־מֹשֶֽׁה: כָּל־הַפְּקֻדִ֡ים אֲשֶׁר֩

פָּקַ֨ד מֹשֶׁ֧ה וְאַהֲרֹ֛ן וּנְשִׂיאֵ֥י יִשְׂרָאֵ֖ל אֶת־הַלְוִיִּ֑ם לְמִשְׁפְּחֹתָ֖ם וּלְבֵ֥ית אֲבֹתָֽם:

מז מִבֶּ֨ן שְׁלֹשִׁ֤ים שָׁנָה֙ וָמַ֔עְלָה וְעַ֖ד בֶּן־חֲמִשִּׁ֣ים שָׁנָ֑ה כָּל־הַבָּ֗א לַעֲבֹ֤ד עֲבֹדַ֣ת

מח עֲבֹדָ֔ה וַעֲבֹדַ֥ת מַשָּׂ֖א בְּאֹ֣הֶל מוֹעֵֽד: וַיִּֽהְי֣וּ פְקֻדֵיהֶ֔ם שְׁמֹנַ֥ת אֲלָפִ֖ים וַחֲמֵ֥שׁ

מט מֵא֖וֹת וּשְׁמֹנִֽים: עַל־פִּ֨י יהו֜ה פָּקַ֤ד אוֹתָם֙ בְּיַד־מֹשֶׁ֔ה אִ֥ישׁ אִ֛ישׁ עַל־עֲבֹֽדָת֖וֹ

וְעַל־מַשָּׂא֑וֹ וּפְקֻדָ֕יו אֲשֶׁר־צִוָּ֥ה יהו֖ה אֶת־מֹשֶֽׁה:

ה שלישי א־ב וַיְדַבֵּ֥ר יהו֖ה אֶל־מֹשֶׁ֥ה לֵּאמֹֽר: צַ֞ו אֶת־בְּנֵ֣י יִשְׂרָאֵ֗ל וִֽישַׁלְּחוּ֙ מִן־הַֽמַּחֲנֶ֔ה

ג כָּל־צָר֖וּעַ וְכָל־זָ֑ב וְכֹ֖ל טָמֵ֣א לָנָ֑פֶשׁ: מִזָּכָ֤ר עַד־נְקֵבָה֙ תְּשַׁלֵּ֔חוּ אֶל־מִח֥וּץ

לַֽמַּחֲנֶ֖ה תְּשַׁלְּח֑וּם וְלֹ֤א יְטַמְּאוּ֙ אֶת־מַ֣חֲנֵיהֶ֔ם אֲשֶׁ֥ר אֲנִ֖י שֹׁכֵ֥ן בְּתוֹכָֽם:

ד וַיַּֽעֲשׂוּ־כֵן֙ בְּנֵ֣י יִשְׂרָאֵ֔ל וַיְשַׁלְּח֣וּ אוֹתָ֔ם אֶל־מִח֖וּץ לַֽמַּחֲנֶ֑ה כַּאֲשֶׁ֨ר דִּבֶּ֤ר יהוה֙

אֶל־מֹשֶׁ֔ה כֵּ֥ן עָשׂ֖וּ בְּנֵ֥י יִשְׂרָאֵֽל:

ה־ו וַיְדַבֵּ֥ר יהו֖ה אֶל־מֹשֶׁ֥ה לֵּאמֹֽר: דַּבֵּר֮ אֶל־בְּנֵ֣י יִשְׂרָאֵל֒ אִ֣ישׁ אֽוֹ־אִשָּׁ֗ה כִּ֤י

יַעֲשׂוּ֙ מִכָּל־חַטֹּ֣את הָֽאָדָ֔ם לִמְעֹ֥ל מַ֖עַל בַּֽיהו֑ה וְאָֽשְׁמָ֖ה הַנֶּ֥פֶשׁ הַהִֽוא:

---

49. אִישׁ אִישׁ עַל עֲבֹדָתוֹ וְעַל מַשָּׂאוֹ וּפְקֻדָיו — *Every one to his service and to his burden and to his appointment.* He appointed every one of them to the service he was to do at the time of encampment and *to his burden* at the time of journeying, so that each would know the weight of his burden; and he would also know פְקֻדָיו, *his appointment*, i.e., he shall know the names of all the vessels (and implements) which he will carry, (for) these were designated by name as it says, *And by name you shall appoint the instruments of the charge of their burden* (v. 32).

V

6. לִמְעֹל מַעַל בַּה׳ — *To commit a trespass against* HASHEM. Tradition teaches that

NOTES

49. אִישׁ אִישׁ עַל עֲבֹדָתוֹ וְעַל מַשָּׂאוֹ וּפְקֻדָיו — *Every one to his service and to his burden and to his appointment.* The phrase וּפְקֻדָיו is translated by other commentators to mean 'their number,' referring to the count of the Levites. The *Sforno*, however, is of the opinion that it applies to the articles and instruments which were in the Levites' charge. Just as a medical practitioner must be able to identify every bone, muscle, and tendon in the human body by name for the purpose of diagnosis and treatment, so were the Levites instructed and trained to identify every item of the *Mishkan* in their charge by name. They were also instructed to have intimate knowledge of the weight of their respective burdens so as to know how many men and wagons should be assigned for transport.

ז וְהִתְוַדּוּ אֶת־חַטָּאתָם אֲשֶׁר עָשׂוּ וְהֵשִׁיב אֶת־אֲשָׁמוֹ בְּרֹאשׁוֹ וַחֲמִישִׁתוֹ יֹסֵף
ח עָלָיו וְנָתַן לַאֲשֶׁר אָשַׁם לוֹ: וְאִם־אֵין לָאִישׁ גֹּאֵל לְהָשִׁיב הָאָשָׁם אֵלָיו
הָאָשָׁם הַמּוּשָׁב לַיהוָה לַכֹּהֵן מִלְּבַד אֵיל הַכִּפֻּרִים אֲשֶׁר יְכַפֶּר־בּוֹ עָלָיו:
ט-י וְכָל־תְּרוּמָה לְכָל־קָדְשֵׁי בְנֵי־יִשְׂרָאֵל אֲשֶׁר־יַקְרִיבוּ לַכֹּהֵן לוֹ יִהְיֶה: וְאִישׁ
אֶת־קֳדָשָׁיו לוֹ יִהְיוּ אִישׁ אֲשֶׁר־יִתֵּן לַכֹּהֵן לוֹ יִהְיֶה:
רביעי יא-יב וַיְדַבֵּר יְהוָה אֶל־מֹשֶׁה לֵּאמֹר: דַּבֵּר אֶל־בְּנֵי יִשְׂרָאֵל וְאָמַרְתָּ אֲלֵהֶם אִישׁ

---

this verse refers to robbery of a proselyte, for indeed, if one robs him he profanes the Name of his God in the eyes of the proselyte who came to find protection under His wings. Therefore, he is called 'one who trespasses against the sacred' and is required to bring a guilt offering, as is the law regarding all who trespass against Him.

8. הָאָשָׁם הַמּוּשָׁב לַה׳ — *The restitution for guilt which is made shall be to* HASHEM. Because when the owner is no longer alive, it is proper to return the stolen goods to the master of the owner — who (in this instance) is God, the Blessed One, as our Sages stated, 'If the slave died, it shall be returned to his master' (*Bava Basra* 51b).

9. וְכָל תְּרוּמָה — *And every heave-offering.* Tradition has it that the offering mentioned here refers to בִּכּוּרִים, *the first fruits,* which are offered to God, the Blessed One, as is the custom to offer the first fruits to the owner of the field, as it says, הִגַּדְתִּי הַיּוֹם לַה׳ אֱלֹהֶיךָ כִּי בָאתִי אֶל הָאָרֶץ אֲשֶׁר נִשְׁבַּע ה׳, *I profess this day to* HASHEM *your God that I have come to the land which* HASHEM *swore* (*Deut.* 26:3). The (Torah) here tells us that just as the stolen property of the proselyte being returned to God is given to the *Kohen* of the מִשְׁמָר, *the watch,* so also are the first fruits, which are offered to God, the Blessed One, given to the *Kohen* of the watch.

10. וְאִישׁ אֶת קֳדָשָׁיו לוֹ יִהְיוּ — *And every man's holy things shall be his* ... but regarding other holy things, namely heave-offerings and tithes, even though they are sanctified to God, they do not belong to any specific *Kohen*, but rather to the *Kohen* to whom the owner chooses to give it.

אִישׁ אֲשֶׁר יִתֵּן לַכֹּהֵן — *Whatsoever any man gives to the Kohen.* But when any owner gives a holy thing to the *Kohen*, it is no longer in the category of 'his holy thing' but ...

לוֹ יִהְיֶה — *It shall be his.* (It belongs) to the *Kohen* who received it, and neither the owner or the other *Kohanim* can expropriate it from him.

NOTES

V

8. הָאָשָׁם הַמּוּשָׁב לַה׳ — *The restitution for guilt which is made shall be to* HASHEM. The Talmud in *Bava Basra* states that one should not accept a פִּקָּדוֹן, *a pledge,* from a slave because there is a probability that it was stolen. However, if one did accept it then he should return it to the slave. If the slave dies then he returns it to his master. And so in our case, where an Israelite has stolen something from a proselyte who subsequently died, it shall be returned to the *Kohanim* who represent God, who is considered the 'Master' of the deceased owner (i.e., the proselyte)

8-10. הָאָשָׁם הַמּוּשָׁב לַה׳ ... וְכָל תְּרוּמָה ... וְאִישׁ אֶת קֳדָשָׁיו לוֹ יִהְיוּ — *The restitution for guilt which is made shall be to* HASHEM ... *And every heave-offering ... And every man's holy things shall be his.* The *Sforno* explains the reason for the juxtaposition of verses 8-10. Seemingly, there is no link between the law of returning a stolen article to the *Kohen* (v. 8), the bringing of the first fruits to the Temple (v. 9) and the offerings of תְּרוּמָה, *heave offering,* and מַעֲשֵׂר, *tithe* (v. 10). The *Sforno,* however, explains the linkage thus: just as the stolen item is returned to the *Kohanim* of that particular watch (מִשְׁמָר), so shall the first fruits be brought to them. However, other

יג אִישׁ כִּי־תִשְׂטֶה אִשְׁתּוֹ וּמָעֲלָה בוֹ מָעַל: וְשָׁכַב אִישׁ אֹתָהּ שִׁכְבַת־זֶרַע
וְנֶעְלַם מֵעֵינֵי אִישָׁהּ וְנִסְתְּרָה וְהִיא נִטְמָאָה וְעֵד אֵין בָּהּ וְהִוא לֹא נִתְפָּשָׂה:
יד וְעָבַר עָלָיו רוּחַ־קִנְאָה וְקִנֵּא אֶת־אִשְׁתּוֹ וְהִוא נִטְמָאָה אוֹ־עָבַר עָלָיו
טו רוּחַ־קִנְאָה וְקִנֵּא אֶת־אִשְׁתּוֹ וְהִיא לֹא נִטְמָאָה: וְהֵבִיא הָאִישׁ אֶת־אִשְׁתּוֹ

---

12. כִּי תִשְׂטֶה אִשְׁתּוֹ — *If his wife goes aside.* (She) deviates from the path of modesty.

וּמָעֲלָה בוֹ מָעַל — *And acts deceitfully against him.* She profaned *the holiness of* H*ASHEM which He loves* (*Malachi* 2:11) inherent in marriage by embracing and kissing (a man) other than her husband and similar acts (of immorality).

13. וְשָׁכַב אִישׁ אֹתָהּ — *And a man lie with her.* For this is the way of the evil inclination to proceed from evil to evil.

וְנֶעְלַם מֵעֵינֵי אִישָׁהּ — *And it be hid from the eyes of the husband.* Although all these incidents preceded (the husband's awareness), it can (still) come about that the matter will be hidden from the eyes of her husband, as though his eyes are dimmed and unseeing, for if he knows and is silent the waters will not examine the woman to determine her guilt at all, as (our Sages) explain (*Sifre*).

וְנִסְתְּרָה — *And she be hidden* ... after all this, and it (then) becomes known to her husband.

14. וְעָבַר עָלָיו רוּחַ קִנְאָה — *And the spirit of jealousy comes over him* ... a pure spirit (prompting him) to warn her, since he knows that she deviated from the path of modesty.

וְקִנֵּא אֶת אִשְׁתּוֹ — *And he is jealous of his wife.* He warned her and said, 'Do not meet secretly with this man.'

אוֹ עָבַר עָלָיו רוּחַ קִנְאָה — *Or if the spirit of jealousy comes upon him.* A spirit which is foolish, without reasonable cause for him to be jealous.

וְהִיא לֹא נִטְמָאָה — *And she is not defiled.* However, she did disregard (lit., transgress) his warning and hid (secretly with that man) nonetheless ...

15. וְהֵבִיא הָאִישׁ אֶת אִשְׁתּוֹ — *Then shall the man bring his wife.* And we shall not say that since he took no action and was silent despite the fact that his wife had deviated from the path of modesty and had acted deceitfully against him, hence, it is an indication of his evil heart, and even though (the truth of the matter is that) it was hidden from his eyes that a man laid with her, we shall pay no heed to his jealousy.

NOTES

offerings, such as תְּרוּמָה and מַעֲשֵׂר can be given to any *Kohen* or Levite whom the owner chooses.

12. וּמָעֲלָה בוֹ מָעַל — *And acts deceitfully against him.* The expression מְעִילָה, *trespass,* is applicable to one's actions vis-a-vis God. Why then does the Torah use this particular phrase regarding a woman who is unfaithful to her husband? The *Sforno* explains that this particular expression was chosen to underscore the seriousness of her action which is, in reality, not only a trespass against her husband, but also against God. This is an example of how a sinful act can be a violation of trust between man and man as well as between man and God. The expression *the holiness ... which He loves* refers to the holiness of matrimony.

14-15. וְעָבַר עָלָיו רוּחַ קִנְאָה ... אוֹ עָבַר עָלָיו רוּחַ קִנְאָה ... וְהֵבִיא הָאִישׁ אֶת אִשְׁתּוֹ — *And the spirit of jealousy comes over him ... or if the spirit of jealousy comes upon him ... Then shall the man bring his wife.* The *Sforno* explains the sequence of these verses in the following manner. The water of bitterness which the *sotah,* the suspected woman, must drink consists of water and ink erased from a special

אֶל־הַכֹּהֵן וְהֵבִיא אֶת־קָרְבָּנָהּ עָלֶיהָ עֲשִׂירִת הָאֵיפָה קֶמַח שְׂעֹרִים לֹא־יִצֹק
עָלָיו שֶׁמֶן וְלֹא־יִתֵּן עָלָיו לְבֹנָה כִּי־מִנְחַת קְנָאֹת הוּא מִנְחַת זִכָּרוֹן מַזְכֶּרֶת
טז־יז עָוֹן: וְהִקְרִיב אֹתָהּ הַכֹּהֵן וְהֶעֱמִדָהּ לִפְנֵי יהוה: וְלָקַח הַכֹּהֵן מַיִם קְדֹשִׁים
בִּכְלִי־חָרֶשׂ וּמִן־הֶעָפָר אֲשֶׁר יִהְיֶה בְּקַרְקַע הַמִּשְׁכָּן יִקַּח הַכֹּהֵן וְנָתַן אֶל־
יח הַמָּיִם: וְהֶעֱמִיד הַכֹּהֵן אֶת־הָאִשָּׁה לִפְנֵי יהוה וּפָרַע אֶת־רֹאשׁ הָאִשָּׁה וְנָתַן
עַל־כַּפֶּיהָ אֵת מִנְחַת הַזִּכָּרוֹן מִנְחַת קְנָאֹת הִוא וּבְיַד הַכֹּהֵן יִהְיוּ מֵי הַמָּרִים
יט הַמְאָרְרִים: וְהִשְׁבִּיעַ אֹתָהּ הַכֹּהֵן וְאָמַר אֶל־הָאִשָּׁה אִם־לֹא שָׁכַב אִישׁ
אֹתָךְ וְאִם־לֹא שָׂטִית טֻמְאָה תַּחַת אִישֵׁךְ הִנָּקִי מִמֵּי הַמָּרִים הַמְאָרְרִים
כ הָאֵלֶּה: וְאַתְּ כִּי שָׂטִית תַּחַת אִישֵׁךְ וְכִי נִטְמֵאת וַיִּתֵּן אִישׁ בָּךְ אֶת־

Similarly, if he is jealous without cause, we will not say that his jealousy is a meaningless thing and ignore it, but we will blot out the scroll and bring (the offering) as it is written in this chapter

19. וְהִשְׁבִּיעַ — *He shall cause* (*her*) *to swear*. He shall tell her to accept the oath and the curse upon herself with this condition.

אִם לֹא שָׁכַב אִישׁ — *If no man have lain* . . . now (presently).

וְאִם לֹא שָׂטִית טֻמְאָה — *And if you have not gone aside to defilement* . . . on other occasions.

הִנָּקִי — *You will be free*. Because it was already stated, כִּי לֹא יְנַקֶּה ה׳ אֵת אֲשֶׁר יִשָּׂא אֶת שְׁמוֹ לַשָּׁוְא, *For HASHEM will not hold him guiltless that takes His Name in vain* (*Exodus* 20:7), (which is interpreted) to mean that even a person who swears truthfully but unnecessarily, as for example, one who swears regarding a known true fact is not held guiltless of that oath. Therefore, it would be proper that you who caused this matter to be in doubt, thereby obligating yourself to swear, should not be held guiltless even if you swear truthfully. Nonetheless, accept these curses on the condition that you will be free of them if you have not gone aside.

NOTES

scroll containing the curses (including God's name). The *Kohen* can only perform an act extreme as that of blotting out God's Name under specially prescribed circumstances. The Torah is teaching us in these verses that even when we might argue that the husband was lax in his concern regarding his wife's behavior or conversely that his jealousy is unfounded, nonetheless we proceed with the ceremony, providing the woman had been warned not to conceal herself (in private) with a particular man and had disregarded that warning.

19. הִנָּקִי — *You will be free.* The Torah teaches us that the severity of taking an oath in the name of God is so great that even if one swears truthfully, but unnecessarily, he is liable to punishment. Hence, the suspected woman (סוֹטָה) would be reluctant to accept the oath and its attendant curse, even though she is innocent of infidelity, since she is responsible for the administering of the oath in God's Name and the blotting out of His Name written in the scroll. The Torah therefore reassures her that she will be held guiltless (clean) if she is indeed innocent of the charge of infidelity. Although the *sotah* is not guilty of an overt immoral act, still by secluding herself with a strange man, she defied her husband and ultimately caused an oath to be administered, and the Name of God in the scroll to be blotted out. Why then is she not punished? The answer is given by the *Sforno* in his commentary on verse 28 in this chapter where he states that God recognizes and appreciates human frailty which causes a person to commit foolish acts, and therefore He is willing to make an exception in this particular case, considering that it will preserve a marriage.

כא שְׁכָבְתּוֹ מִבַּלְעֲדֵי אִישֵׁךְ: וְהִשְׁבִּיעַ הַכֹּהֵן אֶת־הָאִשָּׁה בִּשְׁבֻעַת הָאָלָה וְאָמַר
הַכֹּהֵן לָאִשָּׁה יִתֵּן יהוה אוֹתָךְ לְאָלָה וְלִשְׁבֻעָה בְּתוֹךְ עַמֵּךְ בְּתֵת יהוה אֶת־
כב יְרֵכֵךְ נֹפֶלֶת וְאֶת־בִּטְנֵךְ צָבָה: וּבָאוּ הַמַּיִם הַמְאָרְרִים הָאֵלֶּה בְּמֵעַיִךְ
כג לַצְבּוֹת בֶּטֶן וְלַנְפִּל יָרֵךְ וְאָמְרָה הָאִשָּׁה אָמֵן | אָמֵן: וְכָתַב אֶת־הָאָלֹת
כד הָאֵלֶּה הַכֹּהֵן בַּסֵּפֶר וּמָחָה אֶל־מֵי הַמָּרִים: וְהִשְׁקָה אֶת־הָאִשָּׁה אֶת־מֵי
כה הַמָּרִים הַמְאָרְרִים וּבָאוּ בָהּ הַמַּיִם הַמְאָרְרִים לְמָרִים: וְלָקַח הַכֹּהֵן מִיַּד
הָאִשָּׁה אֵת מִנְחַת הַקְּנָאֹת וְהֵנִיף אֶת־הַמִּנְחָה לִפְנֵי יהוה וְהִקְרִיב אֹתָהּ
כו אֶל־הַמִּזְבֵּחַ: וְקָמַץ הַכֹּהֵן מִן־הַמִּנְחָה אֶת־אַזְכָּרָתָהּ וְהִקְטִיר הַמִּזְבֵּחָה
כז וְאַחַר יַשְׁקֶה אֶת־הָאִשָּׁה אֶת־הַמָּיִם: וְהִשְׁקָהּ אֶת־הַמַּיִם וְהָיְתָה אִם־
נִטְמְאָה וַתִּמְעֹל מַעַל בְּאִישָׁהּ וּבָאוּ בָהּ הַמַּיִם הַמְאָרְרִים לְמָרִים וְצָבְתָה
כח בִטְנָהּ וְנָפְלָה יְרֵכָהּ וְהָיְתָה הָאִשָּׁה לְאָלָה בְּקֶרֶב עַמָּהּ: וְאִם־לֹא נִטְמְאָה
כט הָאִשָּׁה וּטְהֹרָה הִוא וְנִקְּתָה וְנִזְרְעָה זָרַע: זֹאת תּוֹרַת הַקְּנָאֹת אֲשֶׁר תִּשְׂטֶה
ל אִשָּׁה תַּחַת אִישָׁהּ וְנִטְמָאָה: אוֹ אִישׁ אֲשֶׁר תַּעֲבֹר עָלָיו רוּחַ קִנְאָה וְקִנֵּא

---

20. וְאַתְּ — *And you* . . . also accept upon yourself . . .

כִּי שָׂטִית תַּחַת אִישֵׁךְ וְכִי נִטְמֵאת — *Have gone aside, being under your husband, and if you have been defiled* . . . that the oath (curse) will take effect because you went aside and became defiled and for no other reason, and being that the cause is removed and is not valid, the words of the oath (curse) will not take effect.

22. אָמֵן אָמֵן — *Amen, amen.* I accept the two conditions which you stated, (namely) that if I did not go aside I shall be clear, and if I did go aside the curse will take effect.

28. וְנִקְּתָה — *She shall be cleared* . . . from the punishment of the oath which she caused, even though it states, כִּי לֹא יְנַקֶּה ה׳, *For HASHEM will not hold him guiltless;* nonetheless, in this case God, the Blessed One, wanted the woman to be cleared כִּי הוּא יָדַע יִצְרֵנוּ, *for He knows our nature* (*Psalms* 103:14).

29. זֹאת תּוֹרַת הַקְּנָאֹת — *This is the law of jealousy* . . . a jealousy which is justified, and a jealousy which is not justified. This (the Torah) explains by stating . . .

אֲשֶׁר תִּשְׂטֶה אִשָּׁה תַּחַת אִישָׁהּ וְנִטְמָאָה — *When a woman, being under her husband, goes aside and is defiled.* Now this refers to justified jealousy. The (Torah) then additionally states . . .

30. אוֹ אִישׁ אֲשֶׁר תַּעֲבֹר עָלָיו רוּחַ קִנְאָה — *Or when the spirit of jealousy comes upon a man* . . . without proper cause.

NOTES

20. כִּי שָׂטִית תַּחַת אִישֵׁךְ וְכִי נִטְמֵאת — *Have gone aside, being under your husband, and if you have been defiled.* The woman must also be reassured that the oath and curse apply exclusively to the charge of infidelity and not to other transgressions. The sin of infidelity, however, is all inclusive, be it the act she is suspected of now which has brought her to the Temple, or acts of infidelity perpetrated on other occasions — as mentioned in verse 19 and as indicated in the repetition of the word 'Amen' in verse 22. (See tractate *Sotah* 18b)

28. וְנִקְּתָה — *She shall be cleared.* See note on verse 19.

29-30. זֹאת תּוֹרַת הַקְּנָאֹת אֲשֶׁר תִּשְׂטֶה אִשָּׁה תַּחַת אִישָׁהּ וְנִטְמָאָה. אוֹ אִישׁ אֲשֶׁר תַּעֲבֹר עָלָיו רוּחַ קִנְאָה — *This is the law of jealousy when a woman, being under her husband, goes aside and is defiled. Or when the spirit of jealousy comes upon a man.* The word הַקְּנָאֹת, *jealousy,* is written in the plural. The *Sforno* interprets it

אֶת־אִשְׁתּוֹ וְהֶעֱמִיד אֶת־הָאִשָּׁה לִפְנֵי יהוה וְעָשָׂה לָהּ הַכֹּהֵן אֵת כָּל־
לב הַתּוֹרָה הַזֹּאת: וְנִקָּה הָאִישׁ מֵעָוֺן וְהָאִשָּׁה הַהִוא תִּשָּׂא אֶת־עֲוֺנָהּ:
ו א־ב וַיְדַבֵּר יהוה אֶל־מֹשֶׁה לֵּאמֹר: דַּבֵּר אֶל־בְּנֵי יִשְׂרָאֵל וְאָמַרְתָּ אֲלֵהֶם אִישׁ
ג אוֹ־אִשָּׁה כִּי יַפְלִא לִנְדֹּר נֶדֶר נָזִיר לְהַזִּיר לַיהוה: מִיַּיִן וְשֵׁכָר יַזִּיר חֹמֶץ יַיִן
וְחֹמֶץ שֵׁכָר לֹא יִשְׁתֶּה וְכָל־מִשְׁרַת עֲנָבִים לֹא יִשְׁתֶּה וַעֲנָבִים לַחִים

וְקִנֵּא אֶת אִשְׁתּוֹ — *And he is jealous over his wife.* He warns her not to hide (meet secretly), nonetheless . . .

וְעָשָׂה לָהּ הַכֹּהֵן אֵת כָּל הַתּוֹרָה הַזֹּאת — *And the Kohen shall execute upon her all this law* . . . and he will not be concerned about blotting out the scroll.

31. וְנִקָּה הָאִישׁ מֵעָוֺן — *And the man shall be clear from iniquity* . . . even though he suspected an innocent (lit., kosher) woman, because she caused this by violating his warning and (thereby) creating (a situation of) circumstantial evidence, as (our Sages) say, 'David did not pay heed to slander; he saw self-evident things in him,' regarding Mephiboshes (*Shabbos* 56a).

וְהָאִשָּׁה הַהִוא תִּשָּׂא אֶת עֲוֺנָהּ — *And that woman shall bear her iniquity.* If she was defiled she will die, and if she was not defiled she will be degraded in public for impudently violating her husband's warning and hiding herself (secretly with another man).

VI

2. כִּי יַפְלִא — *If he pronounce (a vow).* He separates himself from the vanities and pleasures of man.

לִנְדֹּר נֶדֶר נָזִיר — *Uttering a vow of a nazir* . . . to be removed and separated from the normal pleasures.

לְהַזִּיר לַה׳ — *To consecrate himself to Hashem* . . . to separate himself from all these (pleasures) in order to be totally (committed) to God; to occupy himself in His Torah, to walk in His ways and to cleave to Him.

3. מִיַּיִן וְשֵׁכָר יַזִּיר — *He shall abstain from wine and strong drink* (alternatively: *new wine and old wine*). He must not afflict himself by fasting for that would diminish his heavenly work, as we find in the words (of our Sages) (*Taanis* 11b), nor should he torture his body with 'flagellation of the abstemious' (*Sotah* 20a), as is the custom of hypocrites and idolatrous *Kohanim*. Rather, he shall separate himself (abstain) from wine, for in that manner he will considerably reduce licentiousness and subdue his (evil) inclination, but he will not weaken his strength through this (abstinence) at all.

NOTES

to mean two kinds of jealousy — one justified and the other unjustified. The former is indicated by the expression *when a woman . . . goes aside and is defiled* while the latter is indicated by the opening phrase of verse 30 — *Or when the spirit of jealousy comes upon a man.* Nonetheless, in both instances, it is incumbent upon the *Kohen* to follow the formula of the Torah even though it involves the blotting out of God's Name in the scroll.

31. וְנִקָּה הָאִישׁ מֵעָוֺן וְהָאִשָּׁה הַהִוא תִּשָּׂא אֶת עֲוֺנָהּ — *And the man shall be clear from iniquity and that woman shall bear her iniquity.* The Torah teaches us that the husband shall be held blameless whereas the woman shall be considered guilty, even when she is proven innocent! The *Sforno* explains this anomaly in the following manner: By defying her husband and closeting herself with a particular man, she is guilty of brazenness and hence is held

ד וִיבֵשִׁים לֹא יֹאכֵל: כֹּל יְמֵי נִזְרוֹ מִכֹּל אֲשֶׁר יֵעָשֶׂה מִגֶּפֶן הַיַּיִן מֵחַרְצַנִּים
ה וְעַד־זָג לֹא יֹאכֵל: כָּל־יְמֵי נֶדֶר נִזְרוֹ תַּעַר לֹא־יַעֲבֹר עַל־רֹאשׁוֹ עַד־מְלֹאת
ו הַיָּמִם אֲשֶׁר־יַזִּיר לַיהוה קָדֹשׁ יִהְיֶה גַּדֵּל פֶּרַע שְׂעַר רֹאשׁוֹ: כָּל־יְמֵי הַזִּירוֹ
ז לַיהוָה עַל־נֶפֶשׁ מֵת לֹא יָבֹא: לְאָבִיו וּלְאִמּוֹ לְאָחִיו וּלְאַחֹתוֹ לֹא־יִטַּמָּא
ח לָהֶם בְּמֹתָם כִּי נֵזֶר אֱלֹהָיו עַל־רֹאשׁוֹ: כֹּל יְמֵי נִזְרוֹ קָדֹשׁ הוּא לַיהוָה:
ט וְכִי־יָמוּת מֵת עָלָיו בְּפֶתַע פִּתְאֹם וְטִמֵּא רֹאשׁ נִזְרוֹ וְגִלַּח רֹאשׁוֹ בְּיוֹם
י טָהֳרָתוֹ בַּיּוֹם הַשְּׁבִיעִי יְגַלְּחֶנּוּ: וּבַיּוֹם הַשְּׁמִינִי יָבִא שְׁתֵּי תֹרִים אוֹ שְׁנֵי בְּנֵי
יא יוֹנָה אֶל־הַכֹּהֵן אֶל־פֶּתַח אֹהֶל מוֹעֵד: וְעָשָׂה הַכֹּהֵן אֶחָד לְחַטָּאת וְאֶחָד
לְעֹלָה וְכִפֶּר עָלָיו מֵאֲשֶׁר חָטָא עַל־הַנָּפֶשׁ וְקִדַּשׁ אֶת־רֹאשׁוֹ בַּיּוֹם הַהוּא:
יב וְהִזִּיר לַיהוה אֶת־יְמֵי נִזְרוֹ וְהֵבִיא כֶּבֶשׂ בֶּן־שְׁנָתוֹ לְאָשָׁם וְהַיָּמִים

---

5. תַּעַר לֹא יַעֲבֹר עַל רֹאשׁוֹ — *No razor shall come upon his head.* And thereby he will divert all thoughts of beauty and the arranging of (his) hair.

קָדֹשׁ יִהְיֶה — *He shall be holy* ... separated from material desires.

6. עַל נֶפֶשׁ מֵת לֹא יָבֹא — *He shall not come near a dead body.* He shall not desecrate his holiness by occupying himself with honoring the dead, as is also the case with the *Kohen Gadol.*

8. קָדֹשׁ הוּא לַה׳ — *He is holy to* HASHEM. He will merit to be illuminated by the light of life, to be prepared to understand and to instruct (others), as is fitting for the holy ones of the generation. It is to this, it seems (to me), that Elkanah referred when he said, אַךְ יָקֵם ה׳ אֶת דְּבָרוֹ, *But let* HASHEM *establish his word* (*I Samuel* 1:23), meaning 'I agree to vow that he be a *nazir* and ask of God, the Blessed One, no other thing for the child than that His word be established and that he be holy to God.'

NOTES

up to shame. He, in turn, confronted by her defiant action is left with no other choice than to bring her to the *Kohen,* who will give her the water to drink so as to resolve this matter.

The selection from tractate *Shabbos* cited by the *Sforno* relates the strange behavior of Mephiboshes, the son of Saul, when David returned to his throne after Absalom's revolt failed. David detected that Mephiboshes was not very pleased with the failure of Absalom to overthrow him. Just as David perceived from Mephiboshes's garb and behavior his true attitude and feelings, so the husband of the *sotah* can detect his wife's rebellious nature from her conduct even when she is technically innocent of infidelity.

VI

3. מִיַּיִן וְשֵׁכָר יַזִּיר — *He shall abstain from wine and strong drink.* Although a *nazir* separates himself from certain physical pleasures and refrains from certain behaviors which would impair his state of holiness, the *Sforno* emphasizes that he is not permitted to deny himself more than the Torah has bidden and certainly not to impose afflictions upon himself which are prohibited by the Torah. The Talmud in tractate *Taanis,* which the *Sforno* alludes to, states that 'a scholar is not permitted to fast (beyond the prescribed fasts) because it diminishes his heavenly service.' The other selection cited by the *Sforno* is from tractate *Sotah* where our Sages reject and criticize the practice of those who inflict physical pain upon themselves as a religious act.

8. קָדֹשׁ הוּא לַה׳ — *He is holy to* HASHEM. The *Sforno* interprets the expression קָדֹשׁ הוּא לַה׳, *He is holy to* HASHEM, in the sense of a Divine promise and assurance. He suggests that this was the intent of Samuel's father, Elkanah, when he permitted his son to be dedicated to God's service at a tender age. His only stipulation was that the assurance given by God in this chapter of the *nazir* be fullfilled.

יג הָרִאשֹׁנִים יִפְּלוּ כִּי טָמֵא נִזְרוֹ: וְזֹאת תּוֹרַת הַנָּזִיר בְּיוֹם מְלֹאת יְמֵי נִזְרוֹ
יד יָבִיא אֹתוֹ אֶל־פֶּתַח אֹהֶל מוֹעֵד: וְהִקְרִיב אֶת־קָרְבָּנוֹ לַיהוָה כֶּבֶשׂ
בֶּן־שְׁנָתוֹ תָמִים אֶחָד לְעֹלָה וְכַבְשָׂה אַחַת בַּת־שְׁנָתָהּ תְּמִימָה לְחַטָּאת
טו וְאַיִל־אֶחָד תָּמִים לִשְׁלָמִים: וְסַל מַצּוֹת סֹלֶת חַלֹּת בְּלוּלֹת בַּשֶּׁמֶן וּרְקִיקֵי
טז מַצּוֹת מְשֻׁחִים בַּשָּׁמֶן וּמִנְחָתָם וְנִסְכֵּיהֶם: וְהִקְרִיב הַכֹּהֵן לִפְנֵי יְהוָה וְעָשָׂה
יז אֶת־חַטָּאתוֹ וְאֶת־עֹלָתוֹ: וְאֶת־הָאַיִל יַעֲשֶׂה זֶבַח שְׁלָמִים לַיהוָה עַל סַל
יח הַמַּצּוֹת וְעָשָׂה הַכֹּהֵן אֶת־מִנְחָתוֹ וְאֶת־נִסְכּוֹ: וְגִלַּח הַנָּזִיר פֶּתַח אֹהֶל מוֹעֵד
אֶת־רֹאשׁ נִזְרוֹ וְלָקַח אֶת־שְׂעַר רֹאשׁ נִזְרוֹ וְנָתַן עַל־הָאֵשׁ אֲשֶׁר־תַּחַת זֶבַח
יט הַשְּׁלָמִים: וְלָקַח הַכֹּהֵן אֶת־הַזְּרֹעַ בְּשֵׁלָה מִן־הָאַיִל וְחַלַּת מַצָּה אַחַת
מִן־הַסַּל וּרְקִיק מַצָּה אֶחָד וְנָתַן עַל־כַּפֵּי הַנָּזִיר אַחַר הִתְגַּלְּחוֹ אֶת־נִזְרוֹ:
כ וְהֵנִיף אוֹתָם הַכֹּהֵן ׀ תְּנוּפָה לִפְנֵי יְהוָה קֹדֶשׁ הוּא לַכֹּהֵן עַל חֲזֵה הַתְּנוּפָה
כא וְעַל שׁוֹק הַתְּרוּמָה וְאַחַר יִשְׁתֶּה הַנָּזִיר יָיִן: זֹאת תּוֹרַת הַנָּזִיר אֲשֶׁר יִדֹּר
קָרְבָּנוֹ לַיהוָה עַל־נִזְרוֹ מִלְּבַד אֲשֶׁר־תַּשִּׂיג יָדוֹ כְּפִי נִדְרוֹ אֲשֶׁר יִדֹּר כֵּן
יַעֲשֶׂה עַל תּוֹרַת נִזְרוֹ:
כב־כג וַיְדַבֵּר יְהוָה אֶל־מֹשֶׁה לֵּאמֹר: דַּבֵּר אֶל־אַהֲרֹן וְאֶל־בָּנָיו לֵאמֹר כֹּה תְבָרְכוּ
כד־כה אֶת־בְּנֵי יִשְׂרָאֵל אָמוֹר לָהֶם: יְבָרֶכְךָ יְהוָה וְיִשְׁמְרֶךָ: יָאֵר יְהוָה ׀

---

13. יָבִיא אֹתוֹ — *He shall bring it.* (Our Sages) have already explained (the word *it*) as meaning 'he shall bring himself' (*Sifre*). This is (to be understood as follows): For indeed, (regarding) whoever draws nigh to one who initiates a new action affecting him, it (always) says that he is *brought* to the one superior to him who changes (his status), similar to, 'He who is imprisoned cannot free himself' (*Berachos* 5b). Therefore, regarding the *tumah* and *taharah* of a leper it is written, וְהוּבָא אֶל הַכֹּהֵן, *And he is 'brought' to the Kohen* (*Leviticus* 14:2), and regarding a *sotah*, וְהֵבִיא הָאִישׁ אֶת אִשְׁתּוֹ אֶל הַכֹּהֵן, *And then shall the man 'bring' his wife to the Kohen* (5:15), and also regarding a slave, וְהִגִּישׁוֹ אֲדֹנָיו אֶל הָאֱלֹהִים, *Then his master shall 'bring' him to the judges* (*Exodus* 21:6). However, regarding the *nazir* who, through the act of shaving (his hair), was renewed and changed into a different man — there is no one more honored (esteemed) than he in this regard; rather he shall bring himself (to the Temple).

24. יְבָרֶכְךָ — *May (Hashem) bless you* . . . with wealth and property, for אִם אֵין קֶמַח אֵין תּוֹרָה, *if there is no flour there is no Torah* (*Avos* 3:21).

וְיִשְׁמְרֶךָ — *And guard you* . . . from robbers.

25. יָאֵר ה׳ — *May* HASHEM *shine* (*illuminate*). May He open your eyes through the light of His countenance to see wonders from His Torah and His deeds, after you have attained your needs through His blessings.

NOTES

13. יָבִיא אֹתוֹ — *He shall bring it. Rashi* explains the expression יָבִיא אֹתוֹ, *He shall bring it*, as meaning 'he shall bring himself, based upon the interpretation of our Sages. The *Sforno* interprets this phrase in the same manner, citing three cases where the Torah tells us that the person whose status is about to be affected or changed, whether a leper, a *sotah* or a slave, is brought to one who is in a position to exercise authority over him. In these three cases, the person in authority, i.e., the *Kohen*, the husband or the master actively brings or receives the passive party, i.e., the leper, *sotah* or slave. In the case of the *nazir*, however, *he*

כו-כז פָּנָיו אֵלֶיךָ וִיחֻנֶּךָּ: יִשָּׂא יְהוָה | פָּנָיו אֵלֶיךָ וְיָשֵׂם לְךָ שָׁלוֹם: וְשָׂמוּ
ז חמישי א אֶת־שְׁמִי עַל־בְּנֵי יִשְׂרָאֵל וַאֲנִי אֲבָרְכֵם: וַיְהִי בְּיוֹם כַּלּוֹת
מֹשֶׁה לְהָקִים אֶת־הַמִּשְׁכָּן וַיִּמְשַׁח אֹתוֹ וַיְקַדֵּשׁ אֹתוֹ וְאֶת־כָּל־
ב כֵּלָיו וְאֶת־הַמִּזְבֵּחַ וְאֶת־כָּל־כֵּלָיו וַיִּמְשָׁחֵם וַיְקַדֵּשׁ אֹתָם: וַיַּקְרִיבוּ נְשִׂיאֵי
יִשְׂרָאֵל רָאשֵׁי בֵּית אֲבֹתָם הֵם נְשִׂיאֵי הַמַּטֹּת הֵם הָעֹמְדִים עַל־
ג הַפְּקֻדִים: וַיָּבִיאוּ אֶת־קָרְבָּנָם לִפְנֵי יְהוָה שֵׁשׁ־עֶגְלֹת צָב וּשְׁנֵי־עָשָׂר בָּקָר
עֲגָלָה עַל־שְׁנֵי הַנְּשִׂאִים וְשׁוֹר לְאֶחָד וַיַּקְרִיבוּ אוֹתָם לִפְנֵי הַמִּשְׁכָּן:

---

26. יִשָּׂא ה׳ פָּנָיו אֵלֶיךָ — *May HASHEM lift up His countenance upon you* . . . to (merit) eternal life, similar to, כִּי עִמְּךָ מְקוֹר חַיִּים בְּאוֹרְךָ נִרְאֶה אוֹר, *For with You is the fountain of life; in Your light do we see light* (*Psalms* 36:10), and so (our Sages) say, 'The righteous will sit with their crowns on their heads enjoying the brightness of the Divine Presence' (*Berachos* 17a).

וְיָשֵׂם לְךָ שָׁלוֹם — *And give you peace* . . . the tranquility of peace which is everlasting, unadulterated by punishment, as is fitting for every perfect (complete) (person who merits) eternal life.

VII

1. וְאֶת הַמִּזְבֵּחַ וְאֶת כָּל כֵּלָיו — *And the altar and all the vessels thereof* . . . to set up the altar and all the vessels thereof (i.e., of the Tabernacle), each one in its (proper) place.

וַיִּמְשָׁחֵם וַיְקַדֵּשׁ אֹתָם — *And he anointed them and sanctified them* . . . after setting up each of them properly.

2. הֵם נְשִׂיאֵי הַמַּטֹּת הֵם הָעֹמְדִים עַל הַפְּקֻדִים — *These were the princes of the tribes, these are they that were over them when they were numbered.* And as such, each one of them brought an offering for his tribe and its members because inasmuch as they stood over (i.e., supervised) those who were numbered, each of them sensed that some members of his tribe were suspect of sin, and as princes they agreed to stand in the breach and offer sacrifices to atone on their behalf.

3. עֲגָלָה עַל שְׁנֵי הַנְּשִׂאִים — *A wagon for every two of the princes* . . . as an indication of the brotherhood (existing) between them, through which they would be worthy that the Divine Presence dwell between them, as it says, וַיְהִי בִישֻׁרוּן מֶלֶךְ בְּהִתְאַסֵּף רָאשֵׁי עָם יַחַד, *And there was a king in Jeshurun when the heads of the people were gathered* (*Deuteronomy* 33:5), as opposed to, חָלַק לִבָּם עַתָּה יֶאְשָׁמוּ, *Their heart is divided; now shall they bear their guilt* (*Hosea* 10:2).

NOTES

himself is capable himself of bringing about the termination of his present status and is thus an active, not a passive, party.

VII

2. הֵם נְשִׂיאֵי הַמַּטֹּת הֵם הָעֹמְדִים עַל הַפְּקֻדִים — *These were the princes of the tribes, these are they that were over them when they were numbered.* The Torah tells us that these princes made offerings on behalf of their tribes for two reasons — they were נְשִׂיאִים, *princes*, and they also joined Moses and Aaron when the census was taken (*Bamidbar* 1:4). Consistent with his commentary on that verse, the *Sforno* explains that since each leader recognized the shortcomings of his people, he was able to bring the appropriate sacrifices to atone for those particular sins, and since they were princes they were willing to do so for each felt responsible for his respective tribe.

3. עֲגָלָה עַל שְׁנֵי הַנְּשִׂאִים — *A wagon for every two of the princes.* The princes were certainly

ד-ה וַיֹּאמֶר יְהוָה אֶל־מֹשֶׁה לֵּאמֹר: קַח מֵאִתָּם וְהָיוּ לַעֲבֹד אֶת־עֲבֹדַת אֹהֶל
ו מוֹעֵד וְנָתַתָּה אוֹתָם אֶל־הַלְוִיִּם אִישׁ כְּפִי עֲבֹדָתוֹ: וַיִּקַּח מֹשֶׁה אֶת־הָעֲגָלֹת
ז וְאֶת־הַבָּקָר וַיִּתֵּן אוֹתָם אֶל־הַלְוִיִּם: אֵת | שְׁתֵּי הָעֲגָלוֹת וְאֵת אַרְבַּעַת
ח הַבָּקָר נָתַן לִבְנֵי גֵרְשׁוֹן כְּפִי עֲבֹדָתָם: וְאֵת | אַרְבַּע הָעֲגָלֹת וְאֵת שְׁמֹנַת
ט הַבָּקָר נָתַן לִבְנֵי מְרָרִי כְּפִי עֲבֹדָתָם בְּיַד אִיתָמָר בֶּן־אַהֲרֹן הַכֹּהֵן: וְלִבְנֵי
י קְהָת לֹא נָתָן כִּי־עֲבֹדַת הַקֹּדֶשׁ עֲלֵהֶם בַּכָּתֵף יִשָּׂאוּ: וַיַּקְרִיבוּ הַנְּשִׂאִים אֵת
חֲנֻכַּת הַמִּזְבֵּחַ בְּיוֹם הִמָּשַׁח אֹתוֹ וַיַּקְרִיבוּ הַנְּשִׂיאִם אֶת־קָרְבָּנָם לִפְנֵי
יא הַמִּזְבֵּחַ: וַיֹּאמֶר יהוה אֶל־מֹשֶׁה נָשִׂיא אֶחָד לַיּוֹם נָשִׂיא אֶחָד לַיּוֹם יַקְרִיבוּ
יב אֶת־קָרְבָּנָם לַחֲנֻכַּת הַמִּזְבֵּחַ: וַיְהִי הַמַּקְרִיב
יג בַּיּוֹם הָרִאשׁוֹן אֶת־קָרְבָּנוֹ נַחְשׁוֹן בֶּן־עַמִּינָדָב לְמַטֵּה יְהוּדָה: וְקָרְבָּנוֹ
קַעֲרַת־כֶּסֶף אַחַת שְׁלֹשִׁים וּמֵאָה מִשְׁקָלָהּ מִזְרָק אֶחָד כֶּסֶף שִׁבְעִים שֶׁקֶל

---

5. קַח מֵאִתָּם — *Take it from them* . . . for Moses thought that the burden of all the Levites was to be carried on their shoulders, as was the case of the Kehathites and their burden.

9. וְלִבְנֵי קְהָת לֹא נָתַן כִּי עֲבֹדַת הַקֹּדֶשׁ עֲלֵהֶם — *But to the sons of Kehath he gave none because the service of the holy things belonged to them.* Not the service of the Tent (of Meeting) but the service of the holy. Now behold, God, the Blessed One, said regarding the wagons that they were (to be used) for the service of the Tent of Meeting, which was the burden of the sons of Gershon and the sons of Merari. The burden of the sons of Kehath, however, had no item whatsoever (pertaining) to the structure of the Tent of Meeting, but their burden was (that of) the holy vessels housed in it which is called מִקְדָּשׁ (Sanctuary) as it says, *And the Kehathites, the bearers of the Sanctuary, set forward* (10:21).

10. וַיַּקְרִיבוּ הַנְּשִׂאִים אֵת חֲנֻכַּת הַמִּזְבֵּחַ — *And the princes brought the dedication offerings of the altar.* They sanctified it.

וַיַּקְרִיבוּ הַנְּשִׂיאִם אֶת קָרְבָּנָם לִפְנֵי הַמִּזְבֵּחַ — *And the princes brought their offerings before the altar.* After they sanctified the offerings, they brought them near before the altar.

13-17. וְקָרְבָּנוֹ קַעֲרַת כֶּסֶף אַחַת — *And his offering was one silver dish.* Behold, each one of them brought every kind of offering, and these were: burnt offering, meal offering, sin offering, peace offering and incense, to dedicate the altar, and those

NOTES

wealthy enough so that each one could bring his own wagon. The reason that two shared one wagon was to demonstrate the unity which reigned in their midst, as the *Sforno* explains. The Sanctuary is called מִשְׁכָּן, indicating that the שְׁכִינָה, *the Divine Presence*, dwells therein, and tradition teaches us that it only dwells in the midst of unity but departs when there is strife and friction in Israel.

9. וְלִבְנֵי קְהָת לֹא נָתַן כִּי עֲבֹדַת הַקֹּדֶשׁ עֲלֵהֶם — *But to the sons of Kehath he gave none because the service of the holy things belonged to them.* The Kehathites were not in charge of any part of the Tabernacle itself. They were responsible solely for the holy objects, such as the Ark, table, etc. These are called מִקְדָּשׁ, *Sanctuary.* Therefore, it was not fitting to place any of these sacred items on a wagon. They were to be carried on the shoulders of the Kehathites as a sign of respect.

10. וַיַּקְרִיבוּ הַנְּשִׂאִים אֵת חֲנֻכַּת הַמִּזְבֵּחַ . . . וַיַּקְרִיבוּ הַנְּשִׂיאִם אֶת קָרְבָּנָם לִפְנֵי הַמִּזְבֵּחַ — *And the princes brought the dedication offerings of the altar . . . and the princes brought their offerings before the altar.* The word וַיַּקְרִיבוּ, *and brought*, is repeated twice in this verse. The *Sforno*

יד בְּשֶׁקֶל הַקֹּדֶשׁ שְׁנֵיהֶם ׀ מְלֵאִים סֹלֶת בְּלוּלָה בַשֶּׁמֶן לְמִנְחָה׃ כַּף אַחַת
טו עֲשָׂרָה זָהָב מְלֵאָה קְטֹרֶת׃ פַּר אֶחָד בֶּן־בָּקָר אַיִל אֶחָד כֶּבֶשׂ־אֶחָד
טז-יז בֶּן־שְׁנָתוֹ לְעֹלָה׃ שְׂעִיר־עִזִּים אֶחָד לְחַטָּאת׃ וּלְזֶבַח הַשְּׁלָמִים בָּקָר שְׁנַיִם
אֵילִם חֲמִשָּׁה עַתּוּדִים חֲמִשָּׁה כְּבָשִׂים בְּנֵי־שָׁנָה חֲמִשָּׁה זֶה קָרְבַּן נַחְשׁוֹן
בֶּן־עַמִּינָדָב׃

יח-יט בַּיּוֹם הַשֵּׁנִי הִקְרִיב נְתַנְאֵל בֶּן־צוּעָר נְשִׂיא יִשָּׂשכָר׃ הִקְרִב אֶת־קָרְבָּנוֹ
קַעֲרַת־כֶּסֶף אַחַת שְׁלֹשִׁים וּמֵאָה מִשְׁקָלָהּ מִזְרָק אֶחָד כֶּסֶף שִׁבְעִים שֶׁקֶל
כ בְּשֶׁקֶל הַקֹּדֶשׁ שְׁנֵיהֶם ׀ מְלֵאִים סֹלֶת בְּלוּלָה בַשֶּׁמֶן לְמִנְחָה׃ כַּף אַחַת
כא עֲשָׂרָה זָהָב מְלֵאָה קְטֹרֶת׃ פַּר אֶחָד בֶּן־בָּקָר אַיִל אֶחָד כֶּבֶשׂ־אֶחָד
כב-כג בֶּן־שְׁנָתוֹ לְעֹלָה׃ שְׂעִיר־עִזִּים אֶחָד לְחַטָּאת׃ וּלְזֶבַח הַשְּׁלָמִים בָּקָר שְׁנַיִם
אֵילִם חֲמִשָּׁה עַתֻּדִים חֲמִשָּׁה כְּבָשִׂים בְּנֵי־שָׁנָה חֲמִשָּׁה זֶה קָרְבַּן נְתַנְאֵל
בֶּן־צוּעָר׃

כד-כה בַּיּוֹם הַשְּׁלִישִׁי נָשִׂיא לִבְנֵי זְבוּלֻן אֱלִיאָב בֶּן־חֵלֹן׃ קָרְבָּנוֹ קַעֲרַת־
כֶּסֶף אַחַת שְׁלֹשִׁים וּמֵאָה מִשְׁקָלָהּ מִזְרָק אֶחָד כֶּסֶף שִׁבְעִים שֶׁקֶל
כו בְּשֶׁקֶל הַקֹּדֶשׁ שְׁנֵיהֶם ׀ מְלֵאִים סֹלֶת בְּלוּלָה בַשֶּׁמֶן לְמִנְחָה׃ כַּף אַחַת
כז עֲשָׂרָה זָהָב מְלֵאָה קְטֹרֶת׃ פַּר אֶחָד בֶּן־בָּקָר אַיִל אֶחָד כֶּבֶשׂ־אֶחָד
כח-כט בֶּן־שְׁנָתוֹ לְעֹלָה׃ שְׂעִיר־עִזִּים אֶחָד לְחַטָּאת׃ וּלְזֶבַח הַשְּׁלָמִים בָּקָר שְׁנַיִם
אֵילִם חֲמִשָּׁה עַתֻּדִים חֲמִשָּׁה כְּבָשִׂים בְּנֵי־שָׁנָה חֲמִשָּׁה זֶה קָרְבַּן אֱלִיאָב
בֶּן־חֵלֹן׃

ל-לא בַּיּוֹם הָרְבִיעִי נָשִׂיא לִבְנֵי רְאוּבֵן אֱלִיצוּר בֶּן־שְׁדֵיאוּר׃ קָרְבָּנוֹ קַעֲרַת־
כֶּסֶף אַחַת שְׁלֹשִׁים וּמֵאָה מִשְׁקָלָהּ מִזְרָק אֶחָד כֶּסֶף שִׁבְעִים שֶׁקֶל בְּשֶׁקֶל
לב הַקֹּדֶשׁ שְׁנֵיהֶם ׀ מְלֵאִים סֹלֶת בְּלוּלָה בַשֶּׁמֶן לְמִנְחָה׃ כַּף אַחַת עֲשָׂרָה
לג זָהָב מְלֵאָה קְטֹרֶת׃ פַּר אֶחָד בֶּן־בָּקָר אַיִל אֶחָד כֶּבֶשׂ־אֶחָד בֶּן־שְׁנָתוֹ
לד-לה לְעֹלָה׃ שְׂעִיר־עִזִּים אֶחָד לְחַטָּאת׃ וּלְזֶבַח הַשְּׁלָמִים בָּקָר שְׁנַיִם אֵילִם
חֲמִשָּׁה עַתֻּדִים חֲמִשָּׁה כְּבָשִׂים בְּנֵי־שָׁנָה חֲמִשָּׁה זֶה קָרְבַּן אֱלִיצוּר
בֶּן־שְׁדֵיאוּר׃

---

who serve it, through these various kinds of offerings — except for the guilt offering, because the sin and guilt offerings have one law. (Now) the Torah relates the offering of each (prince) separately to teach us that each of them had intent to atone for the specific transgressions of his tribe which he was aware of. (Now) this (intent was incorporated) into each specific offering so as to make it acceptable for them before God. (Each prince) laid (his hand on the head of the animal) and stood there on behalf of his tribe, as was the case with the מַעֲמָדוֹת (public representatives) and the public sacrifices (*Taanis* 26a).

NOTES

explains that the princes first sanctified their offerings, after which each brought his to the altar. *Rashi* gives a different answer to explain the difficulty presented by this repetition.

13-17. וְקָרְבָּנוֹ קַעֲרַת כֶּסֶף אַחַת — *And his offering was one silver dish.* The Torah records the detailed offering of each prince, even though they were all precisely the same. The *Sforno* explains the reason for this lengthy and seemingly unnecessary repetition.

The citing of the Mishnah in *Taanis* by

לו-לז בַּיּוֹם הַחֲמִישִׁי נָשִׂיא לִבְנֵי שִׁמְעוֹן שְׁלֻמִיאֵל בֶּן־צוּרִישַׁדָּי׃ קָרְבָּנוֹ
קַעֲרַת־כֶּסֶף אַחַת שְׁלֹשִׁים וּמֵאָה מִשְׁקָלָהּ מִזְרָק אֶחָד כֶּסֶף שִׁבְעִים שֶׁקֶל
לח בְּשֶׁקֶל הַקֹּדֶשׁ שְׁנֵיהֶם ׀ מְלֵאִים סֹלֶת בְּלוּלָה בַשֶּׁמֶן לְמִנְחָה׃ כַּף אַחַת
לט עֲשָׂרָה זָהָב מְלֵאָה קְטֹרֶת׃ פַּר אֶחָד בֶּן־בָּקָר אַיִל אֶחָד כֶּבֶשׂ־אֶחָד
מ-מא בֶּן־שְׁנָתוֹ לְעֹלָה׃ שְׂעִיר־עִזִּים אֶחָד לְחַטָּאת׃ וּלְזֶבַח הַשְּׁלָמִים בָּקָר שְׁנַיִם
אֵילִם חֲמִשָּׁה עַתֻּדִים חֲמִשָּׁה כְּבָשִׂים בְּנֵי־שָׁנָה חֲמִשָּׁה זֶה קָרְבַּן שְׁלֻמִיאֵל
בֶּן־צוּרִישַׁדָּי׃

ששי מב-מג בַּיּוֹם הַשִּׁשִּׁי נָשִׂיא לִבְנֵי גָד אֶלְיָסָף בֶּן־דְּעוּאֵל׃ קָרְבָּנוֹ קַעֲרַת־כֶּסֶף אַחַת
שְׁלֹשִׁים וּמֵאָה מִשְׁקָלָהּ מִזְרָק אֶחָד כֶּסֶף שִׁבְעִים שֶׁקֶל בְּשֶׁקֶל הַקֹּדֶשׁ
מד שְׁנֵיהֶם ׀ מְלֵאִים סֹלֶת בְּלוּלָה בַשֶּׁמֶן לְמִנְחָה׃ כַּף אַחַת עֲשָׂרָה זָהָב מְלֵאָה
מה-מו קְטֹרֶת׃ פַּר אֶחָד בֶּן־בָּקָר אַיִל אֶחָד כֶּבֶשׂ־אֶחָד בֶּן־שְׁנָתוֹ לְעֹלָה׃ שְׂעִיר־
מז עִזִּים אֶחָד לְחַטָּאת׃ וּלְזֶבַח הַשְּׁלָמִים בָּקָר שְׁנַיִם אֵילִם חֲמִשָּׁה עַתֻּדִים
חֲמִשָּׁה כְּבָשִׂים בְּנֵי־שָׁנָה חֲמִשָּׁה זֶה קָרְבַּן אֶלְיָסָף בֶּן־דְּעוּאֵל׃

מח-מט בַּיּוֹם הַשְּׁבִיעִי נָשִׂיא לִבְנֵי אֶפְרָיִם אֱלִישָׁמָע בֶּן־עַמִּיהוּד׃ קָרְבָּנוֹ קַעֲרַת־
כֶּסֶף אַחַת שְׁלֹשִׁים וּמֵאָה מִשְׁקָלָהּ מִזְרָק אֶחָד כֶּסֶף שִׁבְעִים שֶׁקֶל בְּשֶׁקֶל
נ הַקֹּדֶשׁ שְׁנֵיהֶם ׀ מְלֵאִים סֹלֶת בְּלוּלָה בַשֶּׁמֶן לְמִנְחָה׃ כַּף אַחַת עֲשָׂרָה
נא זָהָב מְלֵאָה קְטֹרֶת׃ פַּר אֶחָד בֶּן־בָּקָר אַיִל אֶחָד כֶּבֶשׂ־אֶחָד בֶּן־שְׁנָתוֹ
נב-נג לְעֹלָה׃ שְׂעִיר־עִזִּים אֶחָד לְחַטָּאת׃ וּלְזֶבַח הַשְּׁלָמִים בָּקָר שְׁנַיִם אֵילִם
חֲמִשָּׁה עַתֻּדִים חֲמִשָּׁה כְּבָשִׂים בְּנֵי־שָׁנָה חֲמִשָּׁה זֶה קָרְבַּן אֱלִישָׁמָע
בֶּן־עַמִּיהוּד׃

נד-נה בַּיּוֹם הַשְּׁמִינִי נָשִׂיא לִבְנֵי מְנַשֶּׁה גַּמְלִיאֵל בֶּן־פְּדָהצוּר׃ קָרְבָּנוֹ קַעֲרַת־
כֶּסֶף אַחַת שְׁלֹשִׁים וּמֵאָה מִשְׁקָלָהּ מִזְרָק אֶחָד כֶּסֶף שִׁבְעִים שֶׁקֶל בְּשֶׁקֶל
נו הַקֹּדֶשׁ שְׁנֵיהֶם ׀ מְלֵאִים סֹלֶת בְּלוּלָה בַשֶּׁמֶן לְמִנְחָה׃ כַּף אַחַת עֲשָׂרָה
נז זָהָב מְלֵאָה קְטֹרֶת׃ פַּר אֶחָד בֶּן־בָּקָר אַיִל אֶחָד כֶּבֶשׂ־אֶחָד בֶּן־שְׁנָתוֹ
נח-נט לְעֹלָה׃ שְׂעִיר־עִזִּים אֶחָד לְחַטָּאת׃ וּלְזֶבַח הַשְּׁלָמִים בָּקָר שְׁנַיִם אֵילִם
חֲמִשָּׁה עַתֻּדִים חֲמִשָּׁה כְּבָשִׂים בְּנֵי־שָׁנָה חֲמִשָּׁה זֶה קָרְבַּן גַּמְלִיאֵל
בֶּן־פְּדָהצוּר׃

ס-סא בַּיּוֹם הַתְּשִׁיעִי נָשִׂיא לִבְנֵי בִנְיָמִן אֲבִידָן בֶּן־גִּדְעֹנִי׃ קָרְבָּנוֹ קַעֲרַת־כֶּסֶף
אַחַת שְׁלֹשִׁים וּמֵאָה מִשְׁקָלָהּ מִזְרָק אֶחָד כֶּסֶף שִׁבְעִים שֶׁקֶל בְּשֶׁקֶל
סב הַקֹּדֶשׁ שְׁנֵיהֶם ׀ מְלֵאִים סֹלֶת בְּלוּלָה בַשֶּׁמֶן לְמִנְחָה׃ כַּף אַחַת עֲשָׂרָה
סג זָהָב מְלֵאָה קְטֹרֶת׃ פַּר אֶחָד בֶּן־בָּקָר אַיִל אֶחָד כֶּבֶשׂ־אֶחָד בֶּן־
סד-סה שְׁנָתוֹ לְעֹלָה׃ שְׂעִיר־עִזִּים אֶחָד לְחַטָּאת׃ וּלְזֶבַח הַשְּׁלָמִים בָּקָר שְׁנַיִם

NOTES

Sforno is most appropriate. The קָרְבַּן תָּמִיד, *daily sacrifice,* was offered on behalf of all Israel. However, it was incumbent upon the person who brought a sacrifice to be present at the time his sacrifice was offered in the Temple. Now this was not the case regarding the public daily sacrifice. Therefore, the Early Prophets (David and Samuel) instituted 24 מִשְׁמָרוֹת, *watches,* of *Kohanim* and 24 מַעֲמָדוֹת, *posts* (of public representatives), some of whom stood by when the daily sacrifice was offered, while those who were a distance from Jerusalem gathered in the synagogues of their communities to fast and pray and read from

אֵילִם חֲמִשָּׁה֙ עַתֻּדִים חֲמִשָּׁה כְּבָשִׂים בְּנֵי־שָׁנָה חֲמִשָּׁה זֶה קָרְבַּן אֲבִידָן
בֶּן־גִּדְעֹנִי׃
סו־סז בַּיּוֹם֙ הָעֲשִׂירִי נָשִׂיא לִבְנֵי דָן אֲחִיעֶזֶר בֶּן־עַמִּישַׁדָּי׃ קָרְבָּנוֹ קַעֲרַת־כֶּסֶף
אַחַת שְׁלֹשִׁים וּמֵאָה מִשְׁקָלָהּ מִזְרָק אֶחָד֙ כֶּסֶף שִׁבְעִים שֶׁקֶל בְּשֶׁקֶל הַקֹּדֶשׁ
סח שְׁנֵיהֶם ׀ מְלֵאִים סֹלֶת בְּלוּלָה בַשֶּׁמֶן לְמִנְחָה׃ כַּף אַחַת עֲשָׂרָה זָהָב מְלֵאָה
סט־ע קְטֹרֶת׃ פַּר אֶחָד בֶּן־בָּקָר אַיִל אֶחָד כֶּבֶשׂ־אֶחָד בֶּן־שְׁנָתוֹ לְעֹלָה׃ שְׂעִיר־
עא עִזִּים אֶחָד לְחַטָּאת׃ וּלְזֶבַח הַשְּׁלָמִים בָּקָר שְׁנַיִם אֵילִם חֲמִשָּׁה֙ עַתֻּדִים
חֲמִשָּׁה כְּבָשִׂים בְּנֵי־שָׁנָה חֲמִשָּׁה זֶה קָרְבַּן אֲחִיעֶזֶר בֶּן־עַמִּישַׁדָּי׃
שביעי עב־עג בְּיוֹם֙ עַשְׁתֵּי עָשָׂר יוֹם נָשִׂיא לִבְנֵי אָשֵׁר פַּגְעִיאֵל בֶּן־עָכְרָן׃ קָרְבָּנוֹ קַעֲרַת־
כֶּסֶף אַחַת שְׁלֹשִׁים וּמֵאָה מִשְׁקָלָהּ מִזְרָק אֶחָד֙ כֶּסֶף שִׁבְעִים שֶׁקֶל בְּשֶׁקֶל
עד הַקֹּדֶשׁ שְׁנֵיהֶם ׀ מְלֵאִים סֹלֶת בְּלוּלָה בַשֶּׁמֶן לְמִנְחָה׃ כַּף אַחַת עֲשָׂרָה זָהָב
עה מְלֵאָה קְטֹרֶת׃ פַּר אֶחָד בֶּן־בָּקָר אַיִל אֶחָד כֶּבֶשׂ־אֶחָד בֶּן־שְׁנָתוֹ לְעֹלָה׃
עו־עז שְׂעִיר־עִזִּים אֶחָד לְחַטָּאת׃ וּלְזֶבַח הַשְּׁלָמִים בָּקָר שְׁנַיִם אֵילִם חֲמִשָּׁה֙
עַתֻּדִים חֲמִשָּׁה כְּבָשִׂים בְּנֵי־שָׁנָה חֲמִשָּׁה זֶה קָרְבַּן פַּגְעִיאֵל בֶּן־עָכְרָן׃
עח־עט בְּיוֹם֙ שְׁנֵים עָשָׂר יוֹם נָשִׂיא לִבְנֵי נַפְתָּלִי אֲחִירַע בֶּן־עֵינָן׃ קָרְבָּנוֹ
קַעֲרַת־כֶּסֶף אַחַת שְׁלֹשִׁים וּמֵאָה מִשְׁקָלָהּ מִזְרָק אֶחָד֙ כֶּסֶף שִׁבְעִים שֶׁקֶל
פ בְּשֶׁקֶל הַקֹּדֶשׁ שְׁנֵיהֶם ׀ מְלֵאִים סֹלֶת בְּלוּלָה בַשֶּׁמֶן לְמִנְחָה׃ כַּף אַחַת
פא עֲשָׂרָה זָהָב מְלֵאָה קְטֹרֶת׃ פַּר אֶחָד בֶּן־בָּקָר אַיִל אֶחָד כֶּבֶשׂ־אֶחָד
פב־פג בֶּן־שְׁנָתוֹ לְעֹלָה׃ שְׂעִיר־עִזִּים אֶחָד לְחַטָּאת׃ וּלְזֶבַח הַשְּׁלָמִים בָּקָר שְׁנַיִם
אֵילִם חֲמִשָּׁה֙ עַתֻּדִים חֲמִשָּׁה כְּבָשִׂים בְּנֵי־שָׁנָה חֲמִשָּׁה זֶה קָרְבַּן אֲחִירַע
בֶּן־עֵינָן׃
פד זֹאת ׀ חֲנֻכַּת הַמִּזְבֵּחַ בְּיוֹם֙ הִמָּשַׁח אֹתוֹ מֵאֵת נְשִׂיאֵי יִשְׂרָאֵל קַעֲרֹת
כֶּסֶף שְׁתֵּים עֶשְׂרֵה מִזְרְקֵי־כֶסֶף֙ שְׁנֵים עָשָׂר כַּפּוֹת זָהָב שְׁתֵּים עֶשְׂרֵה׃
פה שְׁלֹשִׁים וּמֵאָה הַקְּעָרָה הָאַחַת֙ כֶּסֶף וְשִׁבְעִים הַמִּזְרָק הָאֶחָד כֹּל כֶּסֶף
פו הַכֵּלִים אַלְפַּיִם וְאַרְבַּע־מֵאוֹת בְּשֶׁקֶל הַקֹּדֶשׁ׃ כַּפּוֹת זָהָב שְׁתֵּים־עֶשְׂרֵה֙
מְלֵאֹת קְטֹרֶת עֲשָׂרָה עֲשָׂרָה הַכַּף בְּשֶׁקֶל הַקֹּדֶשׁ כָּל־זְהַב הַכַּפּוֹת עֶשְׂרִים
מפטיר פז וּמֵאָה׃ כָּל־הַבָּקָר לָעֹלָה שְׁנֵים עָשָׂר פָּרִים אֵילִם שְׁנֵים־עָשָׂר֙ כְּבָשִׂים
פח בְּנֵי־שָׁנָה שְׁנֵים עָשָׂר וּמִנְחָתָם וּשְׂעִירֵי עִזִּים שְׁנֵים עָשָׂר לְחַטָּאת׃ וְכֹל
בְּקַר ׀ זֶבַח הַשְּׁלָמִים עֶשְׂרִים וְאַרְבָּעָה פָּרִים אֵילִם שִׁשִּׁים֙ עַתֻּדִים
שִׁשִּׁים כְּבָשִׂים בְּנֵי־שָׁנָה שִׁשִּׁים זֹאת חֲנֻכַּת הַמִּזְבֵּחַ אַחֲרֵי הִמָּשַׁח אֹתוֹ׃

---

84. זאת חֲנֻכַּת הַמִּזְבֵּחַ — *This was the dedication-offering of the altar.* Behold, the dedication of the altar at that time was, in general, a small event compared to the dedication of the First Temple (of Solomon) with it's many vessels, its riches and abundance of sacrifices.

NOTES

the Torah. In this manner it was considered as though all Israel was present during the offering of the daily sacrifice. The *Sforno* indicates that the origin of this custom had its roots in the dedication of the altar, where the princes brought sacrifices on behalf of their tribe and served as אַנְשֵׁי מַעֲמָד, *public representatives.*

פט וּבְבֹא מֹשֶׁה אֶל־אֹהֶל מוֹעֵד לְדַבֵּר אִתּוֹ וַיִּשְׁמַע אֶת־הַקּוֹל מִדַּבֵּר אֵלָיו
מֵעַל הַכַּפֹּרֶת אֲשֶׁר עַל־אֲרֹן הָעֵדֻת מִבֵּין שְׁנֵי הַכְּרֻבִים וַיְדַבֵּר אֵלָיו:

---

89. וּבְבֹא מֹשֶׁה אֶל אֹהֶל מוֹעֵד לְדַבֵּר אִתּוֹ וַיִּשְׁמַע אֶת הַקּוֹל — *And when Moses went into the Tent of Meeting that he might speak with Him, then he heard the Voice.* And even though the event was very small in comparison to the dedication of (the Temple of) Solomon, nonetheless, when Moses went into the Tent of Meeting he heard the same Voice that he had heard prior to the act of the Golden Calf. This did not occur in (the time) of the First Temple and certainly not (in the period) of the Second Temple, for no prophet went into the Temple to prophesize in such a manner that he would attain prophecy at once. (Now) this was because this dedication (of the Sanctuary) was acceptable (to God), as were those who made the offerings, and as was Moses who was the shepherd.

מִדַּבֵּר אֵלָיו — *Speaking to him* . . . to Himself, because כֹּל פָּעַל ה׳ לַמַּעֲנֵהוּ, *HASHEM has made everything for His own purpose* (*Proverbs* 16:4), making known (elucidating) to Himself and thus imparting knowledge and (granting) goodness to others through the generosity of His influence which is without parsimony. Now this action (of God) will become apparent (i.e., have effect) on the recipient according to (the extent of) his preparation (to hear it — i.e., the Voice). With this, (the Torah) explains the manner of every 'saying' (דִּבּוּר) which is stated in the Torah whenever it says *And HASHEM spoke* ◆

NOTES

84-89. זֹאת חֲנֻכַּת הַמִּזְבֵּחַ . . . וּבְבֹא מֹשֶׁה אֶל אֹהֶל מוֹעֵד לְדַבֵּר אִתּוֹ וַיִּשְׁמַע אֶת הַקּוֹל . . . — *This was the dedication-offering of the altar . . . And when Moses went into the Tent of Meeting that he might speak with Him, then he heard the Voice.* The *Sforno* explains the reason for placing this seemingly unrelated verse (89) at the conclusion of the section dealing with the dedication of the altar. He explains that the Torah is teaching us that although the offerings brought in honor of the dedication in the wilderness were insignificant compared to those brought at the dedication of Solomon's Temple, nonetheless this dedication was far superior because Moses heard the Voice of God, a phenomenon not experienced at the time of the dedication of the First and Second Temples in Jerusalem.

89. מִדַּבֵּר אֵלָיו — *Speaking to him.* The word מִדַּבֵּר, *speaking,* as *Rashi* points out is similar to מִתְדַּבֵּר (in the *Hitpael* form), implying that 'he heard the Voice speaking to itself.' The *Sforno* expands upon this, explaining that God, as it were, 'makes known to Himself' (not directly to His prophet) and that the Voice heard by Moses was an overflow of God's words which are received by each prophet according to his own personal powers of perception and understanding. The *Rambam* states in his *Guide* (1:68) that regarding the Almighty, the intellect (שֵׂכֶל), concept (מוּשְׂכָּל) and intelligence (מַשְׂכִּיל) are one. 'God is an intellect which is always in action . . . He comprehends constantly; consequently He and the things comprehended are one and the same thing.' This idea is what the *Sforno* is alluding to when he says, וּבְהַשְׂכִּילוֹ אֶת עַצְמוֹ (elucidating to Himself), i.e., He is always (as the *Guide* puts it) the intellect (דֵּעָה), the intelligence (יוֹדֵעַ), and the concept (יָדוּעַ). The *Rambam* states this principle in *Mishnah Torah* (*Yesodai Hatorah* 2:10) as well. 'Our knowledge and ourselves are separate. But as for the Creator, Blessed is He, His knowledge and His life are One . . . He is One in every aspect . . . God is the One Who knows (יוֹדֵעַ), is known (יָדוּעַ) and is the knowledge (דֵּעָה) of Himself. This is beyond the power of speech to express, beyond the capacity of the ear to hear and of the human mind to apprehend clearly.' The *Sforno* also uses this principle as the basis of his statement that the 'knowledge and goodness' of God are given to man through the generosity of His influence, and it was given to Moses in a far greater measure than to any other human being.

פרשת בהעלתך
Parashas Behaaloscha

ח א־ב וַיְדַבֵּר יְהוָה אֶל־מֹשֶׁה לֵּאמֹר: דַּבֵּר אֶל־אַהֲרֹן וְאָמַרְתָּ אֵלָיו בְּהַעֲלֹתְךָ
ג אֶת־הַנֵּרֹת אֶל־מוּל פְּנֵי הַמְּנוֹרָה יָאִירוּ שִׁבְעַת הַנֵּרוֹת: וַיַּעַשׂ כֵּן אַהֲרֹן
ד אֶל־מוּל פְּנֵי הַמְּנוֹרָה הֶעֱלָה נֵרֹתֶיהָ כַּאֲשֶׁר צִוָּה יְהוָה אֶת־מֹשֶׁה: וְזֶה
מַעֲשֵׂה הַמְּנֹרָה מִקְשָׁה זָהָב עַד־יְרֵכָהּ עַד־פִּרְחָהּ מִקְשָׁה הִוא כַּמַּרְאֶה אֲשֶׁר
הֶרְאָה יְהוָה אֶת־מֹשֶׁה כֵּן עָשָׂה אֶת־הַמְּנֹרָה:

VIII

2. בְּהַעֲלֹתְךָ אֶת הַנֵּרֹת — *When you light the lamps* ... when you kindle the six lamps.

אֶל מוּל פְּנֵי הַמְּנוֹרָה — *Over against the central candlestick* ... which is the central shaft; that is, when you turn the wick (lit., flame) of each of the six lamps toward the center shaft, then ...

יָאִירוּ שִׁבְעַת הַנֵּרוֹת — *The seven lamps shall give light.* All seven (lamps) will illuminate and shed the Divine light upon Israel, (and in this manner) teach them that the light of the right (lamps) and the light of the left (lamps) must turn toward the light of the central shaft, which is the principal part of the menorah. And so it is fitting (to be) the intention of those who turn to the right, i.e., who occupy themselves with (activities of) eternal life and those who turn to the left, i.e., who occupy themselves with (activities of) temporal life, yet assist (the ones on) the right, as it says, 'If not for the leaves, the grapes could not exist' (*Chullin* 92a). All shall have as their purpose the fulfillment of the will of God, the Blessed One, in such a manner that through all of them His intent will be realized, and together they shall exalt His Name, as they accepted upon themselves (at Sinai), to which (the Torah) attests to saying, וַיַּעֲנוּ כָל הָעָם יַחְדָּו וַיֹּאמְרוּ כֹּל אֲשֶׁר דִּבֶּר ה׳ נַעֲשֶׂה, *And all the people answered together and said, 'All that HASHEM has spoken we will do'* (Exodus 19:8) — meaning that together we will fulfill His intent.

4. וְזֶה מַעֲשֵׂה הַמְּנֹרָה מִקְשָׁה — *And this was the work of the menorah, (it should be) beaten (out of one piece).* And this intended purpose (תַּכְלִית) of lighting the lamps *over against the central candlestick* is also the reason for the obligation of making the menorah of *beaten work,* for it thereby teaches (the need for) unity, which is the intended purpose (of the menorah) itself.

NOTES

VIII

2. בְּהַעֲלֹתְךָ אֶת הַנֵּרֹת אֶל מוּל פְּנֵי הַמְּנוֹרָה יָאִירוּ שִׁבְעַת הַנֵּרוֹת — *When you light the lamps over against the central candlestick the seven lamps shall give light.* The Book of *Proverbs* (3:16) states regarding wisdom, *Length of days is in her right hand, in her left hand are riches and honor.* The Talmud in tractate *Shabbos* 63a interprets this verse to mean that those who pursue the study of Torah motivated by a desire to master the wisdom which God shared with us therein, devoting their efforts and energies to the realm of the spirit, are called מַיְימִנִים — 'those who go to the right hand' — and are promised length of days. Those, however, who are called מַשְׂמְאִילִים — 'those who go to the left hand' — i.e., who occupy themselves with worldly affairs, but who nonetheless lend their support to the students of Torah, shall be blessed with 'riches and honor.' This latter group is referred to by our Sages as the 'leaves' that protect the 'grapes', the 'grapes' referring to the Torah scholars. The Talmud in tractate *Chullin* 92a states, 'Let the grapes (the scholars) pray for the leaves (the untutored), for the grapes could not exist if not for the leaves.'

The *Sforno* incorporates both of these Talmudic concepts in his commentary on this

ה־ו וַיְדַבֵּר יְהוָה אֶל־מֹשֶׁה לֵּאמֹר: קַח אֶת־הַלְוִיִּם מִתּוֹךְ בְּנֵי יִשְׂרָאֵל וְטִהַרְתָּ
ז אֹתָם: וְכֹה־תַעֲשֶׂה לָהֶם לְטַהֲרָם הַזֵּה עֲלֵיהֶם מֵי חַטָּאת וְהֶעֱבִירוּ תַעַר
ח עַל־כָּל־בְּשָׂרָם וְכִבְּסוּ בִגְדֵיהֶם וְהִטֶּהָרוּ: וְלָקְחוּ פַּר בֶּן־בָּקָר וּמִנְחָתוֹ סֹלֶת
ט בְּלוּלָה בַשָּׁמֶן וּפַר־שֵׁנִי בֶן־בָּקָר תִּקַּח לְחַטָּאת: וְהִקְרַבְתָּ אֶת־הַלְוִיִּם לִפְנֵי
י אֹהֶל מוֹעֵד וְהִקְהַלְתָּ אֶת־כָּל־עֲדַת בְּנֵי יִשְׂרָאֵל: וְהִקְרַבְתָּ אֶת־הַלְוִיִּם
יא לִפְנֵי יְהוָה וְסָמְכוּ בְנֵי־יִשְׂרָאֵל אֶת־יְדֵיהֶם עַל־הַלְוִיִּם: וְהֵנִיף אַהֲרֹן
אֶת־הַלְוִיִּם תְּנוּפָה לִפְנֵי יְהוָה מֵאֵת בְּנֵי יִשְׂרָאֵל וְהָיוּ לַעֲבֹד אֶת־עֲבֹדַת
יב יְהוָה: וְהַלְוִיִּם יִסְמְכוּ אֶת־יְדֵיהֶם עַל רֹאשׁ הַפָּרִים וַעֲשֵׂה אֶת־הָאֶחָד
יג חַטָּאת וְאֶת־הָאֶחָד עֹלָה לַיהוָה לְכַפֵּר עַל־הַלְוִיִּם: וְהַעֲמַדְתָּ אֶת־הַלְוִיִּם
יד לִפְנֵי אַהֲרֹן וְלִפְנֵי בָנָיו וְהֵנַפְתָּ אֹתָם תְּנוּפָה לַיהוָה: וְהִבְדַּלְתָּ אֶת־הַלְוִיִּם
שני טו מִתּוֹךְ בְּנֵי יִשְׂרָאֵל וְהָיוּ לִי הַלְוִיִּם: וְאַחֲרֵי־כֵן יָבֹאוּ הַלְוִיִּם לַעֲבֹד אֶת־אֹהֶל
טז מוֹעֵד וְטִהַרְתָּ אֹתָם וְהֵנַפְתָּ אֹתָם תְּנוּפָה: כִּי נְתֻנִים נְתֻנִים הֵמָּה לִי מִתּוֹךְ

---

14. וְהִבְדַּלְתָּ אֶת הַלְוִיִּם — *And you shall separate the Levites.* You shall separate the encampment of the Levites who lived at that time (in the wilderness).

וְהָיוּ לִי הַלְוִיִּם — *And the Levites shall be Mine.* They and their offspring shall be prepared to serve Me.

15. וְאַחֲרֵי כֵן יָבֹאוּ הַלְוִיִּם — *And after that shall the Levites go in* . . . who are of the present (in this generation).

16. כִּי נְתֻנִים נְתֻנִים הֵמָּה לִי — *For they are given, they are given unto Me. They are given*, (voluntarily offering) themselves, for they gave themselves over to My service, as the (verse) attests saying, מִי לַה׳ אֵלָי וַיֵּאָסְפוּ אֵלָיו כָּל בְּנֵי לֵוִי, *Whoso is on* HASHEM*'s side let him come to me. And all the sons of Levi gathered themselves together to him* (Exodus 32:26). And they are also *given* . . .

NOTES

verse. The central shaft of the menorah represents the Divine light. The three wicks on the right represent the Torah scholars while the three on the left represent the supporters of Torah. Both are necessary, and together they exalt God's Name, and when they are unified they are able to effectuate the intent of God in His giving the Torah to the people of Israel.

See the *Sforno's* commentary on *Exodus* 25:37 and the explanatory notes on verses 31-37 there for a different interpretation of the right and left wicks. However, both there and in verse 4, the *Sforno* stresses the symbolism of מִקְשָׁה (beaten out of one piece) which teaches the need for unity among all segments of Israel and among the students and supporters of Torah.

14. וְהִבְדַּלְתָּ אֶת הַלְוִיִּם . . . וְהָיוּ לִי הַלְוִיִּם — *And you shall separate the Levites . . . and the Levites shall be Mine.* The *Sforno* explains that there is no redundancy in this verse regarding the special status of the Levites. The first part of the verse refers to the Levites of that generation, while the latter part refers to the appointment of the Levites for all time.

16. כִּי נְתֻנִים נְתֻנִים הֵמָּה לִי — *For they are given, they are given unto Me.* The word נְתֻנִים, *they are given*, is repeated twice in this verse, and also in 3:9. The *Sforno* explains that the first נְתֻנִים refers to the voluntary giving of the Levites by themselves to His service when they responded to the cry of Moses at the time of the sin of the Golden Calf. The second נְתֻנִים refers to the giving of the tithes by the Israelites as compensation for the Levites' service. The latter interpretation is given above in 3:9 as well. However, the first expression *they are given* there refers to the Levites acceptance of direction by the *Kohanim*, to whom they were *given* as subordinates.

בְּנֵי יִשְׂרָאֵל תַּחַת פִּטְרַת כָּל־רֶחֶם בְּכוֹר כֹּל מִבְּנֵי יִשְׂרָאֵל לָקַחְתִּי אֹתָם
יז לִי: כִּי לִי כָל־בְּכוֹר בִּבְנֵי יִשְׂרָאֵל בָּאָדָם וּבַבְּהֵמָה בְּיוֹם הַכֹּתִי כָל־בְּכוֹר
יח בְּאֶרֶץ מִצְרַיִם הִקְדַּשְׁתִּי אֹתָם לִי: וָאֶקַּח אֶת־הַלְוִיִּם תַּחַת כָּל־בְּכוֹר בִּבְנֵי
יט יִשְׂרָאֵל: וָאֶתְּנָה אֶת־הַלְוִיִּם נְתֻנִים | לְאַהֲרֹן וּלְבָנָיו מִתּוֹךְ בְּנֵי יִשְׂרָאֵל

מִתּוֹךְ בְּנֵי יִשְׂרָאֵל — *From among the Children of Israel . . .* who will give the Levites their sustenance through the first tithe in exchange for their (Divine) service so that My service be done through all of them.

תַּחַת פִּטְרַת כָּל רֶחֶם — *Instead of all that open the womb . . .* for (originally) the service was incumbent upon them (i.e., the firstborn).

17. כִּי לִי כָל בְּכוֹר — *For all the firstborn are Mine.* Originally, the (Divine) service was (the responsibility) of the firstborn because they are the most honored in their household and to them (belonged) the rights of the service.

בְּיוֹם הַכֹּתִי כָל בְּכוֹר . . . הִקְדַּשְׁתִּי אֹתָם — *On the day that I smote all the firstborn . . . I sanctified them.* However, the reason that I made it necessary for them (to have) redemption is because on the day that I smote (the Egyptian firstborn) I sanctified them for Myself in that they should not occupy themselves with any ordinary labor at all, just as I prohibited shearing or working with a firstborn animal. And this I did in order to save them through the law (relating to) a sacred (object), for they were not (really) worthy to be saved from the plague of the *messengers of evil* (based on *Psalms* 78:49) since they were the (most) honored among the people and the onus (lit., prisoner's band) of everyone was resting upon them. (Therefore) I said that they are to be redeemed so that they will thereby become non-holy and hence permitted to do ordinary labor.

18. וָאֶקַּח אֶת הַלְוִיִּם תַּחַת כָּל בְּכוֹר — *And I have taken the Levites instead of all the firstborn . . .* only in that generation, as explained above (3:45).

19. וָאֶתְּנָה אֶת הַלְוִיִּם — *And I have given the Levites.* Since they gave of themselves (voluntarily) to My service, (therefore) I have given them to Aaron and his sons for My service.

NOTES

17. כִּי לִי כָל בְּכוֹר . . . בְּיוֹם הַכֹּתִי כָל בְּכוֹר . . . הִקְדַּשְׁתִּי אֹתָם — *For all the firstborn are Mine . . . on the day that I smote all the firstborn . . . I sanctified them.* The role of the firstborn from earliest times, their sanctification in Egypt and the need for their redemption are intertwined. Because of their role of leadership, they bear the responsibility for the behavior — and hence the sins — of all. Therefore, by right they should have been included in the smiting of the firstborn in Egypt. However, by sanctifying them God granted them immunity from annihilation as 'objects of holiness' (הֶקְדֵּשׁ). This, in turn, meant that they were not permitted to occupy themselves with any common (i.e., non-holy) labor or endeavors (חולין); hence, they had to be ultimately redeemed, thereby permitting them to do common labor.

18. וָאֶקַּח אֶת הַלְוִיִּם תַּחַת כָּל בְּכוֹר — *And I have taken the Levites instead of all the firstborn.* In that generation, the Levites redeemed the firstborn. Later, as in our time, it is done with five *shekalim.*

19. וָאֶתְּנָה אֶת הַלְוִיִּם לַעֲבֹד אֶת עֲבֹדַת בְּנֵי יִשְׂרָאֵל בְּאֹהֶל מוֹעֵד — *And I have given the Levites to do the service of the Children of Israel in the Tent of Meeting.* See the *Sforno's* commentary and the notes on verse 16 above. The meaning of this verse is: Being that the Levites voluntarily gave themselves to Me

לַעֲבֹד אֶת־עֲבֹדַת בְּנֵי־יִשְׂרָאֵל בְּאֹהֶל מוֹעֵד וּלְכַפֵּר עַל־בְּנֵי יִשְׂרָאֵל וְלֹא
כ יִהְיֶה בִּבְנֵי יִשְׂרָאֵל נֶגֶף בְּגֶשֶׁת בְּנֵי־יִשְׂרָאֵל אֶל־הַקֹּדֶשׁ: וַיַּעַשׂ מֹשֶׁה וְאַהֲרֹן
וְכָל־עֲדַת בְּנֵי־יִשְׂרָאֵל לַלְוִיִּם כְּכֹל אֲשֶׁר־צִוָּה יהוה אֶת־מֹשֶׁה לַלְוִיִּם
כא כֵּן־עָשׂוּ לָהֶם בְּנֵי יִשְׂרָאֵל: וַיִּתְחַטְּאוּ הַלְוִיִּם וַיְכַבְּסוּ בִּגְדֵיהֶם וַיָּנֶף אַהֲרֹן
כב אֹתָם תְּנוּפָה לִפְנֵי יהוה וַיְכַפֵּר עֲלֵיהֶם אַהֲרֹן לְטַהֲרָם: וְאַחֲרֵי־כֵן בָּאוּ
הַלְוִיִּם לַעֲבֹד אֶת־עֲבֹדָתָם בְּאֹהֶל מוֹעֵד לִפְנֵי אַהֲרֹן וְלִפְנֵי בָנָיו כַּאֲשֶׁר
כג צִוָּה יהוה אֶת־מֹשֶׁה עַל־הַלְוִיִּם כֵּן עָשׂוּ לָהֶם: וַיְדַבֵּר יהוה
כד אֶל־מֹשֶׁה לֵּאמֹר: זֹאת אֲשֶׁר לַלְוִיִּם מִבֶּן חָמֵשׁ וְעֶשְׂרִים שָׁנָה וָמַעְלָה יָבוֹא
כה לִצְבֹא צָבָא בַּעֲבֹדַת אֹהֶל מוֹעֵד: וּמִבֶּן חֲמִשִּׁים שָׁנָה יָשׁוּב מִצְּבָא הָעֲבֹדָה
כו וְלֹא יַעֲבֹד עוֹד: וְשֵׁרֵת אֶת־אֶחָיו בְּאֹהֶל מוֹעֵד לִשְׁמֹר מִשְׁמֶרֶת וַעֲבֹדָה לֹא
יַעֲבֹד כָּכָה תַּעֲשֶׂה לַלְוִיִּם בְּמִשְׁמְרֹתָם:

לַעֲבֹד אֶת עֲבֹדַת בְּנֵי יִשְׂרָאֵל בְּאֹהֶל מוֹעֵד — *To do the service of the Children of Israel in the Tent of Meeting* ... to perform that service which was (originally) fitting for their firstborn.

וּלְכַפֵּר עַל בְּנֵי יִשְׂרָאֵל — *And to make atonement for the Children of Israel.* By receiving the tithes from the Israelites so that they will be able to serve God, the Blessed One, they will atone for Israel, all of who caused the rejection of their firstborn, through the (sin) of the calf.

וְלֹא יִהְיֶה בִּבְנֵי יִשְׂרָאֵל נֶגֶף — *That there be no plague among the Children of Israel* ... Among the Levites and the rest of Israel.

בְּגֶשֶׁת בְּנֵי יִשְׂרָאֵל אֶל הַקֹּדֶשׁ — *Through the Children of Israel coming nigh to the holy.* For then the strangers (i.e., the Israelites) who draw nigh will sin, and the Levites who permit the strangers to come nigh (will also sin) and all of them will be guilty, as it says, *That they die not, neither they, nor you* (18:3)

20. וַיַּעַשׂ מֹשֶׁה וְאַהֲרֹן וְכָל עֲדַת בְּנֵי יִשְׂרָאֵל לַלְוִיִּם — *Thus did Moses and Aaron and all the congregation of the Children of Israel to the Levites.* On behalf of the Levites they lent their assistance in the matter of the shaving of their hair, the washing of their clothes and the offering.

כְּכֹל אֲשֶׁר צִוָּה ה׳ אֶת מֹשֶׁה לַלְוִיִּם — *According to all that HASHEM commanded Moses regarding the Levites* ... as He had commanded Moses to command the Levites that they shall do.

כֵּן עָשׂוּ לָהֶם בְּנֵי יִשְׂרָאֵל — *So did the Children of Israel unto them.* Israel eagerly did this on their behalf so that the will of their Master be done.

22. כַּאֲשֶׁר צִוָּה ה׳ אֶת מֹשֶׁה עַל הַלְוִיִּם — *As HASHEM had commanded Moses concerning the Levites* ... above (chapter 4) where He commanded that their watches were to serve, (to carry) burdens and sing according to (the instructions of) Aaron and his sons — so did Aaron and his sons set them in order in their watches.

NOTES

and My service, I have now given them over to the *Kohanim*, whom they shall serve — a service which originally was meant to be fulfilled by the firstborn.

ט שלישי א וַיְדַבֵּר יְהוָה אֶל־מֹשֶׁה בְמִדְבַּר־סִינַי בַּשָּׁנָה הַשֵּׁנִית לְצֵאתָם מֵאֶרֶץ מִצְרַיִם
ב־ג בַּחֹדֶשׁ הָרִאשׁוֹן לֵאמֹר: וְיַעֲשׂוּ בְנֵי־יִשְׂרָאֵל אֶת־הַפָּסַח בְּמוֹעֲדוֹ: בְּאַרְבָּעָה

IX

1. בַּחֹדֶשׁ הָרִאשׁוֹן — *In the first month.* After he counted the men for the army and set in order the standards and those who carried the Tabernacle so as to bring them into the Land, and he made *tahor* the camp of the *tameim*, as it says, וְהָיָה מַחֲנֶיךָ קָדוֹשׁ, *therefore shall your camp be holy* (*Deut.* 23:15), and (after he eliminated) illegitimate offspring through the matter (i.e., law) of the *sotah* so that the Divine Presence might dwell in the midst of their hosts — the Scripture (text) then relates four good (meritorious) acts which Israel performed through which they would have merited to enter the Land immediately without a struggle, had it not been for (the sin of) the Spies, as Moses our Teacher attested when he said to Chovev, *We are journeying to the place* (10:29). First, (the Torah) relates the dedication of the altar (7:1-8); second, their zealousness in the matter of the dedication of the Levites (8:5-26); third, their zealousness in (bringing) the *Pesach* offering (9:1-14); and fourth, (their) following God, the Blessed One, in the wilderness, even though the cloud would travel (lit., ascend) at unknown (unscheduled) times. At times, (they would travel) after a lengthy period and other times after short periods, in a manner that their encampment and journeying was most difficult for them (9:17-23). Now, in making all this known, (the Torah) relates it according to their degree of acceptance (רָצוֹן) before Him, not according to the (sequence) of time (i.e., chronologically). Therefore, (the Torah) relates here the matter of the dedication of the altar, and the (induction of) the Levites and the (bringing) of the *Pesach* which (all) occurred in the first month (even though the events recorded in) the beginning of the Book (of *Numbers*) (occurred in the) second month, and the matter of their encampments and journeying by the order of God (began) from the day they left Egypt. It is regarding (cases) like these that (our Sages) say, אֵין מוּקְדָּם וּמְאוּחָר בַּתּוֹרָה, *There is no chronological order in the Torah* (*Pesachim* 6b), this being so when the intent is to (teach us) something (through the order of the text), beside the time sequence of the events related.

2. וְיַעֲשׂוּ בְנֵי יִשְׂרָאֵל אֶת הַפָּסַח — *Let the Children of Israel make the Pesach.* Besides (the offerings) which they made (i.e., offered) on the eighth day of מִלּוּאִים (the ceremony of inducting the *Kohanim*) and the dedication (ceremony) of the princes,

NOTES

IX

1. בַּחֹדֶשׁ הָרִאשׁוֹן — *In the first month.* The *Sforno* in the general introduction to his commentary on the Torah mentions among the many criticisms leveled by those who question the paramount, central role that Torah plays in Judaism the lack of chronological order of the events recorded therein. These chapters in the Book of *Numbers* would seem to be a target for these criticisms since the opening chapter of the book is set in the *second* month of the second year after the Exodus from Egypt, while the ninth chapter records God's words to Moses in the *first* month! The *Sforno* reconciles this seeming anomaly, explaining that the Torah, at times, deviates from the chronological order in favor of a different order which contains a purposeful lesson. The original intent of God was to bring the Israelites into the Land of Israel soon after their departure from Egypt, and have them occupy the Land without recourse to war. Hence, at the beginning of this book (בְּמִדְבַּר), which sets out to tell us the story of the Israelites' journey and entrance into the

עָשָׂר־יוֹם בַּחֹדֶשׁ הַזֶּה בֵּין הָעַרְבַּיִם תַּעֲשׂוּ אֹתוֹ בְּמֹעֲדוֹ כְּכָל־חֻקֹּתָיו
ד וּכְכָל־מִשְׁפָּטָיו תַּעֲשׂוּ אֹתוֹ׃ וַיְדַבֵּר מֹשֶׁה אֶל־בְּנֵי יִשְׂרָאֵל לַעֲשֹׂת הַפָּסַח׃
ה וַיַּעֲשׂוּ אֶת־הַפֶּסַח בָּרִאשׁוֹן בְּאַרְבָּעָה עָשָׂר יוֹם לַחֹדֶשׁ בֵּין הָעַרְבַּיִם
ו בְּמִדְבַּר סִינָי כְּכֹל אֲשֶׁר צִוָּה יהוה אֶת־מֹשֶׁה כֵּן עָשׂוּ בְּנֵי יִשְׂרָאֵל׃ וַיְהִי
אֲנָשִׁים אֲשֶׁר הָיוּ טְמֵאִים לְנֶפֶשׁ אָדָם וְלֹא־יָכְלוּ לַעֲשֹׂת־הַפֶּסַח בַּיּוֹם הַהוּא
ז וַיִּקְרְבוּ לִפְנֵי מֹשֶׁה וְלִפְנֵי אַהֲרֹן בַּיּוֹם הַהוּא׃ וַיֹּאמְרוּ הָאֲנָשִׁים הָהֵמָּה
אֵלָיו אֲנַחְנוּ טְמֵאִים לְנֶפֶשׁ אָדָם לָמָּה נִגָּרַע לְבִלְתִּי הַקְרִיב אֶת־קָרְבַּן
ח יהוה בְּמֹעֲדוֹ בְּתוֹךְ בְּנֵי יִשְׂרָאֵל׃ וַיֹּאמֶר אֲלֵהֶם מֹשֶׁה עִמְדוּ וְאֶשְׁמְעָה
מַה־יְצַוֶּה יהוה לָכֶם׃

---

let them also make (i.e., offer) the *Pesach*. They shall not be exempt from offering it because of their rejoicing in the commandments which they kept, as happened at the time of the building of the First Temple, (concerning which) our Sages tell us (*Moed Katan* 9a) that Solomon nullified Yom Kippur because of the rejoicing in the dedication of the Temple.

7. אֲנַחְנוּ טְמֵאִים לְנֶפֶשׁ אָדָם לָמָּה נִגָּרַע — *We are tamei by the dead body of a man; why are we to be kept back?* Since our *tumah* (affects our ability to perform) a commandment, why should that 'lead to a transgression?' (Based on *Avos* 4:2).

בְּמֹעֲדוֹ — *In its appointed season.* (Hence) it is a 'passing commandment.'

NOTES

Land, the Torah tells us first of the preparatory arrangements leading to this goal. The camps were organized, assignments were given to the *Kohanim* and Levites, the camp of Israel was cleansed of *tumah* — all vital aspects of this preparation. These events, although occurring later in time, are recorded first since they are of primary importance for they contain instructions and commandments given by the Almighty. However, there were also other acts performed by the people of Israel which were instrumental in qualifying them to be worthy of God's Providence in bringing them into the Land of Israel in a miraculous manner, i.e., through a bloodless conquest! These were four in number and are recorded in the order of their importance, not in the order of their occurrence. They are: the dedication of the altar, the induction of the Levites, the offering of the *Pesach* sacrifice and the loyal adherence to the cloud which signaled when to journey and when to encamp. Here then is a case in point of what our Sages mean when they state, אֵין מוּקְדָּם וּמְאוּחָר בַּתּוֹרָה, *There is no chronological order in the Torah.*

2. וְיַעֲשׂוּ בְנֵי יִשְׂרָאֵל אֶת הַפָּסַח — *Let the Children of Israel make the Pesach.* Since the word וְיַעֲשׂוּ begins with the prefix *vav*, which links this verse to previous events, the *Sforno* connects it to the other sacrifices and offerings mentioned above, i.e., the offerings brought on the eighth day of מִלוּאִים and those brought by the princes (7:10).

The reason it was necessary for God to tell Moses to command the Children of Israel to bring the *Pesach* lamb is discussed by a number of the commentators (*Rashi, Ramban,* and *Ibn Ezra*). The *Sforno* explains that Israel had to be told that their rejoicing in the dedication of the Sanctuary and the altar did not exempt them from the *mitzvah* of the קָרְבַּן פֶּסַח, *Pesach offering,* as was the case regarding Yom Kippur when King Solomon dedicated the Holy Temple in Jerusalem. The Talmud (*Moed Katan* 9a) tells us that the fourteen days of rejoicing in conjunction with this dedication included Yom Kippur, which was not observed that year as a day of fasting in deference to the rejoicing associated with the dedication of the Temple (*I Kings* 8:65).

7. אֲנַחְנוּ טְמֵאִים לְנֶפֶשׁ אָדָם לָמָּה נִגָּרַע . . . בְּמֹעֲדוֹ . . . — *We are tamei by the dead body of a man; why are we to be kept back . . . in its appointed season.* The Mishnah in *Avos (4:2) states that amone mitzvah leads to another mitzvah and one sin to another sin.* Therefore, these men who, according to tradition, were carrying the

ט־י וַיְדַבֵּר יהוה אֶל־מֹשֶׁה לֵּאמֹר: דַּבֵּר אֶל־בְּנֵי יִשְׂרָאֵל לֵאמֹר אִישׁ אִישׁ
כִּי־יִהְיֶה־טָמֵא ׀ לָנֶפֶשׁ אוֹ בְדֶרֶךְ רְחֹקָה לָכֶם אוֹ לְדֹרֹתֵיכֶם וְעָשָׂה פֶסַח
יא לַיהוה: בַּחֹדֶשׁ הַשֵּׁנִי בְּאַרְבָּעָה עָשָׂר יוֹם בֵּין הָעַרְבַּיִם יַעֲשׂוּ אֹתוֹ עַל־מַצּוֹת
יב וּמְרֹרִים יֹאכְלֻהוּ: לֹא־יַשְׁאִירוּ מִמֶּנּוּ עַד־בֹּקֶר וְעֶצֶם לֹא יִשְׁבְּרוּ־בוֹ
יג כְּכָל־חֻקַּת הַפֶּסַח יַעֲשׂוּ אֹתוֹ: וְהָאִישׁ אֲשֶׁר־הוּא טָהוֹר וּבְדֶרֶךְ לֹא־הָיָה
וְחָדַל לַעֲשׂוֹת הַפֶּסַח וְנִכְרְתָה הַנֶּפֶשׁ הַהִוא מֵעַמֶּיהָ כִּי ׀ קָרְבַּן יהוה לֹא
יד הִקְרִיב בְּמֹעֲדוֹ חֶטְאוֹ יִשָּׂא הָאִישׁ הַהוּא: וְכִי־יָגוּר אִתְּכֶם גֵּר וְעָשָׂה פֶסַח
לַיהוה כְּחֻקַּת הַפֶּסַח וּכְמִשְׁפָּטוֹ כֵּן יַעֲשֶׂה חֻקָּה אַחַת יִהְיֶה לָכֶם וְלַגֵּר
רביעי טו וּלְאֶזְרַח הָאָרֶץ: וּבְיוֹם הָקִים אֶת־הַמִּשְׁכָּן כִּסָּה
הֶעָנָן אֶת־הַמִּשְׁכָּן לְאֹהֶל הָעֵדֻת וּבָעֶרֶב יִהְיֶה עַל־הַמִּשְׁכָּן כְּמַרְאֵה־אֵשׁ
טז־יז עַד־בֹּקֶר: כֵּן יִהְיֶה תָמִיד הֶעָנָן יְכַסֶּנּוּ וּמַרְאֵה־אֵשׁ לָיְלָה: וּלְפִי הֵעָלוֹת
הֶעָנָן מֵעַל הָאֹהֶל וְאַחֲרֵי כֵן יִסְעוּ בְּנֵי יִשְׂרָאֵל וּבִמְקוֹם אֲשֶׁר יִשְׁכָּן־שָׁם
יח הֶעָנָן שָׁם יַחֲנוּ בְּנֵי יִשְׂרָאֵל: עַל־פִּי יהוה יִסְעוּ בְּנֵי יִשְׂרָאֵל וְעַל־פִּי יהוה
יט יַחֲנוּ כָּל־יְמֵי אֲשֶׁר יִשְׁכֹּן הֶעָנָן עַל־הַמִּשְׁכָּן יַחֲנוּ: וּבְהַאֲרִיךְ הֶעָנָן
עַל־הַמִּשְׁכָּן יָמִים רַבִּים וְשָׁמְרוּ בְנֵי־יִשְׂרָאֵל אֶת־מִשְׁמֶרֶת יהוה וְלֹא יִסָּעוּ:

2

14. חֻקָּה אַחַת יִהְיֶה לָכֶם — *You shall have one statute* ... here in the wilderness.

וְלַגֵּר וּלְאֶזְרַח הָאָרֶץ — *For the stranger and for the one that is born in the Land* ... in the Land of Israel.

17. וְאַחֲרֵי כֵן יִסְעוּ — *Then after that they journeyed.* After it (the cloud) ascended, they traveled to that side (direction) where the cloud moved.

וּבִמְקוֹם אֲשֶׁר יִשְׁכָּן שָׁם הֶעָנָן שָׁם יַחֲנוּ — *And in the place where the cloud abode, there they encamped.* The (Torah) relates the merit of Israel concerning their traveling after Him in the wilderness. The first (point of praise) is that they encamped in the place where the cloud stopped, even though it was a place of waste, a howling wilderness (based on *Deut* 32:10).

19. וְשָׁמְרוּ בְנֵי יִשְׂרָאֵל אֶת מִשְׁמֶרֶת ה׳ — *And the Children of Israel kept the charge of* HASHEM. Secondly, the (Torah) relates that they waited for a long time, even though the place (of their encampment) was very poor.

וְלֹא יִסָּעוּ — *And did not journey* ... to scout out a better place for themselves to camp.

NOTES

coffin of Joseph wondered how the performance of such a *mitzvah* could result in the deprivation of another *mitzvah*, especially since the latter could only be performed at an appointed time, and once the time passed could not be retrieved. Perhaps they felt that just as communal *tumah* (טוּמְאָה בְּצִבּוּר) is set aside in order to perform the commandment of the *Pesach* offering, so should *tumah* caused by the performance of a *mitzvah* be set aside, thereby permitting them to participate in the offering of the *Pesach* sacrifice.

17-23. ... וּבִמְקוֹם אֲשֶׁר יִשְׁכָּן שָׁם הֶעָנָן שָׁם יַחֲנוּ וְשָׁמְרוּ בְנֵי יִשְׂרָאֵל אֶת מִשְׁמֶרֶת ה׳ וְלֹא יִסָּעוּ. וְיֵשׁ אֲשֶׁר יִהְיֶה הֶעָנָן יָמִים מִסְפָּר ... עַל פִּי ה׳ יַחֲנוּ וְעַל פִּי ה׳ יִסָּעוּ — *And in the place where the cloud abode, there they encamped ... and the Children of Israel kept the charge of* HASHEM *and did not journey. And sometimes the cloud was a few days ... and at the commandment of* HASHEM *they encamped and at the commandment of* HASHEM *they journeyed.* These verses which relate in detail the journeying of the Israelites in the wilderness come to tell us of Israel's

כ וְיֵשׁ אֲשֶׁר יִהְיֶה הֶעָנָן יָמִים מִסְפָּר עַל־הַמִּשְׁכָּן עַל־פִּי יהוה יַחֲנוּ וְעַל־פִּי
כא יהוה יִסָּעוּ: וְיֵשׁ אֲשֶׁר־יִהְיֶה הֶעָנָן מֵעֶרֶב עַד־בֹּקֶר וְנַעֲלָה הֶעָנָן בַּבֹּקֶר וְנָסָעוּ
כב אוֹ יוֹמָם וָלַיְלָה וְנַעֲלָה הֶעָנָן וְנָסָעוּ: אוֹ־יֹמַיִם אוֹ־חֹדֶשׁ אוֹ־יָמִים בְּהַאֲרִיךְ
הֶעָנָן עַל־הַמִּשְׁכָּן לִשְׁכֹּן עָלָיו יַחֲנוּ בְנֵי־יִשְׂרָאֵל וְלֹא יִסָּעוּ וּבְהֵעָלֹתוֹ יִסָּעוּ:
כג עַל־פִּי יהוה יַחֲנוּ וְעַל־פִּי יהוה יִסָּעוּ אֶת־מִשְׁמֶרֶת יהוה שָׁמָרוּ עַל־פִּי יהוה
בְּיַד־מֹשֶׁה:
י א־ב וַיְדַבֵּר יהוה אֶל־מֹשֶׁה לֵּאמֹר: עֲשֵׂה לְךָ שְׁתֵּי חֲצוֹצְרֹת כֶּסֶף מִקְשָׁה תַּעֲשֶׂה

---

20. וְיֵשׁ אֲשֶׁר יִהְיֶה הֶעָנָן יָמִים מִסְפָּר — *And sometimes the cloud was a few days.* Thirdly, the (Torah) relates that, at times, their encampment was in a place pleasant for themselves and their cattle, and the cloud rested there (only) for a few days, but nonetheless . . .

עַל פִּי ה׳ יַחֲנוּ — *At the commandment of* HASHEM *they encamped . . .* and not because of their love for that place.

וְעַל פִּי ה׳ יִסָּעוּ — *And at the commandment of* HASHEM *they journeyed . . .* although they were leaving that good place.

21. וְיֵשׁ אֲשֶׁר יִהְיֶה הֶעָנָן מֵעֶרֶב עַד בֹּקֶר — *And sometimes the cloud was (fixed) from evening until morning.* Fourth, the (Torah) relates that, at times, the encampment of the cloud was for an undetermined period, in a manner that it was only for a night, which was insufficient preparatory time (to attend) to the needs of encamping and journeying. However, with all this we are told that no journey began at night.

22. אוֹ יֹמַיִם אוֹ חֹדֶשׁ אוֹ יָמִים — *Whether it were two days, a month, or a year.* Fifth, (the Torah) relates that sometimes they had no opportunity to set in order their affairs and that of their cattle, while at other (times) they had already prepared and set in order (their affairs) and they had to depart immediately and break camp (lit., 'dismantle their preparations').

23. עַל פִּי ה׳ יַחֲנוּ — *At the commandment of* HASHEM *they encamped . . .* even for a short period, when they were unable to attain (the proper) ordering of their affairs.

וְעַל פִּי ה׳ יִסָּעוּ — *And at the commandment of* HASHEM *they journeyed . . .* when the cloud was taken up (from over the Tent), even after a lengthy period, after all their affairs and needs had already been set in order.

X

2. עֲשֵׂה לְךָ שְׁתֵּי חֲצוֹצְרֹת כֶּסֶף — *Make for yourself two trumpets of silver.* Since the intent now was to travel and enter the Land immediately, He commanded that trumpets (be made) for *the trumpet signal for the king is among them* (23:21); (this

NOTES

implicit trust in the Almighty. They followed the cloud faithfully and unquestioningly, halting wherever it stopped even if the place was desolate and dangerous. If they encamped in a pleasant and fertile area it was only because God so commanded, and not because they derived pleasure from the congenial surroundings. And even if they were content and happy in a particular location, they left as soon as the cloud moved on. The period of time was irrelevant; whether they had not yet established themselves or had been settled there for some time, they always broke camp and followed the cloud. Such was the total commitment of that generation to the dictates and direction of God.

ג אֹתָם וְהָיוּ לְךָ לְמִקְרָא הָעֵדָה וּלְמַסַּע אֶת־הַמַּחֲנוֹת: וְתָקְעוּ בָּהֵן וְנוֹעֲדוּ
ד אֵלֶיךָ כָּל־הָעֵדָה אֶל־פֶּתַח אֹהֶל מוֹעֵד: וְאִם־בְּאַחַת יִתְקָעוּ וְנוֹעֲדוּ אֵלֶיךָ
ה הַנְּשִׂיאִים רָאשֵׁי אַלְפֵי יִשְׂרָאֵל: וּתְקַעְתֶּם תְּרוּעָה וְנָסְעוּ הַמַּחֲנוֹת הַחֹנִים
ו קֵדְמָה: וּתְקַעְתֶּם תְּרוּעָה שֵׁנִית וְנָסְעוּ הַמַּחֲנוֹת הַחֹנִים תֵּימָנָה תְּרוּעָה
ז־ח יִתְקְעוּ לְמַסְעֵיהֶם: וּבְהַקְהִיל אֶת־הַקָּהָל תִּתְקְעוּ וְלֹא תָרִיעוּ: וּבְנֵי אַהֲרֹן

---

referred to) when the Sanctuary traveled, and when the Holy traveled and when they went forth to battle, as it says, *And when you go to war in your land against the adversary that oppresses you then you shall sound an alarm with the trumpets* (v. 9).

וְהָיוּ לְךָ לְמִקְרָא הָעֵדָה — *And they shall be for you for the calling of the congregation* ... because the calling of the congregation and the princes (was) ...

3. אֶל פֶּתַח אֹהֶל מוֹעֵד — *At the door of the Tent of Meeting.* In the presence of (lit., before) God, He wanted that call to be (through) the trumpets which were in honor of the King.

5. וּתְקַעְתֶּם תְּרוּעָה וְנָסְעוּ הַמַּחֲנוֹת הַחֹנִים קֵדְמָה — *And when you blow an alarm, the camps that lie on the eastern side shall journey.* For together with them, the bearers of the Sanctuary did journey.

6. וּתְקַעְתֶּם תְּרוּעָה שֵׁנִית וְנָסְעוּ הַמַּחֲנוֹת הַחֹנִים תֵּימָנָה — *And when you blow an alarm the second time, the camps that lie to the southern side shall journey* ... for together with them journeyed the bearers of the holy (vessels and furnishings).

תְּרוּעָה יִתְקְעוּ לְמַסְעֵיהֶם — *They shall blow an alarm for their journeys* ... for in their journeying there is (both) a תְּקִיעָה (blast) and a תְּרוּעָה (alarm). (Now) this is because the alarm is for the traveling of the Holy, while the blast (sounded) with it, was meant (as a signal) for them to gather together for their travels, similar to the calling of the congregation and the princes, which was through a blast without an alarm (v. 7).

NOTES

X

2. עֲשֵׂה לְךָ שְׁתֵּי חֲצוֹצְרֹת כֶּסֶף ... וְהָיוּ לְךָ לְמִקְרָא הָעֵדָה — *Make for yourself two trumpets of silver ... and they shall be for you for the calling of the congregation.* The signals sounded on the two trumpets of silver, as the *Sforno* explains, are linked to the kingdom of heaven and the King of Kings. The verse cited from *parashas Balak* (23:21) demonstrates that the תְּרוּעָה *alarm,* is one which heralds the King of the Universe. Hence, it was sounded when the various parts of the Sanctuary set forth on their journey, carried by the sons of Gershon and Merari, as well as the 'Holy' vessels and furnishings, i.e., the ark, table, golden altar and its implements, carried by the sons of Kehath, for the trumpets are meant to be used exclusively for the sacred. As the *Sforno* points out in his commentary on the verse in *Balak* mentioned above, the blast of the trumpets is also a sign of שִׂמְחָה, *joy,* for Israel rejoiced in its King whenever the Sanctuary traveled. The trumpets were also sounded to rally the people to the defense of *Eretz Yisrael*, for this land is the *holy* land, and also to call the congregation and princes to *the door of the Tent of Meeting* in the wilderness, because that gathering was for the sake of the King, as the *Sforno* explains in his commentary on verse 3.

5. וּתְקַעְתֶּם תְּרוּעָה וְנָסְעוּ הַמַּחֲנוֹת הַחֹנִים קֵדְמָה — *And when you blow an alarm, the camps that lie on the eastern side shall journey.* The תְּרוּעָה was sounded twice. The first was to signal the departure of the eastern camps of Judah, Issachar and Zevulun with whom the Gershonites and Merarites, carrying the Sanctuary (i.e., the boards, curtains, etc.), traveled. The second blast was for the southern contingent of Reuben, Simeon and Gad accompanied by the Kehathites, bearing the holy vessels and furnishings. The *Sforno*, unlike

ט הַכֹּהֲנִים יִתְקְעוּ בַּחֲצֹצְרוֹת וְהָיוּ לָכֶם לְחֻקַּת עוֹלָם לְדֹרֹתֵיכֶם: וְכִי־תָבֹאוּ
מִלְחָמָה בְּאַרְצְכֶם עַל־הַצַּר הַצֹּרֵר אֶתְכֶם וַהֲרֵעֹתֶם בַּחֲצֹצְרֹת וְנִזְכַּרְתֶּם
י לִפְנֵי יהוה אֱלֹהֵיכֶם וְנוֹשַׁעְתֶּם מֵאֹיְבֵיכֶם: וּבְיוֹם שִׂמְחַתְכֶם וּבְמוֹעֲדֵיכֶם
וּבְרָאשֵׁי חָדְשֵׁכֶם וּתְקַעְתֶּם בַּחֲצֹצְרֹת עַל עֹלֹתֵיכֶם וְעַל זִבְחֵי שַׁלְמֵיכֶם וְהָיוּ
לָכֶם לְזִכָּרוֹן לִפְנֵי אֱלֹהֵיכֶם אֲנִי יהוה אֱלֹהֵיכֶם:
חמישי יא וַיְהִי בַּשָּׁנָה הַשֵּׁנִית בַּחֹדֶשׁ הַשֵּׁנִי בְּעֶשְׂרִים בַּחֹדֶשׁ נַעֲלָה הֶעָנָן מֵעַל מִשְׁכַּן
יב הָעֵדֻת: וַיִּסְעוּ בְנֵי־יִשְׂרָאֵל לְמַסְעֵיהֶם מִמִּדְבַּר סִינָי וַיִּשְׁכֹּן הֶעָנָן בְּמִדְבַּר
יג־יד פָּארָן: וַיִּסְעוּ בָּרִאשֹׁנָה עַל־פִּי יהוה בְּיַד־מֹשֶׁה: וַיִּסַּע דֶּגֶל מַחֲנֵה בְנֵי־יְהוּדָה
טו בָּרִאשֹׁנָה לְצִבְאֹתָם וְעַל־צְבָאוֹ נַחְשׁוֹן בֶּן־עַמִּינָדָב: וְעַל־צְבָא מַטֵּה בְּנֵי
טז יִשָּׂשכָר נְתַנְאֵל בֶּן־צוּעָר: וְעַל־צְבָא מַטֵּה בְּנֵי זְבוּלֻן אֱלִיאָב בֶּן־חֵלֹן:
יז־יח וְהוּרַד הַמִּשְׁכָּן וְנָסְעוּ בְנֵי־גֵרְשׁוֹן וּבְנֵי מְרָרִי נֹשְׂאֵי הַמִּשְׁכָּן: וְנָסַע דֶּגֶל מַחֲנֵה
יט רְאוּבֵן לְצִבְאֹתָם וְעַל־צְבָאוֹ אֱלִיצוּר בֶּן־שְׁדֵיאוּר: וְעַל־צְבָא מַטֵּה בְּנֵי
כ שִׁמְעוֹן שְׁלֻמִיאֵל בֶּן־צוּרִישַׁדָּי: וְעַל־צְבָא מַטֵּה בְנֵי־גָד אֶלְיָסָף בֶּן־דְּעוּאֵל:

---

11. בַּחֹדֶשׁ הַשֵּׁנִי בְּעֶשְׂרִים בַּחֹדֶשׁ — *In the second month on the twentieth day of the month.* After the *tameim* had offered the second *Pesach* lamb on the fourteenth day of the month, the trumpets were made with which the congregation and princes were called to Moses, who informed them regarding the order of their journeys through the (medium of the) trumpets and the order of the (use of these) trumpets in the Holy and when (going) to battle. And thus the cloud ascended (signaling them) to move forward to Kadesh Barnea, which was the first city in *Eretz Yisrael* they would reach on that road, the road (which went through) the great and dreadful wilderness as it says, וַנִּסַּע מֵחֹרֵב וַנֵּלֶךְ אֵת כָּל הַמִּדְבָּר הַגָּדוֹל וְהַנּוֹרָא ... וַנָּבֹא עַד קָדֵשׁ בַּרְנֵעַ, *And we journeyed from Horeb and went through all that great and dreadful wilderness . . . and we came to Kadesh Barnea* (*Deut.* 1:19).

NOTES

other commentators such as the *Ramban*, is of the opinion that the other two camps (western and northern) did not need, nor did they have, a special alarm to signal their departure. The reason may have been because these camps did not have any items of sanctity traveling with them. The *Ibn Ezra* offers another reason for the absence of a trumpet sound in conjunction with these last two camps. Since the sons of Aaron were given the task of blowing the trumpets (v. 8), and the *Kohanim* had all departed with the first two camps, there was no one available who was permitted to sound the trumpets!

6. תְּרוּעָה יִתְקְעוּ לְמַסְעֵיהֶם — *They shall blow an alarm for their journeys.* There were two kinds of notes sounded by the trumpets. One was תְּקִיעָה (a simple straight blowing) and the second, תְּרוּעָה (an alarm). Now the Torah established that the former was to be used for the gathering of the congregation or the princes (vs. 3 and 4) whereas the latter was to signal the journeying of the *Mishkan* and its sacred vessels. This explains why the breaking of camp and the signal to depart combined both the תְּקִיעָה and תְּרוּעָה, for as the *Sforno* points out, this included a calling together of the people, as well as the dismantling and transporting of the Sanctuary and its contents.

11. בַּחֹדֶשׁ הַשֵּׁנִי בְּעֶשְׂרִים בַּחֹדֶשׁ — *In the second month on the twentieth day of the month.* The narrative now returns to a chronological order of events. The twentieth day of the second month in the second year sets the scene, following all that has been recorded in the first part of this book. All necessary preparations to enter *Eretz Yisrael* had been made: the census, the banners, the purification of the camp of Israel, the consecration of the Levites, the dedication of the altar, the offering of the *Pesach* sacrifice (first and second) and the fashioning of the trumpets. Israel was now

כא-כב וְנָסְעוּ֙ הַקְּהָתִ֔ים נֹשְׂאֵ֖י הַמִּקְדָּ֑שׁ וְהֵקִ֥ימוּ אֶת־הַמִּשְׁכָּ֖ן עַד־בֹּאָֽם: וְנָסַ֞ע דֶּ֣גֶל

כג מַחֲנֵ֧ה בְנֵי־אֶפְרַ֛יִם לְצִבְאֹתָ֖ם וְעַל־צְבָא֔וֹ אֱלִישָׁמָ֖ע בֶּן־עַמִּיהֽוּד: וְעַל־צְבָ֕א

כד מַטֵּ֖ה בְּנֵ֣י מְנַשֶּׁ֑ה גַּמְלִיאֵ֖ל בֶּן־פְּדָהצֽוּר: וְעַל־צְבָ֕א מַטֵּ֖ה בְּנֵ֣י בִנְיָמִ֑ן אֲבִידָ֖ן

כה בֶּן־גִּדְעוֹנִֽי: וְנָסַ֗ע דֶּ֚גֶל מַחֲנֵ֣ה בְנֵי־דָ֔ן מְאַסֵּ֥ף לְכָל־הַֽמַּחֲנֹ֖ת לְצִבְאֹתָ֑ם וְעַל־

כו צְבָא֔וֹ אֲחִיעֶ֖זֶר בֶּן־עַמִּישַׁדָּֽי: וְעַל־צְבָ֕א מַטֵּ֖ה בְּנֵ֣י אָשֵׁ֑ר פַּגְעִיאֵ֖ל בֶּן־עָכְרָֽן:

כז-כח וְעַל־צְבָ֕א מַטֵּ֖ה בְּנֵ֣י נַפְתָּלִ֑י אֲחִירַ֖ע בֶּן־עֵינָֽן: אֵ֛לֶּה מַסְעֵ֥י בְנֵי־יִשְׂרָאֵ֖ל

כט לְצִבְאֹתָ֑ם וַיִּסָּֽעוּ: וַיֹּ֣אמֶר מֹשֶׁ֗ה לְ֠חֹבָב בֶּן־רְעוּאֵ֣ל הַמִּדְיָנִי֮

חֹתֵ֣ן מֹשֶׁה֒ נֹסְעִ֣ים ׀ אֲנַ֗חְנוּ אֶל־הַמָּקוֹם֙ אֲשֶׁ֣ר אָמַ֣ר יְהֹוָ֔ה אֹת֖וֹ אֶתֵּ֣ן לָכֶ֑ם

ל לְכָ֤ה אִתָּ֙נוּ֙ וְהֵטַ֣בְנוּ לָ֔ךְ כִּֽי־יְהֹוָ֥ה דִּבֶּר־ט֖וֹב עַל־יִשְׂרָאֵֽל: וַיֹּ֥אמֶר אֵלָ֖יו לֹ֣א

לא אֵלֵ֑ךְ כִּ֧י אִם־אֶל־אַרְצִ֛י וְאֶל־מֽוֹלַדְתִּ֖י אֵלֵֽךְ: וַיֹּ֕אמֶר אַל־נָ֖א תַּעֲזֹ֣ב אֹתָ֑נוּ כִּ֣י ׀

לב עַל־כֵּ֣ן יָדַ֗עְתָּ חֲנֹתֵ֙נוּ֙ בַּמִּדְבָּ֔ר וְהָיִ֥יתָ לָּ֖נוּ לְעֵינָֽיִם: וְהָיָ֖ה כִּי־תֵלֵ֣ךְ עִמָּ֑נוּ וְהָיָ֣ה ׀

לג הַטּ֣וֹב הַה֗וּא אֲשֶׁ֨ר יֵיטִ֧יב יְהֹוָ֛ה עִמָּ֖נוּ וְהֵטַ֥בְנוּ לָֽךְ: וַיִּסְעוּ֙ מֵהַ֣ר יְהֹוָ֔ה דֶּ֖רֶךְ

שְׁלֹ֣שֶׁת יָמִ֑ים וַֽאֲר֨וֹן בְּרִית־יְהֹוָ֜ה נֹסֵ֣עַ לִפְנֵיהֶ֗ם דֶּ֚רֶךְ שְׁלֹ֣שֶׁת יָמִ֔ים לָת֥וּר

---

30. כִּי אִם אֶל אַרְצִי וְאֶל מוֹלַדְתִּי אֵלֵךְ — *But I will depart to my own land and to my birthplace* . . . for in my advanced age I will not be able to tolerate the climate and food of another country.

31. אַל נָא תַּעֲזֹב אֹתָנוּ — *Please do not leave us.* At least let your sons come with us.

כִּי עַל כֵּן יָדַעְתָּ חֲנֹתֵנוּ בַּמִּדְבָּר — *Seeing that you know how we are to encamp in the wilderness.* For if your children will also leave us, you will profane God in the eyes of the nations who will say, 'If Jethro had observed an authentic presence of Godliness (in the camp of Israel) he and his children would not have left them.' And in this (matter), Moses, Jethro and his sons agreed, for indeed Jethro returned to his land, as it says, וַיְשַׁלַּח מֹשֶׁה אֶת חֹתְנוֹ וַיֵּלֶךְ לוֹ אֶל אַרְצוֹ, *And Moses sent away his father-in-law and he went his way into his own land* (Exodus 18:27), while his children, without a doubt, went with the Israelites, as the Book of Judges attests saying, וּבְנֵי קֵינִי חֹתֵן מֹשֶׁה עָלוּ מֵעִיר הַתְּמָרִים אֶת בְּנֵי יְהוּדָה, *And the children of the Keni, Moses' father-in-law, went up out of the city of palm trees with the children of Judah* (Judges 1:16).

33. דֶּרֶךְ שְׁלֹשֶׁת יָמִים — *Three days' journey* . . . to Eretz Yisrael. Because indeed, in three (phased) journeys they arrived opposite Kadesh Barnea in the wilderness of Paran from whence they sent forth the spies as Moses our Teacher explained, when he said, וַתִּקְרְבוּן אֵלַי כֻּלְּכֶם וַתֹּאמְרוּ נִשְׁלְחָה אֲנָשִׁים, *And you came near unto me every one of you and said, 'Let us send men before us'* (Deut. 1:22), and this was the place

NOTES

ready to enter the Land and so Moses invited his father-in-law and his family to join them.

31. אַל נָא תַּעֲזֹב אֹתָנוּ כִּי עַל כֵּן יָדַעְתָּ חֲנֹתֵנוּ בַּמִּדְבָּר — *Please do not leave us seeing that you know how we are to encamp in the wilderness.* The Sforno explains why Moses insisted that Jethro not forsake them. The original decision of Jethro to leave Midian when he heard of all the miracles wrought by the Almighty during Israel's Exodus from Egypt, and to join the camp of Israel must have had a profound impact upon the people of his time and place who respected his position and reputation. By leaving now and rejecting the invitation of Moses, he would cast aspersion upon the Israelite camp. Moses, therefore, pleads with him that even though Jethro himself is too old to change his abode and adjust to a new land, still and all, by allowing his children to

°ששי לג-לה לָהֶם מְנוּחָה: וַעֲנַן יהוה עֲלֵיהֶם יוֹמָם בְּנָסְעָם מִן־הַמַּחֲנֶה: ז ° וַיְהִי
בִּנְסֹעַ הָאָרֹן וַיֹּאמֶר מֹשֶׁה קוּמָה ׀ יהוה וְיָפֻצוּ אֹיְבֶיךָ וְיָנֻסוּ מְשַׂנְאֶיךָ מִפָּנֶיךָ:

---

of their encampment in the wilderness of Paran mentioned here (in this *sedra*) saying, *and afterward the people journeyed from Chazeros and pitched in the wilderness of Paran* (12:16) and it was there that the spies returned as it says, *And they returned . . . and they came . . . to the wilderness of Paran to Kadesh* (13:25-26). Now that place was called Rismah, as it says, *and they journeyed from Chazeros and pitched in Rismah* (33:18), and there (in that chapter) three journeys are mentioned from the wilderness of Sinai until there and they are: Kivros Hataaveh, and Chazeros and Rismah — for the affair of 'Taverah' (11:3) occurred en route, and not when they were encamped.

וַאֲרוֹן בְּרִית ה׳ נֹסֵעַ לִפְנֵיהֶם דֶּרֶךְ שְׁלֹשֶׁת יָמִים — *And the Ark of the covenant of* H*ASHEM* *went before them on the three days' journey*. During the three days that they traveled those three journeys by the way of הַמִּדְבָּר הַגָּדוֹל וְהַנּוֹרָא, *the great and dreadful wilderness* (*Deut.* 1:19), the Ark *went before them* to secure the way from serpents and scorpions and other (dangerous creatures). However, on all other journeys the Ark traveled *in the midst of the camps* (2:17), similar to the other carryings of the Kehathites (i.e., who carried the Ark on their shoulders).

לָתוּר לָהֶם מְנוּחָה — *To seek out a resting place for them* . . . a secure (safe) camping place in the dreadful wilderness.

34. וַעֲנַן ה׳ עֲלֵיהֶם יוֹמָם — *And the cloud of* H*ASHEM* *was over them by day*. It did not go *before* them, as it did during other journeys, for it was sufficient then for the Ark to prepare the way as it traveled before them. But (the cloud) did hover over them by day during the time they traveled.

35. וַיְהִי בִּנְסֹעַ הָאָרֹן — *And it came to pass when the Ark set forward* . . . to go and enter into *Eretz Yisrael*.

קוּמָה ה׳ וְיָפֻצוּ אֹיְבֶיךָ — *Rise up,* H*ASHEM*, *and let Your enemies be scattered*. Because indeed, had they not sent the spies they would have entered (the Land of Israel) without (recourse to) war, for the nations would have fled כַּעֲזוּבַת הַחֹרֶשׁ וְהָאָמִיר אֲשֶׁר עָזְבוּ מִפְּנֵי בְּנֵי יִשְׂרָאֵל, *as the forsaken portion of the thicket and the uppermost branch which they left because of the Children of Israel* (*Isaiah* 17:9).

וְיָנֻסוּ מְשַׂנְאֶיךָ מִפָּנֶיךָ — *And let them that hate You flee before You* . . . lest Israel come to annihilate them.

NOTES

accompany the Israelites into the Promised Land, the honor of Israel would be safeguarded. Jethro and his sons agreed to this proposal as the *Sforno* proves from the Book of *Judges*. (See also the *Sforno's* commentary to *Exodus* 18:27.)

33. וַאֲרוֹן בְּרִית ה׳ נֹסֵעַ לִפְנֵיהֶם — *And the Ark of the covenant of* H*ASHEM* *went before them*. The Kehathites were charged with the task of carrying the Holy Ark on their shoulders and were therefore not given wagons, as were the Gershonites and Merarites. In chapter 2, where the Torah discusses the order of the camps in their journeying, we are told that the Kehathites traveled בְּתוֹךְ הַמַּחֲנֹת, *in the midst of the camps*, i.e., between the groupings of Judah and Reuben (v. 17). However, during the three days' journey from the 'mountain of God,' the Ark of the covenant went miraculously before the Israelites on its own, without being carried by the Kehathites. As *Rashi* explains in his commentary on this verse, 'They traveled three days' journey in one day because God wished to bring them into the Land immediately.' It was for this reason that

לו וּבְנֻחֹה יֹאמַר שׁוּבָה יהוה רִבְבוֹת אַלְפֵי יִשְׂרָאֵל: נ
יא א וַיְהִי הָעָם כְּמִתְאֹנְנִים רַע בְּאָזְנֵי יהוה וַיִּשְׁמַע יהוה וַיִּחַר אַפּוֹ וַתִּבְעַר־בָּם
ב אֵשׁ יהוה וַתֹּאכַל בִּקְצֵה הַמַּחֲנֶה: וַיִּצְעַק הָעָם אֶל־מֹשֶׁה וַיִּתְפַּלֵּל מֹשֶׁה
ג אֶל־יהוה וַתִּשְׁקַע הָאֵשׁ: וַיִּקְרָא שֵׁם־הַמָּקוֹם הַהוּא תַּבְעֵרָה כִּי־בָעֲרָה בָם

---

36. שׁוּבָה — *Return* (or *'abide'*). Let Your tranquility abide here among us, similar to זֹאת מְנוּחָתִי עֲדֵי עַד, *This is My resting place forever* (*Psalms* 132:14), and although You will reveal Your Divine Presence before Israel to evict their enemies, (nonetheless) the resting place of Your Divine Presence will (abide) in our midst.

ה׳ רִבְבוֹת אַלְפֵי יִשְׂרָאֵל — *HASHEM, unto the ten thousand thousands of Israel.* Similar to, 'HASHEM of the hosts of the thousands of Israel,' as (our Sages) say, 'The term hosts (צְבָאוֹת) only refers to the name hosts of Israel' (*Shevuos* 35b). And (the verse) says *ten thousand thousands,* similar to, רִבֹּתַיִם אַלְפֵי, *twice ten thousand, thousands* (*Psalms* 68:18), for perhaps Israel at that time reached that number, with men, women and children (all included).

XI

1. כְּמִתְאֹנְנִים — *As murmurers* . . . regarding the travail of the road; not that they truly complained in their hearts, for they had no worthwhile reason to murmur. (Rather), they murmured with their words to test (God).

2. וַתִּשְׁקַע הָאֵשׁ — *And the fire sank down* (*abated*) . . . contrary to the nature of fire, so that they might recognize that it was a supernatural wonder, and that it was not a natural fire that had then occurred due to some natural cause.

NOTES

theArk preceded the Israelites on its own and was not carried by the Levites.

33-36. דֶּרֶךְ שְׁלֹשֶׁת יָמִים וַאֲרוֹן בְּרִית ה׳ נֹסֵעַ לִפְנֵיהֶם . . . קוּמָה ה׳ וְיָפֻצוּ אֹיְבֶיךָ וְיָנֻסוּ מְשַׂנְאֶיךָ . . . שׁוּבָה ה׳ רִבְבוֹת אַלְפֵי יִשְׂרָאֵל — *Three days' journey and theArk of the covenant of HASHEM went before them . . . Rise up, HASHEM, and let Your enemies be scattered and let them that hate You flee . . . Return, HASHEM, unto the ten thousand thousands of Israel.* The *Sforno,* as is his wont, explains these verses according to their plain meaning as opposed to the interpretation of other commentators and the Midrashic exegesis of our Sages. He explains these verses thus: Israel was supposed to enter *Eretz Yisrael* in a period of three days, had they not insisted on sending the spies and subsequently believing their defeatist and despairing report. The ark, during this special period, went before them (v. 33) while the cloud hovered over them. Verses 35-36 are, according to him and contrary to other interpretations, inserted in their correct place. They follow logically the sequence of the previous verses. Since the Israelites were about to enter the Promised Land, Moses uttered a prayer that God rise up so that His and Israel's enemies be scattered, for the *Sforno* has already explained that it would not have been necessary for Israel to wage war since the Almighty Himself would have driven out the nations from Canaan. Then the Israelites would have entered to possess the Land and God's presence would have come to rest in their midst.

XI

1. כְּמִתְאֹנְנִים — *As murmurers.* The phrase used by the Torah regarding the murmuring and complaining of the people (כְּמִתְאֹנְנִים) is qualified by the preposition *kaf* (כ״ף הַדִּמְיוֹן), meaning 'as' or 'like'. The *Sforno* therefore interprets it to mean that the people were not expressing their real feelings; it was not a sincere, true outpouring of criticism for there was no basis for them to do so. Hence, it must be understood in the sense of a test of God and Moses by certain elements among the people of Israel, as we see in chapter 78 of *Psalms* from which the *Sforno* quotes at length in his commentary on this chapter. *Ibn Ezra,* indeed, renders the phrase מִתְאֹנְנִים as 'they that

ד אֵשׁ יהוה: וְהָאסַפְסֻף אֲשֶׁר בְּקִרְבּוֹ הִתְאַוּוּ תַּאֲוָה וַיָּשֻׁבוּ וַיִּבְכּוּ גַּם בְּנֵי
ה יִשְׂרָאֵל וַיֹּאמְרוּ מִי יַאֲכִלֵנוּ בָּשָׂר: זָכַרְנוּ אֶת־הַדָּגָה אֲשֶׁר־נֹאכַל בְּמִצְרַיִם
חִנָּם אֵת הַקִּשֻּׁאִים וְאֵת הָאֲבַטִּחִים וְאֶת־הֶחָצִיר וְאֶת־הַבְּצָלִים וְאֶת־
ו־ז הַשּׁוּמִים: וְעַתָּה נַפְשֵׁנוּ יְבֵשָׁה אֵין כֹּל בִּלְתִּי אֶל־הַמָּן עֵינֵינוּ: וְהַמָּן כִּזְרַע־גַּד
ח הוּא וְעֵינוֹ כְּעֵין הַבְּדֹלַח: שָׁטוּ הָעָם וְלָקְטוּ וְטָחֲנוּ בָרֵחַיִם אוֹ דָכוּ בַּמְּדֹכָה
ט וּבִשְּׁלוּ בַּפָּרוּר וְעָשׂוּ אֹתוֹ עֻגוֹת וְהָיָה טַעְמוֹ כְּטַעַם לְשַׁד הַשָּׁמֶן: וּבְרֶדֶת
י הַטַּל עַל־הַמַּחֲנֶה לָיְלָה יֵרֵד הַמָּן עָלָיו: וַיִּשְׁמַע מֹשֶׁה אֶת־הָעָם בֹּכֶה
לְמִשְׁפְּחֹתָיו אִישׁ לְפֶתַח אָהֳלוֹ וַיִּחַר־אַף יהוה מְאֹד וּבְעֵינֵי מֹשֶׁה רָע:
יא וַיֹּאמֶר מֹשֶׁה אֶל־יהוה לָמָה הֲרֵעֹתָ לְעַבְדֶּךָ וְלָמָּה לֹא־מָצָתִי חֵן בְּעֵינֶיךָ
יב לָשׂוּם אֶת־מַשָּׂא כָּל־הָעָם הַזֶּה עָלָי: הֶאָנֹכִי הָרִיתִי אֵת כָּל־הָעָם הַזֶּה אִם־

---

4. וַיָּשֻׁבוּ וַיִּבְכּוּ — *And (the Children of Israel) wept again.* They continued to act as murmurers (in order) to test (God), and now they cried for having left Egypt, as though they rejected the value (i.e., privilege) of having the Divine Presence amongst them, as (the Torah) testifies (v. 20), saying, *because you have rejected HASHEM who is among you, and you have wept before Him saying, 'Why is this that we have come forth from Egypt?'*

מִי יַאֲכִלֵנוּ בָּשָׂר — *Who shall give us flesh to eat?* (This was in order) to test אִם יָכִין שְׁאֵר לְעַמּוֹ, *Can He supply meat for his people?* (*Psalms* 78:20), as the psalmist attested when he said, וַיְנַסּוּ אֵל בִּלְבָבָם לִשְׁאָל אֹכֶל לְנַפְשָׁם, *They tested God in their hearts by requesting food for their craving* (ibid. 18).

11. לָמָה הֲרֵעֹתָ לְעַבְדֶּךָ — *Why have You done evil to Your servant?*. . . by sending me, against my will, to bring this people out of Egypt.

וְלָמָּה לֹא מָצָתִי חֵן בְּעֵינֶיךָ — *And why have I not found favor in Your eyes* . . . when I said, שְׁלַח נָא בְּיַד תִּשְׁלָח, *Send please by the hand of an agent* (*Exodus* 4:13).

לָשׂוּם אֶת מַשָּׂא כָּל הָעָם הַזֶּה עָלָי — *That You put the burden of all this people upon me.* And this You did in order to place the burden of all of them upon me, as though You had no leader other than myself to at least share with me that it might benefit them.

12. הֶאָנֹכִי הָרִיתִי — *Have I conceived.* Behold, a father can lead his sons even though

NOTES

uttered words of wickedness,' since it was not a legitimate complaint.

2. וַתִּשְׁקַע הָאֵשׁ — *And the fire sank down (abated).* Fire normally goes up — here it sank down. This demonstrated that it was not a natural occurrence but a heavenly retribution, as it is indeed identified in verse 3, "the fire of God."

4. וַיָּשֻׁבוּ וַיִּבְכּוּ . . . מִי יַאֲכִלֵנוּ בָּשָׂר — *And (the Children of Israel) wept again . . . Who shall give us meat to eat?* Although the Torah clearly states that the cause of this second complaint, accompanied by weeping, was their inadequate diet, the *Sforno* explains that there were two other motivations implicit in this complaint. One was their regret for having left Egypt, ignoring the fact that their leaving that spiritually contaminated land resulted in having the Divine Presence in their midst which was impossible in the land of Egypt. (See the *Sforno* on *Exodus* 13:21 and *Rashi* on *Exodus* 9:29.) The second was to test God once again to see if He was capable of providing them with meat in the desolate wilderness. Indeed, the *Sifre* states that 'they were looking for a pretext to remove themselves from God.'

11-12. לָמָה הֲרֵעֹתָ לְעַבְדֶּךָ וְלָמָּה לֹא מָצָתִי חֵן בְּעֵינֶיךָ לָשׂוּם אֶת מַשָּׂא כָּל הָעָם הַזֶּה עָלָי. הֶאָנֹכִי הָרִיתִי — *Why have You done evil to Your*

אָנֹכִ֖י יְלִדְתִּ֑יהוּ כִּֽי־תֹאמַ֨ר אֵלַ֜י שָׂאֵ֣הוּ בְחֵיקֶ֗ךָ כַּֽאֲשֶׁ֨ר יִשָּׂ֤א הָֽאֹמֵן֙ אֶת־הַיֹּנֵ֔ק
יג עַ֚ל הָֽאֲדָמָ֔ה אֲשֶׁ֥ר נִשְׁבַּ֖עְתָּ לַֽאֲבֹתָֽיו׃ מֵאַ֤יִן לִי֙ בָּשָׂ֔ר לָתֵ֖ת לְכָל־הָעָ֣ם הַזֶּ֑ה
יד כִּֽי־יִבְכּ֤וּ עָלַי֙ לֵאמֹ֔ר תְּנָה־לָּ֥נוּ בָשָׂ֖ר וְנֹאכֵֽלָה׃ לֹֽא־אוּכַ֤ל אָֽנֹכִי֙ לְבַדִּ֔י
טו לָשֵׂ֖את אֶת־כָּל־הָעָ֣ם הַזֶּ֑ה כִּ֥י כָבֵ֖ד מִמֶּֽנִּי׃ וְאִם־כָּ֣כָה ׀ אַתְּ־עֹ֣שֶׂה לִּ֗י הָרְגֵ֤נִי
נָא֙ הָרֹ֔ג אִם־מָצָ֥אתִי חֵ֖ן בְּעֵינֶ֑יךָ וְאַל־אֶרְאֶ֖ה בְּרָֽעָתִֽי׃

---

they (the father and the sons) have diverse opinions, and this is because they all consider him as one who loves them and who attempts with all his might to benefit them. But these (people) have no trust in me at all, and are suspicious (of me), testing (me) to see what I can do for them.

13. מֵאַיִן לִי בָּשָׂר — *Whence should I have meat.* Behold, without a doubt they (know) that I have no meat to give them, and therefore when they weep to me and say *give us meat* as if it were in my power (to do so), and (as though) through their weeping I will fulfill their desires, this is only (done) to test my leadership by Your command, to (see) what I can attain from You for them.

14. לֹא אוּכַל אָנֹכִי לְבַדִּי — *I am not able alone.* You must join others with me in whom this people will trust.

15. וְאִם כָּכָה אַתְּ עֹשֶׂה לִּי — *And if You treat me thus.* And if You, the Perfect One, withhold perfection of leadership which is fitting to come from You, and (instead You) lead them *thus,* (i.e.,) in a way that is lacking, akin to the leadership of a female, (and all this) for my sake and my honor, and You do not join others with me so as not to mar my honor ...

הָרְגֵנִי נָא הָרֹג אִם מָצָאתִי חֵן בְּעֵינֶיךָ — *Kill me, I pray You, if I have found favor in Your eyes* ... so that You will be able to appoint others, through whom the leadership of the people will be perfect (complete), as (our Sages) state regarding Samuel, that he died before his time so that the kingship of the House of David might be established (*Taanis* 5b).

וְאַל אֶרְאֶה בְּרָעָתִי — *And let me not see my evil* ... the evil of diminished leadership on my account, because that would be more difficult for me (to accept) than death!

NOTES

servant? And why have I not found favor in Your eyes that You put the burden of all this people upon me. Have I conceived. At the end of this *sedrah,* Moses is depicted by the Torah as being 'very meek above all men upon the face of the earth' (12:3) This great humility is manifested in these verses. Moses is convinced that he is unequal to the task of leadership given to him by God. The discontent displayed by Israel is not their fault, rather it is due to their lack of trust in him, which he feels is justified. When he uses the expression *Have I conceived, etc.'* he is not disclaiming any relationship with them, nor is he demonstrating insensitivity to their plight. Rather, he is reiterating his perception of his shortcomings and inability to evoke Israel's trust.

15. וְאִם כָּכָה אַתְּ עֹשֶׂה לִּי הָרְגֵנִי נָא הָרֹג ... וְאַל אֶרְאֶה בְּרָעָתִי — *And if You treat me thus, kill me, I pray You ... and let me not see my evil.* The Hebrew word *You* is written in the feminine form (אַתְּ) instead of the masculine (אַתָּה). *Rashi* explains this as an indication that Moses' strength weakened to become like that of a woman. The difficulty with this explanation is obvious. The term אַתְּ refers to God, not to Moses! The *Sforno*, therefore, explains the word אַתְּ as reflecting a diminishment in the flow of God's blessing of leadership qualities to Moses, similar to the weaker strength of a female as compared to a male. Moses is convinced that this is also due to his shortcoming, and the only reason God does not appoint others to augment — or even replace — his

טז וַיֹּאמֶר יהוה אֶל־מֹשֶׁה אֶסְפָה־לִּי שִׁבְעִים אִישׁ מִזִּקְנֵי יִשְׂרָאֵל אֲשֶׁר יָדַעְתָּ
כִּי־הֵם זִקְנֵי הָעָם וְשֹׁטְרָיו וְלָקַחְתָּ אֹתָם אֶל־אֹהֶל מוֹעֵד וְהִתְיַצְּבוּ שָׁם
יז עִמָּךְ: וְיָרַדְתִּי וְדִבַּרְתִּי עִמְּךָ שָׁם וְאָצַלְתִּי מִן־הָרוּחַ אֲשֶׁר עָלֶיךָ וְשַׂמְתִּי
יח עֲלֵיהֶם וְנָשְׂאוּ אִתְּךָ בְּמַשָּׂא הָעָם וְלֹא־תִשָּׂא אַתָּה לְבַדֶּךָ: וְאֶל־הָעָם
תֹּאמַר הִתְקַדְּשׁוּ לְמָחָר וַאֲכַלְתֶּם בָּשָׂר כִּי בְּכִיתֶם בְּאָזְנֵי יהוה לֵאמֹר מִי
יט יַאֲכִלֵנוּ בָּשָׂר כִּי־טוֹב לָנוּ בְּמִצְרָיִם וְנָתַן יהוה לָכֶם בָּשָׂר וַאֲכַלְתֶּם: לֹא יוֹם
אֶחָד תֹּאכְלוּן וְלֹא יוֹמָיִם וְלֹא ׀ חֲמִשָּׁה יָמִים וְלֹא עֲשָׂרָה יָמִים וְלֹא עֶשְׂרִים
כ יוֹם: עַד ׀ חֹדֶשׁ יָמִים עַד אֲשֶׁר־יֵצֵא מֵאַפְּכֶם וְהָיָה לָכֶם לְזָרָא יַעַן
כִּי־מְאַסְתֶּם אֶת־יהוה אֲשֶׁר בְּקִרְבְּכֶם וַתִּבְכּוּ לְפָנָיו לֵאמֹר לָמָּה זֶּה יָצָאנוּ
כא מִמִּצְרָיִם: וַיֹּאמֶר מֹשֶׁה שֵׁשׁ־מֵאוֹת אֶלֶף רַגְלִי הָעָם אֲשֶׁר אָנֹכִי בְּקִרְבּוֹ
כב וְאַתָּה אָמַרְתָּ בָּשָׂר אֶתֵּן לָהֶם וְאָכְלוּ חֹדֶשׁ יָמִים: הֲצֹאן וּבָקָר יִשָּׁחֵט לָהֶם
וּמָצָא לָהֶם אִם אֶת־כָּל־דְּגֵי הַיָּם יֵאָסֵף לָהֶם וּמָצָא לָהֶם:

---

17. וְנָשְׂאוּ אִתְּךָ — *And they shall carry (the burden of the people) with you.* Since they will also be established (accepted) as prophets, the people will trust your leadership when they see that the elders are with you and concur in your actions.

20. וְהָיָה לָכֶם לְזָרָא — *And it shall be loathsome to you.* For you will eat of it until the excess will cause sickness, as (the verse) testifies, וּבַחוּרֵי יִשְׂרָאֵל הִכְרִיעַ, *And the young men of Israel He bent over* (*Psalms* 78:31) — (i.e., in pain).

לָמָּה זֶּה יָצָאנוּ מִמִּצְרָיִם — *Why is this that we came forth from Egypt?* For there we had a variety of many foods, not only the manna.

21. שֵׁשׁ מֵאוֹת אֶלֶף רַגְלִי — *Six hundred thousand men on foot.* And much meat will be necessary to satisfy them.

וְאַתָּה אָמַרְתָּ בָּשָׂר אֶתֵּן לָהֶם וְאָכְלוּ חֹדֶשׁ יָמִים — *And yet You have said, I will give them meat that they may eat a whole month.* And therefore, the meat you give them must be of a very large amount as it says, וַיַּמְטֵר עֲלֵיהֶם כֶּעָפָר שְׁאֵר וּכְחוֹל יַמִּים עוֹף כָּנָף, *He rained upon them meat like dust, and winged birds like the sands of the seas* (*Psalms* 78:27); (still) nonetheless . . .

22. הֲצֹאן וּבָקָר יִשָּׁחֵט לָהֶם וּמָצָא לָהֶם — *If flocks and herds are slain for them, will they suffice for them?* How will this suffice to remove their complaints since they are only requesting meat in order to test (God), as it says, וַיְנַסּוּ אֵל בִּלְבָבָם, *And they tested God in their hearts* (*Psalms* 78:18). Surely, without a doubt, just as they tested (You) with this (request), so they will test (You) with (requests for) other food without end — and You will not remove their free will, as (our Sages) say, הַכֹּל בִּידֵי שָׁמַיִם חוּץ מִיִּרְאַת שָׁמַיִם, *Everything is in the hands of Heaven except the fear of Heaven* (*Berachos* 33b).

NOTES

leadership, is because of God's concern for his (Moses') honor. Hence, he pleads with God not to deprive Israel of strong leadership, even if it means that he will be removed before his time — as was the prophet Samuel.

22. הֲצֹאן וּבָקָר יִשָּׁחֵט לָהֶם וּמָצָא לָהֶם — *If flocks and herds are slain for them, will they suffice for them?* Moses does not understand how Israel will be cured of their lustful desires unless God removes their desire and appetite,

כג וַיֹּאמֶר יהוה אֶל־מֹשֶׁה הֲיַד יהוה תִּקְצָר עַתָּה תִרְאֶה הֲיִקְרְךָ דְבָרִי
כד אִם־לֹא: וַיֵּצֵא מֹשֶׁה וַיְדַבֵּר אֶל־הָעָם אֵת דִּבְרֵי יהוה וַיֶּאֱסֹף שִׁבְעִים אִישׁ
כה מִזִּקְנֵי הָעָם וַיַּעֲמֵד אֹתָם סְבִיבֹת הָאֹהֶל: וַיֵּרֶד יהוה | בֶּעָנָן וַיְדַבֵּר אֵלָיו
וַיָּאצֶל מִן־הָרוּחַ אֲשֶׁר עָלָיו וַיִּתֵּן עַל־שִׁבְעִים אִישׁ הַזְּקֵנִים וַיְהִי כְּנוֹחַ
כו עֲלֵיהֶם הָרוּחַ וַיִּתְנַבְּאוּ וְלֹא יָסָפוּ: וַיִּשָּׁאֲרוּ שְׁנֵי־אֲנָשִׁים | בַּמַּחֲנֶה שֵׁם הָאֶחָד
| אֶלְדָּד וְשֵׁם הַשֵּׁנִי מֵידָד וַתָּנַח עֲלֵהֶם הָרוּחַ וְהֵמָּה בַּכְּתֻבִים וְלֹא יָצְאוּ
כז הָאֹהֱלָה וַיִּתְנַבְּאוּ בַּמַּחֲנֶה: וַיָּרָץ הַנַּעַר וַיַּגֵּד לְמֹשֶׁה וַיֹּאמַר אֶלְדָּד וּמֵידָד
כח מִתְנַבְּאִים בַּמַּחֲנֶה: וַיַּעַן יְהוֹשֻׁעַ בִּן־נוּן מְשָׁרֵת מֹשֶׁה מִבְּחֻרָיו וַיֹּאמַר אֲדֹנִי
כט מֹשֶׁה כְּלָאֵם: וַיֹּאמֶר לוֹ מֹשֶׁה הַמְקַנֵּא אַתָּה לִי וּמִי יִתֵּן כָּל־עַם יהוה
שביעי ל נְבִיאִים כִּי־יִתֵּן יהוה אֶת־רוּחוֹ עֲלֵיהֶם: וַיֵּאָסֵף מֹשֶׁה אֶל־הַמַּחֲנֶה הוּא
לא וְזִקְנֵי יִשְׂרָאֵל: וְרוּחַ נָסַע | מֵאֵת יהוה וַיָּגָז שַׂלְוִים מִן־הַיָּם וַיִּטֹּשׁ

---

23. הֲיַד ה׳ תִּקְצָר — *Will the hand of HASHEM be too short?* ... to find a way by which they (themselves) will find all lustful food abhorrent, as it says *until it come out of your nostrils* (v. 20).

עַתָּה תִרְאֶה הֲיִקְרְךָ דְבָרִי אִם לֹא — *Now you shall see whether My word shall come to pass or not.* You will see this happen, that they will eat the meat motivated by their desire for pleasure until it comes out of their nostrils, and (then) they will reject it — (all this) without My removing their free will at all; for indeed (then) they will be able to repent out of love and fear if they so desire, as it says, יָדַעְתִּי כִּי כֹל תּוּכָל וְלֹא יִבָּצֵר מִמְּךָ מְזִמָּה, *I know that You can do everything and that no purpose of Yours can be thwarted* (Job 42:2).

28. אֲדֹנִי מֹשֶׁה כְּלָאֵם — *My master Moses, shut them in* ... for he (Joshua) thought that the (reason) they did not present themselves at the Tent was to show that they could prophesize without accepting the spirit of Moses our Teacher (upon themselves).

29. כִּי יִתֵּן ה׳ אֶת רוּחוֹ עֲלֵיהֶם — *That HASHEM would put His spirit upon them* ... without receiving the spirit through me.

31. מִן הַיָּם — *From the sea* ... from the (direction) of the Sea of Reeds which was southward from their location. And this (was so) because the quails passed over the sea from the southern extremity (i.e., direction).

NOTES

thereby denying them freedom of will and choice — something He would never do. Hence, how will this failing of Israel be resolved? Certainly not by indulging them, for that will only encourage them to make more demands.

23. הֲיַד ה׳ תִּקְצָר עַתָּה תִרְאֶה הֲיִקְרְךָ דְבָרִי אִם לֹא — *Will the hand of HASHEM be too short? Now you shall see whether My word shall come to pass or not.* God reassures Moses that they themselves, of their own free will, will overindulge to the point of disgust with their own satiety and this will cure them of their lustful desires for a variety of foods other than the manna. When this occurs they will repent their evil ways.

28-29. אֲדֹנִי מֹשֶׁה כְּלָאֵם ... כִּי יִתֵּן ה׳ אֶת רוּחוֹ עֲלֵיהֶם — *My master Moses, shut them in ... that HASHEM would put His spirit upon them.* Joshua is jealous for Moses' honor and feels that Eldad and Medad were arrogant in not presenting themselves to Moses at the Tent, as though to declare that the spirit of prophecy could rest on them without the intervention and assistance of Moses. However, Moses dismisses the complaint of Joshua and ex-

עַל־הַמַּחֲנֶה כְּדֶרֶךְ יוֹם כֹּה וּכְדֶרֶךְ יוֹם כֹּה סְבִיבוֹת הַמַּחֲנֶה וּכְאַמָּתַיִם
לב עַל־פְּנֵי הָאָרֶץ: וַיָּקָם הָעָם כָּל־הַיּוֹם הַהוּא וְכָל־הַלַּיְלָה וְכֹל ׀ יוֹם הַמָּחֳרָת
וַיַּאַסְפוּ אֶת־הַשְּׂלָו הַמַּמְעִיט אָסַף עֲשָׂרָה חֳמָרִים וַיִּשְׁטְחוּ לָהֶם שָׁטוֹחַ
לג סְבִיבוֹת הַמַּחֲנֶה: הַבָּשָׂר עוֹדֶנּוּ בֵּין שִׁנֵּיהֶם טֶרֶם יִכָּרֵת וְאַף יהוה חָרָה בָעָם
לד וַיַּךְ יהוה בָּעָם מַכָּה רַבָּה מְאֹד: וַיִּקְרָא אֶת־שֵׁם־הַמָּקוֹם הַהוּא קִבְרוֹת
לה הַתַּאֲוָה כִּי־שָׁם קָבְרוּ אֶת־הָעָם הַמִּתְאַוִּים: מִקִּבְרוֹת הַתַּאֲוָה נָסְעוּ הָעָם
חֲצֵרוֹת וַיִּהְיוּ בַּחֲצֵרוֹת:

---

32. הַמַּמְעִיט אָסַף עֲשָׂרָה חֳמָרִים — *He that gathered least gathered ten heaps . . .* for they were all desirous to eat a large amount of them.

33. הַבָּשָׂר עוֹדֶנּוּ בֵּין שִׁנֵּיהֶם — *While the meat was yet between their teeth.* (And) they had as yet not reached the limit where they would reject it.

טֶרֶם יִכָּרֵת — *Before it was cut off . . .* for the time of a full month, which was set by God (v. 20), had not yet been reached.

וַיַּךְ ה׳ בָּעָם — *And HASHEM smote the people . . .* (referring to) those who lusted, who had asked for meat in order to test (God) and were afflicted (at once) through their testing — because the (time period) of *and they shall eat a whole month* was (only) said regarding those who cried, and did not lust (or test) but who said, *Why is this that we came forth from Egypt?* (v. 20). Now they (i.e., the criers) (eventually) cried in (their state) of illness, as it says, *and it shall be loathsome to you* (ibid.).

35. וַיִּהְיוּ בַּחֲצֵרוֹת — *And they stayed in Chazeros.* They remained there for a period of time, similar to, וַיִּהְיוּ שָׁם . . . כְּעֶשֶׂר שָׁנִים, *and remained there . . . about ten years* (*Ruth* 1:2, 4) (and) וַיִּהְיוּ שָׁם כַּאֲשֶׁר צִוַּנִי ה׳, *and remained there as HASHEM commanded me* (*Deut.* 10:5). (The Torah) states that at that time when they tarried there (in Chazeros), the (incident) of Miriam speaking against Moses occurred, and since the Tent of Meeting was then standing, God, the Blessed One, ordered them (i.e., Moses, Miriam and Aaron) to leave their tents and (present themselves) at the Tent of Meeting.

NOTES

presses his hope that God would rest His spirit directly upon all who are worthy to receive the spirit of prophecy, without need for any mediator.

31. מִן הַיָּם — *From the sea.* The term יָם, when used to denote direction, always means west, since the sea lies westward of *Eretz Yisrael.* In this case, however, the *Sforno* explains that it refers to the Sea of Reeds (not the Mediterranean) which lies to the south, since these quails breed in the south.

33. וַיַּךְ ה׳ בָּעָם — *And HASHEM smote the people.* The *Sforno* explains that there were two groupings and each was punished in a different manner. One consisted of those who demanded meat because they wanted to test God. They were smitten immediately as a punishment for their arrogant, blasphemous lack of faith. The other group consisted of those who wept and lamented at the thought of having left Egypt. They were punished at the end of a month when the meat of the quails came out of their nostrils and it became so loathsome to them that they fell ill, as God had promised (v. 20).

35. וַיִּהְיוּ בַּחֲצֵרוֹת — *And they stayed in Chazeros.* The *Sforno* understands this phrase as being an introduction to the following chapter, for the reason they stayed in Chazeros was because of the incident of Miriam (12:15,16).

יב א וַתְּדַבֵּר מִרְיָם וְאַהֲרֹן בְּמֹשֶׁה עַל־אֹדוֹת הָאִשָּׁה הַכֻּשִׁית אֲשֶׁר לָקָח
ב כִּי־אִשָּׁה כֻשִׁית לָקָח: וַיֹּאמְרוּ הֲרַק אַךְ־בְּמֹשֶׁה דִּבֶּר יהוה הֲלֹא גַּם־
ג בָּנוּ דִבֵּר וַיִּשְׁמַע יהוה: וְהָאִישׁ מֹשֶׁה עָנָו מְאֹד מִכֹּל הָאָדָם אֲשֶׁר
ד עַל־פְּנֵי הָאֲדָמָה: וַיֹּאמֶר יהוה פִּתְאֹם אֶל־מֹשֶׁה
וְאֶל־אַהֲרֹן וְאֶל־מִרְיָם צְאוּ שְׁלָשְׁתְּכֶם אֶל־אֹהֶל מוֹעֵד וַיֵּצְאוּ שְׁלָשְׁתָּם:
ה וַיֵּרֶד יהוה בְּעַמּוּד עָנָן וַיַּעֲמֹד פֶּתַח הָאֹהֶל וַיִּקְרָא אַהֲרֹן וּמִרְיָם
ו וַיֵּצְאוּ שְׁנֵיהֶם: וַיֹּאמֶר שִׁמְעוּ־נָא דְבָרָי אִם־יִהְיֶה נְבִיאֲכֶם יהוה בַּמַּרְאָה

XII

2. הֲרַק אַךְ בְּמֹשֶׁה דִּבֶּר ה׳ — *Has HASHEM indeed spoken only to Moses?* Indeed, has Moses alone merited this (status), that the word of God is directed exclusively to him, in addition to the (gift of) prophecy which he merited together with the multitude of Israel at the giving of the Torah?

וַיִּשְׁמַע ה׳ — *And HASHEM heard it.* As (our Sages) say, 'A rabbinical student is different, because the Holy One, Blessed be He, avenges his honor' (*Berachos* 19a).

4. צְאוּ שְׁלָשְׁתְּכֶם — *Go out, you three.* He wanted Moses to know the goodness of God, the Blessed One, Who was scrupulous regarding his (Moses') honor.

6. אִם יִהְיֶה נְבִיאֲכֶם — *If there be a prophet among you.* If Moses were a prophet on the level which you imagined when you said, *Has He not spoken also to us?* (v. 2) . . .

ה׳ בַּמַּרְאָה אֵלָיו אֶתְוַדָּע — *I, HASHEM, will make Myself known to him in a vision.* I would not make Myself known, or reveal Myself to him with this (particular) Divine Name, but (rather) in a vision (מַרְאָה, in the feminine form) — not in a waking state — as was the case with Isaiah when he said, וָאֶרְאֶה אֶת ה׳ יֹשֵׁב עַל כִּסֵּא רָם וְנִשָּׂא, *I saw HASHEM sitting upon a throne, high and exalted* (*Isaiah* 6:1) and also (in the case) of Michayahu (who said,) רָאִיתִי אֶת ה׳ יֹשֵׁב עַל כִּסְאוֹ, *I saw HASHEM sitting on His throne* (*I Kings* 22:19). (Now) all this was, without a doubt, in a prophetic vision and not in a waking state. (Regarding) Balaam also, even though

NOTES

XII

2. הֲרַק אַךְ בְּמֹשֶׁה דִּבֶּר ה׳ — *Has HASHEM indeed spoken only to Moses?* The words אַךְ and רַק both mean 'only'; why then is it necessary to use here two terms of מִיעוּט, *limitation*? The *Sforno* explains that Miriam and Aaron were challenging the exclusive character of Moses' prophetic powers: Is he the 'only' (רַק) one who has merited this level of prophecy? We have also reached this status (אַךְ), where God speaks to us 'alone.'

וַיִּשְׁמַע ה׳ — *And HASHEM heard it.* The Talmudic quote cited by the *Sforno* is meant to explain the significance of this expression. Certainly, God hears and knows all. Therefore, this phrase must mean that He reacted vigorously, defending the honor of Moses. This is in keeping with the statement of our Sages who tell us that if one makes a derogatory remark about a scholar after his death, God avenges his insult.

4. צְאוּ שְׁלָשְׁתְּכֶם — *Go out, you three.* The *Sforno* explains why all three were summoned since God only wanted to speak to Miriam and Aaron.

6-8. ה׳ בַּמַּרְאָה אֵלָיו אֶתְוַדָּע . . . לֹא כֵן עַבְדִּי מֹשֶׁה . . . פֶּה אֶל פֶּה אֲדַבֶּר בּוֹ וּמַרְאֶה וְלֹא בְחִידֹת וּתְמֻנַת ה׳ יַבִּיט וּמַדּוּעַ לֹא יְרֵאתֶם . . . — *I, HASHEM, will make Myself known to him in a vision . . . My servant Moses is not so . . . With him do I speak mouth to mouth in a manifest vision and not in riddles, and the similitude of HASHEM he beholds; wherefore then were you not afraid?* . . . The phrase מַרְאָה, *vision*, appears in verse 6

ז אֵלָיו אֶתְוַדָּע בַּחֲלוֹם אֲדַבֶּר־בּוֹ: לֹא־כֵן עַבְדִּי מֹשֶׁה בְּכָל־בֵּיתִי נֶאֱמָן
ח הוּא: פֶּה אֶל־פֶּה אֲדַבֶּר־בּוֹ וּמַרְאֶה וְלֹא בְחִידֹת וּתְמֻנַת יהוה יַבִּיט וּמַדּוּעַ

---

the (Divine) Word came to him in a waking state, it was not through the special Name (i.e., the Tetragrammaton), as he thought when he said, *Perhaps HASHEM will come to meet me* (23:3), for indeed, this was never accomplished, but it says regarding him, *and God met Balaam* (23:4).

7. לֹא כֵן עַבְדִּי מֹשֶׁה — *My servant Moses is not so.* The (Divine) Word to him is through the special Name (the Tetragrammaton) in a waking state. (Now) this he explains, saying . . .

8. פֶּה אֶל פֶּה אֲדַבֶּר בּוֹ — *With him do I speak mouth to mouth.* His prophecy is without the dulling (lit., the slumbering) of his senses.

וּמַרְאֶה — *In a manifest vision . . .* (written) in the masculine form, which our Sages called אַסְפַּקְלַרְיָה הַמְּאִירָה, *a transparent glass* (*Yevamos* 49b).

וְלֹא בְחִידֹת — *And not in riddles.* (Moses perceived) the (Divine) Word clearly defined without a riddle, unlike Zechariah and other (prophets) who saw riddles and (of Zechariah it is related) parables, and the angel said to him, הֲלוֹא יָדַעְתָּ מָה הֵמָּה אֵלֶּה וָאֹמַר לֹא אֲדֹנִי, *Do you not know what these are? And I said, 'No my Lord'* (*Zechariah* 4:5), and the angel had to explain the parable to him. And there were (prophets) among them who saw the parables and did understand them, similar to, הֵיטַבְתָּ לִרְאוֹת, *You have seen well* (*Jeremiah* 1:12), and Balaam (of whom) it says, *and he took up his parable*, because first he told the parable he had seen and later he explained it.

וּתְמֻנַת ה׳ יַבִּיט — *And the similitude of HASHEM he beholds.* And all this he grasps through God's revelation to him with the special Name, unlike Balaam who only grasped (G-d's message) through the (medium) of the parable and his perception was only through the name of 'Elohim,' not the special Name (the Tetragrammaton).

NOTES

in the feminine form as opposed to מַרְאֶה, used in verse 8, which is the masculine form. The feminine form is a weaker one and denotes a certain deficiency. (See chapter 11:15, the *Sforno's* commentary there, as well as the notes.) Hence, the word מַרְאָה signifies a lesser kind of prophecy than that of מַרְאֶה. There is also a profound difference whether God communicates with a prophet through His particular Name (שֵׁם הֲוַיָ׳ — the Tetragrammaton) or through the Name of אֱלֹהִים (God). Finally, save for a number of exceptions, God speaks to his prophets in visions and parables when the prophet is not in a waking state and in command of his senses; nor is he always capable of grasping the meaning of the parable revealed to him. The exception to these rules was Moses with whom God spoke *mouth to mouth*, i.e., while Moses was in total command of his senses — in a waking state, and *not in riddles*, i.e., it was a sharp, clear and defined communication. Also, the word of God always came to Moses through the particular Name of the Tetragrammaton (שֵׁם הֲוַיָ׳) which denotes a special relationship between the Almighty and the prophet. Even Balaam (whom our Sages compare partially to Moses) who was privileged to hear the Word of God in a waking state never reached the level of receiving prophecy through the particular special Name of God, nor in the form of a מַרְאֶה (in the masculine form), which our Sages explain to mean as the clarity of a transparent glass (אַסְפַּקְלַרְיָה הַמְּאִירָה). Also, all Balaam's prophecies were through the medium of a מָשָׁל, *parable*. Only Moses merited clarity of vision, communication with God in a waking state and the privilege of revelation through His special Name. This is the sense of the *Sforno's* commentary on verses 6, 7 and 8.

ט־י לֹא יְרֵאתֶם לְדַבֵּר בְּעַבְדִּי בְמֹשֶׁה: וַיִּחַר־אַף יְהוָה בָּם וַיֵּלַךְ: וְהֶעָנָן
סָר מֵעַל הָאֹהֶל וְהִנֵּה מִרְיָם מְצֹרַעַת כַּשָּׁלֶג וַיִּפֶן אַהֲרֹן אֶל־מִרְיָם
יא וְהִנֵּה מְצֹרָעַת: וַיֹּאמֶר אַהֲרֹן אֶל־מֹשֶׁה בִּי אֲדֹנִי אַל־נָא תָשֵׁת עָלֵינוּ
יב חַטָּאת אֲשֶׁר נוֹאַלְנוּ וַאֲשֶׁר חָטָאנוּ: אַל־נָא תְהִי כַּמֵּת אֲשֶׁר בְּצֵאתוֹ
יג מֵרֶחֶם אִמּוֹ וַיֵּאָכֵל חֲצִי בְשָׂרוֹ: וַיִּצְעַק מֹשֶׁה אֶל־יְהוָה לֵאמֹר אֵל נָא

וּמַדּוּעַ לֹא יְרֵאתֶם — *Wherefore then were you not afraid?* It is therefore inescapable that this can only be (attributed) to the evil of the heart, for if you (truly) thought (i.e., understood) that I am cognizant of his deeds, than you (must have) thought that I was in error and I desire evil men, which is the opposite of what you should have thought, because I would never have granted him this exalted (position) were he not worthy. Therefore, you should have been afraid to speak thus against such a man. And if perhaps you thought that I (really) am not cognizant of his actions and that you know him better than I do and that I (incorrectly) thought he is worthy of this (status) and (in reality) he is not, then all the more so do you consider God to be in error, (and) as (our Sages) say, 'This (statement) is even worse than the previous one' (*Sifre*).

9. וַיִּחַר אַף ה׳ בָּם — *And the anger of HASHEM was kindled against them ...* (because) they did not humble themselves immediately, as did David when he said to Nathan (the prophet), חָטָאתִי, *I have sinned* (*II Samuel* 12:13).

9-10. וַיֵּלַךְ ... וְהֶעָנָן סָר — *And He departed ... And the cloud was removed ...* indicating, as it were, a distancing of the leper, so that they should send her outside the camp to shame her.

12. אַל נָא תְהִי כַּמֵּת אֲשֶׁר בְּצֵאתוֹ מֵרֶחֶם אִמּוֹ וַיֵּאָכֵל חֲצִי בְשָׂרוֹ — *Please do not be as a dead fetus of whom the flesh is half consumed when he comes out of his mother's womb.* Behold, when a dead fetus is delivered from his mother's womb in such a manner that half his flesh is consumed and impaired, even though it may appear that he becomes more complete through (his) birth by leaving (the womb) and entering a place of complete life, (as compared) to his previous (state) when he was in his mother's womb; nonetheless, (in a sense) he becomes more deficient since half

NOTES

(See the *Sforno's* commentary on *Exodus* 19:9 and the notes.)

וּמַדּוּעַ לֹא יְרֵאתֶם — *Wherefore then were you not afraid?* The Almighty rebukes Miriam and Aaron for questioning either His judgement or His omniscience. 'If I was aware of Moses' shortcomings,' the Almighty argues, 'then I had no right to designate him as the teacher and leader of Israel, and if I was not aware, then it means that I am not all-knowing, and that would be a far more serious accusation on your part.' (See *Rashi's* commentary on this verse.)

9. וַיִּחַר אַף ה׳ בָּם — *And the anger of HASHEM was kindled against them.* The *Sforno* interprets God's anger as being precipitated by a new action — or inaction — on the part of Miriam and Aaron *following* His words of admonition and rebuke. He therefore explains that this anger was evoked through their failure to humble themselves promptly, as David did when he was admonished for his transgression.

12. אַל נָא תְהִי כַּמֵּת אֲשֶׁר בְּצֵאתוֹ מֵרֶחֶם אִמּוֹ וַיֵּאָכֵל חֲצִי בְשָׂרוֹ — *Please do not be as a dead fetus of whom the flesh is half consumed when he comes out of his mother's womb.* To understand the *Sforno's* commentary on this verse, one must preface it with *Rashi's*. explanation

רְפָא נָא לָהּ׃
מפטיר יד וַיֹּאמֶר יהוה אֶל־מֹשֶׁה וְאָבִיהָ יָרֹק יָרַק בְּפָנֶיהָ הֲלֹא תִכָּלֵם שִׁבְעַת יָמִים
טו תִּסָּגֵר שִׁבְעַת יָמִים מִחוּץ לַמַּחֲנֶה וְאַחַר תֵּאָסֵף׃ וַתִּסָּגֵר מִרְיָם מִחוּץ
טז לַמַּחֲנֶה שִׁבְעַת יָמִים וְהָעָם לֹא נָסַע עַד־הֵאָסֵף מִרְיָם׃ וְאַחַר נָסְעוּ הָעָם
מֵחֲצֵרוֹת וַיַּחֲנוּ בְּמִדְבַּר פָּארָן׃

---

his flesh is consumed through that birth. So, you who will leave this wilderness and enter the Chosen Land, thereby (establishing) a better dwelling place for yourself, (still) I pray you, do not be as that dead (fetus) by leaving over half your flesh in the wilderness.

13. אֵל נָא רְפָא נָא לָהּ — *Heal her now, O God, I beseech You.* Please, I ask (of You), cure her now so that we will not have to shame her by sending her outside the camp.

14. הֲלֹא תִכָּלֵם — *She would be shamed.* She is worthy to (suffer) this shame.

15. וְהָעָם לֹא נָסַע — *And the people did not journey.* Even though the cloud was removed from above the Tent, and it is written, וּבְהֵעָלוֹת הֶעָנָן מֵעַל הַמִּשְׁכָּן יִסְעוּ בְּנֵי יִשְׂרָאֵל בְּכֹל מַסְעֵיהֶם, *And whenever the cloud went up from above the Sanctuary the Children of Israel traveled throughout all their journeys* (*Exodus* 40:36), nonetheless (at that time) they did not journey, for they realized that (the cloud) went up then only (in order) to distance the leper (i.e., Miriam).

16. וַיַּחֲנוּ בְּמִדְבַּר פָּארָן — *And they encamped in the wilderness of Paran . . .* in a place in the wilderness which had no name at all but was across from and close to Kadesh Barnea, in order to arrange their affairs so as to enter therein, for this was the first city of *Eretz Yisrael* which they encountered on that road as (the Torah) attests, saying, וַנָּבֹא עַד קָדֵשׁ בַּרְנֵעַ וָאֹמַר אֲלֵכֶם בָּאתֶם עַד הַר הָאֱמֹרִי אֲשֶׁר ה׳ אֱלֹהֵינוּ נֹתֵן לָנוּ . . . עֲלֵה רֵשׁ וכו׳, *And we came to Kadesh Barnea, and I said to you, 'You have come to the hill country of the Emorites, which HASHEM our God gives to us . . . go up, take possession'* (*Deut.* 19-21). And that place was called 'Rismah,' as explained in *Maasei* (33:18).

NOTES

A brother and sister are considered as one flesh. If Moses will not intervene to help his afflicted sister Miriam, then he will be affected as well, for it will be as though half of his own flesh is consumed. The *Sforno*, however, adds a new and different interpretation to the meaning of רֶחֶם, *womb*. He considers it symbolic of the wilderness in which Israel (and Moses) now find themselves. Leaving the wilderness and entering the Land of Israel is comparable to the fetus leaving the mother's womb and entering the real world. However, if Miriam will not be healed and perforce remain behind, then it would be like a dead fetus whose flesh is consumed in the process of birth, for Moses would be leaving part of himself (as a brother) behind in the process of Israel's 'birth' — i.e., their departure from the wilderness and entry into the Promised Land.

15. וְהָעָם לֹא נָסַע — *And the people did not journey.* In verse 10, the *Sforno* explained that the removal of the cloud, which represents the Divine Glory of God, was an indication that Miriam was to leave the camp of Israel for a period of time. Although normally the removal of the cloud was a signal to journey, in this case it was only meant to indicate that the leper (Miriam) be distanced from the camp, as the *Sforno* explains.

פרשת שלח

Parashas Shelach

יג א־ב וַיְדַבֵּר יהוה אֶל־מֹשֶׁה לֵּאמֹר: שְׁלַח־לְךָ אֲנָשִׁים וְיָתֻרוּ אֶת־אֶרֶץ כְּנַעַן
אֲשֶׁר־אֲנִי נֹתֵן לִבְנֵי יִשְׂרָאֵל אִישׁ אֶחָד אִישׁ אֶחָד לְמַטֵּה אֲבֹתָיו תִּשְׁלָחוּ
ג כֹּל נָשִׂיא בָהֶם: וַיִּשְׁלַח אֹתָם מֹשֶׁה מִמִּדְבַּר פָּארָן עַל־פִּי יהוה כֻּלָּם
ד אֲנָשִׁים רָאשֵׁי בְנֵי־יִשְׂרָאֵל הֵמָּה: וְאֵלֶּה שְׁמוֹתָם לְמַטֵּה רְאוּבֵן שַׁמּוּעַ

XIII

2. שְׁלַח לְךָ אֲנָשִׁים — *Send out men for yourself.* Do not permit them to send (men of their own choice), which they intended to do when they said, נִשְׁלְחָה אֲנָשִׁים לְפָנֵינוּ, *we would send men before us* (*Deut.* 1:22), lest they send common men who will not appreciate how praiseworthy the Land is and will disparage it in such a manner that Israel will think that God has misled (them), and (therefore) they will not repent, as they (partially) did, (however) later when they said, חָטָאנוּ לַה׳, *We have sinned against HASHEM* (*Deut.* 1:41). Now, the spies whom Moses sent, although they acted wickedly in turning away the heart of the people due to their (own) lack of faith in Almighty God, nonetheless, they recognized and related the goodness of the Land when they said, *and it is also a (land) which flows with milk and honey* (13:27), which (the Torah) attests (to) saying, וַיִּקְחוּ בְיָדָם מִפְּרִי הָאָרֶץ ... וַיֹּאמְרוּ טוֹבָה הָאָרֶץ, *And they took in their hands from the fruit of the Land . . . and they said, 'The Land is good'* (*Deut.* 1:25) — but they (also) said that it was impossible to conquer. And when Israel realized their sin in not trusting the salvation of God, the Exalted One, and His (ability to be) victorious after having (performed) such wonders for them, they repented and said, חָטָאנוּ לַה׳ אֲנַחְנוּ נַעֲלֶה וְנִלְחַמְנוּ, *We have sinned against HASHEM, we will go up and do battle* (*Deut.* 1:41), and they prayed (to Him) as it says, וַתָּשֻׁבוּ וַתִּבְכּוּ לִפְנֵי ה׳, *You returned and wept before HASHEM* (ibid. verse 45); however, God, the Blessed One, did not accept their prayers because of the desecration of God's Name which they committed, (a transgression) which cannot be atoned for except through death, similar to that which the Torah attests to, saying, וּבְיוֹם פָּקְדִי וּפָקַדְתִּי עֲלֵהֶם חַטָּאתָם, *In the day when I visit, I will visit their sin upon them* (*Exodus* 32:34).

כֹּל נָשִׂיא בָהֶם — *Each a prince among them . . .* those who were the most outstanding in their (respective) tribes, (so as) to (be able to) recognize the quality of the Land.

3. כֻּלָּם אֲנָשִׁים — *They were, all of them, men . . .* men of strength, similar to הֲלוֹא אִישׁ אַתָּה, *Are you not a valiant man* (*I Samuel* 26:15) and also וְחָזַקְתָּ וְהָיִיתָ לְאִישׁ, *Be strong and show yourself a man* (*I Kings* 2:2).

4. וְאֵלֶּה שְׁמוֹתָם — *And these were their names.* They were all men of importance, each a man whose name (reflected) his elevated role. (The Torah) mentions them

NOTES

XIII

2. שְׁלַח לְךָ אֲנָשִׁים — *Send out men for yourself.* The question as to whether Moses was agreeable to sending the spies, and whether God gave His approval, is one that *Rashi* addresses both here and in the Book of *Deuteronomy* (1:22,23). The *Sforno* is of the opinion that God advised Moses to send men of his own choosing who would appreciate the qualities of the Land of Israel. And indeed, they did — for with all their criticism and ambivalence, they did not fail to praise the Land and its fruits. Thanks to this measure of honesty, the Children of Israel eventually repented. Now, we have been taught that there is nothing which stands in the way of repentance. Nonetheless, God did not accept the repentance of Israel following the sin of the spies. The *Sforno* offers two reasons for this excep-

ה־ז בֶּן־זַכּוּר: לְמַטֵּה שִׁמְעוֹן שָׁפָט בֶּן־חוֹרִי: לְמַטֵּה יְהוּדָה כָּלֵב בֶּן־יְפֻנֶּה: לְמַטֵּה
ח־ט יִשָּׂשכָר יִגְאָל בֶּן־יוֹסֵף: לְמַטֵּה אֶפְרָיִם הוֹשֵׁעַ בִּן־נוּן: לְמַטֵּה בִנְיָמִן פַּלְטִי
י־יא בֶּן־רָפוּא: לְמַטֵּה זְבוּלֻן גַּדִּיאֵל בֶּן־סוֹדִי: לְמַטֵּה יוֹסֵף לְמַטֵּה מְנַשֶּׁה גַּדִּי
יב־יג בֶּן־סוּסִי: לְמַטֵּה דָן עַמִּיאֵל בֶּן־גְּמַלִּי: לְמַטֵּה אָשֵׁר סְתוּר בֶּן־מִיכָאֵל:
יד־טז לְמַטֵּה נַפְתָּלִי נַחְבִּי בֶּן־וָפְסִי: לְמַטֵּה גָד גְּאוּאֵל בֶּן־מָכִי: אֵלֶּה שְׁמוֹת
הָאֲנָשִׁים אֲשֶׁר־שָׁלַח מֹשֶׁה לָתוּר אֶת־הָאָרֶץ וַיִּקְרָא מֹשֶׁה לְהוֹשֵׁעַ בִּן־נוּן
יז יְהוֹשֻׁעַ: וַיִּשְׁלַח אֹתָם מֹשֶׁה לָתוּר אֶת־אֶרֶץ כְּנָעַן וַיֹּאמֶר אֲלֵהֶם עֲלוּ זֶה
יח בַּנֶּגֶב וַעֲלִיתֶם אֶת־הָהָר: וּרְאִיתֶם אֶת־הָאָרֶץ מַה־הִוא וְאֶת־הָעָם הַיֹּשֵׁב
יט עָלֶיהָ הֶחָזָק הוּא הֲרָפֶה הַמְעַט הוּא אִם־רָב: וּמָה הָאָרֶץ אֲשֶׁר־הוּא יֹשֵׁב

---

according to their age and not according to the order of the tribes nor the order of the flags, because at that time they were all equal in stature, particularly insofar as the nature of the assignment was concerned.

16. וַיִּקְרָא מֹשֶׁה לְהוֹשֵׁעַ בִּן נוּן יְהוֹשֻׁעַ — *And Moses called Hoshea the son of Nun Joshua.* (The verse) states that he was known in his tribe as a man of strength by the name Hoshea (הוֹשֵׁעַ). (Now) the (reason) he is called (by the name) Joshua (יְהוֹשֻׁעַ) above (11:28) is because Moses our Teacher called him thus as (a mark) of honor, and (also) to pray for him that he be saved (from the plot of the spies) and that he should save others.

17. עֲלוּ זֶה בַּנֶּגֶב — *Go up here in the south* . . . from this side, where we are (located) presently, for you will find it good (easy) to enter (here), and there is no need for us to circle around to another place.

18. וּרְאִיתֶם אֶת הָאָרֶץ מַה הִוא — *And see the Land, what it is like* . . . whether the Land is settled with many (fortified) as well as open cities.

וְאֶת הָעָם הַיֹּשֵׁב עָלֶיהָ — *And the people that dwell therein* . . . to know (determine) if the living conditions are good, as the wise men of medicine have taught regarding the choice of residence, that one should observe the inhabitants of the Land as to whether they are strong, wholesome and healthy or the reverse. And one should also look to see if they are many or a few, for a great number of people and their well-being (lit., strength) indicates whether the climate and produce of the Land are good, while the opposite denotes the reverse.

NOTES

tion to the rule. One is, that only death can atone for the sin of חִלּוּל הַשֵּׁם, *the desecration of God's Name,* which this rejection of the Land of Israel and of God's powers reflected. Secondly, as the *Sforno* explained more fully in *Exodus* 32:34, the sin of the spies preceded by that of the Golden Calf represents an established pattern of habitual transgression; repentance in such a case is of no avail, for 'when a man transgresses and repeats his offense it becomes (as if it were permitted to him' (*Yoma* 86b). The *Sforno* in *Deut.* 1:45 gives an additional reason for God's rejection of their repentance.

4. וְאֵלֶּה שְׁמוֹתָם — *And these were their names.* The *Sforno* disagrees with the *Ramban* who states that they are listed according to their superior qualities of wisdom and leadership. As the *Sforno* says, they were all equal in importance, hence the order must be according to age.

16. וַיִּקְרָא מֹשֶׁה לְהוֹשֵׁעַ בִּן נוּן יְהוֹשֻׁעַ — *And Moses called Hoshea the son of Nun Joshua.* The name Joshua was not initially given to Hoshea now for we find this name used above in chapter 11:28. Still, the Torah tells us here that his name was Hoshea. The *Sforno* ex-

בָּהּ הֲטוֹבָה הִוא אִם־רָעָה וּמָה הֶעָרִים אֲשֶׁר־הוּא יוֹשֵׁב בָּהֵנָּה הַבְּמַחֲנִים
כ אִם בְּמִבְצָרִים: וּמָה הָאָרֶץ הַשְּׁמֵנָה הִוא אִם־רָזָה הֲיֵשׁ־בָּהּ עֵץ אִם־אַיִן
שני כא וְהִתְחַזַּקְתֶּם וּלְקַחְתֶּם מִפְּרִי הָאָרֶץ וְהַיָּמִים יְמֵי בִּכּוּרֵי עֲנָבִים: וַיַּעֲלוּ וַיָּתֻרוּ
כב אֶת־הָאָרֶץ מִמִּדְבַּר־צִן עַד־רְחֹב לְבֹא חֲמָת: וַיַּעֲלוּ בַנֶּגֶב וַיָּבֹא עַד־חֶבְרוֹן

---

19. הֲטוֹבָה הִוא — *Is it good* ... with plentiful, good water, as it says, כִּי ה׳ אֱלֹהֶיךָ מְבִיאֲךָ אֶל אֶרֶץ טוֹבָה אֶרֶץ נַחֲלֵי מָיִם, *For HASHEM your God is bringing you into a good land, a land full of brooks of water* (Deut. 8:7).

הַבְּמַחֲנִים — *Whether open cities* ... whether they dwell in open cities securely, with no fear of war.

אִם בְּמִבְצָרִים — *Or in fortified ones* ... (or) if they dwell in fortified cities because of fear of war, similar to, חָדְלוּ פְרָזוֹן בְּיִשְׂרָאֵל חָדֵלּוּ, *The inhabitants of open cities ceased* (Judges 5:7).

20. הַשְּׁמֵנָה הִוא — *Whether fat* ... with riches and possessions, as it says, אֲשֶׁר לֹא בְמִסְכֵּנֻת תֹּאכַל בָּהּ לֶחֶם, *In which you will not eat bread in parsimony* (Deut. 8:9).

הֲיֵשׁ בָּהּ עֵץ — *Are there trees there* ... vines, figs and pomegranates, oil-producing olives and honey (from dates), (fruits) for which (the Land) was praised (see *Deut.* 8:8).

וְהִתְחַזַּקְתֶּם וּלְקַחְתֶּם מִפְּרִי הָאָרֶץ — *And take courage and take some of the fruit of the Land* ... to take (legal) possession of it (i.e., the Land), and do not fear that they will consider you spies.

וְהַיָּמִים יְמֵי בִּכּוּרֵי עֲנָבִים — *And the time was the season of the ripening of the first grapes.* And although the fruit with which the Land was praised was not as yet fully ripened (lit., perfected); nonetheless, Moses our Teacher was confident that the size and taste of the fruit, even at that time, would suffice to attest to the goodness and praiseworthiness of the Land.

22. וַיָּבֹא עַד חֶבְרוֹן — *And he came to Hebron.* He (Caleb) alone (came) to seclude himself and pray at the graves of the Patriarchs (based on *Sotah* 34b).

NOTES

plains that within his tribe (Ephraim) he was called Hoshea. Moses, however, added the letter *yud*, for two reasons. Originally, it was meant as a mark of honor, and subsequently (as *Rashi* also explains) it served as a prayer that he be saved from the plot of the spies. Since the name יְהוֹשֻׁעַ is *'piel'* (the grammatical intensive form), the *Sforno* interprets it to mean that not only should *he* be saved, but he should also save others.

20. וְהִתְחַזַּקְתֶּם וּלְקַחְתֶּם מִפְּרִי הָאָרֶץ — *And take courage and take some of the fruit of the land.* The term חֲזָקָה means to perform an act for the purpose of taking possession, and by taking of the fruits, they performed such an act, this being the meaning of וְהִתְחַזַּקְתֶּם. Hence, the *Sforno* says that Moses had to encourage them not to be afraid since they were thereby acquiring the ownership of the Land, an act which normally would evoke strong opposition on the part of its inhabitants.

וְהַיָּמִים יְמֵי בִּכּוּרֵי עֲנָבִים — *And the time was the season of the ripening of the first grapes.* The *Sforno* explains why it is necessary for the Torah to tell us precisely the season of the year. Since they were instructed to bring back all the species of *Eretz Yisrael* which are cited as being exceptionally praiseworthy, there was an element of risk involved. When the grapes first ripen, the other fruits are not as yet ready. Still, Moses was confident that the people would recognize the superior quality of these fruits even at an unripe stage.

22. וַיָּבֹא עַד חֶבְרוֹן — *And he came to Hebron.* This commentary of the *Sforno* is not found in

וְשָׁם אֲחִימַן שֵׁשַׁי וְתַלְמַי יְלִידֵי הָעֲנָק וְחֶבְרוֹן שֶׁבַע שָׁנִים נִבְנְתָה לִפְנֵי צֹעַן
כג מִצְרָיִם: וַיָּבֹאוּ עַד־נַחַל אֶשְׁכֹּל וַיִּכְרְתוּ מִשָּׁם זְמוֹרָה וְאֶשְׁכּוֹל עֲנָבִים אֶחָד
כד וַיִּשָּׂאֻהוּ בַמּוֹט בִּשְׁנָיִם וּמִן־הָרִמֹּנִים וּמִן־הַתְּאֵנִים: לַמָּקוֹם הַהוּא קָרָא נַחַל
כה אֶשְׁכּוֹל עַל אֹדוֹת הָאֶשְׁכּוֹל אֲשֶׁר־כָּרְתוּ מִשָּׁם בְּנֵי יִשְׂרָאֵל: וַיָּשֻׁבוּ מִתּוּר
כו הָאָרֶץ מִקֵּץ אַרְבָּעִים יוֹם: וַיֵּלְכוּ וַיָּבֹאוּ אֶל־מֹשֶׁה וְאֶל־אַהֲרֹן וְאֶל־כָּל־
עֲדַת בְּנֵי־יִשְׂרָאֵל אֶל־מִדְבַּר פָּארָן קָדֵשָׁה וַיָּשִׁיבוּ אֹתָם דָּבָר וְאֶת־כָּל־
כז הָעֵדָה וַיַּרְאוּם אֶת־פְּרִי הָאָרֶץ: וַיְסַפְּרוּ־לוֹ וַיֹּאמְרוּ בָּאנוּ אֶל־הָאָרֶץ אֲשֶׁר
כח שְׁלַחְתָּנוּ וְגַם זָבַת חָלָב וּדְבַשׁ הִוא וְזֶה־פִּרְיָהּ: אֶפֶס כִּי־עַז הָעָם הַיֹּשֵׁב
כט בָּאָרֶץ וְהֶעָרִים בְּצֻרוֹת גְּדֹלֹת מְאֹד וְגַם־יְלִדֵי הָעֲנָק רָאִינוּ שָׁם: עֲמָלֵק
יוֹשֵׁב בְּאֶרֶץ הַנֶּגֶב וְהַחִתִּי וְהַיְבוּסִי וְהָאֱמֹרִי יוֹשֵׁב בָּהָר וְהַכְּנַעֲנִי יוֹשֵׁב
ל עַל־הַיָּם וְעַל יַד הַיַּרְדֵּן: וַיַּהַס כָּלֵב אֶת־הָעָם אֶל־מֹשֶׁה וַיֹּאמֶר עָלֹה נַעֲלֶה

---

24. עַל אֹדוֹת הָאֶשְׁכּוֹל אֲשֶׁר כָּרְתוּ מִשָּׁם בְּנֵי יִשְׂרָאֵל — *On account of the cluster of grapes which the Children of Israel cut down there.* The Canaanites were astonished that this grape cluster, which the Children of Israel cut, was considered by them to be so novel and wondrous, for there were many such clusters in the Land as large, or larger, than this (particular) one. To them, i.e., the Canaanites, the inhabitants of the land, this was nothing wondrous at all, hence their wonderment [resulted] in their calling the place *The brook of Eshkol.*

26. אֶל מִדְבַּר פָּארָן קָדֵשָׁה — *Unto the wilderness of Paran to Kadesh* ... to that portion of the wilderness which was across from Kadesh Barnea.

27. וְגַם זָבַת חָלָב וּדְבַשׁ הִוא — *And indeed, it flows with milk and honey.* Not only is it *good* (see verse 19) but it also flows with milk and honey; i.e., it produces, without great effort, much cattle who give plentiful milk, and it produces much honey and royal delights (based on *Genesis* 49:20).

28. אֶפֶס כִּי עַז הָעָם — *But the people are too strong.* But it is impossible to conquer it because the people are fierce, and the cities are fortified, and the inhabitants of the Land are our enemies; the children of Amalek will also do battle against us so that we should not come nigh to their borders.

30. וַיַּהַס כָּלֵב אֶת הָעָם — *Then Caleb stilled the people.* He silenced the people who had already begun to lift up their voices, as (indeed) they later did — as it is said, *And the whole congregation lifted up their voice* (14:1).

אֶל מֹשֶׁה — *Toward Moses.* (He urged them) to listen to what Moses would answer. Perhaps it was then that Moses said what is attested to later when he said, וָאֹמַר אֲלֵכֶם לֹא תַעַרְצוּן וְלֹא תִירְאוּן מֵהֶם, *And I said to you; do not be dismayed and do not fear them* (*Deut.* 1:29), and Caleb strengthened (supported) his words, by stating ...

NOTES

many editions. Compare to *Rashi* here and to the *Sforno* on *Exodus* 3:1.

24. עַל אֹדוֹת הָאֶשְׁכּוֹל — *On account of the cluster of grapes.* The name נַחַל אֶשְׁכּוֹל, *the brook of the grape cluster*, was given by the Canaanites — not the Children of Israel.

26. אֶל מִדְבַּר פָּארָן קָדֵשָׁה — *Unto the wilderness of Paran to Kadesh.* See the commentary of the *Sforno* on chapter 12:16.

30. וַיַּהַס כָּלֵב אֶת הָעָם אֶל מֹשֶׁה — *Then Caleb stilled the people toward Moses.* The expression וַיַּהַס, *and he stilled,* is applicable only

לא וְיָרַשְׁנוּ אֹתָהּ כִּי־יָכוֹל נוּכַל לָהּ׃ וְהָאֲנָשִׁים אֲשֶׁר עָלוּ עִמּוֹ אָמְרוּ לֹא נוּכַל
לב לַעֲלוֹת אֶל־הָעָם כִּי־חָזָק הוּא מִמֶּנּוּ׃ וַיֹּצִיאוּ דִּבַּת הָאָרֶץ אֲשֶׁר תָּרוּ אֹתָהּ
אֶל־בְּנֵי יִשְׂרָאֵל לֵאמֹר הָאָרֶץ אֲשֶׁר עָבַרְנוּ בָהּ לָתוּר אֹתָהּ אֶרֶץ אֹכֶלֶת
לג יוֹשְׁבֶיהָ הִוא וְכָל־הָעָם אֲשֶׁר־רָאִינוּ בְתוֹכָהּ אַנְשֵׁי מִדּוֹת׃ וְשָׁם רָאִינוּ
אֶת־הַנְּפִילִים בְּנֵי עֲנָק מִן־הַנְּפִלִים וַנְּהִי בְעֵינֵינוּ כַּחֲגָבִים וְכֵן הָיִינוּ
יד א בְּעֵינֵיהֶם׃ וַתִּשָּׂא כָּל־הָעֵדָה וַיִּתְּנוּ אֶת־קוֹלָם וַיִּבְכּוּ הָעָם בַּלַּיְלָה הַהוּא׃

עָלֹה נַעֲלֶה — *We will indeed go up.* It is proper for us to go up, for they will not rise up against us to prevent our going up.

וְיָרַשְׁנוּ אֹתָהּ כִּי יָכוֹל נוּכַל לָהּ — *And take possession of it for we are truly able to do so* ... for after we go up there they will flee from our presence, because all the inhabitants of Canaan have already *melted away* (based on *Exodus* 15:15).

31. לֹא נוּכַל לַעֲלוֹת — *We are not able to go up* ... for they will rise up against us and not allow us to go up, as (indeed) it occured after the sin, as it says *and the Amalekites and the Canaanites came down* (14:45).

32. אֶרֶץ אֹכֶלֶת יוֹשְׁבֶיהָ — *A land that consumes its inhabitants.* Even though the people who dwell in it (the Land) are strong, it is not due to the praiseworthiness (i.e., quality) of the Land, but it is because only the strong survive, for they are strong by nature, while the others perish because of the poor climate.

33. בְּנֵי עֲנָק — *The sons of Anak* ... from (their) father's side.

מִן הַנְּפִלִים — *Of the Nephilim* ... from (their) mother's side.

וְכֵן הָיִינוּ בְּעֵינֵיהֶם — *And so were we in their eyes* ... like grasshoppers, or even inferior to them. Therefore, they did not rise up against us for we were not sufficiently important, and it was contemptible in their eyes to do us harm (similar to *Megillas Esther* 3:6).

NOTES

when there are those who are speaking or complaining. This, however, is not mentioned until the beginning of the next chapter (14:1). The *Sforno* therefore explains that at first some did begin to complain, and later the *whole congregation* followed suit. Caleb attempted to silence those who had already begun to raise their voices — but to no avail. Unlike *Rashi*, who bases his interpretation upon the Midrash, the *Sforno* explains the verse to mean that Caleb urged the people to listen to the words of Moses (which are not recorded here but in *parashas Devarim*), and he also made a personal plea to the people.

31. לֹא נוּכַל לַעֲלוֹת — *We are not able to go up.* The *Sforno* explains that their despair and lack of faith precipitated the eventual debacle. Their hopelessness was father to the reality. The *Sforno* expresses this same idea in his commentary on 14:37.

33. בְּנֵי עֲנָק מִן הַנְּפִלִים — *The sons of Anak of the Nephilim.* The word *nephilim* is usually translated 'giants'. It is first mentioned in *Genesis* 6:4. The *Abarbanel*, however, explains the phrase differently. In Hebrew, the word נֵפֶל means an aborted or premature infant. Being that the (human) mother was of average size while the (Anak) father was of giant proportions, the infant could not be carried to term — hence נֵפֶל, or נְפִלִים in the plural. The *Sforno*, following this interpretation, interprets *sons of Anak* as referring to the lineage of their fathers, and *from the Nephilim* as referring to the lineage of the mother — who occasionally did give birth to these huge offspring.

ב וַיִּלֹּנוּ עַל־מֹשֶׁה וְעַל־אַהֲרֹן כֹּל בְּנֵי יִשְׂרָאֵל וַיֹּאמְרוּ אֲלֵהֶם כָּל־הָעֵדָה
ג לוּ־מַתְנוּ בְּאֶרֶץ מִצְרַיִם אוֹ בַּמִּדְבָּר הַזֶּה לוּ־מָתְנוּ: וְלָמָה יהוה מֵבִיא
אֹתָנוּ אֶל־הָאָרֶץ הַזֹּאת לִנְפֹּל בַּחֶרֶב נָשֵׁינוּ וְטַפֵּנוּ יִהְיוּ לָבַז הֲלוֹא טוֹב לָנוּ
ד־ה שׁוּב מִצְרָיְמָה: וַיֹּאמְרוּ אִישׁ אֶל־אָחִיו נִתְּנָה רֹאשׁ וְנָשׁוּבָה מִצְרָיְמָה: וַיִּפֹּל
ו מֹשֶׁה וְאַהֲרֹן עַל־פְּנֵיהֶם לִפְנֵי כָּל־קְהַל עֲדַת בְּנֵי יִשְׂרָאֵל: וִיהוֹשֻׁעַ בִּן־נוּן
ז וְכָלֵב בֶּן־יְפֻנֶּה מִן־הַתָּרִים אֶת־הָאָרֶץ קָרְעוּ בִּגְדֵיהֶם: וַיֹּאמְרוּ אֶל־כָּל־
עֲדַת בְּנֵי־יִשְׂרָאֵל לֵאמֹר הָאָרֶץ אֲשֶׁר עָבַרְנוּ בָהּ לָתוּר אֹתָהּ טוֹבָה הָאָרֶץ

XIV

2. וַיִּלֹּנוּ עַל מֹשֶׁה וְעַל אַהֲרֹן — *And they murmured against Moses and Aaron.* For they were the messengers of God, the Blessed One, sent to bring them forth from Egypt and to save them from all fear of death in the wilderness. (But now) they said that all this was done (in order to) deliver them into the hands of the Emorites.

3. וְלָמָה ה׳ מֵבִיא אֹתָנוּ — *And why does HASHEM bring us.* How have we sinned against Him that He now attempts, through you, to bring us to this (state)? For they thought that all this had occurred by His design, (motivated by) His hatred for them on account of their idolatry in Egypt, or some other reason — as (the Torah) testifies, saying, וַתֹּאמְרוּ בְּשִׂנְאַת ה׳ אֹתָנוּ הוֹצִיאָנוּ מֵאֶרֶץ מִצְרַיִם לָתֵת אֹתָנוּ בְּיַד הָאֱמֹרִי לְהַשְׁמִידֵנוּ, *And you said, 'Because HASHEM hates us He brought us out of the land of Egypt to deliver us into the hand of the Emorites, to destroy us'* (*Deut.* 1:27).

5. וַיִּפֹּל מֹשֶׁה וְאַהֲרֹן עַל פְּנֵיהֶם — *And Moses and Aaron fell on their faces* ... when they saw (that this was) מְעֻוָּת לֹא יוּכַל לִתְקֹן, *something crooked which cannot be made straight* (*Ecclesiastes* 1:15), similar to (the episode of) the Sanhedrin who pressed their faces into the ground when they did not know what to do because of their fear of the king (*Sanhedrin* 19b).

7. הָאָרֶץ אֲשֶׁר עָבַרְנוּ בָהּ לָתוּר אֹתָהּ — *The Land through which we have passed to spy it out* ... to spy out the place and its inhabitants, as it says, *And see the Land, what it is; and the people that dwell therein* (13:18).

טוֹבָה הָאָרֶץ — *The Land is good.* Behold, regarding *the land, what it is,* we testify that it is a place that is exceedingly good, with no blemish, and not as our colleagues testified (when) they said that although it *flows with milk and honey* (13:27), (nonetheless), it *consumes its inhabitants* (13:32). And regarding *the people that dwell therein,* we testify that *they are our bread* (verse 9) and they will not dare oppose us, contrary to the testimony of our colleagues who said *the people are too strong* (13:28).

NOTES

XIV

2. וַיִּלֹּנוּ עַל מֹשֶׁה וְעַל אַהֲרֹן — *And they murmured against Moses and Aaron.* The question is: Why did the people turn against Moses and Aaron, since they themselves claimed it was the Almighty who hated them and was determined to hand them over to the Emorites? The *Sforno* explains that in keeping with the Talmudic dictum that שְׁלוּחוֹ שֶׁל אָדָם כְּמוֹתוֹ, *a messenger of a person is considered to be as him,* Moses and Aaron as the messengers of God were fair target for their murmurings.

5. וַיִּפֹּל מֹשֶׁה וְאַהֲרֹן עַל פְּנֵיהֶם — *And Moses and Aaron fell on their faces.* The *Sforno* explains the reaction of Moses and Aaron as manifesting their sense of inadequacy and despair, similar to the episode related in the Talmud regarding Shimon ben Shetach and King Yanai. The slave of the king had committed murder and Shimon urged the Sanhedrin to

שלישי ח מְאֹד מְאֹד: אִם־חָפֵץ בָּנוּ יהוה וְהֵבִיא אֹתָנוּ אֶל־הָאָרֶץ הַזֹּאת וּנְתָנָהּ לָנוּ
ט אֶרֶץ אֲשֶׁר־הִוא זָבַת חָלָב וּדְבָשׁ: אַךְ בַּיהוה אַל־תִּמְרֹדוּ וְאַתֶּם
אַל־תִּירְאוּ אֶת־עַם הָאָרֶץ כִּי לַחְמֵנוּ הֵם סָר צִלָּם מֵעֲלֵיהֶם וַיהוה אִתָּנוּ

---

8. אִם חָפֵץ בָּנוּ ה׳ — *If HASHEM desires us.* However, the exceeding goodness (of this place) is conditional upon HASHEM's delight in us, as it says, אֶרֶץ אֲשֶׁר ה׳ אֱלֹהֶיךָ דֹּרֵשׁ אֹתָהּ . . . וְהָיָה אִם שָׁמֹעַ תִּשְׁמְעוּ, *A land which HASHEM your God seeks . . . and it shall come to pass if you hearken* (*Deut.* 11:12,13).

וְהֵבִיא אֹתָנוּ אֶל הָאָרֶץ הַזֹּאת — *Then He will bring us into this land* . . . contrary to what our colleagues have testified saying, *We are not able to go up against the people* (13:31), for indeed the inhabitants of the Land will not rise up against us at all, as it says, יִדְּמוּ כָּאָבֶן עַד יַעֲבֹר עַמְּךָ ה׳, *They shall be still as a stone, till Your people pass over, HASHEM* (*Exodus* 15:16). And so it was, for they (the inhabitants) erected no barriers nor made any preparations to prevent the people (of Israel) from going up against them.

וּנְתָנָהּ לָנוּ — *And give it to us* . . . for we saw that there did not arise any spirit in any man to oppose us, and that their intention was to flee.

אֶרֶץ אֲשֶׁר הִוא זָבַת חָלָב וּדְבָשׁ — *A land which flows with milk and honey* . . . (the Land) itself, (on its own), without the labor of those who work the earth, similar to the forests as we find, וְכָל הָאָרֶץ בָּאוּ בַיָּעַר וַיְהִי דְבַשׁ עַל פְּנֵי הַשָּׂדֶה, *And all the people came to the wood and behold, there was a stream of honey on the ground* (*I Samuel* 14:25), and this would have been impossible if the Land or its climate had some blemish.

9. אַךְ בַּה׳ אַל תִּמְרֹדוּ — *Only rebel not against HASHEM.* However, if you want the Land to be on this level of goodness, then do not rebel against God, as it says, וְהָיָה אִם שָׁמֹעַ תִּשְׁמְעוּ . . . וְנָתַתִּי מְטַר אַרְצְכֶם בְּעִתּוֹ . . . וְאָסַפְתָּ, *And it shall come to pass if you will continually hearken . . . then I will send rain to your land in its proper time . . . that you may gather* (*Deut.* 11:13, 14).

וְאַתֶּם אַל תִּירְאוּ אֶת עַם הָאָרֶץ — *And you should not fear the people of the Land.* Behold, if you do not rebel, then God will bring us (into the Land) and you, have no fear . . .

כִּי לַחְמֵנוּ הֵם — *For they are our bread.* Because we observed that they have no intention to rise up against us at all, just as bread does not rise up against those who eat it, as Rahab testified when she said, וְלֹא קָמָה עוֹד רוּחַ בְּאִישׁ מִפְּנֵיכֶם, *Neither did there remain any more courage in any man because of you* (*Joshua* 2:11).

סָר צִלָּם מֵעֲלֵיהֶם — *Their defense is departed from them.* And we saw that they have agreed to abandon every shield and buckler so as to hasten their flight from our

NOTES

bring him to justice, but they were afraid of the king and did nothing. Rather, they 'pressed their faces into the ground' as Moses and Aaron did in the case at hand. The *Sforno* implies that Moses and Aaron were immobilized by the report of the spies and unable to stand up to the people.

7-9. טוֹבָה הָאָרֶץ . . . אִם חָפֵץ בָּנוּ ה׳ . . . וְאַתֶּם אַל תִּירְאוּ אֶת עַם הָאָרֶץ — *The Land is good . . . If HASHEM desires us . . . And you should not fear the people of the Land.* The meaning of these verses, according to the *Sforno*, is as follows: Caleb and Joshua first address themselves to the original purpose of their mission, follow-

י אַל־תִּירָאֻם: וַיֹּאמְרוּ כָּל־הָעֵדָה לִרְגּוֹם אֹתָם בָּאֲבָנִים וּכְבוֹד יהוה נִרְאָה
בְּאֹהֶל מוֹעֵד אֶל־כָּל־בְּנֵי יִשְׂרָאֵל:
יא וַיֹּאמֶר יהוה אֶל־מֹשֶׁה עַד־אָנָה יְנַאֲצֻנִי הָעָם הַזֶּה וְעַד־אָנָה לֹא־יַאֲמִינוּ בִי
יב בְּכֹל הָאֹתוֹת אֲשֶׁר עָשִׂיתִי בְּקִרְבּוֹ: אַכֶּנּוּ בַדֶּבֶר וְאוֹרִשֶׁנּוּ וְאֶעֱשֶׂה אֹתְךָ

presence, similar to, כָּל הַדֶּרֶךְ מְלֵאָה בְגָדִים וְכֵלִים אֲשֶׁר הִשְׁלִיכוּ אֲרָם בְּחָפְזָם, *All the way was full of garments and vessels which Aram had cast away in their haste* (*II Kings* 7:15).

11. עַד אָנָה יְנַאֲצֻנִי — *How far shall (this people) provoke Me?* To what extent of contempt shall I tolerate their contempt of Me?

וְעַד אָנָה לֹא יַאֲמִינוּ בִי — *And to what extent will they not believe in Me?* And to what extent must I perform wonders before they will trust Me and rely upon My word?

12. אַכֶּנּוּ בַדֶּבֶר — *I will smite them with pestilence* ... similar to, וְגַם יַד ה׳ הָיְתָה בָּם לְהֻמָּם מִקֶּרֶב הַמַּחֲנֶה עַד תֻּמָּם, *And also the hand of* HASHEM *was against them to destroy them from the midst of the camp until they were spent* (*Deut.* 2:15).

וְאוֹרִשֶׁנּוּ — *And they will inherit them.* I will cause them to *leave over their possessions to others* (based on *Psalms* 49:11) and they (the others) will inherit them, similar to 'the dead were heirs to the living' (*Bava Basra* 117a) regarding the division of the Land. Thereby He fulfilled (His) vow to those who came out of Egypt, when He said, וְנָתַתִּי אֹתָהּ לָכֶם מוֹרָשָׁה, *And I will give it to you as a heritage* (*Exodus* 6:8).

NOTES

ing which they refute the claims of the other spies. Regarding the Land itself, they insist that it is exceedingly good, and as for the inhabitants, they will not put up any resistance. The former they submit in order to refute the false claim that *Eretz Yisrael* is a land which *consumes its inhabitants*, and the latter they underscore in order to give the Israelites courage and strengthen their trust in God. They stress, however, that their triumphant entry into the Land, as well as the blessings of the Land, depend completely upon their finding favor in God's eyes, which can only be possible if they do not rebel against Him.

9. סָר צִלָּם מֵעֲלֵיהֶם — *Their defense is departed from them.* The *Ramban* and *Ibn Ezra* both interpret צִלָּם (lit., their shadow) in the sense of a person's defense, comparing a warrior's weapons to a protective shadow. *Ibn Ezra* writes, 'If the mighty warrior has no shield with which to protect himself and serve as a shadow for him, his heart is afraid.' The *Sforno* follows their method of interpretation in his commentary as well.

11. עַד אָנָה יְנַאֲצֻנִי ... וְעַד אָנָה לֹא יַאֲמִינוּ בִי — *How far shall (this people) provoke me? And to what extent will they not believe in Me?* The Hebrew phrase אָנָה is interpreted by *Rashi* to mean 'how long;' not 'how far.' The former refers to time while the latter denotes place. (See the *Sifsei Chachamim* on *Rashi* here.) The *Sforno* prefers the latter interpretation — עַד אֵיזֶה גְּבוּל (lit., to what boundary) meaning, how far can My patience be tried and to what outer limits of wonders must I extend myself in order to evoke Israel's trust in Me?

12. וְאוֹרִשֶׁנּוּ — *And they will inherit them. Rashi* explains the word וְאוֹרִשֶׁנּוּ as meaning 'a cutting off or driving out.' He interprets the phrase יוֹרִשֶׁנָּה in verse 24 in a similar manner. The *Sforno*, however, interprets both of these phrases as meaning 'inheritance' or 'bequeathing,' i.e., in the sense of יְרוּשָׁה. The Sages in tractate *Bava Basra* (117a) disagree regarding the division of *Eretz Yisrael* among the tribes of Israel. Rabbi Josiah states that the Land was divided according to those who came out of Egypt (לְיוֹצְאֵי מִצְרַיִם נִתְחַלְּקָה הָאָרֶץ), i.e., it was divided according to the number of men that left Egypt, and not according to the number that entered Canaan. Rabbi Jonathan is of the opinion that the Land was divided according to those who entered it, and not according to

יג לְגוֹי־גָּדוֹל וְעָצוּם מִמֶּנּוּ: וַיֹּאמֶר מֹשֶׁה אֶל־יהוה וְשָׁמְעוּ מִצְרַיִם כִּי־הֶעֱלִיתָ
יד בְכֹחֲךָ אֶת־הָעָם הַזֶּה מִקִּרְבּוֹ: וְאָמְרוּ אֶל־יוֹשֵׁב הָאָרֶץ הַזֹּאת שָׁמְעוּ
כִּי־אַתָּה יהוה בְּקֶרֶב הָעָם הַזֶּה אֲשֶׁר־עַיִן בְּעַיִן נִרְאָה | אַתָּה יהוה וַעֲנָנְךָ
עֹמֵד עֲלֵהֶם וּבְעַמֻּד עָנָן אַתָּה הֹלֵךְ לִפְנֵיהֶם יוֹמָם וּבְעַמּוּד אֵשׁ לָיְלָה:
טו וְהֵמַתָּה אֶת־הָעָם הַזֶּה כְּאִישׁ אֶחָד וְאָמְרוּ הַגּוֹיִם אֲשֶׁר־שָׁמְעוּ אֶת־שִׁמְעֲךָ
טז לֵאמֹר: מִבִּלְתִּי יְכֹלֶת יהוה לְהָבִיא אֶת־הָעָם הַזֶּה אֶל־הָאָרֶץ אֲשֶׁר־נִשְׁבַּע
יז לָהֶם וַיִּשְׁחָטֵם בַּמִּדְבָּר: וְעַתָּה יִגְדַּל־נָא כֹּחַ אֲדֹנָי כַּאֲשֶׁר דִּבַּרְתָּ לֵאמֹר:

---

13. וְשָׁמְעוּ מִצְרַיִם — *When the Egyptians hear.* Moses thought that when God, the Blessed One, said, *I will smite them with pestilence,* the intent was to smite all of them immediately, and so he was moved to ask what will happen to His Great Name, and he said, 'Behold, the Egyptians will immediately hear that You killed these (people) suddenly, and they will say that You did so because You *were not able* (verse 16) to (overcome) the inhabitants of this land (Canaan). This (they will say) because, indeed, they saw that *You brought up this people from their midst in Your might,* and (also) *they have heard that You, HASHEM, are in the midst of this people* (verse 14); (hence) they will not think that their downfall was due to Your leaving them because of their iniquities.'

14. אֲשֶׁר עַיִן בְּעַיִן נִרְאָה אַתָּה ה׳ — *That face to face* (lit., *eye to eye*), *You, HASHEM, were seen* ... the eye of Your Providence (supervision) over them, has already been seen in its reality (by Israel).

וַעֲנָנְךָ עֹמֵד עֲלֵהֶם — *And Your cloud stands over them* ... in the present, as it says, כִּי עֲנַן ה׳ עַל הַמִּשְׁכָּן יוֹמָם וְאֵשׁ תִּהְיֶה לַיְלָה בּוֹ לְעֵינֵי כָל בֵּית יִשְׂרָאֵל בְּכָל מַסְעֵיהֶם, *For the cloud of HASHEM was on the Sanctuary by day, and a fire was on it by night, before the eyes of all the house of Israel throughout all their journeys* (Exodus 40:38).

17. יִגְדַּל נָא כֹּחַ ה׳ — *Let the power of HASHEM be great* ... so as to conquer (overcome) the attribute of justice.

NOTES

the number of those who came out of Egypt (לְבָאֵי הָאָרֶץ נִתְחַלְּקָה הָאָרֶץ). Explaining his opinion, Rabbi Jonathan adds, 'this manner of inheritance is different from all others ... for in the case of all others, the living are heirs to the dead, but in this case, the dead were heirs to the living.' The meaning of this cryptic statement is that those who entered the Land received shares according to their numbers, but these shares were considered to belong to the fathers who came out of Egypt (even though they were dead), and then in turn reverted to and were 'inherited' by the sons. Hence, although the generation that left Egypt was destined to die out, nonetheless, they would still inherit the Land through their children. In this manner, God's promise to the people of Israel in Egypt that *I shall give it to you as a heritage* (Exodus 6:8) was still fulfilled even though that generation did not actually enter the Land.

13-14. וְשָׁמְעוּ מִצְרַיִם ... אֲשֶׁר עַיִן בְּעַיִן נִרְאָה אַתָּה ה׳ וַעֲנָנְךָ עֹמֵד עֲלֵהֶם — *When the Egyptians hear ... That face to face* (lit., *eye to eye*), *You, HASHEM, were seen and Your cloud stands over them.* The meaning of these verses according to the *Sforno* is as follows: The Egyptians had witnessed the greatness and might of the Almighty in Egypt and the Exodus of the Israelites through His Omnipotence. They had also heard of God's Presence in the midst of Israel and were unaware of any reason for Him to abandon them. Were He to slay them all at one time, the reason could only be because He was unable to overcome the inhabitants of Canaan and bring the Israelites into the

יח יהוה אֶרֶךְ אַפַּיִם וְרַב־חֶסֶד נֹשֵׂא עָוֺן וָפָשַׁע וְנַקֵּה לֹא יְנַקֶּה פֹּקֵד עֲוֺן אָבוֹת
יט עַל־בָּנִים עַל־שִׁלֵּשִׁים וְעַל־רִבֵּעִים: סְלַח־נָא לַעֲוֺן הָעָם הַזֶּה כְּגֹדֶל חַסְדֶּךָ
כ וְכַאֲשֶׁר נָשָׂאתָה לָעָם הַזֶּה מִמִּצְרַיִם וְעַד־הֵנָּה: וַיֹּאמֶר יהוה סָלַחְתִּי
כא־כב כִּדְבָרֶךָ: וְאוּלָם חַי־אָנִי וְיִמָּלֵא כְבוֹד־יהוה אֶת־כָּל־הָאָרֶץ: כִּי כָל־
הָאֲנָשִׁים הָרֹאִים אֶת־כְּבֹדִי וְאֶת־אֹתֹתַי אֲשֶׁר־עָשִׂיתִי בְמִצְרַיִם וּבַמִּדְבָּר
כג וַיְנַסּוּ אֹתִי זֶה עֶשֶׂר פְּעָמִים וְלֹא שָׁמְעוּ בְּקוֹלִי: אִם־יִרְאוּ אֶת־הָאָרֶץ אֲשֶׁר

---

18. פֹּקֵד עֲוֺן אָבוֹת עַל בָּנִים — *Visiting the iniquity of the fathers upon the children.* He is long-suffering (containing His anger) until the fourth generation. If they (the children) hold fast to the (evil) deeds of their fathers and even increase (their) wickedness, then their measure becomes full in the third generation and the hope for their repentance is lost and He exacts payment (i.e., punishment) from them. If they hold fast to the (evil) ways of their fathers, but do not increase in their wicked ways, then (God) waits until the fourth generation, and then their measure will be full, for there is no hope that they will repent, and they will perish.

20. סָלַחְתִּי כִּדְבָרֶךָ — *I have pardoned according to your word.* When I said, *I will smite them with pestilence,* I had already forgiven them in the manner which you are (now) saying, because My intent was not to put them to death all together. Rather, (it was) to have them die gradually in the wilderness, and that no man among them would enter the Land.

21. וְאוּלָם חַי אָנִי וְיִמָּלֵא כְבוֹד ה׳ אֶת כָּל הָאָרֶץ — *However, as surely as I live and as the whole earth will be full of the glory of* HASHEM. However, I swear that as it is true that I live and that all the earth will be filled with My glory, so it will be true that all the men who are twenty years (and older) . . .

23. אִם יִרְאוּ אֶת הָאָרֶץ — *Shall surely not see the Land.* They will *not* see the Land, in keeping with (the general principle) that every expression אִם, *if,* when not followed by a double תְּנַאי, *condition,* (is a negative). (This is) similar to, אִם מִחוּט וְעַד שְׂרוֹךְ נַעַל וְאִם אֶקַּח מִכָּל אֲשֶׁר לָךְ, *I will not take so much as a thread or a shoelace, and I will not take anything that is yours* (Genesis 14:23) and חַי ה׳ אִם יוּמָת, *As* HASHEM *lives, he will not be slain* (*I Samuel* 19:6) and other similar verses.

NOTES

Land. This, in turn, would cause His great Name to be desecrated.

17. יִגְדַּל נָא כֹּחַ ה׳ — *Let the power of* HASHEM *be great.* 'HASHEM' represents the attribute of mercy. Moses asks God to strengthen that attribute to the point where it will overcome and override the attribute of justice (God).

18. פֹּקֵד עֲוֺן אָבוֹת עַל בָּנִים — *Visiting the iniquity of the fathers upon the children.* See the *Sforno* on *Exodus* 20:5 and the notes.

20. סָלַחְתִּי כִּדְבָרֶךָ — *I have pardoned according to your word.* The expression סָלַחְתִּי, *I have forgiven,* is in the past tense. The *Sforno* explains this to mean that God was not responding to the argument of Moses. Rather, Moses had misunderstood God's statement of אַכֶּנּוּ בַדֶּבֶר, *I will smite them with pestilence,* for he thought it would take place at once, but God now tells him that the Divine plan, in any event, was to bring about the death of the present generation over a period of many years. Hence, כִּדְבָרֶךָ, *according to your word,* does not mean as *Rashi* says, 'because of what you have said.' The *Sforno's* view is that it means that your request, not to slay all of them immediately, was My original intent. Hence, God does not 'change His mind' — for He is unchanging.

כד נִשְׁבַּ֖עְתִּי לַאֲבֹתָ֑ם וְכָל־מְנַאֲצַ֖י לֹ֥א יִרְאֽוּהָ׃ וְעַבְדִּ֣י כָלֵ֗ב עֵ֣קֶב הָֽיְתָ֞ה ר֤וּחַ
אַחֶ֙רֶת֙ עִמּ֔וֹ וַיְמַלֵּ֖א אַחֲרָ֑י וַהֲבִֽיאֹתִ֗יו אֶל־הָאָ֙רֶץ֙ אֲשֶׁר־בָּ֣א שָׁ֔מָּה וְזַרְע֖וֹ
כה יוֹרִשֶֽׁנָּה׃ וְהָעֲמָלֵקִ֥י וְהַֽכְּנַעֲנִ֖י יוֹשֵׁ֣ב בָּעֵ֑מֶק מָחָ֗ר פְּנ֨וּ וּסְע֥וּ לָכֶ֛ם הַמִּדְבָּ֖ר דֶּ֥רֶךְ
יַם־סֽוּף׃
רביעי כו־כז וַיְדַבֵּ֣ר יְהוֹ֔ה אֶל־מֹשֶׁ֥ה וְאֶֽל־אַהֲרֹ֖ן לֵאמֹֽר׃ עַד־מָתַ֗י לָעֵדָ֤ה הָֽרָעָה֙ הַזֹּ֔את
אֲשֶׁ֛ר הֵ֥מָּה מַלִּינִ֖ים עָלָ֑י אֶת־תְּלֻנּ֞וֹת בְּנֵ֣י יִשְׂרָאֵ֗ל אֲשֶׁ֨ר הֵ֧מָּה מַלִּינִ֛ים עָלַ֖י

וְכָל מְנַאֲצַי לֹא יִרְאוּהָ — *And all those who angered Me shall not see it* . . . and also, their children who are not (included) in this decree since they have not yet reached the age of twenty, all who will anger Me in the future will not see it (the Land), as happened with those who died (as a result) of the episode of Korach (chapter 16), the matter of Pe'or (chapter 25) and the fiery serpents (chapter 21).

24. וְזַרְעוֹ יוֹרִשֶׁנָּה — *And his seed shall inherit it.* He shall bequeath it to his seed unlike the rest of the generation of the wilderness, for although their children inherited from them (their fathers), they (the original members of that wilderness generation) were not the bequeathers. Rather, God, the Blessed One, bequeathed an arrangement in accordance with His commandment to the distributors of the Land, as (the Torah) attests, saying, וְאוֹרִשֶׁנּוּ, *And they will inherit them* (verse 12).

27. עַד מָתַי לָעֵדָה הָרָעָה הַזֹּאת — *How long shall this evil congregation.* Although I have pardoned in accordance with your words (request), and will be forbearing so as not to slay them immediately, nor all at one time; nonetheless, I have not forgiven the congregation of the spies (themselves).

אֲשֶׁר הֵמָּה מַלִּינִים עָלָי — *That keeps murmuring against Me* . . . for they caused others to sin, and (the responsibility for) the sin of the multitude lies with them; hence, I shall not practice forbearance with them at all. And because of this *murmuring of the Children of Israel which they,* i.e., the spies, *keep murmuring against Me, have I heard,* and I (now) set My face (against them) to punish them — therefore . . .

NOTES

23. וְכָל מְנַאֲצַי לֹא יִרְאוּהָ — *And all those who angered Me shall not see it.* Since God had already decreed that this generation would not merit to *see the Land,* why then is it necessary to add the words, *And all those who angered Me shall not see it?* The *Sforno* explains that this latter phrase refers to those who were under twenty years of age at the time of the decree and therefore not included in this decree, but because they were guilty of other transgressions (such as joining the congregation of Korach, etc.) they would also not merit to see the land.

24. וְזַרְעוֹ יוֹרִשֶׁנָּה — *And his seed shall inherit it.* As in verse 12, the *Sforno* differs from *Rashi* who interprets the word יוֹרִשֶׁנָּה to mean 'drive them out.' *Sforno* interprets it to mean 'he will bequeath it'; i.e., Caleb alone, of the generation that went forth from Egypt, will merit to bequeath his portion of the Land to his children, unlike the others who never actually possessed their share in the Land. See verse 12 above and the note there. The *Sforno* apparently finds *Rashi's* explanation difficult since Caleb himself, and not his offspring, drove out the children of Anak from Hebron and its environs (see *Joshua* 14-15).

27. אֲשֶׁר הֵמָּה מַלִּינִים עָלָי — *That keeps murmuring against Me.* Although repentance is always accepted, nonetheless, there are times when one is not assisted from Heaven and this assistance is vital in bringing a person to this end. The *Sforno* interprets this verse as indicating God's determination to prevent the spies from repenting because they were guilty of causing others to sin as well, and our Sages teach us, 'One who influences the masses to sin will not be given the means to achieve repentance' (*Avos* 5:21).

כח שָׁמָֽעְתִּי׃ אֱמֹר אֲלֵהֶם חַי־אָנִי נְאֻם־יהוה אִם־לֹא כַּאֲשֶׁר דִּבַּרְתֶּם בְּאָזְנָי כֵּן
כט אֶעֱשֶׂה לָכֶם׃ בַּמִּדְבָּר הַזֶּה יִפְּלוּ פִגְרֵיכֶם וְכָל־פְּקֻדֵיכֶם לְכָל־מִסְפַּרְכֶם מִבֶּן
ל עֶשְׂרִים שָׁנָה וָמָעְלָה אֲשֶׁר הֲלִינֹתֶם עָלָי׃ אִם־אַתֶּם תָּבֹאוּ אֶל־הָאָרֶץ
אֲשֶׁר נָשָׂאתִי אֶת־יָדִי לְשַׁכֵּן אֶתְכֶם בָּהּ כִּי אִם־כָּלֵב בֶּן־יְפֻנֶּה וִיהוֹשֻׁעַ
לא בִּן־נוּן׃ וְטַפְּכֶם אֲשֶׁר אֲמַרְתֶּם לָבַז יִהְיֶה וְהֵבֵיאתִי אֹתָם וְיָדְעוּ אֶת־הָאָרֶץ
לב-לג אֲשֶׁר מְאַסְתֶּם בָּהּ׃ וּפִגְרֵיכֶם אַתֶּם יִפְּלוּ בַּמִּדְבָּר הַזֶּה׃ וּבְנֵיכֶם יִהְיוּ רֹעִים
בַּמִּדְבָּר אַרְבָּעִים שָׁנָה וְנָשְׂאוּ אֶת־זְנוּתֵיכֶם עַד־תֹּם פִּגְרֵיכֶם בַּמִּדְבָּר׃
לד בְּמִסְפַּר הַיָּמִים אֲשֶׁר־תַּרְתֶּם אֶת־הָאָרֶץ אַרְבָּעִים יוֹם יוֹם לַשָּׁנָה יוֹם לַשָּׁנָה
לה תִּשְׂאוּ אֶת־עֲוֺנֹתֵיכֶם אַרְבָּעִים שָׁנָה וִידַעְתֶּם אֶת־תְּנוּאָתִי׃ אֲנִי יהוה

---

28. אֱמֹר אֲלֵהֶם חַי אָנִי נְאֻם ה׳ אִם לֹא — *Say unto them: As I live, says* H*ASHEM, as you have* (*spoken*). (These are) two negatives in place of a positive. This means to say, that indeed, (it shall be) *as you have spoken in My ears* when you said, *or would we had died in this wilderness* (verse 2) and when you said, *our wives and children will become a prey* (verse 3) and also when the spies said, *a land that consumes its inhabitants* (13:32) — all this will be fulfilled with you!

כֵּן אֶעֱשֶׂה לָכֶם — *So I will do to you* . . . at various (different) times. And to this He swore, as the psalmist attests, saying, וַיִּשָּׂא יָדוֹ לָהֶם לְהַפִּיל אוֹתָם בַּמִּדְבָּר. וּלְהַפִּיל זַרְעָם בַּגּוֹיִם, *And He lifted up His hand against them to throw them down in the wilderness. And to throw down their descendants among the nations* (*Psalms* 106:26, 27), and also Ezekiel (who) says, גַּם אֲנִי נָשָׂאתִי אֶת יָדִי לָהֶם בַּמִּדְבָּר לְהָפִיץ אֹתָם בַּגּוֹיִם, *I lifted up my hand to them also in the wilderness, to scatter them among the nations* (*Ezekiel* 20:23).

33. וְנָשְׂאוּ אֶת זְנוּתֵיכֶם — *And will bear your defections* . . . for you rebelled against Me when you said, *Let us appoint a chief etc.* (verse 4).

34. בְּמִסְפַּר הַיָּמִים — *According to the number of days* . . . that they (the spies) prolonged (their visit), in keeping with your (i.e., the people of Israel's) command, to determine whether it is possible to conquer it (the Land).

יוֹם לַשָּׁנָה — *A day for a year* . . . the Ninth Day of Av, each year, as explained in the last chapter of *tractate Taanis* (30b).

תְּנוּאָתִי — *My removal.* You will recognize how bad it is to nullify My intent, by turning away from it, as it says, *and you will fall by the sword because you turned back from following* H*ASHEM* (verse 43).

NOTES

34. יוֹם לַשָּׁנָה — *A day for a year.* The *Sforno* overcomes the difficulty presented by the expression יוֹם לַשָּׁנָה, *a day for a year,* which would have been better expressed in the reverse שָׁנָה לַיּוֹם, *a year for a day,* by applying the statement of our Sages in tractate *Taanis* 30b to these two words. There, we are told that during the 40-year trek in the wilderness, on the Ninth of Av, the day marking the return of the spies and the consequent 'mourning' of the Children of Israel, every person dug a grave and went to sleep in it. The next morning, those who were still alive arose, while those who died during the night were buried. With this Talmudic interpretation, the *Sforno* explains the expression, יוֹם לַשָּׁנָה, as meaning that on a specific day each year they shall pay for their sin. This will also clarify the reason for the repetition of the phrase יוֹם לַשָּׁנָה — since this occurred each year for forty years.

תְּנוּאָתִי — *My removal.* Although the phrase תְּנוּאָתִי means *My removal* or turning away,

דִּבַּ֫רְתִּי֙ אִם־לֹ֣א ׀ זֹ֣את אֶֽעֱשֶׂ֗ה לְכָל־הָעֵדָ֤ה הָֽרָעָה֙ הַזֹּ֔את הַנּוֹעָדִ֖ים עָלָ֑י
לו בַּמִּדְבָּ֥ר הַזֶּ֛ה יִתַּ֖מּוּ וְשָׁ֥ם יָמֻֽתוּ: וְהָ֣אֲנָשִׁ֔ים אֲשֶׁר־שָׁלַ֥ח מֹשֶׁ֖ה לָת֣וּר
°וַיֵּלֹ֖ינוּ ק אֶת־הָאָ֑רֶץ וַיָּשֻׁ֗בוּ °וַיִּלּ֤ונוּ עָלָיו֙ אֶת־כָּל־הָ֣עֵדָ֔ה לְהוֹצִ֥יא דִבָּ֖ה עַל־הָאָֽרֶץ:
לז־לח וַיָּמֻ֙תוּ֙ הָֽאֲנָשִׁ֔ים מֽוֹצִאֵ֥י דִבַּת־הָאָ֖רֶץ רָעָ֑ה בַּמַּגֵּפָ֖ה לִפְנֵ֥י יהוֹה: וִֽיהוֹשֻׁ֙עַ֙
בִּן־נ֔וּן וְכָלֵ֖ב בֶּן־יְפֻנֶּ֑ה חָיוּ֙ מִן־הָֽאֲנָשִׁ֣ים הָהֵ֔ם הַהֹֽלְכִ֖ים לָת֥וּר אֶת־הָאָֽרֶץ:
לט וַיְדַבֵּ֤ר מֹשֶׁה֙ אֶת־הַדְּבָרִ֣ים הָאֵ֔לֶּה אֶֽל־כָּל־בְּנֵ֖י יִשְׂרָאֵ֑ל וַיִּֽתְאַבְּל֥וּ הָעָ֖ם
מ מְאֹֽד: וַיַּשְׁכִּ֣מוּ בַבֹּ֔קֶר וַיַּֽעֲל֥וּ אֶל־רֹאשׁ־הָהָ֖ר לֵאמֹ֑ר הִנֶּ֗נּוּ וְעָלִ֛ינוּ אֶל־הַמָּק֛וֹם
מא אֲשֶׁר־אָמַ֥ר יהוֹה֖ כִּ֣י חָטָֽאנוּ: וַיֹּ֣אמֶר מֹשֶׁ֔ה לָ֥מָּה זֶּ֛ה אַתֶּ֥ם עֹֽבְרִ֖ים אֶת־פִּ֣י
מב יהוֹ֑ה וְהִ֖וא לֹ֣א תִצְלָֽח: אַל־תַּֽעֲל֗וּ כִּ֣י אֵ֤ין יהוֹה֙ בְּקִרְבְּכֶ֔ם וְלֹא֙ תִּנָּ֣גְפ֔וּ לִפְנֵ֥י

---

36. וְהָאֲנָשִׁים אֲשֶׁר שָׁלַח מֹשֶׁה — *And the men whom Moses had sent . . .* who were loyal to him and then became his enemies.

וַיָּשֻׁבוּ וַיַּלִּינוּ עָלָיו אֶת כָּל הָעֵדָה — *And who, when they returned, caused all the congregation to murmur against him.* (The word עֵדָה) refers to the Sanhedrin and the leaders of the people (who reacted) when they (the spies) said, *for they are stronger than we* (13:31). Now this was done to submit an evil report against the Land, for while the elders were occupied in their murmuring, they (the spies) in turn could submit an evil report against the Land to the multitude. This they could not have done in the presence of the elders who knew and (would) recognize their falsehood.

37. וַיָּמֻתוּ הָאֲנָשִׁים מוֹצִאֵי דִבַּת הָאָרֶץ רָעָה בַּמַּגֵּפָה — *And these men who had brought up the evil report of the Land died by the plague . . .* by the same plague which they said would occur in the land which *consumes its inhabitants* (13:32). Behold, the effect of the climate of the land (in which they now were) became loathsome to them and they died immediately.

41. לָמָּה זֶה אַתֶּם עֹבְרִים אֶת פִּי ה' וְהִוא לֹא תִצְלָח — *Why do you transgress the order of HASHEM, (being that) it will not succeed.* Because, in this manner, you will be considered sinners, not (seeking to satisfy your) desire or for your own pleasure, but rather (in order) to anger (me).

NOTES

and according to the *Sforno's* commentary, the Torah should have written תְּנוּאַתְיכֶם, *Your turning away,* nonetheless, the Torah's choice of expression can be explained thus: When a man turns away from God, the Almighty turns away from him. Your removal, God says, has caused תְּנוּאָתִי, *My removal,* and the withdrawal of My protection from Israel.

36. וַיָּשֻׁבוּ וַיַּלִּינוּ עָלָיו אֶת כָּל הָעֵדָה — *And who, when they returned, caused all the congregation to murmur against him.* The *Sforno* divides the verse into two parts. The first part states that the spies initially incited the leaders of the people, i.e., the Sanhedrin, who are called עֵדָה ('congregation' — a term of importance), by telling them their misgivings re-

garding the inhabitants of the Land who, in their opinion, were too mighty to be conquered. This judgment even the Sanhedrin could accept. The spies then spoke against the Land itself to the masses, deprecating its character and worth — a qualitative judgement which the Sanhedrin would never have accepted. But these leaders were so occupied with murmuring among themselves regarding the might of the inhabitants of Canaan that they were not even present to refute the spies when they spread calumnies about the Land to the multitude.

37. וַיָּמֻתוּ הָאֲנָשִׁים מוֹצִאֵי דִבַּת הָאָרֶץ רָעָה בַּמַּגֵּפָה — *And these men who had brought up the evil report of the Land died by the plague.* The *Sforno* explains the cause of the plague, in

מג אֹיְבֵיכֶֽם: כִּ֣י הָֽעֲמָלֵקִ֤י וְהַֽכְּנַעֲנִי֙ שָׁ֣ם לִפְנֵיכֶ֔ם וּנְפַלְתֶּ֖ם בֶּחָ֑רֶב כִּֽי־עַל־כֵּ֣ן
מד שַׁבְתֶּם֙ מֵֽאַחֲרֵ֣י יהוֹה וְלֹא־יִֽהְיֶ֥ה יהוֹה עִמָּכֶֽם: וַיַּעְפִּ֕לוּ לַֽעֲל֖וֹת אֶל־רֹ֣אשׁ
מה הָהָ֑ר וַֽאֲר֤וֹן בְּרִֽית־יהוֹה֙ וּמֹשֶׁ֔ה לֹא־מָ֖שׁוּ מִקֶּ֥רֶב הַֽמַּחֲנֶֽה: וַיֵּ֤רֶד הָֽעֲמָלֵקִי֙
וְהַֽכְּנַעֲנִ֗י הַיֹּשֵׁ֖ב בָּהָ֣ר הַה֑וּא וַיַּכּ֥וּם וַֽיַּכְּת֖וּם עַד־הַֽחָרְמָֽה:

טו א-ב וַיְדַבֵּ֥ר יהוֹה אֶל־מֹשֶׁ֖ה לֵּאמֹֽר: דַּבֵּר֙ אֶל־בְּנֵ֣י יִשְׂרָאֵ֔ל וְאָֽמַרְתָּ֖ אֲלֵהֶ֑ם כִּ֣י
ג תָבֹ֗אוּ אֶל־אֶ֨רֶץ֙ מֽוֹשְׁבֹ֣תֵיכֶ֔ם אֲשֶׁ֥ר אֲנִ֖י נֹתֵ֥ן לָכֶֽם: וַֽעֲשִׂיתֶ֨ם אִשֶּׁ֤ה לַֽיהוֹה֙
עֹלָ֣ה אֽוֹ־זֶ֗בַח לְפַלֵּא־נֶ֨דֶר֙ א֣וֹ בִנְדָבָ֔ה א֖וֹ בְּמֹֽעֲדֵיכֶ֑ם לַֽעֲשׂ֞וֹת רֵ֤יחַ נִיחֹ֨חַ֙
ד לַֽיהוֹה מִן־הַבָּקָ֖ר א֣וֹ מִן־הַצֹּֽאן: וְהִקְרִ֛יב הַמַּקְרִ֥יב קָרְבָּנ֖וֹ לַֽיהוֹה מִנְחָה֙ סֹ֣לֶת

---

44. וַיַּעְפִּלוּ — *And they persisted.* They hardened their hearts, similar to, וַיְחֲזֵק לֵב פַּרְעֹה וְלֹא שָׁמַע אֲלֵהֶם, *The heart of Pharaoh was hardened and he did not listen to them* (Exodus 7:13).

45. וַיֵּרֶד הָעֲמָלֵקִי — *And the Amalekites came down* . . . and did not permit them to go up.

XV

3-4. . . . רֵיחַ נִיחֹחַ לַה׳ . . . וְהִקְרִיב הַמַּקְרִיב — *A sweet savor to* HASHEM . . . *And he who brings the offering shall bring.* Behold, until (the sin of) the Golden Calf, an offering was *a satisfying aroma* (to God) even without a meal-offering and drink-offering, similar to (the offerings brought by) Abel, Noah and Abraham, and similar to וַיִּשְׁלַח אֶת נַעֲרֵי בְּנֵי יִשְׂרָאֵל וַיַּעֲלוּ עֹלֹת וַיִּזְבְּחוּ זְבָחִים שְׁלָמִים לַה׳ פָּרִים, *And he sent the young men of the Children of Israel and they offered burnt offerings and sacrificed peace-offerings of oxen to* HASHEM (Exodus 24:5), i.e., without (bringing) these (נְסָכִים and מְנָחוֹת). (However) when they sinned with the Golden Calf, (the Torah) required that a meal-offering and drink-offering (be brought) with the daily burnt offering, which is a communal offering; and from the time they sinned (in the incident of) the spies, a meal-offering and drink-offering were also needed to qualify (לְהַכְשִׁיר) an individual offering.

NOTES

keeping with the principle of מִדָּה כְּנֶגֶד מִדָּה, *measure for measure.*

41. לָמָּה זֶּה אַתֶּם עֹבְרִים אֶת פִּי ה׳ וְהִוא לֹא תִצְלָח — *Why do you transgress the order of* HASHEM, *(being that) it will not succeed.* Once Moses told them that their efforts to go up the mountain were doomed to failure, their insistence upon doing so became לְהַכְעִיס, utterly provocative — and the punishment in such cases is swift and harsh.

44. וַיַּעְפִּלוּ — *And they persisted.* See Rashi who, indeed, interprets the root of the word וַיַּעְפִּלוּ as an expression of חוֹזֶק, *insolent force,* characterizing the nature of Israel's persistence. The *Sforno* follows his view.

XV

3-4. רֵיחַ נִיחֹחַ לַה׳ . . . וְהִקְרִיב הַמַּקְרִיב — *A sweet savor to* HASHEM . . . *And he who brings the offering shall bring.* The obligation to bring מְנָחוֹת וּנְסָכִים, *meal-offerings and libations,* as an accompaniment to the קָרְבַּן תָּמִיד, *daily communal offering,* was already ordained in *Exodus* 29 and in regard to the קָרְבַּן מוּסָף, *additional offering,* it is mentioned later in *Numbers* 28. In our present chapter, Israel is commanded to bring נְסָכִים with every קָרְבַּן יָחִיד, *individual offering,* as well. The *Sforno* explains that there were three periods in which the law regarding offerings differed. Originally, no נְסָכִים were necessary. After the sin of the Golden Calf, they were commanded to bring them with communal offerings, and

ה עִשָּׂרוֹן בָּלוּל בִּרְבִעִית הַהִין שָׁמֶן: וְיַיִן לַנֶּסֶךְ רְבִיעִית הַהִין תַּעֲשֶׂה
ו עַל־הָעֹלָה אוֹ לַזָּבַח לַכֶּבֶשׂ הָאֶחָד: אוֹ לָאַיִל תַּעֲשֶׂה מִנְחָה סֹלֶת שְׁנֵי
ז עֶשְׂרֹנִים בְּלוּלָה בַשֶּׁמֶן שְׁלִשִׁית הַהִין: וְיַיִן לַנֶּסֶךְ שְׁלִשִׁית הַהִין תַּקְרִיב
חמישי ח רֵיחַ־נִיחֹחַ לַיהוָה: וְכִי־תַעֲשֶׂה בֶן־בָּקָר עֹלָה אוֹ־זָבַח לְפַלֵּא־נֶדֶר
ט אוֹ־שְׁלָמִים לַיהוָה: וְהִקְרִיב עַל־בֶּן־הַבָּקָר מִנְחָה סֹלֶת שְׁלֹשָׁה עֶשְׂרֹנִים
י בָּלוּל בַּשֶּׁמֶן חֲצִי הַהִין: וְיַיִן תַּקְרִיב לַנֶּסֶךְ חֲצִי הַהִין אִשֵּׁה רֵיחַ־נִיחֹחַ
יא לַיהוָה: כָּכָה יֵעָשֶׂה לַשּׁוֹר הָאֶחָד אוֹ לָאַיִל הָאֶחָד אוֹ־לַשֶּׂה בַכְּבָשִׂים אוֹ
יב־יג בָעִזִּים: כַּמִּסְפָּר אֲשֶׁר תַּעֲשׂוּ כָּכָה תַּעֲשׂוּ לָאֶחָד כְּמִסְפָּרָם: כָּל־הָאֶזְרָח
יד יַעֲשֶׂה־כָּכָה אֶת־אֵלֶּה לְהַקְרִיב אִשֵּׁה רֵיחַ־נִיחֹחַ לַיהוָה: וְכִי־יָגוּר אִתְּכֶם גֵּר
אוֹ אֲשֶׁר־בְּתוֹכְכֶם לְדֹרֹתֵיכֶם וְעָשָׂה אִשֵּׁה רֵיחַ־נִיחֹחַ לַיהוָה כַּאֲשֶׁר תַּעֲשׂוּ
טו כֵּן יַעֲשֶׂה: הַקָּהָל חֻקָּה אַחַת לָכֶם וְלַגֵּר הַגָּר חֻקַּת עוֹלָם לְדֹרֹתֵיכֶם כָּכֶם
טז כַּגֵּר יִהְיֶה לִפְנֵי יהוה: תּוֹרָה אַחַת וּמִשְׁפָּט אֶחָד יִהְיֶה לָכֶם וְלַגֵּר הַגָּר
אִתְּכֶם:
ששי יז־יח וַיְדַבֵּר יהוה אֶל־מֹשֶׁה לֵּאמֹר: דַּבֵּר אֶל־בְּנֵי יִשְׂרָאֵל וְאָמַרְתָּ אֲלֵהֶם
יט בְּבֹאֲכֶם אֶל־הָאָרֶץ אֲשֶׁר אֲנִי מֵבִיא אֶתְכֶם שָׁמָּה: וְהָיָה בַּאֲכָלְכֶם
כ מִלֶּחֶם הָאָרֶץ תָּרִימוּ תְרוּמָה לַיהוָה: רֵאשִׁית עֲרִסֹתֵכֶם חַלָּה
כא תָּרִימוּ תְרוּמָה כִּתְרוּמַת גֹּרֶן כֵּן תָּרִימוּ אֹתָהּ: מֵרֵאשִׁית עֲרִסֹתֵיכֶם
כב תִּתְּנוּ לַיהוָה תְּרוּמָה לְדֹרֹתֵיכֶם: וְכִי תִשְׁגּוּ

---

20. חַלָּה תָּרִימוּ תְרוּמָה — *You shall set apart challah as a heave-offering.* Following the sin of the spies, (the Torah) also instituted (the *mitzvah*) of *challah,* so that they would be worthy that a blessing come to rest in their homes, as it says, וְרֵאשִׁית עֲרִיסוֹתֵיכֶם תִּתְּנוּ לַכֹּהֵן לְהָנִיחַ בְּרָכָה אֶל בֵּיתֶךָ, *You shall give to the Kohen the first of your dough that he may cause a blessing to rest on your house* (*Ezekiel* 44:30), and (as we find) regarding Elijah, עֲשִׂי לִי מִשָּׁם עֻגָה קְטַנָּה בָרִאשֹׁנָה וְהוֹצֵאת לִי . . . כִּי כֹה אָמַר ה׳ . . . כַּד הַקֶּמַח לֹא תִכְלָה, *Make me a little cake of it first and bring it to me . . . for thus says HASHEM . . . the jar of flour shall not be spent* (*I Kings* 17:13, 14).

22. וְכִי תִשְׁגּוּ — *And if you err.* It has already been explained according to tradition, that this verse refers to the inadvertent transgression of idolatry (*Horayos* 8a). Now this (will happen) since it was decreed that *their descendants would be thrown down among the nations* (based on *Psalms* 106:27); therefore, it will not be unusual for them to err regarding idolatry when they return to their land.

NOTES

following the sin of the spies it was incumbent upon every individual who brought an offering to do so as well. As a result of these sins, it was necessary to compensate for them by adding a new dimension of devotion to God in order to make the offerings more acceptable — 'a sweet savor to God.' This interpretation explains why this particular commandment appears here, following the episode of the spies.

20. חַלָּה תָּרִימוּ תְרוּמָה — *You shall set apart challah as a heave-offering.* Just as in verse 4, the *Sforno* gives the reason for the Torah's inclusion of a particular commandment in this chapter.

כג וְלֹא תַעֲשׂוּ אֵת כָּל־הַמִּצְוֺת הָאֵלֶּה אֲשֶׁר־דִּבֶּר יהוה אֶל־מֹשֶׁה: אֵת
כָּל־אֲשֶׁר צִוָּה יהוה אֲלֵיכֶם בְּיַד־מֹשֶׁה מִן־הַיּוֹם אֲשֶׁר צִוָּה יהוה וָהָלְאָה
כד לְדֹרֹתֵיכֶם: וְהָיָה אִם מֵעֵינֵי הָעֵדָה נֶעֶשְׂתָה לִשְׁגָגָה וְעָשׂוּ כָל־הָעֵדָה פַּר
בֶּן־בָּקָר אֶחָד לְעֹלָה לְרֵיחַ נִיחֹחַ לַיהוה וּמִנְחָתוֹ וְנִסְכּוֹ כַּמִּשְׁפָּט
כה וּשְׂעִיר־עִזִּים אֶחָד לְחַטָּת: וְכִפֶּר הַכֹּהֵן עַל־כָּל־עֲדַת בְּנֵי יִשְׂרָאֵל וְנִסְלַח
לָהֶם כִּי־שְׁגָגָה הִוא וְהֵם הֵבִיאוּ אֶת־קָרְבָּנָם אִשֶּׁה לַיהוה וְחַטָּאתָם לִפְנֵי
כו יהוה עַל־שִׁגְגָתָם: וְנִסְלַח לְכָל־עֲדַת בְּנֵי יִשְׂרָאֵל וְלַגֵּר הַגָּר בְּתוֹכָם כִּי
שביעי כז לְכָל־הָעָם בִּשְׁגָגָה: וְאִם־נֶפֶשׁ אַחַת תֶּחֱטָא
כח בִשְׁגָגָה וְהִקְרִיבָה עֵז בַּת־שְׁנָתָהּ לְחַטָּאת: וְכִפֶּר הַכֹּהֵן עַל־הַנֶּפֶשׁ הַשֹּׁגֶגֶת
כט בְּחֶטְאָה בִשְׁגָגָה לִפְנֵי יהוה לְכַפֵּר עָלָיו וְנִסְלַח לוֹ: הָאֶזְרָח בִּבְנֵי יִשְׂרָאֵל
ל וְלַגֵּר הַגָּר בְּתוֹכָם תּוֹרָה אַחַת יִהְיֶה לָכֶם לָעֹשֶׂה בִּשְׁגָגָה: וְהַנֶּפֶשׁ
אֲשֶׁר־תַּעֲשֶׂה ׀ בְּיָד רָמָה מִן־הָאֶזְרָח וּמִן־הַגֵּר אֶת־יהוה הוּא מְגַדֵּף

וְלֹא תַעֲשׂוּ אֵת כָּל הַמִּצְוֺת הָאֵלֶּה אֲשֶׁר דִּבֶּר ה׳ אֶל מֹשֶׁה — *And do not observe all these commandments which* HASHEM *has spoken to Moses.* Since you will err regarding idolatry, hence even though you will (technically) perform all the acts of the commandments you will not be doing those *commandments which God spoke to Moses,* because He, the Blessed One, prefaced all (the commandments) with knowledge (recognition) of His Godliness, as it says, אָנֹכִי ה׳ אֱלֹהֶיךָ, *I am* HASHEM, *your God* (*Exodus* 20:2), and so (our Sages) have stated, 'He who accepts idolatry is as one who denies the entire Torah' (*Sifre*).

30. אֶת ה׳ הוּא מְגַדֵּף — *He has blasphemed* HASHEM . . . and he shall not be granted atonement in this world until he dies, even if he repents out of a fear of punishment. Therefore, the repentance of Israel in regard to (the sin of) the spies was to no avail, as it says, וַתָּשֻׁבוּ וַתִּבְכּוּ לִפְנֵי ה׳ וְלֹא שָׁמַע ה׳ בְּקֹלְכֶם, *And you returned and wept before* HASHEM, *but* HASHEM *did not hearken to your voice* (*Deut.* 1:45)

NOTES

22. וְכִי תִשְׁגּוּ וְלֹא תַעֲשׂוּ אֵת כָּל הַמִּצְוֺת הָאֵלֶּה אֲשֶׁר דִּבֶּר ה׳ אֶל מֹשֶׁה — *And if you err and do not observe all these commandments which* HASHEM *has spoken to Moses.* The *Sforno* explains why this grave sin of idolatry is written in this particular *parashah.* In the previous chapter (14:28), the *Sforno* cites the verse from *Psalms* (106:27) where the sin of the spies and the subsequent retribution (death in the wilderness) is linked to the punishment of exile, when their seed will be 'cast among the nations.' In the Diaspora, it is difficult for the Jew not to be influenced by the culture and beliefs of his host country. Hence, the law concerning idolatry follows the chapter of the spies.

The *Sforno* also explains why the non-observance of *all* the commandments of God will result if one is guilty of idolatry — even בְּשׁוֹגֵג (with no outright intent). A person can *perform* the *mitzvos* and still be deemed as one who has failed to do God's wish (רְצוֹן ה׳). Without recognizing a מְצַוֶּה, *one who commands,* there can be no מִצְוָה, *commandment.* The act of idolatry is a denial of God, and without a total unadulterated belief in the One God, performance of the *mitzvos* is meaningless. See *Rashi* here and in verse 23.

30. אֶת ה׳ הוּא מְגַדֵּף — *He has blasphemed* HASHEM. See note on 14:27 regarding repentance. One who blasphemes can only gain atonement through death. The Talmud (*Yoma* 86a) states that if one is guilty of חִלּוּל הַשֵּׁם (the profaning of God's Name), only death can atone for that sin. See *Rambam, Mishneh Torah, Laws of Teshuvah* 1:4. The *Sforno,*

לא וְנִכְרְתָה הַנֶּפֶשׁ הַהִוא מִקֶּרֶב עַמָּהּ: כִּי דְבַר־יהוה בָּזָה וְאֶת־מִצְוָתוֹ הֵפַר
הִכָּרֵת ׀ תִּכָּרֵת הַנֶּפֶשׁ הַהִוא עֲוֺנָה בָהּ:
לב וַיִּהְיוּ בְנֵי־יִשְׂרָאֵל בַּמִּדְבָּר וַיִּמְצְאוּ אִישׁ מְקֹשֵׁשׁ עֵצִים בְּיוֹם הַשַּׁבָּת:
לג וַיַּקְרִיבוּ אֹתוֹ הַמֹּצְאִים אֹתוֹ מְקֹשֵׁשׁ עֵצִים אֶל־מֹשֶׁה וְאֶל־אַהֲרֹן וְאֶל כָּל־
לד-לה הָעֵדָה: וַיַּנִּיחוּ אֹתוֹ בַּמִּשְׁמָר כִּי לֹא פֹרַשׁ מַה־יֵּעָשֶׂה לוֹ: וַיֹּאמֶר
יהוה אֶל־מֹשֶׁה מוֹת יוּמַת הָאִישׁ רָגוֹם אֹתוֹ בָאֲבָנִים כָּל־הָעֵדָה מִחוּץ
לו לַמַּחֲנֶה: וַיֹּצִיאוּ אֹתוֹ כָּל־הָעֵדָה אֶל־מִחוּץ לַמַּחֲנֶה וַיִּרְגְּמוּ אֹתוֹ בָּאֲבָנִים
וַיָּמֹת כַּאֲשֶׁר צִוָּה יהוה אֶת־מֹשֶׁה:
מפטיר לז-לח וַיֹּאמֶר יהוה אֶל־מֹשֶׁה לֵּאמֹר: דַּבֵּר אֶל־בְּנֵי יִשְׂרָאֵל וְאָמַרְתָּ אֲלֵהֶם
וְעָשׂוּ לָהֶם צִיצִת עַל־כַּנְפֵי בִגְדֵיהֶם לְדֹרֹתָם וְנָתְנוּ עַל־צִיצִת הַכָּנָף
לט פְּתִיל תְּכֵלֶת: וְהָיָה לָכֶם לְצִיצִת וּרְאִיתֶם אֹתוֹ וּזְכַרְתֶּם אֶת־כָּל־
מִצְוֺת יהוה וַעֲשִׂיתֶם אֹתָם וְלֹא תָתֻרוּ אַחֲרֵי לְבַבְכֶם וְאַחֲרֵי עֵינֵיכֶם

---

39. וּרְאִיתֶם אֹתוֹ וּזְכַרְתֶּם אֶת כָּל מִצְוֹת — *And you will see it and remember all the commandments of HASHEM.* You will remember that you are servants of God, the Blessed One, (and that) you accepted His commandments with an oath and a curse. This (shall be) when you see the *tzitzis* which are as the seal of the king (imprinted) on his servants. And thus you will cease to turn ...

אַחֲרֵי לְבַבְכֶם — *After your heart* ... to attain the caprice of your heart in terms of wealth and honor, even if it be through robbery.

וְאַחֲרֵי עֵינֵיכֶם — *And after your eyes* ... to attain the desires of that which you have laid your eyes upon.

NOTES

however, indicates that if one repents, motivated by אַהֲבָה (love, i.e., of God) rather than יִרְאָה (fear of punishment), his repentance will be accepted. Apparently the regret and repentance of the Children of Israel recorded in *Deut.* 1:45 was not in the category of תְּשׁוּבָה מֵאַהֲבָה, *repentance motivated by love.* See the *Sforno's* commentary there.

39. אַחֲרֵי לְבַבְכֶם וְאַחֲרֵי עֵינֵיכֶם אֲשֶׁר אַתֶּם זֹנִים אַחֲרֵיהֶם — *After your heart and after your eyes (in pursuit of) that by which you have been led astray.* The *Sforno* submits that the heart is greedy, propelling man to pursue and satisfy his desired goals even through dishonest, illegal means, while man's eyes are lustful and bring him to partake of forbidden pleasures. Both of these 'agents of the evil inclina-

מ אֲשֶׁר־אַתֶּם זֹנִים אַחֲרֵיהֶם: לְמַעַן תִּזְכְּרוּ וַעֲשִׂיתֶם אֶת־כָּל־מִצְוֺתָי וִהְיִיתֶם
מא קְדֹשִׁים לֵאלֹהֵיכֶם: אֲנִי יהוה אֱלֹהֵיכֶם אֲשֶׁר הוֹצֵאתִי אֶתְכֶם מֵאֶרֶץ
מִצְרַיִם לִהְיוֹת לָכֶם לֵאלֹהִים אֲנִי יהוה אֱלֹהֵיכֶם:

אֲשֶׁר אַתֶּם זֹנִים אַחֲרֵיהֶם — *(In pursuit of) that by which you have been led astray.* You turn your intelligent soul away from the ways of eternal life, to the ways of death and destruction.

40. לְמַעַן תִּזְכְּרוּ — *In order that you may remember* . . . in order that you may be free of vain thoughts, and thereby remember the wonders of Torah and through them recognize the greatness of God and His kindness.

וַעֲשִׂיתֶם אֶת כָּל מִצְוֺתָי — *And do all My commandments* . . . and thus you will do all My commandments out of love and awe (reverence).

וִהְיִיתֶם קְדֹשִׁים לֵאלֹהֵיכֶם — *And be holy to your God* . . . and thus you will be holy before Him, (leading you to) eternal life, as He intended when He said, וְאַתֶּם תִּהְיוּ לִי מַמְלֶכֶת כֹּהֲנִים וְגוֹי קָדוֹשׁ, *And you shall be unto Me a kingdom of Kohanim and a holy nation* (*Exodus* 19:6).

41. אֲנִי ה׳ אֱלֹהֵיכֶם אֲשֶׁר הוֹצֵאתִי אֶתְכֶם — *I am HASHEM your God who brought you out. I am HASHEM,* in the sense that I am *your God* whom you recognize as the One Who is the First Cause and Who is worthy to be served and to Whom prayer should be directed.

הוֹצֵאתִי אֶתְכֶם מֵאֶרֶץ מִצְרַיִם — *Who brought you out of the land of Egypt.* (This I did) so that you shall merit that I be *your God,* (and thus) your ongoing existence will flow from Me, without need for any intermediary. Such existence is unchanging and will in no manner deteriorate, as is true regarding the existence of all everlasting matter.

אֲנִי ה׳ אֱלֹהֵיכֶם — *I am HASHEM your God.* I now command you (to perform) this commandment for this purpose, in order that you may merit this intended (end) — as He said, *and be holy unto your God* (verse 40).

NOTES

tion' lead man astray, causing him to deviate from the right path to a deceitful, devious and destructive one.

40-41. וַעֲשִׂיתֶם אֶת כָּל מִצְוֺתָי וִהְיִיתֶם קְדֹשִׁים לֵאלֹהֵיכֶם . . . אֲנִי ה׳ אֱלֹהֵיכֶם — *And do all My commandments and be holy to your God . . . I am HASHEM your God.* The sense of these verses, according to the *Sforno*, is as follows: God's intention was to grant the people of Israel eternal existence. This was to be effectuated through two means, which the *Sforno* explained above in *Genesis* 17:7 and *Exodus* 19:6. One way was by creating them in such a manner that their existence as a people emanates directly from Him and not through any heavenly intermediary, as is the case with other nations. The second medium was by sanctifying them, because sanctity ensures eternity. The *tzitzis* (fringes) remind Israel of their mission and purpose in the world, and it was in order to fulfill this role that they were delivered from Egypt.

פרשת קרח
Parashas Korach

טז א וַיִּקַּח קֹרַח בֶּן־יִצְהָר בֶּן־קְהָת בֶּן־לֵוִי וְדָתָן וַאֲבִירָם בְּנֵי אֱלִיאָב וְאוֹן
ב בֶּן־פֶּלֶת בְּנֵי רְאוּבֵן: וַיָּקֻמוּ לִפְנֵי מֹשֶׁה וַאֲנָשִׁים מִבְּנֵי־יִשְׂרָאֵל חֲמִשִּׁים
ג וּמָאתָיִם נְשִׂיאֵי עֵדָה קְרִאֵי מוֹעֵד אַנְשֵׁי־שֵׁם: וַיִּקָּהֲלוּ עַל־מֹשֶׁה וְעַל־אַהֲרֹן
וַיֹּאמְרוּ אֲלֵהֶם רַב־לָכֶם כִּי כָל־הָעֵדָה כֻּלָּם קְדֹשִׁים וּבְתוֹכָם יהוה וּמַדּוּעַ
ד-ה תִּתְנַשְּׂאוּ עַל־קְהַל יהוה: וַיִּשְׁמַע מֹשֶׁה וַיִּפֹּל עַל־פָּנָיו: וַיְדַבֵּר אֶל־קֹרַח

XVI

1-2. וַיִּקַּח קֹרַח — *Now, Korach took.* The sense and sequence of the verse is as though it said: And Korach, Dathan and Abiram and On the son of Peleth took two hundred and fifty men who were princes of the congregation and they rose up in the face of Moses with certain of the Children of Israel, after which . . .

3. וַיִּקָּהֲלוּ עַל מֹשֶׁה וְעַל אַהֲרֹן — *And they assembled themselves together against Moses and against Aaron.* Korach, Dathan and Abiram assembled together to complain against Moses and Aaron in the presence of the two hundred and fifty princes of the congregation who had gone there, at the advice of these complainers, at a time when *certain of the Children of Israel* had come (to Moses and Aaron) for judgment (i.e., adjudication). (Now) these two hundred and fifty men gathered there as though they were innocently coming to stand there with Moses. (This was done) so that when Korach, Dathan and Aviram would later assemble against Moses and Aaron, they (the 250) would agree, as one, with the demands of those assembling, in the presence of certain of the Children of Israel who were (also) present there. (Now) they (i.e., Korach et al.) chose a time when a multitude would be there so as to publicize (the event) and to spread (their complaints) throughout the camp in order to increase the number of those who would rise up with them.

כִּי כָל הָעֵדָה — *Being that all the congregation* . . . each and every one of them.

כֻּלָּם קְדֹשִׁים — *Are all holy.* From the sole of the foot unto the head (based on *Isaiah* 1:6), as it says, *And you shall be holy unto your God* (15:40).

וּמַדּוּעַ תִּתְנַשְּׂאוּ — *Why then do you lift yourselves up* . . . in the area of sanctity by prohibiting the firstborn from (officiating) at the service, (while) Moses already served as a *Kohen* during the seven days of consecration, and Aaron and his sons (have been designated) as *Kohanim* forever.

NOTES

XVI

1-3. וַיִּקַּח קֹרַח . . . וַיִּקָּהֲלוּ עַל מֹשֶׁה וְעַל אַהֲרֹן — *Now, Korach took . . . And they assembled themselves together against Moses and against Aaron.* The *Sforno* construes the verb *took* (וַיִּקַּח) as an antecedent of אֲנָשִׁים מִבְּנֵי יִשְׂרָאֵל, *certain of the Children of Israel,* and also of חֲמִשִּׁים וּמָאתָיִם נְשִׂיאֵי עֵדָה, *two hundred and fifty princes of the congregation.* As the *Sforno* explains, the challenge to Moses' authority and Aaron's priesthood was carefully planned. When Korach and his cohorts would appear to rise up against Moses, the princes would be present, together with those who had come to Moses for a decision of law. In this manner, their complaints would be heard and joined in by others, and the fire of rebellion would quickly spread throughout the camp.

3. כֻּלָּם קְדֹשִׁים — *Are all holy.* The *Sforno* interprets the word כֻּלָּם, *are all,* in a literal sense, referring to the total being of each Israelite, for hadn't God stated (in the *parashah* of *tzitzis*) that everyone is holy? And the *parasha* of *tzitzis* was commanded to all Israel! Hence, by what right does Moses strip the firstborn of their right to serve and arrogate this honor to himself, his brother Aaron and Aaron's sons?

וְאֶל־כָּל־עֲדָתוֹ לֵאמֹר בֹּקֶר וְיֹדַע יהוה אֶת־אֲשֶׁר־לוֹ וְאֶת־הַקָּדוֹשׁ וְהִקְרִיב
ו אֵלָיו וְאֵת אֲשֶׁר יִבְחַר־בּוֹ יַקְרִיב אֵלָיו: זֹאת עֲשׂוּ קְחוּ־לָכֶם מַחְתּוֹת קֹרַח
ז וְכָל־עֲדָתוֹ: וּתְנוּ בָהֵן | אֵשׁ וְשִׂימוּ עֲלֵיהֶן | קְטֹרֶת לִפְנֵי יהוה מָחָר וְהָיָה
ח הָאִישׁ אֲשֶׁר־יִבְחַר יהוה הוּא הַקָּדוֹשׁ רַב־לָכֶם בְּנֵי לֵוִי: וַיֹּאמֶר מֹשֶׁה
ט אֶל־קֹרַח שִׁמְעוּ־נָא בְּנֵי לֵוִי: הַמְעַט מִכֶּם כִּי־הִבְדִּיל אֱלֹהֵי יִשְׂרָאֵל אֶתְכֶם
מֵעֲדַת יִשְׂרָאֵל לְהַקְרִיב אֶתְכֶם אֵלָיו לַעֲבֹד אֶת־עֲבֹדַת מִשְׁכַּן יהוה
י וְלַעֲמֹד לִפְנֵי הָעֵדָה לְשָׁרְתָם: וַיַּקְרֵב אֹתְךָ וְאֶת־כָּל־אַחֶיךָ בְנֵי־לֵוִי אִתָּךְ

---

5. וַיְדַבֵּר אֶל קֹרַח וְאֶל כָּל עֲדָתוֹ — *And he spoke to Korach and to all his company.* He informed them that he was aware of their stratagem and the plot of their congregation.

אֶת אֲשֶׁר לוֹ — *Who are His . . .* who (truly) speak on behalf of God, the Blessed One's, honor.

וְאֶת הַקָּדוֹשׁ וְהִקְרִיב אֵלָיו — *And who is holy to come near unto Him . . .* and He will notify (us) who the holy one is that is worthy to offer sacrifices unto Him.

וְאֶת אֲשֶׁר יִבְחַר בּוֹ יַקְרִיב אֵלָיו — *And whom He shall choose to come near unto Him.* He alone will God draw near to Him from the midst of the destruction which will befall the others, as it says, *separate yourselves from among this congregation* (v. 21).

7. הוּא הַקָּדוֹשׁ — *He shall be holy.* He alone, for only one shall merit this (role). This was said so that they would be afraid, repent and not be lost, for (God) does not desire the death (of the wicked) (based on *Ezekiel* 18:32.)

רַב לָכֶם בְּנֵי לֵוִי — *You want too much, sons of Levi.* You, *the men that belong to Korach* (v. 32), take too much upon yourselves, for God will be angry with you all the more, being that you have already been chosen for His service.

9. וְלַעֲמֹד לִפְנֵי הָעֵדָה לְשָׁרְתָם — *And to stand before the congregation to minister to them . . .* to serve God, the Exalted One, through song, and (serving in) His Sanctuary through the labor of carrying and other (labors). Now, He wanted you to perform this service *before the congregation* so as to inform them of their shortcoming, disqualifying them from serving, and that you have been chosen in their stead.

NOTES

5-7. וַיְדַבֵּר אֶל קֹרַח וְאֶל כָּל עֲדָתוֹ . . . אֶת אֲשֶׁר לוֹ וְאֶת הַקָּדוֹשׁ וְהִקְרִיב אֵלָיו וְאֶת אֲשֶׁר יִבְחַר בּוֹ יַקְרִיב אֵלָיו . . . הוּא הַקָּדוֹשׁ — *And he spoke to Korach and to all his company . . . who are His and who is holy to come near unto Him and whom He shall choose to come near unto Him . . . He shall be holy.* The *Sforno* divides the statement of Moses to Korach and his company into three parts. First, he tells them that he is fully cognizant of their evil plot. Secondly, the Almighty will let them know, in no uncertain terms, who truly speaks in His behalf and is competent to offer sacrifices on the altar. Finally, he cautions them that they are courting danger, for the only survivor from the destruction which will befall them will be the one who is worthy. Moses was hopeful that they would heed his warning and repent. The *Sforno* is of the opinion that this is another example of God not wanting to punish the wicked. Rather, His greatest desire is for the transgressor to do *teshuvah.*

9. וְלַעֲמֹד לִפְנֵי הָעֵדָה לְשָׁרְתָם — *And to stand before the congregation to minister to them.* Moses appeals to the Levites to be reasonable. Why do they join the others in claiming that all are holy and why do they demand the

יא וּבִקַּשְׁתֶּם גַּם־כְּהֻנָּה: לָכֵן אַתָּה וְכָל־עֲדָתְךָ הַנֹּעָדִים עַל־יהוה וְאַהֲרֹן
יב מַה־הוּא כִּי תַלּוֹנוּ עָלָיו: וַיִּשְׁלַח מֹשֶׁה לִקְרֹא לְדָתָן וְלַאֲבִירָם בְּנֵי אֱלִיאָב
יג וַיֹּאמְרוּ לֹא נַעֲלֶה: הַמְעַט כִּי הֶעֱלִיתָנוּ מֵאֶרֶץ זָבַת חָלָב וּדְבַשׁ לַהֲמִיתֵנוּ
שני יד בַּמִּדְבָּר כִּי־תִשְׂתָּרֵר עָלֵינוּ גַּם־הִשְׂתָּרֵר: אַף לֹא אֶל־אֶרֶץ זָבַת חָלָב
וּדְבַשׁ הֲבִיאֹתָנוּ וַתִּתֶּן־לָנוּ נַחֲלַת שָׂדֶה וָכָרֶם הַעֵינֵי הָאֲנָשִׁים הָהֵם תְּנַקֵּר
טו לֹא נַעֲלֶה: וַיִּחַר לְמֹשֶׁה מְאֹד וַיֹּאמֶר אֶל־יהוה אַל־תֵּפֶן אֶל־מִנְחָתָם °לֹא

---

11. לָכֵן אַתָּה וְכָל עֲדָתְךָ הַנֹּעָדִים עַל ה׳ — *Therefore, you and all your congregation that are gathered against* HASHEM . . . I say to you, that it is עַל ה׳, *against* HASHEM*!* Let it be known that I cast my burden upon HASHEM (based on *Psalms* 55:23) and He will (no doubt) repay you for His insult, but I will not rise up against you at all.

14. אַף לֹא אֶל אֶרֶץ . . . וַתִּתֶּן לָנוּ — *Moreover, you have not brought us to a land . . . (nor) given us.* Not only have you perpetrated evil against us by taking us out of a land flowing with milk and honey and bringing us into the wilderness, but you also jest with us — for you have not brought us to the Land into which you said (you would bring us) and still you speak (to us) as though you have given us 'an inheritance of fields and vineyards,' by commanding us those commandments which are connected (only) to the Land, when you said, לֹא תְכַלֶּה פְּאַת שָׂדְךָ . . . וּפֶרֶט כַּרְמְךָ לֹא תְלַקֵּט, *You shall not wholly reap the corner of your field . . . nor shall you gather the fallen fruit of your vineyard* (*Leviticus* 19:9, 10), as though it was already ours and we have fields and vineyards in it!

הַעֵינֵי הָאֲנָשִׁים הָהֵם תְּנַקֵּר — *Will you put out the eyes of these men?* Do you think you can put out our eyes (i.e., blindfold us) in such a manner that we will not discern your scheme?

15. אַל תֵּפֶן אֶל מִנְחָתָם — *Turn not to their offering.* Do not accept any kind of offering which they will bring to atone for themselves — the reverse of יָרַח מִנְחָה, *Let Him accept an offering* (*I Samuel* 26:19). This is because I do not forgive my

NOTES

rights of the holy service on behalf of the firstborn? They know full well that they were chosen after the sin of the Golden Calf to replace the firstborn — and this was done openly ('before the congregation'); not in a secret manner.

11. לָכֵן אַתָּה וְכָל עֲדָתְךָ הַנֹּעָדִים עַל ה׳ — *Therefore, you and all your congregation that are gathered upon* HASHEM*.* The expression עַל ה׳ is not interpreted by the *Sforno* as meaning *against* HASHEM but in the sense of *upon* HASHEM, similar to the expression used in *Psalms* 55:23 — הַשְׁלֵךְ עַל ה׳ יְהָבְךָ וכו׳, *Cast your burden upon* HASHEM *and He will sustain you etc.* Hence, Moses is saying that he will do naught to punish them, for he is confident that God will exact retribution for their rebellion against the one who was chosen by the Almighty.

14. אַף לֹא אֶל אֶרֶץ . . . וַתִּתֶּן לָנוּ . . . הַעֵינֵי הָאֲנָשִׁים הָהֵם תְּנַקֵּר — *Moreover, you have not brought us to a land . . . (nor) given us . . . will you put out the eyes of these men?* The *Sforno* explains the sense of the verse in a manner which clarifies the (seemingly) awkward lack of continuity in the phraseology of this verse. The first part is a simple complaint that Moses has not kept his promise to bring them into *Eretz Yisrael.* The second part is a more serious grievance, for Moses has added insult to injury by speaking to them as though they had already inherited the Land and were already obligated to give gifts to the poor from fields and vineyards which were nonexistent! Surely this is a case of mockery on the part of Moses, which Korach and his company refused to accept with equanimity.

15. אַל תֵּפֶן אֶל מִנְחָתָם לֹא חֲמוֹר אֶחָד מֵהֶם נָשָׂאתִי וְלֹא הֲרֵעֹתִי אֶת אַחַד מֵהֶם — *Turn not to their*

טז חֲמ֨וֹר אֶחָ֤ד מֵהֶם֙ נָשָׂ֔אתִי וְלֹ֥א הֲרֵעֹ֖תִי אֶת־אַחַ֥ד מֵהֶֽם׃ וַיֹּ֤אמֶר מֹשֶׁה֙
יז אֶל־קֹ֔רַח אַתָּה֙ וְכָל־עֲדָ֣תְךָ֔ הֱי֖וּ לִפְנֵ֣י יְהוָ֑ה אַתָּ֥ה וָהֵ֛ם וְאַהֲרֹ֖ן מָחָֽר׃ וּקְח֣וּ ׀
אִ֣ישׁ מַחְתָּת֗וֹ וּנְתַתֶּ֤ם עֲלֵיהֶם֙ קְטֹ֔רֶת וְהִקְרַבְתֶּ֞ם לִפְנֵ֤י יְהוָה֙ אִ֣ישׁ מַחְתָּת֔וֹ
יח חֲמִשִּׁ֥ים וּמָאתַ֖יִם מַחְתֹּ֑ת וְאַתָּ֥ה וְאַהֲרֹ֖ן אִ֥ישׁ מַחְתָּתֽוֹ׃ וַיִּקְח֞וּ אִ֣ישׁ מַחְתָּת֗וֹ
וַיִּתְּנ֤וּ עֲלֵיהֶם֙ אֵ֔שׁ וַיָּשִׂ֥ימוּ עֲלֵיהֶ֖ם קְטֹ֑רֶת וַיַּֽעַמְד֗וּ פֶּ֛תַח אֹ֥הֶל מוֹעֵ֖ד וּמֹשֶׁ֥ה
יט וְאַהֲרֹֽן׃ וַיַּקְהֵ֨ל עֲלֵיהֶ֥ם קֹ֙רַח֙ אֶת־כָּל־הָ֣עֵדָ֔ה אֶל־פֶּ֖תַח אֹ֣הֶל מוֹעֵ֑ד וַיֵּרָ֥א
שלישי כ כְבוֹד־יְהוָ֖ה אֶל־כָּל־הָעֵדָֽה׃ וַיְדַבֵּ֣ר יְהוָ֔ה אֶל־מֹשֶׁ֥ה וְאֶֽל־
כא-כב אַהֲרֹ֖ן לֵאמֹֽר׃ הִבָּ֣דְל֔וּ מִתּ֖וֹךְ הָעֵדָ֣ה הַזֹּ֑את וַאֲכַלֶּ֥ה אֹתָ֖ם כְּרָֽגַע׃ וַיִּפְּל֤וּ

insult and You cannot pardon them without this (exculpation), as (our Sages) said, 'Sins committed between man and his fellow man are not atoned for on Yom Kippur unless he appeases his fellow' (*Yoma* 85b), and so Jeremiah says, כִּי כָרוּ שׁוּחָה לְנַפְשִׁי זְכֹר עָמְדִי לְפָנֶיךָ לְדַבֵּר עֲלֵיהֶם טוֹבָה... אַל תְּכַפֵּר עַל עֲוֹנָם וְחַטָּאתָם מִלְּפָנֶיךָ אַל תֶּמְחִי, *For they have dug a pit for my soul. Remember that I stood before You to speak good for them ... forgive not their iniquity, neither blot out their sin from Your sight* (*Jeremiah* 18:20,23).

לֹא חֲמוֹר אֶחָד מֵהֶם נָשָׂאתִי — *I have not taken one ass from them.* I did not benefit from them even as a common man would benefit from his friend, for I did not even borrow an ass from them. Hence, my rulership over them was totally for their benefit and to attend to their affairs; not for mine or for my pleasure, as is the custom of those who are in a position of authority. Their criticism of my leadership is therefore only due to their ingratitude.

וְלֹא הֲרֵעֹתִי אֶת אַחַד מֵהֶם — *Neither have I hurt one of them.* Even the enmity caused by a guilty verdict in court is not applicable to me, for it never happened that they should appear before me for a decision of law in a manner that I should declare them culpable.

16. אַתָּה וְכָל עֲדָתְךָ הֱיוּ לִפְנֵי ה׳ — *You and all your congregation are to be before* HASHEM. You are summoned to judgment before Him.

21. הִבָּדְלוּ — *Separate yourselves* ... so that your merit shall not shield them, similar to יְמַלֵּט אִי נָקִי, *He delivers the one who is not innocent* (*Job* 22:30).

NOTES

offering; I have not taken one ass from them, neither have I hurt one of them. The *Sforno* explains why Moses asked God not to accept their act of repentance. Surely, the power of acceptance or rejection is not in his domain but in the hands of the Almighty. But in truth, a sin committed against one's fellowman may be forgiven by God, but it is not completely exculpated until the injured party is appeased, and Moses states that he is not prepared to forgive his insult, just as we find in the case of Jeremiah. The reason for Moses' anger and adamant refusal to forgive them is, as he explains, because of their profound ingratitude. The *Sforno* interprets the words of Moses as referring to his judicial decisions, for how could we presume that Moses would ever 'hurt' anyone.

21. הִבָּדְלוּ — *Separate yourselves.* The verse from *Job* cited by the *Sforno* proves that the guilty can be saved by the righteous, for as the *Metzudos David* interprets the verse, the meaning is: God delivers those who are not innocent in the merit of those *whose hands are pure* (וְנִמְלַט בְּבֹר כַּפֶּיךָ). Therefore, Moses and Aaron are told to separate themselves from these sinners, for otherwise their presence will protect them from punishment. On the other hand, those who may not be guilty of

עַל־פְּנֵיהֶם וַיֹּאמְרוּ אֵל אֱלֹהֵי הָרוּחֹת לְכָל־בָּשָׂר הָאִישׁ אֶחָד יֶחֱטָא וְעַל
כג-כד כָּל־הָעֵדָה תִּקְצֹף: וַיְדַבֵּר יהוה אֶל־מֹשֶׁה לֵּאמֹר: דַּבֵּר
כה אֶל־הָעֵדָה לֵאמֹר הֵעָלוּ מִסָּבִיב לְמִשְׁכַּן־קֹרַח דָּתָן וַאֲבִירָם: וַיָּקָם מֹשֶׁה
כו וַיֵּלֶךְ אֶל־דָּתָן וַאֲבִירָם וַיֵּלְכוּ אַחֲרָיו זִקְנֵי יִשְׂרָאֵל: וַיְדַבֵּר אֶל־הָעֵדָה
לֵאמֹר סוּרוּ נָא מֵעַל אָהֳלֵי הָאֲנָשִׁים הָרְשָׁעִים הָאֵלֶּה וְאַל־תִּגְּעוּ
כז בְּכָל־אֲשֶׁר לָהֶם פֶּן־תִּסָּפוּ בְּכָל־חַטֹּאתָם: וַיֵּעָלוּ מֵעַל מִשְׁכַּן־קֹרַח דָּתָן
וַאֲבִירָם מִסָּבִיב וְדָתָן וַאֲבִירָם יָצְאוּ נִצָּבִים פֶּתַח אָהֳלֵיהֶם וּנְשֵׁיהֶם וּבְנֵיהֶם
כח וְטַפָּם: וַיֹּאמֶר מֹשֶׁה בְּזֹאת תֵּדְעוּן כִּי־יהוה שְׁלָחַנִי לַעֲשׂוֹת אֵת
כט כָּל־הַמַּעֲשִׂים הָאֵלֶּה כִּי־לֹא מִלִּבִּי: אִם־כְּמוֹת כָּל־הָאָדָם יְמֻתוּן אֵלֶּה
ל וּפְקֻדַּת כָּל־הָאָדָם יִפָּקֵד עֲלֵיהֶם לֹא יהוה שְׁלָחָנִי: וְאִם־בְּרִיאָה יִבְרָא יהוה
וּפָצְתָה הָאֲדָמָה אֶת־פִּיהָ וּבָלְעָה אֹתָם וְאֶת־כָּל־אֲשֶׁר לָהֶם וְיָרְדוּ חַיִּים
לא שְׁאֹלָה וִידַעְתֶּם כִּי נִאֲצוּ הָאֲנָשִׁים הָאֵלֶּה אֶת־יהוה: וַיְהִי כְּכַלֹּתוֹ לְדַבֵּר
לב אֵת כָּל־הַדְּבָרִים הָאֵלֶּה וַתִּבָּקַע הָאֲדָמָה אֲשֶׁר תַּחְתֵּיהֶם: וַתִּפְתַּח הָאָרֶץ
אֶת־פִּיהָ וַתִּבְלַע אֹתָם וְאֶת־בָּתֵּיהֶם וְאֵת כָּל־הָאָדָם אֲשֶׁר לְקֹרַח וְאֵת
לג כָּל־הָרְכוּשׁ: וַיֵּרְדוּ הֵם וְכָל־אֲשֶׁר לָהֶם חַיִּים שְׁאֹלָה וַתְּכַס עֲלֵיהֶם הָאָרֶץ

---

22. הָאִישׁ אֶחָד יֶחֱטָא — *Shall one man sin* ... since he (alone) caused the congregation to assemble against us, as it says, *and Korach assembled all the congregation against them* (v. 19).

24. דַּבֵּר אֶל הָעֵדָה לֵאמֹר הֵעָלוּ מִסָּבִיב — *Speak to the congregation saying: Get up from around.* He explained that when it says *separate yourselves from the congregation* (v. 21), it only referred to the congregation of Korach.

26. פֶּן תִּסָּפוּ — *Lest you be swept away* ... for you are not worthy to be saved if you will be with them when they are smitten.

30. וִידַעְתֶּם כִּי נִאֲצוּ — *Then you will know that (these men) have derided (God)* ... and they are not worthy to receive the (normal) honor given the dead, i.e., to be buried with the rest of the people.

32. וַתִּפְתַּח הָאָרֶץ אֶת פִּיהָ — *And the earth opened its mouth.* The cleft widened to (encompass) the place of their homes.

וְאֵת כָּל הָאָדָם אֲשֶׁר לְקֹרַח — *And all the men that belonged to Korach* ... and all those who joined with Korach in his controversy. Therefore, his sons did not die for they were not drawn after him in this (matter).

וְאֵת כָּל הָרְכוּשׁ — *And all their possessions* ... so they shall gain no merit from the fact that righteous men might derive benefit from their toil, similar to, 'if a sela (coin) fell out of his lap and a poor man found it and used it to purchase food' (*Sifra* cited in *Rashi, Leviticus* 5:17).

NOTES

rebellion, but are also not deemed righteous, would nonetheless be vulnerable to destruction were they to remain in the vicinity of Korach, for we have a principle, 'Woe to the wicked, and woe to his neighbor.' Hence, they are told to distance themselves *lest they be swept away* (v. 26).

32. וְאֵת כָּל הָרְכוּשׁ — *And all their possessions.* The *Sforno* explains the reason for the 'swal-

לד וַיֹּאבְדוּ מִתּוֹךְ הַקָּהָל: וְכָל־יִשְׂרָאֵל אֲשֶׁר סְבִיבֹתֵיהֶם נָסוּ לְקֹלָם כִּי אָמְרוּ
לה פֶּן־תִּבְלָעֵנוּ הָאָרֶץ: וְאֵשׁ יָצְאָה מֵאֵת יהוה וַתֹּאכַל אֵת הַחֲמִשִּׁים וּמָאתַיִם
יז א אִישׁ מַקְרִיבֵי הַקְּטֹרֶת: וַיְדַבֵּר יהוה אֶל־מֹשֶׁה לֵּאמֹר:
ב אֱמֹר אֶל־אֶלְעָזָר בֶּן־אַהֲרֹן הַכֹּהֵן וְיָרֵם אֶת־הַמַּחְתֹּת מִבֵּין הַשְּׂרֵפָה וְאֶת־
ג הָאֵשׁ זְרֵה־הָלְאָה כִּי קָדֵשׁוּ: אֵת מַחְתּוֹת הַחַטָּאִים הָאֵלֶּה בְּנַפְשֹׁתָם וְעָשׂוּ
אֹתָם רִקֻּעֵי פַחִים צִפּוּי לַמִּזְבֵּחַ כִּי־הִקְרִיבֻם לִפְנֵי־יהוה וַיִּקְדָּשׁוּ וְיִהְיוּ לְאוֹת
ד לִבְנֵי יִשְׂרָאֵל: וַיִּקַּח אֶלְעָזָר הַכֹּהֵן אֵת מַחְתּוֹת הַנְּחֹשֶׁת אֲשֶׁר הִקְרִיבוּ
ה הַשְּׂרֻפִים וַיְרַקְּעוּם צִפּוּי לַמִּזְבֵּחַ: זִכָּרוֹן לִבְנֵי יִשְׂרָאֵל לְמַעַן אֲשֶׁר לֹא־יִקְרַב
אִישׁ זָר אֲשֶׁר לֹא מִזֶּרַע אַהֲרֹן הוּא לְהַקְטִיר קְטֹרֶת לִפְנֵי יהוה וְלֹא־יִהְיֶה
כְקֹרַח וְכַעֲדָתוֹ כַּאֲשֶׁר דִּבֶּר יהוה בְּיַד־מֹשֶׁה לוֹ:

---

33. וַתְּכַס עֲלֵיהֶם הָאָרֶץ — *And the earth closed upon them.* (The verse) tells us that this opening (of the earth) was unlike the openings caused by an earthquake which it does not close immediately. In this instance, however, it closed at once, similar to one who opens his mouth to swallow something and closes it after swallowing.

XVII

2. וְאֶת הָאֵשׁ זְרֵה הָלְאָה — *And scatter the fire yonder* . . . but not in the place where the ashes are (normally) poured out (שֶׁפֶךְ הַדֶּשֶׁן) [see *Leviticus* 4:12] because this was an alien (lit. strange) incense.

כִּי קָדֵשׁוּ — *For they have become holy* . . . and it is not fitting to allow them to lie in disgrace.

3. כִּי הִקְרִיבֻם לִפְנֵי ה׳ וַיִּקְדָּשׁוּ — *For they were offered before* HASHEM *and became holy* . . . for they were sanctified as vessels of service (to be used) for other Divine service besides this defective one, and thus they are worthy to be used as a covering in the holy.

NOTES

lowing up' of all their possessions. Were these possessions salvaged and enjoyed by others who were righteous men, then Korach and his company would have gained merit thereby, even though it was not given directly and willingly, for as *Rashi* tells us in *Leviticus* 5:17 that just as one is punished for sinning in error, so he is rewarded for doing good unintentionally.

33. וַתְּכַס עֲלֵיהֶם הָאָרֶץ — *And the earth closed upon them.* The *Sforno* emphasizes that this was indeed a *new thing* (v. 30), for the manner in which it happened was unlike that which occurs in an ordinary earthquake.

XVII

2-3. וְאֶת הָאֵשׁ זְרֵה הָלְאָה כִּי קָדֵשׁוּ . . . כִּי הִקְרִיבֻם לִפְנֵי ה׳ וַיִּקְדָּשׁוּ . . . — *And scatter the fire yonder for they have become holy . . . for they were offered before* HASHEM *and became holy* . . . The שֶׁפֶךְ הַדֶּשֶׁן was a special place outside the three camps when the Israelites were in the wilderness, and outside Jerusalem at the time when the Holy Temple stood. The ashes of certain sacrifices were poured out there. The *Sforno* explains that the fire in the censers of those who challenged Aaron was not to be scattered in that special place since only that which was acceptable and hence sacred could be poured out on the שֶׁפֶךְ הַדֶּשֶׁן. The fire pans of these men, however, were to be treated with care and respect and used *for a covering of the altar* since they were holy. Some commentators say that this was so because the offering was made at the behest of Moses, while others say it was so because these men sincerely believed that it would be acceptable to God. The *Sforno*, however, explains that they were holy because they were meant to be used for Divine service other than this improper one.

ו וַיִּלֹּנוּ כָּל־עֲדַת בְּנֵי־יִשְׂרָאֵל מִמָּחֳרָת עַל־מֹשֶׁה וְעַל־אַהֲרֹן לֵאמֹר אַתֶּם
ז הֲמִתֶּם אֶת־עַם יהוה: וַיְהִי בְּהִקָּהֵל הָעֵדָה עַל־מֹשֶׁה וְעַל־אַהֲרֹן וַיִּפְנוּ
ח אֶל־אֹהֶל מוֹעֵד וְהִנֵּה כִסָּהוּ הֶעָנָן וַיֵּרָא כְּבוֹד יהוה: וַיָּבֹא מֹשֶׁה וְאַהֲרֹן
רביעי ט אֶל־פְּנֵי אֹהֶל מוֹעֵד: וַיְדַבֵּר יהוה אֶל־מֹשֶׁה לֵּאמֹר:
י־יא הֵרֹמּוּ מִתּוֹךְ הָעֵדָה הַזֹּאת וַאֲכַלֶּה אֹתָם כְּרָגַע וַיִּפְּלוּ עַל־פְּנֵיהֶם: וַיֹּאמֶר
מֹשֶׁה אֶל־אַהֲרֹן קַח אֶת־הַמַּחְתָּה וְתֶן־עָלֶיהָ אֵשׁ מֵעַל הַמִּזְבֵּחַ וְשִׂים
קְטֹרֶת וְהוֹלֵךְ מְהֵרָה אֶל־הָעֵדָה וְכַפֵּר עֲלֵיהֶם כִּי־יָצָא הַקֶּצֶף מִלִּפְנֵי יהוה
יב הֵחֵל הַנָּגֶף: וַיִּקַּח אַהֲרֹן כַּאֲשֶׁר ׀ דִּבֶּר מֹשֶׁה וַיָּרָץ אֶל־תּוֹךְ הַקָּהָל וְהִנֵּה
יג הֵחֵל הַנֶּגֶף בָּעָם וַיִּתֵּן אֶת־הַקְּטֹרֶת וַיְכַפֵּר עַל־הָעָם: וַיַּעֲמֹד בֵּין־הַמֵּתִים
יד וּבֵין הַחַיִּים וַתֵּעָצַר הַמַּגֵּפָה: וַיִּהְיוּ הַמֵּתִים בַּמַּגֵּפָה אַרְבָּעָה עָשָׂר אֶלֶף
טו וּשְׁבַע מֵאוֹת מִלְּבַד הַמֵּתִים עַל־דְּבַר־קֹרַח: וַיָּשָׁב אַהֲרֹן אֶל־מֹשֶׁה
אֶל־פֶּתַח אֹהֶל מוֹעֵד וְהַמַּגֵּפָה נֶעֱצָרָה:

---

6. אַתֶּם הֲמִתֶּם — *You have killed . . .* because you told them to be tested through the (burning) of the incense which is only fitting to be burnt by one who offers the daily burnt-offering. You should have tested them with sacrifices that are fitting to be brought by many *Kohanim* together.

13. וַיַּעֲמֹד בֵּין הַמֵּתִים וּבֵין הַחַיִּים — *And he stood between the dead and the living . . .* after he stood there, he remained (there) to protect the sick ones that they should not die; the reverse of (the command to) *separate yourselves from among this congregation* (16:21).

וַתֵּעָצַר הַמַּגֵּפָה — *And the pestilence was stopped.* No one else became ill due to the illness (caused by) the pestilence.

15. וְהַמַּגֵּפָה נֶעֱצָרָה — *And the pestilence was stopped.* Those stricken by the plague were healed.

NOTES

6. אַתֶּם הֲמִתֶּם — *You have killed.* The difficulty posed by this accusation, *you have killed*, is obvious. The punishment was meted out by Heaven, not by Moses! The *Sforno* explains that they were angry at Moses for suggesting a test which exposed them to imminent danger, since bringing the incense was done by only one person who is therefore more vulnerable than he who participates in a service in which many are involved. The wording of the *Sforno* however is puzzling. He states that the burning of the incense is done only by 'one who offers the daily burnt offering.' The Mishnayos in *Yoma* (chapter 2) discuss the lots drawn each morning to determine which *Kohanim* shall participate in the service. Regarding the incense it states that anyone who never had that privilege before is eligible (*Mishnah* 4). However, that privilege has no connection with the offering of the daily sacrifice which involved quite a number of *Kohanim*. Perhaps the text should be emended to read 'by one who offers the incense alone.'

13. וַיַּעֲמֹד בֵּין הַמֵּתִים וּבֵין הַחַיִּים . . . — *And he stood between the dead and the living.* Previously, God had told Moses and Aaron not to stand in the proximity of the rebels for their presence would protect them, which was contrary to God's wishes (16:21). Here, however, in the absence of such an order, Aaron chooses to remain in the midst of the afflicted so as to protect them from the consequences of their accusation — *you have killed the people of HASHEM* (v. 16).

15. וְהַמַּגֵּפָה נֶעֱצָרָה — *And the pestilence was stopped.* The phrase *and the pestilence (plague) was stopped* appears in verse 13 as well, but in a different sequence. In verse 13, it is written וַתֵּעָצַר הַמַּגֵּפָה, whereas in this verse the wording is וְהַמַּגֵּפָה נֶעֱצָרָה. The *Sforno's* interpretation of these two verses is a reconciliation of this variance. In verse 13, it refers to a

חמישי טז-יז וַיְדַבֵּר יְהוָה אֶל־מֹשֶׁה לֵּאמֹר: דַּבֵּר ׀ אֶל־בְּנֵי יִשְׂרָאֵל וְקַח מֵאִתָּם מַטֶּה
מַטֶּה לְבֵית אָב מֵאֵת כָּל־נְשִׂיאֵהֶם לְבֵית אֲבֹתָם שְׁנֵים עָשָׂר מַטּוֹת אִישׁ
יח אֶת־שְׁמוֹ תִּכְתֹּב עַל־מַטֵּהוּ: וְאֵת שֵׁם אַהֲרֹן תִּכְתֹּב עַל־מַטֵּה לֵוִי כִּי מַטֶּה
יט אֶחָד לְרֹאשׁ בֵּית אֲבוֹתָם: וְהִנַּחְתָּם בְּאֹהֶל מוֹעֵד לִפְנֵי הָעֵדוּת אֲשֶׁר אִוָּעֵד
כ לָכֶם שָׁמָּה: וְהָיָה הָאִישׁ אֲשֶׁר אֶבְחַר־בּוֹ מַטֵּהוּ יִפְרָח וַהֲשִׁכֹּתִי מֵעָלַי
כא אֶת־תְּלֻנּוֹת בְּנֵי יִשְׂרָאֵל אֲשֶׁר הֵם מַלִּינִם עֲלֵיכֶם: וַיְדַבֵּר מֹשֶׁה אֶל־בְּנֵי
יִשְׂרָאֵל וַיִּתְּנוּ אֵלָיו ׀ כָּל־נְשִׂיאֵיהֶם מַטֶּה לְנָשִׂיא אֶחָד מַטֶּה לְנָשִׂיא אֶחָד
כב לְבֵית אֲבֹתָם שְׁנֵים עָשָׂר מַטּוֹת וּמַטֵּה אַהֲרֹן בְּתוֹךְ מַטּוֹתָם: וַיַּנַּח מֹשֶׁה
כג אֶת־הַמַּטֹּת לִפְנֵי יְהוָה בְּאֹהֶל הָעֵדֻת: וַיְהִי מִמָּחֳרָת וַיָּבֹא מֹשֶׁה אֶל־אֹהֶל
הָעֵדוּת וְהִנֵּה פָּרַח מַטֵּה־אַהֲרֹן לְבֵית לֵוִי וַיֹּצֵא פֶרַח וַיָּצֵץ צִיץ וַיִּגְמֹל
כד שְׁקֵדִים: וַיֹּצֵא מֹשֶׁה אֶת־כָּל־הַמַּטֹּת מִלִּפְנֵי יְהוָה אֶל־כָּל־בְּנֵי יִשְׂרָאֵל
וַיִּרְאוּ וַיִּקְחוּ אִישׁ מַטֵּהוּ:
ששי כה וַיֹּאמֶר יְהוָה אֶל־מֹשֶׁה הָשֵׁב אֶת־מַטֵּה אַהֲרֹן לִפְנֵי הָעֵדוּת לְמִשְׁמֶרֶת
כו לְאוֹת לִבְנֵי־מֶרִי וּתְכַל תְּלוּנֹּתָם מֵעָלַי וְלֹא יָמֻתוּ: וַיַּעַשׂ מֹשֶׁה כַּאֲשֶׁר צִוָּה
יְהוָה אֹתוֹ כֵּן עָשָׂה:
כז-כח וַיֹּאמְרוּ בְּנֵי יִשְׂרָאֵל אֶל־מֹשֶׁה לֵאמֹר הֵן גָּוַעְנוּ אָבַדְנוּ כֻּלָּנוּ אָבָדְנוּ: כֹּל
יח א הַקָּרֵב ׀ הַקָּרֵב אֶל־מִשְׁכַּן יְהוָה יָמוּת הַאִם תַּמְנוּ לִגְוֹעַ: וַיֹּאמֶר
יְהוָה אֶל־אַהֲרֹן אַתָּה וּבָנֶיךָ וּבֵית־אָבִיךָ אִתָּךְ תִּשְׂאוּ אֶת־עֲוֺן הַמִּקְדָּשׁ

---

24. וַיִּרְאוּ וַיִּקְחוּ אִישׁ מַטֵּהוּ — *And they looked, and every man took his rod* ... to identify the markings of their rods in their homes, for perhaps they were interchanged.

25. וּתְכַל תְּלוּנֹּתָם — *That there may be an end to their murmurings.* This token and sign shall put an end to their murmurings so that they will not continue to complain.

XVIII

1. אַתָּה וּבָנֶיךָ וּבֵית אָבִיךָ אִתָּךְ תִּשְׂאוּ אֶת עֲוֺן הַמִּקְדָּשׁ — *You and your sons and your father's house with you shall bear the iniquity of the Sanctuary* ... that no *tamei* person or stranger enter within its confines, for this (responsibility) rests on all of you and if one enters through your negligence (lit., lack of effort), you will bear his iniquity.

NOTES

complete cessation of the plague, i.e., no one became ill any longer. Hence the verb precedes the noun to indicate that the plague totally ceased, וַתֵּעָצַר הַמַּגֵּפָה — the plague was stopped. In this verse, the noun precedes the verb to indicate that although the victims had been stricken, they were now healed; the meaning is that the *effect* of the plague was stayed and the victims were healed.

24. וַיִּרְאוּ וַיִּקְחוּ אִישׁ מַטֵּהוּ — *And they looked, and every man took his rod.* The rods were taken home for careful examination; why else would they be 'taken' at all?

25. וּתְכַל תְּלוּנֹּתָם — *That there may be an end to their murmurings.* Whenever someone in the future might question the right of Aaron to serve as *Kohen Gadol,* he would be shown the blossoming rod as proof of his being Divinely chosen.

XVIII

1. אַתָּה וּבָנֶיךָ וּבֵית אָבִיךָ אִתָּךְ תִּשְׂאוּ אֶת עֲוֺן הַמִּקְדָּשׁ ... — *You and your sons and your father's house with you shall bear the iniquity of the*

ב וְאַתָּה וּבָנֶיךָ אִתָּךְ תִּשְׂאוּ אֶת־עֲוֺן כְּהֻנַּתְכֶם׃ וְגַם אֶת־אַחֶיךָ מַטֵּה לֵוִי שֵׁבֶט
אָבִיךָ הַקְרֵב אִתָּךְ וְיִלָּווּ עָלֶיךָ וִישָׁרְתוּךָ וְאַתָּה וּבָנֶיךָ אִתָּךְ לִפְנֵי אֹהֶל
ג הָעֵדֻת׃ וְשָׁמְרוּ מִשְׁמַרְתְּךָ וּמִשְׁמֶרֶת כָּל־הָאֹהֶל אַךְ אֶל־כְּלֵי הַקֹּדֶשׁ
ד וְאֶל־הַמִּזְבֵּחַ לֹא יִקְרָבוּ וְלֹא־יָמֻתוּ גַם־הֵם גַּם־אַתֶּם׃ וְנִלְווּ עָלֶיךָ וְשָׁמְרוּ
אֶת־מִשְׁמֶרֶת אֹהֶל מוֹעֵד לְכֹל עֲבֹדַת הָאֹהֶל וְזָר לֹא־יִקְרַב אֲלֵיכֶם׃
ה וּשְׁמַרְתֶּם אֵת מִשְׁמֶרֶת הַקֹּדֶשׁ וְאֵת מִשְׁמֶרֶת הַמִּזְבֵּחַ וְלֹא־יִהְיֶה עוֹד קֶצֶף
ו עַל־בְּנֵי יִשְׂרָאֵל׃ וַאֲנִי הִנֵּה לָקַחְתִּי אֶת־אֲחֵיכֶם הַלְוִיִּם מִתּוֹךְ בְּנֵי יִשְׂרָאֵל
ז לָכֶם מַתָּנָה נְתֻנִים לַיהוָה לַעֲבֹד אֶת־עֲבֹדַת אֹהֶל מוֹעֵד׃ וְאַתָּה וּבָנֶיךָ

וְאַתָּה וּבָנֶיךָ אִתָּךְ תִּשְׂאוּ אֶת עֲוֺן כְּהֻנַּתְכֶם — *And you and your sons with you shall bear the iniquity of your priesthood.* You alone (i.e., the *Kohanim*) are (responsible) to prevent any stranger from participating in the priestly service.

2. וִישָׁרְתוּךָ — *And minister to you . . .* only in regard to that which is in your charge and the charge of your sons.

וְאַתָּה וּבָנֶיךָ אִתָּךְ לִפְנֵי אֹהֶל הָעֵדֻת — *And you and your sons with you before the tent of testimony.* The order shall be thus: You and your sons shall keep the charge in front of the Holy of Holies which is the tent of the ark where the tablets of testimony are located.

3. וְשָׁמְרוּ מִשְׁמַרְתְּךָ וּמִשְׁמֶרֶת כָּל הָאֹהֶל — *And they shall keep your charge and the charge of all the tent.* And the Levites shall keep your charge which is (outside) the Holy of Holies and the charge of the rest of the Sanctuary which is outside the boards of the Sanctuary.

אַךְ אֶל כְּלֵי הַקֹּדֶשׁ — *Only (they shall not come nigh to) the holy furnishings . . .* which are within the Sanctuary, namely the menorah, the table and the golden altar.

וְאֶל הַמִּזְבֵּחַ — *And unto the altar . . .* the outer altar which is the altar of the burnt offering — even though it is outside the boards.

4. וְשָׁמְרוּ אֶת מִשְׁמֶרֶת אֹהֶל מוֹעֵד — *And keep the charge of the Tent of Meeting . . .* within the curtains, which is the entire courtyard.

5. וּשְׁמַרְתֶּם אֵת מִשְׁמֶרֶת הַקֹּדֶשׁ — *And you shall keep the charge of the holy things.* And you, the *Kohanim*, shall keep the charge of the Sanctuary within the boards.

6. לָכֶם מַתָּנָה נְתֻנִים לַה׳ — *For you, they are given as a gift to HASHEM.* They will be obligated to serve, by Your command, all the needs of the Tent of Meeting.

NOTES

Sanctuary. It is the responsibility of both the *Kohanim* and the Kehathites to prevent any stranger from entering the Sanctuary or touching the holy objects. The phrase *your father's house* refers to the sons of Kehath who were Levites. All precautions, however, in connection with the priesthood are the exclusive responsibility of the *Kohanim*.

2. וִישָׁרְתוּךָ — *And minister to you.* The Levites were charged with ministering to the needs of the *Kohanim* in the domain of the sacred service, and not to their personal needs.

3-5. וְשָׁמְרוּ מִשְׁמַרְתְּךָ וּמִשְׁמֶרֶת כָּל הָאֹהֶל . . . וּשְׁמַרְתֶּם אֵת מִשְׁמֶרֶת הַקֹּדֶשׁ — *And they shall keep your charge and the charge of all the tent . . . And you shall keep the charge of the holy things.* The *Sforno* explains that the guarding of the Holy is a joint endeavor of the *Kohanim* and the Levites, with precise parameters; 'the *Kohanim* on the inside, the Levites on the outside' as the *Sifri* puts it.

אִתְּךָ תִּשְׁמְרוּ אֶת־כְּהֻנַּתְכֶם לְכָל־דְּבַר הַמִּזְבֵּחַ וּלְמִבֵּית לַפָּרֹכֶת וַעֲבַדְתֶּם
עֲבֹדַת מַתָּנָה אֶתֵּן אֶת־כְּהֻנַּתְכֶם וְהַזָּר הַקָּרֵב יוּמָת׃
ח וַיְדַבֵּר יהוה אֶל־אַהֲרֹן וַאֲנִי הִנֵּה נָתַתִּי לְךָ אֶת־מִשְׁמֶרֶת תְּרוּמֹתָי לְכָל־
ט קָדְשֵׁי בְנֵי־יִשְׂרָאֵל לְךָ נְתַתִּים לְמָשְׁחָה וּלְבָנֶיךָ לְחָק־עוֹלָם׃ זֶה־יִהְיֶה לְךָ
מִקֹּדֶשׁ הַקֳּדָשִׁים מִן־הָאֵשׁ כָּל־קָרְבָּנָם לְכָל־מִנְחָתָם וּלְכָל־חַטָּאתָם וּלְכָל־
י אֲשָׁמָם אֲשֶׁר יָשִׁיבוּ לִי קֹדֶשׁ קָדָשִׁים לְךָ הוּא וּלְבָנֶיךָ׃ בְּקֹדֶשׁ הַקֳּדָשִׁים
יא תֹּאכְלֶנּוּ כָּל־זָכָר יֹאכַל אֹתוֹ קֹדֶשׁ יִהְיֶה־לָּךְ׃ וְזֶה־לְּךָ תְּרוּמַת מַתָּנָם לְכָל־
תְּנוּפֹת בְּנֵי יִשְׂרָאֵל לְךָ נְתַתִּים וּלְבָנֶיךָ וְלִבְנֹתֶיךָ אִתְּךָ לְחָק־עוֹלָם כָּל־
יב טָהוֹר בְּבֵיתְךָ יֹאכַל אֹתוֹ׃ כֹּל חֵלֶב יִצְהָר וְכָל־חֵלֶב תִּירוֹשׁ וְדָגָן רֵאשִׁיתָם

---

7. תִּשְׁמְרוּ אֶת כְּהֻנַּתְכֶם — *Shall guard your priesthood* . . . that no stranger shall come nigh to the priestly service, as it occurred with Uziyahu (*II Chronicles* 26:16).

וַעֲבַדְתֶּם — *And you shall serve.* And likewise you shall prevent any stranger from the service in which you (alone) serve. Now this (warning) is necessary because, indeed . . .

עֲבֹדַת מַתָּנָה אֶתֵּן אֶת כְּהֻנַּתְכֶם — *I give you the priesthood as a service of gift*. The service of the priesthood which is imposed only upon you, is given and placed as a gift of honor and superiority in the eyes of all men. Therefore, all will desire it; hence you must guard it well.

8. וַאֲנִי הִנֵּה נָתַתִּי לְךָ — *And I, behold, have given you.* You shall keep the charge of the holy things as I commanded you, and I (in turn) give you the priestly gifts written in this chapter.

9. מִן הָאֵשׁ — (*Reserved*) *from the fire.* The entire (offering) is given (to the One) on High, and the *Kohanim* have no part in it until after the (sacrifice) has been burnt (on the altar), for they (only) receive from the 'elevated table' (i.e., the altar), therefore . . .

10. בְּקֹדֶשׁ הַקֳּדָשִׁים תֹּאכְלֶנּוּ — *In a most holy place shall you eat it* . . . within the curtains.

11. תְּרוּמַת מַתָּנָם — *The heave-offering of their gift* . . . that which is given by the 'owners' (the ones who bring the offering) to the *Kohanim* from the holy of 'lesser degree' (קָדָשִׁים קַלִּים), in which the owners have a portion.

NOTES

7. עֲבֹדַת מַתָּנָה אֶתֵּן אֶת כְּהֻנַּתְכֶם — *I give you the priesthood as a service of gift.* The *Sforno* interprets the expression עֲבֹדַת מַתָּנָה as a gift so precious in the eyes of others that they will be tempted to usurp the privilege, as did King Uziyahu who attempted to offer קְטֹרֶת, *incense*, on the golden altar. It was therefore imperative that they exercise caution not to permit others to participate in the priestly service in which they would be interested.

9. מִן הָאֵשׁ — (*Reserved*) *from the fire.* The portion received by the *Kohen* from קָדְשֵׁי קָדָשִׁים (most holy offerings) is not given to him *directly*, as is the case of קָדָשִׁים קַלִּים (offerings of a 'lesser' degree of holiness) where the owner gives it directly to the *Kohen*. In the first case, it is *from the fire*, meaning that the altar is entitled to everything, except that God grants the *Kohanim* a portion from 'His Table.' It therefore follows that this meat can only be eaten in the most holy place, unlike the priestly gifts which are of a lesser degree of holiness that they may be eaten elsewhere.

יג אֲשֶׁר־יִתְּנוּ לַיהוָה לְךָ נְתַתִּים: בִּכּוּרֵי כָּל־אֲשֶׁר בְּאַרְצָם אֲשֶׁר־יָבִיאוּ
יד לַיהוָה לְךָ יִהְיֶה כָּל־טָהוֹר בְּבֵיתְךָ יֹאכְלֶנּוּ: כָּל־חֵרֶם בְּיִשְׂרָאֵל לְךָ יִהְיֶה:
טו כָּל־פֶּטֶר רֶחֶם לְכָל־בָּשָׂר אֲשֶׁר־יַקְרִיבוּ לַיהוָה בָּאָדָם וּבַבְּהֵמָה יִהְיֶה־לָּךְ
אַךְ | פָּדֹה תִפְדֶּה אֵת בְּכוֹר הָאָדָם וְאֵת בְּכוֹר־הַבְּהֵמָה הַטְּמֵאָה תִּפְדֶּה:
טז וּפְדוּיָו מִבֶּן־חֹדֶשׁ תִּפְדֶּה בְּעֶרְכְּךָ כֶּסֶף חֲמֵשֶׁת שְׁקָלִים בְּשֶׁקֶל הַקֹּדֶשׁ
יז עֶשְׂרִים גֵּרָה הוּא: אַךְ בְּכוֹר־שׁוֹר אוֹ־בְכוֹר כֶּשֶׂב אוֹ־בְכוֹר עֵז לֹא תִפְדֶּה
קֹדֶשׁ הֵם אֶת־דָּמָם תִּזְרֹק עַל־הַמִּזְבֵּחַ וְאֶת־חֶלְבָּם תַּקְטִיר אִשֶּׁה לְרֵיחַ
יח־יט נִיחֹחַ לַיהוָה: וּבְשָׂרָם יִהְיֶה־לָּךְ כַּחֲזֵה הַתְּנוּפָה וּכְשׁוֹק הַיָּמִין לְךָ יִהְיֶה: כֹּל
| תְּרוּמֹת הַקֳּדָשִׁים אֲשֶׁר יָרִימוּ בְנֵי־יִשְׂרָאֵל לַיהוָה נָתַתִּי לְךָ וּלְבָנֶיךָ
וְלִבְנֹתֶיךָ אִתְּךָ לְחָק־עוֹלָם בְּרִית מֶלַח עוֹלָם הִוא לִפְנֵי יְהוָה לְךָ וּלְזַרְעֲךָ
כ אִתָּךְ: וַיֹּאמֶר יְהוָה אֶל־אַהֲרֹן בְּאַרְצָם לֹא תִנְחָל וְחֵלֶק לֹא־יִהְיֶה לְךָ
שביעי כא בְּתוֹכָם אֲנִי חֶלְקְךָ וְנַחֲלָתְךָ בְּתוֹךְ בְּנֵי יִשְׂרָאֵל: וְלִבְנֵי לֵוִי
הִנֵּה נָתַתִּי כָּל־מַעֲשֵׂר בְּיִשְׂרָאֵל לְנַחֲלָה חֵלֶף עֲבֹדָתָם אֲשֶׁר־הֵם עֹבְדִים
כב אֶת־עֲבֹדַת אֹהֶל מוֹעֵד: וְלֹא־יִקְרְבוּ עוֹד בְּנֵי יִשְׂרָאֵל אֶל־אֹהֶל מוֹעֵד
כג לָשֵׂאת חֵטְא לָמוּת: וְעָבַד הַלֵּוִי הוּא אֶת־עֲבֹדַת אֹהֶל מוֹעֵד וְהֵם יִשְׂאוּ
כד עֲוֺנָם חֻקַּת עוֹלָם לְדֹרֹתֵיכֶם וּבְתוֹךְ בְּנֵי יִשְׂרָאֵל לֹא יִנְחֲלוּ נַחֲלָה: כִּי
אֶת־מַעְשַׂר בְּנֵי־יִשְׂרָאֵל אֲשֶׁר יָרִימוּ לַיהוָה תְּרוּמָה נָתַתִּי לַלְוִיִּם לְנַחֲלָה
עַל־כֵּן אָמַרְתִּי לָהֶם בְּתוֹךְ בְּנֵי יִשְׂרָאֵל לֹא יִנְחֲלוּ נַחֲלָה:
כה־כו וַיְדַבֵּר יְהוָה אֶל־מֹשֶׁה לֵּאמֹר: וְאֶל־הַלְוִיִּם תְּדַבֵּר וְאָמַרְתָּ אֲלֵהֶם כִּי־תִקְחוּ
מֵאֵת בְּנֵי־יִשְׂרָאֵל אֶת־הַמַּעֲשֵׂר אֲשֶׁר נָתַתִּי לָכֶם מֵאִתָּם בְּנַחֲלַתְכֶם
כז וַהֲרֵמֹתֶם מִמֶּנּוּ תְּרוּמַת יְהוָה מַעֲשֵׂר מִן־הַמַּעֲשֵׂר: וְנֶחְשַׁב לָכֶם תְּרוּמַתְכֶם
כח כַּדָּגָן מִן־הַגֹּרֶן וְכַמְלֵאָה מִן־הַיָּקֶב: כֵּן תָּרִימוּ גַם־אַתֶּם תְּרוּמַת יְהוָה מִכֹּל

---

19. כֹּל תְּרוּמֹת הַקֳּדָשִׁים — *All the heave-offerings of the holy things* . . . such as that which is lifted from the breads of the thanksgiving offering, and the two loaves and *challah* (from the dough).

27. וְנֶחְשַׁב לָכֶם תְּרוּמַתְכֶם — *And your offering which you set apart shall be reckoned to you* . . . to cause a blessing to rest on your household, even though it is

NOTES

27. . . . וְנֶחְשַׁב לָכֶם תְּרוּמַתְכֶם — *And your offering which you set apart shall be reckoned to you.* The expression 'and your offering (i.e., the heave-offering of the Levite's tithe) shall be reckoned as the corn of the threshing floor etc.' is difficult to understand. The *Sforno* offers this explanation. Just as the gift of the Israelite to the *Kohen* brings heavenly blessing to his household and his possessions, so shall the heave-offering from the Levite's tithe

מַעְשְׂרֹתֵיכֶם אֲשֶׁר תִּקְחוּ מֵאֵת בְּנֵי יִשְׂרָאֵל וּנְתַתֶּם מִמֶּנּוּ אֶת־תְּרוּמַת
כט יְהוָה לְאַהֲרֹן הַכֹּהֵן׃ מִכֹּל מַתְּנֹתֵיכֶם תָּרִימוּ אֵת כָּל־תְּרוּמַת יְהוָה
ל מִכָּל־חֶלְבּוֹ אֶת־מִקְדְּשׁוֹ מִמֶּנּוּ׃ וְאָמַרְתָּ אֲלֵהֶם בַּהֲרִימְכֶם אֶת־חֶלְבּוֹ מִמֶּנּוּ
לא וְנֶחְשַׁב לַלְוִיִּם כִּתְבוּאַת גֹּרֶן וְכִתְבוּאַת יָקֶב׃ וַאֲכַלְתֶּם אֹתוֹ בְּכָל־מָקוֹם
אַתֶּם וּבֵיתְכֶם כִּי־שָׂכָר הוּא לָכֶם חֵלֶף עֲבֹדַתְכֶם בְּאֹהֶל מוֹעֵד׃
לב וְלֹא־תִשְׂאוּ עָלָיו חֵטְא בַּהֲרִימְכֶם אֶת־חֶלְבּוֹ מִמֶּנּוּ וְאֶת־קָדְשֵׁי בְנֵי־
יִשְׂרָאֵל לֹא תְחַלְּלוּ וְלֹא תָמוּתוּ׃

---

measured, and (our Sages) have said, 'If he first measured the grain and recited the benediction, his prayer is in vain' (*Taanis* 8b); nonetheless, the offering set apart from the tithe (the tithe of the tithe) shall bring a good blessing in the rest of the tithe, which is considered as *chullin* (non-holy) in the hands of the Levite.

NOTES

bring a blessing to his household, even though (unlike the *terumah* of the Israelite) it is measured, and there is a principle that a blessing does not dwell on that which is 'measured, weighed or counted.' Since the offering of the Levite to the *Kohen* is precise — a tenth from his tenth — one might think that this would prevent the effectiveness of the blessing. Therefore, the Torah reassures the Levite that he shall enjoy the same blessing as that enjoyed by the Israelite who gives from the corn and the wine press.

פרשת חקת
Parashas Chukas

יט א־ב וַיְדַבֵּר יהוה אֶל־מֹשֶׁה וְאֶל־אַהֲרֹן לֵאמֹר: זֹאת חֻקַּת הַתּוֹרָה אֲשֶׁר־צִוָּה
יהוה לֵאמֹר דַּבֵּר | אֶל־בְּנֵי יִשְׂרָאֵל וְיִקְחוּ אֵלֶיךָ פָרָה אֲדֻמָּה תְּמִימָה אֲשֶׁר

XIX

2. זאת חֻקַּת הַתּוֹרָה אֲשֶׁר צִוָּה ה׳ — *This is the statute of the Torah which HASHEM has commanded . . .* when He said, *Sprinkle water of purifying upon them* (8:7).

Now behold, our Sages have stated 'The term *statute* (חוק) is (used) to imply that it is an enactment before Me and you have no right to question it' (*Yoma* 67b), and regarding this Solomon said, אָמַרְתִּי אֶחְכָּמָה וְהִיא רְחוֹקָה מִמֶּנִּי, *I said, 'I will be wise, but it was far from me'* (*Ecclesiastes* 7:23). The major enigma of this (statute) is that (the red cow) makes *tamei* those who are *tahor* while making *tahor* those who are *tamei.* However, as we (examine) and discern the totality of this commandment, *a word secretly came to me and we received a whisper of it* (based on *Job* 4:12). (Now) this is because we found initially that all who occupy themselves with it (i.e, the red cow) from the time of its burning and beyond become *tamei* — namely, the one who burns it and he who casts in the cedarwood, hyssop and scarlet thread as it burns, as well as he who gathers, touches and carries (its ashes). However, he who sprinkles and he who sanctifies remain *tahor*. Secondly, a cardinal rule of the cow is that it must be perfectly red, and the prophet has explained that sin is compared to red, saying, אִם יִהְיוּ חֲטָאֵיכֶם כַּשָּׁנִים כַּשֶּׁלֶג יַלְבִּינוּ, *Though your sins be like scarlet they shall be as white as snow* (*Isaiah* 1:18), and our Sages therefore said that they would 'tie a strip of red wool atop the Temple entrance (on Yom Kippur); if it became white they rejoiced, and if not they were sad' (*Yoma* 67a).

Third, it is proper to consider that since כָּל אִמְרַת אֱלוֹהַּ צְרוּפָה, *every word of God is proven* (*Proverbs* 30:5), then without a doubt, they (are meant) to bring (lit., straighten) all (man's) deeds to the middle path, for either extreme is to be rejected, as it says, וְנֶעְקַשׁ דְּרָכִים יִפּוֹל בְּאֶחָת, *He who takes crooked paths shall fall suddenly* (*Proverbs* 28:18).

NOTES

XIX

2. זאת חֻקַּת הַתּוֹרָה — *This is the statute of the Torah.* The *Sforno* explains the red cow ritual allegorically. The color of the cow, as well as the scarlet thread, symbolize sin, while the cedarwood and hyssop represent pride and humility respectively. Sin, in general, and these two traits in particular, mirror extremes in man's behavior. The golden path is the middle path, eschewing both extremes, as the *Rambam* explains in *Hilchos Daos* (1:3-5). However, when one sins, thereby in effect going to an extreme, he can only correct this deviation by bending to the opposite extreme and eventually he will return to the desired middle. When a Jew sins he defiles his soul and impairs the Divine image which is housed in his body, this body being comparable to God's Sanctuary. Now just as one becomes *tamei* when he comes into contact with a dead person or enters a tent where a dead person lies, so does this likewise happen when he defiles himself by transgressing God's Torah. The degree, however, of his impurity varies. When he deviates at times from the norm, the *Sforno* refers to him as one who only draws nigh to the vanities of this world, but if he becomes immersed in the pursuit of material and physical pleasures, he is guilty of sullying his sacred Jewish soul. As a member of *Klal Yisrael,* he also contaminates the climate of the society of which he is a part. Such a serious infraction requires sincere repentance so as to rehabilitate and purify him.

The מֵי חַטָּאת, *waters of purification,* sprinkled on the one who became *tamei* through a dead body, defines the means of *taharah,* purification, for the sinner as well. This water, which combines extreme elements, i.e., the ashes of the red cow symbolizing sin, and water which is the ultimate in purity, as well as the cedar representing pride, and the hyssop symbolizing humility, will serve to instruct

ג אֵין־בָּהּ מוּם אֲשֶׁר לֹא־עָלָה עָלֶיהָ עֹל: וּנְתַתֶּם אֹתָהּ אֶל־אֶלְעָזָר הַכֹּהֵן
ד וְהוֹצִיא אֹתָהּ אֶל־מִחוּץ לַמַּחֲנֶה וְשָׁחַט אֹתָהּ לְפָנָיו: וְלָקַח אֶלְעָזָר הַכֹּהֵן

Fourth, it is fitting to consider that there is no better way to straighten the crooked and bring it back to the middle path than to (first) bend it to the extreme, as is (true) of bodily ailments, as it says, חַבֻּרוֹת פֶּצַע תַּמְרוּק בְּרָע, *Sharp wounds cleanse away evil* (*Proverbs* 20:30), although inclining to the extreme is in itself to be rejected, and could be destructive to one who is in the middle path, similar to a laxative medication which is beneficial for the ill person and harmful to a healthy person.

Fifth, it is important to consider that the purification effected by the ashes of the cow is applicable only to *tumah* caused by a dead person and to no other kind of *tumah*. Now, it is known that Torah and Mitzvos are (commandments) giving life to those who find them and occupy themselves with them, as it says, כִּי הוּא חַיֵּיכֶם, *For it is your life* (*Deut.* 32:47), and he who turns away from them (to pursue) the vanity of the transitory (lit., perishable) is (in danger) of dying or is altogether dead, as (our Sages) state, 'The wicked even in their lifetime are called dead' (*Berachos* 18b).

Sixth, it is fitting to consider that which our Sages told us, that the cedar wood symbolizes pride (or arrogance) and the hyssop symbolizes the opposite (i.e., humility), and since the scarlet thread is combined with them, it symbolizes (lit., teaches) that both (traits) are sinful, as (the Sages) said, 'He (the scholar) in whom there is pride deserves excommunication, as well as the one in whom there is no pride' (*Sotah* 5a), especially regarding one who must exercise leadership on behalf of the people. And indeed, our Sages have told us that Saul was punished because he was not particular about his honor (*Yoma* 22b), as it says, וַיִּבְזֻהוּ וְלֹא הֵבִיאוּ לוֹ מִנְחָה וַיְהִי כְּמַחֲרִישׁ, *And they despised him and did not bring him presents, but he held his peace* (*I Samuel* 10:27). And the prophet also chastened him when he said, הֲלוֹא אִם קָטֹן אַתָּה בְּעֵינֶיךָ רֹאשׁ שִׁבְטֵי יִשְׂרָאֵל אָתָּה, *Although you are little in your own sight, you are the head of the tribes of Israel* (ibid. 15:17).

NOTES

him of the danger of extremes and thereby bring him back to the golden middle path.

Those occupied in preparing the water of purification, who are themselves not *tamei*, take on this state of impurity for they represent those who are not in need of purification, hence for them the extreme is harmful — unlike the recipient of the water who has already gone to one extreme, and by being lead to the other is ultimately brought back to the middle. The one who sprinkles and sanctifies, however, does not become *tamei* since he represents the wise teacher of Torah who instructs the sinner in the ways of repentance.

The *Sforno* skillfully draws from Scripture, the Talmud and medical science to prove that red and scarlet represent sin; that both pride and humility carried to the extreme are faulty and injurious, and that which is harmful to a healthy person is beneficial to a sick person. In this manner he is able to resolve the anomaly that the red cow is מְטַהֵר טְמֵאִים וּמְטַמֵּא טְהוֹרִים, i.e., *purifies the unclean and defiles the clean.*

The reason that the sprinkling of the מֵי חַטָּאת is used only to make *tahor* a טְמֵא מֵת (one who is defiled by contact with the dead) is linked to the severe punishment imposed by the Torah upon one who is *tamei* in such a manner and enters the Holy. In similar fashion, one who becomes 'impure' through sin defiles himself and must purge his sins through the living waters of Torah and through repentance. The *Sforno* teaches that this is the subtle meaning of the introductory phrase זֹאת חֻקַּת הַתּוֹרָה, *This is the statute of the Torah.*

אֲשֶׁר צִוָּה ה׳ — *Which* HASHEM *has commanded.* The expression *which* HASHEM *has commanded* implies that God had already instructed Moses regarding the מֵי חַטָּאת, *purify-*

ה מִדָּמָהּ בְּאֶצְבָּעוֹ וְהִזָּה אֶל־נֹכַח פְּנֵי אֹהֶל־מוֹעֵד מִדָּמָהּ שֶׁבַע פְּעָמִים׃ וְשָׂרַף
אֶת־הַפָּרָה לְעֵינָיו אֶת־עֹרָהּ וְאֶת־בְּשָׂרָהּ וְאֶת־דָּמָהּ עַל־פִּרְשָׁהּ יִשְׂרֹף׃
ו וְלָקַח הַכֹּהֵן עֵץ אֶרֶז וְאֵזוֹב וּשְׁנִי תוֹלָעַת וְהִשְׁלִיךְ אֶל־תּוֹךְ שְׂרֵפַת הַפָּרָה׃
ז וְכִבֶּס בְּגָדָיו הַכֹּהֵן וְרָחַץ בְּשָׂרוֹ בַּמַּיִם וְאַחַר יָבֹא אֶל־הַמַּחֲנֶה וְטָמֵא הַכֹּהֵן
ח עַד־הָעָרֶב׃ וְהַשֹּׂרֵף אֹתָהּ יְכַבֵּס בְּגָדָיו בַּמַּיִם וְרָחַץ בְּשָׂרוֹ בַּמָּיִם וְטָמֵא
ט עַד־הָעָרֶב׃ וְאָסַף ׀ אִישׁ טָהוֹר אֵת אֵפֶר הַפָּרָה וְהִנִּיחַ מִחוּץ לַמַּחֲנֶה בְּמָקוֹם
י טָהוֹר וְהָיְתָה לַעֲדַת בְּנֵי־יִשְׂרָאֵל לְמִשְׁמֶרֶת לְמֵי נִדָּה חַטָּאת הִוא׃ וְכִבֶּס
הָאֹסֵף אֶת־אֵפֶר הַפָּרָה אֶת־בְּגָדָיו וְטָמֵא עַד־הָעָרֶב וְהָיְתָה לִבְנֵי יִשְׂרָאֵל
יא וְלַגֵּר הַגָּר בְּתוֹכָם לְחֻקַּת עוֹלָם׃ הַנֹּגֵעַ בְּמֵת לְכָל־נֶפֶשׁ אָדָם וְטָמֵא שִׁבְעַת
יב יָמִים׃ הוּא יִתְחַטָּא־בוֹ בַּיּוֹם הַשְּׁלִישִׁי וּבַיּוֹם הַשְּׁבִיעִי יִטְהָר וְאִם־לֹא
יג יִתְחַטָּא בַּיּוֹם הַשְּׁלִישִׁי וּבַיּוֹם הַשְּׁבִיעִי לֹא יִטְהָר׃ כָּל־הַנֹּגֵעַ בְּמֵת בְּנֶפֶשׁ
הָאָדָם אֲשֶׁר־יָמוּת וְלֹא יִתְחַטָּא אֶת־מִשְׁכַּן יהוה טִמֵּא וְנִכְרְתָה הַנֶּפֶשׁ
הַהִוא מִיִּשְׂרָאֵל כִּי מֵי נִדָּה לֹא־זֹרַק עָלָיו טָמֵא יִהְיֶה עוֹד טֻמְאָתוֹ בוֹ׃
יד זֹאת הַתּוֹרָה אָדָם כִּי־יָמוּת בְּאֹהֶל כָּל־הַבָּא אֶל־הָאֹהֶל וְכָל־אֲשֶׁר בָּאֹהֶל
טו יִטְמָא שִׁבְעַת יָמִים׃ וְכֹל כְּלִי פָתוּחַ אֲשֶׁר אֵין־צָמִיד פָּתִיל עָלָיו טָמֵא
טז הוּא׃ וְכֹל אֲשֶׁר־יִגַּע עַל־פְּנֵי הַשָּׂדֶה בַּחֲלַל־חֶרֶב אוֹ בְמֵת אוֹ־בְעֶצֶם אָדָם
יז אוֹ בְקָבֶר יִטְמָא שִׁבְעַת יָמִים׃ וְלָקְחוּ לַטָּמֵא מֵעֲפַר שְׂרֵפַת הַחַטָּאת וְנָתַן
שני יח עָלָיו מַיִם חַיִּים אֶל־כֶּלִי׃ וְלָקַח אֵזוֹב וְטָבַל בַּמַּיִם אִישׁ טָהוֹר וְהִזָּה
עַל־הָאֹהֶל וְעַל־כָּל־הַכֵּלִים וְעַל־הַנְּפָשׁוֹת אֲשֶׁר הָיוּ־שָׁם וְעַל־הַנֹּגֵעַ בַּעֶצֶם
יט אוֹ בֶחָלָל אוֹ בַמֵּת אוֹ בַקָּבֶר׃ וְהִזָּה הַטָּהֹר עַל־הַטָּמֵא בַּיּוֹם הַשְּׁלִישִׁי
וּבַיּוֹם הַשְּׁבִיעִי וְחִטְּאוֹ בַּיּוֹם הַשְּׁבִיעִי וְכִבֶּס בְּגָדָיו וְרָחַץ בַּמַּיִם וְטָהֵר בָּעָרֶב׃
כ וְאִישׁ אֲשֶׁר־יִטְמָא וְלֹא יִתְחַטָּא וְנִכְרְתָה הַנֶּפֶשׁ הַהִוא מִתּוֹךְ הַקָּהָל כִּי
כא אֶת־מִקְדַּשׁ יהוה טִמֵּא מֵי נִדָּה לֹא־זֹרַק עָלָיו טָמֵא הוּא׃ וְהָיְתָה לָהֶם
לְחֻקַּת עוֹלָם וּמַזֵּה מֵי־הַנִּדָּה יְכַבֵּס בְּגָדָיו וְהַנֹּגֵעַ בְּמֵי הַנִּדָּה יִטְמָא
כב עַד־הָעָרֶב׃ וְכֹל אֲשֶׁר־יִגַּע־בּוֹ הַטָּמֵא יִטְמָא וְהַנֶּפֶשׁ הַנֹּגַעַת תִּטְמָא
עַד־הָעָרֶב׃

Therefore, let us say that although this commandment is a statute and we must not criticize it nor question (lit., doubt) whether it is proper or not, for 'every word of God is proven' and doubtless there is some sublime reason (for this *mitzvah)* known to the King who commanded it, and perhaps also to Moses our Teacher and those who are like him — it contains an allusion to the way of repentance necessary for every sinner, (which is) to incline to the opposite extreme of his (evil) deeds, which defile the purity of every (man's) heart, in order to attain the middle path and (thereby) become purified. Now this course, although good and purifying for the sinner, is discreditable and bad and defiling for those whose hearts are pure, as our Sages state (regarding the *nazir*), 'Against which soul did he sin? It must refer to the fact that he denied himself wine' (*Taanis* 11a).

However, the (cleansing) waters (of the red cow) composed of ashes and water, which are two extremes from which combination there evolves a middle path, teaches us that through this middle path the sinner shall be corrected and this is

כ
א וַיָּבֹאוּ בְנֵי־יִשְׂרָאֵל כָּל־הָעֵדָה מִדְבַּר־צִן בַּחֹדֶשׁ הָרִאשׁוֹן וַיֵּשֶׁב הָעָם
ב בְּקָדֵשׁ וַתָּמָת שָׁם מִרְיָם וַתִּקָּבֵר שָׁם: וְלֹא־הָיָה מַיִם לָעֵדָה וַיִּקָּהֲלוּ
ג עַל־מֹשֶׁה וְעַל־אַהֲרֹן: וַיָּרֶב הָעָם עִם־מֹשֶׁה וַיֹּאמְרוּ לֵאמֹר וְלוּ גָוַעְנוּ בִּגְוַע
ד אַחֵינוּ לִפְנֵי יהוה: וְלָמָה הֲבֵאתֶם אֶת־קְהַל יהוה אֶל־הַמִּדְבָּר הַזֶּה לָמוּת

---

called *taharah,* as it says, מִכֹּל חַטֹּאתֵיכֶם לִפְנֵי ה׳ תִּטְהָרוּ, *From all your sins you shall become tahor before* HASHEM (*Leviticus* 16:30). Now, it is fitting to consider that the Almighty decreed that one who comes into contact with a dead person, as well as one who enters the tent (of a dead person), makes *tamei* the Sanctuary of God (if he enters it), and this (teaches us) that indeed, whoever draws nigh to the vanities of the perishable aspects (of this world), without a doubt, will defile the pure heart which is the sanctuary of God's temple called צֶלֶם אֱלֹהִים, *the image of God,* and this impurity is characterized as an error of omission. (However), when one enters the tent of a dead person, similar to, שֹׁכְנֵי בָתֵּי חֹמֶר, *those who dwell in houses of clay* (*Job* 4:19), meaning those who have naught in life save their bodies and who are immersed in the pursuit of the transitory experiences of this world, and whose steps (lit., feet) lead them to death — such a person, without a doubt, defiles the aforementioned מִקְדַּשׁ ה׳, *God's Temple,* by which the people (of Israel) and each individual is meant to be sanctified to God, as it says, וְלִהְיֹתְךָ עַם קָדֹשׁ לַה׳ אֱלֹהֶיךָ, *And that you may be a holy people to* HASHEM *your God* (*Deut.* 26:19). In this case, he defiles himself (in a positive manner) which is considered an error of commission, and all this is contrary to the intent (of God). For these (reasons), it is fitting that only the dead body of an Israelite can cause *tumah* in a tent, because only his physical matter (i.e., body) is chosen and prepared above all others to serve God, the Blessed One, and only he (the Israelite) sins against his honored soul. However, the wise men who instruct the sinners in the way of repentance, who are akin to the one who sprinkles the water and to the one who sanctifies, are not susceptible to any *tumah.*

And thus in the detailed observance of this commandment, as it is written (in the Torah) and as (taught in) tradition, there is an indication of all these (interpretations) which are part of the intention (and purpose) of Torah, without a doubt.

XX

3. וַיָּרֶב הָעָם עִם מֹשֶׁה — *And the people strove with Moses* . . . Behold, their strife with Moses was in their saying . . .

4. וְלָמָה הֲבֵאתֶם אֶת קְהַל ה׳ אֶל הַמִּדְבָּר הַזֶּה — *And why have you brought the assembly of* HASHEM *into this wilderness?* However, they also (did strive) with God, the Blessed One, (as well) as the (Torah) attests to by saying, *Where the Children of Israel strove with* HASHEM (v. 13), and this (striving with God) was (also manifest) in their saying *and wherefore have you made us come up out of Egypt* (v. 5).

NOTES

ing waters. The *Sforno* explains that this refers to the *taharah,* purification, of the Levites at the time of their consecration, recorded above in *parashas Behaloscha* (8:7).

XX

3-4. וַיָּרֶב הָעָם עִם מֹשֶׁה . . . וְלָמָה הֲבֵאתֶם אֶת קְהַל ה׳ אֶל הַמִּדְבָּר הַזֶּה . . . — *And the people strove with Moses . . . And why have you brought the*

ה שָׁם אֲנַחְנוּ וּבְעִירֵנוּ׃ וְלָמָה הֶעֱלִיתֻנוּ מִמִּצְרַיִם לְהָבִיא אֹתָנוּ אֶל־הַמָּקוֹם
ו הָרָע הַזֶּה לֹא ׀ מְקוֹם זֶרַע וּתְאֵנָה וְגֶפֶן וְרִמּוֹן וּמַיִם אַיִן לִשְׁתּוֹת׃ וַיָּבֹא מֹשֶׁה
וְאַהֲרֹן מִפְּנֵי הַקָּהָל אֶל־פֶּתַח אֹהֶל מוֹעֵד וַיִּפְּלוּ עַל־פְּנֵיהֶם וַיֵּרָא
כְבוֹד־יְהוָה אֲלֵיהֶם׃
שלישי [שני] ז־ח וַיְדַבֵּר יְהוָה אֶל־מֹשֶׁה לֵּאמֹר׃ קַח אֶת־הַמַּטֶּה וְהַקְהֵל אֶת־הָעֵדָה אַתָּה
וְאַהֲרֹן אָחִיךָ וְדִבַּרְתֶּם אֶל־הַסֶּלַע לְעֵינֵיהֶם וְנָתַן מֵימָיו וְהוֹצֵאתָ לָהֶם מַיִם
ט מִן־הַסֶּלַע וְהִשְׁקִיתָ אֶת־הָעֵדָה וְאֶת־בְּעִירָם׃ וַיִּקַּח מֹשֶׁה אֶת־הַמַּטֶּה

---

8. קַח אֶת הַמַּטֶּה . . . וְדִבַּרְתֶּם אֶל הַסֶּלַע — *Take the rod . . . and speak unto the rock.* There are many opinions as to the nature of the sin of 'the waters of Meribah' (strife), and many are in doubt as to what the sin of Moses and Aaron was that the (Torah) does write of them, *you believed not* (v. 12), *you trespassed* (*desecrated*) (*Deut.* 32:51) and *you rebelled* (v. 24). Now, if it was the intent of God, the Blessed One, that they should only *speak* to the rock, then what was the purpose of taking the rod, and if the sin was that Moses hit the rock in the absence of any such command of the One who sent him, then what was Aaron's sin?

However, if we consider the matter of the strife it is fitting that we realize that God's command was (given) in such a fashion that they (i.e., Israel) recognize the evil of their strife and confess their sin and repent so that they be healed, for *He does not desire the death* (*of the wicked*) [based on *Ezekiel* 18:32]. And thus we will understand that it was this that Moses and Aaron overlooked, i.e., the intent of God, the Holy One, and for this He punished them. For, indeed, the strife with Moses was in their saying that his leadership was imperfect, being that he brought them to the worst part of the wilderness, while their strife with God, the Blessed One, was in their saying that He took them forth from a good, settled land to a (barren) wilderness. Now to make known to them their wickedness, it was necessary that this miracle (should) inform them that the messenger was functioning (lit., leading them) with perfection and that He who sent him did it for their benefit and not to harm them whatsoever.

Now there are three kinds of miracles related in Holy Scriptures, each (taking place) in one of three ways: One is a hidden miracle, such as rainfall or when one is delivered from illness or travail. This type of miracle can be attained by the righteous through their prayers, similar to, וַיִּתְפַּלֵּל אַבְרָהָם אֶל הָאֱלֹהִים וַיִּרְפָּא אֱלֹהִים אֶת אֲבִימֶלֶךְ וְאֶת אִשְׁתּוֹ וְאַמְהֹתָיו וַיֵּלֵדוּ, *And Abraham prayed to God and God healed Abimelech and his wife and his maidservants and they gave birth* (*Genesis* 20:17); also *And Moses prayed for the people* (21:7). The second is a revealed miracle, which nature cannot achieve in that (particular) manner but it can be brought about after a period of time through much movement. This type of miracle is wrought by

NOTES

assembly of HASHEM *into this wilderness?* . . . Although the verse states that they only strove with Moses for leading them into the wilderness, the *Sforno* explains that they also were critical of God for bringing them forth from Egypt, as we clearly see in verse 13. The *Sforno* explains this point further in his commentary on verse 8.

8. קַח אֶת הַמַּטֶּה . . . וְדִבַּרְתֶּם אֶל הַסֶּלַע — *Take the rod ... and speak unto the rock.* At Rephidim, the Almighty commanded Moses to smite the rock with his rod and bring forth water (*Exodus* 17:6). At Meribah, Moses and Aaron were told to speak to the rock. Still, Moses was also commanded to 'take the rod,' which puzzles the *Sforno*. If they were meant

י מִלִּפְנֵי יהוה כַּאֲשֶׁר צִוָּהוּ: וַיַּקְהִלוּ מֹשֶׁה וְאַהֲרֹן אֶת־הַקָּהָל אֶל־פְּנֵי הַסָּלַע
יא וַיֹּאמֶר לָהֶם שִׁמְעוּ־נָא הַמֹּרִים הֲמִן־הַסֶּלַע הַזֶּה נוֹצִיא לָכֶם מָיִם: וַיָּרֶם
מֹשֶׁה אֶת־יָדוֹ וַיַּךְ אֶת־הַסֶּלַע בְּמַטֵּהוּ פַּעֲמָיִם וַיֵּצְאוּ מַיִם רַבִּים וַתֵּשְׁתְּ
יב הָעֵדָה וּבְעִירָם: וַיֹּאמֶר יהוה אֶל־מֹשֶׁה וְאֶל־אַהֲרֹן יַעַן

God, the Blessed One, through His servants, preceded by certain actions ordered by Him such as הַשְׁלִיכֵהוּ אַרְצָה, *Cast it on the ground* (*Exodus* 4:3) and הָרֵם אֶת מַטְּךָ, *Lift up your rod* (ibid. 14:16) or וְהִכִּיתָ בַצּוּר, *And you shall smite the rock* (ibid. 17:6) and יְרֵה וַיּוֹר, *'Shoot!' and he shot* (*II Kings* 13:17), and other (such examples).

The third kind of miracle is one that nature can, in no way, achieve and this type (of miracle) God, the Exalted One, achieves with His servants only through speech alone, which is an intellectual act and more distinguished than other physical movements, as was the case when the earth opened its mouth, as it says, *And it came to pass when he finished speaking . . . that the ground did cleave asunder* (16:31). And when the sun stood still for Joshua, it says, אָז יְדַבֵּר יְהוֹשֻׁעַ, *And then Joshua spoke* (*Joshua* 10:12). Now, behold that regarding this episode of Meribah, it was imperative to remove the evil complaints of Israel (in such a manner) that the miracle wrought would clarify the excellence of the King who dispatched (Moses) and His ways of goodness while (also) clarifying the excellence of the messenger and *his* goodness, that he was prepared to achieve good for his people (on behalf of) the King. Now, the excellence of the One who sends is elucidated through the third type of miracle, which nature cannot achieve at all in any fashion or at any time, while the excellence of the messenger is (demonstrated) through the second kind of miracle, which is achieved through the appropriate movements of the messenger. Therefore, God, the Blessed One, commanded that the rock be transformed into (a source) of water, as it says, *that it give forth its water*, meaning that the water will come forth from the rock itself, and not be drawn to it from another place. Now this would have been impossible unless the rock changed its form from 'rock' to 'water,' as (the verse) later testifies to by saying, הַמּוֹצִיא לְךָ מַיִם מִצּוּר הַחַלָּמִישׁ, *Who brought forth for you water out of the rock of flint* (*Deut.* 8:15); because if the water would have been brought there miraculously from a different source it would make no difference whether it (gushed forth) from a rock of flint or from anything else!

Now this type of miracle cannot be effectuated by nature through any means or at any time. (Therefore) He commanded that it be done through the speech of His servants, as it says, *and speak unto the rock*, so that Israel shall realize that this miracle is of the third kind, as we have said (above) — namely that the water was

NOTES

only to speak to it, then what need was there for the rod? Secondly, why was it proper to smite the rock at Rephidim, whereas here the water was to be drawn forth through speech?

The *Sforno* explains that there are three kinds of miracles. The first is one that manifests itself through seemingly natural channels. This can result from the prayers of the righteous. The second transforms the laws of nature to a certain degree, yet is still within the realm of the natural. This can only be achieved by God but is done through His servants who cause it to happen by way of some action — which is in keeping with a specific directive of God. The third — and highest — type of miracle is one which completely transcends nature. This is done through the speech of His servant, for speech is an act more intellectual than physical, hence it represents an action, on the part of God, which is supernatural.

As mentioned above, the Children of Israel

לֹא־הֶאֱמַנְתֶּם בִּי לְהַקְדִּישֵׁנִי לְעֵינֵי בְּנֵי יִשְׂרָאֵל לָכֵן לֹא תָבִיאוּ
יג אֶת־הַקָּהָל הַזֶּה אֶל־הָאָרֶץ אֲשֶׁר־נָתַתִּי לָהֶם׃ הֵמָּה מֵי מְרִיבָה אֲשֶׁר־רָבוּ

---

not being drawn from another place, and thus they will recognize (lit., know) the greatness and goodness of the מְשַׁלֵּחַ (Sender) and consider that although He brought them forth from Egypt to a wilderness it was not detrimental to them at all since He was with them and since He was capable of transforming the wilderness into a *pond of water*, (an act) which cannot be achieved through nature; hence, 'if He is here, all are here' (based on *Succah* 53a) and as it is written, הֲמִדְבָּר הָיִיתִי לְיִשְׂרָאֵל, *Have I been a wilderness to Israel* (*Jeremiah* 2:31). With all this, He (also) commanded that after the rock would change over to water, Moses was to bring forth this water with his rod to their tribes, as it says, *with the sceptre and with their staves* (21:18), and for this kind of miracle He said, *Take the rod . . . and bring forth to them water from the rock.* (Now) behold, Moses and Aaron agreed to perform the second category of miracle, and to bring the water to the rock from another (existing) place as they did in Rephidim, as it says, וְהִכִּיתָ בַצּוּר וְיָצְאוּ מִמֶּנּוּ מַיִם, *And you shall smite the rock and water shall come out of it* (*Exodus* 17:6), because they did not trust that God, the Blessed One, would fulfill His word to perform the third type of miracle for Israel, for they thought that Israel were rebels and hence unworthy of God's goodness. Therefore, they performed the second kind of miracle with the rod, which proclaimed the excellence of the messenger, but did not follow the third way by which Israel would have been told of the excellence and goodness of the Sender. Therefore, it is written regarding them . . .

12. לֹא הֶאֱמַנְתֶּם בִּי — *You did not believe in Me.* This means: You had no confidence that I would fulfill that which I had said; (and) מְעַלְתֶּם בִּי, *You trespassed against Me* (*Deut.* 32:51), for you desecrated My honor and did not show those who were striving (against us) their foolishness, and (also) *You rebelled against My word* (v. 24) by not observing My commandment.

NOTES

had challenged both the motivation of God in taking them out of Egypt as well as the authenticity of Moses' leadership. The purpose of this miracle was to establish the beneficence and goodness of God and the legitimacy of His messengers — Moses and Aaron. To establish the former, the third category of miracle was called for; namely, to do it through speech and transform the stone into water — a totally radical change in nature. To establish the credibility of Moses, it was sufficient to perform a miracle of the second kind, which was to bring the water from the rock to the tents of the people, as was the accepted case during their travels in the wilderness (see *Rashi*, Chapter 21:18). For this latter purpose, the rod was necessary. However, Moses and Aaron felt that Israel was not worthy of the highest form of miracle, namely to have God transform the rock into a *direct* source of new water through their speech. Therefore, they smote the rock in order to bring water from an existing well or spring, as had been done at Rephidim. Hence, they were guilty of non-belief, of מְעִילָה, *trespass*, as well as rebellion, as explained by the *Sforno* in verse 12.

12. לֹא הֶאֱמַנְתֶּם בִּי — *You did not believe in Me.* God had told Moses and Aaron that He was prepared to perform a miracle of the third kind. Moses and Aaron (1) did not believe Him; (2) were guilty of מְעִילָה (trespass or unlawful use of sacred property) for they failed to properly utilize their God-given power of teaching to relate to the people God's willingness to care for them in spite of their unworthiness; and (3) they did not observe the direct commandment of God to speak to the rock, which was a rebellious act. In this manner, the *Sforno* explains all three expressions used in the Torah — 'lack of belief' (in this verse), 'trespass' (*Deut.* 32:51) and 'rebellion' (in verse 24).

רביעי יד בְּנֵי־יִשְׂרָאֵל אֶת־יהוה וַיִּקָּדֵשׁ בָּם: וַיִּשְׁלַח מֹשֶׁה מַלְאָכִים
מִקָּדֵשׁ אֶל־מֶלֶךְ אֱדוֹם כֹּה אָמַר אָחִיךָ יִשְׂרָאֵל אַתָּה יָדַעְתָּ אֵת
טו כָּל־הַתְּלָאָה אֲשֶׁר מְצָאָתְנוּ: וַיֵּרְדוּ אֲבֹתֵינוּ מִצְרַיְמָה וַנֵּשֶׁב בְּמִצְרַיִם יָמִים
טז רַבִּים וַיָּרֵעוּ לָנוּ מִצְרַיִם וְלַאֲבֹתֵינוּ: וַנִּצְעַק אֶל־יהוה וַיִּשְׁמַע קֹלֵנוּ וַיִּשְׁלַח
יז מַלְאָךְ וַיֹּצִאֵנוּ מִמִּצְרָיִם וְהִנֵּה אֲנַחְנוּ בְקָדֵשׁ עִיר קְצֵה גְבוּלֶךָ: נַעְבְּרָה־נָּא
בְאַרְצֶךָ לֹא נַעֲבֹר בְּשָׂדֶה וּבְכֶרֶם וְלֹא נִשְׁתֶּה מֵי בְאֵר דֶּרֶךְ הַמֶּלֶךְ נֵלֵךְ לֹא
יח נִטֶּה יָמִין וּשְׂמֹאול עַד אֲשֶׁר־נַעֲבֹר גְּבֻלֶךָ: וַיֹּאמֶר אֵלָיו אֱדוֹם לֹא תַעֲבֹר
יט בִּי פֶּן־בַּחֶרֶב אֵצֵא לִקְרָאתֶךָ: וַיֹּאמְרוּ אֵלָיו בְּנֵי־יִשְׂרָאֵל בַּמְסִלָּה נַעֲלֶה
וְאִם־מֵימֶיךָ נִשְׁתֶּה אֲנִי וּמִקְנַי וְנָתַתִּי מִכְרָם רַק אֵין־דָּבָר בְּרַגְלַי אֶעֱבֹרָה:

---

13. וַיִּקָּדֵשׁ בָּם — *And He was sanctified in them* . . . with those very same waters He was later sanctified at the episode of the valley of Arnon, when Israel was shown that these waters were supernatural, as their song indicates when they said, *And from Nachliel Bamos* (21:19), for the water went upward, higher than their source, which is contrary to the nature of water.

17. דֶּרֶךְ הַמֶּלֶךְ — *The King's highway.* We will travel on the road which the King shall command us (to traverse), as is the custom of every king who grants passage to the army of his friends (lit., 'those with whom he has peaceful relations'), sending a scout with them so that the soldiers will do no damage to the inhabitants of the land as they pass through.

18. פֶּן בַּחֶרֶב אֵצֵא לִקְרָאתֶךָ — *Lest I come out with the sword to meet you* . . . for the masses of the Edomites are bloodthirsty men, and for any minor reason (such as that) caused by an argument or similar incident between the inhabitants and those passing through, the inhabitants will be roused to take up their swords against those passing through.

19. בַּמְסִלָּה נַעֲלֶה — *We will go up by the highway.* Behold, this is possible to occur were we to pass through the cities, but we will only travel on the highway, and there will be no cause to arouse your people to take up arms (lit., sword) against us.

רַק אֵין דָּבָר בְּרַגְלַי — *There is no reason (to object) on my account.* We have naught with us which will instigate a quarrel.

NOTES

13. וַיִּקָּדֵשׁ בָּם — *And He was sanctified in them.* Since Moses and Aaron had not obeyed God's command, how then was *He sanctified* through this well? The *Sforno* explains that the supernatural character of these waters was eventually recognized by Israel in the valley of Arnon, as recorded in 21:16 — *that is the well etc.* — and those waters defied the laws of nature by rising higher than their source.

18-20. פֶּן בַּחֶרֶב אֵצֵא לִקְרָאתֶךָ . . . בַּמְסִלָּה נַעֲלֶה . . . אֶעֱבֹרָה . . . וַיֵּצֵא אֱדוֹם לִקְרָאתוֹ . . . — *Lest I come out with the sword to meet you . . . we will go up by the highway . . . let us pass . . . and Edom came out against him.* The discussion between Israel and Edom presents certain difficulties. Considering that Israel courteously asked permission of the king, why was the response such a threatening, militant one? Secondly, the phraseology is strange; the word פֶּן, *lest,* should have read כִּי, *because.* And finally, once they were refused why did they keep pressing for permission? The *Sforno* resolves these difficulties by explaining the sense of these verses thus: The king stated that he would be amenable to follow protocol and permit Israel passage; however, he could not be responsible for the actions of his people. Israel, however, argued that they would only travel on the outskirts of the inhabited areas

כ־כא וַיֹּאמֶר לֹא תַעֲבֹר וַיֵּצֵא אֱדוֹם לִקְרָאתוֹ בְּעַם כָּבֵד וּבְיָד חֲזָקָה: וַיְמָאֵן ׀
אֱדוֹם נְתֹן אֶת־יִשְׂרָאֵל עֲבֹר בִּגְבֻלוֹ וַיֵּט יִשְׂרָאֵל מֵעָלָיו:
חמישי כב־כג וַיִּסְעוּ מִקָּדֵשׁ וַיָּבֹאוּ בְנֵי־יִשְׂרָאֵל כָּל־הָעֵדָה הֹר הָהָר: וַיֹּאמֶר יְהוָה
[שלישי] כד אֶל־מֹשֶׁה וְאֶל־אַהֲרֹן בְּהֹר הָהָר עַל־גְּבוּל אֶרֶץ־אֱדוֹם לֵאמֹר: יֵאָסֵף אַהֲרֹן
אֶל־עַמָּיו כִּי לֹא יָבֹא אֶל־הָאָרֶץ אֲשֶׁר נָתַתִּי לִבְנֵי יִשְׂרָאֵל עַל
כה אֲשֶׁר־מְרִיתֶם אֶת־פִּי לְמֵי מְרִיבָה: קַח אֶת־אַהֲרֹן וְאֶת־אֶלְעָזָר בְּנוֹ וְהַעַל
כו אֹתָם הֹר הָהָר: וְהַפְשֵׁט אֶת־אַהֲרֹן אֶת־בְּגָדָיו וְהִלְבַּשְׁתָּם אֶת־אֶלְעָזָר בְּנוֹ
כז וְאַהֲרֹן יֵאָסֵף וּמֵת שָׁם: וַיַּעַשׂ מֹשֶׁה כַּאֲשֶׁר צִוָּה יְהוָה וַיַּעֲלוּ אֶל־הֹר הָהָר
כח לְעֵינֵי כָּל־הָעֵדָה: וַיַּפְשֵׁט מֹשֶׁה אֶת־אַהֲרֹן אֶת־בְּגָדָיו וַיַּלְבֵּשׁ אֹתָם
אֶת־אֶלְעָזָר בְּנוֹ וַיָּמָת אַהֲרֹן שָׁם בְּרֹאשׁ הָהָר וַיֵּרֶד מֹשֶׁה וְאֶלְעָזָר מִן־הָהָר:
כט וַיִּרְאוּ כָּל־הָעֵדָה כִּי גָוַע אַהֲרֹן וַיִּבְכּוּ אֶת־אַהֲרֹן שְׁלֹשִׁים יוֹם כֹּל בֵּית
כא א יִשְׂרָאֵל: וַיִּשְׁמַע הַכְּנַעֲנִי מֶלֶךְ־עֲרָד יֹשֵׁב הַנֶּגֶב כִּי בָּא
ב יִשְׂרָאֵל דֶּרֶךְ הָאֲתָרִים וַיִּלָּחֶם בְּיִשְׂרָאֵל וַיִּשְׁבְּ ׀ מִמֶּנּוּ שֶׁבִי: וַיִּדַּר יִשְׂרָאֵל

אֶעֱבֹרָה — *Let us pass* ... for since you refuse to let us pass only because of what you have said, then behold, we can pass, for there is no reason to be concerned at all.

20. וַיֵּצֵא אֱדוֹם לִקְרָאתוֹ — *And Edom came out against him* ... to the boundary.

26. וְהַפְשֵׁט אֶת אַהֲרֹן אֶת בְּגָדָיו — *And remove Aaron's garments from him* ... those garments which are reserved for the *Kohen Gadol* (alone) more so than those used by a common *Kohen*.

וְהִלְבַּשְׁתָּם אֶת אֶלְעָזָר — *And put them upon Elazar* ... who was (already) wearing the four garments of a common *Kohen*. Hence, Aaron remained clothed in the four garments of a common *Kohen*, the linen garments, as was his garb when he entered the Holy of Holies (lit., 'all the way within'), and similar to the appearance of God's angels (when they are seen by) His servants.

XXI

1. וַיִּשְׁבְּ מִמֶּנּוּ שֶׁבִי — *And took from them a prisoner* ... (but) no one was killed.

NOTES

and therefore not incite the populace. The king then showed his true colors and marshaled his forces on the border, thereby demonstrating his enmity toward his 'cousins'.

26. וְהַפְשֵׁט אֶת אַהֲרֹן אֶת בְּגָדָיו וְהִלְבַּשְׁתָּם אֶת אֶלְעָזָר ... — *And remove Aaron's garments from him and put them upon Elazar* ... The *Sforno* explains (similar to *Rashi*) that Moses only removed the four special garments of the *Kohen Gadol* from Aaron, which were then transferred to Elazar. Aaron remained clothed with the four linen garments of the כֹּהֵן הֶדְיוֹט, *the common priest*, which was most fitting. The reason for this was that he was now going to meet his Maker, an act which was akin to his entering the holy of Holies on Yom Kippur, at which time the *Kohen Gadol* removed his gold-embroidered garments, ornaments and vestments, entering only in his white linen clothing. The *Sforno* adds that, indeed, the angels, the messengers of God, always appeared garbed as such in visions to the prophets — hence, it was appropriate for Aaron to leave this world and enter the next dressed in these four garments.

נֶ֤דֶר לַֽיהוָה֙ וַיֹּאמַ֔ר אִם־נָתֹ֨ן תִּתֵּ֜ן אֶת־הָעָ֤ם הַזֶּה֙ בְּיָדִ֔י וְהַֽחֲרַמְתִּ֖י
ג אֶת־עָרֵיהֶֽם: וַיִּשְׁמַ֨ע יְהוָ֜ה בְּק֣וֹל יִשְׂרָאֵ֗ל וַיִּתֵּן֙ אֶת־הַֽכְּנַעֲנִ֔י וַיַּֽחֲרֵ֥ם אֶתְהֶ֖ם
וְאֶת־עָרֵיהֶ֑ם וַיִּקְרָ֥א שֵׁם־הַמָּק֖וֹם חָרְמָֽה:
ד וַיִּסְע֞וּ מֵהֹ֤ר הָהָר֙ דֶּ֣רֶךְ יַם־ס֔וּף לִסְבֹ֖ב אֶת־אֶ֣רֶץ אֱד֑וֹם וַתִּקְצַ֥ר נֶֽפֶשׁ־הָעָ֖ם
ה בַּדָּֽרֶךְ: וַיְדַבֵּ֣ר הָעָ֗ם בֵּֽאלֹהִים֮ וּבְמֹשֶׁה֒ לָמָ֤ה הֶֽעֱלִיתֻ֨נוּ֙ מִמִּצְרַ֔יִם לָמ֖וּת
ו בַּמִּדְבָּ֑ר כִּ֣י אֵ֥ין לֶ֨חֶם֙ וְאֵ֣ין מַ֔יִם וְנַפְשֵׁ֣נוּ קָ֔צָה בַּלֶּ֖חֶם הַקְּלֹקֵֽל: וַיְשַׁלַּ֨ח יְהוָ֜ה
בָּעָ֗ם אֵ֚ת הַנְּחָשִׁ֣ים הַשְּׂרָפִ֔ים וַֽיְנַשְּׁכ֖וּ אֶת־הָעָ֑ם וַיָּ֥מָת עַם־רָ֖ב מִיִּשְׂרָאֵֽל:
ז וַיָּבֹא֩ הָעָ֨ם אֶל־מֹשֶׁ֜ה וַיֹּֽאמְר֣וּ חָטָ֗אנוּ כִּֽי־דִבַּ֤רְנוּ בַֽיהוָה֙ וָבָ֔ךְ הִתְפַּלֵּל֙
ח אֶל־יְהוָ֔ה וְיָסֵ֥ר מֵֽעָלֵ֖ינוּ אֶת־הַנָּחָ֑שׁ וַיִּתְפַּלֵּ֥ל מֹשֶׁ֖ה בְּעַ֥ד הָעָֽם: וַיֹּ֨אמֶר יְהוָ֜ה
אֶל־מֹשֶׁ֗ה עֲשֵׂ֤ה לְךָ֙ שָׂרָ֔ף וְשִׂ֥ים אֹת֖וֹ עַל־נֵ֑ס וְהָיָה֙ כָּל־הַנָּשׁ֔וּךְ וְרָאָ֥ה אֹת֖וֹ
ט וָחָֽי: וַיַּ֤עַשׂ מֹשֶׁה֙ נְחַ֣שׁ נְחֹ֔שֶׁת וַיְשִׂמֵ֖הוּ עַל־הַנֵּ֑ס וְהָיָ֗ה אִם־נָשַׁ֤ךְ הַנָּחָשׁ֙
שׁשׁי י אֶת־אִ֔ישׁ וְהִבִּ֛יט אֶל־נְחַ֥שׁ הַנְּחֹ֖שֶׁת וָחָֽי: וַיִּסְע֖וּ בְּנֵ֣י יִשְׂרָאֵ֑ל וַיַּֽחֲנ֖וּ בְּאֹבֹֽת:

---

3. וַיַּחֲרֵם אֶתְהֶם וְאֶת עָרֵיהֶם — *And they utterly destroyed them and their cities.* They vowed to utterly destroy them when they entered the Land, and so they did, as explained in the Book of *Judges* 1:17.

8. עֲשֵׂה לְךָ שָׂרָף — *Make for yourself a fiery serpent.* The serpent is to be (fashioned) from a material which implies 'burning' (i.e., such as brass) so that they would concentrate on the burning vapor (exhalation) of the serpent's mouth, this being akin to their iniquity and its resultant retribution, and thus they will repent.

9. נְחַשׁ נְחֹשֶׁת — *A serpent of brass.* After he (Moses) understood the intent of his Creator, he agreed to make it of brass and not of gold, so as to remind them (Israel) of their iniquity through (the medium) of the appearance of the material, its name and its form. (This was to teach them) that they had acted as serpents, through the vapor of their mouths, when they spoke against God, His action and His servant.

NOTES

XXI

3. וַיַּחֲרֵם אֶתְהֶם וְאֶת עָרֵיהֶם — *And they utterly destroyed them and their cities.* The word חֵרֶם means 'to destroy,' and also means to dedicate something to a sacred purpose, as *Rashi* explains in his commentary on this verse. However, the vow of the Israelites could not be fulfilled at that time since they were on the east bank of the Jordan while the Canaanites and King Arad were on the west side. The *Sforno*, therefore, explains (as does the *Ramban*) that this vow was taken with the intent of fulfilling it later, when Israel would enter the Land. The Book of *Judges*, indeed, records that they destroyed the Canaanites and called the city (of Arad) Chormah. The Torah relates here what eventually happened.

8-9. . . . . עֲשֵׂה לְךָ שָׂרָף . . . נְחַשׁ נְחֹשֶׁת — *Make for yourself a fiery serpent . . . a serpent of brass.* The Children of Israel were guilty of לָשׁוֹן הָרַע, *slander*, a transgression traditionally attributed to the serpent. Slander consumes the victim — it 'burns' — as these fiery serpents burned and consumed the Israelites. The fashioning of a brass serpent and placing it on a banner aroused the Israelites to examine their sin of slander, thereby bringing them to repentance. This was the purpose served by the *serpent of brass*. It was a means toward an end, not some magical cure. Moses originally thought to make it of gold, because any artifact commanded to be fashioned by God deserves to be made of the most expensive material — similar to the vessels of the Sanctuary. In this case, however, the intention

יא וַיִּסְעוּ מֵאֹבֹת וַיַּחֲנוּ בְּעִיֵּי הָעֲבָרִים בַּמִּדְבָּר אֲשֶׁר עַל־פְּנֵי מוֹאָב מִמִּזְרַח
יב־יג הַשָּׁמֶשׁ: מִשָּׁם נָסָעוּ וַיַּחֲנוּ בְּנַחַל זָרֶד: מִשָּׁם נָסָעוּ וַיַּחֲנוּ מֵעֵבֶר אַרְנוֹן אֲשֶׁר
בַּמִּדְבָּר הַיֹּצֵא מִגְּבֻל הָאֱמֹרִי כִּי אַרְנוֹן גְּבוּל מוֹאָב בֵּין מוֹאָב וּבֵין
יד הָאֱמֹרִי: עַל־כֵּן יֵאָמַר בְּסֵפֶר מִלְחֲמֹת יהוה אֶת־וָהֵב בְּסוּפָה וְאֶת־הַנְּחָלִים
טו־טז אַרְנוֹן: וְאֶשֶׁד הַנְּחָלִים אֲשֶׁר נָטָה לְשֶׁבֶת עָר וְנִשְׁעַן לִגְבוּל מוֹאָב: וּמִשָּׁם
בְּאֵרָה הִוא הַבְּאֵר אֲשֶׁר אָמַר יהוה לְמֹשֶׁה אֱסֹף אֶת־הָעָם וְאֶתְּנָה לָהֶם

---

13. הַיֹּצֵא . . . מֵעֵבֶר אַרְנוֹן — *On the other side of the Arnon . . . that goes out* . . . in that portion of the Arnon, and the wilderness that goes out.

כִּי אַרְנוֹן גְּבוּל מוֹאָב — *For Arnon is the border of Moab* . . . because the border of Moab was (situated) only in that portion which met that of the Emorites, but in the portion where (Israel) entered, Moab had no border (whatsoever).

14. בְּסֵפֶר מִלְחֲמֹת ה׳ אֶת וָהֵב בְּסוּפָה — *In the Book of the Wars of* HASHEM, *Vaheb and Suphah* . . . it will be told of God to (future) generations, together with the (accounts of) His other wars, regarding *Vaheb and Suphah and the brooks of Arnon.* Behold, that part of Arnon where Israel passed through in peace and Sichon at that time did not rise up against them — that this was granted to them *through Suphah* (i.e., a storm wind) in the valley of Arnon where God, the Blessed One stirred up a storm and caused a pouring forth of many waters which prevented Sichon from coming out to rise up against them.

15. וְאֶשֶׁד הַנְּחָלִים — *And the discharge of the brooks.* That Book will also tell about the event of the pouring forth of those brooks *that incline to Shebes-ar and lean upon the border of Moab.* (These waters) reached into the city called *Ar*, across from which the Israelites were, but nonetheless (the waters) did not spread to the place where Israel stood, rather it *leaned up* and pressed up *to the border of Moab.*

16. וּמִשָּׁם בְּאֵרָה — *And from there to B'eer (the well)* . . . And from there, that pouring forth of the brooks inclined to the place of the well, whereof . . .

אָמַר ה׳ לְמֹשֶׁה, אֱסֹף אֶת הָעָם — HASHEM *said to Moses, 'Gather the people together.'* We find that the place of that well, which (enabled it) to deepen in such a way that

NOTES

was to underscore the link between נְחֹשֶׁת, *brass* forged through fire, and נָחָשׁ, *a serpent*, whose venom burns and destroys, as does slander. This is a play on words which is most instructive.

14-15. בְּסֵפֶר מִלְחֲמֹת ה׳ אֶת וָהֵב בְּסוּפָה . . . וְאֶשֶׁד הַנְּחָלִים . . . — *In the Book of the Wars of* HASHEM, *Vaheb and Suphah* . . . *And the discharge of the brooks* . . . When Israel encamped on the other side of Arnon, they were not attacked by the Emorites. This verse explains the reason for this inaction. The word וָהֵב (Vaheb) means *to give* (as *Rashi* states); the word סוּפָה (Suphah) means *storm.* The sense of the verse is: God gave (or granted) Israel peace by preventing Sichon from attacking them through a fierce storm wind and the gushing forth of the brook waters. These strong currents of water reached the city of Ar in the vicinity of the Israelites, yet did not engulf them. Miraculously, the waters did not spread out but 'leaned up,' and hence did not inundate the camp of Israel.

16. וּמִשָּׁם בְּאֵרָה — *And from there to B'eer (the well).* As mentioned above, the rock to which Moses was commanded to speak was transformed into water but did not possess the properties or nature of water. Water always descends, but this supernatural water had the power to *ascend.* When the Israelites beheld this phenomena, they burst into a

יז מָיִם: אָז יָשִׁיר יִשְׂרָאֵל אֶת־הַשִּׁירָה הַזֹּאת עֲלִי בְאֵר
יח עֱנוּ־לָהּ: בְּאֵר חֲפָרוּהָ שָׂרִים כָּרוּהָ נְדִיבֵי הָעָם בִּמְחֹקֵק בְּמִשְׁעֲנֹתָם

---

it could not (normally) elevate itself, was much lower than the place where Israel was now standing at the time of the Song, and since that well came up with them to the high (area) of the other side of Arnon, from whence the brooks poured down, they (then) saw that God, the Blessed One, had given power to those waters to rise upward — and therefore they began their song, and said . . .

17. עֲלִי בְאֵר — *Spring up, O well.* It appears to me that the war with the Ammonites at that time, as our Sages tell us (in *tractate Berachos* 54b), is alluded to in the expression, *The Book of the Wars of* HASHEM (v. 14). (Now) Scripture does not elaborate (lit., explain) the details of the miracles (regarding the well) so as to protect (lit., because of) the honor of Moses and Aaron, for indeed these (miracles) were only necessary to demonstrate to Israel that which was proper for Moses and Aaron to have told them had their actions been complete and in keeping with the command of God, the Blessed One. And this (lesson) was that they should know that the waters brought forth from the rock were not natural waters brought there in a wondrous way from some spring or river, but rather they were supernatural, for the rock had been transformed into a pond of water through the will of its Creator in such a manner that it did not possess the nature of other waters whose movement inclines toward the center, and therefore it went up with them to a place higher than its source — and all the more so since it brought up the limbs of the dead in the course of their movement, as our Sages tell us (ibid.). And therefore, Moses our Teacher does not participate in this song, for its theme was to explain how his action was deficient in (fulfilling) the will of his Creator, may He be Blessed, Who completed it, as it says, *And He was sanctified in them* (20:13) (i.e.,) by demonstrating that these waters had power contrary to the nature of other waters, as already explained (20:8).

18. בְּאֵר חֲפָרוּהָ שָׂרִים — *The well which the princes dug* . . . for this well was not full, as would be (a well) which flowed from a high place.

NOTES

song of praise, 'Spring up, O well.'

17. עֲלִי בְאֵר — *Spring up, O well.* The *Sforno* is of the opinion that the expression *The Boook of the Wars of* HASHEM refers to the destruction of the Emorites who were hiding in caves above the valley through which Israel was marching with the intent of killing them with arrows and stone missiles. As our Sages tell us (and so does *Rashi* in his commentary on verse 15), the mountain opposite the caves had projections which moved miraculously across to this mountain, penetrated the caves and crushed the ambushers to death. This event is alluded to in the phrase *The Wars of* HASHEM. However, the miracle regarding the well where God transformed the rock into a *pond of water* (אֲגַם מָיִם) is alluded to in the song of Israel (*Spring up, O well*) in celebration of the supernatural character of these waters and their ability to flow upward. The *Sforno* points out that Moses did not join in this song (as opposed to the Song of the Sea) because it reflects the deficiency in his faith and his disobedience of God's command, manifested when he smote the rock instead of speaking to it. Had he done so he would have sanctified God's Name. Since he did not, God Himself had to demonstrate the miraculous nature of this well by causing it to go up with Israel to a place higher than its source, and by bringing up the blood and limbs of the Emorites from the valley. Therefore, Moses sadly had no part in the sanctification of God through these waters and it was appropriate that he not share in the song.

יט-כ וּמִמִּדְבָּ֖ר מַתָּנָ֑ה: וּמִמַּתָּנָ֖ה נַחֲלִיאֵ֑ל וּמִנַּחֲלִיאֵ֖ל בָּמֽוֹת: וּמִבָּמ֗וֹת הַגַּיְא֙ אֲשֶׁר֙
בִּשְׂדֵ֣ה מוֹאָ֔ב רֹ֖אשׁ הַפִּסְגָּ֑ה וְנִשְׁקָ֖פָה עַל־פְּנֵ֥י הַיְשִׁימֹֽן:

שביעי כא-כב וַיִּשְׁלַ֤ח יִשְׂרָאֵל֙ מַלְאָכִ֔ים אֶל־סִיחֹ֥ן מֶֽלֶךְ־הָאֱמֹרִ֖י לֵאמֹֽר: אֶעְבְּרָ֣ה בְאַרְצֶ֗ךָ
[רביעי] לֹ֤א נִטֶּה֙ בְּשָׂדֶ֣ה וּבְכֶ֔רֶם לֹ֥א נִשְׁתֶּ֖ה מֵ֣י בְאֵ֑ר בְּדֶ֤רֶךְ הַמֶּ֙לֶךְ֙ נֵלֵ֔ךְ עַ֥ד
כג אֲשֶֽׁר־נַעֲבֹ֖ר גְּבֻלֶֽךָ: וְלֹא־נָתַ֨ן סִיחֹ֣ן אֶת־יִשְׂרָאֵ֮ל עֲבֹ֣ר בִּגְבֻלוֹ֒ וַיֶּאֱסֹ֨ף סִיחֹ֜ן
אֶת־כָּל־עַמּ֗וֹ וַיֵּצֵ֞א לִקְרַ֤את יִשְׂרָאֵל֙ הַמִּדְבָּ֔רָה וַיָּבֹ֖א יָ֑הְצָה וַיִּלָּ֖חֶם
כד בְּיִשְׂרָאֵֽל: וַיַּכֵּ֥הוּ יִשְׂרָאֵ֖ל לְפִי־חָ֑רֶב וַיִּירַ֨שׁ אֶת־אַרְצ֜וֹ מֵֽאַרְנֹ֗ן עַד־יַבֹּק֙
כה עַד־בְּנֵ֣י עַמּ֔וֹן כִּ֣י עַ֔ז גְּב֖וּל בְּנֵ֥י עַמּֽוֹן: וַיִּקַּח֙ יִשְׂרָאֵ֔ל אֵ֥ת כָּל־הֶעָרִ֖ים הָאֵ֑לֶּה
כו וַיֵּ֤שֶׁב יִשְׂרָאֵל֙ בְּכָל־עָרֵ֣י הָֽאֱמֹרִ֔י בְּחֶשְׁבּ֖וֹן וּבְכָל־בְּנֹתֶֽיהָ: כִּ֣י חֶשְׁבּ֔וֹן עִ֗יר
סִיחֹ֛ן מֶ֥לֶךְ הָאֱמֹרִ֖י הִ֑וא וְה֣וּא נִלְחַ֗ם בְּמֶ֤לֶךְ מוֹאָב֙ הָֽרִאשׁ֔וֹן וַיִּקַּ֧ח
כז אֶת־כָּל־אַרְצ֛וֹ מִיָּד֖וֹ עַד־אַרְנֹֽן: עַל־כֵּ֛ן יֹאמְר֥וּ הַמֹּשְׁלִ֖ים בֹּ֣אוּ חֶשְׁבּ֑וֹן תִּבָּנֶ֥ה

וּמִמִּדְבָּר מַתָּנָה — *And from the wilderness to Mattanah ...* and thus it was revealed (lit., explained) that the existence (of the water) was given (by God) (directly) from that rock in the wilderness.

19. וּמִמַּתָּנָה נַחֲלִיאֵל — *And from Mattanah to Nachliel ...* and with (all this), it did not increase or diminish as it went up and came down, as would have occurred (lit., been fitting) according to the nature of water if it had flowed from another place.

25. בְּכָל עָרֵי הָאֱמֹרִי בְּחֶשְׁבּוֹן וּבְכָל בְּנֹתֶיהָ — *In all the cities of the Emorites, in Cheshbon, and in all the towns thereof.* All the towns conquered by Sichon, together with all the other towns of his kingdom, were (considered as) daughter-cities of Cheshbon which was the (principal) city from (days of) yore, similar to (the expression), וְנָתַתִּי אֶתְהֶן לָךְ לְבָנוֹת, *And I will give them to you as daughter-cities* (Ezekiel 16:61).

26. כִּי חֶשְׁבּוֹן עִיר סִיחֹן מֶלֶךְ הָאֱמֹרִי הִוא — *For Cheshbon was the city of Sichon, the king of the Emorites.* The reason we stated that all the cities of the Emorites were daughter-cities of Cheshbon is because Cheshbon was the principal city of the kingdom of Sichon, king of the Emorites prior to the conquest of the cities of the Moabites.

27. עַל כֵּן יֹאמְרוּ הַמֹּשְׁלִים — *Wherefore those who speak in parables say ...* Those who tell the meaning of parables which they saw in a visionary dream, as did Bil'am, when it says, *And he took up his parable* (23:7).

בֹּאוּ חֶשְׁבּוֹן — *Come into Cheshbon.* You, the inhabitants of the Moabite towns, come to Cheshbon and submit to Sichon, for he shall be victorious and rule over you.

NOTES

18-19. בְּאֵר חֲפָרוּהָ שָׂרִים ... וּמִמִּדְבָּר מַתָּנָה. וּמִמַּתָּנָה נַחֲלִיאֵל — *The well which the princes dug ... and from the wilderness to Mattanah. And from Mattanah to Nachliel.* The *Sforno* in his commentary on these verses is strengthening his interpretation regarding the nature of

the waters of the well given in verses 20:8 and 21:16, 17.

26-31. כִּי חֶשְׁבּוֹן עִיר סִיחֹן מֶלֶךְ הָאֱמֹרִי הִוא ... בֹּאוּ חֶשְׁבּוֹן ... וַנִּירָם אָבַד חֶשְׁבּוֹן ... וַיֵּשֶׁב יִשְׂרָאֵל בְּאֶרֶץ הָאֱמֹרִי — *For Cheshbon was the city of*

כח וְתִכּוֹנֵן עִיר סִיחוֹן׃ כִּי־אֵשׁ יָצְאָה מֵחֶשְׁבּוֹן לֶהָבָה מִקִּרְיַת סִיחֹן אָכְלָה עָר

כט מוֹאָב בַּעֲלֵי בָּמוֹת אַרְנֹן׃ אוֹי־לְךָ מוֹאָב אָבַדְתָּ עַם־כְּמוֹשׁ נָתַן בָּנָיו

ל פְּלֵיטִם וּבְנֹתָיו בַּשְּׁבִית לְמֶלֶךְ אֱמֹרִי סִיחוֹן׃ וַנִּירָם אָבַד חֶשְׁבּוֹן עַד־דִּיבֹן

לא-לב וַנַּשִּׁים עַד־נֹפַח אֲשֶׁר עַד־מֵידְבָא׃ וַיֵּשֶׁב יִשְׂרָאֵל בְּאֶרֶץ הָאֱמֹרִי׃ וַיִּשְׁלַח

°וַיּוֹרֶשׁ ק׳ לג מֹשֶׁה לְרַגֵּל אֶת־יַעְזֵר וַיִּלְכְּדוּ בְּנֹתֶיהָ °וַיִּירֶשׁ אֶת־הָאֱמֹרִי אֲשֶׁר־שָׁם׃ וַיִּפְנוּ

וַיַּעֲלוּ דֶּרֶךְ הַבָּשָׁן וַיֵּצֵא עוֹג מֶלֶךְ־הַבָּשָׁן לִקְרָאתָם הוּא וְכָל־עַמּוֹ לַמִּלְחָמָה

מפטיר לד אֶדְרֶעִי׃ וַיֹּאמֶר יְהֹוָה אֶל־מֹשֶׁה אַל־תִּירָא אֹתוֹ כִּי בְיָדְךָ נָתַתִּי אֹתוֹ

וְאֶת־כָּל־עַמּוֹ וְאֶת־אַרְצוֹ וְעָשִׂיתָ לּוֹ כַּאֲשֶׁר עָשִׂיתָ לְסִיחֹן מֶלֶךְ הָאֱמֹרִי

לה אֲשֶׁר יוֹשֵׁב בְּחֶשְׁבּוֹן׃ וַיַּכּוּ אֹתוֹ וְאֶת־בָּנָיו וְאֶת־כָּל־עַמּוֹ עַד־בִּלְתִּי

כב א הִשְׁאִיר־לוֹ שָׂרִיד וַיִּירְשׁוּ אֶת־אַרְצוֹ׃ וַיִּסְעוּ בְּנֵי יִשְׂרָאֵל וַיַּחֲנוּ בְּעַרְבוֹת

מוֹאָב מֵעֵבֶר לְיַרְדֵּן יְרֵחוֹ׃

---

30. וַנִּירָם אָבַד חֶשְׁבּוֹן — *And their dominion and Cheshbon were destroyed.* The dominion (נִיר) and kingdom of Sichon, his fire and his flame (see v. 28), namely the military officers (of Sichon), shall perish. Because after they (the מוֹשְׁלִים) told (parables of) Sichon's victories, they also told of the loss of his kingdom through the Israelites.

31. וַיֵּשֶׁב יִשְׂרָאֵל בְּאֶרֶץ הָאֱמֹרִי — *Thus Israel dwelt in the land of the Emorites.* All this is related to explain that Israel did not dwell in the land of Moab, but (rather) they dwelt in the land of the Emorites, as Yiftach explains, saying, לֹא לָקַח יִשְׂרָאֵל אֶת אֶרֶץ מוֹאָב וְאֶת אֶרֶץ בְּנֵי עַמּוֹן, *Israel did not take away the land of Moab nor the land of the children of Ammon* (*Judges* 11:15).

32. וַיִּלְכְּדוּ בְּנֹתֶיהָ — *And they conquered its towns.* The spies sent by Moses took the daughter-cities of Jazer.

וַיּוֹרֶשׁ — *And drove out.* Moses later drove out the Emorites from Jazer.

NOTES

Sichon, the king of the Emorites . . . come into Cheshbon . . . And their dominion and Cheshbon were destroyed . . . Thus Israel dwelt in the land of the Emorites. The Israelites were prohibited by God from waging war against Moab and Ammon and taking their land away from them (*Deut.* 2:19). They were not enjoined from doing so to the Emorites. These verses come to tell us that many Moabite towns were first conquered by Sichon, the Emorite king, and were subsequently taken from him by Israel. This was permitted since these towns were now his and were no longer considered part of Moab or Ammon. It is precisely this argument which Yiftach used when he spoke to the Ammonites, as recorded in *Judges* 11. The *haftarah* of *parashas Chukas* is taken from this chapter in the Book of *Judges* for this reason.

32. וַיִּלְכְּדוּ בְּנֹתֶיהָ וַיּוֹרֶשׁ — *And they conquered its towns and drove out. They* refers to those who were sent by Moses to spy out Jazer, whereas the expression *and drove out* is singular, implying that Moses was the one who drove out the Emorites from Jazer.

פרשת בלק
Parashas Balak

ב־ג וַיַּרְא בָּלָק בֶּן־צִפּוֹר אֵת כָּל־אֲשֶׁר־עָשָׂה יִשְׂרָאֵל לָאֱמֹרִי: וַיָּגָר מוֹאָב
ד מִפְּנֵי הָעָם מְאֹד כִּי רַב־הוּא וַיָּקָץ מוֹאָב מִפְּנֵי בְּנֵי יִשְׂרָאֵל: וַיֹּאמֶר מוֹאָב
אֶל־זִקְנֵי מִדְיָן עַתָּה יְלַחֲכוּ הַקָּהָל אֶת־כָּל־סְבִיבֹתֵינוּ כִּלְחֹךְ הַשּׁוֹר אֵת
ה יֶרֶק הַשָּׂדֶה וּבָלָק בֶּן־צִפּוֹר מֶלֶךְ לְמוֹאָב בָּעֵת הַהִוא: וַיִּשְׁלַח מַלְאָכִים
אֶל־בִּלְעָם בֶּן־בְּעוֹר פְּתוֹרָה אֲשֶׁר עַל־הַנָּהָר אֶרֶץ בְּנֵי־עַמּוֹ לִקְרֹא־לוֹ
לֵאמֹר הִנֵּה עַם יָצָא מִמִּצְרַיִם הִנֵּה כִסָּה אֶת־עֵין הָאָרֶץ וְהוּא יֹשֵׁב מִמֻּלִי:
ו וְעַתָּה לְכָה־נָּא אָרָה־לִּי אֶת־הָעָם הַזֶּה כִּי עָצוּם הוּא מִמֶּנִּי אוּלַי אוּכַל

XXII

2. וַיַּרְא בָּלָק — *And Balak saw.* (Balak was) a man famed for his military knowledge (prowess) as it says, וְעַתָּה הֲטוֹב טוֹב אַתָּה מִבָּלָק בֶּן צִפּוֹר מֶלֶךְ מוֹאָב, *And now, are you better than Balak the son of Zippor, king of Moab?* (*Judges* 11:25). (Still) he observed that when Israel asked permission to pass through the land of Sichon and he refused, they destroyed him; and they (i.e., Moab) saw that this victory was accomplished without a normal stratagem of war.

3. וַיָּגָר מוֹאָב — *And Moab was afraid.* (This refers to) the mighty ones (leaders) of Moab who did not permit Israel to pass (through their land), as Yiftach stated, וְגַם אֶל מֶלֶךְ מוֹאָב שָׁלַח וְלֹא אָבָה, *And in like manner they sent to the king of Moab, but he would not consent* (*Judges* 11:17).

כִּי רַב הוּא — *Because they were many* . . . (and) not due to their stratagem of battle.

וַיָּקָץ מוֹאָב — *And Moab was seized with dread.* The masses of Moab were *weary of life* (based on *Genesis* 27:46) because of the Children of Israel who plundered them.

4. עַתָּה — *Now* . . . that they have conquered the lands of Sichon and Og.

יְלַחֲכוּ הַקָּהָל אֶת כָּל סְבִיבֹתֵינוּ — *This multitude will lick up all that is around about us* . . . to expand and secure their borders.

וּבָלָק בֶּן צִפּוֹר — *And Balak the son of Zippor* . . . who was known for his strength and as a man of war.

מֶלֶךְ לְמוֹאָב בָּעֵת הַהִוא — *Was King of Moab at that time* . . . and yet, he had no heart to fight the Israelites, as it says, הֲרוֹב רָב עִם יִשְׂרָאֵל אִם נִלְחֹם נִלְחַם בָּם, *Did he ever strive against Israel or did he ever fight against them?* (*Judges* 11:25). And Joshua who said, וַיָּקָם בָּלָק בֶּן צִפּוֹר מֶלֶךְ מוֹאָב וַיִּלָּחֶם בְּיִשְׂרָאֵל, *Then Balak the son of Zippor, King of Moab arose and warred against Israel* (*Joshua* 24:9), was referring to his hiring of Balaam to curse (them) as he explains saying, וַיִּשְׁלַח וַיִּקְרָא לְבִלְעָם, *And he sent and called Balaam* (ibid.).

6. אוּלַי אוּכַל — *Perhaps I shall prevail* . . . after you curse them.

NOTES

XXII

2. וַיַּרְא בָּלָק — *And Balak saw.* See the *Sforno's* commentary on *Exodus* 18:1 where he explains the difference between the expressions וַיַּרְא, *and he saw,* and וַיִּשְׁמַע, *and he heard.*

3. וַיָּגָר מוֹאָב . . . וַיָּקָץ מוֹאָב — *And Moab was afraid . . . and Moab was seized with dread.* The first part of the verse refers to the leadership of Moab who were *afraid.* The second part refers to the people of Moab who were *seized with dread.* In this manner, the *Sforno* explains that these expressions are not redundant.

4-6. וּבָלָק . . . מֶלֶךְ לְמוֹאָב . . . אוּלַי אוּכַל נַכֶּה בּוֹ —

נַכֶּה־בּוֹ וַאֲגָרְשֶׁנּוּ מִן־הָאָרֶץ כִּי יָדַעְתִּי אֵת אֲשֶׁר־תְּבָרֵךְ מְבֹרָךְ וַאֲשֶׁר
ז תָּאֹר יוּאָר: וַיֵּלְכוּ זִקְנֵי מוֹאָב וְזִקְנֵי מִדְיָן וּקְסָמִים בְּיָדָם וַיָּבֹאוּ אֶל־בִּלְעָם
ח וַיְדַבְּרוּ אֵלָיו דִּבְרֵי בָלָק: וַיֹּאמֶר אֲלֵיהֶם לִינוּ פֹה הַלַּיְלָה וַהֲשִׁבֹתִי אֶתְכֶם
ט דָּבָר כַּאֲשֶׁר יְדַבֵּר יהוה אֵלָי וַיֵּשְׁבוּ שָׂרֵי־מוֹאָב עִם־בִּלְעָם: וַיָּבֹא אֱלֹהִים
י אֶל־בִּלְעָם וַיֹּאמֶר מִי הָאֲנָשִׁים הָאֵלֶּה עִמָּךְ: וַיֹּאמֶר בִּלְעָם אֶל־הָאֱלֹהִים

נַכֶּה בוֹ — *That we may smite them.* I [will smite] through battle, and you, through a curse.

אֲשֶׁר תְּבָרֵךְ מְבֹרָךְ — *The one whom you bless is blessed.* Behold, his power was not in blessing but in cursing, by reminding (God) of (man's) iniquity or by anticipating the time (of God's anger), as our Sages say (*Berachos* 7a). Therefore, he (Balak) did not ask him for a blessing to be victorious, or that he might be able to stand up to them; but he said, *I know that he whom you bless is blessed*, for Balaam's honor, to demonstrate that he does not consider him to be one who only does damage.

7. וּקְסָמִים בְּיָדָם — *With all kinds of divination in their hand* . . . the implements of magic, for Balaam was a diviner who knew how to anticipate the time, as it says, וְאֶת בִּלְעָם בֶּן בְּעוֹר הַקּוֹסֵם הָרְגוּ בְנֵי יִשְׂרָאֵל בַּחֶרֶב אֶל חַלְלֵיהֶם, *And Balaam the son of Be'or, the soothsayer, did the Children of Israel slay with the sword among those that were slain* (*Joshua* 13:22).

8. כַּאֲשֶׁר יְדַבֵּר ה׳ אֵלָי — *As* HASHEM *may speak to me* . . . because I will prepare myself for prophecy.

9. מִי הָאֲנָשִׁים הָאֵלֶּה עִמָּךְ — *Who are these men with you?* What are their (dealings) with you that you have prepared yourself for prophecy on their behalf so as to know what to do for them? Are they here with you to inquire regarding the future and (therefore) you wish to know the future so as to be able to tell it to them? Or are they here with you to attain some (desired) specific purpose through your curse, and your intention now is to ask (My) permission as to whether you can fulfill their desire?

NOTES

And Balak . . . was King of Moab . . . perhaps I shall prevail that we may smite them. The *Sforno* explains here, as he does in verse 2, that although Balak was a famous warrior, he was unwilling to confront Israel in battle even though, as king, he had the authority to do so. The reason, therefore, had to be his conviction that Israel was protected by God and that his only hope was to engage Balaam to utilize his powers for cursing this people, thereby weakening them and making them vulnerable. Thereby, he would be able to do battle against them, having a greater chance for victory.

6. אֲשֶׁר תְּבָרֵךְ מְבֹרָךְ — *The one whom you bless is blessed.* The *Sforno* explains why Balak didn't ask Balaam to bless *him* rather than curse Israel. Balaam only had the power to curse but not to bless. Balak's statement that whomsoever Balaam *blesses is blessed* was only said to flatter him. According to our Sages, Balaam's power to curse lay in his ability to determine the exact moment when God's wrath was kindled, at which time he would invoke the Divine anger on his chosen target.

7. וּקְסָמִים בְּיָדָם — *With all kinds of divination in their hand.* See note on verse 6 regarding the importance of Balaam's ability to anticipate the time when God was angry.

9. מִי הָאֲנָשִׁים הָאֵלֶּה עִמָּךְ — *Who are these men with you?* Superficially, this question suggested to Balaam that God was not all-knowing. Indeed, this is the explanation of this question given by *Rashi,* quoting the *Tanchuma.* In *Genesis* 3:9, *Rashi* gives a different explanation, namely that God at times puts a seemingly superfluous question to

יא בָּלָק בֶּן־צִפֹּר מֶלֶךְ מוֹאָב שָׁלַח אֵלָי: הִנֵּה הָעָם הַיֹּצֵא מִמִּצְרַיִם וַיְכַס
אֶת־עֵין הָאָרֶץ עַתָּה לְכָה קָבָה־לִּי אֹתוֹ אוּלַי אוּכַל לְהִלָּחֶם בּוֹ וְגֵרַשְׁתִּיו:
יב וַיֹּאמֶר אֱלֹהִים אֶל־בִּלְעָם לֹא תֵלֵךְ עִמָּהֶם לֹא תָאֹר אֶת־הָעָם כִּי בָרוּךְ
שני [חמישי] יג הוּא: וַיָּקָם בִּלְעָם בַּבֹּקֶר וַיֹּאמֶר אֶל־שָׂרֵי בָלָק לְכוּ אֶל־אַרְצְכֶם כִּי מֵאֵן
יד יְהוָה לְתִתִּי לַהֲלֹךְ עִמָּכֶם: וַיָּקוּמוּ שָׂרֵי מוֹאָב וַיָּבֹאוּ אֶל־בָּלָק וַיֹּאמְרוּ מֵאֵן
טו בִּלְעָם הֲלֹךְ עִמָּנוּ: וַיֹּסֶף עוֹד בָּלָק שְׁלֹחַ שָׂרִים רַבִּים וְנִכְבָּדִים מֵאֵלֶּה:
טז וַיָּבֹאוּ אֶל־בִּלְעָם וַיֹּאמְרוּ לוֹ כֹּה אָמַר בָּלָק בֶּן־צִפּוֹר אַל־נָא תִמָּנַע מֵהֲלֹךְ
יז אֵלָי: כִּי־כַבֵּד אֲכַבֶּדְךָ מְאֹד וְכֹל אֲשֶׁר־תֹּאמַר אֵלַי אֶעֱשֶׂה וּלְכָה־נָּא
יח קָבָה־לִּי אֵת הָעָם הַזֶּה: וַיַּעַן בִּלְעָם וַיֹּאמֶר אֶל־עַבְדֵי בָלָק אִם־יִתֶּן־לִי
בָלָק מְלֹא בֵיתוֹ כֶּסֶף וְזָהָב לֹא אוּכַל לַעֲבֹר אֶת־פִּי יְהוָה אֱלֹהָי לַעֲשׂוֹת
יט קְטַנָּה אוֹ גְדוֹלָה: וְעַתָּה שְׁבוּ נָא בָזֶה גַּם־אַתֶּם הַלָּיְלָה וְאֵדְעָה מַה־יֹּסֵף
כ יְהוָה דַּבֵּר עִמִּי: וַיָּבֹא אֱלֹהִים ׀ אֶל־בִּלְעָם לַיְלָה וַיֹּאמֶר לוֹ אִם־לִקְרֹא לְךָ
בָּאוּ הָאֲנָשִׁים קוּם לֵךְ אִתָּם וְאַךְ אֶת־הַדָּבָר אֲשֶׁר־אֲדַבֵּר אֵלֶיךָ אֹתוֹ
שלישי כא תַעֲשֶׂה: וַיָּקָם בִּלְעָם בַּבֹּקֶר וַיַּחֲבֹשׁ אֶת־אֲתֹנוֹ וַיֵּלֶךְ עִם־שָׂרֵי מוֹאָב:
כב וַיִּחַר־אַף אֱלֹהִים כִּי־הוֹלֵךְ הוּא וַיִּתְיַצֵּב מַלְאַךְ יְהוָה בַּדֶּרֶךְ לְשָׂטָן לוֹ וְהוּא

---

12. לֹא תֵלֵךְ עִמָּהֶם — *You shall not go with them.* You shall not go even though you will not curse them, so that you shall not look at them with an evil eye, as our Sages tell us, 'He cast his eyes upon him and he became a heap of bones' (*Berachos* 58a).

20. אִם לִקְרֹא לְךָ בָּאוּ הָאֲנָשִׁים — *If the men have come to call you* . . . if they have only come to you for consultation, (the phrase לִקְרֹא being) similar to, קְרוּאֵי הָעֵדָה, *the elect of the congregation*, and similar to, וָאֶקְרָאֶה לְךָ לְהוֹדִיעֵנִי מָה אֶעֱשֶׂה, *I have called you that you may make known to me what I shall do* (*I Samuel* 28:15).

קוּם לֵךְ אִתָּם — *Rise up, go with them* . . . to caution them not to sin.

22. כִּי הוֹלֵךְ הוּא — *Because he was going* . . . for it was not a case of others leading him, similar to, וַיָּקָם וַיֵּלֶךְ אַחֲרֶיהָ, *And he arose and followed her* (*II Kings* 4:30); rather he went as an interested party, and as one who was attempting to defy the will of God, the Blessed One, because they had not come for consultation at all.

לְשָׂטָן לוֹ — *For an adversary against him.* The phrase הַשְׂטָנָה, *hindering*, implies

NOTES

a person in order to initiate a conversation. The *Sforno*, however, gives a most plausible reason for the question, *Who are these men*? The Almighty is not asking their identity. Rather, He is asking Balaam what his motivation is in contacting Him at this time. Have these men come to find out what the future holds in store for them, or is their purpose to retain Balaam's services to curse Israel?

12. לֹא תֵלֵךְ עִמָּהֶם — *You shall not go with them.* God prohibits Balaam from going with these men (לֹא תֵלֵךְ) and also from uttering any curse (לֹא תָאֹר). The *Sforno* explains that Balaam was prohibited from going even if he would not curse, for his evil gaze would suffice to bring harm upon Israel. Such was the evil power of Balaam! To prove that casting an evil glance upon a person can destroy him, the *Sforno* cites the story of R' Shesheth, who cast his eye on a Sadducean who had treated him disrespectfully, and as a result became a heap of bones.

20. אִם לִקְרֹא לְךָ בָּאוּ הָאֲנָשִׁים — *If the men have come to call you.* God did not change His mind. He granted permission to Balaam to accompany these men for only one purpose,

כג רֹכֵב עַל־אֲתֹנוֹ וּשְׁנֵי נְעָרָיו עִמּוֹ: וַתֵּרֶא הָאָתוֹן אֶת־מַלְאַךְ יהוה נִצָּב
בַּדֶּרֶךְ וְחַרְבּוֹ שְׁלוּפָה בְּיָדוֹ וַתֵּט הָאָתוֹן מִן־הַדֶּרֶךְ וַתֵּלֶךְ בַּשָּׂדֶה וַיַּךְ בִּלְעָם
כד אֶת־הָאָתוֹן לְהַטֹּתָהּ הַדָּרֶךְ: וַיַּעֲמֹד מַלְאַךְ יהוה בְּמִשְׁעוֹל הַכְּרָמִים גָּדֵר
כה מִזֶּה וְגָדֵר מִזֶּה: וַתֵּרֶא הָאָתוֹן אֶת־מַלְאַךְ יהוה וַתִּלָּחֵץ אֶל־הַקִּיר וַתִּלְחַץ
כו אֶת־רֶגֶל בִּלְעָם אֶל־הַקִּיר וַיֹּסֶף לְהַכֹּתָהּ: וַיּוֹסֶף מַלְאַךְ־יהוה עֲבוֹר וַיַּעֲמֹד
כז בְּמָקוֹם צָר אֲשֶׁר אֵין־דֶּרֶךְ לִנְטוֹת יָמִין וּשְׂמֹאול: וַתֵּרֶא הָאָתוֹן
אֶת־מַלְאַךְ יהוה וַתִּרְבַּץ תַּחַת בִּלְעָם וַיִּחַר־אַף בִּלְעָם וַיַּךְ אֶת־הָאָתוֹן
כח בַּמַּקֵּל: וַיִּפְתַּח יהוה אֶת־פִּי הָאָתוֹן וַתֹּאמֶר לְבִלְעָם מֶה־עָשִׂיתִי לְךָ כִּי
כט הִכִּיתַנִי זֶה שָׁלֹשׁ רְגָלִים: וַיֹּאמֶר בִּלְעָם לָאָתוֹן כִּי הִתְעַלַּלְתְּ בִּי לוּ
ל יֶשׁ־חֶרֶב בְּיָדִי כִּי עַתָּה הֲרַגְתִּיךְ: וַתֹּאמֶר הָאָתוֹן אֶל־בִּלְעָם הֲלוֹא אָנֹכִי

---

opposition to an action, similar to, וַיָּרִיבוּ גַּם עָלֶיהָ וַיִּקְרָא שְׁמָהּ שִׂטְנָה, *And they strove for that (well) also and they called its name* שִׂטְנָה, *enmity* (*Genesis* 26:21). Now, the angel came out to oppose Balaam so that his way would not be a smooth one (lit., 'prepared before him'); so that he might divine, as was his wont, and not force the issue. All this was (done) so that he should not sin and thereby be destroyed (i.e., punished).

וְהוּא רֹכֵב עַל אֲתֹנוֹ וּשְׁנֵי נְעָרָיו עִמּוֹ — *Now he was riding on his ass and his two servants were with him.* Therefore, he did not see the angel, as our Sages say, 'To three, it (the evil spirit) will not show itself or do harm' (*Berachos* 43b).

23. וַתֵּלֶךְ בַּשָּׂדֶה — *And went into the field.* Hence, he left his two servants and the lords of Moab behind and therefore they were not aware of the episode with the ass.

28. וַיִּפְתַּח ה' אֶת פִּי הָאָתוֹן — *And* HASHEM *opened the mouth of the ass.* He gave her the power of speech, similar to, ה' שְׂפָתַי תִּפְתָּח, HASHEM *open my lips* (*Psalms* 51:17). All this occurred so that Balaam should be aroused to repent and be reminded that וּמֵה' מַעֲנֵה לָשׁוֹן, *from* HASHEM *come the utterances of the tongue* (*Proverbs* 16:1), even to one who is unprepared; how much more so that (God) can remove (this power) according to His will from one who is prepared. (Now) all this (happened) so that a man such as he not be destroyed.

NOTES

namely to admonish and advise them and caution them, thereby cautioning them not to sin.

22. לְשָׂטָן לוֹ — *For an adversary against him.* The *Sforno* explains the phrase לְשָׂטָן לוֹ as meaning 'hindrance' or 'opposition,' exercised here by God for the person's good. Man's freedom of choice is never denied him, but often there are signs from heaven which will hopefully cause him to reconsider his ways. Since Balaam was sensitive to these omens, the obstacles placed in his path might influence him to reconsider his evil decision.

וּשְׁנֵי נְעָרָיו עִמּוֹ — *And his two servants were with him.* Although the saying of our Sages cited by the *Sforno* speaks of 'evil spirits,' while in our case it is an angel who stands in Balaam's path, the comparison is apt. Man is not able to see any noncorporeal being when three people are present, whether that being is good or evil.

28. וַיִּפְתַּח ה' אֶת פִּי הָאָתוֹן — *And* HASHEM *opened the mouth of the ass.* In this verse, as well as in verses 22 and 32, the *Sforno* is of the opinion that God was concerned for Balaam's welfare and did not want him to bring calamity on himself. Apparently, Balaam was a man of great spiritual powers which were sadly mischanneled, but nonetheless, it would have been tragic for such a person to be destroyed despite the fact that such great potential was squandered.

אֲתֹנְךָ אֲשֶׁר־רָכַבְתָּ עָלַי מֵעוֹדְךָ עַד־הַיּוֹם הַזֶּה הַהַסְכֵּן הִסְכַּנְתִּי לַעֲשׂוֹת
לא לְךָ כֹּה וַיֹּאמֶר לֹא: וַיְגַל יהוה אֶת־עֵינֵי בִלְעָם וַיַּרְא אֶת־מַלְאַךְ יהוה נִצָּב
לב בַּדֶּרֶךְ וְחַרְבּוֹ שְׁלֻפָה בְּיָדוֹ וַיִּקֹּד וַיִּשְׁתַּחוּ לְאַפָּיו: וַיֹּאמֶר אֵלָיו מַלְאַךְ יהוה
עַל־מָה הִכִּיתָ אֶת־אֲתֹנְךָ זֶה שָׁלוֹשׁ רְגָלִים הִנֵּה אָנֹכִי יָצָאתִי לְשָׂטָן
לג כִּי־יָרַט הַדֶּרֶךְ לְנֶגְדִּי: וַתִּרְאַנִי הָאָתוֹן וַתֵּט לְפָנַי זֶה שָׁלֹשׁ רְגָלִים אוּלַי
לד נָטְתָה מִפָּנַי כִּי עַתָּה גַּם־אֹתְכָה הָרַגְתִּי וְאוֹתָהּ הֶחֱיֵיתִי: וַיֹּאמֶר בִּלְעָם

---

30. הַהַסְכֵּן הִסְכַּנְתִּי — *Was I ever wont to do so . . .* and it would have been fitting for you to consider that since this happened to you outside the manner of my normal behavior, it is to indicate that you will not succeed — for even though there is no (validity) to divination, there is (validity) to a sign (based on *Chullin* 95b).

32. עַל מָה הִכִּיתָ אֶת אֲתֹנְךָ — *Wherefore have you smitten your ass.* Since you saw these signs, you should have realized (concluded) that your mission (lit., 'journey') is unacceptable and will not succeed.

זֶה שָׁלוֹשׁ רְגָלִים — *These three times . . .* and how did you 'stiffen your neck' three times (in an attempt) to force the issue.

הִנֵּה אָנֹכִי יָצָאתִי לְשָׂטָן — *Behold, I went out as an adversary.* Behold, I did whatever was possible to obstruct your journey in this manner for your own good.

כִּי יָרַט הַדֶּרֶךְ לְנֶגְדִּי — *Because your way trembles before me.* The word יָרַט comes from וְרֶטֶט הֶחֱזִיקָה, *And fear* (רֶטֶט) *has gripped her* (*Jeremiah* 49:24), just as וַתָּרַץ אֶת גֻּלְגָּלְתּוֹ, *And crushed* (וַתָּרַץ) *his skull* (*Judges* 9:53) is derived from רָצַץ. (The angel) then says: Behold, I have come forth to hinder you, and this hindrance was by causing the way before me 'to tremble,' similar to, לֹא רָאוּ אֶת הַמַּרְאָה אֲבָל חֲרָדָה גְדֹלָה נָפְלָה עֲלֵיהֶם, *They did not see the vision but a great trembling fell upon them* (*Daniel* 10:7), (but) all this did not suffice to frighten you because you have hardened your heart.

33. וַתִּרְאַנִי הָאָתוֹן וַתֵּט לְפָנַי — *And the ass saw me and turned aside before me.* And with all this, you experienced the turning aside of the ass from me three times; how could you not pay attention to this (strange behavior)?

אוּלַי נָטְתָה מִפָּנַי — *Perhaps she had turned aside from me.* You should have considered that perhaps she turned aside before *me*, for you already knew that God, the Blessed One, has before Him those who advocate good regarding Israel.

כִּי עַתָּה גַּם אֹתְכָה הָרַגְתִּי וְאוֹתָהּ הֶחֱיֵיתִי — *Surely now I would have slain you and saved her alive.* The reason that I said *wherefore have you smitten your ass* (v. 32) in an accusatory manner is because now, indeed, *to you it was shown that you might know* (based on *Deut.* 4:35) that even if I would slay you and spare her (the she-ass) in such

NOTES

30. הַהַסְכֵּן הִסְכַּנְתִּי — *Was I ever wont to do so.* The Talmudic saying cited by the *Sforno* states that although we are not permitted to divine, we should pay attention to a sign which may have validity. For example, if one's business prospers after moving into a house, or after marrying a woman or after the birth of a child, it is a sign that his success is now insured from heaven. The reverse is also true. Balaam should therefore have paid attention to the strange behavior of his she-ass and considered it as a sign of God's displeasure, as the *Sforno* explains in verse 32.

33. אוּלַי נָטְתָה מִפָּנַי — *Perhaps she had turned aside from me.* We find reference made in our

אֶל־מַלְאַךְ יהוה חָטָאתִי כִּי לֹא יָדַעְתִּי כִּי אַתָּה נִצָּב לִקְרָאתִי בַּדָּרֶךְ
לה וְעַתָּה אִם־רַע בְּעֵינֶיךָ אָשׁוּבָה לִּי: וַיֹּאמֶר מַלְאַךְ יהוה אֶל־בִּלְעָם לֵךְ
עִם־הָאֲנָשִׁים וְאֶפֶס אֶת־הַדָּבָר אֲשֶׁר־אֲדַבֵּר אֵלֶיךָ אֹתוֹ תְדַבֵּר וַיֵּלֶךְ
לו בִּלְעָם עִם־שָׂרֵי בָלָק: וַיִּשְׁמַע בָּלָק כִּי־בָא בִלְעָם וַיֵּצֵא לִקְרָאתוֹ אֶל־עִיר
לז מוֹאָב אֲשֶׁר עַל־גְּבוּל אַרְנֹן אֲשֶׁר בִּקְצֵה הַגְּבוּל: וַיֹּאמֶר בָּלָק אֶל־בִּלְעָם
הֲלֹא שָׁלֹחַ שָׁלַחְתִּי אֵלֶיךָ לִקְרֹא־לָךְ לָמָּה לֹא־הָלַכְתָּ אֵלָי הַאֻמְנָם לֹא
לח אוּכַל כַּבְּדֶךָ: וַיֹּאמֶר בִּלְעָם אֶל־בָּלָק הִנֵּה־בָאתִי אֵלֶיךָ עַתָּה הֲיָכֹל אוּכַל
רביעי [ששי] לט דַּבֵּר מְאוּמָה הַדָּבָר אֲשֶׁר יָשִׂים אֱלֹהִים בְּפִי אֹתוֹ אֲדַבֵּר: וַיֵּלֶךְ בִּלְעָם

---

a manner that you would (clearly) recognize that this (entire episode) was not a chance happening at all, nonetheless, you would not have refrained from going. Hence, you are as one who hands himself over to death (in order) to transgress the will of his Maker — and there is no greater apostate than such (a person).

34. חָטָאתִי — *I have sinned* . . . by stiffening my neck (i.e., by being so stubborn).

כִּי לֹא יָדַעְתִּי — *For I knew not* . . . and I should have been more sensitive to it.

וְעַתָּה אִם רַע בְּעֵינֶיךָ — *Now, therefore, if it displeases you* . . . for perhaps you are the angel who is the advocate on behalf of Israel.

אָשׁוּבָה לִּי — *I will return* . . . so as not to do anything against your will, even though God, the Blessed One, gave me permission (to go).

35. לֵךְ עִם הָאֲנָשִׁים — *Go with the men.* Do not go as a בַּעַל דָּבָר, *an interested party*, but as one who goes with them at their request so that you shall not be destroyed.

וְאֶפֶס אֶת הַדָּבָר — *But only the words* . . . and with all (this), I am not apprehensive that you will do anything contrary to my will, for indeed, you will not be able to do except that which I will say to you.

36. וַיֵּצֵא לִקְרָאתוֹ — *And he went out to meet him* . . . to honor him, for he knew that he had an 'arrogant spirit,' which our Rabbis attest to (*Avos* 5:18).

38. הִנֵּה בָאתִי אֵלֶיךָ — *Behold, I have come to you.* Although I would have come to you (initially) in accordance with your request (lit., 'word'), how could I be of any benefit to you? And this is so now, as well.

הֲיָכֹל אוּכַל דַּבֵּר מְאוּמָה — *Am I able to speak anything at all.* Can I speak in the manner of one who speaks of his own will?

הַדָּבָר אֲשֶׁר יָשִׂים אֱלֹהִים בְּפִי אֹתוֹ אֲדַבֵּר — *The word that God puts in my mouth, that shall I speak* . . . similar to, רוּחַ ה׳ דִּבֶּר בִּי, *The spirit of* H*ASHEM* *spoke in me* (*II Samuel* 23:2), and in this manner I shall not (really) be the speaker.

NOTES

prayers to angels who are מְלִיצֵי יֹשֶׁר — advocates on behalf of Israel. The *Sforno* is referring to such a מֵלִיץ both here and in verse 34.

36. וַיֵּצֵא לִקְרָאתוֹ — *And he went out to meet him.* The Mishnah in *Avos* 5:18 teaches us that Balaam possessed three characteristics; an evil eye, a haughty temperament and an insatiable spirit. The *Sforno* refers to these vices in his commentary on this verse and in verse 40. He paraphrases the Mishnah, substituting *arrogant spirit* for *haughty temperament* and *eye of pride* for *insatiable spirit.*

38. הַדָּבָר אֲשֶׁר יָשִׂים אֱלֹהִים בְּפִי — *The word that God puts in my mouth.* The *Rambam* in

מ עִם־בָּלָק וַיָּבֹאוּ קִרְיַת חֻצוֹת: וַיִּזְבַּח בָּלָק בָּקָר וָצֹאן וַיְשַׁלַּח לְבִלְעָם
מא וְלַשָּׂרִים אֲשֶׁר אִתּוֹ: וַיְהִי בַבֹּקֶר וַיִּקַּח בָּלָק אֶת־בִּלְעָם וַיַּעֲלֵהוּ בָּמוֹת בָּעַל
כג א וַיַּרְא מִשָּׁם קְצֵה הָעָם: וַיֹּאמֶר בִּלְעָם אֶל־בָּלָק בְּנֵה־לִי בָזֶה שִׁבְעָה
ב מִזְבְּחֹת וְהָכֵן לִי בָּזֶה שִׁבְעָה פָרִים וְשִׁבְעָה אֵילִים: וַיַּעַשׂ בָּלָק כַּאֲשֶׁר דִּבֶּר
ג בִּלְעָם וַיַּעַל בָּלָק וּבִלְעָם פָּר וָאַיִל בַּמִּזְבֵּחַ: וַיֹּאמֶר בִּלְעָם לְבָלָק הִתְיַצֵּב
עַל־עֹלָתֶךָ וְאֵלְכָה אוּלַי יִקָּרֶה יהוה לִקְרָאתִי וּדְבַר מַה־יַּרְאֵנִי וְהִגַּדְתִּי לָךְ

40. וַיְשַׁלַּח לְבִלְעָם — *And sent to Balaam* ... as a gift of honor besides his (regular) meal, so as to satisfy his 'eye of pride.'

41. וַיַּרְא מִשָּׁם קְצֵה הָעָם — *And he saw from there the utmost part of the people* ... so as to cast his (evil) eye upon them, similar to, וַיִּפֶן אַחֲרָיו וַיִּרְאֵם וַיְקַלְלֵם, *And he turned back and looked at them and cursed them* (*II Kings* 2:24), as opposed to, וַיַּרְאֵהוּ ה׳ אֶת כָּל הָאָרֶץ, *And HASHEM showed him all the land* (*Deut.* 34:1), so that he (Moses) should bless it before his death.

XXIII

1. בְּנֵה לִי בָזֶה — *Build me here.* A place from which I can see them (the Israelites).

3. הִתְיַצֵּב עַל עֹלָתֶךָ — *Stand by your burnt-offering* ... so as to have (proper) intent when every part of it is offered (lit., elevated), akin to, כִּי הַדָּם הוּא בַּנֶּפֶשׁ יְכַפֵּר, *for it is the blood that makes atonement for (man's) life* (*Leviticus* 17:11).

אוּלַי יִקָּרֶה ה׳ לִקְרָאתִי — *Perhaps HASHEM will come to meet me.* Perhaps in my solitude — even though I will not attain a (prophetic) level of (spiritual) elevation (and merit) to be *in the light of the King's countenance* (based on *Proverbs* 16:15) as was the case with Moses, as it says, *in all My house, he is the faithful one* (12:7) —

NOTES

his *Guide* (2:45) lists different degrees of prophecy. He describes the effect of the prophetic spirit upon a person as 'another force which has come upon him and has made him speak.' He writes that it was this kind of רוּחַ הַקֹּדֶשׁ, *holy spirit*, that descended on David, who described this experience when he said, 'The spirit of HASHEM spoke through me and His word was upon my tongue.' This is the verse which the *Sforno* quotes regarding Balaam. The *Rambam*, indeed, proceeds to tell us that 'the powers of Balaam, when he was righteous, also belonged to this kind (i.e., degree) of prophecy' (ibid.). According to the *Sforno* and the *Rambam*, this is the meaning of *The word that God puts in my mouth, that shall I speak.*

41. וַיַּרְא מִשָּׁם — *And he saw from there.* To bless or curse effectively, one must see the object of his blessing or his curse. The *Sforno* explains this in *Genesis* 48:10 regarding Jacob when he wanted to bless Ephraim and Menasseh. When Elisha cursed those who taunted him, it states that 'he turned and *saw* them.' Balaam also *sees* the people of Israel from a high vantage point. Moses, the אוֹהֵב יִשְׂרָאֵל, *lover of Israel*, and אוֹהֵב אֶרֶץ יִשְׂרָאֵל, *lover of the Land of Israel*, is shown the Land before he dies so that his blessing shall be a complete, effective and lasting one. Balaam's power of prophecy is compared to Moses', but he used his gift for evil while Moses used his for good.

XXIII

3. הִתְיַצֵּב עַל עֹלָתֶךָ — *Stand by your burnt-offering.* When a man brings an animal offering to God, he should consider the sacrifice of its parts and the blood offered on the altar as representing his own limbs and blood. This is the significance of the verse from *Leviticus*, quoted by the *Sforno*, to explain why Balaam instructed Balak to *stand by his offering* and associate himself with the sacrifice — its various parts and the blood — so that his wish might be granted.

אוּלַי יִקָּרֶה ה׳ לִקְרָאתִי — *Perhaps HASHEM will come to meet me.* The *Sforno*, in his commen-

ד וַיֵּלֶךְ שֶׁפִי: וַיִּקָּר אֱלֹהִים אֶל־בִּלְעָם וַיֹּאמֶר אֵלָיו אֶת־שִׁבְעַת הַמִּזְבְּחֹת
ה עָרַכְתִּי וָאַעַל פָּר וָאַיִל בַּמִּזְבֵּחַ: וַיָּשֶׂם יהוה דָּבָר בְּפִי בִלְעָם וַיֹּאמֶר שׁוּב
ו אֶל־בָּלָק וְכֹה תְדַבֵּר: וַיָּשָׁב אֵלָיו וְהִנֵּה נִצָּב עַל־עֹלָתוֹ הוּא וְכָל־שָׂרֵי
ז מוֹאָב: וַיִּשָּׂא מְשָׁלוֹ וַיֹּאמַר מִן־אֲרָם יַנְחֵנִי בָלָק מֶלֶךְ־מוֹאָב מֵהַרְרֵי־קֶדֶם
ח לְכָה אָרָה־לִּי יַעֲקֹב וּלְכָה זֹעֲמָה יִשְׂרָאֵל: מָה אֶקֹּב לֹא קַבֹּה אֵל וּמָה
ט אֶזְעֹם לֹא זָעַם יהוה: כִּי־מֵרֹאשׁ צֻרִים אֶרְאֶנּוּ וּמִגְּבָעוֹת אֲשׁוּרֶנּוּ הֶן־עָם
י לְבָדָד יִשְׁכֹּן וּבַגּוֹיִם לֹא יִתְחַשָּׁב: מִי מָנָה עֲפַר יַעֲקֹב וּמִסְפָּר אֶת־רֹבַע
יא יִשְׂרָאֵל תָּמֹת נַפְשִׁי מוֹת יְשָׁרִים וּתְהִי אַחֲרִיתִי כָּמֹהוּ: וַיֹּאמֶר בָּלָק
יב אֶל־בִּלְעָם מֶה עָשִׂיתָ לִי לָקֹב אֹיְבַי לְקַחְתִּיךָ וְהִנֵּה בֵּרַכְתָּ בָרֵךְ: וַיַּעַן

(nonetheless,) it may happen that God will come to meet me as it occurred with Moses at the beginning of his prophetic (experience) before he was elevated to the perfection which he (ultimately) attained, as it says, וַיַּרְא ה׳ כִּי סָר לִרְאוֹת וַיִּקְרָא אֵלָיו אֱלֹהִים, *And* HASHEM *saw that he turned aside to see, and God called to him* (*Exodus* 3:4).

7. וַיִּשָּׂא מְשָׁלוֹ — *And he took up his parable.* He stated the parable which he had seen in his prophetic vision.

וַיֹּאמַר מִן אֲרָם — *And he said: From Aram.* After he related the parable, he interpreted its content and said that the meaning (lit., teaching) of the parable was that Balak brought him from Aram, etc.

9. הֶן עָם לְבָדָד יִשְׁכֹּן — *They are a nation that will dwell alone.* They alone will inhabit the earth at the end of 'the matter' (i.e., 'the end of time'), as it says, ה׳ בָּדָד יַנְחֶנּוּ, HASHEM *alone did lead him* (*Deut.* 32:12); (hence,) how can I annihilate them?

10. תָּמֹת נַפְשִׁי מוֹת יְשָׁרִים — *Let me die that death of the righteous.* Wouldst that my living spirit die now, providing however, that my death be that of the righteous — that (my soul) merit eternal life.

וּתְהִי אַחֲרִיתִי כָּמֹהוּ — *And let my end be like his.* Only let my end and my offspring (lit., the offspring of my bowels) be like (those of) Israel because, indeed, a man's children and offspring are called אַחֲרִיתוֹ, *his posterity*, similar to, יְהִי אַחֲרִיתוֹ לְהַכְרִית, *Let his posterity be cut off* (*Psalms* 109:13), and also, וְלֹא לְאַחֲרִיתוֹ, *And not to his posterity* (*Daniel* 11:4).

NOTES

tary on *Exodus* 3:2, explains at great length the gradual progress of Moses in the realm of prophecy. The least of these prophetic levels was experienced by him at the time of the 'burning bush,' which was his initial encounter with an angel of God. Balaam here expresses the hope that he might merit that God meet him at least on that level.

7. וַיִּשָּׂא מְשָׁלוֹ — *And he took up his parable.* The parable which Balaam related is not recorded in the Torah, only its interpretation as explained by Balaam, i.e., *From Aram Balak brought me, etc.*

9. הֶן עָם לְבָדָד יִשְׁכֹּן — *They are a nation that will dwell alone.* The *Sforno* does not interpret the word הֶן as meaning *Behold*, followed by the observation that Israel is a nation that dwells alone, i.e., separate and distinct from other people. Rather, he interprets the sense of the verse as follows: הֶן, *they*, alone will remain at the end of time (אַחֲרִית הַיָּמִים), for all other nations will be destroyed, as the prophet states, *For I shall make an end to all the nations* (*Jeremiah* 46). See his commentary on *Genesis* 49:1 where he elaborates on this theme, and on *Deut.* 32:12 where he quotes the aforementioned verse from Jeremiah.

חמישי יג וַיֹּאמַר הֲלֹא אֵת אֲשֶׁר יָשִׂים יהוה בְּפִי אֹתוֹ אֶשְׁמֹר לְדַבֵּר: וַיֹּאמֶר אֵלָיו
בָּלָק לְךָ־נָּא אִתִּי אֶל־מָקוֹם אַחֵר אֲשֶׁר תִּרְאֶנּוּ מִשָּׁם אֶפֶס קָצֵהוּ תִרְאֶה
יד וְכֻלּוֹ לֹא תִרְאֶה וְקָבְנוֹ־לִי מִשָּׁם: וַיִּקָּחֵהוּ שְׂדֵה צֹפִים אֶל־רֹאשׁ הַפִּסְגָּה
טו וַיִּבֶן שִׁבְעָה מִזְבְּחֹת וַיַּעַל פָּר וָאַיִל בַּמִּזְבֵּחַ: וַיֹּאמֶר אֶל־בָּלָק הִתְיַצֵּב כֹּה
טז עַל־עֹלָתֶךָ וְאָנֹכִי אִקָּרֶה כֹּה: וַיִּקָּר יהוה אֶל־בִּלְעָם וַיָּשֶׂם דָּבָר בְּפִיו
יז וַיֹּאמֶר שׁוּב אֶל־בָּלָק וְכֹה תְדַבֵּר: וַיָּבֹא אֵלָיו וְהִנּוֹ נִצָּב עַל־עֹלָתוֹ וְשָׂרֵי
יח מוֹאָב אִתּוֹ וַיֹּאמֶר לוֹ בָּלָק מַה־דִּבֶּר יהוה: וַיִּשָּׂא מְשָׁלוֹ וַיֹּאמַר קוּם בָּלָק
יט וּשֲׁמָע הַאֲזִינָה עָדַי בְּנוֹ צִפֹּר: לֹא אִישׁ אֵל וִיכַזֵּב וּבֶן־אָדָם וְיִתְנֶחָם הַהוּא
כ אָמַר וְלֹא יַעֲשֶׂה וְדִבֶּר וְלֹא יְקִימֶנָּה: הִנֵּה בָרֵךְ לָקָחְתִּי וּבֵרֵךְ וְלֹא
כא אֲשִׁיבֶנָּה: לֹא־הִבִּיט אָוֶן בְּיַעֲקֹב וְלֹא־רָאָה עָמָל בְּיִשְׂרָאֵל יהוה אֱלֹהָיו
כב-כג עִמּוֹ וּתְרוּעַת מֶלֶךְ בּוֹ: אֵל מוֹצִיאָם מִמִּצְרָיִם כְּתוֹעֲפֹת רְאֵם לוֹ: כִּי

---

12. הֲלֹא אֵת אֲשֶׁר יָשִׂים ה׳ בְּפִי — *Must I not* (*take heed to speak*) *that which* HASHEM *has put in my mouth* . . . and you already know that He is the God of Israel, and will not speak aught but good regarding Israel.

13. אֲשֶׁר תִּרְאֶנּוּ מִשָּׁם — *From whence you may see them* . . . and you will be able to cast your eye upon them for evil.

אֶפֶס קָצֵהוּ תִרְאֶה וְכֻלּוֹ לֹא תִרְאֶה — *You shall see but part of them and shall not see them all.* Do not (however) cast your (evil) eye upon all of them, for you will not be able to attain your intended (goal) at all, as it says, כִּי אֶעֱשֶׂה כָלָה בְּכָל הַגּוֹיִם . . . וְאֹתְךָ לֹא אֶעֱשֶׂה כָלָה, *for I will make a full end of all the nations* . . . *but I will not make a full end of you* (*Jeremiah* 46:28).

20. וּבֵרֵךְ — *And when He has blessed* . . . and He has already blessed!

21. וּתְרוּעַת מֶלֶךְ בּוֹ — *The trumpet signal for the king is among them.* When the camps journey, they sound the תְּרוּעָה, *trumpet-signal,* as an expression of joy and rejoicing in their God, for the Sanctuary travels (with them).

22. כְּתוֹעֲפֹת רְאֵם לוֹ — *Like the lofty horns of the wild-ox.* (This refers) to the people of Israel who do not devour and eat like a lion, but they push with their horn like a *wild-ox,* for their intent is to expel the nations and to bring themselves into the Land without (resorting) to the slaughter of the nations, as it says, תְּגָרֵשׁ גּוֹיִם וַתִּטָּעֶהָ, *You have cast out nations and planted it* (*Psalms* 80:9), for He does not desire the

NOTES

13. אֶפֶס קָצֵהוּ תִרְאֶה — *You shall see but part of them.* Balak is a pragmatist. He knows that God will never permit Israel to be totally destroyed; hence, if Balaam is overanxious and curses them all, none shall be affected. Balak therefore cautions him to concentrate only on part of the people (קָצֵהוּ); otherwise he will end with 'nothing' (אֶפֶס).

21. וּתְרוּעַת מֶלֶךְ בּוֹ — *The trumpet signal for the king is among them.* The תְּרוּעָה, *trumpet-signal,* is symbolic of the Kingship of heaven. *HASHEM his God is with him* is attested to by the presence of the מִשְׁכָּן, *Sanctuary,* in their midst; hence, they are secure and happy.

22. כְּתוֹעֲפֹת רְאֵם לוֹ — *Like the lofty horns of the wild-ox.* At the very beginning of the Book of *Numbers,* the *Sforno* explains that the original intent of God was to bring Israel into the Land without recourse to war. The reason for the eventual need to destroy the inhabitants of the land of Canaan was due to the sin of the spies which extended the Canaanite stay in the land. During this time, their conduct became totally corrupt, thereby seal-

לֹא־נַחַשׁ בְּיַעֲקֹב וְלֹא־קֶסֶם בְּיִשְׂרָאֵל כָּעֵת יֵאָמֵר לְיַעֲקֹב וּלְיִשְׂרָאֵל
כד מַה־פָּעַל אֵל׃ הֶן־עָם כְּלָבִיא יָקוּם וְכַאֲרִי יִתְנַשָּׂא לֹא יִשְׁכַּב עַד־יֹאכַל
כה טֶרֶף וְדַם־חֲלָלִים יִשְׁתֶּה׃ וַיֹּאמֶר בָּלָק אֶל־בִּלְעָם גַּם־קֹב לֹא תִקֳּבֶנּוּ
כו גַּם־בָּרֵךְ לֹא תְבָרְכֶנּוּ׃ וַיַּעַן בִּלְעָם וַיֹּאמֶר אֶל־בָּלָק הֲלֹא דִּבַּרְתִּי אֵלֶיךָ
ששי [שביעי] כז לֵאמֹר כֹּל אֲשֶׁר־יְדַבֵּר יהוה אֹתוֹ אֶעֱשֶׂה׃ וַיֹּאמֶר בָּלָק אֶל־בִּלְעָם
לְכָה־נָּא אֶקָּחֲךָ אֶל־מָקוֹם אַחֵר אוּלַי יִישַׁר בְּעֵינֵי הָאֱלֹהִים וְקַבֹּתוֹ לִי

---

death (of the wicked). And so our Sages said, '... Joshua sent three letters (to the inhabitants of Canaan): Whoever wishes to leave, let him leave; whoever wishes to make peace, let him make peace; whoever wants to do battle let him do so' (*Jerusalem Talmud, Tractate Sheveis* 6:1). However, they stiffened their necks and did battle, forcing (Israel) to destroy them. Thus, they (Israel) did not deal with them (the nations) at all as a lion who devours, but dealt with them as a wild-ox who either pushes out or conquers, yet does not consume at all.

23. כִּי לֹא נַחַשׁ בְּיַעֲקֹב — *For there is not enchantment with Jacob* ... and the reason He brought Israel forth from Egypt and cast out the nations on their behalf and gave them *the lofty horns of the wild-ox* was because they are דּוֹר דֹּרְשָׁו, *the generation of those who seek Him* (*Psalms* 24:6) and they do not seek after enchantment, as it says, כִּי הַגּוֹיִם הָאֵלֶּה... אֶל מְעֹנְנִים וְאֶל קֹסְמִים יִשְׁמָעוּ וְאַתָּה לֹא כֵן, *For these nations ... hearken unto soothsayers and diviners, but you are not so* (*Deut.* 18:14).

כָּעֵת — *Now* (*lit., this time*) ... at a time when they want to know the future ...

יֵאָמֵר לְיַעֲקֹב וּלְיִשְׂרָאֵל מַה פָּעַל אֵל — *It will be said to Jacob and Israel what God has wrought.* It shall be told to them through prophecy or through some prophet what God, the Blessed One, has decreed. It shall not be told to them what the signs of heaven indicate (lit., teach) or how the constellations will work because they are not under those constellations.

24. כְּלָבִיא יָקוּם — *That rises up as a lioness* ... to battle with those who have not waged war against them at all.

עַד יֹאכַל טֶרֶף — *Until he eats of the prey.* They will eat and consume those nations who are now their prey as it says, *For they are our bread* (14:9).

27. אוּלַי יִישַׁר בְּעֵינֵי הָאֱלֹהִים וְקַבֹּתוֹ לִי מִשָּׁם — *Perhaps it will please God that you may curse for me there* ... because it may be that particular part (of Israel) which is more vulnerable to curses.

NOTES

ing their doom. Here, however, the *Sforno* gives a different reason for the need to resort to physical destruction of the inhabitants. It resulted from the refusal of the nations residing in Canaan to accept the offer of Joshua to leave unharmed or to make peace. Nonetheless, the simile of Balaam is correct; Israel is compared to a רְאֵם, *wild-ox*, and not to a lion, for their original intent was not to devour their enemies but merely to drive them out of the land.

23. כִּי לֹא נַחַשׁ בְּיַעֲקֹב — *For there is not enchantment with Jacob.* The interpretation of the *Sforno* regarding God's communication with Israel through prophets is similar to *Rashi's* explanation. However, he adds the thought that the destiny of Israel is not dictated by the stars, nor is their fate determined by the 'signs of heaven,' as our Sages teach us, אֵין מַזָּל לְיִשְׂרָאֵל, *Israel is not subject to planetary influences* (*Nedarim* 32a).

כח־כט מִשָּׁם: וַיִּקַּח בָּלָק אֶת־בִּלְעָם רֹאשׁ הַפְּעוֹר הַנִּשְׁקָף עַל־פְּנֵי הַיְשִׁימֹן: וַיֹּאמֶר
בִּלְעָם אֶל־בָּלָק בְּנֵה־לִי בָזֶה שִׁבְעָה מִזְבְּחֹת וְהָכֵן לִי בָּזֶה שִׁבְעָה פָרִים
ל וְשִׁבְעָה אֵילִם: וַיַּעַשׂ בָּלָק כַּאֲשֶׁר אָמַר בִּלְעָם וַיַּעַל פַּר וָאַיִל בַּמִּזְבֵּחַ:
כד א וַיַּרְא בִּלְעָם כִּי טוֹב בְּעֵינֵי יהוה לְבָרֵךְ אֶת־יִשְׂרָאֵל וְלֹא־הָלַךְ
ב כְּפַעַם־בְּפַעַם לִקְרַאת נְחָשִׁים וַיָּשֶׁת אֶל־הַמִּדְבָּר פָּנָיו: וַיִּשָּׂא בִלְעָם
ג אֶת־עֵינָיו וַיַּרְא אֶת־יִשְׂרָאֵל שֹׁכֵן לִשְׁבָטָיו וַתְּהִי עָלָיו רוּחַ אֱלֹהִים: וַיִּשָּׂא
ד מְשָׁלוֹ וַיֹּאמַר נְאֻם בִּלְעָם בְּנוֹ בְעֹר וּנְאֻם הַגֶּבֶר שְׁתֻם הָעָיִן: נְאֻם שֹׁמֵעַ
ה אִמְרֵי־אֵל אֲשֶׁר מַחֲזֵה שַׁדַּי יֶחֱזֶה נֹפֵל וּגְלוּי עֵינָיִם: מַה־טֹּבוּ אֹהָלֶיךָ יַעֲקֹב

XXIV

1. לִקְרַאת נְחָשִׁים — *To seek for enchantments.* He ceased attempting to anticipate the time which might be appropriate for curses to take effect upon them because he realized (lit., 'saw') *that it was good in the eyes of God to bless Israel,* and (therefore) there was no hope for him to curse them.

וַיָּשֶׁת אֶל הַמִּדְבָּר פָּנָיו — *And he set his face toward the desert* . . . to bless them with limited blessings which contain (the element) of damage within them, as our Sages say, 'Better the curse which Achiya the Shiloni cursed Israel than the blessing of Balaam' (*Taanis* 20a).

5. מַה טֹּבוּ אֹהָלֶיךָ יַעֲקֹב — *How goodly are your tents, O Jacob.* (This refers to) Houses of Study, similar to, יֹשֵׁב אֹהָלִים, *Dwelling in tents* (*Genesis* 25:27) and to, וְיִשְׁכֹּן בְּאָהֳלֵי שֵׁם, *And he shall dwell in the tents of Shem* (*Genesis* 9:27) as well as, וְהָיָה כָּל מְבַקֵּשׁ ה׳ יֵצֵא אֶל אֹהֶל מוֹעֵד, *Every one that sought* HASHEM *went out to the Tent of Meeting* (*Exodus* 33:7).

NOTES

27. וְקַבֹּתוֹ לִי מִשָּׁם — *That you may curse for me there.* Since Balak has been frustrated in his plan to curse Israel time after time, what does he expect to accomplish by bringing Balaam to another place? The *Sforno* explains that Balak realized that the people of Israel as a whole was impervious to any curse, but he reasoned that sections of the camp of Israel, which could be seen from another place, might be vulnerable.

XXIV

1. וַיָּשֶׁת אֶל הַמִּדְבָּר פָּנָיו — *And he set his face toward the desert.* The blessings of Balaam were uttered with a lack of sincerity because Balaam was, in truth, an enemy of Israel. Our Sages tell us that hidden within each blessing was a curse. The *Sforno* interprets the expression אֶל הַמִּדְבָּר, *toward the desert,* as implying something which is barren and desolate, and symbolically the antithesis of a blessing; hence, any blessing he would pronounce would contain an element of curse within it, even though superficially it was a blessing. The saying of our Sages in tractate *Taanis,* cited by the *Sforno,* is most apt. The Talmud interprets the verse in *Proverbs* 27:6, *Faithful are the wounds of a friend, but the kisses of an enemy are deceptive,* as referring to Achiya the Shiloni who admonished Israel but did so out of love, and to Balaam who blessed them but did so in a spirit of animosity.

5. מַה טֹּבוּ אֹהָלֶיךָ יַעֲקֹב מִשְׁכְּנֹתֶיךָ יִשְׂרָאֵל — *How goodly are your tents, O Jacob, your dwellings, O Israel. Rashi* interprets *tents* as referring to the private tents of Israel, but the *Sforno* is of the opinion that the phrase אֹהֶל, *tent,* be it here or in the various verses cited by him, means the tent of study, while the word מִשְׁכָּן, *dwelling place,* refers to a place of prayer or the Sanctuary. He also explains why the name *Jacob* is associated with אֹהֶל (tent), while the name *Israel* is linked to מִשְׁכָּן (dwelling). The *Sforno* established in his commentary on *Genesis* 32:29, and again in *Genesis* 49:24, that the name *Jacob* indicates that the Jewish people shall remain at the 'end' of time, while *Israel* is indicative of their superior rank as a nation who will prevail over their adversaries, be they 'heavenly' or earthly. Hence, the

ו מִשְׁכְּנֹתֶיךָ יִשְׂרָאֵל: כִּנְחָלִים נִטָּיוּ כְּגַנֹּת עֲלֵי נָהָר כַּאֲהָלִים נָטַע יהוה
ז כַּאֲרָזִים עֲלֵי־מָיִם: יִזַּל־מַיִם מִדָּלְיָו וְזַרְעוֹ בְּמַיִם רַבִּים וְיָרֹם מֵאֲגַג מַלְכּוֹ
ח וְתִנַּשֵּׂא מַלְכֻתוֹ: אֵל מוֹצִיאוֹ מִמִּצְרַיִם כְּתוֹעֲפֹת רְאֵם לוֹ יֹאכַל גּוֹיִם צָרָיו
ט וְעַצְמֹתֵיהֶם יְגָרֵם וְחִצָּיו יִמְחָץ: כָּרַע שָׁכַב כַּאֲרִי וּכְלָבִיא מִי יְקִימֶנּוּ
י מְבָרֲכֶיךָ בָרוּךְ וְאֹרְרֶיךָ אָרוּר: וַיִּחַר־אַף בָּלָק אֶל־בִּלְעָם וַיִּסְפֹּק אֶת־כַּפָּיו

מִשְׁכְּנֹתֶיךָ יִשְׂרָאֵל — *Your dwellings, O Israel.* (This refers to) Houses of Assembly (prayer) and the Sanctuary of God, which are designated for His Name to dwell there and to accept the prayers of worshipers.

Now he said, *how goodly etc.*, for not only do they benefit those who are occupied therein, but they also bring good to the entire nation, as the name 'Jacob' indicates, namely that they shall remain at the end after all others (will disappear), and they shall never cease (to exist), as the name 'Israel' indicates, i.e., that they will strive with *Elohim* and with man (and be victorious).

6. כִּנְחָלִים נִטָּיוּ — *As streams winding their way.* For indeed, Houses of Prayer and Houses of Study are to the masses of Israel as streams which make their way into the fields to water them, and those who dwell in these tents and comprehend the Torah draw and give to drink of their Torah to the masses — and so also are those who pray . . .

כְּגַנֹּת עֲלֵי נָהָר — *As gardens by the riverside . . .* who do not cease to produce fruit, as our Sages say, 'A covenant has been made with the 13 Attributes of Mercy that they will not be turned away empty-handed' (*Rosh Hashanah* 17b).

8. יֹאכַל גּוֹיִם צָרָיו — *He shall devour the nations that are his adversaries . . .* in the distant future, as it says, וְנָקָם יָשִׁיב לְצָרָיו, *and renders vengeance to his adversaries* (*Deut.* 32:43).

וְחִצָּיו יִמְחָץ — *And pierce them through with his arrows . . .* as it says, אַשְׁכִּיר חִצַּי מִדָּם, *I will make my arrows drunk with blood* (*Deut.* 32:42).

9. מְבָרֲכֶיךָ בָרוּךְ — *Blessed be he who blesses you . . .* as was the case with Abraham, for indeed, the remnant of Israel will (attain) the level of Abraham our father, as it says, כִּי יָשׁוּב ה׳ לָשׂוּשׂ עָלֶיךָ לְטוֹב כַּאֲשֶׁר שָׂשׂ עַל אֲבֹתֶיךָ, *For* HASHEM *will again rejoice over you for good as He rejoiced over your fathers* (*Deut.* 30:9).

10. וַיִּסְפֹּק אֶת כַּפָּיו — *And he clapped his hands together.* For he despaired of attaining his desire since he (Balaam) had cursed those who curse (Israel).

NOTES

choice of these names in this verse are most fitting. Through the study of Torah, they will guarantee their survival, and through prayer they will earn God's support and His Providence.

6. כְּגַנֹּת עֲלֵי נָהָר — *As gardens by the river side.* The *Sforno* explains the comparison of those who pray to a garden which produces fruit as referring to the prayer of the י״ג מִדּוֹת הָרַחֲמִים (the Thirteen Attributes of Mercy) recorded in *Exodus* 34:6-7. According to our Sages, God revealed this prayer to Moses and promised him that whenever the Children of Israel would recite this prayer, He would have mercy upon them and forgive them. This תְּפִלָּה is an integral part of our *Selichos* prayers.

10. וַיִּסְפֹּק אֶת כַּפָּיו — *And he clapped his hands together.* Once Balaam proclaimed that anyone who cursed Israel would themselves be cursed (v. 9), it was inconceivable that he would now curse them, so Balak despairs completely of attaining his goal and proceeds to dismiss Balaam.

וַיֹּאמֶר בָּלָק אֶל־בִּלְעָם לָקֹב אֹיְבַי קְרָאתִיךָ וְהִנֵּה בֵּרַכְתָּ בָרֵךְ זֶה שָׁלֹשׁ
יא פְּעָמִים: וְעַתָּה בְּרַח־לְךָ אֶל־מְקוֹמֶךָ אָמַרְתִּי כַּבֵּד אֲכַבֶּדְךָ וְהִנֵּה מְנָעֲךָ
יב יהוה מִכָּבוֹד: וַיֹּאמֶר בִּלְעָם אֶל־בָּלָק הֲלֹא גַּם אֶל־מַלְאָכֶיךָ אֲשֶׁר־שָׁלַחְתָּ
יג אֵלַי דִּבַּרְתִּי לֵאמֹר: אִם־יִתֶּן־לִי בָלָק מְלֹא בֵיתוֹ כֶּסֶף וְזָהָב לֹא אוּכַל
לַעֲבֹר אֶת־פִּי יהוה לַעֲשׂוֹת טוֹבָה אוֹ רָעָה מִלִּבִּי אֲשֶׁר־יְדַבֵּר יהוה אֹתוֹ
שביעי יד אֲדַבֵּר: וְעַתָּה הִנְנִי הוֹלֵךְ לְעַמִּי לְכָה אִיעָצְךָ אֲשֶׁר יַעֲשֶׂה הָעָם הַזֶּה לְעַמְּךָ
טו בְּאַחֲרִית הַיָּמִים: וַיִּשָּׂא מְשָׁלוֹ וַיֹּאמַר נְאֻם בִּלְעָם בְּנוֹ בְעֹר וּנְאֻם הַגֶּבֶר
טז שְׁתֻם הָעָיִן: נְאֻם שֹׁמֵעַ אִמְרֵי־אֵל וְיֹדֵעַ דַּעַת עֶלְיוֹן מַחֲזֵה שַׁדַּי יֶחֱזֶה נֹפֵל
יז וּגְלוּי עֵינָיִם: אֶרְאֶנּוּ וְלֹא עַתָּה אֲשׁוּרֶנּוּ וְלֹא קָרוֹב דָּרַךְ כּוֹכָב מִיַּעֲקֹב וְקָם

---

11. בְּרַח לְךָ — *Flee, you.* בְּרִיחָה, *fleeing,* wherever it is mentioned (in Scriptures) does not mean *fleeing* from a pursuer, but (it means rather) to leave a place (motivated) by fear of future harm.

12. הֲלֹא גַּם אֶל מַלְאָכֶיךָ — *Did I not also* (*speak so*) *to your messengers.* There is no reason (lit., it is not fitting) for you to wonder why I did not fulfill your wish in the hope of receiving honor, for I told the messengers whom you sent to say to me, *For I will promote you unto very great honor* (22:17), that it was not in my hand (to fulfill your request).

14. לְכָה אִיעָצְךָ — *Come and I will advise you . . .* the counsel being that of sending women (to mislead Israel) as it is explained (later in the Torah) when it says, *Behold these caused the Children of Israel, through the counsel of Balaam* (*to break faith etc.*) (31:16).

אֲשֶׁר יַעֲשֶׂה הָעָם הַזֶּה לְעַמְּךָ בְּאַחֲרִית הַיָּמִים — *What this people shall do to your people in the end of days . . .* because, indeed, the evil *which this people shall do to your people* will not happen in your day, and you have nothing to fear. But it shall only (come to pass) *in the end of days* as it says, *And shall smite the corners of Moab* (v. 17) and as it says, אֱדוֹם וּמוֹאָב מִשְׁלוֹחַ יָדָם, *They shall lay their hand upon Edom and Moab* (*Isaiah* 11:14).

17. אֶרְאֶנּוּ — *I see him . . .*that which this people shall do to your people.

דָּרַךְ כּוֹכָב — *There shall step forth a star from Jacob . . .* corporeal and everlasting, as it says, וּמַצְדִּיקֵי הָרַבִּים כַּכּוֹכָבִים לְעוֹלָם וָעֶד, *And they who turn many to righteousness are like the stars forever and ever* (*Daniel* 12:3).

NOTES

11. בְּרַח לְךָ — *Flee, you.* See the *Sforno's* commentary on *Genesis* 31:21, where he explains the difference between the words בְּרִיחָה and נִיסָה, both of which mean 'flight.'

14. לְכָה אִיעָצְךָ — *Come and I will advise you.* The advice given by Balaam to Balak was to have the daughters of Moab seduce the men of Israel and through harlotry entice them to practice idolatry. All this is recorded in the next chapter (25), while in *Mattos* (31:16) the Torah tells us explicitly that this plan was Balaam's, who knew that the God of Israel detests immorality and idolatry.

17. דָּרַךְ כּוֹכָב — *There shall step forth a star from Jacob. Rashi* explains that the *star from Jacob* refers to the Messiah. The *Sforno* explains that the Messiah will be a man (a physical being), yet one who shall be everlasting, which he bases on the verse in *Daniel.* The verse here compares the Messiah to a *star,* as does the verse in *Daniel.* Just as the stars are forever, so shall be the Messiah.

יח שֵׁבֶט מִיִּשְׂרָאֵל וּמָחַץ פַּאֲתֵי מוֹאָב וְקַרְקַר כָּל־בְּנֵי־שֵׁת: וְהָיָה אֱדוֹם יְרֵשָׁה
יט וְהָיָה יְרֵשָׁה שֵׂעִיר אֹיְבָיו וְיִשְׂרָאֵל עֹשֶׂה חָיִל: וְיֵרְדְּ מִיַּעֲקֹב וְהֶאֱבִיד שָׂרִיד

וּמָחַץ פַּאֲתֵי מוֹאָב — *And shall smite the corners of Moab* — Although all the nations will be destroyed through the breath of God, as it says, כִּי אֶעֱשֶׂה כָלָה בְּכָל הַגּוֹיִם, *For I will make a full end of all the nations* (*Jeremiah* 30.11), Edom's and Moab's downfall (lit., 'revenge') will be through the hand of Israel because these two nations were always his enemies and evil neighbors.

18. וְהָיָה אֱדוֹם יְרֵשָׁה — *And Edom shall be a possession* . . . (a possession) for the beasts and birds of the wilderness, as it says, וִירֵשׁוּהָ קָאַת וְקִפּוֹד, *But the pelican and bittern shall possess it* (*Isaiah* 34:11).

וְהָיָה יְרֵשָׁה שֵׂעִיר — *Seir also shall be a possession* . . . (a possession) for Israel, since it is a part of the Kenite, the Kenizzite and the Kadmonite (*Genesis* 15:19).

אֹיְבָיו — *His enemies* . . . and the reason that the avenging of Moab and Edom shall be greater than that of other nations is because they were the perpetual enemies of Israel.

וְיִשְׂרָאֵל עֹשֶׂה חָיִל — *And Israel shall do valiantly* . . . and then Israel shall be able to do valiantly, as it says, וּלְאֹם מִלְאֹם יֶאֱמָץ, *And the one people shall be stronger than the other people* (*Genesis* 25:23).

19. וְיֵרְדְּ מִיַּעֲקֹב — *And out of Jacob shall come he that shall have dominion.* Each one of his descendants shall rule among the nations, as it says, וְהָיָה הַנִּכְשָׁל בָּהֶם בַּיּוֹם הַהוּא כְּדָוִיד, *And he that stumbles among them on that day shall be as David* (*Zechariah* 12:8), and as it says, וְהָיָה שְׁאֵרִית יַעֲקֹב בַּגּוֹיִם בְּקֶרֶב עַמִּים רַבִּים כְּאַרְיֵה בְּבַהֲמוֹת יַעַר כִּכְפִיר בְּעֶדְרֵי צֹאן, *And the remnant of Jacob shall be among the nations, in the midst of many peoples, as a lion among the beasts of the forest, as a young lion among the flocks of sheep* (*Michah* 5:7).

NOTES

17-20. וּמָחַץ פַּאֲתֵי מוֹאָב . . . עֲדֵי אֹבֵד — *And shall smite the corners of Moab . . . shall come to destruction.* The *Sforno's* commentary on these verses does not appear in the מִקְרָאוֹת גְדוֹלוֹת — the standard edition of the Bible, which includes numerous commentaries including that of the *Sforno*. We have, however, translated his commentary on these verses, taken from various manuscripts and published in the Mosad Harav Kook edition 5740. We assume that the censor removed the commentary on these verses because it was considered too harsh an indictment of the Christian world's treatment of the Jews, and depicts too vividly the revenge that Israel will take of them at the end of time. One can surmise that the censor knew that Edom is synonymous with Rome, and in these verses the Torah singles out Edom (Rome) as the eternal enemy of the Jewish people, who will eventually be subdued and conquered by Israel and become its possession (v. 18).

18. וְהָיָה אֱדוֹם יְרֵשָׁה וְהָיָה יְרֵשָׁה שֵׂעִיר — *And Edom shall be a possession, Seir also shall be a possession.* Since Edom and Seir are one and the same, the word *possession* seems to be repetitious. The *Sforno*, however, explains that the first part of the verse refers to its desolation, while the second part refers to the annexation of its land by Israel.

וְיִשְׂרָאֵל עֹשֶׂה חָיִל — *And Israel shall do valiantly. Rashi* explains the phrase *and the one people shall be stronger than the other people* (*Gen.* 25:23) to mean that when one rises the other must fall, relating to the historic conflict between Esau (Edom) and Jacob. The *Sforno* correctly quotes that verse here to explain the link between *and Edom shall be a possession* with *Israel shall do valiantly*. Only when Esau falls shall Israel do valiantly and be victorious over all its enemies.

19. וְיֵרְדְּ מִיַּעֲקֹב — *And out of Jacob shall come he that shall have dominion.* The word וְיֵרְדְּ

כ מֵעִיר: וַיַּרְא֙ אֶת־עֲמָלֵ֔ק וַיִּשָּׂ֥א מְשָׁל֖וֹ וַיֹּאמַ֑ר רֵאשִׁ֤ית גּוֹיִם֙ עֲמָלֵ֔ק וְאַחֲרִית֖וֹ
כא עֲדֵ֥י אֹבֵֽד: וַיַּרְא֙ אֶת־הַקֵּינִ֔י וַיִּשָּׂ֥א מְשָׁל֖וֹ וַיֹּאמַ֑ר אֵיתָן֙ מֽוֹשָׁבֶ֔ךָ וְשִׂ֥ים בַּסֶּ֖לַע
כב־כג קִנֶּֽךָ: כִּ֚י אִם־יִהְיֶ֣ה לְבָ֣עֵֽר קָ֑יִן עַד־מָ֖ה אַשּׁ֥וּר תִּשְׁבֶּֽךָּ: וַיִּשָּׂ֥א מְשָׁל֖וֹ וַיֹּאמַ֑ר
כד א֕וֹי מִ֥י יִחְיֶ֖ה מִשֻּׂמ֥וֹ אֵֽל: וְצִים֙ מִיַּ֣ד כִּתִּ֔ים וְעִנּ֥וּ אַשּׁ֖וּר וְעִנּוּ־עֵ֑בֶר וְגַם־ה֖וּא
כה עֲדֵ֥י אֹבֵֽד: וַיָּ֣קָם בִּלְעָ֔ם וַיֵּ֖לֶךְ וַיָּ֣שָׁב לִמְקֹמ֑וֹ וְגַם־בָּלָ֖ק הָלַ֥ךְ לְדַרְכּֽוֹ:
כה א־ב וַיֵּ֥שֶׁב יִשְׂרָאֵ֖ל בַּשִּׁטִּ֑ים וַיָּ֣חֶל הָעָ֔ם לִזְנ֖וֹת אֶל־בְּנ֥וֹת מוֹאָֽב: וַתִּקְרֶ֣אןָ לָעָ֔ם

וְהֶאֱבִיד שָׂרִיד מֵעִיר — *And shall destroy the remnant from the city* . . . as it says, וְרָמַס וְטָרַף וְאֵין מַצִּיל תָּרֹם יָדְךָ עַל צָרֶיךָ וְכָל אֹיְבֶיךָ יִכָּרֵתוּ, *And tread down and tear and there is none to deliver. Let your hand be lifted up above your adversaries and let all your enemies be cut off* (ibid. vs. 7-8).

20. עֲדֵי אֹבֵד — *Shall come to destruction.* Although the sovereignty of all nations shall be eliminated in the future, as it says, וּשְׁאָר חֵיוָתָא הֶעְדִּיו שָׁלְטָנְהוֹן, *And as for the rest of the nations (lit., beasts), their dominion was taken away* (*Daniel* 7:12), nonetheless, the nations will not be totally destroyed except for these two nations, and they are Amalek who began to battle against Israel, and the Kuthim who completed the destruction of Israel, as it says, *And he also shall come to destruction* (v. 24).

21. אֵיתָן מוֹשָׁבֶיךָ — *Your dwelling place is strong.* You dwelt with Israel in a land which was אֵיתָן, namely in the wilderness, in a land which was unplanted.

וְשִׂים בַּסֶּלַע קִנֶּךָ — *And set your nest in the rock.* Hence, because of this, at the time that they (Israel) will be elevated and strong, your nest shall (also) be with them, as our Sages say, 'He who lives with you in your poverty shall be settled among you in your wealth' (*Yevamos* 24b).

23. אוֹי מִי יִחְיֶה — *Alas, who shall live* . . . similar to, 'Let him (the Messiah) come but let me not see him' (*Sanhedrin* 98b).

XXV

1. וַיָּחֶל הָעָם לִזְנוֹת — *And the people began to commit harlotry.* At the beginning, they did not worship idols at all but (their sole intent was to) commit harlotry; however, they were led to idolatry (lit., it happened to them) as the Torah cautioned (lit.,

NOTES

(and he shall have dominion) is in the singular, hence it must refer to every descendant of Jacob, regardless of how mighty or weak he may appear to be.

20. עֲדֵי אֹבֵד — *Shall come to destruction.* Amalek is also a descendant of Esau. Here again, the *Sforno* emphasizes the eventual total destruction of Esau-Edom.

21. אֵיתָן מוֹשָׁבֶךָ — *Your dwelling place is strong.* The Kenites were the descendants of Jethro, who joined the Israelites in the wilderness and faithfully remained with Israel, sharing their travails and difficulties, even though Jethro himself ultimately returned to his homeland. Therefore, they were given a share in the Land of Israel which was only fitting and proper, as the *Sforno* points out citing the saying of our Sages that he who remains loyal to you in your time of need is entitled to share in your eventual success.

23. אוֹי מִי יִחְיֶה — *Alas, who shall live.* The preceding verses speak of the Messianic period. According to tradition, that period will be a most difficult and painful one, so much so that Ulla said he does not want to be present when the Messiah will arrive! Balaam therefore exclaims, 'Woe, who would want to live during that difficult time?' This, according to the *Sforno*, is the sense of אוֹי מִי יִחְיֶה.

ג לְזִבְחֵי אֱלֹהֵיהֶן וַיֹּאכַל הָעָם וַיִּשְׁתַּחֲווּ לֵאלֹהֵיהֶן: וַיִּצָּמֶד יִשְׂרָאֵל לְבַעַל
ד פְּעוֹר וַיִּחַר־אַף יהוה בְּיִשְׂרָאֵל: וַיֹּאמֶר יהוה אֶל־מֹשֶׁה קַח אֶת־כָּל־רָאשֵׁי
הָעָם וְהוֹקַע אוֹתָם לַיהוה נֶגֶד הַשָּׁמֶשׁ וְיָשֹׁב חֲרוֹן אַף־יהוה מִיִּשְׂרָאֵל:
ה וַיֹּאמֶר מֹשֶׁה אֶל־שֹׁפְטֵי יִשְׂרָאֵל הִרְגוּ אִישׁ אֲנָשָׁיו הַנִּצְמָדִים לְבַעַל פְּעוֹר:
ו וְהִנֵּה אִישׁ מִבְּנֵי יִשְׂרָאֵל בָּא וַיַּקְרֵב אֶל־אֶחָיו אֶת־הַמִּדְיָנִית לְעֵינֵי מֹשֶׁה
מפטיר ז וּלְעֵינֵי כָּל־עֲדַת בְּנֵי־יִשְׂרָאֵל וְהֵמָּה בֹכִים פֶּתַח אֹהֶל מוֹעֵד: וַיַּרְא פִּינְחָס
ח בֶּן־אֶלְעָזָר בֶּן־אַהֲרֹן הַכֹּהֵן וַיָּקָם מִתּוֹךְ הָעֵדָה וַיִּקַּח רֹמַח בְּיָדוֹ: וַיָּבֹא אַחַר
אִישׁ־יִשְׂרָאֵל אֶל־הַקֻּבָּה וַיִּדְקֹר אֶת־שְׁנֵיהֶם אֵת אִישׁ יִשְׂרָאֵל וְאֶת־
ט הָאִשָּׁה אֶל־קֳבָתָהּ וַתֵּעָצַר הַמַּגֵּפָה מֵעַל בְּנֵי יִשְׂרָאֵל: וַיִּהְיוּ הַמֵּתִים בַּמַּגֵּפָה
אַרְבָּעָה וְעֶשְׂרִים אָלֶף:

---

attested) when it prohibited intermarriage with the nations, as it says, וְקָרָא לְךָ וְאָכַלְתָּ מִזִּבְחוֹ. וְלָקַחְתָּ מִבְּנֹתָיו . . . וְזָנוּ בְנֹתָיו . . . וְהִזְנוּ אֶת בָּנֶיךָ אַחֲרֵי אֱלֹהֵיהֶן, *And they will call you to eat of their sacrifice. And you will take of their daughters . . . and their daughters will go astray . . . and make your sons go astray after their gods* (Exodus 34:15-16).

2. וַיֹּאכַל הָעָם וַיִּשְׁתַּחֲווּ לֵאלֹהֵיהֶן — *And the people ate and bowed down to their gods.* For this is the way of the evil inclination, to lead one from evil to evil, as our Sages have testified (*Shabbos* 105b).

4. נֶגֶד הַשָּׁמֶשׁ — *In the face of the sun* . . . so that the people will see the execution of those who worshipped the idols and they will not protest (prevent) and thus they will find atonement for not protesting against these sinners.

8. וַתֵּעָצַר הַמַּגֵּפָה — *And the plague was stayed* . . . (the plague or decree) which God, the Exalted One, had already decreed when He said, *Neither shall any of them that angered Me see it* (14:23).

NOTES

XXV

2. וַיֹּאכַל . . . וַיִּשְׁתַּחֲווּ — *And the people ate and bowed down.* The *Sforno* explains that Israel's transgression developed gradually. It began with harlotry, followed by the eating of pagan sacrifices, and culminated in Israel's bowing down to idols. This is reflected in the saying of our Sages in tractate *Shabbos* 105b: *Such are the wiles of the evil inclination; today he says to him, 'Do this,' tomorrow he tells him, 'Do that,' until he bids him, 'Go and serve idols.'*

4. נֶגֶד הַשָּׁמֶשׁ — *In the face of the sun.* The masses were not guilty of harlotry or idolatry. However, they were guilty of apathy, having witnessed these grave transgressions and failed to object or intervene. Their atonement, in turn, would be attained by permitting the culprits to be hung in public without protest or intervention. The *Sforno* gives a similar explanation in *Exodus* 32:27 regarding the punishment meted out to those who were guilty of worshiping the Golden Calf.

8. וַתֵּעָצַר הַמַּגֵּפָה — *And the plague was stayed.* The *Sforno's* interpretation of the word הַמַּגֵּפָה, *the plague*, written with the definite article 'ה', is to be understood according to his commentary in chapter 14:23. There he explains that the decree of the Almighty regarding those who would not merit to enter the Land extended beyond the generation of the spies, and included those who would be guilty of other transgressions as well, such as the congregation of Korach; those who worshiped Baal Peor and those who were killed by the fiery serpents. *The plague* cited here refers to God's decree in *Parashas Shelach* where He said, *Neither shall any who angered Me see it.* It was that plague which now ceased, for all the episodes mentioned above had already occurred and no other sins would merit such radical punishment.

פרשת פינחס

Parashas Pinchas

י־יא וַיְדַבֵּר יהוה אֶל־מֹשֶׁה לֵּאמֹר: פִּינְחָס בֶּן־אֶלְעָזָר בֶּן־אַהֲרֹן הַכֹּהֵן הֵשִׁיב
אֶת־חֲמָתִי מֵעַל בְּנֵי־יִשְׂרָאֵל בְּקַנְאוֹ אֶת־קִנְאָתִי בְּתוֹכָם וְלֹא־כִלִּיתִי
יב אֶת־בְּנֵי־יִשְׂרָאֵל בְּקִנְאָתִי: לָכֵן אֱמֹר הִנְנִי נֹתֵן לוֹ אֶת־בְּרִיתִי שָׁלוֹם:

---

11. בְּקַנְאוֹ אֶת קִנְאָתִי בְּתוֹכָם — *He was zealous for My sake in their midst.* He avenged (My honor) in the sight of all, so that (although) they (Israel) saw this (despicable act) against which they did not protest, they (still) would find atonement for not having protested against the sinners, and thereby *he turned My wrath away* from them.

12. אֶת בְּרִיתִי שָׁלוֹם — *My covenant of peace ...* from the angel of death, similar to עֹשֶׂה שָׁלוֹם בִּמְרוֹמָיו, *He who makes peace in His heights* (*Job* 25:2). Because, indeed, all diminishment (of life) is caused only (as a result) of opposing conflicting (forces). Now, this (blessing of peace) was fulfilled with Pinchas [Phinehas] who lived much longer than all his contemporaries (lit., the men of his generation), to such an extent that he (even) served (as the *Kohen*) in the Sanctuary of Shiloh at the time (of the episode) of the concubine in Givah (*Judges* 20:28) which, doubtless, occurred after the death of Joshua and the death of הַזְּקֵנִים אֲשֶׁר הֶאֱרִיכוּ יָמִים אַחֲרֵי יְהוֹשֻׁעַ, *the elders who outlived Joshua* (*Joshua* 24:31). And certainly (this is the case) if (Pinchas) lived in the time of Yiftach who wrote to the King of Ammon, בְּשֶׁבֶת יִשְׂרָאֵל בְּחֶשְׁבּוֹן וּבִבְנוֹתֶיהָ ... שְׁלֹשׁ מֵאוֹת שָׁנָה, *While Israel dwelt in Cheshbon and its hamlets ... for three hundred years* (*Judges* 11:26), and our Sages have (also) related to us that Pinchas did not want to go to Yiftach to absolve him from his vow. And this (i.e., Pinchas' longevity) is certainly true according to (the Sage) who says that Elijah and Pinchas are one (and the same) for he (Elijah) still lives and exists.

NOTES

11. בְּקַנְאוֹ אֶת קִנְאָתִי בְּתוֹכָם — *He was zealous for My sake in their midst.* See the *Sforno's* commentary on verse 4 and the note thereon.

12. אֶת בְּרִיתִי שָׁלוֹם — *My covenant of peace.* Angels, although they represent opposing forces and are diverse in their mission and purpose, are still able to exist in peace with one another. We learn this from the verse in *Job* cited by the *Sforno* in his commentary on this verse. The angel of death, however, represents the ultimate force of negation, deprivation and loss which results from opposing, conflicting forces (הִתְנַגְּדוּת הַהֲפָכִים). In other words, the angel of death is the only angel who cannot coexist in peace with the other angels on High. Pinchas, who is the personification of peace, possesses the antidote to death and consequently merits longevity, and perhaps even eternal life. The *Sforno* cites various verses to confirm Pinchas' longevity, as well as the opinion of one Sage that Pinchas and Elijah are the same person which would mean that he still lives and exists (חַי וְקַיָּים)

The episode of the concubine in Givah is recorded in the Book of *Judges* as is that of Yiftach. The former tragic event involved the tribe of Benjamin against whom all of the other tribes did battle after receiving an affirmative answer from the Urim and Tummim (אורים ותומים) through Pinchas. The latter episode is that of Yiftach's daughter who was the first to come out of her father's house upon his return from his victory over Ammon. He had vowed to sacrifice the first one who came forth to greet him, and according to the Midrash, Pinchas refused to go and absolve him from this vow. Since these two events occurred hundreds of years after the conquest of the land, Pinchas, perforce, was a very old man at that time. The tradition that Pinchas and Elijah were one and the same is brought by *Rashi* in tractate *Bava Metzia* (114b) regarding Rabbah bar Abuhu who met Elijah in a cemetery and asked him a halachic question, after which he expressed his amazement that a *Kohen* should be in a

יג וְהָיְתָה לּוֹ וּלְזַרְעוֹ אַחֲרָיו בְּרִית כְּהֻנַּת עוֹלָם תַּחַת אֲשֶׁר קִנֵּא לֵאלֹהָיו
יד וַיְכַפֵּר עַל־בְּנֵי יִשְׂרָאֵל: וְשֵׁם אִישׁ יִשְׂרָאֵל הַמֻּכֶּה אֲשֶׁר הֻכָּה אֶת־הַמִּדְיָנִית
טו זִמְרִי בֶּן־סָלוּא נְשִׂיא בֵית־אָב לַשִּׁמְעֹנִי: וְשֵׁם הָאִשָּׁה הַמֻּכָּה הַמִּדְיָנִית
כָּזְבִּי בַת־צוּר רֹאשׁ אֻמּוֹת בֵּית־אָב בְּמִדְיָן הוּא:
טז-יח וַיְדַבֵּר יהוה אֶל־מֹשֶׁה לֵּאמֹר: צָרוֹר אֶת־הַמִּדְיָנִים וְהִכִּיתֶם אוֹתָם: כִּי
צֹרְרִים הֵם לָכֶם בְּנִכְלֵיהֶם אֲשֶׁר נִכְּלוּ לָכֶם עַל־דְּבַר פְּעוֹר וְעַל־דְּבַר כָּזְבִּי
כו א בַּת־נְשִׂיא מִדְיָן אֲחֹתָם הַמֻּכָּה בְיוֹם־הַמַּגֵּפָה עַל־דְּבַר פְּעוֹר: וַיְהִי אַחֲרֵי
הַמַּגֵּפָה
ב וַיֹּאמֶר יהוה אֶל־מֹשֶׁה וְאֶל אֶלְעָזָר בֶּן־אַהֲרֹן הַכֹּהֵן לֵאמֹר: שְׂאוּ
אֶת־רֹאשׁ | כָּל־עֲדַת בְּנֵי־יִשְׂרָאֵל מִבֶּן עֶשְׂרִים שָׁנָה וָמַעְלָה לְבֵית אֲבֹתָם
ג כָּל־יֹצֵא צָבָא בְּיִשְׂרָאֵל: וַיְדַבֵּר מֹשֶׁה וְאֶלְעָזָר הַכֹּהֵן אֹתָם בְּעַרְבֹת מוֹאָב
ד עַל־יַרְדֵּן יְרֵחוֹ לֵאמֹר: מִבֶּן עֶשְׂרִים שָׁנָה וָמָעְלָה כַּאֲשֶׁר צִוָּה יהוה
שני ה אֶת־מֹשֶׁה וּבְנֵי יִשְׂרָאֵל הַיֹּצְאִים מֵאֶרֶץ מִצְרָיִם: רְאוּבֵן בְּכוֹר יִשְׂרָאֵל בְּנֵי
ו רְאוּבֵן חֲנוֹךְ מִשְׁפַּחַת הַחֲנֹכִי לְפַלּוּא מִשְׁפַּחַת הַפַּלֻּאִי: לְחֶצְרֹן מִשְׁפַּחַת

---

13. תַּחַת אֲשֶׁר קִנֵּא לֵאלֹהָיו — *Because he was zealous for his God* ... and since he fought My battle, I shall save him from strife (caused by) any opposition, and he shall have peace.

וַיְכַפֵּר עַל בְּנֵי יִשְׂרָאֵל — *And made atonement for the Children of Israel* ... by avenging (God's honor) publicly in order that they find atonement for failing to protest against the sinners, and therefore he is worthy (to be granted) an everlasting priesthood through which he will atone for them.

14. וְשֵׁם אִישׁ יִשְׂרָאֵל הַמֻּכֶּה — *The name of the man of Israel who was slain.* And this (reward is given) because he atoned for them in a manner which demanded a willingness to expose oneself to danger by publicly killing a (Jewish) prince and a (heathen) princess.

XXVI

3-4. לֵאמֹר מִבֶּן עֶשְׂרִים שָׁנָה וָמַעְלָה — *Saying,* (*Take the sum of the people*) *from twenty years old and upwards.* Moses and Elazar said to Israel that they should relate and report all individuals who were twenty years of age.

כַּאֲשֶׁר צִוָּה ה' אֶת מֹשֶׁה וּבְנֵי יִשְׂרָאֵל הַיֹּצְאִים מֵאֶרֶץ מִצְרָיִם — *As* HASHEM *commanded Moses and the Children of Israel who went forth out of the land of Egypt* ... as He said at that time: *after their families, by the house of their fathers* (1:2).

NOTES

cemetery. *Rashi* explains that since according to tradition Elijah and Pinchas were one and the same, perforce Elijah (Pinchas) was a *Kohen*.

13. וַיְכַפֵּר עַל בְּנֵי יִשְׂרָאֵל — *And made atonement for the Children of Israel.* The mission of a *Kohen* is to perform the service of God at the altar through which he atones for the sins of the Children of Israel. It is therefore most fitting that Pinchas, who atoned for Israel's transgressions at the risk of his own life, should be granted the covenant of everlasting priesthood.

14. וְשֵׁם אִישׁ יִשְׂרָאֵל הַמֻּכֶּה — *The name of the man of Israel who was slain.* The Torah does not reveal the name of sinners unless it

ז הַחֶצְרוֹנִי לְכַרְמִי מִשְׁפַּחַת הַכַּרְמִי׃ אֵלֶּה מִשְׁפְּחֹת הָרֻאוּבֵנִי וַיִּהְיוּ פְקֻדֵיהֶם
ח-ט שְׁלֹשָׁה וְאַרְבָּעִים אֶלֶף וּשְׁבַע מֵאוֹת וּשְׁלֹשִׁים׃ וּבְנֵי פַלּוּא אֱלִיאָב׃ וּבְנֵי
°קְרִיאֵי ק׳ אֱלִיאָב נְמוּאֵל וְדָתָן וַאֲבִירָם הוּא־דָתָן וַאֲבִירָם °קְרוּאֵי הָעֵדָה אֲשֶׁר הִצּוּ
י עַל־מֹשֶׁה וְעַל־אַהֲרֹן בַּעֲדַת־קֹרַח בְּהַצֹּתָם עַל־יְהוָה׃ וַתִּפְתַּח הָאָרֶץ
אֶת־פִּיהָ וַתִּבְלַע אֹתָם וְאֶת־קֹרַח בְּמוֹת הָעֵדָה בַּאֲכֹל הָאֵשׁ אֵת חֲמִשִּׁים
יא-יב וּמָאתַיִם אִישׁ וַיִּהְיוּ לְנֵס׃ וּבְנֵי־קֹרַח לֹא־מֵתוּ׃ בְּנֵי שִׁמְעוֹן
לְמִשְׁפְּחֹתָם לִנְמוּאֵל מִשְׁפַּחַת הַנְּמוּאֵלִי לְיָמִין מִשְׁפַּחַת הַיָּמִינִי לְיָכִין
יג-יד מִשְׁפַּחַת הַיָּכִינִי׃ לְזֶרַח מִשְׁפַּחַת הַזַּרְחִי לְשָׁאוּל מִשְׁפַּחַת הַשָּׁאוּלִי׃ אֵלֶּה
טו מִשְׁפְּחֹת הַשִּׁמְעֹנִי שְׁנַיִם וְעֶשְׂרִים אֶלֶף וּמָאתָיִם׃ בְּנֵי גָד
לְמִשְׁפְּחֹתָם לִצְפוֹן מִשְׁפַּחַת הַצְּפוֹנִי לְחַגִּי מִשְׁפַּחַת הַחַגִּי לְשׁוּנִי מִשְׁפַּחַת
טז-יז הַשּׁוּנִי׃ לְאָזְנִי מִשְׁפַּחַת הָאָזְנִי לְעֵרִי מִשְׁפַּחַת הָעֵרִי׃ לַאֲרוֹד מִשְׁפַּחַת
יח הָאֲרוֹדִי לְאַרְאֵלִי מִשְׁפַּחַת הָאַרְאֵלִי׃ אֵלֶּה מִשְׁפְּחֹת בְּנֵי־גָד לִפְקֻדֵיהֶם
יט אַרְבָּעִים אֶלֶף וַחֲמֵשׁ מֵאוֹת׃ בְּנֵי יְהוּדָה עֵר וְאוֹנָן
כ וַיָּמָת עֵר וְאוֹנָן בְּאֶרֶץ כְּנָעַן׃ וַיִּהְיוּ בְנֵי־יְהוּדָה לְמִשְׁפְּחֹתָם לְשֵׁלָה מִשְׁפַּחַת
כא הַשֵּׁלָנִי לְפֶרֶץ מִשְׁפַּחַת הַפַּרְצִי לְזֶרַח מִשְׁפַּחַת הַזַּרְחִי׃ וַיִּהְיוּ בְנֵי־פֶרֶץ
כב לְחֶצְרֹן מִשְׁפַּחַת הַחֶצְרֹנִי לְחָמוּל מִשְׁפַּחַת הֶחָמוּלִי׃ אֵלֶּה מִשְׁפְּחֹת יְהוּדָה
כג לִפְקֻדֵיהֶם שִׁשָּׁה וְשִׁבְעִים אֶלֶף וַחֲמֵשׁ מֵאוֹת׃ בְּנֵי יִשָּׂשכָר
כד לְמִשְׁפְּחֹתָם תּוֹלָע מִשְׁפַּחַת הַתּוֹלָעִי לְפֻוָּה מִשְׁפַּחַת הַפּוּנִי׃ לְיָשׁוּב
כה מִשְׁפַּחַת הַיָּשֻׁבִי לְשִׁמְרֹן מִשְׁפַּחַת הַשִּׁמְרֹנִי׃ אֵלֶּה מִשְׁפְּחֹת יִשָּׂשכָר
כו לִפְקֻדֵיהֶם אַרְבָּעָה וְשִׁשִּׁים אֶלֶף וּשְׁלֹשׁ מֵאוֹת׃ בְּנֵי זְבוּלֻן
לְמִשְׁפְּחֹתָם לְסֶרֶד מִשְׁפַּחַת הַסַּרְדִּי לְאֵלוֹן מִשְׁפַּחַת הָאֵלֹנִי לְיַחְלְאֵל
כז מִשְׁפַּחַת הַיַּחְלְאֵלִי׃ אֵלֶּה מִשְׁפְּחֹת הַזְּבוּלֹנִי לִפְקֻדֵיהֶם שִׁשִּׁים אֶלֶף וַחֲמֵשׁ
כח-כט מֵאוֹת׃ בְּנֵי יוֹסֵף לְמִשְׁפְּחֹתָם מְנַשֶּׁה וְאֶפְרָיִם׃ בְּנֵי מְנַשֶּׁה
לְמָכִיר מִשְׁפַּחַת הַמָּכִירִי וּמָכִיר הוֹלִיד אֶת־גִּלְעָד לְגִלְעָד מִשְׁפַּחַת
ל הַגִּלְעָדִי׃ אֵלֶּה בְּנֵי גִלְעָד אִיעֶזֶר מִשְׁפַּחַת הָאִיעֶזְרִי לְחֵלֶק מִשְׁפַּחַת
לא-לב הַחֶלְקִי׃ וְאַשְׂרִיאֵל מִשְׁפַּחַת הָאַשְׂרִאֵלִי וְשֶׁכֶם מִשְׁפַּחַת הַשִּׁכְמִי׃ וּשְׁמִידָע
לג מִשְׁפַּחַת הַשְּׁמִידָעִי וְחֵפֶר מִשְׁפַּחַת הַחֶפְרִי׃ וּצְלָפְחָד בֶּן־חֵפֶר לֹא־הָיוּ
לוֹ בָּנִים כִּי אִם־בָּנוֹת וְשֵׁם בְּנוֹת צְלָפְחָד מַחְלָה וְנֹעָה חָגְלָה מִלְכָּה
לד וְתִרְצָה׃ אֵלֶּה מִשְׁפְּחֹת מְנַשֶּׁה וּפְקֻדֵיהֶם שְׁנַיִם וַחֲמִשִּׁים אֶלֶף וּשְׁבַע
לה מֵאוֹת׃ אֵלֶּה בְנֵי־אֶפְרַיִם לְמִשְׁפְּחֹתָם לְשׁוּתֶלַח מִשְׁפַּחַת
לו הַשֻּׁתַלְחִי לְבֶכֶר מִשְׁפַּחַת הַבַּכְרִי לְתַחַן מִשְׁפַּחַת הַתַּחֲנִי׃ וְאֵלֶּה בְּנֵי
לז שׁוּתָלַח לְעֵרָן מִשְׁפַּחַת הָעֵרָנִי׃ אֵלֶּה מִשְׁפְּחֹת בְּנֵי־אֶפְרַיִם לִפְקֻדֵיהֶם שְׁנַיִם
לח וּשְׁלֹשִׁים אֶלֶף וַחֲמֵשׁ מֵאוֹת אֵלֶּה בְנֵי־יוֹסֵף לְמִשְׁפְּחֹתָם׃ בְּנֵי

NOTES

serves an educational purpose. The *Sforno*, similar to *Rashi*, explains that the reason the Torah records the name of Zimri, prince of the tribe of Simeon, as well as informing us that the woman was a Midianite princess, is to underscore the willingness of Pinchas to defend God's honor, even at the risk of his own life.

בִנְיָמִן לְמִשְׁפְּחֹתָם לְבֶלַע מִשְׁפַּחַת הַבַּלְעִי לְאַשְׁבֵּל מִשְׁפַּחַת הָאַשְׁבֵּלִי
לט לַאֲחִירָם מִשְׁפַּחַת הָאֲחִירָמִי׃ לִשְׁפוּפָם מִשְׁפַּחַת הַשּׁוּפָמִי לְחוּפָם מִשְׁפַּחַת
מ הַחוּפָמִי׃ וַיִּהְיוּ בְנֵי־בֶלַע אַרְדְּ וְנַעֲמָן מִשְׁפַּחַת הָאַרְדִּי לְנַעֲמָן מִשְׁפַּחַת
מא הַנַּעֲמִי׃ אֵלֶּה בְנֵי־בִנְיָמִן לְמִשְׁפְּחֹתָם וּפְקֻדֵיהֶם חֲמִשָּׁה וְאַרְבָּעִים אֶלֶף וְשֵׁשׁ
מב מֵאוֹת׃ אֵלֶּה בְנֵי־דָן לְמִשְׁפְּחֹתָם לְשׁוּחָם מִשְׁפַּחַת הַשּׁוּחָמִי
מג אֵלֶּה מִשְׁפְּחֹת דָּן לְמִשְׁפְּחֹתָם׃ כָּל־מִשְׁפְּחֹת הַשּׁוּחָמִי לִפְקֻדֵיהֶם אַרְבָּעָה
מד וְשִׁשִּׁים אֶלֶף וְאַרְבַּע מֵאוֹת׃ בְּנֵי אָשֵׁר לְמִשְׁפְּחֹתָם לְיִמְנָה
מה מִשְׁפַּחַת הַיִּמְנָה לְיִשְׁוִי מִשְׁפַּחַת הַיִּשְׁוִי לִבְרִיעָה מִשְׁפַּחַת הַבְּרִיעִי׃ לִבְנֵי
מו בְרִיעָה לְחֶבֶר מִשְׁפַּחַת הַחֶבְרִי לְמַלְכִּיאֵל מִשְׁפַּחַת הַמַּלְכִּיאֵלִי׃ וְשֵׁם
מז בַּת־אָשֵׁר שָׂרַח׃ אֵלֶּה מִשְׁפְּחֹת בְּנֵי־אָשֵׁר לִפְקֻדֵיהֶם שְׁלֹשָׁה וַחֲמִשִּׁים אֶלֶף
מח וְאַרְבַּע מֵאוֹת׃ בְּנֵי נַפְתָּלִי לְמִשְׁפְּחֹתָם לְיַחְצְאֵל מִשְׁפַּחַת
מט הַיַּחְצְאֵלִי לְגוּנִי מִשְׁפַּחַת הַגּוּנִי׃ לְיֵצֶר מִשְׁפַּחַת הַיִּצְרִי לְשִׁלֵּם מִשְׁפַּחַת
נ הַשִּׁלֵּמִי׃ אֵלֶּה מִשְׁפְּחֹת נַפְתָּלִי לְמִשְׁפְּחֹתָם וּפְקֻדֵיהֶם חֲמִשָּׁה וְאַרְבָּעִים
נא אֶלֶף וְאַרְבַּע מֵאוֹת׃ אֵלֶּה פְּקוּדֵי בְּנֵי יִשְׂרָאֵל שֵׁשׁ־מֵאוֹת אֶלֶף וָאָלֶף שְׁבַע
מֵאוֹת וּשְׁלֹשִׁים׃
שלישי נב־נג וַיְדַבֵּר יְהוָה אֶל־מֹשֶׁה לֵּאמֹר׃ לָאֵלֶּה תֵּחָלֵק הָאָרֶץ בְּנַחֲלָה בְּמִסְפַּר
נד שֵׁמוֹת׃ לָרַב תַּרְבֶּה נַחֲלָתוֹ וְלַמְעַט תַּמְעִיט נַחֲלָתוֹ אִישׁ לְפִי פְקֻדָיו יֻתַּן

---

54. לָרַב תַּרְבֶּה נַחֲלָתוֹ — *To the numerous you shall increase the inheritance.* (This increase refers to) the quantity of the land (allotted) because the land was divided into twelve portions equal in value, although unequal quantitatively. Rather, a *kor* of inferior quality (was given) as the equivalent of a good piece of land sufficient to sow a *seah*. Now, the tribe that was numerous took a portion larger in area while the tribe that was lesser took a smaller portion in quantity but in value it was equal to the larger portion, as it says, *to the numerous you shall increase the inheritance* (33:54). In this manner, Menasseh and Ephraim received two portions because of Joseph's birthright as a firstborn, as it says, נָתַתִּי לְךָ שְׁכֶם אַחַד עַל אַחֶיךָ, *I have given you one portion, Shechem, above your brothers* (Genesis 48:22), and so it is explained in *I Chronicles* 5:1, וּבְחַלְּלוֹ יְצוּעֵי אָבִיו נִתְּנָה בְּכֹרָתוֹ לִבְנֵי יוֹסֵף בֶּן יִשְׂרָאֵל, *But since he defiled his father's bed, his birthright was given to the sons of Joseph, the son of Israel.* Now, to Simeon, who was the least numerous of all the tribes when they entered the Land, was given the smallest portion in quantity (but) very valuable, and since there was no continuous concentrated tract of land of sufficient value for Simeon's share, his portion was chosen from a number of places in the land of Judah, as it says, מֵחֶבֶל בְּנֵי יְהוּדָה נַחֲלַת בְּנֵי שִׁמְעוֹן, *Out of the portion of the children of Judah was the inheritance of the children of Simeon* (Joshua 19:9), and thus was fulfilled regarding the tribe of Simeon (the prophecy of Jacob), אֲחַלְּקֵם בְּיַעֲקֹב, *I will divide them in Jacob* (Genesis 49:7).

NOTES

XXVI

54. לָרַב תַּרְבֶּה נַחֲלָתוֹ — *To the numerous you shall increase the inheritance. Rashi's* commentary on this verse explains that, in addition to giving a larger portion to the tribe that had a numerous population, the fertility and value of the soil also had to be considered, and thus an inferior piece of land sufficient to sow a *kor* (a measure mentioned in the Mishnah

נה-נו נַחֲלָתוֹ: אַךְ־בְּגוֹרָל יֵחָלֵק אֶת־הָאָרֶץ לִשְׁמוֹת מַטּוֹת־אֲבֹתָם יִנְחָלוּ: עַל־פִּי
נז הַגּוֹרָל תֵּחָלֵק נַחֲלָתוֹ בֵּין רַב לִמְעָט: וְאֵלֶּה פְקוּדֵי הַלֵּוִי
לְמִשְׁפְּחֹתָם לְגֵרְשׁוֹן מִשְׁפַּחַת הַגֵּרְשֻׁנִּי לִקְהָת מִשְׁפַּחַת הַקְּהָתִי לִמְרָרִי
נח מִשְׁפַּחַת הַמְּרָרִי: אֵלֶּה | מִשְׁפְּחֹת לֵוִי מִשְׁפַּחַת הַלִּבְנִי מִשְׁפַּחַת הַחֶבְרֹנִי
מִשְׁפַּחַת הַמַּחְלִי מִשְׁפַּחַת הַמּוּשִׁי מִשְׁפַּחַת הַקָּרְחִי וּקְהָת הוֹלִד
נט אֶת־עַמְרָם: וְשֵׁם | אֵשֶׁת עַמְרָם יוֹכֶבֶד בַּת־לֵוִי אֲשֶׁר יָלְדָה אֹתָהּ לְלֵוִי
ס בְּמִצְרָיִם וַתֵּלֶד לְעַמְרָם אֶת־אַהֲרֹן וְאֶת־מֹשֶׁה וְאֵת מִרְיָם אֲחֹתָם: וַיִּוָּלֵד
סא לְאַהֲרֹן אֶת־נָדָב וְאֶת־אֲבִיהוּא אֶת־אֶלְעָזָר וְאֶת־אִיתָמָר: וַיָּמָת נָדָב
סב וַאֲבִיהוּא בְּהַקְרִיבָם אֵשׁ־זָרָה לִפְנֵי יהוה: וַיִּהְיוּ פְקֻדֵיהֶם שְׁלֹשָׁה וְעֶשְׂרִים
אֶלֶף כָּל־זָכָר מִבֶּן־חֹדֶשׁ וָמָעְלָה כִּי | לֹא הָתְפָּקְדוּ בְּתוֹךְ בְּנֵי יִשְׂרָאֵל °כִּי
סג לֹא־נִתַּן לָהֶם נַחֲלָה בְּתוֹךְ בְּנֵי יִשְׂרָאֵל: אֵלֶּה פְּקוּדֵי מֹשֶׁה וְאֶלְעָזָר הַכֹּהֵן
סד אֲשֶׁר פָּקְדוּ אֶת־בְּנֵי יִשְׂרָאֵל בְּעַרְבֹת מוֹאָב עַל יַרְדֵּן יְרֵחוֹ: וּבְאֵלֶּה
לֹא־הָיָה אִישׁ מִפְּקוּדֵי מֹשֶׁה וְאַהֲרֹן הַכֹּהֵן אֲשֶׁר פָּקְדוּ אֶת־בְּנֵי יִשְׂרָאֵל
סה בְּמִדְבַּר סִינָי: כִּי־אָמַר יהוה לָהֶם מוֹת יָמֻתוּ בַּמִּדְבָּר וְלֹא־נוֹתַר מֵהֶם אִישׁ
כז א כִּי אִם־כָּלֵב בֶּן־יְפֻנֶּה וִיהוֹשֻׁעַ בִּן־נוּן: וַתִּקְרַבְנָה בְּנוֹת

---

55. אַךְ בְּגוֹרָל — *Notwithstanding, by lot.* Although the (land was) divided into larger and smaller portions according to the needs of the tribes and their size, (nonetheless) no portion was given to a tribe except *according to the lot*, and thus each tribe received its portion according to God.

56. עַל פִּי הַגּוֹרָל תֵּחָלֵק נַחֲלָתוֹ — *According to the lot shall the possession be divided* . . . and when the tribe allotted portions according to the number (of individuals) in each family, it was also given *according to the lot*.

NOTES

and Talmud) was regarded as the equivalent of a good piece of land sufficient to plant a *seah*, which is the 30th part of a *kor*. The *Ramban* interprets this verse to mean that each family should receive an allotment proportionate to the number of its members. While each tribe was given an equal share of the land, that share was subdivided among its families, each family receiving a portion according to its number.

The *Sforno*, while following the lead of *Rashi* in his commentary, adds two important points. He explains that since quantity and quality were both taken into account, one can now understand the advantage gained by Menasseh and Ephraim in being considered as two tribes. For one could well ask, even if they were but one tribe, would they not receive land according to their total numbers? However, once we are told that the value of the land is a determinant, the advantage of receiving a portion as a distinct separate tribe becomes apparent. The second point made by the *Sforno* is regarding Simeon. Jacob, in his blessing (*parashas Vayechi*), had said אֲחַלְּקֵם בְּיַעֲקֹב, *I will divide them in Jacob* — and וַאֲפִיצֵם בְּיִשְׂרָאֵל, *and I will scatter them in Israel* (*Genesis* 49:7). The *Sforno* explains that this prophecy was fulfilled, not by denying them a permanent portion in the Land (which was never the intent of Jacob), but by giving them land of superior quality since they were few numerically. Perforce, this had to involve different areas since there was not sufficient contiguous good land to meet the quota of land to which Simeon was entitled, thereby realizing the prophecy of his father.

55. אַךְ בְּגוֹרָל — *Notwithstanding, by lot.* The *Sforno* here reflects the statement of our Sages in *Bava Basra* 122a that although the portions of the land were assigned according to the size of each tribe, nonetheless, it was done through lots, and these lots fell according to רוּחַ הַקֹּדֶשׁ, *the Holy Spirit*. See *Rashi* here who gives a fuller explanation of how these lots fell.

צְלָפְחָד בֶּן־חֵפֶר בֶּן־גִּלְעָד בֶּן־מָכִיר בֶּן־מְנַשֶּׁה לְמִשְׁפְּחֹת מְנַשֶּׁה בֶן־יוֹסֵף
ב וְאֵלֶּה שְׁמוֹת בְּנֹתָיו מַחְלָה נֹעָה וְחָגְלָה וּמִלְכָּה וְתִרְצָה: וַתַּעֲמֹדְנָה לִפְנֵי
מֹשֶׁה וְלִפְנֵי אֶלְעָזָר הַכֹּהֵן וְלִפְנֵי הַנְּשִׂיאִם וְכָל־הָעֵדָה פֶּתַח אֹהֶל־מוֹעֵד
ג לֵאמֹר: אָבִינוּ מֵת בַּמִּדְבָּר וְהוּא לֹא־הָיָה בְּתוֹךְ הָעֵדָה הַנּוֹעָדִים עַל־יְהוָה
ד בַּעֲדַת־קֹרַח כִּי־בְחֶטְאוֹ מֵת וּבָנִים לֹא־הָיוּ לוֹ: לָמָּה יִגָּרַע שֵׁם־אָבִינוּ
ה מִתּוֹךְ מִשְׁפַּחְתּוֹ כִּי אֵין לוֹ בֵּן תְּנָה־לָּנוּ אֲחֻזָּה בְּתוֹךְ אֲחֵי אָבִינוּ: וַיַּקְרֵב
מֹשֶׁה אֶת־מִשְׁפָּטָן לִפְנֵי יְהוָה:
רביעי ו־ז וַיֹּאמֶר יְהוָה אֶל־מֹשֶׁה לֵּאמֹר: כֵּן בְּנוֹת צְלָפְחָד דֹּבְרֹת נָתֹן תִּתֵּן לָהֶם
ח אֲחֻזַּת נַחֲלָה בְּתוֹךְ אֲחֵי אֲבִיהֶם וְהַעֲבַרְתָּ אֶת־נַחֲלַת אֲבִיהֶן לָהֶן: וְאֶל־בְּנֵי
יִשְׂרָאֵל תְּדַבֵּר לֵאמֹר אִישׁ כִּי־יָמוּת וּבֵן אֵין לוֹ וְהַעֲבַרְתֶּם אֶת־נַחֲלָתוֹ
ט־י לְבִתּוֹ: וְאִם־אֵין לוֹ בַּת וּנְתַתֶּם אֶת־נַחֲלָתוֹ לְאֶחָיו: וְאִם־אֵין לוֹ אַחִים
יא וּנְתַתֶּם אֶת־נַחֲלָתוֹ לַאֲחֵי אָבִיו: וְאִם־אֵין אַחִים לְאָבִיו וּנְתַתֶּם
אֶת־נַחֲלָתוֹ לִשְׁאֵרוֹ הַקָּרֹב אֵלָיו מִמִּשְׁפַּחְתּוֹ וְיָרַשׁ אֹתָהּ וְהָיְתָה לִבְנֵי
יִשְׂרָאֵל לְחֻקַּת מִשְׁפָּט כַּאֲשֶׁר צִוָּה יְהוָה אֶת־מֹשֶׁה:
יב וַיֹּאמֶר יְהוָה אֶל־מֹשֶׁה עֲלֵה אֶל־הַר הָעֲבָרִים הַזֶּה וּרְאֵה אֶת־הָאָרֶץ
יג אֲשֶׁר נָתַתִּי לִבְנֵי יִשְׂרָאֵל: וְרָאִיתָה אֹתָהּ וְנֶאֱסַפְתָּ אֶל־עַמֶּיךָ גַּם־
יד אַתָּה כַּאֲשֶׁר נֶאֱסַף אַהֲרֹן אָחִיךָ: כַּאֲשֶׁר מְרִיתֶם פִּי בְּמִדְבַּר־צִן בִּמְרִיבַת

XXVII

3. וְהוּא לֹא הָיָה — *And he was not.* (He was not) a member of Korach's congregation whose sentence was that all their possessions (lit., money) be condemned (חֵרֶם), for Moses our Teacher did condemn it when he said, סוּרוּ נָא מֵעַל אָהֳלֵי הָאֲנָשִׁים הָרְשָׁעִים הָאֵלֶּה וְאַל תִּגְּעוּ בְּכָל אֲשֶׁר לָהֶם פֶּן תִּסָּפוּ, *Depart, I pray you, from the tents of these wicked men, and touch nothing of theirs, lest you be swept away* (16:26); and they were so judged by Heavenly law, as it says, וְאֵת כָּל הָרְכוּשׁ, *and all their goods* (16:32).

כִּי בְחֶטְאוֹ מֵת — *But he died in his own sin.* The sole punishment for his sin was that he would die, but not that his possessions would be denied his heirs.

NOTES

XXVII

3. וְהוּא לֹא הָיָה . . . כִּי בְחֶטְאוֹ מֵת — *And he was not . . . but he died in his own sin.* The Talmud in tractate *Bava Basra* 118b states that 'the murmurers and the company of Korach did not receive a share in the land.' The daughters of Zelaphchad told Moses that their father was not among the company of Korach and therefore, it was not reasonable that his share in the Land should be forfeited due to a different sin which he did commit. According to tradition, he was the man who picked up wood on Shabbos (16:32).

The *Sforno*, as does the *Ramban*, interprets the phrase וְאַל תִּגְּעוּ, *touch nothing,* (16:26) as meaning that all the possessions of Korach's group were to be considered as חֵרֶם, a word which means '*set apart*', be it because the item is hallowed or condemned. Now, this admonition of Moses only applied to the possessions of Korach and his company which were at hand, and not necessarily to their share in the Land of Israel. The *Sforno* therefore adds that they were also judged בְּדִינֵי שָׁמַיִם, *through Heavenly justice*, which caused them to forfeit their portion in the Land. He bases this upon the phrase כָּל הָרְכוּשׁ, *all their goods* or substance (16:32), which is all inclusive and includes their share in *Eretz Yisrael.*

הָעֵדָה לְהַקְדִּישֵׁנִי בַמַּיִם לְעֵינֵיהֶם הֵם מֵי־מְרִיבַת קָדֵשׁ מִדְבַּר־
טו־טז צִן׃ וַיְדַבֵּר מֹשֶׁה אֶל־יהוה לֵאמֹר׃ יִפְקֹד יהוה אֱלֹהֵי
יז הָרוּחֹת לְכָל־בָּשָׂר אִישׁ עַל־הָעֵדָה׃ אֲשֶׁר־יֵצֵא לִפְנֵיהֶם וַאֲשֶׁר יָבֹא
לִפְנֵיהֶם וַאֲשֶׁר יוֹצִיאֵם וַאֲשֶׁר יְבִיאֵם וְלֹא תִהְיֶה עֲדַת יהוה כַּצֹּאן אֲשֶׁר
יח אֵין־לָהֶם רֹעֶה׃ וַיֹּאמֶר יהוה אֶל־מֹשֶׁה קַח־לְךָ אֶת־יְהוֹשֻׁעַ בִּן־נוּן אִישׁ
יט אֲשֶׁר־רוּחַ בּוֹ וְסָמַכְתָּ אֶת־יָדְךָ עָלָיו׃ וְהַעֲמַדְתָּ אֹתוֹ לִפְנֵי אֶלְעָזָר הַכֹּהֵן
כ וְלִפְנֵי כָּל־הָעֵדָה וְצִוִּיתָה אֹתוֹ לְעֵינֵיהֶם׃ וְנָתַתָּה מֵהוֹדְךָ עָלָיו לְמַעַן יִשְׁמְעוּ
כא כָּל־עֲדַת בְּנֵי יִשְׂרָאֵל׃ וְלִפְנֵי אֶלְעָזָר הַכֹּהֵן יַעֲמֹד וְשָׁאַל לוֹ בְּמִשְׁפַּט
הָאוּרִים לִפְנֵי יהוה עַל־פִּיו יֵצְאוּ וְעַל־פִּיו יָבֹאוּ הוּא וְכָל־בְּנֵי־יִשְׂרָאֵל אִתּוֹ

---

17. אֲשֶׁר יֵצֵא לִפְנֵיהֶם — *Who may go out before them* . . . in military affairs.

וַאֲשֶׁר יוֹצִיאֵם — *Who may lead them out* . . . in administering national affairs.

18. אִישׁ אֲשֶׁר רוּחַ בּוֹ — *A man in whom is spirit* . . . who is prepared to receive *the light of the living king's countenance* (based on *Proverbs* 16:15), similar to, וּבְלֵב כָּל חֲכַם לֵב נָתַתִּי חָכְמָה, *And in the hearts of all that are wise-hearted I have put wisdom* (*Exodus* 31:6).

19. וְצִוִּיתָה אֹתוֹ לְעֵינֵיהֶם — *And appoint him in their sight.* Appoint him as a ruler over them in their presence so that they shall accept him and listen to him. The phrase צוּוּי applies to appointment, similar to, וְצִוְּךָ לְנָגִיד, *And appoint you as ruler* (*I Samuel* 25:30) and to, וּלְמִן הַיּוֹם אֲשֶׁר צִוִּיתִי שֹׁפְטִים, *And as since the time that I appointed judges* (*II Samuel* 7:11).

20. וְנָתַתָּה מֵהוֹדְךָ עָלָיו — *And you shall put (some) of your honor upon him.* (This refers to) the glory of kingship (majesty). Give him some authority in your lifetime so that they (Israel) will begin (at once) to conduct themselves (toward him) with honor.

לְמַעַן יִשְׁמְעוּ — *So that they shall hearken* . . . and the reason for appointing him in their sight and granting him honor in your lifetime is so that the entire congregation, namely the Sanhedrin (courts) and the elders of the people, shall hearken to his voice.

NOTES

18. אִישׁ אֲשֶׁר רוּחַ בּוֹ — *A man in whom is spirit.* The Talmud in tractate *Berachos* 55a says, 'The Holy One, Blessed Be He, gives wisdom only to one who already has wisdom.' R' Abbahu derived this concept from *Exodus* 31:6, which is quoted by the *Sforno* in his commentary on this verse. In other words, God's light and inspiration demands a vessel which is capable of receiving it. That is why God assures Moses that Joshua is indeed such a man — one in whom there is spirit and hence, he will be able to receive additional spirit and wisdom.

19. וְצִוִּיתָה אֹתוֹ לְעֵינֵיהֶם — *And appoint him in their sight.* The *Sforno* explains that the term וְצִוִּיתָה in the context of this verse does not mean *'to command,'* but *'to appoint'*. He brings proof from the verses in *Samuel*. See the commentary of the *Sforno* in *Exodus* 6:13 regarding Moses and Aaron where he gives a similar explanation.

20. וְנָתַתָּה מֵהוֹדְךָ עָלָיו — *And you shall put (some) of your honor upon him.* God impresses upon Moses the importance of establishing Joshua's credentials during his own lifetime, because it is only natural that the elders and judges will be slow in accepting the successor of their Master and Teacher. By sharing some of his authority in his lifetime and by honoring Joshua in their presence, Moses will strengthen the hand and establish the authority of his disciple.

כב וְכָל־הָעֵדָה׃ וַיַּעַשׂ מֹשֶׁה כַּאֲשֶׁר צִוָּה יְהוָה אֹתוֹ וַיִּקַּח אֶת־יְהוֹשֻׁעַ וַיַּעֲמִדֵהוּ
כג לִפְנֵי אֶלְעָזָר הַכֹּהֵן וְלִפְנֵי כָּל־הָעֵדָה׃ וַיִּסְמֹךְ אֶת־יָדָיו עָלָיו וַיְצַוֵּהוּ כַּאֲשֶׁר
דִּבֶּר יְהוָה בְּיַד־מֹשֶׁה׃
כח חמישי א־ב וַיְדַבֵּר יְהוָה אֶל־מֹשֶׁה לֵּאמֹר׃ צַו אֶת־בְּנֵי יִשְׂרָאֵל וְאָמַרְתָּ אֲלֵהֶם
ג אֶת־קָרְבָּנִי לַחְמִי לְאִשַּׁי רֵיחַ נִיחֹחִי תִּשְׁמְרוּ לְהַקְרִיב לִי בְּמוֹעֲדוֹ׃ וְאָמַרְתָּ
לָהֶם זֶה הָאִשֶּׁה אֲשֶׁר תַּקְרִיבוּ לַיהוָה כְּבָשִׂים בְּנֵי־שָׁנָה תְמִימִם שְׁנַיִם לַיּוֹם
ד עֹלָה תָמִיד׃ אֶת־הַכֶּבֶשׂ אֶחָד תַּעֲשֶׂה בַבֹּקֶר וְאֵת הַכֶּבֶשׂ הַשֵּׁנִי תַּעֲשֶׂה בֵּין
ה הָעַרְבָּיִם׃ וַעֲשִׂירִית הָאֵיפָה סֹלֶת לְמִנְחָה בְּלוּלָה בְּשֶׁמֶן כָּתִית רְבִיעִת
ו־ז הַהִין׃ עֹלַת תָּמִיד הָעֲשֻׂיָה בְּהַר סִינַי לְרֵיחַ נִיחֹחַ אִשֶּׁה לַיהוָה׃ וְנִסְכּוֹ
ח רְבִיעִת הַהִין לַכֶּבֶשׂ הָאֶחָד בַּקֹּדֶשׁ הַסֵּךְ נֶסֶךְ שֵׁכָר לַיהוָה׃ וְאֵת הַכֶּבֶשׂ
הַשֵּׁנִי תַּעֲשֶׂה בֵּין הָעַרְבָּיִם כְּמִנְחַת הַבֹּקֶר וּכְנִסְכּוֹ תַּעֲשֶׂה אִשֵּׁה רֵיחַ נִיחֹחַ
לַיהוָה׃
ט וּבְיוֹם הַשַּׁבָּת שְׁנֵי־כְבָשִׂים בְּנֵי־שָׁנָה תְּמִימִם וּשְׁנֵי עֶשְׂרֹנִים סֹלֶת מִנְחָה
י בְּלוּלָה בַשֶּׁמֶן וְנִסְכּוֹ׃ עֹלַת שַׁבַּת בְּשַׁבַּתּוֹ עַל־עֹלַת הַתָּמִיד וְנִסְכָּהּ׃
יא וּבְרָאשֵׁי חָדְשֵׁיכֶם תַּקְרִיבוּ עֹלָה לַיהוָה פָּרִים בְּנֵי־בָקָר שְׁנַיִם וְאַיִל אֶחָד

XXVIII

6. עֹלַת תָּמִיד הָעֲשֻׂיָה בְּהַר סִינַי — *A continual burnt-offering which was offered on Mt. Sinai* . . . (offered) prior to (the sin of) the Golden Calf, at which time it did not necessitate נְסָכִים, *drink offerings.*

8. כְּמִנְחַת הַבֹּקֶר וּכְנִסְכּוֹ תַּעֲשֶׂה אִשֵּׁה רֵיחַ נִיחֹחַ — *As the meal-offering of the morning and as the drink offering thereof, you shall present it, a burnt-offering, a sweet savor.* Even though, on that very (same) day, you already brought the *morning* burnt-offering, identical to this second one (i.e., the evening offering), nonetheless this second one will also be (acceptable as) *a sweet savour.*

11. וּבְרָאשֵׁי חָדְשֵׁיכֶם — *And on your New Moons.* Behold, it was a custom among the Israelites to observe Rosh Chodesh (the New Moon) as a semi-holy day (festival), as

NOTES

XXVIII

6. עֹלַת תָּמִיד הָעֲשֻׂיָה בְּהַר סִינַי — *A continual burnt-offering which was offered on Mt. Sinai. Rashi* on verse 4 comments, 'Although this מִצְוָה has already been stated (in תְּצַוֶּה — *Exodus* 29:38), that instruction (to offer a morning and evening sacrifice of a lamb) was intended for the יְמֵי הַמִּלּוּאִים, *days of installation,* but here the command is for all generations.' The *Sforno* gives a different explanation for the repetition, by commenting that although prior to the sin of the Golden Calf the daily sacrifice was indeed brought, it did not include a drink offering. After that transgression, the drink offering was added, and that is the reason for the Torah repeating the instruction here in פָּרָשַׁת פִּנְחָס. Indeed, the verse which follows states, *and the drink offering thereof shall be etc.* (verse 7), which supports the *Sforno's* interpretation.

8. כְּמִנְחַת הַבֹּקֶר וּכְנִסְכּוֹ תַּעֲשֶׂה אִשֵּׁה רֵיחַ נִיחֹחַ — *As the meal-offering of the morning and as the drink offering thereof, you shall present it, a burnt-offering, a sweet savor.* Although the evening sacrifice was identical to that of the morning, hence seemingly a duplication, still it is pleasing to God. As the Sifri quoted by *Rashi* on this verse states, 'רֵיחַ נִיחֹחַ — it causes satisfaction to Me, that I commanded and My will was obeyed.'

11. וּבְרָאשֵׁי חָדְשֵׁיכֶם — *And on your New Moons.* The *Sforno,* citing the episode of David

יב כְּבָשִׂים בְּנֵי־שָׁנָה שִׁבְעָה תְּמִימִם׃ וּשְׁלֹשָׁה עֶשְׂרֹנִים סֹלֶת מִנְחָה בְּלוּלָה
בַשֶּׁמֶן לַפָּר הָאֶחָד וּשְׁנֵי עֶשְׂרֹנִים סֹלֶת מִנְחָה בְּלוּלָה בַשֶּׁמֶן לָאַיִל הָאֶחָד׃
יג וְעִשָּׂרֹן עִשָּׂרוֹן סֹלֶת מִנְחָה בְּלוּלָה בַשֶּׁמֶן לַכֶּבֶשׂ הָאֶחָד עֹלָה רֵיחַ נִיחֹחַ
יד אִשֶּׁה לַיהוָה׃ וְנִסְכֵּיהֶם חֲצִי הַהִין יִהְיֶה לַפָּר וּשְׁלִישִׁת הַהִין לָאַיִל וּרְבִיעִת
טו הַהִין לַכֶּבֶשׂ יָיִן זֹאת עֹלַת חֹדֶשׁ בְּחָדְשׁוֹ לְחָדְשֵׁי הַשָּׁנָה׃ וּשְׂעִיר עִזִּים אֶחָד
ששי טז לְחַטָּאת לַיהוָה עַל־עֹלַת הַתָּמִיד יֵעָשֶׂה וְנִסְכּוֹ׃ וּבַחֹדֶשׁ
יז הָרִאשׁוֹן בְּאַרְבָּעָה עָשָׂר יוֹם לַחֹדֶשׁ פֶּסַח לַיהוָה׃ וּבַחֲמִשָּׁה עָשָׂר יוֹם
יח לַחֹדֶשׁ הַזֶּה חָג שִׁבְעַת יָמִים מַצּוֹת יֵאָכֵל׃ בַּיּוֹם הָרִאשׁוֹן מִקְרָא־קֹדֶשׁ

(the verse) testifies saying, אֲשֶׁר נִסְתַּרְתָּ שָּׁם בְּיוֹם הַמַּעֲשֶׂה, *Where you hid yourself on the day of the deed* (*I Samuel* 20:19), which implies that Rosh Chodesh was not a day of labor to them. Therefore, (this day) is associated with Israel, as it says, '*your* New Moons,' (an expression) not found regarding (other) festivals. It is not written regarding Shabbos, '*your* Sabbaths' (שַׁבַּתְּכֶם), nor (regarding the *bikurim*), 'In the day of *your* first fruits' (בִּכּוּרֵיכֶם), nor (regarding Succos), 'In the day of *your* booths' (סֻכּוֹתֵיכֶם). Now, the reason for this custom (to observe Rosh Chodesh) is because, to a certain extent, the fate (lit., success) of Israel in this world is similar to that of the moon which has no light of its own whatsoever save that which it receives from another (luminary). This is so because prior to the (sin of the) Golden Calf (they were destined to be in a state of) חָרוּת עַל הַלֻּחֹת, *engraved on the Tablets* (*Exodus* 32:16), (interpreted to mean) freedom (חֵרוּת) from the subjugation of (world) kingdoms forever. However, when they sinned with the Golden Calf, (their) crown of kingship was stripped (from them for the time being) and they were not able to employ it continually as do other nations, but it (i.e., kingship) was theirs periodically according to (the extent of) the overflow of Divine Light upon them. Without it (i.e., this light), they walked in darkness and there was no light unto them (based on *Isaiah* 50:10), as is the case of the moon when it does not receive the light (reflection) of the sun — because אֵין מַזָּל לְיִשְׂרָאֵל, *Israel is not subject to the influence of the planets* (*Shabbos* 156a), and they possess no light of their own whatsoever except the light of God, the Blessed One, when they are acceptable (to Him). And therefore, the prophets refer to God, the Blessed One, as the *Light of Israel*, saying, וְהָיָה אוֹר יִשְׂרָאֵל לְאֵשׁ, *And the Light of Israel shall be for a fire* (*Isaiah*

NOTES

and Jonathan, supports his contention that Rosh Chodesh was a semi-holiday when labor was not performed. The verse preceding the one quoted by him states, "And Jonathan said to him, 'Tomorrow is (Rosh) Chodesh' ", after which he refers to the day when David hid from Saul as יוֹם הַמַּעֲשֶׂה, *the day of deed*, i.e., a workday, implying that Rosh Chodesh would not be a day of work.

The *Sforno* proceeds to explain why the New Moon is the only festival in this chapter referred to as *your* Rosh Chodesh, indicating a special link between this day and the people of Israel. The moon has no light of its own, for it reflects the light of the sun. Israel also has no other source of light than that of the אור ה׳, *the light of God* (as we see in *Psalms* 36:10, *by Your light shall we see light*). That light, however, depends upon their conduct and behavior which, if sinful, dims or obscures the light of God, casting them into a state of darkness. The destiny of Israel is totally determined by the degree of their relationship to God. When they obey God's commandments and conduct their lives in accordance with Torah, they sanctify His Name, and are thereby worthy of His Providence, but when they transgress and defect, they bring about חִלּוּל הַשֵּׁם, *desecration of God's Name*, causing Him to turn away from them.

יט כָּל־מְלֶאכֶת עֲבֹדָה לֹא תַעֲשׂוּ: וְהִקְרַבְתֶּם אִשֶּׁה עֹלָה לַיהוָה פָּרִים
בְּנֵי־בָקָר שְׁנַיִם וְאַיִל אֶחָד וְשִׁבְעָה כְבָשִׂים בְּנֵי שָׁנָה תְּמִימִם יִהְיוּ לָכֶם:
כ וּמִנְחָתָם סֹלֶת בְּלוּלָה בַשָּׁמֶן שְׁלֹשָׁה עֶשְׂרֹנִים לַפָּר וּשְׁנֵי עֶשְׂרֹנִים לָאַיִל
כא־כב תַּעֲשׂוּ: עִשָּׂרוֹן עִשָּׂרוֹן תַּעֲשֶׂה לַכֶּבֶשׂ הָאֶחָד לְשִׁבְעַת הַכְּבָשִׂים: וּשְׂעִיר
כג חַטָּאת אֶחָד לְכַפֵּר עֲלֵיכֶם: מִלְּבַד עֹלַת הַבֹּקֶר אֲשֶׁר לְעֹלַת הַתָּמִיד
כד תַּעֲשׂוּ אֶת־אֵלֶּה: כָּאֵלֶּה תַּעֲשׂוּ לַיּוֹם שִׁבְעַת יָמִים לֶחֶם אִשֵּׁה רֵיחַ־נִיחֹחַ
כה לַיהוָה עַל־עוֹלַת הַתָּמִיד יֵעָשֶׂה וְנִסְכּוֹ: וּבַיּוֹם הַשְּׁבִיעִי מִקְרָא־קֹדֶשׁ יִהְיֶה

10:17), and so it is attested to when it is said, ה׳ אוֹרִי וְיִשְׁעִי, *HASHEM is my light and my salvation* (*Psalms* 27:1). Now, when (Israel's) sins separated them (from God) as it says, כִּי אִם עֲוֹנֹתֵיכֶם הָיוּ מַבְדִּלִים בֵּינֵכֶם לְבֵין אֱלֹהֵיכֶם וְחַטֹּאותֵיכֶם הִסְתִּירוּ פָנִים מִכֶּם מִשְּׁמוֹעַ, *But your iniquities have separated between you and your God, and your sins have hid His face from you that He will not hear* (*Isaiah* 59:2), they then walked in darkness, bewildered and driven among the nations, and this, without a doubt, caused a profanation of God's Name, בֶּאֱמֹר לָהֶם עַם ה׳ אֵלֶּה, *that it was said of them, these are the people of HASHEM* (*Ezekiel* 36:20), and consequently, to some extent, it lead to the condition of בְּכָל צָרָתָם לוֹ צָר, *In all their affliction He was afflicted* (*Isaiah* 63:9), as our Sages say, 'The spoiler (שׁוֹדֵד) is come, as it were, upon Me and upon you' (*Gittin* 58a). Now the sin offering of Rosh Chodesh is meant to be an atonement for Israel who cause the diminishment or prevention of the Divine Light (from shining on them), as our Sages state (in the *siddur*) saying וּשְׂעִירֵי חַטָּאת לְכַפֵּר בַּעֲדָם זִכָּרוֹן לְכֻלָּם יִהְיוּ וּתְשׁוּעַת נַפְשָׁם מִיַּד שׂוֹנֵא, *and goats of sin-offering to atone on their behalf. They would serve as a remembrance for them all and a salvation for their soul from the hand of the enemy*, and through this atonement there will be, to an extent, salvation for (their sin) of profanation of God's Name. Therefore (our Sages) said it is for this reason (the Torah) says regarding the goat offering of Rosh Chodesh, חַטָּאת לַה׳, *a sin offering for HASHEM* (v. 15), because this atonement effects the sanctification of His Blessed Name; and this was (also) their intent when they said, "The Holy One, Blessed be He, said, 'Bring an atonement for Me for making the moon smaller' " (*Chullin* 60b). This (in essence) means, 'Bring an atonement for Me so that you may be able to attain Sanctification of My Name which was profaned among the nations as a result of My making the 'moon' smaller when I exiled Israel and concealed My face from them.'

NOTES

Every Rosh Chodesh, the moon is reborn and reflects the light of the sun. This is symbolic of Israel's rebirth as well, when they once again find the light of God by atoning for their sins. Not only do they atone for themselves through the sin offering of Rosh Chodesh, but in a sense, they also atone for God, Who sent them into exile thereby causing the desecration of God's Name. The *Sforno* is interpreting the statement of our Sages in Tractate *Chullin* 60b regarding the diminishment of 'the moon' as meaning the diminishment of Israel's sacred status, by their being sent into *galus* by God. This is radically different than the explanation of other commentators. His interpretation of the phrase חַטָּאת לַה׳, *a sin offering for God*, is also different than theirs, since they explain it literally as meaning 'for God,' i.e., to atone for His unfair treatment of the moon at the time of Creation. The *Sforno*, however, interprets חַטָּאת לַה׳ as a sin offering brought to atone for God's banishment of Israel, which was the prime cause of the desecration of His Holy Name. For this act, He also, as it were, needs atonement.

כו לָכֶם כָּל־מְלֶאכֶת עֲבֹדָה לֹא תַעֲשׂוּ: וּבְיוֹם הַבִּכּוּרִים
בְּהַקְרִיבְכֶם מִנְחָה חֲדָשָׁה לַיהוָה בְּשָׁבֻעֹתֵיכֶם מִקְרָא־קֹדֶשׁ יִהְיֶה לָכֶם
כז כָּל־מְלֶאכֶת עֲבֹדָה לֹא תַעֲשׂוּ: וְהִקְרַבְתֶּם עוֹלָה לְרֵיחַ נִיחֹחַ לַיהוָה
כח פָּרִים בְּנֵי־בָקָר שְׁנַיִם אַיִל אֶחָד שִׁבְעָה כְבָשִׂים בְּנֵי שָׁנָה: וּמִנְחָתָם
סֹלֶת בְּלוּלָה בַשָּׁמֶן שְׁלֹשָׁה עֶשְׂרֹנִים לַפָּר הָאֶחָד שְׁנֵי עֶשְׂרֹנִים לָאַיִל
כט־ל הָאֶחָד: עִשָּׂרוֹן עִשָּׂרוֹן לַכֶּבֶשׂ הָאֶחָד לְשִׁבְעַת הַכְּבָשִׂים: שְׂעִיר עִזִּים אֶחָד
לא לְכַפֵּר עֲלֵיכֶם: מִלְּבַד עֹלַת הַתָּמִיד וּמִנְחָתוֹ תַּעֲשׂוּ תְּמִימִם יִהְיוּ־לָכֶם
וְנִסְכֵּיהֶם:

כט

א וּבַחֹדֶשׁ הַשְּׁבִיעִי בְּאֶחָד לַחֹדֶשׁ מִקְרָא־קֹדֶשׁ יִהְיֶה לָכֶם כָּל־מְלֶאכֶת
ב עֲבֹדָה לֹא תַעֲשׂוּ יוֹם תְּרוּעָה יִהְיֶה לָכֶם: וַעֲשִׂיתֶם עֹלָה לְרֵיחַ נִיחֹחַ לַיהוָה
ג פַּר בֶּן־בָּקָר אֶחָד אַיִל אֶחָד כְּבָשִׂים בְּנֵי־שָׁנָה שִׁבְעָה תְּמִימִם: וּמִנְחָתָם
ד סֹלֶת בְּלוּלָה בַשָּׁמֶן שְׁלֹשָׁה עֶשְׂרֹנִים לַפָּר שְׁנֵי עֶשְׂרֹנִים לָאָיִל: וְעִשָּׂרוֹן
ה אֶחָד לַכֶּבֶשׂ הָאֶחָד לְשִׁבְעַת הַכְּבָשִׂים: וּשְׂעִיר־עִזִּים אֶחָד חַטָּאת לְכַפֵּר
ו עֲלֵיכֶם: מִלְּבַד עֹלַת הַחֹדֶשׁ וּמִנְחָתָהּ וְעֹלַת הַתָּמִיד וּמִנְחָתָהּ וְנִסְכֵּיהֶם
ז כְּמִשְׁפָּטָם לְרֵיחַ נִיחֹחַ אִשֶּׁה לַיהוָה: וּבֶעָשׂוֹר לַחֹדֶשׁ
הַשְּׁבִיעִי הַזֶּה מִקְרָא־קֹדֶשׁ יִהְיֶה לָכֶם וְעִנִּיתֶם אֶת־נַפְשֹׁתֵיכֶם כָּל־מְלָאכָה
ח לֹא תַעֲשׂוּ: וְהִקְרַבְתֶּם עֹלָה לַיהוָה רֵיחַ נִיחֹחַ פַּר בֶּן־בָּקָר אֶחָד אַיִל אֶחָד
ט כְּבָשִׂים בְּנֵי־שָׁנָה שִׁבְעָה תְּמִימִם יִהְיוּ לָכֶם: וּמִנְחָתָם סֹלֶת בְּלוּלָה בַשָּׁמֶן
י שְׁלֹשָׁה עֶשְׂרֹנִים לַפָּר שְׁנֵי עֶשְׂרֹנִים לָאַיִל הָאֶחָד: עִשָּׂרוֹן עִשָּׂרוֹן לַכֶּבֶשׂ
יא הָאֶחָד לְשִׁבְעַת הַכְּבָשִׂים: שְׂעִיר־עִזִּים אֶחָד חַטָּאת מִלְּבַד חַטַּאת
שביעי יב הַכִּפֻּרִים וְעֹלַת הַתָּמִיד וּמִנְחָתָהּ וְנִסְכֵּיהֶם: וּבַחֲמִשָּׁה
עָשָׂר יוֹם לַחֹדֶשׁ הַשְּׁבִיעִי מִקְרָא־קֹדֶשׁ יִהְיֶה לָכֶם כָּל־מְלֶאכֶת עֲבֹדָה לֹא
יג תַעֲשׂוּ וְחַגֹּתֶם חַג לַיהוָה שִׁבְעַת יָמִים: וְהִקְרַבְתֶּם עֹלָה אִשֵּׁה רֵיחַ נִיחֹחַ
לַיהוָה פָּרִים בְּנֵי־בָקָר שְׁלֹשָׁה עָשָׂר אֵילִם שְׁנָיִם כְּבָשִׂים בְּנֵי־שָׁנָה אַרְבָּעָה
יד עָשָׂר תְּמִימִם יִהְיוּ: וּמִנְחָתָם סֹלֶת בְּלוּלָה בַשָּׁמֶן שְׁלֹשָׁה עֶשְׂרֹנִים לַפָּר
הָאֶחָד לִשְׁלֹשָׁה עָשָׂר פָּרִים שְׁנֵי עֶשְׂרֹנִים לָאַיִל הָאֶחָד לִשְׁנֵי הָאֵילִם:

---

26. בְּשָׁבֻעֹתֵיכֶם — *On account of your weeks . . .* because of שְׁבֻעֹת חֻקּוֹת קָצִיר, *the appointed weeks of the harvest* (*Jeremiah* 5:24), which I kept for you. The meaning of the letter ב in the word בְּשָׁבֻעֹתֵיכֶם is the same as (the ב) in בַּנֶּפֶשׁ יְכַפֵּר; *That makes an atonement for the soul* (*Leviticus* 17:11), and בְּדַם עֲשָׂהאֵל, *for the blood of Asa'el* (*II Samuel* 3:27) and בַּלֶּחֶם נִשְׂכָּרוּ, *have hired themselves out for bread* (*I Samuel* 2:5).

NOTES

26. בְּשָׁבֻעֹתֵיכֶם — *On account of your weeks.* On the holiday of Shevuos, two loaves of wheat bread were brought from the new harvest. This 50th day follows the counting of the forty-nine days since Pesach and marks the completion of the seven weeks. Hence, the phrase בְּשָׁבֻעֹתֵיכֶם cannot mean *'on' your feast of weeks* since it was already after the weeks *were out*. The sense of this expression must perforce be, as the *Sforno*

טו-טז וְעִשָּׂרוֹן עִשָּׂרוֹן לַכֶּבֶשׂ הָאֶחָד לְאַרְבָּעָה עָשָׂר כְּבָשִׂים׃ וּשְׂעִיר־עִזִּים אֶחָד
יז חַטָּאת מִלְּבַד עֹלַת הַתָּמִיד מִנְחָתָהּ וְנִסְכָּהּ׃ וּבַיּוֹם הַשֵּׁנִי
פָּרִים בְּנֵי־בָקָר שְׁנֵים עָשָׂר אֵילִם שְׁנָיִם כְּבָשִׂים בְּנֵי־שָׁנָה אַרְבָּעָה
יח עָשָׂר תְּמִימִם׃ וּמִנְחָתָם וְנִסְכֵּיהֶם לַפָּרִים לָאֵילִם וְלַכְּבָשִׂים בְּמִסְפָּרָם
יט כַּמִּשְׁפָּט׃ וּשְׂעִיר־עִזִּים אֶחָד חַטָּאת מִלְּבַד עֹלַת הַתָּמִיד וּמִנְחָתָהּ
כ וְנִסְכֵּיהֶם׃ וּבַיּוֹם הַשְּׁלִישִׁי פָּרִים עַשְׁתֵּי־עָשָׂר אֵילִם שְׁנָיִם
כא כְּבָשִׂים בְּנֵי־שָׁנָה אַרְבָּעָה עָשָׂר תְּמִימִם׃ וּמִנְחָתָם וְנִסְכֵּיהֶם לַפָּרִים
כב לָאֵילִם וְלַכְּבָשִׂים בְּמִסְפָּרָם כַּמִּשְׁפָּט׃ וּשְׂעִיר חַטָּאת אֶחָד מִלְּבַד עֹלַת
כג הַתָּמִיד וּמִנְחָתָהּ וְנִסְכָּהּ׃ וּבַיּוֹם הָרְבִיעִי פָּרִים עֲשָׂרָה אֵילִם
כד שְׁנָיִם כְּבָשִׂים בְּנֵי־שָׁנָה אַרְבָּעָה עָשָׂר תְּמִימִם׃ מִנְחָתָם וְנִסְכֵּיהֶם לַפָּרִים
כה לָאֵילִם וְלַכְּבָשִׂים בְּמִסְפָּרָם כַּמִּשְׁפָּט׃ וּשְׂעִיר־עִזִּים אֶחָד חַטָּאת מִלְּבַד
כו עֹלַת הַתָּמִיד מִנְחָתָהּ וְנִסְכָּהּ׃ וּבַיּוֹם הַחֲמִישִׁי פָּרִים תִּשְׁעָה
כז אֵילִם שְׁנָיִם כְּבָשִׂים בְּנֵי־שָׁנָה אַרְבָּעָה עָשָׂר תְּמִימִם׃ וּמִנְחָתָם וְנִסְכֵּיהֶם
כח לַפָּרִים לָאֵילִם וְלַכְּבָשִׂים בְּמִסְפָּרָם כַּמִּשְׁפָּט׃ וּשְׂעִיר חַטָּאת אֶחָד מִלְּבַד
כט עֹלַת הַתָּמִיד וּמִנְחָתָהּ וְנִסְכָּהּ׃ וּבַיּוֹם הַשִּׁשִּׁי פָּרִים שְׁמֹנָה
ל אֵילִם שְׁנָיִם כְּבָשִׂים בְּנֵי־שָׁנָה אַרְבָּעָה עָשָׂר תְּמִימִם׃ וּמִנְחָתָם וְנִסְכֵּיהֶם
לא לַפָּרִים לָאֵילִם וְלַכְּבָשִׂים בְּמִסְפָּרָם כַּמִּשְׁפָּט׃ וּשְׂעִיר חַטָּאת אֶחָד מִלְּבַד
לב עֹלַת הַתָּמִיד מִנְחָתָהּ וּנְסָכֶיהָ׃ וּבַיּוֹם הַשְּׁבִיעִי פָּרִים שִׁבְעָה
לג אֵילִם שְׁנָיִם כְּבָשִׂים בְּנֵי־שָׁנָה אַרְבָּעָה עָשָׂר תְּמִימִם׃ וּמִנְחָתָם וְנִסְכֵּהֶם
לד לַפָּרִים לָאֵילִם וְלַכְּבָשִׂים בְּמִסְפָּרָם כְּמִשְׁפָּטָם׃ וּשְׂעִיר חַטָּאת אֶחָד מִלְּבַד
מפטיר לה עֹלַת הַתָּמִיד מִנְחָתָהּ וְנִסְכָּהּ׃ בַּיּוֹם הַשְּׁמִינִי עֲצֶרֶת
לו תִּהְיֶה לָכֶם כָּל־מְלֶאכֶת עֲבֹדָה לֹא תַעֲשׂוּ׃ וְהִקְרַבְתֶּם עֹלָה אִשֵּׁה
רֵיחַ נִיחֹחַ לַיהוָה פַּר אֶחָד אַיִל אֶחָד כְּבָשִׂים בְּנֵי־שָׁנָה שִׁבְעָה
לז תְּמִימִם׃ מִנְחָתָם וְנִסְכֵּיהֶם לַפָּר לָאַיִל וְלַכְּבָשִׂים בְּמִסְפָּרָם כַּמִּשְׁפָּט׃
לח-לט וּשְׂעִיר חַטָּאת אֶחָד מִלְּבַד עֹלַת הַתָּמִיד וּמִנְחָתָהּ וְנִסְכָּהּ׃ אֵלֶּה תַּעֲשׂוּ
לַיהוָה בְּמוֹעֲדֵיכֶם לְבַד מִנִּדְרֵיכֶם וְנִדְבֹתֵיכֶם לְעֹלֹתֵיכֶם וּלְמִנְחֹתֵיכֶם
ל א וּלְנִסְכֵּיכֶם וּלְשַׁלְמֵיכֶם׃ וַיֹּאמֶר מֹשֶׁה אֶל־בְּנֵי יִשְׂרָאֵל כְּכֹל אֲשֶׁר־צִוָּה יְהוָה
אֶת־מֹשֶׁה׃

XXIX

35. עֲצֶרֶת תִּהְיֶה לָכֶם — *You shall have a solemn assembly* . . . as explained in (the commentary on) *Parashas Emor* (*Leviticus* 23:36).

NOTES

explains, you shall bring this offering of two loaves in recognition of God's blessing granted to you during these seven weeks which brought you to this harvest. The prefix ל has a variety of meanings. In this verse, it means 'for' (or 'on account of'), as it does in the verses cited by the *Sforno* in support of his interpretation.

פרשת מטות
Parasha Matos

ב וַיְדַבֵּר מֹשֶׁה אֶל־רָאשֵׁי הַמַּטּוֹת לִבְנֵי יִשְׂרָאֵל לֵאמֹר זֶה הַדָּבָר אֲשֶׁר צִוָּה
ג יהוה: אִישׁ כִּי־יִדֹּר נֶדֶר לַיהוה אוֹ־הִשָּׁבַע שְׁבֻעָה לֶאְסֹר אִסָּר עַל־נַפְשׁוֹ
ד לֹא יַחֵל דְּבָרוֹ כְּכָל־הַיֹּצֵא מִפִּיו יַעֲשֶׂה: וְאִשָּׁה כִּי־תִדֹּר נֶדֶר לַיהוה וְאָסְרָה
ה אִסָּר בְּבֵית אָבִיהָ בִּנְעֻרֶיהָ: וְשָׁמַע אָבִיהָ אֶת־נִדְרָהּ וֶאֱסָרָהּ אֲשֶׁר אָסְרָה
עַל־נַפְשָׁהּ וְהֶחֱרִישׁ לָהּ אָבִיהָ וְקָמוּ כָּל־נְדָרֶיהָ וְכָל־אִסָּר אֲשֶׁר־אָסְרָה
ו עַל־נַפְשָׁהּ יָקוּם: וְאִם־הֵנִיא אָבִיהָ אֹתָהּ בְּיוֹם שָׁמְעוֹ כָּל־נְדָרֶיהָ וֶאֱסָרֶיהָ
אֲשֶׁר־אָסְרָה עַל־נַפְשָׁהּ לֹא יָקוּם וַיהוה יִסְלַח־לָהּ כִּי־הֵנִיא אָבִיהָ אֹתָהּ:
ז וְאִם־הָיוֹ תִהְיֶה לְאִישׁ וּנְדָרֶיהָ עָלֶיהָ אוֹ מִבְטָא שְׂפָתֶיהָ אֲשֶׁר אָסְרָה
ח עַל־נַפְשָׁהּ: וְשָׁמַע אִישָׁהּ בְּיוֹם שָׁמְעוֹ וְהֶחֱרִישׁ לָהּ וְקָמוּ נְדָרֶיהָ וֶאֱסָרֶהָ
ט אֲשֶׁר־אָסְרָה עַל־נַפְשָׁהּ יָקֻמוּ: וְאִם בְּיוֹם שְׁמֹעַ אִישָׁהּ יָנִיא אוֹתָהּ וְהֵפֵר
אֶת־נִדְרָהּ אֲשֶׁר עָלֶיהָ וְאֵת מִבְטָא שְׂפָתֶיהָ אֲשֶׁר אָסְרָה עַל־נַפְשָׁהּ וַיהוה
י יִסְלַח־לָהּ: וְנֵדֶר אַלְמָנָה וּגְרוּשָׁה כֹּל אֲשֶׁר־אָסְרָה עַל־נַפְשָׁהּ יָקוּם עָלֶיהָ:
יא־יב וְאִם־בֵּית אִישָׁהּ נָדָרָה אוֹ־אָסְרָה אִסָּר עַל־נַפְשָׁהּ בִּשְׁבֻעָה: וְשָׁמַע אִישָׁהּ
וְהֶחֱרִשׁ לָהּ לֹא הֵנִיא אֹתָהּ וְקָמוּ כָּל־נְדָרֶיהָ וְכָל־אִסָּר אֲשֶׁר־אָסְרָה

XXX

2. זֶה הַדָּבָר אֲשֶׁר צִוָּה ה׳ — *This is the thing which HASHEM has commanded.* When He said at Mt. Sinai, וְלֹא תִשָּׁבְעוּ בִשְׁמִי לַשָּׁקֶר וְחִלַּלְתָּ, *And you shall not swear by My name falsely, so that you profane* (*Leviticus* 19:12), the intent was that when a man takes a vow or swears an oath, 'he shall not profane (break) his word,' because when he profanes his word, he (also) profanes God. However, a woman who is not independent (lit., in her own control) will not have profaned (her vow) if he who has the power (i.e., her father or husband) declares it null and void.

6. וַה׳ יִסְלַח לָהּ — *And HASHEM will forgive her* ... for taking a vow which she is unable to fulfill.

כִּי הֵנִיא אָבִיהָ אֹתָהּ — *Because her father disallowed her* ... and (since) she did not know her father's opinion when she took the vow, (hence) she intended to fulfill it (at the time).

NOTES

XXX

2. זֶה הַדָּבָר אֲשֶׁר צִוָּה ה׳ — *This is the thing which HASHEM has commanded.* The expression, זֶה הַדָּבָר אֲשֶׁר צִוָּה ה׳, *This is the thing which HASHEM has commanded*, normally is used regarding a commandment which one is obligated to fulfill immediately. For example, in *Exodus* 16:16 it is used regarding the manna and in *Exodus* 35:4 regarding the collection of offerings for the Sanctuary. This, however, cannot be the meaning in the context of our *parshah* which deals with vows and oaths. The *Sforno*, therefore, explains that זֶה הַדָּבָר וכו׳ refers to the verse in *Leviticus* 19:12 where we have already been cautioned not to profane the Name of God by swearing falsely. This admonition is now carried over to פָּרָשַׁת נְדָרִים, *the section dealing with vows.* Hence, the phrase זֶה הַדָּבָר serves as a link to the verse in *Leviticus* cited by the *Sforno*. A similar interpretation of this expression can also be found in the *Sforno's* commentary on *Leviticus* 17:2.

6. וַה׳ יִסְלַח לָהּ כִּי הֵנִיא אָבִיהָ אֹתָהּ — *And HASHEM will forgive her because her father disallowed her.* Although she may have acted improperly by taking a vow which she had no power to fulfill, nonetheless since she assumed that her father would agree with her, she honestly intended to keep her word. Therefore, God will forgive her.

יג עַל־נַפְשָׁהּ יָקוּם: וְאִם־הָפֵר יָפֵר אֹתָם | אִישָׁהּ בְּיוֹם שָׁמְעוֹ כָּל־מוֹצָא
שְׂפָתֶיהָ לִנְדָרֶיהָ וּלְאִסַּר נַפְשָׁהּ לֹא יָקוּם אִישָׁהּ הֲפֵרָם וַיהֹוָה יִסְלַח־לָהּ:
יד־טו כָּל־נֶדֶר וְכָל־שְׁבֻעַת אִסָּר לְעַנֹּת נָפֶשׁ אִישָׁהּ יְקִימֶנּוּ וְאִישָׁהּ יְפֵרֶנּוּ: וְאִם־
הַחֲרֵשׁ יַחֲרִישׁ לָהּ אִישָׁהּ מִיּוֹם אֶל־יוֹם וְהֵקִים אֶת־כָּל־נְדָרֶיהָ אוֹ אֶת־כָּל־
טז אֱסָרֶיהָ אֲשֶׁר עָלֶיהָ הֵקִים אֹתָם כִּי־הֶחֱרִשׁ לָהּ בְּיוֹם שָׁמְעוֹ: וְאִם־הָפֵר יָפֵר
יז אֹתָם אַחֲרֵי שָׁמְעוֹ וְנָשָׂא אֶת־עֲוֹנָהּ: אֵלֶּה הַחֻקִּים אֲשֶׁר צִוָּה יְהֹוָה אֶת־
מֹשֶׁה בֵּין אִישׁ לְאִשְׁתּוֹ בֵּין־אָב לְבִתּוֹ בִּנְעֻרֶיהָ בֵּית אָבִיהָ:

לא שני א־ב וַיְדַבֵּר יְהֹוָה אֶל־מֹשֶׁה לֵּאמֹר: נְקֹם נִקְמַת בְּנֵי יִשְׂרָאֵל מֵאֵת הַמִּדְיָנִים
ג אַחַר תֵּאָסֵף אֶל־עַמֶּיךָ: וַיְדַבֵּר מֹשֶׁה אֶל־הָעָם לֵאמֹר הֵחָלְצוּ מֵאִתְּכֶם
ד אֲנָשִׁים לַצָּבָא וְיִהְיוּ עַל־מִדְיָן לָתֵת נִקְמַת־יְהֹוָה בְּמִדְיָן: אֶלֶף לַמַּטֶּה אֶלֶף

---

15. וְאִם הַחֲרֵשׁ יַחֲרִישׁ לָהּ אִישָׁהּ — *But if her husband keeps silent.* Silence on the part of one who has the power to protest is tantamount to admission (consent), for regarding he who is silent (it is as though) he agrees with the action.

16. וְאִם הָפֵר יָפֵר אֹתָם אַחֲרֵי שָׁמְעוֹ — *But if he shall make them null and void after he heard them . . .* after the day he has heard them, at which time he cannot regret or nullify.

וְנָשָׂא אֶת עֲוֹנָהּ — *Then he shall bear her iniquity . . .* as is the law regarding anyone who forces another to transgress, or who misleads and instructs (someone) falsely.

NOTES

15. וְאִם הַחֲרֵשׁ יַחֲרִישׁ לָהּ אִישָׁהּ — *But if her husband keeps silent.* The *Sforno* bases his commentary of this verse on the Talmudic dictum, שְׁתִיקָה כְּהוֹדָאָה, *Silence is like admission,* mentioned in tractate *Bava Metzia* 37b and elsewhere throughout the Talmud. If one who had the power to do so does not protest and is silent, it is considered as a sign of acquiescence. Hence, since her husband has the authority to protest and does not, it is regarded as his having tacitly consented to her vow. This concept of one's failure to protest being regarded as approval is based on an episode recorded in a mishnah in Tractate *Shabbos* 54b. The mishnah relates that R' Elazar ben Azariah's cow used to go out on the Sabbath with a thong between its horn, against the consent of the Rabbis. The Talmud explains that the cow did not actually belong to him but to a neighbor. However, since he did not protest it was considered as his! We learn from this that silence on the part of one who has the power to protest is tantamount to agreement.

The *Sforno* also expresses this idea in his commentary (*Exodus* 32) regarding the culpability of those Israelites who did not participate actively in the sin of the Golden Calf but nonetheless were silent. Conversely, they were forgiven for this sin of omission when they were silent and did not interfere at the time punishment was meted out to the sinners. Similarly, in the episode of Ba'al Peor, non-protest at the time the sinners were executed atoned for the silence of those who failed to object when the sin was first perpetrated (see 25:4, 11).

16. וְאִם הָפֵר יָפֵר . . . וְנָשָׂא אֶת עֲוֹנָהּ — *But if he shall make them null and void . . . then he shall bear her iniquity.* The Torah considers the husband responsible for his wife's broken vow since he forced her to break it or he misled her into believing that her vow was nullified. The *Sforno* explains that the transfer of her iniquity upon him is justified, because we assume that the active transgressor would not have sinned were it not for the intervention of the one who forced or misled. See *Rashi's* commentary on this verse which gives a similar explanation.

ה לַמַּטֶּה לְכֹל מַטּוֹת יִשְׂרָאֵל תִּשְׁלְחוּ לַצָּבָא: וַיִּמָּסְרוּ מֵאַלְפֵי יִשְׂרָאֵל אֶלֶף
ו לַמַּטֶּה שְׁנֵים־עָשָׂר אֶלֶף חֲלוּצֵי צָבָא: וַיִּשְׁלַח אֹתָם מֹשֶׁה אֶלֶף לַמַּטֶּה
לַצָּבָא אֹתָם וְאֶת־פִּינְחָס בֶּן־אֶלְעָזָר הַכֹּהֵן לַצָּבָא וּכְלֵי הַקֹּדֶשׁ וַחֲצֹצְרוֹת
ז הַתְּרוּעָה בְּיָדוֹ: וַיִּצְבְּאוּ עַל־מִדְיָן כַּאֲשֶׁר צִוָּה יהוה אֶת־מֹשֶׁה וַיַּהַרְגוּ
ח כָּל־זָכָר: וְאֶת־מַלְכֵי מִדְיָן הָרְגוּ עַל־חַלְלֵיהֶם אֶת־אֱוִי וְאֶת־רֶקֶם וְאֶת־צוּר
וְאֶת־חוּר וְאֶת־רֶבַע חֲמֵשֶׁת מַלְכֵי מִדְיָן וְאֵת בִּלְעָם בֶּן־בְּעוֹר הָרְגוּ בֶּחָרֶב:
ט וַיִּשְׁבּוּ בְנֵי־יִשְׂרָאֵל אֶת־נְשֵׁי מִדְיָן וְאֶת־טַפָּם וְאֵת כָּל־בְּהֶמְתָּם וְאֶת־כָּל־
י מִקְנֵהֶם וְאֶת־כָּל־חֵילָם בָּזָזוּ: וְאֵת כָּל־עָרֵיהֶם בְּמוֹשְׁבֹתָם וְאֵת כָּל־טִירֹתָם
יא שָׂרְפוּ בָּאֵשׁ: וַיִּקְחוּ אֶת־כָּל־הַשָּׁלָל וְאֵת כָּל־הַמַּלְקוֹחַ בָּאָדָם וּבַבְּהֵמָה:
יב וַיָּבִאוּ אֶל־מֹשֶׁה וְאֶל־אֶלְעָזָר הַכֹּהֵן וְאֶל־עֲדַת בְּנֵי־יִשְׂרָאֵל אֶת־הַשְּׁבִי
וְאֶת־הַמַּלְקוֹחַ וְאֶת־הַשָּׁלָל אֶל־הַמַּחֲנֶה אֶל־עַרְבֹת מוֹאָב אֲשֶׁר עַל־יַרְדֵּן
שלישי [שני] יג יְרֵחוֹ: וַיֵּצְאוּ מֹשֶׁה וְאֶלְעָזָר הַכֹּהֵן וְכָל־נְשִׂיאֵי הָעֵדָה
יד לִקְרָאתָם אֶל־מִחוּץ לַמַּחֲנֶה: וַיִּקְצֹף מֹשֶׁה עַל פְּקוּדֵי הֶחָיִל שָׂרֵי הָאֲלָפִים
טו וְשָׂרֵי הַמֵּאוֹת הַבָּאִים מִצְּבָא הַמִּלְחָמָה: וַיֹּאמֶר אֲלֵיהֶם מֹשֶׁה הַחִיִּיתֶם
טז כָּל־נְקֵבָה: הֵן הֵנָּה הָיוּ לִבְנֵי יִשְׂרָאֵל בִּדְבַר בִּלְעָם לִמְסָר־מַעַל בַּיהוה

XXXI

5. וַיִּמָּסְרוּ — *So there were delivered* . . . unto Moses, from each tribe.

6. וַיִּשְׁלַח אֹתָם מֹשֶׁה אֶלֶף לַמַּטֶּה לַצָּבָא — *And Moses sent them, a thousand of every tribe, to war.* He sent one thousand from each tribe, to gather together for war.

אֹתָם וְאֶת פִּינְחָס — *Them and Pinchas* . . . and after they had gathered, he sent them out all together, and with them he sent Pinchas.

לַצָּבָא וּכְלֵי הַקֹּדֶשׁ וַחֲצֹצְרוֹת הַתְּרוּעָה בְּיָדוֹ — *To the war, with the holy vessels and the trumpets for the alarm in his hand.* He sent him to the war, as the leader and anointed *Kohen* of battle, as well (as entrusting) the holy vessels and trumpets of alarm to him (that they) be under his control.

15. הַחִיִּיתֶם כָּל נְקֵבָה — *Have you kept alive all the females?* Although in regard to battle with all nations except for the seven nations, it is written, רַק הַנָּשִׁים וְהַטַּף וְהַבְּהֵמָה וְכֹל אֲשֶׁר יִהְיֶה בָעִיר כָּל שְׁלָלָהּ תָּבֹז לָךְ, *But the women and the little ones and the animals, and all that is in the city, even all the spoil, shall you take for a prey* (*Deut.* 20:14), (still) you should, at the least, not have permitted those women to live whom you recognized as being the ones who were the cause of your (moral)

NOTES

XXXI

5. וַיִּמָּסְרוּ — *So there were delivered.* The Torah states that they *were delivered*, but does not tell us who they were. The *Sforno*, therefore, explains that each tribe sent a thousand men to Moses, who organized them into a fighting force.

6. וַיִּשְׁלַח אֹתָם מֹשֶׁה אֶלֶף לַמַּטֶּה לַצָּבָא . . . לַצָּבָא וּכְלֵי הַקֹּדֶשׁ . . . בְּיָדוֹ — *And Moses sent them, a thousand of every tribe, to war . . . to the war, with the holy vessels . . . in his hand.* The word לַצָּבָא, *to war*, appears twice in this verse. The *Sforno* explains that the first time it refers to the gathering together of the soldiers in the camp, while the second refers to Pinchas who was sent together with the holy ark and trumpets to act as the כֹּהֵן מְשִׁיחַ מִלְחָמָה, *the anointed Kohen of battle*, as taught in *Deut.* 20:2.

יז עַל־דְּבַר פְּעוֹר וַתְּהִי הַמַּגֵּפָה בַּעֲדַת יהוה: וְעַתָּה הִרְגוּ כָל־זָכָר בַּטָּף
יח וְכָל־אִשָּׁה יֹדַעַת אִישׁ לְמִשְׁכַּב זָכָר הֲרֹגוּ: וְכֹל הַטַּף בַּנָּשִׁים אֲשֶׁר
יט לֹא־יָדְעוּ מִשְׁכַּב זָכָר הַחֲיוּ לָכֶם: וְאַתֶּם חֲנוּ מִחוּץ לַמַּחֲנֶה שִׁבְעַת יָמִים כֹּל
הֹרֵג נֶפֶשׁ וְכֹל ׀ נֹגֵעַ בֶּחָלָל תִּתְחַטְּאוּ בַּיּוֹם הַשְּׁלִישִׁי וּבַיּוֹם הַשְּׁבִיעִי אַתֶּם
כ וּשְׁבִיכֶם: וְכָל־בֶּגֶד וְכָל־כְּלִי־עוֹר וְכָל־מַעֲשֵׂה עִזִּים וְכָל־כְּלִי־עֵץ
כא תִּתְחַטָּאוּ: וַיֹּאמֶר אֶלְעָזָר הַכֹּהֵן אֶל־אַנְשֵׁי הַצָּבָא
כב הַבָּאִים לַמִּלְחָמָה זֹאת חֻקַּת הַתּוֹרָה אֲשֶׁר־צִוָּה יהוה אֶת־מֹשֶׁה: אַךְ
אֶת־הַזָּהָב וְאֶת־הַכָּסֶף אֶת־הַנְּחֹשֶׁת אֶת־הַבַּרְזֶל אֶת־הַבְּדִיל וְאֶת־
כג הָעֹפָרֶת: כָּל־דָּבָר אֲשֶׁר־יָבֹא בָאֵשׁ תַּעֲבִירוּ בָאֵשׁ וְטָהֵר אַךְ בְּמֵי נִדָּה
כד יִתְחַטָּא וְכֹל אֲשֶׁר לֹא־יָבֹא בָּאֵשׁ תַּעֲבִירוּ בַמָּיִם: וְכִבַּסְתֶּם בִּגְדֵיכֶם בַּיּוֹם
רביעי כה הַשְּׁבִיעִי וּטְהַרְתֶּם וְאַחַר תָּבֹאוּ אֶל־הַמַּחֲנֶה: וַיֹּאמֶר יהוה
כו אֶל־מֹשֶׁה לֵּאמֹר: שָׂא אֵת רֹאשׁ מַלְקוֹחַ הַשְּׁבִי בָּאָדָם וּבַבְּהֵמָה אַתָּה
כז וְאֶלְעָזָר הַכֹּהֵן וְרָאשֵׁי אֲבוֹת הָעֵדָה: וְחָצִיתָ אֶת־הַמַּלְקוֹחַ בֵּין תֹּפְשֵׂי

---

stumbling at the suggestion of Balaam.

17. הִרְגוּ כָל זָכָר בַּטָּף — *Kill every male among the young ones.* Although they are not fit for sexual congress; this was done for the purpose of revenge, that there shall not remain sons or son's son (נִין וָנֶכֶד) to Midian.

21. זֹאת חֻקַּת הַתּוֹרָה — *This is the statute of the law.* That which Moses told you regarding the purification (procedure) on the third and seventh day is a law (called) חֻקַּת הַתּוֹרָה, *the statute of the Torah,* of the red cow which makes *tahor* from *tumah* caused by death.

22. אַךְ אֶת הַזָּהָב — *But the gold* . . . but regarding metal vessels, besides *taharah,* it is necessary to purge them (i.e., הַגְעָלָה).

23. וְטָהֵר — *And shall be clean* . . . (cleansed) of the abhorrent (forbidden food) of the idolaters.

אַךְ בְּמֵי נִדָּה יִתְחַטָּא — *Nevertheless it shall be made tahor with the water of sprinkling.* For it still does not become ritually *tahor* with purging by fire (לִבּוּן) even though it now appears as new.

27. וְחָצִיתָ אֶת הַמַּלְקוֹחַ — *And divide the prey into two parts.* Since this battle was one of vengeance (in retaliation) for what had been done to all of them, (God) wanted the promise of וְאָכַלְתָּ אֶת שְׁלַל אֹיְבֶיךָ, *And you shall eat the booty of your enemies* (*Deut.* 20:14), to be fulfilled, similar to that of David and the booty of

NOTES

22-23. אַךְ אֶת הַזָּהָב . . . וְטָהֵר אַךְ בְּמֵי נִדָּה יִתְחַטָּא — *But the gold . . . and shall be clean; nevertheless it shall be purified with the water of sprinkling.* The phrase אַךְ, *but,* implies מִעוּט, *exclusion.* Although purification of these vessels from the defilement caused by a corpse was completed, they still had to be cleansed from the forbidden food which they had absorbed. Some metal vessels can be cleansed by immersion in hot water (הַגְעָלָה) while others must be purged by fire (לִבּוּן). The *Sforno* incorporates these laws in his commentary, adding that even when purged by fire the vessel requires ritual purification although it appears new.

27. וְחָצִיתָ אֶת הַמַּלְקוֹחַ — *And divide the prey into two parts.* The *Sforno* tells us why those who did not participate in the war received a portion of the booty. He explains that since the

כח הַמִּלְחָמָה הַיֹּצְאִים לַצָּבָא וּבֵין כָּל־הָעֵדָה: וַהֲרֵמֹתָ֮ מֶ֣כֶס לַֽיהוה֒ מֵאֵ֖ת אַנְשֵׁ֣י
הַמִּלְחָמָ֣ה הַיֹּצְאִ֣ים לַצָּבָ֑א אֶחָ֣ד נֶ֗פֶשׁ מֵֽחֲמֵ֣שׁ הַמֵּא֑וֹת מִן־הָֽאָדָם֙ וּמִן־הַבָּקָ֔ר
כט וּמִן־הַֽחֲמֹרִ֖ים וּמִן־הַצֹּֽאן: מִמַּֽחֲצִיתָ֖ם תִּקָּ֑חוּ וְנָֽתַתָּ֛ה לְאֶלְעָזָ֥ר הַכֹּהֵ֖ן תְּרוּמַ֥ת
ל יהוה: וּמִמַּֽחֲצִ֨ת בְּנֵֽי־יִשְׂרָאֵ֜ל תִּקַּ֣ח | אֶחָ֣ד | אָחֻ֣ז מִן־הַֽחֲמִשִּׁ֗ים מִן־הָֽאָדָ֤ם
מִן־הַבָּקָר֙ מִן־הַֽחֲמֹרִ֣ים וּמִן־הַצֹּ֔אן מִכָּל־הַבְּהֵמָ֑ה וְנָֽתַתָּ֤ה אֹתָם֙ לַֽלְוִיִּ֔ם
לא שֹֽׁמְרֵ֕י מִשְׁמֶ֖רֶת מִשְׁכַּ֣ן יהוה: וַיַּ֣עַשׂ מֹשֶׁ֔ה וְאֶלְעָזָ֖ר הַכֹּהֵ֑ן כַּֽאֲשֶׁ֛ר צִוָּ֥ה יהוה
לב אֶת־מֹשֶֽׁה: וַיְהִי֙ הַמַּלְק֔וֹחַ יֶ֣תֶר הַבָּ֔ז אֲשֶׁ֥ר בָּֽזְז֖וּ עַ֣ם הַצָּבָ֑א צֹ֗אן שֵׁשׁ־מֵא֥וֹת
לג-לד אֶ֛לֶף וְשִׁבְעִ֥ים אֶ֖לֶף וַֽחֲמֵ֥שֶׁת אֲלָפִֽים: וּבָקָ֕ר שְׁנַ֥יִם וְשִׁבְעִ֖ים אָֽלֶף: וַֽחֲמֹרִ֕ים
לה אֶחָ֥ד וְשִׁשִּׁ֖ים אָֽלֶף: וְנֶ֣פֶשׁ אָדָ֔ם מִן־הַ֨נָּשִׁ֔ים אֲשֶׁ֥ר לֹא־יָֽדְע֖וּ מִשְׁכַּ֣ב זָכָ֑ר
לו כָּל־נֶ֕פֶשׁ שְׁנַ֥יִם וּשְׁלֹשִׁ֖ים אָֽלֶף: וַתְּהִי֙ הַמֶּֽחֱצָ֔ה חֵ֕לֶק הַיֹּֽצְאִ֖ים בַּצָּבָ֑א מִסְפַּ֣ר
לז הַצֹּ֗אן שְׁלֹשׁ־מֵא֥וֹת אֶ֨לֶף֙ וּשְׁלֹשִׁ֣ים אֶ֔לֶף וְשִׁבְעַ֥ת אֲלָפִ֖ים וַֽחֲמֵ֥שׁ מֵאֽוֹת: וַיְהִ֥י
לח הַמֶּ֖כֶס לַֽיהוה֑ מִן־הַצֹּ֕אן שֵׁ֥שׁ מֵא֖וֹת חָמֵ֥שׁ וְשִׁבְעִֽים: וְהַ֨בָּקָ֔ר שִׁשָּׁ֥ה וּשְׁלֹשִׁ֖ים
לט אֶ֑לֶף וּמִכְסָ֥ם לַֽיהוה֖ שְׁנַ֣יִם וְשִׁבְעִֽים: וַֽחֲמֹרִ֕ים שְׁלֹשִׁ֥ים אֶ֖לֶף וַֽחֲמֵ֥שׁ מֵא֑וֹת
מ וּמִכְסָ֥ם לַֽיהוה֖ אֶחָ֥ד וְשִׁשִּֽׁים: וְנֶ֣פֶשׁ אָדָ֔ם שִׁשָּׁ֥ה עָשָׂ֖ר אָ֑לֶף וּמִכְסָם֙ לַֽיהוה֔
מא שְׁנַ֥יִם וּשְׁלֹשִׁ֖ים נָֽפֶשׁ: וַיִּתֵּ֣ן מֹשֶׁ֗ה אֶת־מֶ֨כֶס֙ תְּרוּמַ֣ת יהוה לְאֶלְעָזָ֖ר הַכֹּהֵ֑ן
מב כַּֽאֲשֶׁ֛ר צִוָּ֥ה יהוה אֶת־מֹשֶֽׁה: חמישי וּמִמַּֽחֲצִ֖ית בְּנֵ֣י יִשְׂרָאֵ֑ל אֲשֶׁר֙ חָצָ֣ה מֹשֶׁ֔ה
מג מִן־הָֽאֲנָשִׁ֖ים הַצֹּֽבְאִֽים: וַתְּהִ֛י מֶֽחֱצַ֥ת הָֽעֵדָ֖ה מִן־הַצֹּ֑אן שְׁלֹשׁ־מֵא֥וֹת אֶ֨לֶף֙
מד וּשְׁלֹשִׁ֣ים אֶ֔לֶף שִׁבְעַ֥ת אֲלָפִ֖ים וַֽחֲמֵ֥שׁ מֵאֽוֹת: וּבָקָ֕ר שִׁשָּׁ֥ה וּשְׁלֹשִׁ֖ים אָֽלֶף:
מה-מז וַֽחֲמֹרִ֕ים שְׁלֹשִׁ֥ים אֶ֖לֶף וַֽחֲמֵ֥שׁ מֵאֽוֹת: וְנֶ֣פֶשׁ אָדָ֔ם שִׁשָּׁ֥ה עָשָׂ֖ר אָ֑לֶף: וַיִּקַּ֨ח
מֹשֶׁ֜ה מִמַּֽחֲצִ֣ת בְּנֵֽי־יִשְׂרָאֵ֗ל אֶת־הָֽאָחֻז֙ אֶחָ֣ד מִן־הַֽחֲמִשִּׁ֔ים מִן־הָֽאָדָ֖ם
וּמִן־הַבְּהֵמָ֑ה וַיִּתֵּ֨ן אֹתָ֜ם לַֽלְוִיִּ֗ם שֹֽׁמְרֵי֙ מִשְׁמֶ֨רֶת֙ מִשְׁכַּ֣ן יהוה כַּֽאֲשֶׁ֛ר צִוָּ֥ה
מח יהוה אֶת־מֹשֶֽׁה: וַיִּקְרְבוּ֙ אֶל־מֹשֶׁ֔ה הַפְּקֻדִ֕ים אֲשֶׁ֖ר לְאַלְפֵ֣י הַצָּבָ֑א שָׂרֵ֥י
מט הָֽאֲלָפִ֖ים וְשָׂרֵ֥י הַמֵּאֽוֹת: וַיֹּֽאמְרוּ֙ אֶל־מֹשֶׁ֔ה עֲבָדֶ֣יךָ נָֽשְׂא֗וּ אֶת־רֹ֛אשׁ אַנְשֵׁ֥י
נ הַמִּלְחָמָ֖ה אֲשֶׁ֣ר בְּיָדֵ֑נוּ וְלֹֽא־נִפְקַ֥ד מִמֶּ֖נּוּ אִֽישׁ: וַנַּקְרֵ֞ב אֶת־קָרְבַּ֣ן יהוה אִישׁ֩
אֲשֶׁ֨ר מָצָ֤א כְלִֽי־זָהָב֙ אֶצְעָדָ֣ה וְצָמִ֔יד טַבַּ֖עַת עָגִ֣יל וְכוּמָ֑ז לְכַפֵּ֥ר
נא עַל־נַפְשֹׁתֵ֖ינוּ לִפְנֵ֥י יהוה: וַיִּקַּ֨ח מֹשֶׁ֜ה וְאֶלְעָזָ֧ר הַכֹּהֵ֛ן אֶת־הַזָּהָ֖ב מֵֽאִתָּ֑ם כֹּ֗ל

Amalek, of which it says, הִנֵּה לָכֶם בְּרָכָה מִשְּׁלַל אֹיְבֵי ה', *Behold, a present (blessing)
for you of the spoil of the enemies of HASHEM (I Samuel 30:26).*

32. יֶתֶר הַבַּז אֲשֶׁר בָּזְזוּ עַם הַצָּבָא — *Over and above the booty which the men of war
plundered ...* because the men of war took the property of the houses (entered by
them) for themselves.

50. לְכַפֵּר עַל נַפְשֹׁתֵינוּ — *To atone for our souls ...* (as an expiation) for the episode
of Pe'or, because we did not protest against the sinners.

NOTES

nefarious plot of Bil'am and Balak was aimed at
the undermining of all the Children of Israel, it
was only proper that the prey and booty
realized from this war of vengeance be shared
with all who were the intended victims of
Moab and Midian.

50. לְכַפֵּר עַל נַפְשֹׁתֵינוּ — *To atone for our souls.*
The Talmud (*Shabbos* 64a) explains that
although these soldiers had not sinned overtly,
they were guilty of lustful thoughts which
required atonement. The *Sforno* offers another
explanation consistent with his interpretation

נב כְּלִי מַעֲשֶׂה: וַיְהִי | כָּל־זְהַב הַתְּרוּמָה אֲשֶׁר הֵרִימוּ לַיהוה שִׁשָּׁה עָשָׂר אֶלֶף
נג שְׁבַע־מֵאוֹת וַחֲמִשִּׁים שָׁקֶל מֵאֵת שָׂרֵי הָאֲלָפִים וּמֵאֵת שָׂרֵי הַמֵּאוֹת: אַנְשֵׁי
נד הַצָּבָא בָּזְזוּ אִישׁ לוֹ: וַיִּקַּח מֹשֶׁה וְאֶלְעָזָר הַכֹּהֵן אֶת־הַזָּהָב מֵאֵת שָׂרֵי
הָאֲלָפִים וְהַמֵּאוֹת וַיָּבִאוּ אֹתוֹ אֶל־אֹהֶל מוֹעֵד זִכָּרוֹן לִבְנֵי־יִשְׂרָאֵל לִפְנֵי
יהוה:

לב

ששי [שלישי] א וּמִקְנֶה | רַב הָיָה לִבְנֵי רְאוּבֵן וְלִבְנֵי־גָד עָצוּם מְאֹד וַיִּרְאוּ אֶת־אֶרֶץ
ב יַעְזֵר וְאֶת־אֶרֶץ גִּלְעָד וְהִנֵּה הַמָּקוֹם מְקוֹם מִקְנֶה: וַיָּבֹאוּ בְנֵי־גָד וּבְנֵי
רְאוּבֵן וַיֹּאמְרוּ אֶל־מֹשֶׁה וְאֶל־אֶלְעָזָר הַכֹּהֵן וְאֶל־נְשִׂיאֵי הָעֵדָה
ג לֵאמֹר: עֲטָרוֹת וְדִיבֹן וְיַעְזֵר וְנִמְרָה וְחֶשְׁבּוֹן וְאֶלְעָלֵה וּשְׂבָם וּנְבוֹ וּבְעֹן:
ד הָאָרֶץ אֲשֶׁר הִכָּה יהוה לִפְנֵי עֲדַת יִשְׂרָאֵל אֶרֶץ מִקְנֶה הִוא וְלַעֲבָדֶיךָ
ה מִקְנֶה: וַיֹּאמְרוּ אִם־מָצָאנוּ חֵן בְּעֵינֶיךָ יֻתַּן אֶת־הָאָרֶץ
ו הַזֹּאת לַעֲבָדֶיךָ לַאֲחֻזָּה אַל־תַּעֲבִרֵנוּ אֶת־הַיַּרְדֵּן: וַיֹּאמֶר מֹשֶׁה לִבְנֵי־גָד
°תְּנִיאוּן ק׳ ז וְלִבְנֵי רְאוּבֵן הַאַחֵיכֶם יָבֹאוּ לַמִּלְחָמָה וְאַתֶּם תֵּשְׁבוּ פֹה: וְלָמָּה °תנואון

---

51. וַיִּקַּח מֹשֶׁה — *And Moses took.* He accepted (the gold) from them and weighed it.

כֹּל כְּלִי מַעֲשֶׂה — *All articles made for use.* Every kind of article which was used as a woman's ornament at the episode of Pe'or.

54. וַיִּקַּח מֹשֶׁה — *And Moses took.* After he weighed them, he brought them to the Tent of Meeting.

זִכָּרוֹן לִבְנֵי יִשְׂרָאֵל — *As a remembrance to the Children of Israel* . . . as an atonement for the iniquity of Pe'or.

XXXII

3. עֲטָרוֹת וְדִיבֹן — *Ataroth and Dibon.* Each one of these lands, by itself, was land (fit) for cattle.

6. הַאַחֵיכֶם יָבֹאוּ לַמִּלְחָמָה — *Shall your brothers go to war?* Do you actually think that your brothers will be willing to go to war, so as to conquer (the land)?

וְאַתֶּם תֵּשְׁבוּ פֹה — *And you shall sit here* . . . in (the land) which has already been conquered! There is no doubt that you cannot presume that this will be accepted; (therefore) this (proposal) can only serve to turn away the hearts of your brothers.

NOTES

of verses 4 and 11 in chapter 25, as well as *Exodus* 32:27. Their failure to protest the action of the wicked men who sinned at Pe'or necessitated atonement.

51-54. וַיִּקַּח מֹשֶׁה . . . כֹּל כְּלִי מַעֲשֶׂה . . . וַיִּקַּח מֹשֶׁה . . . זִכָּרוֹן לִבְנֵי יִשְׂרָאֵל — *And Moses took . . . all articles made for use . . . And Moses took . . . as a remembrance to the Children of Israel.* The *Sforno* explains the repetition of the verb וַיִּקַּח, *took*, in these two verses. The first refers to his accepting the ornaments of gold which he then weighed. The second refers to his subsequent act of bringing them into the Tent of Meeting.

The phrase זִכָּרוֹן, *remembrance*, is also used in *Exodus* 30:16 as an expression of atonement. When man remembers his sins and also remembers God, Whom he 'forgot' in the passion of the moment, he finds atonement.

XXXII

3. עֲטָרוֹת וְדִיבֹן — *Ataroth and Dibon.* The expression אֶרֶץ מִקְנֶה, *a land for cattle*, in the next verse is written in the singular because it refers to each of the individual lands enumerated here, i.e., Ataroth, Dibon etc. That is what the *Sforno* alludes to in his commentary on this verse. The phrase הָאָרֶץ אֲשֶׁר הִכָּה ה׳, *the*

ח אֶת־לֵב בְּנֵי יִשְׂרָאֵל מֵעֲבֹר אֶל־הָאָרֶץ אֲשֶׁר־נָתַן לָהֶם יהוה: כֹּה עָשׂוּ
ט אֲבֹתֵיכֶם בְּשָׁלְחִי אֹתָם מִקָּדֵשׁ בַּרְנֵעַ לִרְאוֹת אֶת־הָאָרֶץ: וַיַּעֲלוּ עַד־נַחַל
אֶשְׁכּוֹל וַיִּרְאוּ אֶת־הָאָרֶץ וַיָּנִיאוּ אֶת־לֵב בְּנֵי יִשְׂרָאֵל לְבִלְתִּי־בֹא
י אֶל־הָאָרֶץ אֲשֶׁר־נָתַן לָהֶם יהוה: וַיִּחַר־אַף יהוה בַּיּוֹם הַהוּא וַיִּשָּׁבַע
יא לֵאמֹר: אִם־יִרְאוּ הָאֲנָשִׁים הָעֹלִים מִמִּצְרַיִם מִבֶּן עֶשְׂרִים שָׁנָה וָמַעְלָה אֵת
הָאֲדָמָה אֲשֶׁר נִשְׁבַּעְתִּי לְאַבְרָהָם לְיִצְחָק וּלְיַעֲקֹב כִּי לֹא־מִלְאוּ אַחֲרָי:
יב־יג בִּלְתִּי כָּלֵב בֶּן־יְפֻנֶּה הַקְּנִזִּי וִיהוֹשֻׁעַ בִּן־נוּן כִּי מִלְאוּ אַחֲרֵי יהוה: וַיִּחַר־אַף
יהוה בְּיִשְׂרָאֵל וַיְנִעֵם בַּמִּדְבָּר אַרְבָּעִים שָׁנָה עַד־תֹּם כָּל־הַדּוֹר הָעֹשֶׂה
יד הָרָע בְּעֵינֵי יהוה: וְהִנֵּה קַמְתֶּם תַּחַת אֲבֹתֵיכֶם תַּרְבּוּת אֲנָשִׁים חַטָּאִים
טו לִסְפּוֹת עוֹד עַל חֲרוֹן אַף־יהוה אֶל־יִשְׂרָאֵל: כִּי תְשׁוּבֻן מֵאַחֲרָיו וְיָסַף עוֹד
טז לְהַנִּיחוֹ בַּמִּדְבָּר וְשִׁחַתֶּם לְכָל־הָעָם הַזֶּה: וַיִּגְּשׁוּ אֵלָיו
יז וַיֹּאמְרוּ גִּדְרֹת צֹאן נִבְנֶה לְמִקְנֵנוּ פֹּה וְעָרִים לְטַפֵּנוּ: וַאֲנַחְנוּ נֵחָלֵץ חֻשִׁים
לִפְנֵי בְּנֵי יִשְׂרָאֵל עַד אֲשֶׁר אִם־הֲבִיאֹנֻם אֶל־מְקוֹמָם וְיָשַׁב טַפֵּנוּ בְּעָרֵי
יח הַמִּבְצָר מִפְּנֵי יֹשְׁבֵי הָאָרֶץ: לֹא נָשׁוּב אֶל־בָּתֵּינוּ עַד הִתְנַחֵל בְּנֵי יִשְׂרָאֵל
יט אִישׁ נַחֲלָתוֹ: כִּי לֹא נִנְחַל אִתָּם מֵעֵבֶר לַיַּרְדֵּן וָהָלְאָה כִּי בָאָה נַחֲלָתֵנוּ
אֵלֵינוּ מֵעֵבֶר הַיַּרְדֵּן מִזְרָחָה:
שביעי [רביעי] כ וַיֹּאמֶר אֲלֵיהֶם מֹשֶׁה אִם־תַּעֲשׂוּן אֶת־הַדָּבָר הַזֶּה אִם־תֵּחָלְצוּ לִפְנֵי יהוה
כא לַמִּלְחָמָה: וְעָבַר לָכֶם כָּל־חָלוּץ אֶת־הַיַּרְדֵּן לִפְנֵי יהוה עַד הוֹרִישׁוֹ
כב אֶת־אֹיְבָיו מִפָּנָיו: וְנִכְבְּשָׁה הָאָרֶץ לִפְנֵי יהוה וְאַחַר תָּשֻׁבוּ וִהְיִיתֶם נְקִיִּם
כג מֵיהוה וּמִיִּשְׂרָאֵל וְהָיְתָה הָאָרֶץ הַזֹּאת לָכֶם לַאֲחֻזָּה לִפְנֵי יהוה: וְאִם־לֹא
תַעֲשׂוּן כֵּן הִנֵּה חֲטָאתֶם לַיהוה וּדְעוּ חַטַּאתְכֶם אֲשֶׁר תִּמְצָא אֶתְכֶם:

---

7. וְלָמָּה תְנִיאוּן — *And wherefore will you turn away the heart?* You certainly know how those who discouraged (others) in the previous generation were punished.

17. עַד אֲשֶׁר אִם הֲבִיאֹנֻם — *Until we have brought them.* (The meaning of עַד is) 'while as yet' they have not been brought, similar to, עַד לֹא עָשָׂה אֶרֶץ וְחוּצוֹת, *While as yet he had not made the earth or the fields* (Mishlei 8:26), (and also) עַד אִם כִּלּוּ לִשְׁתּוֹת, *While as yet they had not finished drinking* (Genesis 24:19).

23. הִנֵּה חֲטָאתֶם לַה׳ — *Behold, you have sinned against HASHEM.* In this event, you will reveal at a later time that you have sinned now, (because) you will reveal (lit., make known) that your intent was to perpetrate evil.

25. עֲבָדֶיךָ יַעֲשׂוּ — *Your servants will do.* (We accept) this part of what you say (and agree) to cross over as armed men.

NOTES

land which HASHEM smote (v. 4), is to be understood parenthetically. The Torah tells us that these were the same lands which Israel had conquered, with God's help, from Sichon and Og.

6. הַאַחֵיכֶם יָבֹאוּ לַמִּלְחָמָה וְאַתֶּם תֵּשְׁבוּ פֹה — *Shall your brothers go to war and you shall sit here?* The *Sforno* explains the verse thus: Moses argues that it was inconceivable that the land on the east side of the Jordan, which was conquered by *all* Israel, should be given to a *few* tribes who would then remain there in peace while the rest of Israel would have to wage war to conquer the west side of the Jordan — the Land of Canaan. Now since this

כד־כה בְּנוּ־לָכֶם עָרִים֙ לְטַפְּכֶ֔ם וּגְדֵרֹ֖ת לְצֹנַאֲכֶ֑ם וְהַיֹּצֵ֥א מִפִּיכֶ֖ם תַּעֲשֽׂוּ׃ וַיֹּ֤אמֶר
בְּנֵי־גָד֙ וּבְנֵ֣י רְאוּבֵ֔ן אֶל־מֹשֶׁ֖ה לֵאמֹ֑ר עֲבָדֶ֣יךָ יַעֲשׂ֔וּ כַּאֲשֶׁ֥ר אֲדֹנִ֖י מְצַוֶּֽה׃
כו־כז טַפֵּ֣נוּ נָשֵׁ֔ינוּ מִקְנֵ֖נוּ וְכָל־בְּהֶמְתֵּ֑נוּ יִֽהְיוּ־שָׁ֖ם בְּעָרֵ֥י הַגִּלְעָֽד׃ וַעֲבָדֶ֨יךָ יַעַבְר֜וּ
כח כָּל־חֲל֥וּץ צָבָ֛א לִפְנֵ֥י יְהוָ֖ה לַמִּלְחָמָ֑ה כַּאֲשֶׁ֥ר אֲדֹנִ֖י דֹּבֵֽר׃ וַיְצַ֤ו לָהֶם֙ מֹשֶׁ֔ה
אֵ֚ת אֶלְעָזָ֣ר הַכֹּהֵ֔ן וְאֵ֖ת יְהוֹשֻׁ֣עַ בִּן־נ֑וּן וְאֶת־רָאשֵׁ֛י אֲב֥וֹת הַמַּטּ֖וֹת לִבְנֵ֥י
כט יִשְׂרָאֵֽל׃ וַיֹּ֨אמֶר מֹשֶׁ֜ה אֲלֵהֶ֗ם אִם־יַעַבְר֣וּ בְנֵי־גָ֣ד וּבְנֵי־רְאוּבֵ֣ן ׀ אִ֠תְּכֶ֠ם
אֶת־הַיַּרְדֵּ֞ן כָּל־חָל֤וּץ לַמִּלְחָמָה֙ לִפְנֵ֣י יְהוָ֔ה וְנִכְבְּשָׁ֥ה הָאָ֖רֶץ לִפְנֵיכֶ֑ם וּנְתַתֶּ֥ם
ל לָהֶ֛ם אֶת־אֶ֥רֶץ הַגִּלְעָ֖ד לַאֲחֻזָּֽה׃ וְאִם־לֹ֧א יַעַבְר֛וּ חֲלוּצִ֖ים אִתְּכֶ֑ם וְנֹאחֲז֥וּ
לא בְתֹכְכֶ֖ם בְּאֶ֥רֶץ כְּנָֽעַן׃ וַיַּעֲנ֧וּ בְנֵי־גָ֛ד וּבְנֵ֥י רְאוּבֵ֖ן לֵאמֹ֑ר אֵת֩ אֲשֶׁ֨ר דִּבֶּ֧ר יְהוָ֛ה
לב אֶל־עֲבָדֶ֖יךָ כֵּ֥ן נַעֲשֶֽׂה׃ נַ֣חְנוּ נַעֲבֹ֧ר חֲלוּצִ֛ים לִפְנֵ֥י יְהוָ֖ה אֶ֣רֶץ כְּנָ֑עַן וְאִתָּ֨נוּ֙
לג אֲחֻזַּ֣ת נַחֲלָתֵ֔נוּ מֵעֵ֖בֶר לַיַּרְדֵּֽן׃ וַיִּתֵּ֣ן לָהֶ֣ם ׀ מֹשֶׁ֡ה לִבְנֵי־גָד֩ וְלִבְנֵ֨י רְאוּבֵ֜ן
וְלַחֲצִ֣י ׀ שֵׁ֣בֶט ׀ מְנַשֶּׁ֣ה בֶן־יוֹסֵ֗ף אֶת־מַמְלֶ֙כֶת֙ סִיחֹן֙ מֶ֣לֶךְ הָאֱמֹרִ֔י
וְאֶת־מַמְלֶ֕כֶת ע֖וֹג מֶ֣לֶךְ הַבָּשָׁ֑ן הָאָ֗רֶץ לְעָרֶ֙יהָ֙ בִּגְבֻלֹ֔ת עָרֵ֥י הָאָ֖רֶץ סָבִֽיב׃
לד־לה וַיִּבְנ֣וּ בְנֵי־גָ֔ד אֶת־דִּיבֹ֖ן וְאֶת־עֲטָרֹ֑ת וְאֵ֖ת עֲרֹעֵֽר׃ וְאֶת־עַטְרֹ֥ת שׁוֹפָ֛ן
לו וְאֶת־יַעְזֵ֖ר וְיָגְבְּהָֽה׃ וְאֶת־בֵּ֥ית נִמְרָ֖ה וְאֶת־בֵּ֣ית הָרָ֑ן עָרֵ֥י מִבְצָ֖ר וְגִדְרֹ֥ת
לז־לח צֹֽאן׃ וּבְנֵ֥י רְאוּבֵ֖ן בָּנ֑וּ אֶת־חֶשְׁבּ֖וֹן וְאֶת־אֶלְעָלֵ֑א וְאֵ֖ת קִרְיָתָֽיִם׃ וְאֶת־נְב֞וֹ
וְאֶת־בַּ֧עַל מְע֛וֹן מֽוּסַבֹּ֥ת שֵׁ֖ם וְאֶת־שִׂבְמָ֑ה וַיִּקְרְא֣וּ בְשֵׁמֹ֔ת אֶת־שְׁמ֥וֹת
לט הֶעָרִ֖ים אֲשֶׁ֥ר בָּנֽוּ׃ וַיֵּ֨לְכ֜וּ בְּנֵ֨י מָכִ֧יר בֶּן־מְנַשֶּׁ֛ה גִּלְעָ֖דָה וַיִּלְכְּדֻ֑הָ וַיּ֖וֹרֶשׁ
מפטיר מ אֶת־הָאֱמֹרִ֥י אֲשֶׁר־בָּֽהּ׃ וַיִּתֵּ֤ן מֹשֶׁה֙ אֶת־הַגִּלְעָ֔ד לְמָכִ֖יר בֶּן־מְנַשֶּׁ֑ה וַיֵּ֖שֶׁב
מא בָּֽהּ׃ וְיָאִ֤יר בֶּן־מְנַשֶּׁה֙ הָלַ֔ךְ וַיִּלְכֹּ֖ד אֶת־חַוֺּתֵיהֶ֑ם וַיִּקְרָ֥א אֶתְהֶ֖ן חַוֺּ֥ת יָאִֽיר׃
מב וְנֹ֣בַח הָלַ֔ךְ וַיִּלְכֹּ֥ד אֶת־קְנָ֖ת וְאֶת־בְּנֹתֶ֑יהָ וַיִּקְרָ֧א לָ֦ה נֹ֖בַח בִּשְׁמֽוֹ׃

---

28. וַיְצַו לָהֶם מֹשֶׁה — *So Moses gave charge concerning them.* He commanded (Elazar and Joshua) not to give them the lands of Sichon and Og until after they returned from the conquest of the land (i.e., Canaan) as it states, ... וְנִכְבְּשָׁה הָאָרֶץ, וְאַחַר תָּשֻׁבוּ ... וְהָיְתָה הָאָרֶץ הַזֹּאת לָכֶם, *And the land be conquered ... and you return afterward ... and this land shall be unto you* (v. 22), but not before that. But they did not accept this, and they said, נַחְנוּ נַעֲבֹר חֲלוּצִים ... וְאִתָּנוּ אֲחֻזַּת נַחֲלָתֵנוּ, *We will pass over armed ... and the possession of our inheritance shall remain with us* (v. 32), i.e., it shall be in our possession at the time we cross the Jordan!

33. וַיִּתֵּן לָהֶם מֹשֶׁה — *And Moses gave unto them.* Moses agreed with them in order not to enter into a dispute.

NOTES

is obvious, what then could be the purpose of the demand of the children of Gad and Reuben? It had to be for the purpose of discouraging Israel from crossing the Jordan, as the spies had attempted to do a generation earlier.

28. וַיְצַו לָהֶם מֹשֶׁה — *So Moses gave charge concerning them.* Moses stipulated that these two and a half tribes (Gad, Reuben and half of Menasseh) should not receive title to the land on the east side of the Jordan, even after they joined their brothers in battle, until the task was finished and they returned home. They, however, refused to accept this condition. They were willing to join the army and fight alongside their brothers, but they demanded to take possession of the lands of the Emorites and Bashan — now!

פרשת מסעי
Parashas Masei

לג א אֵלֶּה מַסְעֵי בְנֵי־יִשְׂרָאֵל אֲשֶׁר יָצְאוּ מֵאֶרֶץ מִצְרַיִם לְצִבְאֹתָם בְּיַד־מֹשֶׁה
ב וְאַהֲרֹן׃ וַיִּכְתֹּב מֹשֶׁה אֶת־מוֹצָאֵיהֶם לְמַסְעֵיהֶם עַל־פִּי יהוה וְאֵלֶּה מַסְעֵיהֶם
ג לְמוֹצָאֵיהֶם׃ וַיִּסְעוּ מֵרַעְמְסֵס בַּחֹדֶשׁ הָרִאשׁוֹן בַּחֲמִשָּׁה עָשָׂר יוֹם לַחֹדֶשׁ
הָרִאשׁוֹן מִמָּחֳרַת הַפֶּסַח יָצְאוּ בְנֵי־יִשְׂרָאֵל בְּיָד רָמָה לְעֵינֵי כָּל־
ד מִצְרָיִם׃ וּמִצְרַיִם מְקַבְּרִים אֵת אֲשֶׁר הִכָּה יהוה בָּהֶם כָּל־בְּכוֹר וּבֵאלֹהֵיהֶם
ה־ו עָשָׂה יהוה שְׁפָטִים׃ וַיִּסְעוּ בְנֵי־יִשְׂרָאֵל מֵרַעְמְסֵס וַיַּחֲנוּ בְּסֻכֹּת׃ וַיִּסְעוּ
ז מִסֻּכֹּת וַיַּחֲנוּ בְאֵתָם אֲשֶׁר בִּקְצֵה הַמִּדְבָּר׃ וַיִּסְעוּ מֵאֵתָם וַיָּשָׁב עַל־פִּי
ח הַחִירֹת אֲשֶׁר עַל־פְּנֵי בַּעַל צְפוֹן וַיַּחֲנוּ לִפְנֵי מִגְדֹּל׃ וַיִּסְעוּ מִפְּנֵי הַחִירֹת
וַיַּעַבְרוּ בְתוֹךְ־הַיָּם הַמִּדְבָּרָה וַיֵּלְכוּ דֶּרֶךְ שְׁלֹשֶׁת יָמִים בְּמִדְבַּר אֵתָם
ט וַיַּחֲנוּ בְּמָרָה׃ וַיִּסְעוּ מִמָּרָה וַיָּבֹאוּ אֵילִמָה וּבְאֵילִם שְׁתֵּים עֶשְׂרֵה

XXXIII

1. אֵלֶּה מַסְעֵי — *These are the journeys.* God, Blessed be He, wanted the journeys of the Israelites to be written (in order to) make known their merit in their following Him in the wilderness, *in a land that was not sown* (based on *Jeremiah* 2:2), and in this manner they deserved to enter the land.

2. וַיִּכְתֹּב מֹשֶׁה — *And Moses wrote.* He wrote down their destination and the place of their departure, for sometimes the place they headed for was exceedingly bad and the place from which they departed was good . . .

וְאֵלֶּה מַסְעֵיהֶם לְמוֹצָאֵיהֶם — *And these are their journeys according to their departures* . . . and sometimes the reverse happened (i.e., they departed from a bad place and traveled to a good one). He also wrote down the details of their journeys which entailed going from place to place without prior notice, which was very difficult. Nonetheless, they did not refrain (from journeying), and therefore it is written of each one of them that they journeyed from a certain place and encamped in (another) certain place, to indicate that the journeying and the encampment were (both) difficult.

NOTES

XXXIII

1. אֵלֶּה מַסְעֵי — *These are the journeys.* The reason for recording Israel's stations in the wilderness has preoccupied the commentators of the Torah. *Rashi* explains that the purpose was to publicize the lovingkindness of God Who in forty years kept the various stations down to only forty-two. The *Rambam* in his Guide (3:50) explains the necessity to enumerate the stations of the Israelites in the wilderness so that later generations will know that these places were uninhabited and did not contain any natural resources, and thus they will appreciate that the forty years of Israel's existence in the wilderness was a miraculous one. He also adds another reason, namely, to instruct us that all their journeys were planned and ordered by God, and not disorganized and haphazard.

The *Sforno*, however, submits a different reason for the Torah's recording of these journeys. It is to teach us Israel's faith in God and their readiness to travel at His behest, regardless of any difficulty or their lack of understanding the decision to leave a given place and proceed to another. Because of this willingness to obey God and follow Him, they merited to eventually enter the Promised Land.

2. וְאֵלֶּה מַסְעֵיהֶם לְמוֹצָאֵיהֶם — *And these are their journeys according to their departures.* Compare the *Sforno's* commentary here to his commentary in chapter 9, verses 19-23 and the notes there.

שני י עֵינֹת מַיִם וְשִׁבְעִים תְּמָרִים וַיַּחֲנוּ־שָׁם: וַיִּסְעוּ מֵאֵילִם וַיַּחֲנוּ עַל־יַם־סוּף:
יא-יב וַיִּסְעוּ מִיַּם־סוּף וַיַּחֲנוּ בְּמִדְבַּר־סִין: וַיִּסְעוּ מִמִּדְבַּר־סִין וַיַּחֲנוּ בְּדָפְקָה:
יג-יד וַיִּסְעוּ מִדָּפְקָה וַיַּחֲנוּ בְּאָלוּשׁ: וַיִּסְעוּ מֵאָלוּשׁ וַיַּחֲנוּ בִּרְפִידִם וְלֹא־הָיָה
טו-טז שָׁם מַיִם לָעָם לִשְׁתּוֹת: וַיִּסְעוּ מֵרְפִידִם וַיַּחֲנוּ בְּמִדְבַּר סִינָי: וַיִּסְעוּ מִמִּדְבַּר
יז סִינָי וַיַּחֲנוּ בְּקִבְרֹת הַתַּאֲוָה: וַיִּסְעוּ מִקִּבְרֹת הַתַּאֲוָה וַיַּחֲנוּ בַּחֲצֵרֹת:
יח-כ וַיִּסְעוּ מֵחֲצֵרֹת וַיַּחֲנוּ בְּרִתְמָה: וַיִּסְעוּ מֵרִתְמָה וַיַּחֲנוּ בְּרִמֹּן פָּרֶץ: וַיִּסְעוּ
כא-כב מֵרִמֹּן פָּרֶץ וַיַּחֲנוּ בְּלִבְנָה: וַיִּסְעוּ מִלִּבְנָה וַיַּחֲנוּ בְּרִסָּה: וַיִּסְעוּ מֵרִסָּה וַיַּחֲנוּ
כג-כד בִּקְהֵלָתָה: וַיִּסְעוּ מִקְּהֵלָתָה וַיַּחֲנוּ בְּהַר־שָׁפֶר: וַיִּסְעוּ מֵהַר־שָׁפֶר וַיַּחֲנוּ
כה-כו בַּחֲרָדָה: וַיִּסְעוּ מֵחֲרָדָה וַיַּחֲנוּ בְּמַקְהֵלֹת: וַיִּסְעוּ מִמַּקְהֵלֹת וַיַּחֲנוּ בְּתָחַת:
כז-כט וַיִּסְעוּ מִתָּחַת וַיַּחֲנוּ בְּתָרַח: וַיִּסְעוּ מִתָּרַח וַיַּחֲנוּ בְּמִתְקָה: וַיִּסְעוּ
ל-לא מִמִּתְקָה וַיַּחֲנוּ בְּחַשְׁמֹנָה: וַיִּסְעוּ מֵחַשְׁמֹנָה וַיַּחֲנוּ בְּמֹסֵרוֹת: וַיִּסְעוּ מִמֹּסֵרוֹת
לב-לג וַיַּחֲנוּ בִּבְנֵי יַעֲקָן: וַיִּסְעוּ מִבְּנֵי יַעֲקָן וַיַּחֲנוּ בְּחֹר הַגִּדְגָּד: וַיִּסְעוּ מֵחֹר הַגִּדְגָּד
לד-לה וַיַּחֲנוּ בְּיָטְבָתָה: וַיִּסְעוּ מִיָּטְבָתָה וַיַּחֲנוּ בְּעַבְרֹנָה: וַיִּסְעוּ מֵעַבְרֹנָה
לו וַיַּחֲנוּ בְּעֶצְיֹן גָּבֶר: וַיִּסְעוּ מֵעֶצְיֹן גָּבֶר וַיַּחֲנוּ בְמִדְבַּר־צִן הִוא קָדֵשׁ:
לז-לח וַיִּסְעוּ מִקָּדֵשׁ וַיַּחֲנוּ בְּהֹר הָהָר בִּקְצֵה אֶרֶץ אֱדוֹם: וַיַּעַל אַהֲרֹן
הַכֹּהֵן אֶל־הֹר הָהָר עַל־פִּי יהוה וַיָּמָת שָׁם בִּשְׁנַת הָאַרְבָּעִים לְצֵאת
לט בְּנֵי־יִשְׂרָאֵל מֵאֶרֶץ מִצְרַיִם בַּחֹדֶשׁ הַחֲמִישִׁי בְּאֶחָד לַחֹדֶשׁ: וְאַהֲרֹן
מ בֶּן־שָׁלֹשׁ וְעֶשְׂרִים וּמְאַת שָׁנָה בְּמֹתוֹ בְּהֹר הָהָר: וַיִּשְׁמַע
הַכְּנַעֲנִי מֶלֶךְ עֲרָד וְהוּא־יֹשֵׁב בַּנֶּגֶב בְּאֶרֶץ כְּנָעַן בְּבֹא בְּנֵי יִשְׂרָאֵל:
מא-מג וַיִּסְעוּ מֵהֹר הָהָר וַיַּחֲנוּ בְּצַלְמֹנָה: וַיִּסְעוּ מִצַּלְמֹנָה וַיַּחֲנוּ בְּפוּנֹן: וַיִּסְעוּ
מד מִפּוּנֹן וַיַּחֲנוּ בְּאֹבֹת: וַיִּסְעוּ מֵאֹבֹת וַיַּחֲנוּ בְּעִיֵּי הָעֲבָרִים בִּגְבוּל מוֹאָב:
מה-מו וַיִּסְעוּ מֵעִיִּים וַיַּחֲנוּ בְּדִיבֹן גָּד: וַיִּסְעוּ מִדִּיבֹן גָּד וַיַּחֲנוּ בְּעַלְמֹן דִּבְלָתָיְמָה:
מז-מח וַיִּסְעוּ מֵעַלְמֹן דִּבְלָתָיְמָה וַיַּחֲנוּ בְּהָרֵי הָעֲבָרִים לִפְנֵי נְבוֹ: וַיִּסְעוּ מֵהָרֵי
מט הָעֲבָרִים וַיַּחֲנוּ בְּעַרְבֹת מוֹאָב עַל יַרְדֵּן יְרֵחוֹ: וַיַּחֲנוּ עַל־הַיַּרְדֵּן מִבֵּית
שלישי [חמישי] נ הַיְשִׁמֹת עַד אָבֵל הַשִּׁטִּים בְּעַרְבֹת מוֹאָב: וַיְדַבֵּר יהוה
נא אֶל־מֹשֶׁה בְּעַרְבֹת מוֹאָב עַל־יַרְדֵּן יְרֵחוֹ לֵאמֹר: דַּבֵּר אֶל־בְּנֵי יִשְׂרָאֵל
נב וְאָמַרְתָּ אֲלֵהֶם כִּי אַתֶּם עֹבְרִים אֶת־הַיַּרְדֵּן אֶל־אֶרֶץ כְּנָעַן: וְהוֹרַשְׁתֶּם
אֶת־כָּל־יֹשְׁבֵי הָאָרֶץ מִפְּנֵיכֶם וְאִבַּדְתֶּם אֵת כָּל־מַשְׂכִּיֹּתָם וְאֵת כָּל־צַלְמֵי

40. וַיִּשְׁמַע הַכְּנַעֲנִי — *And the Canaanite heard.* This was also a merit for them because they did not say as their fathers had, *'Let us make a captain and return to Egypt'* (14:4), even when faced by war, but they made a vow to God and fulfilled it (see 21:2,3).

NOTES

40. וַיִּשְׁמַע הַכְּנַעֲנִי — *And the Canaanite heard. Rashi* comments that the news heard by the Canaanites was that of Aaron's death which resulted in the departure of the clouds of glory. Emboldened by this, they attacked the Israelites who did battle against them, as recorded in chapter 21, verses 1-3. The *Sforno* comments that this brave act on the part of Israel demonstrated that this generation possessed great courage and faith which was lacking in the previous one at the time of the spies.

נג מַסֵּכֹתָם֙ תְּאַבֵּ֔דוּ וְאֵ֥ת כָּל־בָּמוֹתָ֖ם תַּשְׁמִֽידוּ׃ וְהֽוֹרַשְׁתֶּ֥ם אֶת־הָאָ֖רֶץ
נד וִישַׁבְתֶּם־בָּ֑הּ כִּ֥י לָכֶ֛ם נָתַ֥תִּי אֶת־הָאָ֖רֶץ לָרֶ֥שֶׁת אֹתָֽהּ׃ וְהִתְנַחַלְתֶּם֩
אֶת־הָאָ֨רֶץ בְּגוֹרָ֜ל לְמִשְׁפְּחֹתֵיכֶ֗ם לָרַ֞ב תַּרְבּ֤וּ אֶת־נַחֲלָתוֹ֙ וְלַמְעַט֙ תַּמְעִ֣יט
אֶת־נַחֲלָת֔וֹ אֶל֩ אֲשֶׁר־יֵ֨צֵא ל֥וֹ שָׁ֛מָּה הַגּוֹרָ֖ל ל֣וֹ יִהְיֶ֑ה לְמַטּ֥וֹת אֲבֹתֵיכֶ֖ם
נה תִּתְנֶחָֽלוּ׃ וְאִם־לֹ֨א תוֹרִ֜ישׁוּ אֶת־יֹשְׁבֵ֣י הָאָרֶץ֮ מִפְּנֵיכֶם֒ וְהָיָ֗ה אֲשֶׁ֤ר תּוֹתִ֙ירוּ֙
מֵהֶ֔ם לְשִׂכִּים֙ בְּעֵ֣ינֵיכֶ֔ם וְלִצְנִינִ֖ם בְּצִדֵּיכֶ֑ם וְצָרְר֣וּ אֶתְכֶ֔ם עַל־הָאָ֕רֶץ אֲשֶׁ֥ר
נו אַתֶּ֖ם יֹשְׁבִ֥ים בָּֽהּ׃ וְהָיָ֗ה כַּאֲשֶׁ֥ר דִּמִּ֛יתִי לַעֲשׂ֥וֹת לָהֶ֖ם אֶעֱשֶׂ֥ה לָכֶֽם׃
לד א־ב וַיְדַבֵּ֥ר יְהוָ֖ה אֶל־מֹשֶׁ֥ה לֵּאמֹֽר׃ צַ֞ו אֶת־בְּנֵ֤י יִשְׂרָאֵל֙ וְאָמַרְתָּ֣ אֲלֵהֶ֔ם
כִּֽי־אַתֶּ֥ם בָּאִ֖ים אֶל־הָאָ֣רֶץ כְּנָ֑עַן זֹ֣את הָאָ֗רֶץ אֲשֶׁ֨ר תִּפֹּ֤ל לָכֶם֙ בְּֽנַחֲלָ֔ה אֶ֥רֶץ
ג כְּנַ֖עַן לִגְבֻלֹתֶֽיהָ׃ וְהָיָ֨ה לָכֶ֧ם פְּאַת־נֶ֛גֶב מִמִּדְבַּר־צִ֖ן עַל־יְדֵ֣י אֱד֑וֹם וְהָיָ֤ה לָכֶם֙

---

53. וְהוֹרַשְׁתֶּם אֶת הָאָרֶץ — *And you shall bequeath the land.* If you remove the inhabitants of the land, then you will merit to have your children inhabit the land. (However) if you do not rid (the land) of them, although you may conquer the land you will not merit to bequeath it to your children.

56. וְהָיָה כַּאֲשֶׁר דִּמִּיתִי לַעֲשׂוֹת לָהֶם אֶעֱשֶׂה לָכֶם — *And it shall come to pass that as I thought to do unto them, so will I do unto you* . . . for undoubtedly, you will go astray after their gods.

XXXIV

2. וְזֹאת הָאָרֶץ אֲשֶׁר תִּפֹּל לָכֶם בְּנַחֲלָה — *This shall be the land that shall fall to you for an inheritance.* It will fall to you by lot (even) before you will completely conquer it; the expression 'to fall' (or 'to cast') is fitting (to be used) regarding a lot, similar to וְעַל לְבוּשִׁי יַפִּילוּ גוֹרָל, *And cast lots for my clothing* (*Psalms* 22:19), and to הִפִּיל פּוּר הוּא הַגּוֹרָל, *He cast a pur, that is the lot* (*Esther* 3:7). (The verse) says זֹאת, *this,* because that which they conquered outside the land did not require (casting of) a lot to be divided. Therefore, Moses divided the land of Sichon and Og without casting lots, as we see in the Book of *Joshua.* This is because the lands of Sichon and Og did not possess the sanctity of *Eretz Yisrael,* as it says, וְאַךְ אִם טְמֵאָה אֶרֶץ אֲחֻזַּתְכֶם, *Howbeit, if the land of your possession be tamei* (*Joshua* 22:19), and was therefore unworthy (to be divided) by lot, which was directed by the Holy Spirit.

NOTES

53. וְהוֹרַשְׁתֶּם אֶת הָאָרֶץ — *And you shall bequeath the land.* The expression וְהוֹרַשְׁתֶּם appears also in the previous verse. The *Sforno* interprets the former one as meaning *to dispossess* or *drive out,* while the present one means *to inherit and bequeath as a possession.* He therefore explains that one is contingent on the other. Only if Israel will drive out the present inhabitants and rid the land of idolatry will they merit to inherit and bequeath the land to future generations. See *Rashi* who interprets this verse in a similar fashion, stating, 'If you drive them out of the land only then shall you dwell in it and be able to remain in it.'

XXXIV

2. וְזֹאת הָאָרֶץ אֲשֶׁר תִּפֹּל לָכֶם בְּנַחֲלָה — *This shall be the land that shall fall to you for an inheritance.* The *Sforno,* as does *Rashi* in his commentary on this verse, explains that the expression אֲשֶׁר תִּפֹּל, *that shall fall,* applies to the casting of lots which determined which area fell to each tribe. Our Sages explain that the lot itself cried out saying, 'I, the lot, have come up for such and such district and for such and such tribe' (*Bava Basra* 122a). As *Rashi* states in *parashas Pinchas* (26:54),

ד גְּבוּל נֶגֶב מִקְצֵה יָם־הַמֶּלַח קֵדְמָה׃ וְנָסַב לָכֶם הַגְּבוּל מִנֶּגֶב לְמַעֲלֵה
°וְהָיוּ ק׳ עַקְרַבִּים וְעָבַר צִנָה °והיה תּוֹצְאֹתָיו מִנֶּגֶב לְקָדֵשׁ בַּרְנֵעַ וְיָצָא חֲצַר־אַדָּר
ה וְעָבַר עַצְמֹנָה׃ וְנָסַב הַגְּבוּל מֵעַצְמוֹן נַחְלָה מִצְרָיִם וְהָיוּ תוֹצְאֹתָיו הַיָּמָּה׃
ו־ז וּגְבוּל יָם וְהָיָה לָכֶם הַיָּם הַגָּדוֹל וּגְבוּל זֶה־יִהְיֶה לָכֶם גְּבוּל יָם׃ וְזֶה־יִהְיֶה
ח לָכֶם גְּבוּל צָפוֹן מִן־הַיָּם הַגָּדֹל תְּתָאוּ לָכֶם הֹר הָהָר׃ מֵהֹר הָהָר תְּתָאוּ
ט לְבֹא חֲמָת וְהָיוּ תּוֹצְאֹת הַגְּבֻל צְדָדָה׃ וְיָצָא הַגְּבֻל זִפְרֹנָה וְהָיוּ תוֹצְאֹתָיו
י חֲצַר עֵינָן זֶה־יִהְיֶה לָכֶם גְּבוּל צָפוֹן׃ וְהִתְאַוִּיתֶם לָכֶם לִגְבוּל קֵדְמָה
יא מֵחֲצַר עֵינָן שְׁפָמָה׃ וְיָרַד הַגְּבֻל מִשְּׁפָם הָרִבְלָה מִקֶּדֶם לָעָיִן וְיָרַד
יב הַגְּבֻל וּמָחָה עַל־כֶּתֶף יָם־כִּנֶּרֶת קֵדְמָה׃ וְיָרַד הַגְּבוּל הַיַּרְדֵּנָה וְהָיוּ
יג תוֹצְאֹתָיו יָם הַמֶּלַח זֹאת תִּהְיֶה לָכֶם הָאָרֶץ לִגְבֻלֹתֶיהָ סָבִיב׃ וַיְצַו
מֹשֶׁה אֶת־בְּנֵי יִשְׂרָאֵל לֵאמֹר זֹאת הָאָרֶץ אֲשֶׁר תִּתְנַחֲלוּ אֹתָהּ בְּגוֹרָל
יד אֲשֶׁר צִוָּה יהוָה לָתֵת לְתִשְׁעַת הַמַּטּוֹת וַחֲצִי הַמַּטֶּה׃ כִּי לָקְחוּ מַטֵּה בְנֵי
הָרְאוּבֵנִי לְבֵית אֲבֹתָם וּמַטֵּה בְנֵי־הַגָּדִי לְבֵית אֲבֹתָם וַחֲצִי מַטֵּה מְנַשֶּׁה
טו לָקְחוּ נַחֲלָתָם׃ שְׁנֵי הַמַּטּוֹת וַחֲצִי הַמַּטֶּה לָקְחוּ נַחֲלָתָם מֵעֵבֶר לְיַרְדֵּן יְרֵחוֹ
קֵדְמָה מִזְרָחָה׃

רביעי [ששי] טז־יז וַיְדַבֵּר יהוָה אֶל־מֹשֶׁה לֵּאמֹר׃ אֵלֶּה שְׁמוֹת הָאֲנָשִׁים אֲשֶׁר־יִנְחֲלוּ לָכֶם
יח אֶת־הָאָרֶץ אֶלְעָזָר הַכֹּהֵן וִיהוֹשֻׁעַ בִּן־נוּן׃ וְנָשִׂיא אֶחָד נָשִׂיא אֶחָד מִמַּטֶּה
יט תִּקְחוּ לִנְחֹל אֶת־הָאָרֶץ׃ וְאֵלֶּה שְׁמוֹת הָאֲנָשִׁים לְמַטֵּה יְהוּדָה כָּלֵב
כ־כא בֶּן־יְפֻנֶּה׃ וּלְמַטֵּה בְּנֵי שִׁמְעוֹן שְׁמוּאֵל בֶּן־עַמִּיהוּד׃ לְמַטֵּה בִנְיָמִן אֱלִידָד
כב־כג בֶּן־כִּסְלוֹן׃ וּלְמַטֵּה בְנֵי־דָן נָשִׂיא בֻּקִּי בֶּן־יָגְלִי׃ לִבְנֵי יוֹסֵף לְמַטֵּה
כד בְנֵי־מְנַשֶּׁה נָשִׂיא חַנִּיאֵל בֶּן־אֵפֹד׃ וּלְמַטֵּה בְנֵי־אֶפְרַיִם נָשִׂיא קְמוּאֵל
כה־כו בֶּן־שִׁפְטָן׃ וּלְמַטֵּה בְנֵי־זְבוּלֻן נָשִׂיא אֱלִיצָפָן בֶּן־פַּרְנָךְ׃ וּלְמַטֵּה בְנֵי־יִשָּׂשכָר
כז נָשִׂיא פַּלְטִיאֵל בֶּן־עַזָּן׃ וּלְמַטֵּה בְנֵי־אָשֵׁר נָשִׂיא אֲחִיהוּד בֶּן־שְׁלֹמִי׃
כח־כט וּלְמַטֵּה בְנֵי־נַפְתָּלִי נָשִׂיא פְּדַהְאֵל בֶּן־עַמִּיהוּד׃ אֵלֶּה אֲשֶׁר צִוָּה יהוָה לְנַחֵל
אֶת־בְּנֵי־יִשְׂרָאֵל בְּאֶרֶץ כְּנָעַן׃

לה חמישי א־ב וַיְדַבֵּר יהוָה אֶל־מֹשֶׁה בְּעַרְבֹת מוֹאָב עַל־יַרְדֵּן יְרֵחוֹ לֵאמֹר׃ צַו אֶת־בְּנֵי
יִשְׂרָאֵל וְנָתְנוּ לַלְוִיִּם מִנַּחֲלַת אֲחֻזָּתָם עָרִים לָשָׁבֶת וּמִגְרָשׁ לֶעָרִים
ג סְבִיבֹתֵיהֶם תִּתְּנוּ לַלְוִיִּם׃ וְהָיוּ הֶעָרִים לָהֶם לָשָׁבֶת וּמִגְרְשֵׁיהֶם יִהְיוּ
ד לִבְהֶמְתָּם וְלִרְכֻשָׁם וּלְכֹל חַיָּתָם׃ וּמִגְרְשֵׁי הֶעָרִים אֲשֶׁר תִּתְּנוּ לַלְוִיִּם מִקִּיר

XXXV

3. לִבְהֶמְתָּם — *For their animals* . . . for riding and (to carry) burdens.

וְלִרְכֻשָׁם — *And for their goods.* Cattle and sheep.

וּלְכֹל חַיָּתָם — *And for all their amenities of life* . . . such as beehives, dovecotes and other such items.

NOTES

'The lot fell by the utterance of the Holy Spirit (רוּחַ הַקֹּדֶשׁ).' Based upon this, the *Sforno* explains the significance of the phrase זֹאת הָאָרֶץ, *this shall be the land.* The word

ה הָעִ֗יר וְח֣וּצָה אֶ֤לֶף אַמָּה֙ סָבִ֔יב: וּמַדֹּתֶ֞ם מִח֣וּץ לָעִ֗יר אֶת־פְּאַת־קֵ֣דְמָה
אַלְפַּ֣יִם בָּֽאַמָּ֡ה וְאֶת־פְּאַת־נֶ֩גֶב֩ אַלְפַּ֨יִם בָּֽאַמָּ֜ה וְאֶת־פְּאַת־יָ֣ם ׀ אַלְפַּ֣יִם
בָּֽאַמָּ֗ה וְאֵ֨ת פְּאַ֥ת צָפ֛וֹן אַלְפַּ֥יִם בָּֽאַמָּ֖ה וְהָעִ֣יר בַּתָּ֑וֶךְ זֶ֚ה יִֽהְיֶ֣ה לָהֶ֔ם מִגְרְשֵׁ֖י
ו הֶֽעָרִֽים: וְאֵ֣ת הֶעָרִ֗ים אֲשֶׁ֤ר תִּתְּנוּ֙ לַֽלְוִיִּ֔ם אֵ֚ת שֵׁשׁ־עָרֵ֣י הַמִּקְלָ֔ט אֲשֶׁ֣ר תִּתְּנ֗וּ
ז לָנֻ֥ס שָׁ֖מָּה הָֽרֹצֵ֑חַ וַֽעֲלֵיהֶ֣ם תִּתְּנ֔וּ אַרְבָּעִ֥ים וּשְׁתַּ֖יִם עִֽיר: כָּל־הֶֽעָרִ֗ים אֲשֶׁ֣ר
ח תִּתְּנוּ֙ לַֽלְוִיִּ֔ם אַרְבָּעִ֥ים וּשְׁמֹנֶ֖ה עִ֑יר אֶתְהֶ֖ן וְאֶת־מִגְרְשֵׁיהֶֽן: וְהֶֽעָרִ֗ים אֲשֶׁ֣ר
תִּתְּנ֜וּ מֵֽאֲחֻזַּ֣ת בְּנֵֽי־יִשְׂרָאֵ֗ל מֵאֵ֤ת הָרַב֙ תַּרְבּ֔וּ וּמֵאֵ֥ת הַמְעַ֖ט תַּמְעִ֑יטוּ אִ֗ישׁ
כְּפִ֤י נַֽחֲלָתוֹ֙ אֲשֶׁ֣ר יִנְחָ֔לוּ יִתֵּ֥ן מֵֽעָרָ֖יו לַֽלְוִיִּֽם:

ששי [שביעי] ט-י וַיְדַבֵּ֥ר יְהֹוָ֖ה אֶל־מֹשֶׁ֥ה לֵּאמֹֽר: דַּבֵּר֙ אֶל־בְּנֵ֣י יִשְׂרָאֵ֔ל וְאָֽמַרְתָּ֖ אֲלֵהֶ֑ם כִּ֤י
יא אַתֶּם֙ עֹֽבְרִ֣ים אֶת־הַיַּרְדֵּ֔ן אַ֖רְצָה כְּנָֽעַן: וְהִקְרִיתֶ֤ם לָכֶם֙ עָרִ֔ים עָרֵ֥י מִקְלָ֖ט
יב תִּֽהְיֶ֣ינָה לָכֶ֑ם וְנָ֥ס שָׁ֨מָּה֙ רֹצֵ֔חַ מַכֵּה־נֶ֖פֶשׁ בִּשְׁגָגָֽה: וְהָי֤וּ לָכֶם֙ הֶֽעָרִ֔ים לְמִקְלָ֖ט
יג מִגֹּאֵ֑ל וְלֹ֤א יָמוּת֙ הָֽרֹצֵ֔חַ עַד־עָמְד֛וֹ לִפְנֵ֥י הָֽעֵדָ֖ה לַמִּשְׁפָּֽט: וְהֶֽעָרִ֖ים אֲשֶׁ֣ר
יד תִּתֵּ֑נוּ שֵׁשׁ־עָרֵ֥י מִקְלָ֖ט תִּֽהְיֶ֥ינָה לָכֶֽם: אֵ֣ת ׀ שְׁלֹ֣שׁ הֶֽעָרִ֗ים תִּתְּנוּ֙ מֵעֵ֣בֶר
טו לַיַּרְדֵּ֔ן וְאֵת֙ שְׁלֹ֣שׁ הֶֽעָרִ֔ים תִּתְּנ֖וּ בְּאֶ֣רֶץ כְּנָ֑עַן עָרֵ֥י מִקְלָ֖ט תִּֽהְיֶֽינָה: לִבְנֵ֣י
יִשְׂרָאֵ֗ל וְלַגֵּ֤ר וְלַתּוֹשָׁב֙ בְּתוֹכָ֔ם תִּֽהְיֶ֛ינָה שֵֽׁשׁ־הֶעָרִ֥ים הָאֵ֖לֶּה לְמִקְלָ֑ט לָנ֣וּס
טז שָׁ֔מָּה כָּל־מַכֵּה־נֶ֖פֶשׁ בִּשְׁגָגָֽה: וְאִם־בִּכְלִ֨י בַרְזֶ֧ל ׀ הִכָּ֛הוּ וַיָּמֹ֖ת רֹצֵ֣חַ ה֑וּא מ֥וֹת
יז יוּמַ֖ת הָֽרֹצֵֽחַ: וְאִ֡ם בְּאֶ֣בֶן יָד֩ אֲשֶׁר־יָמ֨וּת בָּ֥הּ הִכָּ֛הוּ וַיָּמֹ֖ת רֹצֵ֣חַ ה֑וּא מ֥וֹת
יח יוּמַ֖ת הָֽרֹצֵֽחַ: א֡וֹ בִּכְלִ֣י עֵץ־יָד֩ אֲשֶׁר־יָמ֨וּת בּ֤וֹ הִכָּ֨הוּ֙ וַיָּמֹ֔ת רֹצֵ֣חַ ה֑וּא מ֥וֹת
יט יוּמַ֖ת הָֽרֹצֵֽחַ: גֹּאֵ֣ל הַדָּ֔ם ה֥וּא יָמִ֖ית אֶת־הָֽרֹצֵ֑חַ בְּפִגְעוֹ־ב֖וֹ ה֥וּא יְמִיתֶֽנּוּ:
כ-כא וְאִם־בְּשִׂנְאָ֖ה יֶהְדָּפֶ֑נּוּ אֽוֹ־הִשְׁלִ֥יךְ עָלָ֛יו בִּצְדִיָּ֖ה וַיָּמֹֽת: א֣וֹ בְאֵיבָ֞ה הִכָּ֤הוּ
בְיָדוֹ֙ וַיָּמֹ֔ת מֽוֹת־יוּמַ֥ת הַמַּכֶּ֖ה רֹצֵ֣חַ ה֑וּא גֹּאֵ֣ל הַדָּ֗ם יָמִ֛ית אֶת־הָֽרֹצֵ֖חַ
כב בְּפִגְעוֹ־בֽוֹ: וְאִם־בְּפֶ֥תַע בְּלֹֽא־אֵיבָ֖ה הֲדָפ֑וֹ אֽוֹ־הִשְׁלִ֥יךְ עָלָ֛יו כָּל־כְּלִ֖י בְּלֹ֥א
כג צְדִיָּֽה: א֣וֹ בְכָל־אֶ֜בֶן אֲשֶׁר־יָמ֥וּת בָּ֙הּ֙ בְּלֹ֣א רְא֔וֹת וַיַּפֵּ֥ל עָלָ֖יו וַיָּמֹ֑ת וְהוּא֙
כד לֹא־אוֹיֵ֣ב ל֔וֹ וְלֹ֥א מְבַקֵּ֖שׁ רָֽעָתֽוֹ: וְשָֽׁפְטוּ֙ הָֽעֵדָ֔ה בֵּ֚ין הַמַּכֶּ֔ה וּבֵ֖ין גֹּאֵ֣ל הַדָּ֑ם
כה עַ֥ל הַמִּשְׁפָּטִ֖ים הָאֵֽלֶּה: וְהִצִּ֨ילוּ הָֽעֵדָ֜ה אֶת־הָֽרֹצֵ֗חַ מִיַּד֮ גֹּאֵ֣ל הַדָּם֒ וְהֵשִׁ֣יבוּ

---

8. מֵאֵת הָרַב תַּרְבּוּ — *From those that have much you shall take more.* Because (the division of land) was according to value, hence, the smaller portion (given to the Levites) by the tribe which had less, was equal in value to the larger portion given to the Levites by the tribe which received more in quantity (see 26:54).

NOTES

זאת, *this*, is meant to exclude the land conquered by the Israelites on the east side of the Jordan which lacked the sanctity of *Eretz Yisrael*. As such, the lot which was guided by the Holy Spirit in *Eretz Yisrael* was not operative there; hence Moses had the right to divide the land as he saw fit. To support this, the *Sforno* cites the Book of *Joshua*, referring to chapter 13, verse 8, where it is written regarding the inheritance of Gad, Reuven and Menasseh on the east bank of the Jordan, אֲשֶׁר נָתַן לָהֶם מֹשֶׁה, *which Moses gave to them.*

XXXV

8. מֵאֵת הָרַב תַּרְבּוּ — *From those that have much you shall take more.* The *Sforno* explained in his commentary on 26:54 that the twelve portions of land divided among the tribes were not equal in area but were equal in value. In order that the land given by the Israelites to the Levites for cities and open space (מִגְרָשׁ) be equitable, the Torah commands that it not be in proportion to the size of the tribe but to

אֹתוֹ הָעֵדָה אֶל־עִיר מִקְלָטוֹ אֲשֶׁר־נָס שָׁמָּה וְיָשַׁב בָּהּ עַד־מוֹת הַכֹּהֵן
כו הַגָּדֹל אֲשֶׁר־מָשַׁח אֹתוֹ בְּשֶׁמֶן הַקֹּדֶשׁ: וְאִם־יָצֹא יֵצֵא הָרֹצֵחַ אֶת־גְּבוּל עִיר
כז מִקְלָטוֹ אֲשֶׁר יָנוּס שָׁמָּה: וּמָצָא אֹתוֹ גֹּאֵל הַדָּם מִחוּץ לִגְבוּל עִיר מִקְלָטוֹ
כח וְרָצַח גֹּאֵל הַדָּם אֶת־הָרֹצֵחַ אֵין לוֹ דָּם: כִּי בְעִיר מִקְלָטוֹ יֵשֵׁב עַד־מוֹת
כט הַכֹּהֵן הַגָּדֹל וְאַחֲרֵי מוֹת הַכֹּהֵן הַגָּדֹל יָשׁוּב הָרֹצֵחַ אֶל־אֶרֶץ אֲחֻזָּתוֹ: וְהָיוּ
ל אֵלֶּה לָכֶם לְחֻקַּת מִשְׁפָּט לְדֹרֹתֵיכֶם בְּכֹל מוֹשְׁבֹתֵיכֶם: כָּל־מַכֵּה־נֶפֶשׁ לְפִי
לא עֵדִים יִרְצַח אֶת־הָרֹצֵחַ וְעֵד אֶחָד לֹא־יַעֲנֶה בְנֶפֶשׁ לָמוּת: וְלֹא־תִקְחוּ כֹפֶר
לב לְנֶפֶשׁ רֹצֵחַ אֲשֶׁר־הוּא רָשָׁע לָמוּת כִּי־מוֹת יוּמָת: וְלֹא־תִקְחוּ כֹפֶר לָנוּס
לג אֶל־עִיר מִקְלָטוֹ לָשׁוּב לָשֶׁבֶת בָּאָרֶץ עַד־מוֹת הַכֹּהֵן: וְלֹא־תַחֲנִיפוּ
אֶת־הָאָרֶץ אֲשֶׁר אַתֶּם בָּהּ כִּי הַדָּם הוּא יַחֲנִיף אֶת־הָאָרֶץ וְלָאָרֶץ
לד לֹא־יְכֻפַּר לַדָּם אֲשֶׁר שֻׁפַּךְ־בָּהּ כִּי־אִם בְּדַם שֹׁפְכוֹ: וְלֹא תְטַמֵּא
אֶת־הָאָרֶץ אֲשֶׁר אַתֶּם יֹשְׁבִים בָּהּ אֲשֶׁר אֲנִי שֹׁכֵן בְּתוֹכָהּ כִּי אֲנִי יהוה
שֹׁכֵן בְּתוֹךְ בְּנֵי יִשְׂרָאֵל:

לו שביעי א וַיִּקְרְבוּ רָאשֵׁי הָאָבוֹת לְמִשְׁפַּחַת בְּנֵי־גִלְעָד בֶּן־מָכִיר בֶּן־מְנַשֶּׁה
מִמִּשְׁפְּחֹת בְּנֵי יוֹסֵף וַיְדַבְּרוּ לִפְנֵי מֹשֶׁה וְלִפְנֵי הַנְּשִׂאִים רָאשֵׁי אָבוֹת
ב לִבְנֵי יִשְׂרָאֵל: וַיֹּאמְרוּ אֶת־אֲדֹנִי צִוָּה יהוה לָתֵת אֶת־הָאָרֶץ בְּנַחֲלָה

---

25. עד מות הַכֹּהֵן הַגָּדֹל — *Until the death of the Kohen Gadol.* It has already been explained that גָלוּת (exile to a city of refuge) is the punishment for one who kills in error. Now being that there are different kinds of unintentional sins (שוגג), which are disparate because some are closer to being considered accidental (אונס) while others are closer to being considered intentional (מֵזִיד); therefore there are varying periods of exile for one who kills unintentionally. For some, the unintentional act (of killing) is (punished by exile) for a brief period before the *Kohen* dies, while some murderers die in exile before the death of the *Kohen.* This occurs (according to) the judgment of God, Blessed is He, the One Who knows and is a witness (based on *Jeremiah* 29:23), Who punishes the unintentional sinner according to the degree of his error, as it says, וְהָאֱלֹהִים אִנָּה לְיָדוֹ, *but God caused it to come to hand* (*Exodus* 21:13).

NOTES

the value of that particular city and open space.

25. עד מות הַכֹּהֵן הַגָּדֹל — *Until the death of the Kohen Gadol.* The Torah teaches us in the Book of *Exodus* (21:13) that whenever an unpremeditated murder occurs, it is nonetheless considered predestined, as the verse states, וְהָאֱלֹהִים אִנָּה לְיָדוֹ, *but God caused it to come to hand.* Nonetheless, there are degrees of fault involved even when the act is in error and not premeditated (שוגג). At times, it is due to gross negligence which is akin to an intentional act (מֵזִיד), whereas on other occasions it is almost an unavoidable accident (אוֹנֶס). Now since the punishment for all of these acts is the same, namely גָלוּת (exile to a city of refuge), it seems unjust. The *Sforno*, therefore, explains that since the murderer is freed when the *Kohen Gadol* dies, the *length* of his stay in exile will vary considerably. Since the manslaughter is pre-ordained by God, He in His infinite wisdom will arrange it to happen relative to the timing of the eventual death of the *Kohen Gadol*, and thus the length of the murderer's imprisonment will be determined by the degree of his negligence.

בְּגוֹרָל לִבְנֵי יִשְׂרָאֵל וַאדֹנִי צֻוָּה בַיהוָה לָתֵת אֶת־נַחֲלַת צְלָפְחָד אָחִינוּ
ג לִבְנֹתָיו: וְהָיוּ לְאֶחָד מִבְּנֵי שִׁבְטֵי בְנֵי־יִשְׂרָאֵל לְנָשִׁים וְנִגְרְעָה נַחֲלָתָן
מִנַּחֲלַת אֲבֹתֵינוּ וְנוֹסַף עַל נַחֲלַת הַמַּטֶּה אֲשֶׁר תִּהְיֶינָה לָהֶם וּמִגֹּרַל
ד נַחֲלָתֵנוּ יִגָּרֵעַ: וְאִם־יִהְיֶה הַיֹּבֵל לִבְנֵי יִשְׂרָאֵל וְנוֹסְפָה נַחֲלָתָן עַל נַחֲלַת
ה הַמַּטֶּה אֲשֶׁר תִּהְיֶינָה לָהֶם וּמִנַּחֲלַת מַטֵּה אֲבֹתֵינוּ יִגָּרַע נַחֲלָתָן: וַיְצַו מֹשֶׁה
ו אֶת־בְּנֵי יִשְׂרָאֵל עַל־פִּי יְהוָה לֵאמֹר כֵּן מַטֵּה בְנֵי־יוֹסֵף דֹּבְרִים: זֶה הַדָּבָר
אֲשֶׁר־צִוָּה יהוה לִבְנוֹת צְלָפְחָד לֵאמֹר לַטּוֹב בְּעֵינֵיהֶם תִּהְיֶינָה לְנָשִׁים אַךְ
ז לְמִשְׁפַּחַת מַטֵּה אֲבִיהֶם תִּהְיֶינָה לְנָשִׁים: וְלֹא־תִסֹּב נַחֲלָה לִבְנֵי יִשְׂרָאֵל
מִמַּטֶּה אֶל־מַטֶּה כִּי אִישׁ בְּנַחֲלַת מַטֵּה אֲבֹתָיו יִדְבְּקוּ בְּנֵי יִשְׂרָאֵל:
ח וְכָל־בַּת יֹרֶשֶׁת נַחֲלָה מִמַּטּוֹת בְּנֵי יִשְׂרָאֵל לְאֶחָד מִמִּשְׁפַּחַת מַטֵּה אָבִיהָ

XXXVI

2. בְּנַחֲלָה בְּגוֹרָל — *For inheritance by lot.* If any tribe would have a portion within the area of a fellow (tribe), then the lot cast would not be correct regarding the boundaries of the diminished tribe. Also regarding the (tribe) which received this addition, the (lot) will not be correct unless that portion, which belongs to his fellow tribe, is added to his area.

4. וְאִם יִהְיֶה הַיֹּבֵל . . . יִגָּרַע נַחֲלָתָן — *And when the Jubilee shall be . . . their inheritance will be taken away.* Also, since the entire land was not conquered immediately as it says, מְעַט מְעַט אֲגָרְשֶׁנּוּ מִפָּנֶיךָ, *Little by little I will drive them out before you* (*Exodus* 23:30), and each tribe had to conquer its portion; therefore, although an individual may sell his portion to a member of another tribe, that seller would not refrain from striving, together with his tribe, to conquer (the land), being that it would return to him at the Jubilee. However, the members of the tribe will not attempt to conquer the portion of the daughters (who marry outside the tribe) which will not return at the Jubilee, or they will permit the inhabitants of the land to remain there since it now belongs to another tribe, and thus the conquest of their inheritance will be subtracted from the allotted (portion) of our father's tribe.

NOTES

XXXVI

2. בְּנַחֲלָה בְּגוֹרָל — *For inheritance by lot.* As the *Sforno* explains this verse, the thrust of the complaint submitted by the heads of the children of Gilead, son of Machir, was that if the daughters of Zelaphchad were to marry men from a different tribe (other than Menasseh), the allocation of land in Eretz Yisrael by the casting of lots would be frustrated because the land they inherited from their father would eventually be passed on to their children whose tribal relationship would be that of their father — who was a member of another tribe. Since the lot cast was directed by the Holy Spirit, as mentioned above, such a deviation could not be tolerated. This explains why the complainants stressed the fact that it was an *inheritance by lot.*

4. וְאִם יִהְיֶה הַיֹּבֵל . . . יִגָּרַע נַחֲלָתָן — *And when the Jubilee shall be . . . their inheritance will be taken away.* This verse seems to be repetitious, since it has already been established that the concern of the heads of the family of Gilead was that their inheritance would be diminished. The *Sforno*, however, explains that there was an added concern. Since the conquest of *Eretz Yisrael* was not

ט תִּהְיֶ֣ה לְאִשָּׁ֔ה לְמַ֣עַן יִֽירְשׁוּ֙ בְּנֵ֣י יִשְׂרָאֵ֔ל אִ֖ישׁ נַחֲלַ֣ת אֲבֹתָ֑יו: וְלֹֽא־תִסֹּ֤ב
נַחֲלָה֙ מִמַּטֶּ֣ה לְמַטֶּ֣ה אַחֵ֔ר כִּי־אִ֗ישׁ בְּנַחֲלָת֔וֹ יִדְבְּק֖וּ מַטּ֥וֹת בְּנֵ֥י יִשְׂרָאֵֽל:

מפטיר י־יא כַּאֲשֶׁ֛ר צִוָּ֥ה יהו֖ה אֶת־מֹשֶׁ֑ה כֵּ֥ן עָשׂ֖וּ בְּנ֣וֹת צְלָפְחָֽד: וַתִּהְיֶ֜ינָה מַחְלָ֣ה תִרְצָ֗ה
יב וְחָגְלָ֧ה וּמִלְכָּ֛ה וְנֹעָ֖ה בְּנ֣וֹת צְלָפְחָ֑ד לִבְנֵ֤י דֹֽדֵיהֶן֙ לְנָשִֽׁים: מִמִּשְׁפְּחֹ֛ת
בְּנֵֽי־מְנַשֶּׁ֥ה בֶן־יוֹסֵ֖ף הָי֣וּ לְנָשִׁ֑ים וַתְּהִי֙ נַחֲלָתָ֔ן עַל־מַטֵּ֖ה מִשְׁפַּ֥חַת אֲבִיהֶֽן:
יג אֵ֣לֶּה הַמִּצְוֺ֞ת וְהַמִּשְׁפָּטִ֗ים אֲשֶׁ֨ר צִוָּ֧ה יהו֛ה בְּיַד־מֹשֶׁ֖ה אֶל־בְּנֵ֣י יִשְׂרָאֵ֑ל
בְּעַֽרְבֹ֣ת מוֹאָ֔ב עַ֖ל יַרְדֵּ֥ן יְרֵחֽוֹ:

---

10. כֵּן עָשׂוּ בְּנוֹת צְלָפְחָד — *So did the daughters of Zelaphchad.* Their (sole) intent
was to fulfill the will of their Maker, *as* HASHEM *had commanded Moses;* not
because they desired to marry these men.

12. מִמִּשְׁפְּחֹת בְּנֵי מְנַשֶּׁה — *Of the families of the sons of Menasseh.* Since
they saw that it was the intent of God, the Exalted One, not to remove the
inheritance (from tribe to tribe), they chose their cousins (as husbands) from
among all the families (within the tribe) because they were the closest, even
though they were given permission to choose whomsoever they wished from
their tribe.

וַתְּהִי נַחֲלָתָן עַל מַטֵּה מִשְׁפַּחַת אֲבִיהֶן — *And their inheritance remained in the tribe
of the family of their father* ... and thus there was no removal of inheritance
whatsoever, even from family to family (within the tribe of Menasseh).

NOTES

completed when Israel initially entered the
land, it behooved each tribe to complete that
conquest over a period of time — on their
own. Now, if certain parts of their family's
inheritance were transferred to another tribe,
then there would be no motivation for their
fellow tribesmen, who belonged to other
families within the tribe of Menasseh, to
assist them in the completion of the task of
conquering those areas, since these areas no
longer belonged to their tribe. The result
would be a diminishment of their family's
share.

12. מִמִּשְׁפְּחֹת בְּנֵי מְנַשֶּׁה — *Of the families of
the sons of Menasseh.* Although each tribe
was allocated an equal share of land, that
share was subdivided among its families.
This being the case, were the daughters of
Zelaphchad to have married within the tribe
but not within their family, although it
would have satisfied the law now promul-
gated, it would have meant subtracting their
share of land from the family unit. Sensing
this, they decided to marry their cousins,
who were their closest relatives within the
family of their father.

ספר דברים

Devarim/Deuteronomy

Sforno's Introduction

When the ruling King spoke and decreed that Moses, the shepherd of His sheep would not enter the Land due to the transgression of His people, then before the removal of his 'shadow' (i.e., protective shield) from them, he began to explain the Torah after he prefaced (this explanation) by telling and reminding them why this was necessary, i.e., because they were to enter the Land without him, due to their foolishness and sins.[1] When he completed this (reminder), he set aside the cities (of refuge)[2] and began to explain and caution them regarding the commandments in whose merit (i.e., by observing them) they would have longevity in the land of their inheritance.[3] (He also explained) those commandments which they are obligated to do when they enter the Land, such as the writing on the stones[4] and the Covenant of Mt. Gerizim[5] and others which are meant as signs for (all) generations that they not deal treacherously. He also gave them the order of the oath[6] that was to be administered, since they had nullified the Covenant of Horeb through the sin of the spies. (He also) testified regarding them, telling them what the future would bring to them in exile, as well as the future redemption which would come after total despair.[7] And he prayed on their behalf and blessed them by casting his eye for good on their Land. And he told of the coming of the redeemer and their future happiness — all this in his blessing given before he died.[8] And thus, the Torah is completed, with the testimony at its conclusion that no other man ever reached the level of prophecy attained by Moses[9] through whom the true Torah was given, (a Torah) to which naught can be added nor subtracted.

Thus, (in this book) we are told of the Divine lovingkindness which granted Moses prophetic powers (lit., prophetic preparedness), more than that which is (conceivably) possible in the nature of man, in order to grant the true Torah through him, (a Torah) which is unchanging, to which naught can be added or subtracted [10] through any other prophet, as our

1. *Parashas Devarim*.
2. *Deut*. 4:41.
3. *Deut*. 4:44 and 5:30.
4. *Deut*. 27:2.
5. *Deut*. 11:29.
6. *Deut*. 27:15.
7. *Deut*. chapter 30.
8. *Parashas Vezos HaBerachah*
9. *Deut*. 34:10.
10. *Deut*. 4:2.

Sages state, שְׁאֵין נָבִיא רַשָּׁאִי לְחַדֵּשׁ דָּבָר מֵעַתָּה, *A prophet may henceforth* (i.e., after Moses) *make no innovations* (*Shabbos* 104b), and this is what the prophet taught when he said, ה׳ אֲשֶׁר עָשָׂה אֶת מֹשֶׁה וְאֶת אַהֲרֹן, *HASHEM who made Moses and Aaron* (*I Samuel* 12:6), because, indeed, through Moses He gave a level (lit., the wherewithal) of prophecy which surpasses all (such) possible powers in the nature of man, and also with Aaron (He granted) the priesthood so that his seed would be sanctified through it forever.

פרשת דברים
Parasha Devarim

א א אֵלֶּה הַדְּבָרִים אֲשֶׁר דִּבֶּר מֹשֶׁה אֶל־כָּל־יִשְׂרָאֵל בְּעֵבֶר הַיַּרְדֵּן בַּמִּדְבָּר
ב בָּעֲרָבָה מוֹל סוּף בֵּין־פָּארָן וּבֵין־תֹּפֶל וְלָבָן וַחֲצֵרֹת וְדִי זָהָב: אַחַד עָשָׂר
ג יוֹם מֵחֹרֵב דֶּרֶךְ הַר־שֵׂעִיר עַד קָדֵשׁ בַּרְנֵעַ: וַיְהִי בְּאַרְבָּעִים שָׁנָה
בְּעַשְׁתֵּי־עָשָׂר חֹדֶשׁ בְּאֶחָד לַחֹדֶשׁ דִּבֶּר מֹשֶׁה אֶל־בְּנֵי יִשְׂרָאֵל כְּכֹל אֲשֶׁר
ד צִוָּה יהוה אֹתוֹ אֲלֵהֶם: אַחֲרֵי הַכֹּתוֹ אֵת סִיחֹן מֶלֶךְ הָאֱמֹרִי אֲשֶׁר יוֹשֵׁב

I

1. אֵלֶּה הַדְּבָרִים אֲשֶׁר דִּבֶּר מֹשֶׁה אֶל כָּל יִשְׂרָאֵל — *These are the words which Moses spoke to all Israel.* (The verse) says that in every place [which is] mentioned here, these being places where they (Israel) deviated from the path (of proper behavior), and by the decree of God, the Exalted One, they wandered about in the wilderness because of the sin of the spies, Moses said these words to all Israel which are now mentioned, namely:

2. אַחַד עָשָׂר יוֹם מֵחֹרֵב — *It is eleven days journey from Horeb.* The entire thirty-eight years they wandered in the wilderness hither and fro, not following a direct route to a specific place — and whenever they reached a (specific) place, they would wander (again) and retrace their steps or go off on a side (route), but never (travel) in a straight direct path. Moses would then say to them: 'See what you have caused, for it is but *a journey of eleven days from Horeb to Kadesh Barnea by way of Mount Seir* which is the shortest route (followed) by travelers, and God, the Blessed One, brought you to Kadesh Barnea in three days through the great and awful wilderness, but because of your transgressions you wandered all this time.' All this he told them (time and again) so that they might remember and return to God.

3. וַיְהִי בְּאַרְבָּעִים שָׁנָה — *And it came to pass in the fortieth year.* After the (older generation) had already died in the wilderness, *Moses spoke to the Children of Israel,* namely to those who were to enter the Land, *according to all that God had given him as a commandment to them* — he reviewed with them the entire Torah which had been given till now.

4. אַחֲרֵי הַכֹּתוֹ — *After he had smitten . . .* and this he did after (Israel) had attained a degree of tranquility in a settled land.

NOTES

I

1. אֵלֶּה הַדְּבָרִים — *These are the words.* According to the *Sifri,* as quoted in *Rashi* in his commentary on this verse, the places mentioned in this *pasuk* are all "places where they angered God.' This is what the *Sforno* refers to as places where Israel deviated from the path of God and were guilty of misconduct. In each of these places, as they sinned, Moses spoke these words to them, i.e., *it is eleven days journey from Horeb to Kadesh Barnea,* to remind them that due to the sin of the spies they were punished and condemned to wander thirty-eight years in the wilderness. As the *Sforno* explains in the next verse, Moses did this in the hope that they would be encouraged to repent, for this was the real purpose of his reminding them of their sins and admonishing them. Hence, it was not simply a case of reproach but for the purpose of urging them to do *teshuvah;* to repent and mend their ways.

3. וַיְהִי בְּאַרְבָּעִים שָׁנָה — *And it came to pass in the fortieth year.* The *Sforno* explains why the Torah tells us that it came to pass in the 40th year that Moses spoke these words to Israel. He says it was necessary after four decades to instruct the new generation in the teachings of Torah, since the older generation had all died out and the obligation to observe the commandments was now theirs.

ה בְּחֶשְׁבּוֹן וְאֵת עוֹג מֶלֶךְ הַבָּשָׁן אֲשֶׁר־יוֹשֵׁב בְּעַשְׁתָּרֹת בְּאֶדְרֶעִי׃ בְּעֵבֶר
ו הַיַּרְדֵּן בְּאֶרֶץ מוֹאָב הוֹאִיל מֹשֶׁה בֵּאֵר אֶת־הַתּוֹרָה הַזֹּאת לֵאמֹר׃ יהוה
ז אֱלֹהֵינוּ דִּבֶּר אֵלֵינוּ בְּחֹרֵב לֵאמֹר רַב־לָכֶם שֶׁבֶת בָּהָר הַזֶּה׃ פְּנוּ ׀ וּסְעוּ
לָכֶם וּבֹאוּ הַר הָאֱמֹרִי וְאֶל־כָּל־שְׁכֵנָיו בָּעֲרָבָה בָהָר וּבַשְּׁפֵלָה וּבַנֶּגֶב וּבְחוֹף
ח הַיָּם אֶרֶץ הַכְּנַעֲנִי וְהַלְּבָנוֹן עַד־הַנָּהָר הַגָּדֹל נְהַר־פְּרָת׃ רְאֵה נָתַתִּי לִפְנֵיכֶם
אֶת־הָאָרֶץ בֹּאוּ וּרְשׁוּ אֶת־הָאָרֶץ אֲשֶׁר נִשְׁבַּע יהוה לַאֲבֹתֵיכֶם לְאַבְרָהָם

---

5. בְּעֵבֶר הַיַּרְדֵּן בְּאֶרֶץ מוֹאָב הוֹאִיל מֹשֶׁה בֵּאֵר — *Beyond the Jordan in the land of Moab, Moses began to explain.* After they no longer wandered and roved, for the encampment in the plains of Moab was (at the end) of their final journey, and since (Moses), after his beseeching (God), despaired of attaining (his request) to cross over, (therefore) he now began to explain (those areas of Torah) which he thought might be unclear (lit., doubtful) after his death. This explanation began when he later said ה׳ אֱלֹהֵינוּ כָּרַת עִמָּנוּ בְּרִית בְּחֹרֵב, *HASHEM, our God, made a covenant with us in Horeb* (5:2).

לֵאמֹר — *Saying.* Before he began this exposition, wherein he elaborated and cautioned (them) regarding a number of the commandments, he said to Israel that the reason they needed (these words of) explanation and caution at this time was because they were crossing over without him and (therefore) he would not be able to caution them at the appropriate time nor resolve every doubt which might arise. He related how they stumbled through their wicked choices and iniquities (resulting) in his not being able to cross over with them. (This he did) so that they should be careful in the future and not corrupt their ways (lit., affairs).

8. רְאֵה נָתַתִּי לִפְנֵיכֶם אֶת הָאָרֶץ — *Behold, I have set before you the land . . .* (namely) the inhabitants of the land; for they will *melt away before you* (based on *Joshua* 2:9), and will not rise up.

בֹּאוּ וּרְשׁוּ אֶת הָאָרֶץ — *Come and possess the land . . .* (namely) the (geographical) area of these nations, because due to their fears, they (the inhabitants) will turn and flee or die; (all this) without doing battle.

NOTES

4. אַחֲרֵי הַכֹּתוֹ — *After he had smitten.* The *Sforno* explains the reason for the Torah's telling us that this occurred after Moses had smitten Sichon and Og. Following that victory, the Israelites were able to settle down in peace, and were not forced to wander. This newly found tranquility created an atmosphere in which the people were able to listen, concentrate and absorb the teachings of their master.

5. הוֹאִיל מֹשֶׁה בֵּאֵר — *Moses began to explain.* Once Moses is convinced that he will not be permitted to accompany Israel into the Promised Land, he decides (and desires) to expound the Torah, and he attempts to anticipate and resolve all future questions in regard to the law since he will not be present to address these problems when they ultimately arise. This interpretation of the *Sforno* is based on the *Rambam's* introduction to his commentary on the Mishnah. The *Rambam* there states, "In the fortieth year, in the eleventh month, on Rosh Chodesh Shevat, he (Moses) gathered the people and said to them, 'The time of my death has arrived. If there be among you one who heard a *halachah* (law) and has forgotten it, let him come and ask me and I shall explain it . . .' as it is written, 'Moses began to explain.' " The *Rambam*, in turn, is expounding upon the *Sifri*, and indeed he quotes from it in his introduction.

8. נָתַתִּי לִפְנֵיכֶם אֶת הָאָרֶץ בֹּאוּ וּרְשׁוּ אֶת הָאָרֶץ — *I have set before you the land; come and possess the land.* The *Sforno* explains the word אֶרֶץ,

ט לְיִצְחָק וּלְיַעֲקֹב לָתֵת לָהֶם וּלְזַרְעָם אַחֲרֵיהֶם: וָאֹמַר אֲלֵכֶם בָּעֵת הַהִוא
י לֵאמֹר לֹא־אוּכַל לְבַדִּי שְׂאֵת אֶתְכֶם: יְהוָה אֱלֹהֵיכֶם הִרְבָּה אֶתְכֶם וְהִנְּכֶם
שני יא הַיּוֹם כְּכוֹכְבֵי הַשָּׁמַיִם לָרֹב: יְהוָה אֱלֹהֵי אֲבוֹתֵכֶם יֹסֵף עֲלֵיכֶם כָּכֶם אֶלֶף
יב פְּעָמִים וִיבָרֵךְ אֶתְכֶם כַּאֲשֶׁר דִּבֶּר לָכֶם: אֵיכָה אֶשָּׂא לְבַדִּי טָרְחֲכֶם
יג וּמַשַּׂאֲכֶם וְרִיבְכֶם: הָבוּ לָכֶם אֲנָשִׁים חֲכָמִים וּנְבֹנִים וִידֻעִים לְשִׁבְטֵיכֶם
יד וַאֲשִׂימֵם בְּרָאשֵׁיכֶם: וַתַּעֲנוּ אֹתִי וַתֹּאמְרוּ טוֹב־הַדָּבָר אֲשֶׁר־דִּבַּרְתָּ
טו לַעֲשׂוֹת: וָאֶקַּח אֶת־רָאשֵׁי שִׁבְטֵיכֶם אֲנָשִׁים חֲכָמִים וִידֻעִים וָאֶתֵּן אֹתָם
רָאשִׁים עֲלֵיכֶם שָׂרֵי אֲלָפִים וְשָׂרֵי מֵאוֹת וְשָׂרֵי חֲמִשִּׁים וְשָׂרֵי עֲשָׂרֹת
טז וְשֹׁטְרִים לְשִׁבְטֵיכֶם: וָאֲצַוֶּה אֶת־שֹׁפְטֵיכֶם בָּעֵת הַהִוא לֵאמֹר שָׁמֹעַ
יז בֵּין־אֲחֵיכֶם וּשְׁפַטְתֶּם צֶדֶק בֵּין־אִישׁ וּבֵין־אָחִיו וּבֵין גֵּרוֹ: לֹא־תַכִּירוּ פָנִים
בַּמִּשְׁפָּט כַּקָּטֹן כַּגָּדֹל תִּשְׁמָעוּן לֹא תָגוּרוּ מִפְּנֵי־אִישׁ כִּי הַמִּשְׁפָּט לֵאלֹהִים
יח הוּא וְהַדָּבָר אֲשֶׁר יִקְשֶׁה מִכֶּם תַּקְרִבוּן אֵלַי וּשְׁמַעְתִּיו: וָאֲצַוֶּה אֶתְכֶם בָּעֵת
יט הַהִוא אֵת כָּל־הַדְּבָרִים אֲשֶׁר תַּעֲשׂוּן: וַנִּסַּע מֵחֹרֵב וַנֵּלֶךְ אֵת כָּל־הַמִּדְבָּר
הַגָּדוֹל וְהַנּוֹרָא הַהוּא אֲשֶׁר רְאִיתֶם דֶּרֶךְ הַר הָאֱמֹרִי כַּאֲשֶׁר צִוָּה יְהוָה

---

12. טָרְחֲכֶם — *Your cumbrance* . . . quarrels which do not involve monetary claims.

וּמַשַּׂאֲכֶם — *And your burden* . . . in (providing) for the needs of the public.

וְרִיבְכֶם — *And your strife* . . . in matters of law and monetary claims. Now this he related to them to remind them of their transgression, that even though he had told them the good tiding that they would enter the Land without a battle, and that this would be a great accomplishment, bringing honor far greater than all their possessions and affairs (here) in the wilderness, (nonetheless,) they did not cease to strive with one another, so that it became necessary to appoint various levels of judges to the extent that every ten of them needed a private judge. (Now,) this could only be due to the evil in their heart.

19. וַנֵּלֶךְ אֵת כָּל הַמִּדְבָּר הַגָּדוֹל וְהַנּוֹרָא — *And we went through all that great and dreadful wilderness.* A path which no man had traversed because of its many serpents and scorpions and their monstrous size, as it says, נָחָשׁ שָׂרָף וְעַקְרָב, *serpents, fiery serpents and scorpions* (8:15). Our Sages have indeed told us that there were 'serpents like beams and scorpions (as large) as bows' (*Sifre*). All this, God, the Blessed One, did to shorten the way for them so that they could enter the Land at

NOTES

have set before you the land; come and possess the land. The *Sforno* explains the word אֶרֶץ, *land,* in the first part of the verse as meaning 'inhabitants of the land' while אֶרֶץ in the second part refers literally to the land itself. In this manner, there is no redundancy in the verse.

12. טָרְחֲכֶם וּמַשַּׂאֲכֶם וְרִיבְכֶם — *Your cumbrance and your burden and your strife.* The *Sforno's* commentary on this verse explains the seeming parenthetical nature of verses 12 through 18. Since Moses is relating the command of God to go up and conquer the Land, which is frustrated by their insistence upon sending spies, it is difficult to understand the insertion of these verses which speak of Israel's quarrels, contentions and strife resulting in the appointment of judges. The *Sforno,* however, shows the link between the command to enter the Land and the failure of the Israelites to appreciate how insignificant were their cumbrances and quarrels in view of the great gift of *Eretz Yisrael* which awaits them.

19. וַנֵּלֶךְ אֵת כָּל הַמִּדְבָּר הַגָּדוֹל וְהַנּוֹרָא — *And we went through all that great and dreadful wilderness.* The *Sforno* explains that God led

כ אֱלֹהֵינוּ אֹתָנוּ וַנָּבֹא עַד קָדֵשׁ בַּרְנֵעַ: וָאֹמַר אֲלֵכֶם בָּאתֶם עַד־הַר הָאֱמֹרִי
כא אֲשֶׁר־יהוה אֱלֹהֵינוּ נֹתֵן לָנוּ: רְאֵה נָתַן יהוה אֱלֹהֶיךָ לְפָנֶיךָ אֶת־הָאָרֶץ
עֲלֵה רֵשׁ כַּאֲשֶׁר דִּבֶּר יהוה אֱלֹהֵי אֲבֹתֶיךָ לָךְ אַל־תִּירָא וְאַל־תֵּחָת:
שלישי כב וַתִּקְרְבוּן אֵלַי כֻּלְּכֶם וַתֹּאמְרוּ נִשְׁלְחָה אֲנָשִׁים לְפָנֵינוּ וְיַחְפְּרוּ־לָנוּ
אֶת־הָאָרֶץ וְיָשִׁבוּ אֹתָנוּ דָּבָר אֶת־הַדֶּרֶךְ אֲשֶׁר נַעֲלֶה־בָּהּ וְאֵת הֶעָרִים אֲשֶׁר
כג נָבֹא אֲלֵיהֶן: וַיִּיטַב בְּעֵינַי הַדָּבָר וָאֶקַּח מִכֶּם שְׁנֵים עָשָׂר אֲנָשִׁים אִישׁ

---

once, *before their pots could feel the thorns* (based on *Psalms* 58:10) and increase their transgression. But all this was insufficient for, in the interim, they sinned through the 'murmerers' (*Numbers* 11:1) and with 'lusting' (ibid. 11:4) and finally, with the 'spies' (ibid. 13).

21. עֲלֵה רֵשׁ — *Go up, take possession.* For no man will stand before you.

22. וַתִּקְרְבוּן אֵלַי כֻּלְּכֶם — *And you came near to me, every one of you.* Even though you had leaders who were appointed over you to attend to public needs, yet you all came.

נִשְׁלְחָה אֲנָשִׁים — *Let us send men.* We will choose men and send them (to spy out the Land). (However) God, the Exalted One, did not agree to this, and said to Moses, שְׁלַח לְךָ, *You send* (*Numbers* 13:2), i.e., he (Moses) was to choose the men, not they, lest they choose common men who will compound their wickedness. Therefore, Moses chose כֻּלָּם אֲנָשִׁים, *All of them men* (ibid. 13:3), and among them Joshua and Caleb; and even the wicked ones among them, although they acted in an evil manner when they said that it is impossible to conquer it (the Land), still they did not brazenly state that the Land was bad. Rather, they spoke well of it and in such a manner that eventually (the people) repented, as it says, וַתַּעֲנוּ וַתֹּאמְרוּ אֵלַי, חָטָאנוּ לַה׳ . . . וַתָּשֻׁבוּ וַתִּבְכּוּ לִפְנֵי ה׳, *Then you answered and said to me: We have sinned against* HASHEM (1:41) . . . *And you returned and wept before* HASHEM (1:45).

23. וַיִּיטַב בְּעֵינַי הַדָּבָר — *And the thing pleased me well* . . . because I thought you did not doubt the word of God, the Blessed One, that the Land was good and that you

NOTES

Israel through that part of the wilderness which men normally never traversed due to the terrible conditions which prevailed there. This He did so as to shorten their way, in the hope that by reducing their difficult stay in the desert, it would diminish the opportunity to rebel against Moses and God. Unfortunately, this proved to be of no avail. The expression used by the *Sforno*, בְּטֶרֶם יָבִינוּ סִירֹתֵיהֶם אָטָד, 'before their pots could feel the thorns,' symbolizes an uncertain state wherein one is in imminent danger of harm befalling him.

22. וַתִּקְרְבוּן אֵלַי כֻּלְּכֶם — *And you came near to me, every one of you*. The *Sforno* interprets this statement of Moses as one that is critical of Israel's behavior when they approached him en masse. Since they had representatives, it would have been more seemly for these leaders to come and suggest to Moses that he send spies, rather than for all of them to descend upon him with their request.

נִשְׁלְחָה אֲנָשִׁים — *Let us send men*. God did not object as such to sending the spies, but He insisted that Moses be the one to choose them. By selecting men of stature, who were basically decent and pious, there was a better chance that this mission would be beneficial. Although unfortunately this did not materialize, still, the inherent honesty and stature of the spies did not permit them to deny the excellent character of the Land, and as a result there was no total rejection. Consequently, there was subsequent regret on the part of many for losing faith in God and Moses, and they later wept and repented.

23. וַיִּיטַב בְּעֵינַי הַדָּבָר — *And the thing pleased me well*. The *Sforno* links this verse to verse

כד אֶחָד לַשָּׁבֶט: וַיִּפְנוּ וַיַּעֲלוּ הָהָרָה וַיָּבֹאוּ עַד־נַחַל אֶשְׁכֹּל וַיְרַגְּלוּ אֹתָהּ:
כה וַיִּקְחוּ בְיָדָם מִפְּרִי הָאָרֶץ וַיּוֹרִדוּ אֵלֵינוּ וַיָּשִׁבוּ אֹתָנוּ דָבָר וַיֹּאמְרוּ טוֹבָה
כו הָאָרֶץ אֲשֶׁר־יְהוָה אֱלֹהֵינוּ נֹתֵן לָנוּ: וְלֹא אֲבִיתֶם לַעֲלֹת וַתַּמְרוּ אֶת־פִּי
כז יְהוָה אֱלֹהֵיכֶם: וַתֵּרָגְנוּ בְאָהֳלֵיכֶם וַתֹּאמְרוּ בְּשִׂנְאַת יְהוָה אֹתָנוּ הוֹצִיאָנוּ
כח מֵאֶרֶץ מִצְרָיִם לָתֵת אֹתָנוּ בְּיַד הָאֱמֹרִי לְהַשְׁמִידֵנוּ: אָנָה ׀ אֲנַחְנוּ עֹלִים
אַחֵינוּ הֵמַסּוּ אֶת־לְבָבֵנוּ לֵאמֹר עַם גָּדוֹל וָרָם מִמֶּנּוּ עָרִים גְּדֹלֹת וּבְצוּרֹת
כט בַּשָּׁמָיִם וְגַם־בְּנֵי עֲנָקִים רָאִינוּ שָׁם: וָאֹמַר אֲלֵכֶם לֹא־תַעַרְצוּן וְלֹא־
ל תִירְאוּן מֵהֶם: יְהוָה אֱלֹהֵיכֶם הַהֹלֵךְ לִפְנֵיכֶם הוּא יִלָּחֵם לָכֶם כְּכֹל אֲשֶׁר
לא עָשָׂה אִתְּכֶם בְּמִצְרַיִם לְעֵינֵיכֶם: וּבַמִּדְבָּר אֲשֶׁר רָאִיתָ אֲשֶׁר נְשָׂאֲךָ יְהוָה

---

would conquer it, but you wished to select that portion which would be best for you (to settle) now, as you said, וְאֵת הֶעָרִים אֲשֶׁר נָבֹא אֲלֵיהֶן, *And the cities unto which we shall come* (1:22). And this (you wished to do) because you knew that you would not conquer the entire (land) in one year, as it says, לֹא אֲגָרֶשֶׁנּוּ מִפָּנֶיךָ בְּשָׁנָה אֶחָת, *I will not drive them out from before you in one year* (Exodus 23:29).

24. וַיָּבֹאוּ עַד נַחַל אֶשְׁכֹּל — *And came to the valley of Eshkol.* As it says, עֲלוּ זֶה בַּנֶּגֶב, *Go up here in the south* (Numbers 13:17), this being the side where Israel was (then situated), next to Kadesh Barnea, which is in the south of *Eretz Yisrael* as explained (regarding) the boundaries of the land (Numbers 34:4).

25. וַיֹּאמְרוּ טוֹבָה הָאָרֶץ — *And said: 'The Land is good.'* Even the wicked ones admitted that it was good, as they said, וְגַם זָבַת חָלָב וּדְבַשׁ הוּא, *and surely it flows with milk and honey* (Numbers 13:27).

26. וְלֹא אֲבִיתֶם לַעֲלֹת — *Yet, you would not go up.* You revealed your wickedness, (demonstrating) that this mission was not to select that part of the land which would benefit you most (during this initial period) as I had thought and you had indicated. Rather, your intent in sending (the spies) was to determine if you would be able to conquer it. This you did because you did not believe that God could give it to you. Hence, when the spies told you that the people were (very) strong, *you would not go up.*

27. בְּשִׂנְאַת ה' אֹתָנוּ — *Because HASHEM hated us . . .* because we worshiped Egyptian gods.

לָתֵת אֹתָנוּ בְּיַד הָאֱמֹרִי — *To deliver us into the hands of the Emorites.* For, although He is able to conquer the Emorites and kill them, (nonetheless) He will deliver us into their hands in revenge (for our sin).

31. אֲשֶׁר נְשָׂאֲךָ ה' אֱלֹהֶיךָ — *That HASHEM your God bore you . . .* (through this) *great and dreadful wilderness* (v. 19), and if He wanted to exact vengeance of you, He would have abandoned you in the hands of the serpents and scorpions of the wilderness.

NOTES

26. At first, Moses thought that the intention of Israel was good and proper. Since the total conquest of *Eretz Yisrael* would take a considerable amount of time, it was fitting to find the best place to establish a foothold in the Land which would serve as a base for their eventual total conquest. Later, however, he realized that this was not their true intention, for they became convinced that God would not simply *give* them the Land but it would be

אֱלֹהֶיךָ כַּאֲשֶׁר יִשָּׂא־אִישׁ אֶת־בְּנוֹ בְּכָל־הַדֶּרֶךְ אֲשֶׁר הֲלַכְתֶּם עַד־בֹּאֲכֶם
לב-לג עַד־הַמָּקוֹם הַזֶּה: וּבַדָּבָר הַזֶּה אֵינְכֶם מַאֲמִינִם בַּיהוָה אֱלֹהֵיכֶם: הַהֹלֵךְ
לִפְנֵיכֶם בַּדֶּרֶךְ לָתוּר לָכֶם מָקוֹם לַחֲנֹתְכֶם בָּאֵשׁ ׀ לַיְלָה לַרְאֹתְכֶם בַּדֶּרֶךְ
לד אֲשֶׁר תֵּלְכוּ־בָהּ וּבֶעָנָן יוֹמָם: וַיִּשְׁמַע יהוה אֶת־קוֹל דִּבְרֵיכֶם וַיִּקְצֹף וַיִּשָּׁבַע
לה לֵאמֹר: אִם־יִרְאֶה אִישׁ בָּאֲנָשִׁים הָאֵלֶּה הַדּוֹר הָרָע הַזֶּה אֵת הָאָרֶץ
לו הַטּוֹבָה אֲשֶׁר נִשְׁבַּעְתִּי לָתֵת לַאֲבֹתֵיכֶם: זוּלָתִי כָּלֵב בֶּן־יְפֻנֶּה הוּא יִרְאֶנָּה
וְלוֹ־אֶתֵּן אֶת־הָאָרֶץ אֲשֶׁר דָּרַךְ־בָּהּ וּלְבָנָיו יַעַן אֲשֶׁר מִלֵּא אַחֲרֵי יהוה:
לז-לח גַּם־בִּי הִתְאַנַּף יהוה בִּגְלַלְכֶם לֵאמֹר גַּם־אַתָּה לֹא־תָבֹא שָׁם: יְהוֹשֻׁעַ

---

33. לָתוּר לָכֶם מָקוֹם לַחֲנֹתְכֶם — *To seek out a place for you to encamp* ... in that wilderness, as it says, לָתוּר לָהֶם מְנוּחָה, *to seek out a resting place for them* (*Numbers* 10:33). Now, all this teaches His love and compassion for you.

34. אֶת קוֹל דִּבְרֵיכֶם — *The voice of your words.* The voice of unfounded (unjustified) weeping.

37. גַּם בִּי הִתְאַנַּף ה׳ בִּגְלַלְכֶם — *HASHEM was also angry with me for your sakes.* And this happened so as to fulfill (the decree of) בְּכִיָּה לְדוֹרוֹת, *weeping for generations*, as He had designated when He said, אִם לֹא כַּאֲשֶׁר דִּבַּרְתֶּם בְּאָזְנָי כֵּן אֶעֱשֶׂה לָכֶם, *Surely as you have spoken in My ears, so will I do to you* (*Numbers* 14:28), the speaking *in His ears* (referring to) when they said, נָשֵׁינוּ וְטַפֵּנוּ יִהְיוּ לָבַז, *Our wives and our little ones will be a prey* (ibid. 14:3). At this point, (Moses) related the event of his death, even though it would not occur until thirty-eight years later; (still) he incorporated it in the words of the Holy One, Blessed is He, spoken in the second year after they departed from Egypt, for it was then that He said, אִם יִרְאֶה אִישׁ בָּאֲנָשִׁים הָאֵלֶּה, *If any one of these men shall see* (v. 35), and He also said, וְטַפְּכֶם אֲשֶׁר אֲמַרְתֶּם לָבַז יִהְיֶה, *And your little ones that you said would be a prey* (v. 39). The intent (of His words) was that (indeed,) at the end they *would* be a prey, as the Psalmist (i.e., David) explained when he said, וַיִּשָּׂא יָדוֹ לָהֶם לְהַפִּיל אוֹתָם בַּמִּדְבָּר. וּלְהַפִּיל זַרְעָם בַּגּוֹיִם וּלְזָרוֹתָם בָּאֲרָצוֹת, *He swore concerning them that He would overthrow them in the wilderness; and that He would cast out their seed among the nations and scatter them in the lands* (*Psalms* 106:26,27), and so also Ezekiel testified when he said — גַּם אֲנִי נָשָׂאתִי אֶת יָדִי לָהֶם בַּמִּדְבָּר לְהָפִיץ אֹתָם בַּגּוֹיִם, *And I did also swear concerning them in the*

NOTES

necessary for *them* to conquer it. Hence, it was now necessary to determine if the Land could be invaded and the people defeated in battle. The spies' report established that this was not the case, for the inhabitants were too strong and their cities well fortified. Had Israel retained their faith in God, this report would have had no bearing on their entering the Land, but they had lost their trust in the Almighty, and as a result they doomed their generation to perish in the wilderness.

34. אֶת קוֹל דִּבְרֵיכֶם — *The voice of your words.* The *Sforno* notes that the expression קוֹל, *voice*, is added to the phrase דִּבְרֵיכֶם, *your words.* By listening to the *voice*, one can detect the true meaning of another's *words*. Although they cried, and the 'gates of tears are always open' (*Berachos* 32b), in this case it was meaningless, since their tears were unjustified; hence their words were unacceptable.

37. גַּם בִּי הִתְאַנַּף ה׳ בִּגְלַלְכֶם — *HASHEM was also angry with me for your sakes.* The explanation of the *Sforno's* commentary on this verse is as follows: Although the sin of the spies and God's decree took place in the second year after the Exodus, while the death of Moses occurred thirty-eight years later, the two are interwoven. When the Israelites lamented that their 'little ones would be a prey,' it was a self-imposed punishment, although it was one

בִּן־נוּן֙ הָעֹמֵ֣ד לְפָנֶ֔יךָ ה֖וּא יָ֣בֹא שָׁ֑מָּה אֹת֣וֹ חַזֵּ֔ק כִּי־ה֖וּא יַנְחִלֶ֥נָּה

רביעי לט אֶת־יִשְׂרָאֵֽל׃ וְטַפְּכֶם֙ אֲשֶׁ֤ר אֲמַרְתֶּם֙ לָבַ֣ז יִהְיֶ֔ה וּבְנֵיכֶ֗ם אֲשֶׁ֨ר לֹא־יָדְע֤וּ

מ הַיּוֹם֙ ט֣וֹב וָרָ֔ע הֵ֖מָּה יָבֹ֣אוּ שָׁ֑מָּה וְלָהֶ֣ם אֶתְּנֶ֔נָּה וְהֵ֖ם יִירָשֽׁוּהָ׃ וְאַתֶּ֖ם פְּנ֣וּ לָכֶ֑ם

מא וּסְע֥וּ הַמִּדְבָּ֖רָה דֶּ֥רֶךְ יַם־סֽוּף׃ וַתַּעֲנ֣וּ ׀ וַתֹּאמְר֣וּ אֵלַ֗י חָטָ֘אנוּ֮ לַֽיהוָה֒ אֲנַ֤חְנוּ

נַעֲלֶה֙ וְנִלְחַ֔מְנוּ כְּכֹ֥ל אֲשֶׁר־צִוָּ֖נוּ יְהוָ֣ה אֱלֹהֵ֑ינוּ וַֽתַּחְגְּר֗וּ אִ֚ישׁ אֶת־כְּלֵ֣י

מב מִלְחַמְתּ֔וֹ וַתָּהִ֖ינוּ לַעֲלֹ֥ת הָהָֽרָה׃ וַיֹּ֨אמֶר יְהוָ֜ה אֵלַ֗י אֱמֹ֤ר לָהֶם֙ לֹ֣א תַֽעֲלוּ֙

מג וְלֹֽא־תִלָּ֣חֲמ֔וּ כִּ֖י אֵינֶ֣נִּי בְּקִרְבְּכֶ֑ם וְלֹא֙ תִּנָּ֣גְפ֔וּ לִפְנֵ֖י אֹיְבֵיכֶֽם׃ וָאֲדַבֵּ֥ר אֲלֵיכֶ֖ם

מד וְלֹ֣א שְׁמַעְתֶּ֑ם וַתַּמְרוּ֙ אֶת־פִּ֣י יְהוָ֔ה וַתָּזִ֖דוּ וַתַּעֲל֥וּ הָהָֽרָה׃ וַיֵּצֵ֨א הָאֱמֹרִ֜י

הַיֹּשֵׁ֨ב בָּהָ֤ר הַהוּא֙ לִקְרַאתְכֶ֔ם וַיִּרְדְּפ֣וּ אֶתְכֶ֔ם כַּאֲשֶׁ֥ר תַּעֲשֶׂ֖ינָה הַדְּבֹרִ֑ים

מה וַיַּכְּת֥וּ אֶתְכֶ֛ם בְּשֵׂעִ֖יר עַד־חָרְמָֽה׃ וַתָּשֻׁ֥בוּ וַתִּבְכּ֖וּ לִפְנֵ֣י יְהוָ֑ה וְלֹֽא־שָׁמַ֤ע

---

wilderness to scatter them among the nations (*Ezekiel* 20:23). Now, by telling them his personal fate and incorporating it in the words of the Holy One, Blessed is He, he informed them that his being prevented from entering the Land with them would cause the severity of the decree, regarding their little ones becoming a prey for generations, to be increased, and this is what the singer (David) attests to when he says: וַיַּקְצִיפוּ עַל מֵי מְרִיבָה וַיֵּרַע לְמֹשֶׁה בַּעֲבוּרָם . . . לֹא הִשְׁמִידוּ אֶת הָעַמִּים . . . וַיִּתְעָרְבוּ בַגּוֹיִם . . . וַיִּחַר אַף ה׳ בְּעַמּוֹ, *They angered Him also at the waters of Meribah, and it went ill with Moses because of them . . . they did not destroy the peoples . . . but mingled themselves with the nations . . . therefore, the wrath of HASHEM was kindled against His people* (*Psalms* 106: 32,34,35,40).

45. וְלֹא שָׁמַע ה׳ בְּקֹלְכֶם — *But HASHEM did not hearken to your voice* . . . due to the desecration of the Name (חִלּוּל הַשֵּׁם) which they had committed, (a sin) for which repentance is insufficient and which can only be purged through death. Also, this was a decree accompanied by an oath, since Moses and Joshua and Caleb had (all) urged them (lit., awakened them) to repent but they only did so later because they feared punishment. Therefore, their repentance did not suffice to eliminate the punishment decreed in this world, similar to the (episodes) of Cain, and Saul with the Amalekites, and that of Eli's sons.

NOTES

that would not be implemented until many years later when they would be exiled from their land. Now, had Moses entered *Eretz Yisrael* with them, there would have been no exile, which ironically would have been disastrous for Israel because when they ultimately sinned, God's wrath would have been poured out upon them and they would ח״ו have been annihilated. Since Moses did not accompany them into the Land, the wrath of heaven was deflected upon 'the trees and rocks,' and although Israel was exiled, they still survived. In exile, the ominous prediction regarding their children, which God had sworn to fulfill (see the *Sforno* on *Numbers* 14:28 where he quotes the same verses from *Psalms* and *Ezekiel* cited here), was indeed fulfilled but the people of Israel endured. Hence, the fact that Moses did not enter *Eretz Yisrael* was ultimately for the benefit of Israel, which is stated explicitly in chapter 3, verse 26, *and God was angry with me for your sake*. See the *Sforno's* commentary on that verse. This explains why Moses mentions God's anger with him when he reviews the sin of the spies and God's response to it.

45. וְלֹא שָׁמַע ה׳ בְּקֹלְכֶם — *But HASHEM did not hearken to your voice*. The *Sforno* offers two reasons for God's rejection of Israel's repentance. The first is that the sin of חִלּוּל הַשֵּׁם, *the profaning of God's name*, cannot be expiated through repentance. Only death can remove this sin and complete the process of repentance, purging and cleansing, as our Sages teach us in tractate *Yoma* 86a. The second

מו יְהוָה בְּקֹלְכֶם וְלֹא הֶאֱזִין אֲלֵיכֶם: וַתֵּשְׁבוּ בְקָדֵשׁ יָמִים רַבִּים כַּיָּמִים אֲשֶׁר

ב

א יְשַׁבְתֶּם: וַנֵּפֶן וַנִּסַּע הַמִּדְבָּרָה דֶּרֶךְ יַם־סוּף כַּאֲשֶׁר דִּבֶּר יְהוָה אֵלָי וַנָּסָב

חמישי ב אֶת־הַר־שֵׂעִיר יָמִים רַבִּים: וַיֹּאמֶר יְהוָה אֵלַי לֵאמֹר:

ג־ד רַב־לָכֶם סֹב אֶת־הָהָר הַזֶּה פְּנוּ לָכֶם צָפֹנָה: וְאֶת־הָעָם צַו לֵאמֹר אַתֶּם

עֹבְרִים בִּגְבוּל אֲחֵיכֶם בְּנֵי־עֵשָׂו הַיֹּשְׁבִים בְּשֵׂעִיר וְיִירְאוּ מִכֶּם וְנִשְׁמַרְתֶּם

ה מְאֹד: אַל־תִּתְגָּרוּ בָם כִּי לֹא־אֶתֵּן לָכֶם מֵאַרְצָם עַד מִדְרַךְ כַּף־רָגֶל

ו כִּי־יְרֻשָּׁה לְעֵשָׂו נָתַתִּי אֶת־הַר שֵׂעִיר: אֹכֶל תִּשְׁבְּרוּ מֵאִתָּם בַּכֶּסֶף

ז וַאֲכַלְתֶּם וְגַם־מַיִם תִּכְרוּ מֵאִתָּם בַּכֶּסֶף וּשְׁתִיתֶם: כִּי יְהוָה אֱלֹהֶיךָ בֵּרַכְךָ

בְּכֹל מַעֲשֵׂה יָדֶךָ יָדַע לֶכְתְּךָ אֶת־הַמִּדְבָּר הַגָּדֹל הַזֶּה זֶה ׀ אַרְבָּעִים שָׁנָה

וְלֹא הֶאֱזִין אֲלֵיכֶם — *Nor gave ear to you* . . . to postpone (the implementation) or even to cancel the decree regarding the children after the death of the fathers. And thus he admonished them that their repentance was not complete (i.e., sincere), and therefore they accomplished nothing, even with their tears.

II

7. יָדַע לֶכְתְּךָ — *He has known your walking.* He supplied you with all the necessities (of life). The expression יָדַע, *He has known*, is similar to, וַיֵּדַע אֱלֹהִים, *And God knew* (*took cognizance*) (*Exodus* 2:25); יְדַעְתִּיךָ בְשֵׁם, *I have known you by name* (ibid. 33:12); אֲשֶׁר יְדָעוֹ ה׳ פָּנִים אֶל פָּנִים, *Whom* HASHEM *knew face to face* (34:10); מָה אָדָם וַתֵּדָעֵהוּ, *What is man that you recognize him?* (*Psalms* 144:3), and many other such (expressions). This expression (*known*) is said of God, the Exalted One, because all actions (of God), the Blessed One, are effected by Divine knowledge.

NOTES

reason is because God had sworn to punish them for the sin of the spies, and our Sages in tractate *Rosh Hashanah* teach us that a decree from on High that is accompanied by an oath 'cannot be torn asunder' (18a). As mentioned above, the decree denying this generation the right to enter the Land was one to which the Almighty swore (*Numbers* 14:28). The reason for this adamant stand on the part of God was due to their refusal to repent of their own volition. Their subsequent willingness to do so was unacceptable since it was only due to pressure and fear of punishment. The *Sforno* cites three other examples of repentance which were blemished and inadequate: First, that of Cain, who said *my sin is too great to be forgiven*, for he himself realized that he waited too long to voice his regret (see the *Sforno's* commentary in *Genesis* 4:13). The second is that of Saul after he returned from the campaign against Amalek but failed to fulfill his mission completely and as a result his kingship was stripped from him. Although he said, *I have sinned for I have transgressed*, and asked for pardon, his plea was rejected, for here also it was motivated by fear of punishment and was not sufficiently sincere (*I Samuel* 15:24,25). Finally, that of the house of Eli is cited by the *Sforno* where God swore that *the iniquity of the house of Eli will not be purged with sacrifice or offering* (*I Samuel* 3:14) for reasons similar to those explained above.

45. וְלֹא הֶאֱזִין אֲלֵיכֶם — *Nor gave ear to you.* The *Sforno's* interpretation resolves the seeming repetitive nature of the phraseology in this verse. וְלֹא שָׁמַע ה׳, HASHEM *did not hearken*, refers to their repentance, while וְלֹא הֶאֱזִין, *nor gave ear*, refers to God's refusal to postpone the punishment of this generation or to commute the sentence for the next generation.

II

7. יָדַע לֶכְתְּךָ — *He has known your walking.* The *Rambam* in his *Mishneh Torah* (*Hilchos Yesodai Hatorah* 2:10) discusses the concept of God's knowledge. He explains that unlike man whose being and knowledge are separate, since his knowledge is gained from outside himself, God is 'He Who knows, is known and

ח יהוה אֱלֹהֶיךָ עִמָּךְ לֹא חָסַרְתָּ דָּבָר: וַנַּעֲבֹר מֵאֵת אַחֵינוּ בְנֵי־עֵשָׂו הַיֹּשְׁבִים
בְּשֵׂעִיר מִדֶּרֶךְ הָעֲרָבָה מֵאֵילַת וּמֵעֶצְיֹן גָּבֶר וַנֵּפֶן וַנַּעֲבֹר
ט דֶּרֶךְ מִדְבַּר מוֹאָב: וַיֹּאמֶר יהוה אֵלַי אַל־תָּצַר אֶת־מוֹאָב וְאַל־תִּתְגָּר בָּם
מִלְחָמָה כִּי לֹא־אֶתֵּן לְךָ מֵאַרְצוֹ יְרֻשָּׁה כִּי לִבְנֵי־לוֹט נָתַתִּי אֶת־עָר
י־יא יְרֻשָּׁה: הָאֵמִים לְפָנִים יָשְׁבוּ בָהּ עַם גָּדוֹל וְרַב וָרָם כָּעֲנָקִים: רְפָאִים יֵחָשְׁבוּ
יב אַף־הֵם כָּעֲנָקִים וְהַמֹּאָבִים יִקְרְאוּ לָהֶם אֵמִים: וּבְשֵׂעִיר יָשְׁבוּ הַחֹרִים
לְפָנִים וּבְנֵי עֵשָׂו יִירָשׁוּם וַיַּשְׁמִידוּם מִפְּנֵיהֶם וַיֵּשְׁבוּ תַּחְתָּם כַּאֲשֶׁר עָשָׂה
יג יִשְׂרָאֵל לְאֶרֶץ יְרֻשָּׁתוֹ אֲשֶׁר־נָתַן יהוה לָהֶם: עַתָּה קֻמוּ וְעִבְרוּ לָכֶם

לֹא חָסַרְתָּ דָּבָר — *You have lacked nothing.* Hence, they will realize that you are not buying necessary things, but your purchases are motivated (solely) by brotherly feelings, so that they might have benefit (from you). Another reason is that they will come to your (camp) and observe the deeds of God and His wonders.

10. הָאֵמִים לְפָנִים — *The Emim (dwelt there) aforetime.* Because the children of Lot were definitely not the heirs of Abraham according to law, (it is necessary) to state that God also gave them their land as He did to the children of Esau. The proof (lies in the fact) that they both conquered the land (given to them) in a manner contrary to the natural laws (lit., 'custom') of the world.

12. וַיַּשְׁמִידוּם -- *And they destroyed them.* Esau and Moab (both) destroyed and laid waste more territory than they needed for their own settlement, in order to destroy all those who dwelt there previously and deter them from rising up and reclaiming the land. Both Moab and Esau did not settle the entire (original) area of the Horites and the Emim whom they had destroyed. Now being that Mt. Seir reached the border of Moab, near which there was no settlement of the children of Esau, and likewise the border of Moab reached the wilderness next to which there was no settlement of the children of Moab; therefore (it was necessary to) say that, nonetheless, they (the Israelites) were not to cross over the borders of either one of these lands.

כַּאֲשֶׁר עָשָׂה יִשְׂרָאֵל — *As Israel did ...* at the time when the Torah was written, having already conquered the great and mighty kings Sichon and Og in a brief period, contrary to the natural laws of the world.

13. עַתָּה קֻמוּ — *Now rise up.* Now since it is prohibited for you to pass over the border of these two (peoples), קֻמוּ וְעִבְרוּ לָכֶם אֶת נַחַל זָרֶד, *Rise up and bring yourselves over the brook of Zered* (which is beyond the boundary of both these nations), and from there you will be able to pass outside the borders of both until you (reach) the Jordan.

NOTES

is the knowledge (of Himself), all these being One.' This is what the *Sforno* is referring to when he states that the verb *known* is used in the sense that Divine action is effected by Divine knowledge. See the *Sforno's* commentary on *Numbers* 7:89 and the notes there.

לֹא חָסַרְתָּ דָּבָר — *You have lacked nothing.* The previous verse (v. 6) speaks of purchasing food and water from the children of Esau in Seir, followed by this verse which seemingly precludes the necessity to do so, since God had provided Israel with all their needs. The *Sforno* explains that Israel was told to buy food and drink from Esau, not because they were in need of them, but in order that their 'brothers'

יד אֶת־נַחַל זָרֶד וַנַּעֲבֹר אֶת־נַחַל זָרֶד: וְהַיָּמִים אֲשֶׁר־הָלַכְנוּ | מִקָּדֵשׁ בַּרְנֵעַ

עַד אֲשֶׁר־עָבַרְנוּ אֶת־נַחַל זֶרֶד שְׁלֹשִׁים וּשְׁמֹנֶה שָׁנָה עַד־תֹּם כָּל־הַדּוֹר

טו אַנְשֵׁי הַמִּלְחָמָה מִקֶּרֶב הַמַּחֲנֶה כַּאֲשֶׁר נִשְׁבַּע יהוה לָהֶם: וְגַם יַד־יהוה

טז הָיְתָה בָּם לְהֻמָּם מִקֶּרֶב הַמַּחֲנֶה עַד תֻּמָּם: וַיְהִי כַאֲשֶׁר־תַּמּוּ כָּל־אַנְשֵׁי

יז הַמִּלְחָמָה לָמוּת מִקֶּרֶב הָעָם: וַיְדַבֵּר יהוה אֵלַי לֵאמֹר:

יח-יט אַתָּה עֹבֵר הַיּוֹם אֶת־גְּבוּל מוֹאָב אֶת־עָר: וְקָרַבְתָּ מוּל בְּנֵי עַמּוֹן

אַל־תְּצֻרֵם וְאַל־תִּתְגָּר בָּם כִּי לֹא־אֶתֵּן מֵאֶרֶץ בְּנֵי־עַמּוֹן לְךָ יְרֻשָּׁה כִּי

כ לִבְנֵי־לוֹט נְתַתִּיהָ יְרֻשָּׁה: אֶרֶץ־רְפָאִים תֵּחָשֵׁב אַף־הִוא רְפָאִים יָשְׁבוּ־בָהּ

כא לְפָנִים וְהָעַמֹּנִים יִקְרְאוּ לָהֶם זַמְזֻמִּים: עַם גָּדוֹל וְרַב וָרָם כָּעֲנָקִים וַיַּשְׁמִידֵם

כב יהוה מִפְּנֵיהֶם וַיִּירָשֻׁם וַיֵּשְׁבוּ תַחְתָּם: כַּאֲשֶׁר עָשָׂה לִבְנֵי עֵשָׂו הַיֹּשְׁבִים

בְּשֵׂעִיר אֲשֶׁר הִשְׁמִיד אֶת־הַחֹרִי מִפְּנֵיהֶם וַיִּירָשֻׁם וַיֵּשְׁבוּ תַחְתָּם עַד הַיּוֹם

כג הַזֶּה: וְהָעַוִּים הַיֹּשְׁבִים בַּחֲצֵרִים עַד־עַזָּה כַּפְתֹּרִים הַיֹּצְאִים מִכַּפְתֹּר

---

20. אֶרֶץ רְפָאִים תֵּחָשֵׁב אַף הִוא — *That also is considered a land of Rephaim* . . . and without a doubt, the children of Ammon were not capable of destroying them, but God, the Blessed One, did it for them . . .

22. כַּאֲשֶׁר עָשָׂה לִבְנֵי עֵשָׂו — *As He did for the children of Esau.* He drove out the inhabitants because they were dwelling in the land of Seir.

23. וְהָעַוִּים הַיֹּשְׁבִים בַּחֲצֵרִים עַד עַזָּה — *And the Avim that dwelt in villages as far as Gaza.* Although they were the children of Esau or the children of the Philistines to whom Abraham had sworn (that he would do them no harm), still, Israel did not refrain from conquering their land. The reason for this was because Israel did not find the land in their possession, since the Caphtorim, who came out of Caphtor seeking a place to settle (lit., 'to find rest'), were then the majority of its inhabitants having destroyed the Avim. It was from the hands of these Caphtorim that Israel conquered the land.

NOTES

might benefit from their presence and be assured of Israel's good will toward them. An additional reason is that through this contact the inhabitants of Seir would be afforded the opportunity of witnessing the wonders of God manifested in the camp of Israel.

10-22. הָאֵמִים לְפָנִים . . . וַיַּשְׁמִידוּם . . . כַּאֲשֶׁר עָשָׂה יִשְׂרָאֵל . . . אֶרֶץ רְפָאִים . . . כַּאֲשֶׁר עָשָׂה לִבְנֵי עֵשָׂו — *The Emim (dwelt there) aforetime* . . . *and they destroyed them* . . . *as Israel did* . . . *a land of Rephaim* . . . *As He did for the children of Esau.* Land given to a people by God belongs to them by Divine right, and therefore the Israelites were not permitted to wage war against them so as to conquer their territory. The Torah tells us that the children of Esau and the children of Lot (Moab and Ammon) were given Seir, Ar and part of the Rephaim's territory respectively. The conquest of these lands, inhabited by such mighty people as the Emim, Horites and Zamzumim, by the children of Esau and Lot attests to the fact that it was Divinely ordained, just as the conquest of Canaan by the Israelites was a fulfillment of God's promise to Abraham.

23. וְהָעַוִּים הַיֹּשְׁבִים בַּחֲצֵרִים עַד עַזָּה — *And the Avim that dwelt in villages as far as Gaza.* Although the Israelites were forbidden to expropriate any land which belonged to Esau, Moab or Ammon, as mentioned above, if any of these territories were conquered by other nations, Israel was permitted to wage war against them and take the land for themselves. The Torah already told us that this was the reason Israel was permitted to take Cheshbon from Sichon although originally it had belonged to Moab (*Numbers* 21:26). The *Sforno* explains that the same holds true for the land

כד הַשְׁמִידָם וַיֵּשְׁבוּ תַחְתָּם: קוּמוּ סְּעוּ וְעִבְרוּ אֶת־נַחַל אַרְנֹן רְאֵה נָתַתִּי בְיָדְךָ
אֶת־סִיחֹן מֶלֶךְ־חֶשְׁבּוֹן הָאֱמֹרִי וְאֶת־אַרְצוֹ הָחֵל רָשׁ וְהִתְגָּר בּוֹ מִלְחָמָה:
כה הַיּוֹם הַזֶּה אָחֵל תֵּת פַּחְדְּךָ וְיִרְאָתְךָ עַל־פְּנֵי הָעַמִּים תַּחַת כָּל־הַשָּׁמָיִם
כו אֲשֶׁר יִשְׁמְעוּן שִׁמְעֲךָ וְרָגְזוּ וְחָלוּ מִפָּנֶיךָ: וָאֶשְׁלַח מַלְאָכִים מִמִּדְבַּר קְדֵמוֹת
כז אֶל־סִיחוֹן מֶלֶךְ חֶשְׁבּוֹן דִּבְרֵי שָׁלוֹם לֵאמֹר: אֶעְבְּרָה בְאַרְצֶךָ בַּדֶּרֶךְ בַּדֶּרֶךְ
כח אֵלֵךְ לֹא אָסוּר יָמִין וּשְׂמֹאול: אֹכֶל בַּכֶּסֶף תַּשְׁבִּרֵנִי וְאָכַלְתִּי וּמַיִם בַּכֶּסֶף
כט תִּתֶּן־לִי וְשָׁתִיתִי רַק אֶעְבְּרָה בְרַגְלָי: כַּאֲשֶׁר עָשׂוּ־לִי בְּנֵי עֵשָׂו הַיֹּשְׁבִים
בְּשֵׂעִיר וְהַמּוֹאָבִים הַיֹּשְׁבִים בְּעָר עַד אֲשֶׁר־אֶעֱבֹר אֶת־הַיַּרְדֵּן אֶל־הָאָרֶץ
ל אֲשֶׁר־יהוה אֱלֹהֵינוּ נֹתֵן לָנוּ: וְלֹא אָבָה סִיחֹן מֶלֶךְ חֶשְׁבּוֹן הַעֲבִרֵנוּ בּוֹ
כִּי־הִקְשָׁה יהוה אֱלֹהֶיךָ אֶת־רוּחוֹ וְאִמֵּץ אֶת־לְבָבוֹ לְמַעַן תִּתּוֹ בְיָדְךָ כַּיּוֹם
ששי לא הַזֶּה: וַיֹּאמֶר יהוה אֵלַי רְאֵה הַחִלֹּתִי תֵּת לְפָנֶיךָ
לב אֶת־סִיחֹן וְאֶת־אַרְצוֹ הָחֵל רָשׁ לָרֶשֶׁת אֶת־אַרְצוֹ: וַיֵּצֵא סִיחֹן לִקְרָאתֵנוּ
לג הוּא וְכָל־עַמּוֹ לַמִּלְחָמָה יָהְצָה: וַיִּתְּנֵהוּ יהוה אֱלֹהֵינוּ לְפָנֵינוּ וַנַּךְ אֹתוֹ
לד וְאֶת־בָּנָו וְאֶת־כָּל־עַמּוֹ: וַנִּלְכֹּד אֶת־כָּל־עָרָיו בָּעֵת הַהִוא וַנַּחֲרֵם
לה אֶת־כָּל־עִיר מְתִם וְהַנָּשִׁים וְהַטָּף לֹא הִשְׁאַרְנוּ שָׂרִיד: רַק הַבְּהֵמָה בָּזַזְנוּ
לו לָנוּ וּשְׁלַל הֶעָרִים אֲשֶׁר לָכָדְנוּ: מֵעֲרֹעֵר אֲשֶׁר עַל־שְׂפַת־נַחַל אַרְנֹן וְהָעִיר
אֲשֶׁר בַּנַּחַל וְעַד־הַגִּלְעָד לֹא הָיְתָה קִרְיָה אֲשֶׁר שָׂגְבָה מִמֶּנּוּ אֶת־הַכֹּל נָתַן
לז יהוה אֱלֹהֵינוּ לְפָנֵינוּ: רַק אֶל־אֶרֶץ בְּנֵי־עַמּוֹן לֹא קָרָבְתָּ כָּל־יַד נַחַל יַבֹּק
ג א וְעָרֵי הָהָר וְכֹל אֲשֶׁר־צִוָּה יהוה אֱלֹהֵינוּ: וַנֵּפֶן וַנַּעַל דֶּרֶךְ הַבָּשָׁן וַיֵּצֵא עוֹג
ב מֶלֶךְ־הַבָּשָׁן לִקְרָאתֵנוּ הוּא וְכָל־עַמּוֹ לַמִּלְחָמָה אֶדְרֶעִי: וַיֹּאמֶר יהוה אֵלַי
אַל־תִּירָא אֹתוֹ כִּי בְיָדְךָ נָתַתִּי אֹתוֹ וְאֶת־כָּל־עַמּוֹ וְאֶת־אַרְצוֹ וְעָשִׂיתָ לּוֹ
ג כַּאֲשֶׁר עָשִׂיתָ לְסִיחֹן מֶלֶךְ הָאֱמֹרִי אֲשֶׁר יוֹשֵׁב בְּחֶשְׁבּוֹן: וַיִּתֵּן יהוה אֱלֹהֵינוּ
בְּיָדֵנוּ גַּם אֶת־עוֹג מֶלֶךְ־הַבָּשָׁן וְאֶת־כָּל־עַמּוֹ וַנַּכֵּהוּ עַד־בִּלְתִּי הִשְׁאִיר־לוֹ
ד שָׂרִיד: וַנִּלְכֹּד אֶת־כָּל־עָרָיו בָּעֵת הַהִוא לֹא הָיְתָה קִרְיָה אֲשֶׁר לֹא־לָקַחְנוּ
ה מֵאִתָּם שִׁשִּׁים עִיר כָּל־חֶבֶל אַרְגֹּב מַמְלֶכֶת עוֹג בַּבָּשָׁן: כָּל־אֵלֶּה עָרִים
ו בְּצֻרֹת חוֹמָה גְבֹהָה דְּלָתַיִם וּבְרִיחַ לְבַד מֵעָרֵי הַפְּרָזִי הַרְבֵּה מְאֹד: וַנַּחֲרֵם
אוֹתָם כַּאֲשֶׁר עָשִׂינוּ לְסִיחֹן מֶלֶךְ חֶשְׁבּוֹן הַחֲרֵם כָּל־עִיר מְתִם הַנָּשִׁים
ז־ח וְהַטָּף: וְכָל־הַבְּהֵמָה וּשְׁלַל הֶעָרִים בַּזּוֹנוּ לָנוּ: וַנִּקַּח בָּעֵת הַהִוא אֶת־הָאָרֶץ
מִיַּד שְׁנֵי מַלְכֵי הָאֱמֹרִי אֲשֶׁר בְּעֵבֶר הַיַּרְדֵּן מִנַּחַל אַרְנֹן עַד־הַר חֶרְמוֹן:

---

30. כִּי הִקְשָׁה ה׳ אֱלֹהֶיךָ אֶת רוחו — *For HASHEM your God hardened his spirit . . .* not to allow the Israelites to pass his border.

וְאִמֵּץ אֶת לְבָבוֹ — *And made his heart obstinate . . .* to wage war against them.

NOTES

originally inhabited by the Avim, whom they were not permitted to displace, but which now was inhabited by the Caphtorim who were an Egyptian people. Just as Sichon the Emorite took over Cheshbon, so the Caphtorim took over the villages as far as Gaza . . .

30. . . . כִּי הִקְשָׁה ה׳ אֱלֹהֶיךָ . . . וְאִמֵּץ — *For HASHEM your God hardened . . . and made obstinate . . .* The *Sforno* explains that these two expressions, הִקְשָׁה, *hardened,* and אִמֵּץ, *made obstinate,* are not redundant. The former refers to Sichon's refusal to allow

ט־י צִידֹנִים יִקְרְאוּ לְחֶרְמוֹן שִׂרְיֹן וְהָאֱמֹרִי יִקְרְאוּ־לוֹ שְׂנִיר׃ כֹּל ׀ עָרֵי הַמִּישֹׁר
יא וְכָל־הַגִּלְעָד וְכָל־הַבָּשָׁן עַד־סַלְכָה וְאֶדְרֶעִי עָרֵי מַמְלֶכֶת עוֹג בַּבָּשָׁן׃ כִּי
רַק־עוֹג מֶלֶךְ הַבָּשָׁן נִשְׁאַר מִיֶּתֶר הָרְפָאִים הִנֵּה עַרְשׂוֹ עֶרֶשׂ בַּרְזֶל הֲלֹה
הִוא בְּרַבַּת בְּנֵי עַמּוֹן תֵּשַׁע אַמּוֹת אָרְכָּהּ וְאַרְבַּע אַמּוֹת רָחְבָּהּ
יב בְּאַמַּת־אִישׁ׃ וְאֶת־הָאָרֶץ הַזֹּאת יָרַשְׁנוּ בָּעֵת הַהִוא מֵעֲרֹעֵר אֲשֶׁר־עַל־
יג נַחַל אַרְנֹן וַחֲצִי הַר־הַגִּלְעָד וְעָרָיו נָתַתִּי לָרְאוּבֵנִי וְלַגָּדִי׃ וְיֶתֶר הַגִּלְעָד
וְכָל־הַבָּשָׁן מַמְלֶכֶת עוֹג נָתַתִּי לַחֲצִי שֵׁבֶט הַמְנַשֶּׁה כֹּל חֶבֶל הָאַרְגֹּב
יד לְכָל־הַבָּשָׁן הַהוּא יִקָּרֵא אֶרֶץ רְפָאִים׃ יָאִיר בֶּן־מְנַשֶּׁה לָקַח אֶת־כָּל־חֶבֶל
אַרְגֹּב עַד־גְּבוּל הַגְּשׁוּרִי וְהַמַּעֲכָתִי וַיִּקְרָא אֹתָם עַל־שְׁמוֹ אֶת־הַבָּשָׁן חַוֺּת
שביעי טו־טז יָאִיר עַד הַיּוֹם הַזֶּה׃ וּלְמָכִיר נָתַתִּי אֶת־הַגִּלְעָד׃ וְלָרְאוּבֵנִי וְלַגָּדִי נָתַתִּי
מִן־הַגִּלְעָד וְעַד־נַחַל אַרְנֹן תּוֹךְ הַנַּחַל וּגְבֻל וְעַד יַבֹּק הַנַּחַל גְּבוּל בְּנֵי עַמּוֹן׃
יז וְהָעֲרָבָה וְהַיַּרְדֵּן וּגְבֻל מִכִּנֶּרֶת וְעַד יָם הָעֲרָבָה יָם הַמֶּלַח תַּחַת אַשְׁדֹּת
יח הַפִּסְגָּה מִזְרָחָה׃ וָאֲצַו אֶתְכֶם בָּעֵת הַהִוא לֵאמֹר יהוה אֱלֹהֵיכֶם נָתַן לָכֶם
אֶת־הָאָרֶץ הַזֹּאת לְרִשְׁתָּהּ חֲלוּצִים תַּעַבְרוּ לִפְנֵי אֲחֵיכֶם בְּנֵי־יִשְׂרָאֵל
יט כָּל־בְּנֵי־חָיִל׃ רַק נְשֵׁיכֶם וְטַפְּכֶם וּמִקְנֵכֶם יָדַעְתִּי כִּי־מִקְנֶה רַב לָכֶם יֵשְׁבוּ
מפטיר כ בְּעָרֵיכֶם אֲשֶׁר נָתַתִּי לָכֶם׃ עַד אֲשֶׁר־יָנִיחַ יהוה ׀ לַאֲחֵיכֶם כָּכֶם וְיָרְשׁוּ

III

11. כִּי רַק עוֹג מֶלֶךְ הַבָּשָׁן נִשְׁאַר מִיֶּתֶר הָרְפָאִים — *For only Og king of Bashan remained of the remnant of the Rephaim.* Now the reason Og reigned in that district was because he alone *remained of the remnant of the Rephaim,* for in the battle with Amraphel (אַמְרָפֶל) and his allies when the Rephaim were smitten in Ashteros Karnaim, many Rephaim survived, but that remnant was smitten by the children of Ammon as explained above (2:20,21), and from that battle with Ammon he alone remained, and since he was mighty, as are all Rephaim, he became the king.

בְּאַמַּת אִישׁ — *After the cubit of a man* . . . (This means to say) a cubit according to the measurement of each one of those Rephaim. The phrase אִישׁ, *man,* indicates each and every one, similar to אִישׁ לְבִצְעוֹ מִקָּצֵהוּ, *Each one to his gain, one and all* (*Isaiah* 56:11) and וַיַּכּוּ אִישׁ אִישׁוֹ, *And they slew each one his man* (*I Kings* 20:20), and other such similar expressions. (The verse) says that although that bedstead was תֵּשַׁע אַמּוֹת אָרְכָּהּ, *nine cubits the length thereof,* according to the cubit of each of them, and according to the cubit measurement of the average person, it was without a doubt much larger than nine cubits, so we can then understand the great size of those giants and their strength. Yet, nonetheless, the children of Ammon destroyed them by the decree of God, the Blessed One, as explained above (2:21).

NOTES

Israel to pass through his land while the latter speaks of his decision to wage war against them.

III

11. בְּאַמַּת אִישׁ — *After the cubit of a man.* An אַמָּה, *cubit,* is a linear measure equal to the distance from the elbow to the tip of the middle finger. Obviously, the length of that distance depends upon the size of the individual. This is what the *Sforno* means when he says that the nine cubits recorded in the Torah was according to the cubit of each one of these giant-like men. Were this bedstead to have

גַּם־הֵם אֶת־הָאָרֶץ אֲשֶׁר יְהוָה אֱלֹהֵיכֶם נֹתֵן לָהֶם בְּעֵבֶר הַיַּרְדֵּן וְשַׁבְתֶּם
כא אִישׁ לִירֻשָּׁתוֹ אֲשֶׁר נָתַתִּי לָכֶם: וְאֶת־יְהוֹשׁוּעַ צִוֵּיתִי בָּעֵת הַהִוא לֵאמֹר
עֵינֶיךָ הָרֹאֹת אֵת כָּל־אֲשֶׁר עָשָׂה יְהוָה אֱלֹהֵיכֶם לִשְׁנֵי הַמְּלָכִים הָאֵלֶּה
כב כֵּן־יַעֲשֶׂה יְהוָה לְכָל־הַמַּמְלָכוֹת אֲשֶׁר אַתָּה עֹבֵר שָׁמָּה: לֹא תִּירָאוּם כִּי
יְהוָה אֱלֹהֵיכֶם הוּא הַנִּלְחָם לָכֶם:

NOTES

been measured by the measurement of 'elbow to tip of finger' of the average man, it would be far more than nine cubits! The only reason the Torah tells us this interesting, but seemingly non-vital piece of information, is to underscore that the conquest of these people by Ammon was accomplished only through the will of God.

פרשת ואתחנן
Parashas Vaeschanan

כג־כד וָאֶתְחַנַּ֖ן אֶל־יהוֹה בָּעֵ֥ת הַהִ֖וא לֵאמֹֽר׃ אֲדֹנָ֣י יהוֹה אַתָּ֣ה הַחִלּ֗וֹתָ לְהַרְא֤וֹת אֶֽת־עַבְדְּךָ֙ אֶ֨ת־גׇּדְלְךָ֔ וְאֶת־יָדְךָ֖ הַחֲזָקָ֑ה אֲשֶׁ֤ר מִי־אֵל֙ בַּשָּׁמַ֣יִם וּבָאָ֔רֶץ

כה אֲשֶׁר־יַעֲשֶׂ֥ה כְמַעֲשֶׂ֖יךָ וְכִגְבוּרֹתֶֽךָ׃ אֶעְבְּרָה־נָּ֗א וְאֶרְאֶה֙ אֶת־הָאָ֣רֶץ הַטּוֹבָ֔ה

כו אֲשֶׁ֖ר בְּעֵ֣בֶר הַיַּרְדֵּ֑ן הָהָ֥ר הַטּ֛וֹב הַזֶּ֖ה וְהַלְּבָנֹֽן׃ וַיִּתְעַבֵּ֨ר יהוֹה בִּי֙ לְמַ֣עַנְכֶ֔ם וְלֹ֥א שָׁמַ֖ע אֵלָ֑י וַיֹּ֨אמֶר יהוֹה֙ אֵלַ֔י רַב־לָ֕ךְ אַל־תּ֗וֹסֶף דַּבֵּ֥ר אֵלַ֛י ע֖וֹד בַּדָּבָ֥ר

כז הַזֶּֽה׃ עֲלֵ֣ה ׀ רֹ֣אשׁ הַפִּסְגָּ֗ה וְשָׂ֥א עֵינֶ֛יךָ יָ֧מָּה וְצָפֹ֛נָה וְתֵימָ֥נָה וּמִזְרָ֖חָה וּרְאֵ֣ה

כח בְעֵינֶ֑יךָ כִּי־לֹ֥א תַעֲבֹ֖ר אֶת־הַיַּרְדֵּ֥ן הַזֶּֽה׃ וְצַ֥ו אֶת־יְהוֹשֻׁ֖עַ וְחַזְּקֵ֣הוּ וְאַמְּצֵ֑הוּ כִּי־ה֣וּא יַעֲבֹ֗ר לִפְנֵי֙ הָעָ֣ם הַזֶּ֔ה וְהוּא֙ יַנְחִ֣יל אוֹתָ֔ם אֶת־הָאָ֖רֶץ אֲשֶׁ֥ר תִּרְאֶֽה׃

כט וַנֵּ֣שֶׁב בַּגָּ֔יְא מ֖וּל בֵּ֥ית פְּעֽוֹר׃

ד א וְעַתָּ֣ה יִשְׂרָאֵ֗ל שְׁמַ֤ע אֶל־הַֽחֻקִּים֙ וְאֶל־הַמִּשְׁפָּטִ֔ים אֲשֶׁ֧ר אָנֹכִ֛י מְלַמֵּ֥ד אֶתְכֶ֖ם

---

24. אֶת־יָדְךָ הַחֲזָקָה — *And Your strong hand . . .* to alter the nature of the imperishables (i.e., the forces of nature) which none but You can do. Now all this You did in order to bring Israel into the Land (of Canaan) and therefore, it is fitting (that I) attempt to secure their residence in it.

25. אֶעְבְּרָה נָּא — *Let me please cross over . . .* to destroy all the inhabitants of Canaan, so that Israel will never be exiled from it.

וְאֶרְאֶה אֶת־הָאָרֶץ הַטּוֹבָה — *And see the good land.* I will gaze upon it for good (which shall result) from my blessing, bringing everlasting benefit for Israel.

26. וַיִּתְעַבֵּר ה' בִּי לְמַעַנְכֶם — *But HASHEM was angry with me for your sake . . .* because I desired to insure your existence in it so that you should never be exiled from it; (but) He had already sworn to *cast out your seed among the nations* (based on *Psalms* 106:27).

IV

1. וְעַתָּה יִשְׂרָאֵל — *And now Israel.* Since you see that the decree of God, the Blessed One, is to exile you if you sin, be careful not to transgress, but (rather to) observe the commandments without adding or diminishing, for any addition to or diminishment from (the word of God) will bring you to ultimate ruination.

NOTES

24. וְאֶת יָדְךָ הַחֲזָקָה — *And Your strong hand.* The *Sifre* states that יָדְךָ הַחֲזָקָה, *Your strong hand,* refers to the Ten Plagues visited upon Egypt by the Almighty. These מַכּוֹת, *plagues,* in many instances affected and altered the laws of nature, as the *Sforno* points out, hence, they are called God's *strong hand.* The very fact that God was prepared to resort to these supernatural acts reflects the importance He attached to Israel's exodus from Egypt and their ultimate entry into the Promised Land. Moses therefore argues that he be permitted to enter with them so as to insure their permanent possession of the Land.

25. אֶעְבְּרָה נָא וְאֶרְאֶה — *Let me please cross over and see.* Moses presents two arguments to God that He relent and permit him to enter

Eretz Yisrael with his people. One is a practical reason: As a mighty warrior and military leader, he will be able to lead the Israelites in vanquishing the inhabitants of the Land. The second reason is that by viewing the Land from a perspective of 'good,' he will be able to have a positive impact upon it for the 'good' of Israel, and that will have an everlasting and indelible influence upon Israel's security and well-being in the Land. According to the *Sforno's* interpretation, the expression וְאֶרְאֶה, *and see,* is not simply a request *to see,* in the usual sense, but to effectuate a major influence upon Israel's permanent residence and success in *Eretz Yisrael.*

26. וַיִּתְעַבֵּר ה' בִּי לְמַעַנְכֶם — *But HASHEM was angry with me for your sake.* See the *Sforno's*

לַעֲשׂ֑וֹת לְמַ֣עַן תִּֽחְי֗וּ וּבָאתֶם֙ וִֽירִשְׁתֶּ֣ם אֶת־הָאָ֔רֶץ אֲשֶׁ֧ר יְהֹוָ֛ה אֱלֹהֵ֥י
ב אֲבֹתֵיכֶ֖ם נֹתֵ֥ן לָכֶֽם׃ לֹ֣א תֹסִ֗פוּ עַל־הַדָּבָר֙ אֲשֶׁ֤ר אָנֹכִי֙ מְצַוֶּ֣ה אֶתְכֶ֔ם וְלֹ֥א
תִגְרְע֖וּ מִמֶּ֑נּוּ לִשְׁמֹ֗ר אֶת־מִצְוֺת֙ יְהֹוָ֣ה אֱלֹהֵיכֶ֔ם אֲשֶׁ֥ר אָנֹכִ֖י מְצַוֶּ֥ה אֶתְכֶֽם׃
ג עֵֽינֵיכֶם֙ הָרֹא֔וֹת אֵ֛ת אֲשֶׁר־עָשָׂ֥ה יְהֹוָ֖ה בְּבַ֣עַל פְּע֑וֹר כִּ֣י כָל־הָאִ֗ישׁ אֲשֶׁ֤ר הָלַךְ֙
ד אַחֲרֵ֣י בַֽעַל־פְּע֔וֹר הִשְׁמִיד֛וֹ יְהֹוָ֥ה אֱלֹהֶ֖יךָ מִקִּרְבֶּֽךָ׃ וְאַתֶּם֙ הַדְּבֵקִ֔ים בַּֽיהֹוָ֖ה
שני ה אֱלֹהֵיכֶ֑ם חַיִּ֥ים כֻּלְּכֶ֖ם הַיּֽוֹם׃ רְאֵ֣ה ׀ לִמַּ֣דְתִּי אֶתְכֶ֗ם חֻקִּים֙ וּמִשְׁפָּטִ֔ים כַּאֲשֶׁ֥ר

---

2. וְלֹא תִגְרְעוּ מִמֶּנּוּ לִשְׁמֹר — *Neither shall you diminish from it, that you may keep.* One should not think that once the cause (reason) of the prohibition is removed, then it is not sinful to diminish, as King Solomon thought (when he said), אֲנִי אַרְבֶּה וְלֹא אָסוּר, אֲנִי אַרְבֶּה וְלֹא אָשִׁיב, *I will multiply but my heart will not be turned away, I will multiply but not cause the people to return* (*Sanhedrin* 21b).

3. עֵינֵיכֶם הָרֹאוֹת — *Your eyes have seen.* Behold, that which you saw happening regarding Baal-Peor attests to this, for indeed, those who sinned with idolatry did not initially intend to do so, but their original intent was (only) to commit harlotry, as it says, וַיָּחֶל הָעָם לִזְנוֹת, *and the people began to commit harlotry* (*Numbers* 25:1). And although the Torah prohibited this because of the fear that (harlotry) will lead to idolatry, as it says, וְזָנוּ בְנֹתָיו . . . וְהִזְנוּ אֶת בָּנֶיךָ, *and their daughters go astray . . . and make your sons go astray* (*Exodus* 34:16), nonetheless, each one of them thought that it would never happen to him, but behold, the opposite occurred.

כִּי כָל הָאִישׁ אֲשֶׁר הָלַךְ אַחֲרֵי בַעַל פְּעוֹר — *For all the men that followed the Baal-Peor* . . . to cleave unto his daughters, not one of them with all his wisdom was able to avoid stumbling into the sin of idolatry until הִשְׁמִידוֹ ה׳ אֱלֹהֶיךָ, HASHEM *your God destroyed him.*

4. וְאַתֶּם הַדְּבֵקִים בַּה׳ אֱלֹהֵיכֶם חַיִּים כֻּלְּכֶם הַיּוֹם — *But you who did cleave unto* HASHEM *your God are alive every one of you this day.* You were all wise enough to avoid the pitfall of idolatry.

NOTES

commentary in chapter 1, verse 37, and the explanatory note on his commentary for clarification of the *Sforno* on this verse.

IV

2. וְלֹא תִגְרְעוּ מִמֶּנּוּ לִשְׁמֹר — *Neither shall you diminish from it, that you may keep.* The words of our Sages cited by the *Sforno* refer to the prohibitions imposed by the Torah upon a Jewish king. In *Deut.* 17:16,17, the king is admonished not to *multiply horses to himself* lest he cause the people to return to Egypt where horses were obtained. He is also cautioned not to *multiply wives to himself*, lest they turn his heart to sensual passions, as the *Ibn Ezra* explains. In most instances, the Torah does not give explicit reasons for prohibitions. This case here is an exception to the rule, and as a result King Solomon reasoned that if the cause for the Torah's apprehension is removed, so is the prohibition. He was confident that he would not be misled by his many wives nor would he be tempted to return to Egypt to purchase more horses. Unfortunately, he was wrong. This verse is interpreted by the *Sforno* as applying not only to subtracting laws from the Torah but also to any rationalization which will prove to be the cause of one's downfall, as was the case with Solomon.

3. עֵינֵיכֶם הָרֹאוֹת — *Your eyes have seen.* The *Sforno* interprets the citing of the event at Peor by Moses as a perfect example how a seemingly minor infraction which is, nonetheless, a transgression can lead to a far more serious one. To add to, or subtract from, the *mitzvos* and prohibitions of the Torah will result in the unraveling of the fabric of observance in an uncontrollable manner, just as harlotry led to idolatry which is one of the cardinal sins.

צִוַּנִי יְהוָה אֱלֹהָי לַעֲשׂוֹת כֵּן בְּקֶרֶב הָאָרֶץ אֲשֶׁר אַתֶּם בָּאִים שָׁמָּה
ו לְרִשְׁתָּהּ: וּשְׁמַרְתֶּם וַעֲשִׂיתֶם כִּי הִוא חָכְמַתְכֶם וּבִינַתְכֶם לְעֵינֵי הָעַמִּים
אֲשֶׁר יִשְׁמְעוּן אֵת כָּל־הַחֻקִּים הָאֵלֶּה וְאָמְרוּ רַק עַם־חָכָם וְנָבוֹן הַגּוֹי הַגָּדוֹל
ז הַזֶּה: כִּי מִי־גוֹי גָּדוֹל אֲשֶׁר־לוֹ אֱלֹהִים קְרֹבִים אֵלָיו כַּיהוָה אֱלֹהֵינוּ
ח בְּכָל־קָרְאֵנוּ אֵלָיו: וּמִי גּוֹי גָּדוֹל אֲשֶׁר־לוֹ חֻקִּים וּמִשְׁפָּטִים צַדִּיקִם כְּכֹל

---

6. כִּי הִוא חָכְמַתְכֶם — *For this is your wisdom* ... (and) with it you will be able to answer the non-believers with reasoned proof.

7. כִּי מִי גוֹי גָּדוֹל אֲשֶׁר לוֹ אֱלֹהִים קְרֹבִים אֵלָיו — *For what great nation is there that has God so close to him.* It is proper to be particularly (concerned) that you be considered wise and understanding in the eyes of the nations because God, the Blessed One, is nigh unto you בְּכָל קָרְאֵנוּ אֵלָיו, *whensoever we call upon Him*, and this demonstrates that He chose us from all the nations, and if you are considered unwise by the nations it would be a desecration of God, when they would say to you (derisively), עַם ה׳ אֵלֶּה, *These are the people of* HASHEM (*Ezekiel* 36:20).

8. וּמִי גוֹי גָּדוֹל אֲשֶׁר לוֹ חֻקִּים — *And what great nation is there that has statutes.* You are considered wise in the eyes of the nations when you observe the statutes of God and His teachings because there is no other nation in existence which has statutes that demonstrate the existence of God and His ways *and ordinances so righteous*, which do not profit the judges nor reward their officials and scribes, but are solely (to dispense) justice and righteousness, as our Sages say: מִשְׁפָּט לָזֶה וּצְדָקָה לָזֶה, מִשְׁפָּט לָזֶה שֶׁהֶחְזִיר לוֹ אֶת שֶׁלּוֹ וּצְדָקָה לָזֶה שֶׁהוֹצִיא גְזֵלָה מִתַּחַת יָדוֹ, *Justice to one and righteousness to the other. Justice to the one to whom we return his due and righteousness to the other by removing an ill-gotten thing from his possession* (*Sanhedrin* 6b).

NOTES

6. כִּי הִוא חָכְמַתְכֶם — *For this is your wisdom.* The observance of *mitzvos* enables one to understand the profound teachings of Torah which, in turn, molds the mind of the observant Israelite. The result is a person who, with this wisdom gained from the Torah, will be able to convey the truth of Torah in a logical, clear and reasoned manner which the *Sforno* believes is the way to answer the unbeliever (דַע מַה שֶּׁתָּשִׁיב לְאֶפִּיקוֹרֹס).

7. כִּי מִי גוֹי גָּדוֹל — *For what great nation is there.* The prophet Ezekiel teaches us that since Israel is the Chosen People of God, their status, condition and qualities — or lack of them — reflect upon God Himself. The actions of Israel either sanctify Him (קִדּוּשׁ הַשֵּׁם) or profane His great Name (חִלּוּל הַשֵּׁם). When Israel is driven out of the Land because of their sins and scattered among the nations, it causes a חִלּוּל הַשֵּׁם and it is that tragic condition to which Ezekiel addresses himself in the chapter cited by the *Sforno*. This is the reason for Moses' concern that their image among the nations be that of a wise people, for since they are recognized as 'the People of God,' the respect and admiration which they evoke as a result of their wisdom brings glory and praise to the Almighty as well. This perception of Israel as a wise people results from Israel's observance of the Torah's statutes and ordinances, as explained in the following verse.

8. וּמִי גוֹי גָּדוֹל — *And what great nation is there.* The Talmudic selection from Tractate *Sanhedrin* quoted by the *Sforno* is the conclusion of the Sages' interpretation of a verse in *II Samuel* 8:15 which speaks of King David. The verse states, וַיְהִי דָוִד עֹשֶׂה מִשְׁפָּט וּצְדָקָה לְכָל עַמּוֹ, *and David executed judgment and righteousness to all his people*. The Sages comment, 'Are these two not mutually contradictory? — If there is justice, then there cannot be righteousness, and if there is righteousness, then there cannot be justice.' For justice is the strict application of the letter of the law while righteousness implies a charitable, lenient interpretation of the spirit of the law. The

ט הַתּוֹרָה הַזֹּאת אֲשֶׁר אָנֹכִי נֹתֵן לִפְנֵיכֶם הַיּוֹם: רַק הִשָּׁמֶר לְךָ וּשְׁמֹר נַפְשְׁךָ
מְאֹד פֶּן־תִּשְׁכַּח אֶת־הַדְּבָרִים אֲשֶׁר־רָאוּ עֵינֶיךָ וּפֶן־יָסוּרוּ מִלְּבָבְךָ כֹּל יְמֵי
י חַיֶּיךָ וְהוֹדַעְתָּם לְבָנֶיךָ וְלִבְנֵי בָנֶיךָ: יוֹם אֲשֶׁר עָמַדְתָּ לִפְנֵי יהוה אֱלֹהֶיךָ
בְּחֹרֵב בֶּאֱמֹר יהוה אֵלַי הַקְהֶל־לִי אֶת־הָעָם וְאַשְׁמִעֵם אֶת־דְּבָרָי אֲשֶׁר
יִלְמְדוּן לְיִרְאָה אֹתִי כָּל־הַיָּמִים אֲשֶׁר הֵם חַיִּים עַל־הָאֲדָמָה וְאֶת־בְּנֵיהֶם
יא יְלַמֵּדוּן: וַתִּקְרְבוּן וַתַּעַמְדוּן תַּחַת הָהָר וְהָהָר בֹּעֵר בָּאֵשׁ עַד־לֵב הַשָּׁמַיִם
יב חֹשֶׁךְ עָנָן וַעֲרָפֶל: וַיְדַבֵּר יהוה אֲלֵיכֶם מִתּוֹךְ הָאֵשׁ קוֹל דְּבָרִים אַתֶּם
יג שֹׁמְעִים וּתְמוּנָה אֵינְכֶם רֹאִים זוּלָתִי קוֹל: וַיַּגֵּד לָכֶם אֶת־בְּרִיתוֹ אֲשֶׁר צִוָּה
יד אֶתְכֶם לַעֲשׂוֹת עֲשֶׂרֶת הַדְּבָרִים וַיִּכְתְּבֵם עַל־שְׁנֵי לֻחוֹת אֲבָנִים: וְאֹתִי צִוָּה
יהוה בָּעֵת הַהִוא לְלַמֵּד אֶתְכֶם חֻקִּים וּמִשְׁפָּטִים לַעֲשֹׂתְכֶם אֹתָם בָּאָרֶץ
טו אֲשֶׁר אַתֶּם עֹבְרִים שָׁמָּה לְרִשְׁתָּהּ: וְנִשְׁמַרְתֶּם מְאֹד לְנַפְשֹׁתֵיכֶם כִּי לֹא
רְאִיתֶם כָּל־תְּמוּנָה בְּיוֹם דִּבֶּר יהוה אֲלֵיכֶם בְּחֹרֵב מִתּוֹךְ הָאֵשׁ:

---

9. רַק הִשָּׁמֶר לְךָ — *Only take heed to yourself.* Although I have told you that it is fitting that you be considered wise in the eyes of the nations, (nonetheless) take heed (not to be influenced) by the philosophy of their wise men who deny the existence, power and providence of God, the Blessed One, and who attempt to prove all this with reasoned proof.

פֶּן תִּשְׁכַּח אֶת הַדְּבָרִים אֲשֶׁר רָאוּ עֵינֶיךָ — *Lest you forget the things which your eyes saw.* And the reason I cautioned you to take great heed of this is because there is reason to be concerned that you may forget what your own physical eyes saw at Sinai, and (what) your discerning eyes (see) in the interpretation of Torah, wherein you were shown that you may know, with reasoned proof, the opposite of their philosophy.

וְהוֹדַעְתָּם לְבָנֶיךָ — *And make them known to your children.* To those children who did not see (the revelation at Sinai) make it known through reasoned proof.

15. כִּי לֹא רְאִיתֶם כָּל תְּמוּנָה — *For you saw no manner of form ...* and this is the reverse of the doctrine of the Sabians who thought that there is nothing in existence superior to the heavenly bodies (lit. 'causes'), and that they alone preceded (everything) (and are) first and eternal.

NOTES

answer given is that which the *Sforno* quotes in his commentary, namely the execution of both justice *and* righteousness which evokes the admiration and respect of the nations.

9. פֶּן תִּשְׁכַּח ... אֲשֶׁר רָאוּ עֵינֶיךָ — *Lest you forget ... which your eyes saw.* 'To see' is to perceive with the eyes and also to perceive mentally, i.e., to grasp and comprehend. The generation that was delivered from Egypt and received the Torah at Sinai was granted this twofold רְאִיָּה — 'seeing.' They saw the miracles with their own eyes and they were also granted the power of prophecy (as explained in *parashas Yisro*) and a clear comprehension of the Divine. Their children, however, did not see this revelation at Sinai and therefore, it is incumbent upon the previous generation, who did so, to make it *known to their children,* through reasoned proof.

15. כִּי לֹא רְאִיתֶם כָּל תְּמוּנָה — *For you saw no manner of form.* The *Rambam* in his *Guide* (III 29) speaks of the Sabians 'whose doctrine is that there is no deity but the stars.' The *Rambam* continues his discussion of the Sabians and tells us that 'in conformity with these opinions, the Sabians set up statues for the planets: golden ones for the sun and silver ones for the moon.' This is what the *Sforno* is referring to in his commentary on this verse where the Torah reminds Israel that no

טז פֶּן־תַּשְׁחִתוּן וַעֲשִׂיתֶם לָכֶם פֶּסֶל תְּמוּנַת כָּל־סָמֶל תַּבְנִית זָכָר אוֹ נְקֵבָה:
יז תַּבְנִית כָּל־בְּהֵמָה אֲשֶׁר בָּאָרֶץ תַּבְנִית כָּל־צִפּוֹר כָּנָף אֲשֶׁר תָּעוּף
יח בַּשָּׁמָיִם: תַּבְנִית כָּל־רֹמֵשׂ בָּאֲדָמָה תַּבְנִית כָּל־דָּגָה אֲשֶׁר־בַּמַּיִם מִתַּחַת
יט לָאָרֶץ: וּפֶן־תִּשָּׂא עֵינֶיךָ הַשָּׁמַיְמָה וְרָאִיתָ אֶת־הַשֶּׁמֶשׁ וְאֶת־הַיָּרֵחַ
וְאֶת־הַכּוֹכָבִים כֹּל צְבָא הַשָּׁמַיִם וְנִדַּחְתָּ וְהִשְׁתַּחֲוִיתָ לָהֶם וַעֲבַדְתָּם אֲשֶׁר
כ חָלַק יהוה אֱלֹהֶיךָ אֹתָם לְכֹל הָעַמִּים תַּחַת כָּל־הַשָּׁמָיִם: וְאֶתְכֶם לָקַח
יהוה וַיּוֹצִא אֶתְכֶם מִכּוּר הַבַּרְזֶל מִמִּצְרָיִם לִהְיוֹת לוֹ לְעַם נַחֲלָה כַּיּוֹם הַזֶּה:
כא וַיהוה הִתְאַנַּף־בִּי עַל־דִּבְרֵיכֶם וַיִּשָּׁבַע לְבִלְתִּי עָבְרִי אֶת־הַיַּרְדֵּן
כב וּלְבִלְתִּי־בֹא אֶל־הָאָרֶץ הַטּוֹבָה אֲשֶׁר יהוה אֱלֹהֶיךָ נֹתֵן לְךָ נַחֲלָה: כִּי

---

16. תְּמוּנַת כָּל סָמֶל — *The form of any figure* . . . (as was) the practice of those who believed that every existing perishable (thing) began with a primeval cause and so they would fashion a form of that perishable (object) to indicate (i.e., reflect or symbolize) that which they thought was the generator and beginning (i.e., cause) of that form or figure. They would (then) worship that form in order to cause that primeval (force) to influence and have some impact upon them to a degree.

19. אֲשֶׁר חָלַק ה׳ אֱלֹהֶיךָ אֹתָם לְכֹל הָעַמִּים — *Which HASHEM your God has allotted unto all the peoples.* He arranged them in a fitting order to meet the need of each part of the earth according to the diversity of each land and the people who inhabit it. Now this order demonstrates the reverse of the doctrine of those who err, because it shows perforce that there is One who exists who arranges all for a purpose designated by Him, and they exist according to a plan and certainly not by chance, in order to attain some goal (purpose) by their (very) being and their order.

20. וְאֶתְכֶם לָקַח ה׳ — *But HASHEM has taken you* . . . to walk in His ways and to cleave to Him, therefore you are not to pay heed to the conduct of the hosts of heaven and their order, as do other nations.

NOTES

manner of form was seen and therefore they are to make no graven image or the form of any figure.

16. תְּמוּנַת כָּל סָמֶל — *The form of any figure*. The term 'נִמְצָא נִפְסָד — perishable existent' is used by the *Sforno* when referring to that which is 'subject to generation and corruption,' to quote the expression of the *Rambam*. The school of Plato believed (as the *Sforno* states here) that the world of matter (עֲשִׂיָּה), i.e., the material world which we experience and know, reflects the world of emanations (אֲצִילוּת) taking on form (צוּרָה). Hence, as the *Sforno* explains, they believed that every material form (i.e., 'perishable' — for it cannot last) comes from a higher spiritual force. By worshiping this material form, one causes the originator or cause (קַדְמוֹן) to influence the material world in a beneficial manner for man. That is why the Torah cautions us not to be misled into making the form of any figure for this erroneous purpose, since God is the Creator of all and there is no need to worship Him through intermediaries.

19-20. אֲשֶׁר חָלַק ה׳ אֱלֹהֶיךָ לְכֹל הָעַמִּים . . . וְאֶתְכֶם לָקַח ה׳ — *Which HASHEM your God has allotted unto all the peoples. . . But HASHEM has taken you*. The Rambam in his *Guide* 2:20 refutes the theory of spontaneity and chance bringing about the existence of the heavenly bodies. He also emphasizes the elements of cause and purpose in their creation. All this the *Sforno* incorporates into his commentary on these verses, adding that the purpose of God's creation of the various stars and planets was, in some mysterious way, to place the nations of the earth under their influence according to some Divine plan and order. The exception is Israel, regarding whom we are taught, אֵין מַזָּל לְיִשְׂרָאֵל, *Israel's fate is not determined by the stars* (*Shabbos* 156b).

אָנֹכִי מֵת בָּאָרֶץ הַזֹּאת אֵינֶנִּי עֹבֵר אֶת־הַיַּרְדֵּן וְאַתֶּם עֹבְרִים וִירִשְׁתֶּם
כג אֶת־הָאָרֶץ הַטּוֹבָה הַזֹּאת׃ הִשָּׁמְרוּ לָכֶם פֶּן־תִּשְׁכְּחוּ אֶת־בְּרִית יהוה
אֱלֹהֵיכֶם אֲשֶׁר כָּרַת עִמָּכֶם וַעֲשִׂיתֶם לָכֶם פֶּסֶל תְּמוּנַת כֹּל אֲשֶׁר צִוְּךָ יהוה
כד אֱלֹהֶיךָ׃ כִּי יהוה אֱלֹהֶיךָ אֵשׁ אֹכְלָה הוּא אֵל קַנָּא׃
כה כִּי־תוֹלִיד בָּנִים וּבְנֵי בָנִים וְנוֹשַׁנְתֶּם בָּאָרֶץ וְהִשְׁחַתֶּם וַעֲשִׂיתֶם פֶּסֶל
כו תְּמוּנַת כֹּל וַעֲשִׂיתֶם הָרַע בְּעֵינֵי־יהוה אֱלֹהֶיךָ לְהַכְעִיסוֹ׃ הַעִידֹתִי בָכֶם
הַיּוֹם אֶת־הַשָּׁמַיִם וְאֶת־הָאָרֶץ כִּי־אָבֹד תֹּאבֵדוּן מַהֵר מֵעַל הָאָרֶץ אֲשֶׁר
אַתֶּם עֹבְרִים אֶת־הַיַּרְדֵּן שָׁמָּה לְרִשְׁתָּהּ לֹא־תַאֲרִיכֻן יָמִים עָלֶיהָ כִּי
כז הִשָּׁמֵד תִּשָּׁמֵדוּן׃ וְהֵפִיץ יהוה אֶתְכֶם בָּעַמִּים וְנִשְׁאַרְתֶּם מְתֵי מִסְפָּר בַּגּוֹיִם
כח אֲשֶׁר יְנַהֶג יהוה אֶתְכֶם שָׁמָּה׃ וַעֲבַדְתֶּם־שָׁם אֱלֹהִים מַעֲשֵׂה יְדֵי אָדָם עֵץ

---

22. כִּי אָנֹכִי מֵת — *But I must die.* I need to caution you exceedingly since I will not be going over with you, as it says, *For I know that after my death you will deal corruptly* (31:29).

24. אֵשׁ אֹכְלָה הוּא — *A devouring fire.* Fire which consumes fire, and as such will devour the soul with the flesh.

אֵל קַנָּא — *A jealous God.* Because there is naught in existence which is comparable to Him and His existence whatsoever, hence, whoever serves another (deity) gives to him what is only fitting to be offered to (God) alone, and this is comparable to a married woman who gives to another man that which is only fitting for her husband alone, and because of this He is a jealous (God).

25. לְהַכְעִיסוֹ — *To provoke Him* ... to remove the Divine Presence from Israel in order to be like unto the nations of the world and not be subject to the Torah and the commandments of God, the Blessed One.

28. וַעֲבַדְתֶּם שָׁם אֱלֹהִים — *And there you shall serve gods* ... (as the Talmud teaches) 'Israelites who reside outside the Land (of Israel) serve idols, though in pure innocence' (*Avodah Zarah* 8a).

NOTES

24. אֵשׁ אֹכְלָה הוּא — *A devouring fire*. The fire which came forth from heaven and devoured Nadav and Avihu (*Leviticus* 10:2) consumed their souls as well as their bodies, according to our Sages. Such is the nature of the Divine fire. Therefore, the *Sforno* interprets the phrase *a devouring fire* as meaning the devouring of the soul together with the flesh.

אֵל קַנָּא — *A jealous God*. The word קִנְאָה, *jealousy*, is found in the *parashah* of the סוֹטָה, *a woman suspected of infidelity*. The sin of adultery is one wherein a woman grants to a man other than her husband that which is exclusively his. The *Sforno* interprets the phrase אֵל קַנָּא, *a jealous God*, in a similar sense; man's observance, service and worship belongs to God alone. The worship of a פֶּסֶל, *graven image*, or the form of any figure is an act of infidelity; hence the term used is אֵל קַנָּא, similar to the expression used in reference to a husband whose wife is unfaithful.

25. לְהַכְעִיסוֹ — *To provoke Him*. When God is angered by man's misbehavior, the שְׁכִינָה — His Presence — departs. The *Sforno* states this principle here, as well as in *Deut.* 32:16. The source may well be in *Numbers* 12:9 where the Torah tells us that when God became angry with Miriam and Aaron, He departed.

28. וַעֲבַדְתֶּם שָׁם אֱלֹהִים — *And there you shall serve gods*. It is difficult to understand the sense of certainty reflected in this verse, that Israel's presence in exile must lead to idolatry. The *Sforno* therefore cites the saying of our Sages that when Israel dwells outside *Eretz Yisrael*, their cultural and social environment

כט וָאֶבֶן אֲשֶׁר לֹא־יִרְאוּן וְלֹא יִשְׁמְעוּן וְלֹא יֹאכְלוּן וְלֹא יְרִיחֻן: וּבִקַּשְׁתֶּם
מִשָּׁם אֶת־יהוה אֱלֹהֶיךָ וּמָצָאתָ כִּי תִדְרְשֶׁנּוּ בְּכָל־לְבָבְךָ וּבְכָל־נַפְשֶׁךָ:
ל בַּצַּר לְךָ וּמְצָאוּךָ כֹּל הַדְּבָרִים הָאֵלֶּה בְּאַחֲרִית הַיָּמִים וְשַׁבְתָּ עַד־יהוה
לא אֱלֹהֶיךָ וְשָׁמַעְתָּ בְּקֹלוֹ: כִּי אֵל רַחוּם יהוה אֱלֹהֶיךָ לֹא יַרְפְּךָ וְלֹא יַשְׁחִיתֶךָ
לב וְלֹא יִשְׁכַּח אֶת־בְּרִית אֲבֹתֶיךָ אֲשֶׁר נִשְׁבַּע לָהֶם: כִּי שְׁאַל־נָא לְיָמִים
רִאשֹׁנִים אֲשֶׁר־הָיוּ לְפָנֶיךָ לְמִן־הַיּוֹם אֲשֶׁר בָּרָא אֱלֹהִים ׀ אָדָם עַל־הָאָרֶץ
וּלְמִקְצֵה הַשָּׁמַיִם וְעַד־קְצֵה הַשָּׁמָיִם הֲנִהְיָה כַּדָּבָר הַגָּדוֹל הַזֶּה אוֹ הֲנִשְׁמַע

אֲשֶׁר לֹא יִרְאוּן — *Which neither see*. These (idols) have no power of will, as their worshipers thought (and who therefore) crafted images with organs that function (in man) at will, in order to demonstrate that the primeval cause they believed in could activate these organs by their will. Hence, they would worship it and pray to it to attain fulfillment of their requests. However, behold that there is naught which exists except God, the Blessed One, and living man who possesses the power of free will, whereas the action of all others (i.e., living creatures and the elements) are caused by (the laws) of nature as ordered by God, the Blessed One.

29. וּמָצָאתָ — *And you shall find Him* . . . even though there is neither a Temple nor sacred vessels (or furnishings) there.

כִּי תִדְרְשֶׁנּוּ בְּכָל לְבָבְךָ וּבְכָל נַפְשֶׁךָ — *Because you will search for Him with all your heart and soul.* The reason you will find Him is because you will seek Him with all your heart due to the great distress (which you will experience).

30. בְּאַחֲרִית הַיָּמִים — *In the latter days* . . . at the end of days as (the Torah) attests to saying: *And it shall come to pass when all these things are come upon you . . . and you shall return to HASHEM your God and hearken to His voice* (30:1-2).

32. כִּי שְׁאַל נָא — *For ask now.* The proof of what I said that the covenant of the fathers will not be forgotten (v. 31) is in what He did for all of Israel at the (time) of the giving of the Torah when you all merited the attainment of such (a high) level of prophecy. This occurred for the purpose of taking you unto Him as a people because of the covenant with the Patriarchs, since each of you (individually) was certainly not worthy (to attain this exalted status), for although it did occur at times that individuals prophesied, (nonetheless,) this never happened to any other (entire) people.

NOTES

causes them to conduct themselves, albeit innocently, in a non-Jewish manner, which the Torah equates with the serving of strange gods. The *Ramban* interprets this verse in a similar fashion, quoting the Talmud in *Kesubos* 110b where our Sages say, 'Whoever dwells outside the Holy Land is regarded as if he worships idols.'

אֲשֶׁר לֹא יִרְאוּן — *Which neither see.* See the notes or verses 15-16.

32. כִּי שְׁאַל נָא — *For ask now.* The previous verse (31) states that God will not forget the covenant of the fathers (בְּרִית אָבוֹת). In verse 37, Moses tells Israel that all the signs and wonders witnessed by them in Egypt and at Mt. Sinai were wrought because God loved their fathers. The *Sforno*, in his commentary, explains that there is a theme which links all these verses together, namely the merit of בְּרִית אָבוֹת. Because of this covenant, the entire nation was delivered; an entire people was elevated to the highest level of prophecy, and ultimately given a special land conducive to the perfection of man's mind and spirit.

לג כָּמֹהוּ: הֲשָׁמַע עָם קוֹל אֱלֹהִים מְדַבֵּר מִתּוֹךְ־הָאֵשׁ כַּאֲשֶׁר־שָׁמַעְתָּ אַתָּה
לד וַיֶּחִי: אוֹ ׀ הֲנִסָּה אֱלֹהִים לָבוֹא לָקַחַת לוֹ גוֹי מִקֶּרֶב גּוֹי בְּמַסֹּת בְּאֹתֹת
וּבְמוֹפְתִים וּבְמִלְחָמָה וּבְיָד חֲזָקָה וּבִזְרוֹעַ נְטוּיָה וּבְמוֹרָאִים גְּדֹלִים כְּכֹל
לה אֲשֶׁר־עָשָׂה לָכֶם יהוה אֱלֹהֵיכֶם בְּמִצְרַיִם לְעֵינֶיךָ: אַתָּה הָרְאֵתָ לָדַעַת כִּי
לו יהוה הוּא הָאֱלֹהִים אֵין עוֹד מִלְבַדּוֹ: מִן־הַשָּׁמַיִם הִשְׁמִיעֲךָ אֶת־קֹלוֹ לְיַסְּרֶךָּ
לז וְעַל־הָאָרֶץ הֶרְאֲךָ אֶת־אִשּׁוֹ הַגְּדוֹלָה וּדְבָרָיו שָׁמַעְתָּ מִתּוֹךְ הָאֵשׁ: וְתַחַת
כִּי אָהַב אֶת־אֲבֹתֶיךָ וַיִּבְחַר בְּזַרְעוֹ אַחֲרָיו וַיּוֹצִאֲךָ בְּפָנָיו בְּכֹחוֹ הַגָּדֹל
לח מִמִּצְרָיִם: לְהוֹרִישׁ גּוֹיִם גְּדֹלִים וַעֲצֻמִים מִמְּךָ מִפָּנֶיךָ לַהֲבִיאֲךָ לָתֶת־לְךָ

---

34. אוֹ הֲנִסָּה אֱלֹהִים — *Or has God proved himself.* Although it has happened that an individual or individuals have escaped from among the wicked, nonetheless this never happened to an entire nation.

בְּמַסֹּת בְּאֹתֹת — *By trials, by signs* ... which indicate that this did not happen by chance, but by the (deliberate) intent of a פּוֹעֵל רְצוֹנִי, *one according to His will.*

וּבִזְרוֹעַ נְטוּיָה — *And by an outstretched arm* ... prepared to smite again, (thereby) teaching that if the sinner does not repent He will continue to smite (him).

35. אַתָּה הָרְאֵתָ — *To you it was shown.* All this God, the Blessed One, showed you ...

לָדַעַת — *That you might know.* So that you might contemplate and know, without a doubt, כִּי ה׳ הוּא הָאֱלֹהִים — *that HASHEM, He is God;* He is perforce the First Cause.

36. לְיַסְּרֶךָּ — *that He might instruct you* ... to bring you to a (high) level of prophecy at the (time) of the giving of the Torah, similar to (the episode) of Elijah, וְהִנֵּה ... וְרוּחַ גְּדוֹלָה וְחָזָק, *and behold ... and a great strong wind* (*I Kings* 19:11), and also, וְעַל הָאָרֶץ הֶרְאֲךָ אֶת אִשּׁוֹ, *And upon the earth He made you see His great fire,* as we (also) find there, where (the verse) states: וְאַחַר הָרַעַשׁ אֵשׁ, *And after the earthquake a fire* (*I Kings* 19:12).

37. וְתַחַת כִּי אָהַב אֶת אֲבֹתֶיךָ — *And because He loved your fathers* ... and since He did all this because He loved your fathers.

וַיִּבְחַר בְּזַרְעוֹ — *And chose his seed* ... of only one, namely the seed of Jacob.

וַיּוֹצִיאֲךָ בְּפָנָיו — *And brought you out with His Presence* ... through actions which emanate from His Presence (lit. face), i.e., transcending nature; not from His 'back', (which denotes) actions within nature.

38. לְהוֹרִישׁ — *To drive out.* His intent was to deliver you from bondage, (a state wherein) you were not able to contemplate.

NOTES

37. וַיּוֹצִיאֲךָ בְּפָנָיו — *And brought you out with His presence. The expressions* פָּנִים, *face,* and אָחוֹר, *back,* in relationship to God appear in *Exodus* 33:23 where God tells Moses, *You shall see My back, but My face shall not be seen.* The *Sforno* translates the word בְּפָנָיו in our verse literally: God brought us out of Egypt through supernatural means, indicated by the expression *face,* for He graciously showed us His face of concern and love, as opposed to His 'back' which implies acts regulated only by the laws of nature. In *Exodus,* the *Sforno* offers a different interpretation. See his commentary on that verse and the explanatory note.

לט אֶת־אַרְצָם נַחֲלָה כַּיּוֹם הַזֶּה: וְיָדַעְתָּ הַיּוֹם וַהֲשֵׁבֹתָ אֶל־לְבָבֶךָ כִּי יהוה הוּא
מ הָאֱלֹהִים בַּשָּׁמַיִם מִמַּעַל וְעַל־הָאָרֶץ מִתָּחַת אֵין עוֹד: וְשָׁמַרְתָּ אֶת־חֻקָּיו
וְאֶת־מִצְוֹתָיו אֲשֶׁר אָנֹכִי מְצַוְּךָ הַיּוֹם אֲשֶׁר יִיטַב לְךָ וּלְבָנֶיךָ אַחֲרֶיךָ וּלְמַעַן
תַּאֲרִיךְ יָמִים עַל־הָאֲדָמָה אֲשֶׁר יהוה אֱלֹהֶיךָ נֹתֵן לְךָ כָּל־הַיָּמִים:

לָתֶת לְךָ אֶת אַרְצָם — *To give you their land* . . . which is God's land, conducive (lit. 'prepared') to attain the desired perfection (of mind and spirit).

39. וְיָדַעְתָּ הַיּוֹם — *And you shall know this day.* Therefore, it is, without a doubt, fitting that you contemplate and know (all the) contradictory parts (of theological speculation).

וַהֲשֵׁבֹתָ אֶל לְבָבֶךָ — *And bring it back to your heart.* And after such reflection you will place in your heart those parts of these philosophical (searchings) which are true, that being (the certainty . . .).

כִּי ה׳ הוּא הָאֱלֹהִים — *That HASHEM is God.* The well-known, eternal (Master) Who orders (all that is . . .).

בַּשָּׁמַיִם מִמַּעַל וְעַל הָאָרֶץ מִתָּחַת — *In heaven above and upon the earth below* . . . because God's mastery is demonstrated by their order, connection and the purpose manifested by them, which cannot be realized except through them, and thereby it becomes known that there is an Existent who directs (the cosmos) who created all this for a specific purpose, which comes from Him.

אֵין עוֹד — *There is none else* . . . and from all this it is made known that there is none else, because perforce all this cannot be except through the power of some Creator who is separated from matter (incorporeal) and elevated to the greatest possible degree. It is (also) impossible that there is more than one on the same level of elevation among those separated from matter, and therefore there can be none comparable to Him.

40. וְשָׁמַרְתָּ אֶת חֻקָּיו — *And you shall keep His statutes* . . . and when you know Him, without a doubt, you will keep His statutes, as it says, מִי לֹא יִרָאֲךָ מֶלֶךְ הַגּוֹיִם, *Who would not fear You, King of the nations?* (*Jeremiah* 10:7).

וְאֶת מִצְוֹתָיו אֲשֶׁר אָנֹכִי מְצַוְּךָ הַיּוֹם . . . כָּל הַיָּמִים — *And His commandments which I command you this day . . . all the days* . . . because there shall never be any new law (religion).

NOTES

39. וְיָדַעְתָּ הַיּוֹם — *And you shall know this day.* The *Sforno* views this verse as a major fundamental doctrine of Judaism. Following in the path of the *Rambam,* he emphasizes the need to study and contemplate the truth of God's existence, to examine and analyze all alternatives, resulting in the conviction that the Almighty is one, non-corporeal, the First Cause, and the Source of all existence. He submits that proof of a Creator is derived from nature — its order, harmony and manifestation of a higher purpose. His interpretation of the phrase, אֵין עוֹד, *there is none else,* is a succinct summary of the *Rambam's* arguments in his *Guide* (II,1) expressing belief in the unity and uniqueness of God.

40. וְשָׁמַרְתָּ אֶת חֻקָּיו — *And you shall keep his statutes.* The *Sforno* in his interpretation of this verse reflects the Rambam in *Mishneh Torah, Yesodai HaTorah* 2:2, where he states that man is commanded to love and revere God. The way to attain this love and reverence is by contemplating His greatness manifested through His wondrous creation which reveals His infinite and incomparable wisdom. The

שלישי מא-מב אָ֣ז יַבְדִּ֤יל מֹשֶׁה֙ שָׁלֹ֣שׁ עָרִ֔ים בְּעֵ֖בֶר הַיַּרְדֵּ֑ן מִזְרְחָ֖ה שָֽׁמֶשׁ: לָנֻ֣ס שָׁ֣מָּה רוֹצֵ֗חַ

אֲשֶׁ֨ר יִרְצַ֤ח אֶת־רֵעֵ֙הוּ֙ בִּבְלִי־דַ֔עַת וְה֛וּא לֹא־שֹׂנֵ֥א ל֖וֹ מִתְּמ֣וֹל שִׁלְשֹׁ֑ם וְנָ֗ס

מג אֶל־אַחַ֛ת מִן־הֶעָרִ֥ים הָאֵ֖ל וָחָֽי: אֶת־בֶּ֧צֶר בַּמִּדְבָּ֛ר בְּאֶ֥רֶץ הַמִּישֹׁ֖ר לָרֽאוּבֵנִ֑י

מד וְאֶת־רָאמֹ֤ת בַּגִּלְעָד֙ לַגָּדִ֔י וְאֶת־גּוֹלָ֥ן בַּבָּשָׁ֖ן לַֽמְנַשִּֽׁי: וְזֹ֖את הַתּוֹרָ֑ה

מה אֲשֶׁר־שָׂ֣ם מֹשֶׁ֔ה לִפְנֵ֖י בְּנֵ֥י יִשְׂרָאֵֽל: אֵ֚לֶּה הָֽעֵדֹ֔ת וְהַֽחֻקִּ֖ים וְהַמִּשְׁפָּטִ֑ים אֲשֶׁ֨ר

מו דִּבֶּ֤ר מֹשֶׁה֙ אֶל־בְּנֵ֣י יִשְׂרָאֵ֔ל בְּצֵאתָ֖ם מִמִּצְרָ֑יִם: בְּעֵ֨בֶר הַיַּרְדֵּ֜ן בַּגַּ֗יְא מ֚וּל

בֵּ֣ית פְּע֔וֹר בְּאֶ֗רֶץ סִיחֹן֙ מֶ֣לֶךְ הָֽאֱמֹרִ֔י אֲשֶׁ֥ר יוֹשֵׁ֖ב בְּחֶשְׁבּ֑וֹן אֲשֶׁ֨ר הִכָּ֤ה מֹשֶׁה֙

מז וּבְנֵ֣י יִשְׂרָאֵ֔ל בְּצֵאתָ֖ם מִמִּצְרָ֑יִם: וַיִּֽירְשׁ֣וּ אֶת־אַרְצ֗וֹ וְאֶת־אֶ֛רֶץ | ע֥וֹג

מח מֶֽלֶךְ־הַבָּשָׁן֙ שְׁנֵי֙ מַלְכֵ֣י הָֽאֱמֹרִ֔י אֲשֶׁ֖ר בְּעֵ֣בֶר הַיַּרְדֵּ֑ן מִזְרַ֖ח שָֽׁמֶשׁ: מֵֽעֲרֹעֵ֡ר

מט אֲשֶׁ֣ר עַל־שְׂפַת־נַ֣חַל אַרְנֹ֗ן וְעַד־הַ֥ר שִׂיאֹ֛ן ה֖וּא חֶרְמ֑וֹן: וְכָל־הָ֣עֲרָבָ֗ה עֵ֚בֶר

הַיַּרְדֵּ֣ן מִזְרָ֔חָה וְעַ֖ד יָ֣ם הָֽעֲרָבָ֑ה תַּ֖חַת אַשְׁדֹּ֥ת הַפִּסְגָּֽה:

ה רביעי א וַיִּקְרָ֣א מֹשֶׁה֮ אֶל־כָּל־יִשְׂרָאֵל֒ וַיֹּ֣אמֶר אֲלֵהֶ֗ם שְׁמַ֤ע יִשְׂרָאֵל֙ אֶת־הַֽחֻקִּ֣ים

וְאֶת־הַמִּשְׁפָּטִ֔ים אֲשֶׁ֧ר אָֽנֹכִ֛י דֹּבֵ֥ר בְּאָזְנֵיכֶ֖ם הַיּ֑וֹם וּלְמַדְתֶּ֣ם אֹתָ֔ם וּשְׁמַרְתֶּ֖ם

ב-ג לַֽעֲשֹׂתָֽם: יְהֹוָ֣ה אֱלֹהֵ֗ינוּ כָּרַ֥ת עִמָּ֛נוּ בְּרִ֖ית בְּחֹרֵֽב: לֹ֣א אֶת־אֲבֹתֵ֔ינוּ כָּרַ֥ת

---

41. אָז יַבְדִּיל מֹשֶׁה שָׁלֹשׁ עָרִים — *Then Moses separated (set aside) three cities.* After he completed the introduction to his explanation of the Torah, he separated the cities (of refuge) to teach Israel how important (lit. 'distinguished') the fulfillment of the commandments are; that he was so particular to observe even a small part of (this) positive commandment.

44. וְזֹאת הַתּוֹרָה — *And this is the Torah (law).* The analytical portion (חֵלֶק הָעִיּוּנִי).

45. אֵלֶּה הָעֵדֹת — *These are the testimonies.* That portion which is attested to by (reasoned) proof.

47. וַיִּירְשׁוּ אֶת אַרְצוֹ — *And they took his land in possession.* After they conquered inhabited lands and were able to keep the *mitzvos* without fear, he (Moses) began to expound the Torah and commandments and caution (Israel) regarding them.

NOTES

knowledge of all this will bring man to a passionate desire to *know His great Name*.

אֲשֶׁר אָנֹכִי מְצַוֶּךָ ... כָּל הַיָּמִים — *Which I command you ... all the days.* The brief commentary of the *Sforno* on this portion of the verse reflects the ninth principle of the *Rambam's* Thirteen Principles of Faith: 'I believe with complete faith that this Torah will not be exchanged nor will there be another Torah from the Creator, Blessed is His Name.' The *Sforno* derives this from the concluding words of this verse כָּל הַיָּמִים, *all the days,* which revert back to the phrase אֲשֶׁר אָנֹכִי מְצַוֶּךָ, *which I command you,* viz., that which I command you in this Torah is for all days.

41. אָז יַבְדִּיל — *Then Moses separated.* The *Sforno* explains the connection of this act to the preceding verses in this chapter. The philosophical, analytical, theoretical verses of this chapter, as the *Sforno* has explained them, important and vital as they may be, are equaled in importance by the action of Moses in commencing the concrete implementation of the commandment to establish cities of refuge. Although these cities would not be operative until those on the west side of the Jordan were established, nonetheless, Moses set aside these cities. He did so to demonstrate the importance of implementing God's command, be it ever so modest an act, even though it is only a partial, non-operative fulfillment of a *mitzvah!*

ד יְהוָה אֶת־הַבְּרִית הַזֹּאת כִּי אִתָּנוּ אֲנַחְנוּ אֵלֶּה פֹה הַיּוֹם כֻּלָּנוּ חַיִּים: פָּנִים
ה | בְּפָנִים דִּבֶּר יְהוָה עִמָּכֶם בָּהָר מִתּוֹךְ הָאֵשׁ: °אָנֹכִי עֹמֵד בֵּין־יְהוָה וּבֵינֵיכֶם
בָּעֵת הַהִוא לְהַגִּיד לָכֶם אֶת־דְּבַר יְהוָה כִּי יְרֵאתֶם מִפְּנֵי הָאֵשׁ
ו וְלֹא־עֲלִיתֶם בָּהָר לֵאמֹר: אָנֹכִי יְהוָה אֱלֹהֶיךָ אֲשֶׁר
ז הוֹצֵאתִיךָ מֵאֶרֶץ מִצְרַיִם מִבֵּית עֲבָדִים: לֹא יִהְיֶה־לְךָ אֱלֹהִים אֲחֵרִים
ח עַל־פָּנָיַ: לֹא־תַעֲשֶׂה־לְךָ פֶסֶל | כָּל־תְּמוּנָה אֲשֶׁר בַּשָּׁמַיִם מִמַּעַל וַאֲשֶׁר
ט בָּאָרֶץ מִתָּחַת וַאֲשֶׁר בַּמַּיִם | מִתַּחַת לָאָרֶץ: לֹא־תִשְׁתַּחֲוֶה לָהֶם וְלֹא
תָעָבְדֵם כִּי אָנֹכִי יְהוָה אֱלֹהֶיךָ אֵל קַנָּא °פֹּקֵד עֲוֺן אָבוֹת עַל־בָּנִים
י וְעַל־שִׁלֵּשִׁים וְעַל־רִבֵּעִים לְשֹׂנְאָי: וְעֹשֶׂה חֶסֶד לַאֲלָפִים לְאֹהֲבַי וּלְשֹׁמְרֵי
°מִצְוֹתָי ק׳ יא °מצותו: לֹא תִשָּׂא אֶת־שֵׁם־יְהוָה אֱלֹהֶיךָ לַשָּׁוְא כִּי לֹא
יב יְנַקֶּה יְהוָה אֵת אֲשֶׁר־יִשָּׂא אֶת־שְׁמוֹ לַשָּׁוְא: שָׁמוֹר
יג אֶת־יוֹם הַשַּׁבָּת לְקַדְּשׁוֹ כַּאֲשֶׁר צִוְּךָ יְהוָה אֱלֹהֶיךָ: שֵׁשֶׁת יָמִים

V

3. הַיּוֹם כֻּלָּנוּ חַיִּים — *All of us alive this day.* Therefore, you who have made the covenant (with God) and are about to enter the Land, arrange your affairs in such a manner that coming generations who were not present when this covenant was established will (still) fulfill that which you accepted upon yourselves.

4-6. פָּנִים בְּפָנִים — *Face to face* . . . not in a dream or a night vision, but while you were in command of your senses — דִּבֶּר ה׳ עִמָּכֶם, *HASHEM spoke with you* — לֵאמֹר אָנֹכִי ה׳ וכו׳, *saying, I am HASHEM etc.* as explained above. וַיְדַבֵּר אֱלֹהִים אֵת כָּל הַדְּבָרִים הָאֵלֶּה לֵאמֹר: אָנֹכִי ה׳, *And God spoke all these words, saying: I am HASHEM* (*Exodus* 20:1-2). However, my standing *between HASHEM and you* was (for this purpose): לְהַגִּיד לָכֶם אֶת דְּבַר ה׳, כִּי יְרֵאתֶם, *to declare unto you the word of HASHEM because you were afraid.*

12. כַּאֲשֶׁר צִוְּךָ ה׳ אֱלֹהֶיךָ — *As HASHEM your God commanded you* . . . in the manner commanded you at Marah, because indeed, when He charged you regarding the Sabbath there, He informed you that it is not sufficient to sanctify it by abstaining from labor, but also to occupy yourselves with Torah and *mitzvos*, as it says, וְהַיָּשָׁר

NOTES

V

3. הַיּוֹם כֻּלָּנוּ חַיִּים — *All of us alive this day.* Moses stresses that the generation he is speaking to witnessed the giving of Torah at Sinai and heard the voice of God. They are therefore charged with the responsibility of transmitting this evidence to the next generation, so as to insure their compliance with the covenant between God and Israel.

4-6. פָּנִים בְּפָנִים . . . — *Face to face* . . . The first two commandments of the Decalogue, אָנֹכִי ה׳ אֱלֹהֶיךָ, *I am HASHEM your God*, and לֹא יִהְיֶה לְךָ אֱלֹהִים אֲחֵרִים, *You shall have no other gods*, were heard by Israel directly from God. However, the balance of the Ten Commandments was transmitted to them by Moses. Because the people of Israel were afraid to listen to the Almighty directly, they had asked Moses to be their intermediary. The *Sforno* explains that the expression 'face to face' refers to the first two commandments, since God spoke to all the people of Israel in this manner, whereas the statement of Moses, that he stood between God and Israel, refers to the subsequent commandments.

12. כַּאֲשֶׁר צִוְּךָ ה׳ אֱלֹהֶיךָ — *As HASHEM your God commanded you.* The expression *as HASHEM . . . commanded you* must refer to a previous period when God spoke to Israel regarding the Sabbath. The Sages, indeed, comment: כַּאֲשֶׁר

יד תַּעֲבֹד וְעָשִׂיתָ כָּל־מְלַאכְתֶּךָ: וְיוֹם הַשְּׁבִיעִי שַׁבָּת לַיהוָה אֱלֹהֶיךָ
לֹא־תַעֲשֶׂה כָל־מְלָאכָה אַתָּה | וּבִנְךָ־וּבִתֶּךָ וְעַבְדְּךָ־וַאֲמָתֶךָ וְשׁוֹרְךָ
וַחֲמֹרְךָ וְכָל־בְּהֶמְתֶּךָ וְגֵרְךָ אֲשֶׁר בִּשְׁעָרֶיךָ לְמַעַן יָנוּחַ עַבְדְּךָ וַאֲמָתְךָ כָּמוֹךָ:
טו וְזָכַרְתָּ כִּי־עֶבֶד הָיִיתָ | בְּאֶרֶץ מִצְרַיִם וַיֹּצִאֲךָ יְהוָה אֱלֹהֶיךָ מִשָּׁם
בְּיָד חֲזָקָה וּבִזְרֹעַ נְטוּיָה עַל־כֵּן צִוְּךָ יְהוָה אֱלֹהֶיךָ לַעֲשׂוֹת אֶת־יוֹם
טז הַשַּׁבָּת: כַּבֵּד אֶת־אָבִיךָ וְאֶת־אִמֶּךָ כַּאֲשֶׁר צִוְּךָ יְהוָה
אֱלֹהֶיךָ לְמַעַן | יַאֲרִיכֻן יָמֶיךָ וּלְמַעַן יִיטַב לָךְ עַל הָאֲדָמָה אֲשֶׁר־יְהוָה
יז אֱלֹהֶיךָ נֹתֵן לָךְ: לֹא תִרְצַח וְלֹא
תִנְאָף וְלֹא תִגְנֹב וְלֹא־תַעֲנֶה בְרֵעֲךָ עֵד
יח שָׁוְא: וְלֹא תַחְמֹד אֵשֶׁת רֵעֶךָ וְלֹא תִתְאַוֶּה בֵּית רֵעֶךָ
חמישי יט שָׂדֵהוּ וְעַבְדּוֹ וַאֲמָתוֹ שׁוֹרוֹ וַחֲמֹרוֹ וְכֹל אֲשֶׁר לְרֵעֶךָ: אֶת־
הַדְּבָרִים הָאֵלֶּה דִּבֶּר יְהוָה אֶל־כָּל־קְהַלְכֶם בָּהָר מִתּוֹךְ הָאֵשׁ הֶעָנָן
וְהָעֲרָפֶל קוֹל גָּדוֹל וְלֹא יָסָף וַיִּכְתְּבֵם עַל־שְׁנֵי לֻחֹת אֲבָנִים וַיִּתְּנֵם אֵלָי:
כ וַיְהִי כְּשָׁמְעֲכֶם אֶת־הַקּוֹל מִתּוֹךְ הַחֹשֶׁךְ וְהָהָר בֹּעֵר בָּאֵשׁ וַתִּקְרְבוּן אֵלַי
כא כָּל־רָאשֵׁי שִׁבְטֵיכֶם וְזִקְנֵיכֶם: וַתֹּאמְרוּ הֵן הֶרְאָנוּ יְהוָה אֱלֹהֵינוּ אֶת־כְּבֹדוֹ
וְאֶת־גָּדְלוֹ וְאֶת־קֹלוֹ שָׁמַעְנוּ מִתּוֹךְ הָאֵשׁ הַיּוֹם הַזֶּה רָאִינוּ כִּי־יְדַבֵּר
כב אֱלֹהִים אֶת־הָאָדָם וָחָי: וְעַתָּה לָמָּה נָמוּת כִּי תֹאכְלֵנוּ הָאֵשׁ הַגְּדֹלָה הַזֹּאת
כג אִם־יֹסְפִים | אֲנַחְנוּ לִשְׁמֹעַ אֶת־קוֹל יְהוָה אֱלֹהֵינוּ עוֹד וָמָתְנוּ: כִּי מִי
כָל־בָּשָׂר אֲשֶׁר שָׁמַע קוֹל אֱלֹהִים חַיִּים מְדַבֵּר מִתּוֹךְ־הָאֵשׁ כָּמֹנוּ וַיֶּחִי:
כד קְרַב אַתָּה וּשְׁמָע אֵת כָּל־אֲשֶׁר יֹאמַר יְהוָה אֱלֹהֵינוּ וְאַתְּ | תְּדַבֵּר אֵלֵינוּ

בְּעֵינָיו תַּעֲשֶׂה וְהַאֲזַנְתָּ לְמִצְוֹתָיו, *and do that which is right in His eyes and give ear to His commandments* (*Exodus* 15:26).

14-15. לְמַעַן יָנוּחַ עַבְדְּךָ וַאֲמָתְךָ כָּמוֹךָ: וְזָכַרְתָּ כִּי עֶבֶד הָיִיתָ — *That your man-servant and your maid-servant may rest as you do: And you shall remember that you were a slave.* Behold, the commandment that the animal should also rest was given so that the servant should rest, and this *mitzvah* (that the servant should rest) was given in order to remember the Exodus from Egypt whereby the Holy One, Blessed is He, caused the slaves to cease their labors.

16. וּלְמַעַן יִיטַב לָךְ — *And that it may go well with you* . . . even in this world, as our Sages say: דְּבָרִים שֶׁאָדָם אוֹכֵל פֵּרוֹתֵיהֶם בָּעוֹלָם הַזֶּה וְהַקֶּרֶן קַיֶּמֶת לוֹ לָעוֹלָם הַבָּא . . . כִּבּוּד אָב וָאֵם וכו׳, *Precepts whose fruits a person enjoys in This World but whose principal remains intact for him in the World to Come . . . honor due to father and mother, etc.* (*Peah* 1:1).

24. וְאַתְּ תְּדַבֵּר אֵלֵינוּ — *And you shall speak to us* . . . although your speaking (to us) will be inferior in quality to God's speaking (to us).

NOTES

צִוְּךָ בְּמָרָה, 'as He commanded you at Marah' (see *Exodus* 15). The *Sforno*, however, adds that this phrase refers not only to the commandment per se of Sabbath observance, but also to the manner and spirit of its observance, which was alluded to at Marah when the Almighty said *and do what is right etc.*, as the *Sforno* explains here in his commentary.

24. וְאַתְּ תְּדַבֵּר — *And you shall speak*. This

כה אֶת כָּל־אֲשֶׁר יְדַבֵּר יְהוָה אֱלֹהֵינוּ אֵלֶיךָ וְשָׁמַעְנוּ וְעָשִׂינוּ׃ וַיִּשְׁמַע יְהוָה
אֶת־קוֹל דִּבְרֵיכֶם בְּדַבֶּרְכֶם אֵלָי וַיֹּאמֶר יְהוָה אֵלַי שָׁמַעְתִּי אֶת־קוֹל
כו דִּבְרֵי הָעָם הַזֶּה אֲשֶׁר דִּבְּרוּ אֵלֶיךָ הֵיטִיבוּ כָּל־אֲשֶׁר דִּבֵּרוּ׃ מִי־יִתֵּן
וְהָיָה לְבָבָם זֶה לָהֶם לְיִרְאָה אֹתִי וְלִשְׁמֹר אֶת־כָּל־מִצְוֺתַי כָּל־הַיָּמִים
כז לְמַעַן יִיטַב לָהֶם וְלִבְנֵיהֶם לְעֹלָם׃ לֵךְ אֱמֹר לָהֶם שׁוּבוּ לָכֶם לְאָהֳלֵיכֶם׃
כח וְאַתָּה פֹּה עֲמֹד עִמָּדִי וַאֲדַבְּרָה אֵלֶיךָ אֵת כָּל־הַמִּצְוָה וְהַחֻקִּים וְהַמִּשְׁפָּטִים
כט אֲשֶׁר תְּלַמְּדֵם וְעָשׂוּ בָאָרֶץ אֲשֶׁר אָנֹכִי נֹתֵן לָהֶם לְרִשְׁתָּהּ׃ וּשְׁמַרְתֶּם
לַעֲשׂוֹת כַּאֲשֶׁר צִוָּה יְהוָה אֱלֹהֵיכֶם אֶתְכֶם לֹא תָסֻרוּ יָמִין וּשְׂמֹאל׃
ל בְּכָל־הַדֶּרֶךְ אֲשֶׁר צִוָּה יְהוָה אֱלֹהֵיכֶם אֶתְכֶם תֵּלֵכוּ לְמַעַן תִּחְיוּן וְטוֹב
ו א לָכֶם וְהַאֲרַכְתֶּם יָמִים בָּאָרֶץ אֲשֶׁר תִּירָשׁוּן׃ וְזֹאת הַמִּצְוָה הַחֻקִּים
וְהַמִּשְׁפָּטִים אֲשֶׁר צִוָּה יְהוָה אֱלֹהֵיכֶם לְלַמֵּד אֶתְכֶם לַעֲשׂוֹת בָּאָרֶץ אֲשֶׁר
ב אַתֶּם עֹבְרִים שָׁמָּה לְרִשְׁתָּהּ׃ לְמַעַן תִּירָא אֶת־יְהוָה אֱלֹהֶיךָ לִשְׁמֹר

---

29. וּשְׁמַרְתֶּם לַעֲשׂוֹת — *And you shall observe to do* ... and since the matter developed thus, it is proper that you observe (what I shall relate to you).

לֹא תָסֻרוּ יָמִין וּשְׂמֹאל — *You shall not turn aside to the right hand or to the left.* You shall neither add (that) which you think will improve (them) nor diminish from them whatsoever.

30. לְמַעַן תִּחְיוּן וְטוֹב לָכֶם — *That you may live and that it may be well with you* ... so that you may (merit) eternal life, in a good and happy manner.

וְהַאֲרַכְתֶּם יָמִים בָּאָרֶץ אֲשֶׁר תִּירָשׁוּן -- *That you may prolong your days in the land which you shall possess* ... and that you may acquire length of days in the world which is כֻּלּוֹ אָרוּךְ, *wholly long* (based on *Kiddushin* 39b), as a result of your dwelling in the land without pain, free from anxiety and impediments.

VI

1. וְזֹאת הַמִּצְוָה — *Now this is the commandment* ... the intent of (God), the Blessed One, Who commanded these precepts which are linked to the Land (הַתְּלוּיוֹת בָּאָרֶץ) when you enter it (is) ...

2. לְמַעַן תִּירָא אֶת ה׳ אֱלֹהֶיךָ — *That you might fear* HASHEM *your God* ... that you shall remember that the Land is His, and that you are (but) *strangers and settlers with Him* (based on *Leviticus* 25:23).

NOTES

commentary of the *Sforno* is suggested by the feminine form of וְאַתְּ, *and you,* which implies a weaker, lesser level of communication.

29. וּשְׁמַרְתֶּם לַעֲשׂוֹת ... לֹא תָסֻרוּ יָמִין וּשְׂמֹאל — *And you shall observe to do ... you shall not turn aside to the right hand or to the left.* Originally, it was God's intent that Israel should hear all the commandments directly from Him. Had that come to pass, there would have been no doubt in the mind of the people that these commandments were authentic, since they emanated from the Almighty. However, since the subsequent eight commandments were transmitted by Moses, there was a danger that they might question their authenticity.

אֶת־כָּל־חֻקֹּתָיו וּמִצְוֺתָיו אֲשֶׁר אָנֹכִי מְצַוֶּךָ אַתָּה וּבִנְךָ וּבֶן־בִּנְךָ כֹּל יְמֵי
ג חַיֶּיךָ וּלְמַעַן יַאֲרִכֻן יָמֶיךָ׃ וְשָׁמַעְתָּ יִשְׂרָאֵל וְשָׁמַרְתָּ לַעֲשׂוֹת אֲשֶׁר יִיטַב לְךָ
וַאֲשֶׁר תִּרְבּוּן מְאֹד כַּאֲשֶׁר דִּבֶּר יהוה אֱלֹהֵי אֲבֹתֶיךָ לָךְ אֶרֶץ זָבַת חָלָב
וּדְבָשׁ׃

אַתָּה וּבִנְךָ וּבֶן בִּנְךָ — *You, your son and your son's son* ... so that those generations who did not see the great works of God will also fear Him, when they accept these commandments from you who did witness them (i.e., the great deeds of God).

וּלְמַעַן יַאֲרִכֻן יָמֶיךָ — *And that your days may be prolonged* ... and so that these commandments shall grant you life which is כֻּלּוֹ אָרוּךְ, *everlasting.*

3. וְשָׁמַעְתָּ יִשְׂרָאֵל — *And you shall hear, O Israel* ... and being that this is the intended purpose of God, the Blessed One, (because of) His great lovingkindness for you, it is fitting that you listen and understand the intent of God, the Blessed One, regarding all these (*mitzvos*).

וְשָׁמַרְתָּ לַעֲשׂוֹת אֲשֶׁר יִיטַב לְךָ — *And observe to do it that it may be well with you.* You will then attempt to do God's will with love and to find favor (in His eyes), which will insure that it shall be well with you and you will be granted eternal happiness. Also by observing to do it, you will 'increase mightily,' all this resulting from your observance of righteousness and justice done in His honor.

כַּאֲשֶׁר דִּבֶּר ה׳ אֱלֹהֵי אֲבֹתֶיךָ לָךְ אֶרֶץ זָבַת חָלָב וּדְבָשׁ — *As HASHEM the God of your fathers promised you, a land flowing with milk and honey.* As He spoke to you, (He will give you) a land flowing with milk and honey, prepared for those who serve Him for this purpose, that you may earn your livelihood without pain and (thereby) have time for analytical (study) and for (good) deeds, (as well) as being fruitful and multiplying.

NOTES

Therefore, it was necessary for Moses to caution them that they must observe *all* of the commandments, including those they heard through him, and not deviate from them.

30. וְהַאֲרַכְתֶּם יָמִים בָּאָרֶץ אֲשֶׁר תִּירָשׁוּן — *That you may prolong your days in the land which you shall possess.* The *Sforno,* consistent with his oft-expressed views, is of the opinion that man requires tranquility, a sense of well-being and security, in order to develop his intellect and attain spiritual perfection, which in turn insures the attainment of one's portion of eternal life. The expression כּוּלּוֹ אָרוּךְ, *wholly long,* in his commentary is taken from the expression in the Torah regarding the reward given for honoring one's parents (לְמַעַן יַאֲרִיכֻן יָמֶיךָ).

VI

2. לְמַעַן תִּירָא ... וּלְמַעַן יַאֲרִכֻן יָמֶיךָ — *That you might fear ... and that your days may be prolonged.* The *Sforno* explains that the מִצְוֹת הַתְּלוּיוֹת בָּאָרֶץ, the commandments which are associated exclusively with the Land, and are not obligatory outside *Eretz Yisrael,* serve a twofold purpose. One, as stated in this verse, is to impress upon the Israelite that he is but a sojourner in the land which belongs to God alone. The second is to reward him with the blessing of eternal life. As the *Sforno* explains in the next verse, the exceptional character of *Eretz Yisrael,* a land which flows with milk and honey, was given to Israel because it decreased the need for strenuous physical labor while improving those conditions which enhance the mental and spiritual growth of its inhabitants.

ששי ד-ה שְׁמַ֖ע יִשְׂרָאֵ֑ל יהוה אֱלֹהֵ֖ינוּ יהוה ׀ אֶחָֽד: וְאָ֣הַבְתָּ֔ אֵ֖ת יהוה אֱלֹהֶ֑יךָ
וּ בְּכָל־לְבָבְךָ֥ וּבְכָל־נַפְשְׁךָ֖ וּבְכָל־מְאֹדֶֽךָ: וְהָי֞וּ הַדְּבָרִ֣ים הָאֵ֗לֶּה אֲשֶׁ֨ר אֽנֹכִ֜י

---

4. שְׁמַע יִשְׂרָאֵל — *Hear, O Israel.* Contemplate and understand this.

ה' — *HASHEM.* Who gives existence and is the Creator.

אֱלֹהֵינוּ — *Our God.* He is the Chosen One of all who are separated (from matter), and our hope is to attain our desires from Him (alone), not through any intermediary. And being that He is exalted (and superior) in His power of creativity, hence it is fitting to bow down to Him alone. And since our hope lies in Him (alone), without need for any intermediary, it is proper that we pray to and serve Him alone.

ה' אֶחָד — *HASHEM is One.* Now, being that He granted existence from total nothingness (יֵשׁ מֵאַיִן), it is understood (lit. 'explained') that there does not exist any kind similar to Him and that He is separated in kind from all that exists in the world of נִפְסָדִים, *perishables,* and all that exists in the world of the spheres, and all that exists in the world of angels, in such a manner that He is (singular) and alone in His fourth world. Now it seems to me that this is alluded to in the fact that the letter *daled* of the word אֶחָד, *echad,* is larger and that the letter *ayin* of the word שְׁמַע, *hear,* is (also) larger, teaching us that it is fitting that we pay attention and increase our analysis of all this, as our Sages said: ' ... Providing that one prolongs (the utterance) of the (letter) *daled* of *echad'* so that one might concentrate (his thoughts) regarding (all) this.

5. וְאָהַבְתָּ — *And you shall love.* You shall rejoice to do that which is good in His eyes once you discern that there is no nobler goal than this.

NOTES

4. שְׁמַע יִשְׂרָאֵל ה' אֱלֹהֵינוּ — *Hear, O Israel, HASHEM Our God.* The sense of the *Sforno's* commentary regarding this major declaration of faith is: It is imperative that the Israelite contemplate and understand that God is the First Cause, who grants the power of being to every aspect of creation and without Him one cannot conceive of any existence. He is our God in the sense that whereas other nations have their heavenly princes (שָׂרִים) and guardian angels, we Israelites are under His direct supervision and Divine Providence without the need of any intermediary. Hence, we must place all our hopes in Him alone, and pray to and worship Him alone. This is the meaning of the word אֱלֹהֵינוּ — *our God.*

ה' אֶחָד — *HASHEM is One.* (a) According to Kabbalistic doctrine there are four 'worlds': עוֹלָם הָאֲצִילוּת, *the world of emanations;* עוֹלָם הַבְּרִיאָה, *the world of creation;* עוֹלָם הַיְצִירָה, *the world of formation;* and עוֹלָם הָעֲשִׂיָּה, *the world of creative matter.* The aforementioned emanations are also known as the ten סְפִירוֹת, *sefiros,* ranging from כֶּתֶר, *Crown,* to מַלְכוּת, *Kingship,* all these being incorporated in the עוֹלָם הָאֲצִילוּת, which is the most spiritual of the

four 'worlds.' As such, the Almighty is 'near' or 'close by' these ten *sefiros* and the word אֲצִילוּת is derived from אֵצֶל, i.e., 'near,' according to the *Ramban.* The *Sforno* is of the opinion that God is singular and unique in this 'fourth world,' which explains why the letter ד is written large at the end of the word אֶחָד according to the *Mesorah* to call our attention to this concept, being that ד is the numerical equivalent of four. The letter ע is also written large at the end of the word שְׁמַע, implying that we should look and see ('*ayin*' meaning 'eye'), the significance of God's transcendence over the four worlds, for He is the אֵין סוֹף, *the Limitless and Boundless One* — as the Kabbalists refer to God.

(b) The 'world of spheres,' mentioned by the *Sforno,* is part of the 'world of emanations' or of 'creative matter,' depending upon the opinion of various Kabbalistic schools, while the 'world of angels' is part of the 'world of formation.' They are not separate worlds. The *Sforno* refers to עוֹלָם הָעֲשִׂיָּה, *the world of matter,* as the world of הַנִּפְסָדִים, *the perishable* or the *destructible.* This material world is comprised of four basic elements or substances — earth, air, water and fire.

ז מְצַוְּךָ הַיּוֹם עַל־לְבָבֶךָ: וְשִׁנַּנְתָּם לְבָנֶיךָ וְדִבַּרְתָּ בָּם בְּשִׁבְתְּךָ בְּבֵיתֶךָ
ח וּבְלֶכְתְּךָ בַדֶּרֶךְ וּבְשָׁכְבְּךָ וּבְקוּמֶךָ: וּקְשַׁרְתָּם לְאוֹת עַל־יָדֶךָ וְהָיוּ לְטֹטָפֹת
ט־י בֵּין עֵינֶיךָ: וּכְתַבְתָּם עַל־מְזֻזוֹת בֵּיתֶךָ וּבִשְׁעָרֶיךָ: וְהָיָה כִּי־
יְבִיאֲךָ ׀ יְהוָה אֱלֹהֶיךָ אֶל־הָאָרֶץ אֲשֶׁר נִשְׁבַּע לַאֲבֹתֶיךָ לְאַבְרָהָם לְיִצְחָק
יא וּלְיַעֲקֹב לָתֶת לָךְ עָרִים גְּדֹלֹת וְטֹבֹת אֲשֶׁר לֹא־בָנִיתָ: וּבָתִּים מְלֵאִים
כָּל־טוּב אֲשֶׁר לֹא־מִלֵּאתָ וּבֹרֹת חֲצוּבִים אֲשֶׁר לֹא־חָצַבְתָּ כְּרָמִים וְזֵיתִים
יב אֲשֶׁר לֹא־נָטָעְתָּ וְאָכַלְתָּ וְשָׂבָעְתָּ: הִשָּׁמֶר לְךָ פֶּן־תִּשְׁכַּח אֶת־יְהוָה אֲשֶׁר
יג הוֹצִיאֲךָ מֵאֶרֶץ מִצְרַיִם מִבֵּית עֲבָדִים: אֶת־יְהוָה אֱלֹהֶיךָ תִּירָא וְאֹתוֹ
יד תַעֲבֹד וּבִשְׁמוֹ תִּשָּׁבֵעַ: לֹא תֵלְכוּן אַחֲרֵי אֱלֹהִים אֲחֵרִים מֵאֱלֹהֵי הָעַמִּים
טו אֲשֶׁר סְבִיבוֹתֵיכֶם: כִּי אֵל קַנָּא יְהוָה אֱלֹהֶיךָ בְּקִרְבֶּךָ פֶּן־יֶחֱרֶה אַף־יְהוָה
טז אֱלֹהֶיךָ בָּךְ וְהִשְׁמִידְךָ מֵעַל פְּנֵי הָאֲדָמָה: לֹא תְנַסּוּ אֶת־
יז יְהוָה אֱלֹהֵיכֶם כַּאֲשֶׁר נִסִּיתֶם בַּמַּסָּה: שָׁמוֹר תִּשְׁמְרוּן אֶת־מִצְוֺת יְהוָה
יח אֱלֹהֵיכֶם וְעֵדֹתָיו וְחֻקָּיו אֲשֶׁר צִוָּךְ: וְעָשִׂיתָ הַיָּשָׁר וְהַטּוֹב בְּעֵינֵי יְהוָה לְמַעַן

---

6. עַל לְבָבֶךָ — *Upon your heart.* You shall constantly remember to direct your deeds toward this goal.

7. וְשִׁנַּנְתָּם לְבָנֶיךָ — *And you shall teach them diligently to your children.* Teach them by constant review and with sharpness, (resulting in) reasoned proof.

וְדִבַּרְתָּ בָּם — *And you shall talk of them* . . . for by such constant repetition, you (and they) will always remember them.

10-11. אֲשֶׁר לֹא בָנִיתָ: וּבָתִּים מְלֵאִים כָּל טוּב אֲשֶׁר לֹא מִלֵּאתָ — *Which you did not build. And houses full of all good things which you did not fill* . . . for you will acquire wealth without toil.

12. הִשָּׁמֶר לְךָ פֶּן תִּשְׁכַּח — *Beware lest you forget.* For wealth acquired in this fashion, in most cases, results in unrestrained lust, and thus man forgets his Maker.

NOTES

5. וְאָהַבְתָּ — *And you shall love.* Many commentators have pointed out that the phrase *and you shall love* cannot be interpreted as a command, for how can the emotion of love be commanded? The *Sforno* resolves this difficulty by interpreting the phrase וְאָהַבְתָּ as a promise and assurance, i.e., you *will* love. When man arrives at a clear and complete understanding of God, he will then appreciate His greatness and kindness which will bring him sincere joy, and this in turn will evoke a profound feeling of love for God. The *Rambam,* in *Hilchos Teshuvah* 10:2, interprets the word וְאָהַבְתָּ thus: 'Whoever serves God out of love and occupies himself with the study of Torah and the fulfillment of commandments and walks in the path of wisdom . . . ultimately happiness comes to him as a result of his conduct . . . This is the standard which God, through Moses, bids us to achieve, as it is said, וְאָהַבְתָּ אֵת ה׳ אֱלֹהֶיךָ, *And you shall love* HASHEM *your God.'*

6. עַל לְבָבֶךָ — *Upon your heart.* The expression *upon your heart* means to commit something to memory. Israel is urged to take heed of God's words and to remember them ever for the purpose of translating them into action. We find a similar expression in *Proverbs* 3:3, כָּתְבֵם עַל לוּחַ לִבֶּךָ, *Write them* (i.e., the commandments of God) *on the tablet of your heart.* In the next verse, the Torah tells us how to insure memory by constant review and repetition.

11-12. וּבָתִּים מְלֵאִים כָּל טוּב . . . הִשָּׁמֶר לְךָ פֶּן תִּשְׁכַּח — *And houses full of all good things which you did not fill . . . Beware lest you forget.* Wealth so easily acquired is liable to produce unlimited desires in man which eventually result in his rejecting the sovereignty of God.

יִיטַב לָךְ וּבָאתָ וְיָרַשְׁתָּ אֶת־הָאָרֶץ הַטֹּבָה אֲשֶׁר־נִשְׁבַּע יהוה לַאֲבֹתֶיךָ:
יט־כ לַהֲדֹף אֶת־כָּל־אֹיְבֶיךָ מִפָּנֶיךָ כַּאֲשֶׁר דִּבֶּר יהוה: כִּי־
יִשְׁאָלְךָ בִנְךָ מָחָר לֵאמֹר מָה הָעֵדֹת וְהַחֻקִּים וְהַמִּשְׁפָּטִים אֲשֶׁר צִוָּה יהוה
כא אֱלֹהֵינוּ אֶתְכֶם: וְאָמַרְתָּ לְבִנְךָ עֲבָדִים הָיִינוּ לְפַרְעֹה בְּמִצְרָיִם וַיֹּצִיאֵנוּ יהוה
כב מִמִּצְרַיִם בְּיָד חֲזָקָה: וַיִּתֵּן יהוה אוֹתֹת וּמֹפְתִים גְּדֹלִים וְרָעִים | בְּמִצְרַיִם
כג בְּפַרְעֹה וּבְכָל־בֵּיתוֹ לְעֵינֵינוּ: וְאוֹתָנוּ הוֹצִיא מִשָּׁם לְמַעַן הָבִיא אֹתָנוּ לָתֶת
כד לָנוּ אֶת־הָאָרֶץ אֲשֶׁר נִשְׁבַּע לַאֲבֹתֵינוּ: וַיְצַוֵּנוּ יהוה לַעֲשׂוֹת אֶת־כָּל־
הַחֻקִּים הָאֵלֶּה לְיִרְאָה אֶת־יהוה אֱלֹהֵינוּ לְטוֹב לָנוּ כָּל־הַיָּמִים לְחַיֹּתֵנוּ
כה כְּהַיּוֹם הַזֶּה: וּצְדָקָה תִּהְיֶה־לָּנוּ כִּי־נִשְׁמֹר לַעֲשׂוֹת אֶת־כָּל־הַמִּצְוָה הַזֹּאת

---

20. מָה הָעֵדֹת — *What do the testimonies mean?* ... that part (of Torah) which is analytical and is proven testimony (of its truth).

וְהַחֻקִּים וְהַמִּשְׁפָּטִים — *And the statutes and the ordinances.* The part (of Torah) which (demands) deeds.

אֲשֶׁר צִוָּה ה׳ אֱלֹהֵינוּ אֶתְכֶם — *Which HASHEM our God has commanded you* ... the commandments given to the sons of Noach (בְּנֵי נֹחַ) being insufficient.

21. עֲבָדִים הָיִינוּ — *We were slaves.* And being that in our servitude (to Pharaoh) we were incapable of attaining the perfection intended for us (by God), He wondrously delivered us and brought us to the land so that we might be able to acquire that perfection (completeness) (residing) in it.

24. וַיְצַוֵּנוּ ה׳ לַעֲשׂוֹת אֶת כָּל הַחֻקִּים הָאֵלֶּה — *And HASHEM commanded us to do all these statutes* ... so that we might understand through observing them ...

לְיִרְאָה אֶת ה׳ אֱלֹהֵינוּ — *To fear HASHEM our God.* And this will result when we contemplate and recognize His greatness. Now, all this He wanted לְטוֹב לָנוּ כָּל הַיָּמִים, *for our good all the days,* for He desires to perform (deeds of) lovingkindness, not for His own sake (but rather for our benefit).

לְחַיֹּתֵנוּ כְּהַיּוֹם הַזֶּה — *That He might preserve us alive as it is this day.* (This refers to) transitory life (lit., life of the hour), and that there be *righteousness to us* and merit *before Hashem, our God*, (refers to) the everlasting world.

25. וּצְדָקָה תִּהְיֶה לָּנוּ — *And it shall be righteousness unto us* ... and when I said to you *for our good all the days,* I meant to say by that it should be for our good in This World (עוֹלָם הַזֶּה) and in the World to Come (עוֹלָם הַבָּא).

NOTES

20. אֲשֶׁר צִוָּה ה׳ אֱלֹהֵינוּ אֶתְכֶם ... — *Which HASHEM our God has commanded you.* The son is puzzled by the multiplicity of laws given to Israel, whereas the other nations are only required to observe the basic laws of humanity, known as 'the seven laws of the sons of Noah,' viz. not to worship idols, not to blaspheme the name of God, to establish courts of justice, not to kill, not to commit adultery, not to rob and not to eat flesh cut from a living animal. The answer to this question is given in verses 24-25.

24-25. לְטוֹב לָנוּ כָּל הַיָּמִים ... וּצְדָקָה תִּהְיֶה לָּנוּ — *For our good all the days ... And it shall be righteousness unto us.* The *Sforno* interprets כָּל הַיָּמִים, *all the days,* as indicating This World and the World to Come. The expression לְטוֹב לָנוּ, *for our good,* means it is for our benefit and not for the benefit of God. The

ז שביעי א לִפְנֵי יהוָה אֱלֹהֵינוּ כַּאֲשֶׁר צִוָּנוּ: כִּי יְבִיאֲךָ יהוָה אֱלֹהֶיךָ
אֶל־הָאָרֶץ אֲשֶׁר־אַתָּה בָא־שָׁמָּה לְרִשְׁתָּהּ וְנָשַׁל גּוֹיִם־רַבִּים | מִפָּנֶיךָ הַחִתִּי
וְהַגִּרְגָּשִׁי וְהָאֱמֹרִי וְהַכְּנַעֲנִי וְהַפְּרִזִּי וְהַחִוִּי וְהַיְבוּסִי שִׁבְעָה גוֹיִם רַבִּים
ב וַעֲצוּמִים מִמֶּךָּ: וּנְתָנָם יהוָה אֱלֹהֶיךָ לְפָנֶיךָ וְהִכִּיתָם הַחֲרֵם תַּחֲרִים אֹתָם
ג לֹא־תִכְרֹת לָהֶם בְּרִית וְלֹא תְחָנֵּם: וְלֹא תִתְחַתֵּן בָּם בִּתְּךָ לֹא־תִתֵּן לִבְנוֹ
ד וּבִתּוֹ לֹא־תִקַּח לִבְנֶךָ: כִּי־יָסִיר אֶת־בִּנְךָ מֵאַחֲרַי וְעָבְדוּ אֱלֹהִים אֲחֵרִים
ה וְחָרָה אַף־יהוָה בָּכֶם וְהִשְׁמִידְךָ מַהֵר: כִּי־אִם־כֹּה תַעֲשׂוּ לָהֶם מִזְבְּחֹתֵיהֶם
ו תִּתֹּצוּ וּמַצֵּבֹתָם תְּשַׁבֵּרוּ וַאֲשֵׁירֵהֶם תְּגַדֵּעוּן וּפְסִילֵיהֶם תִּשְׂרְפוּן בָּאֵשׁ: כִּי
עַם קָדוֹשׁ אַתָּה לַיהוָה אֱלֹהֶיךָ בְּךָ בָּחַר | יהוָה אֱלֹהֶיךָ לִהְיוֹת לוֹ לְעַם
ז סְגֻלָּה מִכֹּל הָעַמִּים אֲשֶׁר עַל־פְּנֵי הָאֲדָמָה: לֹא מֵרֻבְּכֶם מִכָּל־הָעַמִּים חָשַׁק
ח יהוָה בָּכֶם וַיִּבְחַר בָּכֶם כִּי־אַתֶּם הַמְעַט מִכָּל־הָעַמִּים: כִּי מֵאַהֲבַת יהוָה

VII

6. כִּי עַם קָדוֹשׁ אַתָּה — *For you are a holy people.* And it is not fitting to profane your holiness by marrying women who serve strange gods, thereby giving birth to disqualified offspring, as it says, כִּי חִלֵּל יְהוּדָה קֹדֶשׁ ה׳ אֲשֶׁר אָהֵב וּבָעַל בַּת אֵל נֵכָר, *for Judah has profaned the holiness of HASHEM which he loved, and has married the daughter of a strange god* (*Malachi* 2:11).

בְּךָ בָּחַר ה׳ — *HASHEM has chosen you* . . . but not unfit offspring, as our Sages say, 'The Divine Presence comes to rest only upon families of pure birth in Israel' (*Kiddushin* 70b).

7. לֹא מֵרֻבְּכֶם — *Not because you were more in number* . . . not for the purpose of gaining honor through their large populace (did God choose them).

8. כִּי מֵאַהֲבַת ה׳ אֶתְכֶם — *But out of HASHEM'S love for you* . . . because you are the seed of (those) who loved Him and acknowledged His Name moreso than other nations.

NOTES

phrase לְחַיֹּתֵנוּ כְּהַיּוֹם הַזֶּה, *that He might preserve us alive as it is this day,* refers to man's happiness and fulfillment in This World, while the expression וּצְדָקָה תִּהְיֶה לָּנוּ, *and it shall be righteousness unto us,* implies the merits earned by man in This World which will be rewarded eventually in the eternal, everlasting world.

VII

6. כִּי עַם קָדוֹשׁ אַתָּה — *For you are a holy people*. The *Sforno* interprets the statement as the source for the prohibition of intermarriage. Because Israel is holy, they must not marry gentile women who practice idolatry. The verse from *Malachi* quoted by the *Sforno* proves that such behavior profanes the holiness of God. [This does not mean that the prohibition against intermarriage is limited to women addicted to idolatry. All gentile women are forbidden to Jewish men. The verse only gives this reason as a generalization.]

8. כִּי מֵאַהֲבַת ה׳ אֶתְכֶם — *But out of HASHEM's love for you*. When the Almighty brought Israel forth from Egypt with a mighty hand, they were not worthy on their own to be delivered. It was only because God had sworn to the Patriarchs and he was obligated to keep His oath, as this verse explicitly states. Hence, the *Sforno* interprets this phrase as also referring to the seed of the Patriarchs, especially Abraham, who is called זֶרַע אַבְרָהָם אֹהֲבִי, *The offspring of Abraham who loved Me* (*Isaiah* 41:8). Indeed, the phraseology used by the *Sforno* here is based on the verse in *Isaiah*.

אֶתְכֶם וּמִשָּׁמְרוֹ אֶת־הַשְּׁבֻעָה אֲשֶׁר נִשְׁבַּע לַאֲבֹתֵיכֶם הוֹצִיא יְהוָה אֶתְכֶם
מפטיר ט בְּיָד חֲזָקָה וַיִּפְדְּךָ מִבֵּית עֲבָדִים מִיַּד פַּרְעֹה מֶלֶךְ־מִצְרָיִם׃ וְיָדַעְתָּ כִּי־יְהוָה
אֱלֹהֶיךָ הוּא הָאֱלֹהִים הָאֵל הַנֶּאֱמָן שֹׁמֵר הַבְּרִית וְהַחֶסֶד לְאֹהֲבָיו וּלְשֹׁמְרֵי
י מִצְוֹתָו לְאֶלֶף דּוֹר׃ וּמְשַׁלֵּם לְשֹׂנְאָיו אֶל־פָּנָיו לְהַאֲבִידוֹ לֹא יְאַחֵר לְשֹׂנְאוֹ
יא אֶל־פָּנָיו יְשַׁלֶּם־לוֹ׃ וְשָׁמַרְתָּ אֶת־הַמִּצְוָה וְאֶת־הַחֻקִּים וְאֶת־הַמִּשְׁפָּטִים
אֲשֶׁר אָנֹכִי מְצַוְּךָ הַיּוֹם לַעֲשׂוֹתָם׃

---

9. הָאֵל הַנֶּאֱמָן — *The faithful God* ... who unswervingly (keeps His word) and is unchanging.

9-10. שֹׁמֵר הַבְּרִית ... וּמְשַׁלֵּם לְשֹׂנְאָיו — *Who keeps the covenant ... and repays them who hate Him.* The reason (that we find) רָשָׁע וְטוֹב לוֹ, *a wicked man who prospers* (*Berachos* 7a), is twofold. One part is due to the merit of (his) fathers, as we find by Ishmael, כִּי זַרְעֲךָ הוּא, *because he is your seed* (*Genesis* 21:13), and the second is due to some merit that the wicked person himself possesses, which is insufficient for him to merit everlasting life but is enough for him to be compensated in this world, for 'the Holy One, Blessed is He, does not withhold the reward of any creature' (*Pesachim* 118a).

11. וְשָׁמַרְתָּ ... הַיּוֹם לַעֲשׂוֹתָם — *And you shall keep ... this day to do them.* And let it not trouble you if you do not receive reward for them in This World.

NOTES

9. הָאֵל הַנֶּאֱמָן — *The faithful God*. The word נֶאֱמָן, *faithful*, also means 'something that is sure and secure,' as we find in *Isaiah* 22:23, בְּמָקוֹם נֶאֱמָן, *in a sure place*. The *Sforno* interprets it similarly here.

10. וּמְשַׁלֵּם לְשֹׂנְאָיו — *And repays them who hate Him*. Ishmael is blessed by God to become a nation because he is the son of Abraham. Thus, the wicked may at times prosper in the merit of righteous fathers.

11. הַיּוֹם לַעֲשׂוֹתָם — *This day to do them*. Compare to *Rashi* who comments, 'And tomorrow, in the World to Come, to receive reward for them,' based on *Eruvin* 22b.

פרשת עקב
Parasha‌s Ekev

יב וְהָיָה ׀ עֵקֶב תִּשְׁמְעוּן אֵת הַמִּשְׁפָּטִים הָאֵלֶּה וּשְׁמַרְתֶּם וַעֲשִׂיתֶם אֹתָם
וְשָׁמַר יהוה אֱלֹהֶיךָ לְךָ אֶת־הַבְּרִית וְאֶת־הַחֶסֶד אֲשֶׁר נִשְׁבַּע לַאֲבֹתֶיךָ:

---

12. וְהָיָה עֵקֶב תִּשְׁמְעוּן — *And it shall come to pass because you hearken*. Behold, the King (i.e., the Almighty) has commanded all this in order that you may merit His keeping of the covenant, and His kindness. Thus, (if) you keep this day (i.e., in this world) His *mitzvos* and observe them out of love and not on the condition of receiving reward immediately, He, in turn, will keep the covenant and show His kindness to you.

אֵת הַמִּשְׁפָּטִים — *These ordinances* ... because בְּמִשְׁפָּט יַעֲמִיד אָרֶץ, *(The king) by justice establishes the land* (based on *Proverbs* 29:4).

וּשְׁמַרְתֶּם — *And you will keep*. This refers to Mishnah.

וַעֲשִׂיתֶם אֹתָם — *And you will do them*. And in this manner you will do them correctly.

וְשָׁמַר ה׳ אֱלֹהֶיךָ לְךָ אֶת הַבְּרִית — *and* HASHEM *your God shall keep the covenant with you* ... which He swore when He said, וַהֲקִמֹתִי אֶת בְּרִיתִי בֵּינִי וּבֵינֶךָ וּבֵין זַרְעֲךָ אַחֲרֶיךָ לְדֹרֹתָם לִבְרִית עוֹלָם לִהְיוֹת לְךָ לֵאלֹהִים וּלְזַרְעֲךָ אַחֲרֶיךָ, *And I will establish My covenant between Myself and you and your seed after you, throughout their generations for an everlasting covenant to be a God unto you and to your seed after you* (*Genesis* 17:7). Because He is a God unto us without any intermediary, hence everlasting existence flows from God to Israel, emanating from Him directly without any intermediary as it says, כִּי כָּל אֲשֶׁר יַעֲשֶׂה הָאֱלֹהִים הוּא יִהְיֶה לְעוֹלָם, *Whatever God does shall be forever* (*Ecclesiastes* 3:14), whereas the existence of the perishable without a doubt, emanates from Him through intermediaries.

וְאֶת הַחֶסֶד — *And the lovingkindness*. As it says, וְנָתַתִּי לְךָ וּלְזַרְעֲךָ אַחֲרֶיךָ אֵת אֶרֶץ מְגֻרֶיךָ, *And I will give you and your seed after you the land of your sojournings* (*Genesis* 17:8); because, indeed, the good granted to the righteous in This World is a result of (God's) lovingkindness, and not compensation for their deeds.

NOTES

12. וְהָיָה עֵקֶב תִּשְׁמְעוּן ... וּשְׁמַרְתֶּם ... וְשָׁמַר ה׳ אֱלֹהֶיךָ — *And it shall come to pass because you hearken ... and you will keep ... and* HASHEM *your God shall keep* ... This verse must be understood as a continuation of verses 9 and 11 at the conclusion of *parashas Vaeschanan*. In verse 9, the Torah tells us that the Almighty will faithfully keep the covenant He entered into with Israel, and will also bestow His lovingkindness upon them, providing they keep their part of the covenant by observing His commandments. In verse 11, another concept is introduced with the phrase הַיּוֹם לַעֲשׂוֹתָם, *to do them this day*, and *Rashi* comments, 'But tomorrow, in the World to Come, you will be rewarded.'

The *Sforno* explains that this opening verse of *Ekev* is to be understood as God's reason for keeping the covenant, resulting from Israel's willingness to observe the commandments even though they will not receive reward in This World but in the World to Come. The *Sforno* explains that this postponed reward is due to the fact that the Almighty's covenant with Israel was originally entered into with Abraham, and continues with his offspring in such a manner that our very existence flows *directly* from the Eternal. As such, we are an eternal people, and therefore our just reward which is everlasting must be given in a world which is also everlasting. On the other hand, those whose existence is temporal and perishable (נִפְסָד), coming through intermediary forces, are properly rewarded in this transitory world.

The final point made by the *Sforno* is that since a covenant imposes responsibilities which are binding on both parties, it cannot correctly be termed a *chesed*, an act of mercy or lovingkindness, when one party compen-

יג וַאֲהֵבְךָ וּבֵרַכְךָ וְהִרְבֶּךָ וּבֵרַךְ פְּרִי־בִטְנְךָ וּפְרִי־אַדְמָתֶךָ דְּגָנְךָ וְתִירֹשְׁךָ
וְיִצְהָרֶךָ שְׁגַר־אֲלָפֶיךָ וְעַשְׁתְּרֹת צֹאנֶךָ עַל הָאֲדָמָה אֲשֶׁר־נִשְׁבַּע לַאֲבֹתֶיךָ
יד לָתֶת לָךְ׃ בָּרוּךְ תִּהְיֶה מִכָּל־הָעַמִּים לֹא־יִהְיֶה בְךָ עָקָר וַעֲקָרָה וּבִבְהֶמְתֶּךָ׃
טו וְהֵסִיר יהוה מִמְּךָ כָּל־חֹלִי וְכָל־מַדְוֵי מִצְרַיִם הָרָעִים אֲשֶׁר יָדַעְתָּ לֹא
טז יְשִׂימָם בָּךְ וּנְתָנָם בְּכָל־שֹׂנְאֶיךָ׃ וְאָכַלְתָּ אֶת־כָּל־הָעַמִּים אֲשֶׁר יהוה
אֱלֹהֶיךָ נֹתֵן לָךְ לֹא־תָחוֹס עֵינְךָ עֲלֵיהֶם וְלֹא תַעֲבֹד אֶת־אֱלֹהֵיהֶם
יז כִּי־מוֹקֵשׁ הוּא לָךְ׃ כִּי תֹאמַר בִּלְבָבְךָ רַבִּים הַגּוֹיִם

---

13. וַאֲהֵבְךָ — *And He will love you* . . . being that you are (His) 'children' (created) in His form and image, as our Sages say, חֲבִיבִין יִשְׂרָאֵל שֶׁנִּקְרְאוּ בָנִים לַמָּקוֹם, *Beloved is Israel for they are called children of God* (*Avos* 3:14), and thus the everlasting (nature of the) covenant shall be a felicitous (complete) one.

וּבֵרַכְךָ — *And bless you* . . . with material wealth for transitory life (This World) and thus He shall (insure) the (condition of) goodness and grace which (He promised) when He swore that you would (dwell) in the Land in a blessed (lit. happy) manner.

15. כָּל חֹלִי — *All sickness* . . . even ordinary ailments which afflict (people) through the (heavenly) bodies (lit. order).

הָרָעִים — *The evil* (*diseases*) . . . contagious (ailments).

אֲשֶׁר יָדַעְתָּ — *Which you know* . . . With which (the Egyptians) were smitten at the sea, as explained above (*Exodus* 14:31).

לֹא יְשִׂימָם בָּךְ וּנְתָנָם בְּכָל שֹׂנְאֶיךָ — *Will not put them upon you, but will visit them upon all that hate you.* Although He will visit them upon your enemies, they will not infect you, similar to, יִפֹּל מִצִּדְּךָ אֶלֶף . . . אֵלֶיךָ לֹא יִגָּשׁ, *A thousand shall fall at your side . . . but it shall not come near you* (*Psalms* 91:7).

16. לֹא תָחוֹס עֵינְךָ עֲלֵיהֶם וְלֹא תַעֲבֹד אֶת אֱלֹהֵיהֶם — *Your eye shall not pity them so that you not serve their gods.* If *your eye will not pity them* then *you will not serve their gods,* but if you pity them, then, without a doubt, they will mislead you (into sin).

כִּי מוֹקֵשׁ הוּא לָךְ — *Because it will be a snare unto you.* Because if you do pity them they will be a snare unto you, for they will entice you to worship their gods.

NOTES

sates the other! Why then does the verse speak of God's *chesed* in addition to His covenant? The *Sforno* answers this question by explaining that *chesed* refers to the good granted to us in This World, bestowed by God in His kindness, since the ultimate reward for our good deeds which we have earned will only be given to us in the World to Come.

13. וַאֲהֵבְךָ וּבֵרַכְךָ — *And He will love you and bless you*. God's manifestation of love for us is a reciprocal act evoked by our love for Him. As mentioned in the previous note, these verses are linked to verse 9 where the Torah speaks of those who love Him. Hence this represents an example of מִדָּה כְּנֶגֶד מִדָּה, *measure for measure*. In addition to this love that God, our Heavenly Father, has for us, He will also bless us with material well-being in the Land of Israel. The phrase וּבֵרַכְךָ, *and bless you*, is similar to the opening phrase of the priestly blessing יְבָרֶכְךָ, *May (HASHEM) bless you,* — which is interpreted to mean בְּמָמוֹן, *with wealth* (see *Rashi* and the *Sforno* on *Bamidbar* 6:24).

15. כָּל חֹלִי . . . הָרָעִים — *All sickness . . . the evil (diseases)*. God promised that He would not permit even common illness to be visited upon Israel, nor would the diseases visited upon the

יח הָאֵלֶּה מִמֶּנִּי אֵיכָה אוּכַל לְהוֹרִישָׁם: לֹא תִירָא מֵהֶם זָכֹר תִּזְכֹּר אֵת
יט אֲשֶׁר־עָשָׂה יְהוָה אֱלֹהֶיךָ לְפַרְעֹה וּלְכָל־מִצְרָיִם: הַמַּסֹּת הַגְּדֹלֹת אֲשֶׁר־רָאוּ
עֵינֶיךָ וְהָאֹתֹת וְהַמֹּפְתִים וְהַיָּד הַחֲזָקָה וְהַזְּרֹעַ הַנְּטוּיָה אֲשֶׁר הוֹצִאֲךָ יְהוָה
כ אֱלֹהֶיךָ כֵּן־יַעֲשֶׂה יְהוָה אֱלֹהֶיךָ לְכָל־הָעַמִּים אֲשֶׁר־אַתָּה יָרֵא מִפְּנֵיהֶם: וְגַם
אֶת־הַצִּרְעָה יְשַׁלַּח יְהוָה אֱלֹהֶיךָ בָּם עַד־אֲבֹד הַנִּשְׁאָרִים וְהַנִּסְתָּרִים
כא מִפָּנֶיךָ: לֹא תַעֲרֹץ מִפְּנֵיהֶם כִּי־יְהוָה אֱלֹהֶיךָ בְּקִרְבֶּךָ אֵל גָּדוֹל וְנוֹרָא:
כב וְנָשַׁל יְהוָה אֱלֹהֶיךָ אֶת־הַגּוֹיִם הָאֵל מִפָּנֶיךָ מְעַט מְעָט לֹא תוּכַל כַּלֹּתָם
כג מַהֵר פֶּן־תִּרְבֶּה עָלֶיךָ חַיַּת הַשָּׂדֶה: וּנְתָנָם יְהוָה אֱלֹהֶיךָ לְפָנֶיךָ וְהָמָם
כד מְהוּמָה גְדֹלָה עַד הִשָּׁמְדָם: וְנָתַן מַלְכֵיהֶם בְּיָדֶךָ וְהַאֲבַדְתָּ אֶת־שְׁמָם
כה מִתַּחַת הַשָּׁמָיִם לֹא־יִתְיַצֵּב אִישׁ בְּפָנֶיךָ עַד הִשְׁמִדְךָ אֹתָם: פְּסִילֵי
אֱלֹהֵיהֶם תִּשְׂרְפוּן בָּאֵשׁ לֹא־תַחְמֹד כֶּסֶף וְזָהָב עֲלֵיהֶם וְלָקַחְתָּ לָךְ פֶּן
כו תִּוָּקֵשׁ בּוֹ כִּי תוֹעֲבַת יְהוָה אֱלֹהֶיךָ הוּא: וְלֹא־תָבִיא תוֹעֵבָה אֶל־בֵּיתֶךָ

17-18. כִּי תֹאמַר . . . אֵיכָה אוּכַל לְהוֹרִישָׁם. לֹא תִירָא מֵהֶם — *If you say . . . 'How can I dispossess them? Be not afraid of them.* When you say, 'How can I dispossess them since they are more numerous than I am,' do not say so because you fear them, but because you recognize that this would, indeed, be impossible were it not for God's help, and this is the meaning of *you shall well remember what God your God did to Pharaoh and all Egypt*, who were more numerous and far more mighty than you.

24. וְנָתַן מַלְכֵיהֶם בְּיָדֶךָ וְהַאֲבַדְתָּ אֶת שְׁמָם — *And He shall deliver their kings into your hand, and you shall destroy their name.* Because if one permits the seed of the royal enemy to survive, they will be adversaries for all time, as was the case with Hadad who was a young lad of the seed of the Edomite king and rose up as an adversary against Solomon (see *King* 1, 11:14).

25. פֶּן תִּוָּקֵשׁ בּוֹ — *Lest you be ensnared therein.* Because, at times, it may happen that you will prosper with the silver and gold which were taken from them and you will attribute (this success) to the power of that idol, whence (this silver and gold) was taken.

NOTES

Egyptians at the sea infect them, in spite of their being contagious, for Israel would be immune to them.

17-18. כִּי תֹאמַר . . . אֵיכָה אוּכַל לְהוֹרִישָׁם. לֹא תִירָא מֵהֶם — *If you say . . . How can I dispossess them. Be not afraid of them.* When one asks, 'How can I dispossess them,' there can be two reasons for posing such a question. One is because you fear them, and that would be improper, for it implies a lack of faith in God. The other reason is because you recognize that you cannot hope to dispossess them without God's help. This is proper and commendable, for it demonstrates a recognition of one's inadequacy coupled with trust and faith in the Almighty. The meaning, therefore, of these two verses is to be understood as follows: Let not your doubts and apprehensions be due to your fear of the enemy, rather let it be an acknowledgment that without the help of God, the task is impossible. When you come to this realization, there will, indeed, be no reason for you to fear them.

24. וְהַאֲבַדְתָּ אֶת שְׁמָם — *And you shall destroy their name*. The *Sforno* cites the story of Hadad the Edomite, who escaped when David and Yoab smote the Edomites, as an example of the threat posed by a royal survivor. Ultimately, Hadad returned to his land and became a dangerous adversary of Solomon and Israel.

25. פֶּן תִּוָּקֵשׁ בּוֹ — *Lest you be ensnared therein*. The *Sforno*'s commentary reflects the powerful attraction idolatry held for people in

וְהָיִיתָ חֵרֶם כָּמֹהוּ שַׁקֵּץ ׀ תְּשַׁקְּצֶנּוּ וְתַעֵב ׀ תְּתַעֲבֶנּוּ כִּי־חֵרֶם הוּא׃
ח א כָּל־הַמִּצְוָה אֲשֶׁר אָנֹכִי מְצַוְּךָ הַיּוֹם תִּשְׁמְרוּן לַעֲשׂוֹת לְמַעַן תִּחְיוּן וּרְבִיתֶם
ב וּבָאתֶם וִירִשְׁתֶּם אֶת־הָאָרֶץ אֲשֶׁר־נִשְׁבַּע יהוה לַאֲבֹתֵיכֶם׃ וְזָכַרְתָּ
אֶת־כָּל־הַדֶּרֶךְ אֲשֶׁר הוֹלִיכֲךָ יהוה אֱלֹהֶיךָ זֶה אַרְבָּעִים שָׁנָה בַּמִּדְבָּר לְמַעַן
ג עַנֹּתְךָ לְנַסֹּתְךָ לָדַעַת אֶת־אֲשֶׁר בִּלְבָבְךָ הֲתִשְׁמֹר מִצְוֺתָו אִם־לֹא׃ וַיְעַנְּךָ

---

26. תְּתַעֲבֶנּוּ כִּי חֵרֶם הוּא — *You shall abhor it, for it is a banned thing.* You shall abhor the silver and gold of abomination, כִּי חֵרֶם הוּא, *for it is a banned (accursed) thing,* and not only will it not bring you success but it will destroy the rest of your possessions.

VIII

1. כָּל הַמִּצְוָה אֲשֶׁר אָנֹכִי מְצַוְּךָ הַיּוֹם תִּשְׁמְרוּן לַעֲשׂוֹת — *All the commandment which I command you this day shall you observe to do.* Behold, the purpose of all who worship strange gods (idols) is to attain temporary success which is threefold — length of days, children and money. Now, by observing the commandments you shall attain all of these, therefore take care to do them ...

לְמַעַן תִּחְיוּן — *That you may live.* Because the intent of God, the Blessed One, when He commanded you to fulfill His commandments was that you might attain longevity, albeit in this transitory world.

וּרְבִיתֶם — *And multiply* ... (and) that you shall have many children.

וּבָאתֶם וִירִשְׁתֶּם — *And come and possess* ... and that you shall attain riches and honor through (inheritance) of the land.

2. וְזָכַרְתָּ אֶת כָּל הַדֶּרֶךְ — *And you shall remember the whole way* ... when He provided you with bread to eat and clothes to wear in a miraculous manner.

לְנַסֹּתְךָ — *To test you* ... (to see) if you will do His will (even) when you are able to attain bread and clothing without pain (i.e., without effort).

לָדַעַת אֶת אֲשֶׁר בִּלְבָבְךָ — *To know what was in your heart* ... in order that what is in your heart (the potential) shall be (translated) into the actual, so that every angel may know that your elevated status, superior to that of the ministering angels, is justified. (You, in turn), will come to (recognize) His knowledge, which functions for the good (of man) as is fitting for that which is found in actuality.

NOTES

ancient times. Although these graven images were powerless to prevent their being taken by the Israelites, nonetheless when the gold and silver would bring prosperity to the Israelites there was concern that they might believe it was due to the magical power of these idols!

26. כִּי חֵרֶם הוּא — *For it is a banned thing.* These graven images are not only an abomination but they also bring with them a curse. The gold and silver would not only fail to bring prosperity, but would lead to the destruction of Israel's other possessions.

VIII

1. כָּל הַמִּצְוָה — *All the commandment.* Our Sages teach us that longevity, children and wealth, depend not on *z'chus*, merit, but rather on *mazal*, destiny (*Moed Katan* 28a). The *Sforno*, nonetheless, interprets this verse as meaning that as a consequence of observing *mitzvos*, God will grant these three blessings of life, progeny and wealth. This assurance is meant to wean Israel away from idolatry, being that in those days the worship of gods was considered to be the only way to insure this threefold blessing.

2. לְנַסֹּתְךָ — *To test you*. The intent of God was

וַיַּרְעִבֶךָ וַיַּאֲכִלְךָ אֶת־הַמָּן אֲשֶׁר לֹא־יָדַעְתָּ וְלֹא יָדְעוּן אֲבֹתֶיךָ לְמַעַן
הוֹדִיעֲךָ כִּי לֹא עַל־הַלֶּחֶם לְבַדּוֹ יִחְיֶה הָאָדָם כִּי עַל־כָּל־מוֹצָא פִי־יהוָה
ד יִחְיֶה הָאָדָם: שִׂמְלָתְךָ לֹא בָלְתָה מֵעָלֶיךָ וְרַגְלְךָ לֹא בָצֵקָה זֶה אַרְבָּעִים
ה שָׁנָה: וְיָדַעְתָּ עִם־לְבָבֶךָ כִּי כַּאֲשֶׁר יְיַסֵּר אִישׁ אֶת־בְּנוֹ יהוָה אֱלֹהֶיךָ
ו־ז מְיַסְּרֶךָּ: וְשָׁמַרְתָּ אֶת־מִצְוֺת יהוָה אֱלֹהֶיךָ לָלֶכֶת בִּדְרָכָיו וּלְיִרְאָה אֹתוֹ: כִּי
יהוָה אֱלֹהֶיךָ מְבִיאֲךָ אֶל־אֶרֶץ טוֹבָה אֶרֶץ נַחֲלֵי מָיִם עֲיָנֹת וּתְהֹמֹת יֹצְאִים
ח בַּבִּקְעָה וּבָהָר: אֶרֶץ חִטָּה וּשְׂעֹרָה וְגֶפֶן וּתְאֵנָה וְרִמּוֹן אֶרֶץ־זֵית שֶׁמֶן וּדְבָשׁ:
ט אֶרֶץ אֲשֶׁר לֹא בְמִסְכֵּנֻת תֹּאכַל־בָּהּ לֶחֶם לֹא־תֶחְסַר כֹּל בָּהּ אֶרֶץ אֲשֶׁר

---

5. מְיַסְּרֶךָּ — *Instructs you.* Through His commandments, He grants you instruction befitting (the purpose of reaching) the perfection which is intended by Him.

7. אֶל אֶרֶץ טוֹבָה — *Into a good land* . . . (a land) in which all kinds of excellence and goodness is concentrated, such as cannot be found in any other (geographical) area. (The verses) relate five kinds of (superior) goodness, and regarding each one of them, the word אֶרֶץ, *land*, is used: The first is אֶרֶץ נַחֲלֵי מָיִם עֲיָנֹת וּתְהֹמֹת, *a land of brooks of water, of fountains and depths,* not muddy (lit., bad) pools and canals, i.e., the opposite of וְהַמַּיִם רָעִים וְהָאָרֶץ מְשַׁכָּלֶת, *The water is bad and the ground causes untimely births* (*II Kings* 2:19). The second is . . .

8. אֶרֶץ חִטָּה וּשְׂעֹרָה — *A land of wheat and barley* . . . which are necessary for sustenance. The third is אֶרֶץ זֵית שֶׁמֶן וּדְבָשׁ, *a land of olive trees and honey*, which are royal delicacies. The fourth is . . .

9. אֶרֶץ אֲשֶׁר לֹא בְמִסְכֵּנֻת תֹּאכַל בָּהּ לֶחֶם — *A land wherein you shall not eat bread parsimoniously.* They will find that the price of bread is cheap there, as it says, וַתִּמָּלֵא אַרְצוֹ כֶּסֶף וְזָהָב וְאֵין קֵצֶה לְאֹצְרֹתָיו, *His land is full of silver and gold, neither is*

NOTES

to give you the test of easily attained physical needs, to see whether this would affect your faith. The *Sforno* interprets the phrase *and that He might test you* (v. 16) similarly.

לָדַעַת אֶת אֲשֶׁר בִּלְבָבְךָ — *To know what was in your heart*. The Almighty knows what is in man's heart. An angel does not. The verse here speaks of man's potential (i.e., what is in his heart), which is unknown both to him and to angels as well. When life's demands bring forth the potential into the actual, man's ability and superiority to the angels is revealed — both to the angels and to man himself. This is the sense of the phrase, *to know what was in your heart*. Man's superiority to the angels is also discussed in the *Sforno*'s explanation of עַתָּה יָדַעְתִּי, *for now I know* (*Genesis* 22:12).

When the Torah speaks of God's 'knowledge,' it means His will and creative power. In *Genesis* 1:4, where the Torah uses the expression, *And HASHEM saw that the light was good,* the *Sforno* explains that when God perceives that something is good for the world and its inhabitants, He brings it into existence through His יְדִיעָה, *knowledge*, which is פּוֹעֶלֶת, i.e., 'the efficient cause.' The meaning, therefore, of the expression *to know what was in your heart*, according to *Sforno* is a twofold one. First, that the angels shall recognize your superiority over them, and secondly, that you shall recognize the power of God's knowledge that can alone translate the potential into reality.

5. מְיַסְּרֶךָּ — *Instructs you*. Although the word יָסַר can mean *to inflict pain* and *to chasten*, the *Sforno* interprets it to mean *instruction*, akin to מוּסַר אָבִיךָ, *the instruction of your father* (*Proverbs* 1:8); compare to 4:36.

7-9. אֶל אֶרֶץ טוֹבָה . . . אֶרֶץ חִטָּה וּשְׂעֹרָה . . . אֶרֶץ אֲשֶׁר לֹא בְמִסְכֵּנֻת תֹּאכַל בָּהּ לֶחֶם . . . — *Into a good land . . . A land of wheat and barley . . . A land wherein you shall not eat bread parsimo-*

י אֲבָנֶיהָ בַרְזֶל וּמֵהֲרָרֶיהָ תַּחְצֹב נְחֹשֶׁת: וְאָכַלְתָּ וְשָׂבָעְתָּ וּבֵרַכְתָּ אֶת־
שני יא יְהוָה אֱלֹהֶיךָ עַל־הָאָרֶץ הַטֹּבָה אֲשֶׁר נָתַן־לָךְ: הִשָּׁמֶר לְךָ פֶּן־תִּשְׁכַּח אֶת־
יְהוָה אֱלֹהֶיךָ לְבִלְתִּי שְׁמֹר מִצְוֹתָיו וּמִשְׁפָּטָיו וְחֻקֹּתָיו אֲשֶׁר אָנֹכִי מְצַוְּךָ
יב-יג הַיּוֹם: פֶּן־תֹּאכַל וְשָׂבָעְתָּ וּבָתִּים טֹבִים תִּבְנֶה וְיָשָׁבְתָּ: וּבְקָרְךָ וְצֹאנְךָ יִרְבְּיֻן
יד וְכֶסֶף וְזָהָב יִרְבֶּה־לָּךְ וְכֹל אֲשֶׁר־לְךָ יִרְבֶּה: וְרָם לְבָבֶךָ וְשָׁכַחְתָּ אֶת־יְהוָה
טו אֱלֹהֶיךָ הַמּוֹצִיאֲךָ מֵאֶרֶץ מִצְרַיִם מִבֵּית עֲבָדִים: הַמּוֹלִיכְךָ בַּמִּדְבָּר ׀ הַגָּדֹל
וְהַנּוֹרָא נָחָשׁ ׀ שָׂרָף וְעַקְרָב וְצִמָּאוֹן אֲשֶׁר אֵין־מָיִם הַמּוֹצִיא לְךָ מַיִם מִצּוּר
טז הַחַלָּמִישׁ: הַמַּאֲכִלְךָ מָן בַּמִּדְבָּר אֲשֶׁר לֹא־יָדְעוּן אֲבֹתֶיךָ לְמַעַן עַנֹּתְךָ
יז וּלְמַעַן נַסֹּתֶךָ לְהֵיטִבְךָ בְּאַחֲרִיתֶךָ: וְאָמַרְתָּ בִּלְבָבֶךָ כֹּחִי וְעֹצֶם יָדִי עָשָׂה לִי
יח אֶת־הַחַיִל הַזֶּה: וְזָכַרְתָּ אֶת־יְהוָה אֱלֹהֶיךָ כִּי הוּא הַנֹּתֵן לְךָ כֹּחַ לַעֲשׂוֹת
חָיִל לְמַעַן הָקִים אֶת־בְּרִיתוֹ אֲשֶׁר־נִשְׁבַּע לַאֲבֹתֶיךָ כַּיּוֹם הַזֶּה:

---

there any end of His treasures (*Isaiah* 2:7), because a scarcity of money is more difficult (to accept) than a scarcity of produce, as (our Sages) state, 'This is the case (that we wait to sound the alarm) when money is plentiful and food is scarce but if money is scarce and food is plentiful then the alarm is sounded at once' (*Taanis* 19b). The fifth is אֶרֶץ אֲשֶׁר אֲבָנֶיהָ בַרְזֶל, *a land whose stones are iron*, for in it are found plentiful hard and bright stones, suitable and good for building (purposes).

תַּחְצֹב נְחֹשֶׁת — *You may dig copper*. Brass; good metal which is bright, and fit for building and (also) for vessels.

10. וּבֵרַכְתָּ אֶת ה׳ אֱלֹהֶיךָ — *And bless HASHEM your God* ... that you may remember that all this comes from Him.

15. מִצּוּר הַחַלָּמִישׁ — *Out of the rock of flint* ... which was transformed into water, as it says, הַהֹפְכִי הַצּוּר אֲגַם מָיִם חַלָּמִישׁ לְמַעְיְנוֹ מָיִם, *Who turned the rock into a pool of water, the flint into a fountain of waters* (*Psalms* 114:8).

16. לְמַעַן עַנֹּתְךָ — *That He might afflict you* ... that you shall fulfill (God's will) in a state of affliction with the worry of 'one who has no loaf in his basket.'

וּלְמַעַן נַסֹּתֶךָ — *And that He might test you* ... whether you would do His will when He grants you sustenance without pain (without effort).

לְהֵיטִבְךָ — *To do good for you* ... more so than (what he does for) the ministering angels, as befits one who is tested by Him.

NOTES

niously ... The first mention of אֶרֶץ, *land*, is an introductory one. The Torah tells us that *Eretz Yisrael* is a good land, of superior quality. The repetition of the word אֶרֶץ is meant to underscore the various aspects of excellence which define this superiority — its water, produce, delicacies, plentiful bread and materials for building.

15. מִצּוּר הַחַלָּמִישׁ — *Out of the rock of flint*. The *Sforno* stresses that the water did not come forth *from* the rock, but the rock became *transformed* into water, which is a far-greater miracle.

16. לְמַעַן עַנֹּתְךָ וּלְמַעַן נַסֹּתֶךָ — *That He might afflict you and that He might test you*. There are two kinds of tests given to man — one is נִסָּיוֹן מֵעֹשֶׁר, *the test of riches*, while the second is נִסָּיוֹן מֵעֹנִי, *the test of poverty*. Will man do God's will when he is prosperous and will he obey Him when he is impoverished? Israel was put to both tests in the wilderness when they were given the manna from heaven each day. On the one hand, their sustenance was given without suffering, while on the other

יט וְהָיָה אִם־שָׁכֹחַ תִּשְׁכַּח אֶת־יהוה אֱלֹהֶיךָ וְהָלַכְתָּ אַחֲרֵי אֱלֹהִים אֲחֵרִים
כ וַעֲבַדְתָּם וְהִשְׁתַּחֲוִיתָ לָהֶם הַעִדֹתִי בָכֶם הַיּוֹם כִּי אָבֹד תֹּאבֵדוּן: כַּגּוֹיִם
אֲשֶׁר יהוה מַאֲבִיד מִפְּנֵיכֶם כֵּן תֹּאבֵדוּן עֵקֶב לֹא תִשְׁמְעוּן בְּקוֹל יהוה
אֱלֹהֵיכֶם:

ט

א שְׁמַע יִשְׂרָאֵל אַתָּה עֹבֵר הַיּוֹם אֶת־הַיַּרְדֵּן לָבֹא לָרֶשֶׁת גּוֹיִם גְּדֹלִים
ב וַעֲצֻמִים מִמֶּךָּ עָרִים גְּדֹלֹת וּבְצֻרֹת בַּשָּׁמָיִם: עַם־גָּדוֹל וָרָם בְּנֵי עֲנָקִים אֲשֶׁר
ג אַתָּה יָדַעְתָּ וְאַתָּה שָׁמַעְתָּ מִי יִתְיַצֵּב לִפְנֵי בְּנֵי עֲנָק: וְיָדַעְתָּ הַיּוֹם כִּי יהוה
אֱלֹהֶיךָ הוּא־הָעֹבֵר לְפָנֶיךָ אֵשׁ אֹכְלָה הוּא יַשְׁמִידֵם וְהוּא יַכְנִיעֵם לְפָנֶיךָ
שלישי ד וְהוֹרַשְׁתָּם וְהַאֲבַדְתָּם מַהֵר כַּאֲשֶׁר דִּבֶּר יהוה לָךְ: אַל־תֹּאמַר בִּלְבָבְךָ
בַּהֲדֹף יהוה אֱלֹהֶיךָ אֹתָם ׀ מִלְּפָנֶיךָ לֵאמֹר בְּצִדְקָתִי הֱבִיאַנִי יהוה לָרֶשֶׁת
ה אֶת־הָאָרֶץ הַזֹּאת וּבְרִשְׁעַת הַגּוֹיִם הָאֵלֶּה יהוה מוֹרִישָׁם מִפָּנֶיךָ: לֹא

---

19. וְהָיָה אִם שָׁכֹחַ תִּשְׁכַּח — *And it shall be if you forget* ... and this will occur when you attribute your success to your own might and fail to bless Him for it.

כִּי אָבֹד תֹּאבֵדוּן — *That you will surely perish* ... from two worlds.

20. עֵקֶב לֹא תִשְׁמְעוּן — *Because you will not hearken* ... and all this shall come to pass when you do not bless (God) as commanded above (v. 10).

IX

4. אַל תֹּאמַר בִּלְבָבְךָ בַּהֲדֹף — *Do not say in your heart when HASHEM thrusts out.* When you will see that you are able to conquer them in an unnatural fashion (lit., 'not according to the custom of the world'), and thereby you will recognize that it is due to Divine intervention, do not think mistakenly that *because of my righteousness God brought me in to possess this land,* so that I might possess the Land quickly, and because of my merit He thrust them out quickly.

וּבְרִשְׁעַת הַגּוֹיִם הָאֵלֶּה ה׳ מוֹרִישָׁם מִפָּנֶיךָ — *Because of the wickedness of these nations did HASHEM drive them out before you.* Behold, the reason He battles against them is because of their wickedness, and not in order that you inherit (the Land) quickly.

NOTES

hand, since it could not be stored, each day they were in a state of uncertainty as to whether they would have food the next day. Now, since angels are never put to such tests, it follows that Israel deserves to be the recipient of God's *good* mentioned here.

19. כִּי אָבֹד תֹּאבֵדוּן — *That you will surely perish*. At the beginning of this *sedrah* (7:12), the *Sforno* explains that God's promise to keep the covenant assures Israel's prosperity in This World, and their inheritance of the World to Come. Conversely, if we fail to keep His commandments the loss will be a twofold one. Hence, the double expression אָבֹד תֹּאבֵדוּן (lit., *you will be lost — be lost*) is most fitting.

20. עֵקֶב לֹא תִשְׁמְעוּן — *Because you will not hearken.* This phrase links the beginning of this *parashah* (עֵקֶב תִּשְׁמְעוּן) with the conclusion of the chapter (עֵקֶב לֹא תִשְׁמְעוּן). *If you hearken,* the reward will be twofold and if *you fail to hearken,* your loss will be twofold, as explained above. Now the reason for your refusal to listen to God will be due to your failure to recognize God's Providence and the erroneous assumption that your prosperity is due to your own strength and talent (v. 19).

IX

4. אַל תֹּאמַר ... וּבְרִשְׁעַת הַגּוֹיִם — *Do not say ... because of the wickedness of these*

בְצִדְקָתְךָ וּבְיֹשֶׁר לְבָבְךָ אַתָּה בָא לָרֶשֶׁת אֶת־אַרְצָם כִּי בְּרִשְׁעַת | הַגּוֹיִם
הָאֵלֶּה יהוה אֱלֹהֶיךָ מוֹרִישָׁם מִפָּנֶיךָ וּלְמַעַן הָקִים אֶת־הַדָּבָר אֲשֶׁר נִשְׁבַּע
ו יהוה לַאֲבֹתֶיךָ לְאַבְרָהָם לְיִצְחָק וּלְיַעֲקֹב: וְיָדַעְתָּ כִּי לֹא בְצִדְקָתְךָ יהוה
אֱלֹהֶיךָ נֹתֵן לְךָ אֶת־הָאָרֶץ הַטּוֹבָה הַזֹּאת לְרִשְׁתָּהּ כִּי עַם־קְשֵׁה־עֹרֶף

5. לֹא בְצִדְקָתְךָ וּבְיֹשֶׁר לְבָבְךָ אַתָּה בָא לָרֶשֶׁת — *Not because of your righteousness do you go in to possess.* Because, indeed, your inheriting the Land is not due to your merit, for you are not worthy that God battle on your behalf so that you might inherit quickly.

כִּי בְּרִשְׁעַת הַגּוֹיִם הָאֵלֶּה ה׳ אֱלֹהֶיךָ מוֹרִישָׁם מִפָּנֶיךָ — *But because of the wickedness of these nations,* HASHEM *your God drives them out before you.* He wanted His revenge to be taken from them through you — that you should destroy them for their iniquities, as it says, וַיֹּאמֶר הַשְׁמֵד, *and said: Destroy* (33:27), as opposed to וּבְיַד אָדָם אַל אֶפֹּלָה, *and let me not fall into the hand of man* (*II Samuel*, 24:14).

וּלְמַעַן הָקִים — *And that He may fulfill.* So that by fulfilling His command, you will merit to inherit, akin to כְּכֹל אֲשֶׁר בִּלְבָבִי עָשִׂיתָ לְבֵית אַחְאָב בְּנֵי רְבִעִים יֵשְׁבוּ לְךָ עַל כִּסֵּא יִשְׂרָאֵל, *And you have done to the house of Ahab according to all that was in my heart, your children of the fourth generation shall sit on the throne of Israel* (*II Kings* 10:30). And all this He did to fulfill that which He swore to the Patriarchs.

6. כִּי עַם קְשֵׁה עֹרֶף אָתָּה — *For you are a stiff-necked people.* It is impossible to have righteousness and an upright heart if one is stiff-necked, for he who is stiff-necked follows the stubbornness of his heart and mind, and even though a righteous teacher may demonstrate (lit., 'tell') with clear proof that his thoughts are improper and will lead to loss, (he still refuses to listen). This is (due to the fact) that he does not turn (his attention) to the teacher — as though his neck were hard, akin to an iron sinew, in such a manner that he cannot turn (his neck) in any direction — but follows the stubbornness of his heart as before.

NOTES

nations. There are two reasons the Almighty intervenes in the affairs of people. One is because a nation merits His involvement and aid, while another is because the wickedness of their adversary demands Divine retribution. Moses tells Israel that their conquest of *Eretz Yisrael* is due to the latter reason.

5. לֹא בְצִדְקָתְךָ . . . כִּי בְּרִשְׁעַת . . . וּלְמַעַן הָקִים — *Not because of your righteousness . . . but because of the wickedness . . . and that He may fulfill.* Although this verse seems repetitious, the *Sforno* explains the significance of this statement as follows: As stated above, the Israelites were not worthy that God should battle on their behalf, nonetheless He desired to fulfill the promise made to the Patriarchs regarding the inheritance of the Land by their children. He therefore is willing to use them as His instrument to punish the inhabitants of Canaan, and by doing so they will fulfill His will and merit His aid and intervention. The *Sforno* proves this thesis from the story of Yahu who destroyed the house of Ahab, which fulfilled the intent of the Almighty, and thereby Yahu merited to reign over Israel for four generations.

6. עַם קְשֵׁה עֹרֶף אָתָּה — *You are a stiff-necked people.* A stubborn person is convinced that his way is correct and proper, and rivets his attention upon a course from which he refuses to deviate. Were he flexible in his opinions, he would be willing to consider different viewpoints and other options. One who is stiff-necked, however, cannot turn left or right — he is inflexible. This is the sense of the *Sforno*'s explanation of the simile used in this verse, as well as in *Exodus* 32:9, and verse 13 in this chapter.

ז אָתָּה: זְכֹר אַל־תִּשְׁכַּח אֵת אֲשֶׁר־הִקְצַפְתָּ אֶת־יְהוָה אֱלֹהֶיךָ בַּמִּדְבָּר
לְמִן־הַיּוֹם אֲשֶׁר־יָצָאתָ ׀ מֵאֶרֶץ מִצְרַיִם עַד־בֹּאֲכֶם עַד־הַמָּקוֹם הַזֶּה מַמְרִים
ח הֱיִיתֶם עִם־יְהוָה: וּבְחֹרֵב הִקְצַפְתֶּם אֶת־יְהוָה וַיִּתְאַנַּף יְהוָה בָּכֶם לְהַשְׁמִיד
ט אֶתְכֶם: בַּעֲלֹתִי הָהָרָה לָקַחַת לוּחֹת הָאֲבָנִים לוּחֹת הַבְּרִית אֲשֶׁר־כָּרַת
יְהוָה עִמָּכֶם וָאֵשֵׁב בָּהָר אַרְבָּעִים יוֹם וְאַרְבָּעִים לַיְלָה לֶחֶם לֹא אָכַלְתִּי
י וּמַיִם לֹא שָׁתִיתִי: וַיִּתֵּן יְהוָה אֵלַי אֶת־שְׁנֵי לוּחֹת הָאֲבָנִים כְּתֻבִים בְּאֶצְבַּע
אֱלֹהִים וַעֲלֵיהֶם כְּכָל־הַדְּבָרִים אֲשֶׁר דִּבֶּר יְהוָה עִמָּכֶם בָּהָר מִתּוֹךְ הָאֵשׁ
יא בְּיוֹם הַקָּהָל: וַיְהִי מִקֵּץ אַרְבָּעִים יוֹם וְאַרְבָּעִים לָיְלָה נָתַן יְהוָה אֵלַי
יב אֶת־שְׁנֵי לֻחֹת הָאֲבָנִים לֻחוֹת הַבְּרִית: וַיֹּאמֶר יְהוָה אֵלַי קוּם רֵד מַהֵר מִזֶּה
כִּי שִׁחֵת עַמְּךָ אֲשֶׁר הוֹצֵאתָ מִמִּצְרָיִם סָרוּ מַהֵר מִן־הַדֶּרֶךְ אֲשֶׁר צִוִּיתִם
יג עָשׂוּ לָהֶם מַסֵּכָה: וַיֹּאמֶר יְהוָה אֵלַי לֵאמֹר רָאִיתִי אֶת־הָעָם הַזֶּה וְהִנֵּה
יד עַם־קְשֵׁה־עֹרֶף הוּא: הֶרֶף מִמֶּנִּי וְאַשְׁמִידֵם וְאֶמְחֶה אֶת־שְׁמָם מִתַּחַת
טו הַשָּׁמָיִם וְאֶעֱשֶׂה אוֹתְךָ לְגוֹי־עָצוּם וָרָב מִמֶּנּוּ: וָאֵפֶן וָאֵרֵד מִן־הָהָר וְהָהָר
טז בֹּעֵר בָּאֵשׁ וּשְׁנֵי לוּחֹת הַבְּרִית עַל שְׁתֵּי יָדָי: וָאֵרֶא וְהִנֵּה חֲטָאתֶם לַיהוָה
אֱלֹהֵיכֶם עֲשִׂיתֶם לָכֶם עֵגֶל מַסֵּכָה סַרְתֶּם מַהֵר מִן־הַדֶּרֶךְ אֲשֶׁר־צִוָּה יְהוָה
יז אֶתְכֶם: וָאֶתְפֹּשׂ בִּשְׁנֵי הַלֻּחֹת וָאַשְׁלִכֵם מֵעַל שְׁתֵּי יָדָי וָאֲשַׁבְּרֵם לְעֵינֵיכֶם:
יח וָאֶתְנַפַּל לִפְנֵי יְהוָה כָּרִאשֹׁנָה אַרְבָּעִים יוֹם וְאַרְבָּעִים לַיְלָה לֶחֶם לֹא

---

7. זְכֹר אַל תִּשְׁכַּח — *Remember, forget not* . . . because your constant backsliding which angered (God), similar to *a dog who returns to his vomit* (based on *Proverbs* 26:11), testifies to your being a stiff-necked people. (And this you did) although each time you (suffered) the chastisement of God your God and saw His greatness!

8. וּבְחֹרֵב הִקְצַפְתֶּם — *And in Horeb you angered.* And the proof of the evil nature of your stiffneckedness was that when you angered God at Horeb, His decision to destroy you was only because you were a stiff-necked people, as the Blessed One said, *I have seen this people, and behold, it is a stiff-necked people; leave Me alone that I may destroy them* (9:13,14). And the reason is because (when one) is stiff-necked, it removes all hope of repentance.

15. וְהָהָר בֹּעֵר בָּאֵשׁ — *And the mount burned with fire* . . . and you sinned while *the King was reclining at His table* (based on *Shir Hashirim* 1:12).

NOTES

7-8. זְכֹר אַל תִּשְׁכַּח . . . וּבְחֹרֵב הִקְצַפְתֶּם — *Remember, forget not . . . And in Horeb you angered*. The *Sforno* explains these verses as proof of Israel's stiffneckedness. The verse quoted from *Proverbs* is a colorful one which illustrates the foolish tendency of man to backslide and repeat his sins over and over again even though they are malodorous.

15. וְהָהָר בֹּעֵר בָּאֵשׁ — *And the mount burned with fire*. The *Sforno* explains why Moses found it necessary to tell them that the mount 'was burning.' He wished to emphasize that while the mount was still on fire, meaning that the majestic experience of מַתַּן תּוֹרָה, *the giving of the Torah,* was so fresh, they sinned with the Golden Calf. The expression used by the *Sforno*, בְּעוֹד שֶׁהַמֶּלֶךְ בִּמְסִבּוֹ, *while the King was reclining at His table,* is based on *Shir Hashirim* 1:12. That verse refers to God's presence at Sinai. The Talmud (*Shabbos* 88b) states, 'shameless is the bride that is unfaithful within her bridal canopy.' Our Sages were commenting on Israel's sin of the Golden Calf, which they committed when they were so fresh from their acceptance of the Torah, which was considered as Israel's betrothal to the Almighty.

אָכַלְתִּי וּמַיִם לֹא שָׁתִיתִי עַל כָּל־חַטַּאתְכֶם אֲשֶׁר חֲטָאתֶם לַעֲשׂוֹת הָרַע
יט בְּעֵינֵי יהוה לְהַכְעִיסוֹ: כִּי יָגֹרְתִּי מִפְּנֵי הָאַף וְהַחֵמָה אֲשֶׁר קָצַף יהוה עֲלֵיכֶם
כ לְהַשְׁמִיד אֶתְכֶם וַיִּשְׁמַע יהוה אֵלַי גַּם בַּפַּעַם הַהִוא: וּבְאַהֲרֹן הִתְאַנַּף יהוה
כא מְאֹד לְהַשְׁמִידוֹ וָאֶתְפַּלֵּל גַּם־בְּעַד אַהֲרֹן בָּעֵת הַהִוא: וְאֶת־חַטַּאתְכֶם
אֲשֶׁר־עֲשִׂיתֶם אֶת־הָעֵגֶל לָקַחְתִּי וָאֶשְׂרֹף אֹתוֹ | בָּאֵשׁ וָאֶכֹּת אֹתוֹ טָחוֹן
הֵיטֵב עַד אֲשֶׁר־דַּק לְעָפָר וָאַשְׁלִךְ אֶת־עֲפָרוֹ אֶל־הַנַּחַל הַיֹּרֵד מִן־הָהָר:
כב־כג וּבְתַבְעֵרָה וּבְמַסָּה וּבְקִבְרֹת הַתַּאֲוָה מַקְצִפִים הֱיִיתֶם אֶת־יהוה: וּבִשְׁלֹחַ
יהוה אֶתְכֶם מִקָּדֵשׁ בַּרְנֵעַ לֵאמֹר עֲלוּ וּרְשׁוּ אֶת־הָאָרֶץ אֲשֶׁר נָתַתִּי לָכֶם
וַתַּמְרוּ אֶת־פִּי יהוה אֱלֹהֵיכֶם וְלֹא הֶאֱמַנְתֶּם לוֹ וְלֹא שְׁמַעְתֶּם בְּקֹלוֹ:
כד־כה מַמְרִים הֱיִיתֶם עִם־יהוה מִיּוֹם דַּעְתִּי אֶתְכֶם: וָאֶתְנַפַּל לִפְנֵי יהוה אֵת־
אַרְבָּעִים הַיּוֹם וְאֶת־אַרְבָּעִים הַלַּיְלָה אֲשֶׁר הִתְנַפָּלְתִּי כִּי־אָמַר יהוה
כו לְהַשְׁמִיד אֶתְכֶם: וָאֶתְפַּלֵּל אֶל־יהוה וָאֹמַר אֲדֹנָי יהוה אַל־תַּשְׁחֵת עַמְּךָ
כז וְנַחֲלָתְךָ אֲשֶׁר פָּדִיתָ בְּגָדְלֶךָ אֲשֶׁר־הוֹצֵאתָ מִמִּצְרַיִם בְּיָד חֲזָקָה: זְכֹר
לַעֲבָדֶיךָ לְאַבְרָהָם לְיִצְחָק וּלְיַעֲקֹב אַל־תֵּפֶן אֶל־קְשִׁי הָעָם הַזֶּה וְאֶל־
כח רִשְׁעוֹ וְאֶל־חַטָּאתוֹ: פֶּן־יֹאמְרוּ הָאָרֶץ אֲשֶׁר הוֹצֵאתָנוּ מִשָּׁם מִבְּלִי יְכֹלֶת
יהוה לַהֲבִיאָם אֶל־הָאָרֶץ אֲשֶׁר־דִּבֶּר לָהֶם וּמִשִּׂנְאָתוֹ אוֹתָם הוֹצִיאָם
כט לַהֲמִתָם בַּמִּדְבָּר: וְהֵם עַמְּךָ וְנַחֲלָתֶךָ אֲשֶׁר הוֹצֵאתָ בְּכֹחֲךָ הַגָּדֹל וּבִזְרֹעֲךָ
הַנְּטוּיָה:
י רביעי א בָּעֵת הַהִוא אָמַר יהוה אֵלַי פְּסָל־לְךָ שְׁנֵי־לוּחֹת אֲבָנִים כָּרִאשֹׁנִים וַעֲלֵה
ב אֵלַי הָהָרָה וְעָשִׂיתָ לְּךָ אֲרוֹן עֵץ: וְאֶכְתֹּב עַל־הַלֻּחֹת אֶת־הַדְּבָרִים אֲשֶׁר
ג הָיוּ עַל־הַלֻּחֹת הָרִאשֹׁנִים אֲשֶׁר שִׁבַּרְתָּ וְשַׂמְתָּם בָּאָרוֹן: וָאַעַשׂ אֲרוֹן עֲצֵי
שִׁטִּים וָאֶפְסֹל שְׁנֵי־לֻחֹת אֲבָנִים כָּרִאשֹׁנִים וָאַעַל הָהָרָה וּשְׁנֵי הַלֻּחֹת בְּיָדִי:

---

22. וּבְתַבְעֵרָה וּבְמַסָּה — *And at Taberah and at Massah.* Although you saw that by angering God, the Blessed One, the tablets of law were shattered, and I had to pray and fast forty days on your behalf, (still) you continued to anger (Him) at Taberah and at Massah when you cried in His hearing to test (Him).

וּבְקִבְרֹת הַתַּאֲוָה — *And at Kibros Hataavah* ... when you asked for meat.

X

1. בָּעֵת הַהִוא אָמַר ה׳ אֵלַי פְּסָל לְךָ — *At that time* HASHEM *said to me: 'Hew out.'* Behold, that with all my prayers, the forgiveness (lit., repair) was incomplete, because in place of the (first) tablets which were the work of God, He (now) told me, *Hew out yourself etc.*

NOTES

22. וּבְתַבְעֵרָה וּבְמַסָּה וּבְקִבְרֹת הַתַּאֲוָה — *And at Taberah and at Massah and at Kibros Hataavah.* Taberah refers to the מִתְאֹנְנִים, *the murmurers*, recorded in *Bamidbar* 11:1; Massah to the people's complaint regarding the lack of water (*Exodus* 17:7), and Kibros Hataavah to their request for meat (*Bamidbar* 11:34)

X

1. פְּסָל לְךָ — *'Hew out.'* The *Ramban* states that this verse is a continuation of the admonition recorded in the previous chapter. The *Sforno* interprets this verse in the same vein, pointing out that whereas the first tablets were מַעֲשֵׂה אֱלֹהִים, *the work of God*

ד וַיִּכְתֹּב עַל־הַלֻּחֹת כַּמִּכְתָּב הָרִאשׁוֹן אֵת עֲשֶׂרֶת הַדְּבָרִים אֲשֶׁר דִּבֶּר יהוה
ה אֲלֵיכֶם בָּהָר מִתּוֹךְ הָאֵשׁ בְּיוֹם הַקָּהָל וַיִּתְּנֵם יהוה אֵלָי: וָאֵפֶן וָאֵרֵד
מִן־הָהָר וָאָשִׂם אֶת־הַלֻּחֹת בָּאָרוֹן אֲשֶׁר עָשִׂיתִי וַיִּהְיוּ שָׁם כַּאֲשֶׁר צִוַּנִי
ו יהוה: וּבְנֵי יִשְׂרָאֵל נָסְעוּ מִבְּאֵרֹת בְּנֵי־יַעֲקָן מוֹסֵרָה שָׁם מֵת אַהֲרֹן וַיִּקָּבֵר
ז שָׁם וַיְכַהֵן אֶלְעָזָר בְּנוֹ תַּחְתָּיו: מִשָּׁם נָסְעוּ הַגֻּדְגֹּדָה וּמִן־הַגֻּדְגֹּדָה יָטְבָתָה
ח אֶרֶץ נַחֲלֵי מָיִם: בָּעֵת הַהִוא הִבְדִּיל יהוה אֶת־שֵׁבֶט הַלֵּוִי לָשֵׂאת
אֶת־אֲרוֹן בְּרִית־יהוה לַעֲמֹד לִפְנֵי יהוה לְשָׁרְתוֹ וּלְבָרֵךְ בִּשְׁמוֹ עַד הַיּוֹם
ט הַזֶּה: עַל־כֵּן לֹא־הָיָה לְלֵוִי חֵלֶק וְנַחֲלָה עִם־אֶחָיו יהוה הוּא נַחֲלָתוֹ כַּאֲשֶׁר
י דִּבֶּר יהוה אֱלֹהֶיךָ לוֹ: וְאָנֹכִי עָמַדְתִּי בָהָר כַּיָּמִים הָרִאשֹׁנִים אַרְבָּעִים יוֹם
וְאַרְבָּעִים לַיְלָה וַיִּשְׁמַע יהוה אֵלַי גַּם בַּפַּעַם הַהִוא לֹא־אָבָה יהוה

---

6. וּבְנֵי יִשְׂרָאֵל נָסְעוּ — *And the Children of Israel journeyed.* Although they saw that the prayers of a righteous person (succeeds) in protecting his generation, and that it was (therefore) fitting to lament his passing (,nonetheless the following occurred). Some or most of those who were tending their flocks in the wilderness journeyed to Mossarah, to seek out water and grazing land for their sheep, and while there Aaron died and was buried, and his son Elazar succeeded him. Yet, they did not return to grieve his death, nor to mourn at his burial, nor were they concerned to honor Elazar who became the *Kohen* in his stead, but ...

7. מִשָּׁם נָסְעוּ הַגֻּדְגֹּדָה — *From there, they journeyed to Gudgod* ... to tend their sheep.

וּמִן הַגֻּדְגֹּדָה יָטְבָתָה אֶרֶץ נַחֲלֵי מָיִם — *And from Gudgod to Jotbah, a land of brooks of water.* All the places mentioned here were areas which had abundant brooks to water the sheep, and they did not even consider the loss (lit., harm) suffered by the death of the righteous man (i.e., Aaron), nor (concern themselves) with his honor nor the honor (due) his son.

8. בָּעֵת הַהִוא הִבְדִּיל ה׳ — *At that time,* HASHEM *separated.* Now since God, the Blessed One, already separated one tribe for the sacred service, and you (the people at large) were not considered worthy (enough) to occupy yourselves with (this service), and in spite of this (punishment), I could only attain through my prayers the (willingness of God) not to destroy you. He then said to me ...

NOTES

(Exodus 2:16), these second tablets were the work of man. This indicates that the original קְדוּשָּׁה, *holiness*, was not recaptured.

6-7. וּבְנֵי יִשְׂרָאֵל נָסְעוּ ... מִשָּׁם נָסְעוּ הַגֻּדְגֹּדָה ... אֶרֶץ נַחֲלֵי מָיִם — *And the Children of Israel journeyed ... From there, they journeyed to Gudgod ... a land of brooks of water.* Moses continues to admonish Israel for the insensitivity demonstrated by many when Aaron died and Elazar succeeded him. They were less concerned over Aaron's death then in hurrying on to places with a good supply of water, nor did they feel the need to pay honor to Elazar, the new *Kohen Gadol.*

8. בָּעֵת הַהִוא הִבְדִּיל ה׳ — *At that time,* HASHEM *separated.* The reason Moses inserts the selection of the Levites for the Divine Service at this point was to remind the people that, as a consequence of the sin of the Golden Calf, Israel as a people was no longer considered worthy to serve God through this service as had been God's original intent. Indeed, their transgression was so great that, at best, Moses was only able to prevail upon God not to destroy them (v. 10), but was unable to restore them to the exalted level they had attained at Sinai when they accepted the Torah.

11. קוּם לֵךְ לְמַסַּע ... אֶת הָאָרֶץ אֲשֶׁר נִשְׁבַּעְתִּי — *Arise, go and cause (them) to journey ... the land which I swore.* Continuing the theme of

יא הַשְׁחִיתֶךָ: וַיֹּאמֶר יהוה אֵלַי קוּם לֵךְ לְמַסַּע לִפְנֵי הָעָם וְיָבֹאוּ וְיִירְשׁוּ
אֶת־הָאָרֶץ אֲשֶׁר־נִשְׁבַּעְתִּי לַאֲבֹתָם לָתֵת לָהֶם:
חמישי יב וְעַתָּה יִשְׂרָאֵל מָה יהוה אֱלֹהֶיךָ שֹׁאֵל מֵעִמָּךְ כִּי אִם־לְיִרְאָה אֶת־יהוה
אֱלֹהֶיךָ לָלֶכֶת בְּכָל־דְּרָכָיו וּלְאַהֲבָה אֹתוֹ וְלַעֲבֹד אֶת־יהוה אֱלֹהֶיךָ
יג בְּכָל־לְבָבְךָ וּבְכָל־נַפְשֶׁךָ: לִשְׁמֹר אֶת־מִצְוֺת יהוה וְאֶת־חֻקֹּתָיו אֲשֶׁר אָנֹכִי
יד מְצַוְּךָ הַיּוֹם לְטוֹב לָךְ: הֵן לַיהוה אֱלֹהֶיךָ הַשָּׁמַיִם וּשְׁמֵי הַשָּׁמָיִם הָאָרֶץ
טו וְכָל־אֲשֶׁר־בָּהּ: רַק בַּאֲבֹתֶיךָ חָשַׁק יהוה לְאַהֲבָה אוֹתָם וַיִּבְחַר בְּזַרְעָם

---

11. קוּם לֵךְ לְמַסַּע — *Arise, go and cause (them) to journey*, (לְמַסַּע should be interpreted as) לְמַסִּיעַ, *causing others to journey*, similar to וּלְמַסַּע אֶת הַמַּחֲנוֹת, *and for causing the camps to set forward* (Numbers 10:2).

וְיָבֹאוּ וְיִירְשׁוּ אֶת הָאָרֶץ אֲשֶׁר נִשְׁבַּעְתִּי — *That they may go in and possess the land which I swore ...* because were it not for the oath, you would not be worthy to (possess) it due to your frequent revolts.

12. וְעַתָּה יִשְׂרָאֵל — *And now, Israel.* Therefore, you Israel, attempt now to correct your crookedness henceforth and consider *what God your God requires of you*, for He does not ask anything for His own sake, כִּי אִם לְיִרְאָה, *but to fear* — and this (level) you shall reach when you reflect in such a manner that you will come to recognize His greatness.

וּלְאַהֲבָה אֹתוֹ — *And to love Him.* And this (love) you shall attain when you consider His Goodness. All this He asks לְטוֹב לָךְ, *for your good* (v. 13) — in order that you may merit eternal life.

14. הֵן לַה׳ אֱלֹהֶיךָ הַשָּׁמַיִם — *Behold, unto* HASHEM *your God belong the heavens.* And the proof that He seeks that which is *for your good* is because, indeed, heaven and earth are His, and even though they are exalted and non-perishable — (nonetheless) ...

15. רַק בַּאֲבֹתֶיךָ חָשַׁק ה׳ — *Only in your forefathers did* HASHEM *find pleasure.* And He altered (the laws of) nature of these exalted (creations) on your behalf in the merit of the Patriarchs which without a doubt was done to attain something of

NOTES

the previous verses, Moses tells the people that the Almighty removed Himself from their midst and commanded him to *cause them to journey*, which represented a far lesser degree of הַשְׁגָּחַת ה׳, *Hashem's providence and concern*. Indeed, were it not for the oath He had taken to grant the Land to them as the descendants of the Patriarchs, He would not have allowed them to enter and conquer *Eretz Yisrael*, because of their frequent revolts.

12. וְעַתָּה יִשְׂרָאֵל — *And now, Israel* ... The expression וְעַתָּה, *and now*, links this verse to the previous ones (8-11). The *Sforno* interprets this verse in the following manner: Since you are guilty of many sins and frequent rebellion against God, it is imperative that you mend your ways and alter your attitude. This can only be accomplished by considering the greatness of God which will bring you to יִרְאָה — *awe and reverance* which deters sin — and by considering God's goodness and kindness which brings one to אַהֲבָה — *love of God*.

The next verse states, לְטוֹב לָךְ, *for your good*. Man's attainment of יִרְאַת ה׳, *reverence of God*, and אַהֲבַת ה׳, *love of God*, is for his own benefit, because through these two traits he will merit eternal life. Hence, this is לְטוֹב לָךְ, *for your good*. The *Sforno* explains in the next verse (14) that God's request that Israel revere and love Him is certainly not for His benefit, since He is the Master of heaven and earth. Hence, it can only be for Israel's benefit that they may merit everlasting life.

15. רַק בַּאֲבֹתֶיךָ חָשַׁק ה׳ — *Only in your*

טז אַחֲרֵיהֶ֑ם בָּכֶ֖ם מִכָּל־הָעַמִּ֑ים כַּיּ֖וֹם הַזֶּֽה: וּמַלְתֶּ֕ם אֵ֖ת עָרְלַ֣ת לְבַבְכֶ֑ם
יז וְעָרְפְּכֶ֕ם לֹ֥א תַקְשׁ֖וּ עֽוֹד: כִּ֚י יְהֹוָ֣ה אֱלֹֽהֵיכֶ֔ם ה֚וּא אֱלֹהֵ֣י הָֽאֱלֹהִ֔ים וַֽאֲדֹנֵ֖י
הָֽאֲדֹנִ֑ים הָאֵ֨ל הַגָּדֹ֤ל הַגִּבֹּר֙ וְהַנּוֹרָ֔א אֲשֶׁר֙ לֹא־יִשָּׂ֣א פָנִ֔ים וְלֹ֥א יִקַּ֖ח שֹֽׁחַד:

greater value than heaven and earth, namely the perfect man who is similar to his
Creator, to the greatest extent possible, as it says: בְּצַלְמֵנוּ כִּדְמוּתֵנוּ, *in our image after
our likeness (Genesis 1:26).*

16. וּמַלְתֶּם אֵת עָרְלַת לְבַבְכֶם — *And circumcise therefore the foreskin of your heart.*
Therefore, it is fitting that you remove the foreskin (covering) of your intelligence,
by examining and eliminating the errors (of your thinking) which give birth to false
ideas (philosophies).

וְעָרְפְּכֶם לֹא תַקְשׁוּ עוֹד — *And be no more stiff-necked.* And when you remove the
stiffness of your neck, which prevents you from turning to that which is proper,
you will come to a recognition of your Creator, and realize that it is evil and bitter
to forsake Him. And this (will come about) when you consider . . .

17. כִּי ה׳ אֱלֹהֵיכֶם הוּא אֱלֹהֵי הָאֱלֹהִים — *For HASHEM your God, He is God of gods . . .*
the Eternal (One) over all the eternal ones who are separated from matter, because
the eternal nature of all others stems from His eternity.

וַאֲדֹנֵי הָאֲדֹנִים — *And the Lord of lords . . .* the conductor of all (heavenly) conductors,
these being the celestial spheres (גַּלְגַּלִּים) and their moving forces, whose actions are
all intended to attain the end purpose of His intent, similar to individual labors that
are directed toward the primary goal.

הָאֵל הַגָּדֹל — *The great God.* There is none in existence equal to His level of existence
in *kind.*

הַגִּבֹּר — *The mighty . . .* who grants (establishes and insures) existence, through His
existence, to all that exist, as it says: וְאַתָּה מְחַיֶּה אֶת כֻּלָּם, *and You preserve them all*
(Nehemiah 9:6).

וְהַנּוֹרָא — *And the* awesome (*God*). He oversees (all) to reward and to punish, in such
a manner that it is fitting (for man) to fear His Presence.

NOTES

forefathers did HASHEM find pleasure. The
fact that God disrupted the laws of nature and
altered the nature of heaven and earth proves
how great His love for the Patriarchs was, and
this Divine willingness also indicates the
greatness and exalted nature of the 'perfect
man' on whose behalf the suspension of the
laws of nature took place. This can only be
because 'perfect man' represents and reflects,
at his best, the 'image and likeness' of God and
the angels.

16. וּמַלְתֶּם ... וְעָרְפְּכֶם לֹא תַקְשׁוּ עוֹד — *And
circumcise ... and be no more stiff-necked.*
Moses argues that since man was created in
the image of God, he is good inherently and
also is straightforward in his thinking. Unfortunately, his physical appetites and weak-

nesses divert him from the proper path. It is
therefore imperative for him to remove the
barrier, symbolically called the 'foreskin,'
which exists between him and God and to be
flexible enough to consider his errors and
return to the Almighty.

17. הוּא אֱלֹהֵי הָאֱלֹהִים — *He is God of gods.* The
Sforno painstakingly defines every term used
in this verse to describe God, explaining that
each appellation is distinctive and not repetitious: He is the source of existence; the first
and continuous cause; He is unique, omnipotent and omniscient, and He rewards and
punishes, showing no favoritism. Man, in
turn, is accountable and will reap what he
sows through his actions. Nonetheless, sincere
repentance will grant him salvation.

יח-יט עֹשֶׂה מִשְׁפַּט יָתוֹם וְאַלְמָנָה וְאֹהֵב גֵּר לָתֶת לוֹ לֶחֶם וְשִׂמְלָה: וַאֲהַבְתֶּם
כ אֶת־הַגֵּר כִּי־גֵרִים הֱיִיתֶם בְּאֶרֶץ מִצְרָיִם: אֶת־יהוה אֱלֹהֶיךָ תִּירָא אֹתוֹ
כא תַעֲבֹד וּבוֹ תִדְבָּק וּבִשְׁמוֹ תִּשָּׁבֵעַ: הוּא תְהִלָּתְךָ וְהוּא אֱלֹהֶיךָ אֲשֶׁר־עָשָׂה
כב אִתְּךָ אֶת־הַגְּדֹלֹת וְאֶת־הַנּוֹרָאֹת הָאֵלֶּה אֲשֶׁר רָאוּ עֵינֶיךָ: בְּשִׁבְעִים נֶפֶשׁ
יָרְדוּ אֲבֹתֶיךָ מִצְרָיְמָה וְעַתָּה שָׂמְךָ יהוה אֱלֹהֶיךָ כְּכוֹכְבֵי הַשָּׁמַיִם לָרֹב:
יא א וְאָהַבְתָּ אֵת יהוה אֱלֹהֶיךָ וְשָׁמַרְתָּ מִשְׁמַרְתּוֹ וְחֻקֹּתָיו וּמִשְׁפָּטָיו וּמִצְוֹתָיו
ב כָּל־הַיָּמִים: וִידַעְתֶּם הַיּוֹם כִּי | לֹא אֶת־בְּנֵיכֶם אֲשֶׁר לֹא־יָדְעוּ וַאֲשֶׁר
לֹא־רָאוּ אֶת־מוּסַר יהוה אֱלֹהֵיכֶם אֶת־גָּדְלוֹ אֶת־יָדוֹ הַחֲזָקָה וּזְרֹעוֹ
ג הַנְּטוּיָה: וְאֶת־אֹתֹתָיו וְאֶת־מַעֲשָׂיו אֲשֶׁר עָשָׂה בְּתוֹךְ מִצְרָיִם לְפַרְעֹה
ד מֶלֶךְ־מִצְרַיִם וּלְכָל־אַרְצוֹ: וַאֲשֶׁר עָשָׂה לְחֵיל מִצְרַיִם לְסוּסָיו וּלְרִכְבּוֹ אֲשֶׁר
הֵצִיף אֶת־מֵי יַם־סוּף עַל־פְּנֵיהֶם בְּרָדְפָם אַחֲרֵיכֶם וַיְאַבְּדֵם יהוה עַד הַיּוֹם

אֲשֶׁר לֹא יִשָּׂא פָנִים — *Who favors no person* . . . (including) the unrestrained (wild) son for the sake of his righteous father, even though He is slow to anger in the merit of the father.

וְלֹא יִקַּח שֹׁחַד — *And takes no bribe.* He will not reduce the punishment for a transgression because of the merit of a *mitzvah* which the sinner performed, as our Sages say, שֶׁאֵין מִצְוָה מְכַבָּה עֲבֵרָה *A mitzvah shall not extinguish a transgression* (*Sotah* 21a). And all this teaches us that if we sin, we cannot rely on any merit to save us from punishment — except perfect repentance.

21. הוּא תְהִלָּתְךָ — *He is your glory.* It is praiseworthy that you be a servant of the One Who reigns over all existence.

XI

2. כִּי לֹא אֶת בְּנֵיכֶם — *For (I speak not) to your children.* Therefore, you who did see (the miracles and wonders) must make signs when you enter (the Land) which will bear witness for (future) generations.

וּזְרֹעוֹ הַנְּטוּיָה — *And His outstretched arm* . . . which is prepared to smite whoever returns to sin.

4. וַיְאַבְּדֵם ה׳ עַד הַיּוֹם הַזֶּה — *And HASHEM has destroyed them unto this day* . . . because the drowning of the captains of Egypt and their soldiers (caused) a loss which was felt forty years later since they were the mighty ones, and there were none to replace them.

NOTES

21. הוּא תְהִלָּתְךָ — *He is your glory*. The *Sforno* explains that the verse does not refer to man's praise of God. Rather, it means that Israel is praiseworthy for having been granted the privilege to be the servants of God!

XI

2. כִּי לֹא אֶת בְּנֵיכֶם — *For (I speak not) to your children*. The *Sforno* explains the sequence of verses 2-8 thus: God speaks to this generation that witnessed the greatness of God, His signs and wonders, as well as the punishment of the Egyptians and of those who rebelled against Moses. Since they actually beheld this with their own eyes it is their responsibility to transmit this testimony to their children who did not experience it. This was to be done by writing the words of Torah on great stones when they passed over the Jordan, setting them up on Mt. Ebal as we read in chapter 27:2-4.

4. עַד הַיּוֹם הַזֶּה — *Unto this day*. The *Sforno*

ה־ו הַזֶּה׃ וַאֲשֶׁר עָשָׂה לָכֶם בַּמִּדְבָּר עַד־בֹּאֲכֶם עַד־הַמָּקוֹם הַזֶּה׃ וַאֲשֶׁר עָשָׂה
לְדָתָן וְלַאֲבִירָם בְּנֵי אֱלִיאָב בֶּן־רְאוּבֵן אֲשֶׁר פָּצְתָה הָאָרֶץ אֶת־פִּיהָ
וַתִּבְלָעֵם וְאֶת־בָּתֵּיהֶם וְאֶת־אָהֳלֵיהֶם וְאֵת כָּל־הַיְקוּם אֲשֶׁר בְּרַגְלֵיהֶם
ז בְּקֶרֶב כָּל־יִשְׂרָאֵל׃ כִּי עֵינֵיכֶם הָרֹאֹת אֶת־כָּל־מַעֲשֵׂה יהוה הַגָּדֹל אֲשֶׁר
ח עָשָׂה׃ וּשְׁמַרְתֶּם אֶת־כָּל־הַמִּצְוָה אֲשֶׁר אָנֹכִי מְצַוְּךָ הַיּוֹם לְמַעַן תֶּחֶזְקוּ
ט וּבָאתֶם וִירִשְׁתֶּם אֶת־הָאָרֶץ אֲשֶׁר אַתֶּם עֹבְרִים שָׁמָּה לְרִשְׁתָּהּ׃ וּלְמַעַן
תַּאֲרִיכוּ יָמִים עַל־הָאֲדָמָה אֲשֶׁר נִשְׁבַּע יהוה לַאֲבֹתֵיכֶם לָתֵת לָהֶם
ששי י וּלְזַרְעָם אֶרֶץ זָבַת חָלָב וּדְבָשׁ׃ כִּי הָאָרֶץ אֲשֶׁר
אַתָּה בָא־שָׁמָּה לְרִשְׁתָּהּ לֹא כְאֶרֶץ מִצְרַיִם הִוא אֲשֶׁר יְצָאתֶם מִשָּׁם אֲשֶׁר
יא תִּזְרַע אֶת־זַרְעֲךָ וְהִשְׁקִיתָ בְרַגְלְךָ כְּגַן הַיָּרָק׃ וְהָאָרֶץ אֲשֶׁר אַתֶּם עֹבְרִים
יב שָׁמָּה לְרִשְׁתָּהּ אֶרֶץ הָרִים וּבְקָעֹת לִמְטַר הַשָּׁמַיִם תִּשְׁתֶּה־מָּיִם׃ אֶרֶץ
אֲשֶׁר־יהוה אֱלֹהֶיךָ דֹּרֵשׁ אֹתָהּ תָּמִיד עֵינֵי יהוה אֱלֹהֶיךָ בָּהּ מֵרֵשִׁית הַשָּׁנָה

---

7. כִּי עֵינֵיכֶם הָרֹאֹת אֵת כָּל מַעֲשֵׂה ה׳ — *But your eyes have seen all the work of* HASHEM. Who did such great (deeds) against those who rebelled against Him; to Pharaoh and the Egyptians in Egypt, and at the sea; to the rebels in the wilderness, and to Dathan and Abiram (as well). Hence, it is (incumbent) upon you to caution the children who did not see all this — therefore . . .

8. וּשְׁמַרְתֶּם אֶת כָּל הַמִּצְוָה אֲשֶׁר אָנֹכִי מְצַוְּךָ הַיּוֹם — *And you shall keep all the commandment which I command you this day* . . . the commandment of the stones which you shall erect in the Jordan, and which you shall take from the midst of the Jordan, and write on them the Torah, which shall bear witness for (all) generations (coming) from you, who did see (all these wonders).

9. וּלְמַעַן תַּאֲרִיכוּ יָמִים עַל הָאֲדָמָה — *And that you may prolong your days upon the land* . . . for if your children will not keep the commandments, they will be exiled from (the Land) quickly, (even) before (the period of) וְנוֹשַׁנְתֶּם בָּאָרֶץ, *and you shall have been long in the Land (4:25)*, as (the Torah) testifies, saying, *and the heaven shall be shut up . . . and you perish quickly* (v. 17).

10. כִּי הָאָרֶץ אֲשֶׁר אַתָּה בָא שָׁמָּה לְרִשְׁתָּהּ לֹא כְאֶרֶץ מִצְרַיִם הִוא — *For the land which you go in to possess, is not as the land of Egypt* . . . Which does not require rain.

11. לִמְטַר הַשָּׁמַיִם תִּשְׁתֶּה מָּיִם — *By rain from heaven, it consumes water*. There are insufficient rivers to water the Land, and it needs rainwater.

12. דֹּרֵשׁ אֹתָהּ — *Cares for (it)* . . . observing the deeds of its inhabitants (to see) if they are worthy (to have) rain or not. Therefore, know this that indeed . . .

NOTES

interprets this phrase as meaning that Egypt never recovered from this disaster.

8. וּשְׁמַרְתֶּם אֶת כָּל הַמִּצְוָה — *And you shall keep all the commandment*. See note on verse 2.

9. וּלְמַעַן תַּאֲרִיכוּ יָמִים — *And that you may prolong your days*. The *Sforno*'s quote of וְנוֹשַׁנְתֶּם, *and you shall have been long*, is most significant. Our Sages tell us that the numerical equivalent of this phrase is 852, indicating that Israel was destined to go into exile after that number of years (*Sanhedrin* 35). In our verse, Israel is cautioned that if the *mitzvos* are not observed, the time of exile will be hastened. The *Sforno* aptly concludes by quoting verse 17 where Israel is warned that they will be dispossessed *quickly*, i.e., before the ordained time.

יג וְעַד אַחֲרִית שָׁנָה׃ וְהָיָה אִם־שָׁמֹעַ תִּשְׁמְעוּ אֶל־
מִצְוֺתַי אֲשֶׁר אָנֹכִי מְצַוֶּה אֶתְכֶם הַיּוֹם לְאַהֲבָה אֶת־יהוה אֱלֹהֵיכֶם
יד וּלְעָבְדוֹ בְּכָל־לְבַבְכֶם וּבְכָל־נַפְשְׁכֶם׃ וְנָתַתִּי מְטַר־אַרְצְכֶם בְּעִתּוֹ יוֹרֶה
טו וּמַלְקוֹשׁ וְאָסַפְתָּ דְגָנֶךָ וְתִירֹשְׁךָ וְיִצְהָרֶךָ׃ וְנָתַתִּי עֵשֶׂב בְּשָׂדְךָ לִבְהֶמְתֶּךָ
טז וְאָכַלְתָּ וְשָׂבָעְתָּ׃ הִשָּׁמְרוּ לָכֶם פֶּן־יִפְתֶּה לְבַבְכֶם וְסַרְתֶּם וַעֲבַדְתֶּם אֱלֹהִים
יז אֲחֵרִים וְהִשְׁתַּחֲוִיתֶם לָהֶם׃ וְחָרָה אַף־יהוה בָּכֶם וְעָצַר אֶת־הַשָּׁמַיִם
וְלֹא־יִהְיֶה מָטָר וְהָאֲדָמָה לֹא תִתֵּן אֶת־יְבוּלָהּ וַאֲבַדְתֶּם מְהֵרָה מֵעַל
יח הָאָרֶץ הַטֹּבָה אֲשֶׁר יהוה נֹתֵן לָכֶם׃ וְשַׂמְתֶּם אֶת־דְּבָרַי אֵלֶּה עַל־לְבַבְכֶם
וְעַל־נַפְשְׁכֶם וּקְשַׁרְתֶּם אֹתָם לְאוֹת עַל־יֶדְכֶם וְהָיוּ לְטוֹטָפֹת בֵּין עֵינֵיכֶם׃
יט וְלִמַּדְתֶּם אֹתָם אֶת־בְּנֵיכֶם לְדַבֵּר בָּם בְּשִׁבְתְּךָ בְּבֵיתֶךָ וּבְלֶכְתְּךָ בַדֶּרֶךְ

13-14. אִם שָׁמֹעַ תִּשְׁמְעוּ . . . וְנָתַתִּי מְטַר אַרְצְכֶם — *If you shall hearken . . . that I will give the rain of your land* . . . in a manner that you will find sustenance without pain (effort) and will be able to serve Him. And if not, He will give you no rain at all and you will have no food to sustain you.

17. וַאֲבַדְתֶּם מְהֵרָה — *And you will perish quickly* . . . through famine which is far worse than the sword — therefore, הִשָּׁמְרוּ לָכֶם, *take heed to yourselves* (v. 16).

18. וְשַׂמְתֶּם אֶת דְּבָרַי אֵלֶּה עַל לְבַבְכֶם — *And you shall place these My words on your heart* . . . to reflect upon them.

וְעַל נַפְשְׁכֶם — *And in your soul* . . . to fulfill them willingly.

19. וְלִמַּדְתֶּם אֹתָם אֶת בְּנֵיכֶם — *And teach them to your children* . . . to train your children in the commandments.

לְדַבֵּר בָּם בְּשִׁבְתְּךָ בְּבֵיתֶךָ — *To speak of them when you sit in your house* . . . so as to speak of them constantly.

NOTES

12. דֹּרֵשׁ אֹתָהּ — *Cares for* (it). The commentary of the *Sforno* is best understood by the phrase that follows, *'the eyes of* HASHEM *your God are always upon it.'* Since *Eretz Yisrael* is special, God observes the deeds of its inhabitants, sending or withholding rain according to their actions, be they good or evil. The *Sifri* comments, 'The land of Egypt has water whether its inhabitants fulfill the will of God or not. *Eretz Yisrael* is not so; if they fulfill God's will, they shall dwell in the Land, and if not, they will go into exile.'

13-14. אִם שָׁמֹעַ תִּשְׁמְעוּ . . . וְנָתַתִּי מְטַר אַרְצְכֶם — *If you shall hearken . . . that I will give the rain of your land*. The Torah states that if Israel will *hearken* to God's commandments and *love* Him and *serve* Him, they will be granted rain and the blessing of plenty. The *Sforno* adds that this prosperity will result without great physical exertion so that they will be able to serve Him (וּלְעָבְדוֹ). The alternative is lack of rain and ultimately famine (v. 17).

17. וַאֲבַדְתֶּם מְהֵרָה — *And you will perish quickly*. The statement by the *Sforno* that famine is more severe than the sword is based upon the Talmudic saying, 'Famine is harder than the sword' (*Bava Basra* 8b), which in turn is derived from the verse in *Lamentations* 4:9, *They that were slain with the sword are better than they that were slain with hunger*.

18. עַל לְבַבְכֶם וְעַל נַפְשְׁכֶם — *On your heart and in your soul*. Reflection stems from the heart, while desire comes from the soul.

19. וְלִמַּדְתֶּם . . . לְדַבֵּר בָּם — *And teach them . . . to speak of them*. To teach is not sufficient; one must *train* his children to do the *mitzvos*, for only through practice will it become second nature. The study of Torah, in turn, cannot be sporadic and occasional but must be constant and continual — in one's home, on the road, by day and by night.

כ־כא וּבְשָׁכְבְּךָ וּבְקוּמֶךָ׃ וּכְתַבְתָּם עַל־מְזוּזוֹת בֵּיתֶךָ וּבִשְׁעָרֶיךָ׃ לְמַעַן יִרְבּוּ
יְמֵיכֶם וִימֵי בְנֵיכֶם עַל הָאֲדָמָה אֲשֶׁר נִשְׁבַּע יהוה לַאֲבֹתֵיכֶם לָתֵת לָהֶם
שביעי ומפטיר כב כִּימֵי הַשָּׁמַיִם עַל־הָאָרֶץ׃ כִּי אִם־שָׁמֹר תִּשְׁמְרוּן
אֶת־כָּל־הַמִּצְוָה הַזֹּאת אֲשֶׁר אָנֹכִי מְצַוֶּה אֶתְכֶם לַעֲשֹׂתָהּ לְאַהֲבָה
כג אֶת־יהוה אֱלֹהֵיכֶם לָלֶכֶת בְּכָל־דְּרָכָיו וּלְדָבְקָה־בוֹ׃ וְהוֹרִישׁ יהוה
אֶת־כָּל־הַגּוֹיִם הָאֵלֶּה מִלִּפְנֵיכֶם וִירִשְׁתֶּם גּוֹיִם גְּדֹלִים וַעֲצֻמִים מִכֶּם׃
כד כָּל־הַמָּקוֹם אֲשֶׁר תִּדְרֹךְ כַּף־רַגְלְכֶם בּוֹ לָכֶם יִהְיֶה מִן־הַמִּדְבָּר וְהַלְּבָנוֹן
כה מִן־הַנָּהָר נְהַר־פְּרָת וְעַד הַיָּם הָאַחֲרוֹן יִהְיֶה גְּבֻלְכֶם׃ לֹא־יִתְיַצֵּב אִישׁ
בִּפְנֵיכֶם פַּחְדְּכֶם וּמוֹרַאֲכֶם יִתֵּן ׀ יהוה אֱלֹהֵיכֶם עַל־פְּנֵי כָל־הָאָרֶץ אֲשֶׁר
תִּדְרְכוּ־בָהּ כַּאֲשֶׁר דִּבֶּר לָכֶם׃

---

22. כִּי אִם שָׁמֹר תִּשְׁמְרוּן... לְאַהֲבָה — *For if you shall diligently guard ... to love ...* to occupy yourselves with Torah in order to recognize the lovingkindness of God, the Exalted One, for from this (knowledge) does love flow.

לָלֶכֶת בְּכָל דְּרָכָיו — *To walk in all His ways* ... to conduct yourselves in those ways with which He conducts His world, namely righteousness and justice.

וּלְדָבְקָה בו — *And to cleave to Him* ... that all your actions have as their aim the doing of His will, as it says, בְּכָל דְּרָכֶיךָ דָעֵהוּ, *In all your ways know Him* (*Proverbs* 3:6).

23. וְהוֹרִישׁ ה׳ — *And HASHEM will drive out.* He will grant you a place in which to earn your livelihood without pain, so that you shall be able to do His will.

25. לֹא יִתְיַצֵּב אִישׁ בִּפְנֵיכֶם — *No man shall stand against you* ... even outside the Land.

NOTES

22. כִּי אִם שָׁמֹר תִּשְׁמְרוּן... לְאַהֲבָה... לָלֶכֶת בְּכָל דְּרָכָיו — *For if you shall diligently guard ... to love ... to walk in all His ways*. The *Sforno* at the beginning of this *sedrah* (7:12) interprets the word וּשְׁמַרְתֶּם as meaning 'Mishnah.' Similarly, he explains the term שָׁמֹר תִּשְׁמְרוּן, *to diligently guard*, as meaning the study of Torah which causes man to recognize and appreciate the חַסְדֵי ה׳, *the loving kindness of God*, which, in turn, brings man to the love of God, as we see in the *Sforno*'s commentary on the phrase וּלְאַהֲבָה אֹתוֹ, *and to love Him* (10:12). To walk in the ways of God is always interpreted as meaning to imitate His attributes. *Rashi* gives a similar interpretation, *and Rashi* also explains the expression of שָׁמֹר תִּשְׁמְרוּן as referring to the continuous study of Torah that it not be forgotten.

23. וְהוֹרִישׁ ה׳ — *And HASHEM will drive out*. By driving out the enemy, God will grant Israel the opportunity to realize their material well-being without excessive exertion, thereby enabling them to serve God in tranquility.

25. לֹא יִתְיַצֵּב אִישׁ בִּפְנֵיכֶם — *No man shall stand against you*. In the previous verse, the borders of the Land are delineated; hence the expression in this verse עַל פְּנֵי כָל הָאָרֶץ, *upon all the land*, seems redundant. The *Sforno*, however, explains that the Torah assures the Israelites that they will enter *Eretz Yisrael* unchallenged, for God will cause the nations to fear and dread their might. This fear of the Israelites will extend to the geographical area outside the Land as well. This explains the use of the term כָל הָאָרֶץ which is all inclusive.

פרשת ראה
Parashas Re'eh

כו־כז רְאֵה אָנֹכִי נֹתֵן לִפְנֵיכֶם הַיּוֹם בְּרָכָה וּקְלָלָה: אֶת־הַבְּרָכָה אֲשֶׁר
תִּשְׁמְעוּ אֶל־מִצְוֺת יהוה אֱלֹהֵיכֶם אֲשֶׁר אָנֹכִי מְצַוֶּה אֶתְכֶם הַיּוֹם:
כח וְהַקְּלָלָה אִם־לֹא תִשְׁמְעוּ אֶל־מִצְוֺת יהוה אֱלֹהֵיכֶם וְסַרְתֶּם מִן־הַדֶּרֶךְ
אֲשֶׁר אָנֹכִי מְצַוֶּה אֶתְכֶם הַיּוֹם לָלֶכֶת אַחֲרֵי אֱלֹהִים אֲחֵרִים אֲשֶׁר
כט לֹא־יְדַעְתֶּם: וְהָיָה כִּי יְבִיאֲךָ יהוה אֱלֹהֶיךָ אֶל־הָאָרֶץ
אֲשֶׁר־אַתָּה בָא־שָׁמָּה לְרִשְׁתָּהּ וְנָתַתָּה אֶת־הַבְּרָכָה עַל־הַר גְּרִזִים
ל וְאֶת־הַקְּלָלָה עַל־הַר עֵיבָל: הֲלֹא־הֵמָּה בְּעֵבֶר הַיַּרְדֵּן אַחֲרֵי דֶּרֶךְ מְבוֹא

---

26. רְאֵה — *Behold.* Look and perceive that your affairs (as a people) are not of an intermediate nature (i.e., the mean or average) as is the case with other nations because, indeed, (in your case) *I set before you this day a blessing and a curse,* which are two extremes since the blessing represents good fortune beyond what is sufficient (or adequate) (for it is) exceedingly good, (whereas) the curse is one which brings diminishment and (even a state of) sufficiency becomes unattainable. Both of these (blessing and curse) are לִפְנֵיכֶם, *before you,* i.e., attainable according to your choice.

29. וְנָתַתָּה אֶת הַבְּרָכָה — *And you shall set the blessing.* You shall bless those who guard (observe) the commandments.

וְאֶת הַקְּלָלָה — *And the curse . . .* (upon) those who transgress them.

30. הֲלֹא הֵמָּה בְּעֵבֶר הַיַּרְדֵּן — *Are they not beyond the Jordan.* (This refers to) when you first enter the Land, in order to publicize as you begin to enter (*Eretz Yisrael*) that your dwelling in it will not be in a moderate, average manner but rather it will be either in a successful manner or an accursed one.

NOTES

26. רְאֵה — *Behold.* The fate of other nations is not one marked by full prosperity or complete devastation. Theirs is not a condition of extremes — blessing or curse. Moses cautions Israel that they, however, are unlike other peoples. Their lot as the people of God is destined to be most uncommon; there will be no middle course, for they will either be blessed or cursed! This is the significance of the introductory word רְאֵה, *see* or *behold*, which indicates something new and different, as we find in *Koheles* 1:10, *See, this is new.* The *Sforno* explains that Moses warned the people of Israel that this unique fate which lies in store for them, of extreme good fortune or total diminishment, is dependent upon their choice (לִפְנֵיכֶם); whether they choose to hearken to the commandments of God or not. According to the *Sforno*, for the people of Israel there can no moderate stance because Torah brooks no compromise. God demands total commitment and offers two extreme options — a blessing or a curse. Unlike other commentators, the *Sforno* does not interpret the 'blessing' and 'curse' as referring to those pronounced on Mount Gerizim and Mount Ebal. He does, however, agree that those blessings and curses listed in chapter 27 emphasize the fact that Israel's destiny in *Eretz Yisrael* will be dependent upon their conduct and behavior as the Chosen People. This we must conclude from his commentary on verse 30.

29. וְנָתַתָּה אֶת הַבְּרָכָה . . . וְאֶת הַקְּלָלָה — *And you shall set the blessing . . . and the curse*. The *Sforno* explains that the setting of the blessing on Mt. Gerizim and the curse on Mt. Ebal is not meant to bless or curse these mountains. The purpose is to bless those who keep God's commandments and curse those who violate them. As *Rashi* explains (and the *Sforno* certainly concurs), those who pronounced the blessing were to face Mt. Gerizim after which they were to turn toward Mt. Ebal with the corresponding curse.

30. הֲלֹא הֵמָּה בְּעֵבֶר הַיַּרְדֵּן — *Are they not beyond the Jordan*. See note on verse 26. The *Sforno* emphasizes that the pronouncement of the blessing and curse was to be done immedi-

לא הַשֶּׁמֶשׁ בְּאֶרֶץ הַכְּנַעֲנִי הַיֹּשֵׁב בָּעֲרָבָה מוּל הַגִּלְגָּל אֵצֶל אֵלוֹנֵי מֹרֶה: כִּי
אַתֶּם עֹבְרִים אֶת־הַיַּרְדֵּן לָבֹא לָרֶשֶׁת אֶת־הָאָרֶץ אֲשֶׁר־יְהוָה אֱלֹהֵיכֶם
לב נֹתֵן לָכֶם וִירִשְׁתֶּם אֹתָהּ וִישַׁבְתֶּם־בָּהּ: וּשְׁמַרְתֶּם לַעֲשׂוֹת אֵת כָּל־הַחֻקִּים
יב א וְאֶת־הַמִּשְׁפָּטִים אֲשֶׁר אָנֹכִי נֹתֵן לִפְנֵיכֶם הַיּוֹם: אֵלֶּה הַחֻקִּים וְהַמִּשְׁפָּטִים
אֲשֶׁר תִּשְׁמְרוּן לַעֲשׂוֹת בָּאָרֶץ אֲשֶׁר נָתַן יְהוָה אֱלֹהֵי אֲבֹתֶיךָ לְךָ לְרִשְׁתָּהּ
ב כָּל־הַיָּמִים אֲשֶׁר־אַתֶּם חַיִּים עַל־הָאֲדָמָה: אַבֵּד תְּאַבְּדוּן אֶת־כָּל־
הַמְּקֹמוֹת אֲשֶׁר עָבְדוּ־שָׁם הַגּוֹיִם אֲשֶׁר אַתֶּם יֹרְשִׁים אֹתָם אֶת־אֱלֹהֵיהֶם
ג עַל־הֶהָרִים הָרָמִים וְעַל־הַגְּבָעוֹת וְתַחַת כָּל־עֵץ רַעֲנָן: וְנִתַּצְתֶּם אֶת־
מִזְבְּחֹתָם וְשִׁבַּרְתֶּם אֶת־מַצֵּבֹתָם וַאֲשֵׁרֵיהֶם תִּשְׂרְפוּן בָּאֵשׁ וּפְסִילֵי
ד אֱלֹהֵיהֶם תְּגַדֵּעוּן וְאִבַּדְתֶּם אֶת־שְׁמָם מִן־הַמָּקוֹם הַהוּא: לֹא־תַעֲשׂוּן כֵּן
ה לַיהוָה אֱלֹהֵיכֶם: כִּי אִם־אֶל־הַמָּקוֹם אֲשֶׁר־יִבְחַר יְהוָה אֱלֹהֵיכֶם מִכָּל־
ו שִׁבְטֵיכֶם לָשׂוּם אֶת־שְׁמוֹ שָׁם לְשִׁכְנוֹ תִדְרְשׁוּ וּבָאתָ שָׁמָּה: וַהֲבֵאתֶם שָׁמָּה

XII

1. אֵלֶּה הַחֻקִּים וְהַמִּשְׁפָּטִים אֲשֶׁר תִּשְׁמְרוּן לַעֲשׂוֹת . . . לְרִשְׁתָּהּ כָּל הַיָּמִים — *These are the statutes and ordinances which you shall observe to do . . . to possess it all the days.* Included in these commandments which you must observe, and through the fulfillment of which you shall possess the Land all the days, (is the commandment) to destroy the place of every idol (v. 2), and (also) that you shall not conduct yourself in like manner regarding God, the Exalted One (v. 4), namely, to sacrifice to Him, in every place. Rather, you shall designate a specific place to sacrifice to Him, that place being the one *which HASHEM your God shall choose out of all your tribes* (v. 5).

5. לְשִׁכְנוֹ — *Unto His habitation* . . . where the dwelling place of His name (shall be). This refers to Shiloh or the Holy Temple (in Jerusalem).

תִּדְרְשׁוּ — *Shall you seek.* You shall seek to bow down and sacrifice in that chosen place, similar to אֵלָיו גּוֹיִם יִדְרֹשׁוּ, *to it shall the nations seek* (*Isaiah* 11:10).

וּבָאתָ שָׁמָּה — *And there you shall come.* But the dwelling place of His Name shall not come to you in every place, as is the custom of idolaters and their gods.

NOTES

ately upon entering the land, thereby informing one and all that their dwelling in *Eretz Yisrael* was meant to be unique — either a prosperous or an accursed one. The *Sifri* comments on וְהָיָה, *and it shall be* (which is the opening word in verse 29): אֵין וְהָיָה אֶלָּא מִיַּד, 'The expression וְהָיָה indicates immediacy.' This supports the commentary of the *Sforno* on this verse.

XII

1. אֵלֶּה הַחֻקִּים וְהַמִּשְׁפָּטִים — *These are the statutes and ordinances.* This statement appears to be all inclusive but the following verses command Israel to destroy the idols of the inhabitants of the land, and to refrain from offering sacrifices to God everywhere, indiscriminately. The *Sforno*, therefore, explains the phrase, *These are the statutes etc.*, as meaning that these two commandments are included among the statutes which they are to observe when they enter the land, and in the merit of observing them Israel will possess the land all the days.

5. וּבָאתָ שָׁמָּה — *And there you shall come.* The Sanctuary was to be established in one place, and the people were enjoined to go there to worship and bring sacrifices. The *Sforno* may well be alluding to practices in his time, when he comments almost parenthetically,

עֹלֹתֵיכֶם וְזִבְחֵיכֶם וְאֵת מַעְשְׂרֹתֵיכֶם וְאֵת תְּרוּמַת יֶדְכֶם וְנִדְרֵיכֶם
ז וְנִדְבֹתֵיכֶם וּבְכֹרֹת בְּקַרְכֶם וְצֹאנְכֶם: וַאֲכַלְתֶּם־שָׁם לִפְנֵי יהוה אֱלֹהֵיכֶם
ח וּשְׂמַחְתֶּם בְּכֹל מִשְׁלַח יֶדְכֶם אַתֶּם וּבָתֵּיכֶם אֲשֶׁר בֵּרַכְךָ יהוה אֱלֹהֶיךָ: לֹא
ט תַעֲשׂוּן כְּכֹל אֲשֶׁר אֲנַחְנוּ עֹשִׂים פֹּה הַיּוֹם אִישׁ כָּל־הַיָּשָׁר בְּעֵינָיו: כִּי לֹא־
בָאתֶם עַד־עָתָּה אֶל־הַמְּנוּחָה וְאֶל־הַנַּחֲלָה אֲשֶׁר־יהוה אֱלֹהֶיךָ נֹתֵן לָךְ:
י וַעֲבַרְתֶּם אֶת־הַיַּרְדֵּן וִישַׁבְתֶּם בָּאָרֶץ אֲשֶׁר־יהוה אֱלֹהֵיכֶם מַנְחִיל אֶתְכֶם
שני יא וְהֵנִיחַ לָכֶם מִכָּל־אֹיְבֵיכֶם מִסָּבִיב וִישַׁבְתֶּם־בֶּטַח: וְהָיָה הַמָּקוֹם אֲשֶׁר־יִבְחַר
יהוה אֱלֹהֵיכֶם בּוֹ לְשַׁכֵּן שְׁמוֹ שָׁם שָׁמָּה תָבִיאוּ אֵת כָּל־אֲשֶׁר אָנֹכִי מְצַוֶּה
אֶתְכֶם עוֹלֹתֵיכֶם וְזִבְחֵיכֶם מַעְשְׂרֹתֵיכֶם וּתְרֻמַת יֶדְכֶם וְכֹל מִבְחַר נִדְרֵיכֶם
יב אֲשֶׁר תִּדְּרוּ לַיהוה: וּשְׂמַחְתֶּם לִפְנֵי יהוה אֱלֹהֵיכֶם אַתֶּם וּבְנֵיכֶם וּבְנֹתֵיכֶם
וְעַבְדֵיכֶם וְאַמְהֹתֵיכֶם וְהַלֵּוִי אֲשֶׁר בְּשַׁעֲרֵיכֶם כִּי אֵין לוֹ חֵלֶק וְנַחֲלָה
יג־יד אִתְּכֶם: הִשָּׁמֶר לְךָ פֶּן־תַּעֲלֶה עֹלֹתֶיךָ בְּכָל־מָקוֹם אֲשֶׁר תִּרְאֶה: כִּי אִם־
בַּמָּקוֹם אֲשֶׁר־יִבְחַר יהוה בְּאַחַד שְׁבָטֶיךָ שָׁם תַּעֲלֶה עֹלֹתֶיךָ וְשָׁם תַּעֲשֶׂה
טו כֹּל אֲשֶׁר אָנֹכִי מְצַוֶּךָּ: רַק בְּכָל־אַוַּת נַפְשְׁךָ תִּזְבַּח ׀ וְאָכַלְתָּ בָשָׂר כְּבִרְכַּת
יהוה אֱלֹהֶיךָ אֲשֶׁר נָתַן־לְךָ בְּכָל־שְׁעָרֶיךָ הַטָּמֵא וְהַטָּהוֹר יֹאכְלֶנּוּ כַּצְּבִי
טז־יז וְכָאַיָּל: רַק הַדָּם לֹא תֹאכֵלוּ עַל־הָאָרֶץ תִּשְׁפְּכֶנּוּ כַּמָּיִם: לֹא־תוּכַל לֶאֱכֹל
בִּשְׁעָרֶיךָ מַעְשַׂר דְּגָנְךָ וְתִירֹשְׁךָ וְיִצְהָרֶךָ וּבְכֹרֹת בְּקָרְךָ וְצֹאנֶךָ וְכָל־נְדָרֶיךָ
יח אֲשֶׁר תִּדֹּר וְנִדְבֹתֶיךָ וּתְרוּמַת יָדֶךָ: כִּי אִם־לִפְנֵי יהוה אֱלֹהֶיךָ תֹּאכְלֶנּוּ
בַּמָּקוֹם אֲשֶׁר יִבְחַר יהוה אֱלֹהֶיךָ בּוֹ אַתָּה וּבִנְךָ וּבִתֶּךָ וְעַבְדְּךָ וַאֲמָתֶךָ
יט וְהַלֵּוִי אֲשֶׁר בִּשְׁעָרֶיךָ וְשָׂמַחְתָּ לִפְנֵי יהוה אֱלֹהֶיךָ בְּכֹל מִשְׁלַח יָדֶךָ: הִשָּׁמֶר
כ לְךָ פֶּן־תַּעֲזֹב אֶת־הַלֵּוִי כָּל־יָמֶיךָ עַל־אַדְמָתֶךָ: כִּי־
יַרְחִיב יהוה אֱלֹהֶיךָ אֶת־גְּבֻלְךָ כַּאֲשֶׁר דִּבֶּר־לָךְ וְאָמַרְתָּ אֹכְלָה בָשָׂר

---

7. וַאֲכַלְתֶּם שָׁם לִפְנֵי ה׳ אֱלֹהֵיכֶם וּשְׂמַחְתֶּם — *And there you shall eat before HASHEM your God and rejoice.* עִבְדוּ אֶת ה׳ בְּשִׂמְחָה, *Serve HASHEM with gladness* (*Psalms* 100:2), as befits all who serve with love.

בְּכֹל מִשְׁלַח יֶדְכֶם — *In all to which you put your hand* ... for then you shall make your ways prosperous and you shall have good success (based on *Joshua* 1:8).

20. וְאָמַרְתָּ אֹכְלָה בָשָׂר — *And you shall say, 'I will eat meat'* ... without the need to trouble myself to bring it (the animal) up to the Temple.

NOTES

'As is the custom of idolaters.' It was common for the priest to transport idols or religious articles from place to place wherever their religious adherents gathered.

7. וּשְׂמַחְתֶּם — *And rejoice.* Although fear of the Almighty is of paramount importance in the service of God, it is שִׂמְחָה, *gladness*, which brings man to the love of God.

20. וְאָמַרְתָּ אֹכְלָה בָשָׂר ... לֶאֱכֹל בָּשָׂר ... תֹּאכַל בָּשָׂר — *And you shall say, 'I will eat meat' ... to eat meat ... you may eat meat.* The word בָּשָׂר, *meat*, appears three times in this verse. The first is permissive; once their borders are enlarged and it is difficult to bring every animal to the Sanctuary, permission is granted to slaughter animals for food anywhere. The second is inclusive; although certain parts of the animal must be given to the *Kohen* when a sacrifice is offered, (the shoulder, the two cheeks and the maw,) such is not the case if the animal is חוּלִין, *non-sacred.* The third is exclusive; although restrictions are removed regarding place and priestly gifts when one

כא כִּֽי־תְאַוֶּה נַפְשְׁךָ לֶאֱכֹל בָּשָׂר בְּכָל־אַוַּת נַפְשְׁךָ תֹּאכַל בָּשָׂר: כִּֽי־יִרְחַק
מִמְּךָ הַמָּקוֹם אֲשֶׁר יִבְחַר יהוה אֱלֹהֶיךָ לָשׂוּם שְׁמוֹ שָׁם וְזָבַחְתָּ מִבְּקָרְךָ
וּמִצֹּאנְךָ אֲשֶׁר נָתַן יהוה לְךָ כַּאֲשֶׁר צִוִּיתִךָ וְאָכַלְתָּ בִּשְׁעָרֶיךָ בְּכֹל אַוַּת
כב נַפְשֶׁךָ: אַךְ כַּאֲשֶׁר יֵאָכֵל אֶת־הַצְּבִי וְאֶת־הָאַיָּל כֵּן תֹּאכְלֶנּוּ הַטָּמֵא
כג וְהַטָּהוֹר יַחְדָּו יֹאכְלֶנּוּ: רַק חֲזַק לְבִלְתִּי אֲכֹל הַדָּם כִּי הַדָּם הוּא הַנָּפֶשׁ
כד וְלֹא־תֹאכַל הַנֶּפֶשׁ עִם־הַבָּשָׂר: לֹא תֹּאכְלֶנּוּ עַל־הָאָרֶץ תִּשְׁפְּכֶנּוּ כַּמָּיִם:
כה לֹא תֹּאכְלֶנּוּ לְמַעַן יִיטַב לְךָ וּלְבָנֶיךָ אַחֲרֶיךָ כִּֽי־תַעֲשֶׂה הַיָּשָׁר בְּעֵינֵי יהוה:

כִּי תְאַוֶּה נַפְשְׁךָ לֶאֱכֹל בָּשָׂר — *Because your soul desires to eat meat* ... and also when you desire to eat that portion which is given to the *Kohanim* from the sacrifice.

בְּכָל אַוַּת נַפְשְׁךָ תֹּאכַל בָּשָׂר — *You may eat meat after all the desire of your soul* ... but not the (prohibited) fat or blood even though it is non-sacred.

22. אַךְ כַּאֲשֶׁר יֵאָכֵל אֶת הַצְּבִי — *Howbeit as the deer is eaten* ... not in a hallowed place.

23. רַק חֲזַק לְבִלְתִּי אֲכֹל הַדָּם — *Only be steadfast in not eating the blood.* Even though by eating it you hope to (be accepted) into the company of שֵׁדִים, *demons,* who will reveal the future to you, as our Sages say, 'They know what will happen like ministering angels' (*Chagigah* 16a), (nonetheless) do not eat the blood in order to fraternize with them.

24. לֹא תֹאכְלֶנּוּ עַל הָאָרֶץ תִּשְׁפְּכֶנּוּ כַּמָּיִם — *You shall not eat it; you shall pour it out upon the earth as water.* Treat it in such a manner that it is rendered unfit for consumption, and this (shall be done) by pouring it on the earth as water. Do not store it as wine, oil and other beverages are stored for consumption.

25. לֹא תֹאכְלֶנּוּ . . . כִּי תַעֲשֶׂה הַיָּשָׁר בְּעֵינֵי ה׳ — *You shall not eat it ... when you shall do that which is right in the eyes of* HASHEM. Do not refrain from eating it because you abhor it, but because you are doing what is right in God's eyes, as our Sages say, "Let not man say, 'My soul loathes the meat of swine,' but let him say, 'I desire it but my Father in heaven has decreed (that it is forbidden)' " (*Sifra*).

NOTES

slaughters an animal outside the Sanctuary, nonetheless the prohibition of fat and blood is still applicable.

22. כַּאֲשֶׁר יֵאָכֵל אֶת הַצְּבִי — *As the deer is eaten.* A deer is not qualified to be brought on the altar as a sacrifice. Hence, comparing the animals slaughtered for ordinary consumption to the deer is apt; both can be eaten by the *tamei* as well as the *tahor.*

23. רַק חֲזַק לְבִלְתִּי אֲכֹל הַדָּם — *Only be steadfast in not eating the blood.* The *Sforno* explains why it is necessary for the Torah to strengthen the resolve of the Israelite not to partake of blood. After all, blood is not that appetizing and tempting that we must be urged to be steadfast and resist the desire to eat it. The answer, however, is that there was a belief that through eating blood one could cultivate the companionship of שֵׁדִים, *demons.* This was greatly desired for many believed that these demons possessed great powers which would benefit those who were close to them, as the *Sforno* explains in *Leviticus* 17:7. See his commentary there and the notes on that verse.

25. לֹא תֹאכְלֶנּוּ . . . — *You shall not eat it* .... The *Sforno* explains why this prohibition is repeated, considering that it was already stated in the previous verse. The reason for this apparent redundancy is to teach us that our motivation for abstaining from any practice should not be because it repels us but because God has forbidden it. On the contrary, one should say, 'אֶפְשִׁי וְאֶפְשִׁי, I indeed desire to

כו רַק קָדָשֶׁיךָ אֲשֶׁר־יִהְיוּ לְךָ וּנְדָרֶיךָ תִּשָּׂא וּבָאתָ אֶל־הַמָּקוֹם אֲשֶׁר־יִבְחַר
כז יהוה: וְעָשִׂיתָ עֹלֹתֶיךָ הַבָּשָׂר וְהַדָּם עַל־מִזְבַּח יהוה אֱלֹהֶיךָ וְדַם־זְבָחֶיךָ
כח יִשָּׁפֵךְ עַל־מִזְבַּח יהוה אֱלֹהֶיךָ וְהַבָּשָׂר תֹּאכֵל: שְׁמֹר וְשָׁמַעְתָּ אֵת כָּל־
הַדְּבָרִים הָאֵלֶּה אֲשֶׁר אָנֹכִי מְצַוֶּךָּ לְמַעַן יִיטַב לְךָ וּלְבָנֶיךָ אַחֲרֶיךָ עַד־
שלישי כט עוֹלָם כִּי תַעֲשֶׂה הַטּוֹב וְהַיָּשָׁר בְּעֵינֵי יהוה אֱלֹהֶיךָ: כִּי־
יַכְרִית יהוה אֱלֹהֶיךָ אֶת־הַגּוֹיִם אֲשֶׁר אַתָּה בָא־שָׁמָּה לָרֶשֶׁת אוֹתָם מִפָּנֶיךָ
ל וְיָרַשְׁתָּ אֹתָם וְיָשַׁבְתָּ בְּאַרְצָם: הִשָּׁמֶר לְךָ פֶּן־תִּנָּקֵשׁ אַחֲרֵיהֶם אַחֲרֵי
הִשָּׁמְדָם מִפָּנֶיךָ וּפֶן־תִּדְרֹשׁ לֵאלֹהֵיהֶם לֵאמֹר אֵיכָה יַעַבְדוּ הַגּוֹיִם הָאֵלֶּה
לא אֶת־אֱלֹהֵיהֶם וְאֶעֱשֶׂה־כֵּן גַּם־אָנִי: לֹא־תַעֲשֶׂה כֵן לַיהוה אֱלֹהֶיךָ כִּי
כָל־תּוֹעֲבַת יהוה אֲשֶׁר שָׂנֵא עָשׂוּ לֵאלֹהֵיהֶם כִּי גַם אֶת־בְּנֵיהֶם
יג א וְאֶת־בְּנֹתֵיהֶם יִשְׂרְפוּ בָאֵשׁ לֵאלֹהֵיהֶם: אֵת כָּל־הַדָּבָר אֲשֶׁר אָנֹכִי מְצַוֶּה
אֶתְכֶם אֹתוֹ תִשְׁמְרוּ לַעֲשׂוֹת לֹא־תֹסֵף עָלָיו וְלֹא תִגְרַע מִמֶּנּוּ:
ב־ג כִּי־יָקוּם בְּקִרְבְּךָ נָבִיא אוֹ חֹלֵם חֲלוֹם וְנָתַן אֵלֶיךָ אוֹת אוֹ מוֹפֵת: וּבָא
הָאוֹת וְהַמּוֹפֵת אֲשֶׁר־דִּבֶּר אֵלֶיךָ לֵאמֹר נֵלְכָה אַחֲרֵי אֱלֹהִים אֲחֵרִים אֲשֶׁר

---

30. וְאֶעֱשֶׂה כֵּן גַּם אָנִי — *I will do likewise.* I will also serve God, the Blessed One, with the same means of service with which they (the idolaters) worship their strange gods.

31. כִּי כָל תּוֹעֲבַת ה׳ אֲשֶׁר שָׂנֵא עָשׂוּ לֵאלֹהֵיהֶם — *For every abomination to HASHEM which He hates, have they done to their gods* . . . because among the practices with which they serve strange gods are acts that are repugnant to God, the Blessed One.

XIII

1. לֹא תֹסֵף עָלָיו — *You shall not add thereto* . . . lest you add something which is repugnant as it may well be if you add certain kinds of service to God, the Blessed One, the addition of which, at times, might be repugnant to Him, the Blessed One, such as the burning of children.

וְלֹא תִגְרַע מִמֶּנּוּ — *Nor diminish from it* . . . even if the reason for the commandment no longer applies (lit., is removed) in your eyes, as we find with (King) Solomon when he said, 'I will multiply (women) but not be turned away' (*Sanhedrin* 21b).

NOTES

do it, but I am disciplined and shall refrain because God has forbidden it.' *Rashi* to *Leviticus* 20:26 quotes this concept from the *Sifra.*

30-31. וְאֶעֱשֶׂה כֵּן גַּם אָנִי. כִּי כָל תּוֹעֲבַת ה׳ . . . — *I will do likewise. For every abomination to HASHEM* . . . The *Sforno* explains that the Israelites will not necessarily be tempted to actually serve strange gods but rather to adopt the practices of the idolaters and use them in the service of God. The Torah warns them not to do so because even though there are aspects of religious service common to both idol worship and Divine service, there are also certain abominable acts which are totally repugnant to God, such as offering one's children as fire offerings to their gods, and therefore it is imperative that we reject the adoption of *any* of their practices.

XIII

1. לֹא תֹסֵף עָלָיו — *You shall not add to.* Although this prohibition is recorded in chapter 4:2, it is repeated here to teach us that the addition of any kind of service to God is included, since it may be repugnant to Him.

וְלֹא תִגְרַע מִמֶּנּוּ — *Nor diminish from it.* See the *Sforno's* commentary on 4:2.

ד לֹא־יְדַעְתָּם וְנָעָבְדֵם: לֹא תִשְׁמַע אֶל־דִּבְרֵי הַנָּבִיא הַהוּא אוֹ אֶל־חוֹלֵם
הַחֲלוֹם הַהוּא כִּי מְנַסֶּה יהוה אֱלֹהֵיכֶם אֶתְכֶם לָדַעַת הֲיִשְׁכֶם אֹהֲבִים

---

3. אֲשֶׁר לֹא יְדַעְתָּם — *Which you have not known* ... for which no proof was ever given to establish their existence, because those (forces), which are known (to us) by sense or wonder, are known to function continually and uniformly, in such a manner that (we know) they are natural forces without a (free) will of their own, and therefore it avails naught to pray to them or serve them.

4. לֹא תִשְׁמַע אֶל דִּבְרֵי הַנָּבִיא הַהוּא — *Do not hearken to the words of that prophet.* Do not pay attention to his words to see if there is some substance (to them) because, without a doubt all his words are false, concocted in his heart for evil (purposes) as it says, *Because he has spoken perversion against HASHEM* (v. 6). And (as for) the sign and wonder, it was done through witchcraft, a contrivance or some other (device), and not by the power of any prophecy which (he claims) came to him.

אוֹ אֶל חוֹלֵם הַחֲלוֹם הַהוּא — *Or unto the dreamer of that dream* ... (nor should you) examine to see whether part of his dream is true — but you should know, without doubt, that he did not dream a single thing which he said, but invented it all from his heart in order to lead you astray.

כִּי מְנַסֶּה ה׳ אֱלֹהֵיכֶם אֶתְכֶם — *For HASHEM your God is testing you* ... because, by considering the person who speaks against your God as an enemy, you will be proven in His sight, as one who loves (God).

לָדַעַת — *To know* ... so that as a consequence of your love (of God), proven in actuality, God's knowledge, which always functions for good, will in turn become actual, as is proper whenever one is prepared to receive the overflow of His goodness.

NOTES

3. אֲשֶׁר לֹא יְדַעְתָּם — *Which you have not known.* The attempt to convince people to serve strange gods can only succeed through the introduction of new, *unknown* ones, since those heavenly bodies and other forces of nature already known to man present no danger to man's pure and established belief, being that they are recognized as forces of nature, and as such are the creation of the One God. Since they have no independent power of their own, people realize that there is no purpose in praying to them or serving them.

4. לֹא תִשְׁמַע אֶל דִּבְרֵי הַנָּבִיא הַהוּא אוֹ אֶל חוֹלֵם הַחֲלוֹם הַהוּא — *Do not hearken to the words of that prophet or unto the dreamer of that dream.* The *Sforno* interprets this admonition thus: The Torah is not concerned lest we give total credence to the words of the false prophet and dreamer. The Torah is concerned lest we believe *part* of the dream or a *portion* of his words. We are told here that *all* his words are false and that his dream is totally a figment of his imagination.

כִּי מְנַסֶּה ה׳ אֱלֹהֵיכֶם אֶתְכֶם — *For HASHEM your God is testing you.* The *Sforno's* expression 'as an enemy' is based on *Psalms* 139:21,22: *Do I not hate them, HASHEM, that hate you ... I regard them as my enemies.*

לָדַעַת — *To know.* In a number of places, the *Sforno* explains this word, in regard to God, as meaning knowledge which is manifested in action through the performance of a deed. In general, דַּעַת, *knowledge*, implies potentiality. Regarding God, however, the potentiality and reality are one, unlike man where the intent and the action are separate and distinct. Man may have the potential to do something, but it must be translated into action in order to become *real*. Also, the expression *to know* in its usual sense is inapplicable regarding God, for it implies a lack of knowledge originally, which only becomes known to Him through some action of man.

The *Sforno*, in his commentary on *Genesis* 22:1, *Numbers* 7:89, and *Deuteronomy* 2:7, expresses this thought, as he does in his

ה את־יהוה אֱלֹהֵיכֶם בְּכָל־לְבַבְכֶם וּבְכָל־נַפְשְׁכֶם: אַחֲרֵי יהוה אֱלֹהֵיכֶם
תֵּלֵכוּ וְאֹתוֹ תִירָאוּ וְאֶת־מִצְוֺתָיו תִּשְׁמֹרוּ וּבְקֹלוֹ תִשְׁמָעוּ וְאֹתוֹ תַעֲבֹדוּ וּבוֹ

5. אַחֲרֵי ה׳ אֱלֹהֵיכֶם תֵּלֵכוּ — *After HASHEM your God shall you walk.* Similar to וְהָלַכְתָּ בִּדְרָכָיו, *and walk in His ways* (28:9), and not in new (incorrect) ways that the prophet or dreamer shows (lit., says), with the intent of leading you astray from the (proper) way.

וְאֹתוֹ תִירָאוּ — *And Him shall you fear.* Even though that prophet was already (accepted) among you as an important and revered person, (yet if) he now exaggerates (his prophetic powers), then nullify your reverence of this prophet before the reverence of God, the Blessed One.

וְאֶת מִצְוֺתָיו תִּשְׁמֹרוּ — *And His commandments you shall keep* ... but not new commandments devised by a prophet, especially idolatry which is contradictory to all the commandments of God, the Exalted One, because He commanded His covenant forever, (and) He will not exchange it or change it.

וּבְקֹלוֹ תִשְׁמָעוּ — *And to His voice shall you hearken* ... that which He commands you through His prophets, in order to preserve His Torah and sanctify His name, as we find with Elijah on Mt. Carmel — but (one is not to hearken) to the voice of he who nullifies all the commandments of God, the Exalted One.

וְאֹתוֹ תַעֲבֹדוּ — *And Him shall you serve* ... Him alone and none other with Him, as it says, זֹבֵחַ לָאֱלֹהִים יָחֳרָם, *He that sacrifices unto the gods ... shall be utterly destroyed* (*Exodus* 22:19), as explained there.

NOTES

commentary on this verse. The sense therefore of this verse according to the *Sforno* is: The blandishments of the false prophet put Israel's love of God to the test, not theoretically but practically. By withstanding this test, they are now worthy and prepared to receive the overflow of God's goodness, for *their* act of faith and love causes God's love and goodness to be actuated as well. God's יְדִיעָה, *knowledge*, becomes a פְּעוּלָה, *actuality*, when there are those prepared to receive the beneficial consequences of that knowledge, 'those' being the people of Israel.

5. אַחֲרֵי ה׳ אֱלֹהֵיכֶם תֵּלֵכוּ — *After HASHEM your God shall you walk*. The expression 'to walk in His ways' denotes the practical application of the commandments in deed. Hence, the verse means to say that we are urged to follow the ways (i.e., commandments) only of God, and not new commandments devised by a false prophet which contradict the law of God.

וְאֶת מִצְוֺתָיו תִּשְׁמֹרוּ — *And His commandments you shall keep*. The expression used by the *Sforno*, לֹא יַחֲלִיפֶנּוּ, *He will not exchange it*, is used by the *Rambam* in the 9th principle of his Thirteen Principles of Faith: 'I believe with complete faith that this Torah will not be exchanged.' The phrase וְלֹא יָמִיר, *and not change it*, is based on *Leviticus* 27:33.

וְאֹתוֹ תִירָאוּ — *And Him shall you fear*. The admonition *Him shall you fear* implies that there is a competing fear which is to be rejected. The *Sforno's* commentary clarifies this phrase. Fear only Him, not the great man who heretofore deserved your reverence but who has now forfeited it because of his deviant conduct.

וּבְקֹלוֹ תִשְׁמָעוּ ... וְאֹתוֹ תַעֲבֹדוּ ... וּבוֹ תִדְבָּקוּן — *And to His voice shall you hearken ... and Him shall you serve ... and unto Him you shall cleave*. The *Sforno* explains that these three statements do not repeat a single idea, namely to be loyal to God, but represent three distinct concepts. *Shall you hearken to His voice* means that God will make His will known to us through the voice of His true prophets; *and Him shall you serve* is a warning against שִׁתּוּף, the prohibition of associating other deities with the one true God (i.e., polytheism), while *and unto Him you shall cleave* teaches us that personal animus must never motivate us in the punishment of the false prophet. It must be done only for the purpose of fulfilling God's will.

ו תִדְבָּקוּן׃ וְהַנָּבִיא הַהוּא אוֹ חֹלֵם הַחֲלוֹם הַהוּא יוּמָת כִּי דִבֶּר־סָרָה
עַל־יְהוָה אֱלֹהֵיכֶם הַמּוֹצִיא אֶתְכֶם ׀ מֵאֶרֶץ מִצְרַיִם וְהַפֹּדְךָ מִבֵּית עֲבָדִים
לְהַדִּיחֲךָ מִן־הַדֶּרֶךְ אֲשֶׁר צִוְּךָ יְהוָה אֱלֹהֶיךָ לָלֶכֶת בָּהּ וּבִעַרְתָּ הָרָע
ז מִקִּרְבֶּךָ׃ כִּי יְסִיתְךָ אָחִיךָ בֶן־אִמֶּךָ אוֹ־בִנְךָ אוֹ־בִתְּךָ אוֹ ׀
אֵשֶׁת חֵיקֶךָ אוֹ רֵעֲךָ אֲשֶׁר כְּנַפְשְׁךָ בַּסֵּתֶר לֵאמֹר נֵלְכָה וְנַעַבְדָה אֱלֹהִים
ח אֲחֵרִים אֲשֶׁר לֹא יָדַעְתָּ אַתָּה וַאֲבֹתֶיךָ׃ מֵאֱלֹהֵי הָעַמִּים אֲשֶׁר סְבִיבֹתֵיכֶם
ט הַקְּרֹבִים אֵלֶיךָ אוֹ הָרְחֹקִים מִמֶּךָּ מִקְצֵה הָאָרֶץ וְעַד־קְצֵה הָאָרֶץ׃ לֹא־
תֹאבֶה לוֹ וְלֹא תִשְׁמַע אֵלָיו וְלֹא־תָחוֹס עֵינְךָ עָלָיו וְלֹא־תַחְמֹל וְלֹא־

וּבוֹ תִדְבָּקוּן — *And unto Him you shall cleave.* The purpose of all your actions shall be to do His will, and your animosity toward this (false prophet) shall not be motivated by a prior hatred.

6. יוּמָת כִּי דִבֶּר סָרָה עַל ה׳ — *Shall be put to death, because he spoke untruth about HASHEM.* Although he spoke in the name of God, and not in the name of strange gods, and therefore it would appear that he should not be put to death, similar to the elders' decision regarding Jeremiah when they said, אֵין לָאִישׁ הַזֶּה מִשְׁפַּט מָוֶת, כִּי בְּשֵׁם ה׳ אֱלֹקֵינוּ דִּבֶּר אֵלֵינוּ, *This man is not worthy to die, for he has spoken to us in the name of HASHEM our God* (*Jeremiah* 26:16); however, (in this case) he deserves to die because he spoke an untruth in His name.

לְהַדִּיחֲךָ מִן הַדֶּרֶךְ — *To draw you aside out of the way.* Even though he did not attempt to draw you away from God, since he said in the name of God that you should serve strange gods according to His command, nonetheless he sought *to draw you aside out of the way which God your God had commanded you.*

8. הַקְּרֹבִים אֵלֶיךָ — *Close to you* ... although due to their close proximity you know (full well) their falsity, and (hence) there is no (reason) to fear that you will be misled by them.

אוֹ הָרְחֹקִים מִמֶּךָּ מִקְצֵה הָאָרֶץ — *Or far from you, from one end of the earth* (*to the other end*) ... even though due to the great distance one need not fear that you will go there to serve them.

9. לֹא תֹאבֶה לוֹ — *Do not accede to him* ... by saying that you will investigate and find out whether his claims (lit., words) are correct, that a particular false god does good thus and bad thus.

וְלֹא תִשְׁמַע אֵלָיו — *Nor hearken to him.* In this manner (i.e., by not acceding to him), you will not listen to him, and you will not accept (his invitation) to serve (this

NOTES

6. כִּי דִבֶּר סָרָה עַל ה׳ — *Because he spoke untruth about HASHEM.* The *Sforno* cites the episode recorded in *Jeremiah* 26 regarding the prophet Jeremiah who was sent by God to warn Jerusalem that unless the people mended their ways and returned to God, the Temple and the city would be destroyed. The *Kohanim* and false prophets demanded that Jeremiah be put to death, but the princes of Judah refused to do so asserting that he had spoken in the name of God. The *Sforno* explains that the argument used by the princes of Judah is not applicable to the false prophet, for even though he claims to speak in His name, and not in the name of a false God, nonetheless he utters falsehoods in the name of the true God, unlike Jeremiah who spoke the truth in the name of God.

9. לֹא תֹאבֶה לוֹ וְלֹא תִשְׁמַע אֵלָיו — *Do not accede to him, nor hearken to him.* The Torah cautions the people of Israel not to permit the

י תְּכַסֶּה עָלָיו׃ כִּי הָרֹג תַּהַרְגֶנּוּ יָדְךָ תִּהְיֶה־בּוֹ בָרִאשׁוֹנָה לַהֲמִיתוֹ וְיַד כָּל־
יא הָעָם בָּאַחֲרֹנָה׃ וּסְקַלְתּוֹ בָאֲבָנִים וָמֵת כִּי בִקֵּשׁ לְהַדִּיחֲךָ מֵעַל יהוה אֱלֹהֶיךָ
יב הַמּוֹצִיאֲךָ מֵאֶרֶץ מִצְרַיִם מִבֵּית עֲבָדִים׃ וְכָל־יִשְׂרָאֵל יִשְׁמְעוּ וְיִרָאוּן וְלֹא־
יג יוֹסִפוּ לַעֲשׂוֹת כַּדָּבָר הָרָע הַזֶּה בְּקִרְבֶּךָ׃ כִּי־תִשְׁמַע
יד בְּאַחַת עָרֶיךָ אֲשֶׁר יהוה אֱלֹהֶיךָ נֹתֵן לְךָ לָשֶׁבֶת שָׁם לֵאמֹר׃ יָצְאוּ אֲנָשִׁים
בְּנֵי־בְלִיַּעַל מִקִּרְבֶּךָ וַיַּדִּיחוּ אֶת־יֹשְׁבֵי עִירָם לֵאמֹר נֵלְכָה וְנַעַבְדָה אֱלֹהִים
טו אֲחֵרִים אֲשֶׁר לֹא־יְדַעְתֶּם׃ וְדָרַשְׁתָּ וְחָקַרְתָּ וְשָׁאַלְתָּ הֵיטֵב וְהִנֵּה אֱמֶת נָכוֹן
טז הַדָּבָר נֶעֶשְׂתָה הַתּוֹעֵבָה הַזֹּאת בְּקִרְבֶּךָ׃ הַכֵּה תַכֶּה אֶת־יֹשְׁבֵי הָעִיר הַהִוא
לְפִי־חָרֶב הַחֲרֵם אֹתָהּ וְאֶת־כָּל־אֲשֶׁר־בָּהּ וְאֶת־בְּהֶמְתָּהּ לְפִי־חָרֶב׃
יז וְאֶת־כָּל־שְׁלָלָהּ תִּקְבֹּץ אֶל־תּוֹךְ רְחֹבָהּ וְשָׂרַפְתָּ בָאֵשׁ אֶת־הָעִיר
וְאֶת־כָּל־שְׁלָלָהּ כָּלִיל לַיהוה אֱלֹהֶיךָ וְהָיְתָה תֵּל עוֹלָם לֹא תִבָּנֶה עוֹד׃

'deity'). For if the matter is in doubt whether he is worthy (to be listened to), eventually you will hearken to him, for such doubt can only come from (your) lack of reflection regarding the greatness of God, the Blessed One, and His order in the world.

11. כִּי בִקֵּשׁ לְהַדִּיחֲךָ — *Because he sought to lead you away.* Although he did not (succeed) in doing damage, as (in the case) of those who lead astray the condemned city (עִיר הַנִּדַּחַת), nonetheless he deserves to die because he did seek to lead you away (from God), and by executing him you will attain (the end) that he will not be able to mislead others, but if you do not kill him, perhaps he, or another, will lead others astray and succeed.

12. וְכָל יִשְׂרָאֵל יִשְׁמְעוּ וְיִרָאוּן וְלֹא יוֹסִפוּ — *And all of Israel shall hear and fear and shall do no more* . . . neither he nor any other (person).

16. וְאֶת בְּהֶמְתָּהּ לְפִי חָרֶב — *And the cattle by the sword* . . . to blot out their remembrance, thereby revenging (the honor) of God, the Blessed One, similar to Amalek of whom it is said, תִּמְחֶה אֶת זֵכֶר עֲמָלֵק, *blot out the remembrance of Amalek* (25:19), and so the prophet elaborated when he said, וְהֵמַתָּה מֵאִישׁ עַד אִשָּׁה מֵעֹלֵל וְעַד יוֹנֵק מִשּׁוֹר וְעַד שֶׂה מִגָּמָל וְעַד חֲמוֹר, *but slay both man and woman, infant and suckling, ox and sheep, camel and ass* (*I Samuel*, 15:3).

NOTES

false prophet to entice them into examining the powers of this false god, even though they will not worship him, for by doing so they will be taking the first step that may ultimately lead to their complete defection. He who is firm and resolute in his faith has no doubts and will in no way accede to this false prophet, nor will he give any credence to the possible efficacy of any false god. The sense of this verse, according to the *Sforno*, is: *Do not accede to him* at all, for only by rejecting him immediately and completely will you insure that you will *not hearken to him.*

16. וְאֶת בְּהֶמְתָּהּ לְפִי חָרֶב — *And the cattle by sword.* The Torah states (*Leviticus* 20:15) that if a man lies with a beast, both he and the beast shall be put to death. Our Sages ask, 'If man sinned, how did the animal sin?' (*Sanhedrin* 54b). One of the answers given is, 'So that the animal should not pass by in the market place and people will say, this is the animal who brought about the execution of that person.' By eliminating the animal, we eliminate added shame. The *Sforno* gives a similar explanation here as to why we destroy the cattle of the עִיר הַנִּדַּחַת, *the city drawn away from God.* By erasing everything which can cause people to remember the idolatry of an entire city, we safeguard the honor of God and prevent added desecration of His Name.

יח וְלֹא־יִדְבַּק בְּיָדְךָ מְאוּמָה מִן־הַחֵרֶם לְמַעַן יָשׁוּב יהוה מֵחֲרוֹן אַפּוֹ וְנָתַן־לְךָ
יט רַחֲמִים וְרִחַמְךָ וְהִרְבֶּךָ כַּאֲשֶׁר נִשְׁבַּע לַאֲבֹתֶיךָ: כִּי תִשְׁמַע בְּקוֹל יהוה
אֱלֹהֶיךָ לִשְׁמֹר אֶת־כָּל־מִצְוֹתָיו אֲשֶׁר אָנֹכִי מְצַוְּךָ הַיּוֹם לַעֲשׂוֹת הַיָּשָׁר
יד רביעי א בְּעֵינֵי יהוה אֱלֹהֶיךָ: בָּנִים אַתֶּם לַיהוה אֱלֹהֵיכֶם לֹא
ב תִתְגֹּדְדוּ וְלֹא־תָשִׂימוּ קָרְחָה בֵּין עֵינֵיכֶם לָמֵת: כִּי עַם קָדוֹשׁ אַתָּה לַיהוה

---

18. וְלֹא יִדְבַּק בְּיָדְךָ מְאוּמָה מִן הַחֵרֶם — *And nothing of that which is banned shall cleave to your hand . . .* lest it become a snare, similar to the ornaments of the strange gods of which (the verse) says, *You shall not covet the silver or the gold that is on them, nor take it for yourself, lest you be ensnared therein* (7:25), as it is explained there.

XIV

1. בָּנִים אַתֶּם לַה׳ אֱלֹהֵיכֶם לֹא תִתְגֹּדְדוּ — *You are the children of HASHEM your God; you shall not cut yourselves.* It is not proper (for you) to show extreme concern and pain for the death of a relative, when a more honorable and distinguished relative still remains, in whom there is hope for (ultimate) good. Therefore, since you are children of God, Who is your eternal Father, it is unseemly that you should worry and mourn excessively over the death of anyone.

וְלֹא תָשִׂימוּ קָרְחָה בֵּין עֵינֵיכֶם לָמֵת — *Nor shall you make any baldness between your eyes for the dead.* And also you must not be greatly pained for the harm caused to the deceased in his death . . .

2. כִּי עַם קָדוֹשׁ אַתָּה — *For you are a holy people . . .* destined (to share) in the life of the World to Come, where one hour of spiritual bliss is better than the entire life of This World (based on *Avos* 4:22).

סְגֻלָּה מִכֹּל הָעַמִּים — *A treasure out of all peoples . . .* and therefore, He only prohibits (these practices) to you, but not to the 'sons of Noah' who are not His treasure to the same extent.

NOTES

18. וְלֹא יִדְבַּק בְּיָדְךָ מְאוּמָה מִן הַחֵרֶם — *And nothing of that which is banned shall cleave to your hand*. The prohibition of taking aught from the spoil of the עִיר הַנִּדַּחַת is for the same reason given by the *Sforno* in his commentary on 7:25. If we were to prosper with the precious material taken from the spoil of this banned city we might attribute it to the power of the idols whom the inhabitants served.

XIV

1. בָּנִים אַתֶּם לַה׳ אֱלֹהֵיכֶם לֹא תִתְגֹּדְדוּ וְלֹא תָשִׂימוּ קָרְחָה — *You are the children of HASHEM your God; you shall not cut yourselves, nor shall you make any baldness*. Excessive mourning is caused by two factors. One is deep concern for the fate of the deceased, while the other is the profound sense of loss experienced by the surviving relatives. The Torah comforts Israel on both counts. Since we are a holy people each of us is insured a share in the World to Come, hence there is no reason to be concerned for the welfare of the deceased. As for one's great feeling of loss, since we are God's children, we must find comfort, support and strength in the realization that we still have our Father in heaven, who is our most dear and distiguished 'relative.'

2. סְגֻלָּה מִכֹּל הָעַמִּים — *A treasure out of all peoples*. This expression is interpreted by the *Sforno* to mean that although all mankind is precious to God, the people of Israel are considered to be a special treasure among the human race and therefore, their exalted level requires the observance of these prohibitions. See his commentary on *Exodus* 19:5.

ג-ד הָאֲדָמָה: לֹא תֹאכַל כָּל־תּוֹעֵבָה: זֹאת הַבְּהֵמָה אֲשֶׁר
ה תֹּאכֵלוּ שׁוֹר שֵׂה כְשָׂבִים וְשֵׂה עִזִּים: אַיָּל וּצְבִי וְיַחְמוּר וְאַקּוֹ וְדִישֹׁן וּתְאוֹ
ו וָזָמֶר: וְכָל־בְּהֵמָה מַפְרֶסֶת פַּרְסָה וְשֹׁסַעַת שֶׁסַע שְׁתֵּי פְרָסוֹת מַעֲלַת גֵּרָה
ז בַּבְּהֵמָה אֹתָהּ תֹּאכֵלוּ: אַךְ אֶת־זֶה לֹא תֹאכְלוּ מִמַּעֲלֵי הַגֵּרָה וּמִמַּפְרִיסֵי
הַפַּרְסָה הַשְּׁסוּעָה אֶת־הַגָּמָל וְאֶת־הָאַרְנֶבֶת וְאֶת־הַשָּׁפָן כִּי־מַעֲלֵה גֵרָה
ח הֵמָּה וּפַרְסָה לֹא הִפְרִיסוּ טְמֵאִים הֵם לָכֶם: וְאֶת־הַחֲזִיר כִּי־מַפְרִיס
פַּרְסָה הוּא וְלֹא גֵרָה טָמֵא הוּא לָכֶם מִבְּשָׂרָם לֹא תֹאכֵלוּ וּבְנִבְלָתָם לֹא
ט תִגָּעוּ: אֶת־זֶה תֹּאכְלוּ מִכֹּל אֲשֶׁר בַּמָּיִם כֹּל אֲשֶׁר־לוֹ
י סְנַפִּיר וְקַשְׂקֶשֶׂת תֹּאכֵלוּ: וְכֹל אֲשֶׁר אֵין־לוֹ סְנַפִּיר וְקַשְׂקֶשֶׂת לֹא תֹאכֵלוּ
יא-יב טָמֵא הוּא לָכֶם: כָּל־צִפּוֹר טְהֹרָה תֹּאכֵלוּ: וְזֶה אֲשֶׁר
יג לֹא־תֹאכְלוּ מֵהֶם הַנֶּשֶׁר וְהַפֶּרֶס וְהָעָזְנִיָּה: וְהָרָאָה וְאֶת־הָאַיָּה וְהַדַּיָּה
יד-טו לְמִינָהּ: וְאֵת כָּל־עֹרֵב לְמִינוֹ: וְאֵת בַּת הַיַּעֲנָה וְאֶת־הַתַּחְמָס וְאֶת־הַשָּׁחַף
טז-יז וְאֶת־הַנֵּץ לְמִינֵהוּ: אֶת־הַכּוֹס וְאֶת־הַיַּנְשׁוּף וְהַתִּנְשָׁמֶת: וְהַקָּאָת וְאֶת־
יח-יט הָרָחָמָה וְאֶת־הַשָּׁלָךְ: וְהַחֲסִידָה וְהָאֲנָפָה לְמִינָהּ וְהַדּוּכִיפַת וְהָעֲטַלֵּף: וְכֹל
כ-כא שֶׁרֶץ הָעוֹף טָמֵא הוּא לָכֶם לֹא יֵאָכֵלוּ: כָּל־עוֹף טָהוֹר תֹּאכֵלוּ: לֹא תֹאכְלוּ
כָל־נְבֵלָה לַגֵּר אֲשֶׁר־בִּשְׁעָרֶיךָ תִּתְּנֶנָּה וַאֲכָלָהּ אוֹ מָכֹר לְנָכְרִי כִּי עַם

---

3. לֹא תֹאכַל כָּל תּוֹעֵבָה — *You shall not eat any abominable thing.* Behold, before the Torah was given, the difference between clean (kosher) and unclean (non-kosher) animals was (already) known, as explained regarding Noah; nonetheless, when God, the Blessed One, permitted Noah and his children to consume living creatures, no differentiation was made between the clean and the unclean. However, being that you are a holy treasure out of all the peoples, it is improper for you to be nourished from the unclean and the abominable, (for through such ingestion) you will become similar (to them) in temperament.

21. לֹא תֹאכְלוּ כָל נְבֵלָה -- *You shall not eat anything that dies of itself* . . . even of a clean species.

NOTES

3. לֹא תֹאכַל כָּל תּוֹעֵבָה — *You shall not eat any abominable thing*. In *parashas Noach*, we find mention made of animals which are both clean and unclean (*Genesis* 7:8). After the flood, mankind was permitted to eat the flesh of *all* animals, and no differentiation was made. A distinction was made between them only regarding sacrifices. However, after the Torah was given, the people of Israel were allowed to eat those animals, fowl and fish enumerated in the subsequent verses. The *Sforno* links this verse to the expression in verse 2, סְגֻלָּה מִכֹּל הָעַמִּים, *a treasure out of all peoples.* Since Israel is a special, unique people, they are not permitted to eat that which is considered unclean and abominable by God, lest it affect their character and personality. This is perhaps the origin of the saying, 'You are what you eat.'

21. לֹא תֹאכְלוּ כָל נְבֵלָה — *You shall not eat anything that dies of itself.* Although a נְבֵלָה, *an animal that dies of itself*, is not in itself an abomination, since this term applies to a clean animal as well and is fit for consumption by the stranger and foreigner (נָכְרִי and גֵּר), nonetheless you are not permitted to eat it because you are a holy people and as such, must avoid those foods which might impair the attainment of the perfection intended for you.

21-22. לֹא תְבַשֵּׁל גְּדִי . . . עַשֵּׂר תְּעַשֵּׂר — *You shall not cook a kid . . . You shall surely tithe*. This prohibition appears twice in *Exodus* (23:19 and 34:26). In those two verses, the commandment to bring the first fruits of one's land to the Temple precedes this prohi-

קָדוֹשׁ אַתָּה לַיהוָה אֱלֹהֶיךָ לֹא־תְבַשֵּׁל גְּדִי בַּחֲלֵב אִמּוֹ׃
חמישי כב־כג עַשֵּׂר תְּעַשֵּׂר אֵת כָּל־תְּבוּאַת זַרְעֶךָ הַיֹּצֵא הַשָּׂדֶה שָׁנָה שָׁנָה׃ וְאָכַלְתָּ
לִפְנֵי ׀ יְהוָה אֱלֹהֶיךָ בַּמָּקוֹם אֲשֶׁר־יִבְחַר לְשַׁכֵּן שְׁמוֹ שָׁם מַעְשַׂר דְּגָנְךָ
תִּירֹשְׁךָ וְיִצְהָרֶךָ וּבְכֹרֹת בְּקָרְךָ וְצֹאנֶךָ לְמַעַן תִּלְמַד לְיִרְאָה אֶת־יְהוָה
כד אֱלֹהֶיךָ כָּל־הַיָּמִים׃ וְכִי־יִרְבֶּה מִמְּךָ הַדֶּרֶךְ כִּי לֹא תוּכַל שְׂאֵתוֹ כִּי־יִרְחַק
מִמְּךָ הַמָּקוֹם אֲשֶׁר יִבְחַר יְהוָה אֱלֹהֶיךָ לָשׂוּם שְׁמוֹ שָׁם כִּי יְבָרֶכְךָ יְהוָה
כה אֱלֹהֶיךָ׃ וְנָתַתָּה בַּכָּסֶף וְצַרְתָּ הַכֶּסֶף בְּיָדְךָ וְהָלַכְתָּ אֶל־הַמָּקוֹם אֲשֶׁר יִבְחַר
כו יְהוָה אֱלֹהֶיךָ בּוֹ׃ וְנָתַתָּה הַכֶּסֶף בְּכֹל אֲשֶׁר־תְּאַוֶּה נַפְשְׁךָ בַּבָּקָר וּבַצֹּאן
וּבַיַּיִן וּבַשֵּׁכָר וּבְכֹל אֲשֶׁר תִּשְׁאָלְךָ נַפְשֶׁךָ וְאָכַלְתָּ שָּׁם לִפְנֵי יְהוָה אֱלֹהֶיךָ
כז וְשָׂמַחְתָּ אַתָּה וּבֵיתֶךָ׃ וְהַלֵּוִי אֲשֶׁר־בִּשְׁעָרֶיךָ לֹא תַעַזְבֶנּוּ כִּי אֵין לוֹ חֵלֶק
כח וְנַחֲלָה עִמָּךְ׃ מִקְצֵה ׀ שָׁלֹשׁ שָׁנִים תּוֹצִיא אֶת־כָּל־מַעְשַׂר
כט תְּבוּאָתְךָ בַּשָּׁנָה הַהִוא וְהִנַּחְתָּ בִּשְׁעָרֶיךָ׃ וּבָא הַלֵּוִי כִּי אֵין־לוֹ חֵלֶק וְנַחֲלָה
עִמָּךְ וְהַגֵּר וְהַיָּתוֹם וְהָאַלְמָנָה אֲשֶׁר בִּשְׁעָרֶיךָ וְאָכְלוּ וְשָׂבֵעוּ לְמַעַן יְבָרֶכְךָ

כִּי עַם קָדוֹשׁ אַתָּה לַה׳ אֱלֹהֶיךָ — *For you are a holy people unto* HASHEM *your God.* Although that which dies of itself is suitable for human food, such as for the stranger or foreigner, it is not suitable food (for) a holy people, designated to attain an intended perfection from God, the Blessed One.

לֹא תְבַשֵּׁל גְּדִי — *You shall not cook a kid.* As was the practice of the nations, who thought that through this act, they would increase their cattle, and their possessions and their animals.

22. עַשֵּׂר תְּעַשֵּׂר — *You shall surely tithe.* Because by tithing the grain produce and animals, you will increase your produce and cattle, as our Sages state, עַשֵּׂר בִּשְׁבִיל שֶׁתִּתְעַשֵּׁר, *Tithe so that you will become affluent* (*Shabbos* 119a).

23. לְמַעַן תִּלְמַד לְיִרְאָה אֶת ה׳ — *That you may learn to fear* HASHEM. Because in that place chosen for the Holy Temple, the Great Court (Sanhedrin) will be (present) to achieve understanding and to teach.

NOTES

bition. Here, in the Book of *Deuteronomy*, this prohibition is followed by the commandment of tithing. In his commentary on the two verses in *Exodus*, the *Sforno* explains that whereas the heathens would cook a kid in its mother's milk to appease the gods in the hope of having their flocks and produce blessed, Israel was told to bring their first fruits to God in recognition of His granting them heavenly blessings and due to the merit of this *mitzvah*, He would continue to bless them. Similarly in these verses, the *Sforno* explains that as opposed to the pagans who resort to this act of cooking a kid in its mother's milk, let the Israelite tithe and as a result he will be granted riches. עַשֵּׂר בִּשְׁבִיל שֶׁתִּתְעַשֵּׁר, *tithe so that you will be rewarded with wealth,* is a play on the word עשר, which can be read as עֲשֵׂר, *tithe*, or עֹשֶׁר, *riches*, depending on the use of the letter שׂ or שׁ.

23. לְמַעַן תִּלְמַד לְיִרְאָה — *That you may learn to fear*. The *Sforno* is of the opinion that fear and reverence of God stems from man's knowledge of Him. To gain this knowledge, one needs instruction which he can receive from the teachers of Israel who reside in Jerusalem. Indeed, the purpose of bringing the second tithe to Jerusalem was to afford them the opportunity to learn God's will and His teachings, which, in turn, would bring one to יִרְאַת שָׁמַיִם *the fear of heaven*, as it says, רֵאשִׁית חָכְמָה יִרְאַת ה׳, *The beginning of wisdom is the fear of* HASHEM (*Psalms* 111:10).

טו ששי א יְהוָה אֱלֹהֶיךָ בְּכָל־מַעֲשֵׂה יָדְךָ אֲשֶׁר תַּעֲשֶׂה׃ מִקֵּץ
ב שֶׁבַע־שָׁנִים תַּעֲשֶׂה שְׁמִטָּה׃ וְזֶה דְּבַר הַשְּׁמִטָּה שָׁמוֹט כָּל־בַּעַל מַשֵּׁה יָדוֹ
אֲשֶׁר יַשֶּׁה בְּרֵעֵהוּ לֹא־יִגֹּשׂ אֶת־רֵעֵהוּ וְאֶת־אָחִיו כִּי־קָרָא שְׁמִטָּה לַיהוָה׃
ג־ד אֶת־הַנָּכְרִי תִּגֹּשׂ וַאֲשֶׁר יִהְיֶה לְךָ אֶת־אָחִיךָ תַּשְׁמֵט יָדֶךָ׃ אֶפֶס כִּי לֹא
יִהְיֶה־בְּךָ אֶבְיוֹן כִּי־בָרֵךְ יְבָרֶכְךָ יהוה בָּאָרֶץ אֲשֶׁר יהוה אֱלֹהֶיךָ נֹתֵן־לְךָ
ה נַחֲלָה לְרִשְׁתָּהּ׃ רַק אִם־שָׁמוֹעַ תִּשְׁמַע בְּקוֹל יהוה אֱלֹהֶיךָ לִשְׁמֹר לַעֲשׂוֹת
ו אֶת־כָּל־הַמִּצְוָה הַזֹּאת אֲשֶׁר אָנֹכִי מְצַוְּךָ הַיּוֹם׃ כִּי־יהוה אֱלֹהֶיךָ בֵּרַכְךָ
כַּאֲשֶׁר דִּבֶּר־לָךְ וְהַעֲבַטְתָּ גּוֹיִם רַבִּים וְאַתָּה לֹא תַעֲבֹט וּמָשַׁלְתָּ בְּגוֹיִם
ז רַבִּים וּבְךָ לֹא יִמְשֹׁלוּ׃ כִּי־יִהְיֶה בְךָ אֶבְיוֹן מֵאַחַד אַחֶיךָ
בְּאַחַד שְׁעָרֶיךָ בְּאַרְצְךָ אֲשֶׁר־יהוה אֱלֹהֶיךָ נֹתֵן לָךְ לֹא תְאַמֵּץ אֶת־לְבָבְךָ

XV

2. וְזֶה דְּבַר הַשְּׁמִטָּה — *And this is the manner of the release* (*shemittah*). When God, the Blessed One, said, וְהַשְּׁבִיעִת תִּשְׁמְטֶנָּה, *but the seventh year you shall release* (*Exodus* 23:11), the intent was to institute the release of money (i.e., cancellation of debts).

שָׁמוֹט כָּל בַּעַל מַשֵּׁה יָדוֹ — *Every creditor shall release from his hand* . . . because God, the Blessed One, proclaimed *shemittah*, release when He said, תִּשְׁמְטֶנָּה, *you shall release* (*Exodus* 23:11).

4. אֶפֶס כִּי לֹא יִהְיֶה בְּךָ אֶבְיוֹן — *Howbeit there shall be no needy among you.* Although I told you to *release your hand*, behold there shall be no borrowers among you that will necessitate the release (of debts). This, without a doubt, transpired with the generation that entered the Land *all the days of Joshua and all the days of the elders who outlived Joshua* (*Joshua* 24:31).

NOTES

XV

2. וְזֶה דְּבַר הַשְּׁמִטָּה — *And this is the manner of the release* (*shemittah*). The *Sforno* in his commentary on *Exodus* 23:11, וְהַשְּׁבִיעִת תִּשְׁמְטֶנָּה וּנְטַשְׁתָּהּ, *but the seventh year you shall release and abandon*, interprets the first verb, תִּשְׁמְטֶנָּה, as meaning the release of all debts which are canceled, while the second verb, וּנְטַשְׁתָּהּ, refers to the land that cannot be sown and the produce of that land which may be eaten by all. In his commentary on this verse, he refers back to the verse in *Exodus*, explaining that the word הַשְּׁמִטָּה, *the shemittah* (using the definite article), only refers to the cancellation of debts (i.e., the first verb in *Exodus* 23:11). Indeed, the subsequent verses here specifically refer to cancellation of debts, and not to the *shemittah* of land.

שָׁמוֹט כָּל בַּעַל מַשֵּׁה יָדוֹ — *Every creditor shall release from his hand*. The *Sforno's* comment on this phrase is based on the concluding part of this verse, *'because a release has been proclaimed to* HASHEM.*'*

4. אֶפֶס כִּי לֹא יִהְיֶה בְּךָ אֶבְיוֹן — *Howbeit there shall be no needy among you*. In this verse, we are told that there will be no needy among us. In verse 11, however, the Torah tells us that *the needy will never cease.* To reconcile these two verses, the *Sforno* explains that it all depends upon Israel's obedience, or disobedience, to God's laws. While this answer is given by many other commentators, he expands on this classic answer by citing two verses which reflect different periods in Jewish history. Moses predicted that a time would come when Israel would turn away from God. During such a period the needy would never cease. During the time of Joshua and the Elders, however, when Israel first entered *Eretz Yisrael* the people followed in the ways of God and poverty was unknown. Of such a time the Torah states, *there shall be no needy among you.*

ח וְלֹא תִקְפֹּץ אֶת־יָדְךָ מֵאָחִיךָ הָאֶבְיוֹן: כִּי־פָתֹחַ תִּפְתַּח אֶת־יָדְךָ לוֹ וְהַעֲבֵט
ט תַּעֲבִיטֶנּוּ דֵּי מַחְסֹרוֹ אֲשֶׁר יֶחְסַר לוֹ: הִשָּׁמֶר לְךָ פֶּן־יִהְיֶה דָבָר עִם־לְבָבְךָ
בְלִיַּעַל לֵאמֹר קָרְבָה שְׁנַת־הַשֶּׁבַע שְׁנַת הַשְּׁמִטָּה וְרָעָה עֵינְךָ בְּאָחִיךָ
י הָאֶבְיוֹן וְלֹא תִתֵּן לוֹ וְקָרָא עָלֶיךָ אֶל־יהוה וְהָיָה בְךָ חֵטְא: נָתוֹן תִּתֵּן לוֹ
וְלֹא־יֵרַע לְבָבְךָ בְּתִתְּךָ לוֹ כִּי בִּגְלַל ׀ הַדָּבָר הַזֶּה יְבָרֶכְךָ יהוה אֱלֹהֶיךָ
יא בְּכָל־מַעֲשֶׂךָ וּבְכֹל מִשְׁלַח יָדֶךָ: כִּי לֹא־יֶחְדַּל אֶבְיוֹן מִקֶּרֶב הָאָרֶץ עַל־
כֵּן אָנֹכִי מְצַוְּךָ לֵאמֹר פָּתֹחַ תִּפְתַּח אֶת־יָדְךָ לְאָחִיךָ לַעֲנִיֶּךָ וּלְאֶבְיֹנְךָ
יב בְּאַרְצֶךָ: כִּי־יִמָּכֵר לְךָ אָחִיךָ הָעִבְרִי אוֹ הָעִבְרִיָּה וַעֲבָדְךָ
יג שֵׁשׁ שָׁנִים וּבַשָּׁנָה הַשְּׁבִיעִת תְּשַׁלְּחֶנּוּ חָפְשִׁי מֵעִמָּךְ: וְכִי־תְשַׁלְּחֶנּוּ חָפְשִׁי
יד מֵעִמָּךְ לֹא תְשַׁלְּחֶנּוּ רֵיקָם: הַעֲנֵיק תַּעֲנִיק לוֹ מִצֹּאנְךָ וּמִגָּרְנְךָ וּמִיִּקְבֶךָ אֲשֶׁר
טו בֵּרַכְךָ יהוה אֱלֹהֶיךָ תִּתֶּן־לוֹ: וְזָכַרְתָּ כִּי עֶבֶד הָיִיתָ בְּאֶרֶץ מִצְרַיִם וַיִּפְדְּךָ
טז יהוה אֱלֹהֶיךָ עַל־כֵּן אָנֹכִי מְצַוְּךָ אֶת־הַדָּבָר הַזֶּה הַיּוֹם: וְהָיָה כִּי־יֹאמַר
יז אֵלֶיךָ לֹא אֵצֵא מֵעִמָּךְ כִּי אֲהֵבְךָ וְאֶת־בֵּיתֶךָ כִּי־טוֹב לוֹ עִמָּךְ: וְלָקַחְתָּ
אֶת־הַמַּרְצֵעַ וְנָתַתָּה בְאָזְנוֹ וּבַדֶּלֶת וְהָיָה לְךָ עֶבֶד עוֹלָם וְאַף לַאֲמָתְךָ
יח תַּעֲשֶׂה־כֵּן: לֹא־יִקְשֶׁה בְעֵינֶךָ בְּשַׁלֵּחֲךָ אֹתוֹ חָפְשִׁי מֵעִמָּךְ כִּי מִשְׁנֶה שְׂכַר
שָׂכִיר עֲבָדְךָ שֵׁשׁ שָׁנִים וּבֵרַכְךָ יהוה אֱלֹהֶיךָ בְּכֹל אֲשֶׁר תַּעֲשֶׂה:
שביעי יט כָּל־הַבְּכוֹר אֲשֶׁר יִוָּלֵד בִּבְקָרְךָ וּבְצֹאנְךָ הַזָּכָר תַּקְדִּישׁ לַיהוה אֱלֹהֶיךָ לֹא

---

11. כִּי לֹא יֶחְדַּל אֶבְיוֹן — *For the needy will never cease.* This refers (to the period of), *For I know that after my death you will fall into great corruption* (31:29).

15. וְזָכַרְתָּ כִּי עֶבֶד הָיִיתָ — *And you shall remember that you were a slave.* Not only did He deliver you and free you from bondage but (also) furnished you liberally with the money of those who subjugated you.

18. לֹא יִקְשֶׁה בְעֵינֶךָ — *And this shall not seem hard in your eyes* ... to furnish him liberally when you set him free because he is worthy (to be so compensated), and you will not lack aught (by doing so).

וּבֵרַכְךָ ה׳ אֱלֹהֶיךָ — *And HASHEM your God will bless you.* (Hence) it is from Him that you give it.

19. כָּל הַבְּכוֹר — *All the firstlings.* After (the Torah) explains the various aspects of *chesed*, lovingkindness, regarding grain produce such as the tithe for the poor, and regarding money such as charity, and the release of debts and regarding other possessions through הַעֲנָקָה, the liberal furnishing of a Hebrew slave (when he is

NOTES

15-18. וְזָכַרְתָּ כִּי עֶבֶד הָיִיתָ ... וּבֵרַכְךָ ה׳ אֱלֹהֶיךָ — *And you shall remember that you were a slave ... and HASHEM your God will bless you.* As the *Sforno* explains, these verses were meant to encourage the master to give הַעֲנָקָה, *compensation*, to a slave leaving his service. The Torah first reminds us that we were also slaves and God gave us great treasures when we departed Egypt, treasures taken from our masters! Secondly, we are reassured by the Almighty that He will compensate us for our generosity, hence it will in no way diminish our wealth.

19. כָּל הַבְּכוֹר — *All the firstlings.* The *Sforno's* commentary on this verse is meant to explain the logical order of the remainder of the *parashah*, and the link to the preceding portion (chapter 14:22 to 15:18). He also answers the question, 'Why doesn't the Torah

כ תַעֲבֹד בִּבְכֹר שׁוֹרֶךָ וְלֹא תָגֹז בְּכוֹר צֹאנֶךָ: לִפְנֵי יהוה אֱלֹהֶיךָ תֹאכְלֶנּוּ
כא שָׁנָה בְשָׁנָה בַּמָּקוֹם אֲשֶׁר־יִבְחַר יהוה אַתָּה וּבֵיתֶךָ: וְכִי־יִהְיֶה בוֹ מוּם פִּסֵּחַ
כב אוֹ עִוֵּר כֹּל מוּם רָע לֹא תִזְבָּחֶנּוּ לַיהוה אֱלֹהֶיךָ: בִּשְׁעָרֶיךָ תֹּאכְלֶנּוּ הַטָּמֵא
כג וְהַטָּהוֹר יַחְדָּו כַּצְּבִי וְכָאַיָּל: רַק אֶת־דָּמוֹ לֹא תֹאכֵל עַל־הָאָרֶץ תִּשְׁפְּכֶנּוּ
כַּמָּיִם:
טז א שָׁמוֹר אֶת־חֹדֶשׁ הָאָבִיב וְעָשִׂיתָ פֶּסַח לַיהוה אֱלֹהֶיךָ כִּי בְּחֹדֶשׁ הָאָבִיב

---

freed), it now explains those commandments which represent thanksgiving to God, the Exalted One, and they are: the offering of the firstlings, for it is proper that owners of cattle thank (Him) because our cattle comes from His hand; and the Festival of Matzos, unleavened bread, to thank (Him) for freedom through the sacrifice of the *Pesach* lamb and the matzos; and for the *Aviv* through the *omer* (measure of barley) which is waved; and the Festival of Shevuos to thank Him for keeping שְׁבֻעֹת חֻקּוֹת קָצִיר, *the appointed weeks of the harvest* (*Jeremiah* 5:24), on our behalf; and the Festival of Ingathering (Succos) to thank Him for the ingathering. On each of these (occasions), we are to bring some gift to the Master, as it says, *and they shall not appear before HASHEM empty* (16:16). Therefore, the Torah does not mention in which month, nor the date of the month, they will occur, but mentions the *Aviv*, (and the Festivals of) the Weeks and the Ingathering.

XVI

1. שָׁמוֹר אֶת חֹדֶשׁ הָאָבִיב — *Observe the month of Aviv.* Guard with constant care that Nissan coincide with the month of *Aviv*, by intercalating the months and years so that the lunar and solar year are equal.

וְעָשִׂיתָ פֶּסַח — *And you shall make the Pesach* ... on the eve of the Festival of *matzos.*

כִּי בְּחֹדֶשׁ הָאָבִיב הוֹצִיאֲךָ — *For in the month of Aviv, (God) brought you forth.* His intent and desire was that your departure (from Egypt) be at a time when the renewal of *Aviv* is complete, (a time) of contrast being that (the sign of) the ram, the deity of Egypt, (then goes up) with the sun in its strength (while) the moon's (state) is the opposite.

NOTES

mention the specific month and day of each festival?' He explains that here the Torah is only telling us the rationale for these festivals, namely an expression of our thanks to God, and not the details of their time and manner of observance.

XVI

1. שָׁמוֹר אֶת חֹדֶשׁ הָאָבִיב — *Observe the month of Aviv. Aviv* is the season of the ripening of the ears. Israel is cautioned to take care that Pesach should always coincide with this month. Since Israel's is a lunar year, which is eleven days shorter than the solar year, it is bound to bring about a shifting of its festivals from their proper seasons in the course of time, hence the need to intercalate the year by adding an extra month (*Adar Sheini*) seven times in every cycle of nineteen years. The Torah, therefore, enjoins us to *guard* (שָׁמוֹר) that Nissan fall in the month of *Aviv*, as the *Sforno* explains.

וְעָשִׂיתָ פֶּסַח — *And offer the Pesach.* In the terminology of the Torah, the term פֶּסַח refers to the *Pesach* lamb which is brought on the 14th day of *Nissan* — the eve of חַג הַמַּצּוֹת, *the Festival of Matzos.*

כִּי בְּחֹדֶשׁ הָאָבִיב הוֹצִיאֲךָ ... לָיְלָה — *For in the month of Aviv, (God) brought you forth ... by night.* In ancient times, every nation identified with a certain planet, constellation or sign of

ב הוֹצִיאֲךָ֧ יהוה אֱלֹהֶ֛יךָ מִמִּצְרַ֖יִם לָֽיְלָה: וְזָבַחְתָּ֙ פֶּ֧סַח לַֽיהוה אֱלֹהֶ֛יךָ צֹ֥אן
ג וּבָקָ֖ר בַּמָּקוֹם֙ אֲשֶׁר־יִבְחַ֣ר יהוה לְשַׁכֵּ֥ן שְׁמ֖וֹ שָֽׁם: לֹא־תֹאכַ֤ל עָלָיו֙ חָמֵ֔ץ
שִׁבְעַ֥ת יָמִ֛ים תֹּֽאכַל־עָלָ֥יו מַצּ֖וֹת לֶ֣חֶם עֹ֑נִי כִּ֣י בְחִפָּז֗וֹן יָצָ֙אתָ֙ מֵאֶ֣רֶץ מִצְרַ֔יִם

לָֽיְלָה — *By night*. That contrast was at night, but being that no sacrifice can be offered at night it was necessary to advance it to the day previous to that contrast, and in remembrance of this it was established so for (future) generations.

2. וּבָקָר — *And the herd* . . . for the *chagigah*, festival offering; even though this (i.e., the *chagigah*) was not brought with the *Pesach* (sacrifice) in Egypt.

3. לֹא תֹאכַל עָלָיו חָמֵץ שִׁבְעַת יָמִים — *You shall eat no leavened bread with it; seven days* . . . even though the prohibition of leavened bread at the Egyptian Pesach was only for one day, as our Sages mention (*Pesachim* 96a).

תֹּאכַל עָלָיו מַצּוֹת — *You shall eat unleavened bread with it*. Because, being that it is an offering of remembrance for the redemption which occurred in a brief moment, it is not fitting to eat leavened bread with it, since bread requires (considerable) time to prepare, from the time of the kneading of the dough until it is leavened (based on *Hosea* 7:4).

לֶחֶם עֹנִי — *The bread of affliction* . . . bread which they ate in their affliction, and because of the pressure of their oppressors they had no time to wait for their dough to become leavened.

כִּי בְחִפָּזוֹן יָצָאתָ — *For in haste you came forth*. And the reason (we are told) to recall the haste (connected) with the bread is (to teach us) that in exchange for the haste of affliction you were then (granted) the haste of redemption, similar to, וְהָפַכְתִּי אֶבְלָם לְשָׂשׂוֹן, *I will turn their mourning to joy* (*Jeremiah* 31:12).

NOTES

the zodiac, which was considered their deity. Egypt's constellation was Aries the Ram. According to astrology, each month corresponds to a different sign of the zodiac indicating the ascendancy of a particular planet during that month. The *mazal*, planet, which represents Egypt ascends in the month of Nissan which is *Aviv*. Symbolically, this means that Egypt's strength and influence was then at its zenith. Conversely, the fortune of Israel, which is compared to the moon, is then at its nadir since the full moon appears in successive parts of the heaven each month, and in Nissan it is at the farthest point from the earth (180 degrees) implying that its influence on Israel's affairs is at its lowest point. Hence, logically, the night of the 15th of Nissan was the time least propitious for Israel to leave Egypt. Nonetheless, God ordained that it be done at that time to demonstrate that His power transcends the heavenly forces. Now the proper time to bring the *Pesach* offering should have been that night, but since sacrifices can only be brought during the

day we were commanded to bring the *Pesach* lamb on the 14th day of Nissan, the eve of the 15th.

See *Rashi* in tractate *Rosh Hashanah* 11b for a full description of the 12 constellations and their positions in the zodiac at various times of the year. It is important to note that our Sages teach us that, unlike other nations, אֵין מַזָּל לְיִשְׂרָאֵל, *Israel has no constellation* and is not subject to planetary influences (*Shabbos* 15a). However, we are *compared* to the moon, which explains the *Sforno's* commentary on this verse.

2. וּבָקָר — *And the herd*. The *Sforno* points out here, as he does in subsequent verses (3,4 and 5), that the Torah in the Book of *Deuteronomy* repeats certain laws of Pesach to teach us that there are basic differences between the law of the פֶּסַח in Egypt and of the *Pesach* sacrifice and festival observance in later generations. In this verse, we learn that a *chagigah*, *a festival offering from the herd*, is to be brought and eaten before one partakes of

ד לְמַ֣עַן תִּזְכֹּ֗ר אֶת־י֤וֹם צֵֽאתְךָ֙ מֵאֶ֣רֶץ מִצְרַ֔יִם כֹּ֖ל יְמֵ֥י חַיֶּֽיךָ׃ וְלֹֽא־יֵרָאֶ֨ה לְךָ֥
שְׂאֹ֛ר בְּכָל־גְּבֻלְךָ֖ שִׁבְעַ֣ת יָמִ֑ים וְלֹא־יָלִ֣ין מִן־הַבָּשָׂ֗ר אֲשֶׁ֨ר תִּזְבַּ֥ח בָּעֶ֛רֶב

לְמַעַן תִּזְכֹּר אֶת יוֹם צֵאתְךָ מֵאֶרֶץ מִצְרַיִם כֹּל יְמֵי חַיֶּיךָ — *That you may remember the day you came out of the land of Egypt all the days of your life.* And the reason I commanded (you) to take care that the lunar year be analogous to the solar year through intercalation was in order that Nissan would always be the month of *Aviv*. And (the reason) I did not command you to count (the festival) according to the solar months, which would not necessitate intercalation, was so that you would remember the Exodus from Egypt *all the days of your life,* because each time you intercalate the year or the month, so as to insure that Nissan would be in the month of *Aviv,* you will remember that it is being done because of the Exodus from Egypt.

4. וְלֹא יֵרָאֶה לְךָ שְׂאֹר בְּכָל גְּבֻלְךָ שִׁבְעַת יָמִים — *And there shall be no leaven seen with you in all your borders seven days* ... although this was not necessary at the time of the *Pesach* (offering) in Egypt.

וְלֹא יָלִין מִן הַבָּשָׂר — *Neither shall any of the meat remain.* Do not think that the prohibition of 'remaining' (נוֹתָר) only applied to the *Pesach* sacrifice in Egypt, because they were leaving in haste and (this prohibition) would serve to prevent any (part) of it from remaining in the hands of the non-Israelites (i.e., Egyptians).

NOTES

the *Pesach* lamb on Passover night so that the latter be eaten עַל הַשּׂוֹבַע, *when one is satisfied*, and not ravenously hungry. In this manner he will be able to observe the prohibition against breaking any bones of the *Pesach* offering. In verse 3, the Torah prohibits the eating of leaven for seven days, whereas in Egypt it was only prohibited for one day. In verse 4, the Torah enjoins us to remove leaven in our possession for seven days, an interdiction which did not apply in Egypt. In verse 5, we are told that the *Pesach* can only be brought in the Holy Temple, even though the first *Pesach* sacrifice was brought in Egypt where there was no temple and altar.

3. לֹא תֹאכַל עָלָיו חָמֵץ ... תֹּאכַל עָלָיו מַצּוֹת ... כִּי בְחִפָּזוֹן יָצָאתָ — *You shall eat no leavened bread with it ... you shall eat unleavened bread with it ... for in haste you came forth.* The *Sforno* points out that the characteristics of bread and matzoh are diametrically opposed. For example, the former requires more time for baking, while the latter is baked quickly. The significance of the brief time required to bake matzoh is that it symbolizes the swiftness of God's redemption of Israel from Egypt. This theme of haste is continued in the *Sforno's* explanation of the balance of this verse. When they were slaves, the Israelites had no time to bake bread because their taskmasters gave them little respite from their labors. As compensation for that callous haste, the Almighty redeemed them swiftly, as He shall do once again in the future, as the prophet Malachi says, *And the Lord Whom you seek shall suddenly come to His Temple* (*Malachi* 3:1).

לְמַעַן תִּזְכֹּר — *That you may remember.* The *Sforno* interprets this phrase as referring back to verse 1. The reason Israel is to take care that this festival falls in the month of 'the ripe ears' (*Aviv*) is so that they will always be mindful, when they intercalate the year, that this is being done to insure that this festival is celebrated during the same season that they departed from Egypt. In this manner, even the intercalation of the year (עִבּוּר שָׁנָה) becomes part of the yearly remembrance of that departure.

4. וְלֹא יָלִין מִן הַבָּשָׂר — *Neither shall any of the meat remain.* The laws pertaining to the פֶּסַח הַדּוֹרוֹת, *Pesach of generations*, are different in many respects from those of פֶּסַח מִצְרַיִם, *the Pesach of Egypt*, as explained in the note to verse 2. It is, therefore, necessary for the Torah to tell us that the prohibition of נוֹתָר, *allowing the meat of the sacrifice to remain overnight*, is common to both, even though the circumstances surrounding the *Pesach* in Egypt are not the same as the circumstances of the *Pesach* for generations.

ה בַּיּ֛וֹם הָרִאשׁ֖וֹן לַבֹּֽקֶר׃ לֹ֥א תוּכַ֖ל לִזְבֹּ֣חַ אֶת־הַפָּ֑סַח בְּאַחַ֣ד שְׁעָרֶ֔יךָ
ו אֲשֶׁר־יְהוָ֥ה אֱלֹהֶ֖יךָ נֹתֵ֥ן לָֽךְ׃ כִּ֠י אִֽם־אֶל־הַמָּק֞וֹם אֲשֶׁר־יִבְחַ֨ר יְהוָ֤ה אֱלֹהֶ֙יךָ֙
לְשַׁכֵּ֣ן שְׁמ֔וֹ שָׁ֛ם תִּזְבַּ֥ח אֶת־הַפֶּ֖סַח בָּעָ֑רֶב כְּב֣וֹא הַשֶּׁ֔מֶשׁ מוֹעֵ֖ד צֵאתְךָ֥
ז מִמִּצְרָֽיִם׃ וּבִשַּׁלְתָּ֙ וְאָ֣כַלְתָּ֔ בַּמָּק֕וֹם אֲשֶׁ֥ר יִבְחַ֛ר יְהוָ֥ה אֱלֹהֶ֖יךָ בּ֑וֹ וּפָנִ֣יתָ
ח בַבֹּ֔קֶר וְהָלַכְתָּ֖ לְאֹהָלֶֽיךָ׃ שֵׁ֥שֶׁת יָמִ֖ים תֹּאכַ֣ל מַצּ֑וֹת וּבַיּ֣וֹם הַשְּׁבִיעִ֗י עֲצֶ֙רֶת֙
ט לַֽיהוָ֣ה אֱלֹהֶ֔יךָ לֹ֥א תַעֲשֶׂ֖ה מְלָאכָֽה׃ שִׁבְעָ֥ה שָׁבֻעֹ֖ת
י תִּסְפָּר־לָ֑ךְ מֵהָחֵ֤ל חֶרְמֵשׁ֙ בַּקָּמָ֔ה תָּחֵ֣ל לִסְפֹּ֔ר שִׁבְעָ֖ה שָׁבֻעֽוֹת׃ וְעָשִׂ֜יתָ חַ֤ג
שָׁבֻעוֹת֙ לַיהוָ֣ה אֱלֹהֶ֔יךָ מִסַּ֛ת נִדְבַ֥ת יָדְךָ֖ אֲשֶׁ֣ר תִּתֵּ֑ן כַּאֲשֶׁ֥ר יְבָרֶכְךָ֖ יְהוָ֥ה
יא אֱלֹהֶֽיךָ׃ וְשָׂמַחְתָּ֞ לִפְנֵ֣י ׀ יְהוָ֣ה אֱלֹהֶ֗יךָ אַתָּ֨ה וּבִנְךָ֣ וּבִתֶּךָ֮ וְעַבְדְּךָ֣ וַאֲמָתֶךָ֒
וְהַלֵּוִי֙ אֲשֶׁ֣ר בִּשְׁעָרֶ֔יךָ וְהַגֵּ֛ר וְהַיָּת֥וֹם וְהָאַלְמָנָ֖ה אֲשֶׁ֣ר בְּקִרְבֶּ֑ךָ בַּמָּק֕וֹם אֲשֶׁ֣ר

---

5. לֹא תוּכַל לִזְבֹּחַ אֶת הַפָּסַח — *You may not sacrifice the Pesach offering.* Although the *Pesach* sacrifice in Egypt was offered without altar or Sanctuary, this is not (permitted) to be done in the future.

8. וּבַיּוֹם הַשְּׁבִיעִי עֲצֶרֶת — *And on the seventh day shall be an assembly.* All Israel convened together in the service of God, the Blessed One, and sang a song unto Him on the seventh day of the Festival of Matzos — therefore, that day became sanctified.

לֹא תַעֲשֶׂה מְלָאכָה — *You shall do no work.* Were it not for this (the convening together to sing a song), the seventh day would not be holy at all, similar to the Festival of Succos when the seventh day is not a holy convocation (מִקְרָא קֹדֶשׁ).

9. מֵהָחֵל חֶרְמֵשׁ בַּקָּמָה — *From the time the sickle is first put to the standing (barley).* (This refers to) the standing barley of the *omer*, כִּי הַשְּׂעֹרָה אָבִיב, *for the barley was in the ear* (*Exodus* 9:31), and from the *Aviv* to the harvest you shall count seven weeks, *the appointed (weeks) of the harvest* (based on *Jeremiah* 5:24).

11. וְהַגֵּר וְהַיָּתוֹם וְהָאַלְמָנָה — *The stranger, the orphan and the widow.* They will rejoice during the festival of the harvest with לֶקֶט, *the gleaning*, and the פֵּאָה (*the corner* of the field), which is available at the harvest. These are mentioned in conjunction with this Festival (of Weeks) in *parashas Emor* (*Leviticus* 23:22).

NOTES

8. וּבַיּוֹם הַשְּׁבִיעִי עֲצֶרֶת . . . לֹא תַעֲשֶׂה מְלָאכָה — *And on the seventh day shall be an assembly . . . you shall do no work.* The word עֲצֶרֶת can be translated as 'stoppage' or 'to cease.' If so, it is meant as an injunction against working on the seventh day of the festival, as stated specifically at the conclusion of the verse. The *Sforno*, however, interprets עֲצֶרֶת in this verse as 'an assembly' and thus the term is meant as an explanation of the historic *cause* and *reason* for prohibiting labor on the seventh day of Pesach. Since Israel assembled (עֲצֶרֶת) together at the Sea of Reeds (יַם סוּף) and sang the Song of the Sea (שִׁירַת הַיָּם) on the seventh day, praising God for the miracle of dividing the waters, it was therefore ordained to mark this day by cessation of labor, as is the case when a holy festival is observed.

11. וְהַגֵּר וְהַיָּתוֹם וְהָאַלְמָנָה — *The stranger, the orphan and the widow.* Although the Torah does not mention the gifts for the poor (the 'gleaning' and 'corner' — לֶקֶט וּפֵאָה) in this chapter, they are mentioned in *parashas Emor* (*Leviticus* 23:22) in the same chapter which speaks of Shevuos. The *Sforno* explains that the reason for the rejoicing of the widow, orphan and stranger stated here is because during the wheat harvest they enjoy the מַתְּנַת עֲנִיִּים — the gifts for the poor which are mentioned in *Leviticus*.

יב יִבְחַ֣ר יְהוָ֣ה אֱלֹהֶ֔יךָ לְשַׁכֵּ֥ן שְׁמ֖וֹ שָֽׁם׃ וְזָכַרְתָּ֔ כִּי־עֶ֥בֶד הָיִ֖יתָ בְּמִצְרָ֑יִם וְשָׁמַרְתָּ֣
וְעָשִׂ֔יתָ אֶת־הַחֻקִּ֖ים הָאֵֽלֶּה׃
מפטיר יג-יד חַ֧ג הַסֻּכֹּ֛ת תַּעֲשֶׂ֥ה לְךָ֖ שִׁבְעַ֣ת יָמִ֑ים בְּאָ֨סְפְּךָ֔ מִגָּרְנְךָ֖ וּמִיִּקְבֶֽךָ׃ וְשָׂמַחְתָּ֖ בְּחַגֶּ֑ךָ
אַתָּ֨ה וּבִנְךָ֤ וּבִתֶּ֙ךָ֙ וְעַבְדְּךָ֣ וַאֲמָתֶ֔ךָ וְהַלֵּוִ֗י וְהַגֵּ֛ר וְהַיָּת֥וֹם וְהָאַלְמָנָ֖ה אֲשֶׁ֥ר
טו בִּשְׁעָרֶֽיךָ׃ שִׁבְעַ֣ת יָמִ֗ים תָּחֹג֙ לַיהוָ֣ה אֱלֹהֶ֔יךָ בַּמָּק֖וֹם אֲשֶׁר־יִבְחַ֣ר יְהוָ֑ה כִּ֣י
יְבָרֶכְךָ֞ יְהוָ֣ה אֱלֹהֶ֗יךָ בְּכֹ֤ל תְּבוּאָֽתְךָ֙ וּבְכֹל֙ מַעֲשֵׂ֣ה יָדֶ֔יךָ וְהָיִ֖יתָ אַ֥ךְ שָׂמֵֽחַ׃
טז שָׁל֣וֹשׁ פְּעָמִ֣ים ׀ בַּשָּׁנָ֡ה יֵרָאֶ֨ה כָל־זְכוּרְךָ֜ אֶת־פְּנֵ֣י ׀ יְהוָ֣ה אֱלֹהֶ֗יךָ בַּמָּקוֹם֙
אֲשֶׁ֣ר יִבְחָ֔ר בְּחַ֧ג הַמַּצּ֛וֹת וּבְחַ֥ג הַשָּׁבֻע֖וֹת וּבְחַ֣ג הַסֻּכּ֑וֹת וְלֹ֧א יֵרָאֶ֛ה אֶת־פְּנֵ֥י
יז יְהוָ֖ה רֵיקָֽם׃ אִ֖ישׁ כְּמַתְּנַ֣ת יָד֑וֹ כְּבִרְכַּ֛ת יְהוָ֥ה אֱלֹהֶ֖יךָ אֲשֶׁ֥ר נָֽתַן־לָֽךְ׃

---

12. וְזָכַרְתָּ כִּי עֶבֶד הָיִיתָ — *And you shall remember that you were a slave* . . . at which time you possessed no money of your own because, מַה שֶּׁקָּנָה עֶבֶד קָנָה רַבּוֹ, *Whatever a slave owns, his master owns* (*Pesachim* 88b).

וְשָׁמַרְתָּ וְעָשִׂיתָ אֶת הַחֻקִּים הָאֵלֶּה — *And you shall observe and do these statutes* . . . (namely) the giving of gleanings and the corner of the field (to the needy) in accordance with the will of God who took you forth from there (Egypt) and gave you riches and possessions.

13. בְּאָסְפְּךָ מִגָּרְנְךָ וּמִיִּקְבֶךָ — *When you gather in from the threshing-floor and from your wine-press* . . . when you gather the produce into your house from the threshing floor and from the wine press.

14. וְהַגֵּר וְהַיָּתוֹם וְהָאַלְמָנָה — *And the stranger, and the orphan and the widow.* They will rejoice with פֶּרֶט (grapes fallen off during cutting) and gleanings, and the gifts (for the poor) from the fruit-trees.

15. כִּי יְבָרֶכְךָ — *Because* HASHEM *your God shall bless you.* You will have a bountiful harvest, and the needy will have many gifts (מַתְּנַת עֲנִיִּים).

אַךְ שָׂמֵחַ — *Altogether joyful.* You will be only joyful and no sorrow will intermingle with your joy.

17. אִישׁ כְּמַתְּנַת יָדוֹ — *Every man shall give as he is able.* He should not give away all that he has, thereby becoming dependent upon others, as is the practice of the foolish among the nations, as our Sages say, הַמְּבַזְבֵּז אַל יְבַזְבֵּז יוֹתֵר מֵחֹמֶשׁ, *If a man wishes to spend liberally (for charity), he should not spend more than a fifth* (*Kesubos* 50a).

NOTES

15. אַךְ שָׂמֵחַ — *Altogether joyful*. The word אַךְ denotes מִעוּט — a limitation. What is the Torah limiting in our case? The *Sforno* explains that God assures us that the festival will be limited to joy exclusively, without any intermingling of grief or sorrow.

17. אִישׁ כְּמַתְּנַת יָדוֹ — *Every man shall give as he is able*. The Torah cautions us not to be excessively open handed to such a degree that one impoverishes himelf. As an aside, he criticizes those adherents of other faiths who take a vow of poverty or give away everything they own as a religious act. Judaism frowns on such practices.

פרשת שופטים
Parashas Shoftim

יח שֹׁפְטִים וְשֹׁטְרִים תִּתֶּן־לְךָ בְּכָל־שְׁעָרֶיךָ אֲשֶׁר יהוה אֱלֹהֶיךָ נֹתֵן לְךָ
יט לִשְׁבָטֶיךָ וְשֵׁפְטוּ אֶת־הָעָם מִשְׁפַּט־צֶדֶק: לֹא־תַטֶּה מִשְׁפָּט לֹא תַכִּיר
פָּנִים וְלֹא־תִקַּח שֹׁחַד כִּי הַשֹּׁחַד יְעַוֵּר עֵינֵי חֲכָמִים וִיסַלֵּף דִּבְרֵי צַדִּיקִם:
כ צֶדֶק צֶדֶק תִּרְדֹּף לְמַעַן תִּחְיֶה וְיָרַשְׁתָּ אֶת־הָאָרֶץ אֲשֶׁר־יהוה אֱלֹהֶיךָ נֹתֵן

---

18. שֹׁפְטִים וְשֹׁטְרִים — *Judges and officers.* Following the commandments given to
the masses, He now commands regarding the affairs of the leaders, these being the
judges and kings, *Kohanim* and prophets, through whose correct (behavior) the
affairs of the masses will be improved, and through whose corrupt (behavior) the
(needs of the populace) will be damaged, which the prophet attests to saying, שָׂרֶיהָ
בְקִרְבָּהּ אֲרָיוֹת שֹׁאֲגִים, שֹׁפְטֶיהָ זְאֵבֵי עֶרֶב לֹא גָרְמוּ לַבֹּקֶר. נְבִיאֶיהָ פֹּחֲזִים אַנְשֵׁי בֹּגְדוֹת כֹּהֲנֶיהָ
חִלְּלוּ קֹדֶשׁ חָמְסוּ תוֹרָה, *Her princes within her are roaring lions; her judges are
wolves at evening, they gnaw no bones in the morning. Her prophets are worthless,
treacherous persons; her Kohanim have polluted the Sanctuary, they have
violently perverted Torah* (Zephaniah 3:3,4).

נֹתֵן לְךָ לִשְׁבָטֶיךָ — *Gives to your tribes.* In your gates which He *gives to you* to be
divided among your tribes, but not (the land) which you may conquer outside the
Land (of Israel) which is not divided (among) the tribes, as our Sages state, 'Outside
the Land you seat judges in each district but not in each city' (*Makos* 7a). This
would apply to Syria and other such (neighboring) lands.

מִשְׁפַּט צֶדֶק — *Righteous judgment.* Let the hearing of testimony (lit., claims) be in
such a manner that the judicial decision be righteous. (The judge) must not be
lenient with one and harsh to the other (based on *Kesuvos* 46a).

20. צֶדֶק צֶדֶק תִּרְדֹּף — *Justice, justice shall you follow.* When you choose and
appoint judges, select only those who are the most likely to judge with
righteousness, even though they may not possess other characteristics befitting a

---

NOTES

18. שֹׁפְטִים וְשֹׁטְרִים — *Judges and officers.* The
previous chapters include numerous commandments addressed to the people of Israel as
a whole. For example in *parashas Re'eh,* the
Torah speaks of Israel's responsibility to rid its
land of idolatry. It also commands the estab-
lishment of a central Sanctuary, the prohibition of eating blood, the laws of tithes, the
dietary laws, the nullification of debts at the
end of the seventh year, the punishment of the
false prophet and of a city guilty of idol
worship, as well as discussing the various
festivals. Now, at the beginning of *parashas
Shoftim,* the Torah directs its attention to
personalities rather than concepts, namely to
the king, the judge, the *Kohen* and the prophet
who fill the roles of leadership and authority
in Israel. The *Sforno* emphasizes, as he does in
numerous other places, that the proper behavior of the leader will affect not only the
spiritual state of Jewish society but also its
material well-being.

נֹתֵן לְךָ לִשְׁבָטֶיךָ — *Gives to your tribes.* The
Sforno interprets the word לִשְׁבָטֶיךָ, *to your
tribes* as a מִעוּט, *a limitation.* Only in *Eretz
Yisrael,* which is divided among your tribes,
shall you establish courts in each city, but not
outside the land. This law applies even in
territory which may be conquered by a Jewish
king if that conquest is not sanctioned by the
Sanhedrin, such as Syria which was conquered by King David (See *Bava Basra* 90b
and *Tosfos* there).

מִשְׁפַּט צֶדֶק — *Righteous judgment.* Can there
be a מִשְׁפָּט, *judgment,* which is not צֶדֶק,
righteous? The *Sforno* explains that this does
not refer to the *decision* of the judges but to
their *manner* of judging. It must be *righteous*
in the sense of being impartial and evenhanded.

20. צֶדֶק צֶדֶק תִּרְדֹּף — *Justice, justice shall you
follow.* The *Sforno* interprets the repetition of
the word צֶדֶק, *justice,* to mean that in choosing

כא לָךְ: לֹא־תִטַּע לְךָ אֲשֵׁרָה כָּל־עֵץ אֵצֶל מִזְבַּח יהוה
כב אֱלֹהֶיךָ אֲשֶׁר תַּעֲשֶׂה־לָּךְ: וְלֹא־תָקִים לְךָ מַצֵּבָה אֲשֶׁר שָׂנֵא יהוה

---

judge, such as perfection in matters of possession, and perfection of physical appearance. This is similar to אַל תַּבֵּט אֶל מַרְאֵהוּ וְאֶל גְּבֹהַּ קוֹמָתוֹ, *Look not on his countenance, nor on the height of his stature* (*I Samuel* 16:7).

לְמַעַן תִּחְיֶה וְיָרַשְׁתָּ — *That you may live and inherit (the land).* There is need for this (justice) more so in the Land (of Israel), because the lack of it will impede the possession of (the Land), as it says, בַּעֲוֹן בִּצְעוֹ קָצַפְתִּי וְאַכֵּהוּ, *For the iniquity of his covetousness was I wrathful and smote him* (*Isaiah* 57:17).

21-22. לֹא תִטַּע לְךָ אֲשֵׁרָה . . . וְלֹא תָקִים לְךָ מַצֵּבָה — *You shall not plant an Asherah . . . Neither shall you set up a pillar.* The Torah cites three instances of similar things which are beautiful and appealing to the senses, but are abhorrent (to God) for they are spiritually blemished. The first is an Asherah, which is used to beautify palaces, but nonetheless, is abhorrent if used in a holy place because it is customarily used for idolatrous services. (Similarly) we grant preference to the spirit of righteousness and justice of the judge over his physical perfection, which is material and (appeals) to the physical senses.

Secondly, although a pillar was acceptable prior to the giving of the Torah, as it says, וּשְׁתֵּים עֶשְׂרֵה מַצֵּבָה, *And twelve pillars* (*Exodus* 24:4), the reason being because symbolically it is as though the one who brings an offering stands continually before the Holy, similar to שִׁוִּיתִי ה׳ לְנֶגְדִּי תָמִיד, *I have set* HASHEM *always before me* (*Psalms* 16:8); — (however), they (i.e., the pillars) fell from that (elevated) level when (Israel sinned) with the Golden Calf, as it says, כִּי לֹא אֶעֱלֶה בְּקִרְבְּךָ, *For I will not go up in your midst* (*Exodus* 33:3). Similarly, regarding an elder (i.e., a judge or leader) whose lifetime has not been well spent and who has a bad name due to youthful (indiscretion), (such a judge should be rejected) when you can find an elder whose lifetime has been well spent.

Thirdly, the Torah cites the case of an abhorrent blemish . . .

NOTES

a judge, judicial temperament and a sense of fairness is of paramount importance, more so than a dignified bearing and imposing presence. Appearance is not as important as substance. The verse quoted by the *Sforno* to prove this scale of priorities is most appropriate. When the prophet Samuel went to the house of Jesse to select a king of Israel, he was impressed by the appearance of Eliav, but God cautioned him not to be misled by his physical stature, saying, '*Do not look at his countenance nor the height of his stature because I have rejected him; for it is not as a man sees; for a man looks at the outward appearance but God looks at the heart*' (*I Samuel* 16).

The *Sforno* uses the expression שְׁלֵמוּת הַקִּנְיָן וּשְׁלֵמוּת הַגּוּף, *perfection in matters of possession,* meaning material wealth attained honestly and used properly, and *perfection of physical stature* — which so impressed Samuel when he saw Eliav.

לְמַעַן תִּחְיֶה — *That you may live*. The *Sforno* explains that there is no greater danger to the stability of national life in *Eretz Yisrael* than injustice.

21-22. לֹא תִטַּע לְךָ אֲשֵׁרָה . . . וְלֹא תָקִים לְךָ מַצֵּבָה . . . לֹא תִזְבַּח — *You shall not plant an Asherah . . . Neither shall you set up a pillar . . . You shall not sacrifice*. The *Sforno* cites three examples of judges who are not qualified to serve on a Jewish court and compares them to three prohibitions, namely the planting of an *Asherah,* the setting up of a pillar and the offering of a blemished animal. The first is an example of something which is aesthetically appealing but spiritually objectionable. The second is an example of something which changes with time, and the third is an example

יז א אֱלֹהֶֽיךָ׃ לֹא־תִזְבַּח לַיהוָה אֱלֹהֶיךָ שׁוֹר וָשֶׂה אֲשֶׁר יִהְיֶה
ב בוֹ מוּם כֹּל דָּבָר רָע כִּי תוֹעֲבַת יְהוָה אֱלֹהֶיךָ הוּא׃ כִּֽי־
יִמָּצֵא בְקִרְבְּךָ בְּאַחַד שְׁעָרֶיךָ אֲשֶׁר־יְהוָה אֱלֹהֶיךָ נֹתֵן לָךְ אִישׁ אוֹ־אִשָּׁה
ג אֲשֶׁר יַעֲשֶׂה אֶת־הָרַע בְּעֵינֵי יְהוָֽה־אֱלֹהֶיךָ לַעֲבֹר בְּרִיתֽוֹ׃ וַיֵּלֶךְ וַיַּעֲבֹד
אֱלֹהִים אֲחֵרִים וַיִּשְׁתַּחוּ לָהֶם וְלַשֶּׁמֶשׁ ׀ אוֹ לַיָּרֵחַ אוֹ לְכָל־צְבָא הַשָּׁמַיִם

XVII

1. לֹא תִזְבַּח . . . אֲשֶׁר יִהְיֶה בוֹ מוּם — *You shall not sacrifice . . . wherein is a blemish.* Although the animal is comely to the senses and fat, its worth being a thousand *zuz*, nonetheless, it is disqualified for sacred use because of its blemish, (although) it does not decrease in value. (On the other hand,) if an ox (only) worth a *sela* is unblemished, it is acceptable to be offered (to God). Similarly, if an elder possesses disgraceful vices and you find one who is superior to him in perfection of his attributes, (select him as a judge) even though he is not as rich and (physically) handsome as the other.

2. כִּי יִמָּצֵא בְקִרְבְּךָ — *If there be found in your midst.* After (the Torah) commands the appointment of judges in every city so that each court should judge the inhabitants of its (own) city, it now mentions the judging of an idolater who is not judged in his city but is judged in the city where he served (the strange god). Following this, (the Torah) speaks of differences of opinion (among the judges) of a court, which is also adjudicated in a different city, namely in the place *which* HASHEM *your God shall choose* (v. 8), and so also (the case) of a זָקֵן מַמְרֵא, *a rebellious scholar* (lit., elder).

לַעֲבֹר בְּרִיתוֹ — *Transgressing His covenant* . . . the covenant which was entered into regarding all the commandments, because, indeed, one who serves strange gods (is considered as though) he denies all the commandments and nullifies them.

3. אֱלֹהִים אֲחֵרִים — *Other gods* . . . beings separated from matter, except for God, the Blessed One.

וְלַשֶּׁמֶשׁ אוֹ לַיָּרֵחַ — *Or to the sun or the moon* . . . which are corporeal.

NOTES

of that which may seem to be valuable but is unacceptable by the standards of Torah. Conversely, that which appears to be without great value may be priceless by the Torah's yardstick. The Asherah represents the first, as does a judge who is physically impressive but deficient in virtues. The pillar represents the second, as does a judge whose past is checkered, while a blemished animal represents the third, similar to a judge who is rich and handsome but whose character is flawed.

XVII

2. כִּי יִמָּצֵא בְקִרְבְּךָ — *If there be found in your midst.* The *Sforno* explains the reason for the juxtaposition of these verses (2-13) which deal with the worshiping of other gods, a difference of opinion among judges of a local court and the punishment of an elder who defies the decision of the High Court in Jerusalem. The common denominator is that they are not judged by their local courts but by the court of the city where the transgression occurred or by the Supreme Court in Jerusalem.

לַעֲבֹר בְּרִיתוֹ — *Transgressing His covenant.* Compare to *Rashi* 11:28, who cites the *Sifri*, that he who serves strange gods is considered as one who denies the entire Torah.

3. אֱלֹהִים אֲחֵרִים . . . וְלַשֶּׁמֶשׁ אוֹ לַיָּרֵחַ — *Other gods . . . or to the sun or the moon.* The *Sforno* explains that these are two distinct and separate modes of proscribed worship. The former refers to angels who are spiritual beings while the heavenly bodies are corporeal. Both are prohibited to be considered deities.

ד אֲשֶׁר לֹא־צִוִּיתִי: וְהֻגַּד־לְךָ וְשָׁמָעְתָּ וְדָרַשְׁתָּ הֵיטֵב וְהִנֵּה אֱמֶת נָכוֹן הַדָּבָר
ה נֶעֶשְׂתָה הַתּוֹעֵבָה הַזֹּאת בְּיִשְׂרָאֵל: וְהוֹצֵאתָ אֶת־הָאִישׁ הַהוּא אוֹ
אֶת־הָאִשָּׁה הַהִוא אֲשֶׁר עָשׂוּ אֶת־הַדָּבָר הָרָע הַזֶּה אֶל־שְׁעָרֶיךָ אֶת־הָאִישׁ
ו אוֹ אֶת־הָאִשָּׁה וּסְקַלְתָּם בָּאֲבָנִים וָמֵתוּ: עַל־פִּי | שְׁנַיִם עֵדִים אוֹ שְׁלֹשָׁה
ז עֵדִים יוּמַת הַמֵּת לֹא יוּמַת עַל־פִּי עֵד אֶחָד: יַד הָעֵדִים תִּהְיֶה־בּוֹ בָרִאשֹׁנָה
לַהֲמִיתוֹ וְיַד כָּל־הָעָם בָּאַחֲרֹנָה וּבִעַרְתָּ הָרָע מִקִּרְבֶּךָ:
ח כִּי יִפָּלֵא מִמְּךָ דָבָר לַמִּשְׁפָּט בֵּין־דָּם | לְדָם בֵּין־דִּין לְדִין וּבֵין נֶגַע לָנֶגַע

אֲשֶׁר לֹא צִוִּיתִי — *Which I have not commanded.* Whom I have not appointed, by any designation, (as having) the power of choice that would (permit them) to function according to their own will. Rather, I ordained unto them immutable laws contrary to the thinking of the idolaters who thought that every city had its (heavenly) lord who could do good or evil according to his will, (and) who benefits those who serve him.

5. אֶת הָאִישׁ הַהוּא אוֹ אֶת הָאִשָּׁה הַהִוא — *That man or that woman.* And we do not say that she was seduced and knew nothing, and therefore it is unnecessary to judge her in the gate (of the city) where she served (the strange gods) so as to demonstrate the error of her opinions.

אֶל שְׁעָרֶיךָ — *Unto your gates* . . . the gate (of the city) where the idol was worshiped, to demonstrate that this alien god has no power to save its worshiper who thought that he would be saved by (his god).

6. עַל פִּי שְׁנַיִם עֵדִים אוֹ שְׁלֹשָׁה — *At the mouth of two witnesses or three.* Even in the case of idolatry the entire set of witnesses is disqualified if one of them is found to be (a relative) or unqualified, and we are not to presume that the testimony shall take place through the rest (of the witnesses).

8. כִּי יִפָּלֵא מִמְּךָ דָבָר — *If there arise a matter too hard.* Although you appointed judges for each city so that each court shall judge its city, nevertheless if a doubt arises regarding the traditional teaching, the court of that city shall not decide according to its (own) deliberation, but the decision shall be made according to the deliberation of the majority of the High Court (in Jerusalem). (This is also the case) when (the local court) cannot reach a majority opinion.

NOTES

5. אוֹ אֶת הָאִשָּׁה הַהִוא — *Or that woman.* The *Sforno* explains the reason why the Torah specifically mentions a woman in this verse. Since a woman is more prone to he misled by certain blandishments, signs and wonders, one might think that she is not responsible for her actions, therefore it is necessary to teach us that this is an incorrect assumption. See the *Ramban* who explains this verse in a similar fashion.

אֶל שְׁעָרֶיךָ — *Unto your gates.* The reason that punishment is exacted in the gates of the city where the idol was worshiped is to demonstrate that the idol has no power to save its worshiper.

6. עַל פִּי שְׁנַיִם עֵדִים אוֹ שְׁלֹשָׁה — *At the mouth of two witnesses or three.* According to Rabbinic teaching, the evidence of two witnesses is considered as one unit of testimony and if one witness is disqualified, the testimony is disallowed. So too is the testimony of three or more witnesses considered as a single unit and if one is rendered unfit, the testimony likewise is rejected. Lest one think that given the severity of the sin of idolatry we should waive this technicality and punish the accused, the Torah cautions us not to do so.

8. כִּי יִפָּלֵא מִמְּךָ דָבָר — *If there arise a matter too hard.* The expression מִפִּי הַשְּׁמוּעָה, *traditional teaching*, is based on *Sanhedrin* 88a, in accordance with the opinion of Rabbi Elazar.

דִּבְרֵי רִיבֹת בִּשְׁעָרֶיךָ וְקַמְתָּ וְעָלִיתָ אֶל־הַמָּקוֹם אֲשֶׁר יִבְחַר יהוה אֱלֹהֶיךָ
ט בּוֹ: וּבָאתָ אֶל־הַכֹּהֲנִים הַלְוִיִּם וְאֶל־הַשֹּׁפֵט אֲשֶׁר יִהְיֶה בַּיָּמִים הָהֵם וְדָרַשְׁתָּ
י וְהִגִּידוּ לְךָ אֵת דְּבַר הַמִּשְׁפָּט: וְעָשִׂיתָ עַל־פִּי הַדָּבָר אֲשֶׁר יַגִּידוּ לְךָ
מִן־הַמָּקוֹם הַהוּא אֲשֶׁר יִבְחַר יהוה וְשָׁמַרְתָּ לַעֲשׂוֹת כְּכֹל אֲשֶׁר יוֹרוּךָ:
יא עַל־פִּי הַתּוֹרָה אֲשֶׁר יוֹרוּךָ וְעַל־הַמִּשְׁפָּט אֲשֶׁר־יֹאמְרוּ לְךָ תַּעֲשֶׂה לֹא
יב תָסוּר מִן־הַדָּבָר אֲשֶׁר־יַגִּידוּ לְךָ יָמִין וּשְׂמֹאל: וְהָאִישׁ אֲשֶׁר־יַעֲשֶׂה בְזָדוֹן
לְבִלְתִּי שְׁמֹעַ אֶל־הַכֹּהֵן הָעֹמֵד לְשָׁרֶת שָׁם אֶת־יהוה אֱלֹהֶיךָ אוֹ
יג אֶל־הַשֹּׁפֵט וּמֵת הָאִישׁ הַהוּא וּבִעַרְתָּ הָרָע מִיִּשְׂרָאֵל: וְכָל־הָעָם יִשְׁמְעוּ
שני יד וְיִרָאוּ וְלֹא יְזִידוּן עוֹד: כִּי־תָבֹא אֶל־הָאָרֶץ אֲשֶׁר
יהוה אֱלֹהֶיךָ נֹתֵן לָךְ וִירִשְׁתָּהּ וְיָשַׁבְתָּה בָּהּ וְאָמַרְתָּ אָשִׂימָה עָלַי מֶלֶךְ
טו כְּכָל־הַגּוֹיִם אֲשֶׁר סְבִיבֹתָי: שׂוֹם תָּשִׂים עָלֶיךָ מֶלֶךְ אֲשֶׁר יִבְחַר יהוה

---

12. וְהָאִישׁ אֲשֶׁר יַעֲשֶׂה בְזָדוֹן — *And the man that does presumptuously* ... who issues a halachic decision, in fact, contrary to the decision of the High Court.

וּמֵת הָאִישׁ הַהוּא — *That man shall die* ... through the High Court, and thus *the people shall hear and fear* (v. 13).

14. אָשִׂימָה עָלַי מֶלֶךְ כְּכָל הַגּוֹיִם — *I will set a king over me like all the nations* ... a hereditary monarchy, unlike (the system) of judges where only the judge ruled but not his children after him. Now, they were commanded regarding the appointment of a judge as a king in such a manner when they came to the Land (of Israel), as it says, וְלֹא תִהְיֶה עֲדַת ה׳ כַּצֹּאן אֲשֶׁר אֵין לָהֶם רֹעֶה, *That the congregation of* HASHEM *be not as sheep which have no shepherd* (*Numbers* 27:17). However, (in regard to) appointing a king, such as one (who rules among) the nations who claims the monarchy for himself and his children, (such a reign) is abhorrent to God, the Blessed One. But He did command that if they would stubbornly insist to have such a monarch, they should choose only a fit person, chosen by God, so that he not lead Israel away from their faith. (Also,) he may not be a foreigner, even though he be a fit, decent person and a mighty man of war. Now, when they sinned by requesting a king who would rule, he and his children after him, similar to all other nations, their punishment was through disasters which befell the masses on account of the king, as it says, וּזְעַקְתֶּם בַּיּוֹם הַהוּא מִלִּפְנֵי מַלְכְּכֶם אֲשֶׁר בְּחַרְתֶּם לָכֶם וְלֹא יַעֲנֶה ה׳ אֶתְכֶם בַּיּוֹם הַהוּא, *And you will cry out on that day because of your king who you will have chosen for yourselves, and* HASHEM *will not answer you on that day* (*I Samuel*

NOTES

12. וְהָאִישׁ אֲשֶׁר יַעֲשֶׂה בְזָדוֹן — *And the man that does presumptuously*. The *Sforno's* commentary is based on tractate *Sanhedrin* 86b. Our Sages teach us that a זָקֵן מַמְרֵא, *rebellious scholar*, is only liable to the death penalty if he renders a decision meant to be implemented (הֲלָכָה לְמַעֲשֶׂה) — not a theoretical one.

וּמֵת הָאִישׁ הַהוּא — *That man shall die*. The *Sforno* reflects in his commentary the Talmudic statement (*Sanhedrin* 89a) that the execution of a rebellious scholar is not held in his city but in Jerusalem, at the time when Israel gathers together at the festival period, so that *all the people shall hear and fear*. *Rashi* explains this verse in a similar manner.

14. אָשִׂימָה עָלַי מֶלֶךְ — *I will set a king over me*. The *Sforno's* commentary on this verse explains the Torah's antipathy to the institution of a monarchy in Israel. When Moses asked God to appoint a leader over the Jewish people who would lead them after his demise (*Numbers* 27:16), it was the appointment of a judge that he requested and not a king whose children would inherit the monarchy. Al-

אֱלֹהֶיךָ בּוֹ מִקֶּרֶב אַחֶיךָ תָּשִׂים עָלֶיךָ מֶלֶךְ לֹא תוּכַל לָתֵת עָלֶיךָ אִישׁ
טז נָכְרִי אֲשֶׁר לֹא־אָחִיךָ הוּא: רַק לֹא־יַרְבֶּה־לּוֹ סוּסִים וְלֹא־יָשִׁיב אֶת־הָעָם
מִצְרַיְמָה לְמַעַן הַרְבּוֹת סוּס וַיהוה אָמַר לָכֶם לֹא תֹסִפוּן לָשׁוּב בַּדֶּרֶךְ הַזֶּה
יז עוֹד: וְלֹא יַרְבֶּה־לּוֹ נָשִׁים וְלֹא יָסוּר לְבָבוֹ וְכֶסֶף וְזָהָב לֹא יַרְבֶּה־לּוֹ מְאֹד:
יח וְהָיָה כְשִׁבְתּוֹ עַל כִּסֵּא מַמְלַכְתּוֹ וְכָתַב לוֹ אֶת־מִשְׁנֵה הַתּוֹרָה הַזֹּאת
יט עַל־סֵפֶר מִלִּפְנֵי הַכֹּהֲנִים הַלְוִיִּם: וְהָיְתָה עִמּוֹ וְקָרָא בוֹ כָּל־יְמֵי חַיָּיו לְמַעַן
יִלְמַד לְיִרְאָה אֶת־יהוה אֱלֹהָיו לִשְׁמֹר אֶת־כָּל־דִּבְרֵי הַתּוֹרָה הַזֹּאת
כ וְאֶת־הַחֻקִּים הָאֵלֶּה לַעֲשֹׂתָם: לְבִלְתִּי רוּם־לְבָבוֹ מֵאֶחָיו וּלְבִלְתִּי סוּר
מִן־הַמִּצְוָה יָמִין וּשְׂמֹאול לְמַעַן יַאֲרִיךְ יָמִים עַל־מַמְלַכְתּוֹ הוּא וּבָנָיו בְּקֶרֶב
יח שלישי א יִשְׂרָאֵל: לֹא־יִהְיֶה לַכֹּהֲנִים הַלְוִיִּם כָּל־שֵׁבֶט לֵוִי חֵלֶק
ב וְנַחֲלָה עִם־יִשְׂרָאֵל אִשֵּׁי יהוה וְנַחֲלָתוֹ יֹאכֵלוּן: וְנַחֲלָה לֹא־יִהְיֶה־לּוֹ בְּקֶרֶב
ג אֶחָיו יהוה הוּא נַחֲלָתוֹ כַּאֲשֶׁר דִּבֶּר־לוֹ: וְזֶה יִהְיֶה מִשְׁפַּט
הַכֹּהֲנִים מֵאֵת הָעָם מֵאֵת זֹבְחֵי הַזֶּבַח אִם־שׁוֹר אִם־שֶׂה וְנָתַן לַכֹּהֵן הַזְּרֹעַ
ד וְהַלְּחָיַיִם וְהַקֵּבָה: רֵאשִׁית דְּגָנְךָ תִּירֹשְׁךָ וְיִצְהָרֶךָ וְרֵאשִׁית גֵּז צֹאנְךָ
ה תִּתֶּן־לוֹ: כִּי בוֹ בָּחַר יהוה אֱלֹהֶיךָ מִכָּל־שְׁבָטֶיךָ לַעֲמֹד לְשָׁרֵת בְּשֵׁם־יהוה

8:18), and as it says, אֶתֶּן לְךָ מֶלֶךְ בְּאַפִּי וְאֶקַּח בְּעֶבְרָתִי, *I give you a king in My anger, and take him away in My wrath* (*Hosea* 13:11). The permission granted (to Israel) to appoint a king is similar to the permission granted to take אֵשֶׁת יְפַת תֹּאַר, *the woman of goodly form* (21:11), where (the Torah) indicates that eventually he will hate her and a rebellious son will be born to her, as it happened with David and Absalom.

19. לְמַעַן יִלְמַד לְיִרְאָה אֶת ה׳ — *That he may learn to fear* HASHEM. Through the knowledge of the contemplative portion of (the Torah) which teaches clearly the greatness and providence of God, the Exalted One, he will perforce be brought to the fear (of God).

XVIII

5. כִּי בוֹ בָּחַר ה׳ אֱלֹהֶיךָ מִכָּל שְׁבָטֶיךָ — *For* HASHEM *your God has chosen him out of all your tribes.* It is (therefore) fitting that you give him bread and clothing so that he be able to stand to minister.

NOTES

though the Torah speaks here of a Jewish king, it is a concession made reluctantly, similar in nature to the law of אֵשֶׁת יְפַת תֹּאַר, *the woman of goodly form,* taken captive in battle, who is allowed to be taken as a concubine. Indeed, our Sages say that *the Torah only speaks thus to appease the evil inclination* in man. The *Sforno* explains that a hereditary monarchy will, in most cases, bring in its wake trouble and anguish, as is the case of *the woman of goodly form* who will usually produce a child that will be a בֵּן סוֹרֵר וּמוֹרֶה, *a stubborn rebellious son.* The *Sforno* links these two together — i.e., Jewish monarchy and the captive woman — by citing the example of David's son Absalom who was the son of Maacha, daughter of Ptolemy, king of Geshur, taken captive in battle by David.

19. לְמַעַן יִלְמַד לְיִרְאָה אֶת ה׳ — *That he may learn to fear* HASHEM. Kingship, by its very nature, often leads to corruption of the monarch's moral character, and also limits the freedom of the people over whom he rules. It is therefore imperative for the Torah to teach that the king of Israel be restrained and guided

רביעי ו הוּא וּבָנָיו כָּל־הַיָּמִים׃ וְכִי־יָבֹא הַלֵּוִי מֵאַחַד שְׁעָרֶיךָ מִכָּל־
יִשְׂרָאֵל אֲשֶׁר־הוּא גָּר שָׁם וּבָא בְּכָל־אַוַּת נַפְשׁוֹ אֶל־הַמָּקוֹם אֲשֶׁר־יִבְחַר
ז יְהוָה׃ וְשֵׁרֵת בְּשֵׁם יְהוָה אֱלֹהָיו כְּכָל־אֶחָיו הַלְוִיִּם הָעֹמְדִים שָׁם לִפְנֵי יְהוָה׃
ח־ט חֵלֶק כְּחֵלֶק יֹאכֵלוּ לְבַד מִמְכָּרָיו עַל־הָאָבוֹת׃ כִּי אַתָּה
בָּא אֶל־הָאָרֶץ אֲשֶׁר־יְהוָה אֱלֹהֶיךָ נֹתֵן לָךְ לֹא־תִלְמַד לַעֲשׂוֹת כְּתוֹעֲבֹת
י הַגּוֹיִם הָהֵם׃ לֹא־יִמָּצֵא בְךָ מַעֲבִיר בְּנוֹ־וּבִתּוֹ בָּאֵשׁ קֹסֵם קְסָמִים מְעוֹנֵן
יא וּמְנַחֵשׁ וּמְכַשֵּׁף׃ וְחֹבֵר חָבֶר וְשֹׁאֵל אוֹב וְיִדְּעֹנִי וְדֹרֵשׁ אֶל־הַמֵּתִים׃
יב כִּי־תוֹעֲבַת יְהוָה כָּל־עֹשֵׂה אֵלֶּה וּבִגְלַל הַתּוֹעֵבֹת הָאֵלֶּה יְהוָה אֱלֹהֶיךָ
חמישי יג־יד מוֹרִישׁ אוֹתָם מִפָּנֶיךָ׃ תָּמִים תִּהְיֶה עִם יְהוָה אֱלֹהֶיךָ׃ * כִּי ׀ הַגּוֹיִם הָאֵלֶּה

---

8. לְבַד מִמְכָּרָיו עַל הָאָבוֹת — *Besides that which can be sold* (*i.e., exchanged*) *according to the fathers' houses.* The fathers could only divide among the priestly watches (מִמְכָּרָיו) that which could be sold through an exchange by every watch to their fellow *Kohanim*, namely the offerings of all the days of the year. Every watch (was permitted) to exchange their portion of the regular offerings during the year with their fellow (*Kohanim*) who would give them (in turn) their portion of a week or two (from their watch). However, the festival offerings, for which there could be no exchange and were not included in מִמְכָּרָיו, that which the fathers could divide among the watches, (regarding these we say) חֵלֶק כְּחֵלֶק יֹאכֵלוּ, *they shall have like portions to eat.*

10. לֹא יִמָּצֵא בְךָ — *There shall not be found among you* . . . even one who is from a foreign people such as the בַּעֲלַת אוֹב — necromanceress — who remained in En-dor (*I Samuel* 28:7).

13. תָּמִים תִּהְיֶה — *You shall be wholehearted* . . . perfect and complete with Him. Even when you seek to inquire as to the future you shall inquire of none other than Him, through a prophet or the *Urim and Tumim.*

NOTES

by the laws and discipline of God's Torah. Hopefully, by studying and obeying it, he will learn to fear God, and thus control his appetite for power which tends to corrupt man.

XVIII

8. לְבַד מִמְכָּרָיו עַל הָאָבוֹת — *Besides that which can be sold according to the fathers' houses.* The priestly families were divided into twenty-four watches (מִשְׁמָרוֹת) at the time of Samuel and David, each serving in the Temple for a period of one week. The various מַתְּנוֹת כְּהוּנָּה, *priestly gifts,* belonged to the watch of that week. However, as the *Sforno* points out, they were permited to exchange these gifts with other priestly families, who in turn would repay them with their portion during the week of their service. However, the priestly gifts from the offerings brought during the festivals were not allocated to the *watch* of that week, but belonged to all the *Kohanim* who were in Jerusalem at that time. (See Tractate *Succah* 56a and compare to *Rashi* on this verse.)

10. לֹא יִמָּצֵא בְךָ — *There shall not be found among you.* The *Sforno* interprets the expression *there shall not be found among you* as a cautionary command not to permit such soothsayers and sorcerers to reside in the midst of Israel even if they are aliens and not Israelites. The *Sforno* is of the opinion that the necromanceress of En-dor was not a Jewess, contrary to the commentary of *Radak* in *I Samuel,* chapter 28, who quotes a Midrash that she was the mother of Abner.

13. תָּמִים תִּהְיֶה — *You shall be wholehearted.* The *Urim and Tumim,* cited by the *Sforno,* are mentioned in *Exodus* 28:30. *Urim* means *light* and *Tumim* means *perfect.* The שֵׁם הַמְּפוֹרָשׁ, *the Ineffable Name of God,* was inscribed on some material and placed in the fold of the

אֲשֶׁר אַתָּה יוֹרֵשׁ אוֹתָם אֶל־מְעֹנְנִים וְאֶל־קֹסְמִים יִשְׁמָעוּ וְאַתָּה לֹא כֵן
נָתַן לְךָ יהוה אֱלֹהֶיךָ: נָבִיא מִקִּרְבְּךָ מֵאַחֶיךָ כָּמֹנִי יָקִים לְךָ יהוה אֱלֹהֶיךָ טו
אֵלָיו תִּשְׁמָעוּן: כְּכֹל אֲשֶׁר־שָׁאַלְתָּ מֵעִם יהוה אֱלֹהֶיךָ בְּחֹרֵב בְּיוֹם הַקָּהָל טז
לֵאמֹר לֹא אֹסֵף לִשְׁמֹעַ אֶת־קוֹל יהוה אֱלֹהָי וְאֶת־הָאֵשׁ הַגְּדֹלָה הַזֹּאת
לֹא־אֶרְאֶה עוֹד וְלֹא אָמוּת: וַיֹּאמֶר יהוה אֵלָי הֵיטִיבוּ אֲשֶׁר דִּבֵּרוּ: נָבִיא יז־יח
אָקִים לָהֶם מִקֶּרֶב אֲחֵיהֶם כָּמוֹךָ וְנָתַתִּי דְבָרַי בְּפִיו וְדִבֶּר אֲלֵיהֶם אֵת
כָּל־אֲשֶׁר אֲצַוֶּנּוּ: וְהָיָה הָאִישׁ אֲשֶׁר לֹא־יִשְׁמַע אֶל־דְּבָרַי אֲשֶׁר יְדַבֵּר יט
בִּשְׁמִי אָנֹכִי אֶדְרֹשׁ מֵעִמּוֹ: אַךְ הַנָּבִיא אֲשֶׁר יָזִיד לְדַבֵּר דָּבָר בִּשְׁמִי אֵת כ
אֲשֶׁר לֹא־צִוִּיתִיו לְדַבֵּר וַאֲשֶׁר יְדַבֵּר בְּשֵׁם אֱלֹהִים אֲחֵרִים וּמֵת הַנָּבִיא
הַהוּא: וְכִי תֹאמַר בִּלְבָבֶךָ אֵיכָה נֵדַע אֶת־הַדָּבָר אֲשֶׁר לֹא־דִבְּרוֹ יהוה: כא
אֲשֶׁר יְדַבֵּר הַנָּבִיא בְּשֵׁם יהוה וְלֹא־יִהְיֶה הַדָּבָר וְלֹא יָבֹא הוּא הַדָּבָר אֲשֶׁר כב

14. וְאַתָּה לֹא כֵן נָתַן לְךָ — *But as for you,* (*God*) *has not given you* (*permission*) *as such* ... for the words of the diviners and soothsayers regarding you will not be fulfilled as our Sages say, אֵין מַזָּל לְיִשְׂרָאֵל, *Israel is not affected by planetary influences* (*Shabbos* 156a).

15. אֵלָיו תִּשְׁמָעוּן — *Unto him shall you hearken* ... if he commands you a commandment which is temporary.

21. אֵיכָה נֵדַע אֶת הַדָּבָר — *How shall we know the word* ... when (the prophet) commands the performance of an (extraordinary) temporary commandment, as Elijah did on Mount Carmel (*I Kings*, ch. 18), and as Joshua did when he surrounded Jericho on the Sabbath, and when he commanded the *Kohanim* to carry the ark into the Jordan and stand there until the people crossed over (*Joshua* 6:4-15).

22. וְלֹא יִהְיֶה הַדָּבָר — *If the thing follow not*. Because, even temporarily, no new commandment will be introduced to the masses unless it is accompanied (substantiated) by some sign. For example, (regarding) Joshua, the Jordan divided (*Joshua*, ch. 3) and the walls of Jericho fell (ibid. 6:20). As for Elijah, fire descended from heaven (*I Kings* 18:38). However, regarding the command of the prophet who said to his colleague, הַכֵּינִי נָא, *smite me* (*I Kings* 20:35), that was said to his fellow prophet, who knew it was the word of God; therefore, he was punished when he refused (to obey).

NOTES

חֹשֶׁן, *breastplate*, worn by the *Kohen Gadol*. The will of God was revealed clearly (like the 'light') and His promises 'made perfect,' i.e., verified through the letters inscribed on the breastplate.

14. וְאַתָּה לֹא כֵן נָתַן לְךָ — *But as for you,* (*God*) *has not given you* (*permission*) *as such*. The *Sforno* does not interpret this phrase as meaning 'God, your God has not given you' the right or need to listen to soothsayers and diviners as do other nations. Rather, he explains the sense of the verse thus: Whereas the destiny of other nations is determined by the stars, and therefore they consult stargazers and diviners, the people of Israel are not affected by these heavenly, planetary forces for they are ruled only by God and transcend the מַזָּלוֹת, *planets*. Hence, they are not subject (לֹא כֵן) to the words of the diviners.

21-22. אֵיכָה נֵדַע ... וְלֹא יִהְיֶה הַדָּבָר — *How shall we know ... if the thing follow not*. The *Sforno* interprets these verses as referring to הוֹרָאַת שָׁעָה, *a temporary ruling*, of a Jewish leader, scholar or prophet. He explains that in order to substantiate the validity of such a ruling, it must be accompanied by some

יט א לֹא־דִבְּרוֹ יְהוָה בְּזָדוֹן דִּבְּרוֹ הַנָּבִיא לֹא תָגוּר מִמֶּנּוּ: כִּֽי־
יַכְרִית יְהוָה אֱלֹהֶיךָ אֶת־הַגּוֹיִם אֲשֶׁר יְהוָה אֱלֹהֶיךָ נֹתֵן לְךָ אֶת־אַרְצָם
ב וִירִשְׁתָּם וְיָשַׁבְתָּ בְעָרֵיהֶם וּבְבָתֵּיהֶם: שָׁלוֹשׁ עָרִים תַּבְדִּיל לָךְ בְּתוֹךְ אַרְצְךָ
ג אֲשֶׁר יְהוָה אֱלֹהֶיךָ נֹתֵן לְךָ לְרִשְׁתָּהּ: תָּכִין לְךָ הַדֶּרֶךְ וְשִׁלַּשְׁתָּ אֶת־גְּבוּל
ד אַרְצְךָ אֲשֶׁר יַנְחִילְךָ יְהוָה אֱלֹהֶיךָ וְהָיָה לָנוּס שָׁמָּה כָּל־רֹצֵחַ: וְזֶה דְּבַר
הָרֹצֵחַ אֲשֶׁר־יָנוּס שָׁמָּה וָחָי אֲשֶׁר יַכֶּה אֶת־רֵעֵהוּ בִּבְלִי־דַעַת וְהוּא
ה לֹא־שֹׂנֵא לוֹ מִתְּמֹל שִׁלְשֹׁם: וַאֲשֶׁר יָבֹא אֶת־רֵעֵהוּ בַיַּעַר לַחְטֹב עֵצִים
וְנִדְּחָה יָדוֹ בַגַּרְזֶן לִכְרֹת הָעֵץ וְנָשַׁל הַבַּרְזֶל מִן־הָעֵץ וּמָצָא אֶת־רֵעֵהוּ וָמֵת
ו הוּא יָנוּס אֶל־אַחַת הֶעָרִים־הָאֵלֶּה וָחָי: פֶּן־יִרְדֹּף גֹּאֵל הַדָּם אַחֲרֵי הָרֹצֵחַ
כִּי־יֵחַם לְבָבוֹ וְהִשִּׂיגוֹ כִּי־יִרְבֶּה הַדֶּרֶךְ וְהִכָּהוּ נָפֶשׁ וְלוֹ אֵין מִשְׁפַּט־מָוֶת כִּי
ז לֹא שֹׂנֵא הוּא לוֹ מִתְּמוֹל שִׁלְשׁוֹם: עַל־כֵּן אָנֹכִי מְצַוְּךָ לֵאמֹר שָׁלֹשׁ עָרִים
ח תַּבְדִּיל לָךְ: וְאִם־יַרְחִיב יְהוָה אֱלֹהֶיךָ אֶת־גְּבֻלְךָ כַּאֲשֶׁר נִשְׁבַּע לַאֲבֹתֶיךָ
ט וְנָתַן לְךָ אֶת־כָּל־הָאָרֶץ אֲשֶׁר דִּבֶּר לָתֵת לַאֲבֹתֶיךָ: כִּי־תִשְׁמֹר
אֶת־כָּל־הַמִּצְוָה הַזֹּאת לַעֲשֹׂתָהּ אֲשֶׁר אָנֹכִי מְצַוְּךָ הַיּוֹם לְאַהֲבָה אֶת־יְהוָה
אֱלֹהֶיךָ וְלָלֶכֶת בִּדְרָכָיו כָּל־הַיָּמִים וְיָסַפְתָּ לְךָ עוֹד שָׁלֹשׁ עָרִים עַל הַשָּׁלֹשׁ
י הָאֵלֶּה: וְלֹא יִשָּׁפֵךְ דָּם נָקִי בְּקֶרֶב אַרְצְךָ אֲשֶׁר יְהוָה אֱלֹהֶיךָ נֹתֵן לְךָ נַחֲלָה
וְהָיָה עָלֶיךָ דָּמִים:

XIX

2. שָׁלוֹשׁ עָרִים תַּבְדִּיל — *You shall separate three cities.* After (the Torah) explains the subject of the judges and of the king, the *Kohanim* and the prophets (in the preceding chapters), it now relates the commandments which are the responsibility of the judges and these are: setting aside the cities of refuge, setting the boundaries (of the tribes) (v. 14), the examination of witnesses and the acceptance of their testimony (vs. 15-21). (The *parashah* then speaks of) the commandments which are the responsibility of the king, these being *when you go forth to do battle* (20:1-9), *when you draw close to a city* (20:10-18), *when you shall besiege a city* (20:19-20). (The Torah than proceeds to tell us) of the (responsibility) placed upon the *Kohanim* and judges jointly, namely the matter of the עֶגְלָה עֲרוּפָה — *the heifer whose neck is broken* (21:1-9).

NOTES

special sign, unless the one who is commanded to do a certain act is himself a prophet who is aware that what is being ordered is indeed the word of God.

XIX

2. שָׁלוֹשׁ עָרִים תַּבְדִּיל — *You shall separate three cities*. The *Sforno* explains the continuity of the topics presented from this point until the end of the *sedrah*. The responsibilities of the judges, the king and the *Kohanim* are the unifying theme of these chapters and verses comprising the balance of *parashas Shoftim*. The determination whether a killing was murder or manslaughter, the settling of disputes over boundaries and the subject of witnesses are all matters to be decided by the judges. The waging of war is the responsibility of the king while the ritual of the עֶגְלָה עֲרוּפָה, *the heifer whose neck is broken*, is the responsibility of both the judges and the *Kohanim* (21:4-8).

13. וּבִעַרְתָּ דַם הַנָּקִי מִיִּשְׂרָאֵל . . . וְטוֹב לָךְ — *But you shall do away with the blood of the innocent . . . that it may go well with you*. The *Sforno* explains the phrase *the blood of the innocent* as referring to the Divine punishment which will be visited upon innocent inhabitants of *Eretz*

יא וְכִי־יִהְיֶה אִישׁ שֹׂנֵא לְרֵעֵהוּ וְאָרַב לוֹ וְקָם עָלָיו וְהִכָּהוּ נֶפֶשׁ וָמֵת וְנָס אֶל־
יב אַחַת הֶעָרִים הָאֵל׃ וְשָׁלְחוּ זִקְנֵי עִירוֹ וְלָקְחוּ אֹתוֹ מִשָּׁם וְנָתְנוּ אֹתוֹ בְּיַד
יג גֹּאֵל הַדָּם וָמֵת׃ לֹא־תָחוֹס עֵינְךָ עָלָיו וּבִעַרְתָּ דַם־הַנָּקִי מִיִּשְׂרָאֵל וְטוֹב
ששי יד לָךְ׃ לֹא תַסִּיג גְּבוּל רֵעֲךָ אֲשֶׁר גָּבְלוּ רִאשֹׁנִים בְּנַחֲלָתְךָ
טו אֲשֶׁר תִּנְחַל בָּאָרֶץ אֲשֶׁר יְהוָה אֱלֹהֶיךָ נֹתֵן לְךָ לְרִשְׁתָּהּ׃ לֹא־
יָקוּם עֵד אֶחָד בְּאִישׁ לְכָל־עָוֺן וּלְכָל־חַטָּאת בְּכָל־חֵטְא אֲשֶׁר יֶחֱטָא
טז עַל־פִּי ׀ שְׁנֵי עֵדִים אוֹ עַל־פִּי שְׁלֹשָׁה־עֵדִים יָקוּם דָּבָר׃ כִּי־יָקוּם עֵד־חָמָס
יז בְּאִישׁ לַעֲנוֹת בּוֹ סָרָה׃ וְעָמְדוּ שְׁנֵי־הָאֲנָשִׁים אֲשֶׁר־לָהֶם הָרִיב לִפְנֵי יְהוָה
יח לִפְנֵי הַכֹּהֲנִים וְהַשֹּׁפְטִים אֲשֶׁר יִהְיוּ בַּיָּמִים הָהֵם׃ וְדָרְשׁוּ הַשֹּׁפְטִים הֵיטֵב
יט וְהִנֵּה עֵד־שֶׁקֶר הָעֵד שֶׁקֶר עָנָה בְאָחִיו׃ וַעֲשִׂיתֶם לוֹ כַּאֲשֶׁר זָמַם לַעֲשׂוֹת
כ לְאָחִיו וּבִעַרְתָּ הָרָע מִקִּרְבֶּךָ׃ וְהַנִּשְׁאָרִים יִשְׁמְעוּ וְיִרָאוּ וְלֹא־יֹסִפוּ לַעֲשׂוֹת
כא עוֹד כַּדָּבָר הָרָע הַזֶּה בְּקִרְבֶּךָ׃ וְלֹא תָחוֹס עֵינֶךָ נֶפֶשׁ בְּנֶפֶשׁ עַיִן בְּעַיִן שֵׁן
כ א בְּשֵׁן יָד בְּיָד רֶגֶל בְּרָגֶל׃ כִּי־תֵצֵא לַמִּלְחָמָה עַל־

---

13. וּבִעַרְתָּ דַם הַנָּקִי מִיִּשְׂרָאֵל — *But you shall do away with the blood of the innocent from Israel* . . . the punishment for (shedding) innocent blood, as it says, וְלָאָרֶץ לֹא יְכֻפַּר לַדָּם אֲשֶׁר שֻׁפַּךְ בָּהּ כִּי אִם בְּדַם שֹׁפְכוֹ, *and no expiration can be made for the land for the blood that is shed therein, but by the blood of him that shed it* (Bamidbar 35:33).

וְטוֹב לָךְ — *That it may go well with you.* For the murderer will not be able to murder others, וְהַנִּשְׁאָרִים יִשְׁמְעוּ וְיִרָאוּ, *and those that remain shall hear and fear* (v. 20).

18. וְהִנֵּה עֵד שֶׁקֶר הָעֵד שֶׁקֶר עָנָה בְאָחִיו — *And behold, if the witness is a false witness and has testified falsely against his brother.* His testimony was false and his intent was to testify falsely against his brother. It was not done mistakenly or inadvertently, as is the case of mistaken testimony regarding the hour on a cloudy day, or regarding the intercalation of a month.

XX

1. כִּי תֵצֵא לַמִּלְחָמָה — *When you go forth to battle* . . . outside the Land (of Israel), for were it a מִלְחֶמֶת מִצְוָה, *a war in fulfillment of a commandment*, none would be exempted from military service (lit., return from the order of battle), for even יֵצֵא חָתָן מֵחֶדְרוֹ וְכַלָּה מֵחֻפָּתָהּ, *the bridegroom (would) go forth from his chamber and the bride out of her pavilion* (based on *Joel* 1:16 and tractate *Sotah* 44b).

NOTES

Yisrael if a murderer is not punished. As he proves from the verse in the Book of *Numbers*, when murder goes unpunished, the Land and its inhabitants suffer the consequences, for the blemish of bloodshed is not expiated until the murderer is put to death. Regarding the phrase *that it may go well with you*, the *Sforno* points out that the execution of the murderer will benefit society in a two-fold manner; it will remove a menace from society, and also serve as a deterrent to others.

18. וְהִנֵּה עֵד שֶׁקֶר הָעֵד שֶׁקֶר עָנָה בְאָחִיו — *And behold, if the witness is a false witness and has testified falsely against his brother*. The *Sforno* explains the reason for the repetition of the word שֶׁקֶר, *falsehood*, in this verse. The first refers to the actual testimony of the witness, while the second refers to his motivation.

XX

1. כִּי תֵצֵא לַמִּלְחָמָה — *When you go forth to battle*. The Talmud in tractate *Sotah* (44b)

אֹֽיְבֶ֗ךָ וְֽרָאִ֜יתָ ס֤וּס וָרֶ֙כֶב֙ עַ֚ם רַ֣ב מִמְּךָ֔ לֹ֥א תִירָ֖א מֵהֶ֑ם כִּֽי־יְהוָ֤ה אֱלֹהֶ֙יךָ֙
ב עִמָּ֔ךְ הַמַּֽעַלְךָ֖ מֵאֶ֥רֶץ מִצְרָֽיִם׃ וְהָיָ֕ה כְּקָֽרָבְכֶ֖ם אֶל־הַמִּלְחָמָ֑ה וְנִגַּ֥שׁ הַכֹּהֵ֖ן
ג וְדִבֶּ֥ר אֶל־הָעָֽם׃ וְאָמַ֤ר אֲלֵהֶם֙ שְׁמַ֣ע יִשְׂרָאֵ֔ל אַתֶּ֨ם קְרֵבִ֥ים הַיּ֛וֹם לַמִּלְחָמָ֖ה
עַל־אֹיְבֵיכֶ֑ם אַל־יֵרַ֣ךְ לְבַבְכֶ֗ם אַל־תִּֽירְא֧וּ וְאַֽל־תַּחְפְּז֛וּ וְאַל־תַּֽעַרְצ֖וּ
ד מִפְּנֵיהֶֽם׃ כִּ֚י יְהוָ֣ה אֱלֹֽהֵיכֶ֔ם הַהֹלֵ֖ךְ עִמָּכֶ֑ם לְהִלָּחֵ֥ם לָכֶ֛ם עִם־אֹיְבֵיכֶ֖ם
ה לְהוֹשִׁ֥יעַ אֶתְכֶֽם׃ וְדִבְּר֣וּ הַשֹּׁטְרִים֮ אֶל־הָעָ֣ם לֵאמֹר֒ מִֽי־הָאִ֞ישׁ אֲשֶׁ֨ר
בָּנָ֤ה בַֽיִת־חָדָשׁ֙ וְלֹ֣א חֲנָכ֔וֹ יֵלֵ֖ךְ וְיָשֹׁ֣ב לְבֵית֑וֹ פֶּן־יָמוּת֙ בַּמִּלְחָמָ֔ה וְאִ֥ישׁ
ו אַחֵ֖ר יַחְנְכֶֽנּוּ׃ וּמִֽי־הָאִ֞ישׁ אֲשֶׁר־נָטַ֥ע כֶּ֙רֶם֙ וְלֹ֣א חִלְּל֔וֹ יֵלֵ֖ךְ וְיָשֹׁ֣ב לְבֵית֑וֹ
ז פֶּן־יָמוּת֙ בַּמִּלְחָמָ֔ה וְאִ֥ישׁ אַחֵ֖ר יְחַלְּלֶֽנּוּ׃ וּמִֽי־הָאִ֞ישׁ אֲשֶׁר־אֵרַ֤שׂ אִשָּׁה֙ וְלֹ֣א
ח לְקָחָ֔הּ יֵלֵ֖ךְ וְיָשֹׁ֣ב לְבֵית֑וֹ פֶּן־יָמוּת֙ בַּמִּלְחָמָ֔ה וְאִ֥ישׁ אַחֵ֖ר יִקָּחֶֽנָּה׃ וְיָסְפ֣וּ
הַשֹּׁטְרִים֮ לְדַבֵּ֣ר אֶל־הָעָם֒ וְאָמְר֗וּ מִֽי־הָאִ֤ישׁ הַיָּרֵא֙ וְרַ֣ךְ הַלֵּבָ֔ב יֵלֵ֖ךְ וְיָשֹׁ֣ב
ט לְבֵית֑וֹ וְלֹ֥א יִמַּ֛ס אֶת־לְבַ֥ב אֶחָ֖יו כִּלְבָבֽוֹ׃ וְהָיָ֛ה כְּכַלֹּ֥ת הַשֹּׁטְרִ֖ים לְדַבֵּ֣ר
שביעי י אֶל־הָעָ֑ם וּפָֽקְד֛וּ שָׂרֵ֥י צְבָא֖וֹת בְּרֹ֥אשׁ הָעָֽם׃ כִּֽי־תִקְרַ֣ב

---

5. פֶּן יָמוּת בַּמִּלְחָמָה וְאִישׁ אַחֵר יַחְנְכֶנּוּ — *Lest he die in battle and another man dedicate it.* Perhaps he is guilty of a transgression, the penalty for which is this particular punishment, as explained in the תּוֹכָחָה, *admonition* (28:30). (This, in turn,) will bring harm to his brothers (in battle), for it will turn away their hearts and cause other similar (demoralization).

9. וּפָקְדוּ שָׂרֵי צְבָאוֹת — *And they appointed captains of hosts ...* (only) after the return (exemption) of the returnees, lest one of those chosen as a captain of hosts would be among the ones who return which would cause the hearts of his legion to melt (in fear), as it says, הַךְ הַכַּפְתּוֹר וְיִרְעֲשׁוּ הַסִּפִּים, *Smite the capitals that the thresholds may shake* (*Amos* 9:1).

NOTES

lists three categories of war. One is מִלְחֶמֶת חוֹבָה, *a war of duty*, such as Joshua's conquest of *Eretz Yisrael*. Another is called מִלְחֶמֶת מִצְוָה, *a war in fulfillment of a commandment*, such as the defense of the Land of Israel or a pre-emptive strike against Israel's enemies. Finally, there is מִלְחֶמֶת רְשׁוּת, *an optional war of political nature*, such as the battles of King David against Syria for the purpose of expanding Israel's territory.

The *Sforno* observes that the expression used in this verse כִּי תֵצֵא, *when you go forth*, implies מִלְחֶמֶת רְשׁוּת, an optional war, and only then are the exemptions listed in this *parashah* granted, but were it מִלְחֶמֶת מִצְוָה, a *commanded war*, these exemptions would not be operative, for then everyone must go to war to defend the land and its people.

5. פֶּן יָמוּת בַּמִּלְחָמָה — *Lest he die in battle*. The section of admonition (פָּרָשַׁת הַתּוֹכָחָה) appears in the portion of *Ki Savo*. The Torah there (28:30) speaks of three misfortunes which will befall Israel, and these three experiences are precisely those mentioned in our chapter regarding exemption from military service. One is the betrothal of a woman who is then taken as a wife by another; the second is regarding one who builds a house and another man ultimately dwells in it; and the third speaks of a man who plants a vineyard and another man eventually eats its fruit. The *Sforno* explains that the reason these men are excused is because if one of them were to fall in battle it would be viewed as the fulfillment of the terrible admonition recorded later in the Book of *Deuteronomy* and would arouse fear, dismay and panic in the hearts of the Jewish army. Hence, it is far better that these soldiers be excused, for the sake of the morale of the other soldiers.

9. וּפָקְדוּ שָׂרֵי צְבָאוֹת — *And they appointed captains of hosts*. The *Sforno* explains why the captains were appointed *after* those who were disqualified were discharged. Otherwise,

יא אֶל־עִיר לְהִלָּחֵם עָלֶיהָ וְקָרָאתָ אֵלֶיהָ לְשָׁלוֹם: וְהָיָה אִם־שָׁלוֹם תַּעַנְךָ
יב וּפָתְחָה לָךְ וְהָיָה כָּל־הָעָם הַנִּמְצָא־בָהּ יִהְיוּ לְךָ לָמַס וַעֲבָדוּךָ: וְאִם־לֹא
יג תַשְׁלִים עִמָּךְ וְעָשְׂתָה עִמְּךָ מִלְחָמָה וְצַרְתָּ עָלֶיהָ: וּנְתָנָהּ יהוה אֱלֹהֶיךָ
יד בְּיָדֶךָ וְהִכִּיתָ אֶת־כָּל־זְכוּרָהּ לְפִי־חָרֶב: רַק הַנָּשִׁים וְהַטַּף וְהַבְּהֵמָה וְכֹל
אֲשֶׁר יִהְיֶה בָעִיר כָּל־שְׁלָלָהּ תָּבֹז לָךְ וְאָכַלְתָּ אֶת־שְׁלַל אֹיְבֶיךָ אֲשֶׁר נָתַן
טו יהוה אֱלֹהֶיךָ לָךְ: כֵּן תַּעֲשֶׂה לְכָל־הֶעָרִים הָרְחֹקֹת מִמְּךָ מְאֹד אֲשֶׁר
טז לֹא־מֵעָרֵי הַגּוֹיִם־הָאֵלֶּה הֵנָּה: רַק מֵעָרֵי הָעַמִּים הָאֵלֶּה אֲשֶׁר יהוה אֱלֹהֶיךָ
יז נֹתֵן לְךָ נַחֲלָה לֹא תְחַיֶּה כָּל־נְשָׁמָה: כִּי־הַחֲרֵם תַּחֲרִימֵם הַחִתִּי וְהָאֱמֹרִי
יח הַכְּנַעֲנִי וְהַפְּרִזִּי הַחִוִּי וְהַיְבוּסִי כַּאֲשֶׁר צִוְּךָ יהוה אֱלֹהֶיךָ: לְמַעַן אֲשֶׁר
לֹא־יְלַמְּדוּ אֶתְכֶם לַעֲשׂוֹת כְּכֹל תּוֹעֲבֹתָם אֲשֶׁר עָשׂוּ לֵאלֹהֵיהֶם וַחֲטָאתֶם
יט לַיהוה אֱלֹהֵיכֶם: כִּי־תָצוּר אֶל־עִיר יָמִים רַבִּים לְהִלָּחֵם
עָלֶיהָ לְתָפְשָׂהּ לֹא־תַשְׁחִית אֶת־עֵצָהּ לִנְדֹּחַ עָלָיו גַּרְזֶן כִּי מִמֶּנּוּ תֹאכֵל
כ וְאֹתוֹ לֹא תִכְרֹת הַכִּי הָאָדָם עֵץ הַשָּׂדֶה לָבֹא מִפָּנֶיךָ בַּמָּצוֹר: רַק עֵץ

---

15. הָרְחֹקֹת מִמְּךָ מְאֹד — *Which are very far off from you* ... far from the place where the camp of Israel is situated, because the boundary of Israel is far from it on all sides.

19. לֹא תַשְׁחִית אֶת עֵצָהּ לִנְדֹּחַ עָלָיו גַּרְזֶן — *You shall not destroy its trees, wielding an axe against them.* Do not destroy the tree (just) to wield an axe of destruction upon it, i.e., (for the sole purpose) of doing harm to the inhabitants of that city.

כִּי מִמֶּנּוּ תֹאכֵל — *Because from it you shall eat.* Because the cutting down of trees in a destructive manner is done by armies to harm (the enemy) when they are not certain that they will be victorious and dwell in the land. However, you, who are assured that you will conquer the land and settle in it, must not destroy the fruit-bearing trees.

כִּי מִמֶּנּוּ תֹאכֵל — *Because from it you shall eat.* Without a doubt, you will conquer the land and (ultimately) eat from its trees, provided you do not destroy them.

כִּי הָאָדָם עֵץ הַשָּׂדֶה — *Is then the tree of the field a man?* Is then the tree of the field a man who is capable of submitting to you that the city be besieged on its account, and be forced to surrender because of the siege? This is (obviously) not so, and although it is acceptable to inflict damage upon the inhabitants of a city with implements of war and other kinds of (tactics) so as to besiege the city, since you will not attain (this goal) by destroying the trees, it is improper to destroy them. (Yet, it is still) proper that you destroy the people who dwell in the city.

לָבֹא מִפָּנֶיךָ בַּמָּצוֹר — *To bring under siege before you.* In order that you bring the city under siege before you in a manner that they will (be forced) to give themselves over into your hand.

NOTES

the captain chosen might be discharged for one of the reasons mentioned above, which would have a devastating effect upon the entire army.

19. לֹא תַשְׁחִית אֶת עֵצָהּ . . . כִּי הָאָדָם עֵץ הַשָּׂדֶה — *You shall not destroy its trees ... is then the tree of the field a man?* The *Sforno* interprets this verse, which prohibits the wanton de-

אֲשֶׁר־תֵּדַע כִּי לֹא־עֵץ מַאֲכָל הוּא אֹתוֹ תַשְׁחִית וְכָרָתָּ וּבָנִיתָ מָצוֹר
עַל־הָעִיר אֲשֶׁר־הִוא עֹשָׂה עִמְּךָ מִלְחָמָה עַד רִדְתָּהּ׃

כא
א כִּי־יִמָּצֵא חָלָל בָּאֲדָמָה אֲשֶׁר יהוה אֱלֹהֶיךָ נֹתֵן לְךָ לְרִשְׁתָּהּ נֹפֵל בַּשָּׂדֶה
ב לֹא נוֹדַע מִי הִכָּהוּ׃ וְיָצְאוּ זְקֵנֶיךָ וְשֹׁפְטֶיךָ וּמָדְדוּ אֶל־הֶעָרִים אֲשֶׁר סְבִיבֹת
ג הֶחָלָל׃ וְהָיָה הָעִיר הַקְּרֹבָה אֶל־הֶחָלָל וְלָקְחוּ זִקְנֵי הָעִיר הַהִוא עֶגְלַת בָּקָר
ד אֲשֶׁר לֹא־עֻבַּד בָּהּ אֲשֶׁר לֹא־מָשְׁכָה בְּעֹל׃ וְהוֹרִדוּ זִקְנֵי הָעִיר הַהִוא
אֶת־הָעֶגְלָה אֶל־נַחַל אֵיתָן אֲשֶׁר לֹא־יֵעָבֵד בּוֹ וְלֹא יִזָּרֵעַ וְעָרְפוּ־שָׁם
ה אֶת־הָעֶגְלָה בַּנָּחַל׃ וְנִגְּשׁוּ הַכֹּהֲנִים בְּנֵי לֵוִי כִּי בָם בָּחַר יהוה אֱלֹהֶיךָ
ו לְשָׁרְתוֹ וּלְבָרֵךְ בְּשֵׁם יהוה וְעַל־פִּיהֶם יִהְיֶה כָּל־רִיב וְכָל־נָגַע׃ וְכֹל זִקְנֵי

---

20. רַק עֵץ אֲשֶׁר תֵּדַע כִּי לֹא עֵץ מַאֲכָל הוּא — *Only a tree which you know is not a tree for food.* Although it is a species of tree which is meant for food, if you know that it is old or spoiled (deficient) to such an extent that it cannot produce fruit, and that it is not worthwhile for one to exert himself on its behalf (given its meager productivity), *you may destroy it.*

XXI

4. אֶל נַחַל אֵיתָן — *To a hard* (*rough*) *ravine* . . . where there are no wayfarers.

וְעָרְפוּ . . . אֶת הָעֶגְלָה — *And break the heifer's neck.* This is a death (killing) which is hidden from the eyes of the slain one (i.e., the heifer), to teach us that the killing (of the victim) was, without a doubt, in a place concealed from the eyes of people, and committed by a murderer unknown as a killer to the court, for were he known to them as a murderer, they would have eliminated him (from their midst).

5. לְשָׁרְתוֹ וּלְבָרֵךְ — *To minister unto Him, and to bless* . . . and through them, there will be atonement for the innocent blood and a blessing for the Land.

NOTES

struction of fruit-bearing trees when a city is under siege, as a reasoned two-fold argument. It would be foolhardy to deprive oneself of the produce of the land which is beneficial for the sustenance of its inhabitants, and since Israel is assured of conquering and settling the land, there would be no reason to destroy these fruit-bearing trees. To do so would demonstrate a lack of faith and trust in God's promise that they will conquer *Eretz Yisrael*. Secondly, the Torah argues that a tree, unlike a person, cannot be intimidated into surrendering; hence, what will be accomplished by destroying it? The sense of the words כִּי הָאָדָם עֵץ הַשָּׂדֶה is, 'Certainly a tree is not a person whose destruction can be justified.'

20. רַק עֵץ אֲשֶׁר תֵּדַע כִּי לֹא עֵץ מַאֲכָל הוּא — *Only a tree which you know is not a tree for food*. Based upon the Talmud (*Bava Kama* 91b), the *Sforno* interprets the phrase *which you know is not a tree for food* as meaning: Although it is a fruit-bearing tree, its yield is so meager or its fruit of such inferior quality that even under ordinary circumstances such a tree would be cut down. Therefore, one is permitted to destroy such a tree.

XXI

4. אֶל נַחַל אֵיתָן . . . וְעָרְפוּ . . . אֶת הָעֶגְלָה — *To a hard* (*rough*) *ravine . . . and break the heifer's neck*. The *Sforno* interprets the act of beheading the heifer from the *back* symbolically. Just as the heifer is slain in a manner whereby the one who kills him is not seen, so the murder victim was taken unawares and killed by one whom he did not see, and who was also unknown to the court, and hidden from the eyes of witnesses.

5. לְשָׁרְתוֹ וּלְבָרֵךְ — *To minister unto Him, and to bless*. This phrase seems to be gratuitous in the context of the verse. Why is it necessary to tell us the function of the *Kohen* in connection with the ceremony of the עֶגְלָה עֲרוּפָה? The *Sforno* explains that the Torah is telling us that the *Kohanim* who had been chosen to serve God and bring blessing to the people are

הָעִיר הַהִוא הַקְּרֹבִים אֶל־הֶחָלָל יִרְחֲצוּ אֶת־יְדֵיהֶם עַל־הָעֶגְלָה הָעֲרוּפָה
°שָׁפְכוּ ק׳ מפטיר ז בַנָּחַל: וְעָנוּ וְאָמְרוּ יָדֵינוּ לֹא °שפכה אֶת־הַדָּם הַזֶּה וְעֵינֵינוּ לֹא רָאוּ:
ח כַּפֵּר לְעַמְּךָ יִשְׂרָאֵל אֲשֶׁר־פָּדִיתָ יהוה וְאַל־תִּתֵּן דָּם נָקִי בְּקֶרֶב עַמְּךָ
ט יִשְׂרָאֵל וְנִכַּפֵּר לָהֶם הַדָּם: וְאַתָּה תְּבַעֵר הַדָּם הַנָּקִי מִקִּרְבֶּךָ כִּי־תַעֲשֶׂה
הַיָּשָׁר בְּעֵינֵי יהוה:

וְעַל פִּיהֶם יִהְיֶה כָּל רִיב וְכָל נָגַע — *And according to their word shall every controversy and every plague be . . .* (and) in this manner they are knowledgeable experts in the temperament and ways of man, (being that) they and their fathers have constantly observed human behavior, and perhaps through their knowledge of his ways and deeds, they will recognize who might be sullied by this sin, and (thus) the matter will be revealed.

7. יָדֵינוּ לֹא שָׁפְכוּ — *Our hands have not shed.* We did not allow any known murderer to remain in the land.

וְעֵינֵינוּ לֹא רָאוּ — *Neither have our eyes seen it.* It did not occur in a place where it could be seen, for if there were those who saw (it happen), they would have risen up and testified.

8. כַּפֵּר לְעַמְּךָ — *Grant atonement to Your people.* (May) You grant atonement by the blood of he who shed it, as our Sages say, 'He, who would have been sentenced to execution by the sword, is either delivered to the government or robbers come upon him' (*Kesuvos* 30b).

וְנִכַּפֵּר לָהֶם הַדָּם — *And the blood shall be atoned for them.* It shall be atoned by the law of heaven through the blood of he who shed it, in such a manner that it appears as though he atones by himself.

9. וְאַתָּה תְּבַעֵר — *And you shall purge.* Behold, God the Blessed One, will atone if you do not know who (the killer) is; but if you do know, you must remove him before the law of heaven is effectuated.

NOTES

best fit to make atonement for the shedding of innocent blood.

וְעַל פִּיהֶם — *And according to their word.* The sense of the *Sforno's* interpretation is that since the *Kohanim* in their various duties constantly come into contact with different people, and are aware of people's weaknesses, hence they may be able to detect the murderer.

7. יָדֵינוּ לֹא שָׁפְכוּ — *Our hands have not shed. Rashi* explains that the elders state that the victim was not sent away from the city without food or without being accompanied part of the way. The *Sforno*, however, explains their disclaimer differently. The elders and *Kohanim* proclaim that they did not permit any murderer to remain in the land, but justice was always served and murderers were punished so as to protect society. Hence, this man's blood is not on their hands.

8. כַּפֵּר לְעַמְּךָ — *Grant atonement to Your people*. The Talmud in tractate *Kesuvos* (30b) states that although the Sanhedrin no longer functions, nonetheless, the four forms of capital punishment have not ceased. By this, our Sages mean that a person who is guilty of a crime or transgression punishable by death will be dealt with accordingly through some *apparent* natural method of death. Since a murderer received the punishment of הֶרֶג (execution by the sword) when the court had the authority to impose it, in our case, this man who slew the victim may be executed by the government or killed by robbers — both of whom will do so by the sword. In this manner, he will receive his due through a decree from Heaven.

9. וְאַתָּה תְּבַעֵר — *And you shall purge*. Although the previous verse states that the blood

NOTES

of the victim will be atoned for by the law of heaven, i.e., the murderer will meet his death through Divine justice, nonetheless this is so only if the court cannot ascertain the identity of the killer. If they know his identity they must punish him even though the heifer has been brought and the ritual of atonement performed. The Jerusalem Talmud (*Sotah* 9:6) says: It is written (v. 8), *'and the blood shall be atoned for them,'* (followed by) *'and you shall purge the innocent blood from your midst'* (v. 9). This teaches us that if the murderer is detected after the heifer has been beheaded, nevertheless (the court) shall execute him.

פרשת כי תצא
Parashas Ki Seitzei

י כִּי־תֵצֵא לַמִּלְחָמָה עַל־אֹיְבֶיךָ וּנְתָנוֹ יהוה אֱלֹהֶיךָ בְּיָדֶךָ וְשָׁבִיתָ שִׁבְיוֹ׃
יא־יב וְרָאִיתָ בַּשִּׁבְיָה אֵשֶׁת יְפַת־תֹּאַר וְחָשַׁקְתָּ בָהּ וְלָקַחְתָּ לְךָ לְאִשָּׁה׃ וַהֲבֵאתָהּ
יג אֶל־תּוֹךְ בֵּיתֶךָ וְגִלְּחָה אֶת־רֹאשָׁהּ וְעָשְׂתָה אֶת־צִפָּרְנֶיהָ׃ וְהֵסִירָה
אֶת־שִׂמְלַת שִׁבְיָהּ מֵעָלֶיהָ וְיָשְׁבָה בְּבֵיתֶךָ וּבָכְתָה אֶת־אָבִיהָ וְאֶת־אִמָּהּ
יד יֶרַח יָמִים וְאַחַר כֵּן תָּבוֹא אֵלֶיהָ וּבְעַלְתָּהּ וְהָיְתָה לְךָ לְאִשָּׁה׃ וְהָיָה אִם־לֹא
חָפַצְתָּ בָּהּ וְשִׁלַּחְתָּהּ לְנַפְשָׁהּ וּמָכֹר לֹא־תִמְכְּרֶנָּה בַּכָּסֶף לֹא־תִתְעַמֵּר בָּהּ
טו תַּחַת אֲשֶׁר עִנִּיתָהּ׃ כִּי־תִהְיֶיןָ לְאִישׁ שְׁתֵּי נָשִׁים הָאַחַת
אֲהוּבָה וְהָאַחַת שְׂנוּאָה וְיָלְדוּ־לוֹ בָנִים הָאֲהוּבָה וְהַשְּׂנוּאָה וְהָיָה הַבֵּן הַבְּכֹר
טז לַשְּׂנִיאָה׃ וְהָיָה בְּיוֹם הַנְחִילוֹ אֶת־בָּנָיו אֵת אֲשֶׁר־יִהְיֶה לוֹ לֹא יוּכַל לְבַכֵּר

---

10. כִּי תֵצֵא — *When you go forth (to battle)* . . . outside the Land.

13. וּבָכְתָה אֶת אָבִיהָ וְאֶת אִמָּהּ — *And weep for her father and her mother* . . . so that she relinquish them and thereby find composure (peace of mind) and not think of them any longer, similar to, וְשִׁכְחִי עַמֵּךְ וּבֵית אָבִיךְ, *forget your people and your father's house* (*Psalms* 45:11). But (her) weeping is not for their death, for we would (certainly) not kill her mother.

15. כִּי תִהְיֶיןָ לְאִישׁ שְׁתֵּי נָשִׁים — *If a man have two wives.* Following the military victory, (the Torah) speaks of affairs (affecting) the citizenry of the state. These are: the case of the women and their sons (verse 18) and of livestock (22:1) and ornaments (22:5) and game (22:6) and a building (22:8) and farming and the wearing of garments (22:9-12).

16. לֹא יוּכַל לְבַכֵּר אֶת בֶּן הָאֲהוּבָה עַל פְּנֵי בֶן הַשְּׂנוּאָה הַבְּכֹר — *He may not make the son of the beloved the firstborn before the son of the hated who is the firstborn.* He cannot transfer the birthright of the firstborn from the (rightful) son due to his hatred of this one or the love of that one. However, if he does so because of the

NOTES

10. כִּי תֵצֵא — *When you go forth (to battle).* The expression כִּי תֵצֵא, *when you go forth,* is identical to the phrase used in chapter 20, verse 1. The *Sforno* there comments, as he does here, 'outside the Land,' i.e., of Israel. Just as the rules set forth there regarding military exemptions only apply to a מִלְחֶמֶת רְשׁוּת, *an optional, political war,* so does the law of the אֵשֶׁת יְפַת תֹּאַר, *the woman of goodly form,* only apply to this type of war, as *Rashi* explains in his commentary on this verse. If the battle is conducted in defense of the Land of Israel or to conquer it, then it is a war in fulfillment of a religious imperative (מִלְחֶמֶת מִצְוָה), and under such circumstances neither of these laws (exemption and the woman captive) apply.

13. וּבָכְתָה אֶת אָבִיהָ וְאֶת אִמָּהּ — *And weep for her father and her mother.* The *Ramban* in his commentary on this verse cites the *Rambam* in his *Guide* 3:41, where he explains that 'she should not be forbidden to grieve . . . for those who grieve find solace in weeping and in arousing their sorrow.' The *Sforno* interprets this verse in a similar vein. He also adds that it cannot mean that she weeps for the death of her parents, for her mother was certainly not put to death in battle by the Israelites, even though her father may have fallen in battle. Hence, her grieving is for being taken from her home and family. In all probability, with the passage of time and the catharsis of weeping, she will make peace with her fate.

15. כִּי תִהְיֶיןָ לְאִישׁ — *If a man have.* The *Sforno* explains the continuity of this *parashah.* After discussing the laws of war in chapters 20-21, the Torah now turns its attention to a variety of laws as they affect society in peacetime, these being the law of the firstborn, the disobedient and rebellious son, lost animals and articles, the prohibition of garbing oneself in clothes of the opposite sex, the law of sending away the mother bird before taking the young ones, building a parapet on one's roof, the prohibition of כִּלְאַיִם (mixture of

יז אֶת־בֶּן־הָאֲהוּבָה עַל־פְּנֵי בֶן־הַשְּׂנוּאָה הַבְּכֹר: כִּי אֶת־הַבְּכֹר בֶּן־הַשְּׂנוּאָה
יַכִּיר לָתֶת לוֹ פִּי שְׁנַיִם בְּכֹל אֲשֶׁר־יִמָּצֵא לוֹ כִּי־הוּא רֵאשִׁית אֹנוֹ לוֹ
יח מִשְׁפַּט הַבְּכֹרָה: כִּי־יִהְיֶה לְאִישׁ בֵּן סוֹרֵר וּמוֹרֶה אֵינֶנּוּ
יט שֹׁמֵעַ בְּקוֹל אָבִיו וּבְקוֹל אִמּוֹ וְיִסְּרוּ אֹתוֹ וְלֹא יִשְׁמַע אֲלֵיהֶם: וְתָפְשׂוּ בוֹ
כ אָבִיו וְאִמּוֹ וְהוֹצִיאוּ אֹתוֹ אֶל־זִקְנֵי עִירוֹ וְאֶל־שַׁעַר מְקֹמוֹ: וְאָמְרוּ אֶל־זִקְנֵי
כא עִירוֹ בְּנֵנוּ זֶה סוֹרֵר וּמֹרֶה אֵינֶנּוּ שֹׁמֵעַ בְּקֹלֵנוּ זוֹלֵל וְסֹבֵא: וּרְגָמֻהוּ
כָּל־אַנְשֵׁי עִירוֹ בָאֲבָנִים וָמֵת וּבִעַרְתָּ הָרָע מִקִּרְבֶּךָ וְכָל־יִשְׂרָאֵל יִשְׁמְעוּ
שני כב וְיִרָאוּ: וְכִי־יִהְיֶה בְאִישׁ חֵטְא מִשְׁפַּט־מָוֶת וְהוּמָת
כג וְתָלִיתָ אֹתוֹ עַל־עֵץ: לֹא־תָלִין נִבְלָתוֹ עַל־הָעֵץ כִּי־קָבוֹר תִּקְבְּרֶנּוּ בַּיּוֹם
הַהוּא כִּי־קִלְלַת אֱלֹהִים תָּלוּי וְלֹא תְטַמֵּא אֶת־אַדְמָתְךָ אֲשֶׁר יהוה

---

wickedness of the firstborn son, then it is proper to transfer it (to another son), as our Sages say, 'If his children did not conduct themselves in a proper manner (and that is why he transferred it) he will be remembered for good' (*Bava Basra* 133b). And apparently, this our father Jacob did, as it says, וּבְחַלְּלוֹ יְצוּעֵי אָבִיו נִתְּנָה בְּכֹרָתוֹ לִבְנֵי יוֹסֵף בֶּן יִשְׂרָאֵל, *But since he defiled his father's bed, his birthright was given to the sons of Joseph, the son of Israel* (*I Chronicles* 5:1).

18. סוֹרֵר וּמוֹרֶה — *Disobedient and rebellious* ... because his rebellious (nature) frustrates any hope that he may repent his disobedience.

20. זוֹלֵל וְסֹבֵא — *He is a glutton and a drunkard.* Since a drunkard and glutton becomes impoverished, he (will eventually) rob to satisfy his appetite (lit., 'soul').

23. כִּי קִלְלַת אֱלֹהִים תָּלוּי — *For he that is hung is a reproach to (the image) of God.* Behold, every object that is separated from matter is called *Elohim*, and regarding this species (i.e., man), the essence of the intelligent soul is called צֶלֶם אֱלֹהִים, *the image of God* (*Genesis* 1:27). In a similar manner, the necromanceress said to Saul, אֱלֹהִים רָאִיתִי עֹלִים, *I saw Elohim ascending* (*I Samuel* 28:13). The disgrace brought upon a deceased person after death is shameful to his intelligent soul, which is considered as the essence separated (from matter) that remains after the death of the body, hence it states that it is a reproach to *Elohim*, because allowing the hanging body to remain overnight without burial is shameful to that everlasting essence called *Elohim*.

NOTES

seeds, animals or material) and the commandment of צִיצִית, *fringes*. These are all civil, social and personal regulations and laws.

16. לֹא יוּכַל לְבַכֵּר אֶת בֶּן הָאֲהוּבָה — *He may not make the son of the beloved the firstborn.* The feelings of the father toward the two mothers cannot determine the status of their sons, but the behavior of the sons may well affect their inheritance. The Mishnah cited by the *Sforno* is according to the opinion of R' Simeon ben Gamliel. The Rabbis, however, disagree and are of the opinion that one should not disinherit even a bad son. Note that the *Sforno* in *Genesis* 48:22 gives a different reason for Jacob's decision to grant Joseph a double inheritance which was due Reuben, his firstborn son.

18. סוֹרֵר וּמוֹרֶה — *Disobedient and rebellious.* The *Sforno* explains why the son who is so severely punished is characterized as both *disobedient and rebellious.* Were he not rebellious, there might be hope that he would repent his evil ways. However, his rebellious spirit will prevent him from ever doing so. *Rashi* explains סוֹרֵר as meaning 'turning away from the proper path.'

23. כִּי קִלְלַת אֱלֹהִים תָּלוּי — *For he that is hung is a reproach to (the image) of God.* The *Sforno*

כב

א אֱלֹהֶיךָ נֹתֵן לְךָ נַחֲלָה׃ לֹא־תִרְאֶה אֶת־שׁוֹר אָחִיךָ אוֹ
ב אֶת־שֵׂיוֹ נִדָּחִים וְהִתְעַלַּמְתָּ מֵהֶם הָשֵׁב תְּשִׁיבֵם לְאָחִיךָ׃ וְאִם־לֹא קָרוֹב
אָחִיךָ אֵלֶיךָ וְלֹא יְדַעְתּוֹ וַאֲסַפְתּוֹ אֶל־תּוֹךְ בֵּיתֶךָ וְהָיָה עִמְּךָ עַד דְּרֹשׁ
ג אָחִיךָ אֹתוֹ וַהֲשֵׁבֹתוֹ לוֹ׃ וְכֵן תַּעֲשֶׂה לַחֲמֹרוֹ וְכֵן תַּעֲשֶׂה לְשִׂמְלָתוֹ וְכֵן
תַּעֲשֶׂה לְכָל־אֲבֵדַת אָחִיךָ אֲשֶׁר־תֹּאבַד מִמֶּנּוּ וּמְצָאתָהּ לֹא תוּכַל
ד לְהִתְעַלֵּם׃ לֹא־תִרְאֶה אֶת־חֲמוֹר אָחִיךָ אוֹ שׁוֹרוֹ נֹפְלִים
ה בַּדֶּרֶךְ וְהִתְעַלַּמְתָּ מֵהֶם הָקֵם תָּקִים עִמּוֹ׃ לֹא־יִהְיֶה
כְלִי־גֶבֶר עַל־אִשָּׁה וְלֹא־יִלְבַּשׁ גֶּבֶר שִׂמְלַת אִשָּׁה כִּי תוֹעֲבַת יהוה אֱלֹהֶיךָ
כָּל־עֹשֵׂה אֵלֶּה׃
ו כִּי יִקָּרֵא קַן־צִפּוֹר ׀ לְפָנֶיךָ בַּדֶּרֶךְ בְּכָל־עֵץ ׀ אוֹ עַל־הָאָרֶץ אֶפְרֹחִים אוֹ
בֵיצִים וְהָאֵם רֹבֶצֶת עַל־הָאֶפְרֹחִים אוֹ עַל־הַבֵּיצִים לֹא־תִקַּח הָאֵם עַל־
ז הַבָּנִים׃ שַׁלֵּחַ תְּשַׁלַּח אֶת־הָאֵם וְאֶת־הַבָּנִים תִּקַּח־לָךְ לְמַעַן יִיטַב לָךְ
שלישי ח וְהַאֲרַכְתָּ יָמִים׃ כִּי תִבְנֶה בַּיִת חָדָשׁ וְעָשִׂיתָ מַעֲקֶה

וְלֹא תְטַמֵּא — *That you not defile* ... by causing a spirit of impurity to rest in the place of the unburied dead person.

XXII

3. וְכֵן תַּעֲשֶׂה לְשִׂמְלָתוֹ — *And so shall you do with his garment.* Even though the loss (of a garment) is not as common (as that of animals), do not consider it a deliberate loss (אֲבֵדָה מִדַּעַת).

7. לְמַעַן יִיטַב לָךְ וְהַאֲרַכְתָּ יָמִים — *That it may be well with you and that you may prolong your days.* Behold, by sending away (the mother bird) from the nest, one performs an act of lovingkindness benefiting the masses, (namely) the preservation of the birds of the field who are ownerless property. This is (accomplished) by

NOTES

explains that it is an affront to the soul of man to allow the body which housed that נֶפֶשׁ שִׂכְלִית, *intelligent soul* (also called *Elohim*, reflecting the image of the Divine), to remain in such a disrespectful manner overnight. In his commentary on *Genesis* 1:27, the *Sforno* states that if one attains the level of perfection which is possible to man, then this *image of God* exists even after death. This explains the expression used by the medium of En-dor regarding Samuel when she said, *'I saw Elohim ascending,'* referring to his עֶצֶם נֶפֶשׁ הַשִּׂכְלִית, *the essence of his intelligent soul*, which is immortal. The *Rambam* in his *Guide* (1:70 and 3:27) teaches that the immortality of the soul is achieved by the special knowledge of God attained through man's intellectual power. This is similar to the concept refered to by the *Sforno*, here and in *Genesis*.

XXII

3. וְכֵן תַּעֲשֶׂה לְשִׂמְלָתוֹ — *And so shall you do with his garment*. The first two verses of this chapter speak of livestock that are lost and found. We are commanded to care for these animals and return them to their owner. Now, while it is quite common for animals to wander off, a garment, on the other hand, is rarely *lost* but may well be *abandoned*. If this were the case there is no commandment of הֲשָׁבַת אֲבֵדָה, *return of lost property*, since the owner did so deliberately. This is known as אֲבֵדָה מִדַּעַת, *a conscious loss.* The *Sforno* explains that this is why the Torah uses the word וְכֵן, *'and so' shall you do with his garment;* i.e., do not assume that this article was abandoned and that you are absolved of returning it. Rather, it must be treated as an אֲבֵדָה, *lost property*, and the commandment to return it is applicable.

7. לְמַעַן יִיטַב לָךְ וְהַאֲרַכְתָּ יָמִים — *That it may be well with you and that you may prolong your days*. The Talmud teaches us that there are

ט לְגַגֶּךָ וְלֹא־תָשִׂים דָּמִים בְּבֵיתֶךָ כִּי־יִפֹּל הַנֹּפֵל מִמֶּנּוּ: לֹא־תִזְרַע
כַּרְמְךָ כִּלְאָיִם פֶּן־תִּקְדַּשׁ הַמְלֵאָה הַזֶּרַע אֲשֶׁר תִּזְרָע וּתְבוּאַת
י־יא הַכָּרֶם: לֹא־תַחֲרֹשׁ בְּשׁוֹר־וּבַחֲמֹר יַחְדָּו: לֹא תִלְבַּשׁ
יב שַׁעַטְנֵז צֶמֶר וּפִשְׁתִּים יַחְדָּו: גְּדִלִים תַּעֲשֶׂה־לָּךְ עַל־
יג אַרְבַּע כַּנְפוֹת כְּסוּתְךָ אֲשֶׁר תְּכַסֶּה־בָּהּ: כִּי־יִקַּח אִישׁ
יד אִשָּׁה וּבָא אֵלֶיהָ וּשְׂנֵאָהּ: וְשָׂם לָהּ עֲלִילֹת דְּבָרִים וְהוֹצִא עָלֶיהָ שֵׁם רָע
וְאָמַר אֶת־הָאִשָּׁה הַזֹּאת לָקַחְתִּי וָאֶקְרַב אֵלֶיהָ וְלֹא־מָצָאתִי לָהּ בְּתוּלִים:
טו וְלָקַח אֲבִי הַנַּעֲרָ וְאִמָּהּ וְהוֹצִיאוּ אֶת־בְּתוּלֵי הַנַּעֲרָ אֶל־זִקְנֵי הָעִיר הַשָּׁעְרָה:
טז וְאָמַר אֲבִי הַנַּעֲרָ אֶל־הַזְּקֵנִים אֶת־בִּתִּי נָתַתִּי לָאִישׁ הַזֶּה לְאִשָּׁה וַיִּשְׂנָאֶהָ:
יז וְהִנֵּה־הוּא שָׂם עֲלִילֹת דְּבָרִים לֵאמֹר לֹא־מָצָאתִי לְבִתְּךָ בְּתוּלִים וְאֵלֶּה
יח בְּתוּלֵי בִתִּי וּפָרְשׂוּ הַשִּׂמְלָה לִפְנֵי זִקְנֵי הָעִיר: וְלָקְחוּ זִקְנֵי הָעִיר־הַהִוא
יט אֶת־הָאִישׁ וְיִסְּרוּ אֹתוֹ: וְעָנְשׁוּ אֹתוֹ מֵאָה כֶסֶף וְנָתְנוּ לַאֲבִי הַנַּעֲרָה כִּי

---

sending forth the mother (bird). (The Torah therefore) says that even for such a minor act of lovingkindness, (one will be rewarded) by enjoying the fruits thereof in This World, while the principal remains intact in the World to Come.

8. וְלֹא תָשִׂים דָּמִים בְּבֵיתֶךָ כִּי יִפֹּל הַנֹּפֵל — *That you shall not bring blood upon your house if any man falls from there.* Should it happen that anyone fall from there (i.e., the roof), you will not be (considered) the cause, bringing about that the punishment for (this) blood would be in your house.

13. כִּי יִקַּח אִישׁ אִשָּׁה — *If a man takes himself a wife.* Following the verses regarding society, (the Torah now) speaks of those cautionary laws which are obligatory (to insure) the dwelling of the *Shechinah* (Divine presence) in Israel. (We are to) guard against blemished offspring which causes (the *Shechinah*) to depart, due to unchastity and to the intermingling of disqualified nations (in Israel), (and also) due to the defiling of the camp (of Israel) as it says, *And your camp shall be holy so that He see no unclean thing among you and turn away from your back* (23:15).

NOTES

precepts whose fruits a person enjoys in This World but whose principal remains intact for him in the World to Come (*Shabbos* 127a). Included in these precepts is *gemilas chasadim*, the performance of acts of loving kindness. The *Sforno* interprets the dual expression of לְמַעַן יִיטַב, *that is may be well* and וְהַאֲרַכְתָּ יָמִים, *and that you may prolong your days*, as reflecting this reward of eating the fruits of one's *mitzvos* in this life and also receiving reward in the World to Come. He explains that sending the mother bird away insures the propagation of the birds of the field which benefits all, for whoever wishes can take them since they are not owned by anyone. The Torah considers this a *chesed*, an act of kindness, and therefore promises the reward of טוב, *well-being*, and also that of אֲרִיכוּת יָמִים, *longevity*, which the *Sforno* always interprets to mean the World to Come, i.e., a time of never-ending days.

8. וְלֹא תָשִׂים דָּמִים בְּבֵיתֶךָ כִּי יִפֹּל הַנֹּפֵל — *That you shall not bring blood upon your house if any man fall from there*. The *Sforno* explains the word דָּמִים, *blood*, as meaning the 'punishment for blood' that was shed by the victim who fell from one's roof. Since you built a parapet you are no longer responsible. The sense of the verse is: Make a parapet for your roof and in this manner, you will not be liable for the blood spilled.

13. כִּי יִקַּח אִישׁ אִשָּׁה — *If a man takes himself a wife*. The 'blemished offspring' mentioned by the *Sforno* refers to verses 21-24. The 'intermingling of disqualified nations' refers to chapter 23, verses 4-9 regarding Ammonites and Moabites (prohibited forever), and Edomites and Egyptians (prior to the third generation).

הוֹצִיא֙ שֵׁ֣ם רָ֔ע עַ֖ל בְּתוּלַ֣ת יִשְׂרָאֵ֑ל וְלוֹ־תִהְיֶ֣ה לְאִשָּׁ֔ה לֹא־יוּכַ֥ל לְשַׁלְּחָ֖הּ
כ כָּל־יָמָֽיו׃ וְאִם־אֱמֶ֣ת הָיָ֔ה הַדָּבָ֖ר הַזֶּ֑ה לֹא־נִמְצְא֥וּ בְתוּלִ֖ים
כא לַֽנַּעֲרָֽ׃ וְהוֹצִ֨יאוּ אֶת־הַֽנַּעֲרָ֜ אֶל־פֶּ֣תַח בֵּית־אָבִ֗יהָ וּסְקָלוּהָ֩ אַנְשֵׁ֨י עִירָ֤הּ
בָּֽאֲבָנִים֙ וָמֵ֔תָה כִּֽי־עָשְׂתָ֤ה נְבָלָה֙ בְּיִשְׂרָאֵ֔ל לִזְנ֖וֹת בֵּ֣ית אָבִ֑יהָ וּבִֽעַרְתָּ֥ הָרָ֖ע
כב מִקִּרְבֶּֽךָ׃ כִּֽי־יִמָּצֵ֨א אִ֜ישׁ שֹׁכֵ֣ב ׀ עִם־אִשָּׁ֣ה בְעֻֽלַת־
בַּ֗עַל וּמֵ֙תוּ֙ גַּם־שְׁנֵיהֶ֔ם הָאִ֛ישׁ הַשֹּׁכֵ֥ב עִם־הָאִשָּׁ֖ה וְהָאִשָּׁ֑ה וּבִֽעַרְתָּ֥ הָרָ֖ע
כג מִיִּשְׂרָאֵֽל׃ כִּ֤י יִהְיֶה֙ נַעֲרָ֣ בְתוּלָ֔ה מְאֹרָשָׂ֖ה לְאִ֑ישׁ
כד וּמְצָאָ֥הּ אִ֛ישׁ בָּעִ֖יר וְשָׁכַ֥ב עִמָּֽהּ׃ וְהוֹצֵאתֶ֨ם אֶת־שְׁנֵיהֶ֜ם אֶל־שַׁ֣עַר ׀ הָעִ֣יר
הַהִ֗וא וּסְקַלְתֶּ֨ם אֹתָ֥ם בָּאֲבָנִים֮ וָמֵתוּ֒ אֶת־הַֽנַּעֲרָ֗ עַל־דְּבַר֙ אֲשֶׁ֣ר לֹא־צָעֲקָ֣ה
בָעִ֔יר וְאֶ֨ת־הָאִ֔ישׁ עַל־דְּבַ֥ר אֲשֶׁר־עִנָּ֖ה אֶת־אֵ֣שֶׁת רֵעֵ֑הוּ וּבִֽעַרְתָּ֥ הָרָ֖ע
כה מִקִּרְבֶּֽךָ׃ וְאִם־בַּשָּׂדֶ֞ה יִמְצָ֣א הָאִ֗ישׁ אֶת־הַֽנַּעֲרָ֙
הַמְאֹ֣רָשָׂ֔ה וְהֶחֱזִֽיק־בָּ֥הּ הָאִ֖ישׁ וְשָׁכַ֣ב עִמָּ֑הּ וּמֵ֗ת הָאִ֛ישׁ אֲשֶׁר־שָׁכַ֥ב עִמָּ֖הּ
כו לְבַדּֽוֹ׃ וְלַֽנַּעֲרָ֙ לֹא־תַעֲשֶׂ֣ה דָבָ֔ר אֵ֥ין לַֽנַּעֲרָ֖ חֵ֣טְא מָ֑וֶת כִּ֡י כַּאֲשֶׁר֩ יָק֨וּם אִ֤ישׁ
כז עַל־רֵעֵ֙הוּ֙ וּרְצָח֣וֹ נֶ֔פֶשׁ כֵּ֖ן הַדָּבָ֥ר הַזֶּֽה׃ כִּ֥י בַשָּׂדֶ֖ה מְצָאָ֑הּ צָעֲקָ֗ה הַנַּעֲרָ֙
כח הַמְאֹ֣רָשָׂ֔ה וְאֵ֥ין מוֹשִׁ֖יעַ לָֽהּ׃ כִּֽי־יִמְצָ֣א אִ֗ישׁ נַעֲרָ֤

---

24. אֲשֶׁר עִנָּה אֶת אֵשֶׁת רֵעֵהוּ — *Because he degraded his neighbor's wife.* He oppressed and degraded her from her (status) of fitness and disqualified her from her worthiness (as a wife) to her husband who is his neighbor, similar to נְשֵׁי עַמִּי תְּגָרְשׁוּן מִבֵּית תַּעֲנֻגֶיהָ, *The women of my people you cast out from their pleasant houses* (*Micah* 2:9).

26. אֵין לַנַּעֲרָ חֵטְא מָוֶת — *The girl has no sin worthy of death* . . . even though the end (of the act) was with (her) consent, since the beginning was under duress, she is absolved (of sin) because when she began (to engage) in an unlawful act, her desire compelled her (to continue), as (our Sages) say, "Even if she said, 'Leave him alone, for if he had not (violated me) I would have hired him' " (*Kesuvos* 51b).

כִּי כַּאֲשֶׁר יָקוּם אִישׁ עַל רֵעֵהוּ וּרְצָחוֹ — *For as a man rises up against his neighbor and slays him.* This is not similar to the case of an animal with whom a man lies, of which it is written, וְאֶת הַבְּהֵמָה תַּהֲרֹגוּ, *And you shall slay the animal* (*Lev.* 20:15), because the animal did not resist at all, but this (girl) who was assaulted resisted to the extent of her capability, hence that which occurred to her is akin to that which happens to a murder victim through whom a sin is committed against his will. Therefore, she has no part in this sin at all.

27. צָעֲקָה הַנַּעֲרָ — *The girl cried out.* We judge her favorably.

NOTES

26. אֵין לַנַּעֲרָ חֵטְא מָוֶת — *The girl has no sin worthy of death.* Considering that the verse just stated, *But unto the girl you shall do nothing,* why is it necessary to add these words? The *Sforno* resolves this difficulty by explaining that this is meant to teach us an important principle in Jewish law, namely that תְּחִלָּתָהּ בְּאוֹנֶס וְסוֹפָהּ בְּרָצוֹן פְּטוּרָה, *an act which begins under compulsion, though it terminated with consent, is non-punishable* (*Kesuvos* 51b). This is in accordance with the opinion of *Rava* who says that she is a victim of uncontrollable passion aroused by the act. According to the *Sforno*, the Torah alludes to this reasoning in our verse in saying that she is not considered responsible for her action.

כִּי כַּאֲשֶׁר יָקוּם — *For as a man rises up.* The

כט בְּתוּלָה אֲשֶׁר לֹא־אֹרָשָׂה וּתְפָשָׂהּ וְשָׁכַב עִמָּהּ וְנִמְצָאוּ: וְנָתַן הָאִישׁ הַשֹּׁכֵב
עִמָּהּ לַאֲבִי הַנַּעֲרָ חֲמִשִּׁים כָּסֶף וְלוֹ־תִהְיֶה לְאִשָּׁה תַּחַת אֲשֶׁר עִנָּהּ
כג א לֹא־יוּכַל שַׁלְּחָהּ כָּל־יָמָיו: לֹא־יִקַּח אִישׁ אֶת־אֵשֶׁת אָבִיו
ב וְלֹא יְגַלֶּה כְּנַף אָבִיו: לֹא־יָבֹא פְצוּעַ־דַּכָּה וּכְרוּת שָׁפְכָה
ג בִּקְהַל יְהוָה: לֹא־יָבֹא מַמְזֵר בִּקְהַל יְהוָה גַּם דּוֹר עֲשִׂירִי
ד לֹא־יָבֹא לוֹ בִּקְהַל יְהוָה: לֹא־יָבֹא עַמּוֹנִי וּמוֹאָבִי בִּקְהַל
ה יְהוָה גַּם דּוֹר עֲשִׂירִי לֹא־יָבֹא לָהֶם בִּקְהַל יְהוָה עַד־עוֹלָם: עַל־דְּבַר אֲשֶׁר
לֹא־קִדְּמוּ אֶתְכֶם בַּלֶּחֶם וּבַמַּיִם בַּדֶּרֶךְ בְּצֵאתְכֶם מִמִּצְרָיִם וַאֲשֶׁר שָׂכַר
ו עָלֶיךָ אֶת־בִּלְעָם בֶּן־בְּעוֹר מִפְּתוֹר אֲרַם נַהֲרַיִם לְקַלְלֶךָּ: וְלֹא־אָבָה
יְהוָה אֱלֹהֶיךָ לִשְׁמֹעַ אֶל־בִּלְעָם וַיַּהֲפֹךְ יְהוָה אֱלֹהֶיךָ לְּךָ אֶת־הַקְּלָלָה
ז לִבְרָכָה כִּי אֲהֵבְךָ יְהוָה אֱלֹהֶיךָ: לֹא־תִדְרֹשׁ שְׁלֹמָם וְטֹבָתָם כָּל־יָמֶיךָ
רביעי ח לְעוֹלָם: לֹא־תְתַעֵב אֲדֹמִי כִּי אָחִיךָ הוּא לֹא־תְתַעֵב
ט מִצְרִי כִּי־גֵר הָיִיתָ בְאַרְצוֹ: בָּנִים אֲשֶׁר־יִוָּלְדוּ לָהֶם דּוֹר שְׁלִישִׁי יָבֹא לָהֶם

XXIII

5. אֲשֶׁר לֹא קִדְּמוּ אֶתְכֶם — *They did not (come forth) to meet you.* Both (Ammon and Moab) did not come forth to meet you. However the Moabites did sell them bread and water for money, as it says, *You shall sell me food for money . . . as the children of Esau that dwell in Seir, and the Moabites that dwell in Ar did for me* (2:28,29). The Ammonites did not do so. Nevertheless, the Moabites added transgression to their sin *because they hired against you Balaam,* and therefore . . .

7. לֹא תִדְרֹשׁ שְׁלֹמָם — *You shall not seek their peace* . . . (because) both did not come forth to meet you. Ammon did not even sell you (food) for money, while Moab who did sell (you food) hired Balaam (to curse you).

NOTES

Sforno explains the reason for comparing the act of rape to that of murder. The Torah in *Leviticus* 20:15 commands us to destroy the animal with whom sodomy has been committed. Why then should the betrothed girl, with whom a sin has been committed, be absolved? In what way is she different than the case of the animal with whom a man did lie? The *Sforno* answers that whereas the animal did not resist, it is difficult to imagine that the assaulted girl did not resist, just as we assume that a murder victim does not passively allow himself to be slain. This explains the reason for the Torah's comparison of the rape victim to the murder victim.

27. צָעֲקָה הַנַּעֲרָ — *The girl cried out*. There is no proof that the girl cried out. It is presumed, however, that she did so, for we always give a person the benefit of the doubt and judge one favorably.

XXIII

5-7. אֲשֶׁר לֹא קִדְּמוּ אֶתְכֶם . . . לֹא תִדְרֹשׁ שְׁלֹמָם — *They did not (come forth) to meet you . . . You shall not seek their peace*. Both Ammon and Moab, who were related to the Israelites, refused them hospitality when they journeyed from Egypt to the Promised Land. In one respect, however, the Moabites were more cooperative than the Ammonites. They were at least willing to sell food and water to the Jewish people which the Ammonites refused to do. On the other hand, the Moabites were guilty of hiring Balaam to curse the people of Israel (*Numbers* 22). Hence, each of these nations was guilty of two offenses. Both failed to come forth to meet them and extend a helping hand to the Israelites. In addition the Ammonites refused to even sell them provisions while the Moabites attempted to destroy the people of Israel through Balaam. Therefore, the Torah tells us that we may *not seek*

י בִּקְהַל יְהוָה׃ כִּי־תֵצֵא מַחֲנֶה עַל־אֹיְבֶיךָ וְנִשְׁמַרְתָּ מִכֹּל
יא דָּבָר רָע׃ כִּי־יִהְיֶה בְךָ אִישׁ אֲשֶׁר לֹא־יִהְיֶה טָהוֹר מִקְּרֵה־לָיְלָה וְיָצָא
יב אֶל־מִחוּץ לַמַּחֲנֶה לֹא יָבֹא אֶל־תּוֹךְ הַמַּחֲנֶה׃ וְהָיָה לִפְנוֹת־עֶרֶב יִרְחַץ
יג בַּמָּיִם וּכְבֹא הַשֶּׁמֶשׁ יָבֹא אֶל־תּוֹךְ הַמַּחֲנֶה׃ וְיָד תִּהְיֶה לְךָ מִחוּץ לַמַּחֲנֶה
יד וְיָצָאתָ שָׁמָּה חוּץ׃ וְיָתֵד תִּהְיֶה לְךָ עַל־אֲזֵנֶךָ וְהָיָה בְּשִׁבְתְּךָ חוּץ וְחָפַרְתָּה
טו בָהּ וְשַׁבְתָּ וְכִסִּיתָ אֶת־צֵאָתֶךָ׃ כִּי יְהוָה אֱלֹהֶיךָ מִתְהַלֵּךְ ׀ בְּקֶרֶב מַחֲנֶךָ
לְהַצִּילְךָ וְלָתֵת אֹיְבֶיךָ לְפָנֶיךָ וְהָיָה מַחֲנֶיךָ קָדוֹשׁ וְלֹא־יִרְאֶה בְךָ עֶרְוַת
טז דָּבָר וְשָׁב מֵאַחֲרֶיךָ׃ לֹא־תַסְגִּיר עֶבֶד אֶל־אֲדֹנָיו אֲשֶׁר־

---

15. וְהָיָה מַחֲנֶיךָ קָדוֹשׁ — *And your camp shall be holy* . . . (uncontaminated by) impurity and repulsiveness.

וְלֹא יִרְאֶה בְךָ עֶרְוַת דָּבָר — *So that He see no unclean thing among you* . . . impurity, or body wastes or blemished offspring, as (our Sages) state, 'The Divine Presence (*Shechinah*) only rests upon families of pure birth in Israel' (*Kiddushin* 70b), and (for this reason) they said that all who are recorded in the army list of the kings of the House of David were, without a doubt, of distinguished descent.

וְשָׁב מֵאַחֲרֶיךָ — *And turn away from your back* . . . when you will turn your back on Him and not be concerned for His honor, (by your unseemly conduct) in one of these (areas).

16. לֹא תַסְגִּיר עֶבֶד אֶל אֲדֹנָיו — *You shall not deliver a slave to his master.* After discussing (laws) regarding the army camp, (the Torah) now speaks of matters which occur therein, such as the slave that fled (his master) and the subject of harlots found there (verse 18), so that you may rectify these matters.

NOTES

their peace because their cruel behavior severed their bond of kinship with Israel.

15. וְהָיָה מַחֲנֶיךָ קָדוֹשׁ — *And your camp shall be holy*. The *Sforno* explains that a state of sanctity cannot exist in an environment of טוּמְאָה — impurity — or מְאוּס — that which is abhorrent and loathsome. The former phrase refers to verse 12 which speaks of a man who had a nocturnal emission causing uncleanness. The latter phrase refers to verse 14 which speaks of the need for hygienic practice in the army camp of Israel when they are in the field.

וְלֹא יִרְאֶה בְךָ עֶרְוַת דָּבָר — *So that He see no unclean thing among you*. The Torah teaches us that when the Jewish army goes forth to do battle against their enemies, God accompanies them. His presence in their midst is their source of strength and protection, hence they must refrain from any unseemly behavior which might drive the *Shechinah* away. The *Sforno* explains that עֶרְוַת דָּבָר, usually translated nakedness, means *an unclean thing*, and encompasses impurity in the ritual sense (טוּמְאָה), unhygienic conditions and פְּסוּלֵי זֶרַע, i.e., flaws in the pedigree of Jewish families. Our Sages have taught us that God's Presence in the camp of Israel depends upon the pure geneology of its armed forces. Indeed, the officers' corps of the king's army was so carefully screened that the very fact that one was chosen was proof that there was no blemish in his family tree.

15. וְשָׁב מֵאַחֲרֶיךָ — *And turn away from your back*. The *Sforno* interprets the word אַחֲרֶיךָ as meaning *your back*. He therefore explains the verse thus: When you will be insensitive to your moral conduct on the field of battle, it is tantamount to turning your back on God. He will then, in turn, leave your midst and abandon you.

16. לֹא תַסְגִּיר עֶבֶד — *You shall not deliver a slave*. The *Sforno* clarifies the continuity of these verses (16-18) with the preceding one, which has as its theme the sanctity of the Jewish camp. It apparently was not unusual

יז יִנָּצֵל אֵלֶיךָ מֵעִם אֲדֹנָיו: עִמְּךָ יֵשֵׁב בְּקִרְבְּךָ בַּמָּקוֹם אֲשֶׁר־יִבְחַר בְּאַחַד
יח שְׁעָרֶיךָ בַּטּוֹב לוֹ לֹא תּוֹנֶנּוּ: לֹא־תִהְיֶה קְדֵשָׁה מִבְּנוֹת
יט יִשְׂרָאֵל וְלֹא־יִהְיֶה קָדֵשׁ מִבְּנֵי יִשְׂרָאֵל: לֹא־תָבִיא אֶתְנַן זוֹנָה וּמְחִיר
כֶּלֶב בֵּית יהוה אֱלֹהֶיךָ לְכָל־נֶדֶר כִּי תוֹעֲבַת יהוה אֱלֹהֶיךָ גַּם־
כ שְׁנֵיהֶם: לֹא־תַשִּׁיךְ לְאָחִיךָ נֶשֶׁךְ כֶּסֶף נֶשֶׁךְ אֹכֶל נֶשֶׁךְ

---

20. לֹא תַשִּׁיךְ לְאָחִיךָ — *You shall not give interest to your brother.* After admonishing us to guard against those things which cause the *Shechinah* (Divine Presence) to depart from Israel, (the Torah) now advocates diverse acts of kindness which cause (the *Shechinah*) to dwell in Israel — these being the matters of interest and vows (verse 22), including charity that one is obligated to fulfill promptly since the poor are ever present. (Also included are) the subject of the laborer's eating (rights) (verses 25-26) and the matter of a גֵּט, *bill of divorce*, which should properly be given only because of (a wife's) immoral behavior (chapter 24, verse 1) so as to remove the obstacle of bastardy, but not for other reasons (of incompatibility), as it says, כִּי ה׳ הֵעִיד בֵּינְךָ וּבֵין אֵשֶׁת נְעוּרֶיךָ אֲשֶׁר אַתָּה בָּגַדְתָּה בָּהּ, *Because* HASHEM *has been witness between you and the wife of your youth against whom you dealt treacherously* (*Malachi* 2:14). (Also mentioned are) the kindness due a new wife which is to cheer her (24:5) and the act of kindness by not taking *the lower or the upper millstone for a pledge* (24:6) and guarding against those who harm the public, namely kidnappers who commonly abduct minors (24:7). (Furthermore, we are cautioned) to take heed regarding the plague of leprosy by isolating the lepers so that their affliction does not harm (society) through contagion; and to guard against talebearing and slander (24:9); and the kindness due a borrower (24:10-13), a hired servant (24:14-15) and the poor during the harvest (24:19-21). (Likewise, we are told about) pity shown to the one who receives stripes (25:2-3); and (the compassion shown) to an animal when he treads out the corn, and (concern) for one who dies without offspring that his name not be wiped out (25:5-10).

NOTES

for a slave who accompanied his master into battle to use that opportunity to flee and seek refuge in the enemy's camp. It also was quite common for an army to have 'camp followers', which is alluded to in verse 18. The *Sforno* explains that the Torah cautions us to give sanctuary to the fugitive slave, and also to remove 'camp followers' from the midst of our camp, so as to insure the high moral standards governing a Jewish army.

20. לֹא תַשִּׁיךְ לְאָחִיךָ — *You shall not give interest to your brother*. Similar to his commentary on 21:15 and 22:13, the *Sforno's* intent is to explain the thematic continuity of the balance of this chapter, as well as the chapters which follow. A superficial reading of these verses gives one an impression of a series of disjointed verses. The *Sforno* however teaches us that, beginning with this verse, and continuing through chapter 25, the Torah is presenting a blueprint for moral excellence and ethical behavior, which will insure God's presence in our midst. These precepts are varied and manifold, including, among others, sensitivity to the financial problems confronting a borrower, concern for the laborer and for the poor, proper grounds for divorce, regard for the happiness of one's wife, compassion for a person punished by the court and pity for an animal treading corn. All these are meant to refine one's character and heighten one's sense of righteousness, compassion, and social responsibility. The unifying theme of these varied verses is that of *chesed*, loving-kindness, in the community of Israel, which will cause the *Shechinah* to dwell in their midst.

כא כָּל־דָּבָר אֲשֶׁר יִשָּׁךְ: לַנָּכְרִי תַשִּׁיךְ וּלְאָחִיךָ לֹא תַשִּׁיךְ לְמַעַן יְבָרֶכְךָ
יְהוָה אֱלֹהֶיךָ בְּכֹל מִשְׁלַח יָדֶךָ עַל־הָאָרֶץ אֲשֶׁר־אַתָּה בָא־שָׁמָּה
כב לְרִשְׁתָּהּ: כִּי־תִדֹּר נֶדֶר לַיהוָה אֱלֹהֶיךָ לֹא תְאַחֵר לְשַׁלְּמוֹ
כג כִּי־דָרֹשׁ יִדְרְשֶׁנּוּ יְהוָה אֱלֹהֶיךָ מֵעִמָּךְ וְהָיָה בְךָ חֵטְא: וְכִי תֶחְדַּל לִנְדֹּר
כד לֹא־יִהְיֶה בְךָ חֵטְא: מוֹצָא שְׂפָתֶיךָ תִּשְׁמֹר וְעָשִׂיתָ כַּאֲשֶׁר נָדַרְתָּ לַיהוָה
חמישי כה אֱלֹהֶיךָ נְדָבָה אֲשֶׁר דִּבַּרְתָּ בְּפִיךָ: כִּי תָבֹא בְּכֶרֶם רֵעֶךָ
כו וְאָכַלְתָּ עֲנָבִים כְּנַפְשְׁךָ שָׂבְעֶךָ וְאֶל־כֶּלְיְךָ לֹא תִתֵּן: כִּי
תָבֹא בְּקָמַת רֵעֶךָ וְקָטַפְתָּ מְלִילֹת בְּיָדֶךָ וְחֶרְמֵשׁ לֹא תָנִיף עַל קָמַת
כד א רֵעֶךָ: כִּי־יִקַּח אִישׁ אִשָּׁה וּבְעָלָהּ וְהָיָה אִם־לֹא תִמְצָא־

---

21. לַנָּכְרִי תַשִּׁיךְ — *Unto a stranger you may give interest.* Give him the interest if you made such a condition with him, and do not renege.

וּלְאָחִיךָ לֹא תַשִּׁיךְ — *But to your brother you shall not give interest.* Even though you made such a condition with him and agreed to pay him (interest), it is forbidden for you to give him interest.

לְמַעַן יְבָרֶכְךָ ה׳ אֱלֹהֶיךָ — *So that HASHEM your God may bless you . . .* when you will not act treacherously with the stranger and (thus) not profane the Name of God.

22. כִּי תִדֹּר נֶדֶר לַה׳ אֱלֹהֶיךָ — *When you make a vow to HASHEM your God.* Behold, it is proper that your word be trustworthy with all. However, that which you vow to God your God, not only are you obligated to pay it, but, in addition, the payment must be made without delay.

כִּי דָרֹשׁ יִדְרְשֶׁנּוּ — *For* (*God your God*) *will surely require it* (*of you*). For if you delay payment, He will collect it from you against your will.

וְהָיָה בְךָ חֵטְא — *And it will be* (*reckoned*) *as a sin to you.* And that which you do pay in this manner will still carry with it punishment for the delay.

NOTES

21. לַנָּכְרִי תַשִּׁיךְ — *Unto a stranger you may give interest.* The phrase לַנָּכְרִי תַשִּׁיךְ is translated by some as meaning 'unto a stranger (i.e., a non-Jew) you may lend with interest.' *Rashi*, based on the Talmud (*Bava Metzia* 70), interprets this phrase as adding a prohibition against lending a fellow Jew money on interest (לָאו הַבָּא מִכְּלַל עֲשֵׂה). The *Sforno*, however, interprets this phrase to mean that if a Jew borrowed money from a non-Jew and agreed to pay him interest (which is permissible), he is bound to do so and must not go back on his word.

וּלְאָחִיךָ לֹא תַשִּׁיךְ — *But to your brother you shall not give interest.* This prohibition seems to be a repetition of that which is already written in verse 20. The *Sforno*, however, explains that the purpose of this added prohibition is to teach us that even if there was a mutual agreement between the lender and borrower, nonetheless it is prohibited for one Jew to pay interest to another Jew.

לְמַעַן יְבָרֶכְךָ — *So that HASHEM your God may bless you.* The *Sforno* explains that the blessing of God is not a reward for refraining from paying interest to a fellow Jew or accepting it, but for meeting your obligation by paying the stranger what you have pledged. By so doing, you earn God's blessing because if you were to deal dishonestly in this situation, you would be desecrating His Name.

22. וְהָיָה בְךָ חֵטְא — *And it will be* (*reckoned*) *as a sin to you.* Since God exacts payment for a vow, even against the will of the person who made that vow, why then does the Torah say that, nevertheless, it is reckoned as a sin? The *Sforno* explains that the sin is for the *delay* in redeeming one's pledge, which is an added violation regarding a vow made to God, unlike a vow made to man which does not carry this penalty.

חֵ֖ן בְּעֵינָ֑יו כִּי־מָ֤צָא בָהּ֙ עֶרְוַ֣ת דָּבָ֔ר וְכָ֨תַב לָ֜הּ סֵ֤פֶר כְּרִיתֻת֙ וְנָתַ֣ן בְּיָדָ֔הּ
ב־ג וְשִׁלְּחָ֖הּ מִבֵּיתֽוֹ׃ וְיָצְאָ֖ה מִבֵּית֑וֹ וְהָלְכָ֖ה וְהָיְתָ֥ה לְאִישׁ־אַחֵֽר׃ וּשְׂנֵאָהּ֮ הָאִ֣ישׁ
הָאַחֲרוֹן֒ וְכָ֨תַב לָ֜הּ סֵ֤פֶר כְּרִיתֻת֙ וְנָתַ֣ן בְּיָדָ֔הּ וְשִׁלְּחָ֖הּ מִבֵּית֑וֹ א֣וֹ כִ֤י יָמוּת֙
ד הָאִ֣ישׁ הָאַחֲר֔וֹן אֲשֶׁר־לְקָחָ֥הּ ל֖וֹ לְאִשָּֽׁה׃ לֹֽא־יוּכַ֣ל בַּעְלָ֣הּ הָרִאשׁ֣וֹן
אֲשֶֽׁר־שִׁ֠לְּחָהּ לָשׁ֨וּב לְקַחְתָּ֜הּ לִהְי֧וֹת ל֣וֹ לְאִשָּׁ֗ה אַחֲרֵי֙ אֲשֶׁ֣ר הֻטַּמָּ֔אָה
כִּֽי־תוֹעֵבָ֥ה הִ֖וא לִפְנֵ֣י יְהוָ֑ה וְלֹ֤א תַחֲטִיא֙ אֶת־הָאָ֔רֶץ אֲשֶׁר֙ יְהוָ֣ה אֱלֹהֶ֔יךָ
ששי ה נֹתֵ֥ן לְךָ֖ נַחֲלָֽה׃ כִּֽי־יִקַּ֥ח אִישׁ֙ אִשָּׁ֣ה חֲדָשָׁ֔ה לֹ֤א יֵצֵא֙ בַּצָּבָ֔א
וְלֹא־יַעֲבֹ֥ר עָלָ֖יו לְכָל־דָּבָ֑ר נָקִ֞י יִהְיֶ֤ה לְבֵיתוֹ֙ שָׁנָ֣ה אֶחָ֔ת וְשִׂמַּ֖ח אֶת־אִשְׁתּ֥וֹ
ו־ז אֲשֶׁר־לָקָֽח׃ לֹא־יַחֲבֹ֥ל רֵחַ֖יִם וָרָ֑כֶב כִּי־נֶ֖פֶשׁ ה֥וּא חֹבֵֽל׃ כִּֽי־
יִמָּצֵ֣א אִ֗ישׁ גֹּנֵ֨ב נֶ֤פֶשׁ מֵאֶחָיו֙ מִבְּנֵ֣י יִשְׂרָאֵ֔ל וְהִתְעַמֶּר־בּ֖וֹ וּמְכָר֑וֹ וּמֵת֙ הַגַּנָּ֣ב
ח הַה֔וּא וּבִעַרְתָּ֥ הָרָ֖ע מִקִּרְבֶּֽךָ׃ הִשָּׁ֧מֶר בְּנֶֽגַע־הַצָּרַ֛עַת
לִשְׁמֹ֥ר מְאֹ֖ד וְלַעֲשׂ֑וֹת כְּכֹל֩ אֲשֶׁר־יוֹר֨וּ אֶתְכֶ֜ם הַכֹּהֲנִ֧ים הַלְוִיִּ֛ם כַּאֲשֶׁ֥ר
ט צִוִּיתִ֖ם תִּשְׁמְר֥וּ לַעֲשֽׂוֹת׃ זָכ֕וֹר אֵ֧ת אֲשֶׁר־עָשָׂ֛ה יְהוָ֥ה אֱלֹהֶ֖יךָ לְמִרְיָ֑ם בַּדֶּ֖רֶךְ
י בְּצֵאתְכֶ֥ם מִמִּצְרָֽיִם׃ כִּֽי־תַשֶּׁ֥ה בְרֵעֲךָ֖ מַשַּׁ֣את מְא֑וּמָה לֹֽא־
יא תָבֹ֥א אֶל־בֵּית֖וֹ לַעֲבֹ֥ט עֲבֹטֽוֹ׃ בַּח֖וּץ תַּעֲמֹ֑ד וְהָאִ֗ישׁ אֲשֶׁ֤ר אַתָּה֙ נֹשֶׁ֣ה ב֔וֹ
יב יוֹצִ֥יא אֵלֶ֛יךָ אֶֽת־הָעֲב֖וֹט הַחֽוּצָה׃ וְאִם־אִ֥ישׁ עָנִ֖י ה֑וּא לֹ֥א תִשְׁכַּ֖ב בַּעֲבֹטֽוֹ׃
יג הָשֵׁב֩ תָּשִׁ֨יב ל֤וֹ אֶת־הָעֲבוֹט֙ כְּב֣וֹא הַשֶּׁ֔מֶשׁ וְשָׁכַ֥ב בְּשַׂלְמָת֖וֹ וּבֵֽרְכֶ֑ךָּ וּלְךָ֙
שביעי יד תִּהְיֶ֣ה צְדָקָ֔ה לִפְנֵ֖י יְהוָ֥ה אֱלֹהֶֽיךָ׃ לֹא־תַעֲשֹׁ֥ק שָׂכִ֖יר עָנִ֣י
טו וְאֶבְי֑וֹן מֵאַחֶ֕יךָ א֧וֹ מִגֵּרְךָ֛ אֲשֶׁ֥ר בְּאַרְצְךָ֖ בִּשְׁעָרֶֽיךָ׃ בְּיוֹמוֹ֩ תִתֵּ֨ן שְׂכָר֜וֹ
וְלֹא־תָב֧וֹא עָלָ֣יו הַשֶּׁ֗מֶשׁ כִּ֤י עָנִי֙ ה֔וּא וְאֵלָ֕יו ה֥וּא נֹשֵׂ֖א אֶת־נַפְשׁ֑וֹ

XXIV

4. כִּי תוֹעֵבָה הִוא — *For it is an abomination* ... because this is a (subtle) way of introducing adultery; the husband divorces his wife at the request of the adulterer so that he may take her for a period of time, (after which) her first husband will take her back.

10. מַשַּׁאת מְאוּמָה — *Any matter of loan* ... even a porter's fee or similar (payment for service), if converted into a loan, as our Sages have received the tradition (regarding this prohibition) (*Bava Metzia* 115a).

NOTES

XXIV

4. כִּי תוֹעֵבָה הִוא — *For it is an abomination*. The *Sforno* explains why the Torah is so adamantly opposed to the remarriage of a woman to her first husband, after she has married another man and subsequently been divorced by him. Because of collusion or pressure, this could be but a subterfuge for the transfer of a woman for a limited period of time to another man, which would still be adultery cloaked in 'legitimacy' and therefore an act of abomination in the eyes of God.

10. מַשַּׁאת מְאוּמָה — *Any matter of loan*. The *Sforno* in his commentary is referring to our Sages' interpretation of this verse, *You shall not go into his house to take his pledge*. They exclude from this prohibition the seizing and holding of goods in pledge in order to obtain satisfaction of a claim for services rendered, as opposed to collection of a debt by the lender. The latter is prohibited while the former is permitted. However, if one's obligation for services rendered, such as porterage, rent or repairs was converted into a loan, then it is covered by the prohibition set forth in our verse. This they learn from the expression מְאוּמָה — *any matter* — of loan.

טז וְלֹא־יִקְרָא עָלֶיךָ אֶל־יהוה וְהָיָה בְךָ חֵטְא׃ לֹא־יוּמְתוּ אָבוֹת
יז עַל־בָּנִים וּבָנִים לֹא־יוּמְתוּ עַל־אָבוֹת אִישׁ בְּחֶטְאוֹ יוּמָתוּ׃ לֹא
יח תַטֶּה מִשְׁפַּט גֵּר יָתוֹם וְלֹא תַחֲבֹל בֶּגֶד אַלְמָנָה׃ וְזָכַרְתָּ כִּי עֶבֶד הָיִיתָ

---

16. לֹא יוּמְתוּ אָבוֹת עַל בָּנִים וּבָנִים לֹא יוּמְתוּ עַל אָבוֹת — *The fathers shall not be put to death for the children, neither shall the children be put to death for the fathers . . .* even for the sin of rebellion against the monarchy, where customarily the king executed the children (of the rebels) so that they should not rise up against the monarchy in (a spirit) of enmity, as we find, הָכִינוּ לְבָנָיו מַטְבֵּחַ בַּעֲוֹן אֲבוֹתָם בַּל יָקֻמוּ וְיָרְשׁוּ אָרֶץ וּמָלְאוּ פְנֵי תֵבֵל עָרִים, *Prepare slaughter for his children, for the iniquity of their fathers; that they rise not up and possess the earth, and fill the face of the world with enemies* (*Isaiah* 14:21), the meaning of עָרִים being *enemies*, similar to וַיְהִי עָרֶךָ, *has become your enemy* (*I Samuel* 28:16). Nonetheless, the Torah prohibits our kings to slay (sons) in this manner (lit., this for this), for God has pity on His people. Now, King Amaziah of Judah fulfilled this (law), as it says, וַיְהִי כַּאֲשֶׁר חָזְקָה הַמַּמְלָכָה עָלָיו וַיַּהֲרֹג אֶת עֲבָדָיו הַמַּכִּים אֶת הַמֶּלֶךְ אָבִיו. וְאֶת בְּנֵיהֶם לֹא הֵמִית כִּי כַכָּתוּב בַּתּוֹרָה בְּסֵפֶר מֹשֶׁה אֲשֶׁר צִוָּה ה׳ לֵאמֹר לֹא יָמוּתוּ אָבוֹת עַל בָּנִים וּבָנִים לֹא יָמוּתוּ עַל אָבוֹת, *Now it came to pass when the kingdom was established unto him that he slew his servants who had killed the king, his father. But he did not put their children to death but did according to that which is written in the law in the Book of Moses, as* HASHEM *commanded saying, 'The fathers shall not die for the children and children shall not die for the fathers'* (*II Chronicles* 25:3,4).

17. לֹא תַטֶּה מִשְׁפַּט גֵּר יָתוֹם — *You shall not pervert the justice due to a stranger or to an orphan.* At the time of argument, be careful (in dealing with) these (litigants) that their claims not be 'closed off' due to their humble standing. (Indeed,) under proper circumstances (you should fulfill the precept of) פְּתַח פִּיךָ לְאִלֵּם, *Open your mouth for the dumb* (*Proverbs* 31:8).

NOTES

16. וּבָנִים לֹא יוּמְתוּ עַל אָבוֹת — *Neither shall the children be put to death for the fathers.* The *Sforno* cites the verse from *Isaiah* to prove his thesis that it was common for a king to wipe out the entire family of a rebel leader. The word עָרִים usually means 'cities'; however, in the context of this particular verse it means *enemies,* as the *Sforno* stresses. Other commentators translate the word עָרֶךָ in *I Samuel* 28:16, where Samuel tells Saul that God has become his enemy, to mean 'the supporter of your adversary.' This interpretation would be appropriate for the verse in *Isaiah* as well, for it would mean that the survivors of a man executed by the king for treason would someday vigorously support another rebellion.

The verses cited by the *Sforno* from *Chronicles* relate the story of Amaziah, whose father Joash, King of Judah, was assassinated by his own servants to avenge the blood of the sons of Jehoida, the *Kohen Gadol,* who were slain at his behest. Amaziah, in turn, executed the murderers of his father, but spared the lives of their sons, in accordance with the teaching of the Torah.

17. לֹא תַטֶּה מִשְׁפַּט גֵּר יָתוֹם — *You shall not pervert the justice due to a stranger or to an orphan.* Although the Torah already cautioned the court not 'to twist judgment' (16:19), the *Sforno* explains that this is a special warning to the judge not to embarrass or intimidate people of humble standing in any way, lest it lead to the perversion of justice. Indeed, just the opposite is demanded of the court — to assist unfortunate and humble people in presenting their case properly. This concept is found in the Talmud in a number of cases such as a woman's claim for payment of her *kesubah* (*Kesuvos* 36a), and in suggesting to one in possession of property that he should claim he had a שְׁטָר, *deed,* but lost it (*Bava Basra* 41a) and also in suggesting to a creditor that he write a *pruzbul* which would permit him to collect a debt after the Sabbatical year (*Gittin* 37b). The responsibility of the court to suggest these claims to one

בְּמִצְרַיִם וַיִּפְדְּךָ יְהֹוָה אֱלֹהֶיךָ מִשָּׁם עַל־כֵּן אָנֹכִי מְצַוְּךָ לַעֲשׂוֹת אֶת־הַדָּבָר
יט הַזֶּה: כִּי תִקְצֹר קְצִירְךָ בְשָׂדֶךָ וְשָׁכַחְתָּ עֹמֶר בַּשָּׂדֶה לֹא
תָשׁוּב לְקַחְתּוֹ לַגֵּר לַיָּתוֹם וְלָאַלְמָנָה יִהְיֶה לְמַעַן יְבָרֶכְךָ יְהֹוָה אֱלֹהֶיךָ
כ בְּכֹל מַעֲשֵׂה יָדֶיךָ: כִּי תַחְבֹּט זֵיתְךָ לֹא תְפַאֵר אַחֲרֶיךָ
כא לַגֵּר לַיָּתוֹם וְלָאַלְמָנָה יִהְיֶה: כִּי תִבְצֹר כַּרְמְךָ לֹא תְעוֹלֵל אַחֲרֶיךָ לַגֵּר
כב לַיָּתוֹם וְלָאַלְמָנָה יִהְיֶה: וְזָכַרְתָּ כִּי־עֶבֶד הָיִיתָ בְּאֶרֶץ מִצְרָיִם עַל־כֵּן אָנֹכִי
כה א מְצַוְּךָ לַעֲשׂוֹת אֶת־הַדָּבָר הַזֶּה: כִּי־יִהְיֶה רִיב בֵּין
אֲנָשִׁים וְנִגְּשׁוּ אֶל־הַמִּשְׁפָּט וּשְׁפָטוּם וְהִצְדִּיקוּ אֶת־הַצַּדִּיק וְהִרְשִׁיעוּ
ב אֶת־הָרָשָׁע: וְהָיָה אִם־בִּן הַכּוֹת הָרָשָׁע וְהִפִּילוֹ הַשֹּׁפֵט וְהִכָּהוּ לְפָנָיו כְּדֵי
ג רִשְׁעָתוֹ בְּמִסְפָּר: אַרְבָּעִים יַכֶּנּוּ לֹא יֹסִיף פֶּן־יֹסִיף לְהַכֹּתוֹ עַל־אֵלֶּה מַכָּה
ד־ה רַבָּה וְנִקְלָה אָחִיךָ לְעֵינֶיךָ: לֹא־תַחְסֹם שׁוֹר בְּדִישׁוֹ: כִּי־
יֵשְׁבוּ אַחִים יַחְדָּו וּמֵת אַחַד מֵהֶם וּבֵן אֵין־לוֹ לֹא־תִהְיֶה אֵשֶׁת־הַמֵּת

---

18. וַיִּפְדְּךָ ה׳ אֱלֹהֶיךָ מִשָּׁם — *And* HASHEM *your God redeemed you from there.* He observed your humble situation and acted toward you (leniently) לִפְנִים מִשּׁוּרַת הַדִּין, *not according to the strict letter of the law,* so as to redeem you, as it says, *and He saw our affliction, and our toil and our oppression* (26:7).

22. וְזָכַרְתָּ כִּי עֶבֶד הָיִיתָ — *And you shall remember that you were a slave.* And then (in Egypt) you (also) needed gleanings at harvest time.

XXV

2. וְהִפִּילוֹ הַשֹּׁפֵט — *And the judge shall cause him to be bound.* He shall be bound to a pillar (for flogging).

3. מַכָּה רַבָּה — *With many stripes . . .* which he is unable to bear.

וְנִקְלָה אָחִיךָ — *Then your brother would be degraded.* He may become soiled with excrement or water (urine) due to the great pain.

NOTES

of these parties, if they are otherwise unaware of these suggestions, is based on the verse in *Proverbs* quoted by the *Sforno*, פְּתַח פִּיךָ לְאִלֵּם, *Open your mouth for the dumb.*

18. וַיִּפְדְּךָ ה׳ אֱלֹהֶיךָ — *And* HASHEM *your God redeemed you.* The *Sforno* explains the sequence of verses 17-18 thus: You are obligated to be concerned for, and helpful to, the weak and unfortunate, even to the extent of arguing their case in court. Although this may seem to be bending evenhanded justice, nonetheless, we do not always follow the strict letter of the law, just as God tempered justice in Egypt. We did not deserve redemption, but even so, God saw our difficulties and redeemed us.

XXV

2. וְהִפִּילוֹ הַשֹּׁפֵט — *And the judge shall cause him to be bound. Rashi,* based on the Talmud in *Makos* 22b, explains that the accused is whipped 'neither standing (erect) or sitting but bending over.' The Sages state that he is bound to a pole and leans over it while receiving the stripes. This is alsc the intent of the *Sforno* in his interpretation of the expression וְהִפִּילוֹ הַשֹּׁפֵט, which should not be translated 'cause him to lie down' (A.V.) but '*cause him to be bound* to a pillar.'

3. מַכָּה רַבָּה וְנִקְלָה אָחִיךָ — *With many stripes then your brother would be degraded.* According to our Sages, the accused's physical condition must be evaluated to determine whether he can reasonably and safely receive the full number of thirty-nine lashes. Otherwise, he is only given the maximum amount that he can bear. Were he to be whipped excessively, he may not be able to withstand the lashes, and he may also be unable to

ו הַחוּצָה לְאִישׁ זָר יְבָמָהּ יָבֹא עָלֶיהָ וּלְקָחָהּ לוֹ לְאִשָּׁה וְיִבְּמָהּ: וְהָיָה הַבְּכוֹר
ז אֲשֶׁר תֵּלֵד יָקוּם עַל־שֵׁם אָחִיו הַמֵּת וְלֹא־יִמָּחֶה שְׁמוֹ מִיִּשְׂרָאֵל: וְאִם־לֹא
יַחְפֹּץ הָאִישׁ לָקַחַת אֶת־יְבִמְתּוֹ וְעָלְתָה יְבִמְתּוֹ הַשַּׁעְרָה אֶל־הַזְּקֵנִים
ח וְאָמְרָה מֵאֵין יְבָמִי לְהָקִים לְאָחִיו שֵׁם בְּיִשְׂרָאֵל לֹא אָבָה יַבְּמִי: וְקָרְאוּ־לוֹ
ט זִקְנֵי־עִירוֹ וְדִבְּרוּ אֵלָיו וְעָמַד וְאָמַר לֹא חָפַצְתִּי לְקַחְתָּהּ: וְנִגְּשָׁה יְבִמְתּוֹ
אֵלָיו לְעֵינֵי הַזְּקֵנִים וְחָלְצָה נַעֲלוֹ מֵעַל רַגְלוֹ וְיָרְקָה בְּפָנָיו וְעָנְתָה וְאָמְרָה
י כָּכָה יֵעָשֶׂה לָאִישׁ אֲשֶׁר לֹא־יִבְנֶה אֶת־בֵּית אָחִיו: וְנִקְרָא שְׁמוֹ בְּיִשְׂרָאֵל
יא בֵּית חֲלוּץ הַנָּעַל: כִּי־יִנָּצוּ אֲנָשִׁים יַחְדָּו אִישׁ וְאָחִיו וְקָרְבָה

---

5. וְיִבְּמָהּ — *And he shall remove her 'yevamah' status.* (This word means) he shall remove her status of יְבָמָה, *deceased brother's wife*, and she will become his wife regarding all matters, even (to the point of) necessitating a divorce through a bill of divorcement and her return to him (through remarriage).

6. וְלֹא יִמָּחֶה שְׁמוֹ מִיִּשְׂרָאֵל — *That his name not be blotted out of Israel* . . . for (regarding) the child (born of this union), God, the Exalted One, will consider it as if (the *mitzvah*) of 'be fruitful and multiply' was fulfilled by the deceased, since he was born as a result of the (original) marriage of the deceased, and the deceased's brother (יָבָם) does not have to remarry her. This commandment was rejected by Onen because of the animosity he had toward his brother, and because of this the anger (of God) was poured out on him.

9. כָּכָה יֵעָשֶׂה לָאִישׁ אֲשֶׁר לֹא יִבְנֶה אֶת בֵּית אָחִיו — *So shall it be done to the man who does not build up his brother's house.* He is worthy of this disgrace since he refused to complete the building up of the house which his brother began by marrying (this woman), as our Sages say, "I never called my wife, 'my wife'; but I called my wife, 'my house' " (*Shabbos* 118b).

NOTES

control his bodily functions, thereby causing him public embarrassment and shame. This is not the intent of מַלְקוֹת, *lashes*, which are meant to punish him and not to degrade him.

5. וְיִבְּמָהּ — *And he shall remove her 'yevamah' status.* The word וְיִבְּמָהּ is written after the phrase, וּלְקָחָהּ לוֹ לְאִשָּׁה, *and take her unto himself as a wife*, hence it cannot mean יִבּוּם, the act of levirate marriage. The *Sforno* therefore explains it to mean that he has changed her status from that of יְבָמָה to that of wife by continuing the previous marriage of his brother. A new act of קִידוּשִׁין, *marriage*, is not necessary, and she now becomes his wife in the full sense of the law. To dissolve this relationship, a divorce will be necessary and not *chalitzah* (the ceremony of the removal of the shoe), which is done to dissolve the levirate bonds of a couple that does not perform *yibum*.

6. וְלֹא יִמָּחֶה שְׁמוֹ מִיִּשְׂרָאֵל — *That his name not be blotted out of Israel.* As mentioned in the previous note, when the brother of the deceased takes his sister-in-law in levirate marriage, it is unnecessary to perform another act of קִידוּשִׁין (marriage). This indicates that their relationship is considered to be a continuation of the original marriage, hence the child born of their union is considered as the child of the deceased brother. The *Sforno* brings proof of this by citing the story of Er and Onen, the sons of Judah. After Er's death, Onen refused to impregnate his brother's wife, because he *knew that the seed would not be his* (*Genesis* 38:9). The *Sforno* explains that Onen's refusal was motivated by his hostility toward his brother.

9. בֵּית אָחִיו — *His brother's house.* The *Sforno* interprets the word בֵּית, *house*, as meaning *wife*. The sense of the verse is that this man (the יָבָם), by refusing to perform a levirate marriage (יִבּוּם), failed to continue and complete the marriage of his deceased brother with this woman. She is called בֵּית אָחִיו, *his brother's house*, in keeping with Rabbi Yosi's statement that he always referred to his wife as *his house*,

אֵ֫שֶׁת הָאֶחָ֔ד לְהַצִּ֥יל אֶת־אִישָׁ֖הּ מִיַּ֣ד מַכֵּ֑הוּ וְשָׁלְחָ֣ה יָדָ֔הּ וְהֶחֱזִ֖יקָה בִּמְבֻשָֽׁיו:
יב־יג וְקַצֹּתָ֖ה אֶת־כַּפָּ֑הּ לֹ֥א תָח֖וֹס עֵינֶֽךָ: לֹא־יִהְיֶ֥ה לְךָ֛ בְּכִֽיסְךָ֖
יד אֶ֣בֶן וָאָ֑בֶן גְּדוֹלָ֖ה וּקְטַנָּֽה: לֹא־יִהְיֶ֥ה לְךָ֛ בְּבֵיתְךָ֖ אֵיפָ֣ה וְאֵיפָ֑ה גְּדוֹלָ֖ה וּקְטַנָּֽה:
טו אֶ֣בֶן שְׁלֵמָ֤ה וָצֶ֙דֶק֙ יִֽהְיֶה־לָּ֔ךְ אֵיפָ֧ה שְׁלֵמָ֛ה וָצֶ֖דֶק יִֽהְיֶה־לָּ֑ךְ לְמַ֙עַן֙ יַאֲרִ֣יכוּ
טז יָמֶ֔יךָ עַ֚ל הָאֲדָמָ֔ה אֲשֶׁר־יְהוָ֥ה אֱלֹהֶ֖יךָ נֹתֵ֥ן לָֽךְ: כִּ֧י תוֹעֲבַ֛ת יְהוָ֥ה אֱלֹהֶ֖יךָ
כָּל־עֹ֣שֵׂה אֵ֑לֶּה כֹּ֖ל עֹ֥שֵׂה עָֽוֶל:
מפטיר יז־יח זָכ֕וֹר אֵ֛ת אֲשֶׁר־עָשָׂ֥ה לְךָ֖ עֲמָלֵ֑ק בַּדֶּ֖רֶךְ בְּצֵאתְכֶ֥ם מִמִּצְרָֽיִם: אֲשֶׁ֨ר קָֽרְךָ֜
בַּדֶּ֗רֶךְ וַיְזַנֵּ֤ב בְּךָ֙ כָּל־הַנֶּחֱשָׁלִ֣ים אַֽחֲרֶ֔יךָ וְאַתָּ֖ה עָיֵ֣ף וְיָגֵ֑עַ וְלֹ֥א יָרֵ֖א אֱלֹהִֽים:
יט וְהָיָ֡ה בְּהָנִ֣יחַ יְהוָ֣ה אֱלֹהֶ֣יךָ ׀ לְ֠ךָ֠ מִכָּל־אֹ֨יְבֶ֜יךָ מִסָּבִ֗יב בָּאָ֙רֶץ֙ אֲשֶׁ֣ר־יְהוָֽה
אֱ֠לֹהֶ֠יךָ נֹתֵ֨ן לְךָ֤ נַחֲלָה֙ לְרִשְׁתָּ֔הּ תִּמְחֶה֙ אֶת־זֵ֣כֶר עֲמָלֵ֔ק מִתַּ֖חַת הַשָּׁמָ֑יִם לֹ֖א
תִּשְׁכָּֽח:

---

11. וְקָרְבָה אֵשֶׁת הָאֶחָד לְהַצִּיל אֶת אִישָׁהּ — *And the wife of one approached to save her husband.* Even though it is a religious duty for a יְבָמָה (sister-in-law of the brother — יָבָם) to disgrace the brother of her husband who was not concerned for her husband (to honor his name), (nonetheless) a woman is not permitted to shame (the man) who is fighting with her husband.

14. לֹא יִהְיֶה לְךָ בְּבֵיתְךָ אֵיפָה וְאֵיפָה — *You shall not have in your house two kinds of measures.* After mentioning the ways by which the *Shechinah* (Divine Presence) comes to dwell in Israel, (the Torah now) warns that God not only hates perversion of justice but He also hates the one who has (in his house) implements whose purpose are to perpetrate injustice. (Therefore), it is necessary to remove those articles, lest His spirit abhor us, as it says, *for all that do such things are an abomination to HASHEM your God* (verse 16).

19. תִּמְחֶה אֶת זֵכֶר עֲמָלֵק — *Blot out the remembrance of Amalek . . . ox and sheep, camel and ass*, as was commanded to Saul (*I Samuel* 15:3). (This is commanded) in order to take revenge of Amalek for their arrogant behavior toward God, the Exalted One, (in the manner of those who) act zealously on behalf of His Honor.

NOTES

because she was the principal figure of the household, as *Rashi* explains there (*Shabbos* 118b).

11. וְקָרְבָה אֵשֶׁת הָאֶחָד — *And the wife of one approached*. The *Sforno's* commentary on this verse explains the juxtaposition of this law, regarding the wife who comes to the defense of her husband, to the ceremony of removing the shoe of the יָבָם and spitting on the ground in front of his face (חֲלִיצָה). Though the latter act is prescribed by Jewish law, the former is inexcusable and the woman must pay monetary compensation for the shame she caused to that man.

14. לֹא יִהְיֶה לְךָ בְּבֵיתְךָ אֵיפָה וְאֵיפָה — *You shall not have in your house two kinds of measures.* The *Sforno's* commentary clarifies the meaning of the phrases כָּל עֹשֵׂה אֵלֶּה, *all who do these (things)*, and כֹּל עֹשֵׂה עָוֶל, *all that do unrighteousness*, both found in verse 16. The former refers to the *means* of committing fraud, while the latter refers to the actual *act* of injustice.

19. תִּמְחֶה אֶת זֵכֶר עֲמָלֵק — *Blot out the remembrance of Amalek*. To *blot out the remembrance* denotes total annihilation, including livestock, which the *Sforno* proves from the verse in the Book of *Samuel*. The expression 'arrogant behavior' reflects the teaching of our Sages regarding Amalek. They were the first nation to challenge God's people after the Exodus from Egypt. The *Sforno*, therefore, states that it is incumbent upon Israel to remember what Amalek did, and to avenge God's honor by blotting them out.

פרשת כי תבוא
Parashas KI Savo

כו א וְהָיָה֙ כִּֽי־תָב֣וֹא אֶל־הָאָ֔רֶץ אֲשֶׁר֙ יְהוָ֣ה אֱלֹהֶ֔יךָ נֹתֵ֥ן לְךָ֖ נַחֲלָ֑ה וִֽירִשְׁתָּ֖הּ
ב וְיָשַׁ֥בְתָּ בָּֽהּ׃ וְלָקַחְתָּ֞ מֵרֵאשִׁ֣ית ׀ כָּל־פְּרִ֣י הָאֲדָמָ֗ה אֲשֶׁ֨ר תָּבִ֧יא מֵֽאַרְצְךָ֛
אֲשֶׁ֨ר יְהוָ֧ה אֱלֹהֶ֛יךָ נֹתֵ֥ן לָ֖ךְ וְשַׂמְתָּ֣ בַטֶּ֑נֶא וְהָֽלַכְתָּ֙ אֶל־הַמָּק֔וֹם אֲשֶׁ֤ר יִבְחַר֙
ג יְהוָ֣ה אֱלֹהֶ֔יךָ לְשַׁכֵּ֥ן שְׁמ֖וֹ שָֽׁם׃ וּבָאתָ֙ אֶל־הַכֹּהֵ֔ן אֲשֶׁ֥ר יִהְיֶ֖ה בַּיָּמִ֣ים הָהֵ֑ם
וְאָמַרְתָּ֣ אֵלָ֗יו הִגַּ֤דְתִּי הַיּוֹם֙ לַיהוָ֣ה אֱלֹהֶ֔יךָ כִּי־בָ֙אתִי֙ אֶל־הָאָ֔רֶץ אֲשֶׁ֨ר
ד נִשְׁבַּ֧ע יְהוָ֛ה לַאֲבֹתֵ֖ינוּ לָ֥תֶת לָֽנוּ׃ וְלָקַ֧ח הַכֹּהֵ֛ן הַטֶּ֖נֶא מִיָּדֶ֑ךָ וְהִנִּיח֕וֹ לִפְנֵ֕י

XXVI

2. מֵרֵאשִׁית כָּל פְּרִי הָאֲדָמָה אֲשֶׁר תָּבִיא מֵאַרְצְךָ — *The choicest of all the fruit of the ground which you shall bring in from your land . . .* the choicest of all its fruits, similar to, וְרֵאשִׁית שְׁמָנִים יִמְשָׁחוּ, *and anoint themselves with chief* (רֵאשִׁית) *ointments* (*Amos* 6:6), and נְקֻבֵי רֵאשִׁית הַגּוֹיִם, *who are named chief* (רֵאשִׁית) *of the nations* (ibid. 6:1). Now, the choicest (fruit) are the seven species with which *Eretz Yisrael* is praised, as we learn from tradition (*Bikurim* 1:3). This (verse) is an explanation of that which is written in *Exodus* 23:19, רֵאשִׁית בִּכּוּרֵי אַדְמָתְךָ תָּבִיא, *The choicest first fruits of your land shall you bring.* (The Torah now) explains that when it is written, *the choicest first fruits of your land*, the intent was that you bring the first of the choicest fruits of your land, namely from the seven species for which it is praised.

3. אֶל הַכֹּהֵן אֲשֶׁר יִהְיֶה בַּיָּמִים הָהֵם — *To the Kohen that shall be in those days.* Even though he is not great in wisdom, you shall not refrain from addressing him with honor by saying, ה׳ אֱלֹהֶיךָ, *HASHEM your God*, and although this (expression) is not used except for men of renown such as kings and prophets, nonetheless it is proper to speak to him with deference since when you bring the first fruits to him, it is as though you are offering a gift to God, the Exalted One, Who is the owner of the land.

הִגַּדְתִּי הַיּוֹם — *I have declared this day.* I declared to all through this action (of bringing the first fruits), similar to, כִּי הִגַּדְתָּ הַיּוֹם כִּי אֵין לְךָ שָׂרִים וַעֲבָדִים, *for you have declared this day that you regard neither princes or servants* (*II Samuel* 19:7)

כִּי בָאתִי אֶל הָאָרֶץ — *That I have come to the Land . . .* that I came from another land to this land.

אֲשֶׁר נִשְׁבַּע ה׳ לַאֲבֹתֵינוּ לָתֶת לָנוּ — *Which HASHEM swore to our fathers to give to us . . .* As it says, וְנָתַתִּי לְךָ וּלְזַרְעֲךָ אַחֲרֶיךָ, *And I will give unto you and your seed after you* (*Genesis* 17:8). Therefore, I, the stranger, who came to this land as a sojourner by virtue of His gift, have brought the first fruits as befitting one who gives land to another as a gift or as a tenancy.

NOTES

XXVI

2. מֵרֵאשִׁית כָּל פְּרִי הָאֲדָמָה — *The choicest of all the fruit of the ground. Rashi* points out that the expression *'of* the first' rather than *'the* first' implies that not all fruits are subject to this law of בִּכּוּרִים, *first fruits.* This commandment only applies to the seven species for which *Eretz Yisrael* is praised, i.e., wheat, barley, grapes, figs, pomegrantes, olives and dates, which are listed in *Deut.* 8:8 (See *Bikurim* 1:3). The *Sforno*, however, interprets the word רֵאשִׁית as meaning *choicest* while בִּכּוּרִים means *first.* Our verse is an amplification of the verse in *Exodus* 23:19 where the Torah commands us to bring the choicest first fruits to the Temple in Jerusalem. Indeed, the verses from *Amos* quoted by the *Sforno* in his commentary on this verse are identical to those cited by him in his commentary on the verse in *Exodus.* The usage of the word רֵאשִׁית in *Amos* substantiates that its meaning is not *first* or *beginning* but *choicest.*

3. אֶל הַכֹּהֵן אֲשֶׁר יִהְיֶה . . . אֲשֶׁר נִשְׁבַּע ה׳ לַאֲבֹתֵינוּ לָתֶת לָנוּ — *To the Kohen that shall be . . . which HASHEM swore to our fathers to give to us.* The *Sforno* explains that the first fruits are not

ה מִזְבַּח יהוה אֱלֹהֶיךָ: וְעָנִיתָ וְאָמַרְתָּ לִפְנֵי ׀ יהוה אֱלֹהֶיךָ אֲרַמִּי אֹבֵד אָבִי
ו וַיֵּרֶד מִצְרַיְמָה וַיָּגָר שָׁם בִּמְתֵי מְעָט וַיְהִי־שָׁם לְגוֹי גָּדוֹל עָצוּם וָרָב: וַיָּרֵעוּ
ז אֹתָנוּ הַמִּצְרִים וַיְעַנּוּנוּ וַיִּתְּנוּ עָלֵינוּ עֲבֹדָה קָשָׁה: וַנִּצְעַק אֶל־יהוה אֱלֹהֵי
אֲבֹתֵינוּ וַיִּשְׁמַע יהוה אֶת־קֹלֵנוּ וַיַּרְא אֶת־עָנְיֵנוּ וְאֶת־עֲמָלֵנוּ וְאֶת־לַחֲצֵנוּ:
ח וַיּוֹצִאֵנוּ יהוה מִמִּצְרַיִם בְּיָד חֲזָקָה וּבִזְרֹעַ נְטוּיָה וּבְמֹרָא גָּדֹל וּבְאֹתוֹת
ט וּבְמֹפְתִים: וַיְבִאֵנוּ אֶל־הַמָּקוֹם הַזֶּה וַיִּתֶּן־לָנוּ אֶת־הָאָרֶץ הַזֹּאת אֶרֶץ זָבַת
י חָלָב וּדְבָשׁ: וְעַתָּה הִנֵּה הֵבֵאתִי אֶת־רֵאשִׁית פְּרִי הָאֲדָמָה אֲשֶׁר־נָתַתָּה לִּי

---

4. וְהִנִּיחוֹ לִפְנֵי מִזְבַּח ה׳ אֱלֹהֶיךָ — *And set it down before the altar of* HASHEM *your God* . . . to demonstrate and declare that the first fruits are not brought to the *Kohen* but to God the Blessed One, and He in turn gives them to the *Kohen*, together with the other priestly gifts.

5. אֲרַמִּי אֹבֵד אָבִי — *A wandering Aramean was my father.* Behold, my father Jacob was, for a period, a wandering Aramean (a wanderer in Aram) who had no permanent home, and therefore he was not prepared to establish a nation fit to inherit a land.

6. וַיְעַנּוּנוּ וַיִּתְּנוּ עָלֵינוּ עֲבֹדָה קָשָׁה — *And afflicted us and placed upon us hard labor.* And even after they became a nation, they were unfit to receive any gift because they were slaves, and 'whatsoever a slave possesses belongs to his master' (*Pesachim* 88b).

9. וַיִּתֶּן לָנוּ אֶת הָאָרֶץ הַזֹּאת — *And gave us this land.* And after we came forth into freedom, we had no portion of land wherein to dwell, (but) He gave us this (land), which is a choice land flowing with milk and honey.

10. וְעַתָּה — *And now.* Now that I know how great is Your goodness and kindness to us, that You made us into a nation worthy to inherit a land, and delivered us into freedom in a manner that we are able to receive a gift which will be ours, and You gave us this (land) which is the most lovely of all lands and the choicest of all places.

הִנֵּה הֵבֵאתִי אֶת רֵאשִׁית פְּרִי הָאֲדָמָה אֲשֶׁר נָתַתָּה לִּי ה׳ — *Behold, I have brought the first of the fruit of the land which You,* HASHEM, *have given me.* I have brought the choicest fruit of that land which You gave unto me, to offer thanks to Your Name for it.

NOTES

meant to be a gift for the *Kohen*, but symbolically are an offering of thanksgiving to the Almighty for giving us the Land of Israel. This act is meant to declare our recognition that God is the master of the Land and had He not given us *Eretz Yisrael*, we would have no legitimate right to it. This thought is developed further in the following verses.

5. אֲרַמִּי אֹבֵד אָבִי — *A wandering Aramean was my father. Rashi*, based on Onkelos, interprets this to mean, 'an Aramean (Laban) planned to destroy my father (Jacob).' The *Sforno*, however, as does Ibn Ezra, interprets this expression as meaning, 'While living in Aram, my father Jacob was destitute and without a permanent home.' This statement is included in the *Bikurim* ceremony, to indicate that the forging of Jacob's family into a nation and their eventual inheritance of the Land of Israel was not a natural, logical development, but came to pass because it was the will of the Almighty. This thought is further expanded upon in the *Sforno's* commentary on verses 6 and 9.

10. וְעַתָּה — *And now.* The *Sforno* explains that three concepts are incorporated in this one word וְעַתָּה, *and now*, pronounced by the Israelite when he brings his offering of first fruits to God. They are: 1) that He fashioned us into a nation; 2) that He liberated us so that as free men we were capable of receiving a gift, unlike a slave who has no such legal

יא יְהוָה וְהִנַּחְתּוֹ לִפְנֵי יְהוָה אֱלֹהֶיךָ וְהִשְׁתַּחֲוִיתָ לִפְנֵי יְהוָה אֱלֹהֶיךָ׃ וְשָׂמַחְתָּ
בְכָל־הַטּוֹב אֲשֶׁר נָתַן־לְךָ יְהוָה אֱלֹהֶיךָ וּלְבֵיתֶךָ אַתָּה וְהַלֵּוִי וְהַגֵּר אֲשֶׁר
שני יב בְּקִרְבֶּךָ׃ כִּי תְכַלֶּה לַעְשֵׂר אֶת־כָּל־מַעְשַׂר תְּבוּאָתְךָ
בַּשָּׁנָה הַשְּׁלִישִׁת שְׁנַת הַמַּעֲשֵׂר וְנָתַתָּה לַלֵּוִי לַגֵּר לַיָּתוֹם וְלָאַלְמָנָה וְאָכְלוּ
יג בִשְׁעָרֶיךָ וְשָׂבֵעוּ׃ וְאָמַרְתָּ לִפְנֵי יְהוָה אֱלֹהֶיךָ בִּעַרְתִּי הַקֹּדֶשׁ מִן־הַבַּיִת וְגַם
נְתַתִּיו לַלֵּוִי וְלַגֵּר לַיָּתוֹם וְלָאַלְמָנָה כְּכָל־מִצְוָתְךָ אֲשֶׁר צִוִּיתָנִי לֹא־עָבַרְתִּי

---

13. בִּעַרְתִּי הַקֹּדֶשׁ מִן הַבַּיִת — *I have removed the sacred things from the house.* (Because) of our sins and the wicked deeds of our fathers, the sacred service was denied to the firstborn (of Israel), who were originally deemed worthy to receive the offerings (תְּרוּמָה) and tithes (מַעְשְׂרוֹת), as it says, וָאֲטַמֵּא אוֹתָם בְּמַתְּנוֹתָם בְּהַעֲבִיר כָּל פֶּטֶר רָחַם, *And I defiled them by their gifts in that they caused all that opens the womb to pass (through the fire)* (*Ezekiel* 20:26). This is the וִדּוּי מַעֲשֵׂר, *confession of the tithe*, mentioned by our Sages (*Maaser Shani* 5:10).

וְגַם נְתַתִּיו לַלֵּוִי — *And although I have given it to the Levite.* The meaning of גַם (in this verse) is akin to the meaning of although, similar to, גַּם הָיִיתִי הַלַּיְלָה לְאִישׁ וְגַם יָלַדְתִּי בָנִים, *even if I should be this night with a man and even should I bear sons* (*Ruth* 1:12). Therefore, this is what he says: I confess that my transgression is great (and) I have caused the sacred things to be removed from the house, and although I have given them to the Levites and to others according to Your commandment, (nonetheless) I pray that You look down (from heaven) for good and not for evil, which, considering my transgression, would be fitting.

NOTES

right; and 3) that He gave us this outstanding beautiful land.

13. בִּעַרְתִּי הַקֹּדֶשׁ מִן הַבַּיִת וְגַם נְתַתִּיו לַלֵּוִי — *I have removed the sacred things from the house and although I have given it to the Levite etc.* The expression קֹדֶשׁ, *sacred things*, refers to the מַעֲשֵׂר שֵׁנִי, *second tithe*, and כֶּרֶם רְבָעִי, *the growth of the vineyard in the fourth year*, which must be removed from the house in the fourth year of the Sabbatical cycle. It also refers to מַעֲשֵׂר רִאשׁוֹן, the *first tithe*, and the מַעֲשֵׂר עָנִי, *tithe for the poor*. The Sages call the statement made at the time of בִּעוּר, *removal*, by the term וִדּוּי מַעַשְׂרוֹת, *confession*. Since the term וִדּוּי means 'confession of sins,' it is difficult to understand why this term is applied to a statement of one's fulfillment of his obligations, including the careful observance of the order and manner of the disposal of these tithes (see Rashi's commentary on this verse). The Sforno explains the reason for the term וִדּוּי. The original intent of God was that the firstborn in Israel be the ones to serve Him. Only after the sin of the Golden Calf was this privilege and responsibility transferred to the Levites and *Kohanim* (see *Sforno* on *Numbers* 3:13). Hence, had Israel not sinned, both *terumah* and *maaseros* would not have been given to the *Kohanim* and Levites, but would have remained in each Jewish home for it would have rightfully belonged to the בְּכוֹר, *firstborn*, of each household. The fact that there must be removal is an indication of this failing, an acknowledgement of the sin of Israel in worshiping the Golden Calf. Therefore, this statement is called וִדּוּי — confession. The *Sforno* points out that the word גַם, in our verse, does not mean *also* but *although*. The sense of the phrase וְגַם נְתַתִּיו לַלֵּוִי is that, although I confess that my giving the tithe to the Levite is an admission of the sin of my fathers, nonetheless הַשְׁקִיפָה, *look down*, from heaven and bless me (v. 15), even though I may not be worthy of this heavenly blessing, considering my transgressions and those of my ancestors as well.

The verse in *Ezekiel* cited by the *Sforno* is to be understood in the following manner. The gift which I gave to all Israel originally, namely that the firstborn of each family be sanctified, which also entitled them to receive the offerings and tithes, was defiled through their sins. This included not only the passivity of the firstborn at the time of the sin of the Golden Calf but also the sacrificing of the

יד מִמִּצְוֺתֶיךָ וְלֹא שָׁכָחְתִּי: לֹא־אָכַלְתִּי בְאֹנִי מִמֶּנּוּ וְלֹא־בִעַרְתִּי מִמֶּנּוּ בְּטָמֵא
וְלֹא־נָתַתִּי מִמֶּנּוּ לְמֵת שָׁמַעְתִּי בְּקוֹל יהוה אֱלֹהָי עָשִׂיתִי כְּכֹל אֲשֶׁר
טו צִוִּיתָנִי: הַשְׁקִיפָה מִמְּעוֹן קָדְשְׁךָ מִן־הַשָּׁמַיִם וּבָרֵךְ אֶת־עַמְּךָ אֶת־יִשְׂרָאֵל
וְאֵת הָאֲדָמָה אֲשֶׁר נָתַתָּה לָנוּ כַּאֲשֶׁר נִשְׁבַּעְתָּ לַאֲבֹתֵינוּ אֶרֶץ זָבַת חָלָב
שלישי טז וּדְבָשׁ: הַיּוֹם הַזֶּה יהוה אֱלֹהֶיךָ מְצַוְּךָ לַעֲשׂוֹת אֶת־
הַחֻקִּים הָאֵלֶּה וְאֶת־הַמִּשְׁפָּטִים וְשָׁמַרְתָּ וְעָשִׂיתָ אוֹתָם בְּכָל־לְבָבְךָ
יז וּבְכָל־נַפְשֶׁךָ: אֶת־יהוה הֶאֱמַרְתָּ הַיּוֹם לִהְיוֹת לְךָ לֵאלֹהִים וְלָלֶכֶת בִּדְרָכָיו

---

15. וּבָרֵךְ אֶת עַמְּךָ . . . וְאֵת הָאֲדָמָה אֲשֶׁר נָתַתָּה לָנוּ — *And bless Your people . . . and the land which You have given us* . . . in the manner that *You did swear to our fathers* when You said, אַעֲלֶה אֶתְכֶם מֵעֳנִי מִצְרַיִם אֶל אֶרֶץ, *I will bring you up out of the affliction of Egypt to the Land* (*Exodus* 3:17).

16. הַיּוֹם הַזֶּה — *This day* . . . the day you enter into a covenant with Him. Behold, the covenant is that God, the Blessed One, commands you to do these statutes and judgments for your (own) good, which He has not done with any other people, and you (in turn) accept upon yourself to observe them.

בְּכָל לְבָבְךָ — *With all your heart* . . . that you shall recognize, without any doubt, that it is fitting to do His will.

וּבְכָל נַפְשְׁךָ — *And with all your soul*. That your powerful desires shall not deter you (from serving God), because you recognize the superiority of He who commanded you (to observe His commandments), and their benefit — and thus . . .

17. אֶת ה׳ הֶאֱמַרְתָּ הַיּוֹם — *You have exalted* HASHEM *this day*. When you accepted upon yourself through an oath, which carried with it a curse, to enter into the covenant whereby you would forfeit all material well-being if you would violate it — הֶאֱמַרְתָּ, you thereby exalted and elevated God, the Blessed One, (acknowledging) that the fulfillment of His will would be more honorable to you than all material good.

לִהְיוֹת לְךָ לֵאלֹהִים — *To be unto you Elohim* . . . that He shall be unto you the most honored of all objects separated (from matter), and from Him (emanates) the direction and existence of all your affairs, without any intermediary, as befits (One)

NOTES

firstborn by their fathers to the Moloch. See the commentaries on chapter 20, verse 26 in the Book of *Ezekiel*.

16. בְּכָל לְבָבְךָ וּבְכָל נַפְשְׁךָ — *With all your heart and with all your soul*. The *Sforno* interprets לְבָבְךָ, *your heart*, as referring to man's intellectual powers, while נַפְשְׁךָ, *your soul*, alludes to his normal appetites and desires which must be disciplined and controlled.

17. אֶת ה׳ הֶאֱמַרְתָּ — *You have exalted* HASHEM. The word הֶאֱמַרְתָּ is interpreted in a variety of ways by the commentators. *Rashi* explains it to mean that Israel selected God from among the strange gods — i.e., they singled Him out. The Sages in *Berachos* 6a expound on this expression, stating that we made of God a 'unique entity' or 'the object of our love' (חֲטִיבָה אַחַת), and He, in turn, made us a 'unique entity' in the world. Ibn Ezra translates it as 'to exalt' and the *Sforno*, similarly, interprets it to mean elevation. The sense of the *Sforno's* commentary is: By entering into a covenant with God, we affirmed that the רְצוֹן ה׳, *God's will*, is paramount, and there is naught in this world more important than the fulfillment of God's will. We have elevated Him above all other considerations and all other claims to our time, energies and means.

לִהְיוֹת לְךָ לֵאלֹהִים — *To be unto you Elohim*. The *Sforno* explains that this phrase has a two-fold

יח וְלִשְׁמֹר חֻקָּיו וּמִצְוֹתָיו וּמִשְׁפָּטָיו וְלִשְׁמֹעַ בְּקֹלוֹ: וַיהוָה הֶאֱמִירְךָ הַיּוֹם
יט לִהְיוֹת לוֹ לְעַם סְגֻלָּה כַּאֲשֶׁר דִּבֶּר־לָךְ וְלִשְׁמֹר כָּל־מִצְוֹתָיו: וּלְתִתְּךָ

---

who is Eternal. (Therefore,) in this manner it is fitting that you serve and be subservient to Him alone, as is proper for the One above (i.e., He Who is) your Leader, and that you pray only to Him, being that He alone is your Guide.

וְלָלֶכֶת בִּדְרָכָיו — *And to walk in His ways.* To be like the One Who is honored above all else that exists.

וְלִשְׁמֹעַ בְּקֹלוֹ — *And hearken to His voice* ... as befits His servants.

18. וַה' הֶאֱמִירְךָ הַיּוֹם — *And HASHEM has exalted you this day.* By entering into a covenant with you, (an act) which He has done with no other people, (and thus) He has given you this preeminence.

לִהְיוֹת לוֹ לְעַם סְגֻלָּה — *To be unto Him a treasured people.* So as to realize, through you, that which He desired to attain with human kind [as it says, נַעֲשֶׂה אָדָם בְּצַלְמֵנוּ כִּדְמוּתֵנוּ, *Let us make man in our image after our likeness* (*Genesis* 1:26).]

וְלִשְׁמֹר כָּל מִצְוֹתָיו — *And to keep all His commandments.* And He also gave you preeminence in that He chose you to keep all His commandments through which you will find favor in His eyes. [All other nations are unprepared and unworthy in His (sight) for this (gift of Torah), as our Sages teach us, 'A non-Jew that observes the Sabbath is guilty of a capital (crime)' (*Sanhedrin* 58b), and they are unfit to keep all His commandments except for those which are the Noachide laws.]

NOTES

implication. As he commented at the very beginning of *Genesis* (1:1), the term *Elohim* can also be applied to angels who are separated from matter, and even to judges who reflect Divine intelligence. However, man must recognize that the Almighty is the One Who is unique and from Whom emanates the existence of all — including those who are 'separated from matter' such as the angels. He also stresses that man's destiny is determined and directed by God alone, and only to Him shall one's prayers be addressed. This latter thought is incorporated in the word לְךָ, *unto you.*

וְלָלֶכֶת בִּדְרָכָיו — *And to walk in His ways.* The *Sforno* interprets this phrase in the sense of endeavoring to follow and imitate the ways of God, as the Talmud teaches us, 'As He is gracious and compassionate, so shall you be gracious and compassionate' (*Shabbos* 133b). This concept reflects the teaching of Abba Saul, who interprets the verse in *Exodus* 15:2, זֶה אֵלִי וְאַנְוֵהוּ, *This is my God and I will glorify Him*, as meaning אֲנִי וָהוּא, *I and He*, indicating that man is to emulate the attributes of God. The *Sforno* interprets the phrase לָלֶכֶת בִּדְרָכָיו, *to walk in His ways*, in a similar fashion.

18. ... וַה' הֶאֱמִירְךָ הַיּוֹם לִהְיוֹת לוֹ לְעַם סְגֻלָּה ... וְלִשְׁמֹר כָּל מִצְוֹתָיו — *And HASHEM has exalted you this day to be unto Him a treasured people ... and to keep all His commandments.* It is interesting to note that the text of the *Sforno* in many editions of the מִקְרָאוֹת גְּדוֹלוֹת (the standard version of the *Chumash*) does not include some of his commentary that appears in the Mosad Rav Kook edition, which is based on various manuscripts. It is apparent that the censor deleted certain words, phrases and quotations. For example, the phrase 'which He has done with no other people' (לֹא עָשָׂה כֵן לְכָל גּוֹי) is missing. The quote from *Genesis* 1:26 regarding the creation of man in God's image is also deleted. Finally, the entire paragraph which speaks of the nations being 'unprepared and unworthy ... for the gift of Torah' and the statement of our Sages from tractate *Sanhedrin* 58b is excised. Obviously, the censor did not want to permit the troublesome statements: (a) that the covenant between God and Israel excludes the גּוֹיִם, *the gentile nations*; (b) that only the people of Israel represent the fulfillment of God's goal of creating mankind in His image and likeness; and (c) that only Israel was capable of accepting the yoke of all the commandments, while others are only required to observe the seven basic commandments (שֶׁבַע מִצְוֹת בְּנֵי נֹחַ).

עֶלְי֔וֹן עַ֥ל כָּל־הַגּוֹיִ֖ם אֲשֶׁ֣ר עָשָׂ֑ה לִתְהִלָּ֖ה וּלְשֵׁ֣ם וּלְתִפְאָ֑רֶת וְלִֽהְיֹתְךָ֧
עַם־קָדֹ֛שׁ לַיהוָ֥ה אֱלֹהֶ֖יךָ כַּאֲשֶׁ֥ר דִּבֵּֽר׃
כז רביעי א וַיְצַ֤ו מֹשֶׁה֙ וְזִקְנֵ֣י יִשְׂרָאֵ֔ל אֶת־הָעָ֖ם לֵאמֹ֑ר שָׁמֹר֙ אֶת־כָּל־הַמִּצְוָ֔ה אֲשֶׁ֧ר
ב אָנֹכִ֛י מְצַוֶּ֥ה אֶתְכֶ֖ם הַיּֽוֹם׃ וְהָיָ֗ה בַּיּוֹם֮ אֲשֶׁ֣ר תַּעַבְר֣וּ אֶת־הַיַּרְדֵּן֒ אֶל־הָאָ֕רֶץ
אֲשֶׁר־יְהוָ֥ה אֱלֹהֶ֖יךָ נֹתֵ֣ן לָ֑ךְ וַהֲקֵמֹתָ֤ לְךָ֙ אֲבָנִ֣ים גְּדֹל֔וֹת וְשַׂדְתָּ֥ אֹתָ֖ם בַּשִּֽׂיד׃
ג וְכָתַבְתָּ֣ עֲלֵיהֶ֗ן אֶֽת־כָּל־דִּבְרֵ֛י הַתּוֹרָ֥ה הַזֹּ֖את בְּעָבְרֶ֑ךָ לְמַ֡עַן אֲשֶׁר֩ תָּבֹ֨א
אֶל־הָאָ֜רֶץ אֲשֶׁר־יְהוָ֥ה אֱלֹהֶ֣יךָ ׀ נֹתֵ֣ן לְךָ֗ אֶ֣רֶץ זָבַ֤ת חָלָב֙ וּדְבַ֔שׁ כַּאֲשֶׁ֥ר דִּבֶּ֛ר
ד יְהוָ֥ה אֱלֹהֵֽי־אֲבֹתֶ֖יךָ לָֽךְ׃ וְהָיָה֮ בְּעָבְרְכֶ֣ם אֶת־הַיַּרְדֵּן֒ תָּקִ֜ימוּ אֶת־הָאֲבָנִ֣ים
הָאֵ֗לֶּה אֲשֶׁ֨ר אָנֹכִ֜י מְצַוֶּ֥ה אֶתְכֶ֛ם הַיּ֖וֹם בְּהַ֣ר עֵיבָ֑ל וְשַׂדְתָּ֥ אוֹתָ֖ם בַּשִּֽׂיד׃

---

19. וּלְתִתְּךָ עֶלְיוֹן עַל כָּל הַגּוֹיִם — *And to make you high above all nations ...* to understand and to teach, as it says, וְאַתֶּם תִּהְיוּ לִי מַמְלֶכֶת כֹּהֲנִים, *And you shall be to Me a kingdom of Kohanim* (*Exodus* 19:6).

לִתְהִלָּה וּלְשֵׁם וּלְתִפְאָרֶת — *In praise, in name and in glory ...* to God, the Blessed One, as it says, יִשְׂרָאֵל אֲשֶׁר בְּךָ אֶתְפָּאָר, *Israel in whom I will be glorified* (*Isaiah* 49:3).

וְלִהְיֹתְךָ עַם קָדֹשׁ — *That you may be a holy people ...* everlasting, (bringing you) to the life of the World to Come.

כַּאֲשֶׁר דִּבֵּר — *As He has spoken ...* when He said, וְאַתֶּם תִּהְיוּ לִי מַמְלֶכֶת כֹּהֲנִים, *And you shall be to Me a kingdom of Kohanim and a holy nation* (*Exodus* ibid.).

XXVII

1. וַיְצַו מֹשֶׁה וְזִקְנֵי יִשְׂרָאֵל — *And Moses and the elders of Israel commanded.* He included the elders with him, because they would be present with him when they (Israel) crossed the Jordan River.

NOTES

19. וּלְתִתְּךָ עֶלְיוֹן — *And to make you high*. The *Sforno* carefully defines the various phrases used in this verse. The expression עֶלְיוֹן, *high* or *elevated*, refers to our role as teachers and guides of mankind. The *Kohen* is normally given this mission, therefore he quotes the verse from *Exodus* where God charges us to be *'a kingdom of Kohanim.'* Israel, however, is not to glorify itself because of this special role which God has given to them. Rather, God is glorified through us, as the prophet says.

וְלִהְיֹתְךָ עַם קָדֹשׁ . . . כַּאֲשֶׁר דִּבֵּר — *That you may be a holy people ... as He has spoken*. In addition to being mankind's mentors, a duty expressed in the phrase מַמְלֶכֶת כֹּהֲנִים, *a kingdom of Kohanim*, Israel is also told to be a גּוֹי קָדוֹשׁ, *a holy people* (*Exodus* 19:6) — which is the same as עַם קָדוֹשׁ, the phrase used here. By so doing, they insure their eternal, everlasting existence, for as the *Sforno* explains elsewhere (*Exodus* 19:6), holiness insures נִצְחִיּוּת, *eternity*. All this was already told to Israel prior to the giving of the Torah at Sinai, and this is the meaning of the words כַּאֲשֶׁר דִּבֵּר, *as He has spoken*. Thus, the *Sforno* explains the Torah's precise choice of words in this section.

XXVII

1. וַיְצַו מֹשֶׁה וְזִקְנֵי יִשְׂרָאֵל — *And Moses and the elders of Israel commanded*. The *Sforno* explains why Moses included the elders when he went to command the Israelites regarding the setting up of the great stones after they cross the Jordan, while in verse 9 Moses included the *Kohanim* and Levites when he spoke to the people and urged them to listen to God and observe His commandments. The reason given by the *Sforno* is that the elders, as the leaders of the people, would be directly involved in the setting up of these stones upon which the commandments contained in the Torah were inscribed, while the *Kohanim*, whose function it was to instruct the people in the laws, were better suited to be associated with Moses in this second area of admonishing the people to learn, obey and follow the teachings of the Torah.

ה וּבָנִיתָ שָּׁם מִזְבֵּחַ לַיהוָה אֱלֹהֶיךָ מִזְבַּח אֲבָנִים לֹא־תָנִיף עֲלֵיהֶם בַּרְזֶל׃
ו אֲבָנִים שְׁלֵמוֹת תִּבְנֶה אֶת־מִזְבַּח יְהוָה אֱלֹהֶיךָ וְהַעֲלִיתָ עָלָיו עוֹלֹת לַיהוָה
ז־ח אֱלֹהֶיךָ׃ וְזָבַחְתָּ שְׁלָמִים וְאָכַלְתָּ שָּׁם וְשָׂמַחְתָּ לִפְנֵי יְהוָה אֱלֹהֶיךָ׃ וְכָתַבְתָּ
ט עַל־הָאֲבָנִים אֶת־כָּל־דִּבְרֵי הַתּוֹרָה הַזֹּאת בַּאֵר הֵיטֵב׃ וַיְדַבֵּר
מֹשֶׁה וְהַכֹּהֲנִים הַלְוִיִּם אֶל כָּל־יִשְׂרָאֵל לֵאמֹר הַסְכֵּת ׀ וּשְׁמַע יִשְׂרָאֵל הַיּוֹם
י הַזֶּה נִהְיֵיתָ לְעָם לַיהוָה אֱלֹהֶיךָ׃ וְשָׁמַעְתָּ בְּקוֹל יְהוָה אֱלֹהֶיךָ וְעָשִׂיתָ
חמישי יא אֶת־מִצְוֺתָו וְאֶת־חֻקָּיו אֲשֶׁר אָנֹכִי מְצַוְּךָ הַיּוֹם׃ וַיְצַו מֹשֶׁה
יב אֶת־הָעָם בַּיּוֹם הַהוּא לֵאמֹר׃ אֵלֶּה יַעַמְדוּ לְבָרֵךְ אֶת־הָעָם עַל־הַר גְּרִזִּים
יג בְּעָבְרְכֶם אֶת־הַיַּרְדֵּן שִׁמְעוֹן וְלֵוִי וִיהוּדָה וְיִשָּׂשכָר וְיוֹסֵף וּבִנְיָמִן׃ וְאֵלֶּה
יד יַעַמְדוּ עַל־הַקְּלָלָה בְּהַר עֵיבָל רְאוּבֵן גָּד וְאָשֵׁר וּזְבוּלֻן דָּן וְנַפְתָּלִי׃ וְעָנוּ
טו הַלְוִיִּם וְאָמְרוּ אֶל־כָּל־אִישׁ יִשְׂרָאֵל קוֹל רָם׃ אָרוּר הָאִישׁ

---

7. וְשָׂמַחְתָּ לִפְנֵי ה׳ אֱלֹהֶיךָ — *And you shall rejoice before* H*ASHEM your God . . .* because you will enter into a covenant with Him at that time, on Mount Gerizim and Mount Ebal.

9. וַיְדַבֵּר מֹשֶׁה וְהַכֹּהֲנִים הַלְוִיִּם — *And Moses and the Kohanim the Levites spoke.* He included the *Kohanim* with him to caution (them) regarding the analytical study of Torah, being that the (responsibility) to teach knowledge (of Torah) to the people rested on the *Kohanim*, as it says, *They shall teach Jacob Your ordinances* (33:10).

הַסְכֵּת — *Imagine.* Imagine (portray) in your mind, similar to, אֵת סִכּוּת מַלְכְּכֶם, *Sikkus (the image of) your king* (*Amos* 5:26).

וּשְׁמַע — *And hear.* And consider (observe).

10. וְשָׁמַעְתָּ בְּקוֹל ה׳ אֱלֹהֶיךָ — *And you will hearken to the voice of* H*ASHEM your God.* When you conjure this up (in your mind) and comprehend, then without a doubt you will listen to His voice.

15. אָרוּר הָאִישׁ — *Cursed be the man.* Behold, all the curses were preceded with the language of *blessed be*, as we have received in our tradition (*Sotah* 32a); therefore, it says, *These shall stand to bless the people* (v. 12). However, the Torah only mentions the language of curse, because the main purpose of these imprecations was to curse those who transgressed these (laws) so that they alone should bear the consequences

NOTES

7. וְשָׂמַחְתָּ — *And you shall rejoice.* The *Sforno* explains that the renewed covenant between God and Israel, entered into on Mount Gerizim and Mount Ebal, was indeed an occasion for rejoicing. There can be no greater *simchah* than the realization that the Almighty has chosen Israel as His people, as it says, *This day you have become a people to God your God* (v. 9).

9-10. הַסְכֵּת וּשְׁמַע . . . וְשָׁמַעְתָּ — *Imagine and hear . . . and you will hearken.* The *Sforno* explains the sequence of these two verses. First, you must conjure up the image of God's relationship to Israel and their commitment to Him and impress this upon your mind. Then you must consider and contemplate the meaning of this covenant between Israel and God, its deeper meaning and significance. If you do this, then it will result in your listening to the voice of God. The word וְשָׁמַעְתָּ, *and you will hearken*, is not an additional commandment, but an assurance that the result of הַסְכֵּת, *imagine*, and שְׁמַע, *hear*, will be וְשָׁמַעְתָּ, *and you will hearken*. The *Sforno's* interpretation of the word הַסְכֵּת is unique. *Rashi*, based on *Onkelos*, interprets it as *listen*. S.R. Hirsch translates it as *pay attention*. Our Sages interpret it in a variety of ways (see *Berachos* 63b). The *Sforno*, however, understands it to mean 'imagine in your mind,' let there be a full impact upon you

אֲשֶׁר יַעֲשֶׂה פֶסֶל וּמַסֵּכָה תּוֹעֲבַת יהוה מַעֲשֵׂה יְדֵי חָרָשׁ וְשָׂם בַּסָּתֶר וְעָנוּ
טז כָל־הָעָם וְאָמְרוּ אָמֵן: אָרוּר מַקְלֶה אָבִיו וְאִמּוֹ וְאָמַר
יז כָּל־הָעָם אָמֵן: אָרוּר מַסִּיג גְּבוּל רֵעֵהוּ וְאָמַר
יח כָּל־הָעָם אָמֵן: אָרוּר מַשְׁגֶּה עִוֵּר בַּדָּרֶךְ וְאָמַר
יט כָּל־הָעָם אָמֵן: אָרוּר מַטֶּה מִשְׁפַּט גֵּר־יָתוֹם וְאַלְמָנָה
כ וְאָמַר כָּל־הָעָם אָמֵן: אָרוּר שֹׁכֵב עִם־אֵשֶׁת אָבִיו כִּי גִלָּה כְּנַף אָבִיו וְאָמַר
כא כָּל־הָעָם אָמֵן: אָרוּר שֹׁכֵב עִם־כָּל־בְּהֵמָה וְאָמַר
כב כָּל־הָעָם אָמֵן: אָרוּר שֹׁכֵב עִם־אֲחֹתוֹ בַּת־אָבִיו אוֹ
כג בַת־אִמּוֹ וְאָמַר כָּל־הָעָם אָמֵן: אָרוּר שֹׁכֵב עִם־חֹתַנְתּוֹ
כד וְאָמַר כָּל־הָעָם אָמֵן: אָרוּר מַכֵּה רֵעֵהוּ בַּסָּתֶר
כה וְאָמַר כָּל־הָעָם אָמֵן: אָרוּר לֹקֵחַ שֹׁחַד לְהַכּוֹת נֶפֶשׁ

---

of their wicked acts, but the rest of the people would not be responsible for them. The (reason) for this is that these sins, in the majority of cases, were committed by the leaders of the people and the common people had (no power) to protest, as Ezekiel attests, saying, . . . נְשִׂיאֵי יִשְׂרָאֵל אִישׁ לִזְרֹעוֹ הָיוּ בָךְ לְמַעַן שְׁפָךְ דָּם. אָב וָאֵם הֵקַלּוּ בָךְ, *The princes of Israel, every man for his own power were they within you, for the sake of bloodshed. Father and mother have they slighted within you . . .* (Ezekiel 22:6,7). Now, in that chapter the prophet mentions most, if not all, of these maledictions, and says that these wicked acts were performed in Jerusalem, not that the entire city sinned but those who transgressed were the princes. However, when he mentions the wicked acts of the community, he does accuse the (entire) city, as it says, קָדָשַׁי בָּזִית וְאֶת שַׁבְּתֹתַי חִלָּלְתְּ, *My sanctities you spurned, My Sabbaths you desecrated* (ibid v. 8).

25. לֹקֵחַ שֹׁחַד לְהַכּוֹת — *That takes a bribe to slay . . .* such as Doeg the Edomite and the Ziphim, (who acted) to gain favor in the eyes of the king or to profit.

NOTES

of the realization that you are God's people. The verse cited from *Amos* speaks of people carrying and clutching their idols closely to their hearts. So should Israel be suffused with their belief in God and hold their loyalty to the covenant close to their heart.

15. אָרוּר הָאִישׁ — *Cursed be the man.* The Talmud in tractate *Sotah* 31a describes how the tribes stood on the two mounts of Gerizim and Ebal while the *Kohanim* and Levites stood in the valley between these mountains and pronounced the blessings and curses, beginning in each instance with בָּרוּךְ, *blessed*, followed by אָרוּר, *cursed*. The *Sforno* quotes verse 12 in our chapter, which speaks of blessing, to prove that, indeed, each curse (not mentioned until verse 13) was preceded by a blessing. He explains that the twelve transgressions listed were not evil acts of the community, but those of certain powerful leaders, as we see from the verses cited in *Ezekiel* which mirror all the sins recorded in our *parashah*. Therefore, the Torah curses only the leaders and not the masses, for they were blameless, given their inability to prevent these mighty men from sinning. The wicked acts enumerated both here and in *Ezekiel* are the cardinal sins of bloodshed, idolatry and sexual immorality, as well as oppression of the weak and the accepting of bribes. All these are associated with the ruling class. For these acts, the populace would not be punished, although all Israel is responsible one for another, but that is true only when one has the power to protest and fails to do so (see Tractate *Shabbos* 54b). The *Sforno*, however, points out that those sins mentioned in the Book of *Ezekiel* (but not here), such as desecration of the Sabbath and the spurning of the holy, was practiced by many of the masses and therefore they would also be punished. The prophet indicates this liability and guilt of all the people by using the term עִיר, *city*.

25. לֹקֵחַ שֹׁחַד לְהַכּוֹת — *That takes a bribe to slay*. The *Sforno* realizes that this phrase

כו דָּם נָקִי וְאָמַר כָּל־הָעָם אָמֵן: אָרוּר אֲשֶׁר לֹא־יָקִים
אֶת־דִּבְרֵי הַתּוֹרָה־הַזֹּאת לַעֲשׂוֹת אוֹתָם וְאָמַר כָּל־הָעָם אָמֵן:
כח א וְהָיָה אִם־שָׁמוֹעַ תִּשְׁמַע בְּקוֹל יהוה אֱלֹהֶיךָ לִשְׁמֹר לַעֲשׂוֹת אֶת־כָּל־
מִצְוֹתָיו אֲשֶׁר אָנֹכִי מְצַוְּךָ הַיּוֹם וּנְתָנְךָ יהוה אֱלֹהֶיךָ עֶלְיוֹן עַל כָּל־גּוֹיֵי
ב הָאָרֶץ: וּבָאוּ עָלֶיךָ כָּל־הַבְּרָכוֹת הָאֵלֶּה וְהִשִּׂיגֻךָ כִּי תִשְׁמַע בְּקוֹל יהוה
ג־ד אֱלֹהֶיךָ: בָּרוּךְ אַתָּה בָּעִיר וּבָרוּךְ אַתָּה בַּשָּׂדֶה: בָּרוּךְ פְּרִי־בִטְנְךָ וּפְרִי
ה אַדְמָתְךָ וּפְרִי בְהֶמְתֶּךָ שְׁגַר אֲלָפֶיךָ וְעַשְׁתְּרוֹת צֹאנֶךָ: בָּרוּךְ טַנְאֲךָ
°ששי ו־ז וּמִשְׁאַרְתֶּךָ: בָּרוּךְ אַתָּה בְּבֹאֶךָ וּבָרוּךְ אַתָּה בְּצֵאתֶךָ: °יִתֵּן יהוה אֶת־אֹיְבֶיךָ

---

26. אֲשֶׁר לֹא יָקִים אֶת דִּבְרֵי הַתּוֹרָה הַזֹּאת לַעֲשׂוֹת אוֹתָם — *That does not confirm the words of this Torah to do them . . .* who does not fulfill and confirm that it is proper to do them *all,* but there will be a commandment which he will nullify; this refers to one who is an apostate (even) regarding one thing (commanded by God).

XXVIII

2. וּבָאוּ עָלֶיךָ כָּל הַבְּרָכוֹת הָאֵלֶּה וְהִשִּׂיגֻךָ — *And all these blessings shall come upon you and overtake you . . .* even though you will make no effort to attain them.

כִּי תִשְׁמַע בְּקוֹל ה׳ אֱלֹהֶיךָ — *If you shall listen to the voice of* H*ASHEM your God.* And this (shall come to pass) when your study of Torah will be your main concern (קֶבַע), and your ordinary work subsidiary (עֲרַאי) to it (based on *Berachos* 35b), and therefore the blessings shall overtake you without any effort (on your part). (Now,) behold, the blessings of the First Temple period are mentioned here, and (the Torah) tells us that they will merit them as long as they keep the commandments. (This section continues until) the verse, H*ASHEM will establish you for a holy people to Himself* (v. 9), which refers to the early period of the Second Temple, as our Sages tell us regarding the blessings (in the time) of Simeon the Righteous and the miracles which transpired in the Holy Temple in his lifetime.

NOTES

cannot be interpreted literally, for then he would be guilty of murder, which is far more serious than bribery, hence why mention שחד, *bribe,* at all? He therefore explains that this verse alludes to one whose actions are motivated by a desire to find favor in the eyes of another, which results in bloodshed. He gives two examples, which are recorded in *I Samuel,* chapters 22, 23. Doeg the Edomite informed King Saul that the *Kohanim* in the city of Nob had given David food and assisted him. As a result of this information, the *Kohanim* were executed. The Ziphim told the king that David was hiding in the hills of Hakhilah. In both instances, the reason for informing on David was to gain favor with Saul whose heart was filled with hatred for him. It is this form of bribery that the Torah speaks of and curses.

26. אֲשֶׁר לֹא יָקִים — *That does not confirm.* The *Sforno* interprets this verse to mean that even one who accepts the entire Torah, except for one commandment which he denies and rejects, is guilty of not confirming the words of Torah and is therefore cursed. He bases this concept on the teaching of our Sages that one who professes that the entire Torah is of Divine origin except for one verse is guilty of heresy (*Sanhedrin* 99b). The *Rambam* in *Hilchos Teshuvah* 3:8 lists three כּוֹפְרִים, *heretics;* and included among them is one who denies the validity of 'one verse or one letter' of the Torah.

XXVIII

2. וְהִשִּׂיגֻךָ כִּי תִשְׁמַע בְּקוֹל ה׳ אֱלֹהֶיךָ — *And overtake you if you shall listen to the voice of* H*ASHEM your God.* The difficulty with the word וְהִשִּׂיגֻךָ, *overtake you,* regarding a blessing is obvious. What person flees from a blessing that it should be necessary for the blessing to overtake him? The *Sforno* answers this question, explaining that the sense of the verse is as follows. Normally, one pursues

הַקָּמִים עָלֶיךָ נִגָּפִים לְפָנֶיךָ בְּדֶרֶךְ אֶחָד יֵצְאוּ אֵלֶיךָ וּבְשִׁבְעָה דְרָכִים יָנוּסוּ
לְפָנֶיךָ: יְצַו יהוה אִתְּךָ אֶת־הַבְּרָכָה בַּאֲסָמֶיךָ וּבְכֹל מִשְׁלַח יָדֶךָ וּבֵרַכְךָ ח
בָּאָרֶץ אֲשֶׁר־יהוה אֱלֹהֶיךָ נֹתֵן לָךְ: יְקִימְךָ יהוה לוֹ לְעַם קָדוֹשׁ כַּאֲשֶׁר ט
נִשְׁבַּע־לָךְ כִּי תִשְׁמֹר אֶת־מִצְוֹת יהוה אֱלֹהֶיךָ וְהָלַכְתָּ בִּדְרָכָיו: וְרָאוּ י
כָּל־עַמֵּי הָאָרֶץ כִּי שֵׁם יהוה נִקְרָא עָלֶיךָ וְיָרְאוּ מִמֶּךָּ: וְהוֹתִרְךָ יהוה לְטוֹבָה יא
בִּפְרִי בִטְנְךָ וּבִפְרִי בְהֶמְתְּךָ וּבִפְרִי אַדְמָתֶךָ עַל הָאֲדָמָה אֲשֶׁר נִשְׁבַּע יהוה
לַאֲבֹתֶיךָ לָתֶת לָךְ: יִפְתַּח יהוה ׀ לְךָ אֶת־אוֹצָרוֹ הַטּוֹב אֶת־הַשָּׁמַיִם לָתֵת יב
מְטַר־אַרְצְךָ בְּעִתּוֹ וּלְבָרֵךְ אֵת כָּל־מַעֲשֵׂה יָדֶךָ וְהִלְוִיתָ גּוֹיִם רַבִּים וְאַתָּה
לֹא תִלְוֶה: וּנְתָנְךָ יהוה לְרֹאשׁ וְלֹא לְזָנָב וְהָיִיתָ רַק לְמַעְלָה וְלֹא תִהְיֶה יג
לְמָטָּה כִּי־תִשְׁמַע אֶל־מִצְוֹת ׀ יהוה אֱלֹהֶיךָ אֲשֶׁר אָנֹכִי מְצַוְּךָ הַיּוֹם לִשְׁמֹר
וְלַעֲשׂוֹת: וְלֹא תָסוּר מִכָּל־הַדְּבָרִים אֲשֶׁר אָנֹכִי מְצַוֶּה אֶתְכֶם הַיּוֹם יָמִין יד

---

10. וְרָאוּ כָּל עַמֵּי הָאָרֶץ — *And all the peoples of the earth shall see . . .* as our Sages tell us regarding Alexander who bowed down to Simeon (the Righteous).

11. וְהוֹתִרְךָ ה׳ לְטוֹבָה — *And HASHEM shall make you plenteous in goods.* Your material prosperity will be greater than that of others who (also) succeed materially. With these blessings, which occurred during the period of the Second Temple, this section concludes.

14. וְלֹא תָסוּר מִכָּל הַדְּבָרִים אֲשֶׁר אָנֹכִי מְצַוֶּה אֶתְכֶם הַיּוֹם יָמִין וּשְׂמֹאול — *And you shall not turn aside from any of the words which I command you this day, to the right*

NOTES

success and material blessings. We, however, are promised that this will be unnecessary, for the blessings will find us without any effort on our part, providing we hearken to the voice of God and observe His commandments.

The *Sforno* is of the opinion that these verses of blessing (1-13) refer to the period of the First Temple, before the people of Israel sinned and deviated from the path of God. They refer also to the early period of the Second Temple during the forty years that Simeon the Righteous ministered as the *Kohen* Gadol and many blessings were showered on Israel and numerous miracles occured in the Temple. The Mishnah (*Yoma* 39a) records a number of them including the following: the lot drawn on Yom Kippur with the name of God on it constantly came up in the right hand of the *Kohen*, which was considered an omen of good fortune; the crimson-colored strap tied on Yom Kippur between the horns of the bull turned white signifying that the sins of Israel were forgiven, and the light on the far right of the menorah was never extinguished. During this period of the Second Temple, a blessing was bestowed from on High on the *omer* (the measure of barley offered on the 16th day of Nissan), and upon the שְׁתֵּי הַלֶּחֶם (the two loaves of bread offered on Shevuos) and on the לֶחֶם הַפָּנִים (the 'showbread' which was changed weekly in the Temple). All this occurred only sporadically after Simeon's death.

10. וְרָאוּ כָּל עַמֵּי הָאָרֶץ — *And all the peoples of the earth shall see.* The Sforno interprets the phrase, *that the name of God is called upon you,* as referring to the awe and reverence aroused in powerful leaders of the nations upon seeing the radiance of sanctity shining forth from the pious men of Israel. He cites the episode recorded in *Yoma* 69a regarding Alexander the Macedonian and Simeon the Righteous. The Cutheans demanded that the Temple in Jerusalem be given to them so that they could destroy it. When Simeon the Righteous heard of this wicked plot, he put on his priestly garments and came to see Alexander the Great. When Alexander beheld Simeon approaching, he descended from his carriage and bowed before him. When he was asked why he did so, he responded, 'His image it is which wins for me in all my battles.' Looking at Simeon the *Kohen Gadol*, he saw the 'name of God' radiating from his face, and paid homage to him.

14. וְלֹא תָסוּר מִכָּל הַדְּבָרִים — *And you shall not*

וּשְׂמֹאול לָלֶכֶת אַחֲרֵי אֱלֹהִים אֲחֵרִים לְעָבְדָם:
טו וְהָיָה אִם־לֹא תִשְׁמַע בְּקוֹל יהוה אֱלֹהֶיךָ לִשְׁמֹר לַעֲשׂוֹת אֶת־כָּל־מִצְוֺתָיו
וְחֻקֹּתָיו אֲשֶׁר אָנֹכִי מְצַוְּךָ הַיּוֹם וּבָאוּ עָלֶיךָ כָּל־הַקְּלָלוֹת הָאֵלֶּה וְהִשִּׂיגוּךָ:
טז־יח אָרוּר אַתָּה בָּעִיר וְאָרוּר אַתָּה בַּשָּׂדֶה: אָרוּר טַנְאֲךָ וּמִשְׁאַרְתֶּךָ: אָרוּר
יט פְּרִי־בִטְנְךָ וּפְרִי אַדְמָתֶךָ שְׁגַר אֲלָפֶיךָ וְעַשְׁתְּרֹת צֹאנֶךָ: אָרוּר אַתָּה בְּבֹאֶךָ
כ וְאָרוּר אַתָּה בְּצֵאתֶךָ: יְשַׁלַּח יהוה ׀ בְּךָ אֶת־הַמְּאֵרָה אֶת־הַמְּהוּמָה
וְאֶת־הַמִּגְעֶרֶת בְּכָל־מִשְׁלַח יָדְךָ אֲשֶׁר תַּעֲשֶׂה עַד הִשָּׁמֶדְךָ וְעַד־אֲבָדְךָ
כא מַהֵר מִפְּנֵי רֹעַ מַעֲלָלֶיךָ אֲשֶׁר עֲזַבְתָּנִי: יַדְבֵּק יהוה בְּךָ אֶת־הַדָּבֶר עַד
כב כַּלֹּתוֹ אֹתְךָ מֵעַל הָאֲדָמָה אֲשֶׁר־אַתָּה בָא־שָׁמָּה לְרִשְׁתָּהּ: יַכְּכָה יהוה
בַּשַּׁחֶפֶת וּבַקַּדַּחַת וּבַדַּלֶּקֶת וּבַחַרְחֻר וּבַחֶרֶב וּבַשִּׁדָּפוֹן וּבַיֵּרָקוֹן וּרְדָפוּךָ עַד
כג אָבְדֶךָ: וְהָיוּ שָׁמֶיךָ אֲשֶׁר עַל־רֹאשְׁךָ נְחֹשֶׁת וְהָאָרֶץ אֲשֶׁר־תַּחְתֶּיךָ בַּרְזֶל:
כד יִתֵּן יהוה אֶת־מְטַר אַרְצְךָ אָבָק וְעָפָר מִן־הַשָּׁמַיִם יֵרֵד עָלֶיךָ עַד הִשָּׁמְדָךְ:
כה יִתֶּנְךָ יהוה ׀ נִגָּף לִפְנֵי אֹיְבֶיךָ בְּדֶרֶךְ אֶחָד תֵּצֵא אֵלָיו וּבְשִׁבְעָה דְרָכִים
כו תָּנוּס לְפָנָיו וְהָיִיתָ לְזַעֲוָה לְכֹל מַמְלְכוֹת הָאָרֶץ: וְהָיְתָה נִבְלָתְךָ לְמַאֲכָל
כז לְכָל־עוֹף הַשָּׁמַיִם וּלְבֶהֱמַת הָאָרֶץ וְאֵין מַחֲרִיד: יַכְּכָה יהוה בִּשְׁחִין מִצְרַיִם
כח °וּבעפלים וּבַגָּרָב וּבֶחָרֶס אֲשֶׁר לֹא־תוּכַל לְהֵרָפֵא: יַכְּכָה יהוה בְּשִׁגָּעוֹן °ובטחורים ק׳
כט וּבְעִוָּרוֹן וּבְתִמְהוֹן לֵבָב: וְהָיִיתָ מְמַשֵּׁשׁ בַּצָּהֳרַיִם כַּאֲשֶׁר יְמַשֵּׁשׁ הָעִוֵּר

---

or to the left. They shall not change the commandments of God, the Blessed One, especially regarding the judgments, nor exchange the other commandments with secular customs and with *commandments learned by rote* (מִצְוַת אֲנָשִׁים מְלֻמָּדָה — *Isaiah* 29:13). This is especially so when these are done in honor of the ancients who instituted these customs and not in honor of their Maker, nor for the purpose of strengthening the observance of His commandments. [For in such a manner you will *go after other gods to serve them*, and even more serious than this (practice) is the institution of a new religion in honor of the ancients who were considered as Elohim — judges in the land.] Now the curses and punishments up to the verse, *HASHEM will bring you and your king* (v. 36), occurred during the (period) of the Second Temple, in the days of the Greeks and others, until the kings of the House of the Hasmoneans besieged one another, and one of them (Aristobulos) was exiled

NOTES

turn aside from any of the words. The תּוֹכָחָה, *admonition,* is written in the Book of *Leviticus* and repeated in our *parashah.* A cursory examination of the two will reveal a number of differences. Our Sages tell us that the admonition recorded in *Leviticus* came directly from God, while the one recorded in our *parashah* was uttered by Moses in his own name. In the former, Israel is addressed in the plural, while in the latter they are addressed in the singular (*Megillah* 31b). The chastisements uttered by Moses are more numerous than those uttered in the name of God (*Bava Basra* 88b). The early Bible commentators are of the opinion that these chastisements are not simply admonitions and warnings, but a prophetic vision of events which would transpire during various periods. The *Ramban* states that the תּוֹכָחָה in *Leviticus* speaks of the First Temple period, while the admonition in *Ki Savo* alludes to the period of the Second Temple. The *Abarbanel,* on the other hand, does not divide the two chapters of curses and punishments in this manner, but is of the opinion that they are part of one whole, covering the period from the destruction of the First Temple to the ultimate exile from the Land following the destruction of the Second Temple.

The *Sforno,* in his commentary on *Leviticus*

בָּאֲפֵלָה וְלֹא תַצְלִיחַ אֶת־דְּרָכֶיךָ וְהָיִיתָ אַךְ עָשׁוּק וְגָזוּל כָּל־הַיָּמִים וְאֵין
°יִשְׁכָּבֶנָּה ק׳ ל מוֹשִׁיעַ׃ אִשָּׁה תְאָרֵשׂ וְאִישׁ אַחֵר °ישגלנה בַּיִת תִּבְנֶה וְלֹא־תֵשֵׁב בּוֹ כֶּרֶם
לא תִּטַּע וְלֹא תְחַלְּלֶנּוּ׃ שׁוֹרְךָ טָבוּחַ לְעֵינֶיךָ וְלֹא תֹאכַל מִמֶּנּוּ חֲמֹרְךָ גָּזוּל
לב מִלְּפָנֶיךָ וְלֹא יָשׁוּב לָךְ צֹאנְךָ נְתֻנוֹת לְאֹיְבֶיךָ וְאֵין לְךָ מוֹשִׁיעַ׃ בָּנֶיךָ
וּבְנֹתֶיךָ נְתֻנִים לְעַם אַחֵר וְעֵינֶיךָ רֹאוֹת וְכָלוֹת אֲלֵיהֶם כָּל־הַיּוֹם וְאֵין לְאֵל
לג יָדֶךָ׃ פְּרִי אַדְמָתְךָ וְכָל־יְגִיעֲךָ יֹאכַל עַם אֲשֶׁר לֹא־יָדָעְתָּ וְהָיִיתָ רַק עָשׁוּק
לד-לה וְרָצוּץ כָּל־הַיָּמִים׃ וְהָיִיתָ מְשֻׁגָּע מִמַּרְאֵה עֵינֶיךָ אֲשֶׁר תִּרְאֶה׃ יַכְּכָה יהוה
בִּשְׁחִין רָע עַל־הַבִּרְכַּיִם וְעַל־הַשֹּׁקַיִם אֲשֶׁר לֹא־תוּכַל לְהֵרָפֵא מִכַּף רַגְלְךָ
לו וְעַד קָדְקֳדֶךָ׃ יוֹלֵךְ יהוה אֹתְךָ וְאֶת־מַלְכְּךָ אֲשֶׁר תָּקִים עָלֶיךָ אֶל־גּוֹי אֲשֶׁר
לז לֹא־יָדַעְתָּ אַתָּה וַאֲבֹתֶיךָ וְעָבַדְתָּ שָּׁם אֱלֹהִים אֲחֵרִים עֵץ וָאָבֶן׃ וְהָיִיתָ
לח לְשַׁמָּה לְמָשָׁל וְלִשְׁנִינָה בְּכֹל הָעַמִּים אֲשֶׁר־יְנַהֶגְךָ יהוה שָׁמָּה׃ זֶרַע רַב
לט תּוֹצִיא הַשָּׂדֶה וּמְעַט תֶּאֱסֹף כִּי יַחְסְלֶנּוּ הָאַרְבֶּה׃ כְּרָמִים תִּטַּע וְעָבָדְתָּ וְיַיִן
מ לֹא־תִשְׁתֶּה וְלֹא תֶאֱגֹר כִּי תֹאכְלֶנּוּ הַתֹּלָעַת׃ זֵיתִים יִהְיוּ לְךָ בְּכָל־גְּבוּלֶךָ
מא וְשֶׁמֶן לֹא תָסוּךְ כִּי יִשַּׁל זֵיתֶךָ׃ בָּנִים וּבָנוֹת תּוֹלִיד וְלֹא־יִהְיוּ לָךְ כִּי יֵלְכוּ
מב-מג בַּשֶּׁבִי׃ כָּל־עֵצְךָ וּפְרִי אַדְמָתֶךָ יְיָרֵשׁ הַצְּלָצַל׃ הַגֵּר אֲשֶׁר בְּקִרְבְּךָ יַעֲלֶה
מד עָלֶיךָ מַעְלָה מָּעְלָה וְאַתָּה תֵרֵד מַטָּה מָּטָּה׃ הוּא יַלְוְךָ וְאַתָּה לֹא תַלְוֶנּוּ
מה הוּא יִהְיֶה לְרֹאשׁ וְאַתָּה תִּהְיֶה לְזָנָב׃ וּבָאוּ עָלֶיךָ כָּל־הַקְּלָלוֹת הָאֵלֶּה

---

at the behest of Pompeius to Rome. From that verse, and until the verse, *You shall be plucked from off the land* (v. 63), (the Torah) refers to the period (culminating with) the destruction of the Temple at the hands of the Romans. From (that verse) on are the admonitions occurring in exile and related to it.

Now he begins the curse and rebuke (תּוֹכָחָה) saying, *It shall come to pass, if you will not listen to the voice of HASHEM your God to observe and do all His commandments and His statutes which I command you this day* (v. 15), this doubtless being when the observance of the *mitzvos* of the Torah were exchanged for various customs, and justice retrogressed. Now after (the Torah) says, *HASHEM will bring you and your king* (v. 36), which is the second part (of the תּוֹכָחָה), it repeats (the reason), *because you did not listen to the voice of HASHEM your God to keep His commandments and His statutes which He commanded you* (v. 45) —

NOTES

26:16-33, interprets those verses as referring to the period following the leadership of Deborah, the destruction of the Sanctuary at Shiloh, the exile of the Ten Tribes and finally, the destruction of the First Temple. He interprets the later verses (ibid. 42-45) as alluding to the Second Temple and the return from Babylonia to the land of Israel. In his commentary on our *parashah*, the *Sforno* interprets the blessings at the beginning of this chapter as applying to the early period of the Second Temple, a time when blessings and miracles would occur and the prosperity of Israel would be very great. The curses and punishments, according to him, would take place at a later period, after the death of Simeon the *Kohen Gadol*, when Israel would sin and deviate from the path of God. During that period, a variety of תַּקָּנוֹת, *ordinances*, would be instituted, necessitated by the weakening of Israel's commitment to the law and an erosion of their faith in the Almighty. Toward the end of the Second Temple period, a number of Biblical rituals and ceremonies would also be suspended, due to the misconduct of the Jewish people. The Mishnah (*Sotah* 47a) states: 'When adulterers multiplied, the ceremony of the bitter waters (מֵי סוֹטָה) was discontinued and when murderers multiplied, the ceremony of the breaking of the heifer's neck, (עֶגְלָה עֲרוּפָה), was discon-

וּרְדָפוּךָ וְהִשִּׂיגוּךָ עַד הִשָּׁמְדָךְ כִּי־לֹא שָׁמַעְתָּ בְּקוֹל יהוה אֱלֹהֶיךָ לִשְׁמֹר
מו מִצְוֹתָיו וְחֻקֹּתָיו אֲשֶׁר צִוָּךְ: וְהָיוּ בְךָ לְאוֹת וּלְמוֹפֵת וּבְזַרְעֲךָ עַד־עוֹלָם:
מז תַּחַת אֲשֶׁר לֹא־עָבַדְתָּ אֶת־יהוה אֱלֹהֶיךָ בְּשִׂמְחָה וּבְטוּב לֵבָב מֵרֹב כֹּל:
מח וְעָבַדְתָּ אֶת־אֹיְבֶיךָ אֲשֶׁר יְשַׁלְּחֶנּוּ יהוה בָּךְ בְּרָעָב וּבְצָמָא וּבְעֵירֹם וּבְחֹסֶר
מט כֹּל וְנָתַן עֹל בַּרְזֶל עַל־צַוָּארֶךָ עַד הִשְׁמִידוֹ אֹתָךְ: יִשָּׂא יהוה עָלֶיךָ גּוֹי
נ מֵרָחֹק מִקְצֵה הָאָרֶץ כַּאֲשֶׁר יִדְאֶה הַנָּשֶׁר גּוֹי אֲשֶׁר לֹא־תִשְׁמַע לְשֹׁנוֹ: גּוֹי
נא עַז פָּנִים אֲשֶׁר לֹא־יִשָּׂא פָנִים לְזָקֵן וְנַעַר לֹא יָחֹן: וְאָכַל פְּרִי בְהֶמְתְּךָ
וּפְרִי־אַדְמָתְךָ עַד הִשָּׁמְדָךְ אֲשֶׁר לֹא־יַשְׁאִיר לְךָ דָּגָן תִּירוֹשׁ וְיִצְהָר שְׁגַר
נב אֲלָפֶיךָ וְעַשְׁתְּרֹת צֹאנֶךָ עַד הַאֲבִידוֹ אֹתָךְ: וְהֵצַר לְךָ בְּכָל־שְׁעָרֶיךָ עַד
רֶדֶת חֹמֹתֶיךָ הַגְּבֹהֹת וְהַבְּצֻרוֹת אֲשֶׁר אַתָּה בֹּטֵחַ בָּהֵן בְּכָל־אַרְצֶךָ וְהֵצַר
נג לְךָ בְּכָל־שְׁעָרֶיךָ בְּכָל־אַרְצְךָ אֲשֶׁר נָתַן יהוה אֱלֹהֶיךָ לָךְ: וְאָכַלְתָּ
פְרִי־בִטְנְךָ בְּשַׂר בָּנֶיךָ וּבְנֹתֶיךָ אֲשֶׁר נָתַן־לְךָ יהוה אֱלֹהֶיךָ בְּמָצוֹר וּבְמָצוֹק
נד אֲשֶׁר־יָצִיק לְךָ אֹיְבֶךָ: הָאִישׁ הָרַךְ בְּךָ וְהֶעָנֹג מְאֹד תֵּרַע עֵינוֹ בְאָחִיו
נה וּבְאֵשֶׁת חֵיקוֹ וּבְיֶתֶר בָּנָיו אֲשֶׁר יוֹתִיר: מִתֵּת ׀ לְאַחַד מֵהֶם מִבְּשַׂר בָּנָיו
אֲשֶׁר יֹאכֵל מִבְּלִי הִשְׁאִיר־לוֹ כֹּל בְּמָצוֹר וּבְמָצוֹק אֲשֶׁר יָצִיק לְךָ אֹיִבְךָ
נו בְּכָל־שְׁעָרֶיךָ: הָרַכָּה בְךָ וְהָעֲנֻגָּה אֲשֶׁר לֹא־נִסְּתָה כַף־רַגְלָהּ הַצֵּג
עַל־הָאָרֶץ מֵהִתְעַנֵּג וּמֵרֹךְ תֵּרַע עֵינָהּ בְּאִישׁ חֵיקָהּ וּבִבְנָהּ וּבְבִתָּהּ:
נז וּבְשִׁלְיָתָהּ הַיּוֹצֵת ׀ מִבֵּין רַגְלֶיהָ וּבְבָנֶיהָ אֲשֶׁר תֵּלֵד כִּי־תֹאכְלֵם בְּחֹסֶר־כֹּל
נח בַּסָּתֶר בְּמָצוֹר וּבְמָצוֹק אֲשֶׁר יָצִיק לְךָ אֹיִבְךָ בִּשְׁעָרֶיךָ: אִם־לֹא תִשְׁמֹר
לַעֲשׂוֹת אֶת־כָּל־דִּבְרֵי הַתּוֹרָה הַזֹּאת הַכְּתֻבִים בַּסֵּפֶר הַזֶּה לְיִרְאָה
נט אֶת־הַשֵּׁם הַנִּכְבָּד וְהַנּוֹרָא הַזֶּה אֵת יהוה אֱלֹהֶיךָ: וְהִפְלָא יהוה אֶת־מַכֹּתְךָ

---

meaning that you did (however) keep that which was commanded or instituted as customs by others (which are) not in (keeping) with His Torah, as our Sages have told us that they ceased giving תְּרוּמָה, *the heave offering*, and מַעַשְׂרוֹת, *tithes*, which necessitated Jochanan the *Kohen Gadol* to institute the law of דְּמַאי (the produce of an *am haaretz* which had to be tithed), and Hillel had to institute the *pruzbul* because 'the door was being closed' to borrowers for fear of the Sabbatical year (cancellation of debts). Also, due to the increase of iniquity at the end of the Second Temple period, the ritual of the water of the suspected adulteress (סוֹטָה) and the ceremony of the heifer whose neck was broken (עֶגְלָה עֲרוּפָה) were discontinued (*Sotah* 47a), and the Sanhedrin ceased to function (ibid. 48a), in a manner that all justice was nullified, as our Sages tell us, *Men of violence grew powerful* (ibid. 49a), and thus, they and their possessions were confiscated (lost). [Similar to the condition prevalent today in all our exiles and our debasement, when wealthy people, especially those who are liable according to (Torah) law, reject the Torah of God, the

NOTES

tinued.' The Sanhedrin ceased to function when 'men of violence grew powerful' (ibid. 49a). All this, according to the *Sforno*, is reflected in this *parashah*.

It is interesting to note that the *Sforno's* commentary, as printed in the מִקְרָאוֹת גְּדוֹלוֹת (the standard edition of the *Chumash*), was apparently censored and a number of sentences which appear in the Mosad Rav Kook edition were eliminated, since they refer in one case to the Christian faith and in another to powerful, rich Jews of his generation. These

ס וְאֶת מַכּוֹת זַרְעֶךָ מַכּוֹת גְּדֹלֹת וְנֶאֱמָנוֹת וָחֳלָיִם רָעִים וְנֶאֱמָנִים: וְהֵשִׁיב בְּךָ
סא אֵת כָּל־מַדְוֵה מִצְרַיִם אֲשֶׁר יָגֹרְתָּ מִפְּנֵיהֶם וְדָבְקוּ בָּךְ: גַּם כָּל־חֳלִי
וְכָל־מַכָּה אֲשֶׁר לֹא כָתוּב בְּסֵפֶר הַתּוֹרָה הַזֹּאת יַעְלֵם יהוה עָלֶיךָ עַד
סב הִשָּׁמְדָךְ: וְנִשְׁאַרְתֶּם בִּמְתֵי מְעָט תַּחַת אֲשֶׁר הֱיִיתֶם כְּכוֹכְבֵי הַשָּׁמַיִם לָרֹב
סג כִּי־לֹא שָׁמַעְתָּ בְּקוֹל יהוה אֱלֹהֶיךָ: וְהָיָה כַּאֲשֶׁר־שָׂשׂ יהוה עֲלֵיכֶם לְהֵיטִיב
אֶתְכֶם וּלְהַרְבּוֹת אֶתְכֶם כֵּן יָשִׂישׂ יהוה עֲלֵיכֶם לְהַאֲבִיד אֶתְכֶם וּלְהַשְׁמִיד
סד אֶתְכֶם וְנִסַּחְתֶּם מֵעַל הָאֲדָמָה אֲשֶׁר־אַתָּה בָא־שָׁמָּה לְרִשְׁתָּהּ: וֶהֱפִיצְךָ
יהוה בְּכָל־הָעַמִּים מִקְצֵה הָאָרֶץ וְעַד־קְצֵה הָאָרֶץ וְעָבַדְתָּ שָּׁם אֱלֹהִים
סה אֲחֵרִים אֲשֶׁר לֹא־יָדַעְתָּ אַתָּה וַאֲבֹתֶיךָ עֵץ וָאָבֶן: וּבַגּוֹיִם הָהֵם לֹא תַרְגִּיעַ
וְלֹא־יִהְיֶה מָנוֹחַ לְכַף־רַגְלֶךָ וְנָתַן יהוה לְךָ שָׁם לֵב רַגָּז וְכִלְיוֹן עֵינַיִם
סו וְדַאֲבוֹן נָפֶשׁ: וְהָיוּ חַיֶּיךָ תְּלֻאִים לְךָ מִנֶּגֶד וּפָחַדְתָּ לַיְלָה וְיוֹמָם וְלֹא תַאֲמִין
סז בְּחַיֶּיךָ: בַּבֹּקֶר תֹּאמַר מִי־יִתֵּן עֶרֶב וּבָעֶרֶב תֹּאמַר מִי־יִתֵּן בֹּקֶר מִפַּחַד
סח לְבָבְךָ אֲשֶׁר תִּפְחָד וּמִמַּרְאֵה עֵינֶיךָ אֲשֶׁר תִּרְאֶה: וֶהֱשִׁיבְךָ יהוה ׀ מִצְרַיִם
בָּאֳנִיּוֹת בַּדֶּרֶךְ אֲשֶׁר אָמַרְתִּי לְךָ לֹא־תֹסִיף עוֹד לִרְאֹתָהּ וְהִתְמַכַּרְתֶּם שָׁם
סט לְאֹיְבֶיךָ לַעֲבָדִים וְלִשְׁפָחוֹת וְאֵין קֹנֶה: אֵלֶּה דִבְרֵי
הַבְּרִית אֲשֶׁר־צִוָּה יהוה אֶת־מֹשֶׁה לִכְרֹת אֶת־בְּנֵי יִשְׂרָאֵל בְּאֶרֶץ מוֹאָב
מִלְּבַד הַבְּרִית אֲשֶׁר־כָּרַת אִתָּם בְּחֹרֵב:

כט שביעי א וַיִּקְרָא מֹשֶׁה אֶל־כָּל־יִשְׂרָאֵל וַיֹּאמֶר אֲלֵהֶם אַתֶּם רְאִיתֶם אֵת כָּל־אֲשֶׁר
עָשָׂה יהוה לְעֵינֵיכֶם בְּאֶרֶץ מִצְרַיִם לְפַרְעֹה וּלְכָל־עֲבָדָיו וּלְכָל־אַרְצוֹ:
ב הַמַּסּוֹת הַגְּדֹלֹת אֲשֶׁר רָאוּ עֵינֶיךָ הָאֹתֹת וְהַמֹּפְתִים הַגְּדֹלִים הָהֵם:
ג וְלֹא־נָתַן יהוה לָכֶם לֵב לָדַעַת וְעֵינַיִם לִרְאוֹת וְאָזְנַיִם לִשְׁמֹעַ עַד הַיּוֹם

Blessed One, and the laws of His mouth, and through the medium of gentiles and their courts boldly pervert (justice) in their disputes with others.] And with these (verses), the cause of the destruction of the Second Temple is explained, and the continuance of the Exile due to the continuance of its cause.

68. וְהִתְמַכַּרְתֶּם — *And you shall attempt to sell.* You will attempt to do a variety of labors to sustain yourself in the midst of the nations.

וְאֵין קֹנֶה — *And none will purchase.* Not one of them will want (to pay for) your labors, so that you will be unable to earn a livelihood from it.

XXIX

3. וְלֹא נָתַן ה׳ לָכֶם לֵב לָדַעַת — *But HASHEM has not given you a heart to know.* Even

NOTES

sentences are bracketed in this edition, and the perceptive reader can see why the censor chose to delete them.

68. וְהִתְמַכַּרְתֶּם וְאֵין קֹנֶה — *And you shall attempt to sell and none will purchase.* The *Sforno* explains that even at a time when slavery would no longer prevail, this verse will still be relevant. The meaning of the verse is that the attitude of gentile society toward the Jew will be such, that any attempt by Jews to earn an honest livelihood will be thwarted by the refusal of their gentile neighbors to utilize their services or patronize their business establishments. This will be motivated by their animosity toward Israel.

XXIX

3. וְלֹא נָתַן ה׳ לָכֶם לֵב לָדַעַת — *But HASHEM has*

ד הַזֶּה: וָאוֹלֵךְ אֶתְכֶם אַרְבָּעִים שָׁנָה בַּמִּדְבָּר לֹא־בָלוּ שַׂלְמֹתֵיכֶם מֵעֲלֵיכֶם
ה וְנַעַלְךָ לֹא־בָלְתָה מֵעַל רַגְלֶךָ: לֶחֶם לֹא אֲכַלְתֶּם וְיַיִן וְשֵׁכָר לֹא שְׁתִיתֶם
מפטיר ו לְמַעַן תֵּדְעוּ כִּי אֲנִי יְהוָה אֱלֹהֵיכֶם: וַתָּבֹאוּ אֶל־הַמָּקוֹם הַזֶּה וַיֵּצֵא סִיחֹן
ז מֶלֶךְ־חֶשְׁבּוֹן וְעוֹג מֶלֶךְ־הַבָּשָׁן לִקְרָאתֵנוּ לַמִּלְחָמָה וַנַּכֵּם: וַנִּקַּח אֶת־אַרְצָם
ח וַנִּתְּנָהּ לְנַחֲלָה לָראוּבֵנִי וְלַגָּדִי וְלַחֲצִי שֵׁבֶט הַמְנַשִּׁי: וּשְׁמַרְתֶּם אֶת־דִּבְרֵי
הַבְּרִית הַזֹּאת וַעֲשִׂיתֶם אֹתָם לְמַעַן תַּשְׂכִּילוּ אֵת כָּל־אֲשֶׁר תַּעֲשׂוּן:

---

though He, the Exalted One, attempted through His teachings and wonders to give you *a heart to know* as it says, וּלְמַעַן תְּסַפֵּר . . . וִידַעְתֶּם כִּי אֲנִי ה׳, *That you may tell . . . that you may know that I am HASHEM* (*Exodus* 10:2), (nonetheless) this intended (goal) was not realized because of your numerous insubordinations.

4. וָאוֹלֵךְ אֶתְכֶם — *And I led you.* However, after you have seen the many kindnesses done on your behalf in the wilderness *that you might know* (v. 5), and now that He brought you to the land of Sichon and Og where you have an inheritance in the land so that you can (now) establish in them the intended (purpose of your settlement), it is proper that from now on you should apply your heart to know.

8. וּשְׁמַרְתֶּם אֶת דִּבְרֵי הַבְּרִית הַזֹּאת — *And you shall observe the words of this covenant* . . . which you shall accept upon yourselves on Mount Gerizim and Mount Ebal.

לְמַעַן תַּשְׂכִּילוּ אֵת כָּל אֲשֶׁר תַּעֲשׂוּן — *That you may succeed in all your doings* . . . that you achieve, through your deeds, the intended purpose (of Israel) and (attain) eternal life and temporal life.

NOTES

not given you a heart to know. The verse cannot be understood as meaning that God did not give them the *ability* to understand. Rather, it means that they did not have the *will* to do so. The *Sforno* proves this point by citing the verse in *Exodus* 10:2, where the Almighty tells Moses that He purposely hardened Pharaoh's heart so that He might show His signs and wonders to Israel for the express purpose of educating generations of Israel that they *may know* that He is God. In spite of this effort, the people of Israel did not reach that level of knowledge until *this day* — forty years later! The *Sforno's* commentary explains the link between this verse and the previous two verses (1-2) which speak of the deeds wrought by God in Egypt and the signs and wonders witnessed by Israel.

4. וָאוֹלֵךְ אֶתְכֶם — *And I led you*. The *Sforno* links this verse with the following one (v. 5) which concludes with the words, *that you might know that I am HASHEM your God*. Moses argues that even if the many miracles and wonders in Egypt did not succeed in implanting the knowledge of God in the hearts of Israel, surely it is now time, as they consider the providential care for them in the wilderness (vs. 4-5), and after acquiring the territories of Sichon and Og, that they acknowledge God's greatness and their obligation to accept and observe His commandments.

8. אֵת כָּל אֲשֶׁר תַּעֲשׂוּן — *In all your doings*. The *Sforno* takes note of the word כָּל, *all*, which is all-inclusive. He interprets the verse to mean that by keeping the covenant, Israel will merit success in This World and reward in the World to Come. See the *Sforno's* commentary on the phrase לְטוֹב לָנוּ כָּל הַיָּמִים, *for our good all the days* (6:24), where he also explains it to mean This World and the Eternal One.

פרשת נצבים

Parasha Nitzavim

ט אַתֶּם נִצָּבִים הַיּוֹם כֻּלְּכֶם לִפְנֵי יהוה אֱלֹהֵיכֶם רָאשֵׁיכֶם שִׁבְטֵיכֶם זִקְנֵיכֶם
י וְשֹׁטְרֵיכֶם כֹּל אִישׁ יִשְׂרָאֵל: טַפְּכֶם נְשֵׁיכֶם וְגֵרְךָ אֲשֶׁר בְּקֶרֶב מַחֲנֶיךָ מֵחֹטֵב
יא עֵצֶיךָ עַד שֹׁאֵב מֵימֶיךָ: לְעָבְרְךָ בִּבְרִית יהוה אֱלֹהֶיךָ וּבְאָלָתוֹ אֲשֶׁר יהוה
שני יב אֱלֹהֶיךָ כֹּרֵת עִמְּךָ הַיּוֹם: לְמַעַן הָקִים־אֹתְךָ הַיּוֹם | לוֹ לְעָם וְהוּא יִהְיֶה־לְּךָ

---

9. אַתֶּם נִצָּבִים הַיּוֹם כֻּלְּכֶם לִפְנֵי ה׳ אֱלֹהֵיכֶם — *You are standing this day, all of you, before* HASHEM *your God.* And whoever might mislead me cannot mislead Him, and it is according to His understanding (of your sincerity) that you accept (the covenant) upon yourselves.

רָאשֵׁיכֶם שִׁבְטֵיכֶם זִקְנֵיכֶם וְשֹׁטְרֵיכֶם — *Your leaders, elders (judges) and your officers.* Your *leaders* who are שִׁבְטֵיכֶם, i.e., those who (are entrusted with) the scepter of one who rules. (This refers) to those who are princes and chiefs in whose hands is the scepter of a ruler; and *your elders* — these are the judges; and *your officers* have the power to force the litigants (to accept the court's decision). It is incumbent upon these leaders to instruct the masses (as to) what is beneficial to accept upon themselves and what they should reject.

10. טַפְּכֶם נְשֵׁיכֶם — *Your little children and your wives* . . . for it is proper that their deeds be in accordance with the consent of their fathers and husbands.

מֵחֹטֵב עֵצֶיךָ עַד שֹׁאֵב מֵימֶיךָ — *From the hewer of your wood to the drawer of your water* . . . from the first of the hewers to the last of the drawers, similar to, מֵעֹלֵל וְעַד יוֹנֵק מִשּׁוֹר וְעַד שֶׂה מִגָּמָל וְעַד חֲמוֹר, *from infant to suckling, from ox to sheep, from camel to ass* (*I Samuel* 15:3).

11. לְעָבְרְךָ בִּבְרִית — *So that you pass over into the covenant.* You stand (here) with all this order and (united) consent, prepared to pass over into the covenant, and thus it is apparent that you are all desirous to accept (this covenant) upon yourselves wholeheartedly.

11-12. אֲשֶׁר ה׳ אֱלֹהֶיךָ כֹּרֵת עִמְּךָ הַיּוֹם. לְמַעַן הָקִים אֹתְךָ הַיּוֹם לוֹ לְעָם — *Which* HASHEM *your God makes with you this day, that He may establish you this day unto Himself for a people.* Behold, the intent of God, the Blessed One, in entering the

NOTES

9. לִפְנֵי ה׳ אֱלֹהֵיכֶם — *Before* HASHEM *your God*. Since God's presence is everywhere, obviously Israel stands 'before God.' The *Sforno* explains that Moses cautioned them that God knows the innermost thoughts of man, and therefore, when they enter into the covenant with Him, they cannot do so with their lips alone, while rejecting it in their hearts, as he explains in verses 17-18. Man can be deceived — not so God.

רָאשֵׁיכֶם שִׁבְטֵיכֶם — *Your leaders, elders (judges) and your officers*. *Rashi* interprets this phrase (רָאשֵׁיכֶם שִׁבְטֵיכֶם) as meaning 'the heads of your tribes.' The *Sforno*, however, explains it to mean 'your heads who are leaders that wield the scepter of rulership.' The word שֵׁבֶט is translated as 'scepter' (*Genesis* 49:10), and in our verse the word שִׁבְטֵיכֶם doesn't mean 'your tribes' but 'your scepters.' According to the *Sforno*, three categories of leadership are listed in this verse: leaders who have authority; judges and officers who enforce the law.

10. טַפְּכֶם נְשֵׁיכֶם — *Your little children and your wives*. Whereas the leaders of Israel have the responsibility to instruct the adult community, the guidance of women and children is the responsibility of their husbands and parents.

11-12. לְעָבְרְךָ בִּבְרִית . . . לְמַעַן הָקִים אֹתְךָ הַיּוֹם לוֹ לְעָם — *So that you pass over into the covenant . . . that He may establish you this day unto Himself for a people*. The preceding two verses (9-10), together with these two, are meant to indicate that the whole nation, from the most

לֵאלֹהִ֔ים כַּאֲשֶׁ֖ר דִּבֶּר־לָ֑ךְ וְכַאֲשֶׁ֤ר נִשְׁבַּע֙ לַאֲבֹתֶ֔יךָ לְאַבְרָהָ֥ם לְיִצְחָ֖ק

יג וּֽלְיַעֲקֹֽב׃ וְלֹ֥א אִתְּכֶ֖ם לְבַדְּכֶ֑ם אָנֹכִ֗י כֹּרֵת֙ אֶת־הַבְּרִ֣ית הַזֹּ֔את וְאֶת־הָאָלָ֖ה

יד הַזֹּֽאת׃ כִּי֩ אֶת־אֲשֶׁ֨ר יֶשְׁנ֜וֹ פֹּ֗ה עִמָּ֙נוּ֙ עֹמֵ֣ד הַיּ֔וֹם לִפְנֵ֖י יהו֣ה אֱלֹהֵ֑ינוּ וְאֵ֨ת

שלישי טו אֲשֶׁ֥ר אֵינֶ֛נּוּ פֹּ֖ה עִמָּ֥נוּ הַיּֽוֹם׃ כִּֽי־אַתֶּ֣ם יְדַעְתֶּ֔ם אֵ֥ת אֲשֶׁר־יָשַׁ֖בְנוּ בְּאֶ֣רֶץ

טז מִצְרָ֑יִם וְאֵ֥ת אֲשֶׁר־עָבַ֖רְנוּ בְּקֶ֣רֶב הַגּוֹיִ֑ם אֲשֶׁ֖ר עֲבַרְתֶּֽם׃ וַתִּרְאוּ֙ אֶת־

יז שִׁקּ֣וּצֵיהֶ֔ם וְאֵ֖ת גִּלֻּלֵיהֶ֑ם עֵ֣ץ וָאֶ֔בֶן כֶּ֥סֶף וְזָהָ֖ב אֲשֶׁ֥ר עִמָּהֶֽם׃ פֶּן־יֵ֣שׁ בָּכֶ֡ם אִ֣ישׁ

אֽוֹ־אִשָּׁ֡ה א֣וֹ מִשְׁפָּחָה֩ אוֹ־שֵׁ֨בֶט אֲשֶׁר֩ לְבָב֨וֹ פֹנֶ֤ה הַיּוֹם֙ מֵעִם֙ יהו֣ה אֱלֹהֵ֔ינוּ

לָלֶ֣כֶת לַעֲבֹ֔ד אֶת־אֱלֹהֵ֖י הַגּוֹיִ֣ם הָהֵ֑ם פֶּן־יֵ֣שׁ בָּכֶ֗ם שֹׁ֛רֶשׁ פֹּרֶ֥ה רֹ֖אשׁ וְלַעֲנָֽה׃

---

covenant is to establish you unto Himself for a people so that He shall be unto you as a God and thereby you will acquire eternal life. Now being that the purpose of this covenant is so distinguished, your acceptance should be with complete wholeheartedness.

14. וְאֵת אֲשֶׁר אֵינֶנּוּ פֹּה עִמָּנוּ הַיּוֹם — *And also with them who are not here with us this day.* They refers to future generations. Therefore, you must inform them that the gift of the Land and other (possessions) is given to you on the condition that you keep the covenant, and contingent upon that condition (is the fact that) they will inherit the Land from you.

15. כִּי אַתֶּם יְדַעְתֶּם אֵת אֲשֶׁר יָשַׁבְנוּ — *For you know how we dwelt . . .* and therefore it is fitting to be apprehensive . . .

17. פֶּן יֵשׁ בָּכֶם אִישׁ אוֹ אִשָּׁה — *Lest there should be among you man or woman.* Lest their hearts have been seduced by the vanities of the nations, when they dwelt among them, and they will consider nullifying the acceptance of the covenant. Therefore, I have said that all of you stand before God, who examines the innermost thoughts in the heart (of man), and you cannot mislead Him.

פֶּן יֵשׁ בָּכֶם שֹׁרֶשׁ פֹּרֶה רֹאשׁ וְלַעֲנָה — *Lest there be among you a root which will bear as fruit a poisonous herb and wormwood . . .* (one) who thinks to lead many astray by accepting his destructive opinions.

NOTES

superior elements to the lowest class, eagerly awaited the opportunity to enter into a covenant with God. This was because they understood the special privilege and status granted to them as the people of God. Hence, their acceptance of the covenant was without reservation or qualification. He calls this שְׁלֵמוּת, *a perfect, complete* acceptance. See the *Sforno's* commentary on *Leviticus* 26:12.

14. וְאֵת אֲשֶׁר אֵינֶנּוּ פֹּה — *And also with them who are not here.* How can those *who are not here this day* be parties to this covenant? The *Sforno* explains that those who were present were obligated to instruct future generations that the possession of the Land of Israel was contingent upon their continued obedience to the covenant.

15. כִּי אַתֶּם יְדַעְתֶּם — *For you know.* The *Sforno* interprets this verse as an introduction to the following verses. The reason the Torah cautions Israel to be concerned and wary of certain elements in their midst, whose heart may turn them away from God, is because Israel's exposure to idolatrous practice in Egypt may have adversely influenced them, and made them susceptible to idolatry.

17. שֹׁרֶשׁ פֹּרֶה רֹאשׁ וְלַעֲנָה — *A root which will bear as fruit a poisonous herb and wormwood.* The *Ramban* explains that the root of evil was already present among some in this generation, and the fear expressed here is that this root might develop into poisonous fruit. The *Sforno's* commentary reflects this explanation of the *Ramban*.

יח וְהָיָ֡ה בְּשָׁמְעוֹ֩ אֶת־דִּבְרֵ֨י הָאָלָ֜ה הַזֹּ֗את וְהִתְבָּרֵ֤ךְ בִּלְבָבוֹ֙ לֵאמֹר֙ שָׁל֣וֹם
יִהְיֶה־לִּ֔י כִּ֛י בִּשְׁרִר֥וּת לִבִּ֖י אֵלֵ֑ךְ לְמַ֛עַן סְפ֥וֹת הָרָוָ֖ה אֶת־הַצְּמֵאָֽה:
יט לֹא־יֹאבֶ֣ה יְהוָה֮ סְלֹ֣חַֽ לוֹ֒ כִּ֣י אָ֠ז יֶעְשַׁ֨ן אַף־יְהוָ֤ה וְקִנְאָתוֹ֙ בָּאִ֣ישׁ הַה֔וּא
וְרָ֤בְצָה בּוֹ֙ כָּל־הָ֣אָלָ֔ה הַכְּתוּבָ֖ה בַּסֵּ֣פֶר הַזֶּ֑ה וּמָחָ֤ה יְהוָה֙ אֶת־שְׁמ֔וֹ מִתַּ֖חַת
הַשָּׁמָֽיִם: כ וְהִבְדִּיל֤וֹ יְהוָה֙ לְרָעָ֔ה מִכֹּ֖ל שִׁבְטֵ֣י יִשְׂרָאֵ֑ל כְּכֹל֙ אָל֣וֹת הַבְּרִ֔ית
כא הַכְּתוּבָ֕ה בְּסֵ֥פֶר הַתּוֹרָ֖ה הַזֶּֽה: וְאָמַ֞ר הַדּ֣וֹר הָאַֽחֲר֗וֹן בְּנֵיכֶם֙ אֲשֶׁ֣ר יָק֣וּמוּ
מֵאַ֣חֲרֵיכֶ֔ם וְהַ֨נָּכְרִ֔י אֲשֶׁ֥ר יָבֹ֖א מֵאֶ֣רֶץ רְחוֹקָ֑ה וְרָא֞וּ אֶת־מַכּ֤וֹת הָאָ֨רֶץ֙ הַהִ֔וא
כב וְאֶת־תַּ֣חֲלֻאֶ֔יהָ אֲשֶׁר־חִלָּ֥ה יְהוָ֖ה בָּ֑הּ גָּפְרִ֣ית וָמֶ֘לַח֮ שְׂרֵפָ֣ה כָל־אַרְצָהּ֒ לֹ֤א
תִזָּרַע֙ וְלֹ֣א תַצְמִ֔חַ וְלֹא־יַעֲלֶ֥ה בָ֖הּ כָּל־עֵ֑שֶׂב כְּֽמַהְפֵּכַ֞ת סְדֹ֤ם וַעֲמֹרָה֙ אַדְמָ֣ה

---

18. וְהִתְבָּרֵךְ בִּלְבָבוֹ — *That he bless himself in his heart.* He will accept the curse with his mouth but *bless himself in his heart* by nullifying it.

לֵאמֹר שָׁלוֹם יִהְיֶה לִּי כִּי בִּשְׁרִרוּת לִבִּי אֵלֵךְ — *Saying, 'I shall have peace though I walk in the stubborness of my heart.'* The expression, *bless himself in his heart,* means, that he will say, 'Although I accept the curse with my mouth, I nullify it in my heart and thereby *I shall have peace.'*

לְמַעַן סְפוֹת הָרָוָה אֶת הַצְּמֵאָה — *That the watered (soul) be added (linked) to the thirsty (ones).* The reason that he will accept the curse with his mouth is so that he might add his soul, which is watered and saturated with (the fulfillment of) all desires, to the congregation of God that thirsts (for the spiritual), and is separated from the physical, material desires. (This is all) so that he may rejoice (together) with them in their blessings.

19. לֹא יֹאבֶה ה' סְלֹחַ לוֹ — HASHEM *will not be willing to pardon him* ... for profaning the oath and curse which he accepted with his mouth, even though he nullified it in his heart.

22. גָּפְרִית וָמֶלַח ... כְּמַהְפֵּכַת סְדֹם וַעֲמֹרָה ... אֲשֶׁר הָפַךְ ה' — *Brimstone and salt ... like the overthrow of Sodom and Amorah ... which* HASHEM *overthrew.* They will recognize that this is not an accident but the finger of God, for it is similar to that which He did in Sodom, where it was evident that He destroyed it.

NOTES

18. לְמַעַן סְפוֹת הָרָוָה אֶת הַצְּמֵאָה — *That the watered (soul) be added (linked) to the thirsty (ones).* The commentators have interpreted this difficult passage in a variety of ways. Some interpret רָוָה, *watered,* as meaning 'drunkenness,' implying a condition of irresponsibility, while conversely others interpret it as a metaphor for the righteous. Similarly, the phrase צְמֵאָה, *dry* or *thirsty,* is interpreted as being descriptive of an act לְתַאֲבוֹן, i.e., a transgression motivated by desire; alternatively, others explain it to be a metaphor for the wicked. The verb סְפוֹת is translated by some as 'swept away' while the Ibn Ezra translates it to mean 'to add.' The *Sforno* agrees with this interpretation of the verb סְפוֹת but explains the words רָוָה and צְמֵאָה as

meaning one whose desires are fulfilled and appetites satiated (רָוָה), as opposed to one who is thirsty because he suppresses his lusts and appetites (צְמֵאָה). The sense of the verse is that there will be those who will accept the oath and curse with their lips but in reality spurn and reject it. The only reason they make a pretense of accepting the covenant is because they wish to *be added* to the congregation of Israel and enjoy the blessings of God, Who will bless Israel in the merit of those who discipline and deny themselves (which the Torah terms צְמֵאָה *thirsty*). At the same time they, the wicked, indulge themselves in all their desires (which the Torah calls רָוָה). Their hope, however, will be frustrated, as the Torah states in the next verse.

°וּצְבוֹיִם ק׳ כג °וצביים אֲשֶׁר הָפַךְ יהוה בְּאַפּוֹ וּבַחֲמָתוֹ: וְאָמְרוּ כָּל־הַגּוֹיִם עַל־מֶה עָשָׂה
כד יהוה כָּכָה לָאָרֶץ הַזֹּאת מֶה חֳרִי הָאַף הַגָּדוֹל הַזֶּה: וְאָמְרוּ עַל אֲשֶׁר עָזְבוּ
אֶת־בְּרִית יהוה אֱלֹהֵי אֲבֹתָם אֲשֶׁר כָּרַת עִמָּם בְּהוֹצִיאוֹ אֹתָם מֵאֶרֶץ
כה מִצְרָיִם: וַיֵּלְכוּ וַיַּעַבְדוּ אֱלֹהִים אֲחֵרִים וַיִּשְׁתַּחֲווּ לָהֶם אֱלֹהִים אֲשֶׁר
כו לֹא־יְדָעוּם וְלֹא חָלַק לָהֶם: וַיִּחַר־אַף יהוה בָּאָרֶץ הַהִוא לְהָבִיא עָלֶיהָ
כז אֶת־כָּל־הַקְּלָלָה הַכְּתוּבָה בַּסֵּפֶר הַזֶּה: וַיִּתְּשֵׁם יהוה מֵעַל אַדְמָתָם בְּאַף
כח וּבְחֵמָה וּבְקֶצֶף גָּדוֹל וַיַּשְׁלִכֵם אֶל־אֶרֶץ אַחֶרֶת כַּיּוֹם הַזֶּה: הַנִּסְתָּרֹת
לַיהוה אֱלֹהֵינוּ וְהַנִּגְלֹת לָנוּ וּלְבָנֵינוּ עַד־עוֹלָם לַעֲשׂוֹת אֶת־כָּל־דִּבְרֵי
ל רביעי [שני] א הַתּוֹרָה הַזֹּאת: וְהָיָה כִי־יָבֹאוּ עָלֶיךָ כָּל־הַדְּבָרִים הָאֵלֶּה

---

23. וְאָמְרוּ כָּל הַגּוֹיִם — *And all the nations shall say* . . . when (Israel) will be exiled among them.

25. אֱלֹהִים אֲשֶׁר לֹא יְדָעוּם — *Gods that they knew not* . . . whose existence was unknown to them in every way, (while) forsaking their God who is the authentic God, whose existence, omnipotence and providence has been proven.

וְלֹא חָלַק לָהֶם — *And that He had not alloted to them.* For they will see (realize) that there is no constellation (or planet) which controls their fate, as it says, *Which HASHEM your God has allotted unto all the peoples . . . but you HASHEM have taken . . . to be unto Him a people* (4:19,20).

28. הַנִּסְתָּרֹת לַה׳ אֱלֹהֵינוּ — *The hidden things belong to HASHEM our God.* Although I said that *you stand this day, all of you, before HASHEM* (verse 9), and that no person can mislead Him, and that He will punish the betrayer, behold this applies only to that which is hidden (unknown to man).

וְהַנִּגְלֹת לָנוּ וּלְבָנֵינוּ עַד עוֹלָם — *But the revealed things belong to us and our children forever.* But (as for) revealed (sins), it is incumbent upon us and our children (to punish the sinner) and it is proper that *we do all the words of this law,* to exact revenge from the sinners and do unto them the judgment that is written.

NOTES

22. כְּמַהְפֵּכַת סְדֹם וַעֲמֹרָה . . . אֲשֶׁר הָפַךְ ה׳ — *Like the overthrow of Sodom and Amorah . . . which HASHEM overthrew.* From the nature of the destruction and the catastrophe visited upon *Eretz Yisrael*, it will be evident that it was an act of God, similar to that which happened to Sodom. The verse does not have to be understood in the literal sense of *brimstone and salt;* rather it is meant in the sense of destruction which is not accidental but is the result of Divine punishment. This will be as apparent as the brimstone and fire showered upon Sodom (*Genesis* 19:24).

25. וְלֹא חָלַק לָהֶם — *And that He had not allotted to them.* The *Sforno* in his commentary on 4:19,20 explains that whereas the destiny of all other nations is affected by planetary influences, Israel is unaffected by 'the hosts of heaven and their order.' See the note on those verses which clarify this concept, based on the opinion of our Sages, that the nations of the earth are under the influence of stars, planets and constellations but Israel is not, as we are taught, אֵין מַזָּל לְיִשְׂרָאֵל, (*Shabbos* 156a), *Israel's fate is not determined by the stars.* This is the thrust of the *Sforno's* commentary on the phrase וְלֹא חָלַק לָהֶם — God has not allotted to Israel heavenly forces to control their destiny.

28. הַנִּסְתָּרֹת לַה׳ אֱלֹהֵינוּ וְהַנִּגְלֹת לָנוּ — *The hidden things belong to HASHEM our God but the revealed things belong to us.* Similar to other commentators (*Rashi, Rashbam, Ibn Ezra*), the *Sforno* explains this verse in the following manner: The terrible Divine retribution mentioned in the preceding verses apply only to those who violate the covenant in secret, hidden from the sight of man and

הַבְּרָכָה וְהַקְּלָלָה אֲשֶׁר נָתַתִּי לְפָנֶיךָ וַהֲשֵׁבֹתָ אֶל־לְבָבֶךָ בְּכָל־הַגּוֹיִם אֲשֶׁר
ב הִדִּיחֲךָ יהוה אֱלֹהֶיךָ שָׁמָּה: וְשַׁבְתָּ עַד־יהוה אֱלֹהֶיךָ וְשָׁמַעְתָּ בְקֹלוֹ כְּכֹל
ג אֲשֶׁר־אָנֹכִי מְצַוְּךָ הַיּוֹם אַתָּה וּבָנֶיךָ בְּכָל־לְבָבְךָ וּבְכָל־נַפְשֶׁךָ: וְשָׁב יהוה

XXX

1. וַהֲשֵׁבֹתָ אֶל לְבָבֶךָ — *And you will ponder in your heart.* When you carefully examine and consider the conflicting aspects (of your concepts and actions), and call them all to mind so as to distinguish truth from falsehood, then you will recognize (realize) how far you have distanced yourself from God, the Blessed One, in your opinions and behavior which are contrary to His Torah.

בְּכָל הַגּוֹיִם — *Among all the nations* ... while you are still in exile.

2. וְשַׁבְתָּ עַד ה׳ אֱלֹהֶיךָ — *And you shall return unto* HASHEM *your God.* Your return (repentance) will be exclusively to do the will of your Creator, and it is this repentance of which our Sages say, שֶׁמַּגַּעַת עַד כִּסֵּא הַכָּבוֹד, *It reaches to the Throne of Glory* (*Yoma* 86a).

וְשָׁמַעְתָּ בְקֹלוֹ כְּכֹל אֲשֶׁר אָנֹכִי מְצַוְּךָ הַיּוֹם — *And you shall listen to His voice according to all that I command you this day* ... and not as *commandments of men performed by rote* (*Isaiah* 29:13), as you have done heretofore.

אַתָּה וּבָנֶיךָ — *You and your children.* The younger members of the generation will also recognize this (truth), as it says, כִּי כּוּלָּם יֵדְעוּ אוֹתִי לְמִקְּטַנָּם וְעַד גְּדוֹלָם, *For they shall all know Me, from the least of them to the greatest of them* (*Jeremiah* 31:33).

בְּכָל לְבָבְךָ — *With all your heart.* You will have no doubts regarding this.

וּבְכָל נַפְשֶׁךָ — *And with all your soul.* The lustful spirit will not deter you, for you will recognize the importance of the matter.

NOTES

known only to God. But those who defy the commandments openly must be tried and punished by the community, for the responsibility of bringing them to justice rests upon the whole nation.

XXX

1. וַהֲשֵׁבֹתָ אֶל לְבָבֶךָ בְּכָל הַגּוֹיִם — *And you will ponder in your heart among all the nations.* As a result of the experiences of Israel in exile, they will at some time realize that their defection from God and His Torah has caused them to be cursed and oppressed. This, in turn, will result in serious self-examination which the Torah calls 'the pondering of the heart,' and which the *Sforno* interprets as one's consideration of the inner conflict between good and evil, the truth and falsehood in man's heart, which he always attempts to resolve. Repentance will follow when man recognizes the folly of his ways and chooses to return to God. The *Sforno* stresses that this reflection and repentance will come to pass while Israel is still in exile, for it is in the merit of this repentance that Israel will be redeemed. See his commentary on verse 11.

2. וְשַׁבְתָּ עַד ה׳ אֱלֹהֶיךָ . . . אַתָּה וּבָנֶיךָ . . . בְּכָל לְבָבְךָ . . . וּבְכָל נַפְשֶׁךָ . . . — *And you shall return unto* HASHEM *your God . . . you and your children . . . with all your heart and with all your soul . . .* The *Sforno* carefully interprets each phrase in this verse. The word עַד, *unto,* is used by the prophet *Hosea* (14:2) when he calls upon Israel to repent — שׁוּבָה יִשְׂרָאֵל עַד ה׳ אֱלֹהֶיךָ, *Return, O Israel unto* HASHEM *your God.* The Talmud in *Yoma* (86a), commenting on this verse, states: 'Great is repentance for it reaches unto the Throne of Glory.' The *Sforno* interprets the term עַד as implying that the repentance spoken of in our verse is similar to the *teshuvah* of which *Hosea* speaks. Such sincere repentance can only result from a substantial meaningful hearkening to God's voice; not a superficial one. He therefore explains that Israel, at the time of their return, will not perform *mitzvos* in a perfunctory fashion but will do so with a profound appreciation of their significance. This return to God will be a total one, including

אֱלֹהֶיךָ אֶת־שְׁבוּתְךָ וְרִחֲמֶךָ וְשָׁב וְקִבֶּצְךָ מִכָּל־הָעַמִּים אֲשֶׁר הֱפִיצְךָ יְהוָה
ד אֱלֹהֶיךָ שָׁמָּה׃ אִם־יִהְיֶה נִדַּחֲךָ בִּקְצֵה הַשָּׁמָיִם מִשָּׁם יְקַבֶּצְךָ יְהוָה אֱלֹהֶיךָ
ה וּמִשָּׁם יִקָּחֶךָ׃ וֶהֱבִיאֲךָ יְהוָה אֱלֹהֶיךָ אֶל־הָאָרֶץ אֲשֶׁר־יָרְשׁוּ אֲבֹתֶיךָ
ו וִירִשְׁתָּהּ וְהֵיטִבְךָ וְהִרְבְּךָ מֵאֲבֹתֶיךָ׃ וּמָל יְהוָה אֱלֹהֶיךָ אֶת־לְבָבְךָ
וְאֶת־לְבַב זַרְעֶךָ לְאַהֲבָה אֶת־יְהוָה אֱלֹהֶיךָ בְּכָל־לְבָבְךָ וּבְכָל־נַפְשְׁךָ
חמישי [שלישי] ז לְמַעַן חַיֶּיךָ׃ וְנָתַן יְהוָה אֱלֹהֶיךָ אֵת כָּל־הָאָלוֹת הָאֵלֶּה עַל־אֹיְבֶיךָ
ח וְעַל־שֹׂנְאֶיךָ אֲשֶׁר רְדָפוּךָ׃ וְאַתָּה תָשׁוּב וְשָׁמַעְתָּ בְּקוֹל יְהוָה וְעָשִׂיתָ
ט אֶת־כָּל־מִצְוֹתָיו אֲשֶׁר אָנֹכִי מְצַוְּךָ הַיּוֹם׃ וְהוֹתִירְךָ יְהוָה אֱלֹהֶיךָ בְּכֹל ׀

---

3. וְשָׁב וְקִבֶּצְךָ — *And return and gather you . . .* through the ingathering of the exiles.

6. וּמָל ה׳ אֱלֹהֶיךָ אֶת לְבָבְךָ וְאֶת לְבַב זַרְעֶךָ לְאַהֲבָה — *And* HASHEM *your God will circumcise your heart and the heart of your children to love.* He will open your eyes so that you might turn away from errors which confuse (man's) understanding and knowledge of the truth. (This shall occur) when you attempt to cleave to Him in such a manner that you will recognize His goodness and perforce love Him. This you shall do *that you may live* forevermore.

7. עַל אֹיְבֶיךָ וְעַל שֹׂנְאֶיךָ — *Upon your enemy and upon those who hate you . . .* upon them that rise up against you and those who harbor hatred for you in their heart, as it says, כִּי אֶעֱשֶׂה כָלָה בְּכָל הַגּוֹיִם, *for I will make a full end of all the nations* (*Jeremiah* 30:11).

8. וְאַתָּה תָשׁוּב — *And you shall be at ease.* You shall rest, similar to בְּשׁוּבָה וָנַחַת, *In ease and rest* (*Isaiah* 30:15). This will (come to pass) when Messiah the Righteous One will reveal himself following the destruction of the nations; that is, they will be destroyed but you will survive in ease and rest and no longer be exiled, as the prophet explains, saying, אִם תָּשׁוּב יִשְׂרָאֵל . . . אֵלַי תָּשׁוּב . . . וְלֹא תָנוּד, *If you will return, O Israel . . . return to Me . . . and you will not wander* (*Jeremiah* 4:1).

וְעָשִׂיתָ אֶת כָּל מִצְוֹתָיו אֲשֶׁר אָנֹכִי מְצַוְּךָ הַיּוֹם — *And do all His commandments which I command you this day . . .* for the faith (religion) will never be changed (lit., made new).

9-10. וְהוֹתִירְךָ ה׳ — *And* HASHEM *will make you plenteous.* He will grant you success greater than all former successes.

NOTES

young and old alike, and it will represent total commitment to *mitzvos*, performed with one's entire *heart and soul.*

6. וּמָל ה׳ אֱלֹהֶיךָ — *And* HASHEM *your God will circumcise.* As explained above (6:5), love of God cannot be commanded, nor can reverence, as our Sages state, הַכֹּל בִּידֵי שָׁמַיִם חוּץ מִיִּרְאַת שָׁמַיִם, *All is in the hands of heaven except for fear of heaven* (*Berachos* 33b). The *Sforno*, therefore, explains this verse as meaning that the Almighty will assist man to open his eyes to the truth, and sensitize him to an awareness of God's preeminent role in the universe and to His goodness. This, in turn, will bring man, of his own free will, to the love and fear of God.

7. עַל אֹיְבֶיךָ וְעַל שֹׂנְאֶיךָ — *Upon your enemy and upon those who hate you.* Two words are used in this verse — אוֹיֵב, *one who persecutes*, and שׂוֹנֵא, *one who hates.* The *Sforno* explains the former to mean one who manifests his enmity through overt action, whereas the latter is applicable to one who harbors hatred for Israel in his heart.

8. וְאַתָּה תָשׁוּב — *And you shall be at ease.* In verse 2 we read וְשַׁבְתָּ, *and you shall return,* meaning repentance. Hence the phrase וְאַתָּה

מַעֲשֵׂה יָדֶךָ בִּפְרִי בִטְנְךָ וּבִפְרִי בְהֶמְתְּךָ וּבִפְרִי אַדְמָתְךָ לְטֹבָה כִּי ׀ יָשׁוּב
י יְהוָה לָשׂוּשׂ עָלֶיךָ לְטוֹב כַּאֲשֶׁר־שָׂשׂ עַל־אֲבֹתֶיךָ: כִּי תִשְׁמַע בְּקוֹל יְהוָה
אֱלֹהֶיךָ לִשְׁמֹר מִצְוֹתָיו וְחֻקֹּתָיו הַכְּתוּבָה בְּסֵפֶר הַתּוֹרָה הַזֶּה כִּי תָשׁוּב
ששי יא אֶל־יְהוָה אֱלֹהֶיךָ בְּכָל־לְבָבְךָ וּבְכָל־נַפְשֶׁךָ: כִּי
הַמִּצְוָה הַזֹּאת אֲשֶׁר אָנֹכִי מְצַוְּךָ הַיּוֹם לֹא־נִפְלֵאת הִוא מִמְּךָ וְלֹא רְחֹקָה

לְטֹבָה . . . הַכְּתוּבָה בְּסֵפֶר הַתּוֹרָה הַזֶּה — *For good . . . which are written in this book of the law* . . . as it says, וְהִתְהַלַּכְתִּי בְּתוֹכְכֶם וְהָיִיתִי לָכֶם לֵאלֹהִים, *And I will walk among you and will be your God and you shall be My people.* Now this He shall do when *He will again rejoice over you for good as He rejoiced over your fathers* (*Leviticus* 26:12), but it will not be in the merit of the fathers, rather because your repentance will be with all your heart and all your soul, in such a manner that all your iniquities will be counted as though they were merits (based on *Yoma* 86b). Thereby, you will find favor before Me as did your fathers.

11. כִּי הַמִּצְוָה הַזֹּאת — *For this commandment.* Now the reason I stated, *You will ponder it in your heart among all the nations* (verse 1), is that it is necessary for you to repent while still in exile so that through (this repentance) you will be saved. This is because, indeed, the commandment of repentance which I command you this day (is in your hands alone), as it says in *parashas Vayikra* regarding all sins, וְאָשֵׁם, *and be guilty,* or וְאָשָׁמוֹ, *and his guilt offering*. The intent of this is that man shall come to recognize his transgression (and confess to it) as it explicitly states subsequently, וְהָיָה כִי יֶאְשַׁם לְאַחַת מֵאֵלֶּה וְהִתְוַדָּה אֲשֶׁר חָטָא עָלֶיהָ, *And it shall be when he is guilty of one of these things that he shall confess that wherein he has sinned* (*Leviticus* 5:5), and also when it says, אִישׁ אוֹ אִשָּׁה כִּי יַעֲשׂוּ מִכָּל חַטֹּאת הָאָדָם . . . וְאָשְׁמָה הַנֶּפֶשׁ הַהִוא. וְהִתְוַדּוּ אֶת חַטָּאתָם . . . , *When a man or a woman shall commit any sin that men commit . . . and that soul shall be guilty. Then they shall confess their sin* (*Numbers* 5:6,7) . . .

לֹא נִפְלֵאת הִוא מִמְּךָ — *Is not beyond your understanding* . . . that you should have need for prophets (to explain the way of repentance).

וְלֹא רְחֹקָה הִוא — *Nor is it far away* . . . that there be need for the wise men of the generation, who are far away, to expound it for you, in such a manner that you may

NOTES

תָּשׁוּב cannot mean 'and you shall return' which would be repetitious. The *Sforno* therefore explains it as meaning a promise and assurance that Israel will survive and be at rest, dwelling tranquilly in their land, never again to be forced into exile.

אֲשֶׁר אָנֹכִי מְצַוְּךָ הַיּוֹם — *Which I command you this day.* One of the fundamentals of the Jewish faith is the principle that the Torah given to us by God through Moses 'will never be exchanged nor will there be another Torah,' as stated by *Maimonides* in his 9th Principle of Faith. The *Sforno* reads this basic concept into the words of this verse. He may well be implying that the addition of the word הַיּוֹם, *today,* is meant to reflect the saying of our Sages that *each day* Torah is to be considered as new and fresh, בְּכָל יוֹם יִהְיוּ בְעֵינֶיךָ כַּחֲדָשִׁים, *each day it shall be new in your eyes,* therefore it is unnecessary for it to be exchanged.

9. וְהוֹתִירְךָ ה׳ — *And* HASHEM *will make you plenteous.* The expression וְהוֹתִירְךָ, *will make you plenteous,* also appears in chapter 28, verse 11. The *Sforno*'s interpretation there is similar to the one he gives here; however, in *Ki Savo,* the verse compares Israel's prosperity to that of other nations, while here Israel's present success is compared to their own previous successes.

9-10. לְטֹבָה . . . הַכְּתוּבָה בְּסֵפֶר הַתּוֹרָה הַזֶּה — *For good . . . which are written in this book of the law.* The *Sforno* links these two verses together.

יב הִוא: לֹא בַשָּׁמַיִם הִוא לֵאמֹר מִי יַעֲלֶה־לָּנוּ הַשָּׁמַיְמָה וְיִקָּחֶהָ לָּנוּ וְיַשְׁמִעֵנוּ
יג אֹתָהּ וְנַעֲשֶׂנָּה: וְלֹא־מֵעֵבֶר לַיָּם הִוא לֵאמֹר מִי יַעֲבָר־לָנוּ אֶל־עֵבֶר הַיָּם
יד וְיִקָּחֶהָ לָּנוּ וְיַשְׁמִעֵנוּ אֹתָהּ וְנַעֲשֶׂנָּה: כִּי־קָרוֹב אֵלֶיךָ הַדָּבָר מְאֹד בְּפִיךָ
שביעי ומפטיר טו וּבִלְבָבְךָ לַעֲשֹׂתוֹ: רְאֵה נָתַתִּי לְפָנֶיךָ הַיּוֹם אֶת־
[רביעי] טז הַחַיִּים וְאֶת־הַטּוֹב וְאֶת־הַמָּוֶת וְאֶת־הָרָע: אֲשֶׁר אָנֹכִי מְצַוְּךָ הַיּוֹם לְאַהֲבָה

---

be able to do it while still in exile; and this he explains by saying ...

12. לֹא בַשָּׁמַיִם הִוא — *It is not in heaven.* There is no aspect of repentance which necessitates the amplification (lit., telling) of a prophet.

13. וְלֹא מֵעֵבֶר לַיָּם הִוא — *Neither is it beyond the sea.* You also have no need for the wise men of the generation, who are far away, to expound it for you in such a manner that it will be possible for you (to do it) in exile. Hence, it is not difficult for you (to perform), as (sometimes) occurs with a commandment that needs the interpretation of the wise men of the generation to clarify doubts which arise (regarding its observance), or (certain *mitzvos*) which cannot possibly be fulfilled in exile.

14. בְּפִיךָ וּבִלְבָבְךָ לַעֲשׂתוֹ — *In your mouth and in your heart that you may do it* ... to recognize your sin in your heart, that you sinned against God, the Blessed One, and to regret it and confess to it by words of your mouth.

15. אֶת הַחַיִּים — *Life* ... forever.

וְאֶת הַטּוֹב — *And good* ... the sweetness of this transitory world.

וְאֶת הַמָּוֶת — *And death* ... forever.

וְאֶת הָרָע — *And evil* ... suffering in this transitory world.

NOTES

He is of the opinion that the greatest good which God can grant Israel is for Him to dwell in their midst, thereby demonstrating that He is the God of Israel and they are His people. This blessing of טוֹב, *good,* will result from Israel's sincere return to God, as stated at the conclusion of verse 10. The *Sforno* stresses that God's joy will be evoked by the actions of Israel and their wholehearted repentance, and not because of זְכוּת אָבוֹת, *the merits of the fathers.*

11-14. ... כִּי הַמִּצְוָה הַזֹּאת ... לֹא נִפְלֵאת הִוא מִמְּךָ ... בְּפִיךָ וּבִלְבָבְךָ לַעֲשׂתוֹ — *For this commandment ... is not beyond your understanding ... in your mouth and in your heart that you may do it.* The *Sforno* interprets the phrase הַמִּצְוָה הַזֹּאת, *this commandment*, as referring to the *mitzvah* of תְּשׁוּבָה, repentance. His commentary on this verse and verses 12-14 must be joined together, the sense of these verses being: Man's ability to repent is a privilege and gift granted to him by God. It is an act which can be performed by anyone and is not conditional upon place or time, nor does it require great wisdom or knowledge. When man sins, he can atone for that sin through sincere regret for having transgressed, combined with confession to God, and by accepting upon himself never to sin again (חֲרָטָה, וִדּוּי, קַבָּלָה). There is no need for a prophet or a wise man to reveal to him or teach him how this is to be done for it is totally within the capacity of man. The sequence of repentance is explained by the *Sforno* in verse 14; recognition of one's sins, regret, and confession which must be expressed. See the *Rambam* in *Hilchos Teshuvah* 1:1 and 2:2,3 where these principles are clearly stated. The *Sforno* explains that the Torah in verse 11 makes two statements regarding the nature of repentance — one that it is not beyond man's understanding necessitating the guidance of a prophet, and second that it is not beyond comprehension, necessitating the teaching and interpretation of a wise man. These two ideas are then expanded upon in verses 12-13, while verse 14 teaches us that each person possesses the ability to repent.

אֶת־יְהוָה אֱלֹהֶיךָ לָלֶכֶת בִּדְרָכָיו וְלִשְׁמֹר מִצְוֺתָיו וְחֻקֹּתָיו וּמִשְׁפָּטָיו וְחָיִיתָ
יז וְרָבִיתָ וּבֵרַכְךָ יְהוָה אֱלֹהֶיךָ בָּאָרֶץ אֲשֶׁר־אַתָּה בָא־שָׁמָּה לְרִשְׁתָּהּ׃ וְאִם־
יִפְנֶה לְבָבְךָ וְלֹא תִשְׁמָע וְנִדַּחְתָּ וְהִשְׁתַּחֲוִיתָ לֵאלֹהִים אֲחֵרִים וַעֲבַדְתָּם׃
יח הִגַּדְתִּי לָכֶם הַיּוֹם כִּי אָבֹד תֹּאבֵדוּן לֹא־תַאֲרִיכֻן יָמִים עַל־הָאֲדָמָה אֲשֶׁר
יט אַתָּה עֹבֵר אֶת־הַיַּרְדֵּן לָבוֹא שָׁמָּה לְרִשְׁתָּהּ׃ הַעִדֹתִי בָכֶם הַיּוֹם אֶת־
הַשָּׁמַיִם וְאֶת־הָאָרֶץ הַחַיִּים וְהַמָּוֶת נָתַתִּי לְפָנֶיךָ הַבְּרָכָה וְהַקְּלָלָה וּבָחַרְתָּ
כ בַּחַיִּים לְמַעַן תִּחְיֶה אַתָּה וְזַרְעֶךָ׃ לְאַהֲבָה אֶת־יְהוָה אֱלֹהֶיךָ לִשְׁמֹעַ בְּקֹלוֹ
וּלְדָבְקָה־בוֹ כִּי הוּא חַיֶּיךָ וְאֹרֶךְ יָמֶיךָ לָשֶׁבֶת עַל־הָאֲדָמָה אֲשֶׁר נִשְׁבַּע
יְהוָה לַאֲבֹתֶיךָ לְאַבְרָהָם לְיִצְחָק וּלְיַעֲקֹב לָתֵת לָהֶם׃

---

16. וְחָיִיתָ — *Then you shall live* . . . forever.

18. אָבֹד תֹּאבֵדוּן — *You will surely perish* . . . forever.

19. וּבָחַרְתָּ בַּחַיִּים — *Therefore choose life* . . . everlasting life.

19-20. לְמַעַן תִּחְיֶה אַתָּה וְזַרְעֶךָ. לְאַהֲבָה אֶת ה׳ אֱלֹהֶיךָ — *That you may live, you and your seed. To love* HASHEM *your God*. And I said that you should choose life, not as one who serves for the sake of receiving a reward, rather, I said (i.e., meant) that you should choose only what is *real* life, by desiring (to utilize) transitory life for this purpose alone, namely to love God your God, recognizing His goodness and greatness.

וּלְדָבְקָה בוֹ — *And to cleave to Him* . . . that all your actions be in His name.

כִּי הוּא חַיֶּיךָ — *For that is your life* . . . the cleaving to Him results in everlasting life.

וְאֹרֶךְ יָמֶיךָ לָשֶׁבֶת עַל הָאֲדָמָה — *And the length of your days that you may dwell on the land*. And this will also bring you length of days to dwell on the land in this transitory life, through which you will merit everlasting life, as a result of careful examination and performance of good deeds (i.e., *mitzvos*), as our Sages say, הַתְקֵן עַצְמְךָ בַּפְּרוֹזְדוֹר כְּדֵי שֶׁתִּכָּנֵס לַטְּרַקְלִין, *Prepare yourself in the anteroom that you may enter the banquet hall* (*Avos* 4:21).

NOTES

15-19. אֶת הַחַיִּים וְאֶת הַטּוֹב . . . וְחָיִיתָ . . . אָבֹד תֹּאבֵדוּן . . . וּבָחַרְתָּ בַּחַיִּים לְמַעַן תִּחְיֶה אַתָּה וְזַרְעֶךָ — *Life and good . . . then you shall live . . . you will surely perish . . . therefore choose life that you may live, you and your seed*. The *Sforno* explains these verses in alternate sequence. Moses speaks to Israel of the transitory and the permanent, of this world and eternity. 'Life' in the context of these verses refers to eternal life while 'death' is eternal death. 'Good' and 'evil' refer to man's condition in this world.

20. לְאַהֲבָה אֶת ה׳ אֱלֹהֶיךָ — *To love* HASHEM *your God*. Since the term חַיִּים, *life*, as mentioned in the previous note, refers to everlasting life, it is necessary to clarify that the phrase לְמַעַן תִּחְיֶה, *that you may live* (verse 19), refers to life in *this world* and is linked to the words in this verse *to love* HASHEM *your God* (verse 20). The *Sforno* explains that life in this world is of great importance and paramount value, providing man utilizes it for fulfillment of God's will and appreciates and acknowledges God's kindness and goodness which is manifested in this world.

כִּי הוּא חַיֶּיךָ וְאֹרֶךְ יָמֶיךָ — *For that is your life and the length of your days*. The *Sforno* amplifies the concept that one's life experience in this world has impact upon everlasting life in the World to Come. By cleaving to God, Israel will be granted length of days in *Eretz Yisrael*, enabling them to serve God through Torah study and *mitzvos*, thereby meriting eternal life.

פרשת וילך
Parashas Vayelech

לא א־ב וַיֵּלֶךְ מֹשֶׁה וַיְדַבֵּר אֶת־הַדְּבָרִים הָאֵלֶּה אֶל־כָּל־יִשְׂרָאֵל׃ וַיֹּאמֶר אֲלֵהֶם
בֶּן־מֵאָה וְעֶשְׂרִים שָׁנָה אָנֹכִי הַיּוֹם לֹא־אוּכַל עוֹד לָצֵאת וְלָבוֹא
ג וַיהוָה אָמַר אֵלַי לֹא תַעֲבֹר אֶת־הַיַּרְדֵּן הַזֶּה׃ יְהוָה אֱלֹהֶיךָ הוּא ׀ עֹבֵר

XXXI

1. וַיֵּלֶךְ מֹשֶׁה — *And Moses went.* He roused himself to do so, similar to וַיֵּלֶךְ אִישׁ מִבֵּית לֵוִי, *And there went a man out of the house of Levi* (*Exodus* 2:1), and וַיֵּלֶךְ וַיַּעֲבֹד, *And he went and served* (17:3) and other (such verses). This (is to say) that after he concluded the matter of completing the covenant (between God and Israel), he roused himself to comfort Israel regarding his death, so that the joy of the covenant which was meant to be accepted with rejoicing — as it states יִשְׂמַח יִשְׂרָאֵל בְּעֹשָׂיו, *Let Israel rejoice in Him who made them* (*Psalms* 149:2), and as it says, וְזָבַחְתָּ שְׁלָמִים וְאָכַלְתָּ שָּׁם וְשָׂמַחְתָּ לִפְנֵי ה׳ אֱלֹהֶיךָ, *And you shall sacrifice peace-offerings and shall eat there and you shall rejoice before* H*ASHEM your God* (27:7) — should not be impaired [lit., confounded] (by the sorrow of Moses' imminent death).

2. בֶּן מֵאָה וְעֶשְׂרִים שָׁנָה אָנֹכִי הַיּוֹם — *I am a hundred and twenty years old this day.* And therefore do not grieve over my death, for according to nature I should no longer be able to live.

לֹא אוּכַל עוֹד לָצֵאת וְלָבוֹא — *I can no longer go out and come in.* And even were I to live, I would not be able to go out and come in on your behalf in my old age.

וַה׳ אָמַר אֵלַי לֹא תַעֲבֹר — *And* H*ASHEM has said to me, you shall not cross over.* And even were I able to go out and come in , behold God has said to me that I am not to go over (the Jordan), therefore it is better for you that I die, so that you will be able to go over (into the land).

3. ה׳ אֱלֹהֶיךָ הוּא עֹבֵר לְפָנֶיךָ — H*ASHEM your God, He will go over before you.* Nor should you grieve over the fact that you will have lost my leadership, because indeed, H*ASHEM your God will go over before you,* and thereby you will merit a leadership which is far better than mine.

NOTES

1. וַיֵּלֶךְ מֹשֶׁה — *And Moses went*. The word וַיֵּלֶךְ, *and went,* in the context of this verse lends itself to various interpretations. Where did Moses go? The verses that follow record his words but not any departure from one place and arrival at another. Some commentators say that he walked vigorously before the people to demonstrate that his powers and vitality were unimpaired. Others say that Moses went to each tribe separately to bid them farewell. The *Midrash Tanchuma* states, *The term* וַיֵּלֶךְ *implies admonition.* The *Sforno,* however, explains this word as indicating arousal, animation, or stirring oneself to action. Moses felt it necessary to comfort and encourage the people of Israel who were devastated by the knowledge that he was leaving them forever. His imminent death threatened to cast them into a state of despair, whereas they should have been in a state of great joy and happiness, having entered into a covenant with God. He therefore roused himself to strengthen their resolve and elevate their spirits, reassuring them that God would not forsake them and will lead them to *Eretz Yisrael* under the leadership of Joshua.

2. בֶּן מֵאָה וְעֶשְׂרִים שָׁנָה . . . וַה׳ אָמַר אֵלַי — *I am a hundred and twenty years old . . . and* H*ASHEM has said to me*. Moses gives three reasons why they should not mourn his passing exceedingly: (1) He has lived a long life; (2) even were he to continue to live, his advanced age would prevent him from maintaining his vigorous leadership; (3) since the heavenly decree was that he would not be permitted to enter *Eretz Yisrael,* then were he to continue to live, it would delay their crossing over into the Promised Land.

לְפָנֶיךָ הוּא־יַשְׁמִ֤יד אֶת־הַגּוֹיִם הָאֵ֨לֶּה֙ מִלְּפָנֶ֔יךָ וִירִשְׁתָּ֑ם יְהוֹשֻׁ֕עַ ה֥וּא עֹבֵ֖ר

שני ד לְפָנֶ֔יךָ כַּאֲשֶׁ֖ר דִּבֶּ֥ר יְהוֹה: וְעָשָׂ֤ה יְהוֹה֙ לָהֶ֔ם כַּאֲשֶׁ֣ר עָשָׂ֗ה לְסִיח֥וֹן וּלְע֛וֹג

ה מַלְכֵ֥י הָאֱמֹרִ֖י וּלְאַרְצָ֑ם אֲשֶׁ֥ר הִשְׁמִ֖יד אֹתָֽם: וּנְתָנָ֤ם יְהוֹה֙ לִפְנֵיכֶ֔ם וַעֲשִׂיתֶ֣ם

ו לָהֶ֔ם כְּכָל־הַמִּצְוָ֖ה אֲשֶׁ֥ר צִוִּ֖יתִי אֶתְכֶֽם: חִזְק֣וּ וְאִמְצ֔וּ אַל־תִּֽירְא֤וּ

וְאַל־תַּֽעַרְצ֖וּ מִפְּנֵיהֶ֑ם כִּ֣י | יְהוֹ֣ה אֱלֹהֶ֗יךָ ה֚וּא הַהֹלֵ֣ךְ עִמָּ֔ךְ לֹ֥א יַרְפְּךָ֖ וְלֹ֥א

שלישי [חמישי] ז יַֽעַזְבֶֽךָּ.   וַיִּקְרָ֨א מֹשֶׁ֜ה לִיהוֹשֻׁ֗עַ וַיֹּ֤אמֶר אֵלָיו֙ לְעֵינֵ֣י כָל־

יִשְׂרָאֵ֔ל חֲזַ֣ק וֶֽאֱמָ֔ץ כִּ֣י אַתָּ֗ה תָּבוֹא֙ אֶת־הָעָ֣ם הַזֶּ֔ה אֶל־הָאָ֔רֶץ אֲשֶׁ֨ר

ח נִשְׁבַּ֤ע יְהוֹה֙ לַאֲבֹתָ֖ם לָתֵ֣ת לָהֶ֑ם וְאַתָּ֖ה תַּנְחִילֶ֥נָּה אוֹתָֽם: וַֽיהוֹ֞ה ה֣וּא |

הַהֹלֵ֣ךְ לְפָנֶ֗יךָ ה֚וּא יִהְיֶ֣ה עִמָּ֔ךְ לֹ֥א יַרְפְּךָ֖ וְלֹ֣א יַעַזְבֶ֑ךָּ לֹ֥א תִירָ֖א וְלֹ֥א תֵחָֽת:

ט וַיִּכְתֹּ֣ב מֹשֶׁה֮ אֶת־הַתּוֹרָ֣ה הַזֹּאת֒ וַֽיִּתְּנָ֗הּ אֶל־הַכֹּֽהֲנִים֙ בְּנֵ֣י לֵוִ֔י הַנֹּשְׂאִים֙

יְהוֹשֻׁעַ הוּא עֹבֵר לְפָנֶיךָ כַּאֲשֶׁר דִּבֶּר ה' — *Joshua shall go over before you, as* HASHEM *has spoken* . . . because indeed Joshua is not the leader, but he goes over before you at the command of God, the Exalted One, Who is (the actual) leader.

6. לֹא יַרְפְּךָ — *He will not fail you.* Because He will strengthen your hands in time of war.

וְלֹא יַעַזְבֶךָּ — *And He will not forsake you.* Afterward, for He will not remove (lit., 'diminish') His watchful eye (providence) from you, and those surrounding you will not rise up (against you).

7. כִּי אַתָּה תָבוֹא — *For you shall go* (with this people) . . . even though I was not privileged to do so.

9. אֶת הַתּוֹרָה הַזֹּאת — *This law.* (This refers to) the פָּרָשַׁת הַמֶּלֶךְ, *the section relating to the king*, which he now commanded to be read at הַקְהֵל (the assembly held every seven years).

וַיִּתְּנָהּ אֶל הַכֹּהֲנִים בְּנֵי לֵוִי — *And gave it to the Kohanim the sons of Levi.* For from their hand the king shall receive it to be read, as we learned, *The deputy hands it to the Kohen Gadol, and the Kohen Gadol (hands it) to the king* (Sotah 41a).

NOTES

3. ה' אֱלֹהֶיךָ הוּא עֹבֵר . . . יְהוֹשֻׁעַ הוּא עֹבֵר — HASHEM *your God, He will go over* . . . *Joshua shall go over.* The verse seems to be self-contradictory. First we are told that God will go over before Israel and then we are told that Joshua will bring them across! The *Sforno* explains that God is the actual leader, whereas Joshua is but His messenger.

6. לֹא יַרְפְּךָ וְלֹא יַעַזְבֶךָּ — *He will not fail you and He will not forsake you.* The *Sforno* explains that these two expressions 'to fail' and 'to forsake' are not redundant. The first speaks of a time of war while the second refers to a period of peace, which nonetheless requires the protection of God to secure Israel's well-being in the land.

7. כִּי אַתָּה תָבוֹא — *For you shall go. Sforno* stresses the significance of the added word אַתָּה,

you. Moses says to Joshua: 'You will merit to cross over the Jordan River and lead Israel into the Promised Land, a privilege denied to me.'

9. אֶת הַתּוֹרָה הַזֹּאת — *This law.* Rashi and *Ramban* understand this to mean the entire Torah, which was entrusted to the tribe of Levi to deposit in the Ark next to the tablets of law (v. 24). This interpretation, however, presents a problem, since here the *Kohanim* are mentioned, whereas in verse 24 the Levites are mentioned. Ibn Ezra attempts to resolve this difficulty by explaining that the *Kohanim* were responsible to teach the Torah to Israel and that the expression in verse 24, 'the Levites' is an abbreviation for *the Kohanim the sons of Levi* written in our verse. The *Sforno*, however, defines the term אֶת הַתּוֹרָה הַזֹּאת, *this law,* as meaning the special section relating to

רביעי י אֶת־אֲרוֹן בְּרִית יהוה וְאֶל־כָּל־זִקְנֵי יִשְׂרָאֵל: וַיְצַו מֹשֶׁה אוֹתָם לֵאמֹר מִקֵּץ
יא | שֶׁבַע שָׁנִים בְּמֹעֵד שְׁנַת הַשְּׁמִטָּה בְּחַג הַסֻּכּוֹת: בְּבוֹא כָל־יִשְׂרָאֵל לֵרָאוֹת
אֶת־פְּנֵי יהוה אֱלֹהֶיךָ בַּמָּקוֹם אֲשֶׁר יִבְחָר תִּקְרָא אֶת־הַתּוֹרָה הַזֹּאת נֶגֶד
יב כָּל־יִשְׂרָאֵל בְּאָזְנֵיהֶם: הַקְהֵל אֶת־הָעָם הָאֲנָשִׁים וְהַנָּשִׁים וְהַטַּף וְגֵרְךָ אֲשֶׁר
בִּשְׁעָרֶיךָ לְמַעַן יִשְׁמְעוּ וּלְמַעַן יִלְמְדוּ וְיָרְאוּ אֶת־יהוה אֱלֹהֵיכֶם וְשָׁמְרוּ
יג לַעֲשׂוֹת אֶת־כָּל־דִּבְרֵי הַתּוֹרָה הַזֹּאת: וּבְנֵיהֶם אֲשֶׁר לֹא־יָדְעוּ יִשְׁמְעוּ

הַנֹּשְׂאִים אֶת אֲרוֹן — *Who carry the Ark* ... who carried (the Ark) when special miracles occurred.

וְאֶל כָּל זִקְנֵי יִשְׂרָאֵל — *And to the elders of Israel* ... from whose hand the *Kohanim* would receive the Torah at the Assembly, as we learn, 'The *chazan* (attendant) of the synagogue gives it to the head of the synagogue, and the head of the synagogue to the deputy' (*Sotah* 41a).

12. לְמַעַן יִשְׁמְעוּ — *That they may hear* ... (that) the wise men of the people may understand.

וּלְמַעַן יִלְמְדוּ — *And that they may learn* ... so that they who do not understand shall (in turn) learn from them.

וְיָרְאוּ אֶת ה׳ אֱלֹהֵיכֶם — *To fear* HASHEM *your God* ... by understanding (appreciating) His greatness, as reflected in the reasoned proof of His Torah.

13. וּבְנֵיהֶם אֲשֶׁר לֹא יָדְעוּ — *And their children who have not known* ... who were incapable of asking when they were little ones.

יִשְׁמְעוּ — *May hear* ... a (superficial) hearing of the ear, i.e., they will hear that something is being said.

NOTES

the monarchy, i.e., that which was read by the king at the *Hakhel* ceremony. This was given to the *Kohanim* rather than to the Levites, for as the Mishnah teaches us (*Sotah* 41a), the *Kohen Gadol* would hand the Scroll to the king to be read on that occasion. The king would read selections from the Book of *Deuteronomy* including the section dealing with the monarchy (פָּרָשַׁת הַמֶּלֶךְ).

הַנֹּשְׂאִים אֶת אֲרוֹן — *Who carry the Ark.* Normally the Ark of the covenant was carried by the Kehathites of the tribe of Levi and not by the *Kohanim.* Our Sages tell us that 'on three occasions the *Kohanim* carried the Ark; when they crossed the Jordan, when they walked around Jericho and when they deposited the Ark in its place (in the holy Temple)' (*Sotah* 33b). The *Sforno's* commentary reflects this saying of our Sages.

וְאֶת כָּל זִקְנֵי יִשְׂרָאֵל — *And to the elders of Israel.* Consistent with his explanation that "this law" refers to the Scroll read by the king at *Hakhel,* the *Sforno* explains the reason for including the elders of Israel. Since they were also involved in the ceremony of handing the Torah to the king on this occasion (*Sotah* 41a), Moses gave it to them, as well as to the *Kohanim.*

12. לְמַעַן יִשְׁמְעוּ וּלְמַעַן יִלְמְדוּ — *That they may hear and that they may learn.* The previous verse (11) already states that the Torah was to be read by the king to Israel, בְּאָזְנֵיהֶם, *in their ears.* Why then is it necessary to state in this verse לְמַעַן יִשְׁמְעוּ, *that they may hear?* The *Sforno* explains that the previous verse speaks of listening superficially, without necessarily absorbing and understanding. Our verse speaks of the intelligent listener who understands the significance of the Torah's words, and in turn can teach it to others.

13. וּבְנֵיהֶם אֲשֶׁר לֹא יָדְעוּ יִשְׁמְעוּ וְלָמְדוּ — *And their children who have not known may hear and learn.* The *Sforno* continues the interpretation of this verse in the same vein as that of the previous verse. The young children assembled at the time of *Hakhel,* who are incapable of appreciating the words read by the king, will nonetheless sense that something of

וְלָמְדוּ לְיִרְאָה אֶת־יְהוָה אֱלֹהֵיכֶם כָּל־הַיָּמִים אֲשֶׁר אַתֶּם חַיִּים עַל־
הָאֲדָמָה אֲשֶׁר אַתֶּם עֹבְרִים אֶת־הַיַּרְדֵּן שָׁמָּה לְרִשְׁתָּהּ:
חמישי [ששי] יד וַיֹּאמֶר יהוה אֶל־מֹשֶׁה הֵן קָרְבוּ יָמֶיךָ לָמוּת קְרָא אֶת־יְהוֹשֻׁעַ וְהִתְיַצְּבוּ
טו בְּאֹהֶל מוֹעֵד וַאֲצַוֶּנּוּ וַיֵּלֶךְ מֹשֶׁה וִיהוֹשֻׁעַ וַיִּתְיַצְּבוּ בְּאֹהֶל מוֹעֵד: וַיֵּרָא יהוה
טז בָּאֹהֶל בְּעַמּוּד עָנָן וַיַּעֲמֹד עַמּוּד הֶעָנָן עַל־פֶּתַח הָאֹהֶל. וַיֹּאמֶר יהוה
אֶל־מֹשֶׁה הִנְּךָ שֹׁכֵב עִם־אֲבֹתֶיךָ וְקָם הָעָם הַזֶּה וְזָנָה ׀ אַחֲרֵי ׀ אֱלֹהֵי
נֵכַר־הָאָרֶץ אֲשֶׁר הוּא בָא־שָׁמָּה בְּקִרְבּוֹ וַעֲזָבַנִי וְהֵפֵר אֶת־בְּרִיתִי אֲשֶׁר
יז כָּרַתִּי אִתּוֹ: וְחָרָה אַפִּי בוֹ בַיּוֹם־הַהוּא וַעֲזַבְתִּים וְהִסְתַּרְתִּי פָנַי מֵהֶם וְהָיָה
לֶאֱכֹל וּמְצָאֻהוּ רָעוֹת רַבּוֹת וְצָרוֹת וְאָמַר בַּיּוֹם הַהוּא הֲלֹא עַל כִּי־אֵין
יח אֱלֹהַי בְּקִרְבִּי מְצָאוּנִי הָרָעוֹת הָאֵלֶּה: וְאָנֹכִי הַסְתֵּר אַסְתִּיר פָּנַי בַּיּוֹם

וְלָמְדוּ — *And learn.* When they grow older, they will inquire and learn from those who do understand.

17. וַעֲזַבְתִּים — *And I will forsake them* . . . into the hands of their enemies who will prevail over them.

וְהִסְתַּרְתִּי פָּנַי מֵהֶם — *And I will hide my face from them.* After they will be (given over into) the hands of the nations who will deal with them in an ill fashion and afflict them, I will avert my merciful eye from them as though I do not see their troubles.

עַל כִּי אֵין אֱלֹהַי בְּקִרְבִּי מְצָאוּנִי הָרָעוֹת הָאֵלֶּה — *These evils have come upon me because my God is not in my midst.* Because He removed His *Shechinah,* Divine Presence, from our midst, all these (evils) have befallen us. And by so thinking, you will not turn to Him in prayer or repent.

18. וְאָנֹכִי הַסְתֵּר אַסְתִּיר פָּנַי — *And I will surely hide My face.* It is not as they thought when they said that I am not in their midst, because (in reality) wherever they may be, My *Shechinah* is to be found there, as our Sages said, 'Wherever Israel was exiled, the *Shechinah* was with them' (*Megillah* 29a). Rather, I shall but *hide* my face (and refrain) from saving them.

NOTES

importance is transpiring. Eventually, they will inquire and learn as they mature, for their curiosity and desire to know will have been aroused. Hence, their attendance at *Hakhel* will serve an important purpose. The *Sforno's* explanation clarifies the question, 'Why should the little ones come?' to which the Sages answer, 'To reward those who bring them' (*Chagigah* 3). The bringing of the little ones must serve some purpose for which the adults will be rewarded. The *Sforno's* commentary illuminates the practical benefit of their presence at *Hakhel.* This experience will ultimately cause them to pursue the teachings of Torah when they mature and will be old enough to understand. And it is for enabling the children to have this experience that their parents are rewarded.

17-18. וְהִסְתַּרְתִּי פָּנַי מֵהֶם . . . עַל כִּי אֵין אֱלֹהַי בְּקִרְבִּי . . . וְאָנֹכִי הַסְתֵּר אַסְתִּיר . . . כִּי פָנָה אֶל אֱלֹהִים אֲחֵרִים — *And I will hide my face from them . . . because my God is not in my midst . . . and I will surely hide . . . because they turned to other gods*. The expression הַסְתָּרַת פָּנִים means 'the concealment of God's face,' which the *Sforno* explains as the removal of His merciful concern for the people of Israel, as though He is averting His eyes and refuses to look at their troubles. This does not mean, however, that God has left their midst as Israel may think (*because God is not in our midst*). The *Sforno* quotes the statement of our Sages, which is a fundamental belief of our faith, that the *Shechinah*, Divine Presence, accompanies Is-

יט הַהוּא עַל כָּל־הָרָעָה אֲשֶׁר עָשָׂה כִּי פָנָה אֶל־אֱלֹהִים אֲחֵרִים: וְעַתָּה כִּתְבוּ
לָכֶם אֶת־הַשִּׁירָה הַזֹּאת וְלַמְּדָהּ אֶת־בְּנֵי־יִשְׂרָאֵל שִׂימָהּ בְּפִיהֶם לְמַעַן
ששי [שביעי] כ תִּהְיֶה־לִּי הַשִּׁירָה הַזֹּאת לְעֵד בִּבְנֵי יִשְׂרָאֵל: כִּי־אֲבִיאֶנּוּ אֶל־הָאֲדָמָה ׀
אֲשֶׁר־נִשְׁבַּעְתִּי לַאֲבֹתָיו זָבַת חָלָב וּדְבַשׁ וְאָכַל וְשָׂבַע וְדָשֵׁן וּפָנָה
כא אֶל־אֱלֹהִים אֲחֵרִים וַעֲבָדוּם וְנִאֲצוּנִי וְהֵפֵר אֶת־בְּרִיתִי: °וְהָיָה כִּי־תִמְצֶאןָ
אֹתוֹ רָעוֹת רַבּוֹת וְצָרוֹת וְעָנְתָה הַשִּׁירָה הַזֹּאת לְפָנָיו לְעֵד כִּי לֹא תִשָּׁכַח
מִפִּי זַרְעוֹ כִּי יָדַעְתִּי אֶת־יִצְרוֹ אֲשֶׁר הוּא עֹשֶׂה הַיּוֹם בְּטֶרֶם אֲבִיאֶנּוּ
כב אֶל־הָאָרֶץ אֲשֶׁר נִשְׁבָּעְתִּי: וַיִּכְתֹּב מֹשֶׁה אֶת־הַשִּׁירָה הַזֹּאת בַּיּוֹם הַהוּא
כג וַיְלַמְּדָהּ אֶת־בְּנֵי יִשְׂרָאֵל: וַיְצַו אֶת־יְהוֹשֻׁעַ בִּן־נוּן וַיֹּאמֶר חֲזַק וֶאֱמָץ כִּי
אַתָּה תָּבִיא אֶת־בְּנֵי יִשְׂרָאֵל אֶל־הָאָרֶץ אֲשֶׁר־נִשְׁבַּעְתִּי לָהֶם וְאָנֹכִי אֶהְיֶה
כד עִמָּךְ: וַיְהִי ׀ כְּכַלּוֹת מֹשֶׁה לִכְתֹּב אֶת־דִּבְרֵי הַתּוֹרָה־הַזֹּאת עַל־סֵפֶר עַד
°שביעי כה־כו תֻּמָּם: ° וַיְצַו מֹשֶׁה אֶת־הַלְוִיִּם נֹשְׂאֵי אֲרוֹן בְּרִית־יהוה לֵאמֹר: לָקֹחַ אֵת

עַל כָּל הָרָעָה אֲשֶׁר עָשָׂה — *For all the evil which they have done* . . . to themselves.

כִּי פָנָה אֶל אֱלֹהִים אֲחֵרִים — *Because they turned to other gods.* Because when troubles befell them due to their sins, they did not turn to Me to help them (through) prayer and repentance, but (instead), they turned to those who serve other gods to be rescued through them.

21. כִּי יָדַעְתִּי אֶת יִצְרוֹ אֲשֶׁר הוּא עֹשֶׂה הַיּוֹם — *For I know their inclinations which they form this day.* They do not anticipate entering the Land so as to serve Me, which is My intent, as it says, וַיִּתֵּן לָהֶם אַרְצוֹת גּוֹיִם . . . בַּעֲבוּר יִשְׁמְרוּ חֻקָּיו, *And He gave them the lands of the nations . . . that they might keep His statutes* (*Psalms* 105:44,45). Rather, they look to it (the Land) to satisfy the (base) desires of their souls, and because of this (attitude) the prophesied evil will come to pass, as it says, *But Jeshurun waxed fat and kicked* (32:15).

23. וַיְצַו אֶת יְהוֹשֻׁעַ — *And He appointed Joshua.* God, the Blessed One, then appointed Joshua as ruler, similar to, צִוִּיתִי שֹׁפְטִים, *I appointed judges* (*II Samuel* 7:11), and וְצִוְּךָ לְנָגִיד, *And have appointed you ruler* (*I Samuel* 25:30) and such similar (verses).

24. עַל סֵפֶר עַד תֻּמָּם — *In a book until they were finished* . . . including the portion of *Haazinu* and the portion of *V'zos HaBeracha*.

NOTES

rael into their various exiles. This error on the part of Israel will deter them from repenting, and therefore it is necessary for God to reassure them that although He has permitted their enemies to prevail and has hidden His face, nonetheless, He has not left them and therefore their prayers will still be heard and their repentance accepted.

21. כִּי יָדַעְתִּי אֶת יִצְרוֹ — *For I know their inclinations.* Moses laments that instead of Israel entering *Eretz Yisrael* to realize and develop their spiritual potential, which was the primary purpose of God's granting them the Land, they will settle in it to enjoy material wealth and physical comfort.

23. וַיְצַו אֶת יְהוֹשֻׁעַ — *And He appointed Joshua.* As the *Sforno* pointed out in his commentary on *Exodus* 6:13 regarding Moses and Aaron — וַיְצַוֵּם אֶל בְּנֵי יִשְׂרָאֵל, *And He charged them over the Children of Israel*, the meaning is He *appointed* them as leaders. So too, in our verse, the word וַיְצַו does not mean *He commanded* but rather, *He appointed* Joshua as a ruler (see also *Sforno, Genesis* 36:31).

סֵפֶר הַתּוֹרָה הַזֶּה וְשַׂמְתֶּם אֹתוֹ מִצַּד אֲרוֹן בְּרִית־יהוה אֱלֹהֵיכֶם וְהָיָה־שָׁם
כז בְּךָ לְעֵד: כִּי אָנֹכִי יָדַעְתִּי אֶת־מֶרְיְךָ וְאֶת־עָרְפְּךָ הַקָּשֶׁה הֵן בְּעוֹדֶנִּי חַי

---

26. וְהָיָה שָׁם בְּךָ לְעֵד — *That it remain there as a witness against you.* It will bear testimony that I knew you would forsake the Torah of God, the Blessed One, and therefore, I had to place a Torah Scroll in a (secure) place where no man could enter, except for the *Kohen Gadol*, and he only once a year. This Scroll will bear testimony that all that is written in the Torah, which is in the hands of the righteous of the generation, are the words which were spoken to Moses at Sinai, without (any) addition or diminishment, and thus no doubts will arise among you regarding them (i.e., the words of Torah). However, as for the Scroll found by Chilkeyahu (*II Kings* 22:8), it would seem to me that it was the Scroll given by Moses to the *Kohanim* who carried the Ark of the Covenant of God, as mentioned above, which contained only the portion of the king (פָּרָשַׁת הַמֶּלֶךְ). In it, Joshua (also) wrote the covenant which he renewed with Israel in Shechem (*Joshua* 24:25,26) when they accepted to serve God, the Exalted One, in truth and integrity (תָמִים), (meaning) with contemplation and deed. When Josiah read from this Scroll and realized that they had strayed from it, he trembled and inquired of God (for guidance) therein (i.e., in regard to this defection).

NOTES

24. עַל סֵפֶר עַד תֻּמָּם — *In a book until they were finished.* The *Sforno* explains that the reference here is to the completion of the entire Torah from beginning to end, including the two portions of *Ha'azinu* and *V'zos HaBerachah*, which appear following this *sedrah*. The שִׁירָה, *song* or *poem*, mentioned in verse 30 however, which includes the same expression עַד תֻּמָּם, *until they were finished*, only refers to the song of *Haazinu*, which Moses recited to the people prior to his death.

26. וְהָיָה שָׁם בְּךָ לְעֵד — *That it remain there as a witness against you*. The Midrash says that on the day Moses passed away, he wrote thirteen Torah Scrolls. He gave one to each of the twelve tribes and the thirteenth he delivered into the hands of the Levites for safekeeping. They placed it *on the side of the Ark of the covenant*. The *Sforno* explains that this was done so that there would always be an authentic, authoritative copy of the Torah in a secure place thus preventing any attempt to falsify it or to produce a counterfeit one. The Levites were entrusted with this Torah for it was they who carried the Ark. However, the Scroll mentioned in verse 9, which contained the פָּרָשַׁת הַמֶּלֶךְ, *the portion of the king*, was entrusted to the *Kohanim*, for the reason given by the *Sforno* in his commentary on that verse. In the opinion of the *Sforno*, it is this latter Torah which Chilkeyahu the *Kohen Gadol* discovered in the reign of King Josiah, as recorded in *II Kings* 22:8, and not the 13th Torah mentioned by the Midrash. In that chapter, we read that Josiah ordered that the Temple be repaired and in the process a Torah Scroll was found which had been hidden in defiance of King Ahaz's order that all Torah Scrolls be burned. When this Sefer Torah was read to Josiah, he rent his clothes, for he realized that Israel was guilty of violating God's teachings. Subsequently, he gathered the people and read from the Scroll and renewed the covenant between Israel and God. The *Sforno* is of the opinion that this particular Scroll contained only 'the portion of the king' which was read by the king at *Hakhel*. This public assembly took place every seven years at the conclusion of the Succos festival following each Sabbatical year.

The basis for the *Sforno's* thesis may well be the Mishnah in tractate *Sotah* (41a), which states that included in the פָּרָשַׁת הַמֶּלֶךְ are the blessings and curses as recorded in *parashas Ki Savo* (chapter 27). Josiah was deeply alarmed when he read these curses, and the fact that he later read from this Scroll to the people whom he had assembled, and also renewed the covenant between Israel and God, is reasonable proof that it was indeed the פָּרָשַׁת הַמֶּלֶךְ which had been found, since the 'blessing and curses' are the prelude to the covenant between Israel and God, as stated in *Nitzavim* (29:11).

The *Sforno* is also of the opinion that when Joshua, before his death, renewed the

מפטיר כח עִמָּכֶם הַיּוֹם מַמְרִים הֱיִתֶם עִם־יהוה וְאַף כִּי־אַחֲרֵי מוֹתִי: הַקְהִילוּ אֵלַי
אֶת־כָּל־זִקְנֵי שִׁבְטֵיכֶם וְשֹׁטְרֵיכֶם וַאֲדַבְּרָה בְאָזְנֵיהֶם אֵת הַדְּבָרִים הָאֵלֶּה
כט וְאָעִידָה בָּם אֶת־הַשָּׁמַיִם וְאֶת־הָאָרֶץ: כִּי יָדַעְתִּי אַחֲרֵי מוֹתִי כִּי־הַשְׁחֵת
תַּשְׁחִתוּן וְסַרְתֶּם מִן־הַדֶּרֶךְ אֲשֶׁר צִוִּיתִי אֶתְכֶם וְקָרָאת אֶתְכֶם הָרָעָה
בְּאַחֲרִית הַיָּמִים כִּי־תַעֲשׂוּ אֶת־הָרַע בְּעֵינֵי יהוה לְהַכְעִיסוֹ בְּמַעֲשֵׂה
ל יְדֵיכֶם: וַיְדַבֵּר מֹשֶׁה בְּאָזְנֵי כָּל־קְהַל יִשְׂרָאֵל אֶת־דִּבְרֵי הַשִּׁירָה הַזֹּאת
עַד תֻּמָּם:

---

28. וַאֲדַבְּרָה בְאָזְנֵיהֶם אֵת הַדְּבָרִים הָאֵלֶּה — *That I may speak these words in their ears* . . . the song of *Ha'azinu.*

וְאָעִידָה בָּם אֶת הַשָּׁמַיִם וְאֶת הָאָרֶץ — *And call heaven and earth to witness against them* . . . as it says, *Give ear, O heavens etc.* (32:1).

29. כִּי יָדַעְתִּי — *For I know.* I shall relate with this song, and bear testimony against you, that I knew you would act in such a manner that evil would be brought upon you. (This was) in order that you shall not attribute future (events) simply to chance but rather you will attribute it to your corrupt behavior, and (thereby) consider returning (to God), similar to, וָאַגִּיד לְךָ מֵאָז בְּטֶרֶם תָּבוֹא הִשְׁמַעְתִּיךָ פֶּן תֹּאמַר עָצְבִּי עָשָׂם, *Therefore I have declared it to you from of old, before it came to pass I announced it to you, lest you say my idol has done them* (*Isaiah* 48:5).

30. אֶת דִּבְרֵי הַשִּׁירָה הַזֹּאת עַד תֻּמָּם — *The words of this song, until they were complete* . . . including the portion of *For HASHEM will judge* (32:36) and *For I lift up My hand* (32:40), even though these are not part of the words of the testimony.

NOTES

covenant between the people and God, he recorded it *in the book of God's Torah* (*Joshua* 24:26), namely, the Scroll of פָּרָשַׁת הַמֶּלֶךְ. This is his theory even though the Talmud (*Makos* 11a) tells us that one Sage is of the opinion that this act of writing by Joshua refers to the last eight verses of the Torah. Since they speak of Moses' death, Moses could not have written them. Thus, God bid Joshua to write these verses. Another Sage states that it refers to the list of cities of refuge recorded in the Book of *Joshua.* Nonetheless, the *Sforno* is of the opinion that Joshua would never have added anything to the Torah itself, but did feel free to add the confirmation of the covenant in his time to the special book of פָּרָשַׁת הַמֶּלֶךְ. When Josiah read of the renewal of the covenant in the time of Joshua, he decided to do likewise, as recorded in *II Kings* 23.

29. כִּי יָדַעְתִּי — *For I know.* The tendency of people is to attribute events to blind chance — a happenstance. Moses cautions the people to avoid this error, and to recognize that their fate is always the consequence of their behavior, and a heavenly judgment from God. The poem of *Ha'azinu* foretells the history of Israel and thereby bears testimony to God's Providence and His Divine system of reward and punishment.

פרשת האזינו
Parasahs Ha'azinu

לב א הַאֲזִינוּ הַשָּׁמַיִם וַאֲדַבֵּרָה וְתִשְׁמַע הָאָרֶץ אִמְרֵי־פִי׃
ב יַעֲרֹף כַּמָּטָר לִקְחִי תִּזַּל כַּטַּל אִמְרָתִי
כִּשְׂעִירִם עֲלֵי־דֶשֶׁא וְכִרְבִיבִים עֲלֵי־עֵשֶׂב׃
ג כִּי שֵׁם יהוה אֶקְרָא הָבוּ גֹדֶל לֵאלֹהֵינוּ׃

XXXII

2. יַעֲרֹף כַּמָּטָר לִקְחִי — *My Torah shall drop as the rain.* Behold, my teaching (lit., my Torah) shall drop and stream as the rain unto those who understand and are prepared to receive the flow from the fount of wisdom.

תִּזַּל כַּטַּל אִמְרָתִי — *My speech shall flow gently like the dew.* And it (i.e., my Torah) shall also grant some knowledge to the common man, according to its apparent (lit., revealed) teaching, for although it is small in quantity it is exceedingly good, similar to the dew. In such a manner, it (the teaching of Moses) shall be as *the stormy showers upon the herbage,* (meaning) that the intelligent ones shall see the wonders in it (i.e., the Torah); *and as the drops of rain upon the grass,* (meaning) that the common people will also attain some knowledge from it, learning to recognize their Creator to some extent through its (study). Therefore to you, Israel, who have received it, (I now say) . . .

3. כִּי שֵׁם ה׳ אֶקְרָא — *When I proclaim the name of* HASHEM. Behold, a קוֹרֵא שֵׁם ה׳, *one who proclaims the name of God,* is he who prays, as it says קָרָאתִי שִׁמְךָ ה׳ מִבּוֹר תַּחְתִּיּוֹת, *I called upon your name,* HASHEM, *out of the nethermost pit* (*Lamentations* 3:55); and also וּשְׁמוּאֵל בְּקֹרְאֵי שְׁמוֹ קֹרְאִים אֶל ה׳ וְהוּא יַעֲנֵם, *and Samuel among those who call upon His Name; they called upon* HASHEM *and He answered them* (*Psalms* 99:6). (Moses) therefore says: When I pray regarding the ingathering of the exiles, saying, *As an eagle that stirs up her nest* (v. 11), and also regarding the coming of Messiah saying, HASHEM *alone did lead him* (v. 12), and also at the conclusion of the song, when I say, *Sing aloud, you nations, of His people* (v. 43), you who know of His greatness through reasoned proof, as explained in His Torah . . .

הָבוּ גֹדֶל לֵאלֹהֵינוּ — *Give greatness to our God.* Do not attribute any change to Him (as a result) of what will be related in this song regarding the future of Israel, or (think) that He will become an enemy to them (i.e., Israel), because you know, through proof from His Torah, that He is *the Rock* who is unchanging, and His hand is (never) incapable of saving, (nor) His ear incapable of hearing. Also, you shall not attribute to Him iniquity, considering that you know with certainty that *His work is perfect* (v. 4) as is (His) existence, and nothing can be added to it (i.e., *His work*) nor can anything be subtracted from it, and thus (we) know . . .

NOTES

ZZZII

2. כַּמָּטָר . . . כַּטַּל — *As the rain . . . like the dew.* Moses uses the simile of מָטָר, *rain*, and also of טַל, *dew*. Linked to the former is the expression שְׂעִירִם, which *Rashi* explains as meaning a stormy wind, whereas the phrase רְבִיבִים, meaning drops of rain, is linked to the latter. The *Sforno* explains the verse thus: God's Torah can be comprehended by simple folk as well as by scholars, but their understanding and grasp of its teachings and profound wisdom are on different levels. The common, average individual understands the Torah's instruction superficially. He absorbs and appreciates it within certain limitations. The Torah compares this to dew and drops of rain. However, the intelligent, advanced student of Torah plummets the depths and unravels its profound mysteries; this is compared to the

ד הַצּוּר תָּמִים פָּעֳלוֹ כִּי כָל־דְּרָכָיו מִשְׁפָּט
אֵל אֱמוּנָה וְאֵין עָוֶל צַדִּיק וְיָשָׁר הוּא:
ה שִׁחֵת לוֹ לֹא בָּנָיו מוּמָם דּוֹר עִקֵּשׁ וּפְתַלְתֹּל:
ו הַ לַיהוָה תִּגְמְלוּ־זֹאת עַם נָבָל וְלֹא חָכָם

---

4. כִּי כָל דְּרָכָיו מִשְׁפָּט — *For all His ways are justice.* His ways of goodness and His attributes of law are all just, without any doubt.

אֵל אֱמוּנָה — *A God of faithfulness.* He will faithfully (fulfill) that which He swore to the Patriarchs, i.e., to be good to (their) descendants in the merit of their fathers.

וְאֵין עָוֶל — *And without iniquity* . . . when He brings punishment.

צַדִּיק — *Righteous.* He loves righteousness, and because of His righteousness He will not cast off His people in exile.

וְיָשָׁר הוּא — *And right is He* . . . never denying the reward of any human being. (He) repays His enemies before Him, and therefore prolongs (their existence) and is good to the nations in This World.

5. שִׁחֵת לוֹ לֹא בָּנָיו מוּמָם דּוֹר עִקֵּשׁ וּפְתַלְתֹּל — *A generation crooked and perverse, that are not His children, has corrupted His ways* (*and this is*) *their blemish.* But a generation (that is) crooked and perverse are not His children, who are (characterized by) perfection, for behold, their blemish (manifested) through the (sin) of the calf corrupted the intent of God, the Exalted One, as it says כִּי שִׁחֵת עַמְּךָ, *for your people have dealt corruptly* (*Exodus* 32:7). Because He indeed intended to sanctify Israel and to sanctify His Name through them in His world, that they should be luminaries for human kind, to understand and to instruct, as it says כִּי לִי כָּל הָאָרֶץ וְאַתֶּם תִּהְיוּ לִי מַמְלֶכֶת כֹּהֲנִים, *For all the earth is Mine; and you shall be unto Me a kingdom of Kohanim* (ibid 19:5,6), (but) they perverted all this through idolatry.

6. הַלְה׳ תִּגְמְלוּ זֹאת — *Do you thus repay* HASHEM*?* Considering that His intent was to elevate you above all the nations, is it then proper that you repay Him thus, impairing His intent by desecrating his Holy Name, and thereby preventing the attainment of (His) purpose which He intended (when) He said, נַעֲשֶׂה אָדָם בְּצַלְמֵנוּ כִּדְמוּתֵנוּ, *Let us make man in our image after our likeness* (*Genesis* 1:26).

עַם נָבָל — *A vile people.* Contemptible, in that you are ingrates who repay with evil (the One) Who does good, as opposed to the honored noble (generous) One, Who does good even to those who never did good unto Him.

NOTES

rain and the stormy wind, because it overwhelms the mind and permeates the soul of wise men who are capable of appreciating the wonders of God's teaching.

3-4. כִּי שֵׁם ה׳ אֶקְרָא . . . כִּי כָל דְּרָכָיו מִשְׁפָּט . . . צַדִּיק וְיָשָׁר הוּא — *When I proclaim the name of* HASHEM *. . . for all His ways are justice . . . righteous and right is He*. The *Sforno* interprets the sense of these two verses thus: Although you may well surmise from my prayer and song that trouble will befall the people of Israel, including persecution and exile, do not despair, for God is unchanging as a Rock and He is unswerving in His love for Israel, ever committed to preserve them. He is also a God of justice and faithfulness, Who rewards the righteous and punishes the wicked. This may not be perceived by man at the beginning, but God is patient — as we must also be — and eventually there is Divine accountability, be it for evil or for good. Compare this commentary to *Rashi* on verse **4**.

5. שִׁחֵת לוֹ — *Has corrupted His ways.* The expression שִׁחֵת is used in this verse and also at

הֲלוֹא־הוּא֙ אָבִ֣יךָ קָּנֶ֔ךָ הוּא עָשְׂךָ֖ וַֽיְכֹנְנֶֽךָ׃
שני ז זְכֹר֙ יְמ֣וֹת עוֹלָ֔ם בִּ֖ינוּ שְׁנ֣וֹת דֹּר־וָדֹ֑ר

וְלֹא חָכָם — *And unwise.* (Unwise) in statesmanship so as to understand what the end result will be and what will (eventually) be attained.

הֲלוֹא הוּא אָבִיךָ קָּנֶךָ — *Is He not your father that has acquired you?* (He) is not a natural father who causes existence by chance, but a father by choice Who granted you existence that you might be His possession, prepared to attain His desire through you, and that you shall be His treasured people. (And thus) He made you into a nation, because (otherwise) you would not have been considered a nation at all.

וַיְכֹנְנֶךָ — *And prepared you.* He gave you preparatory (powers) that you might be predisposed through them to be a treasured (chosen) people unto Him.

7. זְכֹר יְמוֹת עוֹלָם — *Remember the days of old.* After he completed the introductory section of the song wherein he proclaimed his intent to tell of the righteousness of the Exalted God; that He is a faithful God Who does good for Israel, Who has 'blessed and will not reverse it' (based on *Numbers* 23:20), and that there is no iniquity in the measure of His judgment against them, Moses (now) begins to explain this by relating the (events) of the past and the future, telling us (the following): First, the intent of God, the Blessed One, was to attain this goal (purpose) through all of humankind 'in days of old and the years of many generations,' and when this did not succeed, God did great wonders with Israel by elevating them to the heights, as He shall do at the 'end of days' with the remnants (of Israel) whom He will call upon.

Second, He gave them an appropriate place in which to serve Him in joy and goodness of heart, with an abundance (of material blessings), but they rebelled and

NOTES

the episode of the Golden Calf. It indicates turning away from the correct and proper way. The *Sforno* interprets our verse as referring to the sin of idolatry at Mt. Sinai, which vitiated the plan of God for Israel — to be a light unto the nations. See the *Sforno's* commentary on *Exodus* 19:5,6 where he explains that mankind as a whole is precious to God, but Israel is His unique treasure whose mission it is to instruct mankind in the ways of God. Through their sinful actions, they thwarted His plan and frustrated His intent, as the *Sforno* states in the next verse.

6. עַם נָבָל וְלֹא חָכָם . . . אָבִיךָ קָּנֶךָ . . . וַיְכֹנְנֶךָ — *A vile people and unwise . . . your father that has acquired you . . . and prepared you.* Similar to other commentators, among them the *Ramban*, the *Sforno* interprets the word נָבָל to mean one whose vile nature is manifested in a lack of gratitude for past favors and לֹא חָכָם, *unwise*, as one who has demonstrated his failure to understand that any future assistance from the same source is jeopardized by such ingratitude. The word קָּנֶךָ, *that has acquired you*, qualifying the word אָבִיךָ, *your father*, is explained as meaning a conscious choice by God to acquire Israel as His people and prepare them to be an עַם סְגוּלָה, *a treasured people* (*Exodus* 19:5). Unlike *Rashi* who interprets וַיְכֹנְנֶךָ as being derived from the root כֵּן, *base*, the *Sforno* interprets it in the sense of הֲכָנָה, *preparation.*

7. זְכֹר יְמוֹת עוֹלָם — *Remember the days of old.* The Talmud (*Rosh Hashanah* 31a) explains why specific psalms were chanted by the Levites each day in the Temple as part of the morning service. At the *Mussaf* service on *Shabbos* they would recite the *parashah* of *Haazinu*, which was divided into six parts and recited over a period of six weeks.

The *Sforno* explains the division of the *parashah* into six sections in the following manner. Verses 1-6 are the introductory remarks of Moses where he assures Israel that God is faithful and concerned for their welfare. This section beginning with the letter ה׳ was read in the Temple as one unit and in the synagogue today is the portion read by the *Kohen*. The second section, read by the Levi (verses 7-12), begins with the letter ז׳ and

שְׁאַל אָבִ֙יךָ֙ וְיַגֵּ֔דְךָ   זְקֵנֶ֖יךָ וְיֹ֥אמְרוּ לָֽךְ:

ח בְּהַנְחֵ֤ל עֶלְיוֹן֙ גּוֹיִ֔ם   בְּהַפְרִיד֖וֹ בְּנֵ֣י אָדָ֑ם

יַצֵּב֙ גְּבֻלֹ֣ת עַמִּ֔ים   לְמִסְפַּ֖ר בְּנֵ֥י יִשְׂרָאֵֽל:

---

repaid evil for good. And he who frustrated this intent (of God) is, without a doubt, deserving of severe punishment.

Third, because of the magnitude of their sins they fell into the net of the wicked and were deserving of complete destruction, were it not for the desecration of God's honor which prevented it.

Fourth, he informs (us) the cause (reason) for which they will be redeemed at the end of days.

Fifth, he describes the manner of (Israel's) redemption, and the revenge that God, the Blessed One, (will exact) against the oppressors of His people. (Now) these are the (various) parts of *parashas Haazinu* mentioned by our Sages (*Rosh Hashanah* 31a) who designated (special) signs for them: הזי״ו ל״ך (these being the first letters of these six sections). He therefore says, *Remember the days of old*, and you will understand the goodness of His ways and how He intended to benefit humankind in general, when you recall how at first He was good to Adam at the beginning of time (lit., the days of old), placing him in the Garden of Eden, but (Adam) spoiled the state of (his affairs). Secondly, *Consider the years of many generations* and you will understand how, prior to the flood, He was good to many generations but they corrupted (their ways); and thirdly, (His goodness) from the time of the flood to (the generations of) dispersal, and (how) they perverted (their ways).

8. יַצֵּב גְּבֻלֹת עַמִּים — *He set the borders of the peoples.* And He set the borders of the peoples (at the time of) the Separation (הַפְּלָגָה) but did not destroy them completely which, in reality, they deserved.

לְמִסְפַּר בְּנֵי יִשְׂרָאֵל — *According to the number of the Children of Israel . . .* for the sake of the Children of Israel who were few in number, but who would ultimately come forth from those people — and the proof of this is . . .

NOTES

discusses God's original plan for mankind. This plan was frustrated as a result of man's transgressions, resulting in the Almighty's choice of one people (Israel) through whom He hoped to effectuate His original plan for mankind. The third section (verses 15-18) tells us that a special land (*Eretz Yisrael*) was given to Israel, and was blessed with material and spiritual goodness, but they rebelled against Him and were consequently punished. This unit begins with the letter י and is שְׁלִישִׁי — the third *aliyah* read on *Shabbos Haazinu*. The fourth unit, (verses 19-28) beginning with the letter ו, speaks of Israel's punishment which was tempered lest their destruction cause a חִלּוּל הַשֵּׁם, *profanation of God's Name.* The fifth section, beginning with the letter ל (verses 29-39), speaks of God's concern and compassion for Israel, His revenge against the nations who had persecuted the Jewish people,

and of Israel's ultimate redemption. The sixth and concluding unit (verses 40-43) begins with the letter כ and tells us the manner of God's revenge and of the redemption of Israel. The Sages refer to these six units as הזי״ו ל״ך, an acrostic composed of the first letter of each of the first words of the six portions. The *Sforno* in his commentary lists only five sections since he considers the first part of האזינו as an introduction and not part of the body of the poem. The *Rambam* explains that this *parashah* was read at the Temple *Mussaf* service on the Sabbath because 'they are words encouraging the people to repent.' (See *Orach Chaim* 428:5 and the *Mishnah Berurah* 11.)

8. יַצֵּב גְּבֻלֹת עַמִּים לְמִסְפַּר בְּנֵי יִשְׂרָאֵל — *He sets the borders of the peoples, according to the number of the Children of Israel.* The *Sforno* reflects the commentary of *Rashi* who states,

ט כִּי חֵלֶק יהוה עַמּוֹ יַעֲקֹב חֶבֶל נַחֲלָתוֹ:
י יִמְצָאֵהוּ בְּאֶרֶץ מִדְבָּר וּבְתֹהוּ יְלֵל יְשִׁמֹן
יְסֹבְבֶנְהוּ יְבוֹנְנֵהוּ יִצְּרֶנְהוּ כְּאִישׁוֹן עֵינוֹ:

---

9. כִּי חֵלֶק ה׳ עַמּוֹ — *For the portion of* H*ASHEM is His people* . . . because God, the Blessed One, has no portion among humankind except for His people, because all other nations are children of strange gods. Hence, it is clear that were it not for His people who were destined to come forth from those nations, He would have destroyed them due to the (sin) of the (Generation) of Separation.

יַעֲקֹב חֶבֶל נַחֲלָתוֹ — *Jacob the lot of His inheritance.* For he and his children are servants of God, the Exalted One, but among the nations of the world, (even) if there is to be found among them a righteous (pious) one, it is not passed on to his children.

10. יִמְצָאֵהוּ בְּאֶרֶץ מִדְבָּר — *He found him in a desert land.* He found the heart of His portion (Israel), trustworthy before Him in the desert, as it says, לֶכְתֵּךְ אַחֲרַי בַּמִּדְבָּר, *Going after Me in the wilderness* (*Jeremiah* 2:2).

יְסֹבְבֶנְהוּ — *He compassed it about* . . . i.e., the mountain of Sinai, as it says, וְהִגְבַּלְתָּ אֶת הָעָם סָבִיב, *And you shall set bounds for the people round about* (*Exodus* 19:12).

יְבוֹנְנֵהוּ — *He instructed him.* As it says, וְהַתּוֹרָה וְהַמִּצְוָה אֲשֶׁר כָּתַבְתִּי לְהוֹרֹתָם, *And the Torah and the commandment which I have written that you may teach them* (ibid. 24:12).

יִצְּרֶנְהוּ — *He protected him* . . . from the bondage of Egypt and the angel of death, [as the Sages say, (The verse) חָרוּת עַל הַלֻּחֹת, *engraved on the tablets* (*Exodus* 32:16), (implies) freedom from the angel of death and freedom from the bondage of the nations].

כְּאִישׁוֹן עֵינוֹ — *As the pupil of his eye* . . . just as He guarded the pupil of man's eye when He formed him, by surrounding the eye with a cloak of skin (the eyelid) that it not be damaged, being that it is prone to be injured.

NOTES

'He let them (the peoples) remain in existence and did not destroy them because of the number of the Children of Israel that were to descend from Shem's sons in the future.'

9. כִּי חֵלֶק ה׳ עַמּוֹ יַעֲקֹב חֶבֶל נַחֲלָתוֹ — *For the portion of* H*ASHEM is His people; Jacob the lot of His inheritance*. The *Sforno* may well be explaining the reason for the choice of the word חֵלֶק, *portion*, in the first part of the verse, and חֶבֶל, *rope*, in the second part. Although the *Sforno* in *Genesis* and *Exodus* emphasizes that all humanity is cherished by God, this love is removed when they serve strange gods. When this occurs, only *His people* (Israel) who are loyal to Him are considered to be *His portion* among the nations. And if one should demur and argue that there are among the nations those who also believe in the One God, nonetheless there is no continuity and later generations generally defect. The nation of Jacob, however, in which the belief in the One God is transmitted from father to son, ties each subsequent generation to the preceding one by חֶבֶל, *a strong rope*, as it were. Hence they alone are His inheritance.

10. יִמְצָאֵהוּ — *He found him*. Israel was not 'lost' that it should be necessary for them to be found by God! The *Sforno* explains that the word *found* refers to the 'heart' or character of this people which proved to be trustworthy, similar to the expression, *You found his heart faithful before you* (*Nechemiah* 9:8), which refers to Abraham.

יִצְּרֶנְהוּ — *He protected him*. The Mosad Harav Kook edition adds, 'As our Sages say: *Engraved upon the tablets* (*Exodus* 32:16), i.e.,

יא כְּנֶשֶׁר יָעִיר קִנּוֹ — עַל־גּוֹזָלָיו יְרַחֵף
יִפְרֹשׂ כְּנָפָיו יִקָּחֵהוּ — יִשָּׂאֵהוּ עַל־אֶבְרָתוֹ:
יב יְהוָה בָּדָד יַנְחֶנּוּ — וְאֵין עִמּוֹ אֵל נֵכָר:
שלישי יג יַרְכִּבֵהוּ עַל־°בָּמוֹתֵי אָרֶץ — וַיֹּאכַל תְּנוּבֹת שָׂדָי

°בָּמֳתֵי ק׳

---

11. כְּנֶשֶׁר יָעִיר קִנּוֹ — *As an eagle stirs up his nest.* May it be His will that He will do (for you) in the future that which He planned to do at Sinai had (Israel) not sinned with the calf. And (indeed) God, the Blessed One, accepted his prayer, as it says, אֶשְׁרְקָה לָהֶם וַאֲקַבְּצֵם כִּי פְדִיתִים, *I will whistle to them and gather them, for I have redeemed them* (Zechariah 10:8).

עַל גּוֹזָלָיו יְרַחֵף — *Hovering over her young . . .* as it says: הִנֵּה אֶשָּׂא אֶל גּוֹיִם יָדִי וְאֶל עַמִּים אָרִים נִסִּי וְהֵבִיאוּ בָנַיִךְ בְּחֹצֶן, *Behold, I will lift up my hand to the nations and set up my standard to the peoples, and they shall bring your sons in their arms* (Isaiah 49:22).

יִפְרֹשׂ כְּנָפָיו יִקָּחֵהוּ — *Spreading out her wings, takes them . . .* as it says, וְאַתֶּם תְּלֻקְּטוּ לְאַחַד אֶחָד בְּנֵי יִשְׂרָאֵל, *And you shall be gathered up one by one, O Children of Israel* (ibid. 27:12).

יִשָּׂאֵהוּ עַל אֶבְרָתוֹ — *Bearing them on her pinions . . .* as it says, מִי אֵלֶּה כָּעָב תְּעוּפֶינָה, *Who are these who fly as a cloud* (ibid. 60:8).

12. ה׳ בָּדָד יַנְחֶנּוּ — *HASHEM alone did guide him.* As it says, כִּי אֶעֱשֶׂה כָלָה בְּכָל הַגּוֹיִם . . . וְאֹתְךָ לֹא אֶעֱשֶׂה כָלָה, *For I will make full end of all the nations . . . but I will not make a full end of you* (Jeremiah 46:28).

וְאֵין עִמּוֹ אֵל נֵכָר — *And there is no strange god with Him . . .* as it says, כִּי אָז אֶהְפֹּךְ אֶל עַמִּים שָׂפָה בְרוּרָה לִקְרֹא כֻלָּם בְּשֵׁם ה׳, *For then I will convert the peoples to a purer language, that they may all call upon the name of HASHEM* (Zephaniah 3:9), and, as it says, אֱלֹהֵי כָל הָאָרֶץ יִקָּרֵא, *He is called the God of the whole world* (Isaiah 54:5).

13. יַרְכִּבֵהוּ עַל בָּמֳתֵי אָרֶץ — *He made him ride on the high places of the earth.* This He will do because He did not attain His desired (goal) through the giving of the Torah mentioned above (v. 10), so He will (now) seek again to perfect them by giving them the Land בַּעֲבוּר יִשְׁמְרוּ חֻקָּיו, *that they might observe His statutes* (Psalms 105:45), and by making them ride on a portion of the earth which is superior in location and in quality over all other lands, as it says, צְבִי הִיא לְכָל הָאֲרָצוֹת, *which is an ornament for all the lands* (Ezekiel 20:6). And this (will occur) now, when they enter the Land.

וַיֹּאכַל תְּנוּבֹת שָׂדָי — *And he ate the produce of the fields . . .* (produce) for which they did not exert themselves as it says, כְּרָמִים וְזֵיתִים אֲשֶׁר לֹא נְטַעְתֶּם אַתֶּם אֹכְלִים, *of vineyards and oliveyards which you did not plant do you eat* (Joshua 24:13).

NOTES

freedom from the angel of death and the bondage of Egypt.' The *Sforno's* intent is to teach us that Torah grants freedom (a play on words — חָרוּת, *engraved*, and חֵרוּת, *freedom*) from the angel of death, and freedom from the bondage of the nations (based on *Eruvin* 54a and the *Tanchuma*).

11. כְּנֶשֶׁר יָעִיר קִנּוֹ — *As an eagle stirs up his nest*. As the *Sforno* explained in his commentary on verse 3, Moses is reviewing the history of the Jewish people, of early mankind, and is prophesying about the future in this song. He is also *praying* to God on behalf of Israel. This verse is an example of how he entreats God for

וַיֵּנִקֵהוּ דְבַשׁ מִסֶּלַע	וְשֶׁמֶן מֵחַלְמִישׁ צוּר:
יד חֶמְאַת בָּקָר וַחֲלֵב צֹאן	עִם־חֵלֶב כָּרִים
וְאֵילִים בְּנֵי־בָשָׁן וְעַתּוּדִים	עִם־חֵלֶב כִּלְיוֹת חִטָּה
טו וְדַם־עֵנָב תִּשְׁתֶּה־חָמֶר:	וַיִּשְׁמַן יְשֻׁרוּן וַיִּבְעָט
שָׁמַנְתָּ עָבִיתָ כָּשִׂיתָ	וַיִּטֹּשׁ אֱלוֹהַ עָשָׂהוּ
טו וַיְנַבֵּל צוּר יְשֻׁעָתוֹ:	יְקַנְאֻהוּ בְּזָרִים

14. וְדַם עֵנָב תִּשְׁתֶּה חָמֶר — *And you did drink wine of the pure blood of the grape.* The juice of the grape was fit to be drunk without need for excessive labor to produce it; hence, they were provided for without pain, and this was done for them by God, the Blessed One, in order that they might have (ample) opportunity to occupy themselves with Torah and *mitzvos.*

15. וַיִּשְׁמַן יְשֻׁרוּן וַיִּבְעָט — *But Jeshurun grew fat and kicked.* Behold, even those who are the scholars and philosophers (בַּעֲלֵי עִיּוּן) among them who are called יְשֻׁרוּן, derived from אֲשׁוּרֶנּוּ וְלֹא קָרוֹב, *I behold him but not close* (*Numbers* 24:17), acted as animals that kick those who give them food.

שָׁמַנְתָּ עָבִיתָ כָּשִׂיתָ — *You are waxen fat, grown thick and covered with fatness.* Behold, you Jeshurun, the congregation of Torah adherents and men who are scholars and philosophers, have turned to material pleasures and *grown thick,* (incapable) of understanding subtle truths, as it says, וְגַם אֵלֶּה בַּיַּיִן שָׁגוּ וּבַשֵּׁכָר תָּעוּ כֹּהֵן וְנָבִיא, *But these also reel through wine and stagger through strong drink, the Kohen and the prophet* (*Isaiah* 28:7). (You are also) *covered with fatness* as it says, כִּי טַח מֵרְאוֹת עֵינֵיהֶם מֵהַשְׂכִּיל לִבֹּתָם, *for He has shut their eyes that they cannot see and their hearts that they cannot understand* (ibid. 44:18).

וַיִּטֹּשׁ אֱלוֹהַּ עָשָׂהוּ — *Then he forsook God who made him.* Therefore, the multitude forsook God Who made *them.*

וַיְנַבֵּל צוּר יְשֻׁעָתוֹ — *And was contemptuous to the Rock of his salvation.* They (treated Him) with contempt, because they progressed from evil to evil.

NOTES

his people; in effect saying, 'May it be Your will that You spread Your wings over Your children and bear them on Your pinions as an eagle carries its young.'

13-14. יַרְכִּבֵהוּ עַל בָּמֳתֵי אָרֶץ ... וְדַם עֵנָב תִּשְׁתֶּה חָמֶר — *He made him ride on the high places of the earth . . . and you did drink wine of the pure blood of the grape.* The *Sforno* does not mean to imply that had Israel attained the desired perfection through their acceptance of the Torah they would not have been given the Land. God had already promised *Eretz Yisrael* to Abraham and his seed. What the *Sforno* means is that although the prime factor in fashioning Israel into a people was the Torah, which is universal, their flowering and development as a people of Torah could only be realized in the Land of Israel which is especially conducive to the implementation of its *mitzvos* and the mastering of its wisdom. Although Israel had sinned at Sinai and did not reach the level of holiness hoped for, nonetheless the Almighty brought them into the holy land for the very purpose of reaching that original goal. They were to observe His statutes and reach the heights of sanctity and ultimate perfection, as indicated by the verses quoted from *Psalms* and *Ezekiel.* God brought Israel into a land which possessed material plenty and was so blessed that one could attain his material needs with little effort, thereby allowing them time for the study of Torah and the fulfillment of its *mitzvos.*

15. וַיִּשְׁמַן יְשֻׁרוּן וַיִּבְעָט ... וַיִּטֹּשׁ אֱלוֹהַּ עָשָׂהוּ — *But Jeshurun grew fat and kicked . . . then he forsook God who made him.* When those who are intelligent, refined leaders of the people set a bad example, the masses will follow their lead

יז בְּתוֹעֵבֹת יַכְעִיסֻהוּ: יִזְבְּחוּ לַשֵּׁדִים לֹא אֱלֹהַ
אֱלֹהִים לֹא יְדָעוּם חֲדָשִׁים מִקָּרֹב בָּאוּ
יח לֹא שְׂעָרוּם אֲבֹתֵיכֶם: צוּר יְלָדְךָ תֶּשִׁי
רביעי יט וַתִּשְׁכַּח אֵל מְחֹלְלֶךָ: וַיַּרְא יהוה וַיִּנְאָץ
כ מִכַּעַס בָּנָיו וּבְנֹתָיו: וַיֹּאמֶר אַסְתִּירָה פָנַי מֵהֶם

---

16. בְּתוֹעֵבֹת יַכְעִיסֻהוּ — *With abomination they provoked Him to anger* ... causing the *Shechinah* to leave Israel, (and thus causing them) to become as the nations of the world.

17. לַשֵּׁדִים לֹא אֱלֹהַ — *To demons, no-gods* ... who are not everlasting (immortal), as our Sages say regarding demons, *'They perish similar to humans'* (*Chagigah* 16a).

אֱלֹהִים לֹא יְדָעוּם חֲדָשִׁים מִקָּרֹב בָּאוּ — *Gods whom they knew not, to new gods that newly arrived.* When they would see a certain species of whose existence they heretofore had no knowledge, they thought that there was some ancient primeval cause (i.e., power) unique to that creature (which created it), and they would therefore worship it (i.e., that power).

18. צוּר יְלָדְךָ תֶּשִׁי — *Of the Rock Who begot you, you are unmindful.* And also, you Jeshurun, the scholarly and philosophical ones, by turning to the pleasures (of life), forgot your wisdom and the knowledge of His greatness.

וַתִּשְׁכַּח אֵל מְחֹלְלֶךָ — *And you have forgotten God that formed you* ... who was good to you, as it says, אָנֹכִי הוּא מְנַחֶמְכֶם ... וַתִּשְׁכַּח ה׳ עֹשֶׂךָ נוֹטֶה שָׁמַיִם, *I am He Who comforts you ... and you have forgotten* HASHEM *your Maker Who stretches forth the heavens* (*Isaiah* 51:12,13).

19. וַיִּנְאָץ מִכַּעַס בָּנָיו וּבְנֹתָיו — *And He abhorred them because of the provocation of His sons and of His daughters.* And after He did not attain the perfection (of Israel) in the Land, He chose a third (way), namely to refine them in Exile. He did this by shaming and making loathsome His sons and daughters through His anger with no mercy shown for the young ones, nor for the honor of the daughters.

NOTES

and even compound the evil ways of their superiors. Those who are called יְשֻׁרוּן — the scholars and intellectuals — 'wax fat' and become materialistic, thereby becoming coarse and insensitive. The masses retrogress further; they forsake God and treat all that is important and sacred with contempt. This is the meaning of the *Sforno's* comment, 'from evil to evil.'

17. לַשֵּׁדִים לֹא אֱלֹהַ — *To demons, no-gods*. See the *Sforno's* commentary on *Genesis* 1:1.

17-18. חֲדָשִׁים מִקָּרֹב בָּאוּ ... צוּר יְלָדְךָ תֶּשִׁי — *To new gods that newly arrived ... Of the Rock Who begot you, you are unmindful. Rashi* interprets this verse to mean that they would worship gods unknown to other nations, gods which were certainly unknown to their own ancestors. The *Sforno*, however, interprets this verse to mean that when they would observe any exotic creature whose existence they were unaware of heretofore, their initial amazement was transformed ultimately into reverence, not for the creature itself but for the force and power who created it. This they attributed not to the Creator but to some primeval, unique force whom they deified by worshiping his handiwork, namely this exotic creature. Verses 16 and 17 speak of the masses who abandoned God and became idolaters, whereas verse 18 addresses itself to יְשֻׁרוּן, the scholars who do not reject God but whose wisdom is adulterated by their pursuit of physical pleasures and material riches. Their 'forgetting' is a twofold one; they forget what they have learned and also are unmindful of past history. That is why the verse uses two words for 'forgetfulness' — תֶּשִׁי and וַתִּשְׁכַּח.

19. וַיִּנְאָץ מִכַּעַס בָּנָיו וּבְנֹתָיו — *And He abhorred*

אֶרְאֶה מָה אַחֲרִיתָם כִּי דוֹר תַּהְפֻּכֹת הֵמָּה
כא בָּנִים לֹא־אֵמֻן בָּם: הֵם קִנְאוּנִי בְלֹא־אֵל
כִּעֲסוּנִי בְּהַבְלֵיהֶם וַאֲנִי אַקְנִיאֵם בְּלֹא־עָם
כב בְּגוֹי נָבָל אַכְעִיסֵם: כִּי־אֵשׁ קָדְחָה בְאַפִּי

---

20. אַסְתִּירָה פָנַי מֵהֶם — *I will hide My face from them* ... from the sons and the daughters.

אֶרְאֶה מָה אַחֲרִיתָם — *I will see what their end shall be.* I see that there is no hope that they will eventually repent.

כִּי דוֹר תַּהְפֻּכֹת הֵמָּה — *For they are a perverse generation.* They had a change of heart, turning aside from the ways of God, the Blessed One.

בָּנִים לֹא אֵמֻן בָּם — *Children in whom there is no faith* ... for they did not learn truth from their fathers.

21. הֵם קִנְאוּנִי בְלֹא אֵל — *They have moved Me to jealousy with a no-god.* The fathers moved Me to jealousy with a *no-god* (during the period of) the First Temple.

כִּעֲסוּנִי בְּהַבְלֵיהֶם — *Provoked Me to anger with their vanities...* (during the period of) the Second Temple.

וַאֲנִי אַקְנִיאֵם בְּלֹא עָם — *And I will move them to jealousy with a no-people* ... (during the time) of the First Temple, which was destroyed by the Chaldeans of whom it is said, הֵן אֶרֶץ כַּשְׂדִּים זֶה הָעָם לֹא הָיָה, *Behold the land of Kasdim* (*Chaldea*) *this people was not* (*Isaiah* 23:13).

בְּגוֹי נָבָל אַכְעִיסֵם — *I will provoke them to anger with a vile people* ... (at the time of) the Second Temple, which was destroyed by a kingdom that was unworthy and which had no alphabet or language.

22. כִּי אֵשׁ קָדְחָה בְאַפִּי — *For a fire is kindled in My anger* ... when I afflicted them so that they should repent.

NOTES

them because of the provocation of His sons and of His daughters. The expression 'a third way' used by the *Sforno* means that the Almighty had already tried two previous methods of instruction in the hope of perfecting Israel; one was by giving them the Torah and the second was by bringing them into the Land of Israel. Both of these methods had failed, so He now attempts Exile as a way to purge, cleanse and refine them.

20. אֶרְאֶה מָה אַחֲרִיתָם — *I will see what their end shall be*. This expression in the view of the *Sforno* does not mean as *Rashi* explains, 'what will come upon them in the end.' Rather, the Almighty says 'I see' (akin to רוֹאֶה אֲנִי) that even in the end there will be no improvement (the word מָה is to be understood as אֶפֶס, *naught*, for they will not repent.

21. הֵם קִנְאוּנִי ... כִּעֲסוּנִי ... וַאֲנִי אַקְנִיאֵם ... בְּגוֹי נָבָל אַכְעִיסֵם — *They have moved Me to jealousy ... provoked Me to anger ... and I will move them to jealousy ... I will provoke them to anger with a vile people*. The *Sforno* sees a symmetry in this verse, where the concluding portion which speaks of God's response and retribution corresponds to the initial part of the verse which speaks of Israel's provocation. They moved God to jealousy during the period of the First Temple by serving idols who were no-gods; therefore He responded by bringing about their destruction through a people who were nonentities. In the time of the Second Temple, they provoked the Almighty with their vanities, therefore He, in turn, punished them through a people who were uncultured, a vile people who were used by God to destroy a people guilty of vanity.

22. כִּי אֵשׁ קָדְחָה בְאַפִּי ... וַתְּלַהֵט מוֹסְדֵי הָרִים — *For a fire is kindled in My anger ... and set on fire the leaders of the people*. The sense of this

וַתִּיקַד עַד־שְׁאוֹל תַּחְתִּית   וַתֹּאכַל אֶרֶץ וִיבֻלָהּ
כג וַתְּלַהֵט מוֹסְדֵי הָרִים׃   אַסְפֶּה עָלֵימוֹ רָעוֹת
כד חִצַּי אֲכַלֶּה־בָּם׃   מְזֵי רָעָב וּלְחֻמֵי רֶשֶׁף
וְקֶטֶב מְרִירִי   וְשֶׁן־בְּהֵמֹת אֲשַׁלַּח־בָּם
כה עִם־חֲמַת זֹחֲלֵי עָפָר׃   מִחוּץ תְּשַׁכֶּל־חֶרֶב
וּמֵחֲדָרִים אֵימָה   גַּם־בָּחוּר גַּם־בְּתוּלָה
כו יוֹנֵק עִם־אִישׁ שֵׂיבָה׃   אָמַרְתִּי אַפְאֵיהֶם
כז אַשְׁבִּיתָה מֵאֱנוֹשׁ זִכְרָם׃   לוּלֵי כַּעַס אוֹיֵב אָגוּר

וַתִּיקַד עַד שְׁאוֹל תַּחְתִּית — *And shall burn to the nethermost parts of the earth.* They rebelliously added to their sin in such a manner that My anger was sufficiently kindled to bring them down to the nethermost abyss, as it says of Achaz, וּבְעֵת הָצֵר לוֹ וַיּוֹסֶף לִמְעוֹל בַּה׳, *And in the time of his distress he trespassed still more against* HASHEM (*II Chronicles* 28:22).

וַתְּלַהֵט מוֹסְדֵי הָרִים — *And set on fire the leaders of the people.* He will remove from them all the leaders of the people, as it says, מֵסִיר מִירוּשָׁלַםִ וּמִיהוּדָה מַשְׁעֵן וּמַשְׁעֵנָה . . . גִּבּוֹר וְאִישׁ מִלְחָמָה . . . וְנָבִיא . . . וְיוֹעֵץ, *He takes away from Jerusalem and from Judah the stay and the staff . . . the mighty man and the man of war . . . the prophet . . . and the counselor* (*Isaiah* 3:1-3).

25. וּמֵחֲדָרִים אֵימָה גַּם בָּחוּר גַּם בְּתוּלָה — *And terror within,* (*shall destroy*) *both the young man and the virgin.* And from within, the terror shall destroy the young men and the virgins.

26. אָמַרְתִּי אַפְאֵיהֶם — *I said I will leave over a corner.* I will leave over some פֵּאָה (corner) while destroying the rest of them, similar to that which I shall do at the end of days, since I did not attain (through them) the perfection (I had hoped for), be it through the giving of the Torah, or *Eretz Yisrael*, or through Exile, as it says, כִּי בְּהַר צִיּוֹן וּבִירוּשָׁלַםִ תִּהְיֶה פְלֵיטָה כַּאֲשֶׁר אָמַר ה׳ וּבַשְּׂרִידִים אֲשֶׁר ה׳ קֹרֵא, *For in mount Zion and in Jerusalem there shall be those that escape, as* HASHEM *has said, and among the remnant those whom* HASHEM *shall call* (*Joel* 3:5).

27. לוּלֵי כַּעַס אוֹיֵב אָגוּר — *Were it not for the heaped-up wrath of the enemy.* Because of the wrath of the nations (directed) against this remnant (of Israel), there is concern . . .

NOTES

verse acording to the *Sforno* is as follows: Affliction is meant to arouse people and thus bring them to repentance, but at times the more one suffers the greater becomes one's resistance to repentance, as we find in the case of King Achaz who increased his trespassing at the time of his distress. This stubbornness added fuel to the fire of God's wrath, resulting in the punishment of the people's leaders whom God holds responsible for the evil ways of the masses.

26. אָמַרְתִּי אַפְאֵיהֶם — *I said I will leave over a corner. Rashi* also explains the phrase אַפְאֵיהֶם to mean, 'I would make them as פֵּאָה — as grain left in the corner of the field.' However, he interprets this to mean that God will cast away Israel as הֶפְקֵר, something which is free to all devoid of ownership. The *Sforno*, however, interprets this phrase as one of encouragement and hope. Although large numbers of Israel shall be destroyed, God assures us that there will always be a saving remnant whom the Torah characterizes as פֵּאָה — that *corner* of the field which *remains*! So it shall be at the end of days.

פֶּן־יְנַכְּרוּ צָרֵימוֹ פֶּן־יֹאמְרוּ יָדֵינוּ רָמָה
כח וְלֹא יהוה פָּעַל כָּל־זֹאת: כִּי־גוֹי אֹבַד עֵצוֹת הֵמָּה
חמישי כט וְאֵין בָּהֶם תְּבוּנָה: לוּ חָכְמוּ יַשְׂכִּילוּ זֹאת
ל יָבִינוּ לְאַחֲרִיתָם: אֵיכָה יִרְדֹּף אֶחָד אֶלֶף

פֶּן יְנַכְּרוּ צָרֵימוֹ — *Lest their adversaries estrange them* . . . lest they draw away the hearts of this remnant to become estranged (from God) as they (i.e., the adversaries) are.

פֶּן יֹאמְרוּ — *Lest they should say* . . . to that remnant.

יָדֵנוּ רָמָה — *Our hand is high* . . . (capable of) exterminating Israel as a nation, and you will (then) remain few in number.

וְלֹא ה׳ פָּעַל כָּל זֹאת — *And HASHEM has not done all this.* And you should not believe that you can escape through His (help). However, being that Israel is numerous and widely dispersed among many nations, not *all* of the nations will attempt to do so (i.e., to mislead them), as our Sages said: 'What is the meaning of the verse, צִדְקֹת פִּרְזוֹנוֹ בְּיִשְׂרָאֵל, *even the righteous acts of His rule in Israel* (*Judges* 5:11)? The Holy One, Blessed is He, showed righteousness (mercy) to Israel by scattering them among the nations' (*Pesachim* 87b).

28. כִּי גוֹי אֹבַד עֵצוֹת הֵמָּה — *For they are a nation void of counsel* . . . the various (peoples) of the world.

29. לוּ חָכְמוּ יַשְׂכִּילוּ זֹאת — *Were they wise they would understand this* . . . that Israel fell into their hands in such an unnatural fashion, because of their (i.e., Israel's) sins!

יָבִינוּ לְאַחֲרִיתָם — *They would consider their latter end.* And thus the nations would understand what *their* latter end will be as a result of their many rebellious transgressions.

30. אֵיכָה יִרְדֹּף אֶחָד אֶלֶף — *How can one man chase a thousand.* They should have understood that it is unnatural for one to pursue a thousand . . .

NOTES

27. פֶּן יְנַכְּרוּ צָרֵימוֹ . . . וְלֹא ה׳ פָּעַל כָּל זֹאת — *Lest their adversaries estrange them . . . and HASHEM has not done all this.* The word יְנַכְּרוּ comes from the root נֵכָר, *a stranger. Rashi* therefore interprets this phrase to mean that the enemy will attribute their success against Israel to a strange power and not to God. The *Sforno* however interprets this phrase to mean that the nations will attempt to wean Israel away from God and estrange them from the true God to become idolaters as they are. However, God will not permit this to happen, for even in Exile the Jewish people will not be concentrated in one place, and although some nations will indeed attempt to exterminate Israel, others will not, and thus their dispersal will prove to be their salvation. That is why our Sages say that the righteousness of God is manifested in the fact that Israel is scattered far and wide; hence though one part of the Jewish people may be subjected to persecution and even destruction, other parts will be spared and they will become the saving remnant.

28. כִּי גוֹי אֹבַד עֵצוֹת הֵמָּה — *For they are a nation void of counsel.* The *Sforno*, as do most commentators, explains that the word 'nation' refers to the peoples of the world, not to Israel. It is interesting to note that in the מִקְרָאוֹת גְּדוֹלוֹת (standard version) the phrase 'peoples of the world' reads 'Babylonians.' This is but one example of revisions and excisions made by the censor in this *parashah*, lest the *Sforno's* commentary reflect in an adverse manner upon the church and government of

וּשְׁנַיִם יָנִיסוּ רְבָבָה אִם־לֹא כִּי־צוּרָם מְכָרָם
לא וַיהוָה הִסְגִּירָם: כִּי לֹא כְצוּרֵנוּ צוּרָם
לב וְאֹיְבֵינוּ פְּלִילִים: כִּי־מִגֶּפֶן סְדֹם גַּפְנָם

אם לא כי צורם מכרם — *Unless their Rock had sold them.* (It is) He who does battle against them and has removed their strength. Therefore, their might has become warped and they are (weak) as women.

31. כי לא כצורנו צורם — *For their rock is not as our Rock.* And this occurred without a doubt because their rock is not like our Rock, because indeed every nation succeeds during the time that its (heavenly) prince or *mazal* (planet) rules, and that heavenly prince will never be transformed into an enemy of his people. However, they will eventually fall when their heavenly prince no longer rules (lit., is turned away), and the prince of another people comes to power, according to the order which God, the Blessed One, has decreed. Therefore, they will never be destroyed in such an unnatural manner that one will pursue a thousand.

ואיבינו — *And our enemies.* Although there are nations who are the enemies of God and the enemies of His people, as the (Torah) attests, *Were it not for the heaped-up wrath of the enemy* (v. 27), and as it says, *With the head of the wild bands of the enemy* (v. 42) — they are פלילים, *men of judgment,* thinkers and intelligent men (in the area) of political science, as it says, והאבדתי חכמים מאדום, *And I will destroy the wise men out of Edom* (*Ovadiah* 1:8), which implies that there are (wise men among them). (See *Eichah Rabbah* 2:13.) [Why, then, are they so blind regarding Israel?]

32. כי מגפן סדם גפנם — *For their vine is the vine of Sodom.* The reason they lack understanding regarding this matter is because they are proud of their great tranquility and turn their attention to the attainment of their physical pleasures, as did the people of Sodom. In order to realize this they (rejected and) abhored all acts of kindness, as the prophet attests saying, הנה זה היה עון סדם אחותך גאון שבעת לחם ושלות השקט היה לה ולבנותיה ויד עני ואביון לא החזיקה, *Behold this was the iniquity of your sister Sodom; she and her daughters had pride, surfeit of bread and abundance of idleness and yet she did not strengthen the hand of the poor and needy* (*Ezekiel* 16:49).

NOTES

Italy and other European nations of the 16th century.

29-30. לו חכמו ... יבינו לאחריתם ... איכה ירדף אחד אלף — *Were they wise ... they would consider their latter end ... How can one man chase a thousand.* The sense of the *Sforno's* commentary is that had God not decided to punish and weaken Israel, the nations of the world would be powerless against them. Hence it is not their strength but the weakness of Israel generated by God which accounts for the abnormal vulnerability of the Jewish people and the unnatural superiority of their enemies.

31. כי לא כצורנו צורם ואיבינו — *For their rock is not as our Rock, and our enemies.* Unlike Israel, whose fate and destiny are determined solely by God and not by any planetary influence, that of the nations of the world is controlled by constellations and planets, and as such their rise and fall follows a steady, even course. Only Israel is subject to abrupt, sudden changes in their status which result from their actions and their relationship to God. His Providence is present to protect His people when they are worthy, or when God forbid undeserving, to punish them. Hence their downfall is marked by abnormal events — as is their success and ultimately their redemption. All this, the nations, who normally are wise and perceptive, fail to understand. The reason for this unusual lack of comprehension is given in the next verse.

וּמִשַּׁדְמֹ֣ת עֲמֹרָ֑ה עֲנָבֵ֙מוֹ֙ עִנְּבֵי־ר֔וֹשׁ
לג אַשְׁכְּלֹ֥ת מְרֹרֹ֖ת לָֽמוֹ׃ חֲמַ֥ת תַּנִּינִ֖ם יֵינָ֑ם
לד וְרֹ֥אשׁ פְּתָנִ֖ים אַכְזָֽר׃ הֲלֹא־ה֖וּא כָּמֻ֣ס עִמָּדִ֑י
לה חָת֖וּם בְּאוֹצְרֹתָֽי׃ לִ֤י נָקָם֙ וְשִׁלֵּ֔ם
לְעֵ֖ת תָּמ֣וּט רַגְלָ֑ם כִּ֤י קָרוֹב֙ י֣וֹם אֵידָ֔ם

עֲנָבֵמוֹ עִנְּבֵי רוֹשׁ — *Their grapes are grapes of gall.* And from this vine shall grow *grapes of gall,* (meaning) evil deeds which harm society, and all this results from their efforts to attain unjust gains, and because they shed innocent blood in order to rule haughtily.

אַשְׁכְּלֹת מְרֹרֹת לָמוֹ — *Their clusters are bitter.* And thus they develop evil and false opinions, speaking against God perversely, saying, *God will not see* (based on *Psalms* 94:7).

33. חֲמַת תַּנִּינִם יֵינָם — *Their wine is the fierceness of crocodiles.* And behold, stored in those clusters of the grapes is to be found wine which is *fierce as crocodiles,* meaning punishment which they deserve according to the attribute of justice. It will be guarded (within the grapes) until God, the Blessed One, will bring it forth and cause them to drink (this wine of punishment) as it says, פּוּרָה דָּרַכְתִּי לְבַדִּי, *I have trodden the winepress alone* (*Isaiah* 63:3).

34. הֲלֹא הוּא כָּמֻס עִמָּדִי — *Is this not laid up with Me?* ... as it says, כִּי יוֹם נָקָם בְּלִבִּי, *For the day of vengeance is in my heart* (ibid. 63:4).

חָתוּם בְּאוֹצְרֹתָי — *And sealed up among My treasures* ... as it says, כִּי סְתֻמִים וַחֲתֻמִים הַדְּבָרִים, *for the words are closed up and sealed* (*Daniel* 12:9).

35. לִי נָקָם — *To Me belongs vengeance.* It is incumbent upon Me to take revenge from my enemies.

וְשִׁלֵּם — *And recompense.* And also to repay measure for measure.

לְעֵת תָּמוּט רַגְלָם — *When their foot slides* ... when their measure is full and they fall and break.

NOTES

32. עֲנָבֵמוֹ עִנְּבֵי רוֹשׁ אַשְׁכְּלֹת מְרֹרֹת לָמוֹ — *Their grapes are grapes of gall, their clusters are bitter.* The *Sforno* explains that these two phrases are not redundant. The first refers to evil actions and deeds, while the second speaks of false concepts and ideas which fashion their evil, corrupt ideology. Within these clusters of grapes, the wine of God's wrath and punishment is stored, as the *Sforno* explains in the next verse (33).

33. חֲמַת תַּנִּינִם יֵינָם — *Their wine is the fierceness of crocodiles.* In the standard version of *Sforno* in the מִקְרָאוֹת גְּדוֹלוֹת, the entire section beginning from the word 'punishment' has been excised by the censor. It does appear in the Mosad Harav Kook edition which is based upon a number of original manuscripts. The prophesy of Moses regarding the eventual Divine retribution against the nations who persecuted Israel was considered unacceptable by the censor, who in most cases was a convert to Christianity. Such deletions abound in this *parashah* and among them are parts of the commentary on verses 34, 35, and 36. Especially significant among the omissions is the *Sforno's* commentary on verse 37, which is totally removed from the standard edition of the מִקְרָאוֹת גְּדוֹלוֹת, as is the concluding part of verse 41, all of 42 and a major part of 43. Careful examination of the *Sforno's* commentary on these verses, which we have included in brackets in this edition, will readily reveal what aroused the ire of the censor.

35. לִי נָקָם . . . לְעֵת תָּמוּט רַגְלָם — *To Me belongs vengeance ... when their foot slides. Rashi* in his commentary on this verse states, 'So far

לו וְחָשׁ עֲתִדֹת לָמוֹ׃ כִּי־יָדִין יהוה עַמּוֹ
וְעַל־עֲבָדָיו יִתְנֶחָם כִּי יִרְאֶה כִּי־אָזְלַת יָד
לז וְאֶפֶס עָצוּר וְעָזוּב׃ וְאָמַר אֵי אֱלֹהֵימוֹ
לח צוּר חָסָיוּ בוֹ׃ אֲשֶׁר חֵלֶב זְבָחֵימוֹ יֹאכֵלוּ
יִשְׁתּוּ יֵין נְסִיכָם יָקוּמוּ וְיַעְזְרֻכֶם

[כִּי קָרוֹב יוֹם אֵידָם — *For the day of their calamity is at hand.* Because, indeed, the day of calamity for the nations is nigh when *HASHEM will judge His people* (v. 36), as it says, וּבָרוֹתִי מִכֶּם הַמֹּרְדִים וְהַפּוֹשְׁעִים, *And I will purge out from among you the rebels, and the transgressors* (*Ezekiel* 20:38), because the other nations will then quickly be destroyed.]

36. וְעַל עֲבָדָיו יִתְנֶחָם — *And repent Himself for His servants.* He will repent Himself for the evil He properly (visited) upon His people, and will have mercy upon them, (in the merit) of His servants who are among them, as it says, כֵּן אֶעֱשֶׂה לְמַעַן עֲבָדַי לְבִלְתִּי הַשְׁחִית הַכֹּל, *So will I do for My servant's sake, that I may not destroy them all* (*Isaiah* 65:8).

כִּי יִרְאֶה כִּי אָזְלַת יָד — *When He sees that their power is gone.* And the reason that He will then repent Himself of the evil properly (visited) upon His people, doing so (in the merit) of His servants [even though this was not done all the days of Exile — is because He will observe that Israel (will have reached) the ultimate affliction and oppression in their Exile, in such a manner that they can no longer exist in it (i.e., Exile), as was the case in Egypt where it says, *And He saw our affliction, and our toil and our oppression* (26:7)].

וְאֶפֶס עָצוּר וְעָזוּב — *And there is nothing retained or left.* And He shall see that they have no money retained in their homes or left in the field.

[**37.** וְאָמַר — *And He shall say.* God, the Blessed One, will say to Israel . . .

אֵי אֱלֹהֵימוֹ — *Where are their gods?* . . . (the gods) of the nations of the world, because then indeed the mastery of the heavenly and temporal princes (the heavenly representatives of the nations) will be removed, as it says, יִפְקֹד ה׳ עַל צְבָא הַמָּרוֹם בַּמָּרוֹם וְעַל מַלְכֵי הָאֲדָמָה עַל הָאֲדָמָה, *HASHEM will punish the host of the high ones on high and the kings of the earth upon the earth* (*Isaiah* 24:21).

38. יָקוּמוּ וְיַעְזְרֻכֶם — *Let them rise up and help you.* And similarly, the Almighty will say to Israel, 'Where are the nations and their kings who will rise up and protect (lit., 'assist') you from My judgment, as you thought when you were in exile, relying upon their protection?']

NOTES

Moses exhorted them (i.e., Israel) with words of reproof . . . from here onwards (i.e., starting with verse 36) he consoles them with a statement of comfort.' The *Sforno*, however, interprets the previous verses, as well as this one, as referring to the nations of the world who will be punished by God for their wickedness towards Israel. God will take revenge from His enemies when their measure is full and as the day of reckoning draws near He will judge His people and have mercy upon them, as the next verse (36) states.

36. וְעַל עֲבָדָיו יִתְנֶחָם כִּי יִרְאֶה כִּי אָזְלַת יָד וְאֶפֶס עָצוּר וְעָזוּב — *And repent Himself for His servants when He sees that their power is gone and there is nothing retained or left.* Although the majority of the people of Israel are worthy of punishment, God will save them in the merit of the righteous ones among them. He

לט יְהִי עֲלֵיכֶם סִתְרָה: רְאוּ ׀ עַתָּה כִּי אֲנִי אֲנִי הוּא
וְאֵין אֱלֹהִים עִמָּדִי אֲנִי אָמִית וַאֲחַיֶּה
מָחַצְתִּי וַאֲנִי אֶרְפָּא וְאֵין מִיָּדִי מַצִּיל:
ששי מ כִּי־אֶשָּׂא אֶל־שָׁמַיִם יָדִי וְאָמַרְתִּי חַי אָנֹכִי לְעֹלָם:
מא אִם־שַׁנּוֹתִי בְּרַק חַרְבִּי וְתֹאחֵז בְּמִשְׁפָּט יָדִי

---

39. רְאוּ עַתָּה כִּי אֲנִי אֲנִי הוּא — *See now that I, even I, am He* ... who brought punishment upon you in Exile.

וְאֵין אֱלֹהִים עִמָּדִי — *And there is no god with Me* ... and it did not emanate from the power of princes above or heavenly hosts.

אֲנִי אָמִית וַאֲחַיֶּה — *I kill and I make alive* ... as it says, וְהַעֲלֵיתִי אֶתְכֶם מִקִּבְרוֹתֵיכֶם, *And cause you to come up out of your graves* (*Ezekiel* 37:12).

מָחַצְתִּי — *I wound* ... with the punishment of being a fugitive and wanderer, as it says, וְהִכָּה ה׳ אֶת יִשְׂרָאֵל כַּאֲשֶׁר יָנוּד הַקָּנֶה בַּמַּיִם, *For* HASHEM *will smite Israel as a reed is shaken in the water* (*I Kings* 14:15).

וַאֲנִי אֶרְפָּא — *And I heal* ... as it says, בְּיוֹם חֲבֹשׁ ה׳ אֶת שֶׁבֶר עַמּוֹ וּמַחַץ מַכָּתוֹ יִרְפָּא, *On the day that* HASHEM *binds up the breach of His people and heals the wound of their bruise* (*Isaiah* 30:26).

40. כִּי אֶשָּׂא אֶל שָׁמַיִם יָדִי — *For I lift My hand to heaven* ... to take an oath, similar to, וַיָּרֶם יְמִינוֹ וּשְׂמֹאלוֹ אֶל הַשָּׁמַיִם, *When He lifted up his right hand and his left hand to heaven* (*Daniel* 12:7).

וְאָמַרְתִּי חַי אָנֹכִי לְעֹלָם — *And say, I live for ever.* I shall swear, just as I live forever, similar to His saying, וַיִּשָּׁבַע בְּחֵי הָעוֹלָם, *And swore by the One Who lives forever* (ibid.).

41. אִם שַׁנּוֹתִי — *If I sharpen.* Although I sharpened the luster of My sword against Israel during the period of Exile, I did not (sharpen) the *edge* of My sword.

וְתֹאחֵז בְּמִשְׁפָּט יָדִי — *And My hand take hold of judgment* ... and even though My hand will afterward *take hold of judgment* against them, *for* HASHEM *will*

NOTES

will do so not only in their merit but because Israel will have reached the limit of their endurance and if not rescued they would, God forbid, be wiped away. The expression עָצוּר, *guarded* or *retained*, is applicable to one's monetary wealth, kept in one's home, whereas the word עָזוּב, *forsaken*, is applicable to one's property in the field.

37-38. וְאָמַר אֵי אֱלֹהֵימוֹ ... יָקוּמוּ וְיַעְזְרֻכֶם — *And He shall say, Where are their gods ... let them rise up and help you.* The Almighty says to Israel: In Exile, you placed your faith and trust in the gods of the nations of the world, as well as in the nations themselves. Now you will realize that these gods are worthless and the nations upon whom you relied are powerless. *Sforno* interprets these verses as a straightforward statement, unlike *Rashi* who interprets it as a mocking rebuke.

39. אֲנִי אָמִית וַאֲחַיֶּה מָחַצְתִּי וַאֲנִי אֶרְפָּא — *I kill and I make alive, I wound and I heal.* The *Sforno* finds in this verse a source from the Torah for our belief in תְּחִיַּת הַמֵּתִים, *the resurrection of the dead*, linking this assurance to the verse in *Ezekiel* which speaks of the dry bones brought back to life. He also is of the opinion that the 'wounding' mentioned in this verse refers to the wandering of Israel in Exile, which is the severest wound that can be inflicted upon a people. However, God comforts them and promises to heal this historic hurt by redeeming them and returning them to their land.

41. אִם שַׁנּוֹתִי — *If I sharpen.* When a warrior

אָשִׁיב נָקָם֙ לְצָרָ֔י	וְלִמְשַׂנְאַ֖י אֲשַׁלֵּֽם׃
מב אַשְׁכִּ֤יר חִצַּי֙ מִדָּ֔ם	וְחַרְבִּ֖י תֹּאכַ֣ל בָּשָׂ֑ר
מִדַּ֤ם חָלָל֙ וְשִׁבְיָ֔ה	מֵרֹ֖אשׁ פַּרְע֥וֹת אוֹיֵֽב׃
מג הַרְנִ֤ינוּ גוֹיִם֙ עַמּ֔וֹ	כִּ֥י דַם־עֲבָדָ֖יו יִקּ֑וֹם

pronounce judgment on His people (v. 36); nonetheless . . .

[אָשִׁיב נָקָם לְצָרָי — *I will render vengeance to My adversaries* . . . the vengeance which they dealt upon Israel, as it says, יַעַן עֲשׂוֹת אֱדוֹם בִּנְקֹם נָקָם לְבֵית יְהוּדָה, *Because Edom has dealt against the house of Judah by taking vengeance* (*Ezekiel* 25:12), I shall bring the same vengeance upon them, as it says, וְנָתַתִּי אֶת נִקְמָתִי בֶּאֱדֹם בְּיַד עַמִּי יִשְׂרָאֵל, *And I will lay my vengeance upon Edom by the hand of My people Israel* (ibid. v. 14).

וְלִמְשַׂנְאַי אֲשַׁלֵּם — *And will repay those who hate Me* . . . the payment of 'measure for measure' as it says, כַּאֲשֶׁר עָשִׂיתָ יֵעָשֶׂה לָּךְ גְּמֻלְךָ יָשׁוּב בְּרֹאשֶׁךָ, *As you have done it shall be done to you, may your recompense return upon your head* (*Obadiah* 1:15).

42. אַשְׁכִּיר חִצַּי מִדָּם וְחַרְבִּי תֹּאכַל בָּשָׂר — *I will make My arrows drunk with blood, and my sword shall devour flesh* . . . as it says, כִּי בָאֵשׁ ה׳ נִשְׁפָּט וּבְחַרְבּוֹ אֶת כָּל בָּשָׂר, *For by fire will* HASHEM *execute judgment and with his sword upon all flesh* (*Isaiah* 66:16).

מִדַּם חָלָל וְשִׁבְיָה — *With the blood of the slain and of the captives* . . . as it says, וְרַבּוּ חַלְלֵי ה׳, *And the slain of* HASHEM *shall be many* (ibid.).]

43. הַרְנִינוּ גוֹיִם — *Rejoice, O nations.* You, the arrows and sword of God, *make the nations rejoice*, for they will all recognize that God is just in Whom there is no wrong (based on *Psalms* 92), as it says, יִשְׂמְחוּ וִירַנְּנוּ לְאֻמִּים כִּי תִשְׁפֹּט עַמִּים מִישֹׁר, *let the nations be glad and sing for joy, for You shall judge the peoples with equity* (*Psalms* 67:5).

עַמּוֹ — *His people* . . . and cause His people to rejoice, that they shall give thanks with the voice of song, because . . .

NOTES

whets his sword it can be for one of two reasons — to shine it so that it might glow, or to sharpen it for use against his enemy. God reassures Israel that although He brandished His sword against them in Exile, it was meant to caution and frighten them so that they would return to Him, but the intent was not to destroy them.

אָשִׁיב נָקָם לְצָרָי וְלִמְשַׂנְאַי אֲשַׁלֵּם — *I will render vengeance to My adversaries and will repay those who hate Me.* These are two expressions, each with a distinct meaning. The vengeful actions of the nations against Israel will be redirected against *them* by God, and the evil inflicted by Israel's enemies upon them will be repaid — measure for measure. Hence two words — אָשִׁיב and אֲשַׁלֵּם — are used to indicate this twofold retribution.

43. הַרְנִינוּ גוֹיִם עַמּוֹ — *Rejoice, O nations, His people*. *Rashi* explains this phrase as meaning that the nations will praise 'His people' for cleaving to Him amidst all their troubles. The *Sforno*, however, links the verb הַרְנִינוּ, *exult with singing*, to the words 'nations' and 'His people.' The nations will sing a song of praise and recognition to God attesting to His just ways. Israel will sing a song of thanksgiving for their deliverance, for the avenging of the blood of their martyrs and for the just punishment meted out to the enemies of Israel. Here again, for obvious reasons, the censor deleted much of the *Sforno*'s commentary on this verse.

וְנָקָם יָשִׁיב לְצָרָיו   וְכִפֶּר אַדְמָתוֹ עַמּוֹ׃

שביעי מד וַיָּבֹא מֹשֶׁה וַיְדַבֵּר אֶת־כָּל־דִּבְרֵי הַשִּׁירָה־הַזֹּאת בְּאָזְנֵי הָעָם הוּא וְהוֹשֵׁעַ
מה בִּן־נוּן׃ וַיְכַל מֹשֶׁה לְדַבֵּר אֶת־כָּל־הַדְּבָרִים הָאֵלֶּה אֶל־כָּל־יִשְׂרָאֵל׃
מו וַיֹּאמֶר אֲלֵהֶם שִׂימוּ לְבַבְכֶם לְכָל־הַדְּבָרִים אֲשֶׁר אָנֹכִי מֵעִיד בָּכֶם הַיּוֹם
מז אֲשֶׁר תְּצַוֻּם אֶת־בְּנֵיכֶם לִשְׁמֹר לַעֲשׂוֹת אֶת־כָּל־דִּבְרֵי הַתּוֹרָה הַזֹּאת׃ כִּי

[דַם עֲבָדָיו יִקּוֹם וְנָקָם יָשִׁיב לְצָרָיו — *The blood of His servants will He avenge and He will render vengeance to His adversaries.* The rejoicing of His people will be for the vengeance of His servant's blood, and for (the punishment) imposed on His adversaries, because of that which they did to Israel in a vengeful manner.]

וְכִפֶּר אַדְמָתוֹ — *And He will atone for His land . . .* (when the Land) will have been left desolate by them, (because) of that which was done therein.

עַמּוֹ — *And His people.* And He will also atone for His people for all (the sins) they have done in Exile (in) desecrating the Name of God and similar (sins). (This atonement will be) because of their sufferings in Exile, in such a manner that the *Shechinah* will return (and dwell) in their midst, as it says, יַחְדָּו יְרַנֵּנוּ כִּי עַיִן בְּעַיִן יִרְאוּ בְּשׁוּב ה׳ צִיּוֹן, *Together shall they sing, for they shall see, eye to eye, HASHEM returning to Zion* (*Isaiah* 52:8).

46. אֲשֶׁר אָנֹכִי מֵעִיד בָּכֶם הַיּוֹם — *Which I testify among you this day . . .* through the song of *Haazinu* by which I testify and caution Israel that just as God, the Blessed One, gave them sustenance without suffering so that they might serve Him, so will He destroy them if they frustrate His intent.

אֲשֶׁר תְּצַוֻּם אֶת בְּנֵיכֶם — *Which you shall command your children.* At the end of your days, you shall make mention of all these words to your children in your last will and testament and command them to guard their souls, lest they become corrupted, just as David (before his death) commanded his son Solomon.

לִשְׁמֹר לַעֲשׂוֹת — *To observe to do . . .* so that the children will observe and do.

NOTES

וְכִפֶּר אַדְמָתוֹ עַמּוֹ — *And He will atone for His land and His people.* Two phases of atonement are implied in this verse. The first concerns the fact that when Israel dwelt in the Land, they failed to observe the Sabbatical and Jubilee years properly. As a result of this transgression they were exiled, and expiation for this sin came only because *Eretz Yisrael* lay desolate for many years. See *Leviticus* 26:34 and the *Sforno's* commentary there. The *Sforno* alludes to this when he states that atonement for the Land was attained through its desolation. The word עַמּוֹ, *His people*, conveys a second thought. The people of Israel sinned in Exile through actions which profaned God's Holy Name. The expiation for these sins will come through their great suffering in their state of exile. The atonement for both of these sins, that of rejecting the laws of *Shemittah* in *Eretz Yisrael* and the transgressions committed in Exile, will eventually result in the return of the Divine Presence to Israel.

46. אֲשֶׁר אָנֹכִי מֵעִיד בָּכֶם הַיּוֹם — *Which I testify among you this day.* The testimony of *Haazinu* is such that Israel would do well to hearken to it most carefully. It is a poem of promise and warning. In verses 13-14, they are told that God will grant them a land filled with material good which they have not worked for and even later the earth will produce its blessings with a minimum of toil. However, by the same token, they are cautioned that if they fail to keep the covenant with God they will be severely punished.

אֲשֶׁר תְּצַוֻּם אֶת בְּנֵיכֶם — *Which you shall command your children.* The *Sforno*

לֹא־דָבָר רֵק הוּא מִכֶּם כִּי־הוּא חַיֵּיכֶם וּבַדָּבָר הַזֶּה תַּאֲרִיכוּ יָמִים
עַל־הָאֲדָמָה אֲשֶׁר אַתֶּם עֹבְרִים אֶת־הַיַּרְדֵּן שָׁמָּה לְרִשְׁתָּהּ:
מפטיר מח־מט וַיְדַבֵּר יהוה אֶל־מֹשֶׁה בְּעֶצֶם הַיּוֹם הַזֶּה לֵאמֹר: עֲלֵה אֶל־הַר הָעֲבָרִים הַזֶּה
הַר־נְבוֹ אֲשֶׁר בְּאֶרֶץ מוֹאָב אֲשֶׁר עַל־פְּנֵי יְרֵחוֹ וּרְאֵה אֶת־אֶרֶץ כְּנַעַן אֲשֶׁר
נ אֲנִי נֹתֵן לִבְנֵי יִשְׂרָאֵל לַאֲחֻזָּה: וּמֻת בָּהָר אֲשֶׁר אַתָּה עֹלֶה שָׁמָּה וְהֵאָסֵף
נא אֶל־עַמֶּיךָ כַּאֲשֶׁר־מֵת אַהֲרֹן אָחִיךָ בְּהֹר הָהָר וַיֵּאָסֶף אֶל־עַמָּיו: עַל אֲשֶׁר
מְעַלְתֶּם בִּי בְּתוֹךְ בְּנֵי יִשְׂרָאֵל בְּמֵי־מְרִיבַת קָדֵשׁ מִדְבַּר־צִן עַל אֲשֶׁר
נב לֹא־קִדַּשְׁתֶּם אוֹתִי בְּתוֹךְ בְּנֵי יִשְׂרָאֵל: כִּי מִנֶּגֶד תִּרְאֶה אֶת־הָאָרֶץ וְשָׁמָּה
לֹא תָבוֹא אֶל־הָאָרֶץ אֲשֶׁר־אֲנִי נֹתֵן לִבְנֵי יִשְׂרָאֵל:

---

47. כִּי הוּא חַיֵּיכֶם — *Because it is your life* . . . eternal perfection, (the condition) in which one lives after the death of the body.

49. וּרְאֵה אֶת אֶרֶץ — *And see the land* . . . so as to grant your blessing therein.

50. וּמֻת בָּהָר — *And accept your death in the mount.* Accept death upon yourself as an atonement for having acted faithlessly.

וְהֵאָסֵף אֶל עַמֶּיךָ — *And be gathered to your people.* And thus, you will be gathered in the bond of life, (together) with those who are as fitting and proper as you are.

NOTES

interprets the word תְּצַוֻּם as meaning not only *to command* but also in the sense of צַוָּאָה — a last will and testament. What is said by a father to his children on his deathbed is of the utmost importance, and children will treat such instructions with great seriousness and respect. By adjuring one's children before passing away to keep the Torah and observe its *mitzvos*, the probability of their doing so is greatly enhanced.

49. וּרְאֵה אֶת אֶרֶץ — *And see the land.* In *Genesis* 48:10, the *Sforno* comments on Jacob's inability to see Ephraim and Menasseh due to his blindness, and states that one must see the object of his blessing in order for that blessing to be effective. He cites as an example the fact that Balak brought Bilaam to the heights to see the camp of Israel in order to curse them, because a blessing and curse are closely related! He also cites *Deut.* 34:1 where God shows Moses the Land of Israel for the purpose of blessing it. The *Sforno's* comment on this verse echoes this idea.

50. וּמֻת בָּהָר — *And accept your death.* The word does not mean *die.* Rather it means *accept death* as a consequence of the sin you committed when you smote the rock rather than speaking to it in defiance of God. When one accepts punishment willingly, it atones for the sin committed.

וְהֵאָסֵף אֶל עַמֶּיךָ — *And be gathered to your people.* See *Sforno* on *Genesis* 25:8 and the note.

פרשת וזאת הברכה

Parashas V'zos HaBerachah

לג א וְזֹ֣את הַבְּרָכָ֗ה אֲשֶׁ֨ר בֵּרַ֥ךְ מֹשֶׁ֛ה אִ֥ישׁ הָאֱלֹהִ֖ים אֶת־בְּנֵ֣י יִשְׂרָאֵ֑ל לִפְנֵ֖י מוֹתֽוֹ׃
ב וַיֹּאמַ֗ר יְהֹוָ֞ה מִסִּינַ֤י בָּא֙ וְזָרַ֤ח מִשֵּׂעִיר֙ לָ֔מוֹ הוֹפִ֙יעַ֙ מֵהַ֣ר פָּארָ֔ן וְאָתָ֖ה

XXXIII

1. וְזֹאת הַבְּרָכָה אֲשֶׁר בֵּרַךְ מֹשֶׁה — *And this is the blessing wherewith Moses blessed* . . . when God, the Blessed One, showed him all the Land (of Israel) before his death, so that he might bless the Land and Israel (who dwelt) therein, as was the intent (of Moses) when he said, אֶעְבְּרָה נָּא וְאֶרְאֶה, *Let me go over, please* (3:25). And this was also God's intent when He said to him, וּרְאֵה אֶת הָאָרֶץ, *And behold the Land* (*Numbers* 27:12). (Now) this is that blessing which he (Moses) did bless (Israel and the Land).

2. וַיֹּאמַר — *And he said.* Before he began the blessing (proper), which begins with *Iron and brass shall be your locks* (verse 25), he recited this introduction and prayed for the tribes, so that his blessing might come to pass; because, indeed, words of blessing are always said when speaking (directly) to the (one) who is being blessed, as it says אָמוֹר לָהֶם, *You shall say to them* (*Numbers* 6:23). (Now) all his words from *iron and brass* until *shall tread upon their high places* (verse 29) were (spoken) with Israel, but his previous words (i.e., verses 2-24) were (directed) to God, beseeching Him on behalf of His people.

ה׳ — *God!* (This is) an expression of calling.

מִסִּינַי בָּא וְזָרַח . . . אֵשׁ דָּת לָמוֹ — *HASHEM came from Sinai and rose . . . a fiery law unto them.* He mentioned the merit of Israel in order that his prayer be accepted and that his blessing should rest upon (them). He said to God, the Blessed One, 'Behold, You came from Sinai and rose and shined from various places unto Israel (radiating) the holines of the fiery law.' (This) refers to the speculative-theoretical part of the Torah (חֵלֶק הָעִיוּנִי) which emanates from the *myriad of holiness,* (meaning) the 'right side of holiness,' because indeed (that portion) was given through a mirror of clarity (אַסְפַּקְלַרְיָה הַמְּאִירָה).

NOTES

XXXIII

1. וְזֹאת הַבְּרָכָה — *And this is the blessing*. This expression implies that a specific previously mentioned blessing is being referred to. The *Sforno* therefore explains that when God showed Moses the Land, as stated in a number of places (*Numbers* 27:12, *Deut.* 32:49, 34:4), and when Moses requested permission to cross over and see the Land (*Deut.* 3:25), the purpose was to see it and bless it. As explained in *Genesis* 48:10, and in the note on verse 49 in the previous chapter, one must see the object or the recipient of the blessing for the blessing to be effective. This then is *the blessing* which was given by Moses, in keeping with his and God's desire.

2. וַיֹּאמַר — *And he said*. A blessing is always given in the presence of the recipient, in a direct manner. It is for this reason that one must see the object of his blessing, as mentioned in the previous note. The *Sforno* points out that all the verses preceding verse 25 are not written in the second person. Only verses 25 through 29 are to be considered a בְּרָכָה, *a blessing*, whereas the opening verses are to be understood as praise of God and prayers uttered by Moses on behalf of the tribes that they may be worthy to receive God's blessing. Also, these opening verses speak of individual tribes, while the verses of actual blessing (25-29) are directed to the people of Israel collectively.

מִסִּינַי בָּא וְזָרַח . . . — *HASHEM came from Sinai and rose etc. Rashi* in his commentary states: '(Moses) began with praise of the Omnipotent . . . but in the praise of God there is also mention of Israel's merit.' The *Sforno* reflects

°אֵשׁ דָּת ק׳ ג מֵרִבְבֹת קֹדֶשׁ מִימִינוֹ °אֵשְׁדָּת לָמוֹ: אַף חֹבֵב עַמִּים כָּל־קְדֹשָׁיו בְּיָדֶךָ וְהֵם
ד תֻּכּוּ לְרַגְלֶךָ יִשָּׂא מִדַּבְּרֹתֶיךָ: תּוֹרָה צִוָּה־לָנוּ מֹשֶׁה מוֹרָשָׁה קְהִלַּת יַעֲקֹב:

---

3. אַף חֹבֵב עַמִּים — *Although He loves the peoples.* Although You love (all) people, as You said, וִהְיִיתֶם לִי סְגֻלָּה מִכָּל הָעַמִּים, *And you shall be My own treasure from among all peoples* (*Exodus* 19:5), and thus You made it known that all humanity is considered as a treasure to You, as (our Sages) state, חָבִיב אָדָם שֶׁנִּבְרָא בְצֶלֶם, *Precious is man who was created in the Image* (*Avos* 3:18), still כָּל קְדֹשָׁיו בְּיָדֶךָ, *all His holy ones are in Your hand;* You have stated that all His holy ones sanctified by the holiness of the fiery law are in Your hand akin to a bag of silver. [For they (i.e., Israel) are more precious to You than all other human beings as it says, וְאַתֶּם תִּהְיוּ לִי מַמְלֶכֶת כֹּהֲנִים וְגוֹי קָדוֹשׁ, *And you shall be unto Me a kingdom of Kohanim and a holy nation* (*Exodus* 19:6), and as our Sages state, חֲבִיבִין יִשְׂרָאֵל שֶׁנִּקְרְאוּ בָנִים לַמָּקוֹם, *Beloved are Israel for they are called children of the Omnipresent* (*Avos* 3:14).]

וְהֵם תֻּכּוּ — *And they (pray) with broken spirit . . .* (תֻּכּוּ) meaning broken, similar to וְאִישׁ תְּכָכִים, *A man who breaks (the oppressor)* (*Proverbs* 29:13). They prayed with a broken, contrite spirit.

לְרַגְלֶךָ — *At your feet.* At Your footstool on Sinai (based on *Psalms* 99:5).

3.-4. יִשָּׂא מִדַּבְּרֹתֶיךָ . . . תּוֹרָה צִוָּה לָנוּ מֹשֶׁה — *He will bear Your words . . . the Torah that Moses commanded us.* They said to God, the Blessed One, 'Moses *will bear Your words* to us, which is the Torah commanded to us.' The phrase מִדַּבְּרֹתֶיךָ is used (as opposed to דְּבָרֶיךָ), similar to (the verse), וַיִּשְׁמַע אֶת הַקּוֹל מִדַּבֵּר אֵלָיו, *And he heard the Voice speaking to him* (*Numbers* 7:89).

מוֹרָשָׁה קְהִלַּת יַעֲקֹב — *An inheritance of the congregation of Jacob.* And this shall be an inheritance to the congregation of Jacob, accepted by us and our children as an inheritance.

NOTES

this latter part of *Rashi's* interpretation, after which he proceeds to explain that the light of revelation at Sinai which shone upon Israel was of such a nature that it emanated from the strongest source of holiness, the 'right' which represents strength as opposed to the 'left,' representing the speculative-theoretical part of Torah which becomes clear and understandable when one reaches the exalted level of פָּנִים אֶל פָּנִים, *face to face*, as Israel did at Sinai. (See the *Sforno* on *Exodus* 19:9.) The word רִבְבוֹת comes from רְבָבָה, *ten thousand*, which represents a myriad of light. The phrase אֶלֶף, *a thousand*, is a lesser degree of God's radiance, hence, the former is called יָמִין, *right*, while the latter is referred to as שְׂמֹאל, *left*.

3. אַף חֹבֵב עַמִּים — *Although He loves the peoples.* In his commentary on *Exodus*, chapter 19, the *Sforno* stresses the importance and dignity of mankind in general, although he also underscores the unique, special role played by Israel. Man is beloved, but Israel alone are called the children of God. He repeats this concept here, adding one moving thought: The people of Israel, called *His holy ones*, are so precious that they are not even placed in the king's treasure house but are held in *His hand!* It is interesting to note that in the מִקְרָאוֹת גְּדוֹלוֹת, that part of the *Sforno's* commentary which states, 'For they are more precious to you etc.', the quote from *Exodus* 19:6 as well as the Mishnah in *Avos* are deleted. The censor apparently could not accept such an expression of elitism.

מִדַּבְּרֹתֶיךָ — *Your words. Sforno* explains the word מִדַּבֵּר similar to *Rashi*, as meaning to speak to oneself (מִתְדַּבֵּר); see the *Sforno's* commentary on *Numbers* 7:89 and the note there. God speaks, as it were, to Himself but makes it audible and understandable to Moses so that he, in turn, might transmit the word of God to Israel. Hence, the word מִדַּבְּרֹתֶיךָ and not דְּבָרֶיךָ.

ה־ו וַיְהִ֥י בִישֻׁר֖וּן מֶ֑לֶךְ בְּהִתְאַסֵּף֙ רָ֣אשֵׁי עָ֔ם יַ֖חַד שִׁבְטֵ֥י יִשְׂרָאֵֽל׃ יְחִ֥י רְאוּבֵ֖ן
ז וְאַל־יָמֹ֑ת וִיהִ֥י מְתָ֖יו מִסְפָּֽר׃ וְזֹ֣את לִֽיהוּדָה֮ וַיֹּאמַר֒ שְׁמַ֤ע

5. וַיְהִי בִישֻׁרוּן מֶלֶךְ — *And there was a King in Jeshurun.* And then He Who was King in Jeshurun, namely God the Blessed One, Who was King among those who delved into and held fast to the Torah...

בְּהִתְאַסֵּף רָאשֵׁי עָם — *When the heads of the people gathered* ... at the time of the giving of the Torah, as it says, *All the heads of your tribes and your elders came near to me* (5:20), and as it says, *HASHEM our God has shown us His glory* (ibid. v. 21).

יַחַד שִׁבְטֵי יִשְׂרָאֵל — *All the tribes of Israel together.* He was then King over all the tribes of Israel together, for it was then that they accepted and affirmed His Kingship, as it says, *and you shall speak unto us all that HASHEM our God speaks to you and we will hear it and do it* (ibid. v. 24).

6. יְחִי רְאוּבֵן — *Let Reuben live.* Even though Reuben chose an unclean land on the other side of the Jordan which was not the land of God, as it says, וְאַךְ אִם טְמֵאָה אֶרֶץ אֲחֻזַּתְכֶם, *Howbeit, if the land of your possession is unclean* (*Joshua* 22:19), and therefore it is not so conducive (lit., prepared) in which to merit everlasting life, nonetheless let his heart live forever.

וְאַל יָמֹת וִיהִי מְתָיו מִסְפָּר — *And not die, nor his number be diminished* (lit., few). And let him not die in this world in such a manner that his men be few, similar to וַאֲנִי מְתֵי מִסְפָּר, *And I am few in number* (*Genesis* 34:30). (And may this be) even though it is written, *That your days may be multiplied ... upon the land* (11:21).

7. וְזֹאת לִיהוּדָה — *And this for Judah.* And this request I also ask and pray on behalf of the land of Judah, wherein the inheritance of Simeon is scattered (as well), that they do not perish in battle — because they went forth to battle together.

NOTES

5. וַיְהִי בִישֻׁרוּן מֶלֶךְ ... יַחַד שִׁבְטֵי יִשְׂרָאֵל — *And there was a King in Jeshurun ... all the tribes of Israel together*. The *Sforno*, in his commentary on 32:15, translates the term יְשֻׁרוּן as meaning those who are of superior intelligence and understanding. The sense of our verse is: God, Who was initially recognized as King by these men of excellence (Jeshurun), was subsequently recognized and accepted as King by the tribes of Israel at large when they experienced the revelation at Sinai. However, the *Sforno* himself gives a different interpretation of this verse in his commentary on *Numbers* 7:3. There he explains it to mean that only when unity reigns among the leaders of Israel is God their King.

6. יְחִי רְאוּבֵן — *Let Reuben live*. *Rashi* interprets this phrase as referring to This World; and *and let him not die* as alluding to the World to Come. The *Sforno* interprets these phrases in reverse fashion: The former speaks of חַיֵּי עוֹלָם, *everlasting life*, which is endangered because Reuben will not reside in *Eretz Yisrael*, a land that is more conducive to insure the spiritual reward of eternal life, while the latter phrase refers to long life here on earth. This prayer was necessary for Reuben, since the blessing of lengthy days (אֲרִיכַת יָמִים) was bestowed in *Eretz Yisrael* and not Trans-Jordan where his tribe resided.

7. וְזֹאת לִיהוּדָה — *And this for Judah*. Both *Rashi* and the *Sforno* explain that the prayer for Simeon, who is not mentioned explicitly in this *parashah*, is alluded to in this verse. The *Sforno*, however, reads it into the phrase, *And this for Judah*, while *Rashi* finds the allusion in the phrase, *Hear, HASHEM, the voice of Judah*. *Sforno* apparently interprets וְזֹאת, *and this*, as a רִבּוּי — a word meant to expand upon the term לִיהוּדָה; hence, it is meant to add Simeon to Judah, which is a reasonable interpretation since Simeon took his portion from amongst Judah's lot (see *Rashi*) and they went forth to do battle together.

יהוה קוֹל יְהוּדָה וְאֶל־עַמּוֹ תְּבִיאֶנּוּ יָדָיו רָב לוֹ וְעֵזֶר מִצָּרָיו תִּהְיֶה:
שני ח וּלְלֵוִי אָמַר תֻּמֶּיךָ וְאוּרֶיךָ לְאִישׁ חֲסִידֶךָ אֲשֶׁר נִסִּיתוֹ בְּמַסָּה תְּרִיבֵהוּ
ט עַל־מֵי מְרִיבָה: הָאֹמֵר לְאָבִיו וּלְאִמּוֹ לֹא רְאִיתִיו וְאֶת־אֶחָיו לֹא
י הִכִּיר וְאֶת־בָּנוֹ לֹא יָדָע כִּי שָׁמְרוּ אִמְרָתֶךָ וּבְרִיתְךָ יִנְצֹרוּ: יוֹרוּ מִשְׁפָּטֶיךָ

ויאמר שמע ה׳ קול יהודה — *And he said, 'Hear, HASHEM, the voice of Judah.'* Besides his saying, וְזֹאת לִיהוּדָה, *and this for Judah*, he also said, *Hear, HASHEM, the voice of Judah,* when he will beseech you in (time of) war or other (times of need).

יָדָיו רָב לוֹ וְעֵזֶר מִצָּרָיו תִּהְיֶה — *You will be his hands, contend for him and help him against his adversaries.* (May) You be *his hands* to battle on his behalf and also contend for him and exact revenge (on his behalf), and also be a help against his enemies when they do battle against him.

8. תֻּמֶּיךָ וְאוּרֶיךָ לְאִישׁ חֲסִידֶךָ — *Your Tumim and Urim* (*You gave*) *to the leader of Your pious ones.* Behold, the *Tumim* and *Urim* You did give to Aaron who was the אִישׁ, *man*, and head of the pious tribe, namely the tribe of Levi. Thus it became evident that he (i.e., Aaron) spoke, inspired by the Holy Spirit, and the *Shechinah* dwelt on him, as our Sages state, 'No Kohen is inquired of (by the Israelites) through the *Urim* and *Tumim* who does not speak by means of the Holy Spirit and upon whom the *Shechinah* does not rest' (*Yoma* 73b).

אֲשֶׁר נִסִּיתוֹ בְּמַסָּה — *Whom You did prove at the time of testing.* The tribe of Levi did not test Him at those times when Israel tested God, the Blessed One, as it says, וַיְנַסּוּ אֹתִי זֶה עֶשֶׂר פְּעָמִים, *You have tested Me these ten times* (*Numbers* 14:22), and therefore the decree (against) the spies was not issued against them.

תְּרִיבֵהוּ עַל מֵי מְרִיבָה — *And with whom You strove at the waters of Meribah.* You eliminated their two leaders, Moses and Aaron, because of the waters of strife.

9. הָאֹמֵר לְאָבִיו — *Who said of his father . . .* in the matter of the (Golden) Calf.

וְאֶת בָּנוֹ לֹא יָדָע כִּי שָׁמְרוּ אִמְרָתֶךָ — *Nor regarded his own children, for they observed Your word.* He was not concerned for the safety (lit., life) of his sons in the

NOTES

יָדָיו רָב לוֹ וְעֵזֶר מִצָּרָיו תִּהְיֶה — *You will be his hands, contend for him and help him against his adversaries*. The *Sforno* explains that these three terms refer to three different circumstances when God's assistance is requested and needed. יָדָיו, *His hands*, refers to God's intervention on behalf of Judah and Simeon when they do battle; רָב לוֹ, *contend for him*, is a request that God avenge Judah when he may have suffered defeat, while עֵזֶר, *help*, speaks of lending assistance in his defense when the enemy attacks Judah.

8. לְאִישׁ חֲסִידֶךָ — *To the leader of Your pious ones*. The term אִישׁ, *man*, in the singular is difficult to understand in the context of this verse. The *Sforno*, however, explains it as referring to Aaron who was the head of the tribe of Levi and who was so worthy that God would make His wishes known through him as the leader of the pious ones.

אֲשֶׁר נִסִּיתוֹ בְּמַסָּה תְּרִיבֵהוּ עַל מֵי מְרִיבָה — *Whom You did prove at the time of testing and with whom You strove at the waters of Meribah.* Unlike the Israelites who tested God on ten different occasions, the Levites never put God or Moses to the test. The one time this tribe faltered was, ironically, when their great leaders, Moses and Aaron, failed to carry out God's directive *at the waters of Meribah.*

9. וְאֶת בָּנוֹ לֹא יָדָע כִּי שָׁמְרוּ אִמְרָתֶךָ — *Nor regarded his own children, for they observed Your word*. The commentators are hard put to explain this phrase since the 'sons' of the tribe were also Levites, and none of them were guilty of idolatry during the episode of the Golden Calf (see *Rashi's* explanation here).

לְיַעֲקֹב וְתוֹרָתְךָ לְיִשְׂרָאֵל יָשִׂימוּ קְטוֹרָה בְּאַפֶּךָ וְכָלִיל עַל־מִזְבְּחֶךָ:
יא בָּרֵךְ יהוה חֵילוֹ וּפֹעַל יָדָיו תִּרְצֶה מְחַץ מָתְנַיִם קָמָיו וּמְשַׂנְאָיו מִן־
יב יְקוּמוּן: לְבִנְיָמִן אָמַר יְדִיד יהוה יִשְׁכֹּן לָבֶטַח עָלָיו חֹפֵף

wilderness, so that he might observe Your word, i.e., the commandment regarding the circumcision of the sons, even though many of them perished, as our Sages say, 'Because the North wind did not blow upon them' (*Yevamos* 72a).

וּבְרִיתְךָ יִנְצֹרוּ — *And they kept Your covenant* . . . as our Sages say, 'The tribe of Levi did not participate in the idolatry (of the Golden Calf)' (*Yoma* 66b), and this was true both in Egypt and in the wilderness.

10. יוֹרוּ מִשְׁפָּטֶיךָ לְיַעֲקֹב — *May they be worthy to teach Your laws to Jacob.* Since they are a proper, fit tribe, grant them favor and good understanding that they may teach Your laws to Jacob, as our Sages say, 'If the *Rav* is like unto a messenger of God, the Lord of Hosts, they will seek Torah from his mouth' (*Moed Katan* 17a).

11. בָּרֵךְ ה׳ חֵילוֹ — *Bless, HASHEM, his substance.* Bless their property in such a manner that a minimum of effort will suffice, so that they will have time to understand and teach (Torah).

וּפֹעַל יָדָיו תִּרְצֶה — *And accept the work of his hands.* (May) their service in the Sanctuary be acceptable to You.

מִן יְקוּמוּן — *That they not rise again* . . . that those who (challenge them) not be able to rise up against them, such as occurred with Korach and Uzziah.

12. יְדִיד ה׳ — *The beloved of HASHEM.* As our Sages state, Benjamin died בְּעֶטְיוֹ שֶׁל נָחָשׁ, *through the serpent's machinations* (*Shabbos* 55b). Moses mentions this merit to God.

יִשְׁכֹּן לָבֶטַח עָלָיו — *Shall dwell securely with Him.* He will not rebel against his king (as did) the ten tribes.

NOTES

The *Sforno*, however, interprets this phrase as extolling the sacrificial commitment of the Levites to the *mitzvah* of בְּרִית מִילָה, *circumcision,* which they performed even in the wilderness even though the environmental and climatic conditions were not suitable for circumcision. See the *Sforno* (*Exodus* 32:29) on the phrase, כִּי אִישׁ בִּבְנוֹ, *for every man through his son,* and the note there. The *Sforno's* interpretation clarifies the subsequent expression, *for they observed Your word,* i.e., they observed Your word (commandment) regarding circumcision, even under the most difficult circumstances.

10. יוֹרוּ מִשְׁפָּטֶיךָ — *May they be worthy to teach Your laws.* As mentioned above, these verses are not a blessing but a prayer to God. Hence, the phrase יוֹרוּ מִשְׁפָּטֶיךָ is interpreted by the *Sforno* not as a statement or a blessing that they will teach the laws of God to the people; rather it is a devout wish that they be granted the qualities and character of the ideal Torah teacher, one whose piety and sincerity is such that people will seek him out and listen to him, as though he were a messenger of God.

11. בָּרֵךְ ה׳ חֵילוֹ וּפֹעַל יָדָיו תִּרְצֶה — *Bless, HASHEM, his substance and accept the work of his hands.* Although the tribe of Levi did not receive a portion in *Eretz Yisrael*, nonetheless, they were given 48 cities in which to dwell and also open land around these cities. Their primary mission was to serve in God's Temple and to be the teachers of His law. Hence the prayer was that they be spared arduous and time-consuming labor so that they might be free to pursue their calling. See the *Sforno's* commentary on *Genesis* 49:13 regarding the gifts given to the *Kohanim* and Levites.

מִן יְקוּמוּן — *That they rise not again.* Korach challenged the legitimacy of Aaron's priesthood. King Uzziah entered the Holy to offer incense on the golden altar even though he

שלישי יג עָלָיו כָּל־הַיּוֹם וּבֵין כְּתֵפָיו שָׁכֵן: וּלְיוֹסֵף אָמַר מְבֹרֶכֶת
יד יְהוָה אַרְצוֹ מִמֶּגֶד שָׁמַיִם מִטָּל וּמִתְּהוֹם רֹבֶצֶת תָּחַת: וּמִמֶּגֶד תְּבוּאֹת שָׁמֶשׁ
טו־טז וּמִמֶּגֶד גֶּרֶשׁ יְרָחִים: וּמֵרֹאשׁ הַרְרֵי־קֶדֶם וּמִמֶּגֶד גִּבְעוֹת עוֹלָם: וּמִמֶּגֶד אֶרֶץ
יז וּמְלֹאָהּ וּרְצוֹן שֹׁכְנִי סְנֶה תָּבוֹאתָה לְרֹאשׁ יוֹסֵף וּלְקָדְקֹד נְזִיר אֶחָיו: בְּכוֹר

---

13. מְבֹרֶכֶת ה' אַרְצוֹ — *Blessed of* HASHEM *is his land.* Behold, the portion of Joseph is naturally blessed.

מִמֶּגֶד שָׁמַיִם מִטָּל — *From the dew of heaven precious things* (*shall come*). And behold, I pray that the blessing (of his land) shall also be through the choice fruits which ripen due to the power of heaven (through the medium) of dew, even without rain — and *from the deep* and *the choice fruits of the sun* (verse 14).

16. וּרְצוֹן שֹׁכְנִי סְנֶה — *And by the will of Him that dwelt in the bush . . .* and also by the will of God Who revealed Himself in the bush, thereby demonstrating to Israel that עִמּוֹ אָנֹכִי בְצָרָה, *I will be with him in trouble* (*Psalms* 91:15). All this . . .

תָּבוֹאתָה לְרֹאשׁ יוֹסֵף — *Let* (*the blessing*) *come upon the head of Joseph.* Besides those blessings which he receives together with the congregation (of Israel), let blessings come from God on high on his head (i.e., directly), without any intermediary.

וּלְקָדְקֹד נְזִיר אֶחָיו — *And upon the crown of the head of him that is prince among his brothers.* Indeed, he is worthy of all this because he was a prince who wore the crown of kingship in the midst of his brothers and conducted himself with lovingkindness toward all of them.

17. בְּכוֹר שׁוֹרוֹ — *The firstborn* (*called*) *His ox.* And he, Joseph, is the firstborn (called) the ox of *He Who dwelt in the bush.* For although kingship belongs to Judah, and he is called 'lion,' following him in rank will be Joseph, just like the ox comes after the lion, as our Sages say, 'The king of the wild animals is the lion; the king of the cattle is the ox' (*Chagigah* 13b). And thus the tribe of Joseph was first

NOTES

was not a *Kohen;* he became a leper as a consequence of this willful illegal act. Moses prays that the authority and special rank of the Levites and *Kohanim* not be challenged but accepted as the will of God who chose them to act as His servants.

12. יְדִיד ה' — *The beloved of* HASHEM. The Talmud (*Shabbos* 55b) tells us that there were four righteous men who never sinned and hence never would have died. Their deaths were due to the decree of death issued by God as a consequence of Adam and Eve's eating of the fruit of the Tree of Knowledge at the instigation of the serpent. This is the meaning of עֶטְיוֹ שֶׁל נָחָשׁ, *the serpent's machinations.* Benjamin was one of the four and is therefore called *the beloved of God.* The other three were Amram the father of Moses, Jesse the father of David and Caleb the son of David.

16. וּרְצוֹן שֹׁכְנִי סְנֶה — *And by the will of Him That dwelt in the bush.* Moses invokes the 'will of God' Who revealed Himself to Moses in the bush (*Exodus* 3:2). The *Sforno* explains that he chose to recall an event which symbolizes God's concern for Israel in times of trouble because similarly, God was with Joseph during his time of trouble in Egypt.

תָּבוֹאתָה לְרֹאשׁ יוֹסֵף וּלְקָדְקֹד נְזִיר אֶחָיו — *Let* (*the blessing*) *come upon the head of Joseph and upon the crown of the head of him that is prince among his brothers.* The *Sforno,* in *Genesis* 49:25, explains that when Jacob blessed Joseph he asked that God bless him Himself, without an intermediary. This is the highest level of Divine blessing. He interprets the prayer of Moses regarding Joseph in a similar vein. Moses adds the thought that since Joseph conducted himself toward his brothers לִפְנִים מִשּׁוּרַת הַדִּין, *beyond that which the law of God required of him,* he earned this

שׁוֹרוֹ הָדָר לוֹ וְקַרְנֵי רְאֵם קַרְנָיו בָּהֶם עַמִּים יְנַגַּח יַחְדָּו אַפְסֵי־אָרֶץ וְהֵם
רביעי יח רִבְבוֹת אֶפְרַיִם וְהֵם אַלְפֵי מְנַשֶּׁה: וְלִזְבוּלֻן אָמַר שְׂמַח
יט זְבוּלֻן בְּצֵאתֶךָ וְיִשָּׂשכָר בְּאֹהָלֶיךָ: עַמִּים הַר־יִקְרָאוּ שָׁם יִזְבְּחוּ זִבְחֵי־צֶדֶק
כ כִּי שֶׁפַע יַמִּים יִינָקוּ וּשְׂפֻנֵי טְמוּנֵי חוֹל: וּלְגָד אָמַר בָּרוּךְ

---

among the tribes, after the tribe of Judah, as it says, כְּדַבֵּר אֶפְרַיִם רְתֵת, *When Ephraim spoke there was trembling* (*Hosea* 13:1).

הָדָר לוֹ — *Glory is his.* Although he does not possess הוד, *the majesty of kingship*, he is worthy of הָדָר, *glory and elevated rank.*

בָּהֶם עַמִּים יְנַגַּח יַחְדָּו — *With them he shall gore the nations all together.* Together with the ruling tribe (Judah) he will gore and destroy many peoples as it says, וְסָרָה קִנְאַת אֶפְרַיִם וְצֹרְרֵי יְהוּדָה יִכָּרֵתוּ . . . וְעָפוּ בְכָתֵף פְּלִשְׁתִּים יָמָּה יַחְדָּו יָבֹזּוּ אֶת בְּנֵי קֶדֶם, *The envy of Ephraim shall depart and the adversaries of Judah shall be cut off . . . And they shall fly on the shoulders of the Philistines toward the sea; they shall spoil the children of the east together* (*Isaiah* 11:13,14).

19. עַמִּים הַר יִקְרָאוּ — *They shall call peoples to the mountain.* Issachar and Zebulun will call (draw) the nations of the world to the 'good mountain' (Jerusalem) through their various wares that are unattainable among the nations.

שָׁם יִזְבְּחוּ זִבְחֵי צֶדֶק — *There they shall offer sacrifices of righteousness.* The merchants of the nations, who all their days sacrificed זִבְחֵי מֵתִים, *sacrifices of the dead* (based on *Psalms* 106:28), will also bring sacrifices of righteousness when they come to the 'good mountain.'

כִּי שֶׁפַע יַמִּים יִינָקוּ — *For they shall suck the abundance of the seas.* Issachar and Zebulun will have all sorts of merchandise which come from the sea, and some which are hidden in the sand, such as the blood (or juice) of the snail and milk glass made from glass sand.

20. בָּרוּךְ מַרְחִיב גָּד — *Blessed be He that enlarges Gad.* For he was given a larger portion than all the other tribes in Trans-Jordan because the land of Sichon and Og was larger quantitatively, even though it was not flowing with milk and honey as was the (west) side of the Jordan (i.e., *Eretz Yisrael* proper).

NOTES

special privilege to be the recipient of God's *direct* blessing.

17. בְּכוֹר שׁוֹרוֹ הָדָר לוֹ — *The firstborn* (*called*) *His ox, glory is his. Rashi* states that there is a usage of the word בְּכוֹר that denotes 'greatness and sovereignty' rather than 'firstborn.' He also says that the simile *ox* refers to Joshua who was descended from Joseph and was indeed, strong and mighty as an ox. The *Sforno*, however, explains the word בְּכוֹר in the sense that Joseph was first among the tribes, second only to Judah insofar as kingship was concerned. Judah is compared to a lion who is the king of the beasts; Joseph to an ox who is king of the domestic animals. He also draws a fine distinction between the word הָדָר, *glory*, and הוד, *majesty*. The latter is Judah's exclusively, but Joseph possesses the former — hence, the phrase in this verse הָדָר לוֹ, *glory is his.*

19. עַמִּים הַר יִקְרָאוּ — *They shall call peoples to the mountain.* Zebulun is a seafaring tribe with access to a variety of treasures which are cherished and desired by all. Since both Zebulun and Issachar come into contact with merchants of many nations, they are able to attract many strangers to Jerusalem and awaken their interest in the Almighty to such an extent that these heathens will eventually bring sacrifices to the Holy Temple.

20-21. בָּרוּךְ מַרְחִיב גָּד כְּלָבִיא שָׁכֵן . . . וַיַּרְא

כא מַרְחִ֣יב גָּ֑ד כְּלָבִ֣יא שָׁכֵ֔ן וְטָרַ֥ף זְר֖וֹעַ אַף־קָדְקֹֽד׃ וַיַּ֤רְא רֵאשִׁית֙ ל֔וֹ כִּי־שָׁ֛ם
חֶלְקַ֥ת מְחֹקֵ֖ק סָפ֑וּן וַיֵּתֵא֙ רָ֣אשֵׁי עָ֔ם צִדְקַ֤ת יהוה֙ עָשָׂ֔ה וּמִשְׁפָּטָ֖יו
חמישי כב עִם־יִשְׂרָאֵֽל׃ וּלְדָ֣ן אָמַ֔ר דָּ֖ן גּ֣וּר אַרְיֵ֑ה יְזַנֵּ֖ק
כג מִן־הַבָּשָֽׁן׃ וּלְנַפְתָּלִ֣י אָמַ֔ר נַפְתָּלִי֙ שְׂבַ֣ע רָצ֔וֹן וּמָלֵ֖א בִּרְכַּ֣ת יהוה יָ֥ם וְדָר֖וֹם

כְּלָבִיא שָׁכֵן — *He dwells as a lioness.* He is worthy of this enlarged territory because he dwells among the nations as a lion, (capable) of conquering all those around him.

21. וַיַּרְא רֵאשִׁית לוֹ — *And he saw* (*chose*) *the first part for himself.* And he was also worthy to receive this (particular portion) because when Gad chose the land of Sichon and Og, (he knew) it was not as holy as Trans-Jordan, but his intent was to obtain something essential to him, for there in the land of Sichon and Og, the *portion of the lawgiver was reserved*, the portion where the lawgiver, namely Moses, was to be buried.

וַיֵּתֵא רָאשֵׁי עָם — *And there he came, the head of the people.* And there, in the land of Sichon and Og, the lawgiver came at the head of the people to conquer the land.

צִדְקַת ה׳ עָשָׂה וּמִשְׁפָּטָיו עִם יִשְׂרָאֵל — *He executed the righteousness of* HASHEM *and His ordinances with Israel.* And there the lawgiver executed *the righteousness of God* with Israel by explaining His Torah, and there he exhorted Israel and discussed the judgments and laws of God with them, as did Samuel when he said, הִתְיַצְּבוּ וְאִשָּׁפְטָה אִתְּכֶם ... אֵת כָּל צִדְקוֹת ה׳, *Now stand there and I will judge with you ... concerning all the righteous acts of* HASHEM (*I Samuel* 12:7).

22. גּוּר אַרְיֵה יְזַנֵּק מִן הַבָּשָׁן — *A lion's whelp that leaps forth from the Bashan.* Behold, the lion does not (usually) spring forth from the Bashan, which is a choice fertile place for cattle, as it says, אַבִּירֵי בָשָׁן, *strong bulls of Bashan* (*Psalms* 22:13) and פָּרוֹת הַבָּשָׁן, *cows of Bashan* (*Amos* 4:1), unless he is confident that he will find prey outside the Bashan. So Dan will be confident that he can conquer his surroundings and (therefore) he will go out against them, secure (in his success).

23. נַפְתָּלִי שְׂבַע רָצוֹן וּמָלֵא בִּרְכַּת ה׳ יָם וְדָרוֹם יְרָשָׁה — *Naphtali, satisfied with favor, and full with the blessings of* HASHEM, *you possess the west and the south.* You, Naphtali, who possess the west and south, are satisfied and full of God's blessings, and I need not pray that your land be blessed, because in this portion are the fruits of Genossar, the first to ripen, and from them are brought בִּכּוּרִים, *the first fruits,* which are accepted with favor by Him (i.e., God).

NOTES

... רֵאשִׁית לוֹ ... צִדְקַת ה׳ עָשָׂה ... — *Blessed be He that enlarges Gad, he dwells as a lioness ... And he saw* (*chose*) *the first part for himself ... he executed the righteousness of* HASHEM. The *Sforno* explains that Gad was worthy to be granted a larger portion of land than any other tribe because of two reasons. First, his strength and valor enabled him to conquer and protect a vast territory on the border. Second, his motivation to acquire this particular area was an honorable and praiseworthy one, namely to be privileged to have Moses buried in his portion. The concluding part of verse 21, *he executed the righteousness, etc.*, speaks not of Gad but of Moses, who is interred in the portion of Gad. See *Sotah* 13, the *Sifri* and *Rashi* on this verse (21).

כד יְרֵשָׁה׃ וּלְאָשֵׁר אָמַר בָּרוּךְ מִבָּנִים אָשֵׁר יְהִי רְצוּי
כה-כו אֶחָיו וְטֹבֵל בַּשֶּׁמֶן רַגְלוֹ׃ בַּרְזֶל וּנְחֹשֶׁת מִנְעָלֶיךָ וּכְיָמֶיךָ דָּבְאֶךָ׃ אֵין
חתן תורה כז כָּאֵל יְשֻׁרוּן רֹכֵב שָׁמַיִם בְּעֶזְרֶךָ וּבְגַאֲוָתוֹ שְׁחָקִים׃ מְעֹנָה אֱלֹהֵי קֶדֶם

---

24. בָּרוּךְ מִבָּנִים אָשֵׁר — *Blessed be Asher by sons (his brothers).* Behold, Asher will be blessed above all others in that he will *be the favored of his brethren.* Although (normally) there is jealousy of brothers toward their rich (brother) and even a degree of animosity, but the opposite (will be true) of the tribe of Asher.

וְטֹבֵל בַּשֶּׁמֶן רַגְלוֹ — *And he dips his foot in oil.* (He is favored) because he sells (lit., 'gives') oil cheaply to his brothers since he has such an abundance of (olive oil).

25-26. בַּרְזֶל וּנְחֹשֶׁת מִנְעָלֶךָ וּכְיָמֶיךָ דָּבְאֶךָ. אֵין כָּאֵל יְשֻׁרוּן — *Iron and brass shall be your locks, and as your early days so shall your strength be. There is none like God, Jeshurun.* After he concludes his prayer for the tribes, he begins to bless Israel collectively, saying, 'You, Jeshurun, being that there is none like (your) God Who is immutable and omnipotent, Who rules over all, your kingdom will be different from other kingdoms on two counts: First, no nation will enter your land to do battle and none will covet your land for fear of you, as indeed it was, כֹּל יְמֵי יְהוֹשֻׁעַ וְכֹל יְמֵי הַזְּקֵנִים אֲשֶׁר הֶאֱרִיכוּ יָמִים אַחֲרֵי יְהוֹשֻׁעַ, *All the days of Joshua and all the days of the elders that outlived Joshua* (*Joshua* 24:31) — as if the Land was locked with bars of iron and brass. Second, your kingdom will not rise and fall as do the kingdoms of the nations of the world who ascend when their מַזָּל, *constellation*, rises, and descend when it falls, because they are subject to the hosts of heaven. You, however, כְּיָמֶיךָ, *as your days*, referring to the days of youth when you first entered the Land, דָּבְאֶךָ, *so shall your strength be*, referring to the days of your old age *when you will beget children and children's children and become old in the Land* (based on 4:25). This blessing of mine shall come to pass since *there is none like God* who conducts your affairs.

רֹכֵב שָׁמַיִם בְּעֶזְרֶךָ — *Who rides upon the heaven and is your Help.* Indeed, God Who is your Helper, He rides upon the heaven, (meaning that) He is supreme, ruling over them (i.e., the planets and constellations) as opposed to the opinion of the Sabians who said that there is none superior (lit., more honored) than the heavens (and their hosts). Therefore, a kingdom which is established by Him does not ascend or decline when the constellations rise and fall.

26-27. וּבְגַאֲוָתוֹ שְׁחָקִים. מְעֹנָה — *And in His majesty on the skies. The dwelling place.* And in His supremacy He rides the skies; this refers to the daily sphere which contains no star or form and its moving (force) is an invisible power, similar to the dwelling place (den) of the lion in which there is great hidden strength.

אֱלֹהֵי קֶדֶם — *The ancient God* . . . the ancient, primeval God, whereas all others are created (lit., renewed) by Him.

NOTES

24. בָּרוּךְ מִבָּנִים אָשֵׁר — *Blessed be Asher by sons (his brothers).* The *Sforno* does not translate the word מִבָּנִים as *above sons*, which is the accepted translation, but *by sons.* Asher will be blessed by the other tribes, the *sons* of Jacob, for he will be generous and gracious in sharing his blessing of oil with all of them.

25-26. בַּרְזֶל וּנְחֹשֶׁת מִנְעָלֶךָ וּכְיָמֶיךָ דָּבְאֶךָ. אֵין כָּאֵל יְשֻׁרוּן רֹכֵב שָׁמַיִם בְּעֶזְרֶךָ — *Iron and brass shall be your locks, and as your early days so shall your strength be. There is none like God, Jeshurun, Who rides upon the heaven and is your help.* As the *Sforno* said in his commentary on verse 2, the blessings of Moses (as opposed to his prayer)

כח וּמִתַּחַת זְרֹעֹת עוֹלָם וַיְגָרֶשׁ מִפָּנֶיךָ אוֹיֵב וַיֹּאמֶר הַשְׁמֵד: וַיִּשְׁכֹּן יִשְׂרָאֵל

וּמִתַּחַת זְרֹעֹת עוֹלָם — *And underneath (the heavens,) the everlasting might.* And below the heavens, He is the God of might Who directs all existing (things) of the world, (meaning) that which exists but perishes with the passage of time such as the quality of the (primary) elements and the (forces) of nature which nourish, promote growth and reproduction, and the formative power in plant life and living creatures.

וַיְגָרֶשׁ מִפָּנֶיךָ אוֹיֵב וַיֹּאמֶר הַשְׁמֵד — *And He thrust out the enemy from before you and said, 'Destroy.'* And behold, He drove out the enemies before you who were the inhabitants of the Land, and He said to you, 'Destroy!' Because you did not conquer the Land by your sword that you should think when your strength leaves you, with the passage of time, or when other (enemies) replace them, that they will overpower you. Because indeed He was the One Who cast them out and how shall others enter (the Land) against His will?

NOTES

begin with these verses. The opening section of the second verse (26) is interpreted by the *Sforno* as an introduction in retrospect to the previous verse (25). Moses addresses Israel using the title Jeshurun and begins by stating that the God of Israel is unique, all-powerful and everlasting. As such, the kingdom He established for them in *Eretz Yisrael* will be secure and safe under His protection and, unlike other nations and kingdoms, their destiny as a people will not be dependent upon the heavenly hosts, planets and constellations which comprise the zodiac. As such, just as God is everlasting and unchanging, so shall Israel be an eternal people and retain their youthful vigor.

The theory of the Sabians, that there is no Divine power superior to the heavenly hosts, is mentioned by Maimonides in his *Guide* and refuted by him, as does the *Sforno* in a number of places in his commentary. Here he reads this refutation into the phrase, *Who rides upon the heaven*, i.e., the Almighty transcends and rules over the stars and planets. Since Israel has no מַזָּל, but is totally dependent upon God and ruled by Him, hence there shall be no national rise and decline for them as is the case with other nations, whose rise and fall correspond to that of their heavenly representatives.

26-27. וּבְגַאֲוָתוֹ שְׁחָקִים: מְעֹנָה — *And in His majesty on the skies. The dwelling place*. The *Rambam* (*Mishnah Torah, Yesodai HaTorah* 3:1-7) states that there are nine גַּלְגַּלִּים, *spheres*, which encircle the universe, eight of which contain stars or planets that move and control them, such as Mercury, Venus, Mars, Jupiter and Saturn. The ninth sphere, however, which encompasses the universe and revolves around the earth every twenty-four hours, 'has no division nor any of these forms nor any star,' as do the other eight. This ninth sphere is called the גַּלְגַּל חוֹזֵר, *revolving sphere*, which is all-encompassing. According to Maimonides, each sphere 'has a soul and is endowed with knowledge and intelligence,' but since the ninth sphere has neither star nor form (צוּרָה) within it, its force is hidden and apparently moved, guided and controlled by the direct influence of the Almighty.

The *Sforno*, in his commentary here, reflects this theory of the *Rambam*, while linking the conclusion of verse 26 (וּבְגַאֲוָתוֹ שְׁחָקִים) with the first word (מְעֹנָה) of verse 27. The meaning of his commentary is that the Almighty rides upon the heaven and traverses the skies by guiding the ninth sphere with His direct power. This sphere is called the *daily sphere*, since it revolves around the planet earth from east to west every twenty-four hours. This force of God is concealed in the sense that, unlike the other eight spheres which contain stars and planets moving them, the ninth sphere contains none. The *Sforno* compares this hidden power to a lion in his den who is not seen, but everyone is aware that there is great strength lurking in his 'dwelling place.' This imagery of a lion in his den is found in *Psalms* 10:9, *He lies in wait secretly like a lion in his den*. The phrase מְעֹנָה is used regarding the lion's den as we find in the verse, *Where is the den of the lions* (*Nachum* 2:12). The meaning of the concluding portion of verse 26, linked with the beginning of verse 27, is 'God in His majesty and power is manifested in the daily sphere, which is the ninth sphere, and this power is invisible, as is the power of the lion in his den or dwelling place.' (I am indebted to Dr. Sid Leiman for his assistance in the preparation of this note.)

אֱלֹהֵי קֶדֶם — *The ancient God*. In Jewish

כט בֶּטַח בָּדָד עֵין יַעֲקֹב אֶל־אֶרֶץ דָּגָן וְתִירוֹשׁ אַף־שָׁמָיו יַעַרְפוּ טָל: אַשְׁרֶיךָ

28. וַיִּשְׁכֹּן יִשְׂרָאֵל בֶּטַח — *And Israel dwells securely* ... as it says, וְהָאָרֶץ שָׁקְטָה מִמִּלְחָמָה, *And the Land had rest from war* (*Joshua* 11:23).

בָּדָד עֵין יַעֲקֹב אֶל אֶרֶץ דָּגָן וְתִירוֹשׁ אַף שָׁמָיו יַעַרְפוּ טָל — *The fountain of Jacob (shall dwell) alone upon a land of corn and wine, also His heavens shall drop down dew.* May it be Your will at the end of days (that) *the Fountain of Jacob*, Who is *the Lord that you seek* (based on *Malachi* 3:1), and Who (will be) the Fountain of Israel at the end (lit., the heel) of time, and (regarding Whom the verse states,) *His heavens shall drop dew*, that there will flow an abundance of dew *upon a land of corn and wine*. This indicates that the teaching of the Messiah will drop as the dew which all rejoice in and the heavens shall also (literally) flow with abundant dew *upon the land of corn and wine*, as was the case at the time of the six days of creation before the sin of Adam, כִּי לֹא הִמְטִיר . . . וְאָדָם אַיִן לַעֲבֹד . . . וְאֵד יַעֲלֶה . . . וְהִשְׁקָה, *For (God) had not caused it to rain . . . and there was not a man to till . . . but a mist went up . . . and watered* (*Genesis* 2:5,6), in such a manner that the earth itself will (produce) corn and wine when the dew will drop down and bless it. In this way, its inhabitants will attain their livelihood without pain as was the (original) intent before the sin, that Adam's needs would be met (without great toil), as our Sages say, 'There will come a time when *Eretz Yisrael* will produce baked cakes and silk garments' (*Shabbos* 30b).

29. אַשְׁרֶיךָ יִשְׂרָאֵל — *Happy are you, O Israel.* And then you will reach that (degree) of happiness which is the highest level (of contentment) possible for a people (to attain).

NOTES

tradition, God is referred to as קַדְמוֹנוֹ שֶׁל עוֹלָם, *the One Who preceded the world.* The word *ancient*, when applied to the Almighty, does not mean 'old' or that which existed many eons ago. God is above time and place. As the *Sforno* states, God is primeval and He is the One Who brought all the forces and powers of the universe into existence, hence, He is referred to as קֶדֶם.

וּמִתַּחַת זְרֹעֹת עוֹלָם — *And underneath (the heavens,) the everlasting might.* The expression זְרֹעֹת עוֹלָם translates literally as *the arms of the world.* God, as it were, holds the world in His arms — guiding, directing and protecting it. As the *Sforno* states, this concern and control of God *underneath the heavens* extends to all the forces of nature which guarantee the continuity of the בְּרִיאָה, *creation.*

וַיְגָרֶשׁ . . . וַיֹּאמֶר הַשְׁמֵד — *And He thrust out . . . and said, 'Destroy.'* Israel is depicted as being the instrument of God in the conquest of *Eretz Yisrael.* God is the true conqueror while Israel is but the medium chosen by Him to drive out the inhabitants of Canaan, whom they will replace. Hence, there is no fear that eventually the Jews will in turn be replaced by others, for they are not subject to the normal pattern of rise, decline and fall as are other nations since God is the source of their strength and security.

28. בָּדָד עֵין יַעֲקֹב . . . אַף שָׁמָיו יַעַרְפוּ טָל — *The fountain of Jacob (shall dwell) alone . . . also His heavens shall drop down dew.* The *Sforno* explains why this verse, which he interprets as being a prayer instead of a blessing , uses the term עֵין יַעֲקֹב, *fountain of Jacob*, rather than יִשְׂרָאֵל, *Israel.* As the *Sforno* points out in *Genesis* 25:26, the name יַעֲקֹב, which stems from עָקֵב, *heel*, implies אַחֲרִית הַיָּמִים, *the end of days.* In our verse, the word *fountain*, the source of life-giving and refreshing waters, refers to מָשִׁיחַ, *the Messiah*, whose teachings will be readily understood, accepted and appreciated by one and all. He explains the phrase יַעַרְפוּ טָל, *shall drop down as dew*, as having a two-fold meaning. One is symbolic, referring to the Messiah and his teachings, while the second is a literal one, promising that Israel will at that time in their history be granted פַּרְנָסָה, *livelihood*, which will be easily acquired, permitting them to pursue the study and mastery of Torah.

יִשְׂרָאֵל מִי כָמוֹךָ עַם נוֹשַׁע בַּיהוָה מָגֵן עֶזְרֶךָ וַאֲשֶׁר־חֶרֶב גַּאֲוָתֶךָ וְיִכָּחֲשׁוּ
לד א אֹיְבֶיךָ לָךְ וְאַתָּה עַל־בָּמוֹתֵימוֹ תִדְרֹךְ: וַיַּעַל מֹשֶׁה מֵעַרְבֹת
מוֹאָב אֶל־הַר נְבוֹ רֹאשׁ הַפִּסְגָּה אֲשֶׁר עַל־פְּנֵי יְרֵחוֹ וַיַּרְאֵהוּ יהוָה אֶת־
ב כָּל־הָאָרֶץ אֶת־הַגִּלְעָד עַד־דָּן: וְאֵת כָּל־נַפְתָּלִי וְאֶת־אֶרֶץ אֶפְרַיִם וּמְנַשֶּׁה
ג וְאֵת כָּל־אֶרֶץ יְהוּדָה עַד הַיָּם הָאַחֲרוֹן: וְאֶת־הַנֶּגֶב וְאֶת־הַכִּכָּר בִּקְעַת יְרֵחוֹ
ד עִיר הַתְּמָרִים עַד־צֹעַר: וַיֹּאמֶר יהוה אֵלָיו זֹאת הָאָרֶץ אֲשֶׁר נִשְׁבַּעְתִּי

מִי כָמוֹךָ — *Who is like unto you?* No other people will be found like unto you (in this respect), as it says, וְאִשְּׁרוּ אֶתְכֶם כָּל הַגּוֹיִם, *And all nations shall call you happily blessed* (*Malachi* 3:12).

עַם נוֹשַׁע בַּה׳ — *A people saved by HASHEM.* Your salvation will not be secured by the battles you wage but rather God will do battle on your behalf.

מָגֵן עֶזְרֶךָ — *The shield of your help.* He is the One Who helped you in Exile, (insuring) that you not be annihilated, as it says, לוּלֵי ה׳ שֶׁהָיָה לָנוּ . . . אֲזַי הַמַּיִם שְׁטָפוּנוּ . . . עֶזְרֵנוּ בְּשֵׁם ה׳ . . . *If not for HASHEM Who was with us . . . then the waters would have overwhelmed us . . . Our help is in the Name of HASHEM* (*Psalms* 124:2,4,8).

וַאֲשֶׁר חֶרֶב גַּאֲוָתֶךָ — *And the sword of your majesty.* His will be the sword that will be elevated over the nations when He battles against them as it says, כִּי בָאֵשׁ ה׳ נִשְׁפָּט, וּבְחַרְבּוֹ אֶת כָּל בָּשָׂר, *For by fire will HASHEM execute judgment, and with His sword upon all flesh* (*Isaiah* 66:16).

וְיִכָּחֲשׁוּ אֹיְבֶיךָ לָךְ — *And your enemies shall submit to you.* Those who shamed you (in the past) will now submit to you when you will be honored, as it says, וְהִשְׁתַּחֲווּ עַל כַּפּוֹת רַגְלַיִךְ כָּל מְנַאֲצָיִךְ, *And those who despised you shall bow down at the soles of your feet* (*Isaiah* 60:14).

וְאַתָּה עַל בָּמוֹתֵימוֹ תִדְרֹךְ — *And you shall tread upon their high places.* Even their kings will humble themselves (before) you, as it says, וְהָיוּ מְלָכִים אֹמְנַיִךְ . . . אַפַּיִם אֶרֶץ יִשְׁתַּחֲווּ לָךְ, *And kings shall be your foster parents . . . they shall bow down to you with their faces toward the earth* (*Isaiah* 49:23).

NOTES

29. אַשְׁרֶיךָ יִשְׂרָאֵל מִי כָמוֹךָ — *Happy are you, O Israel; who is like unto you?* Moses is not praising or complimenting Israel, rather he is stating a fact regarding their future. He asserts that ultimately they will reach a level of happiness that will be unique and unsurpassed by other nations, and this special condition will be recognized by all the nations, as Malachi prophesied.

עַם נוֹשַׁע בַּה׳ מָגֵן עֶזְרֶךָ וַאֲשֶׁר חֶרֶב גַּאֲוָתֶךָ — *A people saved by HASHEM, the shield of your help and the sword of your majesty.* The *Sforno* explains these three distinct phrases in the following manner: Israel's salvation is not secured by their own military might but through God Who battles on their behalf. In fact, through the years in Exile, were it not for the fact that God was their *shield of help,* they would have been destroyed. And at that time in Israel's history, when they will again do battle against their enemies at the conclusion of their exile, God will serve as their *sword of majesty.*

וְיִכָּחֲשׁוּ אֹיְבֶיךָ לָךְ וְאַתָּה עַל בָּמוֹתֵימוֹ תִדְרֹךְ — *And your enemies shall submit to you and you shall tread upon their high places.* The *Sforno* explains that these two concluding phrases refer to the high regard, esteem and respect that the nations and their leaders will have for the people of Israel. Those nations who were their enemies, mocking and shaming them over the years, will eventually submit to them and be subservient to them, and the leaders of those nations will likewise humble themselves before Israel.

לְאַבְרָהָם לְיִצְחָק וּלְיַעֲקֹב לֵאמֹר לְזַרְעֲךָ אֶתְּנֶנָּה הֶרְאִיתִיךָ בְעֵינֶיךָ וְשָׁמָּה
ה־ו לֹא תַעֲבֹר: וַיָּמָת שָׁם מֹשֶׁה עֶבֶד־יהוה בְּאֶרֶץ מוֹאָב עַל־פִּי יהוה: וַיִּקְבֹּר
אֹתוֹ בַגַּי בְּאֶרֶץ מוֹאָב מוּל בֵּית פְּעוֹר וְלֹא־יָדַע אִישׁ אֶת־קְבֻרָתוֹ עַד
ז הַיּוֹם הַזֶּה: וּמֹשֶׁה בֶּן־מֵאָה וְעֶשְׂרִים שָׁנָה בְּמֹתוֹ לֹא־כָהֲתָה עֵינוֹ וְלֹא־נָס
ח לֵחֹה: וַיִּבְכּוּ בְנֵי יִשְׂרָאֵל אֶת־מֹשֶׁה בְּעַרְבֹת מוֹאָב שְׁלֹשִׁים יוֹם וַיִּתְּמוּ יְמֵי
ט בְכִי אֵבֶל מֹשֶׁה: וִיהוֹשֻׁעַ בִּן־נוּן מָלֵא רוּחַ חָכְמָה כִּי־סָמַךְ מֹשֶׁה אֶת־יָדָיו
עָלָיו וַיִּשְׁמְעוּ אֵלָיו בְּנֵי־יִשְׂרָאֵל וַיַּעֲשׂוּ כַּאֲשֶׁר צִוָּה יהוה אֶת־מֹשֶׁה:

XXXIV

4. הֶרְאִיתִיךָ בְעֵינֶיךָ — *I have caused you to see it with your eyes* . . . so that you may bless it.

וְשָׁמָּה לֹא תַעֲבֹר — *But you shall not go over there* . . . lest your blessing will (firmly) take hold in such a manner that (the Land) will not be destroyed at the end, as it was decreed (to occur) when their measure (of evil) would be full.

6. וַיִּקְבֹּר אֹתוֹ — *And he was buried.* If he (Moses) buried himself, as is the opinion of some of our Sages, then (we must say) that his separated soul did it, because he died on the mountain on the top of Pisgah, from whence he saw the Land, as it states, *And Moses died there* (v. 5), whereas the burial was in the valley.

8-9. וַיִּתְּמוּ יְמֵי בְכִי אֵבֶל מֹשֶׁה. וִיהוֹשֻׁעַ בִּן נוּן מָלֵא רוּחַ חָכְמָה — *The days of weeping in the mourning for Moses ended. And Joshua the son of Nun was full of the spirit of wisdom* . . . because in the days of weeping, there is no wisdom and no counsel.

כַּאֲשֶׁר צִוָּה ה׳ אֶת מֹשֶׁה — *As* HASHEM *commanded Moses* . . . according to all that God had commanded Moses, as it says, וְשָׁאַל לוֹ בְּמִשְׁפַּט הָאוּרִים לִפְנֵי ה׳ עַל פִּיו יֵצְאוּ וְעַל פִּיו יָבֹאוּ הוּא וְכָל בְּנֵי יִשְׂרָאֵל אִתּוֹ וְכָל הָעֵדָה, *They shall inquire of him by the judgment of the Urim before* HASHEM*; at his word shall they go out and at his word they shall come in, both he and all the Children of Israel with him and all the congregation* (*Numbers* 27:21).

NOTES

XXXIV

4. הֶרְאִיתִיךָ בְעֵינֶיךָ — *I have caused you to see it with your eyes*. See *Genesis* 48:10 and the note there; also *Numbers* 27:12 and *Deut.* 32:49.

וְשָׁמָּה לֹא תַעֲבֹר — *But you shall not go over there*. Rabbinic tradition has it that whatever Moses himself did was destined to last forever. Had he himself entered the Land of Israel and conquered it, *Eretz Yisrael* would never have been destroyed, nor would the Jewish people have been exiled from it. The *Sforno* established this concept above in chapter 1:37 and chapter 3:25. God, however, had decreed that if Israel sinned they would be punished with Exile, hence, Moses was not permitted to enter the Land since this would frustrate the Divine plan. In some ways this was also beneficial to the Jewish people, for had the Land not been destroyed and the people exiled, then when their sins would multiply greatly and God could no longer be forbearing with them, they would be subject to total annihilation. Hence, their exile allowed them to survive as a people and God's wrath was poured out on the Land, and in the case of the Temple, on 'the wood and stones.'

6. וַיִּקְבֹּר אֹתוֹ — *And he was buried*. See *Rashi's* commentary on this verse.

8-9. וַיִּתְּמוּ יְמֵי בְכִי אֵבֶל מֹשֶׁה: וִיהוֹשֻׁעַ בִּן נוּן מָלֵא רוּחַ חָכְמָה — *The days of weeping in the mourning for Moses ended. And Joshua the son of Nun was full of the spirit of wisdom*. The Sages have taught us that the *Shechinah*, the Divine Presence, including the gift

וְלֹא־קָם נָבִיא עוֹד בְּיִשְׂרָאֵל כְּמֹשֶׁה אֲשֶׁר֙ יְדָע֣וֹ יהוה פָּנִ֖ים אֶל־פָּנִֽים׃

10. וְלֹא קָם נָבִיא עוֹד בְּיִשְׂרָאֵל כְּמֹשֶׁה — *And there did not arise a prophet in Israel like Moses since.* No other prophet ever reached his level of prophecy and thus it is clear that no prophet is permitted to institute new laws, as our Sages say, 'One *Beis Din* cannot annul the ordinances of another unless it is superior to it in number and in wisdom' (*Megillah* 2a).

אֲשֶׁר יְדָעוֹ ה׳ — *Whom* HASHEM*'s knowledge (he absorbed).* Behold, when a prophet prophesies, without a doubt, he acquires an added (dimension) of intellectual light, emanating from the light (radiance) of the King's countenance, as it says, וְהִתְנַבִּיתָ עִמָּם וְנֶהְפַּכְתָּ לְאִישׁ אַחֵר, *And you shall prophesy with them and shall be turned into another man* (*I Samuel* 10:6). That is also why (the prophet) tells us of the lovingkindness shown by God to His people (and it therefore) says, וָאָקִים מִבְּנֵיכֶם לִנְבִיאִים, *And I will rise up your sons for prophets* (*Amos* 2:11). Now, being that all actions of God, the Blessed One, are executed solely through His own knowledge of self, it says, אֲשֶׁר יְדָעוֹ, *Whom* (HASHEM'S) *knowledge*, teaching (us) that He acted upon him through His knowledge for good, similar to, מָה אָדָם וַתֵּדָעֵהוּ, *What is man that you make him to know* (*Psalms* 144:3), and וָאֵדָעֲךָ בְּשֵׁם, *and I know you by name* (*Exodus* 33:17), and וַיֵּדַע אֱלֹהִים, *And God knew* (ibid. 2:25) and יוֹדֵעַ ה׳ דֶּרֶךְ צַדִּיקִים, HASHEM *knows the way of the righteous* (*Psalms* 1:6) and many such similar (passages).

פָּנִים אֶל פָּנִים — *Face to face . . .* while he still made use of his senses (faculties).

NOTES

of prophecy, can only dwell upon a person when a spirit of joy prevails (*Shabbos* 30b). Depression and sadness caused by mourning inhibits the powr of prophecy and the gift of Divinely inspired wisdom as well. The *Sforno* therefore links together the concluding phrase of verse 8 with the opening statement of verse 9. Only after the days of weeping and mourning were over could Joshua be the recipient of *the spirit of wisdom.*

10. וְלֹא קָם נָבִיא — *And there did not arise a prophet.* The *Sforno* stresses that the Torah given by Moses is a permanent and unchanging one. The claim by the Church that Christianity was the 'New Israel' supplanting the old, and that the New Testament replaced the Tanach, had to be refuted. Maimonides, his contemporaries and many who followed, such as the *Sforno*, emphasized the everlasting character of God's covenant with Israel and the unchanging nature of Torah. (See the *Rambam's* ninth Principle of Faith.) *Sforno* interprets the opening phrase of this verse, *And there did not arise a prophet like Moses,* as an added argument against the attempt made by those who would amend the original covenant and the Torah given through Moses our Teacher. Since a later court that is inferior to a previous one has no power to override the decision of that court, and since no prophet ever arose who was the equal, let alone the superior, of Moses, how then could any *prophet* abrogate the teachings of Moses and legitimately establish a new covenant or testament? It is for this reason that the Torah emphasizes that no prophet ever rose to his level.

אֲשֶׁר יְדָעוֹ ה׳ — *Whom* HASHEM*'s knowledge.* The *Sforno* explains this expression as meaning that the Almighty, whose knowledge is not external to Himself, but rather 'He . . . and His knowledge are One' (*Rambam, Mishnah Torah, Hilchos Teshuvah* 5:5), acted upon Moses until he became influenced and instructed by this Divine knowledge, thereby expanding his own knowledge. See the *Sforno's* commentary on *Numbers* 7:89 and *Deut.* 2:7 and the notes on those verses for further clarification.

פָּנִים אֶל פָּנִים — *Face to face.* See the *Sforno* on *Exodus* 19:19 and 33:11 and the notes on those verses regarding the meaning of פָּנִים אֶל פָּנִים, *face to face.*

יא לְכָל־הָאֹתֹת וְהַמּוֹפְתִים אֲשֶׁר שְׁלָחוֹ יהוה לַעֲשׂוֹת בְּאֶרֶץ מִצְרָיִם לְפַרְעֹה
יב וּלְכָל־עֲבָדָיו וּלְכָל־אַרְצוֹ׃ וּלְכֹל הַיָּד הַחֲזָקָה וּלְכֹל הַמּוֹרָא הַגָּדוֹל אֲשֶׁר
עָשָׂה מֹשֶׁה לְעֵינֵי כָּל־יִשְׂרָאֵל׃

---

11. לְכָל הָאֹתֹת — *In all the signs.* And this knowledge (of God) *face to face* was granted to him when God sent him to perform signs and wonders in Egypt, because indeed the vision revealed to him at the bush did not take place in this manner as it says, כִּי יָרֵא מֵהַבִּיט אֶל הָאֱלֹהִים, *For he was afraid to look upon God* (*Exodus* 3:6) as compared to, וּתְמֻנַת ה׳ יַבִּיט, *And the similitude of* HASHEM *he beholds* (*Numbers* 12:8).

12. וּלְכֹל הַיָּד הַחֲזָקָה — *And in all that mighty hand . . .* which God wrought through him, changing the nature of permanent (aspects of creation), such as the splitting of the (waters) of the Sea (of Reeds) (*Exodus* 14:21) and the earth opening its mouth (*Numbers* 16:31) and bringing down manna from heaven (*Exodus* 16:4) and other such (phenomena).

וּלְכֹל הַמּוֹרָא הַגָּדוֹל — *And in all the great awesomeness . . .* of the giving of the Torah.

אֲשֶׁר עָשָׂה מֹשֶׁה לְעֵינֵי כָּל יִשְׂרָאֵל — *Which Moses performed in the sight of all Israel.* When they (Israel) stood from afar at the time the Torah was given, they saw how Moses drew nigh to the thick darkness (*Exodus* 20:18), because he then attained the highest level of prophecy (characterized as) *face to face*, and Moses then became נוֹרָא, *awesome*, through the 'rays of glory.'

לְעֵינֵי כָּל יִשְׂרָאֵל — *In the sight of all Israel . . .* as it says, וַיַּרְא אַהֲרֹן וְכָל בְּנֵי יִשְׂרָאֵל אֶת מֹשֶׁה וְהִנֵּה קָרַן עוֹר פָּנָיו וַיִּירְאוּ מִגֶּשֶׁת אֵלָיו, *And when Aaron and all the Children of Israel saw Moses, and behold the skin of his face sent forth beams, they were afraid to come near him* (*Exodus* 34:30).

NOTES

11-12. לְכָל הָאֹתֹת . . . וּלְכֹל הַיָּד הַחֲזָקָה . . . וּלְכֹל הַמּוֹרָא הַגָּדוֹל אֲשֶׁר עָשָׂה מֹשֶׁה לְעֵינֵי כָּל יִשְׂרָאֵל — *In all the signs . . . and in all that mighty hand . . . and in all the great awesomeness which Moses performed in the sight of all Israel. Rashi* interprets *mighty hand* as referring to the giving of the Torah, while *and in all the great awesomeness* refers to the miracles and mighty deeds wrought by God in the terrible wilderness. *Sforno*, however, interprets *mighty hand* to mean the supernatural acts of God in Egypt and at the Sea of Reeds, executed through the hand of Moses, while *the great awsomeness* refers to the giving of the Torah. The latter occasion caused Israel to be in awe of Moses who drew nigh to Sinai when all others stood from afar, and who ultimately came down to the people with 'rays of glory' shining from his face. The *Sforno*, in his commentary on verse 11, links the unique stature of Moses and his ability to communicate with God *face to face* (verse 10) with his worthiness to be chosen to perform signs and wonders in Egypt at the behest of God. This level of prophecy was not reached at once but evolved gradually, for at the bush he had not as yet attained such an exalted station, but with time he merited to speak with God while still in command of his faculties.